Bibliographies of Studies in Victorian Literature

Compiled by

Robert A. Donovan

Charles T. Dougherty

Ronald E. Freeman

Donald J. Gray

Oscar Maurer

Robert C. Slack

William D. Templeman

Michael Timko

Richard C. Tobias

Francis G. Townsend

Austin Wright

Bibliographies of Studies in Victorian Literature

For the Ten Years 1955-1964

Edited by Robert C. Slack

UNIVERSITY OF ILLINOIS PRESS
Urbana, Chicago, and London, 1967

❧ PREFACE

The present volume collects and reproduces the annual Victorian Bibliographies for the years 1955 through 1964 published in *Modern Philology* (1956-57) and in *Victorian Studies* (1958-65). This is a sequel to two previous volumes published by the University of Illinois Press: *Bibliographies of Studies in Victorian Literature for the Thirteen Years 1932-1944,* edited by William D. Templeman and published in 1945; and *Bibliographies of Studies in Victorian Literature for the Ten Years 1945-1954,* edited by Austin Wright and published in 1956.

The annual Victorian Bibliography is a project of the Victorian Literature Group of the Modern Language Association of America, and it is prepared by a Bibliography Committee appointed by that group. Professor William D. Templeman, who was principally responsible for the inauguration of the project, served as its editor for the first thirteen years.

In this reprint the periodical pagination of each annual bibliography has been preserved at the top of the page, to permit use of cross references in the original issues. Continuous pagination appears at the bottom of the pages. Index entries and footnotes in the Introduction refer to the continuous pagination of this volume.

In editing the present volume and throughout the years of preparing the annual bibliographies I have had recurrent reasons to be grateful for the advice and help of Professor Austin Wright, editor of the previous volume covering the years 1945-54. Also I am deeply grateful to Professor Francis G. Townsend, my predecessor as editor of the annual bibliographies, and to the hard-working members of the Bibliography Committee, who are named in the Introduction. Special thanks are due to the editors of *Modern Philology* and *Victorian Studies* for giving the annual bibliographies a home, as well as to Professor Donald D. Jackson of the University of Illinois Press for making this publication possible. Finally, I am grateful for the patience of my wife and family during the countless hours demanded by the Victorian Bibliography.

ROBERT C. SLACK
Carnegie Institute of Technology

❧ INTRODUCTION

Since its beginning in 1932, the annual Victorian Bibliography has stated that it aims "to list the noteworthy publications" which have a bearing on Victorian literature. The precise meaning of this statement has been subject to periodic review by the Bibliography Committee, and will no doubt continue to be as long as the Bibliography appears. In the decade covered by this volume, the Committee came more and more to feel that it should endeavor to make the listings as inclusive as possible and not omit anything of more than marginal significance. If such omissions have occurred, they have been inadvertent. The Committee was encouraged in its pursuit of broader inclusiveness by the editorial policy of *Victorian Studies,* to which the Bibliography was transferred from *Modern Philology* in 1958. Previous to this transfer, the Bibliography had been more selective, and it contained a number of lengthy review comments by members of the Committee. Since the transfer, the number of entries has increased markedly, especially in Section II, concerned with the economic, political, religious, and social environment. The result is that this volume contains almost 50 per cent more entries than did the previous ten-year collection (for 1945-54); but the amount of comment by members of the Committee has been significantly reduced.

The annual bibliographies included in this collection have had a succession of three editors: Austin Wright, Carnegie Institute of Technology, edited the bibliography for 1955; Francis G. Townsend, Florida State University, edited the bibliographies for 1956, 1957, and 1958; the present editor, Robert C. Slack, Carnegie Institute of Technology, has edited the annual bibliographies for 1959 through 1964. The other members of the Bibliography Committee, whose faithful and dedicated labor deserves far more than mere acknowledgment, have been:

William D. Templeman, University of Southern California	1955-58
Oscar Maurer, University of Texas	1955-64
Robert A. Donovan, Cornell University and State University of New York	1956-63
Charles T. Dougherty, St. Louis University	1956-64
Donald J. Gray, Indiana University	1957-64
Richard C. Tobias, University of Pittsburgh	1959-64
Ronald E. Freeman, University of Southern California	1959-64
Michael Timko, Queens College	1961-64

Within the ten years covered, special contributions to the preparation of the bibliographies have been made by: Carl J. Weber, Colby College (all years); T. J. Truss, University of Mississippi (1958); and John Filor, Indiana University (1962). Without the many hours of labor freely given by all the persons named in this paragraph, the present volume could not have come into existence. The world of Victorian scholarship has reason to be grateful to these scholars.

As this collection testifies, Victorian scholarship is thriving and healthy. The mass of material represented is both cheering and intimidating. Any scholar is pleased to engage in a field in which there is so much stir and active interest; yet the prospect of becoming acquainted with a significant amount of this vast production grows more and more remote. The present volume contains slightly over 7,900 entries, not counting book reviews. Since this collection approaches comprehensiveness, a detailed study of it can give a reasonably accurate apprehension of number, shape, and direction in Victorian scholarship.[1] Considering the sheer welter of the material, some apprehension of shape and direction is eminently desirable. In the ten years 1955-64, the Victorian Bibliography has averaged some 790 entries per year. This represents a truly impressive mountain of paper and ink, to say nothing of the hours of toil and eyestrain that it represents for scholars. The massive bulk of this material cries aloud for some kind of analytic distribution.

An elementary breakdown occurs in the Bibliography itself. Each annual bibliography is divided into four sections. Section I, by far the smallest, is of particular interest to bibliographers; it lists bibliographies of relevance to the Victorian period, such as the annual bibliography of nineteenth-century studies which appears in *PMLA* and the listings of recent publications which appear in the *Victorian News Letter,* as well as various checklists, reviews of the year's work in *Victorian Poetry* or in *Nineteenth Century Literature,* and descriptions of library collections. This small section comprises only about 3 per cent of the total number of entries.

Section II is concerned with the environment — economic, political, religious, or social. Entries here range from such concerns as Josef Altholz' book on *The Liberal Catholic Movement in England*[2] or Paul Scherer's dissertation on "British Policy with Respect to the Unification of Germany, 1848-1871"[3] to such items as Jenifer Hart's article "Reform of the Borough Police, 1835-1856"[4] or a book by Marion Giordan called *The Victorian Book of Dreams,*[5] a collection of popular interpretations compiled from various nineteenth-century dream-books. As a result of encouragement by the editors of *Victorian Studies,* this section has trebled in quantity, and over the ten years it has contained almost 29 per cent of the entries.

A third concern of the Bibliography is reflected in Section III, averaging some 90 items per year, dealing with movements of ideas or with literary forms and theory. This comparatively small section (less than 12 per cent of the entries) contains listings of great interest and importance. Here are included such perceptive critical successes as Wayne Booth's *The Rhetoric of Fiction,*[6] such thoughtful studies as J. Hillis Miller's *The Disappearance of God*[7] and Morse Peckham's exciting *Beyond the Tragic Vision.*[8] Also included in this section are the vast variety of special-interest subjects that are somehow covered by the giant umbrella called "literary history" — such articles as Robert L. Peters' "Whistler and the English Poets of the 1890's"[9] or Michael R. Booth's "The Drunkard's Progress: Nineteenth-Century Temperance Drama."[10]

Section IV, devoted to individual Victorians of distinction, contains the greatest number of entries, some 56 per cent of the total. A poll of readers of *Victorian Studies* in 1963 confirmed what everybody knew, that Section IV is the heart of the Bibliography; that its users turn first and oftenest to this area, and that they consider it the most valuable part of the whole Bibliography. A fuller examination of this section will be the concern of the remainder of this essay.

---

[1] Some of the material here presented was utilized in a talk given at the 1965 Conference of the Pennsylvania Council of Teachers of English, University Park, Pa.; the talk subsequently appeared in the *PCTE Bulletin* for December, 1965.
[2] The entry appears on p. 279.　　[3] See p. 371.　　[4] See p. 5.　　[5] See p. 365.
[6] See p. 293.　　[7] See p. 335.　　[8] See p. 296.　　[9] See p. 89.　　[10] See p. 373.

But first, it may be of interest to the users of this volume if I summarize the number of entries in each section of the Bibliography for the ten years involved. This summary appears in Table 1.

TABLE 1. *Number of Entries per Section, 1955-64*

Year	I Bibliographical	II Social Environment	III Ideas & Literary Forms	IV Individual Writers or Figures	Total
1955	26	78	57	391	552
1956	34	102	91	376	603
1957	22	194	116	428	760
1958	27	218	121	394	760
1959	29	201	103	468	801
1960	26	262	110	443	841
1961	27	303	97	445	872
1962	25	329	83	443	880
1963	30	324	63	542	959
1964	20	270	71	533	894
Total	266	2281	912	4463	7922

One question that is of prime interest is which Victorian writers have been attracting the most attention during the past decade. Do the dozen writers at the top of the list include the cosmopolitan Thackeray, any one of the magnetic Brontës, the voluble Carlyle, the versatile Ruskin? From time to time one meets with generalizations by Victorian scholars, based no doubt on informed guesses. But only an editor of bibliographies would have the temperament that would lead him to sit down and actually count the number of studies concerning each Victorian. Yet there is no other way to arrive at the facts.

The twelve writers who head the list might all be expected to rank high. The surprising thing is not the names that do appear there, but certain names that do not appear. Here are the dozen individual Victorians who have the highest number of entries in the ten-year period:

Dickens	621	Conrad	247
Shaw	456	Tennyson	217
Yeats	305	Eliot	193
Hardy	295	Darwin	182
Arnold	274	Hopkins	157
Browning	249	Newman	154

As a *family*, the Brontës might be placed in the tenth position, but neither Emily nor Charlotte alone comes close to Newman. Scholars who wish to know how other writers fared may be interested in the next eight names on the list: Carlyle (122), Mill (109), Thackeray (106), Wilde (88), Meredith (87), Emily Brontë (76), Housman (73), and Charlotte Brontë (71). In all cases I have included cross-referenced entries in the count.

Among the twelve writers at the top are three who (I feel) should be eliminated from detailed consideration as true Victorians, even though they are included prominently in the bibliographies. One is George Bernard Shaw, who, though he began his writing career in the 1880's, belongs essentially to our century; we must recall that he outlived Scott Fitzgerald by ten years. The other two are Joseph Conrad and William Butler Yeats, both of whom are claimed by the literary history of the twentieth century. These three have been eliminated from further consideration, and the top group is thus reduced to nine.

In this top nine, three writers fall handily into each of three categories. Three of them are thought of principally as novelists (though one is significantly important in another area); three are thought of principally as poets; and three are most frequently studied as writers of expository prose (though, once again, one of these is important in another category).

Without doubt, Number One favorite among all the Victorians is Charles Dickens. Better than one out of nine titles concerned with any Victorian writer listed in Section IV during the past ten years pertains to Dickens. He receives more than twice as much attention as any other one of the top nine. This is a remarkable testament to the enduring vitality of the fictional universe that he created.

What sort of things are written about Dickens? Is there any way of characterizing the more than 600 studies published in the past ten years? Are they, for instance, dominated by an approach that for some time we have been calling the New Criticism — that is, do they consist to a large degree of studies of single works, filled with close textual analysis and a careful examination of imagery? Or do they follow other paths, standard approaches of scholars of literature for generations: a concern with the biography of the writer or with the intellectual or social history of the times in which he lived? It has seemed to me that the clearest way to discover the answers to these questions, and to arrive at a fact-based apprehension of the character of recent Dickensian scholarship in particular and of Victorian scholarship in general, is to determine the chief categories into which this vast body of scholarship divides itself.[11]

With apologies for all the shortcomings of this approach — and there are many — I have found that an examination of the scholarship has yielded a half-dozen reasonably distinct categories.

DICKENS SCHOLARSHIP

Editions & Bibliography	26
Biography & Letters	176
Sources; Comparisons with Other Writers	47
Literary or Intellectual History	197
Concern with a Single Work	93
General Aesthetic Considerations	82

There are the new scholarly editions of the writer's work, such as Kenneth Joshua Fielding's edition of *The Speeches of Charles Dickens*,[12] and there are bibliographical listings, such as Sister Mary Callista Carr's *Catalogue of the Dickens Collection at the University of Texas*.[13] New scholarly editions and items of bibliographical concern I have grouped as a single category. It is a small one: only about 4 per cent of the Dickens entries fall within it.

---

[11] The titles of many studies are named in the paragraphs which follow. By selecting these titles rather than others, I imply no judgments on their quality. These were chosen because they especially clearly help to illustrate the nature of the category under discussion.

[12] See p. 223.   [13] See p. 262.

A second group of studies consists of biographies and biographical material, including the letters. In the past ten years no biography of Dickens has been published that rivals Edgar Johnson's monumental study of his life and work that appeared in 1952. But there has been a charming pictorial biography with text by J. B. Priestly.[14] A selection of the letters of Dickens has been edited by F. W. Dupee.[15] Of course, there have been other books and a whole spate of articles concerned with the life and letters; indeed, this group constitutes a good quarter of all the work on Dickens. The number of entries in this category has been swollen, certainly, by the enthusiastic concern of the Dickens Society for every scrap of information about the life of their idol, which they publish in *The Dickensian.*

A third group of entries also deals with an area of concern to traditional scholarship: literary or intellectual history. Into this category fall such books as Philip Collins' *Dickens and Crime,*[16] and such articles as Monroe Engel's "The Politics of Dickens' Novels,"[17] or Walter S. Lazenby's dissertation "Stage Versions of Dickens's Novels in America to 1900."[18] This group of studies is slightly the largest, about 32 per cent of the total; this and the biographical studies form 60 per cent of the entries in the Bibliography. Add the other quite traditional scholarly studies — the new editions, the bibliographical materials, and the hunt for sources or comparisons with other writers — and we find that well over two-thirds of the work published about Charles Dickens is squarely in the camp of traditional scholarship.

How much has been the sort of study that is frequently associated with the New Critics? Almost all the rest. About a third consists of either critical concerns with a single work, like Louis Crompton's "Satire and Symbolism in *Bleak House*"[19] or Joseph A. Hynes's "Image and Symbol in *Great Expectations*";[20] or it consists of wider aesthetic considerations which go beyond a single work, such as George H. Ford's *Dickens and His Readers*[21] or Michael Steig's dissertation "Erotic Themes in Dickens' Novels."[22]

Number Two of the top nine is also a novelist, though his reputation as a poet has constantly been growing; this is Thomas Hardy.

DICKENS AND HARDY SCHOLARSHIP

	Dickens	Hardy
Editions & Bibliography	26	23
Biography & Letters	176	77
Sources; Comparisons with Other Writers	47	23
Literary or Intellectual History	197	49
Concern with a Single Work	93	70
General Aesthetic Considerations	82	53

When we look at the pattern of entries for Hardy we find some marked contrasts with the pattern for Dickens. The largest difference comes in the area that I believe is identifiable with the interests of the New Criticism — in the studies stressing critical concern with a single work, such as James L. Roberts' "Legend and Symbol in Hardy's 'The Three Strangers' "[23] or Frederick P. W. McDowell's "Hardy's 'Seemings or Personal Impressions': The Symbolic Use of Image and

---

[14] See p. 264.   [15] See p. 223.   [16] See p. 303.   [17] See p. 55.   [18] See p. 304.
[19] See p. 139.   [20] See p. 344.   [21] See p. 20.   [22] See p. 385.   [23] See p. 308.

Contrast in 'Jude the Obscure' ";[24] as well as studies involving wider aesthetic considerations than focus upon a single work, such as James F. Scott's dissertation "The Gothic Element in the Fiction of Thomas Hardy"[25] or Russell Hoffman's dissertation "The Idea of the Unconscious in the Novels of Thomas Hardy."[26] A full 42 per cent of the Hardy scholarship falls within these areas of concern, as compared with 28 per cent of the Dickens scholarship which reflects similar interests.

One wonders why there is this disparity, why Hardy is receiving a higher percentage of close technical analysis. My suspicion is that this sort of interest in Hardy was given a great stimulus by Albert Guerard's book on Hardy's fiction published in 1949. Among other things, Guerard opened our eyes to the elements of grotesquerie and even absurdity that lie close behind the world of Hardy's fiction. He suggested a whole new area for aesthetic exploration.

The higher percentage of studies in these areas does not mean that every other area of Hardy studies is at a low ebb. There has always been a strong interest in the biography of Hardy; indeed, almost as high a percentage of interest as in Dickens biography. The dean of Hardy biographers, Carl J. Weber, has produced two books.[27] One contains Hardy's letters to his wife, Emmie; the other, which I have found particularly wonderful, is an edition of Hardy's love poems with a long biographical introduction relating these lyrics to Hardy's strange and touching relationship to the wife who was once the girl with the corn-silk hair that he loved long ago in the land of King Arthur — who later appeared as a limited, self-proud, prudish, dumpy wife — and who, after her death, endured a transformation in Hardy's imagination, so that she became the beloved of years ago. The love poems provide a striking, and indeed startling, demonstration of how poetry arises out of life.

The third writer on the list is Matthew Arnold, who gets about equal attention as a critic and as a poet.

ARNOLD SCHOLARSHIP

Editions & Bibliography	35
Biography & Letters	42
Sources; Comparisons with Other Writers	33
Literary or Intellectual History	100
Concern with a Single Work	24
General Aesthetic Considerations	40

The two categories that stand out immediately are the first, pertaining to new scholarly editions and to bibliography, and the fourth, studies usually classified as literary or intellectual history.

The first category is strengthened by R. H. Super's edition of *The Complete Prose Works of Matthew Arnold*[28] which began appearing in 1960. There have also appeared a concordance to the poems and several books of selections. In the last few decades, Victorian scholars have been crying out for definitive texts. It is difficult for an outsider to believe the astounding number of textual corruptions in the books of only a century ago. Arnold's texts are receiving responsible attention now.

---

[24] See p. 227. [25] See p. 227. [26] See p. 387. [27] See p. 348. [28] See p. 216.

The other area of scholarship that claims many Arnold scholars is literary or intellectual history. Because of Arnold's own involvement with the mainstream of culture, a high percentage of these studies tend more toward intellectual history. Three books deal with Arnold's relationship with Romanticism,[29] and we find lengthy studies such as Charles K. Kenosian's dissertation "The Position of Matthew Arnold in the Religious Dilemma of His Time."[30]

Numbers Four and Five on the list of most-studied Victorians are the two major poets of the age, Robert Browning slightly ahead of Tennyson.

BROWNING AND TENNYSON SCHOLARSHIP

	Browning	Tennyson
Editions & Bibliography	7	14
Biography & Letters	34	28
Sources; Comparisons with Other Writers	24	29
Literary or Intellectual History	63	65
Concern with a Single Work	84	50
General Aesthetic Considerations	37	31

The Browning work is especially rich in explications or critical examinations of single poems. In the ten years, eleven doctoral dissertations[31] studied a single work (though I must confess that eight of them dealt with *The Ring and the Book*). I might say that six other dissertations[32] plus nine books by mature scholars[33] have been concerned with aesthetic considerations involving wider areas of Browning's poetry. Almost half of the works concerned with Browning fall into these two categories.

By comparison, Tennyson scholarship reflects more interest in the traditional concerns of literary history, as in Howard Mumford Jones's "The Generation of 1830."[34] This is not to say that there are not several studies of individual works; almost a quarter of the entries fall into this category — studies such as Clyde de L. Ryals' "The Moral Paradox of the Hero in *Idylls of the King*"[35] and Edward Stokes's "The Metrics of *Maud*."[36]

The five authors already mentioned account for some 70 per cent of the scholarship devoted to the top nine. I shall review the records of the other four more briefly. Number Six in totals is George Eliot with 193. Number Seven is Darwin, whose name on this list of writers of belles lettres may be unexpected;

---

[29] See Jamison, William Alexander, p. 133; James, David Gwilym, p. 257; Gottfried, Leon, p. 337.

[30] See p. 216.

[31] See Katope, Christopher G., p. 16; Henry, Marjorie Ruth, p. 93; Williams, Luster J., p. 94; Wishmeyer, William Hood, p. 94; Johnson, Agnes Boswell, p. 135; Garriott, Harold M., p. 218; Kemper, Frances C., p. 299; Columbus, Robert R., p. 339; Stevens, Lewis R., p. 340; Nelson, Charles E., p. 380; Sullivan, Mary Rose, p. 380.

[32] See Lloyd-Jones, Richard, p. 51; Rivers, Charles Leo, p. 176; Barnett, Howard A., p. 218; Blair, Carolyn L., p. 259; Buhl, Paulina E., p. 259; Docherty, Helen A., p. 299.

[33] See Federle, Walter, p. 16; Langbaum, Robert, p. 88; King, Roma A., Jr., p. 94; Foakes, Reginald Anthony, p. 128; Honan, Park, p. 259; Rivers, Charles, p. 260; Kenmare, Dallas, p. 300; Whitla, William, p. 340; Crowell, Norton B., p. 379.

[34] See p. 169. [35] See p. 356. [36] See p. 397.

but the Committee has recognized since the beginning that Darwin produced some of the most significant literature of the mid–ninteenth century, and has naturally included his name in Section IV of the Bibliography. It is interesting to see, however, that Darwin receives less attention than the preceding six writers of belles lettres. Number Eight is Gerard Manley Hopkins, the Victorian who, ever since the flourishing of the New Critical approach, has attracted so many explications of his complex and difficult poems. Each year "The Wind-hover" exerts its magnetic force upon another scholar and we have a new account of what it is really about. Number Nine is Cardinal John Henry New-man — above any one of the Brontës, Carlyle, Mill, Thackeray, Wilde — to say nothing of Meredith, the Rosettis, and Swinburne.

This list of the top nine may be a surprise, in some ways; but here it is. These top nine, out of some 81 authors catalogued each year, account for almost a third of all the scholarship devoted to Victorian writers. Table 2 summarizes the full number of entries in the bibliographies for the top nine for the past ten years.

Table 3 transmutes the figures into *percentages* rather than numbers. This tabulation is a fairer and more accurate representation of the distinctions that I have been making. For instance, in the Dickens column, it is clear that 31.8 per cent of the studies devoted to Dickens fall within the category of literary or intellectual history; that 26.1 per cent of the studies related to Hardy are associated with biography and letters; and that the major category for Arnold (36.5 per cent) is also devoted to literary or intellectual history.

It is clear that the single major area of studies concerned with George Eliot falls within literary or intellectual history, but it is significant that the combined total of studies concerned with single works or with general aesthetic considerations comprises 43 per cent of the work on Eliot. Fairly representative of the latter category are W. J. Harvey's *The Art of George Eliot*[37] and the dissertation of Rowland L. Collins, "The Present Past: The Origin and Exposition of Theme in the Prose Fiction of George Eliot."[38]

Darwin, it is obvious, is interesting chiefly as a subject for intellectual history. I would cite as illustrations such works as Asa Gray's *Darwiniana: Essays and Reviews Pertaining to Darwinism*[39] and John C. Greene's *Darwin and the Modern World View.*[40]

As I have already suggested, the greatest number of studies of Hopkins are concerned with single poems. Second to this group is the broad category which, clearly, ranks high with every writer, literary or intellectual history. Good illustrations are William Henry Walsh's *The Use of Imagination: Educational Thought and the Literary Mind*[41] or John Wain's *Gerard Manley Hopkins: An Idiom of Desperation.*[42]

Newman, as one would suspect, is most frequently studied for his association with the religious stirring of the Oxford Movement; or he is of interest for the profound spiritual quest which led to his conversion to Catholicism. Thus we see that 52.6 per cent of the Newman studies fall into the category of intellectual history, and the next highest percentage into that of biography. Meriol Trevor's

---

[37] See p. 265. [38] See p. 305. [39] See p. 342. [40] See p. 261. [41] See p. 172.
[42] See p. 308.

TABLE 2. *The Nine Leaders*

	Dickens	Hardy	Arnold	Browning	Tennyson	Eliot	Darwin	Hopkins	Newman	Total
Editions & Bibliography	26	23	35	7	14	8	16	11	22	162
Biography & Letters	176	77	42	34	28	22	21	12	41	453
Sources; Comparisons with Other Writers	47	23	33	24	29	23	22	16	4	221
Literary or Intellectual History	197	49	100	63	65	55	122	34	81	766
Concern with a Single Work	93	70	24	84	50	41	0	55	5	422
General Aesthetic Considerations	82	53	40	37	31	44	1	29	1	318
Total	621	295	274	249	217	193	182	157	154	2342

TABLE 3. *The Nine Leaders (per cent)*

	Dickens	Hardy	Arnold	Browning	Tennyson	Eliot	Darwin	Hopkins	Newman	10-Year Average
Editions & Bibliography	4.4	7.8	12.8	2.8	6.5	4.1	8.8	7.0	14.3	6.9
Biography & Letters	28.3	26.1	15.3	13.7	12.9	11.4	11.5	7.6	26.6	19.3
Sources; Comparisons with Other Writers	7.4	7.8	11.9	9.6	13.4	11.9	12.1	10.2	2.6	9.4
Literary or Intellectual History	31.8	16.6	36.5	25.3	30.0	28.5	67.0	21.7	52.6	32.7
Concern with a Single Work	15.0	23.7	8.8	33.7	23.0	21.2	0.0	35.0	3.2	18.0
General Aesthetic Considerations	13.2	18.0	14.6	14.9	14.3	22.8	0.5	18.5	0.6	13.6

two-volume life of Newman, *The Pillar of the Cloud* and *Light in Winter*,[43] has set the pace for an unusual number of biographical studies.

Table 3 completes a bibliographer's report on the vast moving glacier of Victorian scholarship. I have tried, by counting and categorizing and computing percentages, to make one corner of it seem a little tidy and comprehendable. But all the way along in this effort I have had an uneasy feeling — the feeling that must be shared by all bibliographers in the mid-1960's — of being the last man before the triumphal march of the computers.

ROBERT C. SLACK
Carnegie Institute of Technology

---

[43] See p. 351.

CONTENTS

VICTORIAN BIBLIOGRAPHY FOR 1955

Edited by AUSTIN WRIGHT

THIS bibliography has been prepared by a committee of the Victorian Literature Group of the Modern Language Association of America: Austin Wright, chairman, Carnegie Institute of Technology; William D. Templeman, University of Southern California; Francis G. Townsend, Ohio State University; Robert C. Slack, Yale University (Visiting); and Oscar Maurer, University of Texas. It attempts to list the noteworthy publications of 1955 (including reviews of these and earlier items) that have a bearing on English literature of the Victorian period, and similar publications of earlier date that have been inadvertently omitted from the preceding Victorian bibliography. Unless otherwise stated, the date of publication is 1955. Reference to a page in the bibliography for 1954, in *Modern Philology*, May, 1955, is made by the following form: See VB 1954, 260. Some cross-references are given, though not all that are possible. For certain continuing bibliographical works the reader should consult VB 1941, the last annual bibliography in which such works are listed in full.

KEY TO ABBREVIATIONS

AHR = *American Historical Review*
AL = *American Literature*
AM = *Atlantic Monthly*
APSR = *American Political Science Review*
APSS = *Annals of the American Academy of Political and Social Science*
BA = *Books Abroad*
BBDI = *Bulletin of Bibliography and Dramatic Index*
BLR = *Bodleian Library Record*
BPLQ = *Boston Public Library Quarterly*
BSP = *Papers of the Bibliographical Society of America*
CE = *College English*

CHJ = *Cambridge Historical Journal*
CJ = *Cambridge Journal*
CR = *Contemporary Review*
CWd = *Catholic World*
DA = *Dissertation Abstracts*
DUJ = *Durham University Journal*
EC = *Essays in Criticism*
EHR = *English Historical Review*
EJ = *English Journal*
ELH = *Journal of English Literary History*
ESt = *English Studies*
Ex = *Explicator*
HJ = *Hibbert Journal*
HLB = *Harvard Library Bulletin*
HLQ = *Huntington Library Quarterly*
HTB = *New York Herald Tribune Book Review*
JAA = *Journal of Aesthetics and Art Criticism*
JEGP = *Journal of English and Germanic Philology*
JEH = *Journal of Economic History*
JHI = *Journal of the History of Ideas*
JMH = *Journal of Modern History*
JP = *Journal of Philosophy*
JPE = *Journal of Political Economy*
KR = *Kenyon Review*
LJ = *Library Journal*
LQ = *Library Quarterly*
LQHR = *London Quarterly and Holborn Review*
LR = *Library Review*
M & L = *Music and Letters*
MLJ = *Modern Language Journal*
MLN = *Modern Language Notes*
MLQ = *Modern Language Quarterly*
MLR = *Modern Language Review*
N = *Nation*
N & Q = *Notes and Queries*
NCF = *Nineteenth-Century Fiction*
NEQ = *New England Quarterly*
NER = *National and English Review*
New R = *New Republic*
NS = *New Statesman and Nation*
NYTBR = *New York Times Book Review*
ParR = *Partisan Review*
PLC = *Princeton University Library Chronicle*
PMLA = *Publications of the Modern Language Association of America*
PQ = *Philological Quarterly*
PSQ = *Political Science Quarterly*
QJS = *Quarterly Journal of Speech*
QQ = *Queen's Quarterly*

1

QR   = Quarterly Review
RES   = Review of English Studies
RoR   = Romantic Review
S   = Spectator
SAQ   = South Atlantic Quarterly
SeR   = Sewanee Review
SP   = Studies in Philology
SR   = Saturday Review
StI   = Studies: An Irish Quarterly Review
TC   = Twentieth Century
TLS   = Times Literary Supplement
TQ   = University of Toronto Quarterly
USQBR   = United States Quarterly Book Review
VNL   = Victorian News Letter
VQR   = Virginia Quarterly Review
YR   = Yale Review

I. BIBLIOGRAPHICAL MATERIAL

"American Bibliography for 1954." *PMLA*, LXX, No. 2, 145–56; English Language and Literature, "X. Nineteenth Century" and "XI. Contemporary," ed. Allan G. Chester and M. A. Shaaber.

[Buckler, William E.]. "Doctoral Theses in the Victorian Period." *VNL*, No. 8 (autumn), pp. 7–8.

Cohen, I. Bernard, and Strelsky, Katharine (eds.). "Eightieth Critical Bibliography of the History of Science and Its Cultural Influences (to 1 January 1954)." *Isis*, XLVI, 111–220.

Derby, J. Raymond (ed.). "The Romantic Movement: A Selective and Critical Bibliography for the Year 1954." *PQ*, XXXIV, 97–176.

Ed. "Additions to the Parrish Collection [of Victorian Novelists]." *PLC*, XVI (1954), 37–39.

Fielding, K. J. "The John Rylands Library, Manchester." *VNL*, No. 8 (autumn), pp. 6–7.
This library is rich in MSS of the Victorian period. The most important new accession: 600 letters and papers relating to Ruskin, including over 500 letters of Ruskin, written 1873–89.

Humphries, Charles, and Smith, William C. *Music Publishing in the British Isles, from the Earliest Times to the Middle of the Nineteenth Century: A Dictionary of Engravers,* Printers, Publishers, and Music Sellers, with a Historical Introduction. London: Cassell, 1954. Pp. 360.
Rev. by Jill Vlasto in *Library*, 5th ser., X, 290–92; in *TLS*, Oct. 1, 1954, p. 632.

Matthews, William (comp.). *British Autobiographies: An Annotated Bibliography of British Autobiographies Published or Written before 1951.* Berkeley: Univ. of California Pr. Pp. 376.

Maurer, Oscar. "Recent Publications: A Selected List." *VNL*, No. 8 (autumn), pp. 9–12.

Maurer, Oscar. "Victorian Periodicals at Tx U." *Libr. Chronicle of Univ. of Texas,* V, No. 3, 18–23.
A survey of the collection of Victorian periodicals at the University of Texas Library—"one of the best on this side of the Atlantic."

Nissen, Claus. *Die illustrierten Vogelbücher, ihre Geschichte und Bibliographie.* Stuttgart: Hiersemann, 1953. Pp. 223.
Rev. favorably by G. W. Cottrell, Jr., in *Isis*, XLVI, 370–71.

Potter, Esther. "English Knitting and Crochet Books of the Nineteenth Century." *Library,* X, 25–40, 103–19.
The second instalment (pp. 103–19) is a bibliography.

The Rosenwald Collection: A Catalogue of Illustrated Books and Manuscripts, of Books from Celebrated Presses, and of Bindings and Maps, 1150–1950, the Gift of Lessing J. Rosenwald to the Library of Congress. Library of Congress: Washington, D.C., 1954. Pp. vi+292.
Rev. by Phyllis M. Giles in *Library*, X, 64–65; in *TLS*, Nov. 12, 1954, p. 728. Includes Whistleriana and a complete set of Kelmscott Press books.

Sadleir, Michael. "The Sadleir Library." *Book Collector,* IV, 115–21.
On a notable collection of Victorian fiction.

Sarton, George (ed.). "Critical Bibliography of the History and Philosophy of Science and of the History of Civilization." *Isis*, XLII (1951), 309–95 (77th bibliography); XLIII

(1952), 128–208 (78th); XLIV (1953), 102–204 (79th).

Singer, Armand Edwards. *A Bibliography of the Don Juan Theme: Versions and Criticism.* Morgantown: Univ. of West Virginia Bulletin, 1954 (Ser. 54, No. 10-1). Pp. 174.

The Sterling Library: A Catalogue of the Printed Books and Literary Manuscripts Collected by Sir Louis Sterling, Hon. D. Lit., and Presented by Him to the University of London. Privately printed, London (Wm. H. Robinson and Maggs Bros.), 1954. Pp. xviii+614.

Rev. by G. L. K. in *Library*, X, 72–73; in *TLS*, Aug. 13, 1954, p. 520. The collection ranges from the fifteenth through the twentieth centuries.

Stewart, James D., with Muriel E. Hammond and Erwin Saenger (eds.). *British Union-Catalogue of Periodicals: A Record of the Periodicals of the World, from the Seventeenth Century to the Present Day, in British Libraries.* Vol. I: *A–C.* London: Butterworth. Pp. xxi+691.

Thornton, John L., and Tully, R. I. J. *Scientific Books, Libraries, and Collectors: A Study of Bibliography and the Book Trade in Relation to Science.* London: Library Assoc., 1954. Pp. x+288.

Tooley, R. V. *English Books with Coloured Plates, 1790 to 1860: A Bibliographical Account of the Most Important Books Illustrated by English Artists in Colour Aquatint and Colour Lithography.* London: Batsford, 1954. Pp. viii+424.

Rev. by P. H. M. in *Library*, X, 134–37; in *TLS*, Dec. 17, 1954, p. 828.

Townsend, Francis G. (comp.). "Recent Publications: A Selected List." *VNL*, No. 7 (April), pp. 10–19.

Townsend, Francis G. "Victorian Studies, 1952–1955: A Catalogue of Complaints and Compliments." *VNL*, No. 8 (autumn), pp. 1–3.

Untermeyer, Louis. *Makers of the Modern World: The Lives of Ninety-two Writers, Artists, Scientists, Statesmen, Inventors, Philosophers, Composers, and Other Creators Who Formed the Pattern of Our Century.* New York: Simon & Schuster. Pp. xx+809.

Rev. briefly in *HTB*, Sept. 25, p. 11; by E. M. Oboler in *LJ*, Apr. 1, p. 799; by G. W. Johnson in *NYTBR*, Apr. 28, p. 7; by Edgar Johnson in *SR*, Oct.. 1, p. 22. Victorians: Darwin, Marx, Hardy, Hopkins, Shaw, Housman, Yeats, Wells.

[Weber, Carl J.]. "The Colby College Press." *Colby Libr. Quart.*, IV, 6–16.

Contains a list of publications of the Press, including works about or by Hardy, Housman, Dickens.

Wright, Austin (ed.). "Victorian Bibliography for 1954." *MP*, LII, 233–61.

The Year's Work in English Studies, Vol. XXXIV (1953). Ed. for the English Assoc. by Frederick S. Boas and Beatrice White. London: Oxford Univ. Pr., 1955. "The Nineteenth Century and After," I and II, pp. 255–312; "Bibliographica," pp. 313–24.

II. ECONOMIC, POLITICAL, RELIGIOUS, AND SOCIAL ENVIRONMENT

Allen, H. C. *Great Britain and the United States: A History of Anglo-American Relations (1783–1952).* New York: St Martin's Pr. Pp. 1024.

Rev. favorably by G. C. Osborn in *APSS*, CCCII, 153–54; in *Current Hist.*, XXVIII, 319; by Marcus Cunliffe in *EHR*, LXIX, 467–69; by Crane Brinton in *HTB*, May 1, p. 3; by Richard W. Van Alstyne in *Mississippi Valley Hist. Rev.*, XLII, 363–64; briefly in *QQ*, CCXCIII, 421; by Geoffrey Brunn in *SR*, June 4, p. 17; in *TLS*, May 20, p. 261.

Banks, J. A. *Prosperity and Parenthood: A Study of Family Planning among the Victorian Middle Classes.* New York: Grove Pr. Pp. vi+240.

Rev. by John Mogey in *Amer. Jour. Sociol.*, LXI, 172; by E. Grebenik in *Economica*, new ser., XXII, 270–71.

Barker, Felix. "The Life and Strange Death of Eleanor Marx." *Cornhill Mag.*, CLXVIII, 167–79.

Daughter of Karl Marx.

Briggs, Asa. *Victorian People*. . . . See VB 1954, 236.

Rev. favorably by Noel Annan in *Adelphi*, XXXI, 226–31; by Richard D. Altick in *HTB*, Oct. 30, p. 6; by George Dangerfield in *N*, Nov. 19, p. 446; by Roger Fulford in *NER*, CLXIV, 109–10; by John Raymond in *NS*, Jan. 8, pp. 47–48; by Hans Kohn in *NYTBR*, Oct. 30, p. 41; briefly in *QR*, CCXCIII, 274–75; favorably by George Woodcock in *SR*, Feb. 4, 1956, pp. 32–34.

Chadwick, Owen. *The Founding of Cuddesdon College*. Oxford: Cuddesdon College.

Founded in 1854 by Samuel Wilberforce: a controversial episode in the Victorian Church of England.

Chevenix-Trench, C. G. "A Scottish School in the '90s." *Blackwood's*, CCLXXVIII, 108–14.

Clements, Roger V. "British Investment and American Legislative Restrictions in the Trans-Mississippi West, 1880–1900." *Mississippi Valley Hist. Rev.*, XLII, 207–28.

Court, W. H. B. *A Concise Economic History of Britain from 1750 to Recent Times*. London: Cambridge Univ. Pr., 1954. Pp. viii+368.

Rev. favorably by Walter M. Stern in *Economica*, new ser., XXII, 272–73; by A. J. Youngson in *Econ. Jour.*, LXV, 131–33; by Henry Hamilton in *EHR*, LXIX, 336–37; briefly in *QR*, CCXCIII, 129; by William Hornby in *S*, Jan. 21, p. 80; by Herbert Heaton in *SR*, Jan. 8, p. 20.

Davidson, Maurice. *The Royal Society of Medicine: The Realization of an Ideal (1805–1955)*. London: Royal Society of Medicine. Pp. 201.

Rev. in *TLS*, Aug. 12, p. 455.

Disher, Maurice Willson. *Victorian Song from Dive to Drawing Room*. New York: Macmillan. Pp. 256.

Rev. by Arthur Marshall in *NS*, Nov. 5, p. 584; by Leo Lerman in *NYTBR*, Feb. 12, 1956, p. 22; by George Woodcock in *SR*, Feb. 4, 1956, pp. 32–34; in *TLS*, Nov. 11, p. 667.

Downer, Alan. "The Reminiscences of William Charles Macready." *PLC*, XVII, 51–52.

The manuscript of the reminiscences contains unpublished material on Macready's early life.

Ellis, Cuthbert Hamilton. *British Railway History: An Outline from the Accession of William IV to the Nationalisation of Railways*. Vol. I: *1830–1876*. New York. Macmillan. Pp. 443.

Rev. in *NS*, Jan. 8, p. 51; by A. N. Marlow in *S*, Feb. 25, p. 236.

Elton, Lord. *General Gordon* . . . [in America, *Gordon of Khartoum*. New York: Knopf, 1954]. . . . See VB 1954, 236.

Rev. by Rodney Gilbert in *HTB*, Jan. 23, p. 4; by J. C. Shipman in *LJ*, Dec. 15, 1954, p. 2440; by Keith Hutchison in *N*, July 2, p. 17; by Cecil Woodham-Smith in *NYTBR*, Jan. 16, p. 6; by H. M. Champness in *S*, Oct. 29, 1954, p. 529; by J. L. Godfrey in *SAQ*, LIV, 556–57; by George Dangerfield in *SR*, Jan. 29, p. 17; unfavorably by Michael Edwardes in *TC*, CLVIII, 87–89; by Harry Champness in *YR*, XLIV, 612–16.

Evans, Joan. *The Endless Web: John Dickinson and Company, Ltd., 1804–1954*. London: Cape.

Rev. by William Hornby in *S*, Dec. 16, p. 848; in *TLS*, Dec. 23, p. 784. The history of a well-known paper-making firm.

Faber, Geoffrey Cust. *Oxford Apostles: A Character Study of the Oxford Movement*. London: Penguin. Pp. 442.

Gernsheim, Helmut, and Gernsheim, Alison. *Roger Fenton, Photographer of the Crimean War: His Photographs and His Letters from the Crimea, with an Essay on His Life and Work*. London: Secker, 1954. Pp. 106.

Rev. by Gladys Scott Thomson in *Apollo*, LXI, 124–25; in *TLS*, Jan. 14, p. 27.

Glasgow, Eric. "The Establishment of the *Northern Star* Newspaper." *History*, XXXIX, 54–67.

On the leading Chartist journal, 1837 ff.

Glasstone, Victor. "The Comedy Theatre." *Theatre Notebook*, X, 17–20.

Brief history of the Comedy Theatre in Panton Street, Haymarket, 1881 to the present.

Glover, Willis B. *Evangelical Nonconformists and Higher Criticism in the Nineteenth Century*. London: Independent Pr. Pp. 296.

Rev. in *TLS*, May 6, suppl. p. iv.

Gooch, G. P. "Victorian Memories." *CR*, Vol. CLXXXVIII. ("I, II. England in the 'Eighties," pp. 235–41, 307–11; "III. Cambridge in the 'Nineties," pp. 382–87.) (To be continued.)

Gordon, Scott. "The London *Economist* and the High Tide of Laissez Faire." *JPE*, LXIII, 461–88.

This major article documents the inextricable connection between belief in the beauty of a providentially ordered nature and belief in a providential order in human affairs which laws can only hinder. The principal writers who promulgated the laissez faire doctrine among the bourgeois intellectuals of the 1840's and 1850's were James Wilson and Thomas Hodgskin.—F. G. T.

Guest, Ivor. "Parodies of *Giselle* on the English Stage (1841–1871)." *Theatre Notebook*, IX, 38–46.

Guest, Ivor. *The Romantic Ballet in England.* London: Phoenix, 1954. Pp. 176.

Rev. by I. K. F. in *Theatre Notebook*, IX, 54–56; in *TLS*, Nov. 19, 1954, p. 732. Concerned especially with the ballet in England to 1858.

Habakkuk, H. J. "Family Structure and Economic Change in Nineteenth-Century Europe." *JEH*, XV, 1–12.

The effect of inheritance laws in England and on the Continent.

Harden, Anne. "A Diary of the Indian Mutiny." *N & Q*, new ser., II, 352–56.

Excerpts from the diary of Mrs. Helena Angelo, wife of a lieutenant of the 16th Native Infantry, May–July, 1857.

Hart, Jenifer. "Reform of the Borough Police, 1835–1856." *EHR*, LXIX, 411–27.

The traditional view has been that the metropolitan police forced an exodus of criminals from London to the towns, which led to an improvement of the borough police in 1835, which in turn caused an exodus of criminals to the rural areas, which led to legislation to improve the county police in 1839. Actually, the borough police forces were organized slowly and somewhat inefficiently. The true cause for the bill to improve the rural police, introduced July 24, 1839, was Chartist agitation.—F. G. T.

Henderson, W. O. *Britain and Industrial Europe, 1750–1870: Studies in British Influ-* ence on the Industrial Revolution in Western Europe. Liverpool: Liverpool Univ. Pr., 1954. Pp. vii+255.

Rev. by Herbert Heaton in *AHR*, LX, 399–400; briefly in *Economica*, new ser., XXII, 96; by Arthur Birnie in *Scottish Hist. Rev.*, XXXIV, 167–68; in *TLS*, Aug. 13, 1954, p. 511.

Herd, Harold. *Seven Editors.* London: Allen. Pp. 126.

Rev. in *TLS*, Sept. 9, p. 522. Includes chapters on William Hone, William Maginn, and Albany Fonblanque.

Hill, Richard. "The Gordon Literature." *DUJ*, XLVII, 97–101.

England has had other heroes whose deaths inspired bad poetry and worse prose, but Gordon literature surpasseth all others in barbarism. Nor are modern books, such as those by the Hansons, Lord Elton, and Charles Beatty, much of an improvement. They are more sophisticated, but they are guilty of the same error, namely, an abysmal ignorance of Egypt and the Sudan. Even scholarly Egyptian works on the subject seem unknown to English biographers.—F. G. T.

Hitchcock, Henry Russell. *Early Victorian Architecture in Britain. . . .* See VB 1954, 237.

Rev. by H. H. in *Connoisseur*, CXXXVI, 60–61; favorably by Graham Hough in *NS*, Feb. 26, pp. 293–94; by John Betjeman in *S*, May 6, pp. 591–92; by Wayne Andrews in *SR*, Jan. 1, p. 67; in *TLS*, June 3, p. 300; in *USQBR*, XI, 45.

Jasper, R. C. D. *Prayer Book Revision in England, 1800–1900.* London: S.P.C.K., 1954. Pp. 148.

Rev. by Claude Jenkins in *EHR*, LXIX, 157–58; in *TLS*, May 6, suppl. p. xii.

Joll, James. *The Second International.* London: Weidenfeld. Pp. 240.

Rev. in *TLS*, Aug. 12, p. 453. A history of the group, 1889–1914.

Jones, L. E. *A Victorian Boyhood.* New York: St Martin's Pr. Pp. 244.

Rev. briefly by Karl Brown in *LJ*, Apr. 1, p. 795; by K. John in *NS*, Feb. 12, p. 216; by Isabel Quigley in *S*, Feb. 11, p. 162; in *TLS*, Feb. 18, p. 99.

Kendall, James. *Michael Faraday, Man of Simplicity.* New York: Roy. Pp. 196.

Rev. in *TLS*, Feb. 18, p. 102.

Laver, James. *Victorian Vista.* . . . See VB 1954, 237 (incorrectly listed under "Lauer").

Rev. by Carlos Baker in *NYTBR*, Nov. 27, p. 10; by George Woodcock in *SR*, Feb. 4, 1956, pp. 32–34.

Leconfield, Lady Maud (ed.). *Three Howard Sisters: Selections from the Writings of Lady Caroline Lascelles, Lady Dover, and Countess Gower, 1825 to 1833.* Revised and completed by John Gore. London: Murray.

Rev. in *TLS*, Apr. 29, p. 194.

Lee, Arthur Gould (ed.). *The Empress Frederick Writes to Sophie: Letters, 1889–1901.* London: Faber. Pp. 360.

Rev. by Kay Dick in *S*, Sept. 16, pp. 370–71; in *TLS*, Aug. 5, p. 442. Letters of Queen Victoria's eldest daughter to her favorite child, later Queen of Greece.

Lennon, E. James. "The Pro-Northern Movement in England, 1861–1865." *QJS*, XLI, 27–37.

Lillibridge, G. D. *Beacon of Freedom: The Impact of American Democracy upon Great Britain, 1830–1870.* Philadelphia: Univ. of Pennsylvania Pr. Pp. xvi+159.

Rev. by F. H. Herrick in *AHR*, LXI, 174; by Arthur Mann in *Mississippi Valley Hist. Rev.*, XLII, 324–26; in *TLS*, Sept. 23, p. 554.

Lipman, V. D. *Social History of the Jews in England, 1850–1950.* London: Watts, 1954.

Rev. by Irene Marinoff in *CR*, CLXXXVIII, 131–32; by Charles Johnson in *EHR*, LXIX, 342–43; in *TLS*, Feb. 11, p. 93.

Mackenzie-Grieve, Averil. *Clara Novello, 1818–1908.* London: Bles. Pp. 338.

Rev. by P. M. Y. in *M & L*, XXXVI, 278–79; by Kay Dick in *S*, Sept. 16, pp. 370–71; in *TLS*, June 10, p. 314. Between 1832 and 1860 she was "the greatest of English singers."

Macqueen-Pope, W. *Back Numbers.* London: Hutchinson.

Rev. in *TLS*, Apr. 29, p. 205. A nostalgic defense of Victorianism in general.

Masters, David. *The Plimsoll Mark.* London: Cassell.

Rev. by Norman Mackenzie in *NS*, Dec. 31, p. 886. Biography of a Victorian reformer, Samuel Plimsoll (1824–98).

Morley, Malcolm. "Early Theatres in Marylebone." *Theatre Notebook*, X, 16–17.

Brief history of the Marylebone Theatre, later the West London (1832–93).

Mumby, F. A., and Stallybrass, Frances. *From Swan Sonnenschein to George Allen and Unwin Ltd.* London: Allen. Pp. 100.

Rev. by Grace Banyard in *CR*, CLXXXVIII, 137; in *TLS*, Aug. 19, p. 484. Important chapters in the history of Victorian publishing.

Murphy, Howard R. "The Ethical Revolt against Christian Orthodoxy in Early Victorian England." *AHR*, LX, 800–817.

Shows convincingly that the Victorian religious crisis was produced by a conflict between certain cherished dogmas and the "meliorist ethical bias" of the age. Illustrated by early works of Francis William Newman, J. A. Froude, and George Eliot. A valuable contribution.—F. G. T.

Parker, W. M. "Dean Milman and *The Quarterly Review*." *QR*, CCXCIII, 30–43.

Pearl, Cyril. *The Girl with the Swansdown Seat.* London: Muller. Pp. 270.

Rev. favorably by V. S. Pritchett in *NS*, Aug. 20, pp. 218–19. According to the reviewer, a good account of Victorian whores and their homes.

Petrie, Sir Charles. *The Carlton Club.* London: Eyre. Pp. 224.

Rev. by Christopher Hollis in *NER*, CXLV, 110–11; in *NS*, July 23, p. 113; in *QR*, CCXCIII, 549–50; by J. H. Plumb in *S*, July 15, p. 101; in *TLS*, July 15, p. 394. History of a famous Tory club.

Pope-Hennessy, James. *Lord Crewe, 1854–1945: The Likeness of a Liberal.* London: Constable.

Rev. by John Raymond in *NS*, Nov. 26, pp. 710–12; by Norman St. John-Stevas in *S*, Dec. 23, pp. 875–76; in *TLS*, Dec. 16, p. 758. Biography of the son of Monckton Milnes, Lord Houghton.

Postgate, Raymond. *The Story of a Year: 1848.* New York: Oxford Univ. Pr. Pp. 286.

Rev. briefly by Eric Gillett in *NER*, CXLV, 285–86; by A. J. P. Taylor in *NS*, Oct. 22, p. 517;

by Keith Hutchison in *NYTBR*, Feb. 19, 1956, p. 3; in *TLS*, Nov. 4, p. 651.

Potter, J. "The British Timber Duties, 1815–60." *Economica*, new ser., XXII, 122–36.

At one time the import duty on Baltic timber was so high that ships actually carried it to Canada so it could be called Canadian timber and then brought it back across the Atlantic to Great Britain for well under the cost of a direct shipment from the Baltic plus the duty. The result was an artificially high price which encouraged the use of iron. At the same time, ships in the Canadian timber trade, which made the western trip almost empty, carried emigrants to North America for as little as 25s. in the 1830's.

R. "Portraits of Victorian Celebrities." *N & Q*, new ser., II, 83–84.

Ratcliffe, S. K. *The Story of South Place*. London: Watts. Pp. 84.

Rev. in *TLS*, Mar. 11, p. 153. A history of the chapel which evolved, under W. J. Fox, Moncure Conway, and others, from liberal theology to free thought.

Reid, J. H. Stewart. *The Origins of the British Labour Party*. Minneapolis: Univ. of Minnesota Pr.

Rev. briefly by Rudolph Heimanson in *LJ*, Nov. 1, pp. 2509–10.

Rupp, E. G. "Victorian Humanity: The Influence of Victorian Nonconformity." *Listener*, Mar. 17, pp. 469–71.

Sanders, Charles Richard. *The Strachey Family*. . . . See VB 1954, 239.

Rev. in *Economist*, CLXX (1954), 946; by Ross H. McLean in *Emory Univ. Quart.*, IX (1953), 252–53; by E. D. O'Brien in *Illus. London News*, Feb. 27, 1954, p. 334; by George H. Ford in *MLN*, LXX, 67–68; by Richard Hughes in *S*, Feb. 5, 1954, pp. 156–57; by Thomas H. English in *South Atlantic Bull.*, XX (1954), 14; in *TLS*, Jan. 29, 1954, p. 73 (leading article, "Ink in the Blood"); by Curtis C. Davis in *Virginia Mag. Hist. and Biog.*, LXII (1954), 352–53.

Saunders, Edith. *The Age of Worth, Couturier to the Empress Eugénie*. Bloomington, Ind.: Indiana Univ. Pr. Pp. ix+218.

Rev. briefly by Katherine Tappert Willis in *LJ*, Sept. 15, p. 1910. Biography of the Englishman who dominated European fashion in the nineteenth century.

Schumpeter, J. A. *History of Economic Analysis*. New York: Oxford Univ. Pr., 1954. Pp. xxv+1260.

Rev. favorably by A. W. Coats in *Economica*, new ser., XXII, 171–74; in a review article by Lionel Robbins in *Quart. Jour. Econ.*, LXIX, 1–22; by E. J. Hobsbawm in *Sci. & Soc.*, XIX, 71–75. Part III deals with the period 1780–1870, covering the "English Classical school."

Simmons, J. S. G. "The Duke of Wellington and the Vice-Chancellorship [of Oxford] in 1844." *BLR*, V (1954), 37–52.

Has much reference to the Tractarians, including John Henry Newman.

Simons, Richard B. "T. R. Malthus on British Society." *JHI*, XVI, 60–75.

A notable study of the author of the "Malthusian" birth-control movement and the man who also inspired, "by Darwin's explicit statement," the doctrine of the survival of the fittest—used in turn by Bagehot to justify competition and, as modified by T. H. Green, to justify social legislation intended to provide an even start for all.—W. D. T.

Snyder, Louis L. (ed.). *Fifty Major Documents of the Nineteenth Century*. New York: Van Nostrand. Pp. 191.

A selection of official documents and of contemporary eyewitness accounts of major events of the century.

Speaight, George. *The History of the English Puppet Theatre*. New York: DeGraff. Pp. 350.

Rev. by Waldo S. Lanchester in *Theatre Notebook*, X, 30–31. One chapter is entitled "Marionettes of the 19th Century."

Stranks, C. J. *Dean Hook*. London: Mowbray.

Rev. by Ronald Leicester in *DUJ*, XLVII, 129–30; in *TLS*, Jan. 7, p. 2.

Taffs, Winifred. "The General Election of 1868." *CR*, CLXXXVIII, 178–82.

Gladstone versus Disraeli in the first election held after the Tory Reform Bill.

Taylor, A. J. "The Miners' Association of Great Britain and Ireland, 1842–48: A Study in the Problem of Integration." *Economica*, new ser., XXII, 45–60.

A short, well-written account of the rise to national power of the Miners' Association established at Wakefield in 1842, of the great strike in Northumberland and Durham in 1844, and of the reasons for its failure and the virtual dissolution of the union in 1848.—F. G. T.

Taylor, A. J. P. *The Struggle for Mastery in Europe: 1848–1918.* (*Oxford History of Modern Europe*, Vol. II.) New York: Oxford Univ. Pr., 1954. Pp. xxxvi+638.

Rev. by Hans Kohn in *APSS*, CCXCVIII, 230–31; by Douglas Woodruff in *Dublin Rev.*, CCXXIX, 216–19; by Louis Barron in *LJ*, Feb. 15, p. 459; briefly in *N*, Apr. 23, p. 353; by Asa Briggs in *NS*, Nov. 6, 1954, p. 586; by Fritz Stern in *PSQ*, LXX, 112; by Henry Fairlie in *S*, Nov. 19, 1954, p. 628; by Gordon A. Craig in *SR*, July 16, p. 28; in *TLS*, Nov. 26, 1954, p. 749.

Taylor, Basil. *Animal Painting in England from Barlow to Landseer.* London: Penguin. Pp. 136.

Rev. in *TLS*, May 6, p. 232.

Terris, Ellaline [Lady Hicks]. *Just a Little Piece of String.* London: Hutchinson.

Rev. by Arthur Marshall in *NS*, Nov. 5, p. 584; in *TLS*, Nov. 4, p. 652. An actress' autobiography, with reminiscences of Shaw, Barrie, and others.

Thomas, Brinley. *Migration and Economic Growth: A Study of Great Britain and the Atlantic Economy.* New York: Cambridge Univ. Pr., 1954. Pp. xxv+362.

Rev. by Rowland T. Berthoff in *AHR*, LX, 340–42; by A. K. Cairncross in *Economica*, new ser., XXII, 174–76; by Ian Bowen in *EHR*, LXIX, 291–92; by Bert F. Hoselitz in *JMH*, XXVII, 423–25; in *TLS*, June 4, 1954, p. 359. Mainly a study of the migration between Great Britain and the United States in the last century.

Thomson, Lady Ethel. *Clifton Lodge.* London: Hutchinson.

Rev. by William Plomer in *Listener*, Mar. 24, p. 531; by Richard Lister in *NS*, Apr. 2, p. 479; by Pansy Pakenham in *S*, Mar. 25, pp. 361–62; in *TLS*, Apr. 29, p. 212. Memories of a late Victorian childhood.

Trewin, J. C. *Mr. Macready: A Nineteenth-Century Tragedian and His Theatre.* London: Harrap. Pp. 272.

Rev. in *Mercure de France*, No. 1107, p. 535; by Montague Slater in *NS*, Nov. 12, pp. 636–37; by John Wain in *S*, Sept. 9, pp. 339–40; in *TLS*, Sept. 9, p. 524.

Wearmouth, R. F. *Methodism and the Struggle of the Working Classes, 1850–1900.* Leicester: Backus. Pp. 286.

Rev. in *TLS*, May 6, suppl. p. iv.

Webb, Robert Kiefer. *The British Working Class Reader, 1790–1848: Literacy and Social Tension.* New York: Columbia Univ. Pr. Pp. 192.

Rev. by G. D. H. Cole in *EHR*, LXIX, 499–500; briefly by Dorothy Kuhn Oko in *LJ*, Oct. 1, p. 2174; by Asa Briggs in *NS*, Mar. 5, p. 332; in *TLS*, Mar. 4, p. 135. Examines the degree of working-class literacy during this period and considers the reading matter produced for working-class consumption.

Webb, R. K. "A Whig Inspector." *JMH*, XXVII, 352–64.

Hugh Seymour Tremenheere, an active inspector and royal commissioner in several fields in the forties, fifties, and sixties.

Williamson, Chilton. "Bentham Looks at America." *PSQ*, LXX, 543–51.

Bentham heartily approved of the United States in so far as it had thrown off the restraints of precedent and become a nation where the majority ruled, but he deplored America's judicial adherence to the common law.

Woodiwiss, John C. "Nineteenth-Century Profiles." *Apollo*, LXI, 12–14.

Complexities in silhouettes.

Woodruff, Philip. *The Men Who Ruled India.* Vol. II: *The Guardians.* . . . See VB 1954, 239.

Rev. by M. N. Chatterjee in *Antioch Rev.*, XV, 118–21; briefly in *APSR*, XLIX, 253; in *Current Hist.*, XXVIII, 63; by Harry Lindsay in *HJ*, LIII, 202; by J. L. Mish in *LJ*, Dec. 15, 1954, p. 2446; in *TLS*, Feb. 18, p. 102; by R. L. Park in *YR*, XLIV, 446.

III. MOVEMENTS OF IDEAS AND LITERARY FORMS

Allen, Louis. "The Authorship of the Letter to the *Univers.*" *N & Q*, new ser., II, 124–26.

A letter which was part of the uproar in the wake of Tract 90.

Allen, Walter. *The English Novel: A Short Critical History.* New York: Dutton. Pp. 454.

Rev. by Roger Becket in *HTB*, Aug. 7, p. 3; briefly in *NCF*, X, 246–47; briefly by John R. Willingham in *LJ*, July, p. 1578; by Giles Romilly in *NS*, Oct. 30, 1954, p. 550; by H. T. Moore in *NYTBR*, Aug. 7, p. 4; briefly in *QR*, CCXCIII, 136–37; by John Wain in *S*, Oct. 22, 1954, p. 500; by H. C. Webster in *SR*, Sept. 10, p. 39; in *TLS*, Nov. 19, 1954, p. 739.

Allen, Walter. *Six Great Novelists*. London: Hamilton.

Rev. briefly by Jane Bacon in *Dickensian*, LI, 189; in *NS*, Mar. 12, p. 366. Includes treatment of Dickens, Stevenson, Conrad.

Appleman, Phillip Dean. "Darwin and the Literary Critics." *DA*, XV, 1618.

The body of the dissertation gives "detailed examinations of the effect of evolution on three Victorian critics, John Addington Symonds, Walter Pater, and Sir Leslie Stephen."

Assad, Thomas Joseph. "The Near East and the Late Victorians: An Approach to Sir Richard Francis Burton, Wilfrid Scawen Blunt, and Charles Montague Doughty." *Summ. Doct. Diss., Univ. of Wisconsin*, XV, 593–95.

Baetzhold, Howard George. "Mark Twain's Attitudes toward England." *Summ. Doct. Diss., Univ. of Wisconsin*, XV, 595–97.

Includes treatment of Arnold, Browning, Carlyle, Dickens, Basil Hall, Kipling, Harriet Martineau, Walter Scott.

Beach, Joseph Warren. "Modern Fiction and the Threshold of Morality." In Walter R. Agard and Others, *The Humanities for Our Time* (Univ. of Kansas Pr., 1949), pp. 67–86. (Inadvertently omitted earlier.)

Bishop, George Reginald. "Sainte-Beuve and the Poetic Art." *DA*, XV, 411.

Blotner, Joseph L. *The Political Novel*. ("Doubleday Short Studies in Political Science.") New York: Doubleday. Pp. xii+100.

Includes brief treatment of Conrad, Disraeli, George Eliot, Meredith, Trollope, Mrs. Ward.

Boner, Harold A. *Hungry Generations: The Nineteenth-Century Case against Malthusianism*. New York: King's Crown Pr. Pp. viii+234.

Rev. by J. A. Beegle in *Amer. Soc. Rev.*, XX, 500; by Frank H. Hankins in *APSS*, CCC, 156–57; by Lloyd Sorenson in *Comp. Lit.*, VII, 368–71; by Robert Bierstedt in *SR*, Aug. 13, p. 25.

Bowra, Sir Cecil Maurice. *Inspiration and Poetry*. New York: St Martin's Pr. Pp. 266.

Rev. by Geoffrey Brereton in *NS*, July 2, pp. 18–19; by William Barrett in *NYTBR*, Aug. 14, p. 4; by Donat O'Donnell in *S*, July 8, p. 53; in *TLS*, June 17, p. 334. Includes short studies of Pater and the lyrical poetry of Hardy.

Bredsdorff, Elias. *H. C. Andersen og England* Copenhagen: Rosenkilde.

Rev. in *TLS*, Feb. 4, p. 71. Discusses Andersen's knowledge of English literature, his dealings with English publishers and translators, his reputation in English literary circles, and his reception by contemporary reviewers.

Bredsdorff, Elias. "Hans Andersen and Scotland." *Blackwood's*, CCLXXVII, 297–312.

An account of Andersen's visit to Scotland in 1847.

Coleman, Marion Moore. *Adam Mickiewicz in English, 1827–1955*. Cambridge Springs, Pa.: Alliance College, 1954.

Rev. by Florian Smieja in *Slavonic and East European Rev.*, XXXIII, 589—a revised and enlarged ed. of a work that appeared in 1940, treating the translations from a Polish author.

Dahl, Curtis. "The Victorian Wasteland." *CE*, XVI, 341–47.

"Wasteland" imagery in Tennyson, Browning, Arnold, Swinburne, and Thomson.

Dale, E. Hilda. *La Poésie française en Angleterre, 1850–1890*. Paris: Didier, 1954. Pp. 147.

Rev. by C. M. Bowra in *French Studies*, IX, 170–72; by Julie Stevenson in *Rev. des sciences humaines*, No. 80, p. 545.

Daniel, Maggie Browne. "A Study of William Dean Howells' Attitude toward and Criticism of the English and Their Literature." *Summ. Doct. Diss., Univ. of Wisconsin*, XV, 603–4.

Includes treatment of Arnold, C. Brontë, Dickens, Eliot, Hardy, C. Kingsley, Kipling, Macaulay, Meredith, Morris, Reade, Tennyson, Thackeray, Trollope.

Dorson, Richard M. "The First Group of British Folklorists." *Jour. Amer. Folklore*, LXVIII, 1–8, 333–40.

Four pioneer British folklorists: Thomas Crofton Croker (1798–1854); Thomas Keightley (1789–1872); Thomas Wright (1810–77); Francis Douce (1757–1834).

Dyson, A. E. "The Technique of Debunking." *TC*, CLVII, 244–56.

Dyson examines how Strachey's rhetoric distorts the truth, although every quotation and every fact can be documented. Dyson concludes that Strachey was a fine novelist but a horrible biographer. This essay is a good place to send students afflicted with Stracheyism.—F. G. T.

Fischer, Walther. *Deutscher Kultureinfluss am Viktorianischen Hofe bis zur Gründung des Deutschen Reiches (1870)*. ("Geissener Beiträge zur deutschen Philologie," No. 97.) Geissen, 1951.

Rev. by Edgar Mertner in *Anglia*, LXII, 495–97.

Graves, Robert. "These Be Your Gods, O Israel!" *EC*, V, 129–50.

Treats several Victorian poets and more recent ones. See comments in *EC*, V, 293–98.

Hale, J. R. *England and the Italian Renaissance: The Growth of Interest in Its History and Art*. London: Faber, 1954. Pp. 216.

Rev. by Alwin Thaler in *Shakespeare Quart.*, VI, 178–79; in *TLS*, June 18, 1954, p. 392. Includes treatment of Ruskin, Symonds, etc.

Hopkins, Kenneth. *The Poets Laureate*. London: Lane, 1954. Pp. 295.

Rev. briefly in *Adelphi*, XXXI, 202–3; by J. Loiseau in *Études anglaises*, VIII, 171–72; by Gerald D. MacDonald in *LJ*, Feb. 1, p. 366; by Naomi Lewis in *NS*, Jan. 29, pp. 150–51; by DeLancey Ferguson in *NYTBR*, Mar. 13, p. 4; briefly in *QR*, CCXCIII, 277–78; in *TLS*, June 14, p. 26.

Hughes, Arthur. "Science in English Encyclopaedias, 1704–1875. IV. Theories of the Earth." *Ann. Sci.*, XI, 74–92.

For the Victorian, an excellent short account of theories of the Deluge before Lyell.

Irvine, William. *Apes, Angels, and Victorians: The Story of Darwin, Huxley, and Evolution*. New York: McGraw-Hill. Pp. 399.

Rev. by Carl H. Ketcham in *Arizona Quart.*, XI, 263–64; by J. C. Gregory in *CR*, CLXXXVIII, 418; by Joseph Wood Krutch in *HTB*, Apr. 3, p. 5; by W. E. Swinton in *Lit. Guide*, LXX, 8–9; briefly by Elizabeth M. Cole in *LJ*, Apr. 15, p. 882; in *N*, Apr. 30, p. 380; briefly by Eric Gillett in *NER*, CXLV, 108; by Francis Huxley in *NS*, Aug. 6, pp. 165–66; by I. B. Cohen in *NYTBR*, Apr. 3, p. 1; by C. Collins in *S*, Sept. 23, pp. 397–98; by Ruth Moore in *SR*, Apr. 23, p. 16; in *TLS*, Aug. 19, p. 471; in *USQBR*, XI, 313; by W. R. Leslie in *VQR*, XXXI, 480–82; by L. E. Eiseley in *YR*, XLIV, 632–34. Important for biography of Darwin, biography of Huxley, and intellectual history.

Jelavich, Barbara. "The British Traveller in the Balkans: The Abuses of Ottoman Administration in the Slavonic Provinces." *Slavonic and East European Rev.*, XXXIII, 396–413.

Carefully annotated; considers several Victorian travel books on the Balkans; one note directs the student wishing a biography of travel books on the Near East to see F. W. Hasluck, *Christianity and Islam under the Sultans* (Oxford, 1952), I, xxi–lxiv, and Shirley Howard Weber, *Voyages and Travels in the Near East Made during the XIX Century* (Princeton, 1952).

Keller, Ernst. *Kulturbilder aus Viktorianischen Autobiographien*. ("Schweizer anglistische Arbeiten," Vol. XXIX.) Bern, 1951.

Rev. by W. Fischer in *Anglia*, LXXIII, 246–47.

Koziol, Herbert. "Zur Aufnahme deutscher Literaturwerke in England." *Anglia*, LXXIII, 207–12.

Leavis, Q. D. "A Note on Literary Indebtedness: Dickens, George Eliot, Henry James." *Hudson Rev.*, VIII, 423–28.

Three uses of the "Roman scene" in fiction to illustrate two kinds of indebtedness.

Lemaître, Henri. *Le Paysage anglais à l'aquarelle, 1760–1851*. Paris: Bordas. Pp. 464.

Rev. by Brinsley Ford in *Études anglaises*, VIII, 372–75, as a major work of art criticism.

Liptzin, Solomon. *The English Legend of Heinrich Heine*. . . . See VB 1954, 241.

Rev. by Harry Pfund in *Amer.-German Rev.*, XXI (April–May), 33; by Bayard Morgan in *Comp. Lit.*, VII, 177–78; by Herman Salinger in

Monatshefte, XLVII, 411; by J. H. Scholte in *Neophilologus*, XXXIX, 234–35; in *USQBR*, XI, 61. Mentions Matthew Arnold, Buchanan, Carlyle, Dowden, George Eliot, Pater, Rossetti, William Sharp, etc.

Low, D. M., and Others (eds.). *A Century of Writers*. London: Chatto & Windus.

Rev. by Grace Banyard in *CR*, CLXXXVIII, 215; by J. I. M. Stewart in *London Mag.*, II, 102–8; by Walter Allen in *NS*, Aug. 13, p. 189; in *TLS*, Aug. 19, p. 471. A centenary volume containing reprints of some of the famous Chatto and Windus books and a short history of the firm by Oliver Warner.

Mack, Mary Peter. "The Fabians and Utilitarianism." *JHI*, XVI, 76–88.

"The fact is that the briefest comparison between Benthamite Utilitarianism and Fabian Socialism brings to light some striking parallels"; mentions J. S. Mill.

McKinley, Erskine. "The Problem of 'Underdevelopment' in the English Classical School." *Quart. Jour. Econ.*, LXIX, 235–52.

The school includes economists from Adam Smith to the two Mills.

Marsh, George L. *A Flight of Lame Ducks.* Microfilm PR 159, University of Chicago Library.

On some nineteenth-century authors who were popular in their own day but not thereafter: Lady Morgan, Pierce Egan, James and Horace Smith, Theodore Hook, Cornelius Webbe, Felicia Hemans, William Maginn, J. H. Reynolds, Letitia Elizabeth Landon, W. H. Ainsworth, Caroline Norton.

Miner, Earl Roy. "The Japanese Influence on English and American Literature, 1850 to 1950." *DA*, XV, 1075.

Includes treatment of numerous Victorians; "Japan unsettled the firm if ambivalent Victorian beliefs, leading Sir Edwin Arnold, Kipling, and Meredith to re-examine Victorian assumptions"; "Japan was central" to the poetry of Yeats and Pound.

Muldrow, Blanche. "The American Theater as Seen by British Travellers, 1790–1860." *Summ. Doct. Diss., Univ. of Wisconsin*, XV, 584–86.

Nevins, Allan. "The Biographer and the Historian." In Agard vol. (see III, Beach, above), pp. 45–66. (Inadvertently omitted earlier.)

Nicoll, Allardyce. *A History of English Drama, 1660–1900.* Vol. IV: *Early Nineteenth-Century Drama, 1800–1850.* Cambridge: Cambridge Univ. Pr. Pp. 668.

Rev. by Grace Banyard in *CR*, CLXXXVIII, 214; by George Freedley in *LJ*, Oct. 1, p. 2180; in *TLS*, Aug. 12, p. 456. Second edition, the revision concerned chiefly with the list of plays appended to the text.

Oppel, Horst. *Der Einfluss der englischen Literatur auf die Deutsche.* Berlin, Bielefeld, and Munich: Erich Schmidt, 1954.

Rev. by A. Gillies in *MLR*, L, 354–55.

Orel, Harold. "English Critics and the Russian Novel, 1850–1917." *Slavonic and East European Rev.*, XXXIII, 456–69.

A noteworthy, documented consideration: "The major attitudes of Victorian critics . . . indicate clearly that a window had been opened . . . one of the most important literary experiences accessible to English readers during the late 19th and early 20th centuries."—W. D. T.

Orel, Harold. "The First Russian Novels in Victorian England," *NCF*, IX (1954), 228–31.

Raymond, John. "Strachey's Eminent Victorians." *NS*, Apr. 16, pp. 545–46.

Raymond contends that the portraits are perfect as art but do not represent the sitters. Under the heading "Strachey and Bloomsbury" (*NS*, Apr. 23, p. 578), Gavin Lambert defends, and Harold Binns condemns, Strachey as a biographer. In "Eminent Victorians" (*NS*, Apr. 30, p. 616), Norman St. John–Stevas documents the story of Cardinal Manning's deathbed remarks to Cardinal Vaughan.

Shain, Charles Edward. "A British Image of America: A Survey of America and the Americans as They Appeared in the English Novel, 1830–1890." *DA*, XV, 830.

Shumaker, Wayne. *English Autobiography: Its Emergence, Materials, and Form.* ("University of California Publications: English Studies," No. 8.) Berkeley: Univ. of California Pr., 1954. Pp. 262.

Rev. in *USQBR*, XI, 211. Includes studies of autobiographies of John Stuart Mill, Anthony Trollope, and George Moore.

Souffrin, Eileen. "La Source des *Thèmes anglaises* de Mallarmé." *Rev. de litt. comp.*, XXIX, 107–8.

H. G. Bohn's *Handbook of Proverbs* (1855) is the unacknowledged source of Mallarmé's *Thèmes*.

Stanton, Stephen Sadler. "English Drama and the French Well-made Play, 1815–1915." *DA*, XV, 2194–95.

Bulwer-Lytton, Shaw, Wilde, Pinero.

Tillotson, Kathleen. *Novels of the Eighteen-forties.* . . . See VB 1954, 242.

Rev. in *Dublin Mag.*, XXXI, 54–55; by J. Blondel in *Études anglaises*, VIII, 80–81; by Gordon S. Haight in *JEGP*, LIV, 438–40; by Robert B. Heilman in *NCF*, IX, 308–12; briefly in *Periodical*, XXXI, 39; by John Holloway in *RES*, new ser., VI, 430–32.

Tindall, William York. *The Literary Symbol.* New York: Columbia Univ. Pr. Pp. 278.

Rev. briefly in *HTB*, Oct. 23, p. 11; briefly by J. R. Willingham in *LJ*, August, p. 1689; in *USQBR*, XI, 469. Includes treatment of Hopkins and Yeats.

Townsend, J. Benjamin. *"The Yellow Book."* *PLC*, XVI, 101–3.

Townsend, Naomi Johnson. "Edmund Burke: Reputation and Bibliography, 1850–1954." *DA*, XV, 1861.

Includes reference to Macaulay, Arnold, Morley, Dilke.

Underwood, V. P. "Rimbaud et l'Angleterre." *Rev. de litt. comp.*, XXIX, 5–35.

Wain, John (ed.). *Interpretations*. London, Routledge.

Rev. by W. Empson in *NS*, Dec. 10, pp. 799–800. A collection of close analyses of poems by, among others, Yeats, Lionel Johnson, and Hopkins.

Wallace, Irving. *The Fabulous Originals: Lives of Extraordinary People Who Inspired Memorable Characters in Fiction.* New York: Knopf. Pp. 316.

Rev. by DeLancey Ferguson in *HTB*, Oct. 23, p. 4; by Earle Walbridge in *LJ*, August, p. 1690, and in *SR*, Oct. 15, p. 30; by Horace Reynolds in *NYTBR*, Oct. 16, p. 6. (See also an extract under the title "The Anatomy of Inspiration" in *Publishers' Weekly*, Sept. 10, pp. 974–80.) Originals for characters of Bulwer-Lytton, Collins, Dickens, Doyle, Meredith, Stevenson, etc.

West, E. J. "Irving in Shakespeare—Interpretation or Creation?" *Shakespeare Quart.*, VI, 415–22.

Wood, Herbert George. *Belief and Unbelief since 1850.* London: Cambridge Univ. Pr. Pp. viii+144.

Rev. briefly in *N & Q*, new ser., II, 550–51; by Kevin Smith in *StI*, XLIV, 482–83; in *TLS*, June 10, p. 320.

Worth, George John. "Maupassant in England." *DA*, XV, 128.

IV. INDIVIDUAL AUTHORS

Acton. Fasnacht, G. E. "Acton on Books and Reading." *TLS*, May 6, p. 244.

Based on MS notes made by Acton in compiling a list of "The Hundred Best Books."

Fasnacht, G. E. "The Riddle of Acton's Personality." *TLS*, Jan. 14, p. 25.

Hill, Roland. "Lord Acton and the Catholic Reviews." *Blackfriars*, XXXVI, 469–82.

On Acton's connection with *Atlantis*, *The Home and Foreign Review*, and other "liberal" Catholic periodicals.

Kochan, Lionel. *Acton on History.* New York: British Book Centre. Pp. 184.

Rev. by Crane Brinton in *APSS*, CCXCIX, 176–77; by David Mathew in *Blackfriars*, XXXVI, 300–301; by Hans Kohn in *NYTBR*, May 22, p. 3; in *TLS*, Jan. 7, p. 7.

Adams-Acton, M. H. Stirling, A. M. W. *Victorian Sidelights: From the Papers of the Late Mrs. Adams-Acton.* London: Benn, 1954.

Rev. in *TLS*, Mar. 4, p. 131. Random reminiscences of Marion Hamilton, a popular novelist and writer of children's books, wife of a well-known mid-Victorian sculptor.

Ainsworth. Bevan, Bryan. "Harrison Ainsworth." *CR*, CLXXXVIII, 96–100.

Arnold, Sir Edwin (see III, Miner).

Arnold, Matthew (see also III, Baetzhold, Dahl, Daniel, Townsend). Allott, Kenneth. *Matthew Arnold.* ("Writers and Their Work" ser., No. 60.) London: Longmans. Pp. 44.

Rev. by John Jones in *NS*, Dec. 31, pp. 887–88; in *TLS*, May 27, p. 290.

Allott, Kenneth. "Matthew Arnold: Two Unpublished Letters." *N & Q*, new ser., II, 356–57.

Armytage, W. H. G. "Matthew Arnold and a Reviewer." *RES*, new ser., VI, 297.

Prints a hitherto unpublished letter from Arnold to Norman MacColl, editor of the *Athenaeum*, thanking him for the excellent review of *Mixed Essays*.

Bevington, Merle M. "Matthew Arnold and John Bright: A Typographical Error and Some Ironic Consequences." *PMLA*, LXX, 543–48.

Arnold's misquotation of Bright in *Culture and Anarchy* was due to a misquotation in the *Times* report of Bright's speech.

De Vries, Jan. "Der Mythos von Balders Tod." *Ark. f. nord. Filol.*, LXX, 41–60.

On the religious implications of the myth.

Dougherty, Charles T. "Matthew Arnold's 'Barbarians.' " *N & Q*, new ser., II, 401–2.

Eells, John Shepard, Jr. *The Touchstone of Matthew Arnold.* New York: Bookman Associates. Pp. 280.

Rev. briefly by Earle F. Walbridge in *LJ*, July, p. 1591.

Jamison, William Alexander. "Arnold and the Romantics." *DA*, XV, 586.

Jump, J. D. *Matthew Arnold.* ("Men and Books" ser.) London: Longmans. Pp. 185.

Rev. by Grace Banyard in *CR*, CLXXXVIII, 214; by John Jones in *NS*, Dec. 31, pp. 887–88; briefly in *QR*, CCXCIII, 555.

Knight, G. Wilson. "*The Scholar Gipsy*: An Interpretation." *RES*, new ser., VI, 53–62.

In an important article Knight attempts to show the relevance of the concluding simile to the whole poem and of the whole poem to one of the central problems of Western culture. The Greeks are the bearers of the Apollonian consciousness, and the Tyrian trader is the seeker after the Dionysian, to use Nietzsche's terms. This article compels attention but not agreement.—F. G. T.

Lowe, Robert L. "Matthew Arnold and Percy William Bunting: Some New Letters, 1884–1887." *Studies in Bibliography, Univ. of Virginia*, VII, 199–207.

Fourteen letters to the editor of the *Contemporary Review*.

Lowe, Robert L. "Matthew Arnold's Poetic Theory: A History." *DA*, XV, 826.

Lowe, Robert L. "Two Arnold Letters." *MP*, LII, 262–64.

A valuable letter from Arnold to his younger brother and a brief note to Sidney Colvin.

Madden, William Anthony. "The Religious and Aesthetic Ideas of Matthew Arnold." *DA*, XV, 1620.

Maxwell, J. C. " 'One Who Most Has Suffered': Arnold and Leopardi?" *RES*, new ser., VI, 182–83.

On a much disputed passage in *The Scholar-Gipsy*.

Mengers, Marie C. "Matter versus Man: Or Régnier's Lyrical Integration, Hugo's Dream of Triumph, and Arnold's Abdication." *French Rev.*, XXVIII, 293–99.

Contrasts the integration of Man and Nature in Henri de Régnier's "Le Sang de Marsyas" with the Romantic vision of Man conquering Nature in Hugo and the northern pessimism of Arnold. Shows that Régnier did have Hugo in mind and suggests that he might have had Arnold in mind, because he had read English authors and "Arnold could easily have been one of the authors."—F. G. T.

Raleigh, John Henry. "The Growth of a Tradition: Arnold in America, 1865–1910, and the Aftermath." *DA*, XV, 589–90.

Three major critics participated in the evolution of an Arnoldian tradition in America: Henry James, W. C. Brownell, Stuart Sherman.

Brontë Society, Transactions and Other Publications of.

Vol. XII, No. 5 (Part 65), has items: Andrews, Sir Linton, "Charlotte Brontë: The Woman and the Feminist" (pp. 351–60); Brontë, Charlotte, "La Chenille [the original *devoir* written by Charlotte for M. Heger, and a translation by Phyllis Bentley]" (pp. 362–65); Brontë, Charlotte, "La Mort de Moise [the original *devoir* written by Charlotte for M. Heger and a translation by Phyllis Bentley]" (pp. 366–75); Brontë, Charlotte, "La Chute des feuilles [the original *devoir de style* written by Charlotte for M. Heger, together with the comments made on the MS by M. Heger, and a translation by Phyllis Bentley]" (pp. 376–83); [between pp. 380 and 381 are two pictures, one a drawing by Jennifer Highsted of Wycoller Hall, the original of Ferndean Manor in *Jane Eyre*, as it is today; the other, a photograph of the house Thorpe Underwood, where Anne Brontë went as governess]; Brontë, Emily, "Lettre [the short *devoir*, corrected by M. Heger, and a translation by Phyllis Bentley]" (pp. 384–85); Charlier, Gustave, "Brussels Life in 'Villette': A Visit to the Salon in 1842 [extracts translated by Phyllis Bentley from Professor Charlier's volume *Passages* (Brussels, 1947)]" (pp. 386–90); Huguenin, Charles A., "Brontëana at Princeton University: The Parrish Collection" (pp. 391–400); Hopewell, Donald, "Charlotte Brontë after a Hundred Years" (pp. 401–5); Crowther, George, "The Rev. Patrick Brontë's Tax Returns [the discovery of tax returns of the township of Haworth for the years 1829 and 1831]" (pp. 406–8); "Two Letters from Charlotte Brontë [to George Smith, Mar. 29, 1853, and to Laetitia Wheelwright, June 3, 1850]" (pp. 409–10); "Two Letters from Branwell [both to J. Frobisher, the first undated, the second dated Mar. 21, 1845]" (pp. 410–11); Weir, Edith M., "Somerset Maugham and Emily Brontë: Theories That Do Not Fit the Facts" (pp. 414–18); W., E. M., "More Reprints of Brontë Classics [comments on three new editions]" (pp. 419–20); [between pp. 428 and 429 appears a four-page facsimile of a letter from Charlotte Brontë to Mrs. Gaskell, Nov. 15, 1853].

Crompton, Margaret. *Passionate Search: A Life of Charlotte Brontë.* London: Cassell.

Rev. favorably by Eric Gillett in *NER*, CXLIV, 344–45; unfavorably by Irving Wardle in *NS*, Dec. 3, p. 762; by J. G. Watson in *S*, Dec. 2, pp. 773–74; in *TLS*, Dec. 23, p. 778.

Duthie, E. L. "Charlotte Brontë and Constantin Heger." *CR*, CLXXXVII, 169–73.

Lehman, B. H. "Of Material, Subject, and Form: *Wuthering Heights*." In B. H. Lehman and Others, *The Image of the Work: Essays in Criticism* (Univ. of California Pr.), pp. 3–17.

Martin, N. D. S. "Two Unpublished Letters of Charlotte Brontë." *BLR*, V, 222–23.

Short letters to W. S. Williams.

Maugham, William Somerset. *The Art of Fiction: An Introduction to Ten Novels and Their Authors.* New York: Doubleday. Pp. 318. See VB 1948, 255.

Rev. by Sylvère Monod in *Études anglaises*, VIII, 173–74; by John Brooks in *Harper's*, CCX (May), 84–86; in *HTB*, June 12, p. 9; briefly by Earle F. Walbridge in *LJ*, Apr. 1, p. 784; in *New R*, May 16, p. 45; by Robert Cantwell in *NYTBR*, Apr. 24, p. 4; in *SR*, May 28, p. 18. Includes treatment of *David Copperfield* and *Wuthering Heights*.

Melton, James. "The Brontë Parsonage Museum." *Connoisseur*, CXXXV, 106–7.

Ratchford, Fannie E. (ed.). *Gondal's Queen: A Novel in Verse.* Austin: Univ. of Texas Pr. Pp. 207.

Rev. briefly in *NCF*, X, 245; by J. G. Watson in *S*, Dec. 2, pp. 773–74; in *TLS*, Nov. 11, p. 672; in *USQBR*, XI, 474. Emily's poems are set in the context of the Gondal story and considered as dramatic. "No coward soul is mine," for example, is spoken by a Gondalan facing a crisis in the Republican-Royalist conflict.

Shannon, Edgar F., Jr. "The Present Tense in *Jane Eyre*." *NCF*, X, 141–45.

The author uses the device "to convey either rising emotional tension or a new departure in the story."

Spark, Muriel, and Stanford, Derek. *Emily Brontë. . . .* See VB 1954, 245.

Rev. by Elizabeth Wilson, in *English*, X, 147–48; by J. Blondel in *Études anglaises*, VIII, 269–70.

Brownings (see also III, Baetzhold, Dahl; **Carlyle:** Sanders; **Jerdan:** Duncan). Akamine, Yayoi. " 'Robert Browning, you writer of plays.' " *Athenaeum*, I (1954), 33–39. [Pub. by the Athenaeum Soc., Tokyo, Japan.]

Badger, Kingsbury. " 'See the Christ Stand!': Browning's Religion." *Boston Univ. Studies in English*, I, 53–73.

A wide-ranging, well-documented consideration; involves concern with general background, Browning's life, and interpretation of many specific poems; noteworthy.—W. D. T.

Broughton, Leslie Nathan, *et al. Robert Browning: A Bibliography.* . . . See VB 1954, 245.

Rev. favorably by L. Bonnerot in *Études anglaises*, VIII, 349–50; by Douglas Bush in *MLN*, LXX, 219–20.

DeVane, William Clyde. *A Browning Handbook.* 2d ed. New York: Appleton. Pp. 602.

Noted in *CE*, XVII, 129; in *Publishers' Weekly*, Mar. 12, p. 1507.

Dietrichson, Jan W. "Obscurity in the Poetry of Robert Browning." *Edda*, LV, 173–91.

Duffin, Henry Charles. "Mysticism in Browning." *HJ*, LIII, 372–76.

Described as "a chapter in a forthcoming book entitled *Amphibian: A Reconsideration of Browning.*"

Federle, Walter. *Robert Brownings dramatisches Experiment.* Zürich: Pfaffikon, 1954.

Rev. by Ludwig Borinski in *Euphorion*, XLIX, 378–79.

Glen, Margaret Eleanor. "The Meaning and Structure of *Pippa Passes.*" *TQ*, XXIV, 410–26.

Sees the theme of the poem as "the irony of God's ways when regarded from man's point of view."

Katope, Christopher G. "Patterns of Imagery in Robert Browning's *The Ring and the the Book.*" *DA*, XV, 403–4.

McCarthy, Barbara P. (ed.). *Elizabeth Barrett to Mr. Boyd: Unpublished Letters of Elizabeth Barrett Browning to Hugh Stuart Boyd.* ("Wellesley College Publications.") New Haven: Yale Univ. Pr. Pp. xxxix+299.

Rev. by P. S. O'Hegarty in *Dublin Mag.*, XXXI, 43–44.

McCarthy, Barbara P. " 'The Pestilence': by Elizabeth Barrett Browning." *N & Q*, new ser., II, 223–24.

Maurois, André. *Robert et Elizabeth Browning.* Paris: Grasset.

Rev. by Marcel Thiébaut in *Rev. de Paris*, LXII, 141–45; briefly in *Rev. de la pensée française*, Nos. 7–8 (July–August), p. 90.

Musgrove, S. "Unpublished Letters of Thomas De Quincey and Elizabeth Barrett Browning." *Auckland Univ. College Bull.*, No. 44, English Ser., No. 7, 1954.

Rev. briefly by H. M. Margoliouth in *RES*, new ser., VI, 218. Prints five letters from Elizabeth Barrett Browning to her friend Mrs. Martin. These letters are now in the Grey collection, Auckland City Library.

Priestley, F. E. L. "A Reading of *La Saisiaz.*" *TQ*, XXV, 47–59.

Raymond, William O. " 'The Jewelled Bow': A Study in Browning's Imagery and Humanism." *PMLA*, LXX, 115–31.

Thale, Jerome. "Browning's 'Popularity' and the Spasmodic Poets." *JEGP*, LIV, 348–54.

"Hobbs, Nobbs, Stokes, and Nokes" identified with Bailey, Alexander Smith, and Dobell.

Bulwer-Lytton (see III, Stanton, Wallace).

Burton (see III, Assad).

Butler. Harkness, Stanley B. *The Career of Samuel Butler, 1835–1902: A Bibliography.* London: Lane. Pp. 160.

Rev. in *TLS*, Apr. 29, p. 228. Does not supersede A. J. Hoppe's bibliography of Butler (1925) but provides much useful material on his reputation during his lifetime and since his death.

Carlyle (see also III, Baetzhold; **Arnold: Tillotson; Jerdan: Duncan; Milman:** Parker). Eidson, John Olin. "Charles Stearns Wheeler: Emerson's 'Good Grecian.' " *NEQ*, XXVII (1954), 472–83.

A brief biography of Charles Stearns Wheeler, who assisted Emerson in editing Carlyle's early work for American publication. On December 25, 1840, Wheeler wrote to Tennyson, offering to see the American edition of his works through the press, an offer which jolted Tennyson into bringing out the 1842 *Poems.* Wheeler, as Tennyson's agent, procured from Ticknor the sum of $150 for the copyright of his work.—F. G. T.

Fain, John Tyree. "Word Echoes in *Past and Present.*" *VNL*, No. 8 (autumn), pp. 5–6.

A study of Carlyle's repetitive devices.

Fish, Howard M., Jr. "Five Emerson Letters." *AL*, XXVII, 25–30.

Contains five hitherto unpublished letters of Emerson to Scottish friends, one of them Jane Welsh Carlyle.

Moore, Carlisle. "*Sartor Resartus* and the Problem of Carlyle's 'Conversion.' " *PMLA*, LXX, 662–81.

Biographical and critical evidence that Carlyle's "crisis" in Leith Walk was not in itself a conversion but that the "Centre of Indifference" in *Sartor* symbolizes truly the eight-year period during which he evolved and consolidated his convictions.

Morris, John William. "Thomas Carlyle's Influence on George Meredith's Theory of Literature." *DA*, XV, 574–75.

Nobbe, Susanne H. (ed.). "Four Unpublished Letters of Thomas Carlyle." *PMLA*, LXX, 876–84.

To Geraldine Jewsbury. Three of the letters, written in 1840, are of special interest as giving Carlyle's counsel to Miss Jewsbury in her spiritual struggles.

Sanders, Charles Richard. "Carlyle's Letters." *Bull. John Rylands Libr.*, XXXVIII, 199–224.

Valuable and fascinating account of work done and being done on Carlyle correspondence, especially at Duke University. Work at Duke on a file of Carlyle's letters was begun in 1952 and, though not completed, shows "significant data." In the master file (5,687 letters are now noted) is a card for each letter of which any trace has been found. Unpublished letters total 3,053. Of the 2,634 letters recorded in print, 805 are in Dyer's list of scattered letters; many of the remainder have been incompletely printed. The guess is made that eventually at least 8,000 autograph letters will be found. Professor Sanders gives many statistics of interest and numerous valuable interpretive comments on the style, contents, and varying significance of Carlyle's correspondence. He contends that the letters reveal accurately not only Carlyle but also the events of the time, with comments and pen-portraits. Sanders mentions many Victorians,

among them Forster, Browning, Tennyson, Landor, Froude, Dickens, Mill, Macaulay, Milnes, Hunt, Sterling, Macready. This is a notable account of important work in progress.—W. D. T.

Shine, Hill. *Carlyle's Early Reading, to 1834.* . . . See VB 1954, 246.

Rev. briefly by Marjorie King in *MLR*, L, 109; favorably by Geoffrey Tillotson in *RES*, new ser., VI, 210–11.

Watt, W. Montgomery. "Carlyle on Muhammad." *HJ*, LIII, 247–54.

Carlyle's conception of Muhammad in *Heroes* is valid, reversing the Christian idea of Islam as "the great enemy."

Carroll. Greenacre, Phyllis. *Swift and Carroll: A Psychoanalytic Study of Two Lives.* New York: International Univs. Pr. Pp. 306.

Rev. briefly by Carvel Collins in *CE*, XVII, 195–96; briefly by Paul Pickrel, in *Harper's*, CCXI (October), 94; briefly by Louis Barron in *LJ*, Sept. 1, p. 1809; briefly in *NCF*, X, 245–46; in *USQBR*, XI, 442–43.

Hudson, Derek. *Lewis Carroll.* . . . See VB 1954, 246.

Rev. by John Heath-Stubbs in *Blackfriars*, XXXVI, 605; by Jeanne Métailler in *Études anglaises*, VIII, 163–64; by DeLancey Ferguson in *HTB*, Jan. 23, p. 3; briefly by Earle F. Walbridge in *LJ*, Jan. 15, p. 152; by Jacob Korg in *N*, Mar. 19, p. 244; by Edgar Johnson in *SR*, Feb. 26, p. 16.

Weaver, Warren. "The Mathematical Manuscripts of Lewis Carroll." *PLC*, XVI (1954), 1–9.

Clare. Unwin, Rayner. *The Rural Muse.* London: Allen, 1954. Pp. 202.

Rev. by B. Ifor Evans in *Adelphi*, XXXI, 190–92; in *TLS*, Oct. 29, 1954, p. 688. Includes a study of Clare.

Collier. Race, Sydney. "John Payne Collier and the Stationers' Registers." *N & Q*, new ser., II, 492–95 (to be continued).

Contends that Collier composed ballads which he alleged were from early sources.

Collins (see also III, Wallace). Davis, Nuel Pharr. "The Early Life and Literary Career of Wilkie Collins." *DA*, XV, 822–23.

Colvin (see **Arnold, Matthew:** Lowe).

Conrad (see also III, Allen, Blotner; **Ford:** Gose, Harris). Chaikin, Milton. "Zola and Conrad's 'The Idiots.' " *SP*, LII, 504–7.

Feder, Lillian. "Marlow's Descent into Hell." *NCF*, IX, 280–92.

Marlow's journey in *Heart of Darkness* parallels the traditional epic descent into Hades.

Gillon, Adam. "Isolation in the Life and Works of Joseph Conrad." *DA*, XIV (1954), 1409.

Harkness, Bruce. "Conrad on Galsworthy: The Time Scheme of *Fraternity*." *Modern Fiction Studies*, I (May), 12–18.

Holland, Michael; Curle, Richard. "Conrad's Favourite Novel." *TLS*, Oct. 7, p. 589; Oct. 14, p. 605.

Though Conrad regarded *Nostromo* as his greatest creative effort, the novel of his own which he liked best was *The Nigger of the Narcissus*.

Lee, Richard Eugene. "The Political and Social Ideas of Joseph Conrad." *DA*, XV, 1073.

Modern Fiction Studies: A Critical Quarterly Published by the Modern Fiction Club of Purdue University. Vol. I, No. 1 (February), is a special number on Conrad, containing articles as follows: Carroll, Wesley, "The Novelist as Artist" (pp. 2–8); Haugh, Robert F., "Conrad's *Chance*: 'Progression d'effet' " (pp. 9–15); Lynskey, Winifred, "The Role of the Silver in *Nostromo*" (pp. 16–21); Wills, John Howard, "Adam, Axel, and 'Il Conde' " (pp. 22–25); Wright, Walter F., " 'The Truth of My Own Sensations' " (pp. 26–29); Beebe, Maurice, "Criticism of Conrad: A Selected Checklist" (pp. 30–45).

Thale, Jerome. "Marlow's Quest." *TQ*, XXIV, 351–58.

Sees Conrad's *Heart of Darkness* as a story of a grail quest.

Visiak, E. H. *The Mirror of Conrad*. London: Laurie. Pp. 255.

Rev. favorably by Don M. Wolfe in *EJ*, XLIV, 541–42; by Eric Gillett in *NER*, CXLV, 164; by John Holloway in *S*, Sept. 23, p. 396; in

TLS, Sept. 23, p. 558. Stresses a biographical interpretation by showing how Conrad's fiction embodies the events of his active sea life.

Worth, George J. "Conrad's Debt to Maupassant in the Preface to *The Nigger of the Narcissus*." *JEGP*, LIV, 700–704.

Cunningham-Graham, R. B. Tschiffely, A. F. *Tornado Cavalier*. London: Harrap. Pp. 144.

A biography.

Darwin (see also I, Untermeyer; III, Appleman, Irvine). Eiseley, Loren C. "Was Darwin Wrong about the Human Brain?" *Harper's* (November), CCXI, 66–70.

Keith, Sir Arthur. *Darwin Revalued*. London: Watts. Pp. 294.

Rev. briefly in *NS*, Sept. 17, p. 342; in *TLS*, Aug. 19, p. 471.

Moore, Ruth E. *Charles Darwin*. ("Great Lives in Brief" ser.) New York: Knopf, 1954.

Rev. by John T. Winterich in *HTB*, Mar. 20, p. 11; briefly by Elizabeth M. Cole in *LJ*, Jan. 1, p. 65; by Keith Hutchison in *N*, May 28, p. 468; by H. S. Commager in *NYTBR*, Feb. 13, p. 3; by E. H. Colbert in *SR*, Jan. 29, p. 18.

Ritter, William Emerson. *Charles Darwin and the Golden Rule*. Ed. by Edna Watson Bailey. New York: Storm, 1954. Pp. xxi + 400.

Rev. by Ashley Montagu in *Isis*, XLVI, 385–86; rev. unfavorably as an outmoded account of the relationship between religion and science by Karl P. Schmidt in *Scient. Month.*, LXXXI, 152.

Yonge, C. M. "Darwin to Bikini." *NS*, Sept. 10, pp. 293–94.

Tells how Darwin arrived at his theory of atoll formation and how research at Bikini has partly substantiated and partly refuted his theory. See also G. F. S. Hills, "Darwin to Bikini" (*NS*, Sept. 17, p. 328), which holds that Darwin's theory was correct.

Dickens (see also I, Weber; III, Allen, Daniel, Leavis, Wallace; **Brontës:** Maugham; **Carlyle:** Sanders; **Shaw:** Drew). Addison, William. *In the Steps of Charles Dickens*. London: Rich. Pp. 256.

Noticed in *TLS*, July 22, p. 419. An illustrated account of the scenes of Dickens' novels.

Adrian, Arthur A. "Dickens and the Brick-and-Mortar Sects." *NCF*, X, 188–201.

Reasons for Dickens' dislike of the Nonconformists.

Barnett, George L. "Corporal Trim's Hat." *N & Q*, new ser., II, 403–4.

An action in *Old Curiosity Shop* reminiscent of a similar action in Sterne's *Tristram Shandy*.

Benjamin, Edwin B. "The Structure of *Martin Chuzzlewit*." *PQ*, XXXIV, 39–47.

[Buckler, William E.] "The Pilgrim Trust and the Dickens Letters." *VNL*, No. 8 (autumn), p. 7.

On the definitive edition (about 10,000 letters) begun by Humphry House and being continued by Graham Hough.

Butt, John. "*Bleak House* in the Context of 1851." *NCF*, X, 1–21.

Chancery reform, criticism of Parliament, and questions of sanitation were themes which the *Times* emphasized in 1851; several characters in *Bleak House* are of the time value.

Connolly, Thomas E. "Technique in *Great Expectations*." *PQ*, XXXIV, 48–55.

Dickensian (quarterly), Vol. LI (Nos. 313–16). . . . See VB 1932, 422.

Items as follows: Adrian, A., "The Demise of the Strange Gentleman" (pp. 158–60); Aylmer, F., "*All Right on the Night* [rev. of book by V. C. Clinton-Baddeley]" (pp. 41–42); Aylmer, F., "Dickens and Ellen Ternan" (pp. 85–86); Aylmer, F., "John Forster and Dickens's Book of Memoranda" (pp. 19–23); Bacon, J., "One of Six [rev. of *Six Great Novelists*, by Walter Allen—his essay on Dickens 'shows much knowledge,' and he regards Dickens as 'the greatest genius amongst English novelists']" (p. 189); Bacon, J., "*Thackeray the Novelist* [rev. of book by Geoffrey Tillotson]" (p. 84); Birch, D., "A Forgotten Book [Dickens' *A Child's History of England*]" (pp. 121–26, 154–57); Blakeney, T., "Problems of *Edwin Drood*" (pp. 182–85); Bleifuss, W., "The Re-examination of *Edwin Drood*" (pp. 24–29); Brend, G., "A Re-examination of *Edwin Drood*" (pp. 87–88); Butt, J., "*A Christmas Carol*: Its Origin and Design" (pp. 15–18); Carlton, W., "Dickens and the Ross Family" (pp. 58–66); Carlton, W., "Dickens's Insurance Policies" (pp. 133–37); Carlton, W., "Who Was Dickens's French Employer?" (pp. 149–54); "Charles

Chaplin on 'The Immortal Memory of Charles Dickens' " (pp. 111–14); Collins, P., "Bruce Castle: A School Dickens Admired" (pp. 174–81); Fielding, K., "Dickens's Novels and Miss Burdett-Coutts" (pp. 30–34); Fielding, K., "In Memoriam: Humphry House" (pp. 115–17); Gibson, F., "Hats in Dickens" (pp. 108–10); Greaves, J., "*The Bedside Dickens* [rev. of anthology comp. by J. W. Garrod]" (pp. 43–44); Greaves, J., "*Bransby Williams* [rev. of autobiog. by Williams]" (pp. 42–43); Grubb, G., "Dickens the Paymaster Once More" (pp. 72–78); Hill, T., "Notes on *Barnaby Rudge*" (pp. 93–96, 137–41); Hulse, B., "Dostoevsky for Dickensians" (pp. 66–71); Johnson, E., "The Paradox of Dickens [corrections for pp. 149–58 of Vol. L]" (p. 23); Major, G., "Topography and Other Matters [rev. of *In the Steps of Charles Dickens*, by William Addison]" (p. 188); Mason, L., "*The Dickensian*: A Tale of Fifty Years" (pp. 4–12); Morley, M., "Plays from the Christmas Numbers of *Household Words*" (pp. 127–32, 169–73); Morley, M., "The Stage Story of *A Tale of Two Cities*" (pp. 34–40); Morley, M., "Stages of *Great Expectations*" (pp. 79–83); Pakenham, P., "The Memorandum Book, Forster & *Edwin Drood*" (pp. 117–21); Pakenham, P., "Somerset Maugham on Dickens" (pp. 83–84); "Recent Dickensiana" (pp. 18, 57, 126, 185); Staples, L., "*David Copperfield* with the Scott Antarctic Expedition" (pp. 100–101); Starr, H., "Dickens's Parody of Gray's *Elegy* [first printing of the entire 12-stanza poem]" (pp. 186–87); Wagenknecht, E., "Why *The Dickensian*?" (pp. 12–13); Walker, S., "The Artistry of Dickens as an English Novelist" (pp. 102–8).

Engel, Monroe. "Dickens on Art." *MP*, LIII, 25–38.

Dickens' theory of the art of writing, derived mainly from his comments on contributions to his magazines.

Engel, Monroe. "The Novel of Reality: An Illustrative Study of the Genesis, Method, and Intent of *Our Mutual Friend*." *DA*, XV, 1612–13.

Fielding, K. J. "Charles Dickens and His Wife: Fact or Forgery?" *Études anglaises*, VIII, 212–22.

Fielding re-examines the question of the authenticity of a letter purportedly from Mrs. Helen Thomson (Mrs. Dickens' aunt) to her friend Mrs. Stark, dated Aug. 20, 1858. Dexter and Johnson rejected the letter as a forgery.

Recent discoveries in the records of Mrs. Dickens' solicitor show that the writer had information about the whereabouts of Mrs. Dickens in June, 1858, that even Dexter and Johnson knew nothing about. Even so, the letter may still be a forgery, but, Fielding concludes, it cannot be summarily dismissed. The text of the letter is here printed in full. Most interesting is the denunciation of Georgina for usurping her sister's place.—F. G. T.

Fielding, K. J. "Dickens and the Hogarth Scandal." *NCF*, X, 64–74.

New papers concerned with Dickens' separation from his wife.

Fielding, K. J. "Dickens and the Royal Literary Fund—1858." *RES*, new ser., VI, 383–94.

Having failed to reform the Royal Literary Fund, which actually needed no reform, Dickens decided to ruin it, but failed. His unwarranted assaults on the society were one more symptom of the bitterness provoked by his personal problems, a bitterness which increasingly affected his writing.—F. G. T.

Fielding, K. J. "The Piracy of *Great Expectations*." *N & Q*, new ser., II, 495–96.

Ford, George H. *Dickens and His Readers: Aspects of Novel-Criticism since 1836.* ("University of Cincinnati Publications.") Princeton, N.J.: Princeton Univ. Pr.

Rev. by Edward Stone in *CE*, XVII, 124–25; briefly by Hudson Rogers in *EJ*, XLIV, 434; by Franklin P. Rolfe in *NCF*, X, 242–45; briefly by Malcolm Ross in *QQ*, XLII, 469; in *TLS*, Jan. 6, 1956, p. 3; in *USQBR*, XI, 466; by Edgar Johnson in *VQR*, XXXI, 644–48; in *YR*, XLV, xxxii–xxxiv.

Fraser, Russell. "A Charles Dickens Original." *NCF*, IX, 301–7.

Nathaniel Bentley as the original of Miss Havisham.

Friedman, Norman. "Versions of Form in Fiction—*Great Expectations* and *The Great Gatsby*." *Accent*, XIV (1954), 246–64.

Grubb, Gerald G. "Some Unpublished Correspondence of Dickens and Chapman and Hall." *Boston Univ. Studies in English*, I, 98–127.

Letters hitherto unpublished, from the Victoria and Albert Museum Library, the Pierpont Morgan Library, the New York Public Library, and the University of North Carolina Library; throw notable light on Dickens' finances and publishing affairs.—W. D. T.

Haight, Gordon S. "Dickens and Lewes on Spontaneous Combustion." *NCF*, X, 53–63.

G. H. Lewes' fruitless attempt to have Dickens recant on the subject.

Jean, Raymond. "De Nerval et quelques humoristes anglais." *Rev. de litt. comp.*, XXIX, 99–104.

De Nerval on Swift, Sterne, and Dickens.

Johnson, Edgar. "The Present State of Dickensian Studies." *VNL*, No. 7 (April), pp. 4–9.

A useful survey of recent scholarship and of areas that still require investigation.

Lane, William G. "R. H. Barham and Dickens's Clergyman of *Oliver Twist*." *NCF*, X, 159–62.

Denies that Barham was the model for the irreverent clergyman in chap. v.

Majut, Rudolf. "Some Literary Affiliations of Georg Büchner with England." *MLR*, L, 30–43.

Points out similarities between Leonce-Valerio in *Leonce und Lena* and Weller-Pickwick and between Woyzeck (in *Woyzeck*) and Toby Veck, but concludes that Büchner probably did not know Dickens' work and that the similarities are due to the *Zeitgeist*.

Mannheim, Leonard F. "The Law as 'Father.'" *Amer. Imago*, XII, 17–23.

The objects of filial acceptance and Oedipal regression are the good John Jarndyce and the evil Krook, both connected with the law. You see, the Father is disguised as the Law, and then the Law is symbolized in the human figure—the anthropomorphic viewpoint, of course. Jarndyce lives in Bleak House, but Bleak House is really not a bad house at all—in fact, it is like the Father's house in which there are many mansions.—F. G. T.

Miller, J. Hillis. "The World View of *Bleak House*." *VNL*, No. 7 (April), p. 10. [Summary of a paper.]

Murphy, Theresa. "Interpretation in the Dickens Period." *QJS*, XLI, 243–49.

Nisbet, Ada B. "Poe and Dickens." *NCF*, IX, 313–14.

Dickens may be the original of the visitor satirized in Poe's "The System of Dr. Tarr and Prof. Fether."

Reinhold, Heinz. "Charles Dickens' Roman *A Tale of Two Cities* und das Publikum." *Germanisch-romanische Monatsschrift*, new ser., V, 319–27.

Stone, Harry. "An Added Note on Dickens and Miss Havisham." *NCF*, X, 85–86.

Tedlock, E. W., Jr. "Kafka's Imitation of *David Copperfield.*" *Comp. Lit.*, VII, 52–62.

Kafka's *Amerika* shows Dickens' influence.

Trilling, Lionel. *The Opposing Self: Nine Essays in Criticism*. New York: Viking. Pp. 232.

Rev. by David Daiches in *HTB*, Apr. 3, p. 4; briefly by Beatrice B. Libaire in *LJ*, Feb. 1, pp. 368–69; by Perry Miller in *N*, Mar. 5, p. 203; favorably by Eric Gillett in *NER*, CXLV, 163–64; unfavorably by A. Alvarez in *NS*, Aug. 13, pp. 193–94; by Harry Levin in *NYTBR*, Feb. 13, p. 3; by John Wain in *S*, July 29, pp. 171–72; by H. M. Jones in *SR*, Feb. 12, pp. 11–12; in *TLS*, Aug. 29, p. 492. A chapter on *Little Dorrit* (pp. 50–65) points out Dickens' deep personal involvement in the character of Clennam.

Dilke (see III, Townsend).

Disraeli (see also II, Taffs; III, Blotner). Parsons, Olive Wrenchel. "The Ideas of Benjamin Disraeli, Lord Beaconsfield." *DA*, XIV (1954), 2072.

Dobell (see also **Brownings:** Thale). Thale, Jerome. "Sydney Dobell's *Roman:* The Poet's Experience and His Work." *Amer. Imago*, XII, 87–113.

After his nervous breakdown in the 1840's, Dobell wrote *The Roman*, a dramatic poem celebrating revolt and liberty. Most interesting is Thale's equating of father with Austrian aggression and mother with oppressed Italy, an equation which suggests why more Victorians than just Dobell were so emotional about 1848. In the case of Dobell, I think Thale's evidence and the arguments he bases on it are conclusive. —F. G. T.

Domett. Horsman, E. A. (ed.). *The Diary of Alfred Domett, 1872–1885.* . . . See VB 1954, 249.

Rev. by Jean-Roger Poisson in *Études anglaises*, VIII, 79–80; by Henry Gifford in *RES*, new ser., VI, 102–4.

Horsman, E. A., and Benson, Lillian Rea (eds.). *The Canadian Journal of Alfred Domett: Being an Extract from a Journal of a Tour in Canada, the United States, and Jamaica, 1833–35.* London, Ontario: Univ. of Western Ontario Pr.

Noticed in *TLS*, Oct. 7, p. 594.

Doughty (see III, Assad).

Doyle (see also III, Wallace). Krogman, Wilton Marion. "Sherlock Holmes as an Anthropologist." *Scient. Month.*, LXXX, 155–62.

It is easy for the modern to dismiss Holmes's anthropology as "elementary," says Krogman, professor of physical anthropology at the University of Pennsylvania, but, despite some rather startling gaps in his knowledge, the great detective was well informed by the standards of his time.

Watson, John Gillard. "The Religion of Sherlock Holmes." *Lit. Guide*, LXX, 12–14.

The Holmes of the great period belongs among the eminent Victorian rationalists.

Eden. Dunbar, Janet. *Golden Interlude: The Edens in India, 1836–1842.* London: Murray. Pp. 342.

Rev. in *NS*, Sept. 10, p. 307; in *TLS*, Oct. 7, p. 590.

Eliot (see also II, Murphy; III, Blotner, Leavis). Arthos, John. "George Eliot: 'The Art of Vision.' " *Riv. di lett. mod.*, III (1952), 260–70. (Inadvertently omitted earlier.)

Barry, James Donald. "The Literary Reputation of George Eliot." *DA*, XV, 1851.

Treats English and American criticism of her novels from 1857 to the present.

Haight, Gordon S. (ed.). *The George Eliot Letters.* Vols. I–III. . . . See VB 1954, 249.

Rev. by Melvin W. Askew in *BA*, XXIX, 476; by I. R. Browning in *EC*, V, 265–74; by Sonya Rudikoff in *Hudson Rev.*, VIII, 294–302 (long, enthusiastically favorable review article, "A Strong Sense of Self"); by Geoffrey Tillotson in *SeR*, LXIII, 494–500; in *USQBR*, XI, 7; by Joan Bennett in *YR*, XLIV, 298–301.

Haight, Gordon S. (ed.). *The George Eliot Letters*. Vols. IV–VII. New Haven: Yale Univ. Pr. Pp. 502; 475; 440; x+535.

Rev. by Samuel C. Chew in *HTB*, Dec. 18, pp. 1, 8; by Lionel Trilling in *NYTBR*, Dec. 18, pp. 1, 11.

Haight, Gordon S. "The Tinker Collection of George Eliot Manuscripts." *Yale Univ. Libr. Gaz.*, XXIX, 148–50.

Hardwick, Elizabeth. "George Eliot's Husband." *ParR*, XXII, 260–64.

Character sketches of George Eliot and G. H. Lewes.

Hardy, Barbara. "Imagery in George Eliot's Last Novels." *MLR*, L, 6–14.

Hussey, Maurice. "Structure and Imagery in *Adam Bede*." *NCF*, X, 115–29.

Jones, William M. "From Abstract to Concrete in *Adam Bede*." *CE*, XVII, 88–89.

The novel is a lengthy example supporting the general statements of Dinah's sermon in chapter ii.

Kaminsky, Alice R. "George Eliot, George Henry Lewes, and the Novel." *PMLA*, LXX, 997–1013.

Concludes that Lewes was a primary influence on George Eliot's theory of the novel, especially as to realism, psychological characterization, and the social and moral significance of fiction.

Moldstad, David Franklin. "Evangelical Influences on George Eliot." *Summ. Doct. Diss., Univ. of Wisconsin*, XV, 620–21.

O'Brien, Kate. "George Eliot: A Moralizing Fabulist." *Essays by Divers Hands: Being the Transactions of the Royal Society of Literature*, XXVII, 34–46.

Rust, James D. "George Eliot on *The Blithedale Romance*." *BPLQ*, VII, 207–15.

A criticism of Hawthorne's novel appeared in the *Westminster Review* in October, 1852. It is here attributed, with reason, to Marian Evans; throws interesting light on the early development of her thought concerning the art of fiction.

She contends that realism per se is not enough, that Hawthorne treats Zenobia too harshly, and that he had not sufficiently shown the moral effect of Brook Farm upon his characters. Rust suggests interestingly that George Eliot may have shown (by the impact of society upon the individual) in *Middlemarch* what she wished Hawthorne had done in *The Blithedale Romance*. —W. D. T.

Schneider, Robert Lee. "George Eliot: Her Search for Order." *DA*, XIV (1954), 2073.

Spivey, Ted Ray. "Two Visions of Character and Fate: A Study of Themes and Major Characters in the Novels of Thomas Hardy and George Eliot." *DA*, XV, 127.

Steiner, F. George. "A Preface to *Middlemarch*," *NCF*, IX, 262–79.

An attempt to determine the stature of the novel.

Steinhoff, William R. "Intent and Fulfillment in the Ending of *The Mill on the Floss*." In B. H. Lehman and Others, *The Image of the Work: Essays in Criticism* (Univ. of California Pr.), pp. 231–51.

Thale, Jerome. "*Adam Bede*: Arthur Donnithorne and *Zeluco*." *MLN*, LXX, 263–65.

Fonblanque, Albany (see II, Herd).

Ford. Gose, Elliott Bickley. "Passion and the Tradition: A Critical Appraisal of Ford Madox Ford." *DA*, XV, 123.

The first chapter of the dissertation treats the collaboration of Ford and Joseph Conrad.

Harris, Markham. "A Memory of Ford Madox Ford." *Prairie Schooner*, XXIX, 252–63.

Includes allusions to Joseph Conrad.

Froude (see II, Murphy; **Carlyle:** Sanders).

Fullerton. Lochhead, Marion. "Two Minor Victorian Novelists: Lady Georgiana Fullerton and Mrs. Norton." *QR*, CCXCIII, 477–85.

Digests the principal novels of Norton and Fullerton, adding occasional critical comments. They wrote full-blown melodrama—dark lovers, cads, and babes separated by shipwreck—but they manage to be readable. "Indeed, having read their books one may, for a time, find modern fiction anaemic."

Gilbert. Troubridge, Sir St. Vincent. "Another Gilbert 'Borrowing.'" *Theatre Notebook*, X, 20–21.

The source for Gilbert's opera *The Grand Duke*.

Gissing. Donnelly, Mabel Collins. *George Gissing.* . . . See VB 1954, 250.

Rev. by R. C. Gordon in *Comp. Lit.*, VII, 67–68; by Clifford Collins in *S*, Mar. 18, p. 337.

Korg, Jacob. "Division of Purpose in George Gissing." *PMLA*, LXX, 323–36.

Gissing's allegiance divided between social reform and art.

Gladstone (see also II, Taffs; **Manning:** Chapeau). *The British Museum Catalogue of Additions to the Manuscripts: The Gladstone Papers.* London: Trustees of the Museum, 1953.

Rev. by M. R. D. Foot in *EHR*, LXX, 688.

Magnus, Philip. *Gladstone.* . . . See VB 1954, 250.

Rev. favorably in *Blackwood's*, CCLXXVII, 190–92; by David Mathew in *Dublin Rev.*, CCXXIX, 362–63; by Nowell C. Smith in *English*, X, 149–50; favorably by R. B. McCallum in *EHR*, LXIX, 292–94; by Leon O'Broin in *Month*, XIII, 174–76; by David Owen in *PSQ*, LXX, 297–98; by Charles Daniel Smith in *QJS*, XLI, 306–7; by W. L. Burn in *TC*, CLVII, 54–65 (long review article, "Lord M. and Mr. G."); by C. H. Driver in *YR*, XLIV, 584–92.

Parker, W. M. "Gladstone as a *Quarterly Review* Contributor." *QR*, CCXCIII, 464–76.

Contains excerpts from hitherto unpublished Gladstone letters and a brief account of Gladstone's contributions to *QR*. Notes especially Gladstone's firm grasp of the subtlest details of ecclesiastical politics and policy.

Gosse, P. H. Stageman, Peter. *A Bibliography of the First Editions of Philip Henry Gosse, F.R.S.* Includes introductory essays by Sacheverell Sitwell and Geoffrey Lapage. Cambridge: Golden Head Pr.

Rev. in *TLS*, Sept. 30, p. 580.

Green, T. H. (see II, Simons).

Gurney. Garmonsway, G. N. "Anna Gurney: Learned Saxonist." In *Essays and Studies*

1955, collected for the English Assoc. by D. M. Low (London), new ser., VIII, 40–57.

Hall, Basil (see III, Baetzhold).

Hallam. Pearce, Helen. "Homage to Arthur Henry Hallam." In B. H. Lehman and Others, *The Image of the Work: Essays in Criticism* (Univ. of California Pr.), pp. 113–33.

Hardy (see also I, Untermeyer, Weber; III, Bowra, Daniel; **Eliot:** Spivey). Baker, James R. "Thematic Ambiguity in *The Mayor of Casterbridge.*" *Twentieth Cent. Lit.*, I, 13–16.

Hardy refuses to indicate whether man's suffering is due to the antagonism of circumstance or to his moral flaws.

Bartlett, Phyllis. "Hardy's Shelley." *Keats-Shelley Jour.*, IV, 15–29.

Shelley's influence, especially on *The Dynasts*.

Bartlett, Phyllis. "'Seraph of Heaven': A Shelleyan Dream in Hardy's Fiction." *PMLA*, LXX, 624–35.

Hardy's Shelleyan heroine, from *The Poor Man and the Lady* to *Jude the Obscure*.

Brown, Douglas. *Thomas Hardy.* . . . See VB 1954, 251.

Rev. by S. Sebaoun in *Études anglaises*, VIII, 166; briefly in *NCF*, X, 165–66.

De la Mare, Walter. "Meeting Thomas Hardy." *Listener*, Apr. 28, pp. 756–57.

De la Mare, Walter. "Thomas Hardy." *Dorset Year Book, 1955–1956*, pp. 140–43.

Ervine, St. John. "Portrait of Thomas Hardy." *Listener*, Sept. 8, pp. 371–72.

Hardy, Evelyn. *Thomas Hardy.* . . . See VB 1954, 251.

Rev. by S. Sebaoun in *Études anglaises*, VIII, 165–66; by Frederick B. Adams, Jr., in *NCF*, X, 75–78; by G. Robert Stange in *Poetry*, LXXXV, 356–61.

Hardy, Evelyn (ed.). *Thomas Hardy's Notebooks.* London: Hogarth.

Rev. by Geoffrey Grigson in *NS*, Dec. 10, pp. 804–6; in *TLS*, Dec. 9, p. 735.

Jonsson, Snaebjorn. "Thomas Hardy og Tess." *Lesbok Morgunbladsins* (Reykjavik, Iceland), Oct. 2, pp. 540–45.

Matchett, William H. "*The Woodlanders*, or Realism in Sheep's Clothing." *NCF*, IX, 241–61.

In this novel, Hardy attempted to mold "a realistic intention to the requirements of a sentimental form."

Morcos, Louis. "*The Dynasts* and the Bible." *Bull. of English Studies 1955* (Cairo, Egypt, Univ.), pp. 29–65.

Morcos, Louis. "The 'Immanent Will' in Thomas Hardy." *Institutionis linguarum paginae* (Cairo, Egypt, 1955), pp. 143–58.

Morcos, Louis. "The Manuscript of Thomas Hardy's *The Dynasts*." *Annuals of the Faculty of Arts* (Ain Shams Univ., Cairo, Egypt), III, 1–37.

Pilkington, F. "Religion in Hardy's Novels." *CR*, CLXXXVIII, 31–35.

Purdy, Richard Little. *Thomas Hardy: A Bibliographical Study.* . . . See VB 1954, 251.

Rev. by Carl J. Weber in *BSP*, XLIX, 85–89 (see also comment by Frederick B. Adams, Jr., on pp. 285–87); by Frederick B. Adams, Jr., in *Book Collector*, II, 82–84; briefly in *CE*, XVII, 122; in *Dublin Mag.*, XXXI, 53–54; by Michael Sadleir in *Library*, X, 137–39; by Henry Reed in *Listener*, Dec. 2, 1954, p. 975; by Carl J. Weber in *MP*, LII, 282–84; by Frederick B. Adams, Jr., in *NCF*, X, 78–79; briefly in *Periodical*, XXXI, 77–78; in *TLS*, Mar. 11, p. 54.

Sorensen, Morten. "*Tess* in Icelandic." *Colby Libr. Quart.*, IV, 63.

Templeman, William D. "Hardy's Wife-selling Incident and a Letter by Warren Hastings." *HLQ*, XVIII, 183–87.

[Weber, Carl J.] "Autograph Letters." *Colby Libr. Quart.*, IV, 69–71.

The text of three letters by Hardy, annotated.

Weber, Carl J. "Hardy Notes." *Colby Libr. Quart.*, IV, 84–86.

Recent acquisitions, including an autograph letter to John Morley, June 25, 1883.

Weber, Carl J. "Hermann Lea's Recollections of Thomas Hardy." *Dorset Year Book, 1955–1956*, pp. 39–48 (with illustrations).

Yarmolinsky, Avrahm. "Hardy behind the Iron Curtain." *Colby Libr. Quart.*, IV, 64–66.

Henty. Davies, Godfrey. "G. A. Henty and History." *HLQ*, XVIII, 159–67.

Hone, William (see II, Herd).

Hood. Hobman, D. L. "Thomas Hood." *CR*, CLXXXVIII, 397–401.

Hook, W. F. Stranks, C. J. *Dean Hook.* London: Mowbrays, Ltd., 1954. Pp. 120.

Rev. favorably by Ronald Leicester in *DUJ*, XLVII, 129–30.

Hopkins (see also I, Untermeyer; III, Tindall, Wain). Adorita, Sister Mary. "Hopkins's 'wings that spell' in *The Wreck of the Deutschland*." *MLN*, LXX, 345–47.

Donoghue, Denis. "The Bird as Symbol: Hopkins's Windhover." *StI*, XLV, 291–99.

Donoghue, Denis. "Technique in Hopkins." *StI*, XLIV, 446–56.

Grigson, Geoffrey. *Gerard Manley Hopkins.* ("Writers and Their Work" ser., No. 59.) London: Macmillan. Pp. 34.

Rev. by Christopher Devlin in *NS*, Mar. 26, p. 447.

Hartman, Geoffrey T. *The Unmediated Vision.* . . . See VB 1954, 252.

Rev. in *TLS*, July 22, p. 414; in *USQBR*, XI, 207–8.

Hill, Archibald A. "An Analysis of *The Windhover*: An Experiment in Structural Method." *PMLA*, LXX, 968–78.

Humiliata, Sister Mary. "Hopkins and the Prometheus Myth." *PMLA*, LXX, 58–68.

Miller, J. Hillis. "The Creation of the Self in Gerard Manley Hopkins." *ELH*, XXII, 293–319.

Morris, David. *The Poetry of Gerard Manley Hopkins and T. S. Eliot in the Light of the Donne Tradition.* ("Swiss Studies in English," No. 33.) Berne: A. Francke, 1953. Pp. 144.

Rev. unfavorably by Roger Sharrock in *MLR*, L, 242–43.

Rooney, William Joseph. " 'Spelt from Sibyl's Leaves'—a Study in Contrasting Methods of Evaluation." *JAA*, XIII, 507–19.

Examines several analyses of the Hopkins poem and defends the "structuralist" approach.

Wasmuth, Ewald. "G. M. Hopkins' Ästhetik." *Neue Rundschau*, LXVI, 590–604.

Housman (see also I, Untermeyer, Weber). Haber, Tom Burns. "A. E. Housman's Poetry in Book-Titles." *BSP*, XLIX, 69–77.

Haber, Tom Burns (ed.). *The Manuscript Poems of A. E. Housman: Eight Hundred Lines of Hitherto Uncollected Verse from the Author's Notebooks*. Minneapolis: Univ. of Minnesota Pr. Pp. xvi+146.

Rev. briefly in *CE*, XVI, 393; by Douglas Lochhead in *Dalhousie Rev.*, XXXV, 182, 184; briefly in *EJ*, XLIV, 178; unfavorably by Janet Adam Smith in *NS*, Apr. 30, pp. 619–20; favorably by DeLancey Ferguson in *NYTBR*, Aug. 7, p. 4; by S. E. Smethurst in *QQ*, LXII, 278–80; by John Wain in *S*, Mar. 26, pp. 359–60; by Helen Bevington in *SAQ*, LIV, 565–66; unfavorably in *TLS*, Apr. 29, pp. 189–91 (see also reply and counterreply, July 1, p. 365).

Marlow, A. N. "The Earliest Influences on *A Shropshire Lad*." *RES*, new ser., VI, 166–73.

The influences are the Rev. J. E. Bode, *Ballads from Herodotus;* George Augustus Simcox, *Poems and Romances;* and a volume by scholars of Shrewsbury School, *Sabrinae Corolla*.

Reynolds, Reginald. "The Third Housman." *English*, X, 208–14.

On *The Life of Sir Aglovale de Galis* by Clemence Housman, A. E. Housman's sister.

Werner, W. L., and Dudley, Fred A. "Housman's 'Terence, This Is Stupid Stuff.' " *Ex*, XIV, Item 2.

White, William. "Housman: A Father-Son Collaboration." *MLN*, LXX, 103–4.

An early translation from Horace by A. E. Housman.

White, William. "An Unrecorded Housman MS Item." *BSP*, XLIX, 78–79.

Howitt. Lee, Amice. *Laurels and Rosemary: The Life of William and Mary Howitt*. New York: Oxford Univ. Pr. Pp. 350.

Rev. in *Mercure de France*, CCCXXV, 534; by Kathleen Tillotson in *S*, July 15, p. 104; in *TLS*, June 24, p. 344.

Hughes. Davidson, William W. "*Tom Brown's School Days*, by Thomas Hughes." *Georgia Rev.*, IX, 238–41.

Huxley (see also III, Irvine). Hallam, George W. "Source of the Word 'Agnostic.' " *MLN*, LXX, 265–69.

Ingram. Miller, John Carl. "Poe's English Biographer, John Henry Ingram: A Biographical Account and a Study of His Contributions to Poe Scholarship." *DA*, XIV (1954), 2070–71.

Jefferies. Williamson, Geoffrey. "The Eye of Richard Jefferies." *Lit. Guide*, LXX, 18–19.

Jerdan. Duncan, Robert Wayne. "William Jerdan and the *Literary Gazette*." *DA*, XV, 1396–97.

Refers to Browning and Carlyle, etc. The London *Literary Gazette* was edited by Jerdan from 1817 to 1850.

Jerrold, D. W. (see **Marryat:** McElderry).

Johnson (see also III, Wain). Roseliep, Rev. Raymond. "Some Letters of Lionel Johnson." *DA*, XV, 418.

Ninety-four letters written 1885–98; they continue "from where the one other published selection of his letters ended."

Kingsley, C. (see III, Daniel).

Kipling (see also III, Baetzhold, Daniel, Miner). Birkenhead, Earl of. "The Young Rudyard Kipling." *Essays by Divers Hands: Being the Transactions of the Royal Society of Literature*, XXVII, 65–88.

Maintains that Kipling's childhood troubles did not permanently affect his character.

Carrington, C. E. *The Life of Rudyard Kipling*. New York: Doubleday. Pp. xxi+433.

Rev. by Edward Weeks in *AM*, CXCVI (November), 86; by Carl T. Naumburg in *HTB*, Nov. 20, p. 3; briefly by Earle F. Walbridge in *LJ*, Nov. 1, pp. 2502–3; by John Raymond in *NS*, Nov. 19, pp. 677–78; by DeLancey Ferguson in *NYTBR*,

Nov. 20, p. 5; by John Wain in *S*, Dec. 2, pp. 770–72; by Edgar Johnson in *SR*, Nov. 19, pp. 18–19; by Betty Miller in *TC*, CLVIII, 585–86; in *TLS*, Nov. 25, pp. 697–99.

Escarpit, Robert. *Rudyard Kipling*. Paris: Hachette.

Rev. by Gabriel Venaissin in *Critique*, XI, 589–94.

Weygandt, Ann M. "A Study of Kipling's Use of Historical Material in 'Brother Square-Toes' and 'A Priest in Spite of Himself.' " *Delaware Notes*, XXVII (1954), 83–106.

Landor (see also **Carlyle**: Sanders). Super, R. H. *The Publication of Landor's Works.* . . . See VB 1954, 253.

Rev. by H. A. Smith in *MLR*, L, 528–29; favorably by Bonamy Dobrée in *RES*, new ser., VI, 326–28.

Super, R. H. *Walter Savage Landor.* . . . See VB 1954, 253.

Rev. briefly in *HTB*, Feb. 27, p. 12; by J. H. Buckley in *JEGP*, LIV, 285–87; briefly by Earle F. Walbridge in *LJ*, Sept. 15, 1954, p. 1587; by G. J. Becker in *MLQ*, XVI, 274; favorably by H. A. Smith in *MLR*, L, 528–29; in *TLS*, May 27, pp. 277–78; in *USQBR*, XI, 16.

Lang. Maurer, Oscar. "Andrew Lang and *Longman's Magazine*, 1882–1905." *Univ. of Texas Studies in English*, XXXIV, 152–78.

Lear. Dyson, A. E. "Method in Madness: A Note on Edward Lear." *English*, X, 221–24.

In Lear's poems the romantic attitude is combined with a parody of itself.

Murphy, Ray (ed.). *Edward Lear's Indian Journal: Watercolours and Extracts from [His] Diary, 1873–1875.* New York: Coward. Pp. 240.

Rev. by Carlos Baker in *NYTBR*, May 29, pp. 10–11.

Lee-Hamilton. Lyon, Harvey T. "When Paris Was in Flames." *Colby Libr. Quart.*, IV, 73–78.

Concerning letters of the half-brother of Vernon Lee.

Lewes (see **Dickens**: Haight; **Eliot**: Hardwick, Kaminsky).

Livingstone. Debenham, Frank. *The Way to Ilala: David Livingstone's Pilgrimage*. New York: Longmans. Pp. 336.

Rev. by Walter Elliot in *NS*, Sept. 24, pp. 370–71.

Simmons, Jack. *Livingstone in Africa*. ("Teach Yourself History" ser.) London: English Univs. Pr. Pp. 180.

Rev. by Walter Elliot in *NS*, Sept. 24, pp. 370–71; briefly in *QR*, CCXCIII, 555–56.

Lytton, Robert ("Owen Meredith"). Reece, Byron Herbert. "*Lucile*, by Owen Meredith." *Georgia Rev.*, IX, 107–9.

Macaulay (see III, Daniel, Townsend; **Carlyle**: Sanders).

Maginn, William (see II, Herd).

Manning. Chapeau, Alphonse-Louis-Eugène. *La Vie anglicane de Manning*. Univ. of Paris diss. *Les Lettres de Manning à Gladstone (1837–1851)*. Thèse complémentaire, Univ. of Paris.

Rev. in *Ann. de l'Univ. de Paris*, XXV, 410–12.

Marryat. McElderry, B. R., Jr. "Three Earlier Treatments of the *Billy Budd* Theme." *AL*, XXVII, 251–57.

Melville is known to have borrowed Jerrold's *The Mutiny at the Nore* from the New York Society Library while he was working on *Billy Budd*. Jerrold's *Black-eyed Susan* was one of the most popular plays in nineteenth-century New York. Marryat was one of the best-known writers of sea stories, and his novel, *The King's Own*, was acknowledged as a source for Jerrold's *The Mutiny at the Nore*. All three of these Victorian works contain scenes in which a man unjustly condemned praises the force which condemns him.

Scott, Kenneth W. "Monsieur Violet." *TLS*, Oct. 1, 1954, p. 632. (See also letters by Oliver Warner and Joan Evans, Oct. 8, 1954, p. 641.)

On plagiarism by Marryat.

Martineau (see III, Baetzhold).

Meredith (see also III, Blotner, Daniel, Miner, Wallace; **Carlyle**: Morris). Benish, John Roland. "George Meredith and

Samuel Alexander: An Intellectual Kinship of Poet and Philosopher." *DA*, XV, 1395.

Daniels, Elizabeth Adams. "George Meredith's Women: A Study of Changing Attitudes in Victorian England." *DA*, XV, 1069–70.

Hart, John Edward. "George Meredith: The Quest of Self, a Study in Mythical Pattern and Symbol." *DA*, XIV (1954), 2345–46.

Stevenson, Lionel. "Meredith's Atypical Novel: A Study of *Rhoda Fleming.*" In B. H. Lehman and Others, *The Image of the Work: Essays in Criticism* (Univ. of California Pr.), pp. 89–109.

Identifies a mediocre short story, "The Parish Clerk's Story," in *Once a Week* for Feb. 23, 1861, as written by Meredith; shows how from it he developed *Rhoda Fleming;* and shows that *Rhoda Fleming* marks a significant step in the maturing of the author's skill as a novelist.

Stevenson, Lionel. *The Ordeal of George Meredith.* . . . See VB 1954, 254.

Rev. by C. L. Cline in *JEGP*, LIV, 441; by S. K. Winther in *MLQ*, XVI, 274–75.

Mill (see also III, Mack, Shumaker; **Carlyle:** Sanders). Britton, Karl. *John Stuart Mill.* . . . See VB 1954, 255.

Rev. by R. J. Spilsbury in *Mind*, LXIV, 571; by J. O. Urmson in *Philos. Quart.*, V, 374–75.

Ellery, John Blaise. "The Collected Speeches of John Stuart Mill with Introduction and Notes." *Summ. Doct. Diss., Univ. of Wisconsin*, XV, 570–71.

Freed, Lan. "Principia ethica." *NS*, Apr. 16, p. 536.

In the issue of April 9, Stuart Hampshire had commented on Moore's criticism, in *Principia ethica*, of J. S. Mill's idea of the good. Freed replies here that Moore simply did not understand Mill's position. In his reply (*NS*, Apr. 23, pp. 579–80), Stuart Hampshire defends both his own original article and Moore's interpretation of Mill.

Packe, Michael St. John. *The Life of John Stuart Mill.* . . . See VB 1954, 255.

Rev. by Patrick J. McCarthy in *Arizona Quart.*, XI, 71–73; by Harold A. Larrabee in *JP*, LII, 549–52; by Dwight N. Lindley in *Philos. Rev.*,

LXIV, 660–63; by Richard Clements in *QQ*, LXII, 466–68; in *VQR*, XXXI, lxxii–lxxiii; by Emery Neff in *YR*, XLIV, 448–51.

Raphael, D. Daiches. "Fallacies in and about Mill's Utilitarianism." *Philosophy*, XXX, 344–57.

Stigler, George J. "The Nature and Role of Originality in Scientific Progress." *Economica*, new ser., XXII, 293–302.

Schumpeter characterized J. S. Mill as the fairest of economists, but he is usually dismissed by economists, as a literary figure, deficient in originality. Stigler singles out six important ideas contributed to economics by Mill. Why, then, are these original contributions overlooked? Because Mill was interested in the advancement of knowledge, not in advancing either himself or a set of his own theories. He advanced these original ideas without even calling attention to their originality; consequently, few in his day or ours have recognized what the science of economics owes to him.—F. G. T.

Strong, E. W. "William Whewell and John Stuart Mill: Their Controversy about Scientific Knowledge." *JHI*, XVI, 209–31.

Milman. Parker, W. M. "Dean Milman and *The Quarterly Review.*" *QR*, CCXCIII, 30–43.

Really a short, interesting biography of Henry Hart Milman. Contains excerpts from hitherto unpublished letters of Milman and Carlyle.

Mitford. Duncan-Jones, C. M. (ed.). *Miss Mitford and Mr. Harness.* London: S.P.C.K.

Rev. in *TLS*, Dec. 16, p. 762. Based on unpublished letters and diaries.

Moore (see also III, Shumaker). Brown, Malcolm. *George Moore: A Reconsideration.* Seattle: Univ. of Washington Pr. Pp. 235.

Rev. by Mary Colum in *NYTBR*, Dec. 11, p. 4; favorably by Leon Edel in *SR*, Jan. 7, 1956, p. 10.

Chaikin, Milton. "The Composition of George Moore's *A Modern Lover.*" *Comp. Lit.*, VII, 259–64.

French influences on Moore's first novel.

Chaikin, Milton. "The Influence of French Realism and Naturalism on George Moore's Early Fiction." *DA*, XV, 1068.

Perkins, William Arthur. "George Moore's Realistic Novels: Roots, Achievements, Influence." *DA*, XIV (1954), 2350–51.

Shumaker, Wayne. "The Autobiographer as Artist: George Moore's *Hail and Farewell.*" In B. H. Lehman and Others, *The Image of the Work: Essays in Criticism* (Univ. of California Pr.), pp. 159–85.

Morley (see III, Townsend; **Hardy:** Weber).

Morris (see also I, *Rosenwald;* III, Daniel). Kegel, Charles H. "William Morris's *A Dream of John Ball:* A Study in Reactionary Liberalism." *Papers of the Michigan Acad. of Science, Arts, and Letters*, XL, 303–12.

In this source study, Kegel finds that Morris relied for his medieval materials mainly on Froissart, partly on Knighton and Walsingham. For the economic interpretation of these materials, Morris was indebted to James E. Thorold Rogers.

Maurer, Oscar. "Morris's Treatment of Greek Legend in *The Earthly Paradise.*" *Univ. of Texas Studies in English*, XXXIII (1954), 103–18.

Schmidt-Kunsemüller, Friedrich Adolf. *William Morris und die neuere Buchkunst.* Wiesbaden: Harrassowitz.

Rev. by S. H. Steinberg in *Library*, 5th ser., X, 298–301.

Smith, H. "The Economics of Socialism Reconsidered." *Econ. Jour.*, LXV, 411–21.

Thompson, E. P. *William Morris: Romantic to Revolutionary.* London: Lawrence. Pp. 908.

Rev. favorably by Norman Mackenzie in *NS*, July 16, pp. 74–76; unfavorably in *TLS*, July 15, p. 391. A study of Morris from the Marxian point of view.

Newman, F. W. (see II, Murphy).

Newman, J. H. (see also II, Simmons). Allen, Louis. "Two Letters from the Newman Archives." *DUJ*, XLVII, 57–67.

A very fine editorial job by Allen brings out the full meaning of these hitherto unpublished letters to Newman, one from Albany Christie, dated Aug. 11, 1844, and written at Malines; the other from J. D. Dalgairns, dated Dec. 19, 1845, and written at Langres.

Culler, A. Dwight. *The Imperial Intellect: A Study of Newman's Educational Ideal.* New Haven, Conn.: Yale Univ. Pr. Pp. 327.

Dinwiddy, Hugh. "Cardinal Newman—the Literary Aspect." *Dublin Rev.*, CCXXIX, 90–97.

Gwynn, Denis. "Some Afterthoughts on the Newman Centenary Celebrations." *Univ. Rev.* (Dublin), I, No. 2 (autumn, 1954), 3–9.

Hosey, Joseph Francis. "Physical Science in Newman's Thought." *DA*, XIV (1954), 1411.

O'Meara, J. J. "Augustine and Newman: Comparison in Conversion." *Univ. Rev.* (Dublin), I, No. 1 (summer, 1954), 27–36.

Pond, Kathleen. "Letters from Newman and Others to Sir Peter LePage Renouf." *Dublin Rev.*, CCXXIX, 321–33, 446–56.

Letters mainly from Ambrose Phillipps and Newman to a prominent convert.

Svaglic, Martin J. "Newman and the Oriel Fellowship." *PMLA*, LXX, 1014–32.

A valuable account, using unpublished material, of a crucial episode in Newman's early life.

Norton, C. (see **Fullerton:** Lochhead).

Oliphant. Keith, Sara. "Margaret Oliphant." *N & Q*, new ser., II, 126–27.

Suggests attributing eight novels to Mrs. Margaret Oliphant instead of to her brother.

Ouida. Stirling, Monice. "La dernière romancière." Translated by Pierre Bandet. *Rev. de Paris*, LXII (December), 111–21.

An interesting biographical sketch of Maria-Louise Ramé, better known as Ouida, who was sure that her girlhood dreams of great wealth and the one great passion would be realized. The wealth she acquired early, but not the lover, so in her middle years she took to assuming that men loved her, and in her old age she kept dogs in incredible numbers. Her books are ridiculous, but they are still readable.—F. G. T.

Pardoe. Szladits, Lola L. "A Victorian Literary Correspondence: Letters from Julia Pardoe to Sir John Philippart, 1841–1860." *Bull. New York Pub. Libr.*, LIX, 367–78.

Pater (see III, Appleman, Bowra). Cecil, Lord David. *Walter Pater: The Scholar-Artist.* Cambridge: Cambridge Univ. Pr.

The Rede Lecture, delivered in May, 1955.

West, Paul. "Walter Pater and 'The Voices of Silence.' " *Adelphi*, XXXI, 355–63.

Peacock. Salz, Paulina June. "Peacock's Use of Music in His Novels." *JEGP*, LIV, 370–79.

Peacock uses musical forms in the structures of his plots and in the rhythms of his prose.

Philippart, Sir John (see **Pardoe:** Szladits).

Phillipps (see **Newman:** Pond).

Pinero (see also III, Stanton). England, Denzil. "Pinero: A Centenary." *CR*, CLXXXVII, 313–18.

Planché. Nadeau, Albert Henry. "James Robinson Planché, Craftsman of Extravaganza." *DA*, XV, 1676.

Reade (see also III, Daniel). Allen, Eliot Dinsmore. "The Literary Reputation of Charles Reade." *DA*, XV, 409.

The bibliography of this dissertation "attempts to give a considerably fuller list both of Reade's own writings, published and in manuscript, and of writings about Reade, than is found elsewhere."

Bankson, Douglas Henneck. "Charles Reade's Manuscript Notecards for *Hard Cash*." *DA*, XIV (1954), 2341.

Reynolds (see also III, Marsh). Marsh, George L. (ed.). *The Poetical Works of John Hamilton Reynolds*. Microfilm PR 158, University of Chicago Library.

Ros. Loudan, Jack. *O Rare Amanda! The Life of Amanda McKittrick Ros.* London: Chatto.

Rev. by Eric Gillett in *NER*, CXLIV, 43–44; favorably by G. W. Stonier in *NS*, Jan. 8, p. 48. Judging from the reviews, the works of Amanda McKittrick Ros will shortly be revived as prime examples of bad Victorian fiction.— F. G. T.

Rossettis. Chewning, Harris. "William Michael Rossetti and the Shelley Renaissance." *Keats-Shelley Jour.*, IV, 81–96.

Cooper, Robert Maxwell. "Dante Gabriel Rossetti: Lost on Both Sides, a Study of His Background, Criticism, and Poetry." *DA*, XV, 415.

Garlitz, Barbara. "Christina Rossetti's *Sing-Song* and Nineteenth-Century Children's Poetry." *PMLA*, LXX, 539–43.

Stresses the moral import of many of Christina Rossetti's children's poems.

Kühnelt, H. H. "Die Bedeutung der italienischen Malerei für den Dichter Dante Gabriel Rossetti." *Anglia*, LXXII, 438–54.

Sawtell, Margaret. *Christina Rossetti*. London: Mowbrays.

Ruskin (see also I, Fielding; III, Hale). Bradley, John Lewis (ed.). *Ruskin's Letters from Venice, 1851–52*. ("Yale Studies in English," Vol. CXXIX.) New Haven: Yale Univ. Pr. Pp. xx+330.

Rev. by Alfred Frankfurter in *NYTBR*, Nov. 6, p. 36. Unpublished letters from Ruskin to his father are especially important as indicating changes in his religious attitudes.

Burd, Van Akin. "The Winnington Letters." *VNL*, No. 8 (autumn), pp. 4–5.

On a projected edition of 225 letters written 1859–70 between Ruskin and Miss Margaret Bell and her girl pupils at Winnington Hall in Cheshire.

Dougherty, Charles. "Ruskin's Views on Non-representational Art." *College Art Jour.*, XV, 112–18.

In one of the best articles on Ruskin in recent years, Dougherty marshals evidence to show that, although Ruskin was well aware of the formal qualities of a work of art, he did not believe that a painter can ignore external reality. The beauty of a work of art resides in its formal qualities, but its truth rests in its grasp of external reality. Roger Fry declared that in the work of art a man's head is of no more significance than a pumpkin, to which Ruskin's reply would have been about as follows: "The artist who sees no more in a man's head than he does in a pumpkin has never *seen* a man's head at all, whatever he may mean by his 'vision.' " —F. G. T.

Evans, Joan. *John Ruskin*. . . . See VB 1954, 256.

Rev. briefly by James R. Wilson in *BA*, XXIX, 475; briefly by P. Fontaney in *Études anglaises*, VIII, 349; by E. D. H. Johnson in *MLN*, LXX, 533–35; in *VQR*, XXXI, lxxv; by Emery Neff in *YR*, XLIV, 448–51.

Morris, Bertram. "Ruskin on the Pathetic Fallacy, or on How a Moral Theory of Art May Fail." *JAA*, XIV, 248–66.

A valuable article with a somewhat misleading title. Morris contrasts Ruskin's moral theory of art with twentieth-century theories of "pure" art (Fry, Bell).

Salomon, Louis B. "The Pound-Ruskin Axis." *CE*, XVI, 270–76.

Parallels, in attitude and subject matter, between two headstrong reformers.

Skelton, Robin. "John Ruskin, the Final Years: A Survey of the Ruskin Correspondence in the John Rylands Library." *Bull. John Rylands Libr.*, XXXVII, 562–86.

Treats newly acquired correspondence with Mrs. Fanny Talbot and her son Quartus. His letters to Miss Blanche Atkinson are "too important for summary treatment" in this article. Talbot correspondence gives many new facts about the Guild of St. George and Ruskin's last years.

Salt. Flanagan, John T. "Henry Salt and His Life of Thoreau." *NEQ*, XXVIII, 237–46.

Publishes for the first time thirteen letters from Salt to Richard Bentley.

Schreiner. Davidson, Basil. "In Memory of Olive Schreiner." *NS*, Mar. 26, pp. 426–28.

Recalls Olive Schreiner's bitter criticism of racial relations in South Africa.

Hobman, D. L. *Olive Schreiner: Her Friends and Times.* London: Watts. Pp. 192.

Rev. in *TLS*, Mar. 25, p. 176.

Plomer, William. "Olive Schreiner: Her Life and Ideals." *Listener*, Mar. 24, pp. 521–22.

Renier, Olive. "A South African Rebel." *Listener*, Apr. 7, pp. 613–14.

Shaw (see also I, Untermeyer; II, Terris; III, Stanton). *Advice to a Young Critic and Other Letters.* Notes and introd. by E. J. West. New York: Crown, 1955. Pp. 208. (Incorrectly listed in VB 1954, 256.)

Rev. briefly by Earle F. Walbridge in *LJ*, Dec. 1, p. 2769.

Anon. "Shaw's Last Known Play: Should It Be Published?" *Manchester Guardian Weekly*, Oct. 27, p. 14.

On a fragmentary manuscript entitled "Why She Would Not."

Cecchi, Emilio. "L'Eclisse di Shaw." *Nuova antol.*, XC, 217–24.

Connolly, Thomas E. "Shaw's St. Joan." *Ex*, XIV, Item 18.

Coxe, Louis O. "*You Never Can Tell:* G. B. Shaw Reviewed." *Western Humanities Rev.*, IX, 313–25.

Drew, Arnold P. "*Pygmalion* and *Pickwick*." *N & Q*, new ser., II, 221–22.

Parallel scenes.

Gassner, John. "The Practicality of Impractical Criticism." *Theatre Arts*, XXXIX (February), 22–23, 95–96.

Shaw commended for routing "Nice-Nellyism from the British stage."

Kaye, Julian Bertram. "Bernard Shaw and the Nineteenth-Century Tradition." *DA*, XV, 269.

Lüdeke, H. "Some Remarks on Shaw's History Plays." *ESt*, XXXVI, 239–46.

Mander, Raymond, and Mitchenson, Joe. *Theatrical Companion to Shaw: A Pictorial Record of the First Performances of the Plays of George Bernard Shaw.* Introd. by Sir Barry Jackson. New York: Pitman. Pp. 343.

Rev. briefly in *CE*, XVII, 59; by George Freedley in *LJ*, June 1, p. 1396; in *N & Q*, new ser., II, 414; by Gerard Fay in *S*, Feb. 11, p. 166; by John Gassner in *Theatre Arts*, XXXIX (July), 9–10; by I. K. F. in *Theatre Notebook*, IX, 80.

O'Casey, Sean. "Shaw's Corner." *Shavian*, No. 4, new ser., pp. 2–5.

Purcell, Victor. "Shaw, Russell, Toynbee, and the Far East." *Shavian*, No. 4, new ser., pp. 15–19.

Sharp, William Leslie. "The Relation of Dramatic Structure to Comedy in the Plays of George Bernard Shaw." *DA*, XIV (1954), 1007–8.

Shattuck, Charles H. "Bernard Shaw's 'Bad Quarto.'" *JEGP*, LIV, 651–53.

On the 1893 edition of *Widower's Houses.*

Shaw Bulletin

No. 7 (January, 1955) has items: "The Blanco Posnet Controversy," including Shaw, Bernard: "Blanco Posnet Banned by the Censor," Joyce, James: "Shaw's Battle with the Censor," Yeats, William Butler: "The Religion of Blanco" (pp. 1–9); Woolf, Virginia, "Virginia Woolf on Shaw"

(p. 9); Griffin, Alice, "The New York Critics and 'Saint Joan'" (pp. 10–15); Batson, Eric J., "Hyperion and the Yahoos" (pp. 16–18); Honan, William, "A Presentational 'Saint Joan'" (pp. 19–21); Code, Grant, "Shaw at Hedgerow" (pp. 22–24); Fry, Christopher, "Nearer a Spiritual Positive" (p. 24).

No. 8 (May, 1955) has items: Barzun, Jacques, "Shaw and Rousseau: No Paradox" (pp. 1–6); L'Donnell, Norbert F., "On the 'Unpleasantness' of *Pygmalion*" (pp. 7–10); Henderson, Archibald, "Shaw's Novels: And Why They Failed" (pp. 11–18); Batson, Eric J., "The Quintessence of Winstenism" (pp. 19–21); Grendon, Felix, "Theatre Notes: The Phoenix's Dilemma" (pp. 22–24).

No. 9 (September, 1955) has items: Nethercot, Arthur H., "G. B. S. and Annie Besant" (pp. 1–14); Scully, Frank, "The Ghost Talks" (pp. 15–18); Laurence, Dan H., "Shaw's Final Curtain" (pp. 19–21); Seabrook, Alexander, "Footlights on Shaw" (pp. 22–24).

Shaw, Frank. "We Were Both Shaw." *Shavian*, No. 4, new ser., pp. 1–2.

Smith, J. Percy. "A Shavian Tragedy: The Doctor's Dilemma." In B. H. Lehman and Others, *The Image of the Work: Essays in Criticism* (Univ. of California Pr.), pp. 187–207.

Stoppel, Hans. "Shaw and Sainthood." *ESt*, XXXVI, 49–63.

West, E. J. "Some Uncollected Shaviana on Theatre and Drama." *Shavian*, No. 5, new ser., pp. 24–26.

Zerke, Carl Frederick. "George Bernard Shaw's Ideas on Acting." *DA*, XIV (1954), 1850–51.

Simcox (see **Housman:** Marlow).

Smith, Alex (see **Brownings:** Thale).

Smith, Sydney. Lane, William G. "Additional Letters of Sydney Smith." *HLB*, IX, 397–402.

Includes four letters from Smith to R. H. Barham.

Spencer. Taylor, Arthur J. "The Originality of Herbert Spencer." *Univ. of Texas Studies in English*, XXXIV, 101–6.

Stephen (see also III, Appleman). Baldanza, Frank. "*To the Lighthouse* Again." *PMLA*, LXX, 548–52.

Leslie Stephen exorcised (as Mr. Ramsay) by Virginia Woolf.

Stevenson (see also III, Allen, Wallace). Booth, Bradford A. "The Letters of Robert Louis Stevenson." *VNL*, No. 8 (autumn), pp. 3–4.

A definitive and scholarly edition in progress.

Ed. "Robert Louis Stevenson [books and MSS acquired in 1954]." *PLC*, XVI, 100–101.

Jordan, John E. (ed.). *Robert Louis Stevenson's Silverado Journal*. Privately printed, San Francisco: Book Club of California, 1954. Pp. lxxii+95.

MacArthur, W. P. "The Appin Murder." *Scottish Hist. Rev.*, XXXIV, 183–88.

Lends support to Lord Cameron's conclusion —see VB 1954, 258.

Neider, Charles (ed.). *Our Samoan Adventure: With a Three-Year Diary by Mrs. Stevenson Now Published for the First Time, Together with Rare Photographs from Family Albums*. New York: Harper. Pp. xxii+264.

Rev. by J. C. Furnas in *HTB*, Sept. 11, p. 4; briefly by Earle F. Walbridge in *LJ*, Sept. 15, p. 1919; by DeLancey Ferguson in *NYTBR*, Sept. 18, p. 10; by H. M. Jones in *SR*, Sept. 17, p. 22; in *USQBR*, XI, 445.

Swinburne (see also III, Dahl). Lang, Cecil Y. "Some Swinburne Manuscripts." *Jour. Rutgers Univ. Libr.*, XVIII (1954), 1–11.

Includes photographic reproduction of the first draft of three stanzas of *Atalanta in Calydon*.

Mayfield, John S. "Two Presentation Copies of Swinburne's *Atalanta in Calydon*." *BSP*, XLIX, 360–65.

Miller, F. De Wolfe. "Lowell the Author of 'Bayard Taylor's' Review of *Laus Veneris*." *AL*, XXVII, 106–9.

Cites a hitherto unpublished letter from C. P. Cranch to Lowell which shows clearly that Lowell was the author of the important article on *Laus Veneris* in the *North American Review* for January, 1867. This review has been attributed to Bayard Taylor since Cushing's index (1878).— F. G. T.

Symonds (see also III, Appleman, Hale). Cochrane, Marie Davis. "John Addington Symonds: Critic of Literature and Art." *Summ. Doct. Diss., Univ. of Wisconsin*, XV, 599–600.

Symons. Lhombreaud, Roger. "Arthur Rimbaud et l'un de ses commentateurs anglais: Arthur Symons." *Rev. de litt. comp.*, XXXIX, 88–91.

Tennyson (see also III, Dahl, Daniel, Hopkins; **Carlyle:** Eidson, Sanders). "The Christ of Ammergau." *TC*, CLVII, 2–3. (See *TLS*, Feb. 18, p. 110.)

This poem, twenty lines long, was recently discovered among the papers of James Knowles, founder of the *Nineteenth Century*, along with Knowles's account of how Tennyson composed it in 1870, as a comment on the Vatican Council.

Allott, Miriam. "James Russell Lowell: A Link between Tennyson and Henry James." *RES*, new ser., VI, 399–401.

Both James and Tennyson made use of a legend told them by Lowell.

Allott, Miriam. " 'The Lord of Burleigh' and Henry James's 'A Landscape Painter.' " *N & Q*, new ser., II, 220–21.

Claims Tennyson's poem is the source of James's story.

Burchell, Samuel C. "Tennyson's Dark Night." *SAQ*, LIV, 75–81.

"*In Memoriam* now finally merits the serious attention of modern critics."

Engelberg, Edward. "The Beast Image in Tennyson's *Idylls of the King*." *ELH*, XXII, 287–92.

Structural unity and dramatic intensity in the *Idylls* are increased by the progressive violence of the beast imagery.

Lerner, Laurence D. "In Memoriam 1955." *EC*, V, 152.

A perceptive comment, in verse, on Tennyson's language.

Miller, Betty. "Tennyson and the Sinful Queen." *TC*, CLVIII, 355–63.

This is without doubt the finest essay on Tennyson in recent years. The reading of Milton's *Samson Agonistes* made a profound impression on the twelve-year-old Tennyson. For the rest of his life he feared he was going blind,

and he associated sexual intercourse with the loss of power, as in the case of Merlin, who, after the storm had spent its passion and left the ravaged woodland at peace, confided his secret to Vivien, and slept. "*I* am Merlin/Who follow the Gleam." Why is it that in the early poetry of Tennyson the woman so often waits in solitude for the lover who is strangely absent?

Malory, contends Betty Miller, fascinated Tennyson because of the attachment of man for man in the *Morte d'Arthur* and the distinct subordination of women. But whereas Malory attributed the tragedy to Arthur's incest, Tennyson suppressed the Oedipus echoes and blamed the fall of the ideal on a woman's lust.—F. G. T.

Munsterberg, Margaret. "Letters from Lady Tennyson." *BPLQ*, VII, 175–91.

Some eighty letters from Emily, Lady Tennyson, to Mr. and Mrs. Gatty, November, 1858—February, 1873, recently acquired by the library. The Gattys are not named in the *Memoir* by Hallam or in the biography by Charles. Yet the letters bear witness to a "cordial and sympathetic friendship" between the two families.

Pierce, Anne Longfellow. "A Visit to Farringford." *Boston Univ. Studies in English*, I, 96–98.

T., G. "Tennyson and 'The Revenge.' " *N & Q*, new ser., II, 152.

A possible source.

Thackeray (see also III, Daniel). Baker, Joseph E. "*Vanity Fair* and the Celestial City." *NCF*, X, 89–98.

Ray, Gordon N. *Thackeray: The Uses of Adversity, 1811–1846*. New York: McGraw-Hill. Pp. xiii+537.

Rev. by DeLancey Ferguson in *HTB*, Oct. 9, p. 3; briefly by Earle F. Walbridge in *LJ*, Oct. 14, p. 2240; by Jacob Korg in *N*, Dec. 31, p. 580; favorably by Leon Edel in *New R*, Nov. 7, p. 17; by Edgar Johnson in *NYTBR*, Oct. 9, pp. 14–15; favorably by William Irvine in *SR*, Dec. 24, pp. 25, 29; favorably in *TLS*, Jan. 20, 1956, p. 29 (leading article, "Vindicating Thackeray").

Ray, Gordon N. "Thackeray's *Book of Snobs*." *NCF*, X, 22–33.

Thackeray was bearing witness to the existing state of English society, not unconsciously revealing a blemish in his moral nature, when he took snobbery as his guide in surveying English life.

Ray, Gordon N. (ed.). *William Makepeace Thackeray's Contributions to the Morning Chronicle*. Urbana: Univ. of Illinois Pr. Pp. 213.

Thirty-five reviews identified by Ray show the development of Thackeray's ideas about fiction. Rev. briefly by R. K. Barksdale in *CE*, XVII, 195.

Schöne, Annemarie. "W. M. Thackeray, *The Rose and the Ring*: Feenmärchen oder Non-sense-Dichtung?" *Arch. f. d. Studium der neueren Sprachen*, CXCI, 273–84.

Classifies the tale as belonging mainly to the category of nonsense.

Sherbo, Arthur. "A Suggestion for the Origin of Thackeray's Rawdon Crawley." *NCF*, X, 211–16.

Asserts that George James Cholmondeley is the original of Rawdon.

Spilka, Mark. "A Note on Thackeray's Amelia." *NCF*, X, 202–10.

The portrait of Amelia in the first half of the novel is "a dramatic fraud."

Tillotson, Geoffrey. *Thackeray the Novelist.* . . . See VB 1954, 259.

Rev. in *Adelphi*, XXXI, 204–6; by M. W. Askew in *BA*, XXIX, p. 350; briefly in *CE*, XVI, 521; by Arundell Esdaile in *English*, X, 148–49; by Lettice Cooper in *London Mag.*, II, 96–100; by Lionel Stevenson in *NCF*, X, 80–83; briefly in *N & Q*, new ser., II, 138; briefly in *QR*, CCXCIII, 137; by Paull F. Baum in *SAQ*, LIV, 426–28; by Gordon S. Haight in *YR*, XLIV, 610–12.

Thomas. Thomas, Jevan Brandon. *Charley's Aunt's Father*. London: Saunders. Pp. 232.

Rev. by Bernard Gutteridge in *NS*, Nov. 5, p. 592. A life of Brandon Thomas.

Thomson (see III, Dahl).

Trollope (see also III, Blotner, Daniel, Shumaker). Cockshut, A. O. J. *Anthony Trollope: A Critical Study*. London: Collins. Pp. 256.

Rev. by V. S. Pritchett in *NS*, Oct. 1, pp. 399–400; by John Holloway in *S*, Sept. 23, p. 396; in *TLS*, Sept. 23, pp. 549–50.

Ed. "Trollope's 'Did He Steal It?' " *PLC*, XVII, 47.

On a copy of Trollope's play and other items from the collection of Miss Muriel Trollope.

Houston, Maude C. "Structure and Plot in *The Warden*." *Univ. of Texas Studies in English*, XXXIV, 107–13.

Maxwell, Constantia. "Anthony Trollope and Ireland." *Dublin Mag.*, XXXI, 6–16.

Walt, James, "Trollope's Literary Apprenticeship." *DA*, XV, 2219–20.

Ward (see also III, Blotner). Suckow, Ruth. "*Robert Elsmere*." *Georgia Rev.*, IX, 344–48.

Waterton. Irwin, R. A. (ed.). *The Letters of Charles Waterton of Walton Hall near Wakefield*. . . . London: Rockliff. Pp. 159.

Rev. by Francis Huxley in *NS*, Sept. 24, p. 374; in *TLS*, July 8, p. 383.

Whewell (see also Mill: Strong). Whitmore, Charles E. "The Language of Science." *Scient. Month.*, LXXX, 185–91.

Recalls how Faraday besought Whewell's aid in devising a terminology to express new concepts in electromagnetism. To Whewell we owe such terms as "anode," "cathode," and "ion," which Faraday found highly useful in expression.

White, W. H. Beresford, Rosemary. " 'Mark Rutherford' and Hero-Worship." *RES*, new ser., VI, 264–72.

Replies to Wilfred H. Stone's charge that White, having lost his faith in God, used literary celebrities as surrogates. On p. 272, Stone repeats his charge and refers Beresford to his recent book (see below).

Low, Florence B. "Walks and Talks with Mark Rutherford." *CR*, CLXXXVII, 405–9.

Maclean, Catherine Macdonald. *Mark Rutherford: A Biography of William Hale White*. London: Macdonald. Pp. 416.

Rev. by Sylva Norman in *CR*, CLXXXVIII, 283–84; by John Rowland in *HJ*, LIII, 414–15; by Maurice Cranston in *London Mag.*, II, 84–88; in *N & Q*, new ser., II, 504–5; favorably by John Raymond in *NS*, Sept. 3, pp. 273–74; briefly in *QR*, CCXCIII, 553–54; in *TLS*, June 17, p. 332.

Stone, Wilfred. *Religion and the Art of William Hale White*. . . . See VB 1954, 260.

Rev. by L. R. Miller in *LJ*, Oct. 15, p. 2338; briefly in *NCF*, IX, 318; favorably by John Raymond in *NS*, Sept. 3, pp. 273–74; in *TLS*, June 17, p. 332.

Wilde (see also III, Stanton). *Adam.* A composite number (Nos. 244, 245, 246) of this periodical is devoted to reminiscences of Wilde by surviving contemporaries, including Lady Emily Lutyens, Sir Max Beerbohm, and Laurence Housman.

Rev. in *TLS*, Mar. 25, p. 186.

Ebermayer, Erich. *Das ungewöhnliche Leben des Oscar Wilde.* Bonn: Athenäum, 1954. Pp. 324.

Rev. unfavorably by Richard Exner in *BA*, XXIX, 446–47. The gravity of Exner's charges makes this an important review. "Ebermayer stresses the famous trial of 1895, taking his material (again in part verbatim and entirely unacknowledged) from *The Trials of Oscar Wilde* (1948)."

Furnell, John. *The Stringed Lute: An Evocation in Dialogue of Oscar Wilde.* London: Rider.

Holland, Vyvyan. *Son of Oscar Wilde....* See VB 1954, 260.

Rev. by Angus Wilson in *London Mag.*, II, 71–78; in *Mercure de France*, CCCXXV, 149; by Shane Leslie in *Month*, XIII, 49–52; by Julian Blackburn in *QQ*, LXII, 292–93.

Horodisch, Abraham. *Oscar Wilde's Ballad of Reading Gaol: A Bibliographical Study.* New Preston, Conn.: Aldus Book Co., 1954. Pp. 126.

Noted in *Publishers' Weekly*, Feb. 12, p. 1105.

Ojala, Aatos. *Aestheticism and Oscar Wilde.* Part I: *Life and Letters.* Helsinki: Academia Scientiarum Fennica, 1954. Pp. 231.

Rev. in *Dublin Mag.*, XXXI, 43–44; by Marjorie Thompson in *MLR*, L, 570–71.

O'Neill, Michael J. "Unpublished Lecture Notes of a Speech by Oscar Wilde at San Francisco." *Univ. Rev.* (Dublin), I, No. 4 (Spring, 1955), 29–32.

Thomas, J. D. "Oscar Wilde's Pose and Poetry." *Rice Institute Pamphlet*, XLII, No. 3, 32–52.

Vordtriede, Werner. "A Dramatic Device in *Faust* and *The Importance of Being Earnest*." *MLN*, LXX, 584–85.

Yeats (see also I, Untermeyer; III, Miner, Tindall, Wain). *The Autobiography of William Butler Yeats....* See VB 1954, 260.

Rev. by Kathleen Raine in *Listener*, Mar. 24, p. 540; by Jacques Vallette in *Mercure de France*, CCCXXV, 141–44; by Wulstan Phillipson in *Month*, XIV, 309–10; by Eric Gillett in *NER*, CLXIV, 229–30; by G. S. Fraser in *NS*, May 21, pp. 723–24; briefly in *QR*, CCXCIII, 558; in *TLS*, Apr. 29, p. 201.

The Letters of W. B. Yeats.... See VB 1954, 260.

Rev. by Hazard Adams in *Accent*, XV, 234–37; briefly in *CE*, XVI, 466; in *Dublin Mag.*, XXXI, 52–53; briefly in *EJ*, XLIV, 246; by H. W. Häusermann in *ESt*, XXXVI, 284–86; favorably by M. L. Cazamian in *Études anglaises*, VIII, 50–60; by Maurice Dolbier in *Harper's*, CCX (April), 98; by Babette Deutsch in *HTB*, Mar. 6, p. 3; by Robert Phelps in *KR*, XVII, 495–500; briefly by Mary H. Ziprids in *LJ*, Feb. 15, p. 451; briefly in *N*, July 9, p. 29; by Leon Edel in *New R*, Mar. 14, pp. 21–22; by Mary Colum in *NYTBR*, Feb. 20, p. 7; in *QR*, CCXCIII, 279–80; by DeLancey Ferguson in *SR*, May 14, p. 12; by Cleanth Brooks in *YR*, XLIV, 618–20.

Adams, Hazard. *Blake and Yeats: The Contrary Vision.* ("Cornell Studies in English," Vol. XL.) Ithaca: Cornell Univ. Pr. Pp. 339.

Beerbohm, Sir Max. "First Meetings with William Butler Yeats." *Listener*, Jan. 6, pp. 15–16.

Blenner-Hassett, Roland. "Yeats' Use of Chaucer." *Anglia*, LXXII, 455–62.

Block, Haskell M. "Yeats's *The King's Threshold*: The Poet and Society." *PQ*, XXXIV, 206–18.

Campbell, Harry M. "Yeats's 'Sailing to Byzantium.'" *MLN*, LXX, 585–89.

Davie, Donald. "Yeats and Pound." *Dublin Mag.*, XXXI, 17–21.

Ellmann, Richard. *The Identity of Yeats....* See VB 1954, 261.

Rev. by Hazard Adams in *Accent*, XV, 234–37; briefly in *CE*, XVI, 327–28; briefly in *EJ*, XLIV, 120; by Sally Appleton in *Thought*, XXX, 319–20; by Reuben A. Brower in *YR*, XLIV, 290–92.

Gleckner, Robert F. "Blake and Yeats." *N & Q*, new ser., II, 38.

Irish Writing, No. 31 (summer). A special issue (ed. by S. J. White) devoted to Yeats contains items as follows: Allt, Peter, "Lady Gregory and Yeats' Cult of Aristocracy" (pp. 19–23); Bradford, Curtis, "*The Speckled Bird*: A Novel by W. B. Yeats" (pp. 9–19); Davie, Donald, "Yeats, Berkeley, and Romanticism" (pp. 36–41); Iremonger, Valentin, "Yeats as a Playwright" (pp. 51–57); Kenner, Hugh, "The Sacred Book of the Arts" (pp. 24–35); Ure, Peter, "Yeats's 'Demon and Beast' " (pp. 42–50).

Rev. by Anthony Hartley in *S*, Dec. 2, p. 778.

Margolis, Joseph. "Yeats' 'Leda and the Swan.' " *Ex*, XIII, Item 34.

Moore, Virginia. *The Unicorn: William Butler Yeats' Search for Reality.* . . . See VB 1954, 261.

Rev. by Charles C. Walcutt in *Arizona Quart.*, XI, 170–73; briefly by Stanley K. Coffman, Jr., in *BA*, XXIX, 226; by Russell Krauss in *Ed. Forum*, XIX, 250–51; by W. D. Templeman in *Personalist*, XXXVI, 424–25; by Reuben A. Brower in *YR*, XLIV, 290–92.

Noon, William. "Yeats and the Human Body." *Thought*, XXX, 188–98.

Parkinson, Thomas. "The World of Yeats' 'Nineteen Hundred and Nineteen.' " In B. H. Lehman and Others, *The Image of the Work: Essays in Criticism* (Univ. of California Pr.), pp. 211–27.

Paul, David. "Yeats and the Irish Mind." *TC*, CLVIII, 66–75.

Despite its generalizations on something called "the Irish mind," this essay is an excellent specimen of the much maligned art of appreciation.

In retrospect, Yeats seems one of the few poets of the last century whose life and work form a coherent unit, in which even the political wrangling and theatrical bickering had their proper function in guarding him from sterility. In retrospect he seems more rational than the rationalists, the poet of greatest intellectual stature since Baudelaire. Nevertheless, his poetry was always too spare. His condescension to Keats is coarse, because "it is so obvious a mask for his own envy of a luxuriance he could never command."— F. G. T.

Rao, K. Bhaskaro. "The Impact of Theosophy on the Poetry of W. B. Yeats." *Aryan Path*, XXVI, 545–52.

Rubenstein, J. S. "Three Misprints in Yeats's *Collected Poems*." *MLN*, LXX, 184–86.

Rutherford, Andrew. "Yeats's 'Who Goes with Fergus?' " *Ex*, XIII, Item 41.

Sees the poem as a call to revelry, Fergus as an Irish Dionysos.

Suss, Irving David. "Yeatsian Drama and the Dying Hero." *SAQ*, LIV, 369–80.

Taylor, Estella Ruth. *The Modern Irish Writers: Cross Currents of Criticism*. Lawrence: Univ. of Kansas Pr., 1954. Pp. 176.

Rev. briefly by Robert H. Sproat in *QJS*, XLI, 204. About writers of the Irish renaissance, including Yeats.

Wildi, Max. "The Influence and Poetic Development of W. B. Yeats." *ESt*, XXXVI, 246–53.

Witt, Marion. "An Unknown Yeats Poem." *MLN*, LXX, 26.

On "The Glove and the Cloak" (1897).

VICTORIAN BIBLIOGRAPHY FOR 1956

Edited by FRANCIS G. TOWNSEND

THIS bibliography has been prepared by a committee of the Victorian Literature Group of the Modern Language Association of America: Francis G. Townsend, chairman, Florida State University; William D. Templeman, University of Southern California; Robert C. Slack, Carnegie Institute of Technology; Oscar Maurer, University of Texas; Robert A. Donovan, Cornell University; and Charles T. Dougherty, St. Louis University. It attempts to list the noteworthy publications of 1956 (including reviews of these and earlier items) that have a bearing on English literature of the Victorian period, as well as similar publications of earlier date that have been inadvertently omitted from the preceding Victorian bibliographies. Unless otherwise stated, the date of publication is 1956. Reference to a page in the bibliography for 1955, in *Modern Philology*, May, 1956, is made by the following form: See VB 1955, 260. Some cross-references are given, though not all that are possible. For certain continuing bibliographical works the reader should consult VB 1941, the last annual bibliography in which such works are listed in full. Bibliographical entries are made to conform as closely as possible with the British National Bibliography for books first published in Great Britain, and with the Library of Congress Catalog for books first published in the United States.

This is the last Victorian Bibliography to appear in *Modern Philology*. On behalf of Group X of the Modern Language Association of America, the editor extends thanks to the editors and publishers of *Modern Philology* for their help and their hospitality over these many years. The Victorian Bibliography for 1957 will appear in the newly founded journal, *Victorian Studies*, published by Indiana University.

KEY TO ABBREVIATIONS

AHR	= *American Historical Review*
AL	= *American Literature*
AM	= *Atlantic Monthly*
APSR	= *American Political Science Review*
APSS	= *Annals of the American Academy of Political and Social Science*
BA	= *Books Abroad*
BBDI	= *Bulletin of Bibliography and Dramatic Index*
BLR	= *Bodleian Library Record*
BPLQ	= *Boston Public Library Quarterly*
BSP	= *Papers of the Bibliographical Society of America*
CE	= *College English*
CHJ	= *Cambridge Historical Journal*
CJ	= *Cambridge Journal*
CR	= *Contemporary Review*
CWd	= *Catholic World*
DA	= *Dissertation Abstracts*
DUJ	= *Durham University Journal*
EC	= *Essays in Criticism*
EHR	= *English Historical Review*
EJ	= *English Journal*
ELH	= *Journal of English Literary History*
ESt	= *English Studies*
Ex	= *Explicator*
HJ	= *Hibbert Journal*
HLB	= *Harvard Library Bulletin*
HLQ	= *Huntington Library Quarterly*
HTB	= *New York Herald Tribune Book Review*
JAA	= *Journal of Aesthetics and Art Criticism*
JEGP	= *Journal of English and Germanic Philology*
JEH	= *Journal of Economic History*
JHI	= *Journal of the History of Ideas*
JMH	= *Journal of Modern History*
JP	= *Journal of Philosophy*
JPE	= *Journal of Political Economy*
KR	= *Kenyon Review*
LJ	= *Library Journal*
LQ	= *Library Quarterly*

234

LQHR = *London Quarterly and Holborn Review*
LR   = *Library Review*
M & L = *Music and Letters*
MLJ   = *Modern Language Journal*
MLN   = *Modern Language Notes*
MLQ   = *Modern Language Quarterly*
MLR   = *Modern Language Review*
MP   = *Modern Philology*
N   = *Nation*
N & Q = *Notes and Queries*
NCF   = *Nineteenth-Century Fiction*
NEQ   = *New England Quarterly*
NER   = *National and English Review*
New R = *New Republic*
NS   = *New Statesman and Nation*
NYTBR = *New York Times Book Review*
ParR = *Partisan Review*
PLC   = *Princeton University Library Chronicle*
PMLA = *Publications of the Modern Language Association of America*
PQ   = *Philological Quarterly*
PSQ   = *Political Science Quarterly*
QJS   = *Quarterly Journal of Speech*
QQ   = *Queen's Quarterly*
QR   = *Quarterly Review*
RES   = *Review of English Studies*
RoR   = *Romanic Review*
S   = *Spectator*
SAQ   = *South Atlantic Quarterly*
SeR   = *Sewanee Review*
SP   = *Studies in Philology*
SR   = *Saturday Review*
StI   = *Studies: An Irish Quarterly Review*
TC   = *Twentieth Century*
TLS   = *Times Literary Supplement*
TQ   = *University of Toronto Quarterly*
USQBR = *United States Quarterly Book Review*
VNL   = *Victorian News Letter*
VQR   = *Virginia Quarterly Review*
YR   = *Yale Review*

I. BIBLIOGRAPHICAL MATERIAL

Alden, John. "An Outstanding Gift of Manuscripts." *BPLQ*, VIII, 104–8.

Lists letters by Arthur Conan Doyle and George Henry Lewes.

"American Bibliography for 1955." *PMLA*, LXXI, No. 2, 147–58; English Language and Literature, "X. Nineteenth Century" and "XI. Contemporary," ed. Allan G. Chester and M. A. Shaaber.

Babb, James T., Blanck, Jacob, and Jones, Howard Mumford. *Books and Publishing*

Lecture Series. Vol. I: *1953–1954*. Boston: School of Library Science, Simmons College, 1954. Pp. i+30.

Rev. by Gerald D. McDonald in *LQ*, XXV, 402. The lecture by Jacob Blanck is titled "A Twentieth-Century Look at Nineteenth-Century Children's Books."

[Buckler, William E.]. "Doctoral Theses in the Victorian Period." *VNL*, No. 9 (Spring), p. 11.

[Buckler, William E.]. "Forthcoming Publications." *VNL*, No. 10 (Autumn), pp. 20–22.

Carter, John. *Books and Book-Collectors*. London: Hart-Davis. Pp. 196.

Rev. by A. N. L. Munby in *NS*, Dec. 8, p. 764.

Cohen, I. Bernard, and Strelsky, Katharine (eds.). "Eighty-first Critical Bibliography of the History of Science and Its Cultural Influences (to 1 January 1956)." *Isis*, XLVII, 247–360.

Colby, Robert A. "Anonymous and Pseudonymous Authors." *VNL*, No. 10 (Autumn), pp. 17–18.

Colby, Robert A. "The Charles A. Stonehill Collection, Hunter College Library." *VNL*, No. 9 (Spring), p. 10.

Cole, Sonia. *Counterfeit*. London: J. Murray, 1955. Pp. vii+209.

Rev. by R. P. in *NS*, Jan. 7, p. 22. Contains a new account of Gosse and Wise, with reference to a short story about a literary forger and his accomplice, published by Kipling in 1932.

Derby, J. Raymond (ed.). "The Romantic Movement: A Selective and Critical Bibliography for the Year 1955." *PQ*, XXXV, 97–174.

Doyle, A. I. "Martin Joseph Routh and His Books in Durham University Library." *DUJ*, XLVIII, 100–107.

Faverty, Frederic E. (ed.). *The Victorian Poets: A Guide to Research*. Cambridge: Harvard Univ. Pr. Pp. 292.

Rev. by Thomas A. Kirby in *CE*, XVIII, 60; by Robert A. Donovan in *MLQ*, XVII, 370–71; briefly by Betty Miller in *TC*, CLX, 576–80.
A review of bibliography, scholarship, and criticism in the field of the Victorian poets. This

book is of great value to students and scholars. Twenty-four double-columned pages of index add to its ready usefulness. The work was sponsored by the Victorian Literature Group of the Mod. Lang. Assoc. of America. Nine notable American scholars have contributed, with justifiable variations in procedure, chapters as follows: "General Materials" (Jerome H. Buckley); "Alfred, Lord Tennyson" (Paull Franklin Baum); "Robert Browning" (William Clyde DeVane); "Elizabeth Barrett Browning, Edward FitzGerald, Arthur Hugh Clough" (A. McKinley Terhune); "Matthew Arnold" (Frederic E. Faverty); "Algernon Charles Swinburne" (Clyde K. Hyder); "The Pre-Raphaelites" (Howard Mumford Jones); "Gerard Manley Hopkins" (John Pick); "The Later Victorian Poets" (Lionel Stevenson). These studies not only indicate the substance of the scholarly and critical work that has been done but also suggest, from time to time, numerous topics for further work. Graduate students as well as more experienced scholars will find this book informative and stimulating.—W. D. T.

Gordan, John D. "What's in a Name? Authors and Their Pseudonyms." *Bull. New York Pub. Libr.*, LX, 107–28.

A collection of pseudonymous books from the Berg Collection, containing many by Victorian authors, including Arnold, the Brontës, Dickens, Wilde, Dodgson, Newman, Ford, Ruskin, Bulwer-Lytton, Thackeray, the Tennysons.

Gulick, Charles Adams. *History and Theories of Working-Class Movements: A Select Bibliography.* Compiled by Charles A. Gulick, Roy A. Ockert, and Raymond J. Wallace. Berkeley: Bureau of Business and Economic Research, Univ. of California Pr., 1955. Pp. xix+364.

Rev. briefly by J. N. W. in *College and Research Libr.*, XVII, 337.

Keith, Sarah. "Mudie's Circulating Library." *NCF*, XI, 156–57.

Low, David Morrice, and others (comps.). *A Century of Writers, 1855–1955.* London: Chatto & Windus, 1955. Pp. 736.

Rev. briefly by E. Poulenard in *Études anglaises*, IX, 268.

Macdonald, Angus, and Pettit, Henry J. (eds.). *Annual Bibliography of English Language*

and Literature. Vol. XXIV: *1943–4.* Pp. xvi+304. Vol. XXV: *1945.* Pp. xv+158. Vol. XXVII: *1947.* Pp. xv+243. London: Cambridge Univ. Pr. for the Modern Humanities Research Assoc.

Rev. in *N & Q*, new ser., III, 459–60.

Matthews, William (comp.). *British Autobiographies.* . . . See VB 1955, 240.

Rev. briefly by E. G. in *College and Research Libr.*, XVII, 340; briefly by Katherine Tappert Willis in *LJ*, LXXXI, 197; briefly in *TLS*, Feb. 3, p. 74.

Maurer, Oscar. "Recent Publications: A Selected List." *VNL*, No. 9 (Spring), pp. 12–16; No. 10 (Autumn), pp. 22–24.

Munby, Alan Noel Latimer. *The Formation of the Phillipps Library from 1841 to 1872.* ("Phillipps Studies," No. 4.) Cambridge: Cambridge Univ. Pr. Pp. xvi+227.

Rev. by William B. Todd in *BSP*, L, 393–96; Vol. IV rev. by Michael Sadleir in *Library*, XI, 289–90 ("for the 19th century not only a biographical dictionary of practically everyone who bought, sold, or collected a book, but an encyclopedia of the customs of the trade").

Ratchford, Fannie E. "Rare Book Collections." *Libr. Chronicle of Univ. of Texas*, V, No. 4, 42–49.

Russo, François. *Histoire des sciences et des techniques: bibliographie.* Paris: Hermann, 1954. Pp. 186.

Rev. briefly by P.-M. Schuhl in *Rev. philos.*, CXLVI, 401.

Singer, Armand E. "Supplement to a Bibliography of the Don Juan Theme: Versions and Criticism." *Univ. of West Virginia Bull.: Philological Papers*, X, 1–36.

Stewart, James D., with Muriel E. Hammond and Erwin Saenger (eds.). *British Union-Catalogue of Periodicals.* . . . See VB 1955, 241.

Rev. briefly by T. P. Fleming in *College and Research Libr.*, XVII, 189–90; by K. L. in *College and Research Libr.*, XVII, 335; in *TLS*, Feb. 3, p. 76.

Stone, George Winchester, Jr. (ed.). "1955 Research in Progress in the Modern Languages and Literatures." *PMLA*, LXXI, 267–345.

Taylor, F. "The John Rylands Library, Manchester." *VNL*, No. 10 (Autumn), pp. 16–17.

Lists some of the family collections of interest to Victorians.

Taylor, Robert H. "The Singular Anomalies." *PLC*, XVII, 71–76.

Remarks on the extraordinary careers of the lady novelists represented in the Parrish Collection now at Princeton; brief treatment is given to the Brontës, George Eliot, Mrs. Gaskell, Mrs. Craik, Charlotte Yonge, Mrs. Henry Wood, Miss Braddon, Ouida, etc.

Trewin, John Courtenay. *Verse Drama since 1800.* ("Reader's Guides," 2d ser., No. 8.) Cambridge: Cambridge Univ. Pr., for the National Book League. Pp. 27.

Rev. by Jack Reading in *Theatre Notebook*, XI, 35–36.

Wainwright, Alexander D. "The Morris L. Parrish Collection of Victorian Novelists." *PLC*, XVII, 59–67.

Walbridge, Earle F. "Drames à clef: A List of Plays with Characters Based on Real People." I. "English Drama." *Bull. New York Pub. Libr.*, LX, 159–74.

Wright, Austin (ed.). *Bibliographies of Studies in Victorian Literature for the Ten Years 1945–1954.* Urbana: Univ. of Illinois Pr. Pp. 310.

Wright, Austin (ed.). "Victorian Bibliography for 1955." *MP*, LIII, 239–73.

The Year's Work in English Studies, Vol. XXXV (1954). Ed. for the English Assoc. by Beatrice White. London: Oxford Univ. Pr., 1956. "The Nineteenth Century," treated by Geoffrey Bullough and P. M. Yarker, pp. 180–210; "The Twentieth Century," by Marjorie Thomson, pp. 211–25; "Bibliographica," by John Crow, pp. 241–54.

II. ECONOMIC, POLITICAL, RELIGIOUS, AND SOCIAL ENVIRONMENT

Allen, H. C. *Great Britain and the United States.* . . . See VB 1955, 241.

Rev. by Alexander DeConde in *SAQ*, LV, 99–102.

Armstrong, William A. "The Art of the Minor Theatres in 1860." *Theatre Notebook*, X, 89–94.

Armstrong, William A. "Madame Vestris: A Centenary Appreciation." *Theatre Notebook*, XI, 11–18.

Armytage, W. H. G. "The Journalistic Activities of J. Goodwin Barmby between 1841 and 1848." *N & Q*, new ser., III, 166–69.

Ausubel, Herman. *The Late Victorians: A Short History.* New York: Van Nostrand, 1955. Pp. 188.

Rev. briefly by Gordon Goodman in *JMH*, XXVIII, 97–98.

Baetzhold, Howard G. "Mark Twain: England's Advocate." *AL*, XXVIII, 328–46.

On Mark Twain's visits in England, 1872–74, and his reactions thereto.

Barkeley, Richard. *The Empress Frederick, Daughter of Queen Victoria.* London: Macmillan. Pp. xiii+322.

Rev. by Erich Eyck in *CR*, CXC, 305–6; by Felix E. Hirsch in *LJ*, LXXXI, 1995; by Percy Cradock in *NS*, Aug. 18, p. 195; by Hans Kohn in *NYTBR*, Aug. 12, p. 12; by Helen Beal Woodward in *SR*, Aug. 11, pp. 24–25; in *TLS*, Aug. 17, pp. 481–82. Biography of "Vicky," Queen Victoria's eldest daughter.

Bearce, George D., Jr. "Lord William Bentinck: The Application of Liberalism to India." *JMH*, XXVIII, 234–46.

Beard, Harry R. "Some Notes on John Braham (1774?–1856) at the St. James's Theatre." *Theatre Notebook*, X, 86–89.

Bell, Sir George. *Soldier's Glory: Being "Rough Notes of an Old Soldier."* Ed. Brian Stuart. London: Bell. Pp. x+325.

Rev. in *TLS*, Apr. 20, p. 234. Includes personal reminiscences of the Crimean War.

Best, G. F. A. "The Religious Difficulties of National Education in England, 1800–70." *CHJ*, XII, 155–73.

Bill, E. G. W. "The Declaration of Students of the Natural and Physical Sciences, 1865." *BLR*, V, 262–67.

Blanch, Lesley. *The Wilder Shores of Love. . . .* See VB 1954, 235.

Rev. by F. Moreux in *Études anglaises*, IX, 278.

Blaug, Mark. "The Empirical Content of Ricardian Economics." *JPE*, LXIV, 41–58.

Bloom, Ursula. *Victorian Vinaigrette*. London: Hutchinson. Pp. 208.

Rev. by Cyril Ray in *S*, Apr. 13, p. 505; briefly in *TLS*, Mar. 9, p. 154. Based on the author's family papers.

Boas, F. S. "Some Oxford Memories, 1881–1886." *Essays and Studies, 1956* (Vol. IX, new ser., for the English Assoc.), pp. 113–21.

Includes memories of Jowett, Sir Edward Grey, Sir Sidney Lee, J. W. Mackail, Anthony Hope Hawkins, Charles E. Mallet, Walter Pater.

Briggs, Asa. *Friends of the People: The Centenary History of Lewis's*. London: Batsford. Pp. iii+242.

Rev. by W. John Morgan in *NS*, Aug. 4, pp. 142–43. Mostly about David Lewis, who introduced the department store and modern publicity to Victorian England.

Briggs, Asa. *Victorian People. . . .* See VB 1955, 242.

Rev. by F. H. Herrick in *AHR*, LXI, 694; by Fraser Neiman in *Amer. Scholar*, XXV, 249–50; in *APSR*, L, 249; by W. P. Hall in *APSS*, CCCIII, 224; by F. H. Underhill in *Canadian Hist. Rev.*, XXXVII, 64; by F. Gunther Eyck in *JMH*, XXVIII, 398–99; briefly in *NCF*, X, 327–28; by George Woodcock in *SR*, XXXIX, 33; by Hiram M. Stout in *VQR*, XXXII, 283–86; in *YR*, XLV, No. 3, xiv–xvi.

Brose, Olive J. "The Survival of the Church of England as by Law Established—1828–1860." *DA*, XVI, 1669.

Bulman, Joan. *Jenny Lind: A Biography*. London: Barrie. Pp. xi+326.

Rev. by Arthur Marshall in *NS*, Dec. 15, pp. 794–95.

Clifford, Sir Henry. *Henry Clifford, V.C.: His Letters and Sketches from the Crimea*. Ed. Bernard Paget. London: Joseph. Pp. 288.

Rev. in *Manchester Guardian*, Feb. 24, p. 6; by Michael Howard in *NS*, Mar. 3, p. 190; by Cecil Woodham-Smith in *NYTBR*, Sept. 23,

p. 6; by David Stone in *S*, Mar. 23, p. 382; in *TLS*, Feb. 17, p. 97.

Cockburn, John. *The Hungry Heart: A Romantic Biography of James Keir Hardie*. London: Jarrolds. Pp. 286.

Rev. by J. E. MacColl in *CR*, CXC, 306–7; by Paul Johnson in *NS*, Sept. 29, pp. 380–81; in *TLS*, Sept. 28, p. 563.

Cohen, John Michael. *The Life of Ludwig Mond*. London: Methuen. Pp. xv+295.

Rev. by Charles Wilson in *S*, Sept. 14, pp. 356–57. On a notable Victorian industrial scientist and entrepreneur.

Coleman, D. C. "Industrial Growth and Industrial Revolutions." *Economica*, new ser., XXIII, 1–22.

The term "Industrial Revolution" is losing its meaning through overextension. It should be reserved for the designation of the great change from an agricultural to an industrial economy, as in the classic case of Great Britain at the end of the eighteenth century.

Court, W. H. B. *A Concise Economic History of Britain from 1750 to Recent Times. . . .* See VB 1955, 242.

Rev. by W. Woodruff in *JMH*, XXVIII, 278–79; briefly by Robert S. Smith in *SAQ*, LV, 132.

Courtney, Marie-Thérèse. *Edward Martyn and the Irish Theatre*. New York: Vantage Pr. Pp. 188.

Cowles, Virginia. *Edward VII and His Circle*. London: H. Hamilton. Pp. 378. (American title, *Gay Monarch*.)

Rev. by G. P. Gooch in *CR*, CXC, 177–79; by Geoffrey Bruun in *HTB*, Oct. 21, p. 3; by Ralph Partridge in *NS*, July 7, p. 21; by Virgilia Peterson in *NYTBR*, Oct. 21, p. 3; in *TLS*, July 27, p. 444.

Deghy, Guy, and Waterhouse, Keith. *Café Royal: Ninety Years of Bohemia*. London: Hutchinson, 1955. Pp. 221.

Rev. by Gerald Hamilton in *S*, Jan. 13, p. 54; in *TLS*, Jan. 20, p. 33. On a well-known late Victorian restaurant and its associations, especially with Wilde and his circle.

Disher, M. Willson. *Melodrama: Plots That Thrilled*. London: Rockliff, 1954. Pp. 210.

Rev. by F. Moreux in *Études anglaises*, IX, 87.

Disher, Maurice Willson. *Victorian Song from Dive to Drawing Room*. . . . See VB 1955, 242.

Rev. by P. L. Miller in *LJ*, LXXXI, 467; by Gerard Fay in *Manchester Guardian*, Nov. 25, 1955, p. 13; by Leo Lerman in *NYTBR*, Feb. 12, p. 22; by George Woodcock in *SR*, Feb. 4, p. 34.

Dutton, Ralph. *The Victorian Home: Some Aspects of Nineteenth-Century Taste and Manners*. London: Batsford, 1954. Pp. x+206.

Rev. by Henri Lemaitre in *Études anglaises*, IX, 371–72.

Elliott-Binns, L. E. *English Thought, 1860–1900: The Theological Aspect*. London: Longmans, Green. Pp. ix+388.

Rev. by R. H. Fuller in *Christian Century*, LXXIII, 555; by H. G. Wood in *HJ*, LIV, 406–7; favorably by Lee Ash in *LJ*, LXXXI, 830; by Alastair MacIntyre in *Manchester Guardian*, Feb. 15, p. 11; by Alec Vidler in *S*, Feb. 17, p. 224; by Raymond Mortimer in *Sunday Times*, Feb. 5, p. 5; in *TLS*, Mar. 30, suppl., p. ii.

Forster, E. M. *Marianne Thornton, 1797–1887: A Domestic Biography*. London: Edward Arnold. Pp. 301.

Rev. by C. J. Rolo in *AM*, CXCVII, 76–77; by Edward Wagenknecht in *Chicago Sunday Tribune*, May 20, p. 2; by Harold Hobson in *Christian Science Monitor*, May 17, p. 7; by Paul Pickrel in *Harper's*, CCXII (June), 80–82; by M. E. Chase in *HTB*, May 20, p. 1; by E. F. Walbridge in *LJ*, LXXXI, 1517–18; by Noel Annan in *Manchester Guardian*, May 25, p. 4; by Ivor Brown in *New R*, May 28, pp. 17–19; favorably by Naomi Lewis in *NS*, May 12, pp. 534–36; by Eudora Welty in *NYTBR*, May 27, p. 5; by Graham Hough in *S*, May 11, p. 663; by George Woodcock in *SR*, May 26, p. 19; by Betty Miller in *TC*, CLX, 87–88; in *TLS*, May 11, p. 282.

Glover, Willis B., Jr. *Evangelical Nonconformists and Higher Criticism in the Nineteenth Century*. . . . See VB 1955, 242.

Rev. favorably by Robert McAfee Brown in *Rev. of Religion*, XX, 237–38.

Gooch, G. P. "Victorian Memories." *CR*, Vols. CLXXXIX, CXC. (For I, II, III see VB 1955, 243.) ("IV, V. Cambridge in the 'Nineties," CLXXXIX, 24–28, 101–6; "VI.

Berlin in the 'Nineties," pp. 159–64; "VII. Lord Acton," pp. 204–9; "VIII. Paris in the 'Nineties," pp. 278–83; "IX. The End of the Century," pp. 344–48; "X. Servants of Humanity," CXC, 17–22; "XI, XII. The South African War," pp. 148–54.)

Gross, Felix. *Rhodes of Africa*. London: Cassell. Pp. xi+433.

Rev. by R. H. S. Crossman in *NS*, Nov. 3, pp. 554–55. According to Crossman, readable but unreliable.

Halévy, Élie. *Thomas Hodgskin*. Trans. and ed. A. J. Taylor. London: Benn. Pp. viii+9+197.

Rev. in *TLS*, Mar. 23, p. 175. Biography of a pioneer British Socialist, first published in 1903.

Harris, David. "European Liberalism in the Nineteenth Century." *AHR*, LX, 501–26.

Hewett, Osbert Wyndham. *Strawberry Fair: A Biography of Frances, Countess Waldegrave, 1821–1879*. London: J. Murray. Pp. xiii+279.

Rev. by Jacques Vallette in *Mercure de France*, CCCXXVII, 137; by Nancy Mitford in *NS*, Feb. 11, pp. 160–61; by Brian Inglis in *S*, Mar. 9, p. 321; in *TLS*, Feb. 10, p. 83. The life of a famous Victorian beauty and hostess.

Hill, William Thomson. *Octavia Hill: Pioneer of the National Trust and Housing Reformer*. London: Hutchinson. Pp. 208.

Rev. briefly by Kay Dick in *S*, May 25, p. 739; in *TLS*, Jan. 27, p. 51.

Hobman, D. L. "A Victorian Diarist." *CR*, CLXXXIX, 41–45.

Hoffmann, Walther G. *British Industry, 1700–1950*. Trans. W. H. Chaloner and W. O. Henderson. Oxford: Blackwell, 1955. Pp. xxiii+338.

Rev. by Phyllis Deane in *Econ. Jour.*, LXVI, 493–500; by W. Ashworth in *Economica*, new ser., XXIII, 183–85; by A. H. John in *EHR*, LXXI, 654–55; by J. F. Wright in *JEH*, XVI, 356–64; by G. M. Meier in *PSQ*, LXXI, 462–63. An important work, now translated for the first time.

Hudson, Winthrop S. "Survey of Recent Literature: British Church History." *Church Hist.*, XXV, 258–61.

A valuable review article, asserting that "after long neglect, the nineteenth century [church] is beginning to receive serious attention from historical scholars."—O. M.

Hutchison, T. W. "Bentham as an Economist." *Econ. Jour.*, LXVI, 288–306.

Jaeger, Muriel. *Before Victoria*. London: Chatto & Windus. Pp. xi+212.

Rev. by Pansy Pakenham in *S*, June 29, p. 895; in *TLS*, June 15, p. 356. A social historian examines the change from late-eighteenth-century to Victorian attitudes.

Jasper, Rev. R. C. D. *Prayer Book Revision in England, 1800–1900.* . . . See VB 1955, 243.

Rev. by Pierre Janelle in *Études anglaises*, IX, 187.

Kennedy, Aubrey Leo (ed.). *"My Dear Duchess": Social and Political Letters to the Duchess of Manchester, 1858–1869*. London: J. Murray. Pp. vii+254.

Rev. unfavorably by Brian Inglis in *S*, Mar. 9, p. 322; in *TLS*, Mar. 9, p. 151.

Laver, James. *Victorian Vista*. . . . See VB 1955, 244.

Rev. by Edward Wagenknecht in *Chicago Sunday Tribune*, Jan. 1, p. 5; by R. D. Altick in *HTB*, Jan. 29, p. 6; briefly in *NCF*, XI, 79.

Levin, Harvey J. "Standards of Welfare in Economic Thought." *Quart. Jour. Econ.*, LXX, 117–38.

Lillibridge, G. D. *Beacon of Freedom.* . . . See VB 1955, 244.

Rev. by Frank Thistlethwaite in *JMH*, XXVIII, 285–86.

Lochhead, Marion. *Their First Ten Years: Victorian Childhood*. London: J. Murray. Pp. xii+247.

Rev. by Irene Slade in *S*, Aug. 17, p. 244; in *TLS*, July 27, p. 444. The life of children in early, mid-, and late Victorian years.

Mann, Arthur. "British Social Thought and American Reformers of the Progressive Era." *Mississippi Valley Hist. Rev.*, XLII, 672–92.

Late-century rejection of British economic orthodoxy.

Medlicott, W. N. *Bismarck, Gladstone, and the Concert of Europe*. London: Athlone Pr. Pp. xiv+353.

Rev. by Winifred Taffs in *CR*, CXC, 371–72; in *TLS*, Sept. 28, p. 563.

Meenai, S. A. "Robert Torrens—1780–1864." *Economica*, new ser., XXIII, 49–61.

Meynell, Viola (ed.). *The Best of Friends: Further Letters to Sydney Carlyle Cockerell*. London: Hart-Davis. Pp. x+11+308.

Rev. by John Raymond in *NS*, Jan. 28, pp. 107–8; in *TLS*, Feb. 3, p. 62.

Millhauser, Milton. "The Literary Impact of Vestiges of Creation." *MLQ*, XVII, 213–26.

Chambers' book, a precursor not of Darwin but of Huxley and Spencer, had little influence on belles-lettres but considerable effect on the literature of intellectual controversy.

Morgan, Margery M., and May, Frederick. "The Early Plays of Harley Granville Barker." *MLR*, LI, 324–38.

On Barker's collaboration with Berte Thomas in the nineties.

Morton, Arthur Leslie, and Tate, George. *The British Labour Movement, 1770–1920: A History*. London: Lawrence & Wishart. Pp. 313.

Rev. by Paul Johnson in *NS*, Sept. 29, pp. 380–81.

Nettel, Reginald. *Sing a Song of England: A Social History of Traditional Song*. London: Phoenix House, 1954. Pp. 286.

Rev. by C. K. Miller in *LJ*, LXXXI, 1805; in *TLS*, Dec. 31, 1954, p. 854.

Nicolson, Harold. *Good Behaviour: Being a Study of Certain Types of Civility*. Garden City, N.Y.: Doubleday. Pp. 293.

Rev. by Wayne Andrews in *SR*, Apr. 7, p. 10. Two chapters on Victorian manners.

Pearl, Cyril. *The Girl with the Swansdown Seat*. . . . See VB 1955, 244.

Rev. by Louis Barron in *LJ*, LXXXI, 631; by Hollis Alpert in *SR*, Apr. 7, p. 11.

Pelling, Henry. *America and the British Left from Bright to Bevan*. London: Black. Pp. xi+174.

Rev. by A. J. P. Taylor in *NS*, Oct. 27, pp. 523–24.

Pelling, Henry. *The Origins of the Labour Party, 1880–1900.* . . . See VB 1954, 238.

Rev. by William O. Aydelotte in *JMH*, XXVIII, 290.

Pope-Hennessy, James. *Lord Crewe, 1854–1945.* . . . See VB 1955, 244.

Rev. by G. P. Gooch in *CR*, CLXXXIX, 55–56.

Postgate, Raymond. *The Story of a Year: 1848.* . . . See VB 1955, 244.

Rev. by Priscilla Robertson in *Amer. Scholar,* XXV, 352–54; by R. D. Altick in *HTB*, Feb. 19, p. 5; briefly by Karl Brown in *LJ*, LXXXI, 191; by D. R. in *Manchester Guardian,* Nov. 4, 1955; by Hazel Hawthorne in *N*, Feb. 25, p. 164; by Keith Hutchison in *NYTBR*, Feb. 19, p. 3; by William B. Willcox in *SR*, Feb. 18, p. 51; in *TLS*, Nov. 4, 1955, p. 651.

Prebble, John. *The High Girders.* London: Secker & Warburg. Pp. ix+221.

Rev. by Michael Crampton in *NS*, Dec. 29, pp. 846–47. According to the reviewer, a readable account of the jerry-built Tay Bridge and its collapse within less than two years, a great blow to Victorian pride.

Purdom, Charles Benjamin. *Harley Granville Barker: Man of the Theatre, Dramatist and Scholar.* Cambridge: Harvard Univ. Pr. Pp. 322.

Rev. by Gerard Fay in *Manchester Guardian,* Dec. 16, 1955, p. 6; by T. C. Worsley in *NS*, Dec. 3, p. 765; by Maurice Evans in *NYTBR*, May 13, p. 19; in *Theatre Arts,* XL (June), 8; by Alec Clunes in *Theatre Notebook,* X, 126–28; in *TLS*, Dec. 2, 1955, p. 716.

Raymond, John. "The Fall of the House of Ushers." *NS*, Dec. 8, pp. 749–50.

Mr. Raymond dearly loves biographies of the Victorian headmasters. In this interesting article he discusses some of the more startling. We shall never see their like again.—F. G. T.

Reid, J. H. Stewart. *The Origins of the British Labour Party.* . . . See VB 1955, 245.

Rev. by Philip Poirier in *AHR*, LXI, 956; by A. B. Ulam in *APSR*, L, 576; by Rudolph Heimanson in *LJ*, LXXXI, 2509; by L. Davis in *PSQ*, LXXI, 464–65.

Reppert, James D. "William Macmath and F. J. Child." *PMLA*, LXXI, 510–20.

Richardson, Joanna. *Rachel.* London: Reinhardt. Pp. xii+222.

Rev. by Peter Wildeblood in *NS*, Sept. 22, pp. 353–54. Account of a Victorian actress who fascinated Charlotte Brontë and Queen Victoria.

Rienaecker, Victor. "Some Early English Water-Colour Painters." *Apollo,* LXIV, 72–75.

Robbins, Lionel. "A Letter from David Ricardo." *Economica,* new ser., XXIII, 172–74.

Rosenfeld, Sybil. "A Project for an Iron Theatre." *Theatre Notebook,* XI, 19–20.

Scott, John William Robertson. *"We" and Me: Memories of Our Eminent Editors I Worked with, a Discussion by Editors of the Future of Editing, and a Candid Account of the Founding and Editing, for Twenty-one Years, of My Own Magazine.* London: W. H. Allen. Pp. 240.

Rev. by Ralph Partridge in *NS*, Aug. 4, p. 142; by Brian Inglis in *S*, Sept. 21, p. 396; in *TLS*, June 1, p. 326. Reminiscences of W. T. Stead, H. W. Massingham, J. A. Spender, Ernest Parke, and other late Victorian editors.

Scott, Richenda. *Elizabeth Cadbury, 1858–1951.* London: Harrap, 1955. Pp. 200.

Rev. in *TLS*, Jan. 27, p. 51. The biography of a social reformer.

Smith, Roland. "The Manchester Chamber of Commerce and the Increasing Foreign Competition to Lancashire Cotton Textiles, 1873–1896." *Bull. John Rylands Libr.,* XXXVIII, 507–34.

Speaight, George. *History of the English Puppet Theatre.* . . . See VB 1955, 245.

Rev. by George Freedley in *LJ*, LXXXI, 2795; in *N & Q*, new ser., III, 183; in *TLS*, July 29, 1955, p. 424.

Spring, David. "Ralph Sneyd: Tory Country Gentleman." *Bull. John Rylands Libr.,* XXXVIII, 534–55.

A fascinating account of "the uneventful life" (1793–1870) of an obscure country gentleman, based on many new letters and some other sources. Sneyd was no mediocrity: he had "a mind that reaches all subjects and understands all thoughts"—a mind of richness and vigor. Such an account gives evidence that broad and derogatory generalizations about the country gentlemen of England in the nineteenth century are dangerous.—W. D. T.

Spring, David and Eileen. "The Fall of the Grenvilles, 1844–1848." *HLQ*, XIX, 165–90.

Sraffa, Piero (ed.), with the collaboration of M. H. Dobb. *The Works and Correspondence of David Ricardo*. Vol. X: *Biographical Miscellany*. Cambridge: Cambridge Univ. Pr., for the Royal Economic Soc., 1955. Pp. x+424.

Rev. briefly in *Economica*, new ser., XXIII, 197.

Stark, W. (ed.). *Jeremy Bentham's Economic Writings*. Vol. III. London: Allen & Unwin, for the Royal Economic Soc., 1954. Pp. 601.

Rev. by B. F. Hoselitz in *JPE*, LXIV, 272–73.

Symons, Julian. *Horatio Bottomley: A Biography*. London: Cresset Pr., 1955. Pp. 287.

A notorious and flamboyant financier and editor, 1860–1933.

Taylor, A. J. "The Third Marquis of Londonderry and the North-eastern Coal Trade." *DUJ*, XLVIII (1955), 21–27.

An account of the ruthlessly selfish nineteenth-century peer who was one of the two most important coal-owners of northern England.

Taylor, A. J. P. *The Struggle for Mastery in Europe: 1848–1918*. . . . See VB 1955, 246.

Rev. by E. C. Helmreich in *JMH*, XXVIII, 304–5.

Thomson, Gladys Scott. *Woburn and the Russells*. Derby: Pilgrim Pr. Pp. 64.

Threlkeld, Budge. "A Study of the Management of Charles Kean at the Princess's Theatre, 1850–1859." *DA*, XVI, 182–83.

Trevelyan, George Macaulay. *Illustrated History of England*. Illustrations selected by St. John Gore. London: Longmans, Green. Pp. xxiv+758.

Rev. by Asa Briggs in *NS*, Mar. 10, pp. 220–21. The birthday edition of this classic work contains, according to the reviewer, nothing new, although the illustrations are of real value in themselves.

Treves, Giuliana Artom. *The Golden Ring: The Anglo-Florentines, 1847–1862*. Trans. Sylvia Sprigge. London: Longmans, Green. Pp. xi+221. (See VB 1954, 239.)

Rev. by Jon Wynne-Tyson in *Apollo*, LXIV, 227; by Betty Miller in *NS*, Oct. 27, pp. 524–25; by D. S. Carne-Ross in *S*, Dec. 28, p. 939; in *TLS*, Nov. 2, p. 652.

Trewin, J. C. *Mr. Macready*. . . . See VB 1955, 246.

Rev. by Guy Boas in *English*, XI, 23; by Charles H. Shattuck in *Theatre Notebook*, X, 57–58.

Vessey, John Henry. *Mr. Vessey of England: Being the Incidents and Reminiscences of Travel in a Twelve Weeks' Tour through the United States and Canada in the Year 1859*. Ed. Brian Waters. New York: Putnam. Pp. 184.

Rev. by John Cournos in *Commonweal*, Oct. 12, p. 54; briefly by D. S. Truesdale in *LJ*, LXXXI, 1990; by D. W. Brogan in *SR*, Sept. 15, p. 16.

Wadham, Juliana. *The Case of Cornelia Connelly*. London: Collins. Pp. 319.

Rev. by Antonia White in *NS*, Oct. 20, pp. 496–97. A startling biography of a Victorian nun, a storm center in her time.

Webb, R. K. *The British Working Class Reader, 1790–1848*. . . . See VB 1955, 246.

Rev. favorably by D. N. Levine in *Amer. Jour. Sociol.*, LXI, 635; briefly by R. G. Cowherd in *APSS*, CCCIV, 177–78; by Richard D. Altick in *BSP*, L, 97–100.

Wibberley, Leonard. *The Trouble with the Irish (or the English, Depending on Your Point of View)*. New York: Holt. Pp. 254.

Rev. by Crane Brinton in *HTB*, Dec. 30, p. 7; by M. H. Zipprich in *LJ*, LXXXI, 1191.

Williams, David. *The Rebecca Riots: A Study in Agrarian Discontent*. Cardiff: Wales Univ. Pr. 1955. Pp. x+377.

Rev. by H. A. Marquand in *Econ. Jour.*, LXVI, 524–25; by T. C. Barker in *Economica*, new ser., XXIII, 284–85. The events leading up to the riots in West Wales in 1839 and 1842–43.

Williams, R. E. T. "The Grand Tour in 1854." *N & Q*, new ser., III, 306–9.

Letters by Edward Lance Tarbuck written to his mother while he was making a tour of Europe.

Williams, R. W. (ed.). *A Century of "Punch."* London: Heinemann. Pp. 352.

Rev. in *Booklist*, LII, 184; briefly by Alice S. Plaut in *LJ*, LXXXI, 1192.

Wills, Geoffrey. "Some Past Collectors— Henry George Bohn (1796–1884)." *Apollo*, LXIII, 54.

Wills, Geoffrey. "Some Past Collectors—J. E. Taylor (1830–1905).'' *Apollo*, LXIV, 153.

Brief biographical note on the proprietor of the *Manchester Guardian*, liberal, and art collector.

Wingfield-Stratford, Esmé. *The Squire and His Relations*. London: Cassell. Pp. xii+424.

Rev. by Ralph Partridge in *NS*, Aug. 11, p. 168.

Wortham, Hugo. *Victorian Eton and Cambridge: Being Life and Times of Oscar Browning*. New ed. London: Barker. Pp. vii+327.

Rev. favorably by Noel Annan in *NS*, Apr. 21, p. 426; in *TLS*, Feb. 24, p. 119.

Young, Agnes Freda, and Ashton, Elwyn Thomas. *British Social Work in the Nineteenth Century*. ("International Library of Sociology and Social Reconstruction.") London: Routledge & K. Paul. Pp. vii+264.

Rev. by Charles Wilson in *S*, Oct. 26, pp. 579–80.

III. MOVEMENTS OF IDEAS AND LITERARY FORMS

Adams, Norman O. W., Jr. "Byron and the Early Victorians: A Study of His Poetic Influence (1824–1855)." *DA*, XVI, 336–37.

Examines Byron's influence on five major poets (Tennyson, the Brownings, Clough, Arnold) and eleven representative minor poets (E. Brontë, L. Landon, F. Hemans, Caroline Norton, J. Edmund Reade, W. Praed, E. Bulwer-Lytton, Philip James Bailey, Alexander Smith, Sidney Dobell, W. E. Aytoun). Includes "evidences whenever they appear of a deviation from or a rejection of Byron's influence," with possible explanation therefor.

Andrews, John S. "The Reception of Gotthelf in British and American Nineteenth-Century Periodicals." *MLR*, LI, 543–54.

Armytage, W. H. G. "Technology and Utopianism: J. A. Etzler in England, 1840–44." *Ann. Sci.*, XI (1955), 129–36.

Baker, Donald Whitelaw. "Themes of Terror in Nineteenth Century English Fiction: The Shift to the Internal." *DA*, XVI, 118–19.

Among the Victorians treated in the dissertation here summarized are the Brontës, Bulwer-Lytton, Collins, Dickens, DuMaurier, Eliot, Gissing, Hardy, LeFanu, Wilde.

Bock, Kenneth Elliott. *The Acceptance of Histories: Toward a Perspective for Social Science*. Berkeley: Univ. of California Pr. Pp. 132.

Rev. by J. E. Sawyer in *AHR*, LXII, 173; by H. O. Engelmann in *Amer. Sociol. Rev.*, XXI, 634. Contains a review of the "Nineteenth Century Science of History."

Boner, Harold A. *Hungry Generations: The Nineteenth-Century Case against Malthusianism.* . . . See VB 1955, 247.

Rev. briefly by J. J. Spengler in *SAQ*, LV, 131; briefly by Francis J. Weiss in *Scient. Month.*, LXXXII, 49.

Bostrom, Irene. "India in English Fiction, 1770–1860." *DA*, XVI, 1135.

Includes special attention to Philip Meadows Taylor and Thackeray.

Bowra, Sir Cecil Maurice. *Inspiration and Poetry.* . . . See VB 1955, 247.

Rev. by Bernard Gicovate in *Comp. Lit.*, VIII, 168–70.

Brooks, Cleanth (ed.). *Tragic Themes in Western Literature*. New Haven: Yale Univ. Pr., 1955. Pp. 178.

Rev. very favorably by E. Poulenard in *Études anglaises*, IX, 87–88.

Brown, Ivor. "Fame That Endures Is for Authors a Sometime Thing." *NYTBR*, Mar. 11, p. 5.

On literary reputations; includes Trollope, Hardy, and Yeats among the "ins" and Thackeray among the "outs."

Browse, Lillian. *William Nicholson*. London: Hart-Davis. Pp. 144.

Rev. by John Piper in *NS*, Aug. 4, p. 138. Biography of the late Victorian painter, copiously illustrated.

Bullough, Geoffrey. "Changing Views of the Mind in English Poetry." ("Warton Lecture on English Poetry.") *Proc. British Acad., 1955*, XLI, 61–83.

Includes mention of J. S. Mill, Henry Maudsley, T. H. Huxley, Walter Pater, J. A. Symonds, W. E. Henley, Oscar Wilde, Alice Meynell.

Burns, Wayne. "The Genuine and Counterfeit: A Study in Victorian and Modern Fiction." *CE*, XVIII, 143–50.

Dickens and C. Brontë were more "genuine" than Trollope or Reade because their forceful individuality broke through conventional forms. The modern novelist, in order to do "genuine" work, must be even more on his own.

Butler, Harry Lee. "The Balzacian Hero." *DA*, XVI, 1903–4.

Butterfield, Herbert. *Man on His Past: The Study of the History of Historical Scholarship.* Cambridge: Cambridge Univ. Pr., 1955. Pp. xvii+238.

Rev. by H. L. Short in *HJ*, LIV, 309; by Burleigh T. Wilkins in *JMH*, XXVIII, 390–91; by F. E. Hirsch in *LJ*, LXXXI, 2862; by A. Goodwin in *Manchester Guardian*, Nov. 8, 1955, p. 4; by Ernest Nagel in *N*, Mar. 3, p. 184; by Noel Annan in *NS*, Jan. 14, p. 49; in *TLS*, Dec. 2, 1955, p. 715; by P. G. Lucas in *Universities Quart.*, X, 185–89.

A great historian reflects on the history of historiography with considerable reference to Acton.—F. G. T.

Carothers, Francis B., Jr. "The Development of Shelley Criticism, 1810–1916: A Study of Conditions That Have Influenced His Critical Reputation." *Univ. of Southern California Abstr. of Diss. . . . 1954* (1955), pp. 85–88.

Cazamian, Madeleine L. *Le Roman et les idées en Angleterre, 1860–1914.* Vol. III: *Les Doctrines d'action et d'aventure, 1880–1914.* Paris: Les Belles Lettres, 1955. Pp. 499.

Rev. briefly by W. Gordon Milne in *BA*, XXX, 180; by J. H. Buckley in *MLN*, LXXI, 391–93. Chapters on Conrad and Galsworthy; briefer treatment of Mrs. Humphry Ward, Kipling, Olive Schreiner, and Chesterton.

Colby, Robert A. " 'How It Strikes a Contemporary': The *Spectator* as Critic." *NCF*, XI, 182–206.

Criticism of George Eliot, Kingsley, Collins, Dickens, Reade, George Moore, Hardy, Meredith, and others as it appeared in the *Spectator* under the literary editorship of Richard Holt Hutton.

Cole, G. D. H. *Marxism and Anarchism (1850–1890). . . .* See VB 1954, 240.

Rev. briefly by Nikita D. Roodkowsky in *CWd*, CLXXXII, 398.

Cole, George Douglas Howard. *The Second International, 1889–1914.* ("History of Socialist Thought" ser., Vol. III.) 2 vols. London: Macmillan. Pp. xvii+518; viii+519.

Rev. by A. J. P. Taylor in *NS*, Apr. 14, pp. 391–92; by Bertram D. Wolfe in *NYTBR*, Apr. 29, p. 6; by Robert Blake in *S*, Mar. 30, p. 414; in *TLS*, p. 364.

Cope, Jackson I. "An Early Analysis of 'the Victorian Age' in Literature." *MLN*, LXXI, 14–17.

George Lillie Craik, in 1861, was among the first to survey the "Victorian" age as a socio-literary phenomenon.

Culler, A. Dwight. "Method in the Study of Victorian Prose." *VNL*, No. 9 (Spring), pp. 1–4. See also R. C. Schweik, "Method in the Study of Victorian Prose: A Criticism," and A. Dwight Culler, "A Rejoinder" in *VNL*, No. 10 (Autumn), pp. 15–16.

Daiches, David. *Critical Approaches to Literature.* Englewood Cliffs, N.J.: Prentice-Hall. Pp. 404.

Rev. by John R. Willingham in *LJ*, LXXXI, 915–16; by J. W. Krutch in *SR*, June 30, p. 17.

Daiches, David. *Literary Essays.* Edinburgh and London: Oliver & Boyd. Pp. vii+225.

Rev. by John Holloway in *S*, July 13, p. 72; in *TLS*, June 29, p. 391. Includes study of "Christopher North," pp. 122–31.

Dale, E. Hilda. *La Poésie française en Angleterre, 1850–1890. . . .* See VB 1955, 247.

Rev. by P. Mansell Jones in *MLR*, LI, 119–21; by Jean Bruneau in *Rev. de litt. comp.*, XXIX, 576–77.

Davie, Donald. *Purity of Diction in English Verse.* . . . See VB 1953, 241.

Rev. by J. G. Ritz in *Études anglaises*, IX, 269–70.

DeBaun, Vincent C. *"Temple Bar:* Index of Victorian Middle-Class Thought." *Jour. Rutgers Univ. Libr.*, XIX (December, 1955), 6–16.

Study of the monthly magazine *Temple Bar*, 1860–1906, an imitation of the *Cornhill Magazine;* it began with a circulation of about 30,000.

Enkvist, Nils Erik. "The *Octoroon* and English Opinions of Slavery." *Amer. Quart.*, VIII, 166–70.

Essays by Divers Hands: Being the Transactions of the Royal Society of Literature. New ser. Vol. XXVIII. London: Oxford Univ. Pr. Pp. xiii+157.

Rev. by James Reeves in *NS*, July 28, pp. 114–15. Contains an essay on Tennyson by Viscount Esher.

Friedeman, William Evan. "The Pre-Raphaelites and Their Critics: A Tentative Approach toward the Aesthetic of Pre-Raphaelitism." *DA*, XVI, 1441.

Geyl, Pieter. *Debates with Historians.* London: Batsford, 1955. Pp. viii+241.

Rev. by R. H. Palmer in *AHR*, LXI, 599; briefly by Walter P. Hall in *APSS*, CCCIII, 220; by J. J. Heslin in *LJ*, LXXXI, 78; by A. J. P. T. in *Manchester Guardian*, Aug. 9, p. 4; by J. W. N. Watkins in *S*, Mar. 9, p. 317; by Harold T. Parker in *SAQ*, LV, 505–6; in *TLS*, Sept. 9, p. 523.

Geyl, Pieter. *Use and Abuse of History.* London: Oxford Univ. Pr. Pp. vi+97.

Rev. together with the preceding title by Michael Howard in *NS*, July 14, pp. 49–50.

Givens, Stuart Ray. "Great Britain and the American Periodical Press, 1889–1895." *DA*, XVI, 1891–92.

Gooch, G. P. "Some Great English Historians." *CR*, CXC, 344–49.

On Hallam, Macaulay, Carlyle, Froude, and others.

Groom, Bernard. *The Diction of Poetry from Spenser to Bridges.* Toronto: Univ. of Toronto Pr. Pp. viii+284.

Chapters on the major Victorians.

Heintzelman, Arthur W. "Cruikshank's Drawings for *The Drunkard's Children." BPLQ*, VIII, 160–62.

On two drawings for his book of illustrations entitled *The Drunkard's Children* (1848).

Henn, Thomas Rice. *The Harvest of Tragedy.* London: Methuen. Pp. xv+304.

Rev. favorably by Geoffrey Brereton in *NS*, Oct. 13, p. 458.

Hughes, Leo. *A Century of English Farce.* Princeton: Princeton Univ. Pr. Pp. vi+307.

Iknayan, Marguerite May. "The Idea of the Novel in France: The Critical Reaction, 1815–1848." *DA*, XVI, 1455.

Irvine, William. *Apes, Angels, and Victorians.* . . . See VB 1955, 248.

Rev. by Jane Hale in *Amer. Scholar*, XXV, 121; by Bentley Glass in *Isis*, XLVII, 91–93.

Johnson, Edgar. *One Mighty Torrent: The Drama of Biography.* New York: Macmillan, 1955. Pp. 591.

Rev. by Donald J. Winslow in *QJS*, XLII, 82. This is a reprint of the 1937 book with "only the benefit of another proofreading."

Kegel, Charles H. "An Undergraduate Magazine, 1856 Style." *Basic College Quart.*, Winter, pp. 27–32.

Evaluates *The Oxford and Cambridge Magazine* and finds it saturated with medievalism, the Tennysonian melancholy, and the revolutionary theories of Carlyle and Ruskin.

Kinsley, James (ed.). *Scottish Poetry: A Critical Survey.* London: Cassell, 1955. Pp. ix+330.

Rev. by P. Henderson in *TC*, CLIX, 406–8.

Lehman, B. H., and Others. *The Image of the Work: Essays in Criticism.* Berkeley: Univ. of California Pr., 1955. Pp. viii+265.

Rev. by Jean Noël in *Études anglaises*, IX, 172–73.

Levi, Albert William. "The Idea of Socrates: The Philosophic Hero in the Nineteenth Century." *JHI*, XVII, 89–108.

Inquires into the question of what the life of Socrates meant to four representative philosophers of the nineteenth century: J. S. Mill, Nietzsche, Hegel, and Kierkegaard.

Leyburn, Ellen Douglass. *Satiric Allegory: Mirror of Man.* New Haven: Yale Univ. Pr. Pp. vii+142.

Contains treatment of *Erewhon.*

Liptzin, Solomon. *The English Legend of Heinrich Heine.* . . . See VB 1955, 248.

Rev. by Ludwig Borinski in *Euphorion,* L, 479; favorably by H. Salinger in *German Quart.,* XXIX, 55–56; by Ernst Feise in *JEGP,* LV, 482–83; by Herman Salinger in *MLQ,* XVII, 177–78.

Lochhead, Marion. "Literature versus Celibacy." *QR,* CCXCIV, 207–17.

Rather whimsical article points out that a married clergy in England made possible (1) all the novelists who are born of such marriages, (2) all the portraits of clergymen's wives in English novels. More seriously, the vicarage provides the "absolute centre" of the society portrayed in the nineteenth-century domestic novel.—C. T. D.

Low, D. M. (ed.). *Essays and Studies of 1955.* Vol. VIII. ("Essays and Studies Collected for the English Association.") London: J. Murray, 1955. Pp. 114.

Rev. by J. Loiseau in *Études anglaises,* IX, 349–50. Contains an essay on W. H. Mallock's *The New Paul and Virginia.*

Maccoby, Simon. *English Radicalism, 1762–1785: The Origins.* London: Allen & Unwin, 1955. Pp. 536. *English Radicalism, 1786–1832: From Paine to Cobbett.* London: Allen & Unwin, 1955. Pp. 559.

Rev. briefly by Henry James in *LJ,* LXXXI, 533.

"Michael Faraday's Researches in Spiritualism." *Scient. Month.,* LXXXIII, 145–50.

A reprint, with introductory remarks, of Faraday's paper in the *Athenaeum,* July 2, 1853, describing his experimental investigation of table-moving and concluding that no supernatural agency was involved in the phenomenon.

Murry, John Middleton. *Unprofessional Essays.* London: Cape. Pp. 191.

Rev. by Rayner Heppenstall in *NS,* Apr. 7, p. 348. Contains an essay entitled "Clare Revisited."

Nicoll, Allardyce. *A History of English Drama, 1660–1900.* Vol. IV. . . . See VB 1955, 249.

Rev. briefly by Paull F. Baum in *SAQ,* LV, 261.

Nicolson, Sir Harold. *The English Sense of Humour, and Other Essays.* London: Constable. Pp. 208.

Rev. by Richard Mayne in *NS,* May 5, p. 490; unfavorably by Kingsley Amis in *S,* May 4, p. 625; in *TLS,* Apr. 27, p. 254. Includes essays on Swinburne and Baudelaire, on the humor of *Punch,* and on Tennyson's two brothers.

O'Connor, Frank. *A Mirror in the Roadway: A Study of the Modern Novel.* New York: Knopf. Pp. 316.

Rev. by Horace Reynolds in *Christian Science Monitor,* Sept. 27, p. 5; by M. E. Chase in *HTB,* Oct. 7, p. 3; by Louis Barron in *LJ,* LXXXI, 1987; by V. S. Pritchett in *NYTBR,* Sept. 23, p. 5; by H. M. Jones in *SR,* Sept. 22, p. 12. An illuminating treatment of Dickens, Thackeray, Trollope, and Hardy from the point of view that "the nineteenth-century novel is a European art." Chapters on French and Russian novelists.

Parrott, Thomas Marc, and Martin, Robert Bernard. *A Companion to Victorian Literature.* New York: Scribner's, 1955. Pp. 308.

Rev. favorably by Clarice Short in *Western Humanities Rev.,* X, 395–96.

Pevsner, Nikolaus. *The Englishness of English Art: An Expanded and Annotated Version of the Reith Lectures Broadcast in October and November, 1955.* London: Architectural Pr. Pp. 208.

Rev. briefly by Robert L. Enequist in *LJ,* LXXXI, 1997; unfavorably by John Berger in *NS,* Apr. 14, pp. 382–83 (see also J. A. Spencer, "The Englishness of English Art," *NS,* Apr. 21, p. 420).

Phelps, Gilbert. *The Russian Novel in English Fiction.* ("University Library, English Literature" ser.) London: Hutchinson. Pp. 206.

Rev. in *Listener,* Sept. 20, p. 433. On the reception in England and the United States of the Russian novel in translation, and the influence of Russian novelists on English and American writers.

Plumb, John Harold (ed.). *Studies in Social History: A Tribute to G. M. Trevelyan.* London: Longmans, Green, 1955. Pp. xv+287.

Rev. by Grace Banyard in *CR*, CLXXXIX, 70; by Robert L. Schuyler in *NYTBR*, Mar. 18, p. 26. Includes an essay by K. Clark on "The Romantic Element, 1830 to 1850," and by Noel Annan on "The Intellectual Aristocracy" (the families of Arnold, Stephen, Trevelyan, and others).

Pollard, Hugh M. *Pioneers of Popular Education, 1760–1850.* London: J. Murray. Pp. xiii+297.

Rev. in *TLS*, Oct. 12, p. 604.

Praz, Mario. *The Hero in Eclipse in Victorian Fiction.* Trans. Angus Davidson. London: Oxford Univ. Pr. Pp. 478.

Rev. by Bradford A. Booth in *JEGP*, LV, 655–58; unfavorably by J. O. Perry in *KR*, XVIII, 497–504; briefly by Herbert Cahoon in *LJ*, LXXXI, 1521; in *Manchester Guardian*, Mar. 29, p. 6; in *N & Q*, new ser., III, 413–14; by Gordon N. Ray in *NCF*, XI, 152–55; unfavorably by Angus Wilson in *NS*, Apr. 21, pp. 426–27; by J. H. Buckley in *NYTBR*, Aug. 5, p. 14; by Lord David Cecil in *S*, Apr. 20, p. 549; in *TLS*, June 15, p. 360; by Edgar Johnson in *VQR*, XXXII, 632–35; by Martin Price in *YR*, XLVI, 300–302. On the diminishing stature of the hero in the novels of Dickens, Thackeray, Trollope, and George Eliot.

Roberts, Harold A. "The Heroes of Postman's Park." *N & Q*, new ser., III, 542–45

Tablets made by G. F. Watts to commemorate heroic courage of common people.

Rowell, George. *The Victorian Theatre: A Survey.* London: Oxford Univ. Pr. Pp. xiii+ 203.

Rev. briefly by George Freedley in *LJ*, LXXXI, 2616; briefly by Colin Chandler in *LR*, Winter, p. 580. Includes a chronology of plays and the "fullest bibliography of the Victorian theatre yet published."

Russell, Bertrand. *Portraits from Memory and Other Essays.* London: Allen & Unwin. Pp. 228.

Rev. briefly by Beatrice B. Libaire in *LJ*, LXXXI, 2689; by Jacques Vallette in *Mercure*

de France, CCCXXVIII, 730–33; by Kingsley Martin in *NS*, Sept. 29, pp. 378–79; by T. V. Smith in *NYTBR*, Nov. 4, p. 5; by John Holloway in *S*, Oct. 5, pp. 460–61; in *TLS*, Nov. 2, p. 643. Includes essays on Mill, Shaw, Conrad, and others.

Schorer, Mark (ed.). *Society and Self in the Novel.* ("English Institute Essays," 1955.) New York: Columbia Univ. Pr. Pp. xviii+ 155.

Rev. by Herbert Cahoon in *LJ*, LXXXI, 1989. Includes an essay by G. Arthur Craig on nineteenth-century English fiction.

Scully, Vincent Joseph. *The Shingle Style: Architectural Theory and Design from Richardson to the Origins of Wright.* ("History of Art" ser., "Yale Historical Publications.") New Haven: Yale Univ. Pr., 1955. Pp. 181.

Rev. briefly in *LJ*, LXXXI, 90.

Sells, Arthur Lytton. *Animal Poetry in French and English Literature and the Greek Tradition.* ("Indiana Univ. Publications, Humanistic Ser.," No. 35.) Bloomington: Indiana Univ. Pr., 1955. Pp. xxxiv+329.

Rev. by Richard T. Bruère in *Class. Phil.*, LI, 207–9.

Shumaker, Wayne. *English Autobiography: Its Emergence, Materials and Form.* . . . See VB 1955, 249.

Rev. by Louis Rocher in *Études anglaises*, IX, 177.

Simon, Walter M. "History for Utopia: Saint-Simon and the Idea of Progress." *JHI*, XVII, 311–31.

Smith, Janet Adam. "That One Talent." *NS*, Oct. 13, pp. 455–56.

A review article based on John L. Sweeney's edition of Henry James's *The Painter's Eye*. James had some notion of what was wrong with Victorian art, although in 1876 he preferred the school of Millais and Holman Hunt to the French Impressionists.

Speaight, Robert. *William Poel and the Elizabethan Revival.* . . . See VB 1954, 242.

Rev. favorably by L. Bonnerot in *Études anglaises*, IX, 151.

Strong, Leonard Alfred George. *Personal Remarks.* London: Nevill, 1953. Pp. viii+9+ 264.

Rev. briefly by L. Bonnerot in *Études anglaises*, IX, 78–79.

Tate, Allen. *The Man of Letters in the Modern World: Selected Essays, 1928–1955*. New York: Meridian Books, 1955. Pp. 352.

Rev. unfavorably by John Jones in *NS*, Dec. 29, pp. 845–46.

Taylor, Alan John Percivale. *Englishmen and Others*. London: H. Hamilton. Pp. vii+192.

Rev. by Ralph Partridge in *NS*, Nov. 3, pp. 560–61; by Charles Wilson in *S*, Nov. 2, pp. 614–15; in *TLS*, Nov. 30, p. 706. Includes essays on Macaulay, Carlyle, Disraeli, and Bright.

Thomson, Patricia. *The Victorian Heroine: A Changing Ideal, 1837–1873*. London: Oxford Univ. Pr. Pp. 178.

Rev. by Norman St. John-Stevas in *Listener*, Dec. 6, p. 947.

Thrane, James Robert. "The Rise of Higher Criticism in England, 1800–1870." *DA*, XVI, 1457.

This study undertakes to outline the Continental origins, going back to the seventeenth century, of Higher Criticism ("the critical study of the text, character and origins of Biblical documents"); and then to show in some detail the frequently stormy progress of Higher Criticism in England, both as an independent science and as a shaping force in Victorian literature and opinion. The summary indicates a useful and important dissertation.—W. D. T.

Tillotson, Geoffrey. "Victorian Novelists and Near-Novelists." *SeR*, LXIV, 663–75.

A notable review article, surveying recent work on Dickens, Thackeray, Eliot, Trollope, and the Brownings.—O. M.

Tillotson, Kathleen. *Novels of the Eighteen-forties*. . . . See VB 1954, 242.

Rev. by Edith C. Batho in *MLR*, LI, 247–48.

Tindall, William York. *The Literary Symbol*. . . . See VB 1955, 250.

Rev. briefly by Peter Seng in *CE*, XVIII, 175.

Trilling, Lionel. *A Gathering of Fugitives*. Boston: Beacon Pr. Pp. 167.

Rev. by Leon Edel in *New R*, Nov. 19, p. 25; by R. G. Davis in *NYTBR*, Nov. 4, p. 5. Critical essays, including one on Dickens.

Turner, James. *The Dolphin's Skin: Six Studies in Eccentricity*. London: Cassell. Pp. xxii+218.

Rev. in *N & Q*, new ser., III, 551.

Underwood, V. *Verlaine et l'Angleterre*. Ouvrage publié avec le concours du Centre nationale de la recherche scientifique et de l'University College (Université de Londres). Paris: Librairie Nizet. Pp. 510.

Rev. by René Taupin in *RoR*, XLVII, 209–12.

Wain, John (ed.). *Interpretations*. . . . See VB 1955, 250.

Rev. by J. G. Ritz in *Études anglaises*, IX, 354–55; by Kennedy Williamson in *Poetry Rev.*, XLVII, 108; by F. N. Lees in *Universities Quart.*, X, 397–401.

Waller, John O. "The American Civil War and Some English Men of Letters: Carlyle, Mill, Ruskin, Arnold, Kingsley, Hughes, Trollope, Thackeray, and Dickens." *Univ. of Southern California Abstr. of Diss.*. . . . *1954* (1955), pp. 91–94.

Ward, A. C. *Illustrated History of English Literature*. Vol. III: *Blake to Bernard Shaw*. London: Longmans, Green, 1955. Pp. xi+325.

Rev. briefly by Michel Poirer in *Études anglaises*, IX, 263; favorably by Jacques Vallette in *Mercure de France*, CCCXXVII, 134–35; unfavorably by Kingsley Amis in *S*, Jan. 20, pp. 89–90.

Wethered, Herbert Newton. *The Curious Art of Autobiography: From Benvenuto Cellini to Rudyard Kipling*. London: Johnson. Pp. vii +237.

Rev. by V. S. Pritchett in *NS*, May 26, pp. 601–2; in *Theatre Arts*, XL (November), 12; in *TLS*, June 22, p. 375. Includes studies of Trollope, Newman, Conrad, and Kipling.

Wilkie, J. S. "Galton's Contribution to the Theory of Evolution with Special Reference to His Use of Models and Metaphors." *Ann. Sci.*, XI, 194–205.

Galton's contribution to the theory of evolution was made incidentally in his studies of heredity, largely through metaphor. His central ideas are: "(1) The importance of discontinuous variations in evolution. (2) The notion of stability of type, or organic stability. (3) A suggestion, contained in the metaphors, that the apparatus responsible for inheritance is rather loosely structured."

Willey, Basil. *More Nineteenth-Century Studies: A Group of Honest Doubters*. London: Chatto & Windus. Pp. 304.

Rev. by Graham Hough in *S*, Dec. 7, pp. 836–37; in *TLS*, Nov. 16, p. 680. Includes essays on Tennyson, Jowett, Froude, Morley, Francis Newman, and William Hale White.

Wilson, Colin. *The Outsider*. London: Gollancz. Pp. 288.

Rev. by C. J. Rolo in *AM*, October, p. 96; by Edward Wagenknecht in *Chicago Sunday Tribune*, Sept. 9, p. 3; by Robert Peel in *Christian Science Monitor*, Sept. 6, p. 4; by H. J. Muller in *HTB*, Sept. 2, p. 5; by Harold Lancour in *LJ*, LXXXI, 1999; by William Cooper in *N*, Aug. 25, p. 162; by Newton Arvin in *NYTBR*, Sept. 9, p. 6; by Kingsley Amis in *S*, June 15, p. 830; by J. W. Krutch in *SR*, Sept. 8, p. 37; in *TLS*, June 8, p. 342; by Helen Adams in *Universities Quart.*, XI, 90–100.

Wölcken, Fritz. *Der literarische Mord: Eine Untersuchung über die englische und amerikanische Detektiv-Literatur*. Nuremberg: Nest-Verlag, 1953. Pp. 348.

Rev. by Victor Lange in *Anglia*, LXXIII (N.S., Vol. XLI), 535–37. References to Ainsworth, Collins, Doyle, LeFanu.

Woods, George Benjamin, and Buckley, Jerome Hamilton (eds.). *Poetry of the Victorian Period*. Rev. ed. Chicago: Scott, Foresman, 1955. Pp. 1,107.

IV. INDIVIDUAL AUTHORS

Acton (see also III, Butterfield). Kochan, Lionel. *Acton on History*. . . . See VB 1955, 250.

Rev. by H. Butterfield in *EHR*, LXXI, 127–28; by Karl J. Weintraub in *JMH*, XXVIII, 389–90.

Arnold (see also I, Faverty, Gordan; III, Adams, Plumb). Allott, Kenneth. "An Arnold-Clough Letter: References to Carlyle and Tennyson." *N & Q*, new ser., III, 267.

Broadbent, J. B. "Milton and Arnold." *EC*, VI, 404–17.

Donovan, Robert A. "The Method of Arnold's *Essays in Criticism*." *PMLA*, LXXI, 922–31.

Finds the *Essays* have a remarkably well-integrated plan.

Eells, John Shepard, Jr. *The Touchstones of Matthew Arnold*. . . . See VB 1955, 251.

Rev. by F. L. Mulhauser in *MLN*, LXXI, 453–54; in *TLS*, May 11, p. 284.

Gollin, Richard M. "A Testimonial Letter from Matthew Arnold." *N & Q*, new ser., III, 123–24.

Johnson, W. Stacy. "Parallel Imagery in Arnold and Clough." *ESt*, XXXVII, 1–11.

Argues the thesis that Arnold and Clough consciously echoed each other's imagery to conduct a kind of poetic debate on a variety of topics which interested them both. The argument is unconvincing, partly because the resemblances in imagery often seem factitious, partly because it involves some wholly unfounded hypotheses about the dating of poems.—R. A. D.

Jump, J. D. *Matthew Arnold*. . . . See VB 1955, 251.

Rev. by Joan Bennett in *MLR*, LI, 252–53; by J. P. Curgenven in *RES*, new ser., VII, 323–24; in *TLS*, May 11, p. 284 (and see a letter by James Reeves, June 1, p. 329).

Krieger, Murray. " 'Dover Beach' and the Tragic Sense of Eternal Recurrence." *Univ. of Kansas City Rev.*, XXIII, 73–79.

Excellent and thorough analysis of the poem in terms of versification, structure, diction, and imagery. The introductory argument, that Arnold achieves "a concept of time as existential rather than as chronologically historical . . . by transcending his period completely and foreseeing the intellectual crisis which is so peculiarly of our own century," rests on the strange, but too common, view that an idea was held by Marvell, Keats, and Virginia Woolf lies completely outside the Victorian consciousness—even when it turns up in a Victorian poem.—C. T. D.

Lloyd-Jones, Richard. "Common Speech—a Poetic Effect for Hopkins, Browning, and Arnold." *DA*, XVI, 957.

Super, R. H. "Arnold's 'Tyrian Trader' in Thucydides." *N & Q*, new ser., III, 397.

Super, R. H. "The Authenticity of the First Edition of Arnold's *Alaric at Rome* (1840)." *HLQ*, XIX, 306–9.

Townsend, Francis G. "*Literature and Dogma*: Matthew Arnold's Letters to George Smith." *PQ*, XXV, 195–98.

Beerbohm (see also II, Meynell). Cecil, David. "Max Beerbohm." *NS*, Nov. 17, p. 626,

Announces that he has been asked by Lady Beerbohm to write the life of Max Beerbohm.

Hyde, H. Montgomery. "An Afternoon with Max." *S*, Oct. 5, pp. 445–47.

Nicholson, Jenny. "Grazie per tutto." *S*, June 1, pp. 754–55.

An account of Beerbohm's last days.

Waugh, Evelyn. "Max Beerbohm: A Lesson in Manners." *AM*, CXCVIII, 75–76.

Besant. Boege, Fred W. "Sir Walter Besant: Novelist." *NCF*, X, 249–80; XI, 32–60.

Biographical material on several phases of Besant's active career and an evaluation of his fiction: "his best work belongs clearly in the realm of literature."

Blackmore. Dunn, Waldo Hilary. *R. D. Blackmore, the Author of Lorna Doone: A Biography.* New York: Longmans, Green. Pp. 316.

Rev. by E. W. Martin in *English*, XI, 108; by DeLancey Ferguson in *HTB*, July 22, p. 5; by H. I'A. F. in *Manchester Guardian*, June 15, p. 6; by William E. Buckler in *NCF*, XI, 218–22; by Carlos Baker in *NYTBR*, Sept. 2, p. 6; by Derek Hudson in *S*, June 8, p. 801; in *TLS*, May 25, p. 314.

Borrow (see also III, Wethered). Fréchet, R. *George Borrow.* Paris: Didier.

Rev. by Jacques Vallette in *Mercure de France*, CCCXXVII, 321. A doctoral thesis.

Brontës (see also I, Gordan; III, Adams, Baker, Burns, Lehman). Bengtsson, Frans S. *Folk som sjöng.* Stockholm: Norstedt. Pp. 319.

Rev. briefly by Frederic Fleisher in *BA*, XXX, 351. A collection of twenty-six essays, including pieces on Emily Brontë, Carlyle, Doyle, and Thackeray.

Blondel, Jacques. *Emily Brontë: expérience spirituelle et création poétique.* Paris: Presses Universitaires de France, 1955. Pp. 452.

Rev. by G. D. Klingopulos in *Études anglaises*, IX, 264–66.

Brontë Society, Transactions and Other Publications of.

Vol. XIII, No. 1 (Part 66), has items: Hopewell, Donald, "Two Literary Ladies: Mrs. Gaskell and Miss Brontë" (pp. 3–9); Huguenin, Charles A., "Charlotte Brontë's Juvenile Poem"

[an 84-line poem dated 1831] (pp. 10–13); Fielding, K. J., "The Brontës and 'The North American Review'—a Critic's Strange Guesses" (pp. 14–18); Hustwick, Wade, "Branwell Brontë and Freemasonry—What the Records of His Lodge Reveal" (pp. 19–23); Duthie, E. L., "Delacroix and 'Jane Eyre'—Two Quoted Passages" [from Delacroix's *Journal*] (pp. 24–27); "Plan To Improve Brontë Museum" (pp. 32 ff.); "Letter from Charlotte" [to Lady Kay Shuttleworth, May 29, 1850] (p. 39); Vint, W. T., "The Brontë Parsonage Museum" [report for 1955; lists additions to museum and library] (pp. 48–51).

Girdler, Lew. "Charlotte Brontë's *Shirley* and Scott's *The Black Dwarf.*" *MLN*, LXXI, 187.

Suggests that Charlotte Brontë borrowed the surname of her heroine from Scott.

Lewis, C. Day. *Notable Images of Virtue.* Toronto: Ryerson Pr., 1954. Pp. 77.

Prints a series of three lectures given at Queen's University in 1954 on the concern of three poets (Emily Brontë, George Meredith, and W. B. Yeats) with the problems of freedom, responsibility, and human dignity. Rev. by John Margeson in *Dalhousie Rev.*, XXXVI, 185 ("What is most refreshing and most important about these lectures is their acceptance of large and great themes as proper subjects for discussion in the criticism of poetry").—W. D. T.

Martin, N. D. S. "Two Unpublished Letters of Charlotte Brontë." *BLR*, V (1955), 222–23. See also Kathleen Tillotson, "Charlotte Brontë," p. 231.

The second letter records the first step in the publication of *Villette.*

Mathison, John K. "Nelly Dean and the Power of *Wuthering Heights.*" *NCF*, XI, 106–29.

Poli, Sara. "La Fortuna di Charlotte Brontë." *English Miscellany* (Rome), 1955, pp. 63–107.

Ratchford, Fannie E. (ed.). *Gondal's Queen: A Novel in Verse. . . .* See VB 1955, 253.

Rev. by Autrey Nell Wiley in *BBDI*, XXI, 175; unfavorably by Margaret Lane in *NS*, Mar. 31, pp. 318–19; by Mildred G. Christian in *VNL*, No. 10 (Autumn), pp. 13–15.

Brownings (see also I, Faverty, Singer; III, Adams, G. Tillotson; **Arnold:** Lloyd-Jones).

Beall, Chandler B. "A Dantean Simile in Browning." *MLN*, LXXI, 492–93.

"Worm into fly," in *Cleon*, traced to a passage in the *Purgatorio*.

Corrigan, Beatrice (trans. and ed.). *Curious Annals: New Documents Relating to Browning's Roman Murder Story*. Toronto: Toronto Univ. Pr. Pp. 142.

Rev. in *TLS*, Sept. 28, p. 570.

DeVane, W. C. *A Browning Handbook*. . . . See VB 1955, 254.

Rev. by Geoffrey Bullough in *English*, XI, 70–71; in *TLS*, Feb. 24, p. 115.

Duffin, Henry Charles. *Amphibian: A Reconsideration of Browning*. London: Bowes & Bowes. Pp. 317.

Rev. by Sylva Norman in *CR*, CXC, 188–89; by Geoffrey Bullough in *English*, XI, 70–71; by René Lalou in *Études anglaises*, IX, 352–53; by W. O. Raymond in *QQ*, LXIII, 309–10; in *QR*, CCXCIV, 267–68; by Geoffrey Tillotson in *SeR*, LXIV, 664–66; in *TLS*, Feb. 24, p. 115. A critical study. "Amphibian" in the title implies the intermixture of poetic and prosaic elements in Browning's writings.

Federle, Walter. *Robert Brownings dramatisches Experiment*. . . . See VB 1955, 254.

Rev. by W. Iser in *RES*, new ser., VII, 107.

Going, William T. "The Ring and the Brownings." *MLN*, LXXI, 493–95.

Elizabeth Barrett's short lyric "A Ring" suggested as source for the central metaphor in *The Ring and the Book*.

Harrison, Thomas P. "Birds in the Poetry of Browning." *RES*, new ser., VII, 393–405.

Birds were important to Browning not only as a source of incidental imagery but also as providing what he called "the feathered parallel" to human life.

Jeffrey, Lloyd N. "Browning as Psychologist: Three Notes." *CE*, XVII, 345–48.

Knickerbocker, Kenneth L. "A Tentative Apology for Browning." *Tennessee Studies in Literature*. ("University of Tennessee Studies in the Humanities," No. 1.) Pp. 75–82.

Takes issue with Richard D. Altick's recent article in the *Yale Review*, which marks the nadir of Browning's reputation as a thinker.

Knickerbocker observes that recent critics find fault with Browning's thought but seldom suggest what he should have thought. Given Browning's beliefs, he is quite as profound as most major poets. Most objections to Browning's thought are pitched on the low level of personal disagreement.

Incidentally, Knickerbocker criticizes William E. Buckler for a statement which I made.—F. G. T.

Langbaum, Robert. "*The Ring and the Book:* A Relativist Poem." *PMLA*, LXXI, 131–54.

A careful demonstration of how the poem "achieves its meaning through meeting the conditions of modern psychological and historical relativism." Suggests that the necessity for meeting such conditions may explain the decline of the long poem in modern culture.—R. C. S.

Lowe, Robert Liddell. "Robert Browning to Percy William Bunting: An Unpublished Letter." *N & Q*, new ser., III, 539–41.

The poet would not contribute a memorial piece on General Gordon to Bunting's *Contemporary Review*.

McAleer, Edward C. "Browning's 'Cleon' and Auguste Comte." *Comp. Lit.*, VIII, 142–45.

McCarthy, Barbara P. (ed.). *Elizabeth Barrett to Mr. Boyd*. . . . See VB 1955, 254.

Rev. in *HTB*, Feb. 19, p. 12; by H. I'A. Fausset in *Manchester Guardian*, Mar. 9, p. 6; in *N & Q*, new ser., III, 230; by Peter Quennell in *S*, Apr. 6, p. 453; in *TLS*, Mar. 16, p. 162; in *USQBR*, XII, 1.

McNeir, Waldo F. "Lucrezia's 'Cousin' in Browning's 'Andrea del Sarto.'" *N & Q*, new ser., III, 500–502.

Raymond, W. O. "Truth in *The Ring and the Book*." *VNL*, No. 10 (Autumn), pp. 12–13.

Ruffin, D. "Browning's Childe Roland and Chaucer's House of Fame." *Essays in Honor of Walter Clyde Curry*. Nashville: Vanderbilt Univ. Pr. Pp. 298.

Schweik, Robert C. "Bishop Blougram's Miracles." *MLN*, LXXI, 416–18.

On contemporary miracles (winking virgins, etc.) as seen by Newman and Wiseman.

Sewter, A. C. "The Barretts at Hope End: Some Unpublished Portraits, Sketches, and Letters." *Connoisseur*, XXXVII, 179–81.

Letters and pictures by the artist William Artaud, who stayed with the Barretts in 1818.

Taplin, Gardner B. "Mrs. Browning's Poems of 1850." *BPLQ*, VIII, 181–94.

Chapter from a book to be published by Yale University Press.

Butler (see also III, Leyburn). Harkness, Stanley B. *The Career of Samuel Butler.* . . . See VB 1955, 254.

Rev. by J.-B. Fort in *Études anglaises*, IX, 68–70 (although he points out the merits of the bibliography, Fort detects some startling errors); briefly in *NCF*, XI, 159–60.

Linde, Ilse Dusoir. "*The Way of All Flesh* and *A Portrait of the Artist as a Young Man: A Comparison.*" *VNL*, No. 9 (Spring), pp. 7–10.

Carlyle (see also III, Geyl, Gooch, Taylor; **Arnold:** Allott; **Brontës:** Bengtsson; **Tennyson:** Krause). Duckett, Margaret. "Carlyle, 'Columbus,' and Joaquin Miller." *PQ*, XXXV, 443–47.

Miller's best-known poem may have been inspired by a passage in *Past and Present*.

Dunn, Waldo H. (ed.). "Carlyle's Last Letters to Froude." *TC*, CLIX, 44–53, 255–63, 591–97; CLX, 241–46.

Eighteen letters to Froude and Mrs. Froude, dated 1864–75. "They reveal Carlyle's confidence in Froude, and his admiration for him and his work. . . . They make clear that Froude was Carlyle's chosen literary executor and biographer."

Kegel, Charles H. "An Uncertain Biographical Fact." *VNL*, No. 10 (Autumn), p. 19.

Attempts to date the first meeting of Carlyle and Ruskin between September, 1846, and June, 1847.

Pearsall, Robert. "Carlyle and Emerson: Horses and Revolutions." *SAQ*, LV, 179–91.

Sanders, Charles Richard. "The Question of Carlyle's Conversion." *VNL*, No. 10 (Autumn), pp. 10–12.

Slater, Joseph Locke. "An Introduction to the Correspondence of Carlyle and Emerson." *DA*, XVI, 753–54.

Worth, George J. "Three Carlyle Documents." *PMLA*, LXXI, 542–44.

Carroll (see also I, Gordan, Ratchford). Bond, W. H. "The Publication of *Alice's Adventures in Wonderland.*" *HLB*, X, 306–24.

Greenacre, Phyllis. *Swift and Carroll.* . . . See VB 1955, 255.

Rev. by Florence Becker Lennon in *Humanist*, new ser., XVI, 145–46.

Weaver, Warren. "The Parrish Collection of Carrolliana." *PLC*, XVII, 85–91.

Clare (see also I, Singer; III, Murry). Tibble, John William and Anne. *John Clare: His Life and Poetry.* London: Heinemann. Pp. xi+216.

Rev. by Naomi Lewis in *NS*, May 5, pp. 492–93.

Clough (see also I, Faverty; III, Adams, Thrane; **Arnold:** Allott, Johnson). Bertram, James. "The Ending of Clough's *Dipsychus.*" *RES*, new ser., VII, 59–60.

Considers the probability that Clough wrote a serious ending in verse but substituted the humorous and abrupt prose ending in the published work.

Collins (see also III, Baker, Colby). Ashley, Robert P. "The Wilkie Collins Collection." *PLC*, XVII, 81–84.

Davis, Nuel Pharr. *The Life of Wilkie Collins.* Introd. by Gordon Ray. Urbana: Univ. of Illinois Pr. Pp. 360.

Rev. by DeLancey Ferguson in *HTB*, Dec. 23, p. 3.

Conrad (see also III, Cazamian, Russell, Wethered). Davis, Harold Edmund. "Method and Form in the Novels of Joseph Conrad." *DA*, XVI, 1682.

Gullason, Thomas A. "Conrad's 'The Lagoon.' " *Ex*, XIV, Item 23.

Hackett, Francis. "Back to Conrad." *New R*, Aug. 6, pp. 20–21.

On *Nostromo*.

Moser, Thomas. " 'The Rescuer' Manuscript: A Key to Conrad's Development—and Decline." *HLB*, X, 325–55.

Schwab, Arnold T. "Joseph Conrad's American Friend: Correspondence with James Huneker." *MP*, LII (1955), 222–32.

Sickels, Eleanor M. "Conrad's 'The Lagoon.' " *Ex*, XV, Item 17.

Stallman, R. W. "Conrad and *The Great Gatsby*." *Twentieth Century Literature*, I (Spring, 1955), 5–12.

Vidan, Ivo. "One Source of Conrad's *Nostromo*." *RES*, new ser., VII, 287–93.

Conrad's debt to G. F. Masterman's *Seven Eventful Years in Paraguay*.

Visiak, E. H. *The Mirror of Conrad*. . . . See VB 1955, 256.

Rev. briefly by B. H. Carroll, Jr., in *EJ*, XLV, 500; by Arnold T. Schwab in *NCF*, XI, 235–37; by Walter M. Teller in *NYTBR*, Nov. 25, p. 24.

Warner, John Riley. "The Ethics of Joseph Conrad." *DA*, XVI, 1458.

Corelli. Scott, William Stuart. *Marie Corelli: The Story of a Friendship*. London: Hutchinson, 1955. Pp. 208.

Rev. by Arthur Marshall in *NS*, Feb. 4, pp. 129–30; by Gerald Hamilton in *S*, Feb. 17, p. 222; in *TLS*, Feb. 3, p. 70.

De Vere. Winckler, Paul A., and Stone, William V. "Aubrey Thomas de Vere, 1814–1902: A Bibliography." *VNL*, No. 10 (Autumn), suppl. 1, pp. 1–4.

Dickens (see also I, Gordan; III, Baker, Burns, Colby, Praz, Strong, G. Tillotson, Trilling; **Reade:** Fielding; **Tennyson:** Sharrock). Addison, William. *In the Steps of Charles Dickens*. . . . See VB 1955, 256.

Rev. briefly and unfavorably by Sylvère Monod in *Études anglaises*, IX, 168.

Bovill, E. W. "Tony Weller's Trade." *N & Q*, new ser., III, 324–28, 527–31.

Bowen, W. H. *Charles Dickens and His Family: A Sympathetic Study*. Cambridge: Heffer. Pp. xiii+182.

Clark, William Ross. "The Hungry Mr. Dickens." *Dalhousie Rev.*, XXXVI, 250–57.

Dickens, Charles. *Mrs. Gamp*. New York: New York Pub. Libr. Pp. 61.

A prepublication notice, *Bull. New York Pub. Libr.*, LX, 474–75. A photographic facsimile of Dickens' reading, *Mrs. Gamp*, which he used on the rostrum.

Dickensian (quarterly), Vol. LII (Nos. 317–20). . . . See VB 1932, 422.

Items as follows: Adrian, A., "Charles Dickens and Dean Stanley" (pp. 152–56); Bland, D., "The 'Lost' Sentence in *Dombey & Son* Once More" (pp. 142–43); Brend, G. "*Edwin Drood* and the Four Witnesses" (pp. 20–24); Butt, J., "A Century of Dickens Criticism [rev. of *Dickens and His Readers*, by George Ford]" (pp. 91–93); Carlton, W., "*Charles Dickens and His Family* [rev. of book by W. H. Bowen]" (pp. 174–76); Carlton, W., "Dickens in the Jury Box" (pp. 65–69); Carlton, W., "A Pickwick Lawsuit in 1837" (pp. 33–38); Collins, P., " 'Keep Household Words Imaginative' " (pp. 117–23); Drew, A., "Structure in *Great Expectations*" (pp. 123–27); DuCann, C., "Dickens on the Death Penalty" (pp. 149–51); Fielding, K., "The Recent Reviews; Dickens in 1858" (pp. 25–32); Gibson, F., "The Idyllic in Dickens" (pp. 59–64); Grubb, G., "Dickens and Chorley" (pp. 100–109); Grubb, G., "Dickens Rejects" (pp. 89–90); Hill, T., "Notes on *Barnaby Rudge*" (pp. 136–40, 185–88); Lane, L., "The Devil in *Oliver Twist*" (pp. 132–36); Matthews, W., "Religious Movements in the Lifetime of Charles Dickens" (pp. 52–59); Morley, M., "*All the Year Round* Plays" (pp. 128–31, 177–80); Morley, M., "Enter *Our Mutual Friend*" (pp. 39–43); Morley, M., "Plays and Sketches by Boz" (pp. 81–88); Murphy, T., "*A Child's History of England*" (pp. 157–61); Murray, D., "Immortal Memory [speech at Dickens Fellowship Dinner, Feb. 7, 1956]" (pp. 113–16); Pakenham, P., "*The Hero in Eclipse in Victorian Fiction* [rev. of book by Mario Praz]" (pp. 173–74); Pakenham, P., "The Way to Dingley Dell" (p. 163); Pakenham, P., "The Wisdom of Humphry House [rev. of *All in Due Time*]" (pp. 93–94); Pechey, R., "Dickensian Nomenclature" (pp. 180–82); Postlethwaite, F., "William Cobbett on Dickens" (pp. 109–12); Schoeck, R., "Acton on Dickens" (pp. 77–80); Staples, L., "The Ghost of a French *Hamlet*" (pp. 71–76); Staples, L., "The Angus Fletcher Bust of Dickens" (pp. 5–6); Tillotson, K., "Dickens and a Story by John Poole" (pp. 69–70); Wagenknecht, E., "Dickens in Longfellow's Letters and Journals" (pp. 7–19); Whitley, A., "Two Hints for *Bleak House*" (pp. 183–84).

Engel, Monroe. "The Politics of Dickens' Novels." *PMLA*, LXXI, 945–74.

Fielding, K. J. "Mill and Gradgrind." *NCF*, XI, 148–51.

Ford, George H. *Dickens and His Readers*. . . . See VB 1955, 258.

Rev. by Heinz Reinhold in *Anglia*, LXXIV (N.S., Vol. XLII), 141–43; briefly but favorably by Sylvère Monod in *Études anglaises*, IX, 169; favorably by Bradford Booth in *MP*, LIV, 71–72; by William D. Templeman in *Personalist*, XXXVII, 419–20; by Kingsley Amis in *S*, Jan. 6, pp. 22–23; by Merle M. Bevington in *SAQ*, LV, 243–44; by Geoffrey Tillotson in *SeR*, LXIV, 671–73; by P. A. W. Collins in *Universities Quart.*, X, 283–86; by Royal A. Gettmann in *VNL*, No. 10 (Autumn), pp. 4–5.

Grenander, M. E. "The Mystery and the Moral: Point of View in Dickens's *Bleak House*." *NCF*, X, 301–5.

Griffith, Ben W. "Two Misdated Dickens Letters." *N & Q*, new ser., III, 122–23.

Haight, Gordon S. "Dickens and Lewes." *PMLA*, LXXI, 166–79.

House, Humphry. *All in Due Time: The Collected Essays and Broadcast Talks*. London: Hart-Davis, 1955. Pp. 306.

Rev. briefly by J. S. Buchanan in *LR*, Spring, p. 289.

Johannsen, Albert (ed.). *Phiz Illustrations from the Novels of Charles Dickens*. Chicago: Univ. of Chicago Pr. Pp. 453.

Reproductions of 516 etchings for seven of Dickens' novels.

"News from the Field." *College and Research Libr.*, XVII, 85–88.

Contains a brief description of a Dickens collection given to the Cornell University Library by William G. Mennen.

Rust, James D. "Dickens and the Americans: An Unnoticed Letter." *NCF*, XI, 70–72.

Shaffer, Ellen. "Portrait of a Philadelphia Collector: William McIntire Elkins (1882–1947)." *BSP*, L, 115–68.

Contains much about the Dickens collection.

Winters, Warrington W. "Unusual Mental Phenomena in the Life and Works of Charles Dickens." *Summ. Ph.D. Theses . . . Minnesota*, V (1951), 147–51. (Inadvertently omitted earlier.)

Disraeli (see also III, Taylor). Hackett, Francis. "Disraeli as a Novelist." *New R*, Dec. 17, pp. 27–28.

Jerman, B. R. "Disraeli's Audience." *SAQ*, LV, 463–72.

A biographical sketch of Sarah Disraeli.

Eliot (see also III, Baker, Colby, Lehman, Praz, Thrane, G. Tillotson). Beaty, Jerome. "*Middlemarch* from Notebook to Novel: A Study of George Eliot's Creative Method." *DA*, XVI, 1138.

Begins with a detailed chronological account of the writing of *Middlemarch*, 1869–72. Proceeds to indicate use of source materials, early versions, revisions, variety of publishing. Indicates, finally, "that . . . contrary to her own, commonly accepted description of writing her best work as if inspired, 'without blur or erasure' —to George Eliot writing was truly a process: she constantly revised, while she was writing, after reading passages over, in proof." This summary shows that the dissertation is unusually noteworthy.—W. D. T.

Beebe, Maurice. " 'Visions Are Creators': The Unity of *Daniel Deronda*." *Boston Univ. Studies in English*, I (1955), 166–77.

Creeger, George R. "An Interpretation of *Adam Bede*." *ELH*, XXIII, 218–38.

A highly perceptive analysis of Eliot's use of symbolism in *Adam Bede*, especially her unconventional handling of the oppositions of country versus city, fertility versus wasteland, Loamshire versus Stoneyshire, as aids to characterization.—O. M.

Haight, Gordon S. (ed.). *The George Eliot Letters*. Vols. I–III. . . . See VB 1955, 259.

Rev. by Barbara Hardy in *MLR*, LI, 249–52; by R. H. Super in *MP*, LIII, 285–89; by Graham Hough in *RES*, new ser., VII, 435–36.

Haight, Gordon S. (ed.). *The George Eliot Letters*. Vols. IV–VII. . . . See VB 1955, 260.

Rev. by Edward Wagenknecht in *Chicago Sunday Tribune*, Jan. 22, p. 4; by W. W. Cunningham in *Christian Science Monitor*, Feb. 2, p. 7; by K. T. Willis in *LJ*, LXXXI, 451–52; briefly in *NCF*, XI, 77–78; by V. S. Pritchett in *NS*, July 21, p. 79 ("She lies entombed in seven volumes of the dullest letters in English literature"); by John Bayley in *S*, Aug. 10, p. 210; by Geoffrey Tillotson in *SeR*, LXIV, 667–70; by DeLancey Ferguson in *SR*, Apr. 7, p. 18; in *TLS*, Aug. 10, pp. 469–70; in *USQBR*, XII, 136; by Gordon N. Ray in *VQR*, XXXII, 302–5.

Haight, Gordon S. "George Eliot's Theory of Fiction." *VNL*, No. 10 (Autumn), pp. 1–3.

Hardy, Barbara. "Mr. Browning and George Eliot." *EC*, VI, 121–23.

Takes exception to part of a review of *The George Eliot Letters*.

Huzzard, John Amos. "George Eliot and Italy: A Comprehensive Study of *Romola*." *DA*, XVI, 1454–55.

Includes, among other items, accounts (1) of George Eliot's theory of the historical novel and (2) of the critical reputation of *Romola* from 1863 to the present.

Paris, Bernard J. "Toward a Revaluation of George Eliot's *The Mill on the Floss*." *NCF*, XI, 18–31.

Rust, James D. "The Art of Fiction in George Eliot's Reviews." *RES*, new ser., VII, 164–72.

Stone, Wilfred H. "Hale White and George Eliot." *TQ*, XXV, 437–51.

Ford (see also I, Gordan). Gose, Elliott B., Jr. "Reality to Romance: A Study of Ford's *Parade's End*." *CE*, XVII, 445–50.

Gilbert (see also I, Walbridge). Lauterbach, Charles E. "Taking Gilbert's Measure." *HLQ*, XIX, 196–202.

Gissing (see also III, Baker). Adams, Ruth M. "George Gissing and Clara Collet." *NCF*, XI, 72–77.

Gladstone (see also II, Medlicott). Battiscombe, Georgina. *Mrs. Gladstone: The Portrait of a Marriage*. London: Constable. Pp. x+251.

Rev. by Jane Hodge in *History Today*, VI, 857–58; by Ralph Partridge in *NS*, Nov. 24, p. 676; briefly by Betty Miller in *TC*, CLX, 576–80; in *TLS*, Nov. 2, p. 648.

Magnus, Philip. *Gladstone*. . . . See VB 1955, 261.

Rev. by John F. Glaser in *JMH*, XXVIII, 286–88; by W. B. Hamilton in *SAQ*, LV, 98–99.

Gosse (see also I, Carter, Cole). Waugh, Alec. "Edmund Gosse." *VQR*, XXXII, 69–78.

An account of Churton Collins' notorious attack on Gosse.

Grosart. Delafons, John. "A. B. Grosart, 'a Prince of Editors': Tribute to a Victorian Scholar." *Bull. New York Pub. Libr.*, LX, 444–54.

Haggard. Baker, Carlos. "A Great Rider Haggard Accession." *PLC*, XVII, 272–73.

"Rider Haggard." *TLS*, June 22, p. 377.

Hallam (see III, Gooch, Lehman).

Hardy (see also I, Faverty; III, Baker, Brown, Colby, Sells, Strong; **Kipling:** Miller). Bailey, James Osler. *Thomas Hardy and the Cosmic Mind: A New Reading of "The Dynasts."* Chapel Hill: Univ. of North Carolina Pr. Pp. 223.

Bellman, Samuel I. "How 'New' a Woman Was Hardy's Sue Bridehead?" *Colby Libr. Quart.*, IV, 137–39.

Earlier portraits of the "emancipated woman."

Bellman, Samuel Irving. "Man as Alien: The Isolation Theme in Thomas Hardy." *DA*, XVI, 960–61.

Chaikin, Milton. "A Possible Source of Hardy's *The Well-beloved*." *MLN*, LXXI, 496–97.

Hardy may have borrowed the pattern of his novel from Maupassant's *Fort comme la mort*.

Clifford, Emma. "*War and Peace* and *The Dynasts*." *MP*, LIV, 33–44.

A thorough, but inconclusive, study of Hardy's use of material from *War and Peace* in *The Dynasts*, based chiefly on a careful collation of the two works and on Hardy's own references to his sources in the Draft Manuscript of a portion of *The Dynasts* now in the County Museum at Dorchester. By demonstrating that Hardy's borrowings were confined to unimportant details, the author seems to be arguing the negative conclusion that Hardy was *not* influenced by Tolstoi in the larger conception of his work.—R. A. D.

Gerber, Helmut E. "Hardy's 'A Tragedy of Two Ambitions.'" *Ex*, XIV, Item 55.

Structure, symbol, and irony in a short story.

Green, David Bonnell. "A Source for Hardy's 'The Duchess of Hamptonshire.'" *N & Q*, new ser., III, 86.

Hackett, Francis. "A Call to Arms." *New R*, Nov. 5, pp. 21–22.

On *The Dynasts*.

Hansford, Frederick E. "Recollections . . ." (of the Hardy Players in Dorchester). *Dor-*

set *Year Book, 1956–57* (Weymouth, England, 1956), pp. 23 and 25–26.

Hardy, Evelyn. "Some Unpublished Poems by Thomas Hardy." *London Mag.*, III, 28–35.

Hardy, Evelyn. *Thomas Hardy.* . . . See VB 1955, 261.

Rev. by G. W. Sherman in *Sci. & Soc.*, XX, 169–70.

Hardy, Evelyn (ed.). *Thomas Hardy's Notebooks.* . . . See VB 1955, 261.

Rev. by Bernard Jones in *Books and Bookmen*, I, 32; briefly in *NCF*, XI, 237; by Kay Dick in *S*, Jan. 13, p. 56.

Hardy, Thomas. "Boys Will Be Boys." *Dorset Year Book, 1956–57*, p. 107.

Facsimile of a letter now in the Colby College Library.

Hardy, Thomas. "Five (Previously) Unpublished Poems." *London Mag.*, III, 35–39.

Holmes, Laurence R. "Hardy's 'Her Father.'" *Ex*, XIV, Item 53.

Humphry, James, III. "The Three Sowers." *Colby Libr. Quart.*, IV, 105–8.

Three distinguished collectors of books by Thomas Hardy, and a gift of Hardiana.

Hynes, Samuel Lynn. "The Poetry of Thomas Hardy." *DA*, XVI, 1256.

Johnson, S. F. "Burke and Hardy." *TLS*, Dec. 7, p. 731.

Suggests Hardy's indebtedness to Burke's *Sublime and Beautiful*.

Johnstone, H. F. V. "Giles Dugdale." *Dorset Year Book, 1956–57*, pp. 129–32.

Lewis, C. Day. "The Lyrical Poetry of Thomas Hardy." ("Warton Lecture on English Poetry.") *Proc. British Acad., 1951*, Vol. XXXVII, 155–74. (Inadvertently omitted earlier.)

Moynahan, Julian. "*The Mayor of Casterbridge* and the Old Testament's First Book of Samuel: A Study of Some Literary Relationships." *PMLA*, LXXI, 118–30.

Extensive parallels between the Henchard-Farfrae rivalry and the Saul-David conflict; the biblical conflict seen as a kind of framing action for the novel's main dramatic situation.

Neiman, Gilbert. "Thomas Hardy, Existentialist." *Twentieth Century Literature*, January, pp. 207–14.

"Other Recent Acquisitions." *Colby Libr. Quart.*, IV, 118–20.

Describes markings and marginal notations made by Hardy which appear in his personal copy of Lucretius' *On the Nature of Things*.

Purdy, Richard L. *Thomas Hardy: A Bibliographical Study.* . . . See VB 1955, 262.

Rev. by G. W. Sherman in *Sci. & Soc.*, XX, 380–81.

Reichard, Hugo M. "Hardy's *Tess of the d'Urbervilles.*" *Ex*, XIV, Item 42.

Starr, William T. "Romain Rolland and Thomas Hardy." *MLQ*, XVII, 99–103.

Influences and echoes of Hardy, especially of *Jude*, in Rolland's *Jean-Christophe*.

Warren, F. C. "Wool and Bindon Abbey." *Dorset Year Book, 1956–57*, pp. 57–59.

Weber, Carl J. "Forty Years in an Author's Life: A Dozen Letters (1876–1915) from Thomas Hardy." *Colby Libr. Quart.*, IV, 108–17.

Most of these letters are here published for the first time.

Weber, Carl J. "Napoleonic Echoes." *Colby Libr. Quart.*, IV, 101–2.

An autograph letter of Hardy to Rev. L. E. F. Filleul.

Weber, Carl J. "R. Grosvenor Bartelot's Hardy Scrap-Book." *Colby Libr. Quart.*, IV, 130–37.

Souvenirs of an acquaintance with Hardy collected by the Rev. Bartelot and pasted into his copy of *A Laodicean*.

Weber, Carl J. " 'What's in a Name?'—or in a Signature?" *Manuscripts*, VIII, 185–88.

Henley (see also I, Faverty). Armstrong, R. L. "Henley's 'The Ways of Death.'" *Ex*, XIV, Item 21.

Hope. Putt, S. Gorley. "The Prisoner of *The Prisoner of Zenda*: Anthony Hope and the Novel of Society." *EC*, VI, 38–59.

Hopkins (see also I, Faverty; **Arnold:** Lloyd-Jones). Abbott, Claude Colleer (ed.).

Further Letters of Gerard Manley Hopkins, Including His Correspondence with Coventry Patmore. 2d ed. rev. and enl. London: Oxford Univ. Pr. Pp. xlvii+465. Rev. by Graham Hough in *S*, Dec. 28, pp. 936–37; in *TLS*, Dec. 21, p. 763. A new edition, including a large number of hitherto unpublished letters, mainly to his mother.

Ayers, R. W. "Hopkins' 'The Windhover': A Further Simplification." *MLN*, LXXI, 577–84.
"As a skate's heel sweeps smooth on a bowbend" is taken to refer to the movement of a predatory fish (*Raja batis*).

Baird, Sister Mary Julian. "Blake, Hopkins and Thomas Merton." *CWd*, CLXXXIII, 46–49.
A rather superficial account of the spiritual influence of Blake and Hopkins on Merton.—R. A. D.

Downes, David Anthony. "The Ignatian Spirit in Gerard Manley Hopkins." *DA*, XVI, 535.

Doyle, Francis G. "Note on Hopkins's Windhover." *StI*, XLV, 88–91.

Duncan-Jones, E. E. "R. W. Dixon's 'Terrible Crystal.'" *N & Q*, new ser., III, 267.
A biblical phrase used by Dixon to describe Hopkins' poetry.

Guidi, Augusto. "Milton e Hopkins." *English Miscellany* (Rome), 1955, pp. 31–43.

Hartman, Geoffrey H. *The Unmediated Vision.* . . . See VB 1955, 262.
Rev. briefly by Stewart C. Wilcox in *BA*, XXX, 443; by H. M. Margoliouth in *RES*, new ser., VII, 436–37.

Kelly, Hugh. "The Windhover—and Christ." *StI*, XLV, 188–93.

King, Anne R. "Hopkins' 'Windhover' and Blake." *ESt*, XXXVII, 245–52.
Conjectures that Hopkins' poem may have been influenced by one of Blake's water-color illustrations of Milton's "L'Allegro."

Ritz, Jean-Georges. "The Windhover de G. M. Hopkins." *Études anglaises*, IX, 14–22.

Sherwood, H. C. "Hopkins's 'Spelt from Sibyl's Leaves.'" *Ex*, XV, Item 5.

Weatherhead, A. Kingsley. "G. M. Hopkins: The Windhover." *N & Q*, new ser., III, 354.

Whitlock, Baird W. "Gerard Hopkins' 'Windhover.'" *N & Q*, new ser., III, 169–71.

Housman (see also I, Faverty). Bailey, D. R. Schackleton. "Maniliana." *Class. Quart.*, XLIX, 81–86.
Challenges, but very respectfully, some of Housman's verdicts in his edition of Manilius.

Haber, Tom Burns (ed.). *The Manuscript Poems of A. E. Housman.* . . . See VB 1955, 263.
See a correspondence on "The Text of Housman's Poetry" in *TLS:* letters by John Carter, June 15, p. 361; by the reviewer of Haber (Apr. 29, 1955), June 22, p. 377; by T. B. Haber, July 20, p. 435.

Haber, Tom Burns. "New Housman Lucretiana." *Class. Jour.*, LI, 386–90.

Haber, Tom Burns. "Parallels in Juvenal and Housman." *Class. Jour.*, LII, 123–24.

Haber, Tom Burns. "A Unique 'Shropshire Lad.'" *BSP*, L, 198–200.

Rockwell, Kiffin Ayres. "A. E. Housman, Poet-Scholar." *Class. Jour.*, LII, 145–48.

Stevenson, John W. "The Pastoral Setting in the Poetry of A. E. Housman." *SAQ*, LV, 487–500.
A defense of Housman against Garrod's charge of "false pastoralism." The author explores the uses which Housman makes of the pastoral mode's "clash between style and theme" and the opportunities it affords to view the complex world from the simple world.

White, William. "Misprints in *A Shropshire Lad*." *BBDI*, XXI, 200.

Howitt. Lee, Amice. *Laurels and Rosemary.* . . . See VB 1955, 263.
Rev. briefly by Louis Rocher in *Études anglaises*, IX, 263–64; by Carl R. Woodring in *JEGP*, LV, 514–16.

Hudson. Landry, Rudolph J. "The Source of the Name 'Rima' in 'Green Mansions.'" *N & Q*, new ser., III, 545–46.
"Rima" is a structure in the larynx of a bird.

Hughes. Steer, Barbara D. G. "Dr. Hayman of Rugby, and Thomas Hughes." *N & Q,* new ser., III, 38.

Usborne, Richard. "A Re-reading of 'Tom Brown.'" *S,* Aug. 17, p. 229.

An attack on this "classic" as a thoroughly unpleasant book, influential for the bad.

Huxley. Bibby, Cyril. "T. H. Huxley's Idea of a University." *Universities Quart.,* X, 377–89.

Huxley's views in relation to those of Arnold and especially of Newman. Based partly on unpublished material: a valuable article.—O. M.

Patrick, J. Max. "The Portrait of Huxley in Mallock's *New Republic.*" *NCF,* XI, 61–69.

Jefferies. Hyde, William J. "Richard Jefferies and the Naturalistic Peasant." *NCF,* XI, 207–17.

An analysis of Jefferies' achievement with the rural scene and the peasant character.

Johnson, Lionel (see I, Faverty).

Kingsley (see also III, Colby). Adrian, Arthur A. "Charles Kingsley Visits Boston." *HLQ,* XX, 94–97.

Kingsley's visit in 1874 as recorded by his Boston hostess, Mrs. J. T. Fields.

Allen, Richard Eilers. "Charles Kingsley and the Industrial Revolution." *DA,* XVI, 1680.

Andrews, John S. "Shockheaded Peter." *N & Q,* new ser., III, 265–66.

Kingsley's references to *Struwwelpeter.*

Kipling (see also I, Cole, Faverty; III, Cazamian, *Essays,* Sells, Wethered). Carrington, C. E. *The Life of Rudyard Kipling.* . . . See VB 1955, 263.

Rev. by Derek Stanford in *CR,* CLXXXIX, 314; briefly by K. W. Hunt in *EJ,* XLV, 231; by Gilbert Thomas in *English,* XI, 23–24; unfavorably by C. A. Bodelsen in *ESt,* XXXVII, 88–89; by Graham Greene in *London Mag.,* III, 68–70; briefly in *NCF,* X, 325; by Donald L. Hill in *VNL,* No. 10 (Autumn), pp. 6–8.

Colvert, James B. "The Origins of Stephen Crane's Literary Creed." *Univ. of Texas Studies in English,* XXXIV, 179–88.

Contends plausibly that Crane owed to Kipling the basic principles of his artistic beliefs;

he read *The Light That Failed* before 1892, and in it is developed explicitly a whole literary credo exactly paralleling Crane's. "In advocating and following closely the principles that art is grounded in actual experience, that absolute honesty in the artist is an indispensable virtue, that all experience, including the ugly and the unpleasant, is material for the artist, Crane, through Kipling, anticipated the 'cult of experience' in American fiction."—W. D. T.

Hollis, Christopher. "Kim and the Apolitical Man." *New R,* Sept. 24, pp. 16–17.

"In our time art and life are impoverished by the predominance of political debate."

Léaud, F. "Du nouveau sur Rudyard Kipling." *Études anglaises,* IX, 141–46.

Mainly devoted to a review of Carrington's *Rudyard Kipling: His Life and Work.*

Lochhead, Douglas. "The Kipling Room." *Dalhousie Rev.,* XXXVI, 117–19.

Dalhousie University is now equipped to house the Stewart Collection (see Yeats's article, below), and endowment now provides a special librarian.

MacKendrick, Paul. "Kipling and the Nature of the Classical." *Class. Jour.,* LII, 67–76.

Classical attitudes in Kipling's life and in his work.

Miller, Betty. "Kipling's First Novel." *Cornhill Mag.,* CLXVIII, 405–12.

On *The Light That Failed.*

Yeats, A. W. "Kipling, Twenty Years After." *Dalhousie Rev.,* XXXVI, 59–64.

A review article based on Carrington's biography of Kipling.

Yeats, A. W. "The Stewart Kipling Collection and Some Notes on Its Significance." *Dalhousie Rev.,* XXXVI, 112–15.

James McGregor Stewart has given to Dalhousie University his Kipling collection. Built over a period of fifty years, the collection brings together under one roof more of the magazine printings of Kipling's works than exist in any other library; some of these are unique. Nearly twelve hundred first editions and association copies of books are included, many newspapers and pirated printings, and MSS, etc. This collection is clearly of great importance.—W. D. T.

Landor. Peterson, Doris Evyline. "Landor's Treatment of His Source Materials in the Imaginary Conversations Greek and Roman." *Summ. Ph.D. Theses . . . Minnesota*, V (1951), 142–47. (Inadvertently omitted earlier.)

Super, R. H. *Walter Savage Landor. . . .* See VB 1955, 264.

Rev. by Marvin B. Perry, Jr., in *CE*, XVII, 320; favorably by Ernest Bernbaum in *MP*, LIII, 210–12; by Bonamy Dobrée in *RES*, new ser., VII, 94–96.

Lang. Maurer, Oscar. "Andrew Lang and *Longman's Magazine*, 1882–1905." *Univ. of Texas Studies in English*, XXXIV, 152–78.

Considers Lang and *Longman's* as a phenomenon in the history of criticism and in the development of the late Victorian literary periodical. This illuminating and carefully documented study mentions many authors, major and minor, of the latter part of the Victorian period.—W. D. T.

Lear. Shusterman, David. "An Edward Lear Letter to Wilkie Collins." *MLN*, LXXI, 262–64.

LeFanu (see also III, Baker, Wölcken). Shroyer, Frederick Benjamin. "A Critical Survey of Representative Works by Joseph Sheridan LeFanu and of Comments upon His Work." *Univ. of Southern California Abstr. of Diss. . . . 1955.* pp, 59–61.

Lewes (see I, Alden; **Dickens:** Haight).

Livingstone. Debenham, Frank. *The Way to Ilala: David Livingstone's Pilgrimage. . . .* See VB 1955, 264.

Rev. in *HTB*, May 27, p. 9; by P. J. M. in *Manchester Guardian*, July 29, 1955, p. 4; by Stuart Cloete in *NYTBR*, May 13, p. 4; by Clifford Collins in *S*, June 24, 1955, p. 805.

Lockhart. Lochhead, Marion. *John Gibson Lockhart. . . .* See VB 1954, 253.

Rev. briefly by Sylvère Monod in *Études anglaises*, IX, 66.

Lytton. Lutyens, Lady Emily. *The Birth of Rowland: An Exchange of Letters in 1865 between Robert Lytton and His Wife.* London: Hart-Davis. Pp. x+11+248.

Macaulay (see also III, Geyl, Gooch, Taylor). Grant, J. S. "The Remarkable Macaulays." *Scots Mag.*, new ser., LXV, 169–73.

On the Macaulays of Lewis, violent forebears of the historian.

Plumb, J. H. "Thomas Babington Macaulay." *TQ*, XXVI, 17–31.

Brief revaluation and high praise.

[Weber, Carl J.]. "A Centennial Reminder of Macaulay." *Colby Libr. Quart.*, IV, 97–98.

A recently discovered autograph of a letter by Macaulay.

Macdonald. Ragg, Laura M. "George Macdonald and His Household: Some Personal Recollections." *English*, XI, 59–63.

Mallock (see III, Low).

Meredith (see also I, Faverty, Ratchford; III, Colby, Lehman; **Brontës:** Lewis). Bynner, Witter. "A Young Visit with George Meredith." *VQR*, XXXII, 229–45.

Cooper, Lane (ed.). *An Essay on Comedy and the Uses of the Comic Spirit.* Ithaca: Cornell Univ. Pr. Pp. ix+326.

Kessler, Jascha. "Meredith's Spiritual Laughter." *Western Humanities Rev.*, X, 65–74.

Full of provocative comments on Meredith's ideas.—C. T. D.

Lindsay, Jack. *George Meredith: His Life and Work.* London: J. Lane. Pp. 420.

Rev. by V. S. Pritchett in *NS*, May 19, p. 573 (see also a reply by Jack Lindsay, May 26, p. 600); by Graham Hough in *S*, May 4, p. 627; briefly and unfavorably by Betty Miller in *TC*, CLX, 180–81; in *TLS*, June 22, p. 371. A biographical and critical study, written from the Marxist point of view.

Sawin, H. Lewis. "George Meredith: A Bibliography of Meredithiana, 1920–1953." *BBDI*, XXI, 186–91, 215–16.

Stevenson, Lionel. *The Ordeal of George Meredith. . . .* See VB 1955, 265.

Rev. by F. Léaud in *Études anglaises*, IX, 68.

Meynell (see also I, Faverty). Meynell, Sir Francis. "Memories of My Mother." *Poetry Rev.*, XLVII, 142–46, 214–18.

Includes references to many Victorian figures·

Mill (see also II, Blaug, Levin; III, Russell, Shumaker, Wethered). De Tocqueville, Alexis. *Œuvres complètes.* Édition définitive publiée sous la direction de J.-P. Mayer. Vol. VI: *Correspondance anglaise: Correspondance d'Alexis de Tocqueville avec Henry Reeve et John Stuart Mill.* Texte établi et annoté par J.-P. Mayer et Gustave Rudler. Introduction par J.-P. Mayer. Paris: Gallimard, 1954. Pp. 354.

Rev. by J. A. Lukacs in *JMH*, XXVIII, 281–84. Contains newly discovered letters from John Stuart Mill to De Tocqueville.

Harris, Abram L. "John Stuart Mill's Theory of Progress." *Ethics*, LXVI, 157–75.

In contrast with Marx, Mill regarded human progress as moral development.

Mueller, Iris Wessel. *John Stuart Mill and French Thought.* Urbana: Univ. of Illinois Pr. Pp. viii+275.

Rev. by Harry E. Barnes in *APSS*, CCCVII, 181–83 ("A substantial contribution to the history of economic, political, and social thought during the second third of the nineteenth century"); in *USQBR*, XII, 185.

Packe, Michael St. John. *The Life of John Stuart Mill.* . . . See VB 1955, 265.

Rev. by D. Owen in *AHR*, LX, 598–99; by William D. Templeman in *Personalist*, XXXVII, 278–79; by John W. Bicknell in *Sci. & Soc.*, XX, 170–73.

Patterson, Jerry E. "A Letter of John Stuart Mill." *Yale Univ. Libr. Gaz.*, XXX, 163–66.

Prints a long letter from Mill, Sept. 1, 1865, to Judge Dickson of Ohio, on what should be done about the states of the South after the Civil War.

Rees, John Collwyn. *Mill and His Early Critics.* Leicester: University College. Pp. 63.

Discussed in *TLS*, June 8, p. 345.

Russell, Bertrand. "John Stuart Mill." (Lecture on a Master Mind.) *Proc. British Acad., 1955,* XLI, 43–59.

Milnes. Pope-Hennessy, James. *Monckton Milnes.* 2 vols. New York: Farrar, Straus & Cudahy, 1955. Pp. 327, 272.

Rev. by Roger Becket, *HTB*, Feb. 19, p. 10; by Carlos Baker in *NYTBR*, Jan. 29, p. 16.

Volume I, *The Years of Promise*, was originally published by Constable (London) in 1949; Vol. II, *The Flight of Youth*, in 1951.

Mitford. Duncan-Jones, C. M. (ed.). *Miss Mitford and Mr. Harness.* . . . See VB 1955, 265.

Rev. by Grace Banyard in *CR*, CLXXXIX, 72.

Moore (see also III, Colby, Lehman, Shumaker). Brown, Malcolm. *George Moore: A Reconsideration.* . . . See VB 1955, 265.

Rev. by Keith McGary in *Antioch Rev.*, XVI, 395–400; briefly by John P. Hughes in *BA*, XXX, 332; briefly by Jean Noël in *Études anglaises*, IX, 171; by Edwin Gilcher in *MLQ*, XVII, 172–73; by Arnold T. Schwab in *NCF*, X, 310–14; by Frank D. Curtin in *QQ*, LXIII, 153–54; in *TLS*, Oct. 5, p. 579; by N. J. Endicott in *TQ*, XXVI, 107–8.

Chaikin, Milton. "Balzac, Zola, and George Moore's *A Drama in Muslin.*" *Rev. de litt. comp.*, XXIX (1955), 540–43.

Chaikin, Milton. "A French Source for George Moore's *A Mere Accident.*" *MLN*, LXXI, 28–30.

Moore's debt to Zola's *La Faute de l'Abbé Mouret.*

Cunard, Nancy. *GM: Memories of George Moore.* London: Hart-Davis. Pp. 206.

Rev. by Walter Allen in *NS*, Oct. 6, p. 428 (see also Nancy Cunard, "George Moore," *NS*, Dec. 15, p. 791); by Graham Hough in *S*, Oct. 5, pp. 456–57; in *TLS*, Oct. 5, p. 579.

Polansky, Aaron. "Three Books by George Moore." *Colby Libr. Quart.*, IV, 144–45.

Morley (see also III, Willey). Gooch, G. P. "Two Elder Statesmen. I. Lord Morley." *CR*, CXC, 216–20.

Moore, Dwain Earl. "John Morley as Critic of Public Address." *DA*, XVI, 401–2.

Morris (see also I, Faverty; III, Fredeman, Kegel). Bunge, Mario. "On William Morris' Socialism." *Sci. & Soc.*, XX, 142–44.

Rutherford, Andrew, and Jamieson, Paul F. "Morris's 'The Nymph's Song to Hylas' ('A Garden by the Sea')." *Ex*, XIV, Item 36.

Newman (see also I, Gordan; III, Strong, Wethered). *Autobiographical Writings*. Ed. Henry Tristram. London: Sheed & Ward. Pp. xi+338.

Rev. by Christopher Hollis in *S*, Dec. 14, pp. 869–70. Newman's Journal and the Memoir which he drew up from it at the end of his life.

Faith and Prejudice, and Other Unpublished Sermons. Ed. Birmingham Oratory. New York: Sheed & Ward. Pp. 128.

Rev. briefly by Richard P. Breaden in *LJ*, LXXXI, 1913. As the title indicates, these are hitherto unpublished sermons and, according to the reviewer, "welcome additions" to Newman's works.

Baum, Paull F. "The Road to Palermo." *SAQ*, LV, 192–97.

An account of the writing of "Lead, Kindly Light."

Boekraad, A. *The Personal Conquest of Truth According to J. H. Newman*. Louvain: Éditions Nauwelaerts, 1955. Pp. 327.

Rev. in *TLS*, Sept. 7, pp. 517–19. (Thesis-Pontificia Università Gregoriana, Rome.)

Cameron, James Munro. *John Henry Newman*. ("British Book News: Bibliographical Ser. of Supplements," No. 72.) London: Longmans, Green. Pp. 44.

Rev. by Jacques Vallette in *Mercure de France*, CCCXXVIII, 159.

Colby, R. A. "Newman on Aristotle's Poetics." *MLN*, LXXI, 22–27.

Newman's marginal notes in a copy of Aristotle.

Culler, A. Dwight. *The Imperial Intellect.* . . . See VB 1955, 266.

Rev. by F. D. Wilhelmsen in *Commonweal*, Dec. 23, 1955, p. 310; briefly but favorably by Paul Pickrel in *Harper's*, CCXII (January), 90; by W. O. L. S. in *Manchester Guardian*, Aug. 7, p. 2; in *TLS*, Sept. 7, pp. 517–19; in *USQBR*, XII, 198; by Edwin R. Clapp in *Western Humanities Rev.*, X, 186–87; by A. S. Ryan in *YR*, XLV, 597–600.

Dibble, Romuald A. *John Henry Newman: The Concept of Infallible Doctrinal Authority*. Washington: Catholic Univ. of America Pr., 1955. Pp. xix+319.

Lewin, E. P. S. "A Newman Letter." *TLS*, Oct. 12, p. 601.

Newman to his solicitor, 1852, outlining his proposed speech at the Achilli trial. See also an explanatory comment by C. Stephen Dessain, *TLS*, Oct. 19, p. 617.

Svaglic, Martin J. "Charles Newman and His Brothers." *PMLA*, LXXI, 370–85.

The erratic life of a younger brother of John Henry Newman.

Tristram, Henry (ed.). *Textes Newmaniens*. Vol. II: *Écrits autobiographiques*. Révision, notes et avant-propos par Louis Bouyer. Paris: Desclée & Brouwer.

Rev. in *TLS*, Sept. 7, pp. 517–19.

Oliphant. Dearden, Seton. "Laurence Oliphant." *Cornhill Mag.*, CLXIX, 1–32.

Rev. in *TLS*, Nov. 16, p. 678. A biographical sketch of a Victorian eccentric, novelist, war correspondent, and mystic.

Henderson, Philip. *The Life of Laurence Oliphant: Traveller, Diplomat, and Mystic*. London: Hale.

Rev. in *TLS*, Nov. 16, p. 678.

Ryan, A. P. "Laurence Oliphant: A Rich Victorian Eccentric." *Listener*, May 31, pp. 714–16.

Pater (see also II, Boas). Bertocci, Angelo P. "French Criticism and the Pater Problem." *Boston Univ. Studies in English*, I (1955), 178–94.

Recent criticism sees Pater not as hedonist and "aesthete" but as a romantic, struggling for religious and intellectual synthesis.

Cecil, Lord David. *Walter Pater.* . . . See VB 1955, 266.

Rev. briefly by Germain J. d'Hangest in *Études anglaises*, IX, 70–71; briefly in *N & Q*, new ser., III, 183; in *TLS*, Feb. 3, p. 69.

Patmore (see also I, Faverty). Beaumont, Ernest. "Coventry Patmore's Philosophy of Womanhood." *Downside Rev.*, LXXIV, 362–82.

How Patmore's mystical concept of woman transcends such categories as those of Simone de Beauvoir.

Marshall, George O., Jr. "Marginalia on Coventry Patmore." *Libr. Chronicle of Univ. of Texas*, V, No. 4, 32–33.

A copy of Champney's *Memoirs* contains marginalia by a friend of Patmore's first wife.

Oliver, Edward James. *Coventry Patmore*. New York: Sheed & Ward. Pp. 211.

Rev. by Bette Richart in *Commonweal*, May 11, p. 161; by Ruth M. Ames in *CWd*, CLXXXIII, 395–96; briefly by T. F. Smith in *LJ*, LXXXI, 1272; by Richard Sullivan in *NYTBR*, May 13, p. 24; by Graham Hough in *S*, Dec. 28, pp. 936–37; by Robert Halsband in *SR*, May 26, p. 33.

Phillipps, Ambrose. Dougherty, Charles T. "Hero without Trumpets." *Columbia*, March, pp. 14–15, 45.

Popular and inspirational biographical sketch. —C. T. D.

Reade. Fielding, K. J. "Charles Reade and Dickens—a Fight against Piracy." *Theatre Notebook*, X, 106–11.

Martin, Robert B. "The Reade Collection." *PLC*, XVII, 77–80.

Robertson (see I, Walbridge).

Rossettis (see also I, Faverty; III, Fredeman). Mason, Ellsworth. "Arnault, Leopardi, Rossetti: Three Men on a Poem." *Italica*, XXX (1953), 223–26. (Inadvertently omitted earlier.)

Shows that Rossetti's "The Leaf" is not a translation, as Rossetti indicated it was, from Leopardi but actually a translation from Antoine-Vincent Arnault's *Fables* (1812).

Sawtell, Margaret. *Christina Rossetti.* . . . See VB 1955, 267.

Rev. by Evelyn D. Bangay in *Poetry Rev.*, XLVII, 234; by Austin Clarke in *S*, Jan. 6, p. 27; in *TLS*, Jan. 20, p. 38.

Shalkhauser, Marian. "The Feminine Christ." *VNL*, No. 10 (Autumn), pp. 19–20.

An interpretation of "Goblin Market."

Shalkhauser, Marian Doris. "The Poetry and Prose of Christina Rossetti." *Summ. Doct. Diss.*, *Univ. of Wisconsin*, XVI, 557–58.

Thale, Jerome. "The Third Rossetti." *Western Humanities Rev.*, X, 277–84.

Critical biographical sketch of William Michael Rossetti.

Ruskin (see also I, Faverty, Gordan, Singer; III, Fredeman). Allott, Miriam. "A Ruskin Echo in *The Wings of the Dove*." *N & Q*, new ser., III, 87.

Armytage, W. H. G. "Ruskin as Utopist." *N & Q*, new ser., III, 219–24.

Autret, Jean. *L'Influence de Ruskin sur la vie, les idées et l'œuvre de Marcel Proust*. Geneva: Librairie Droz, 1955. Pp. 180.

Rev. by Stanley Jones in *MLR*, LI, 605. A doctoral dissertation, University of Chicago.

Bradley, John Lewis (ed.). *Ruskin's Letters from Venice.* . . . See VB 1955, 267.

Rev. by Terence Mullaly in *Apollo*, LXIV, 94; by Mary Stocks in *Manchester Guardian*, May 18, p. 6; by V. S. Pritchett in *NS*, Oct. 20, p. 489; in *TLS*, June 8, p. 346; in *USQBR*, XII, 142.

Burd, Van Akin. "Ruskin's Quest for a Theory of the Imagination." *MLQ*, XVII, 60–72.

New light on the crucial Italian journey of 1845, based on unpublished letters.

Dougherty, Charles T. "Ruskin's Moral Argument." *VNL*, No. 9 (Spring), pp. 4–7.

Evans, Joan, and Whitehouse, John Howard (eds.). *The Diaries of John Ruskin (1835–1847)*. Oxford: Oxford Univ. Pr. Pp. xii+364.

Rev. by Gladys Scott Thomson in *Apollo*, LXIV, 226; by Sir Kenneth Clark in *Listener*, Oct. 11, p. 565; briefly by Douglas P. Bliss in *LR*, Winter, p. 519; by Peter Quennell in *S*, Oct. 5, pp. 453–54.

Evans, Joan. *John Ruskin.* . . . See VB 1955, 267.

Rev. by C. H. Salter in *RES*, new ser., VII, 96–97.

Fain, John Tyree. *Ruskin and the Economists*. Nashville: Vanderbilt Univ. Pr. Pp. 164.

A valuable supplement (and in some degree a corrective) to J. A. Hobson. Fain concludes that Ruskin's indictment of orthodox political economy is unjustified when applied to the work of its best exponents (e.g., Mill) but is valid when applied to the popularizations and abuses of that doctrine. Includes a stimulating analysis of *Unto This Last*.—O. M.

Fogle, French. "Unpublished Letters of Ruskin and Millais, 1854–1855." *HLQ*, XX, 39–51.

Retells the Ruskin-Effie-Millais story, employing four previously unpublished letters by Millais and one by Ruskin.

Livingstone, R. W. "Ruskin." (Lecture on a Master Mind.) *Proc. British Acad., 1945*, XXXI, 85–102. (Inadvertently omitted earlier.)

Lloyd, Michael. "Hawthorne, Ruskin, and the Hostile Tradition." *English Miscellany* (Rome), 1955, pp. 109–33.

The "hostile tradition" is that of English condemnation of the Italians as ignorant, idle, frivolous, immoral.

Pritchett, V. S. "The Most Solitary Victorian." *NS*, Oct. 20, pp. 489–90.

In this review article based on the books by Quennell, Bradley, Evans, and Whitehouse, Pritchett explores the monstrous egoism and terrible solitude of Ruskin, which was the price he paid for those incredible purple passages which are still masterpieces of prose technique. Of Carlyle and Ruskin as reformers, Pritchett says: "These prophets addressed not the outer but the inner life and populated it with images, set moving the confused spirit of possibility."

Quennell, Peter. *John Ruskin.* ("British Book News: Bibliographical Ser. of Supplements," No. 76.) London: Longmans, Green. Pp. 36.

Rev. by Jacques Vallette in *Mercure de France,* CCCXXVIII, 535.

Viljoen, Helen Gill. *Ruskin's Scottish Heritage: A Prelude.* Urbana: Univ. of Illinois Pr. Pp. 284.

Rev. by Donald Smalley in *CE*, XVIII, 60–61; in *HTB*, Aug. 26, p. 9; by Van Akin Burd in *MLQ*, XVII, 369–70; in *N & Q*, new ser., III, 368; in *TLS*, Aug. 17, p. 488; by Charles T. Dougherty in *VNL*, No. 10 (Autumn), pp. 9–10.

Shaw (see also I, Ratchford, Singer, Walbridge; II, Meynell; III, Brooks, Henn, Lehman, Russell). *Advice to a Young Critic.* . . . See VB 1955, 268.

Rev. by Rod Nordell in *Christian Science Monitor*, Jan. 19, p. 7; by W. P. Eaton in *HTB*, Jan. 29, p. 6; by E. F. Walbridge in *LJ*, LXXXI,

2769; by Brooks Atkinson in *NYTBR*, Feb. 12, p. 7; by Albert E. Johnson in *QJS*, XLII, 427; in *TLS*, June 29, 388; in *USQBR*, XII, 142.

Albert, Sidney P. "Bernard Shaw: The Artist as Philosopher." *JAA*, XIV, 419–38.

Shaw's debt to Plato, Kant, and Hegel and the transmutations of philosophical ideas effected by his comic art.

Barnet, Sylvan. "Bernard Shaw on Tragedy." *PMLA*, LXXI, 888–99.

Because of his belief in creative evolution, Shaw felt that the tragic dramatist had a limited view.

Batson, Eric J. "Pygmalion." *NS*, Dec. 22, pp. 818–19.

Deplores the limitations on the presentation of *Pygmalion* because of the musical adaptation, *My Fair Lady*. See also "London Diary." *NS*, Dec. 15, p. 778.

Benedictine Nuns, Stanbrook. *In a Great Tradition: Tribute to Dame Laurentia McLachlan, Abbess of Stanbrook.* London: J. Murray. Pp. xiii+313.

Rev. by Antonia White in *NS*, Oct. 20, pp. 496–97. A biography of Dame Laurentia McLachlan, the Benedictine nun who was Shaw's friend and correspondent.

Driberg, Tom. "Honouring the Sage." *NS*, July 28, p. 103.

Reviews the B.B.C.'s handling of the Shaw centenary.

"Editorial." *Theatre Notebook*, X, 101–2.

A centenary note, dealing mainly with Shaw's dramatic criticism.

Ervine, St. John Greer. *Bernard Shaw: His Life, Work, and Friends.* London: Constable. Pp. xii+628.

Rev. by C. J. Rolo in *AM*, October, p. 98; by Edward Wagenknecht in *Chicago Sunday Tribune*, Sept. 23, p. 2; by Harold Hobson in *Christian Science Monitor*, Sept. 27, p. 5; by J. H. M. Scott in *CR*, CXC, 376–77; briefly by Kellogg W. Hunt in *EJ*, XLV, 569; by Robert Greacen in *English*, XI, 111–12; by Paul Pickrel in *Harper's*, CCXIII (October), 8; by Walter Kerr in *HTB*, Sept. 23, p. 1; by George Freedley in *LJ*, LXXXI, 1985; by Jacques Vallette in *Mercure de France*, CCCXXVIII, 529–32; by Kingsley Martin in *NS*, July 28, pp. 107–8 (contains

Jung's analysis of Shaw as a man who had evaded the passions, not mastered them); by Brooks Atkinson in *NYTBR*, Sept. 23, p. 1; by Brian Inglis in *S*, July 27, p. 147; by Carlos Baker in *SR*, Oct. 6, p. 32; by H. F. Rubinstein in *TC*, CLX, 268–69; by Elliot Norton in *Theatre Arts*, XL (December), 8, 11; in *TLS*, July 27, p. 441.

Forter, Elizabeth Tusten. "A Study of the Dramatic Technique of Bernard Shaw." *Summ. Doct. Diss., Univ. of Wisconsin*, XVI, 537–39.

Undertakes to analyze certain techniques of relating theme and form in the twenty-nine major plays by Shaw.

Frank, Joseph. "*Major Barbara*—Shaw's 'Divine Comedy.'" *PMLA*, LXXI, 61–74.

An analysis of the play as an epitome of Shaw's career, stressing its points of comparison with Dante's poem.

Gow, Ronald, "Keir Hardie and G. B. S." *NS*, Aug. 18, p. 188.

Substantiates the story that Shaw advised the first Labour M.P.'s not to behave like gentlemen.

Henderson, Archibald. *George Bernard Shaw: Man of the Century*. New York: Appleton-Century-Crofts. Pp. xxxii+969. De luxe 1st ed. in two vols.

Rev. by Walter Prichard Eaton in *HTB*, Dec. 2, p. 12; by Brooks Atkinson in *NYTBR*, Dec. 16, p. 4; by J. W. Krutch in *SR*, Dec. 8, p. 18.

King, Carlyle. "GBS and Music." *QQ*, LXIII, 165–78.

Lane, Margaret. "The Nun and the Dramatist." *NS*, July 28, pp. 108–9.

A review of the Shaw letters to Dame Laurentia McLachlan, abbess of Stanbrook, published in the Summer, 1956, issue of the *Cornhill*.

Laurence, Dan H. "The Facts about *Why She Would Not*." *Theatre Arts*, XL (August), 20–21, 89–90.

Lederer, Moritz. "In Memoriam George Bernard Shaw." *Deutsche Rundschau*, LXXXII, 762–65.

Lerner, Alan Jay. *My Fair Lady: A Musical Play in Two Acts*. New York: Coward-McCann. Pp. 186.

Text of Broadway musical version of *Pygmalion*.

"My Fair Lady." *Theatre Arts*, XL (May), 18–19.

Review of the musical adaptation of *Pygmalion*.

"The Nun and the Dramatist: Dame Laurentia McLachlan and George Bernard Shaw." By a Nun of Stanbrook. *Cornhill Mag.*, CLXVIII, 415–58.

A somewhat abridged version of this correspondence appeared in *AM*, July, pp. 27–34, and August, pp. 69–76, under the title "The Nun and the Dramatist: George Bernard Shaw to the Abbess of Stanbrook."

O'Hare, John. "How the Play Reached Publication." *Theatre Arts*, XL (August), 22–23. On *Why She Would Not*.

Pearson, Hesketh. "Beerbohm Tree, Mrs. Pat and G. B. S." *Theatre Arts*, XL (December), 29–31, 82–85.

An account of the stormy rehearsals for the first production of *Pygmalion*.

Priestley, J. B. "Thoughts on Shaw." *NS*, July 28, pp. 96–97.

Shaw was never able to rise to an emotional acceptance of his own intellectual beliefs. That gave him the detachment so essential to the creation of the Shavian play and the repellent hardness which is its chief defect.

Raymond, John. "Storm in a Teacup." *NS*, Feb. 18, pp. 174–75.

A review of Lionel Harris' production of *Misalliance*.

Robinson, Wayne. "Alfred Doolittle Still Stops the Show." *Theatre Arts*, XL (June), 68–69.

The character as played by Stanley Holloway in *My Fair Lady*.

"Saint Joan." *Theatre Arts*, XL (November), 80–81.

Review of Cambridge Drama Festival production.

Saturday Review. G. B. S. One Hundredth Anniversary: 1856–1956. July 21.

Anniversary issue with items as follows: Masefield, John, "Lines for a One Hundredth Birthday: George Bernard Shaw" (p. 7); Daiches,

David, "GBS: Spokesman for Vitality" (pp. 8–10); "Shaw as Wells Saw Him [a premature 'obituary' by H. G. Wells]" (p. 10); "Bibliography" (p. 11); Grunfeld, Fred, "Discography: GBS on Records" (p. 11); Krutch, J. W., "An Open Letter to George Bernard Shaw" (pp. 12–13); "GBS [two pages of pictures]" (pp. 14–15).

Schirmer-Inhoff, Ruth. "*Saint Joan* — die Quelle und ihre Bearbeitung." *Anglia*, LXXIV, 102–32.

Argues that Joan is almost unique among Shaw's characters in that she is more than a theatrical device for expressing his ideas. Her three-dimensional quality is attributed to Shaw's reliance on the official records of the trial.

Scott, Robert Lee. "Bernard Shaw's Rhetorical Drama: A Study of Rhetoric and Poetic in Selected Plays." *DA*, XVI, 402–3.

Shaw Bulletin

No. 10 (November, 1956) has items: Henderson, Archibald, "Biographer's Breviary" (pp. 1–3); Lerner, Alan Jay, "*Pygmalion* and *My Fair Lady*" (pp. 4–7); "Eastern Eyes on Bernard Shaw"—Hiralal Amritlal Shah, "Bernard Shaw in Bombay" (pp. 8–19), and Lusin (trans. Capt. Martin R. Ring, U.S.A.F.), "Lusin Looks at Bernard Shaw" (pp. 11–13); "A Continuing Check-List of Shaviana" (pp. 13–15); "Centenary Year Theatre Notes"—by Felix Grendon on a recent production of *Village Wooing* (pp. 15–17), by Dan H. Laurence on a revival of *The Admirable Bashville* (pp. 17–18), by Richard Watts, Jr., on Siobhan McKenna's Saint Joan (pp. 18–19); Weintraub, Stanley, "Bernard Shaw's Boswells" (pp. 20–22); Hughes, Robert J., "Bernard Shaw Day in Chicago" (pp. 23–24).

Valency, Maurice. "Shaw the Durable Dramatist." *Theatre Arts*, XL (July), 66–68, 86–87.

Shaw succeeded through "melodrama with a built-in debunking mechanism."

W., T. C. "*The Doctor's Dilemma* at the Saville." *NS*, Oct. 13, p. 452.

An unfavorable review of Julian Amyes's production.

Weales, Gerald. "Shaw Pleasant and Unpleasant." *New R*, Dec. 3, pp. 21–23.

Unfavorable review of current productions of *Major Barbara* and *The Apple Cart*.

Winsten, Stephen. *Jesting Apostle: The Life of Bernard Shaw*. London: Hutchinson. Pp. 231.

Rev. by Kingsley Martin in *NS*, July 28, pp. 107–8; by Brian Inglis in *S*, July 27, p. 147; by H. F. Rubinstein in *TC*, CLX, 268–69; in *TLS*, July 27, p. 441.

Worsley, T. C. "The Comic Muse." *NS*, Nov. 17, pp. 621–22.

Contains an unfavorable (to Shaw) review of the Winter Garden production of *The Devil's Disciple*.

Worsley, T. C. "Revivals." *NS*, Aug. 11, pp. 158–59.

Includes an unfavorable review of the centenary production of *Caesar and Cleopatra*.

Worsley, T. C. "Shavian Comedy." *NS*, July 28, p. 103.

A review of a performance of *Major Barbara* turns into a general discussion of Shaw. What is becoming clear, says Worsley, is that, as the issues which Shaw debated become more remote, the arguments between the characters become clashes of temperament rather than social propaganda. The theories, the doctrines, and the follies are only the external, the dramatic, embodiment of timeless types of humanity.

Smiles. Smiles, Aileen. *Samuel Smiles and His Surroundings*. London: Hale. Pp. 255.

Rev. by Charles Wilson in *S*, Sept. 14, p. 356; in *TLS*, July 27, p. 444 (and see comment by W. N. Leak, Aug. 3, p. 463). On the life of the author of *Self-help*, the patron saint of Victorian Philistinism.—O. M.

Smith, Sydney. Smith, Nowell C. (ed.). *Selected Letters of Sydney Smith*. ("World's Classics," No. 548.) London: Oxford Univ. Pr. Pp. 353.

Rev. by Peter Quennell in *S*, Aug. 24, pp. 264–65; a selection appears in *Periodical*, XXXI, 224–27.

Spencer. Taylor, Arthur J. "The Originality of Herbert Spencer: A Footnote to 'Herbert Spencer and His Father.'" *Univ. of Texas Studies in English*, XXXIV, 101–6.

Stephen (see III, Plumb).

Stevenson (see also I, Faverty, Ratchford). Ferguson, DeLancey, and Waingrow, Marshall (eds.). *R. L. S.: Stevenson's Letters to Charles Baxter*. New Haven: Yale Univ. Pr. Pp. xxvi+385.

Rev. by Richard D. Altick in *HTB*, June 17, p. 7; briefly by Earle F. Walbridge in *LJ*, LXXXI, 1522; by Bradford A. Booth in *NCF*, XI, 229–32; by J. C. Furnas in *NYTBR*, May 27, p. 4; by H. M. Jones in *SR*, June 9, p. 19.

Neider, Charles (ed.). *Our Samoan Adventure.* . . . See VB 1955, 269.

Rev. briefly by Thomas C. Livingstone in *LR*, Autumn, p. 512; by Bradford A. Booth in *NCF*, X, 322–23; by Janet Adam Smith in *NS*, June 9, pp. 562–63; in *TLS*, May 18, p. 293; in *YR*, XLV No. 2, xxii–xxviii.

Randall, David A. "The Stevenson Collection." *PLC*, XVII, 92–95.

"Robert Louis Stevenson." *PLC*, XVII, 105–6.

New accessions: books, letters, and other MSS.

Swinburne (see also I, Faverty, Ratchford; III, Nicolson). Foss, Kenelm (ed.). *A Swinburne Anthology: Verse, Drama, Prose, Criticism, Selected, with a Biographical Introduction.* London: Richards. Pp. 254.

Rev. briefly by R. D. Macleod in *LR*, Spring, p. 291.

Milstead, John. "Swinburne's Elemental Imagery." *DA*, XVI, 748.

Synge. Bourget-Pailleron, Robert. "Revue dramatique." *Rev. des deux mondes*, Mar. 15, pp. 350–55.

Contains a review of a performance of *Le Baladin du monde occidental*, translated by Jacques Panigel. Bourget-Pailleron found it impossible to appreciate unless one understood the Irish. In fact, he got no more out of the play than if it had been performed in English.

Talfourd. Watson, Vera. "Thomas Noon Talfourd and His Friends." *TLS*, Apr. 20, p. 244; Apr. 27, p. 260.

Based on an examination of several hundred unpublished letters and some volumes of Talfourd's private diary.

Taylor (see III, Bostrom).

Tennyson (see also I, Gordan; III, Adams, *Essays*, Nicolson, Willey; **Arnold:** Allott). Beck, Warren. "Clouds upon Camelot." *EJ* XLV, 447–54.

A brief survey of the reputation of Tennyson's poetry in general and of *The Idylls of the*

King in particular, ending with the proposal that, since their defects are more palpable than their poetic virtues, the *Idylls* be replaced in the curriculum by selected short lyrics.

Eidson, John Olin. "The Reception of Tennyson's Plays in America." *PQ*, XXXV, 435–43.

The plays lowered the level of Tennyson's American reputation sharply during the seventies, starting a downward curve from which his fame has never recovered.

Greenberg, Robert A. "A Possible Source of Tennyson's 'Tooth and Claw,' " *MLN*, LXXI, 491–92.

The well-known image in *In Memoriam* may have been suggested by a passage in *Past and Present*.

"Harvard Buys Tennyson Manuscripts." *LJ*, LXXXI, 888–89.

Announces the purchase by the Houghton Library of 350 Tennyson poems in first drafts and revisions.

Hendrick, George. "Enoch Arden in Texas: A Critical Rhapsody." *Libr. Chronicle of Univ. of Texas*, V, No. 4, 26–31.

A previously unpublished critique of the poem, delivered in 1871.

James, D. G. "Wordsworth and Tennyson" ("Warton Lecture on English Poetry"). *Proc. British Acad., 1950*, XXXVI, 113–29. (Inadvertently omitted earlier.)

A comparative study of *The Prelude* and *In Memoriam*, both published in 1850; at the end James declares that "Wordsworth is greater than Tennyson. . . . It is hardly possible to stand today where Tennyson stood. . . . But it is possible to go back to Wordsworth." This is a provocative lecture.—W. D. T.

Johnson, E. D. H. *The Alien Vision of Victorian Poetry.* . . . See VB 1954, 258.

Rev. unfavorably by Paul Turner in *ESt*, XXXVII, 32–35.

Krause, Anna. "Unamuno and Tennyson." *Comp. Lit.*, VIII, 122–35.

Indicates many "arresting points of contact" between the Spaniard and the Englishman and incidentally calls attention to the influence of Carlyle's *Sartor resartus* on Unamuno, as shown in Carlos Clavería's *Temas de Unamuno* (1953).

Millhauser, Milton. "Tennyson: Artifice and Image." *JAA*, XIV, 333–38.

Argues that Tennyson's compromise with the respectable conventionalities of Victorian opinion led him to substitute artifice for the "stubborn sincerities" of *In Memoriam* and "The Two Voices."

Shannon, Edgar F., Jr., and Bond, W. H. "Literary Manuscripts of Alfred Tennyson in the Harvard College Library." *HLB*, X, 254–74.

An article of importance; includes a review of the principal depositories (and their holdings) of Tennyson MSS, letters, and printed matter in the United States and in England.—W. D. T.

Shannon, Edgar Finley, Jr. *Tennyson and the Reviewers.* . . . See VB 1954, 259.

Rev. favorably by L. Bonnerot in *Études anglaises*, IX, 67–68.

Sharrock, Roger. "A Reminiscence of *In Memoriam* in *David Copperfield*" *N & Q*, new ser., III, 502.

Stanford, William Bedell. *The Ulysses Theme: A Study in the Adaptability of a Traditional Hero.* Oxford: Blackwell, 1954. Pp. x+292.

Rev. by Thomas Cutt in *Class. Jour.*, LII, 143–44; by J. A. Davison in *Class. Rev.*, new ser., VI, 9–12.

Tennyson, Sir Charles. *Six Tennyson Essays.* . . . See VB 1954, 259.

Rev. by L. Bonnerot in *Études anglaises*, IX, 66–67.

Thackeray (see also I, Faverty, Gordan; III, Bostrom, Brown, Praz, G. Tillotson; **Brontës:** Bengtsson). Bishop, Morchard. "Emily Fotheringay and Ellen Ternan." *TLS*, Jan. 27, p. 60.

Identifies Dickens' mistress with Arthur Pendennis' early love.

Johnson, Edgar. "The Garrick Club Affair. II." *PMLA*, LXXI, 256–59.

Charges Gordon Ray with overstating Thackeray's case in Professor Ray's article of this title in *PMLA*, September, 1954. The answer by Gordon Ray (listed below) follows this statement.

Metzdorf, Robert F. "M. L. Parrish and William Makepeace Thackeray." *PLC*, XVII, 68–70.

Ray, Gordon N. "The Garrick Club Affair. III." *PMLA*, LXXI, 259–63.

Gordon Ray answers Edgar Johnson's charges, noted above.

Ray, Gordon N. *Thackeray: The Uses of Adversity.* . . . See VB 1955, 270.

Rev. by L. L. Schücking in *Anglia*, LXXIV, 143–49; by Lionel Stevenson in *CE*, XVII, 370; by F. S. Boas in *English*, XI, 109–10; by Lionel Stevenson in *JEGP*, LV, 516–19; by John Lewis Bradley in *MLQ*, XVII, 275–76; by Kathleen Tillotson in *NCF*, X, 306–9; favorably by V. S. Pritchett in *NS*, Jan. 7, pp. 17–18; in *QR*, CCXCIV, 264–65; by Geoffrey Tillotson in *SeR*, LXIV, 673–74; by Betty Miller in *TC*, CLIX, 400–401; in *USQBR*, XII, 7; by Joseph Warren Beach in *VQR*, XXXII, 296–300.

Ray, Gordon N. (ed.). *William Makepeace Thackeray's Contributions to the Morning Chronicle.* . . . See VB 1955, 271.

Rev. by L. L. Schücking in *Anglia*, LXXIV, 143–49; by Edward Wagenknecht in *Chicago Sunday Tribune*, Oct. 9, 1955; by Robert F. Metzdorf in *JEGP*, LV, 335–37; by John Lewis Bradley in *MLQ*, XVII, 275–76; by John E. Tilford, Jr., in *NCF*, X, 319–21; by Geoffrey Tillotson in *SeR*, LXIV, 674; in *TLS*, Feb. 17, p. 98.

Tillotson, Geoffrey. *Thackeray the Novelist.* . . . See VB 1955, 271.

Rev. by E. F. Shannon, Jr., in *MLN*, LXXI, 134–36; by Lilian Haddakin in *MLR*, LI, 105–6; by Robert A. Colby in *MP*, LIII, 212–13; by R. George Thomas in *RES*, new ser., VII, 209–11.

Worth, George J. "Thackeray and James Hannay: Three New Letters." *JEGP*, LV, 414–16.

Thompson, Francis (see I, Faverty).

Thomson, James (see I, Faverty).

Trollope (see also III, Brown, Burns, Praz, Shumaker, G. Tillotson, Wethered). *Barchester Towers.* Ed. Sir Michael Sadleir. ("Everyman's Library.") London: Dent.

Includes a new introduction, "Anthony Trollope's Clergy," by Sir Michael Sadleir.

"Anthony Trollope." *PLC*, XVII, 106–7.

New accessions of MSS and books.

Cockshut, A. O. J. *Anthony Trollope.* . . . See VB 1955, 271.

Rev. by Sylva Norman in *CR*, CLXXXIX, 139–40; by Frances Winwar in *NYTBR*, Dec. 23, p. 6; in *QR*, CCXLIV, 138; by Geoffrey Tillotson in *SeR*, LXIV, 674–75; by W. L. Burn in *TC*, CLIX, 33–43; by Bradford A. Booth in *VNL*, No. 10 (Autumn), pp. 5–6.

Coyle, William. "Trollope as Social Anthropologist." *CE*, XVII, 392–97.

An analysis, in anthropological terminology, of the class structure and social organization of Barsetshire.

Donovan, Robert A. "Trollope's Prentice Work." *MP*, LIII, 179–86.

An analysis of a representative early novel, *The Kellys and the O'Kellys*, to support the conclusion that it conforms to the typical pattern of the Trollopean novel of manners.

Hackett, Francis. "The Trollope Problem." *New R*, Oct. 18, pp. 22–23.

Houston, Maud. "Structure and Plot in *The Warden*." *Univ. of Texas Studies in English*, XXXIV, 107–13.

Contends that *The Warden* is well plotted and well constructed; submits a well-reasoned refutation of "the myth" that plot was unimportant to Trollope.—W. D. T.

Tingay, Lance. "The Publication of Trollope's First Novel." *TLS*, Mar. 30, p. 200.

On an early misleading attribution of *The Macdermots* to Mrs. Trollope. See also a letter on Thomas Newby, Trollope's publisher, by Sylva Norman, *TLS*, Apr. 6, p. 207; and on the reputation of *The Macdermots* by John Hagan, May 4, p. 269.

Tingay, Lance O. "Trollope's Popularity: A Statistical Approach." *NCF*, XI, 223–29.

Ward (see III, Cazamian).

White, W. H. (see also III, Willey; Eliot: Stone). Maclean, Catherine Macdonald. *Mark Rutherford*. . . . See VB 1955, 271.

Rev. by Gilbert Thomas in *English*, XI, 23–24; by H. A. Smith in *MLR*, LI, 253–55.

Stock, Irvin. *William Hale White (Mark Rutherford): A Critical Study*. Introd. by Lionel Trilling. New York: Columbia Univ. Pr. Pp. xii+268.

Rev. by William D. Templeman in *CE*, XVIII, 128; by Sylva Norman in *CR*, CXC,

312–13; in *Manchester Guardian*, May 18, p. 6; briefly in *NCF*, XI, 237–38; by John Holloway in *S*, June 1, p. 766; in *TLS*, June 8, p. 346.

Stone, Wilfred. *Religion and the Art of William Hale White*. . . . See VB 1955, 271.

Rev. by M. L. Cazamian in *Études anglaises*, IX, 169–70; by H. A. Smith in *MLR*, LI, 253–55.

Wilde (see also I, Faverty, Gordan; II, Deghy; III, Baker). *The Importance of Being Earnest: A Trivial Comedy for Serious People, in Four Acts, as Originally Written*. Ed. Sarah Augusta Dickson. 2 vols. New York: New York Public Libr. Pp. 184, 372.

Rev. by Theodore Bolton in *BSP*, L, 205–8; see also D[avid]. V. E[rdman]., "The Importance of Publishing 'Earnest,' " *Bull. New York Pub. Libr.*, LX, 368–72, and "Penultimate Earnest," LX, 422–23; by William W. Appleton in *SR*, May 12, p. 21; in *Theatre Arts*, XL (December), 11–12. Reproduces the original manuscript and the corrected typescript of the play.

Bourget-Pailleron, Robert. "Revue dramatique." *Rev. des deux mondes*, Jan. 1, pp. 148–59.

Reviews favorably Parisian performances of *L'Eventail de Lady Windermere*, adapted by Michelle Lahaye, and *Un Mari idéal*.

Broad, Lewis. *The Friendships and Follies of Oscar Wilde*. . . . See VB 1954, 260.

Rev. briefly by Hugh Corbett in *BA*, XXX, 89.

Brown, R. D. "Suetonius, Symonds, and Gibbon in *The Picture of Dorian Gray*." *MLN*, LXXI, 264.

Foster, Richard. "Wilde as Parodist: A Second Look at *The Importance of Being Earnest*." *CE*, XVIII, 18–23.

The play parodies standard romantic characters, themes, and plot situations and thereby accomplishes sharp social satire.

Furnell, John. *The Stringed Lute*. . . . See VB 1955, 272.

Noticed in *TLS*, Feb. 17, p. 106.

Merle, R. *Oscar Wilde ou la "destinée" de l'homosexuel*. Paris: Gallimard, 1955. Pp. 213.

Rev. by J. France in *Études anglaises*, IX, 71.

Ojala, Aatos. *Aestheticism and Oscar Wilde.* . . . See VB 1955, 272.

Rev. by Robert L. Schneider in *JEGP*, LV, 348–49; by W. Iser in *RES*, new ser., VII, 215–16.

Peckham, Morse. "What Did Lady Windermere Learn?" *CE*, XVIII, 11–14.

Claims Lady Windermere does not learn her lesson, since she is one who cannot tell the difference between ideals and illusions.

Reinert, Otto. "Satiric Strategy in *The Importance of Being Earnest.*" *CE*, XVIII, 14–18.

Finds that tone and plot have been successfully integrated, forming a play which has coherent meaning.

Yeats (see also I, Ratchford, Singer; III, Brown, Henn, Lehman, Strong, Tate; **Brontës:** Lewis). *Collected Poems.* Definitive ed., with the author's final revisions. New York: Macmillan. Pp. xv+480.

The Letters of W. B. Yeats. . . . See VB 1955, 272.

Rev. favorably by F. W. Dupee in *ParR*, XXIII, 108–11; by Curtis B. Bradford in *VQR*, XXXII, 157–60.

A Vision. A reissue with the author's final revisions. New York: Macmillan. Pp. 305.

Rev. briefly in *CE*, XVIII, 62.

Adams, Hazard. *Blake and Yeats.* . . . See VB 1955, 272.

Rev. briefly by Calvin D. Linton in *Amer. Scholar*, XXV, 378; by William Van O'Connor in *CE*, XVIII, 127; in *USQBR*, XII, 170–71; by Sven Armens in *Western Rev.*, XII, 69–76; in *YR*, XLV, No. 4, vi–viii.

"Books and Manuscripts of W. B. Yeats." *TLS*, May 4, p. 276.

On an exhibition commemorating the seventieth anniversary of Yeats's first book, held at Trinity College, Dublin.

Cazamian, M. L. (trans.). *Yeats: poèmes choisis.* Paris: Aubier–Éditions Montaigne, 1954. Pp. 383.

Rev. by René Fréchet in *Études anglaises*, IX, 180–82.

Ellmann, Richard. *The Identity of Yeats.* . . . See VB 1955, 272.

Rev. by George Whalley in *QQ*, LXII, 617–21.

Henn, T. R. "The Accent of Yeats' 'Last Poems.'" *Essays and Studies, 1956*, new ser., IX (for the English Assoc.), 56–72.

Kenner, Hugh. "Unpurged Images." *Hudson Rev.*, VIII (1956), 609–17.

Review article on *The Letters of W. B. Yeats*, ed. Allan Wade; *The Identity of Yeats*, by Richard Ellmann; *The Unicorn: William Butler Yeats' Search for Reality*, by Virginia Moore. Kenner's final remark is: "There is still room for a book on Yeats which examines what he had to say."

Moore, Virginia. *The Unicorn: William Butler Yeats' Search for Reality.* . . . See VB 1955, 273.

Rev. by George Whalley in *QQ*, LXII, 617–21.

"News from the Field." *College and Research Libr.*, XVII, 174–77.

Contains a brief description of a Yeats collection formed by P. S. O'Hegarty which has come to the University of Kansas.

Rosenthal, M. L. "Sources in Myth and Magic." *N*, June 23, pp. 533–35.

Sickels, Eleanor M. "Yeats' 'I am of Ireland.'" *Ex*, XV, Item 10.

Ure, Peter. "Yeats's Supernatural Songs." *RES*, new ser., VII, 38–51.

Wakefield, Dan. "Sailing to Byzantium, Yeats and the Young Mind." *N*, June 23, 531–32.

Yonge. Mare, Margaret, and Percival, Alicia. *Victorian Best-Seller.* . . . See VB ι948, 272.

Rev. by Léonie Villard in *Études anglaises*, IX, 167–68.

VICTORIAN BIBLIOGRAPHY FOR 1957

Francis G. Townsend, editor

THIS BIBLIOGRAPHY has been prepared by a committee of the Victorian Literature Group of the Modern Language Association of America: Francis G. Townsend, chairman, Florida State University; William. D. Templeman, University of Southern California; Robert C. Slack, Carnegie Institute of Technology; Oscar Maurer, University of Texas; Robert A. Donovan, Cornell University; Charles T. Dougherty, St. Louis University, and Donald J. Gray, Indiana University. It attempts to list the noteworthy publications of 1957 (including reviews of these and earlier items) that have a bearing on the Victorian period, as well as similar publications of earlier date that have been inadvertently omitted from the preceding Victorian bibliographies. Unless otherwise stated, the date of publication is 1957. Reference to a page in the bibliography for 1956, in *Modern Philology,* May, 1957, is made by the following form: See VB 1956, 260. Some cross-references are given, though not all that are possible. For certain continuing bibliographical works the reader should consult VB 1941, the last annual bibliography in which such works are listed in full. Bibliographical entries are made to conform as closely as possible with the British National Bibliography for books first published in Great Britain, and with the Library of Congress Catalog for books first published in the United States.

The editor wishes to thank Professor Carl J. Weber of Colby College for his assistance with the Hardy section of the bibliography in this as in so many preceding years.

KEY TO ABBREVIATIONS

AHR = *American Historical Review*
AL = *American Literature*
AM = *Atlantic Monthly*
APSR = *American Political Science Review*
APSS = *Annals of the American Academy of Political and Social Science*
ArQ = *Arizona Quarterly*
BA = *Books Abroad*
BBDI = *Bulletin of Bibliography*

BLR = *Bodleian Library Record*
BPLQ = *Boston Public Library Quarterly*
BSP = *Papers of the Bibliographical Society of America*
CE = *College English*
CHJ = *Cambridge Historical Journal*
CJ = *Cambridge Journal*
CR = *Contemporary Review*
CWd = *Catholic World*
DA = *Dissertation Abstracts*
DUJ = *Durham University Journal*
EC = *Essays in Criticism*
EHR = *English Historical Review*
EJ = *English Journal*
ELH = *Journal of English Literary History*
ESt = *English Studies*
Ex = *Explicator*
HJ = *Hibbert Journal*
HLB = *Harvard Library Bulletin*
HLQ = *Huntington Library Quarterly*
HTB = *New York Herald Tribune Book Review*
JAA = *Journal of Aesthetics and Art Criticism*
JEGP = *Journal of English and Germanic Philology*
JEH = *Journal of Economic History*
JHI = *Journal of the History of Ideas*
JMH = *Journal of Modern History*
JP = *Journal of Philosophy*
JPE = *Journal of Political Economy*
KR = *Kenyon Review*
LJ = *Library Journal*
LQ = *Library Quarterly*
LQHR = *London Quarterly and Holborn Review*
LR = *Library Review*
M & L = *Music and Letters*
MLJ = *Modern Language Journal*
MLN = *Modern Language Notes*
MLQ = *Modern Language Quarterly*
MLR = *Modern Language Review*
MP = *Modern Philology*
N = *Nation*
N & Q = *Notes and Queries*
NCF = *Nineteenth-Century Fiction*
NEQ = *New England Quarterly*

NER = National and English Review
New R = New Republic
NS = New Statesman and Nation
NYTBR = New York Times Book Review
PAPS = Proceedings of the American
Philological Society
ParR = Partisan Review
PLC = Princeton University Library
Chronicle
PMLA = Publications of the Modern
Language Association of America
PQ = Philological Quarterly
PSQ = Political Science Quarterly
QJS = Quarterly Journal of Speech
QQ = Queen's Quarterly
QR = Quarterly Review
RES = Review of English Studies
RoR = Romantic Review
S = Spectator
SAQ = South Atlantic Quarterly
SeR = Sewanee Review
SP = Studies in Philology
SR = Saturday Review
StI = Studies: An Irish Quarterly
Review
TC = Twentieth Century
TLS = Times Literary Supplement
TQ = University of Toronto Quarterly
VNL = Victorian News Letter
VQR = Virginia Quarterly Review
VS = Victorian Studies
YR = Yale Review

I. BIBLIOGRAPHICAL MATERIAL

"Annual Bibliography for 1956." *PMLA*, LXXII, No. 2, 218-38; English Language and Literature, "X. Nineteenth Century" and "XI. Contemporary," ed. Charles C. Mish, J. Max Patrick, and John G. Allee, Jr.

Bell, Marion V., and Bacon, Jean C. *Poole's Index: Date and Volume Key.* ("ACRL Monographs," No. 19.) Chicago: Association of College and Reference Libraries. Pp. 61.
Described in *BBDI*, XXII, 55. A key to the use of Poole's Index, covering 1802-1906.

"Bibliographie der an Deutschen und Österreichischen Universitäten 1952-1955 Angenommen Anglistischen Dissertationen." *Anglia*, LXXIV (1956), 385-412.

A *Bibliography of Parliamentary Debates of*

Great Britain. London: H.M.S.O., 1956. Pp. 62.
Briefly described in *College and Research Libr.*, XVIII, 311.

Bullock, Alan, and Taylor, A. J. P. (eds.). *A Select List of Books on European History, 1815-1914.* 2d ed. Oxford: Clarendon Pr. Pp. 79.

Carter, John. *Books and Book-collectors.* . . .
See VB 1956, 235.
Rev. by James Wells in *LQ*, XXVII, 346-68.

Collins, P. A. W. *Dickens's Periodicals: Articles on Education, An Annotated Bibliography.* ("Vaughan College Papers," No. 3.) Leicester: The Univ. of Leicester. Pp. iii + 36.
Lists articles on education which appeared in *Household Words* and *All the Year Round.*

Dickson, Sarah Augusta. "The Arents Collection of Books in Parts and Associated Literature." *Bull. New York Pub. Libr.*, LXI, 267-80.
Included in the collection of books originally issued in parts are works of Dickens, Thackeray, Trollope, Lever, Lytton, Ainsworth, the Brontë sisters, George Eliot, and others.

Faverty, Frederic E. (ed.). *The Victorian Poets: A Guide to Research.* . . . See VB 1956, 235.
Rev. by Desmond Powell in *ArQ*, XIII, 170-71; by A. C. Ames in *Chicago Sunday Tribune*, July 1, p. 3; by M. G. Parks in *Dalhousie Rev.*, XXXVI, 429-31; by George H. Ford in *JEGP*, LVI, 640-42; by Geoffrey Tillotson in *MLR*, LII, 596; by R. H. Super in *MP*, LV, 63-65; in *TLS*, Feb. 1, p. 66.

Fogle, Stephen F. "A Right Noble Beginning." *VNL*, No. 12 (Autumn), pp. 21-22.
An appraisal of the new journal, *Victorian Studies.* See also the notice of *Victorian Studies* in *TLS*, Oct. 18, p. 625.

Gordan, John D. "New in the Berg Collection: 1952-1956." *Bull. New York Pub. Libr.*, LXI, 303-11, 353-63.
Descriptive Catalogue of materials—MSS and unusual printed pieces, predominantly by or pertaining to nineteenth-century writers — which have been added to the Berg Collection from 1952 to 1956. Represented are Browning, Dickens, Hardy, Shaw, Tennyson, Yeats, and others.

Leclaire, Lucien. *Le Roman régionaliste dans les Îles Britanniques.* . . . See VB 1954, 234.

Rev. by Gwyn Jones in *RES*, new ser., VIII, 102-4.

Maurer, Oscar (ed.). "Recent Publications: A Selected List." *VNL*, No. 11 (Spring), pp. 27-31; No. 12 (Autumn), pp. 30-32.

Nurmi, Martin K. (ed.). "The Romantic Movement: A Selective and Critical Bibliography for the Year 1956." *PQ*, XXXVI, 97-182.

Pettit, Henry, and Macdonald, Angus (eds.). *Annual Bibliography of English Language and Literature.* Vol. XXVIII: *1948.* Pp. xiii + 259. Vol. XXIX: *1949.* Pp. xiv + 293. London: Cambridge Univ. Pr. for the Modern Humanities Research Assoc.

Sitwell, Sacheverell, and Blunt, Wilfrid. *Great Flower Books, 1700-1900: A Bibliographical Record of Two Centuries of Finely-illustrated Flower Books.* London: Collins, 1956. Pp. x + 94.
Rev. by J. S. L. Gilmour in *Library*, XII, 215-16; briefly by Elizabeth C. Hall in *LJ*, LXXXII, 1541.

Stewart, James D., with Muriel E. Hammond and Erwin Saenger (eds.). *British Union-Catalogue of Periodicals: A Record of the Periodicals of the World, from the Seventeenth Century to the Present Day, in British Libraries.* Vol. II: *D-K;* Vol. III: *L-R.* London: Butterworth, 1956, 1957. Pp. xxxi + 677; xxxi + 767.
Vol. II rev. briefly in *LR*, Spring, p. 54; in *TLS*, Apr. 26, p. 264; Vol. III rev. briefly by R. D. Macleod in *LR*, Winter, pp. 265-66. For Vol. I see VB 1955, 241.

Townsend, Francis G. (ed.). "Victorian Bibliography for 1956." *MP*, LIV, 234-69.

Travel in Aquatint and Lithography, 1770-1860, from the Library of J. R. Abbey: A Bibliographical Catalogue. 2 vols. London: Curwen Pr., privately printed, 1956, 1957. Pp. xiii + 299; xiv + 301.
Vol. I rev. by A. Hyatt Mayor in *BSP*, LI, 177-78; Vols. I and II by I. A. Williams in *Library*, XII, 276-79. Williams' review also covers the first two volumes of this catalogue (see VB 1952, 245 and VB 1953, 234).

Watson, George (ed.). *The Cambridge Bibliography of English Literature.* Vol. V: *Supplement: A. D. 600-1900.* London: Cambridge Univ. Pr. Pp. xiv + 710.
Rev. briefly in *LR*, Winter, p. 268; in *TLS*, Oct. 4, p. 600.

Wright, Austin (ed.). *Bibliographies of Stud-ies in Victorian Literature for the Ten Years 1945-1954.* . . . See VB 1956, 237.
Rev. by John D. Gordan in *LJ*, LXXXII, 2343; by Wallace A. Bacon in *QJS*, XLIII, 96-97.

The Year's Work in English Studies, Vol. XXXVI (1955). Ed. for the English Assoc. by Beatrice White. London: Oxford Univ. Pr., 1957. "The Nineteenth Century: Books," treated by Geoffrey Bullough, pp. 190-205; "The Nineteenth Century: Periodicals," by P. M. Yarker, pp. 205-17; "The Twentieth Century," by Marjorie Thompson, pp. 218-26.

II. ECONOMIC, POLITICAL, RELIGIOUS, AND SOCIAL ENVIRONMENT

Adam and Charles Black, 1807-1957; Some Chapters in the History of a Publishing House. London: A. and C. Black. Pp. 116.
Rev. in *TLS*, Dec. 6, p. 748. Sesquicentennial history of a notable firm of Scottish publishers which moved from Edinburgh to London in 1889.

Adams, W. S. *Edwardian Portraits.* London: Secker & Warburg. Pp. vii + 228.
Rev. by Arthur Marshall in *NS*, Nov. 30, p. 738; in *TLS*, Nov. 29, p. 718. Essays on Edwardian period, Baden-Powell, Leverhulme, W. S. Blunt, and Edward VII.

Alexander, Michael. *The True Blue: The Life and Adventures of Colonel Fred Burnaby, 1842-1885.* London: Hart-Davis. Pp. 215.
Rev. by Philip Henderson in *Listener*, Dec. 5, pp. 943-44; by K. John in *NS*, Dec. 7, pp. 786-87; in *TLS*, Dec. 13, p. 754.

Armytage, W. H. G. *Sir Richard Gregory, His Life and Work.* London: Macmillan. Pp. xi + 241.
Rev. by C. P. Snow in *NS*, Feb. 9, pp. 175-76; in *TLS*, Feb. 1, p. 69. Biography of a scientist on the editorial board of *Nature* 1893-1937.

Arnstein, Walter L. "The Bradlaugh Case: A Reappraisal." *JHI*, XVIII, 254-69.
Political and religious repercussions of the notorious fight for admission to Parliament by an atheist, republican, and advocate of birth control.

Balleine, G. R. *Past Finding Out: The Tragic Story of Joanna Southcott and Her Successors.* London: S.P.C.K., 1956. Pp. xi + 151.
Rev. by Winthrop S. Hudson in *Church*

Hist., XXVI, 391-92; briefly by Eleanor T. Smith in *LJ*, LXXXII, 72.

Bayer, Theodor A. *England und der neue Kurs, 1890-1895: auf Grund unveröffentlichter Akten.* Tübingen: Mohr, 1955. Pp. 128.

Rev. by Klaus Epstein in *JMH*, XXIX, 392-93.

Beatty, Charles. *De Lesseps of Suez.* London: Eyre and Spottiswoode, 1956. Pp. 334.

Rev. by Clay Gowran in *Chicago Sunday Tribune*, Feb. 10, p. 3; by J. G. Harrison in *Christian Science Monitor*, Feb. 6, p. 9; by H. W. Baehr in *HTB*, Feb. 10, p. 8; by Asa Briggs in *Manchester Guardian*, Aug. 17, 1956, p. 3; by D. W. Brogan in *NYTBR*, Feb. 10, p. 3; by Charles Wilson in *S*, Aug. 10, 1956, p. 209; by Leo Gershoy in *SR*, Feb. 23, p. 23; in *TLS*, Aug. 17, 1956, p. 484; unfavorably by J. D. Fage in *VS*, I, 100-102.

Beer, Samuel H. "The Representation of Interests in British Government: Historical Background." *APSR*, LI, 613-50.

Discussion of certain political attitudes in Britain over the past two hundred years.

Betjeman, John. "City and Suburban." *S*, Aug. 23, pp. 244-45.

On the founding of a "Victorian Group" to preserve the best in nineteenth-century architecture. Lists three useful "rules for looking at Victorian buildings."

Blake, George. *The Ben Line: The History of Wm. Thomson & Co. of Leith and Edinburgh, and of the Ships Owned and Managed by Them, 1825-1955.* London: Nelson, 1956. Pp. ix + 222.

Bloom, Ursula. *The Elegant Edwardian.* London: Hutchinson. Pp. 241.

Rev. in *TLS*, Oct. 4, p. 590. Biography of Rev. Harvey Bloom, with material on Marie Corelli.

Bolgar, R. R. "Victor Cousin and Nineteenth-Century Education." *CJ*, II (March, 1949), 357-68.

Treats of England, France, Holland, Germany. (Inadvertently omitted earlier.)

Bourne, Kenneth. "Great Britain and the Cretan Revolt, 1866-1869." *Slavonic and East European Rev.*, XXXV, 74-94.

Boykin, Edward (ed.). *Victoria, Albert, and Mrs. Stevenson.* New York: Rinehart. Pp. x + 309.

Rev. by Ellen Hart Smith in *HTB*, Mar. 31, p. 7; by K. T. Willis in *LJ*, LXXXII, 663; by George Curry in *VS*, I, 205-6. Letters of Sallie Cole Stevenson from 1836 to 1841, when her husband was Minister to the Court of St. James.

Briggs, Asa. *Friends of the People. . . .* See *VB* 1956, 238.

Rev. in *Listener*, Jan. 10, p. 75; in *TLS*, Apr. 19, p. 238.

Briggs, Asa. *Victorian People. . . .* See *VB* 1956, 238.

Rev. by Joseph Finkelstein in *JEH*, XVII, 314-16.

Broeker, Galen. "The Problem of Law and Order in Ireland, 1812-1836." *DA*, XVII, 1989-90.

Brook, Michael. "A Chartist Flag." *N & Q*, new ser., IV, 314.

Brown, E. H. Phelps, and Hopkins, Sheila V. "Seven Centuries of the Prices of Consumables, Compared with Builders' Wagerates." *Economica*, new ser., XXIII (1956), 296-314.

The figures and tables in this article give a startling picture of the tremendous betterment in the workers' lot throughout the Victorian era.

Bullock, Alan, and Shock, Maurice (eds.). *The Liberal Tradition from Fox to Keynes.* ("British Political Tradition" ser., No. 8.) London: Black, 1956. Pp. xviii + 289.

Rev. by J. H. Burns in *History*, XLII, 274-75; by D. W. Brogan in *S*, Oct. 26, 1956, pp. 577-78; in *TLS*, Nov. 23, 1956, p. 690.

Burnell, Richard Desborough. *Henley Regatta: A History.* London: Oxford Univ. Pr. Pp. xii + 298.

Rev. by Ralph Partridge in *NS*, June 15, p. 774. Covers every regatta from 1839 to 1956.

Burt, Alfred LeRoy. *The Evolution of the British Empire and Commonwealth from the American Revolution.* Boston: Heath, 1956. Pp. 950.

Bury, Adrian. "Joseph Crawhall." *Apollo*, LXVI, 112-16.

Crawhall, 1861-1913, was a gifted painter of animals and birds.

Cardwell, D. S. L. *The Organisation of Science in England.* London: Heinemann. Pp. ix + 204.

Rev. by W. L. Francis in *Economica*, new ser., XXIV, 273-74; by Phyllis Deane in *Econ. Jour.*, LXVII, 737-38; in *TLS*, Mar. 1, p. 132; by Frank Greenaway in *Universities Quart.*, XI, 408-12.

Carpenter, Minnie Lindsay. *William Booth, Founder of the Salvation Army.* London: Epworth Pr. Pp. 128.

Carson, R. A. G. "Some Aspects of the Victorian Medal." *Connoisseur*, CXL, 102-4. A note on commemorative medals produced in Victorian times.

Carter, George Stuart. *A Hundred Years of Evolution.* Sidgwick and Jackson. Pp. x + 206.

Rev. in *TLS*, Oct. 11, p. 613. An account of the various stages through which evolutionary theory has passed since the mid-nineteenth century.

Cecil, Lord David. *Melbourne.* . . . See VB 1954, 236.

Rev. favorably by L. Malarmey in *Études anglaises*, X, 277-80.

Checkland, S. G. "Marshall and the Wages-Wealth Paradox." *Econ. Jour.*, LXVII, 330-33.

Clarke, R. O. "The Dispute in the British Engineering Industry 1897-98: An Evaluation." *Economica*, new ser., XXIV, 128-37.

Cohen, Ethel A. Waley (ed.). *A Young Victorian in India.* London: Cape. Pp. 242.

Rev. in *TLS*, May 3, p. 271. Letters written by H. M. Kisch, civil servant in India, between 1874 and 1889.

Cooper, Leonard. *Havelock.* London: Lane. Pp. 192.

Rev. in *TLS*, Aug. 16, p. 498.

Coppard, A. E. *It's Me, O Lord! An Abstract & Brief Chronicle of Some of the Life with Some of the Opinions of A. E. Coppard; Written by Himself.* London: Methuen. Pp. 252.

Rev. favorably by Betty Miller in *NS*, Mar. 16, p. 348.

Corry, B. A. "A Testimonial from Ricardo." *Economica*, new ser., XXIV, 71-72.

Reproduces a letter first printed in *The Bolton Chronicle*, November 17, 1832, in which Ricardo endorsed the candidacy of Robert Torrens for a seat in the House of Commons.

Corti, Egon Caesar Conte. *The English Empress.* Trans. E. M. Hodgson. London: Cassell. Pp. xiii + 406.

Rev. by Gerald Hamilton in *S*, May 17, pp. 657-58; in *TLS*, Apr. 5, p. 204. Life of Empress Frederick, daughter of Victoria, with extracts from Victoria's correspondence.

Courtney, Marie-Thérèse. *Edward Martyn and the Irish Theatre.* . . . See VB 1956, p. 238.

Rev. in *TLS*, Mar. 1, p. 124; by David Greene in *VS*, I, 207.

Cowherd, Raymond G. *The Humanitarians and the Ten Hour Movement in England.* (Harvard Graduate School of Business Administration, "Kress Library of Business and Economics," No. 10). Cambridge, Mass.: Harvard Univ. Pr., 1956. Pp. 27.

Rev. briefly in *Economica*, new ser., XXIV, 183.

Cowherd, Raymond Gibson. *The Politics of English Dissent: The Religious Aspects of Liberal and Humanitarian Reform Movements from 1815 to 1848.* New York: New York Univ. Pr., 1956. Pp. 242.

Rev. by David Owen in *AHR*, LXII, 615-16; by Chester Kirby in *APSS*, CCX, 176-77; by R. T. Handy in *Christian Century*, LXXIV, 762; by F. R. Salter in *JMH*, XXIX, 270; briefly by Carlos T. Flick in *SAQ*, LVI, 409.

Craig, Eward Gordon. *Index to the Story of My Days: Some Memoirs of Edward Gordon Craig, 1872-1907.* London: Hulton Pr. Pp. vii + 308.

Rev. by John Piper in *NS*, Oct. 5, p. 436; by Janet Leeper in *S*, Oct. 18, p. 523; in *TLS*, Oct. 25, p. 642. Craig finished his acting career in 1899, then worked as a producer-designer, for Yeats, among others.

Crapster, Basil L. "Scotland and the Conservative Party in 1876." *JMH*, XXIX, 355-60. An analysis of Disraeli's failure to convert Scotland to Conservatism.

Crawford, Floyd Wardlaw. "Some Aspects of the Political and Economic Problems of Woman in English Society, 1884-1901." *DA*, XVII, 348.

Cruise O'Brien, Conor. *Parnell and His Party, 1880-90.* Oxford: Clarendon Pr. Pp. xiii + 373.

Rev. by John V. Kelleher in *APSS*, CCXIV, 187-88; by Robert Rhodes James in *History Today*, VII, 417-18; in *N & Q*, new ser., IV, 274-75; by Asa Briggs in *NS*, Apr. 27, pp. 546-47; by D. W. Brogan in *S*, May 3, pp. 589-90; favorably in *TLS*, Apr. 12, p. 219; by Lawrence McCaffery in *VS*, I, 192-93.

De Banke, Cecile. *Hand over Hand.* London: Hutchinson. Pp. 263.

Rev. by Margaret Lane in *NS*, July 27, p. 123. Cecile de Banke's autobiography tells of her early years in the East End of London in the 1890's.

Dennis, Geoffrey. *Till Seven.* London: Eyre & Spottiswoode. Pp. 208.

Rev. briefly by A. D. in *NS*, Aug. 3, p.

155. Autobiography of a childhood in Manchester in the nineties.

Derry, T. K., and Jarman, T. L. *The Making of Modern Britain: Life and Work from George III to Elizabeth II.* London: Murray, 1956. Pp. 308.
Rev. by D. R. in *Manchester Guardian*, Feb. 10, 1956, p. 6; in *TLS*, Feb. 3, 1956, p. 66.

Disher, Maurice Willson. *Pharaoh's Fool.* London: Heinemann. Pp. xi + 252.
Rev. in *TLS*, Apr. 5, p. 204. Life of Giovanni Belzoni, Regency and early Victorian actor, adventurer, impresario of Egyptian Hall.

Duhamel, Jean. "L'Amour Inconnu de Lady Hester Stanhope." *Rev. des deux mondes,* Nov. 15, pp. 297-309.

Edwards, Robert Dudley, and Williams, Thomas Desmond (eds.). *The Great Famine: Studies in Irish History 1845-52.* Dublin: Browne & Nolan. Pp. xx + 517.
Rev. by Norman Gash in *History*, XLII, 155-56; by Louis Schreiber in *LJ*, LXXXII, 1883; by Cecil Woodham-Smith in *NYTBR*, Aug. 4, p. 14; by D. W. Brogan in *S*, Mar. 8, pp. 317-18; favorably in *TLS*, Apr. 26, p. 252. Essays on Irish famine of 1845-51.

Elliott-Binns, L. E. *English Thought, 1860-1900.* . . . See VB 1956, 239.
Rev. briefly by Claude Jenkins in *EHR*, LXXII, 195; by J. Morris Le Bour'his in *Études anglaises*, X, 178-79.

Eyck, Frank. "Fresh Light on the Constitutional Monarchy." *Listener*, June 20, pp. 993-94.
New evidence from the Windsor archives on Prince Albert's role in the relations between the Queen and Sir Robert Peel, 1841.

Ferriday, Peter. *Lord Grimthorpe, 1816-1905.* London: Murray. Pp. xiii + 230.
Rev. in *TLS*, Nov. 8, p. 670. Biography of a Victorian parliamentary lawyer, low churchman, advocate of marriage with deceased wife's sister, and inventor of a patent lavatory door-latch which could be opened from the inside only after the stool had been flushed.

Findlater, Richard [Kenneth Bruce Findlater Bain]. *Six Great Actors: David Garrick, John Philip Kemble, Edmund Kean, W. C. Macready, Henry Irving, Sir Johnston Forbes-Robertson.* London: Hamish Hamilton. Pp. 192.
Rev. by Michael Redgrave in *NS*, Nov. 2, pp. 577-78.

Finnberg, Florence Faith. "The Social and Political Thought of Victor Hugo, as Revealed in *L'Evenement*, a Newspaper Published under His Aegis from July 30-31, 1848, to December 1, 1851." *DA*, XV (1955), 2525. (Inadvertently omitted earlier.)

Forster, E. M. *Marianne Thornton.* . . . See VB 1956, 239.
Rev. briefly by R. S. Sayers in *Economica*, new ser., XXIII (1956), 384-85.

Forsyth, Gerald. "WILHELM: A Noted Victorian Theatrical Designer." *Theatre Notebook*, XI, 55-58.
Wilhelm's real name was John Charles Pitcher. Besides designing for the theatre, he was prominent as a painter in watercolor.

Fox, Richard Michael. *Jim Larkin: The Rise of the Underman.* London: Lawrence & Wishart. Pp. 183.
Rev. by Norman Mackenzie in *NS*, Feb. 16, p. 210. Biography of a labor leader.

Freeman, T. W. *Pre-Famine Ireland: A Study in Historical Geography.* Manchester: Manchester Univ. Pr. Pp. viii + 352.
Rev. briefly in *TLS*, Sept. 20, p. 566.

Fulford, Roger. *Votes for Women.* London: Faber. Pp. i + 343.
Rev. by Jane Hodge in *History Today*, VII, 339-40; by Emily Lutyens in *NER*, CXLVIII, 254-55; by Letitia Fairfield in *NS*, Apr. 13, pp. 490-91; briefly by Betty Miller in *TC*, CLXI, 592-94; favorably in *TLS*, Apr. 12, p. 224; by George Dangerfield in *VS*, I, 198-99.

Gartner, Lloyd P. "The Jewish Immigrant in England 1870-1914." *DA*, XVII, 1539-40.

Gilbert, Michael. *The Claimant.* London: Constable. Pp. viii + 224.
Rev. by Gerald Hamilton in *S*, Sept. 6, p. 314; in *TLS*, June 28, p. 396. Account of life and trial of the Tichborne Claimant.

Gillespie, C. "L'Ouevre d'Élie Halévy: Appreciation critique." *Rev. de métaphysique et de morale*, LXII, 157-86.
This important article examines Halévy's method of analysis, which was to examine a multiplicity of contradictions and trace them back to a single underlying contradiction central to a whole system of thought. In the case of the Utilitarians the contradiction lay in assuming a natural identification of interests in economics, and an artificial identification of interests in politics. In the case of nineteenth-century liberalism, only the heavy moral restraint imposed on the individual by

Evangelicalism made political liberty and orderly progress possible.

Goddard, Henry. *Memoirs of a Bow Street Runner*. New York: Morrow. Pp. 253.

Rev. by Vivian Mercier in *Commonweal*, Apr. 5, p. 21; by W. H. Hughes in *NS*, Feb. 16, p. 213; by Rex Stout in *NYTBR*, Mar. 24, p. 16; by Christopher Pulling in *S*, Mar. 1, p. 291; in *TLS*, Dec. 7, 1956, p. 724. Goddard served fifteen years as a Bow Street runner, then nine years as Chief Constable of Northampton, before becoming a prosperous private detective. He died in 1883.

Godden, Geoffrey A. "Hannah B. Barlow." *Apollo*, LXVI, 22-23.

Hannah Barlow was an artist in pottery decoration with Messrs. Doulton of Lambeth in the last third of the century.

Graves, Robert. *They Hanged My Saintly Billy*. London: Cassell. Pp. xi + 269.

Rev. by C. J. Rolo in *AM*, CC, 88; by Paul Pickrel in *Harper's*, CCXV (July), 88-89; by James Sandoe in *HTB*, May 26, p. 5; by Hesketh Pearson in *Listener*, May 23, pp. 849-50; by Donald Malcolm in *New R*, July 1, p. 21; unfavorably by Ralph Partridge in *NS*, May 25, pp. 679-80 (see reply by Graves, June 15, p. 768); by Erle Stanley Gardner in *NYTBR*, May 26, p. 5; by Jenny Nasmyth in *S*, July 12, pp. 70-71; by John T. Winterich in *SR*, June 22, p. 26; in *TLS*, May 31, p. 336. Account of William Palmer, the convicted poisoner, whom Graves believes innocent —that is, of the crime for which he was hanged.

Graveson, Ronald Harry, and Crane, Francis Roger (eds.). *A Century of Family Law, 1857-1957*. London: Sweet and Maxwell. Pp. xviii + 459.

Noticed in *TLS*, Mar. 29, p. 198. An account of the developments in the legal status of wives and children since the establishment of the Divorce Court in 1857.

Gray, Malcolm. *The Highland Economy, 1750-1850*. Edinburgh: Oliver and Boyd. Pp. viii + 280.

Rev. by Phyllis Deane in *Econ. Jour.*, LXVII, 738-40.

Greenwall, Harry James. *Northcliffe: Napoleon of Fleet Street*. London: Wingate. Pp. xii, 13-240.

Rev. unfavorably in *TLS*, Oct. 18, p. 627.

Greenwood, George A. *Taylor of Batley*. London: Parrish. Pp. 188.

Noticed briefly in *TLS*, June 7, p. 354. Biography of a Yorkshire woolen manufacturer and Liberal M.P. who died recently at the age of 102.

Grinnell-Milne, Duncan. *Baden-Powell at Mafeking*. London: Bodley Head. Pp. xii + 237.

Rev. in *TLS*, Mar. 1, p. 131.

Gross, Felix, *Rhodes of Africa.* . . . See VB 1956, 239.

Rev. by George Shepperson in *History*, XLII, 258; briefly by Louis Barron in *LJ*, LXXXII, 1765; by Hans Kohn in *NYTBR*, Sept. 8, p. 10; by John Barkham in *SR*, Sept. 14, pp. 53-54; in *TLS*, Dec. 28, 1956, p. 778.

Grylls, R. Glynn. "The Correspondence of F. G. Stephens," *TLS*, Apr. 5, p. 216; "The Pre-Raphaelite Brotherhood," *TLS*, Apr. 12, p. 232.

Letters to Stephens, one of the original seven members of the Brotherhood, from artists and literary men: Patmore, Rossetti, Holman Hunt and others.

Guest, Ivor. *Clara Webster: A Victorian Ballet Girl*. London: Black. Pp. vii + 136.

Hales, Edward Elton Young. *Mazzini and the Secret Societies: The Making of a Myth*. London: Eyre & Spottiswoode, 1956. Pp. 226.

Rev. favorably by Paul Johnson in *NS*, Jan. 5, pp. 20-21.

Halévy, Élie. *Thomas Hodgskin.* . . . See VB 1956, 239.

Rev. by T. W. Hutchinson in *Economica*, new ser., XXIV, 88-89; by Asa Briggs in *History*, XLII, 154-55.

Halfpenny, Eric. "Letters from Lincoln's Inn, 1846-9." *Library*, XII, 256-69.

Correspondence concerning the preparation of a catalogue of the C. Purton Cooper gift of books to the library of the Inn.

Hall, A. R. "A Note on the English Capital Market as a Source of Funds for Home Investment before 1914." *Economica*, new ser., XXIV, 59-66.

Lavington's study of the English capital market before 1914 has led to a widely accepted belief that the machinery for home new issues was inadequate, and that the imperfect organization of the capital market was one of the reasons for the deficiencies in British industry before 1914. Hall questions this belief.

Hearder, H. "Napoleon III's Threat to Break off Diplomatic Relations with England during the Crisis over the Orsini Attempt in 1858." *EHR*, LXXII, 474-81.

Hedman, Edwin Randolph. "Early French Feminism: From the Eighteenth Century to 1848." *DA*, XVII, 2253.

Helgesen, Moira Anne. "Forgues: Nineteenth

Century Anglophile." *DA,* XVII, 629-30.

Higonnet, René P. "Bank Deposits in the United Kingdom, 1870-1914." *Quart. Jour. Econ.,* LXXI, 329-67.

Hilton, George W. "The British Truck System in the Nineteenth Century." *JPE,* LXV, 237-56.

After a study of the Midland handmade nail trade and the collieries, Hilton concludes that Sidney and Beatrice Webb were probably right when they assigned as the main motive for trucking the effort to circumvent an established wage rate.

Hilton, Richard. *The Indian Mutiny.* London: Hollis & Carter, Pp. xii + 232.

Rev. by Paul Johnson in *NS,* May 4, pp. 581-82; by Colin Welch in *S,* June 7, pp. 754-55; in *TLS,* May 3, p. 270 ("compact and highly readable").

Hobsbawm, E. J. "Methodism and the Threat of Revolution in Britain." *History Today,* VII, 115-24.

Takes issue with the opinion that Methodism helped to keep England from revolution between 1789 and 1848 by pointing out that Methodism was relatively weak in industrial areas, and where it was strong, radicalism was not checked.

Howarth, Patrick. *Questions in the House: The History of a Unique British Institution.* London: J. Lane, 1956. Pp. 220.

Rev. by Betty Kemp in *EHR,* LXXII, 383-84.

Hughes, Emrys. *Keir Hardie.* London: Allen & Unwin, 1956. Pp. 248.

Rev. by Norman MacKenzie in *NS,* Feb. 16, p. 210; by Robert Blake in *S,* Mar. 22, p. 379; in *TLS,* Feb. 1, p. 62; by Asa Briggs in *VS,* I, 183-85 ("adds little to the assessments of Hardie that have already been made").

"Indian Mutiny." *S,* Aug. 2-30.

A series of articles compiled from the *Spectator* of 1857, as follows: "Cartridges and Chuprassies," Aug. 2, pp. 156-57; "Item: Twenty New Ropes," Aug. 9, pp. 185-86; "The Pomp of Tamerlane," Aug. 16, pp. 212-13; "Nana Sahib," Aug. 23, pp. 243-44; "Poor Jessie Brown," Aug. 30, pp. 271-72.

Jaeger, Muriel. *Before Victoria. . . .* See VB 1956, 240.

Rev. favorably by Léonie Villard in *Études anglaises,* X, 264-66; by C. H. D. Howard in *History,* XLII, 259-60.

James, Robert Rhodes. "Charles Stewart Parnell 1846-1891." *History Today,* VII, 11-17.

Particularly emphasizes his development

of Parliamentary obstruction tactics.

James, Robert Rhodes. "Radical Joe." *History Today,* VII, 618-26.

The career and principles of Joseph Chamberlain to 1886, when he broke with the Liberals over Home Rule. Some previously unpublished letters from the Salisbury collection are used.

Johnson, Albert E. "Greatest of Juliets." *Theatre Arts,* XLI (August), 63-64, 95-96.

The story of Adelaide Neilson.

Johnson, L. G. *General T. Perronet Thompson, 1783-1869.* London: Allen & Unwin. Pp. 295.

Rev. favorably in *TLS,* June 28, p. 395; by Norman McCord in *VS,* I, 199-200. Biography of a Radical politician and writer.

Jones, Howard Mumford. "The Greatness of the Nineteenth Century." *HLB,* XI, 5-20.

Jones, William Devereux. *Lord Derby and Victorian Conservatism.* Athens, Ga.: Univ. of Georgia Pr., 1956. Pp. xi + 367.

Rev. by Walter P. Hall in *APSS,* CCCXII, 165; unfavorably by Robert Blake in *History Today,* VII, 485; by Madeline R. Robinton in *JMH,* XXIX, 385-86; favorably by Asa Briggs in *NS,* Mar. 9, pp. 315-16; by Brian Inglis in *S,* Jan. 18, p. 87; by W. H. B. Court in *VS,* I, 102-3.

Jopling, L. M. "Indian Mutiny." *NS,* June 1, p. 708.

Objects to Pannikar's statement that the Mutiny left the British in India forever fearful of the Indians.

Kaplan, Louis. "Sources for the Study of European Labor and Socialism (1840-1914) at Wisconsin." *College and Research Libr.,* XVIII, 141-43, 152.

Kearney, Hugh F. "The Great Famine." *StI,* XLV, 184-63.

Surveys treatment of the Irish famine by historians.

Kelsall, Roger Keith. *Higher Civil Servants in Britain, from 1870 to the Present Day.* London: Routledge and Paul, 1955: Pp. 233.

Rev. by Theodore Caplow in *Amer. Jour. Sociol.,* LXIII, 331.

Lack, David. *Evolutionary Theory and Christian Belief: The Unresolved Conflict.* London: Methuen. Pp. 128.

Rev. in *TLS,* Sept. 27, p. 579. An account of the controversies which followed the publication of the Darwin-Wallace studies, 1858-59, and their aftermath.

Larkin, Emmet. "The Stuff of Which History

Is Made." *VNL*, No. 12 (Autumn), pp. 16-18.
A review article based on Edwards and Williams' *The Great Famine*.

Leasor, James. *The Red Fort: The Story of the Indian Mutiny of 1857*. New York: Reynal. Pp. 383.
Rev. by Taliaferro Boatwright in *HTB*, May 5, p. 7; by M. C. in *NS*, Mar. 9, p. 317; by Cecil Woodham-Smith in *NYTBR*, Apr. 21, pp. 1, 20; by J. M. White in *S*, Feb. 15, p. 215; by Joseph Hitrec in *SR*, Apr. 20, p. 35.

Leslie, Shane (ed.). *Edward Tennyson Reed, 1860-1933: A Memoir Compiled by Shane Leslie from an Incomplete Autobiography, with a Choice of his Caricatures Made by Kenneth Bird*. London: Heinemann. Pp. xii + 155.
Rev. in *TLS*, Nov. 29, p. 718. A life of the artist who succeeded Charles Keene on the staff of *Punch*.

Lever, Tresham (ed.). *The Letters of Lady Palmerston*. London: Murray. Pp. xii + 376.
Rev. by Grace Banyard in *CR*, CXCII, 352; unfavorably by Ralph Partridge in *NS*, Dec. 28, p. 885; by Karl Miller in *S*, Oct. 11, pp. 489-90; in *TLS*, Nov. 15, p. 683 (according to reviewer, this selection is supplementary rather than complete).

Lewis, W. David. "Three Religious Orators and the Chartist Movement." *QJS*, XLIII, 62-68.
Three ministers who espoused the Chartist cause, Joseph Raynor Stephens, Charles Kingsley, and Frederick W. Robertson.

MacGregor, Geddes. *The Tichborne Imposter*. Philadelphia: Lippincott. Pp. 288.
Rev. by R. L. Duffus in *NYTBR*, Aug. 18, p. 5; by Allen Churchill in *SR*, Sept. 14, pp. 58-59.

McGregor, Oliver Ross. *Divorce in England*. London: Heinemann. Pp. xi + 220.
Rev. by Alec Vidler in *S*, Sept. 27, p. 404.

Mairet, P. A. *Pioneer of Sociology: The Life and Letters of Patrick Geddes*. London: Lund Humphries. Pp. xx + 226.
Rev. in *TLS*, Nov. 1, p. 659.

Marlowe, John. *The Puritan Tradition in English Life*. London: Cresset Pr. Pp. 148.
Rev. by V. S. Pritchett in *NS*, Jan. 26, pp. 103-4; in *TLS*, Feb. 1, p. 62. Discusses the Victorian middle class as the acme of Puritan tradition.

Maurer, Oscar. " 'Punch' on Slavery and Civil War in America." *VS*, I, 5-28.
Although against slavery from its early radical days, in the 1860's *Punch* reflected upper middle-class sympathy with the Confederacy and, until his assassination, its distrust of Lincoln. Mr. Maurer's article is well documented by cartoons and poems.

Medlicott, W. N. *Bismarck, Gladstone, and the Concert of Europe*. . . . See VB 1956, 240.
Rev. by E. Malcolm Carroll in *AHR*, LXII, 890-91; briefly in *APSR*, LI, 875; by F. H. Hinsley in *CHJ*, XIII, 94-96; by Elizabeth Wiskemann in *History Today*, VII, 63-64; by Robert A. Spencer in *JMH*, XXIX, 271-72.

Meek, Ronald Lindley. *Studies in the Labour Theory of Value*. London: Lawrence & Wishart, 1956. Pp. 310.
Rev. by T. W. Hutchison in *Economica*, new ser., XXIV, 163-64; by H. D. Dickinson in *Econ. Jour.*, LXVII, 499-504.

Meeks, Carroll. *The Railroad Station*. New Haven: Yale Univ. Pr., 1956. Pp. xxvi + 203.
Rev. by S. L. in *NS*, Apr. 20, pp. 522-23; favorably by Nikolaus Pevsner in *VS*, I, 78-81.

Melton, James. "Elizabethan Furniture in Early Victorian Times." *Apollo*, LXVI, 170-73.
Revival of interest in old English furniture in early Victorian times.

Miesle, Frank Leland. "The Staging of Pantomime Entertainments on the London Stage: 1715-1808." *DA*, XV (1955), 2341. (Inadvertently omitted earlier.)

Miles, Wyndham D. "Provost Smith's Mauve Tie." *The Library Chronicle of the Friends of the Univ. of Pennsylvania Library*, XXIII, 37-41.
One of the prized possessions of the University of Pennsylvania Library is a mauve tie, a memento of William Henry Perkin, who in 1856, at the age of eighteen, took out "English Patent No. 1984," covering a process for producing mauve dye. Perkin opened a factory the next year and became a major figure in the development of chemical industry. At the age of thirty-six he sold his business interests and returned to his real love, research.

Minchinton, W. E. *The British Tinplate Industry*. Oxford: Clarendon Pr. Pp. xvi + 286.
Rev. by H. A. Marquand in *Econ. Jour.*, LXVII, 732-33.

Moraud, Marcel Ian. *Une Irlandaise libérale en France sous la Restauration: Lady*

Morgan (1775-1859). Paris: Didier, 1954. Pp. 204.
Rev. by René Fréchet in *Études anglaises*, X, 83-84.

Morris, Owen James. *Grandfather's London*. London: Putnam, 1956. Pp. 127.
Rev. briefly by Ida Darlington in *LR*, Spring, p. 66; by Jacques Vallette in *Mercure de France*, CCCXXXIII, 163. Documentary photographs of London in the 1880's.

Mount, Charles Merrill. *John Singer Sargent: A Biography*. London: Cresset Pr. Pp. xii + 371.
Rev. by Ralph Partridge in *NS*, May 18, pp. 644-46; by John Berger in *S*, May 17, p. 654; in *TLS*, May 10, p. 284.

Oliver, Roland. *Sir Harry Johnston and the Scramble for Africa*. London: Chatto & Windus. Pp. xv + 368.
Rev. by Thomas Hodgkin in *NS*, Nov. 23, pp. 701-2; by Isaac Schapera in *S*, Nov. 1, p. 586; in *TLS*, Nov. 8, pp. 665-66 ("Surely it will take its place among the best biographies of this decade"). A biography of the empire-building contemporary of Rhodes and Lugard.

Palmer, A. W. "The Anglo-Russian Entente." *History Today*, VII, 748-54.
As background to an account of the entente which protected British interests in the Near East and helped Russia to regain European prestige lost during the Sino-Japanese war, Mr. Palmer briefly but competently sketches Anglo-Russian relations during the entire nineteenth century.—D. G.

Panikkar, K. M. "The Indian Mutiny." *NS*, May 11, p. 598.

Pares, Richard, and Taylor, Alan John Percivale (eds.). *Essays Presented to Sir Lewis Namier*. London: Macmillan, 1956. Pp. viii + 542.
Rev. by Howard Robinson in *AHR*, LXII, 370-71; by J. H. Plumb in *CHJ*, XIII, 91-92. Contains some nineteenth century studies.

Pearson, Hesketh. *Beerbohm Tree: His Life and Laughter*. London: Methuen, 1956. Pp. xiv + 250.
Rev. briefly by Eric Gillett in *NER*, CXLVII (1956), 319-24; by T. C. Worsley in *NS*, Nov. 10, 1956, pp. 595-96; by Harold Clurman in *NYTBR*, Feb. 10, p. 6; by Gerard Fay in *S*, Feb. 8, p. 185; by W. W. Appleton in *SR*, Apr. 6, p. 16; in *TLS*, Nov. 23, 1956, p. 692.

Pelling, Henry. *America and the British Left*. . . . See VB 1956, 240.

Rev. by Mary E. Murphy in *APSS*, CCCXI, 197-98; by Asa Briggs in *History*, XLII, 257-58; in *Mississippi Valley Hist. Rev.*, XLIV, 581-82; by Anthony Hartley in *S*, Dec. 21, 1956, p. 911; by Samuel Bernstein in *Sci. and Soc.*, XXI, 269-70; favorably in *TLS*, Jan. 25, p. 42; by Philip Poirer in *VS*, I, 193-94; in *YR*, XLVII, xvi-xvii.

Perham, Margery. *Lugard: The Years of Adventure, 1858-1898: The First Part of the Life of Frederick Dealtry Lugard, Later Lord Lugard of Abinger*. London: Collins, 1956. Pp. xv + 750.
Rev. by J. D. Hargreaves in *CHJ*, XIII, 198-200 ("a contribution, of the highest importance, to the history of British empire in Africa"); by A. P. Thornton in *History Today*, VII, 129-31; by Philip Curtin in *VS*, I, 103-4.

Pevsner, Nikolaus. *London*. Vol. I. *The Cities of London and Westminster*. Harmondsworth: Penguin Books. Pp. 640.
Rev. by G. W. Stonier in *NS*, June 15, pp. 776-77. Much information about Victorian London.

Piper, David. "English XIXth Century Conversation Pieces." *Apollo*, LXV, 163-68.
The art of nineteenth-century group-portrait painting.

Plumb, J. H. (ed.). *Studies in Social History*. . . . See VB 1956, 247.
Rev. by Gladys Scott Thomson in *EHR*, LXXII, 203-4.

Pollard, Sidney. "British and World Shipbuilding, 1890-1914: A Study in Comparative Costs." *JEH*, XVII, 426-44.

Pollock, J. G. *Way to Glory: The Life of Havelock of Lucknow*. London: Murray. Pp. x + 270.
Rev. in *Listener*, Oct. 31, p. 709.

Prebble, John. *The High Girders*. . . . See VB 1956, 241.
Rev. by Walter Havighurst in *Chicago Sunday Tribune*, Feb. 10, p. 3; by P. J. Searles in *HTB*, Jan. 13, p. 3; by Henry James in *LJ*, LXXXII, 550; by Walter Lord in *NYTBR*, Jan. 13, p. 3; by Borden Deal in *SR*, Jan. 12, p. 15; briefly in *TLS*, Feb. 8, p. 86; unfavorably by R. K. Webb in *VS*, I, 106.

Pressnell, Leslie Sedden. *Country Banking in the Industrial Revolution*. Oxford: Clarendon Pr., 1956. Pp. xvi + 591.
Rev. by David Spring in *AHR*, LXII, 614-15; by S. G. Checkland in *JPE*, LXI, 364-65.

Prestige, George Leonard. *St. Paul's in its Glory: A Candid History of the Cathedral*,

1831-1911. London: S. P. C. K., 1955. Pp. xix + 262.
Rev. briefly by G. F. A. Best in *EHR*, LXXII, 382.

Price, R. G. G. *A History of Punch*. London: Collins. Pp. 384.
Rev. by Francis Williams in *NS*, Aug. 24, p. 230; by Bernard Levin (whose review is an attack on *Punch*) in *S*, Aug. 30, p. 279; in *TLS*, Sept. 27, p. 574. Five of Price's chapters deal with the Victorian years of *Punch* under its first four editors, 1841-1906.

Prouty, Roger. *The Transformation of the Board of Trade, 1830-1855. A Study of the Administrative Reorganization in the Heyday of Laissez Faire*. London: Heinemann. Pp. viii + 123.
Rev. briefly in *Econ. Jour.*, LXVII, 780; in *TLS*, Nov. 8, p. 676. Study of the regulation of industry by the Board of Trade from 1830 to 1855.

Purdom, Charles Benjamin. *Harley Granville Barker.* . . . See VB 1956, 241.
Rev. by E. J. West in *QJS*, XLIII, 84-85.

Radzinowicz, Leon. *A History of English Criminal Law and its Administration from 1750*. Vol. II: *The Clash between Private Initiative and Public Interest in the Enforcement of the Law*. Pp. xix + 751. Vol. III: *Cross-currents in the Movement for Reform of the Police*. Pp. xix + 688. London: Stevens & Sons, 1956.
Rev. briefly by Joseph L. Andrews in *LJ*, LXXXII, 982-83.

Ray, Cyril. "Pre-Wolfenden." *S*, Sept. 27, p. 389.
The Victorian demi-monde as revealed by *The Man of Pleasure's Illustrated Pocket-Book, 1850*.

Records of the Borough of Nottingham: Being a Series of Extracts from the Archives of the Corporation of Nottingham. Vol. IX. *1836-1900*. Nottingham: Central Library, 1956. Pp. xix + 462.
Rev. briefly by W. G. Hoskins in *EHR*, LXXII, 382-83. Catalogue of daily life in a large industrial town, 1836-1900.

Redford, Arthur. *Manchester Merchants and Foreign Trade*. Vol. II: *1850-1939*. ("Manchester University Economic History Ser.," No. 15.) Manchester: Manchester Univ. Pr., 1956. Pp. xxii + 307.
Rev. by W. Ashworth in *Economica*, new ser., XXIV, 90-91; by Francis E. Hyde in *EHR*, LXII, 341-42; by T. C. Barker in *JEH*, XVII, 270-71.

Rees, C. B. *100 Years of the Hallé*. London: MacGibbon and Kee. Pp. 175.
Rev. in *TLS*, Nov. 1, p. 652.

Reynolds, E. E. *Baden-Powell*. 2d ed., rev. New York: Oxford Univ. Pr. Pp. viii + 270. Rev. in *TLS*, Mar. 1, p. 131.

Riggs, Robert E. "Peel and Disraeli: Architects of a New Conservative Party." *Western Humanities Rev.*, XI, 183-87.

Robson, Robert. *The Cotton Industry in Britain*. London: Macmillan. Pp. xx + 364.

Rogin, Leo. *The Meaning and Validity of Economic Theory: A Historical Approach*. New York: Harper, 1956. Pp. xvii + 697.
Rev. by A. W. Coats in *Economica*, new ser., XXIV, 164-66; by A. J. Youngson in *Econ. Jour.*, LXVII, 708-9; by Donald F. Gordon in *JPE*, LXV, 167-68. Contains adverse comments on Ricardo and some praise of Malthus as an economist, with a chapter on Mill.

Rolt, Lionel Thomas Caswall. *Isambard Kingdom Brunel: A Biography*. London: Longmans, Green. Pp. xv + 345.
Rev. by Adrian Brunel in *History Today*, VII, 636-37; by Eric Gillett in *NER*, CXLIX, 81; by A. J. P. Taylor in *NS*, Aug. 17, p. 204; by Charles Wilson in *S*, July 19, p. 115. Biography of the Victorian engineer who designed the ship, *Great Eastern*, and also the Great Western railway.

St. Clair, Oswald. *A Key to Ricardo*. London: Routledge & Kegan Paul. Pp. xxv + 363.
Rev. by N. H. Dobb in *Econ. Jour.*, LXVII, 498-99.

Saul, S. B. "The Economic Significance of 'Constructive Imperialism'." *JEH*, XVII, 173-92.

Saville, John. *Rural Depopulation in England and Wales 1851-1951*. London: Routledge & K. Paul. Pp. xvi + 253.
Noticed briefly in *TLS*, May 10, p. 295.

Schrier, Arnold. "Ireland and the American Emigration, 1850-1900." *DA*, XVII, 615.

Semmel, Bernard. "Sir William Ashley as 'Socialist of the Chair'." *Economica*, new ser., XXIV, 343-53.
Ashley brought from Oxford to Toronto, then to Harvard, then to Birmingham, the theories of the German historical school.

Sen, Surrendra Neth. *Eighteen Fifty-Seven*. London: Luzac. Pp. xxviii + 466.
Rev. by James Cameron in *NS*, Oct. 19, pp. 506-7. A general history of the Indian Mutiny.

Sen, Surrendra Nath. "The Indian Mutiny. I. The 'Mutiny' Reconsidered." *Listener,* May 16, pp. 783-84. See also H. T. Lambrick, "The Indian Mutiny. II. The Bengal Army and the Mutiny," May 23, pp. 813-15, and A. R. Mallick, "The Indian Mutiny. III. The Muslims and the 'Mutiny'," May 23, pp. 875-76.

Shepard, Ernest Howard. *Drawn From Memory.* Philadelphia: Lippincott. Pp. 190.
Rev. briefly in *LJ,* LXXXII, 3255; in *TLS,* Dec. 13, p. 754. Reminiscences by a *Punch* illustrator of his boyhood in the London of the 1880's.

Shepperson, Wilbur Stanley. *British Emigration to North America: Projects and Opinions in the Early Victorian Period.* Minneapolis: Univ. of Minnesota Pr. Pp. xvi + 302.
Rev. by W. C. Smith in *APSS,* CCCXIII, 187; by Helen I. Cowan in *JMH,* XXIX, 384-85; by G. S. Pryde in *Manchester Guardian,* Mar. 1, p. 6; by Roger V. Clements in *Mississippi Valley Hist. Rev.,* XLIV, 552-53. A study of the economic causes, official policies, and popular attitudes concerning British emigration during the late Georgian and early Victorian era.

Shock, Maurice. "Gladstone's Invasion of Egypt, 1882." *History Today,* VII, 351-57.

Smith, Colin Leonard. *The Embassy of Sir William White at Constantinople, 1886-1891.* London: Oxford Univ. Pr. Pp. xii + 183.
Rev. in *TLS,* Dec. 6, p. 734.

Spain, Nancy. *The Beeton Story.* 3d ed. London: Ward, Lock, 1956. Pp. 190.
Rev. in *TLS,* Jan. 4, p. 14. This new edition of a book originally entitled Mrs. Beeton and her Husband (see VB 1948, 249) contains new material on Samuel Beeton, an enterprising Victorian publisher of books and periodicals.

Spearman, Diana. *Democracy in England.* London: Rockliff. Pp. xviii + 238.
Rev. unfavorably by A. J. P. Taylor in *NS,* June 1, p. 714; in *TLS,* July 5, p. 407 ("scholarly, balanced and detached"). History of democracy in England since the first Reform Bill.

Stephenson, Lady. "Memories of Queen Victoria's Jubilees." *Listener,* July 4, pp. 13-14.

Stewart, Cecil. *The Stones of Manchester.* London: Edward Arnold, 1956. Pp. 144.

Rev. in *TLS,* June 14, p. 370. A study of the architecture, architects, and society of nineteenth-century Manchester.

Stigler, George J. "Perfect Competition, Historically Contemplated." *JPE,* LXV, 1-17.
A brief survey of the concept of competition, from Adam Smith to the present, with brief discussions of the theories of Cairnes, Jevons, Edgeworth, and Marshall.

Tappe, E. D. "General Gordon in Rumania." *Slavonic and East European Rev.,* XXXV, 566-72.

Taylor, A. J. P. *Englishmen and Others.* London: Hamish Hamilton, 1956. Pp. vii + 192.
Rev. by C. L. Mowat in *VS,* I, 98-99. Includes essays on Palmerston, Bright, Disraeli, and Cobbett.

Taylor, A. J. P. *The Trouble Makers: Dissent Over Foreign Policy, 1792-1939.* London: Hamish Hamilton. Pp. 207.
Rev. in *TLS,* June 21, p. 382.

Taylor, Overton H. *Economics and Liberalism: Collected Papers.* ("Harvard Economic Studies," Vol. XCVI.) Cambridge, Mass.: Harvard Univ. Pr., 1955. Pp. 321.
Rev. by Kurt Kloppholz in *Economica,* new ser., XXIV, 78-79.

Thomson, A. A. *The Great Cricketer.* London: Hale. Pp. 224.
Rev. in *TLS,* May 17, p. 307; by T. W. Hutchison in *VS,* I, 204. A biography of W. G. Grace.

Thornton, John L., and Wiles, Anna. "William Odling, 1829-1921." *Ann. Sci.,* XII (1956), 288-95.
A bibliography of the nineteenth-century chemist.

Towner, Donald C. "The Leeds Pottery and Its Wares." Part IV. *Apollo,* LXV, 169-72.
Part IV deals with nineteenth-century products of the Leeds Pottery.

Torr, Dona. *Tom Mann and His Times.* Vol. I: *1856-1890.* London: Lawrence and Wishart, 1956. Pp. 356.
Rev. by Norman MacKenzie in *NS,* Feb. 16, p. 210; by Asa Briggs in *VS,* I, 83-85; in *TLS,* Jan. 4, p. 10. This first part of a two-part biography carries the story of a notable Victorian labor leader up to 1889.

Travers, Morris W. *A Life of Sir William Ramsey.* London: Arnold, 1956. Pp. viii + 308.
Rev. in *TLS,* Feb. 22, p. 116; by A. R. Hall in *VS,* I, 187-89 ("of great value to

all who are attentive to the scientific and educational currents of its subject's lifetime"). A biography of the English chemist (1852-1916), discoverer of inert gasses and Nobel prize winner.

Tropp, Asher. *The School Teachers: The Growth of the Teaching Profession in England and Wales from 1800 to the Present Day.* London: Heinemann. Pp. viii + 286.
Rev. by John Roach in *CHJ*, XIII, 196-98; by F. R. Salter in *Econ. Jour.*, LXVII, 528-30; by M. C. Farquhar in *LJ*, LXXXII, 746. An account of the elementary school teachers since 1815.

Troughton, Marion. "Americans in Britain." *CR*, CXCII, 338-42.
Nineteenth-century impressions recorded by Washington Irving, Mrs. Stowe, Hawthorne, and Lowell.

Urwin, G. G. "Alfred Bunn 1796-1860: A Revaluation." *Theatre Notebook*, XI, 96-102.
A prominent theatre manager who tried unsuccessfully to make English opera pay.

Wade, E. K. *27 Years with Baden-Powell.* London: Blanford Pr. Pp. 160.
Rev. in *TLS*, Mar. 1, p. 131.

Wadham, Juliana. *Case of Cornelia Connelly.* . . . See VB 1956, 242.
Rev. in *CWd*, June, p. 240; by Chad Walsh in *HTB*, Apr. 21, p. 3; in *Listener*, Jan. 24, p. 164; by N. K. Burger in *NYTBR*, Apr. 21, p. 23; in *TLS*, Nov. 2, 1956, p. 653.

Walker, Frank Fish. "British Liberalism: Some Philosophic Origins. The Contributions of Adam Smith, Thomas Robert Malthus, Jeremy Bentham, and Herbert Spencer." *DA*, XVII, 2996-97.

Wallace, Elisabeth. *Goldwin Smith: Victorian Liberal.* Toronto: Toronto Univ. Pr. Pp. xii + 297.

Wearmouth, R. F. *Methodism and the Struggle of the Working Classes.* . . . See VB 1955, 246.
Rev. briefly by Edward Hughes in *DUJ*, L, 47.

Webb, R. K. "The Victorian Reading Public." *Universities Quart.*, XII, 24-44.

Weber, Bernard C. "An Unpublished Letter of Robert Owen to Viscount Palmerston (1847)." *N & Q*, new ser., IV, 486-87.
The letter deals with the Irish situation.

Weisskopf, Walter A. *The Psychology of Economics.* Chicago: Univ. of Chicago Pr., 1955. Pp. viii + 266.

Rev. by T. W. Hutchison in *Economica*, new ser., XXIV, 268; by Eli Ginzberg in *JPE*, LXV, 168-69. A Freudian analysis of the economic theories of Ricardo, Malthus, and Marshall.

Whates, Harold Grant. *The Birmingham Post, 1857-1957: A Centenary Retrospect.* Birmingham: Birmingham Post and Mail. Pp. xvi + 255.
Rev. in *TLS*, Dec. 20, p. 775.

White, Hope Costley. *Willoughby Hyett Dickinson, 1859-1943.* Gloucester: John Bellows, privately printed. Pp. 170.
Rev. in *TLS*, Feb. 15, p. 94. A biography of a Liberal politician.

White, Jon Manchip. "The Indian Mutiny." *History Today*, VII, 301-7, 373-80, 450-57.

Wickham, Edward Ralph. *Church and People in an Industrial City.* London: Lutterworth Pr. Pp. 292.
Rev. by John Raymond in *NS*, Dec. 21, pp. 856-57. Account of the religious life of Sheffield during the last two centuries.

Williams, David. *The Rebecca Riots.* . . . See VB 1956, 242.
Rev. by A. H. John in *EHR*, LXII, 339-41; by R. K. Webb in *JEH*, XVII, 84-85; by Francis H. Herrick in *JMH*, XXIX, 143-44.

Winther, Oscar O. "Promoting the American West in England, 1865-1890." *JEH*, XVI (1956), 506-13.

Woodruff, Douglas. *The Tichborne Claimant: A Victorian Mystery.* London: Hollis & Carter. Pp. xx + 479.
Rev. by DeLancey Ferguson in *HTB*, July 28, p. 5; by Letitia Fairfield in *NS*, June 22, pp. 813-14 (see also her correction of errors in this review, June 29, p. 841); by R. L. Duffus in *NYTBR*, Aug. 18, p. 5; by Evelyn Waugh in *S*, June 21, p. 816; by Allen Churchill in *SR*, Sept. 14, pp. 58-59; in *TLS*, June 28, p. 396 ("patient, devoted and altogether admirable").

Wordsworth, Andrew. "Portrait of a Greatuncle." *Listener*, Aug. 29, pp. 314-15.
On Charles Wordsworth (1806-92), Bishop of St. Andrews.

Wortham, Hugo. *Victorian Eton and Cambridge.* . . . See VB 1956, 243.
Rev. by Kenneth Rose in *NER*, CXLVI (1956), 179-81.

Young, A. F., and Ashton, E. T. *British Social Work in the Nineteenth Century.* . . . See VB 1956, 243.
Rev. by R. A. Lewis in *History*, XLII,

254-55.

Young, G. M., and Handcock, W. D. (eds.). *English Historical Documents.* Vol. XII, Part I: *1833-1874.* London: Eyre and Spottiswoode, 1956. Pp. xxiii + 1017.

Rev. by Norman Gash in *CHJ*, XIII, 194-96; by David Owen in *JMH*, XXIX, 268-69; unfavorably by Asa Briggs in *NS*, Mar. 2, p. 286; favorably in *TLS*, Jan. 25, p. 44; by Charles F. Mullett in *VS*, I, 90-91.

III. MOVEMENTS OF IDEAS AND LITERARY FORMS

Aiken, Henry David (ed.). *The Age of Ideology: The Nineteenth Century Philosophers.* Boston: Houghton-Mifflin. Pp. 283.

Rev. favorably by Albert William Levi in *VS*, I, 81-83. Selections, with commentary, from Kant, Mill, Comte, Marx, Spencer, and others.

Allen, Jeremiah Mervin. "The British Military Novel: 1825-1850." *DA*, XVII, 2265.

Includes mention of G. R. Gleig, W. H. Maxwell, C. J. Lever, George Wood, Thomas Hamilton, William Maginn.

Altick, Richard D. *The English Common Reader: A Social History of the Mass Reading Public, 1800-1900.* Chicago: Univ. of Chicago Pr. Pp. ix + 430.

Rev. by DeLancey Ferguson in *HTB*, Aug. 4, p. 5; by R. R. McClarren in *LJ*, LXXXII, 1522; briefly in *NCF*, XII, 256; by F. L. Mott in *NYTBR*, July 7, p. 5; by John T. Winterich in *SR*, Oct. 5, pp. 12-13.

Andrews, John S. "A Few 'Intermediaries' of German Literature in 19th-Century Britain." *N & Q*, new ser., IV, 315-16.

Andrews, John S. "The Reception of Fontane in Nineteenth-Century Britain." *MLR*, LII, 403-6.

Baylen, Joseph O., and Hogan, Patrick G. "W. T. Stead on the Art of Public Speaking." *QJS*, XLIII, 128-36.

Bayley, John. *The Romantic Survival. A Study in Poetic Evolution.* London: Constable. Pp. vii + 231.

Rev. by Peter Ure in *Listener*, July 25, pp. 133-35; by Jacques Vallette in *Mercure de France*, CCCXXXI, 162; by Angus McIntyre in *NER*, CXLVIII, 305-6; by John Jones in *NS*, Apr. 13, p. 492; by Graham Hough in *S*, Apr. 12, p. 490; in *TLS*, Apr. 5, p. 208; by Wallace Douglas in *VS*, I, 202-3. Traces the evolution and influence of romantic ideas and practice through the last 150 years.

Beck, Martha Ryan. "A Comparative Study of Prompt Copies of 'Hamlet' Used by Garrick, Booth, and Irving." *DA*, XVII, 1412.

Bentley, Eric. *A Century of Hero-Worship: A Study of the Idea of Heroism in Carlyle and Nietzsche, with Notes on Wagner, Spengler, Stefan George and D. H. Lawrence.* 2d. ed. Boston: Beacon Pr. Pp. 271.

Rev. briefly by Beatrice B. Libaire in *LJ*, LXXXII, 1878.

Beringouse, A. F. "Journey through *The Waste Land.*" *SAQ*, LVI, 79-90.

Illuminating account, contending that Eliot owes much to FitzGerald's translation of the *Rubáiyát* and to Thomson's *The City of Dreadful Night;* the final sentence states that "it is only by means of the Victorians that readers are able to travel freely through *The Waste Land.*"—W. D. T.

Blair, Walter. "The French Revolution and Huckleberry Finn." *MP*, LV, 21-35.

Discusses the influence on Mark Twain of Carlyle's *French Revolution* and Dickens' *Tale of Two Cities.*

Blake, John B. "Scientific Institutions since the Renaissance: Their Role in Medical Research." *PAPS*, CI, 31-62.

Includes very interesting discussion of how scientific research was supported in Victorian England: "although scientific societies proliferated, science still depended on privately financed research and institutions."

Bock, Kenneth E. *The Acceptance of Histories. . . .* See VB 1956, 243.

Rev. by Roscoe Hinkle in *VS*, I, 97-98.

Bøe, Alf. *From Gothic Revival to Functional Form.* ("Oslo Studies in English," No. 6.) Oslo: Oslo Univ. Pr. Pp. ix + 184. A study of theories of design in nineteenth-century England.

Boner, Harold A. *Hungry Generations. . . .* See VB 1956, 243.

Rev. by Conway Zirkle in *Isis*, XLVII (1956), 434-38.

Browne, Ray B. "Shakespeare in the Nineteenth-Century Songsters." *Shakespeare Quart.*, VIII, 207-18.

The songbooks studied were published in 1834, 1846, 1867.

Cairns, Paul Edward. "William Archer as Critic of Modern English Drama, 1882-1914." *DA*, XVII, 140-41.

Mentions Pinero, Henry A. Jones, Ibsen, Wilde, Barrie, Shaw.

Carson, William G. B. "*As You Like It* and the Stars: Nineteenth-Century Prompt

Books." *QJS*, XLIII, 117-27.

How the play was presented by Macready, Kean and Phelps.

Cecil, David. *The Fine Art of Reading, and Other Literary Studies*. London: Constable. Pp. ix + 221.

Rev. by Robert N. Linscott in *Amer. Scholar*, XXVI, 514-15; by Edward Wagenknecht in *Chicago Sunday Tribune*, June 23, p. 2; by Rod Nordell in *Christian Science Monitor*, June 19, p. 11; by David Daiches in *HTB*, July 21, p. 4; briefly by Beatrice B. Libaire in *LJ*, LXXXII, 1525; briefly in *NCF*, XII, 255; by Eric Gillett in *NER*, CXLIX, 135; by Ivor Brown in *New R*, July 15, p. 20; unfavorably by Walter Allen in *NS*, July 27, pp. 121-22; by DeLancey Ferguson in *NYTBR*, June 9, p. 7; by Peter Quennell in *S*, Aug. 2, pp. 167-68; by Carlos Baker in *SR*, Sept. 28, pp. 22-23; in *TLS*, Sept. 13, p. 546. Includes Lord David's Rede Lecture on Pater (see VB 1956, 261) and an essay on Conrad.

Clark, Jeanne Gabriel. "London in English Literature, 1880-1955." *DA*, XVII, 1761.

Includes treatment of Gissing, Moore, Symons, Henley, Conrad.

Clive, John. *Scotch Reviewers: The Edinburgh Review, 1802-1815*. Cambridge, Mass.: Harvard Univ. Pr. Pp. 224.

Rev. in *TLS*, June 7, p. 347 ("If one is looking for the reading matter which formed the climate of opinion in the reforming 1830's and 1840's, it will be found in the *Edinburgh Review* of Jeffrey, Horner, Brougham, and Sydney Smith").

Cole, George Douglas Howard. *The Second International. . . .* See VB 1956, 244.

Rev. by William Ebenstein in *APSS*, CCCIX, 190-91; favorably by Bert F. Hoselitz in *JPE*, LXV, 459-60.

Coveney, Peter. *Poor Monkey: The Child in Literature*. London: Rockliff. Pp. xiv + 297.

Rev. by Naomi Lewis in *NS*, Nov. 16, pp. 667-68; by Peter Quennell in *S*, Dec. 27, p. 901. Attitudes toward children reflected in poetry and fiction from the Romantic Revival to the twentieth century.

Daiches, David. *Critical Approaches to Literature. . . .* See VB 1956, 244.

Rev. briefly by John L. Bradley in *BA*, XXXI, 307.

Dalziel, Margaret. *Popular Fiction 100 Years Ago: An Unexplored Tract of Literary History*. London: Cohen & West. Pp. vii + 188.

Rev. in *TLS*, Dec. 13, p. 756. A study of the themes and popular appeal of fiction

serialized in journals like the *Family Herald*, which had predominantly working-class readers.

Davidson, Donald. *Still Rebels, Still Yankees, and Other Essays*. Baton Rouge: Louisiana State Univ. Pr. Pp. 284.

Rev. briefly by Virgil C. Lutes in *LJ*, LXXXII, 978.

DeBaun, Vincent Claud. "*Temple Bar:* Index of Victorian Middle-Class Thought." *DA*, XVII, 2607-8.

The 420-page dissertation here summarized will serve students of the period 1860-1906, showing much about the tastes, problems, and aspirations of the times among the middle class: trend to Conservatism politically, to religious tolerance, to literary realism. Many notable authors contributed. Early translations from Tolstoi, Turgenev, Chekhov, Daudet, and Balzac were printed. A useful study.—W. D. T.

Deneau, Daniel P. "Notes on the Image and the Novel." *VNL*, No. 12 (Autumn), pp. 27-29.

Concentrates on George Eliot.

DeSelincourt, Aubrey. *Six Great Poets*. London: Hamish Hamilton, 1956. Pp. 247.

Rev. by J. Loiseau in *Études anglaises*, X, 68-69. The six poets are Chaucer, Pope, Wordsworth, Shelley, Tennyson, and Browning.

Duncan, Robert W. "Byron and the London Literary Gazette." *Boston Univ. Studies in English*, II (1956), 240-50.

Eliot, T. S. *On Poetry and Poets*. London: Faber. Pp. 262.

Rev. by John Raymond in *NS*, Sept. 14, pp. 321-22; by R. L. Sleight in *S*, Oct. 11, p. 486; by John C. Kelly in *StI*, XLVI, 486-88; in *TLS*, Oct. 18, p. 624. Includes essays on Kipling and Yeats.

Engelman, Herta. "The Ideal English Gentlewoman in the Nineteenth Century: Her Education, Conduct, and Sphere." *DA*, XVI (1956), 2445-46.

Enkvist, Erik. *American Humour in England before Mark Twain. . . .* See VB 1953, 241.

Rev. by Lars Åhnebrink in *ESt*, XXXVIII, 226-27.

Fackler, Miriam Ernestine. "Death: Idea and Image in Some Later Victorian Lyrists." *DA*, XVII, 621-22.

Includes mention of C. Rossetti, F. Thompson, Hardy.

Fairchild, Hoxie Neale. *Religious Trends in English Poetry.* Vol. IV: *1830-1880, Chris-*

tianity and Romanticism in the Victorian Era. New York: Columbia Univ. Pr. Pp. x + 592.

Rev. by Robert B. Martin in *CE*, XIX, 90; briefly in *HTB*, Oct. 6, p. 12; by Hugh Fausset in *Manchester Guardian*, Sept. 3, p. 6; favorably by Douglas Bush in *VS*, I, 185-87.

Garbaty, Thomas Jay. "*The Savoy*, 1896: A Re-Edition of Representative Prose and Verse, with a Critical Introduction, and Biographical and Critical Notes." *DA*, XVII, 3014-15.

This 744-page dissertation employs numerous unpublished letters by Ernest Dowson, Arthur Symons, Stephane Mallarmé, Hubert Crackenthorpe, William Sharp, etc.; treats the Celtic Revival, occultism, the influence of French writers; uses unpublished MSS and letters as it gives biographical and critical sketches of 19 contributors, including Shaw, Conrad, Yeats, Dowson, etc. This is a critical edition of "the major English literary periodical in the Eighteen-Nineties."—W. D. T.

Gettmann, Royal A. "Colburn-Bentley and the March of Intellect." *Studies in Bibliography*, IX, 197-213.

Gooch, G. P. "Some Great English Historians. II." *CR*, CXC, 19-24. (For Part I see VB 1956, 245.)

On Lecky, Seeley, Acton, Maitland, Bury, Trevelyan, and Toynbee.

Gray, Donald Joseph. "Victorian Verse Humor: 1830-1870." *DA*, XVII, 1083.

Includes treatment of Bulwer-Lytton, Bailey, Austin, Hood, Barham, Beeton, Brough, Aytoun, Martin, Thackeray, Calverley, Lear, Carroll, Gilbert.

Groom, Bernard. *The Diction of Poetry.* . . . See VB 1956, 245.

Rev. by Burns Martin in *Dalhousie Rev.*, XXXVI, 419-21; by John Arthos in *JEGP*, LVI, 473-76; by V. de S. Pinto in *N & Q*, new ser., IV, 364-65; by Wilhelmina Gordon in *QQ*, LXIV, 151-52; briefly in *TLS*, Jan. 25, pp. 54-55.

Gurewitch, Morton L. "European Romantic Irony." *DA*, XVII, 1554.

Includes mention of Carlyle, Leopardi, Musset, Heine, Gautier, Stendhal, Flaubert, Baudelaire, etc.

Haines, George. *German Influence Upon English Education and Science, 1800-1866.* ("Connecticut College Monograph," No. 6.) New London, Conn.: Connecticut College. Pp. 107.

Rev. unfavorably by R. K. Webb in *JMH*, XXIX, 426.

Hammer, Carl, Jr. "Nineteenth Century German Drama in English." *German Quart.*, XXX, 32-36.

Harris, Truett Wilson. "Victorien Sardow in the Modern Theater." *DA*, XVI (1956), 2458.

Includes treatment of influence of Sardow on G. B. Shaw.

Harrison, J. F. C. "The Victorian Gospel of Success." *VS*, I, 155-64.

Originally "a means of personal and social advance for the working classes," in the 1850's self-help was used by the middle class to strengthen "independent citizenship as opposed to ideas of collective or communal responsibility for social ills."

Hemmings, F. W. J. "The Origin of the Terms *Naturalisme, Naturaliste.*" *French Studies*, VIII (1954), 109-21.

"Had it not been for Zola's 'plugging' of the word . . . in the late 'seventies, naturalism would probably never have become so momentous a word . . . in France and in most other countries," including England.

Hicks, John H. "The Critical History of Tristram Shandy." *Boston Univ. Studies in English*, II (1956), 65-84.

Hillegas, Mark Robert. "The Cosmic Voyage and the Doctrine of Inhabited Worlds in Nineteenth-Century English Literature." *DA*, XVII, 2001-2.

Hitchcock, Henry-Russell. "High Victorian Gothic." *VS*, I, 47-71.

Gothic architecture in England from the 1850's to the 1870's was eclectic, polychromatic, "realistic" in its use of crude, structural detail, and reflected the influence of Ruskin rather than Pugin.

Hoggart, Richard. *The Uses of Literacy: Aspects of Working-class Life, with Special Reference to Publications and Entertainments.* London: Chatto & Windus. Pp. 319.

Rev. briefly by George Adelman in *LJ*, LXXXII, 1887; favorably by J. F. C. Harrison in *NS*, Mar. 2, pp. 283-84. A study of popular magazines, songs, and postcards of the 1890-1920 era, as compared with the same forms of popular art today.

Holroyd, Stuart. *Emergence from Chaos.* London: Gollancz. Pp. 222.

Rev. by John Jones in *NS*, July 20, p. 90. Contains a brief but, according to the review, excellent sketch of Yeats.

Houghton, Walter Edwards. *The Victorian*

Frame of Mind, 1830-1870. New Haven: Yale Univ. Pr. Pp. xvii + 467.

Rev. by Fraser Neiman in *Amer. Scholar,* XXVII, 126-28; briefly in *NCF,* XII, 256; by Perry Miller in *NEQ,* XXX, 407-9; by George Woodcock in *SR.* July 27, p. 19; in *TLS,* Dec. 27, p. 786; by Geoffrey Tillotson in *VS,* I, 184-85; by W. C. DeVane in *YR,* XLVII, 108-12. Deriving his data from literature in the broad sense (letters, diaries, sermons, and tracts as well as poetry and fiction), Houghton explores general Victorian ideas about life, rather than formal doctrines ("isms"). The result is richly informative for all students of Victorian literature and history.—O. M.

Howe, Irving. *Politics and the Novel.* New York: Horizon Pr. Pp. 251.

Rev. by Otto Friedrich in *Amer. Scholar,* XXVI, 515; by Melvin Maddocks in *Christian Science Monitor,* Apr. 25, p. 7; by J. M. Duffy in *Commonweal,* May 10, p. 159; by Lewis Dabney in *N,* June 15, p. 529; briefly in *NCF,* XII, 174; by Donald Malcolm in *New R,* Apr. 29, p. 19; by Frank O'Connor in *NYTBR,* Mar. 31, p. 4; by Hilton Kramer in *ParR,* XXIV, 441-46.

Kaufman, Marjorie Ruth. "Henry James's Comic Discipline: The Use of the Comic in the Structure of His Early Fiction." *DA,* XV (1955), 2534. (Inadvertently omitted earlier.)

Includes treatment of influence upon James of some Victorians, especially Tennyson and Browning.

Kegel, Charles Herbert. "Medieval-Modern Contrasts Used for a Social Purpose in the Work of William Cobbett, Robert Southey, A. Welby Pugin, Thomas Carlyle, John Ruskin, and William Morris." *DA,* XV (1955), 2526-27. (Inadvertently omitted earlier.)

Keller, Ernest. *Kulturbilder aus Viktorianischen Autobiographien....* See VB 1955, 248.

Rev. briefly by Sylvère Monod in *Études anglaises,* X, 64-65.

Kelly, Thomas. *George Birkbeck: Pioneer of Adult Education.* Liverpool: Liverpool Univ. Pr. Pp. 380.

Rev. in *TLS,* Aug. 23, p. 510 ("scholarly and illuminating").

Kermode, Frank. *Romantic Image.* London: Routledge & K. Paul. Pp. xi + 171.

Rev. by J. G. Weightman in *NS,* June 22, pp. 812-13; by John C. Kelly in *StI,* XLVI, 492-93; in *TLS,* May 17, p. 304 ("extremely important").

Kochman, Andrew John. "Realism in the Early and Middle Nineteenth Century British Theatre." *DA,* XVII, 693-94.

Langbaum, Robert. *The Poetry of Experience: The Dramatic Monologue in Modern Literary Tradition.* London: Chatto & Windus. Pp. 246.

Rev. by Donald Hall in *Amer. Scholar,* XXVII, 130; by A. W. Phinney in *Christian Science Monitor,* July 25, p. 5; by Chad Walsh in *HTB,* Aug. 4, p. 6; by Philip Larkin in *Manchester Guardian,* July 23, p. 4; by John Jones in *NS,* Aug. 3, p. 153; by John Bayley in *S,* July 26, p. 143; in *TLS,* Aug. 2, p. 472.

Lauterbach, Charles E., and Lauterbach, Edward S. "The Nineteenth Century Three-Volume Novel." *BSP,* LI, 262-302.

This history of the three-decker includes statistical studies of over one hundred such novels.

Lawrence, Elwood P. *Henry George in the British Isles.* East Lansing, Mich.: Michigan State Univ. Pr. Pp. 203.

Lewis, Naomi. *A Visit to Mrs. Wilcox.* London: Cresset Pr. Pp. viii + 246.

Rev. by Eric Gillett in *NER,* CXLIX, 283; by K. John in *NS,* Nov. 2, p. 576; favorably in *TLS,* Nov. 22, p. 707. Includes essays on the Brownings, Mrs. Gaskell, Clare, Tennyson, Charlotte Mew, Tupper, Charlotte Yonge, Wilkie Collins, and Lady Ritchie.

Liptzin, Sol. "The English Reception of Heine." *VNL,* No. 11 (Spring), pp. 14-16.

Loomis, Emerson Robert. "The Anti-Gothic English Novel." *DA,* XVII, 3003.

The anti-Gothic writers "helped to prepare the way for the nineteenth century novel."

Lorch, Fred W. "Mark Twain's Public Lectures in England in 1873." *AL,* XXIX, 297-304.

English response to Twain's humor.

Maas, John. *The Gingerbread Age: A View of Victorian America.* New York: Rinehart. Pp. 212.

Rev. unfavorably by Richard Janson in *VS,* I, 201-2. A survey, profusely illustrated, of Victorian architecture in America from 1840 to 1880.

Madsen, Stephan Tschudi. *Sources of Art Nouveau.* Trans. Ragnar Christopherson. New York: Wittenborn, 1956. Pp. 488.

Rev. by A. S. Plaut in *LJ,* LXXXII, 1240; by Georgine Oeri in *SR,* May 11, p. 18; favorably by James Grady in *VS,* I, 189-

92. Effect of new art (including ideas of Beardsley and Ruskin) on curlicued decoration and on lesser crafts—household ornament and on appliances—in the 1890's and early twentieth century.

Metzger, Lore. "*Faust* in England: 1800-1850." *DA*, XVI (1956), 2152.

Miles, Josephine. *Eras and Modes in English Poetry*. Berkeley: Univ. of California Pr. Pp. 233.
Includes chapters on "The Classical Mode of the Late Nineteenth Century," Hopkins, and Yeats.

Morgan, Edwin. "Women and Poetry." *CJ*, III (August, 1950), 643-73. (Inadvertently omitted earlier.)
Includes treatment of E. Brontë, E. B. Browning.

Newman, Charles. *The Evolution of Medical Education in the Nineteenth Century*. New York: Oxford Univ. Pr. Pp. x + 340.
Rev. by John L. Thornton in *N & Q*, new ser., IV, 413-14; in *TLS*, Oct. 18, p. 629.

O'Connor, Frank. *The Mirror in the Roadway.* . . . See VB 1956, 246.
Rev. by John Peter in *KR*, XIX, 153-58; by David Paul in *Listener*, May 23, pp. 845-46; by Jacques Vallette in *Mercure de France*, CCCXXXI, 322; briefly in *NCF*, XI, 317; by Tom Hopkinson in *S*, June 14, p. 783; by Dorothy Van Ghent in *YR*, XLVI, 440-42.

Pankhurst, Richard K. P. *The Saint Simonians, Mill and Carlyle*. London: Sidgwick & Jackson. Pp. x + 154.

Passmore, John Arthur. *A Hundred Years of Philosophy*. London: Duckworth. Pp. 523.
Rev. in *TLS*, Sept. 20, p. 565 ("a masterpiece of digestion and exposition"). A study of philosophical movements and ideas from 1843 to the present.

Paulus, Gretchen. "Beerbohm Tree and 'The New Drama'." *TQ*, XXVII, 103-15.
On Tree's production of *An Enemy of the People*, 1893.

Perkin, H. J. "The Origins of the Popular Press." *History Today*, VII, 425-34.
Discounts the idea that the popular press had its origins in the Education Act of 1870; before mid-century ballads, sensational serial novels, and Sunday papers like *Bell's* and *Reynold's* found a literate working-class audience.

Peters, Robert L. "Whistler and the English Poets of the 1890's." *MLQ*, XVIII, 251-61.
The influence of Whistler's "impressions," "nocturnes," and "harmonies" on Wilde, Symons, Henley, and others.

Phelps, Gilbert. *The Russian Novel in English Fiction.* . . . See VB 1956, 246.
Rev. by Howard Sergeant in *CR*, CXCII, 349-50; by V. S. Pritchett in *NS*, Apr. 6, pp. 448-49; favorably by Harold Orel in *VS*, I, 197-98.

Phelps, Gilbert. "Russian Realism and English Fiction." *CJ*, III (February, 1950), 277-91. (Inadvertently omitted earlier.)
Mentions Gissing, Moore, Stevenson, Gosse, and many other Victorians.

Pipes, Bishop Newton, Jr. "The Poetry and Drama of the English Romantics and Early Victorians as Seen by the *Revue des Deux Mondes*, 1838-1848." *DA*, XVII, 364.

Pratt, William C., Jr. "Revolution without Betrayal: James, Pound, Eliot and the European Tradition." *DA*, XVII, 2600.

Praz, Mario. *The Hero in Eclipse in Victorian Fiction.* . . . See VB 1956, 247.
Rev. by R. J. Schoeck in *America*, Sept. 8, 1956, pp. 538-40; by John Holloway in *MLN*, LXXII, 293-95; by John Holloway in *MLR*, LII, 428-29; by George H. Ford in *MP*, LIV, 215-16.

Proctor, Mortimer R. *The English University Novel*. ("University of California Publications, English Studies," No. 15.) Berkeley: Univ. of California Pr. Pp. ix + 228.
Rev. by Noel Annan in *JEGP*, LVI, 642-46; by David Robertson, Jr. in *VS*, I, 204-5.

Rathbun, John Wilbert. "The Development of Historical Literary Criticism in America, 1800-1860." *DA*, XVI (1956), 2448.
Shows some influence of Carlyle, etc.

Reinhold, Ernest. "The Reception of Franz Grillparzer's Works in England during the Nineteenth Century." *DA*, XVII, 146.

Richardson, Mary Kathleen. *Sudden Splendor*. New York: Sheed & Ward. Pp. 242.
The biography of a nineteenth-century English convert to Catholicism who later became Superior General of the Order of the Sacred Heart.

Roach, John. "Liberalism and the Victorian Intelligentsia." *CHJ*, XIII, 58-81.
A valuable contribution to the political and intellectual history of the later Victorian Age. By examining with special care the political opinions of "old liberals" like J. F. Stephen and Sir Henry Maine, the author demonstrates impressively that during the second half of the nineteenth century Victorian intellectuals were evincing a growing distrust of popular government, a distrust which manifested itself

most clearly in the controversy over Gladstone's Home Rule Bill of 1886.—R. A. D.

Roll-Hansen, Diderik. *The Academy, 1869-1879; Victorian Intellectuals in Revolt.* Copenhagen: Rosenkilde and Bagger. Pp. 237.
Rev. briefly in *QR*, CCXCV, 480-81; by Gordon Haight in *VS*, I, 194-96.

Roppen, Georg. *Evolution and Poetic Belief: A Study in Some Victorian and Modern Writers.* ("Oslo Studies in English," No. 5.) Oslo: Oslo Univ. Pr., 1956. Pp. xi + 475.
Rev. briefly in *TLS*, June 14, p. 370. A study of evolutionary motifs in some Victorian and modern English poets and writers, from the younger Tennyson and Browning to H. G. Wells. "Whereas previous scholarship has stressed the influence of Darwin, the present author maintains that his writers have, almost exclusively, been neo-Lamarckians—inspired by a faith in creative and purposive evolution."

Rose, Edgar Smith. "James Gibbons Huneker: Critic of the Seven Arts." *DA*, XVII, 1343.
Treats the influence upon a famous American critic of Pater, Wilde, Swinburne.

Rosenblum, Robert. "British Painting vs. Paris." *ParR*, XXIV, 95-100.
Rosenblum, commenting on the Museum of Modern Art's survey of British painting of the last century and a half, notes that the Pre-Raphaelites attracted the most attention, because they were in such violent collision with Parisian values. "In short, these paintings demonstrated that in the 1850's, in the white heat of their fervor, the pre-Raphaelites were able to persuade us that their alien values were genuine." Constable and Turner, of course, proved revelations to many unfamiliar with the British tradition, which Rosenblum happily describes as the "marriage of precise fact and intense feeling, . . ."—F. G. T.

Rowell, George. *The Victorian Theatre.* . . . See VB 1956, 247.
Rev. by Sybil Rosenfeld in *MLR*, LII, 595; by John H. McDowell in *QJS*, XLIII, 206-7; briefly in *Theatre Arts*, XLI (April), 94; by St. Vincent Troubridge in *Theatre Notebook*, XI, 63-64; in *TLS*, Mar. 8, p. 148.

Ryals, Clyde de L. "Decadence in British Literature before the *Fin de Siècle*." *DA*, XVII, 3004.
Attempts to show that the so-called Decadent Movement was not entirely the result of borrowings from the French; finds decadent elements in the works of Keats, Tennyson, Rossetti, Swinburne, and especially Pater.

Sampson, Ronald Victor. *Progress in the Age of Reason: The Seventeenth Century to the Present Day.* Cambridge, Mass.: Harvard Univ. Pr., 1956. Pp. 259.
Rev. favorably in *TLS*, Mar. 29, p. 193. Discusses the idea and its influence from the seventeenth century to the present.

Sanders, Charles Richard. *Lytton Strachey: His Mind and Art.* New Haven: Yale Univ. Pr. Pp. 381.

Schorer, Mark (ed.). *Society and Self in the Novel.* . . . See VB 1956, 247.
Rev. briefly by Harriet Zinnes in *BA*, XXXI, 427; by Michael Harrington in *Commonweal*, Jan. 25, p. 444; by Maxwell Geismar in *N*, Nov. 10, 1956, p. 408; briefly in *NCF*, XII, 94.

Shawe-Taylor, Desmond. "The Kingdom Revived." *NS*, June 8, pp. 733-34.
A critical essay on Elgar's position in the contemporary concert hall. Only *Gerontius* and the *Enigma Variations* hold permanent place in the repertory.

Shumaker, Wayne. *English Autobiography.* . . . See VB 1956, 247.
Rev. by Harold E. Briggs in *Personalist*, XXXVIII, 218-19.

Sterling, Elwyn Franklin. "The Theory of Long Prose Fiction in France, 1750-1830." *DA*, XVII, 1771.

Svaglic, Martin J. "Method in the Study of Victorian Prose: Another View." *VNL*, No. 11 (Spring), pp. 1-5.

Thomson, Patricia. *The Victorian Heroine.* . . . See VB 1956, 248.
Rev. by Phyllis Bentley in *Brontë Society Transactions*, XIII, 153-54; by Mario Praz in *MLR*, LII, 593-95; by Charles Wilson in *S*, Jan. 25, p. 120; briefly by Betty Miller in *TC*, CLXI, 501-2; in *TLS*, Jan. 11, p. 21.

Tylecote, Mabel. *The Mechanics' Institutes of Lancashire and Yorkshire before 1851.* Manchester: Manchester Univ. Pr. Pp. x + 346.

Underwood, V. P. *Verlaine et l'Angleterre.* . . . See VB 1956, 248.
Rev. by Antoine Fongaro in *Rev. de litt. comp.*, XXXI, 134-38.

Wain, John. *Preliminary Essays.* London: Macmillan. Pp. x + 196.
Rev. by Jacques Vallette in *Mercure de France*, CCCXXXI, 543; favorably by John Raymond in *NS*, Aug. 10, p. 179; by R. George Thomas in *RES*, new ser., VIII,

451-54; by Donat O'Donnell in S, Aug. 16, pp. 223-24. Includes essays on Tennyson, Browning, Hopkins, Housman, and Yeats.

Wallis, Nevile (ed.). *A Victorian Canvas: The Memoirs of W. P. Frith, R. A.* London: Bles. Pp. 238.

Rev. by Raymond Postgate in NS, Dec. 14, pp. 829-30; by Peter Quennell in S, Nov. 8, p. 622; in TLS, Nov. 15, p. 684. Frith's *My Autobiography* (1887) and *Further Reminiscences* (1888) condensed and illustrated.

West, Rebecca. *The Court and the Castle: Some Treatments of a Recurrent Theme.* New Haven: Yale Univ. Pr. Pp. 319.

Rev. by R. B. Dooley in CWd, CLXXXVI, 233; by Paul Pickrel in Harper's, CCXV (November), 84-86; by Marvin Lowenthal in HTB, Nov. 10, p. 1; by Louis Barron in LJ, LXXXII, 2541; by Dachine Rainer in New R, Nov. 25, p. 18; by Newton Arvin in NYTBR, Nov. 3, p. 28; by J. W. Krutch in SR, Oct. 26, p. 21. Contains material on many major Victorian novelists.

Willey, Basil. *More Nineteenth-Century Studies: A Group of Honest Doubters.* . . . See VB 1956, 248.

Rev. by J. F. Glaser in AHR, LXIII, 184; by Jerome H. Buckley in CE, XIX, 90; favorably by L. Cazamian in *Études anglaises*, X, 266-67; by J. B. Brebner in JMH, XXIX, 269-70; by H. I'A. F. in *Manchester Guardian*, Jan. 18, p. 4; by R. V. Sampson in VS, I, 76-78; by W. C. DeVane in YR, XLVII, 108-12.

Wimsatt, William K., and Brooks, Cleanth. *Literary Criticism: A Short History.* New York: Knopf. Pp. 755.

Rev. briefly by J. P. Pritchard in BA, XXXI, 425; by Perry Miller in *Christian Science Monitor*, Apr. 25, p. 7; by H. T. Moore in NYTBR, Aug. 4, p. 4; by Marie Hochmuth in QJS, XLIII, 312-13.

Wittrock, Verna Dorothy. "The Re-Emergence of Realism in the Minor English Domestic Novel, 1824-1850." DA, XVII, 1344.

Includes mention of Harriet Martineau, W. and M. Howitt, Catherine Gore, Frances Trollope, Mary Sherwood, Harriet Mozley, Elizabeth Sewell, Lady Georgiana Fullerton, Charlotte Yonge, Frederika Bremer, Anne Marsh-Caldwell.

Wong, Helene Har Lin. "The Late Victorian Theatre: As Reflected in *The Theatre*, 1878-1897." DA, XV (1955), 2347. (Inadvertently omitted earlier.)

Wood, Herbert George. *Belief and Unbelief since 1850.* . . . See VB 1955, 250.

Rev. by George A. Foote in Isis, XLVII (1956), 427-28.

Worth, George J. "The English 'Maupassant' School of the 1890's: Some Reservations." MLN, LXXII, 337-40.

Wright, H. G. *Boccaccio in England: From Chaucer to Tennyson.* London: Athlone Pr. Pp. xiv + 495.

Young, Percy M. (ed.). *Letters of Edward Elgar, and Other Writings.* London: Bles, 1956. Pp. xxiii + 371.

Rev. by Desmond Shawe-Taylor in NS, Mar. 16, p. 344; by Colin Mason in S, Feb. 15, p. 215. A selection, covering the period 1882-1933.

Zabel, Morton Dauwen. *Craft and Character: Texts, Method, and Vocation in Modern Fiction.* New York: Viking Pr. Pp. xv + 331.

Rev. by Oscar Cargill in *Chicago Rev.*, XI, pp. 99-102; by Milton Rugoff in HTB, July 21, p. 6; by Rose Macaulay in Listener, Oct. 3, p. 530; briefly in NCF, XII, 172; by Horace Gregory in NYTBR, July 21, p. 10; by David Daiches in SR, Apr. 13, p. 42; favorably in TLS, Sept. 13, p. 546. Discusses Dickens, Hardy, Butler, Conrad, and "the terms of the appeal" from the nineteenth to the twentieth century.

IV. INDIVIDUAL AUTHORS

ARNOLD, MATTHEW (see also III, Fairchild, Wimsatt).

Christensen, Merton A. "Thomas Arnold's Debt to German Theologians: A Prelude to Matthew Arnold's *Literature and Dogma*." MP, LV, 14-20.

An admirably succinct and lucid account of Thomas Arnold's debt to the German biblical critics who, like Schleiermacher, "mediated" between the destructive attacks of rationalist critics and the uniformed fervor of the Pietists.—R. A. D.

Donovan, Robert A. "Philomela: A Major Theme in Arnold's Poetry." VNL, No. 12 (Autumn), pp. 1-6.

Dyson, A. E. "The Last Enchantments." RES, new ser., VIII, 257-65.

In this highly rewarding analysis of *The Scholar Gipsy* Dyson replies to G. Wilson Knight's "*The Scholar Gipsy:* An Interpretation" (see VB 1955, 251).—O. M.

Eells, John Shepard, Jr. *The Touchstones of Matthew Arnold.* . . . See VB 1956, 249.
Rev. by Asa Briggs in Sci. and Soc., XXI, 187-89.

Holloway, John. "Milton and Arnold." *EC*, VII, 226-28.

Johnson, Wendell Stacy. "Matthew Arnold's Poetic Imagery." *DA*, XVII, 3016-17.

Müller-Schwefe, Gerhard. *Das persönliche Menschenbild Matthew Arnolds in der dichterischen Gestaltung.* Tübingen: M. Niemeyer, 1955. Pp. 292.

Rev. by W. H. G. Armytage in *RES*, new ser., VIII, 349-50.

Neiman, Fraser. "Some Newly Attributed Contributions of Matthew Arnold to the *Pall Mall Gazette*." *MP*, LV, 84-92.

An important contribution to Arnold's bibliography.

Neiman, Fraser. "The Zeitgeist of Matthew Arnold." *PMLA*, LXXII, 977-96.

How Arnold used the term "Zeitgeist" and the meanings it had for him.

Perrine, Laurence. "Arnold's *The Scholar Gipsy* and *Thyrsis*." *Ex*, XV, Item 33.

Further argument against the proposition that the Gipsy Scholar symbolizes escape from responsibility.

Raleigh, John Henry. *Matthew Arnold and American Culture.* Berkeley: Univ. of California Pr. Pp. xii + 301.

Spector, Robert Donald. "Eliot, Pound, and the Conservative Tradition." *History of Ideas News Letter*, III (April), 2-5.

Modern poets are in Arnold's tradition of social criticism, but Arnold remained truly concerned while the social criticism of modern poets takes the form of the rejection of society.

Templeman, William D. "Matthew Arnold and the American Way." *Ed. Forum*, XXI, 429-36.

Application of Arnold's "Civilization in the United States" to modern pressure for conformity.

Tillotson, Kathleen. "Matthew Arnold and Carlyle." *Proc. British Acad.*, 1956, Vol. XLII, 133-53.

An important study, well documented; examines the complexity of Arnold's response to the great influence of Carlyle, "his acceptance and his rebellion"; throws light on some of Arnold's poems; and shows the very great impact of Carlyle on Arnold's "Emerson" lecture.—W. D. T.

Woodward, Frances J. *The Doctor's Disciples.* . . . See VB 1954, 243.

Rev. briefly by L. C. B. in *Études anglaises*, X, 160-61.

Worth, Peter. "A Source of Excellence: Two of Matthew Arnold's Terms Adapted."

Prairie Schooner, XXXI, 219-27.

BARHAM (see also III, Gray).

Gettmann, Royal A. "Barham and Bentley." *JEGP*, LVI, 337-46.

On Barham's work for *Bentley's Miscellany*, especially the *Ingoldsby Legends*. Based on unpublished letters.

BARING-GOULD. Purcell, William. *Onward Christian Soldier: A Life of Sabine Baring-Gould, 1834-1924.* London: Longmans. Pp. vii + 188.

Rev. briefly in *LJ*, LXXXII, 1970; by Eric Gillett in *NER*, CXLVIII, 248; by Andrew Wordsworth in *NS*, Apr. 13, pp. 493-94; by Karl Miller in *S*, May 24, p. 686; in *TLS*, Apr. 12, p. 223.

BARRIE (see also III, Cairns).

When Wendy Grew Up: An Afterthought, London: Nelson. Pp. 32.

Rev. unfavorably by Naomi Lewis in *NS*, Dec. 28, pp. 880-81. A hitherto unpublished scene, an epilogue to *Peter Pan*, which was performed only once, at the end of the last performance of the third season, 1907-1908.

Grotjahn, Martin. "The Defenses against Creative Anxiety in the Life and Work of James Barrie." *Amer. Imago*, XIV, 143-48.

Skinner, John. "James M. Barrie, or The Boy Who Wouldn't Grow Up." *Amer. Imago*, XIV, 111-41.

BEERBOHM. *Mainly on the Air.* Enl. ed. London: Heinemann. Pp. 192.

Rev. by Richard Mayne in *NS*, Dec. 21, pp. 857-58; by Bernard Levin in *S*, Dec. 13, p. 839; in *TLS*, Dec. 27, p. 787. A new edition with several additional essays.

Pearson, Hesketh. "The Incomparable Max." *Theatre Arts*, XLI (August), 16-17, 84-85.

Raymond, John. "The Unmaximilian Max." *NS*, June 8, p. 736.

Searle, Ronald. "Note on Max Beerbohm." *NER*, CXLVIII, 299.

Stanford, Derek. "Sir Max Beerbohm." *Dublin Mag.*, new ser., XXXI (October-December, 1956), 34-38.

BLUNT (see II, Adams).

BORROW. Meyers, Robert Rex. "George Borrow: His Reputation, Motifs, and Stylistic Techniques." *DA*, XVII, 2269-70.

BOUCICAULT. Rohrig, Gladys May. "An Analysis of Certain Acting Editions and Promptbooks of Plays by Dion Boucicault." *DA*, XVII, 1155.

BRAY. *A Voyage from Utopia.* Ed. M. F. Lloyd-Prichard. London: Lawrence & Wishart. Pp. 192.
Rev. by J. F. C. Harrison in *NS*, Mar. 30, pp. 416-17; in *TLS*, Feb. 22, p. 111. A hitherto unpublished Utopia, written in 1840-41, by a pre-Marx Socialist.

BRONTËS (see also I, Dickson; III, Morgan).

Bentley, Phyllis. *The Brontës.* ("Novelist's Series," No. 2.) London: Barker. Pp. 127. Originally published, London, Home & Van Thal, 1947.

Blondel, Jacques. *Emily Brontë: expérience spirituelle et création poétique.* . . . See VB 1956, 250.
Rev. by Francis J. Carmody in *NCF*, XII, 169-70.

Bluestone, George. *Novels into Film.* Baltimore: Johns Hopkins Pr. Pp. 237.
Rev. by Edward Kessler in *Amer. Scholar*, XXVI, 515; by E. F. Walbridge in *LJ*, LXXXII, 1523-24. *Wuthering Heights* is included.

Brontë Society, Transactions and Other Publications of.
Vol. XIII, No. 2 (Part 67), has items: Lewis, C. Day, "The Poetry of Emily Brontë [Her poetry gives us an image of man's inveterate, vain yearning for freedom.] (pp. 83-99); Ratchford, Fannie E., "The Loneliness of a Brontë Cousin" [Eliza Jane Kingston] (pp. 100-10); Marsdèn, Hilda, "The Scenic Background of Wuthering Heights" (pp. 111-30); Oram, Eanne, "Emily and F. D. Maurice, Some Parallels of Thought" (pp. 131-40); "Letters from Charlotte to Francis Bennoch" [3 new letters transcribed, with one facsimile] (pp. 140-44); Stollard, Mary L., "The Pupils of the Brontës" (pp. 145-48); Holgate, Ivy, "The Cottage in the Wood" [photo. and account of the locale of Mr. Brontë's tale] (pp. 149-52); "A Brontë T. V. Programme" (pp. 155-56); "The 63rd Annual Meeting" (pp. 157-67); "The Brontë Parsonage Museum" [report for 1956; lists additions to museum and library] (pp. 168-71).

Crandall, Norma. *Emily Brontë; A Psychological Portrait.* Rindge, N. H.: Richard R. Smith. Pp. 160.
Rev. briefly by Beatrice B. Libaire in *LJ*, XXXII, 3200.

Korg, Jacob. "The Problem of Unity in *Shirley*." *NCF*, XII, 125-36.

Werkmeister, Lucyle. "The Great Brontë Robbery." *Prairie Schooner*, XXXI, 237-46.

Willis, Irene Cooper. *The Brontës.* London: Duckworth. Pp. 144.

Woodring, Carl R. "The Narrators of *Wuthering Heights*." *NCF*, XI, 298-305.

BROUGHAM. Hawes, Frances. *Henry Brougham.* London: Cape. Pp. 326.
Rev. by W. H. Hughes in *NS*, July 13, p. 57; by J. H. Plumb in *S*, June 7, pp. 757-58; in *TLS*, June 7, p. 347; by N. Gash in *VS*, I, 206.

BROWNINGS (see also I, Gordan; III, De Selincourt, Fairchild, Kaufman, Langbaum, Lewis, Morgan, Roppen, Wain).

Altick, Richard D. "Browning's 'Karshish' and Saint Paul." *MLN*, LXXII, 494-96.

Corrigan, Beatrice (trans. and ed.). *Curious Annals: New Documents Relating to Browning's Roman Murder Story.* . . . See VB 1956, 251.
Rev. briefly by John Henry Raleigh in *BA*, XXXI, 419; by Charles T. Dougherty in *MLN*, LXXII, 295-97.

Dahl, Curtis. "*Neblaretai* and *Rattei* in Browning's *Aristophanes' Apology*." *MLN*, LXXII, 271-73.

DeVane, William Clyde. *A Browning Handbook.* . . . See VB 1956, 251.
Rev. by W. O. Raymond in *MLN*, LXXII, 452-53.

Dudley, Fred A. "*Hy, Zy, Hine*." Research Studies of the State College of Washington, XXV (*Bundy-Kies Festschrift*), 63-68.

Duffin, Henry Charles. *Amphibian: A Reconsideration of Browning.* . . . See VB 1956, 251.
Rev. briefly by Floyd Zulli, Jr. in *BA*, XXXI, 81; by H. J. McLachlan in *HJ*, LV, 193-94; by Donald Smalley in *MLN*, LXXII, 137-38; by W. C. DeVane in *MLR*, LII, 265-66.

Federle, Walter. *Robert Brownings dramatisches Experiment* . . . . See VB 1955, 254.
Rev. by W. O. Raymond in *Études anglaises*, X, 164-65.

Henry, Marjorie Ruth. "The Pope in *The Ring*." *DA*, XVII, 2010.
Proposes a new reading of parts of *The Ring and the Book*, especially the Book of the Pope; contends that the Pope "is not just Browning's mouthpiece, and that he is a questioning, fallible old man"; tries to place the Pope back properly "in the ring of prejudiced speakers." This is notable.—W. D. T.

Hill, Archibald A. "Pippa's Song: Two Attempts at Structural Criticism." *Univ. of Texas Studies in English*, XXXV (1956), 51-56.

Jerman, B. R. "Browning's Witless Duke." *PMLA*, LXXII, 488-93.

A reading of "My Last Duchess": the Duke has no hidden message for the envoy, but simply reveals himself as a vain and not too perceptive patron of art.

Kenmare, Dallas. *The Browning Love Story*. London: Peter Owen. Pp. 199.

Abridgement of Browning-Elizabeth Barrett correspondence condensed from the 1200 pp. of the original edition to just under 200. Noticed in *TLS*, Mar. 8, p. 150.

King, Roma A., Jr. *The Bow and the Lyre: The Art of Robert Browning*. Ann Arbor, Mich.: Univ. of Michigan Pr. Pp. 162.

McAleer, Edward C. "Pasquale Villari and the Brownings." *BPLQ*, IX, 40-47.

Correspondence between the Brownings and one of the very few Italians they knew.

Miller, Betty. "The Séance at Ealing: A Study in Memory and Imagination." *Cornhill Mag.*, CLXIX, 317-24.

Detailed record of the Brownings' relations with Daniel Home, the medium celebrated as Mr. Sludge.

Pepperdene, Margaret W. "Browning's 'Fra Lippo Lippi', 70-75." *Ex*, XV, Item 34.

Perrine, Laurence, and Everett, Edwin M. "Browning's 'Fra Lippo Lippi', 70-75." *Ex*, XVI, Item 18.

Praz, Mario. "Browning's 'A Grammarian's Funeral'." *TLS*, Dec. 6, p. 739.

A letter from Professor Praz points out a passage in Heinrich Stromer's description of the death of Erasmus as a possible source for Browning's description of the Grammarian's death. See also a rejoinder by H. H. Brown, *TLS*, Dec. 27, p. 787.

Szladits, Lola L. "Browning's French Nightcap." *Bull. New York Pub. Libr.*, LXI, 458-67.

Taplin, Gardner B. *The Life of Elizabeth Barrett Browning*. New Haven: Yale Univ. Pr. Pp. xv + 482.

Rev. by A. O. J. Cockshut in *Manchester Guardian*, July 5, p. 7; as the authoritative biography by Betty Miller in *NS*, July 6, pp. 25-26; by Isabel Quigley in *S*, July 12, pp. 58-59; by Merle M. Bevington in *SAQ*, LVI, 529-30; by Gordon N. Ray in *SR*, May 4, p. 25; in *TLS*, July 26, pp. 449-50; by W. O. Raymond in *VS*, I, 96-97.

Williams, Luster J. "Figurative Imagery in *The Ring and the Book*: A Study in Browning's Poetic Technique." *DA*, XVI (1956), 2153-54.

Windolph, Francis Lyman. *Reflections of the Law in Literature*. Philadelphia: Univ of Pennsylvania Pr., 1956. Pp. 83.

Rev. briefly by Albrecht B. Strauss in *BA*, XXXI, 311-12. Legal matters in *The Ring and the Book*, *The Merchant of Venice*, and *Phineas Redux*.

Wishmeyer, William Hood. "The Myth in *The Ring and the Book*." *DA*, XVII, 3026.

BULWER-LYTTON (see also I, Dickson; III, Gray).

Fradin, Joseph Irwin. "The Novels of Edward Bulwer-Lytton." *DA*, XVI (1956), 2148-49.

Liljegren, S. B. *Bulwer-Lytton's Novels and "Isis Unveiled."* ("Essays and Studies on Engl. Lang. and Lit.," XVIII.) Upsala; Cambridge, Mass.: Harvard Univ. Pr. Pp. 60.

Contends impressively that Mme. Blavatski, the founder of the Theosophical Society, drew heavily upon the novels of Bulwer-Lytton.—W. D. T.

BURTON. Bishop, Jonathan. "The Identities of Sir Richard Burton: The Explorer as Actor." *VS*, I, 119-35.

Burton's role-playing (Anglo-Indian, Moslem, diplomat, explorer, scholar) and the over-statement of his prose style express his inability to decide who he was: "His life remains essentially putative and rhetorical, a theatrical gesture exploiting the attitudes it rejects."

BUTLER (see also III, Zabel).

Wilson, Angus. "The Revolt of Samuel Butler." *AM*, CC, 190-98.

On Butler's "Anti-Victorianism," its virtues and its defects.

CARLYLE (see also III, Bentley, Blair, Gurewitch, Kegel, Pankhurst, Rathbun; ARNOLD: Tillotson).

Symons, Julian (ed.). *Carlyle: Selected Works, Reminiscences, and Letters*. London: Hart-Davis, 1956. Pp. 784.

Rev. by J. Donald Adams in *NYTBR*, Nov. 24, p. 2; by Peter Quennell in *S*, Feb. 10, 1956, p. 188; in *TLS*, Feb. 3, 1956, pp. 61-62 (and see a reply by Symons, Feb. 10, p. 85). A selection designed, according to the editor, "to show the stages in which an unorthodox Radical became an advocate of extreme authoritarian rule."

Adrian, Arthur. "Dean Stanley's Report of Conversations with Carlyle." *VS,* I, 72-74.
Hitherto unpublished notes of Carlyle's opinions about English government. despotism, the past, and Goethe.

Burd, Van Akin. "Ruskin's Antidote for Carlyle's Purges." *Boston Univ. Studies in English,* III, 51-57.

Gordon, Robert C. "A Victorian Anticipation of Recent Scott Criticism." *PQ,* XXXVI, 272-75.
Julia Wedgwood's refutation of Carlyle's view of Scott.

"Letters of Ruskin and Carlyle." *Bull. John Rylands Libr.,* XL, 3-4.

Lindberg, John Monson. "Symbolic Presentation of Ideas in Carlyle." *DA,* XVII, 622.

Moore, Carlisle. "Carlyle *Resartus.*" *VNL,* No. 12 (Autumn), pp. 11-13.

Moore, Carlisle. "The Persistence of Carlyle's 'Everlasting Yea'." *MP,* LIV, 187-96.

Origo, Iris. *A Measure of Love.* London: Cape. Pp. 256.
Rev. by DeLancey Ferguson in *HTB,* Nov. 10, p. 3; by K. John in *NS,* Nov. 2, p. 576; by Peter Quennell in *NYTBR,* Nov. 10, p. 5; by John Davenport in *S,* Oct. 4, p. 447; in *TLS,* Nov. 8, p. 674.

Roellinger, Francis X., Jr. "The Early Development of Carlyle's Style." *PMLA,* LXXII, 936-51.

Sanders, Charles Richard. "The Victorian Rembrandt: Carlyle's Portraits of His Contemporaries." *Bull. John Rylands Libr.,* XXXIX, 521-57.

CARROLL (see also III, Gray).

Green, Roger Lancelyn. "The Griffin and the Jabberwock." *TLS,* Mar. 1, p. 136.
On the relation between "Jabberwocky" and Menella Smedley's "The Shepherd of the Giant Mountains," translated from Fouqué.

Green, Roger Lancelyn. "Lewis Carroll's First Publication." *TLS,* Sept. 13, p. 552.
Two poems, hitherto unidentified, by Carroll in the *Oxonian Advertiser,* April, 1854. See a letter on this article by Dorothy Wormald, *TLS,* Oct. 11, p. 609.

Priestley, J. B. "The Walrus and the Carpenter." *NS,* Aug. 10, p. 168.

CLARE (see also III, Lewis).

Harrison, Thomas P. "Birds in the Poetry of

John Clare." *Peterborough Museum Society Occasional Papers,* No. 1. Peterborough: The Museum.

CLOUGH (see also III, Fairchild).

Mulhauser, Frederick L. (ed.). *The Correspondence of Arthur Hugh Clough.* 2 vols. Oxford: Clarendon Pr. Pp. xxiii + 320; v + 321.
Rev. by Rose Macaulay in *Listener,* Dec. 5, p. 937; in *TLS,* Dec. 6, p. 738.

Timko, Michael. "The Lyrics of Arthur Hugh Clough: Their Background and Form." *DA,* XVI (1956), 2449.

COBDEN. Briggs, Asa. "Cobden and Bright." *History Today,* VII, 495-503.

COLLIER. Race, Sydney. "John Payne Collier and His Fabrications." *N & Q,* new ser., IV, 309-12.

Race, Sydney. "John Payne Collier and the Percy Society." *N & Q,* new ser., IV, 395-97.

COLLINS (see also III, Lewis).

Davis, Nuel Pharr. *The Life of Wilkie Collins. . . .* See VB 1956, 252.
Rev. by Edward Wagenknecht in *Chicago Sunday Tribune,* Jan. 20, p. 9; by Frederick T. Wood in *ESt,* XXXVIII, 180-82; by DeLancey Ferguson in *HTB,* Dec. 23, 1956, p. 3; by Lionel Stevenson in *JEGP,* LVI, 505-7; by Lauriat Lane in *MLN,* LXXII, 549-50; by Robert P. Ashley in *NCF,* XII, 248-50; in *N & Q,* new ser., IV, 183; by R. D. Altick in *SR,* Feb. 23, p. 21; in *TLS,* Jan. 25, p. 48; by Bradford Booth in *VS,* I, 93-94 ("there is little that is new and much that is subject to corrective interpretation").

Hart, Francis Russell. "Wilkie Collins and the Problem of Biographical Evidence." *VNL,* No. 12 (Autumn), pp. 18-21.

"Manuscripts of Wilkie Collins [library acquisitions]." *PLC,* XVIII, 85.

CONRAD (see also II, Swinnerton; III, Cecil, Clark, Garbaty, Howe, Zabel).

Bache, William B. "*Nostromo* and 'The Snows of Kilimanjaro'." *MLN,* LXXII, 32-34.

Baines, Jocelyn. "The Young Conrad in Marseilles." *TLS,* Dec. 6, p. 748.
A hitherto unpublished letter from Conrad's uncle and guardian gives an account of the young Conrad's early struggles and attempted suicide.

Brown, Dorothy Snodgrass. "The Irony of Joseph Conrad." *DA,* XVI (1957), 2148.

Conrad, Borys. "A Famous Father and His Son." *NYTBR*, Dec. 1, pp. 7, 74.

Curle, Richard. *Joseph Conrad and His Characters*. London: Heinemann. Pp. 254. Rev. by John Bayley in *S*, Dec. 13, pp. 840-41; in *TLS*, Nov. 29, p. 723.

Dowden, Wilfred S. "The Light and the Dark: Imagery and Thematic Development in Conrad's *Heart of Darkness*." *Studies in English Honoring George Wesley Whiting* (Rice Institute Pamphlet, Vol. XLIV, No. 1), 33-51.

Duffin, Henry Charles. "Conrad: A Centenary Survey." *CR*, CXCII, 319-23.

Evans, Robert O. "Conrad: A Nautical Image." *MLN*, LXXII, 98-99.

Haugh, Robert F. *Joseph Conrad: Discovery in Design*. Norman, Okla.: Univ. of Oklahoma Pr. Pp. 173.

Housley, Robert W. "Suspense." *NS*, May 18, p. 642.

Notes that Conrad's unfinished novel, *Suspense*, corresponds closely with the real person, the Contesse de Boigne.

Jean-Aubry, Gerard. *The Sea Dreamer: A Definitive Biography of Joseph Conrad*. Trans. by Helen Sebba. London: Allen & Unwin. Pp. 321.

Rev. by C. J. Rolo in *AM*, CXCIX, 81-83; by Edward Wagenknecht in *Chicago Sunday Tribune*, Feb. 3, p. 3; by Francis Russell in *Christian Science Monitor*, Jan. 31, p. 5; by David Daiches in *HTB*, Feb. 3, p. 5; by Edith Lenel in *LJ*, LXXXI, 2947; by Sir David W. Bone in *LR*, Winter, p. 280; briefly in *NCF*, XII, 173; by Eric Gillett in *NER*, CXLIX, 134; by V. S. Pritchett in *NS*, Aug. 24, p. 229; by Carlos Baker in *NYTBR*, Feb. 3, pp. 1, 24; by Jocelyn Baines in *S*, July 26, p. 139; by J. W. Krutch in *SR*, Feb. 9, p. 12; in *TLS*, July 26, p. 454.

"Joseph Conrad." *TLS*, Dec. 6, p. 739.

Karl, Frederick Robert. "Joseph Conrad: A Modern Victorian (A Study in Novelistic Technique)." *DA*, XVII, 1764.

Kaye, Julian B. "Conrad's *Under Western Eyes* and Mann's *Doctor Faustus*." *Comp. Lit.*, IX, 60-65.

Levin, Gerald Henry. "Conrad and the 'Atmosphere of Authenticity': An Inquiry into the Structure and Meaning of *Chance*," *DA*, XVII, 1340-41.

Lohf, Kenneth A., and Sheehy, Eugene Paul (eds.). *Joseph Conrad at Mid-Century: Editions and Studies, 1895-1955*. Minneapolis, Minn.: Univ. of Minnesota Pr.

Pp. xiii + 114.

Rev. by Leo Gurko in *Amer. Scholar*, XXVII, 128-30; briefly in *NCF*, XII, 254; in *TLS*, Nov. 29, p. 723.

Maser, Frederick E. "The Philosophy of Joseph Conrad." *HJ*, LVI, 69-78.

Maxwell, J. C. "Conrad: A Misdated Letter." *N & Q*, new ser., IV, 314-15.

Milosz, Czeslaw. "Joseph Conrad in Polish Eyes." *AM*, CC, 219-28.

Moser, Thomas. *Joseph Conrad: Achievement and Decline*. Cambridge, Mass.: Harvard Univ. Pr. Pp. 227.

Rev. by Leo Gurko in *Amer. Scholar*, XXVII, 128-30; by Edward Wagenknecht in *Chicago Sunday Tribune*, July 28, p. 2; in *Christian Science Monitor*, July 18, p. 5; by J. R. Willingham in *LJ*, LXXXII, 1673; briefly in *NCF*, XII, 254; by David Daiches in *NYTBR*, June 30, p. 5; by Jocelyn Baines in *S*, Nov. 1, p. 583; in *TLS*, Nov. 29, p. 723.

Mudrick, Marvin. "The Artist's Conscience and *The Nigger of the Narcissus*." *NCF*, XI, 288-97.

Visiak, E. H. *The Mirror of Conrad* . . . . See VB 1956, 253.

Rev. by Bruce Harkness in *JEGP*, LVI, 507-9; by Thomas Moser in *MLN*, LXXII, 297-300; by Joseph Wood Krutch in *SR*, Feb. 9, p. 12.

DARWIN. *The Darwin Reader*. Ed. Marston Bates and Philip S. Humphrey. New York: Scribner, 1956, Pp. ix + 470.

Rev. by Ward Shepard in *Amer. Scholar*, XXVI, 380; briefly in *HTB*, Jan. 27, p. 12; by John Pfeiffer in *NYTBR*, Feb. 3, p. 14; in *TLS*, Nov. 15, p. 693; by B. J. Loewenberg in *VS*, I, 106-7.

The Expression of the Emotions in Man and Animals. Ed. Margaret Mead. New York: Philosophical Library, 1955. Pp. xi + 372.

Moore, Ruth E. *Charles Darwin* . . . . See VB 1955, 256.

Rev. in *TLS*, July 5, p. 410.

DAVIDSON. Macleod, Robert Duncan. *John Davidson: A Study in Personality*. London: W. & R. Holmes. Pp. 35.

Rev. briefly by Sir Harold Williams in *LR*, Autumn, p. 208.

DICKENS (see also I, Collins, Dickson, Gordan; III, Blair, Coveney, West, Zabel).

Mrs. Gamp; A Facsimile of the Author's Prompt Copy. Ed. John D. Gordan. New York: New York Public Libr., 1956.

Pp. xvii + 120.
Rev. briefly by C. P. Snow in *NS,* July 27, p. 120. Copy of script Dickens used for his readings in 1858.

Adrian, Arthur A. *Georgina Hogarth and the Dickens Circle.* London: Oxford Univ. Pr. Pp. xvi + 320.
Rev. by Pamela Hansford Johnson in *NS,* Nov. 30, pp. 735-36; unfavorably by Karl Miller in *S,* Dec. 13, p. 842; unfavorably in *TLS,* Nov. 29, p. 722.

Bergler, Edmund. "*Little Dorrit* and Dickens' Intuitive Knowledge of Psychic Masochism." *Amer. Imago,* XIV, 371-88.
Extends Trilling's discussion of the "genetic pattern" of psychic masochism in *Little Dorrit* by providing a "clinical analysis" of Amy Dorrit and Miss Wade.

Blissett, William. "Dylan Thomas." *QQ,* LXIII (1956), 45-58.

Bovill, E. W. "Tony Weller's Trade" [concluded]. *N & Q,* new ser., IV, 155-59, 260-63, 451-53.

Bredsdorff, Elias. *Hans Andersen and Charles Dickens: A Friendship and Its Dissolution.* Rev. translation. Cambridge: Heffer, 1956. Pp. 140.
Rev. by H. Reinhold in *Anglia,* LXXV, 122-24; by C. A. Bodelsen in *ESt,* XXXVIII, 178-80; briefly by Sylvère Monod in *Études anglaises,* X, 65; by George H. Ford in *NCF,* XII, 166-68; by Ernest Bernbaum in *Scandinavian Studies,* XXIX, 97-100; in *TLS,* Apr. 12, p. 226. Correspondence between the two men and Andersen's diary during his English visit, here translated into English for the first time.

Butt, John, and Tillotson, Kathleen. *Dickens at Work.* London: Methuen. Pp. 238.
Rev. by Grace Banyard in *CR,* CXCII, 239; as a "significant contribution" by Ada Nisbet in *NCF,* XII, 239-45; by Eric Gillett in *NER,* CXLIX, 81; favorably by C. P. Snow in *NS,* July 27, pp. 119-20; ("To those brought up to believe that the conscious aesthetic of the novel began with Flaubert and Henry James, it will be a little startling to see how technically sophisticated Dickens and his contemporaries were. They were not primitives — in fact, only an ass could ever have thought they were."); by W. W. Robson in *S,* Aug. 2, p. 168; in *TLS,* July 26, p. 459; by P. A. W. Collins in *Universities Quart.,* XII, 104-10. A study, fully documented, of Dickens' methods of composition, with especial emphasis on the effect of serial publication on his work.

Carlton, William J. "The Third Man at Newgate." *RES,* new ser., VIII, 403-7.

N. P. Willis's recollections of a visit with Dickens to Newgate Prison in 1835, dismissed as fabrication by Forster and Ley, are shown to be authentic.

Carter, John Archer, Jr. "Dickens and Education: The Novelist as Reformer." *DA,* XVII, 628-29.

Clark, William R. "The Rationale of Dickens' Death Rate." *Boston Univ. Studies in English,* II (1956), 125-39.

Coolidge, Archibald Cary. "Serialization in the Novels of Charles Dickens." *DA,* XVI (1956), 2455-56.

Eoff, Sherman. "*Oliver Twist* and the Spanish Picaresque Novel." *SP,* LIV, 440-47.
An attempt to relate *Oliver Twist* to the Spanish picaresque tradition of the 16th and 17th centuries. The comparison seems pointless, however, since the author says nothing of Dickens' knowledge of the tradition that is here made his point of departure.—R. A. D.

Friedman, Norman. "The Shadow and the Sun: Notes Toward a Reading of *Bleak House.*" *Boston Univ. Studies in English,* III, 147-66.

Griffith, Ben W., Jr. "Dickens the Philanthropist: An Unpublished Letter." *NCF,* XII, 160-63.

Johannsen, Albert (ed.). *Phiz: Illustrations from the Novels of Charles Dickens. . . .*
See VB 1956, 254.
Rev. briefly in *NCF,* XII, 92-93; in *TLS,* Mar. 29, p. 190; by Beatrice Corrigan in *VS,* I, 98-99.

Johnson, Edgar. "Dickens and Shaw: Critics of Society." *VQR,* XXXIII, 66-79.
Parallels between "the greatest British writer of the nineteenth century" and "the greatest British writer of our own time," as artists and as social critics.

Karl, Frederick R. "Conrad's Debt to Dickens." *N & Q,* new ser., IV, 398-400.

Low, Donald R. "The Speeches, Lectures, and Readings of Charles Dickens and William M. Thackeray in the United States, 1842-1868." *DA,* XVI (1956), 2555-56.

Miller, Melvin Hall. "The Collected Speeches of Charles Dickens with Introduction and Notes." *DA,* XVII, 3124-25.
Part Two of this dissertation includes the text of 128 speeches which Dickens delivered on 93 occasions. Topical and literary allusions have been identified in footnotes. The dissertation (798 pp.) includes what is called "the most complete collection of Dickens' speeches ever

made." Notable.—W. D. T.

Monod, Sylvère. "Alain, lecteur de Dickens." *Mercure de France*, CCCXXXI, 108-21.
A review-article on Alain's *En lisant Dickens* (Paris, 1954).

Monod, Sylvère. "L'Expression dans *Our Mutual Friend* Manière ou Maniérisme?" *Étude anglaises*, X, 37-48.

"New Letters from Charles Dickens to John Forster." *Boston Univ. Studies in English*, II (1956), 140-93.
Three sections make up this item: (1) "How the Letters Were Found" (pp. 140-49), by K. J. Fielding; (2) "The Significance of the Letters" (pp. 150-55), by Gerald G. Grubb; and (3) "The Letters Themselves" (pp. 156-93), ed. by Gerald G. Grubb. More than forty letters, 1837-41, found in the offices of a firm of solicitors in London, in 1937.

Rathburn, Robert Charles. "Dickens' Periodical Essays and Their Relationships to the Novels." *DA*, XVII, 2002.

Shaffer, Ellen. "The Rare Book Department of the Free Library of Philadelphia." *College and Research Libr.*, XVIII, 284-89.
Contains brief descriptions of the "Charles Dickens Collection" and the "D. Jacques Benoliel Collection of Dickens Letters" available in the Free Library of Philadelphia.

Spilka, Mark. "Dickens and Kafka: A Mutual Interpretation." *DA*, XVI (1956), 2462-63.

Stange, G. Robert. "Dickens and the Fiery Past: *A Tale of Two Cities* Reconsidered." *EJ*, XLVI, 381-90.

Stone, Harry. "Charles Dickens and Harriet Beecher Stowe." *NCF*, XII, 188-202.
Includes a hitherto unpublished letter of Dickens asserting his own moral purpose in writing fiction.

Stone, Harry. "Dickens' Use of His American Experiences in *Martin Chuzzlewit*." *PMLA*, LXXII, 464-78.

Stuart, Dorothy Margaret. "Sarah Gamp." *CR*, CXCII, 205-8.

Tillotson, Kathleen. "Dickens's Count Smorltork." *TLS*, Nov. 22, p. 712.
Identifies the foreign visitor in *Pickwick* as Friedrich von Raumer, Professor of History at the University of Berlin.

Troughton, Marion. "Dickens as Editor." *CR*, CXCI, 87-91.

V. R. "An American 'Pickwick'." *N & Q*, new ser., IV, 123-24.
Reproduces a dedication, written by Dickens.

Wagenknecht, Edward. "*Great Expectations* and Ellen Glasgow." *Boston Univ. Studies in English*, III, 57-60.

DOUGHTY. Fairley, Barker. "The Dawn in Britain after Fifty Years." *TQ*, XXVI, 149-64.
A critical and appreciative account. This poem was in Doughty's mind as early as 1865. It is here called "a Victorian poem" —for "At what other time in English literature . . . could this sense of history have flowered in its threefold aspect of scholarly, patriotic, and philosophical?"

Rope, Rev. H. E. G. "A Note on Doughty's *Dawn in Britain*." *Nine*, IV, No. 2 (April, 1956), 23-25.

DOYLE. Weil-Nordon, P. "Sir Arthur Conan Doyle et la France." *Études anglaises*, X, 109-14.
The historical novels of Doyle show him as clearly a Francophile, yet he is known in France almost exclusively as the creator of Sherlock Holmes, perhaps because his romances have never been adequately translated.

ELIOT (see also I, Dickson; III, Coveney, Deneau).

Beaty, Jerome. "George Eliot's Notebook for an Unwritten Novel." *PLC*, XVIII, 175-82.

Beaty, Jerome. "History by Indirection: The Era of Reform in *Middlemarch*." *VS*, I, 173-79.
Eliot's characteristic method in this novel is to introduce historical political events as part of the every-day affairs of her characters.

Beaty, Jerome. "Visions and Revisions: Chapter LXXXI of *Middlemarch*." *PMLA*, LXXII, 662-79.
Contrary to the report of John Cross that George Eliot said she wrote this scene in *Middlemarch* "without alteration or erasure," her notebook and the MS give evidence of careful revision.

Colby, Robert A. "An American Sequel to *Daniel Deronda*." *NCF*, XII, 231-35.

Goldberg, Hannah. "George Henry Lewes and *Daniel Deronda*." *N & Q*, new ser., IV, 356-58.
Claims Lewes influenced George Eliot's *Daniel Deronda* and may even have been the prototype for Deronda.

Haight, Gordon S. (ed.). *The George Eliot Letters*. Vols. IV to VII. . . . See VB 1956,

254.
Rev. by Barbara Hardy in *MLR*, LII, 266-70.

Hardy, Barbara. "The Image of the Opiate in George Eliot's Novels." *N & Q*, new ser., IV, 487-90.

Heilman, Robert B. "Return to Raveloe: Thirty-five Years After." *EJ*, XLVI, 1-10.

Huzzard, John A. "The Treatment of Florence and Florentine Characters in George Eliot's *Romola*." *Italica*, XXXIV, 158-65.

Hyde, William J. "George Eliot and the Climate of Realism." *PMLA*, LXXII, 147-64. George Eliot's critical theory of realism aimed at "the accurate representation of the commonplace," and avoided the eccentrically ugly or the superhumanly virtuous. This theory, expressed in the *Westminster Review* during the 1850's, she put into practice in her novels.

Stang, Richard. "The Literary Criticism of George Eliot." *PMLA*, LXXII, 952-61.

Stump, Reva Juanita. "Vision as Imagery, Theme, and Structure in George Eliot's Novels." *DA*, XVII, 2018.

Thale, Jerome. "Image and Theme: *The Mill on the Floss*." *Univ. of Kansas City Rev.*, XXIII, 227-34.

FARADAY. *The Chemical History of a Candle*. New York: Crowell. Pp. 158.
Rev. by M. S. Libby in *HTB*, Sept. 1, p. 6; briefly by H. Seymour in *LJ*, LXXXII, 2197. An illustrated reprint of six lectures for young people first given in England in 1848.

FITZ GERALD (see also III, Beringouse). Hanford, James Holly. "FitzGerald's 'Rubáiyát'." *PLC*, XIX, 60-62.
Prints a letter from the great Orientalist Lord Strangford about the first edition.

Arberry, A. J. *FitzGerald's Salámán and Absál*. London: Cambridge Univ. Pr., 1956. Pp. vii + 206.
Rev. briefly by Paul Selver in *Poetry Rev.*, XLVIII, 108-9; briefly by Merle M. Bevington in *SAQ*, LVI, 535; in *TLS*, Mar. 29, p. 186. Reprints two versions of Fitz-Gerald's translation and letters concerning its publication.

Terhune, A. McKinley. "Edward FitzGerald." *VNL*, No. 12 (Autumn), pp. 22-23.

GASKELL (see also III, Lewis).
Shusterman, David. "William Rathbone Greg and Mrs. Gaskell." *PQ*, XXXVI, 268-72.

GILBERT (see also III, Gray).
Baily, Leslie. *The Gilbert & Sullivan Book*.

Rev. ed. New York: Coward-McCann. Pp. xvi + 475.
Rev. by T. H. Wenning in *HTB*, April 14, p. 3; by William Lichtenwanger in *Music Libr. Assn. Notes*, XIV, 373. Revised edition of work first published in 1952.

Pearson, Hesketh. "Further Quarrels of W. S. Gilbert." *Listener*, Sept. 5, pp. 347-48. Based on Gilbert's private papers.

Pearson, Hesketh. *Gilbert: His Life and Strife*. London: Methuen. Pp. 276.
Rev. by Eric Gillett in *NER*, CXLIX, 237; by Arthur Marshall in *NS*, Nov. 30, p. 738; in *TLS*, Nov. 8, p. 666.

Pearson, Hesketh. "The Private Papers of W. S. Gilbert." *Theatre Arts*, XLI (December), 70-71, 84-87.

Pearson, Hesketh. "The Quarrel between Gilbert and Sullivan." *Listener*, Aug. 29, pp. 307-8.

GISSING (see also III, Clark, Phelps).
Donnelly, Mabel Collins. *George Gissing: Grave Comedian*. . . . See VB 1955, 261.
Rev. by M. L. Cazamian in *Études anglaises*, X, 66-67.

Gettmann, Royal A. "Bentley and Gissing." *NCF*, XI, 306-14. Relations between Gissing and his publisher were not as unsympathetic as has been generally thought.

"Propos de la Quinzaine." *Rev. des deux mondes*, Nov. 15, p. 375.

Young, Arthur C. "Gissing's *Veranilda*." *N & Q*, new ser., IV, 359.

GLADSTONE (see also II, Adams).
Battiscombe, Georgina. *Mrs. Gladstone: The Portrait of a Marriage*. . . . See VB 1956, 255.
Rev. by J. A. Arndt in *Christian Science Monitor*, May 29, p. 5; by Winifred Taffs in *CR*, CXCI, 117-18; by Paul Pickrel in *Harper's*, CCXIV (June), 80-82; by C. D. Bowen in *HTB*, May 26, p. 3; by Roger Fulford in *Manchester Guardian*, Nov. 30, 1956, p. 13; briefly by Eric Gillett in *NER*, CXLVII (1956), 255-60; by Louise Hall Tharp in *SR*, June 29, p. 18; in *TLS*, Nov. 2, 1956, p. 648; by John L. Glaser in *VS*, I, 199.

GOSSE (see also III, Phelps). White, William. "Sir Edmund Gosse on Walt Whitman." *VS*, I, 180-82.

HARDY (see also I, Gordan; III, Fackler, Fairchild, Zabel).
Auden, W. H. "My First Master." *Periodical*, XXXI, 300-2.

Hardy was Auden's first master. Extract from *Making, Knowing, and Judging.*

Bailey, James Osler. *Thomas Hardy and the Cosmic Mind.* . . . See VB 1956, 255.

Rev. by Jacob Korg in *CE*, XIX, 91; by A. Dwight Culler in *JEGP*, LVI, 646-49; briefly in *NCF*, XI, 319; briefly in *TLS*, Mar. 29, p. 198.

Brogan, Howard O. "Science and Narrative Structure in Austen, Hardy, and Woolf." *NCF*, XI, 276-87.

Clifford, Emma. "The 'Trumpet-Major Note-book' and *The Dynasts.*" *RES*, new ser., VIII, 149-61.

Goldberg, M. A. "Hardy's Double-Visioned Universe." *EC*, VII, 374-82.

Goodheart, Eugene. "Thomas Hardy and the Lyrical Novel." *NCF*, XII, 215-25.

States that Hardy was not a Jamesian sort of novelist, since he did not place a high value on the social setting; that Hardy was essentially a Romantic poet. The author contends that Hardy's denial of the validity of social appearance is "a nihilistic tendency, undermining the very assumptions on which the novel rests."

Green, David Bonnell. " 'The Eve of St. Agnes' and *A Pair of Blue Eyes.*" *N & Q*, new ser., IV, 153.

Haber, Grace Stevenson. "Echoes from Carlyle's 'Goethe's "Helena" ' in *The Mayor of Casterbridge.*" *NCF*, XII, 89-90.

"Hardy's Drawings for a Child." *TLS*, July 19, p. 448.

Hillyer, Robert. "Speaking of Books." *NYT-BR*, Feb. 3, p. 2.

Hoopes, Kathleen R. "Illusion and Reality in *Jude the Obscure.*" *NCF*, XII, 154-57.

Jude's idealized expectations (called here his "ghosts" or "phantoms") repeatedly crushed by harsh reality.

MacKay, Harper. "Five Poems by Thomas Hardy." *Colby Libr. Quart.*, IV, 187-88.

Mallory, Thomas Oliver, Jr. "The Devil and Thomas Hardy: A Study of the Manifestations of Supernatural Evil in Hardy's Fiction." *DA*, XVII, 2012-13.

Peterson, Edith Hamilton-Moodie. " 'Symmetric History': A Study of Thought Patterns in the Prose Works of Thomas Hardy." *DA*, XVII, 2599.

Sanders, E. N. "Another Hardy Scrap-book." *Colby Libr. Quart.*, IV, 173-77.

A copy of *The Return of The Native*, containing clippings, and other material, including four letters by Hardy, here printed.

Shirreff, A. G. " 'The Eve of St. Agnes' and *A Pair of Blue Eyes.*" *N & Q*, new ser., IV, 502.

Slack, Robert C. "The Text of Hardy's *Jude the Obscure.*" *NCF*, XI, 261-75.

An account of the two revisions made of the text of *Jude* after it had been published as a novel in 1895.

[Weber, Carl J.] "An Unrecorded Hardy Item." *Colby Libr. Quart.*, IV, 177-78.

George Bazile's French translation of "An Imaginative Woman," which appeared in 1912.

Weber, Carl J. "Hardy's Copy of Schopenhauer." *Colby Libr. Quart.*, IV, 217-24.

From markings in Hardy's copy of the book it is clear that Hardy read and pondered Schopenhauer's *Four-fold Root of the Principle of Sufficient Reason.*

[Weber, Carl J.] "Recent Gifts to the Library" *Colby Libr. Quart.*, IV, 186-88.

Weber, Carl J. "Thomas Hardy." *VNL*, No. 12 (Autumn), p. 23-24.

Yamamoto, Bunnosuke (ed.). *Bibliography of Thomas Hardy in Japan.* Tokyo: Shinozaki Shorin. Pp. ix + 294.

Mostly books, by and about Hardy, translated into Japanese.

HENLEY (see also III, Clark, Peters).

Braunlich, Alice F. "Some Sources of Henley's Echoes." *MLN*, LXXII, 341-42.

Influences of Shakespeare, Tennyson, Thomson, Schiller, and Johnson.

HOOD (see also III, Gray).

Whitley, Alvin. "Thomas Hood and 'The Times'." *TLS*, May 17, p. 309.

On the sources of "The Song of the Shirt" and "The Bridge of Sighs." See also a letter on this subject from P. F. Morgan, *TLS*, June 7, p. 349.

HOPKINS (see also III, Fairchild, Miles, Wain).

Abbott, Claude Colleer (ed.). *Further Letters of Gerard Manley Hopkins.* . . . See VB 1956, 256.

Rev. briefly by Ruth Ames in *CWd*, CLXXV, 155; by T. A. Birrell in *ESt*, XXXVIII, 225-26; by A. O. J. Cockshut in *Manchester Guardian*, Jan. 1, p. 4; briefly by Eric Gillett in *NER*, CXLVIII, 85-88; briefly by Robert Armstrong in *Poetry Rev.*, XLVIII, 109-10; briefly in *QR*, July, 363-64; by Hugh Kelly in *StI*, XLV, 121-23; briefly by Betty Miller in *TC*, CLXI, 306; by John Pick in *VS*, I, 91-93.

Gardner, W. H. "Hopkins's Spiritual Diaries." *TLS*, Mar. 29, p. 193.
A letter describing the destruction by the poet's surviving sister of his notebook of meditations.

Harrison, Thomas P. "The Birds of Gerard Manley Hopkins." *SP*, LIV, 448-63.
In the early poems Hopkins is concerned with rendering the bird as object; in the later poems, without sacrificing the element of inscape, he turns to symbolic values and externally imposed meanings.

Lisca, Peter. "The Return of 'The Windhover'." *CE*, XIX, 124-26.
Another exegesis of the poem.

Litzinger, Boyd. "Hopkins' *The Habit of Perfection*." *Ex*, XVI, Item 1.
Religious vows and the Sacrament of Extreme Unction as structural devices.

Martin, Philip M. *Mastery and Mercy: A Study of Two Religious Poems, The Wreck of the Deutschland by G. M. Hopkins and Ash Wednesday by T. S. Eliot.* London: Oxford Univ. Pr. Pp. xii + 149.
Rev. in *TLS*, June 28, p. 399.

Matchett, William H. "An Analysis of 'The Windhover'." *PMLA*, LXXII, 310-11.
A critical note on Archibald A. Hill's analysis of "The Windhover," in *PMLA*, LXX, 968-78.

Nowell-Smith, Simon. "Bridges, Hopkins, and Dr. Daniel." *TLS*, Dec. 13, p. 764.
On Bridges' plans for publication of Hopkins' poems, prior to 1893.

Peel, J. H. B. "The Echoes in the Booming Voice." *NYTBR*, Oct. 20, pp. 40-41.
A comparison concluding that "the difference between Hopkins and Dylan Thomas is fundamentally the difference between a major and minor poet." See letters provoked by this article from Lloyd Frankenberg and others, *NYTBR*, Nov. 10, p. 34.

Ratliff, John D. "Hopkins' 'The May Magnificat'." *Ex*, XVI, Item 17.

Schoeck, R. J. "Influence and Originality in Hopkins." *Renascence*, IX (1956), 77-84.

Spira, Theodor. "Gerard Manley Hopkins: Zu einer Deutschen Neuerscheinung." *Anglia*, LXXIV (1956), 333-34.
A study of the problems of rendering Hopkins in German, illustrated by reference to the translations by Ursula Clemen, Irene Behn, and Karl Horst.

HOUSMAN (see also III, Wain).

Drew, Fraser Bragg, and Sieller, William Vincent. "A. E. Housman's Comments on Morris, Masefield, Wilde, Douglas and Saintsbury." *Colby Libr. Quart.*, IV, 194-201.
Marginal comments in books from the library of A. E. Housman.

Gross, Seymour. "Housman and Pindar." *N & Q*, new ser., IV, 128-29.

Haber, Tom Burns (ed.). *The Manuscript Poems of A. E. Housman. . . .* See VB 1956, 257.
Rev. by G. B. A. Fletcher in *RES*, new ser., VIII, 104-6.

Peterson, Spiro. "Housman's 'On Wenlock Edge'." *Ex*, XV, Item 46.

Watson, George L. *A. E. Housman: A Divided Life.* London: Hart-Davis. Pp. 235.
Rev. unfavorably by Stephen Spender in *Listener*, May 23, pp. 841-42; by Jacques Vallette in *Mercure de France*, CCCXXXI, 538-40: by Eric Gillett in *NER*, CXLIX, 32; by V. S. Pritchett in *NS*, May 18, pp. 643-44; by Peter Quennell in *S*, June 7, p. 753; unfavorably in *TLS*, Aug. 16, pp. 489-90.

White, William. "A. E. Housman: A Critical and Bibliographical Review of Books about the Poet, 1936-55." *JEGP*, LVI, 242-50.

White, William. "Willa Cather and A. E. Housman." *N & Q*, new ser., IV, 313-14.

HUNT. Houtchens, Lawrence Huston, and Houtchens, Carolyn Washburn (eds.). *Leigh Hunt's Literary Criticism.* With an essay on evaluation by Clarence DeWitt Thorpe. New York: Columbia Univ. Pr., 1956. Pp. xii + 732.
Rev. by R. G. Cox in *Manchester Guardian*, Mar. 12, p. 4; in *NS*, Mar. 23, p. 390; in *TLS*, May 3, p. 272; by Richard D. Altick in *VS*, I, 84-87.

HUTTON. Mackerness, E. D. "R. H. Hutton and the Victorian Lay Sermon." *Dalhousie Rev.*, XXXVII, 259-67.

HUXLEY. Bibby, Cyril. "The Prince of Controversialists." *TC*, CLXI, 268-76.

Blinderman, Charles S. "The Oxford Debate and After." *N & Q*, new ser., IV, 126-28.

Blinderman, C. S. "Thomas Henry Huxley." *Scient. Month.*, LXXXIV, 171-82.
A biographical sketch including a good deal of unpublished material from the Huxley Papers in the Imperial College of Science and Technology in London.

JEFFERIES. *Field and Farm: Essays Now First Collected, with Some from MSS.*

Ed. Samuel J. Looker. London: Phoenix House. Pp. 191.
Rev. in *Listener*, Aug. 15, p. 248. Hitherto uncollected essays and articles.

JONES (see also III, Cairns).

Thompson, Marjorie. "Henry Arthur Jones and Wilson Barrett: Some Correspondence 1879-1904." *Theatre Notebook*, XI, 42-50.

JOWETT. Faber, Sir Geoffrey. *Jowett: A Portrait with Background*. London: Faber. Pp. 456.
Rev. by Eric Gillett in *NER*, CXLIX, p. 238; favorably by John Raymond in *NS*, Nov. 2, pp. 571-72; by Rose Macaulay in *S*, Nov. 8, p. 617; in *TLS*, Oct. 25, pp. 633-34.

KEBLE. Reed, John Thomas. "A Critical Analysis of the Literary Theories of John Keble." *DA*, XVII, 3003-4.

KINGSLEY. Campbell, Olwen. *Mary Kingsley: A Victorian in the Jungle*. London: Methuen. Pp. 196.
Rev. in *TLS*, Nov. 22, p. 707.

Howard, Cecil. *Mary Kingsley*. London: Hutchinson. Pp. 231.
Rev. by Eric Gillett in *NER*, CXLIX, 190-91; by V. S. Pritchett in *NS*, Sept. 14, pp. 322-23; in *TLS*, Nov. 22, p. 707.

KIPLING (see also III, Eliot).

Bushnell, Nelson S. "Kipling's Ken of India." *TQ*, XXVII, 62-78.

Carrington, C. E. *The Life of Rudyard Kipling*. . . . See VB 1956, 258.
Rev. by Eric Gillett in *NER*, CLXVI (1956), 109-14; by J. M. S. Tompkins in *RES*, new ser., VIII, 332-34.

Murphy, Carol. "Kipling: Crust and Core." *Approach*, Fall, pp. 29-32.

Rao, Kanatur Bhaskara. "Rudyard Kipling's India." *DA*, XVII, 2014-15.

Weygandt, Ann M. "A Study of Kipling's Use of Historical Material in 'Brother Square-Toes' and 'A Priest in Spite of Himself.'" *Delaware Notes*, 27th ser. (Newark: Univ. of Delaware, 1954), pp. 83-106.

LANDOR. Super, R. H. *Walter Savage Landor: A Biography*. . . . See VB 1956, 259.
Rev. favorably by P. Vitoux in *Études anglaises*, X, 62-64.

LIVINGSTONE. Anstruther, Ian. *I Presume: Stanley's Triumph and Disaster*. London:

Bles, 1956. Pp. xiii + 208.
Rev. by M. H. Bradley in *Chicago Sunday Tribune*, Feb. 10, p. 3; by Leila Flower in *Christian Science Monitor*, July 12, 1956, p. 7; by F. T. Marsh in *HTB*, Feb. 10, p. 5; by M. S. Byam in *LJ*, LXXXII, 1232; by A. J. Hanna in *Manchester Guardian*, Apr. 13, 1956, p. 6; by Eric Gillett in *NER*, CXLVI (1956), 223-28; by James Stern in *NYTBR*, Feb. 10, p. 3; by Walter Clemons in *S*, Apr. 20, 1956, p. 554; by Bennett Epstein in *SR*, Sept. 14, pp. 54-55; in *TLS*, Apr. 13, 1956, p. 219; by J. D. Fage in *VS*, I, 100-2. Biography of Henry M. Stanley. American edition titled: *Dr. Livingstone, I Presume?* New York: Dutton.

Farwell, Byron. *The Man Who Presumed: A Biography of Henry M. Stanley*. New York: Holt. Pp. 334.
Rev. by R. W. Henderson in *LJ*, LXXXII, 1884; by James Stern in *NYTBR*, Sept. 8, p. 10; by Bennett Epstein in *SR*, Sept. 14; p. 54.

Gelfand, Michael. *Livingstone the Doctor*. Oxford: Blackwell. Pp. xix + 333.

Maurice, Albert (ed.). *H. M. Stanley: Unpublished Letters*. London: Chambers. Pp. xvi + 183.
Rev. briefly and unfavorably by Thomas Hodgkin in *NS*, June 22, p. 818.

Northcott, Cecil. *Livingstone in Africa*. "World Christian Books," No. 18.) London: Lutterworth Pr. Pp. 83.

Seaver, George. *David Livingstone: His Life and Letters*. New York: Harper. Pp. 650.
Rev. by R. C. Nelson in *Christian Science Monitor*, Nov. 15, p. 9; by Stuart Cloete (and pronounced "definitive") in *NYTBR*, Nov. 3, p. 3; by Isaac Schapera in *S*, Nov. 1, p. 586; in *TLS*, Nov. 22, p. 702 ("a diligent, careful, conscientious study, which makes the best of all available material").

LYTTON. Lutyens, Lady Emily. *The Birth of Rowland*. . . . See VB 1956, 259.
Rev. by Peter Quennell in *S*, Jan. 18, p. 88; in *TLS*, Jan. 11, p. 20.

MAITLAND (see also III, Gooch).

Cam, Helen M. (ed.). *Selected Historical Essays of F. W. Maitland*. London: Cambridge Univ. Pr. Pp. xxix + 278.

Maitland, Ermengard. *F. W. Maitland: A Child's Eye View*. London: Bernard Quaritch. Pp. 16.
Rev. briefly in *TLS*, June 7, p. 354.

MARRYAT. Zanger, Jules. "Marryat, Monsieur Violet, and Edward La Salle." *NCF*,

XII, 226-31.

MARTINEAU (see also III, Wittrock).

Wheatley, Vera. *The Life and Work of Harriet Martineau*. London: Secker & Warburg. Pp. 421.
Rev. by Jane Hodge in *History Today*, VII, pp. 713-15; by R. D. Altick in *HTB*, Oct. 20, p. 10: by Mary Stocks in *Manchester Guardian*, Aug. 30, p. 4; by Betty Miller in *NS*, Aug. 31, pp. 253-54; by Jenny Nasmith in *S*, Sept. 20, p. 371; very favorably in *TLS*, Oct. 4, p. 592.

MEREDITH (see also BEERBOHM: Beerbohm).

Austin, Deborah S. "Meredith on the Nature of Metaphor." *TQ*, XXVII, 96-102.

Bartlett, Phyllis. "George Meredith: Early Manuscript Poems in the Berg Collection." *Bull. New York Pub. Libr.*, LXI, 396-415.
An interleaved copy of Meredith's *Poems*, 1851, in which appear 41 poems in his handwriting, some of them later published, some still uncollected. Each of his entries is described in this article.

Cline, C. L. "The Letters of George Meredith." *Libr. Chronicle of Univ. of Texas*, VI, 30-32.

Friedman, Norman. "The Jangled Harp: Symbolic Structure in *Modern Love*." *MLQ*, XVIII, 9-26.

Harrison, Thomas P. "Meredith as Poet of Birds." *Bird Notes* (London), XXVII, 249-54.

Landis, Joseph C. "George Meredith's Comedy." *Boston Univ. Studies in English*, II (1956), 17-35.

Lindsay, Jack. *George Meredith: His Life and Work*. . . . See VB 1956, 259.
Rev. by F. Léaud in *Études anglaises*, X, 65-66.

Watson, Robert. "George Meredith's *Sandra Belloni*." *ELH*, XXIV, 321-35.
Sentimentalism equated with estrangement from nature, as the theme of Meredith's third novel.

MILL (see also II, Rogin; III, Aiken, Pankhurst).

Atkinson, R. F. "J. S. Mill's 'Proof' of the Principle of Utility." *Philosophy*, XXXII, 158-67.
Replies to recent defenses of Mill's proof by E. W. Hall, Raphael, and others, and maintains that they are fallacious.

Borchard, Ruth. *John Stuart Mill: The Man.* London: Watts. Pp. 156.

Rev. briefly by Betty Miller in *TC*, CLXI, 592-94.

Lindley, Dwight N. "John Stuart Mill: The Second Greatest Influence." *VNL*, No. 11 (Spring), pp. 25-26.

Mineka, Francis E. (ed.). "John Stuart Mill: Letters on the French Revolution of 1830." *VS*, I, 137-54.
Four letters, one hitherto unpublished and two until now not definitely ascribed to Mill, which reveal the enthusiasm with which Mill first regarded the revolution.

Mueller, Iris W. *John Stuart Mill and French Thought.* . . . See VB 1956, 260.
Rev. by C. H. Van Duzer in *AHR*, LXII, 385-86; by A. Dwight Culler in *JEGP*, LVI, 293-94.

Packe, Michael St. John. *The Life of John Stuart Mill.* . . . See VB 1956, 260.
Rev. by Harold T. Parker in *SAQ*, LVI, 247-49.

Rees, John Collwyn. *Mill and His Early Critics.* . . . See VB 1956, 260.
Rev. by J. H. Burns in *History*, XLII, 275; by F. A. Hayek in *JMH*, XXIX, 184.

Robbins, Lionel. "Packe on Mill." *Economica*, new ser., XXIV, 250-59.
Robbins notes Packe's Stracheyan tendency towards inventing colorful details which no evidence can either prove or disprove. He contends that Hayek and Packe have given us a very full picture, but have not changed the view of Mill which we had from the *Autobiography* and from Bain.

MOORE (see also III, Clark, Phelps; BEERBOHM: Beerbohm).

Letters to Lady Cunard, 1895-1933. Ed. Rupert Hart-Davis. London: Hart-Davis. Pp. 208.
Rev. by Eric Gillett in *NER*, CXLIX, 237-38; by Richard Mayne in *NS*, Sept. 21, p. 362; by Thomas Hogan in *S*, Sept. 30, p. 372; in *TLS*, Sept. 20, p. 562.

Chaikin, M. "George Moore's *A Mummer's Wife* and Zola." *Rev. de litt. comp.*, XXXI, 85-88.
That *A Mummer's Wife* (1885) is an imitation of Zola is well known, and it has been called the first British novel in the naturalistic mode. This study shows how very great was Moore's dependence on Zola.

Cunard, Nancy. *G. M.: Memories of George Moore.* . . . See VB 1956, 260.
Rev. by Jean Noël in *Études anglaises*, X, 268; by DeLancey Ferguson in *HTB*, Aug. 11, p. 9; by Kay Dick in *Manchester*

Guardian, Oct. 5, 1956; briefly in *NCF,* XII, 173-74; by Bernard Wall in *TC,* CLXI, 80-82.

MORRIS (see also I, McLean; III, Anshen, Kegel, Wimsatt; BEERBOHM: Beerbohm).

Dewsnap, Terence. "Symmetry in the Early Poetry of William Morris." *N & Q,* new ser., IV, 132-33.

Macleod, Robert Duncan. *William Morris as Seen by His Contemporaries.* London: W & R Holmes. Pp. 23.

"A William Morris Exhibition." *TLS,* Aug. 2, p. 476.

"The Typographical Adventures of William Morris," an exhibition sponsored by the William Morris Society in London.

NEWMAN. *Autobiographical Writings.* . . . See VB 1956, 261.

Rev. in *Listener,* Feb. 14, p. 174; by W. C. Heiser in *LJ,* LXXXII, 1058; by F. F. McGrath in *Manchester Guardian,* Mar. 5, p. 4; by J. M. Cameron in *NS,* Feb. 16, pp. 209-10; by Chad Walsh in *NYTBR,* Mar. 31, p. 14; by Christopher Hollis in *S,* Dec. 14, 1956, p. 869; favorably by A. Dwight Culler in *VS,* I, 88-90.

Catholic Sermons of Cardinal Newman. Ed. Birmingham Oratory. London: Burns & Oates. Pp. 134.

Rev. by Fr. Zeno in *Dublin Rev.,* CCXXXI, 369-73; by Jacques Vallette in *Mercure de France,* CCCXXXIII, 532; in *TLS,* Mar. 15, p. 165. First publication of sermons delivered at Birmingham.

Spark, Muriel, and Stanford, Derek (eds.). *The Letters of John Henry Newman.* London: Owen. Pp. 251.

Rev. by Fr. Zeno in *Dublin Rev.,* CCXXXI, 369-73; by John Raymond in *NS,* July 6, pp. 27-28; by Sean O'Faolain in *S,* July 5, p. 21; in *TLS,* Aug. 16, p. 496.

Tillotson, Geoffrey (ed.). *Newman: Prose and Poetry.* London: Hart-Davis. Pp. 842.

Rev. by F. F. McGrath in *Manchester Guardian,* Mar. 5, p. 4; by Jacques Vallette in *Mercure de France,* CCCXXXIII, 340; by J. M. Cameron in *NS,* Feb. 16, pp. 209-10; unfavorably by Graham Hough in *S,* Mar. 22, p. 380; in *TLS,* Feb. 1, p. 63.

Boekraad, A. *The Personal Conquest of Truth According to J. H. Newman.* . . . See VB 1956, 261.

Rev. briefly by Kurt F. Reinhardt in *BA,* XXXI, 87-88.

Cameron, James Munro. *John Henry Newman.* . . . See VB 1956, 261.

Rev. by A. Koszul in *Études anglaises,* X, 165-66.

Chadwick, Owen. *From Bossuet to Newman: The Idea of Doctrinal Development.* London: Cambridge Univ. Pr. Pp. xii + 254.

Rev. by Howard Root in *S,* Dec. 6, p. 803; in *TLS,* Dec. 6, p. 744; and reply by Maurice Bévenot, S. J., Dec. 27, p. 787.

Culler, A. Dwight. *The Imperial Intellect.* . . . See VB 1956, 261.

Rev. by Walter E. Houghton in *JEGP,* LVI, 149-51; by Martin J. Svaglic in *MP,* LV, 66-70 ("The best work on Newman in almost twenty-five years"); by Barry Ulanov in *Rev. of Religion,* XXII, 89-91; by Paul Andrews in *StI,* XLV, 373-75.

Culler, A. Dwight. "John Henry Newman." *VNL,* No. 12 (Autumn), pp. 24-26.

Dessain, C. Stephen. "Newman's First Conversion." *StI,* XLV, 44-59.

Davis, H. Francis. "Newman on Educational Method." *Dublin Rev.,* CCXXX, 101-13.

Kenny, Terence. *The Political Thought of John Henry Newman.* London: Longmans. Pp. x + 208.

Rev. by Fr. Zeno in *Dublin Rev.,* CCXXXI, 369-73; by Jacques Vallette in *Mercure de France,* CCCXXXI, 321; by John Raymond in *NS,* July 6, pp. 27-28; by Sean O'Faolain in *S,* July 5, p. 21; by Paul Andrews in *StI,* XLV, 373-75; in *TLS,* Aug. 16, p. 496.

Mackerness, E. D. "John Henry Newman's 'Religious Music'." *LQHR,* CLXXXII, 130-36.

An analysis of Newman's pulpit oratory. Concludes that in his Catholic sermons Newman "voluntarily compromised a part of his primal integrity."

Noel, Elisabeth Ann. "An Edition of Poems by John Henry Cardinal Newman." *DA,* XVII, 356-57.

Summarizes a dissertation that gives "the first critical edition of Newman's poetry," consisting of an introduction, the texts of all the poems known to have been written by Newman, together with textual notes recording the significant variants which occur in the MSS and editions used by the editor, etc. It is stated that more than half of Newman's two hundred poems were written between Nov., 1832, and June, 1833. This is clearly a notable contribution.—W. D. T.

Rea, (Father) David F. "Newman: Supremely Literary." *VNL,* No. 12 (Autumn), pp. 13-16.

Townsend, Francis G. "Newman and the Problem of Critical Prose." *VNL,* No. 11

(Spring), pp. 22-25.

Fr. Zeno. *John Henry Newman: Our Way to Certitude. An Introduction to Newman's Psychological Discovery, the Illative Sense and His "Grammar of Assent".* Leiden: E. J. Brill. Pp. xiv + 279.
Rev. by H. Francis Davis in *Dublin Rev.,* CCXXXI, 373-75.

OLIPHANT. Henderson, Philip. *The Life of Laurence Oliphant: Traveller, Diplomat, and Mystic.* . . . See VB 1956, 261.
Rev. briefly by Eric Gillett in *NER,* CXLVIII, 31-36; by N. L. in *NS,* Jan. 19, p. 78.

OUIDA. Stirling, Monica. *The Fine and the Wicked: The Life and Times of Ouida.* London: Gollancz. Pp. 223.
Rev. by Christopher Sykes in *S,* Dec. 20, p. 876; unfavorably in *TLS,* Dec. 2, p. 774.

PATER (see also III, Cecil, Rose, Ryals; BEERBOHM: Beerbohm).
Cecil, Lord David. *Walter Pater.* . . . See VB 1956, 261.
Rev. by V. de S. Pinto in *RES,* new ser., VIII, 218.
Wellek, René. "Walter Pater's Literary Theory and Criticism." *VS,* I, 29-46.
West, Paul. "A Narrowed Humanism: Pater and Malraux." *Dalhousie Rev.,* XXXVII, 278-84.

PATMORE (see also II, Grylls; III, Fairchild).
De La Mare, Walter. "Metrical Technique." *NER,* CXLVI (1956), 89-97; 156-67.
Includes discussion of Patmore's ideas about the meters of prose and poetry.
Oliver, Edward James. *Coventry Patmore.* . . . See VB 1956, 262.
Rev. briefly in *N & Q,* new ser., IV, 46; in *TLS,* Jan. 25, p. 50; by John Keating in *VS,* I, 206-7.
Reid, John Cowie. *The Mind and Art of Coventry Patmore.* London: Routledge and K. Paul. Pp. viii + 358.
Rev. by A. O. J. Cockshut in *Manchester Guardian,* Apr. 9, p. 8; by Richard Sullivan in *NYTBR,* Sept. 8, p. 14; briefly by Betty Miller in *TC,* CLXI, 501-2; in *TLS,* May 24, p. 320; by John Keating in *VS,* I, 206-7.

PATTISON. Green, Vivian Hubert Howard. *Oxford Common Room: A Study of Lincoln College and Mark Pattison.* London:

Edward Arnold. Pp. 336.
Rev. in *TLS,* Dec. 20, p. 774.

ROLFE. Woolf, Cecil. *Baron Corvo: A Bibliography of Frederick Rolfe.* London: Hart-Davis. Pp. 136.
Rev. in *TLS,* Jan. 18, p. 40.

ROSSETTIS (see also II, Grylls; III, Fackler, Ryals; BEERBOHM: Beerbohm).
Doughty, Oswald (ed.). *The Poems of Dante Gabriel Rossetti.* London: Dent. Pp. xxiv + 328.
Rev. in *TLS,* Aug. 9, p. 484; by P. F. Baum in *VS,* I, 203-4.
Doughty, Oswald. *Dante Gabriel Rossetti.* ("British Book News: Bibliographical Ser. of Supplements," No. 85.) London: Longman, Green. Pp. 32.
Noticed by Jacques Vallette in *Mercure de France,* CCCXXXIII, 534.
Ray, S. N. "The First Literary Friendship of D. G. Rossetti." *N & Q,* new ser., IV, 453-54.

RUSKIN (see also III, Hitchcock, Kegel, Wimsatt; CARLYLE: Burd).
Adams, Richard P. "Architecture and the Romantic Tradition." *Amer. Quart.,* IX, 46-62.
Autret, Jean. *L'Influence de Ruskin sur la vie, les idées et l'oeuvre de Marcel Proust.* . . . See VB 1956, 262.
Rev. by Harry Levin in *French Rev.,* XXX, 417; unfavorably by L. A. Bisson in *French Studies,* XI, 188-89; by Douglas W. Alden in *RoR,* XLVII, 155-56.
Evans, Joan, and Whitehouse, John Howard (eds.). *The Diaries of John Ruskin (1835-1847).* . . . See VB 1956, 262.
Rev. by Bertram Morris in *JAA,* XV, 491-92; by Jacques Vallette in *Mercure de France,* CCCXXXIX, 148-49; briefly by Eric Gillett in *NER,* CXLVII (1956), 319-24; in *SR,* Feb. 16, p. 50; briefly by Betty Miller in *TC,* CLXI, 82-83; in *TLS,* Mar. 22, p. 176; by John Bradley in *VS,* I, 100-101.
Evans, Joan. "John Ruskin as Artist." *Apollo,* LXVI, 139-45.
Fain, John Tyree. *Ruskin and the Economists.* . . . See VB 1956, 262.
Rev. by Scott Gordon in *JPE,* LXV, 461; by Charles T. Dougherty in *MLN,* LXXII, 626-27.
Kegel, Charles H. "Ruskin's St. George in America." *Amer. Quart.,* IX, 412-20.
Interesting history of the "Ruskin Co-op-

erative Association" in Tennessee.—
C. T. D.

Maslenikov, Oleg A. "Ruskin, Bely, and the Solov'yovs." *Slavonic and East European Rev.*, XXXV, 15-24.

Bely knew Ruskin's works through Mme. Solov'yov and he drew many images and perhaps the theme of his *Third Symphony: The Return* from Ruskin.

Spence, Margaret E. "The Guild of St. George: Ruskin's Attempt to Translate His Ideas into Practice." *Bull. John Rylands Libr.*, XL, 147-201.

"This St. George's work was to John Ruskin the prime task of his life. . . . It may be that too many of his critics have paused to mock, pity, and rebuke . . ." This impressive article quotes from various unpublished letters.—W. D. T.

Viljoen, Helen Gill. *Ruskin's Scottish Heritage*. . . . See VB 1956, 263.

Rev. by Francis G. Townsend in *JEGP*, LVI, 295-98; by S. O. A. Ullmann in *MLN*, LXXII, 225-28; by Robert A. Colby in *MP*, LIV, 210-12.

RUSSELL. *My Indian Mutiny Diary*. Ed. Michael Edwardes. London: Cassel. Pp. xxvii + 288.

Rev. by H. Baerlein in *CR*, CXCII, 121; by Alan Hodge in *History Today*, VII, 483; by Paul Johnson in *NS*, June 8, pp. 743-44; by Colin Welch in *S*, June 7, pp. 754-55; in *TLS*, June 14, p. 362.

SCHREINER. Gregg, Lyndall. *Memories of Olive Schreiner*. London: Chambers. Pp. 78.

Rev. in *TLS*, Dec. 13, p. 754.

Kindilien, Carlin T. "Stephen Crane and the 'Savage Philosophy' of Olive Schreiner." *Boston Univ. Studies in English*, III, 97-107.

SHARP (see also III, Garbaty).

Iorio, John J. "A Victorian Controversy: William Sharp's Letters on 'Motherhood'." *Colby Libr. Quart.*, IV, 178-84.

SHAW (see also I, Gordan; III, Cairns, Garbaty, Harris; DICKENS: Johnson).

Bernard Shaw's Letters to Granville Barker. Ed. C. B. Purdom. London: Phoenix House. Pp. viii + 206.

Rev. by Gordon Gould in *Chicago Sunday Tribune*, Jan. 27, p. 3; by W. P. Eaton in *HTB*, Feb. 17, p. 9; by Gerard Fay in *Manchester Guardian*, Apr. 12, p. 6; by Jacques Vallette in *Mercure de France*, CCCXXXIII, 337; by T. C. Worsley in *NS*, Mar. 30, pp. 415-16; briefly by Ger-

ard Fay in *S*, June 7, p. 759; by Warren S. Smith in *The Shaw Bulletin*, II, No. 1, 21-24; by D. E. Solem in *Theatre Arts*, XLI (May), 16, 89; in *TLS*, Mar. 29, p. 190; by H. M. Jones in *VS*, I, 165-72.

My Dear Dorothea: A Practical System of Moral Education for Females Embodied in a Letter to a Young Person of That Sex. London: Phoenix House. Pp. 55.

Rev. by Edward Wagenknecht in *Chicago Sunday Tribune*, May 26, p. 8; by Rod Nordell in *Christian Science Monitor*, May 2, p. 7; by Walter Kerr in *HTB*, Apr. 28, p. 1; by E. F. Walbridge in *LJ*, LXXXII, 1534-35; by Lewis Nichols in *NYTBR*, Apr. 28, p. 12; by Mark Bennett in *The Shaw Bulletin*, II, No. 2, 17-18; in *TLS*, Nov. 16, 1956, p. 682; by H. M. Jones in *VS*, I, 165-72.

Barber, George S. "Shaw's Contributions to Music Criticism." *PMLA*, LXXII, 1005-17.

Barrett, William. "A Plausible Irishman." *ParR*, XXIV, 101-5.

Barrett says that contemporary playwrights have no idea of how to make a statement and no statements to make anyway, which is one way of accounting for the current Shaw boom. After everything has been said against Shaw, and almost everything has, it is still true that he was a master craftsman. His delight in ideas as toys gave him a passable substitute for dramatic objectivity. Barrett compares Shaw with O'Neill. Shaw seldom creates psychological tension or a powerfully emotional scene, but through the blarney comes a real feeling for people; O'Neill, on the other hand, can create the tensions and produce the profundity, but his attitude toward people remains cerebral and remote.

Benedictine Nuns, Stanbrook. *In a Great Tradition*. . . . See VB 1956, 263.

Rev. by Ruth A. Ames in *CWd*, CLXXXV, 475-76; by Aelred Graham in *HTB*, June 23, p. 6; by Peter Quennell in *NYTBR*, June 30, p. 4.

Bourget-Pailleron, Robert. "Revue dramatique." *Rev. des deux mondes*, Feb. 1, pp. 531-36.

Contains a review of César et Cléopâtre, translated from Shaw by Henriette Hamon, with the collaboration of Jean Marsan.

Cathey, Kenneth Clay. "George Bernard Shaw's Drama of Ideas." *DA*, XVII, 2606.

Collins, P. A. W. "Shaw on Shakespeare." *Shakespeare Quarterly*, VIII, 1-13.

Collis, John Stewart. "The Two Bernard Shaws." *Dublin Mag.*, new ser., XXXI,

(July-September, 1956), 36-40.
Shaw is "a sea of confusing lucidity."

Couchman, Gordon W. "Here Was A Caesar: Shaw's Comedy Today." *PMLA*, LXXII, 272-85.

Diesel, Leota. "The Traveling 'Fair Lady'." *Theatre Arts*, XLI (October), 63-64, 94.

Ervine, St. John Greer. *Bernard Shaw.* . . . See VB 1956, 263.
Rev. briefly by Roger B. Dooley in *CWd*, CLXXXIV, 313; by Kenneth Muir in *EC*, VII, 217-21; briefly by Eric Gillett in *NER*, CXLVII (1956), 143-48; by Walter Pritchard Eaton in *VQR*, XXXIII, 124-27.

Eyrignoux, T. "Le Centenaire de la Naissance de Bernard Shaw." *Études anglaises*, X, 123-27.
Eyrignoux discusses Shaw's reputation at present, and expresses disappointment at St. John Ervine's, *Bernard Shaw: His Life, Work, and Friends.*

Gordan, John D. "Bernard Shaw: 1856-1956; An Exhibition from the Berg Collection." *Bull. New York Pub. Libr.*, LXI, 117-38, 192-207, 250-59.
Rev. in *TLS*, Feb. 1, p. 72. This was published as a separate pamphlet (pp. 51) by the New York Public Library.

Henderson, Archibald. *George Bernard Shaw: Man of the Century.* . . . See VB 1956, 264.
Rev. by Edward Wagenknecht in *Chicago Sunday Tribune*, Dec. 9, 1956, p. 3; by E. F. Melvin in *Christian Science Monitor*, Dec. 27, 1956, p. 7; by Ward Morehouse in *Theatre Arts*, XLI, 62; by Walter Pritchard Eaton in *VQR*, XXXIII, 124-27.

Jones, Howard Mumford. "Shaw as a Victorian." *VS*, I, 165-72.
Rev. of biographies by Ervine, Henderson, and Winsten (see VB 1956, 263, 264, 265). Connects Shaw's radicalism, rationalism, hero-worship, and dramatic technique with their Victorian origins.

Krabbe, Henning. *Bernard Shaw on Shakespeare and English Shakespearean Acting. Pubs. of the Univ. of Aarhus*, XXVII, Supp. B. Aarhus, Denmark: University Pr., 1955. Pp. 66.
Rev. by St. Vincent Troubridge in *Shakespeare Quarterly*, VIII, 101-4.

"Major Barbara". *Theatre Arts*, XLI (January), 21-22.
Review of the Producers' Theatre production directed by Charles Laughton.

McDowell, Frederick P. W. "Victorian Shaw." *VNL*, No. 11 (Spring), pp. 16-19.

McDowell, Frederick P. W. "The World, God, and World Bettering: Shaw's *Buoyant Billions*." *Boston Univ. Studies in English*, III, 167-76.

Moffett, John. "When Shaw to Savage Spoke." *NER*, CXLIX, 27-29.
How Shaw, during his visit to New Zealand in 1934, gave impetus to a program to give free milk to schoolchildren.

O'Donnell, Norbert F. "Shaw, Bunyan, and Puritanism." *PMLA*, LXXII, 520-33.

Perrine, Laurence. "Shaw's *Arms and the Man.*" *Ex*, XV, Item 54.
On Sergius as the consistent disillusioned romantic.

Rypins, Stanley. "Bernard Shaw Remembered." *VQR*, XXXIII, 80-92.

Schlauch, Margaret. "Symbolic Figures and the Symbolic Technique of George Bernard Shaw." *Sci. and Soc.*, XXI, 210-21.

Shaw Bulletin —
Vol. II, No. 1 (January, 1957) has items: 'Leaves from a Prison Diary,' an early Shaw book review (pp. 1-3); "Shavian News Notes" (pp. 3-4); "A Continuing Check-list of Shaviana" (pp. 4, 24-25); Rice, Elmer, "Extemporaneous Remarks Made at a Luncheon at the Hotel Savoy, London Given by the British Society of Authors and Composers, On the Centenary of George Bernard Shaw's Birth, July 26, 1956" (pp. 5-7); Rockman, Robert E., "Dickens and Shaw: Another Parallel" (pp. 8-10); Weintraub, Stanley, "Bernard Shaw, Charles Lever and *Immaturity*" (pp. 11-15); "Theatre Notes" — by Maxwell Steinhardt on Laughton's version of *Major Barbara* (pp. 15-16), by Felix Grendon on the Maurice Evans production of *The Apple Cart*; "G. B. S. — Published and Recorded" — by Mark Bennett on the Cambridge Drama Festival recording of *Saint Joan* (pp. 19-20), by Ozy on a book by Tullah Innes Hanley called *The Strange Triangle of G. B. S.* (pp. 20-21), by Warren S. Smith a review of *Bernard Shaw's Letters to Granville Barker* edited by C. B. Purdom (pp. 21-24).
No. 2 (May, 1957) has items: "Archibald Henderson, Shavian Biographer Extraordinary: An Eightieth Birthday Salute" — by Brooks Atkinson "Henderson and Shaw: Plain Facts and Brilliant Answers" (pp. 1-3), by Lucile Kelling "Archibald Henderson: A Selected Bibliography of His Writings on Shaw, Drama and Theatre" (pp. 3-8); Weintraub, Stanley, "The Garnetts, The Fabians and *The Paradox Club*" (pp. 9-12); "Shavian News Notes" (pp. 13-14); "A Continuing

Check-list of Shaviana" (pp. 14, 24-25); Miller, Henry, "An American's Point of View re *The Strange Triangle of G. B. S.* — A Rebuttal" (pp. 15-16); Bennett, Mark, "G. B. S.'s Advice to Children of All Ages," a review of Shaw's *My Dear Dorothea* (pp. 17-18); "Theatre Notes" — by Ozy on the Elizabeth and William Landis production of *In Good King Charles's Golden Days* (pp. 19-20); by Felix Grendon on a Shaw evening at the Grolier Club, two short plays, *The Fascinating Foundling* and *Why She Would Not* (pp. 20-22); "Shavian Dead Letter File" (pp. 23-24).

No. 3 (September, 1957), has items: Starr, William T., "Romain Rolland and George Bernard Shaw" (pp. 1-6); "Biographer's Blunders Corrected: G. B. S. on Edward McNulty's 'George Bernard Shaw as a Boy'" (pp. 7-10); "Shavian News Notes" (pp. 10, 25); Han, Tien, "Bernard Shaw: Master of Realist Drama [A Chinese Communist Perspective]" (pp. 11-15); McDowell, Frederick P. W., "Guildenstern Among the Biographers," a review of Stephen Winsten's *Jesting Apostle: The Private Life of Bernard Shaw* (pp. 16-20); Smith, Warren S., "The Nun and the Dramatist," a review of *In a Great Tradition: Tribute to Dame Laurentia McLachlan, Abbess of Stanbrook* (pp. 21-23); "A Continuing Check-list of Shaviana" (pp. 24-25).

"Shaw and the Actor." *Theatre Arts*, XLI (March), 29-30, 88-89.

Players Rex Harrison and Siobhan McKenna answer questions about Henry Higgins and Saint Joan.

Silverman, Albert H. "Bernard Shaw's Shakespeare Criticism." *PMLA*, LXXII, 722-36.

Shaw's criticism of Shakespeare explained as "dogma consistent with his antitragic, antiromantic criticism of art and life."

Smoker, Barbara. "The £ s d of G. B. S." *NS*, Feb. 23, pp. 227-28.

An account of the current condition of Shaw's estate.

Smoker, Barbara. "Shaw and the Alphabet." *NS*, Jan. 26, pp. 94-96.

Vielleux, Jere Shanor. "An Analysis of the Rhetorical Situation and Rhetorical Character Types in Selected Plays of George Bernard Shaw." *DA*, XVII, 2089.

Weintraub, Stanley. "Bernard Shaw, Novelist." *DA*, XVII, 369-70.

West, E. J. "G. B. S. and the Rival Queens — Duse and Bernhardt." *QJS*, XLIII, 365-73.

Winsten, Stephen. *Jesting Apostle: The Private Life of Bernard Shaw.* . . . See VB 1956, 265.

Rev. by Stanley Weintraub in *CE*, XIX, 87; by Edward Wagenknecht in *Chicago Sunday Tribune*, July 14, p. 2; by E. F. Melvin in *Christian Science Monitor*, June 6, p. 7; briefly by George Freedley in *LJ*, LXXXII, 3214; briefly by Eric Gillett in *NER*, CXLVII (1956), 143-48; by Frederick P. W. McDowell in *The Shaw Bulletin*, II, No. 3, 16-20; by Edmund Fuller in *SR*, July 27, p. 18; in *TLS*, July 27, p. 441.

SMILES. Smiles, Aileen. *Samuel Smiles and His Surroundings.* . . . See VB 1956, 265.

Rev. by F. W. Gray in *Dalhousie Rev.*, XXXVI, 433-35; by Louis Rocher in *Études anglaises*, X, 267-68.

SMITH, SYDNEY. Auden, W. H. (ed.). *Selected Writings of Sydney Smith.* London: Faber. Pp. xx + 396.

Rev. by W. H. Hughes in *NS*, Dec. 28, p. 882; in *TLS*, Oct. 11, p. 604.

Smith, Nowell C. (ed.). *Selected Letters of Sydney Smith.* . . . See VB 1956, 265.

Rev. favorably by André Parreaux in *Études anglaises*, X, 61-63.

STEPHEN. Appleman, Philip. "Evolution and Two Critics of Art and Literature." *Proc. of the Third International Congress on Aesthetics*, pp. 237-40.

Sheen, Edwin Drummond. "Leslie Stephen, Man of Letters and Critic of Literature." *DA*, XVII, 2003-4.

Tolleson, Floyd Clyde, Jr. "The Relation Between Leslie Stephen's Agnosticism anad Voltaire's Deism." *DA*, XV (1955), 2218-19.

Ullmann, S. O. A. (ed.). *Men, Books, and Mountains: Essays of Leslie Stephen.* London: Hogarth Pr., 1956. Pp. 247.

Rev. by John Bayley in *S*, Jan. 11, pp. 58-59; in *TLS*, Feb. 15, p. 98; by John Bicknell in *VS*, I, 103. Previously uncollected essays, mainly from *Cornhill* and *National Review*.

Wellek, René. "Leslie Stephen's Stature as a Literary Critic." *VNL*, No. 11 (Spring), pp. 19-22.

STEVENSON (see also III, Phelps).

Jordan, John E. (ed.). *Robert Louis Stevenson's Silverado Journal.* . . . See VB 1955, 269.

Rev. by Lionel Stevenson in *MLN*, LXXII, 62-64.

Aldington, Richard. *Portrait of a Rebel: The*

Life and Work of Robert Louis Stevenson. London: Evans. Pp. 245. Rev. unfavorably by Janet Adam Smith in *NS*, Oct. 12, pp. 470-71; by Iain Hamilton in *S*, Sept. 27, p. 402; in *TLS*, Oct. 4, p. 594.

Chamson, André. "R. – L. Stevenson et les Cévennes." *Rev. des deux mondes*, Apr. 1, pp. 422-29.

Ferguson, DeLancey, and Waingrow, Marshall (eds.). *R. L. S.: Stevenson's Letters to Charles Baxter.* . . . See VB 1956, 265. Rev. by A. Dwight Culler in *JEGP*, LVI, 292-93; by Compton Mackenzie in *S*, Feb. 8, p. 180; briefly by Betty Miller in *TC*, CLXI, 265; in *TLS*, Mar. 15, p. 160.

J. P. H. "*Treasure Island* at the Theatre Royal, Stratford." *NS*, Jan. 5, p. 13. The adaption was by Joan Littlewood.

McKay, George L. (comp.). *A Stevenson Library: Catalogue of a Collection of Writings by and about Robert Louis Stevenson Formed by Edwin J. Beinecke.* Vol. III: *Autograph Letters by Robert Louis Stevenson and His Wife.* New Haven: Yale Univ. Libr. (For Vol. I see VB 1951, 270; Vol. II see VB 1953, 262.) Pp. 351. Rev. in *TLS*, Mar. 15, p. 160.

Neider, Charles (ed.). *Our Samoan Adventure.* . . . See VB 1956, 266. Rev. by Eric Gillett in *NER*, CXLVI (1956), 281-88.

Poston, Lawrence, III. " 'Markheim' and Chesterton's 'The Hammer of God'." *NCF*, XII, 235-36.

Stevenson, Robert. "Robert Louis Stevenson's Musical Interests." *PMLA*, LXXII, 700-704.

SURTEES. Noakes, Aubrey. *Horses, Hounds and Humans.* London: Oldbourne Pr. Pp. 184. Rev. by V. S. Pritchett in *NS*, June 1, pp. 709-10. Biography of Surtees.

SWINBURNE (see also III, Fairchild, Rose, Ryals; BEERBOHM: Beerbohm).

Connolly, Thomas E. "Swinburne on 'The Music of Poetry'." *PMLA*, LXXII, 680-88.

Lang, Cecil Y. "A Manuscript, a Mare's-Nest, and a Mystery." *Yale Univ. Libr. Gazette*, XXXI, 163-71.

Noyes, Alfred. "Dinner at the Pines: Reminiscences of Swinburne." *Listener*, Mar.

28, pp. 507-8.

Viljoen, Helen Gill. "Swinburne's 'Boo'." *VNL*, No. 12 (Autumn), p. 29.

SYMONDS (see also STEPHEN: Appleman).

Losa, Mary Jane. "John Addington Symonds: Nineteenth-Century Historian of the Italian Renaissance." *DA*, XVII, 2012.

TALFOURD. Watson, Vera. "The Journals of Thomas Noon Talfourd." *TLS*, Feb. 8, p. 88. An account of five volumes of Talfourd's journals for the years 1842-44, 1846, and 1852-54.

TAYLOR, SIR HENRY. *The Statesman.* With a New Introductory Essay by Leo Silberman. Cambridge: Heffer. Pp. lvi + 134. Rev. by Henry Fairlie in *S*, Oct. 25, p. 552; in *TLS*, Oct. 25, p. 641. A guide for politicians and senior civil servants first published in 1836.

TENNYSON (see also I, Gordan; III, De Selincourt, Fairchild, Kaufman, Langbaum, Lewis, Roppen, Ryals, Wain).

Johnson, W. Stacy. "The Theme of Marriage in Tennyson." *VNL*, No. 12 (Autumn), pp. 6-8.

Lucas, F. L. *Tennyson.* ("British Book News: Bibliographical Ser. of Supplements," No. 83.) London: Longmans, Green. Pp. 40. Rev. by Jacques Vallette in *Mercure de France*, CCCXXXIII, 163; briefly by Betty Miller in *TC*, CLXI, 592-94.

Robson, W. W. "The Dilemma of Tennyson." *Listener*, June 13, pp. 963-65. Discusses the problem of the discrepancy between Tennyson "the responsible social being, the admirably serious and 'committed' Victorian intellectual," and Tennyson "the most un-strenuous, lonely, and poignant of poets."

Sanders, Charles Richard. "Tennyson and the Human Hand." *VNL*, No. 11 (Spring), pp. 5-14.

Shannon, Edgar F., Jr. "Alfred Tennyson." *VNL*, No. 12 (Autumn), pp. 26-27.

Stanford, W. B. *The Ulysses Theme.* . . . See VB 1956, 267. Rev. by Northrop Frye in *Comp. Lit.*, IX, 181-82.

Tennyson, Sir Charles. "The Idylls of the King." *TC*, CLXI, 277-86. The genesis of the poem.

Tennyson, Sir Charles. *Stars and Markets.* London: Chatto & Windus. Pp. 263.

Rev. by Eric Gillett in *NER,* CXLIX, 198; by Betty Miller in *NS,* Mar. 16, p. 348; by Iain Hamilton in *S,* Apr. 5, p. 446; in *TLS,* Mar. 22, p. 180 (and see a letter by Sir Charles, March 29, p. 193). Memoirs, inclding early memories of his grandfather, the Poet Laureate.

THACKERAY (see also I, Dickson; III, Gray; DICKENS: Low).

Fraser, Russell A. "Pernicious Casuistry: A Study of Character in *Vanity Fair.*" *NCF,* XII, 137-47.

Krishnaswami, P. R. *In Thackeray's Workshop.* Madras: T. Sundara Roghavan, 1956. Pp. 124.

Rev. by L. B. in *Études anglaises,* X, 163-64.

Rader, Ralph Wilson. "Thackeray's Injustice to Fielding." *JEGP,* LVI, 203-12.

Argues that Thackeray's unfavorable lecture on Fielding was occasioned by a sense of guilt at his own real or imagined shortcomings.

Ray, Gordon N. *Thackeray: The Uses of Adversity.* . . . See VB 1956, 267.

Rev. by L. Bonnerot in *Études anglaises,* X, 162-63; by J. H. Buckley in *MLN,* LXXII, 60-62; favorably by George H. Ford in *MP,* LIV, 207-10; by Eric Gillett in *NER,* CXLVI (1956), 109-14; by Henry Gifford in *RES,* new ser., VIII, 325-26; by P. F. Baum in *SAQ,* LVI, 135-36.

Ray, Gordon N. (ed.). *William Makepeace Thackeray's Contributions to the Morning Chronicle.* . . . See VB 1956, 267.

Rev. by L. Bonnerot in *Études anglaises,* X, 161-62; by Lionel Stevenson in *MP,* LIV, 205-7.

Solomon, Eric. "An Interview with Thackeray." *N & Q,* new ser., IV, 397-98.

An interview conducted by the American novelist John Esten Cooke in 1855.

Tilford, John E., Jr. "The Untimely Death of Rachel Esmond." *NCF,* XII, 148-53. Thackeray's inconsistency about the date of Rachel's death.

THOMPSON, FRANCIS (see also III, Fackler).

Pope, Myrtle Pihlman. "Francis Thompson: Poet as Critic." *DA,* XVII, 2599-2600.

Thomson, Paul van Kuykenball. "A Study of Certain Notebooks and Manuscripts of Francis Thompson in Relation to His Poetic Theory and Critical Procedure." *DA,* XVII, 139.

Wilson, W. G. "Francis Thompson's Outlook on Science." *CR,* CXCII, 263-66.

TROLLOPE (see also I, Dickson; III, West; BROWNINGS: Windolph).

Cockshut, A. O. J. *Anthony Trollope.* . . . See VB 1956, 267.

Rev. by Donald Smalley in *NCF,* XII, 90-92.

WARD. Coghlan, Kathryn Alberta. "Mrs. Humphry Ward, Novelist and Thinker." *DA,* XVII, 2606-7.

Willey, Basil. "How *Robert Elsmere* Struck Some Contemporaries." *Essays and Studies,* 1957, new ser., X (for the English Assoc.), 53-68.

WARREN. Yorks, Samuel Augustus. "Samuel Warren: An Early Contributor to Victorian Literature." *DA,* XVI (1956), 2171-72.

WHITE, W. H. Maclean, Catherine Macdonald. *Mark Rutherford.* . . . See VB 1956, 258.

Rev. by Rosemary Beresford in *RES,* new ser., VIII, 330-32.

WILDE (see also III, Cairns, Peters, Rose, Wimsatt).

The Importance of Being Earnest. . . . Ed. Sarah Augusta Dickson. See VB 1956, 268.

Rev. in *TLS,* Mar. 1, p. 136.

Cargill, Oscar. "Mr. James's Aesthetic Mr. Nash." *NCF,* XII, 177-87. Evidence that Gabriel Nash, in *The Tragic Muse,* is drawn from Oscar Wilde.

Finzi, John Charles (comp.). *Oscar Wilde and His Literary Circle: A Catalogue of Manuscripts and Letters in the William Andrews Clark Memorial Library.* Berkeley: Univ. of California Pr. Pp. xxxiv + 242.

Miserocchi, Manlio. "Attraverso il centenario di G. B. Shaw quello di O. Wilde." *Nuova Antologia,* CCCCLXX, 377-86.

Ojala, Aatos. *Aestheticism and Oscar Wilde.* Part 2: *Literary Style.* Helsinki: Finnish Academy of Science and Letters, 1955. Pp. 270.

Part 1 rev. by Herbert Huscher in *Anglia,* LXXIV (1956), 382-85; Parts 1 and 2 rev. by Hans Joachim-Lang in *Euphorion,* LI, 97-100. For Part I see VB 1955, 272.

YEATS (see also I, Gordan; III, Bayley,

Craig, Davidson, Eliot, Garbaty, Holroyd, Miles, Wain; BEERBOHM: Beerbohm).

Collected Poems. . . . See VB 1956, 269.
Rev. by B. R. McElderry in *Personalist,* XXXVIII, 314-15.

The Variorum Edition of the Poems of W. B. Yeats. Ed. Peter Allt and Russell Alspach. New York: Macmillan. Pp. xxxv + 884.
Rev. by Horace Reynolds in *Christian Science Monitor,* Oct. 31, p. 11; in *HTB,* Nov. 17, p. 12; by Horace Gregory in *NYTBR,* Dec. 22, pp. 5, 18; by Winfield T. Scott in *SR,* Dec. 7, pp. 47-50.

A Vision. . . . See VB 1956, 269.
Rev. by W. H. Davenport in *Personalist,* XXXVIII, 315.

Adams, Hazard. *Blake and Yeats.* . . . See VB 1956, 269.
Rev. briefly by John P. Hughes in *BA,* XXXI, 80; by Thomas Partinson in *MP,* LIV, 281-84; by V. G. Kiernan in *Sci. and Soc.,* XXI, 185-87.

Adams, Hazard. "The William Butler Yeats Collection at Texas." *Libr. Chronicle of Univ. of Texas,* VI, 33-38.

Adams, Hazard. "Yeats's Country of the Young." *PMLA,* LXXII, 510-19.
Yeats's rejected version of a play on which he and Lady Gregory originally collaborated. Lady Gregory's version of the story appeared as *The Travelling Man.*

Beerbohm, Max. "First Meetings with William Butler Yeats." *AM,* CC, 70-72.
This article appeared in *Listener,* Jan. 6, 1955, pp. 15-16.

Denton, Marilyn Jewell. "The Form of Yeats' Lyric Poetry." *DA,* XVII, 3012.
This dissertation suggests that Yeats gave far more attention to poetic form than is generally recognized. The writer consulted Yeats's MS notebooks and "found passages illustrating his method of composing poems"; with Mrs. Yeats's assistance, transcribed those which illustrated Yeats's concern with form. She discusses in detail his indebtedness to certain poets, including William Morris. She lists Yeats's poems according to their verse forms. She discusses his scattered writings about poetic form. A noteworthy study. —W. D. T.

Donoghue, Denis. "Yeats and the Clean Outline." *SeR,* LXV, 202-25.

F., G. S. "Yeats Exhibition at Reading University." *NS,* June 1, p. 706.

Franklin, Laura Mabel. "The Development of Yeats's Poetic Diction." *DA,* XVI (1956), 2456-57.

Hethmon, Robert Henry, Jr. "The Theatre's Anti-Self: A Study of the Symbolism of Yeats' Unpopular Plays." *DA,* XVII, 917.

Less, F. N. "Yeats's 'Byzantium', Dante, and Shelley." *N & Q,* new ser., IV, 312-13.

Mazzaro, Jerome L. "Apple Imagery in Yeats' 'The Song of Wandering Aengus'." *MLN,* LXXII, 342-43.
Argues that the imagery should be interpreted mythologically rather than personally.

Mazzaro, Jerome L. "Yeats' 'The Second Coming'." *Ex,* XVI, Item 6.
On the falcon as a symbol of chaos.

Miner, Earl Roy. "A Poem by Swift and W. B. Yeats's *Words upon the Window-pane.*" *MLN,* LXXII, 273-75.

Moore, John Rees. "Evolution of Myth in the Plays of W. B. Yeats." *DA,* XVII, 1556-57.

O'Brien, James Howard. "Theosophy and the Poetry of George Russell (AE), William Butler Yeats, and James Stephens." *DA,* XVI (1956), 2167-68.

Pirkhofer, A. M. "Zur Bildersprache von Blake und Yeats." *Anglia,* LXXV, 224-33.

Reid, Benjamin Lawrence. "W. B. Yeats and Generic Tragedy." *DA,* XVII, 2615.

Srigley, M. B. "The Mathematical Muse." *Dublin Mag.,* new ser., XXXI, (July-September, 1956), 13-21.
A most interesting article; it argues (following Spengler) that "each scientific interpretation of the universe is the rationalization of an epoch's dream, and that this rationalization is always expressed mathematically." Poetry "humanizes" the mathematical vision. Yeats saw the need of modern poetry to grasp the Einsteinian vision and to "humanize" it.—C. T. D.

Unterecker, John Eugene. "A Study of the Function of Bird and Tree Imagery in the Works of W. B. Yeats." *DA,* XVII, 637-38.

Warschausky, Sidney. "W. B. Yeats as Literary Critic." *DA,* XVII, 1559-60.

Wilson, F. A. O. "Patterns in Yeats's Imagery: The Herne's Egg." *MP,* LV, 46-52.
A suggestive analysis of the symbolism of *The Herne's Egg* in the light of Yeats's two principal sources: the Indian philosophy of Purohit Swami and Balzac's *Seraphita.*—R. A. D.

YONGE (see also III, Lewis).

Lochhead, Marion. "The Victorian Young Lady." *QR,* CCXCV, 323-33.

VICTORIAN BIBLIOGRAPHY FOR 1958

Francis G. Townsend, editor

THIS BIBLIOGRAPHY has been prepared by a committee of the Victorian Literature Group of the Modern Language Association of America: Francis G. Townsend, chairman, Florida State University; William D. Templeman, University of Southern California; Robert C. Slack, Carnegie Institute of Technology; Oscar Maurer, University of Texas; Robert A. Donovan, Cornell University; Charles T. Dougherty, St. Louis University, and Donald J. Gray, Indiana University. It attempts to list the noteworthy publications of 1958 (including reviews of these and earlier items) that have a bearing on the Victorian period, as well as similar publications of earlier date that have been inadvertently omitted from the preceding Victorian bibliographies. Unless otherwise stated, the date of publication is 1958. Reference to a page in the bibliography for 1957, in *Victorian Studies,* June, 1958, is made by the following form: See VB 1957, 260. Some cross-references are given, though not all that are possible. For certain continuing bibliographical works the reader should consult VB 1941, the last annual bibliography in which such works are listed in full. Bibliographical entries are made to conform as closely as possible with the British National Bibliography for books first published in Great Britain, and with the Library of Congress Catalog for books first published in the United States.

Several members of the Victorian Literature Group have made special contributions to VB 1958. The editor wishes to express his gratitude for such assistance to Professors Carl J. Weber of Colby College, T. J. Truss

of the University of Mississippi, and Richard C. Tobias, of the University of Pittsburgh.

Next year's VB will be edited by Professor Robert C. Slack, of the Carnegie Institute of Technology. Communications should be addressed to him.

KEY TO ABBREVIATIONS

AHR = American Historical Review
AL = American Literature
AM = Atlantic Monthly
APSR = American Political Science Review
APSS = Annals of the American Academy of Political and Social Science
ArQ = Arizona Quarterly
BA = Books Abroad
BB = Bulletin of Bibliography
BLR = Bodleian Library Record
BPLQ = Boston Public Library Quarterly
BSP = Papers of the Bibliographical Society of America
CE = College English
CHJ = Historical Journal (formerly *Cambridge Historical Journal*)
CJ = Cambridge Journal
CR = Contemporary Review
CWd = Catholic World
DA = Dissertation Abstracts
DUJ = Durham University Journal
EC = Essays in Criticism
EHR = English Historical Review
EJ = English Journal
ELH = Journal of English Literary History
ESt = English Studies
Ex = Explicator
HJ = Hibbert Journal

HLB = *Harvard Library Bulletin*
HLQ = *Huntington Library Quarterly*
HTB = *New York Herald Tribune Book Review*
JAA = *Journal of Aesthetics and Art Criticism*
JEGP = *Journal of English and Germanic Philology*
JEH = *Journal of Economic History*
JHI = *Journal of the History of Ideas*
JMH = *Journal of Modern History*
JP = *Journal of Philosophy*
JPE = *Journal of Political Economy*
KR = *Kenyon Review*
LJ = *Library Journal*
LQ = *Library Quarterly*
LQHR = *London Quarterly and Holborn Review*
LR = *Library Review*
M & L = *Music and Letters*
MLJ = *Modern Language Journal*
MLN = *Modern Language Notes*
MLQ = *Modern Language Quarterly*
MLR = *Modern Language Review*
MP = *Modern Philology*
N = *Nation*
N & Q = *Notes and Queries*
NCF = *Nineteenth-Century Fiction*
NEQ = *New England Quarterly*
NER = *National and English Review*
New R = *New Republic*
NS = *New Statesman*
NYTBR = *New York Times Book Review*
PAPS = *Proceedings of the American Philological Society*
ParR = *Partisan Review*
PLC = *Princeton University Library Chronicle*
PMLA = *Publications of the Modern Language Association of America*
PQ = *Philological Quarterly*
PSQ = *Political Science Quarterly*
QJS = *Quarterly Journal of Speech*
QQ = *Queen's Quarterly*
QR = *Quarterly Review*
RES = *Review of English Studies*
RoR = *Romanic Review*
S = *Spectator*
SAQ = *South Atlantic Quarterly*
SeR = *Sewanee Review*
SP = *Studies in Philology*
SR = *Saturday Review*
StI = *Studies: An Irish Quarterly Review*

TC = *Twentieth Century*
TLS = *Times Literary Supplement*
TQ = *University of Toronto Quarterly*
VNL = *Victorian News Letter*
VQR = *Virginia Quarterly Review*
VS = *Victorian Studies*
YR = *Yale Review*

I. BIBLIOGRAPHICAL MATERIAL

"Annual Bibliography for 1957." *PMLA,* LXXIII, No. 2, 173-91; English Language and Literature, "IX. Nineteenth Century" and "X. Twentieth Century," ed. Charles C. Mish, Seymour B. Chatman, Harrison T. Meserole, and J. Max Patrick.

Cam, Gilbert A. "A Survey of the Literature on Investment Companies 1864-1957." *Bull. New York Pub. Libr.,* LXII, 57-74.

Clark, Alexander P. "The Manuscript Collections of the Princeton University Library." *PLC,* XIX, 159-90.
Mentions (pp. 164-70, 184) items by Macready, Herschel, Barrie, Hardy, Collins, Bulwer-Lytton, Mrs. Craik, William Black, Lewis Carroll, George Eliot, C. Kingsley, Hughes, Reade, Stevenson, Trollope, Dickens, Meredith, Lewes, Du Maurier, P. J. Bailey, Mrs. Gaskell, "Ouida," the Brontës, Yonge, Thackeray, Madame Vestris, Coventry Patmore, Allingham, Bridges, Carlyle, Ruskin, Housman, Yeats.

Cohen, I. Bernard, and Strelsky, Katharine (eds.). "Eighty-second Critical Bibliography of the History of Science and Its Cultural Influences (to 1 January 1957)." *Isis,* XLVIII (1957), 189-280.

Cohen, I. Bernard, and Strelsky, Katharine (eds.). "Eighty-third Critical Bibliography of the History of Science and Its Cultural Influences (to 1 January 1958)." *Isis,* XLIX, 179-296.

Dickson, Sarah Augusta. *The Arents Collection of Books in Parts and Associated Literature.* New York: New York Public Libr., 1957. Pp. 88.
Rev. by Alexander Wainwright in *Book Collector,* VII, 435-36; by Theodore Bolton in *BSP,* LII, 224-26. Collection includes sporting, comic, travel books, and novels by Dickens, Thackeray, Trollope, Ainsworth, etc. as they appeared serially; MSS and letters of Dickens, Thackeray, and others; drawings by Leech, Cruikshank, and others.

Everyman's Dictionary of Literary Biography, English and American. Compiled after John W. Cousin by D. C. Browning. Everyman's Reference Library. London: Dent. Pp. xi + 752. Rev. by Earle F. Walbridge in *LJ*, LXXXIII, 1552-53; in *TLS*, 31 Jan., p. 62.

Faverty, Frederic E. (ed.). *The Victorian Poets: A Guide to Research.* . . . See VB 1957, 384. Rev. by William E. Buckler in *Comp. Lit.*, X, 159-62 (this favorable review is especially valuable for its specific indication of the research topics recommended in this important book); by J. D. Jump in *RES*, n.s. IX, 122; by William E. Buckler in *VNL*, Fall (No. 14), pp. 19-22.

Jones, Claude E. "Modern Books Dealing with the Novel in English: A Check List." *BB*, XXII, 85-87.

Leary, Lewis (ed.). *Contemporary Literary Scholarship.* New York: Appleton. Pp. 474.

Macdonald, Angus, and Pettit, Henry (eds.). *Annual Bibliography of English Language and Literature.* Vol. XXVI: *1946.* London: Cambridge Univ. Pr. for the Modern Humanities Research Assoc. Pp. xiv + 130.

McLean, Ruari. *Modern Book Design from William Morris to the Present Day.* London: Faber. Pp. xii + 116. Rev. in *TLS*, 19 Dec., p. 744.

Maurer, Oscar (ed.). "Recent Publications: A Selected List." *VNL*, No. 13 (Spring), pp. 30-32; No. 14 (Fall), pp. 29-32.

"Notes on Sales." *TLS*, 19 Dec., p. 754. On the sale of the last library formed by the late Michael Sadleir.

Nowell-Smith, Simon. "Michael Sadleir: A Handlist." *Library*, XIII, 132-38. A selective list containing volumes and periodical contributions of importance, many of which concern Victorian literature.

Nurmi, Martin K. (ed.). "The Romantic Movement: A Selective and Critical Bibliography for the Year 1957." *PQ*, XXXVII, 129-244.

"Research in Progress in the Modern Languages and Literature, 1958." *PMLA*, LXXIII, No. 2, 63-69; English Language and Literature, "IX. Nineteenth Century" and "X. Contemporary," ed. Louise Lindemann.

Stewart, James D., with Muriel E. Hammond

and Erwin Saenger (eds.). *British Union-Catalogue of Periodicals.* . . . See VB 1957, 385. Vol. IV: S-Z. London: Butterworth. Pp. xxxi + 630. Vol. III rev. in *TLS*, 14 Feb., p. 92; Vol. IV by R. D. Macleod in *LR*, XVI, 473-74. For Vol. I see VB 1955, 241; Vols. II and III, VB 1957, 385.

Taylor, Robert H. "The J. Harlin O'Connell Collection." *PLC*, XIX, 150-52. Acquisition by Princeton of a collection of 1890-1900 material; already described in part by O'Connell in *PLC*, II (1941), 121-32, this collection includes twenty letters from Wilde, fourteen from Beardsley, seven from Beerbohm, eighteen from Dowson, eleven from G. Moore, etc., and many magazines, "even those numbers of *Kottabos* to which Wilde contributed when at Trinity College, Dublin."

Topsfield, L. T. (ed.). *The Year's Work in Modern Language Studies.* Vol. XVIII. London: Cambridge Univ. Pr. Pp. viii + 652. Rev. briefly in *TLS*, 31 Jan., p. 66.

Townsend, Francis G. "An Introduction to the Victorian Bibliography." *VS*, I, 352-54.

Townsend, Francis G. (ed.). "Victorian Bibliography for 1957." *VS*, I, 383-422.

Watson, George (ed.). *The Cambridge Bibliography of English Literature.* Vol. V: *Supplement.* . . . See VB 1957, 385. Rev. by George L. McKay in *BSP*, LII, 68-70; briefly by J. N. W. in *College and Research Libr.*, XIX, 27-28; by L. W. Hanson in *Library*, XIII, 208-10; by Herbert Cahoon in *LJ*, LXXXIII, 61; by R. D. Altick in *SR*, 22 Mar., p. 46.

[Weber, Carl J.] "A Former Colby Librarian Comments Authoritatively on Rare Books." *Colby Libr. Quart.*, IV, 252-60.

[Weber, Carl J.] "Some Noteworthy Recent Gifts." *Colby Libr. Quart.*, IV, 279-84. Description of gifts to the Colby College Library, including a privately printed edition of Hardy's *An Indiscretion in the Life of an Heiress*, reprints of two Hardy poems, a letter by Ruskin, three letters of Laurence Housman, additions to the papers of Vernon Lee.

Wing, Donald G., and Gallup, Donald. "The Blum Library: From A'Beckett to Zangwill." *Yale Univ. Libr. Gazette*, XXXIII, 41-43. Acquisitions, including first editions and MSS of many Victorians—Arnold (thirty-one letters, all written to James Knowles), Barrie, Borrow (MSS, supposedly unpublished), Conrad, Gissing, Hardy, Meredith, Yeats, G. Moore, Wilde; letters by Lewis Carroll, Wilkie Collins; etc.

The Year's Work in English Studies, Vol. XXXVII (1956). Ed. for the English Assoc. by Beatrice White and T. S. Dorsch. London: Oxford Univ. Pr., 1958. "The Nineteenth Century," treated by G. Bullough and P. M. Yarker, pp. 202-228; "The Twentieth Century," by Marjorie Thompson, pp. 229-240.

II. ECONOMIC, POLITICAL, RELIGIOUS, AND SOCIAL ENVIRONMENT

Addis, John P. *The Crawshay Dynasty: A Study in Industrial Organization and Development, 1765-1867.* Cardiff: Univ. of Wales Pr., 1957.
Rev. by Richard W. Hale, Jr. in *AHR*, LXIII, 471-72; by W. H. B. Court in *History*, XLIII, 251-52; by W. Woodruff in *JMH*, XXX, 390-91. History of a notable firm of Welsh iron and steel manufacturers.

Allchin, Arthur Macdonald. *The Silent Rebellion: Anglican Religious Communities, 1845-1900.* London: S. C. M. Pp. 256.

Almedingen, Edith Martha von. *Life of Many Colours: The Story of Grandmother Ellen.* London: Hutchinson. Pp. 256.
Rev. by Mary Ross in *HTB*, 4 May, p. 7; by Walter Allen in *NS*, 29 Mar., p. 415; by Virgilia Peterson in *NYTBR*, 11 May, p. 4; by Peter Vansittart in *S*, 28 Mar., p. 406; by L. B. Johnson in *SR*, 31 May, p. 25; in *TLS*, 7 Mar., p. 124. Chronicle of author's Victorian English grandmother.

Arlott, John. "Blundering into Beauty." *Listener*, 2 Oct., pp. 512-14.
On Staffordshire portrait figures in the Victorian age.

Armytage, W. H. G. "Alcott House: An Anglo-American Educational Experiment." *Educational Theory*, VIII, 129-43.
Alcott House was a school founded by James Pierrepont Greaves and based on Pestalozzian principles.

Armytage, W. H. G. "The Chartist Land Colonies 1846-1848." *Agricultural History*, XXXII, 87-96.

Armytage, W. H. G. "John Minter Morgan's Schemes, 1841-1855." *International Rev. of Social History*, III, 26-42.
Morgan's neo-Owenite schemes concerned

the establishment of self-supporting villages supervised by the Established Church. Prof. Armytage also considers some other mid-century proposals for and experiments in Christian association.

Arundell, Dennis. *The Critic at the Opera.* London: Benn, 1957. Pp. xiv + 424.
Rev. by Winton Dean in *M & L*, XXXIX, 286-89. Part III contains "press notices of the first English performances of well-known operas between 1800 and 1914."

Baillie, Eileen. *The Shabby Paradise.* London: Hutchinson. Pp. 223.
Rev. in *TLS*, 22 Aug., p. 468. Family and parish life of an East End vicar at the turn of the century.

Balston, Thomas. *Staffordshire Portrait Figures of the Victorian Age.* London: Faber. Pp. 93.
Rev. in *TLS*, 7 Nov., p. 644.

Bealey, Frank, and Pelling, Henry. *Labour and Politics, 1900-1906.* London: Macmillan. Pp. xi + 314.
Rev. by Asa Briggs in *NS*, 16 Aug., pp. 197-98; in *TLS*, 15 Aug., p. 455. A history, based on unpublished records, of the Labour Representation Committee, precursor of the Labour Party.

Bell, Enid Moberly. *A History of the Church Schools Company, 1883-1958.* London: S. P. C. K. Pp. 89.
Rev. briefly in *TLS*, 16 May, p. 274.

Bernstein, Samuel. "Some Recent Historical Literature: From the Enlightenment to the Commune." *Sci. and Soc.*, XXII, 330-55.

Berthrong, Merrill Gray. "Disarmament in European Diplomacy, 1816-1870." *DA*, XIX, 783.

Blaug, Mark. "The Classical Economists and the Factory Acts—A Re-examination." *Quart. Jour. Econ.*, LXXII, 211-16.

Bloomfield, Paul. "R. S. Rintoul, 1787-1858." *S*, 18 Apr., p. 481.
On the first editor (1828-58) of the *Spectator*.

Blow, Sydney. *Through Stage Doors: Or, Memories of Two in the Theatre.* Edinburgh: Chambers. Pp. 236.
Rev. briefly by T. C. W. in *NS*, 6 Dec., p. 820. This actor's autobiography has stories about various late Victorians, including Ruskin.

Bodenheimer, F. S. "Canon Henry Baker Tristram of Durham (1822-1906)." *DUJ*, XLIX (1957), 95-97.
A biographical sketch of the Victorian

naturalist and divine.

Bradshaw, Percy V. *"Brother Savages and Guests": A History of the Savage Club 1857-1957.* London: W. H. Allen. Pp. xiv + 162.

Rev. by "A Brother Savage" in *LR,* XVI, 488. The history of the Savage Club from founding in mid-nineteenth-century to the present.

[Bristol University Drama Department.]. "Bristol University Theatre Collection." *Theatre Notebook,* XII, 96-98.

Playbills, programmes, prompt-books, etc., many of which are from the Victorian theatre.

Broad, Lewis. *Advocates of the Golden Age: Their Lives and Cases.* London: Long. Pp. 288.

Rev. in *TLS,* 17 Oct., pp. 598-99. On four famous late Victorian barristers: Marshall Hall, Edward Carson, Rufus Isaacs, and F. E. Smith.

Brown, Ivor (ed.). *A Book of England: with 110 Photographs from "The Times."* London: Collins. Pp. 511.

Rev. in *Booklist,* LV (1 Sept.), p. 19; by N. E. Taylor in *Christian Science Monitor,* 28 Aug., p. 7; by G. H. in *Manchester Guardian,* 27 June, p. 6; in *TLS,* 25 July, p. 424. Covers ten centuries of English history.

Brown, Lucy. *The Board of Trade and the Free Trade Movement, 1830-42.* Oxford: Clarendon Pr. Pp. 245.

Rev. briefly in *TLS,* 14 Nov., p. 663.

Bruce, Maurice. *The Shaping of the Modern World, 1870-1939.* Vol. I: *1870-1914.* London: Hutchinson. Pp. xiii + 970.

Rev. by W. O. Henderson in *History,* XLIII, 252-53; by H. R. Trevor-Roper in *NYTBR,* 10 Aug., p. 6; by C. N. Parkinson in *SR,* 9 Aug., p. 28; in *TLS,* 14 Feb., p. 82.

Buechler, John. "The Roxburghe Club." *College and Research Libr.,* XIX, 19-23.

A brief history of the bibliophilic club from 1812 to the present.

Burgoyne, Elizabeth. *Gertrude Bell: From Her Personal Papers, 1889-1914.* London: Ernest Benn. Pp. 320.

Rev. by Elizabeth Monroe in *NS,* 23 Aug., p. 229; in *TLS,* 1 Aug., p. 437.

Cairncross, A. K. "The English Capital Market before 1914." *Economica,* n.s. XXV, 142-46.

Disputes A. R. Hall's finding that the English capital market was adequate as a

source of funds for home investment before 1914. The large issues on the stock exchange were, in a great number of cases, for the purchase by large corporations of flourishing businesses which had been privately owned. Investment in new assets was relatively small.

Cardwell, D. S. L. *The Organisation of Science in England....* See VB 1957, 386.

Rev. by W. H. G. Armytage in *EHR,* LXXIII, 374; by S. Lilley in *VS,* I, 290-92.

Carter, George Stuart. *A Hundred Years of Evolution....* See VB 1957, 387.

Rev. by Marston Bates in *Amer. Scholar,* XXVII, 254-55; by John C. Greene in *JMH,* XXX, 282-83; by Ashley Montagu in *SR,* 4 Jan., p. 25.

Champion, Harold. "Thomas Cook." *S,* 21 Nov., p. 671.

On the Victorian founder of the grouptour.

Churchill, Winston S. *A History of the English-Speaking Peoples.* Vol. IV: *The Great Democracies.* London: Cassell. Pp. xi + 322.

Rev. by David Harris in *AHR,* LXIV, 71-72; by J. G. Harrison in *Christian Science Monitor,* 20 Mar., p. 15; by Paul Kiniery in *CWd,* CLXXXVII, 153; by Crane Brinton in *HTB,* 16 Mar., p. 3; by J. D. Marshall in *LJ,* LXXXIII, 836; by Geoffrey Barraclough in *Manchester Guardian,* 21 Mar., p. 6; by V. S. Pritchett in *NS,* 29 Mar., p. 413; by Harold Nicholson in *NYTBR,* 16 Mar., p. 1; by D. M. Smith in *S,* 21 Mar., p. 365; by Allan Nevins in *SR,* 19 Apr., p. 25; in *TLS,* 21 Mar., p. 145.

Clark, Ronald William. *The Royal Albert Hall.* London: H. Hamilton. Pp. xii + 263.

Rev. by Eric Gillett in *NER,* CL, 256; favorably by Arthur Marshall in *NS,* 10 May, pp. 609-10; in *TLS,* 2 May, p. 244.

Clarke, Arthur Charles. *Voice Across the Sea.* New York: Harper. Pp. 208.

Rev. in *Booklist,* LV (1 Sept.), p. 12; by R. C. Cowen in *Christian Science Monitor,* 2 Sept., p. 9; by H. W. Baehr in *HTB,* 24 Aug., p. 6; by M. B. Wenger in *LJ,* LXXXIII, 2156; by J. N. Leonard in *NYTBR,* 7 Sept., p. 37. On early efforts to talk across the Atlantic.

Coleman, Donald Cuthbert. *The British Paper Industry, 1495-1860: A Study in Industrial Growth.* Oxford: Clarendon Pr. Pp. xvi + 367.

Conacher, J. B. "Peel and the Peelites, 1846-1850." *EHR,* LXXIV, 431-52.

Peel's position in these years, in which he occasionally supported a government to which he was in opposition, prepared the way for a coalition with the Whigs.

Cope, Sir Zachary. *Florence Nightingale and the Doctors*. London: Museum Pr. Pp. x + 163.

Rev. briefly by Henrietta B. Miller in *LR*, XVI, 361; in *TLS*, 23 May, p. 285. A study of Miss Nightingale's influence on the education and practice of army doctors.

Corry, B. A. "The Theory of the Economic Effects of Government Expenditure in English Classical Political Economy." *Economica*, n.s. XXV, 34-48.

During the Napoleonic Wars various unorthodox explanations of the price rise and general prosperity were advanced which contended that extraordinary demand was created by government expenditures. After 1815 Malthus, Blake, Tooke, and Barton argued that the collapse was due to a failure of demand. Their early Keynesian arguments failed because of the general acceptance of Smith's theory that saving is spending, because savings are automatically invested. Furthermore, of all these economists only Blake so much as mentions the existence of resources unused because of a failure of demand.

Cowherd, Raymond G. *The Politics of English Dissent*. . . . See VB 1957, 387.

Rev. by A. Briggs in *EHR*, LXXIII, 168-69; by R. W. Greaves in *History*, XLIII, 64-65.

Craig, Edward Gordon. *Index to the Story of My Days: Some Memoirs of Edward Gordon Craig*. . . . See VB 1957, 387.

Rev. by I. K. F. in *Theatre Notebook*, XII, 74-75.

Cranston, Maurice. "Robert Owen: Socialist Visionary." *Listener*, 27 Nov., pp. 877-78.

"Critic." "London Diary." *NS*, 7 June, pp. 718-20.

An evaluation of Graham Wallas, answered by Lord Samuel, "Graham Wallas," *NS*, 14 June, p. 767.

Crowther, Sir Geoffrey. *The Wealth and Poverty of Nations*. Claremont: Claremont College, 1957. Pp. 48.

Rev. briefly in *APSR*, LII, 894. Considers nineteenth-century England, in this study of disparity of wealth in three "countries."

Cruise O'Brien, Conor. *Parnell and His Party*. . . . See VB 1957, 387.

Rev. by James B. Christoph in *APSR*, LII, 565-66; by W. L. Burn in *CHJ*, I,

83-85; by F. S. L. Lyons in *History*, XLIII, 155-56; by F. S. L. Lucas in *Irish Hist. Studies*, XI, 64-69 ("incomparably the best book we have on the subject"); by D. J. McDougall in *JMH*, XXX, 147-48.

Deghy, Guy. *Paradise in the Strand: The Story of Romano's*. London: Richards Pr. Pp. 256.

Rev. in *TLS*, 7 Mar., p. 131. Romano's was a restaurant popular with the half-world of late Victorian London.

DeTocqueville, Alexis. *Journeys to England and Ireland*. Trans. George Lawrence and K. P. Mayer; ed. J. P. Mayer. London: Faber. Pp. 243.

Rev. by A. J. P. Taylor in *NS*, 12 July, pp. 51-52. First English translation.

Dolmetsch, Mabel. *Personal Recollections of Arnold Dolmetsch*. London: Routledge & K. Paul. Pp. viii + 198.

Rev. in *TLS*, 28 Feb., p. 116. On a distinguished musician and craftsman (1858-1940) influential in the '90s and after.

Dudley, Ernest. *The Gilded Lily: The Life and Loves of the Fabulous Lily Langtry*. London: Odhams. Pp. 224.

Rev. unfavorably by Ralph Partridge in *NS*, 29 Nov., pp. 768-69.

Duff, David. *The Shy Princess: The Life of Her Royal Highness Princess Beatrice, the Youngest Daughter and Constant Companion of Queen Victoria*. London: Evans. Pp. 310.

Rev. in *TLS*, 26 Dec., p. 747.

Dunsheath, Percy, and Miller, Margaret. *Convocation in the University of London: The First Hundred Years*. London: Athlone Pr. Pp. 204.

Rev. in *TLS*, 23 May, p. 286; by R. C. Latham in *Universities Rev.*, XXXI, 25-26; by John Roach in *VS*, II, 181-82. Account of how graduates of London University acquired a voice in its affairs.

Easton, John. *The De La Rue History of British and Foreign Postage Stamps, 1855-1901*. London: Faber. Pp. xxiii + 846.

Rev. in *TLS*, 19 Sept., p. 524. A history of a firm of printers of stamps.

Edwardes, Michael. *The Necessary Hell: John and Henry Lawrence and the Indian Empire*. London: Cassell. Pp. xxi + 213.

Rev. by Peter Mayne in *NS*, 31 May, pp. 703-4; by Peter Vansittart in *S*, 30 May, p. 709; unfavorably in *TLS*, 16 May, p. 267.

Edwards, Ralph, and Ramsey, Leonard Gerald Gwynne (eds.). The "Connoisseur" Period Guides to the Houses, Decoration, Furnishing and Chattels of the Classic Periods. The Early Victorian Period, 1830-1860. London: Connoisseur. Pp. xii + 180.

Rev. briefly by Paul von Khrum in LJ, LXXXIII, 3155.

Edwards, Robert Dudley, and Williams, Thomas Desmond (eds.). The Great Famine. . . . See VB 1957, 388.

Rev. by Helen F. Mulvey in AHR, LXIII, 402-4; by W. L. Burn in EHR, LXXIII, 316-18; by Nicholas Mansergh in Irish Hist. Studies, XI, 60-64; by Charles F. Mullett in JMH, XXX, 257-58; by W. O. Aydelotte in VS, I, 374-76.

Engels, Friedrich. The Condition of the Working Class in England. Trans. and ed. W. O. Henderson and W. H. Chaloner. Oxford: Blackwell. Pp. xxxi + 386.

Rev. by Asa Briggs in NS, 22 Mar., pp. 379-80 (see also George F. Peel, "The Chimney of the World," NS, 29 Mar., p. 408, for an answer concerning Sir Robert); by F. C. Mather in VS, II, 179-80.

Eyre, John Vargas. Henry Edward Armstrong, 1848-1937: The Doyen of British Chemists and Pioneer of Technical Education. London: Butterworth. Pp. xix + 325.

Rev. in TLS, 3 Oct., p. 566. Biography of a Victorian chemist.

Fay, Gerald. The Abbey Theatre: Cradle of Genius. London: Hollis & Carter. Pp. 190.

Rev. in TLS, 28 Nov., p. 684. Account concentrating on the early years.

Ferguson, Thomas. Scottish Social Welfare, 1864-1914. London: Livingstone. Pp. xi + 610.

Rev. by Karl Miller in S, 29 Aug., p. 286; briefly in TLS, 22 Aug., p. 475.

Fox, Alan. A History of the National Union of Boot and Shoe Operatives, 1874-1957. Oxford: Blackwell. Pp. viii + 684.

Forbes-Robertson, Beatrice. "Memories of Henry Irving and Ellen Terry." Listener, 23 Oct., pp. 645-46.

Fortescue, Chichester Samuel Parkinson. ". . . and Mr. Fortescue:" A Selection from the Diaries from 1851 to 1862 of Chichester Fortescue, Lord Carlingford, K.P. Ed. Osbert Wyndham Hewett. London: Murray. Pp. xi + 209.

Rev. By Ralph Partridge in NS, 1 Nov.,

pp. 607-8; in TLS, 14 Nov., p. 654. Chichester Fortescue was supposedly the original of Trollope's Phineas Finn.

Freeman, T. W. Pre-Famine Ireland. . . . See VB 1957, 388.

Rev. by John Vaizey in Econ. Jour., LXVIII, 820-22; by René Fréchet in Études anglaises, XI, 366-67; by H. D. Jordan in JMH, XXX, 394-95; by W. O. Aydelotte in VS, I, 374-76.

Fussell, G. E. "William Bland, Jun., of Hartlip, Near Sittingbourne." N & Q, n.s. V, 449-50.

The writer of a book on farming.

Galbraith, John S. The Hudson's Bay Company as an Imperial Factor, 1821-1869. Berkeley: Univ. of California Pr., 1957. Pp. viii + 500.

Rev. by A. L. Burt in Mississippi Valley Hist. Rev., XLV, 137-38; in TLS, 18 July, p. 406.

Germon, Maria. Journal of the Siege of Lucknow. Ed. Michael Edwardes. London: Constable. Pp. xvi + 136.

Rev. favorably by Peter Mayne in NS, 31 May, pp. 703-4; in TLS, 18 Apr., p. 206.

Gilbert, Michael. The Claimant. . . . See VB 1957, 388.

Rev. by A. de Montmorency in CR, CXCIII, 107-8; by Norman St.-John Stevas in VS, I, 284-86.

Glaser, John F. "English Nonconformity and the Decline of Liberalism." AHR, LXIII, 352-63.

Gooch, Brison D. "The Crimean War in Selected Documents and Secondary Works since 1940." VS, I, 271-79.

Gooch, G. P. Under Six Reigns. London: Longmans. Pp. vii + 344.

Gray, Malcolm. The Highland Economy, 1750-1850. . . . See VB 1957, 389.

Rev. by Donald G. MacRae in Economica, n.s. XXV, 265-66; by W. H. B. Court in History, XLIII, 250-51; by I. M. M. MacPhail in Scottish Hist. Rev., XXVII, 67-70.

Green, E. R. R. "The Fenians." History Today, VIII, 698-705.

The Fenians involved America in a struggle for freedom, thereby founding a base for later movements.

Grenville, J. A. S. "Goluchowski, Salisbury, and the Mediterranean Agreements, 1895-1897." Slavonic and East European Rev., XXXVI, 340-69.

Gross, Felix. Rhodes of Africa. . . . See VB 1957, 389.

Rev. by Arthur N. Cook in *JMH*, XXX, 171; by J. D. Fage in *VS*, II, 82-84.

Guest, Ivor. *Adeline Genée, A Lifetime of Ballet under Six Reigns.* London: A. and C. Black. Pp. xvii + 307.

Biography of ballerina of Edwardian Empire Theatre.

Guest, Ivor. *Clara Webster: A Victorian Ballet Girl.* . . . See VB 1957, 389.

Rev. by G. B. L. Wilson in *Theatre Notebook*, XII, 143-44; briefly in *TLS*, 21 Feb., p. 106; by G. B. L. Wilson in *VS*, I, 297-98.

Haber, L. F. *The Chemical Industry During the Nineteenth Century: A Study of the Economic Aspects of Applied Chemistry in Europe and North America.* Oxford: Clarendon Pr. Pp. x + 292.

Rev. favorably by Charles Wilson in *Econ. Jour.*, LXVIII, 811-13 ("indispensable for a balanced knowledge of industrial development in the nineteenth century"); by T. C. Barker in *Economica*, n.s. XXV, 358-59; in *TLS*, 21 Feb., p. 104; by D. C. Coleman in *VS*, II, 78-80.

Hague, D. C. "Alfred Marshall and the Competitive Firm." *Econ. Jour.*, LXVIII, 673-90.

Hall, A. R. "The English Capital Market before 1914—A Reply." *Economica*, n.s. XXV, 339-43.

In answer to Cairncross, Hall points out that between 1949-53 capital raising by English industry through the new issue market came to only fifteen per cent of company investment in tangible assets and stocks. Even at the lowest estimate, the comparable figure before 1914 was ten per cent.

Hall, Douglas. "Manchester in 1857." *Connoisseur*, CXL, 237-40.

Description of an exhibition of "The Art Treasures of the United Kingdom, collected at Manchester in 1857."

Hall, Helena (ed.). *A Dictionary of the Sussex Dialect and Collection of Provincialisms in Use in the County of Sussex,* by the Rev. W. D. Parish. Chichester: R. G. Acford. Pp. xxii + 186.

Rev. by Philippa Revill in *N & Q*, n.s. V, 457-58. Originally printed in 1875.

Herd, Harold. *A Press Gallery.* London: Fleet Publications. Pp. 144.

Rev. in *TLS*, 3 Oct., p. 556. Includes sketches of William Gifford of the *Quarterly Review* and Henry Cust, editor (1893-1896) of the *Pall Mall Gazette.*

Hewitt, Osbert Wyndham. "Without the Passion of Love." *Listener,* 23 Jan., pp. 155-56.

On Sir Walter and Lady Trevelyan of Wallington, friends of Ruskin and the Pre-Raphaelites.

Hewitt, Margaret. *Wives and Mothers in Victorian Industry: A Study of the Effects of the Employment of Married Women in Victorian Industry.* London: Rockcliff. Pp. x + 245.

Hill, A. G. "The Englishman's Library, 1839-1846." *N & Q,* n.s. V, 511-18.

A publishing effort which throws light "on the aims and sympathies of the Tractarians."

Holt, Edgar. *The Boer War.* London: Putnam. Pp. 317.

Rev. by Eric Gillett in *NER*, CLI, 32-33; favorably by Michael Howard in *NS*, 14 June, p. 784; by Cyril Ray in *S*, 13 June, pp. 781-82; in *TLS*, 4 July, p. 371; by G. B. Pyrah in *VS*, II, 184-85.

Holt, Edgar. "Garnet Wolseley, Soldier of Empire." *History Today,* VIII, 706-13.

Wolseley served the Army as a reformer, and the Empire as an efficient and usually successful wager of "small" wars.

Houghton, R. W. "A Note on the Early History of Consumer's Surplus." *Economica,* n.s. XXV, 49-57.

Points out that Jules Dupuit's "utilité relative" was Marshall's surplus utility, and that the general belief that Dupuit's theory had no effect on economic thought ignores its influence on the Austrians, Auspitz and Lieben.

Hughes, J. R. T., and Reiter, Stanley. "The First 1,945 British Steamships." *Jour. of Amer. Statistical Association,* LIII, 360-81.

Analysis of data about main characteristics of British steamships between 1814 and 1860 indicates that economic expansion of the 1850's was accompanied by the rapid development of a steam merchant fleet.

Hurst, Peter Geoffrey. *The Age of Jean de Reszke: Forty Years of Opera, 1874-1914.* London: C. Johnson. Pp. 256.

Rev. by Grace Banyard in *CR*, CXCIV, 303-4.

Imlah, Albert Henry. *Economic Elements in the Pax Britannica: Studies in British Foreign Trade in the Nineteenth Century.* Cambridge, Mass.: Harvard Univ. Pr. Pp. xiv + 224.

Inglis, K. S. "The Labour Church Movement." *International Rev. of Social History,* III, 445-60.

Traces the decline of the Labour Church Movement—organized by John Trevor in 1891—to the secularization and confusion resulting from different attempts to use it for political ends.

Jackman, Sydney W. *Galloping Head: The Life of the Right Honourable Sir Francis Bond Head, Bart., P. C., 1793-1875, Late Lieutenant-Governor of Upper Canada.* London: Phoenix House. Pp. 191.
Rev. in *TLS,* 27 June, p. 358.

James, Henry. *The Art of Travel: Scenes and Journeys in America, England, France and Italy from the Travel Writings of Henry James.* Ed. Morton Dauwen Zabel. Garden City, N. Y.: Doubleday. Pp. iv + 567.
Rev. by Herbert Barrows in *Antioch Rev.,* XVIII, 515; by Edward Wagenknecht in *Chicago Sunday Tribune,* 22 June, p. 2; by Carlyle Morgan in *Christian Science Monitor,* 19 June, p. 7; by E. F. Walbridge in *LJ,* LXXXIII, 1926; by Granville Hicks in *SR,* 19 July, p. 22.

James, Robert Rhodes. "Lord Randolph [Churchill] Resigns, December 1886." *History Today,* VIII, 762-69, 864-70.

Jenkins, Roy. *Sir Charles Dilke: A Victorian Tragedy.* London: Collins. Pp. 447.
Rev. by Angus Macintyre in *NER,* CLI, 248-50; favorably by John Strachey in *NS,* 1 Nov., pp. 596-97 (and see Leslie Plummer, 8 Nov., p. 637); by Christopher Hollis in *S,* 24 Oct., p. 540; in *TLS,* 31 Oct., p. 619 (and see Ivor Bulmer-Thomas, 7 Nov., p. 631). Biography of the brilliant Liberal whose career was cut short by the Crawford scandal.

Jewkes, John, Sawers, David, and Stillerman, Richard. *The Sources of Invention.* London: Macmillan. Pp. xii + 428.
Rev. by J. C. Allen in *Econ. Jour.,* LXVIII, 554-56 (according to the reviewer, this brilliant series of studies of inventors and inventions destroys the popular idea that the individual genius invented in the last century, whereas in this century invention depends on organized research); by Asa Briggs in *NS,* 1 Mar., pp. 276-77; in *TLS,* 21 Feb., p. 104.

Johnson, L. G. *General T. Perronet Thompson, 1783-1869.* . . . See VB 1957, 390.
Rev. by John Roach in *History,* XLIII, 63-64.

Jones, A. G. E. "The Banks of Bath." *N & Q,* n.s. V, 277-83.
Banking houses in Bath from the eighteenth to the twentieth century.

Jones, Wilbur Devereux. *Lord Derby and*

Victorian Conservatism. . . . See VB 1957, 390.
Rev. by George Curry in *AHR,* LXIII, 665-66.

Kamm, Josephine. *How Different from Us: A Biography of Miss Buss & Miss Beale.* London: J. Lane. Pp. 272.
Rev. favorably by Mary Scrutton in *NS,* 20 Sept., pp. 386-87; by Stevie Smith in *S,* 17 Oct., p. 528; in *TLS,* 26 Sept., p. 540. Biographies of Dorothea Beale and Frances Mary Buss, pioneering headmistresses of Victorian girls' public schools.

Kegel, Charles H. "William Cobbett and Malthusianism." *JHI,* XIX, 348-62.
Includes reference to the influence of Cobbett on Carlyle, Morris, and Ruskin—cf. Kegel's unpublished dissertation (Michigan State Univ., 1955).

Keller, Paul. *Dogmengeschichte des Wohlstandspolitischen Interventionismus.* Winterthur: P. G. Keller, 1955. Pp. x + 367.
Rev. favorably by Lucien Foldes in *Economica,* n.s. XXV, 175-76. Among other things, examines the development of interventionist doctrines in the English classical school—Malthus, McCulloch, Sidgwick, and J. S. Mill.

Kelly, Edith, and Kelly, Thomas (eds.). *A Schoolmaster's Notebook, Being an Account of a Nineteenth-Century Experiment in Social Welfare, by David Winstanley of Manchester, Schoolmaster.* Remains, historical and literary, connected with the Palatine counties of Lancaster and Chester. 3rd ser., Vol. VIII. Manchester: Chetham Society, 1957. Pp. 128.
Rev. by W. H. G. Armytage in *EHR,* LXXIII, 733. Notes on Miles Platting in Manchester, in which Sir Benjamin Heywood established schools, friendly societies, a Mechanics' Institute, public baths, etc. for hand-loom weavers.

King, A. Hyatt. "The Royal Music Library." *Book Collector,* VII, 241-52.
Includes discussion of Albert's part in enlarging the library.

Kirk, George. "Lord Cromer of Egypt—A Retrospect." *HLB,* XII, 392-409.

Kirk-Smith, Harold. *William Thompson, Archbishop of York: His Life and Times, 1819-90.* London: S. P. C. K. Pp. 190.
Rev. in *TLS,* 19 Sept., p. 533.

Kovalev, Y. V. (ed.). *An Anthology of Chartist Literature.* London: Central Books, 1957. Pp. 413.
Rev. by F. C. Mather in *VS,* II, 178-80.

Kovalev, Y. V. "The Literature of Chartism." *VS*, II, 117-38.
Translation, by J. C. Dumbreck and Michael Beresford, with a brief introduction by W. H. Chaloner, of an introduction to the anthology mentioned above, which is used in Russian schools.

Lack, David. *Evolutionary Theory and Christian Belief*. . . . See VB 1957, 390.
Rev. by C. C. Gillispie in *VS*, II, 166-69.

Large, David. "The Third Marquess of Londonderry and the End of the Regulation 1844-45." *DUJ*, LI, 1-9.
Londonderry was the "proximate cause" of the breakdown of the monopoly in the northeastern coal trade.

Le Hardy, William (ed.). *Calendar to the Sessions Books, Sessions Minute Books and Other Sessions Records, with Appendixes*. Vol. X: *1833 to 1843*. Hertfordshire County Records Series. Hertford: Clerk of the Peace. Pp. xxxii + 650.
Rev. in *N & Q*, n.s. V, 455-56.

Leonard, A. G. K. "St. Lubbock's Day." *CR*, CXCIV, 87-90.
On Sir John Lubbock and the Bank Holiday Act of 1871.

Lorwin, Val R. "Working-Class Politics and Economic Development in Western Europe." *AHR*, LXIII, 338-51.
A general article with some reference to Victorian England.

McCord, Norman. *The Anti-Corn Law League, 1838-1846*. London: Allen & Unwin. Pp. 227.
Rev. by E. J. Hobsbawm in *NS*, 26 July, p. 121; in *TLS*, 1 Aug., p. 436; by N. H. Gibbs in *VS*, II, 180-81.

MacDonagh, Oliver. "Delegated Legislation and Administrative Discretions in the 1850's: A Particular Study." *VS*, II, 29-44.
The particular study of how delegated legislation compromised mid-century laissez-faire concerns the authority given to officers who inspected and approved the storage of cargo in iron ships.

Macfie, A. L. "On Psychological Treatment for the Classics." *Econ. Jour.*, LXVIII, 25-33.
A review-article based on W. A. Weisskopf's *The Psychology of Economics*.

Mack, Mary Peter. "The Political Odyssey of Jeremy Bentham." *DA*, XIX, 833-34.

Mackerness, E. D. "Frances Parthenope, Lady Verney (1819-1890)." *JMH*, XXX, 131-36.

The accomplishments of the sister of Florence Nightingale.

Maclean, Sir Fitzroy. *A Person From England and Other Travellers*. London: Cape. Pp. 384.
Rev. by Eric Shipton in *NS*, 1 Nov., pp. 604-5; in *TLS*, 12 Dec., p. 715. Stories of British travellers and agents in nineteenth-century Turkestan.

Macqueen-Pope, Walter. *Give Me Yesterday: A Backward Glance down the Years*. London: Hutchinson, 1957. Pp. 308.
Rev. in *TLS*, 10 Jan., p. 15. Memoirs of the late Victorian, Edwardian period.

Macqueen-Pope, Walter. *St. James's: Theatre of Distinction*. London: W. H. Allen. Pp. 256.
Rev. briefly in *TLS*, 28 Mar., p. 175.

Magnus, Sir Philip. *Kitchener: Portrait of an Imperialist*. London: J. Murray. Pp. xiii + 410.
Rev. favorably by Paul Johnson in *NS*, 25 Oct., pp. 564-66 ("the cumulative effect is all the more appalling in that Sir Philip virtually refrains from comment and allows the deadly facts to speak for themselves"); see also W. Lyon Blease, "Kitchener as Commander," *NS*, 1 Nov., p. 594; in *TLS*, 31 Oct., pp. 617-18.

Majumdar, Ramesh Chandra. *The Sepoy Mutiny and the Revolt of 1857*. Calcutta: K. L. Mukhopadhyay, 1957. Pp. 289.
Rev. by S. A. Shah in *Sci. and Soc.*, XXII, 375-77.

Majumdar, Tapas. *The Measurement of Utility*. London: Macmillan. Pp. xiv + 149.
Rev. by W. E. Armstrong in *Economica*, n.s. XXV, 351-52. Extensive treatment of Marshall.

Mander, Raymond, and Mitchenson, Joe. *The British Theatre*. Picture Histories Series. London: Hutton Pr., 1957. Pp. 160.
Rev. by George Freedley in *LJ*, LXXXIII, 95; in *N & Q*, n. s. V, 129-30; by Mordecai Gorelek in *Theatre Arts*, XLII (April), p. 89; by Phyllis Hartnoll in *Theatre Notebook*, XII, 75-76.

Marsh, David Charles. *The Changing Social Structure of England and Wales, 1871-1951*. International Library of Sociology and Social Reconstruction. London: Routledge & K. Paul. Pp. xiv + 266.
Rev. by Peter Townsend in *S*, 26 Dec., p. 924.

Marshall, Herbert, and Stock, Mildred. *Ira Aldridge: The Negro Tragedian*. London: Rockliff. Pp. viii + 355.

Rev. in *TLS*, 5 Dec., p. 702. Biography of the American negro who achieved a considerable reputation in mid-nineteenth-century England.

Masterman, Neville. J. *Viriamu Jones 1856-1901, Pioneer of the Modern University.* Llandybie: Christopher Davies, 1957. Pp. 32.
Appreciation of the first Principal of University College at Cardiff.

Maxwell, James A. "Some Marshallian Concepts, Especially the Representative Firm." *Econ. Jour.*, LXVIII, 691-98.

Maynard, Douglas H. "The Forbes-Aspinwall Mission." *Mississippi Valley Hist. Rev.*, XLV, 67-89.
Concerning the Union mission to buy vessels in Britain during the Civil War.

Medlicott, W. N. *Bismarck, Gladstone, and the Concert of Europe.* . . . See VB 1957, 391.
Rev. by Erich Eyck in *History*, XLIII, 258-59; by Charles Webster in *Slavonic and East European Rev.*, XXXVI, 256-57.

Meier, Hugo A. "American Technology and the Nineteenth-Century World." *Amer. Quart.*, X, 116-30.
The development of American independence of the technology of England and the Continent.

Mitchell, Rosamund Joscelyne, and Leys, Mary Dorothy Rose. *A History of London Life.* London: Longmans. Pp. xii + 302.
Rev. by Raymond Postgate in *NS*, 31 May, p. 704; by Peter Quennell in *NYTBR*, 10 Aug., p. 6; by Cyril Ray in *S*, 16 May, p. 631; in *TLS*, 30 May, p. 295. Includes chapters on London of Edwin Chadwick, of Albert, and of Dickens.

Mongan, Agnes. "The Fogg Art Museum's Collection of Drawings." *HLB*, XII, 196-209.
Includes mention of many Pre-Raphaelite drawings, and many by Ruskin and Turner.

Moody, T. W. "The Irish University Question in the Nineteenth Century." *History*, XLIII, 90-109.
Political and religious controversies on higher education in Ireland, 1793-1908.

Morris, John Henry, and Williams, Lawrence John. *The South Wales Coal Industry, 1841-1875.* Cardiff: Univ. of Wales Pr. Pp. xii + 289.

Mortimer, Roger. *The Jockey Club.* London: Cassell. Pp. 184.
Rev. by Ralph Partridge in *NS*, 11 Oct., pp. 500-501; in *TLS*, 12 Sept., p. 516. A

history of this influential and aristocratic group, with emphasis on the activities of Lord George Bentinck and other Victorians.

Myint, H. "The 'Classical Theory' of International Trade and the Underdeveloped Countries." *Econ. Jour.*, LXVIII, 317-37.
Finds Adam Smith's "vent for surplus" theory of trade relevant to world conditions today, in spite of the criticisms of J. S. Mill and later writers.

Nadel, George. *Australia's Colonial Culture: Ideas, Men and Institutions in Mid-Nineteenth Century Eastern Australia.* Cambridge, Mass.: Harvard Univ. Pr. Pp. xiii + 304.
Rev. briefly in *TLS*, 4 July, p. 383; by Michael Roe in *VS*, II, 175-76.

O'Brien, Brian [pseud.] *She Had a Magic: The Story of Mary Slessor.* London: Cape. Pp. 256.
Biography of Scottish missionary to Africa.

Oliver, Roland. *Sir Harry Johnston and the Scramble for Africa.* . . . See VB 1957, 392.
Rev. by D. J. McDougall in *Canadian Hist. Rev.*, XXXIX, 318-19; by A. Sillery in *CR*, CXCIII, 163-64; by George Shepperson in *EHR*, LXXIII, 319-21; by J. D. Hargreaves in *History*, XLIII, 163-64; by J. D. Hargreaves in *History Today*, VIII, 61-63; by J. D. Fage in *VS*, II, 82-84.

Oliver, W. H. "Robert Owen and the English Working-Class Movements." *History Today*, VIII, 787-96.
Owen's ideas had their effect on cooperative retail societies, labour exchanges, and other socialistic and industrial experiments.

Pannell, Charles. "Disorder in the House." *NS*, 15 Feb., pp. 192-94.
An M. P. recalls the rowdy days when only "gentlemen" sat in Parliament, and the great unwashed were excluded.

Paul, Rodman W. "The Wheat Trade between California and the United Kingdom." *Mississippi Valley Hist. Rev.*, XLV, 391-412.
Concerned chiefly with the last half of the nineteenth century.

Pemberton, W. Baring. "Orsini's Bomb." *Blackwood's*, CCLXXXIII, 17-26.
The crisis in Anglo-French relations brought about by the attempt on the Emperor Napoleon III in 1858.

Perham, Margery. *Lugard.* . . . See VB 1957, 392.
Rev. by D. J. McDougall in *Canadian Hist. Rev.*, XXXIX, 318-19; by George Shepper-

son in *EHR*, LXXIII, 116-20.

Perkins Centenary, London: 100 Years of Synthetic Dyestuffs. London: Pergamon Pr. Pp. xii + 136.

Phillips, A. W. "The Relation between Unemployment and the Rate of Change of Money Wage Rates in the United Kingdom, 1861-1957." *Economica,* n.s. XXV, 283-99.

Poirier, Philip Patrick. *The Advent of the British Labour Party.* London: Allen and Unwin. Pp. 288.
Rev. by Asa Briggs in *NS*, 16 Aug., pp. 197-98; by D. W. Brogan in *S*, 13 June, p. 777; in *TLS*, 15 Aug., p. 455.

Ponsonby, Doris Almon. *The Lost Duchess: The Story of the Prince Consort's Mother.* London: Chapman and Hall. Pp. 172.
Rev. in *TLS*, 17 Oct., p. 590. On Princess Louise, mother of the Prince Consort.

Poolman, Kenneth. *The "Alabama" Incident.* London: Kimber. Pp. 203.
Rev. unfavorably in *TLS*, 26 Dec., p. 754. A crucial case in Anglo-American diplomatic relations in the 'sixties and 'seventies.

Price, R. G. G. *A History of Punch.* . . . See VB 1957, 393.
Rev. by Oscar Maurer in *VS*, I, 301.

Prouty, Roger. *The Transformation of the Board of Trade.* . . . See VB 1957, 393.
Rev. by H. D. Jordan in *AHR*, LXIII, 472; briefly and unfavorably in *Economica,* n.s. XXV, 88; by Lucy Brown in *EHR*, LXXIII, 733-34; by A. R. Schoyen in *JEH*, XVIII, 223-24; by H. W. Parris in *JMH*, XXX, 66-67.

Purdom, Charles Benjamin. *Harley Granville Barker.* . . . See VB 1957, 383.
Rev. by A. J. Farmer in *Études anglaises,* X (1957), 304-9.

"Queen Victoria Came to Stoneleigh." *Connoisseur,* CXLI (June), 47-49.

R., S. "An Earl's Court Exhibition." *N & Q,* n.s. V, 303-4.
A guide to the exhibition of 1893.

Rae, Isobel. *The Strange Story of Dr. James Barry, Army Surgeon, Inspector-General of Hospitals, Discovered on Death to Be a Woman.* London: Longmans. Pp. ix + 124.

Rasmussen, P. Nørregaard. "A Note on the History of the Balanced Budget Multiplier." *Econ. Jour.,* LXVIII, 154-56.
The theory first appeared in Ricardo's *Principles.*

Read, Donald. *Peterloo: The "Massacre" and Its Background.* Manchester: Manchester Univ. Pr. Pp. ix + 235.
Rev. by Raymond Postgate in *NS*, 12 Apr., pp. 480-81.

Reckitt, Maurice B. "When Did 'Victorianism' End?" *VS*, I, 268-71.
According to Reckitt, in 1887.

Redford, Arthur. *Manchester Merchants and Foreign Trade.* . . . See VB 1957, 393.
Rev. by Robert B. Eckles in *AHR*, LXIII, 474.

Reynolds, E. E. *Baden-Powell.* . . . See VB 1957, 393.
Rev. by Kenneth Kirkwood in *VS*, I, 298-300.

Richmond, Arthur. "On Meeting Some Famous Victorians." *Listener,* 31 July, pp. 159-60.
Anecdotes of Pater, Morris, Stevenson and others by the son of W. B. Richmond.

Ridley, Viscountess (ed.). *Cecilia: The Life and Letters of Cecilia Ridley, 1819-1845.* London: Hart-Davis. Pp. 215.
Rev. by Ralph Partridge in *NS*, 1 Nov., pp. 607-8; in *TLS*, 10 Oct., p. 572.

Roberts, Benjamin Charles. *The Trades Union Congress, 1868-1921.* London: Allen & Unwin. Pp. 408.
Rev. by H. R. G. Greaves in *NS*, 5 July, p. 24.

Roberts, David. "Tory Paternalism and Social Reform in Early Victorian England." *AHR*, LXIII, 323-37.
". . . recent historians and new conservatives alike have romanticized nineteenth-century conservatism. It was not as benevolent, as generous, nor as heroic as they imagine."

Roberts, R. O. "Bank of England Branch Discounting, 1826-59." *Economica,* n.s. XXV, 230-45.
Traces the operations of the Branch Bank at Swansea, and the reasons for its failure to yield profits.

Rodkey, F. S. "Ottoman Concern about Western Economic Penetration in the Levant, 1849-1856." *JMH*, XXX, 348-53.

Rodrigo, Robert. *The Racing Game: A History of Flat Racing.* London: Phoenix House. Pp. 224.
Rev. in *TLS*, 7 Nov., p. 644.

Rolt, Lionel Thomas Caswall. *Isambard Kingdom Brunel.* . . . See VB 1957, 393.
Rev. by R. J. Forbes in *VS*, I, 381-82.

Rolt, Lionel Thomas Caswall. *Thomas Tel-*

ford. London: Longmans. Pp. xv + 211.

Rev. by E. W. Martin in *History Today*, VIII, 508-9; by Eric Gillett in *NER*, CLI, 33; by W. John Morgan in *NS*, 16 Aug., p. 202; by Peter Vansittart in *S*, 30 May, p. 709; in *TLS*, 16 May, p. 264.

Rosenthal, Harold. *Two Centuries of Opera at Covent Garden.* London: Putnam. Pp. xv + 849.

Rev. by Eric Blom in *M & L*, XXXIX, 408-9; by Desmond Shawe-Taylor in *NS*, 5 July, pp. 22-23; by Bernard Levin in *S*, 11 July, pp. 67-68; by Walter White in *Theatre Notebook*, XIII, 33-35; in *TLS*, 27 June, p. 364. A valuable chronicle, with chapters on Italian opera in London in the 'thirties and 'forties and a survey of the great opera productions from the days of Malibran to the present.—O. M.

Rothenstein, Sir John. *The Tate Gallery.* London: Thames & Hudson. Pp. 196.

Rev. by Bryan Robertson in *Listener*, 4 Dec., p. 939; in *TLS*, 19 Dec., p. 732.

Rowse, Alfred Leslie. *The Later Churchills.* London: Macmillan. Pp. xv + 528.

Rev. by C. V. Wedgwood in *HTB*, 27 Apr., p. 1; by J. D. Marshall in *LJ*, LXXXIII, 1545; by Raymond Postgate in *N*, 26 Apr., p. 357; by Eric Gillett in *NER*, CLI, 72-73; by John Raymond in *NS*, 28 June, pp. 838-39; by Geoffrey Bruun in *NYTBR*, 27 Apr., p. 7; by L. B. Wright in *SR*, 3 May, p. 16.

Saville, John. *Rural Depopulation in England and Wales.* . . . See VB 1957, 393.

Rev. by W. Ashworth in *Economica*, n.s. XXV, 80-81.

Savory, Douglas. "Eighty Years Ago." *CR*, CXCIV, 126-30.

Parish life in Suffolk in the 'seventies and 'eighties.

Sayers, Richard Sidney. *Central Banking after Bagehot.* Oxford: Clarendon Pr., 1957. Pp. 149.

Rev. by R. F. Henderson in *Econ. Jour.*, LXVIII, 114-16; by J. R. T. Hughes in *JEH*, XVIII, 220-21.

Sayers, Richard Sidney. *Lloyds Bank in the History of English Banking.* London: Oxford Univ. Pr., 1957. Pp. xiv + 381.

Rev. by Ralph Hawtrey in *Econ. Jour.*, LXVIII, 357-59; by Nicholas Lane in *History Today*, VIII, 363; in *TLS*, 31 Jan., p. 64.

Schoyen, Albert Robert. *The Chartist Challenge: A Portrait of George Julian Harney.* London: Heinemann. Pp. viii + 300.

Rev. by W. H. Chaloner in *History Today*, VIII, 511-12; favorably by Asa

Briggs in *NS*, 26 Apr., pp. 542-43; by Geoffrey Barraclough in *S*, 25 Apr., p. 531; by Henry Pelling in *VS*, II, 89.

Schrier, Arnold. *Ireland and the American Emigration, 1850-1900.* Minneapolis: Univ. of Minnesota Pr. Pp. x + 210.

Rev. briefly by J. F. Moran in *LJ*, LXXXIII, 2174; briefly in *Mississippi Valley Hist. Rev.*, XLV, 532-33.

Schwarz, Heinrich. "An Exhibition of Victorian Calotypes." *VS*, I, 354-56.

Sen, S. N. *Eighteen-Fifty-Seven.* . . . See VB 1957, 393.

Rev. by Daniel Thorner in *VS*, I, 364-67.

Shepperson, Wilbur Stanley. *British Emigration to North America.* . . . See VB 1957, 394.

Rev. by Fred London in *Canadian Hist. Rev.*, XXXIX, 158-59; by D. C. Harvey in *Dalhousie Rev.*, XXXVIII, 129; by W. P. Morrell in *EHR*, LXXIII, 735-36; by A. L. Burt in *JEH*, XVIII, 122-23.

Singer, Charles, et al. (eds.). *The History of Technology; Vol. IV: The Industrial Revolution, c. 1750 to c. 1850; Vol. V: The Late Nineteenth Century, c. 1850 to c. 1900.* Oxford: Clarendon Pr. Pp. xxxiii + 728; xxxviii + 888.

Vol. IV rev. by Asa Briggs in *NS*, 20 Dec., pp. 885-86; in *TLS*, 25 July, p. 426.

Sitwell, Dame Edith. *English Eccentrics.* New York: Vanguard Pr., 1957. Pp. 376.

Rev. by R. F. Deen in *Commonweal*, 28 Feb., p. 573; by DeLancey Ferguson in *HTB*, 29 Dec., 1957, p. 4; by K. T. Willis in *LJ*, LXXXIII, 3206; by Leo Lerman in *NYTBR*, 29 Dec., 1957, p. 5. This new and enlarged edition of a book published in 1950 contains material on the Carlyles and Herbert Spencer.

Smith, Colin Leonard. *The Embassy of Sir William White.* . . . See VB 1957, 394.

Rev. by Arthur Leon Horniker in *AHR*, LXIV, 154; at length by F. H. Hinsley in *CHJ*, I, 76-81; by Patrick Ground in *History Today*, VIII, 139-40; by John B. Wolf in *JMH*, XXX, 280.

Smith, J. Maynard. *The Theory of Evolution.* Pelican Biology Series. London: Penguin Books. Pp. 320.

Rev. in *TLS*, 12 Sept., p. 515. Darwinism up to date.

Speaight, George. "Illustrations of Minor Theatres." *Theatre Notebook*, XII, 94-96. Water-color drawings of London theatres in the early 1830's.

Spearman, Diana. *Democracy in England.* . . . See VB 1957, 394.

Rev. by William S. Livingston in *APSR*, LII, 566-67; unfavorably by H. R. Winkler in *APSS*, CCCXVII, 174.

Stephenson, Jim Bob. "Percy Fitzgerald, Critic and Prophet, 1834-1925." *DA*, XVIII, 1903.

His analysis of English theatre, 1868 to 1910, in periodicals and other published works; taken together these writings are of wide scope and "encompass the whole range of English theatre history."

Stewart, Cecil. *The Stones of Manchester.* . . . See VB 1957, 394.

Rev. by T. S. R. Boase in *VS*, I, 295-96.

Taine, Hippolyte Adolphe. *Notes on England.* Trans. Edward Hyams. London: Thames & Hudson, 1957. Pp. xxxi + 296.

Rev. by George Curry in *JMH*, XXX, 396; by Mina Curtiss in *N*, 19 Apr., p. 348; by J. Newman in *New R*, 31 Mar., p. 21; by V. S. Pritchett in *NS*, 20 July, 1957, p. 86; by Peter Quennell in S, 26 July, 1957, p. 138; in *TLS*, 15 Nov., 1957, p. 692.

Taylor, A. J. P. *Englishmen and Others.* . . . See VB 1957, 394.

Rev. by E. Malcolm Carroll in *AHR*, LXIII, 722.

Taylor, A. J. P. *The Trouble Makers: Dissent Over Foreign Policy.* . . . See VB 1957, 394.

Rev. by William L. Neumann in *AHR*, LXIII, 723; by Eugene E. Pfaff in *Amer. Scholar*, XXVIII, 110-12; by W. L. Burns in *History*, XLIII, 61-63.

Taylor, Frank Sherwood. *A History of Industrial Chemistry.* London: Heinemann, 1957. Pp. xvi + 467.

Rev. by Aaron Ihde in *Isis*, XLIX, 352.

Taylor, Gordon Rattray. *The Angel Makers: A Study in the Psychological Origins of Historical Change.* London: Heinemann. Pp. xviii + 388.

Rev. in *TLS*, 11 July, p. 390 (an "infuriating" but also a "stimulating and courageous" book). An analysis of the psychological basis of society in the period 1650-1850.

Tholfsen, Trygve R. "The Chartist Crisis in Birmingham." *International Rev. of Social History*, III, 461-80.

Considers causes (O'Connorite violence and official panic) of the single disruption of the usually harmonious class relationships in nineteenth-century Birmingham.

Thompson, D. "John Tyndall and the Royal Institution." *Ann. of Sci.*, XIII (1957), 9-21.

A biographical sketch of "one of the great popularizers of scientific knowledge."

Thompson, Ruth D'Arcy. *D'Arcy Wentworth Thompson: The Scholar-Naturalist, 1860-1948.* London: Oxford Univ. Pr. Pp. xi + 244.

Rev. in *TLS*, 4 July, p. 380 ("recalls to memory not a man alone but a whole era when scientists were scholars and scholars gentlemen").

Thomson, A. A. *Odd Men In: A Gallery of Cricket Eccentrics.* London: Museum Pr. Pp. 184.

Stories of great men of nineteenth-century cricket.

Thomson, David. *Europe Since Napoleon.* London: Longmans, 1957. Pp. xviii + 909.

Rev. by W. O. Henderson in *History*, XLIII, 252-53; by Harold T. Parker in *SAQ*, LVII, 149-50.

Turberville, Arthur Stanley. *The House of Lords in the Age of Reform, 1784-1837: With an Epilogue on Aristocracy and the Advent of Democracy, 1837-1867.* London: Faber. Pp. 519.

Rev. by Asa Briggs in *History Today*, VIII, 728-29; in *TLS*, 15 Aug., p. 461.

Turner, E. S. *Call the Doctor: A Social History of Medical Men.* London: Joseph. Pp. 320.

Rev. favorably by D. A. P. in *NS*, 22 Nov., p. 738. A social history of doctors since the Medical Registration Act.

Vane-Tempest-Stewart, Edith, Marchioness of Londonderry. *Frances Anne: The Life and Times of Frances Anne, Marchioness of Londonderry, and Her Husband, Charles, Third Marquess of Londonderry.* London: Macmillan. Pp. xiii + 316.

Rev. by Jane Hodge in *History Today*, VIII, 509; by Eric Gillett in *NER*, CLI, 33; in *TLS*, 6 June, p. 312.

Vernon, Anne. *A Quaker Business Man: The Life of Joseph Rowntree, 1836-1925.* London: Allen & Unwin. Pp. 208.

Ward, John M. *Earl Grey and the Australian Colonies, 1846-1857: A Study of Self-Government and Self-Interest.* London: Cambridge Univ. Pr. Pp. xiii + 496.

Waterhouse, Ellis. "The Art of David Wilkie." *Listener*, 13 Nov., p. 788.

Watkin, Edward Ingram. *Roman Catholicism in England From the Reformation to 1950.* Home Univ. Library of Modern Knowledge. London: Oxford Univ. Pr., 1957. Pp. xi + 244.

Rev. by Gervase Mathew in *Blackfriars*, XXXIX, 143-44; by William Kilbourn in *JMH*, XXX, 393-94; in *StI*, XLVII, 340.

Whitridge, Arnold. "The American Slave-Trade." *History Today*, VIII, 462-72. Anglo-American friction in decades when England sought right of search on the high seas in order to suppress slave-trade, then conducted almost entirely by ships registered under the American flag.

Whyte, John Henry. *The Independent Irish Party, 1850-9*. Oxford Historical Series, British Series. London: Oxford Univ. Pr. Pp. xiii + 201.
Rev. by F. S. L. Lyons in *VS*, II, 177-78.

Wilde, Richard H. *Joseph Chamberlain and the South African Republic, 1895-1899: A Study in the Formulation of Imperial Policy*. Pretoria, Union of South Africa: Reprinted by Cape Times, Ltd. from the Archives Year Book for South African History, 1957. Pp. 154.
Rev. by John S. Galbraith in *JMH*, XXX, 164-65.

Wilson, Charles, and Reader, William. *Men and Machines: A History of D. Napier & Son, Engineers, Ltd., 1808-1958*. London: Weidenfeld & Nicholson, Pp. 187.

Wilson, Mardis Glen, Jr. "Charles Kean: A Study in Nineteenth Century Production of Shakespearean Tragedy (Volumes I and II)." *DA*, XVIII, 1535.

Woodruff, Douglas. *The Tichborne Claimant*. . . . See VB 1957, 395.
Rev. by A. de Montmorency in *CR*, CXCIII, 107-8; by P. G. Walsh in *StI*, XLVII, 214-15; by Norman St.-John Stevas in *VS*, I, 284-86.

Woodruff, William. *The Rise of the British Rubber Industry during the Nineteenth Century*. Liverpool: Liverpool Univ. Pr. Pp. xvii + 246.

Wrench, Sir John Evelyn. *Alfred Lord Milner: The Man of No Illusions, 1854-1925*. London: Eyre & Spottiswoode. Pp. 398.
Rev. by Edgar Holt in *History Today*, VIII, 726-27; by Lord Altrincham in *NER*, CLI, 109-11; by R. H. S. Crossman in *NS*, 23 Aug., pp. 226-27; in *TLS*, 19 Sept., pp. 521-22 ("in no sense an adequate, let alone a worthy, biography").

Würgler, Hans. *Malthus als Kritiker der Klassik*. Winterthur: P. G. Keller, 1957. Pp. xxiv + 200.
Rev. by T. W. Hutchinson in *Economica*, n.s. XXV, 263.

Yearley, Clifton K., Jr. *Britons in American Labor: A History of the Influence of the United Kingdom Immigrant on American Labor, 1820-1914*. The Johns Hopkins University Studies in Historical and Political Science, Series LXXV, Number 1. Baltimore: Johns Hopkins Pr., 1957. Pp. 332.
Rev. by Rowland Berthoff in *AHR*, LXIII, 750; by Frank Thistlethwaite in *Amer. Quart.*, X, 495-96; by J. P. Mackintosh in *EHR*, LXXIII, 731; by D. K. Oko in *LJ*, LXXXIII, 1097; by George B. Engberg in *Mississippi Valley Hist. Rev.*, XLV, 138-39.

Young, G. M., and Handcock, W. D. (eds.). *English Historical Documents*. . . . See VB 1957, 396.
Rev. by Asa Briggs in *EHR*, LXXIII, 734-35; by A. J. Taylor in *History*, XLIII, 63.

III. MOVEMENTS OF IDEAS AND LITERARY FORMS

Abrams, M. H. "Belief and Disbelief." *TQ*, XXVII, 117-36.

Adam and Charles Black, 1807-1957. . . . See VB 1957, 385.
Rev. by Royal A. Gettman in *VS*, II, 172-73.

Altick, Richard D. *The English Common Reader*. . . . See VB 1957, 396.
Rev. by L. B. Wright in *AHR*, LXIII, 401-2; by Rutherford D. Rogers in *College and Research Libr.*, XIX, 86-89; by Charles S. Blinderman in *JEGP*, LVII, 560-61; by Norbert J. Gossman in *JMH*, XXX, 67-68; by Cyprian Blagden in *Library*, XIII, 74-75; by Fred B. Millett in *LQ*, XXVIII, 80-82; by J. H. Buckley in *MLN*, LXXIII, 132-33; by R. A. Colby in *MP*, LV, 213-15; in *N & Q*, n.s. V, 272; by B. R. McElderry, Jr., in *Personalist*, XXXIX, 312-13; by M. S. Wilkins in *PSQ*, LXXIII, 633-35; in *TLS*, 14 Feb., p. 88; favorably by George H. Ford in *VNL*, No. 13 (Spring), pp. 11-12; by R. K. Webb in *VS*, I, 286-88.

Altick, Richard D. "From Aldine to Everyman: Cheap Reprint Series of the English Classics 1830-1906." *Studies in Bibliography: Papers of the Bibliographical Society of the University of Virginia*, XI, 3-24.

Altick, Richard D. "The Vision behind the Metaphor." *VNL*, No. 13 (Spring), pp. 9-10.

In this review article based on Leon Edel's *Literary Biography*, Altick surveys briefly the present state of Victorian biography and makes suggestions for future studies.

Alvarez, Alfred. *The Shaping Spirit: Studies in Modern English and American Poets.* London: Chatto & Windus. Pp. 191.
Rev. briefly by Paul C. Wermuth in *LJ*, LXXXIII, 3420. American title, *Stewards of Excellence;* includes treatment of Yeats.

Armstrong, A. MacC. "Samuel Wilberforce *v.* T. H. Huxley: A Retrospect." *QR*, CCXCVI, 426-37.

Ashby, Sir Eric. *Technology and the Academics: An Essay on Universities and the Scientific Revolution.* London: Macmillan. Pp. vii + 118.
Rev. in *TLS*, 17 Oct., p. 593. Includes study of the effect on traditional education of demands for technical education in the nineteenth century.

Best, G. F. A. "The Cambridge University 19th-Century Group." *VS*, I, 267-68.
Description of informal group of scholars in different disciplines who meet to discuss aspects of Victorian life and thought.

Betjeman, John (ed.). *Collins Guide to English Parish Churches, Including the Isle of Man.* Pride of Britain Series. London: Collins. Pp. 24.
Rev. by Andrew Wordsworth in *NS*, 6 Dec., pp. 818-19.

Bøe, Alf. *From Gothic Revival to Functional Form.* . . . See VB 1957, 396.
Rev. by Ellis Waterhouse in *EHR*, LXXIII, 372-73; in *TLS*, 4 July, p. 372.

Bogan, Louise. *Selected Criticism.* London: Owen. Pp. 404.
Rev. by Richard Mayne in *NS*, 22 Mar., pp. 383-84. Originally published, New York: Noonday Pr., 1955. Essays on Yeats and Hopkins.

Brocklehurst, J. Brian. "The Studies of J. B. Cramer and His Predecessors." *M & L*, XXXIX, 256-61.
Study of the *Eighty-four Studies* of this nineteenth-century musician.

Buckler, William Earl (ed.). *Prose of the Victorian Period.* Riverside Editions. Boston: Houghton-Miflin. Pp. xxxi + 570.
Introductory essay discusses the esthetics of Victorian prose.

Cary, Joyce. *Art and Reality.* The Clark Lectures, 1956. London: Cambridge Univ. Pr. Pp. 182.

Rev. briefly by Paul C. Wermuth in *LJ*, LXXXIII, 2420; by G. S. Fraser in *NS*, 16 Aug., p. 201. Includes Cary's estimate of Dickens.

Cazamian, Madeleine L. *Le Roman et les Idées en Angleterre.* . . . See VB 1956, 244.
Rev. by Irène Simon in *Études anglaises*, XI, 72-74.

Clapham, John. "Dvořák and the Philharmonic Society." *M & L*, XXXIX, 122-134.
Letters from the musician to the London society, 1883-1899.

Clarke, I. F. "The Nineteenth-Century Utopia." *QR*, CCXCVI, 80-91.

Clive, John. "More or Less Eminent Victorians: Some Trends in Recent Victorian Biography." *VS*, II, 5-28.
Includes consideration of recent biographies of Manning, Thomas Arnold, Florence Nightingale, Monckton Milnes, Jowett, Mill, Leslie Stephen, and Dickens.

Cohen, Herman. "Hugh Blair's Theory of Taste." *QJS*, XLIV, 265-74.

Cotgrove, Stephen Frederick. *Technical Education and Social Change.* London: Allen & Unwin. Pp. x + 221.
Rev. briefly in *TLS*, 1 Aug., p. 439. Study of technical education, its motives and influences, from the Mechanics' Institute to the present.

Coveney, Peter. *Poor Monkey: The Child in Literature.* . . . See VB 1957, 397.
Rev. by Charles Tomlinson in *SeR*, LXVI, 490-94; briefly in *TLS*, 10 Jan., p. 24; by Barbara Garlitz in *VS*, II, 89-90.

Curran, Eileen Mary. "The *Foreign Quarterly Review* (1827-1846): A British Interpretation of Modern European Literature." *DA*, XIX, 137-38.
The *Foreign Quarterly* was the first successful English review to consider foreign literature. This study traces its history and its criticism of continental literature. An appendix identifies the anonymous reviewers; another gives sketches of obscure reviewers.

Dalziel, Margaret. *Popular Fiction 100 Years Ago.* . . . See VB 1957, 397.
Rev. by Sylvère Monod in *Études anglaises*, XI, 364; by Robert S. Walker in *LR*, XVI, 401-2; by Miriam Allott in *MLR*, LIII, 577-78; by Ruari McLean in *TC*, CLXIII, 392-94; by Arnold Kettle in *Universities Quart.*, XII, 336-40; by W. L. G. James in *VS*, II, 182-83.

Davis, Frank. "The Age of Victoria." *Illustrated London News*, CCXXXII (March 15), 444.

On Victorian painting.

Dunsany, Lord. "Four Poets: AE, Kipling, Yeats, Stephens." *AM,* CCI, 77-80.

Eliot, T. S. *On Poetry and Poets.* . . . See VB 1957, 397.

Rev. favorably by Kathleen Nott in *ParR,* XXV, 139-44; by Hugh Kenner in *Poetry,* XCII, 121-26; by J. V. Cunningham in *VQR,* XXXIV, 126-29.

Ellegård, Alvar. "Public Opinion and the Press: Reactions to Darwinism." *JHI,* XIX, 379-87.

Ellegård, Alvar. "The Readership of the Periodical Press in Mid-Victorian Britain." *Göteborgs Universitets Årsskrift,* LXIII (1957), 3-41.

Rev. by Cyprian Blagden in *Library,* XIII, 308-9. A valuable statistical survey, indicating size and character of the various publics and special interest groups appealed to by over one hundred periodicals (especially 1860-1870).–O. M.

English Libraries, 1800-1850: Three Lectures Delivered at University College, London. London: H. K. Lewis. Pp. 78.

Rev. briefly in *TLS,* 1 Aug., p. 439. Contains essays by Simon Nowell-Smith on Carlyle and London Library, by W. A. Mumford on George Birkbeck and Mechanics' Institute, by C. B. Oldman on Sir Anthony Panizzi and the British Museum.

Enright, Elizabeth. "The Hero's Changing Face." *Bull. New York Pub. Libr.,* LXII, 241-48.

Discusses changing fashions in the heroes and heroines of children's fiction from the time of the brothers Grimm to the present.

Fairchild, Hoxie Neale. *Religious Trends in English Poetry.* Vol. IV. . . . See VB 1957, 397.

Rev. briefly by Harry W. Rudman in *BA,* XXXII, 80-81; by A. Dwight Culler in *JEGP,* LVII, 830-32.

Farr, Dennis Larry Ashwell. *William Etty.* London: Routledge & K. Paul. Pp. xiii + 217.

Rev. by Lawrence Gowing in *NS,* 28 June, p. 843.

Flanagan, Thomas J. B. "The Irish Novelists: 1800-1850." DA, XIX, 326.

Includes treatment of Lady Morgan, John Banim, Crofton Croker, Eyre Evans Crowe, Gerald Griffin, William Carleton.

Foakes, Reginald Anthony. *The Romantic Assertion: A Study in the Language of Nineteenth Century Poetry.* New Haven: Yale Univ. Pr. Pp. 186.

Rev. by Ralph Lawrence in *English,* XII, 106-7; by Jacques Vallette in *Mercure de France,* CCCXXXIV, 543; in *TLS,* 8 Aug., p. 448. On the course of romanticism in English poetry through the nineteenth century; a study of imagery. Includes discussions of Tennyson, Browning, Arnold, Thomson, and Hardy.

Ford, Boris (ed.). *From Dickens to Hardy.* Pelican Guide to English Literature, Vol. VI. Harmondsworth: Penguin Books. Pp. 512.

Rev. briefly in *LJ,* LXXXIII, 2405; by David Craig in *S,* 21 Nov., p. 726; in *TLS* ("Victorians under fire"), 31 Oct., p. 626.

Friedman, Norman. "Criticism and the Novel." *Antioch Rev.,* XVIII, 343-70.

Stresses importance of plot-action in analyzing a novel; includes analyses of novels by Hardy and Conrad.

Groom, Bernard. *The Diction of Poetry.* . . . See VB 1957, 398.

Rev. by L. B. in *Études anglaises,* XI, 266; by A. N. Jeffares in *MLR,* LIII, 100-101; by Edwin Morgan in *RES,* n.s. IX, 346-47.

Groshong, James Willard. "G. B. S. and Germany: The Major Aspects." *DA,* XVIII, 588.

Haines, George, IV. *German Influence on English Education.* . . . See VB 1957, 398.

Rev. by Herman Ausubel in *AHR,* LXIII, 473-74; by W. H. G. Armytage in *EHR,* LXXIII, 365-66.

Haines, George, IV. "German Influence upon Scientific Instruction in England, 1867-1887." *VS,* I, 215-44.

From mid-century on, scientists, educators, and a few businessmen aware that Germany's system of technical and scientific education was creating a formidable trade rival, fought for and eventually effected reforms in the universities, the introduction of laboratory instruction, and the extension of technical education. A thoroughly documented study, acutely relevant to the present status of Western science and education.

Hanbury, Harold Greville. *The Vinerian Chair and Legal Education.* Oxford: Blackwell. Pp. 256.

Rev. briefly in *TLS,* 5 Sept., p. 503. History of the Vinerian professorship of law at Oxford, the chair occupied by, among others, Albert Venn Dicey.

Hitchcock, Henry Russell. *Architecture: Nineteenth and Twentieth Centuries.* Pelican History of Art Series, No. Z15. Harmondsworth: Penguin Books. Pp. xxix + 498.

Rev. as a masterpiece by John Summerson in *NS*, 13 Dec., p. 856; in *TLS*, 26 Dec., p. 748 ("a wonderful array of knowledge").

Houghton, Walter E. *The Victorian Frame of Mind.* . . . See VB 1957, 398.
Rev. briefly by Melvin W. Askew in *BA*, XXXII, 446; by David Owen in *Canadian Historical Rev.*, XXXIX, 327-30; by John Roach in *History*, XLIII, 154-55; by Alice Kogan Chandler in *History of Ideas Newsletter*, III (1957), 84-86.

Howarth, Herbert. *The Irish Writers, 1880-1940: Literature under Parnell's Star.* London: Rockliff. Pp. x + 318.
Study of George Moore, Lady Gregory, A. E., Synge, and Joyce.

Howells, W. D. "Novel-Writing and Novel-Reading: An Impersonal Explanation," ed. William M. Gibson. *Bull. New York Pub. Libr.*, LXII, 15-34.
The first publication of an important lecture by Howells which contains critical statements on most of the major Victorian novelists.

Howes, Alan B. *Yorick and the Critics: Sterne's Reputation in England, 1760-1868.* Yale Studies in English, Vol. CXXXIX. New Haven: Yale Univ. Pr. Pp. x + 186.

Irwin, Raymond. *The Origins of the English Library.* London: Allen & Unwin. Pp. 256.
Rev. by A. N. L. Munby in *NS*, 16 Aug., p. 202.

Johnson, John Curtis. "The *Academy*, 1869-1896: Center of Informed Critical Opinion." *DA*, XIX, 1382-83.

Kelly, Thomas. *George Birkbeck.* . . . See VB 1957, 399.
Rev. by W. H. G. Armytage in *VS*, I, 294.

Kenner, Hugh. *Gnomon: Essays on Contemporary Literature.* New York: McDowell, Obolensky. Pp. 300.
Rev. unfavorably by Steven Marcus in *ParR*, XXV, 591-94. Contains an essay on Yeats.

Kermode, Frank. *Romantic Image.* . . . See VB 1957, 399.
Rev. by Thomas Parkinson in *SeR*, LXVI, 678-85; by A. Alvarez in *Universities Quart.*, XII, 206-16; by Robert Louis Peters in *VNL*, No. 14 (Fall), pp. 18-19; by M. H. Abrams in *VS*, II, 75-77.

Kogan, Herman. *The Great EB: The Story of the Encyclopaedia Britannica.* Chicago: Univ. of Chicago Pr. Pp. 338.

Rev. by Eugene P. Sheehy in *College and Research Libr.*, XIX, 513; by David M. Glixon in *SR*, 31 May, p. 11.

Kroeber, A. L. "Parts of Speech in Periods of Poetry." *PMLA*, LXXIII, 309-14.
Victorian poets are included in this study.

Langbaum, Robert. *The Poetry of Experience.* . . . See VB 1957, 399.
Rev. by Graham Hough in *VS*, I, 77-78.

Lawrence, Elwood P. *Henry George in the British Isles.* . . . See VB 1957, 399.
Rev. by Joseph Schiffman in *AL*, XXX, 385-86; by Leon D. Epstein in *APSR*, LII, 903-4; by Alfred F. Havighurst in *APSS*, CCCXVII, 174-75; by David Roberts in *JMH*, XXX, 258-59; by Daniel Aaron in *VS*, I, 377-78.

Lindley, Dwight Newton. "The Saint-Simonians, Carlyle, and Mill: A Study in the History of Ideas." *DA*, XIX, 320.

Lochhead, Marion. "Some Aspects of Victorian Boyhood." *QR*, CCXCVI, 319-30.
Life in the great public schools.

MacDonagh, Oliver. "The Nineteenth-Century Revolution in Government: A Reappraisal." *CHJ*, I, 52-67.
The "revolution" consisted, generally speaking, of "the substitution of a dynamic for a static concept of administration." An important article.—R. A. D.

McGehee, Judson Dodds. "The Nature Essay as a Literary Genre: An Intrinsic Study of the Works of Six English and American Nature Writers." *DA*, XIX, 1388-89.
Includes treatment of W. H. Hudson.

Mack, Maynard, et al. "A Mirror for the Lamp." *PMLA*, LXXIII, 45-71.
Nominations by members of the MLA for outstanding and influential articles published 1885-1958; the nominations for "English-Victorian" are commented on pp. 64-65.

Maison, Margaret M. "Tom Brown and Company: Scholastic Novels of the 1850's." *English*, XII, 100-3.

Melchiori, Giorgio. *The Tightrope Walkers: Studies of Mannerism in Modern English Literature.* New York: Macmillan, 1956. Pp. 277.
Rev. by H. E. Briggs in *Personalist*, XXXIX, 314-15 (includes discussion of G. M. Hopkins).

Miles, Josephine. *Eras and Modes in English Poetry.* . . . See VB 1957, 400.
Rev. by Hugh Kenner in *Poetry*, XCII, 121-26; in *TLS*, 12 Sept., p. 512.

Miner, Earl Roy. *The Japanese Tradition in*

British and American Literature. Princeton: Princeton Univ. Pr. Pp. 312.
Includes chapters on Victorian image of and influences from Japan.

Morland, M. A. "Nietzsche and the Nineties." *CR,* CXCIII, 209-12.
Nietzsche's influence on John Davidson, Havelock Ellis, and others.

Newman, Charles. *The Evolution of Medical Education.* . . . See VB 1957, 400.
Rev. by George A. Foote in *AHR,* LXIII, 1044; by Douglas Guthrie in *EHR,* LXXIII, 371; by James E. O'Neill in *JMH,* XXX, 395-96; by Richard H. Shryock in *VS,* I, 293-94.

Nowell-Smith, Simon. *The House of Cassell, 1848-1958.* London: Cassell. Pp. x + 299.
Rev. by Grace Banyard in *CR,* CXCIII, 167-68; by Eric Gillett in *NER,* CL, 82; by Walter Allen in *NS,* 8 Mar., p. 311; by Ruari McLean in *TC,* CLXIII, 392-94; in *TLS,* 31 Jan., p. 62; by Royal A. Gettman in *VS,* II, 172-73.

Pankhurst, Richard. *The Saint Simonians, Mill, and Carlyle.* . . . See VB 1957, 400.
Rev. by G. D. H. Cole in *EHR,* LXXIII, 368-69; by John Roach in *History,* XLIII, 154-55.

Partridge, Monica. "Alexander Herzen and the English Press." *Slavonic and East European Rev.,* XXXVI, 453-70.

Pennington, D. H. "Cromwell and the Historians." *History Today,* VIII, 598-605.
Includes discussion of Carlyle, Dickens, Gardiner, and other Victorian chroniclers of Cromwell's career.

Pfeifer, Edward Justin. "The Reception of Darwinism in the United States, 1859-1880." *DA,* XVIII, 1024-25.

Phelps, Gilbert. "The Early Phases of British Interest in Russian Literature." *Slavonic and East European Rev.,* XXXVI, 418-33.
Surveys publications and translations 1557-1912.

Phelps, Gilbert. *The Russian Novel in English Fiction.* . . . See VB 1957, 400.
Rev. by Richard Hare in *Slavonic and East European Rev.,* XXXVI, 572-73.

Pinto, Vivian de Sola, and Rodway, Allan Edwin (eds.). *The Common Muse: An Anthology of Popular British Ballad Poetry, XVth-XXth Century.* London: Chatto & Windus, 1957. Pp. xii + 470.
Rev. briefly by Mary E. Knapp in *BA,* XXXII, 194-95; by Tristram P. Coffin in *Jour. Amer. Folklore,* LXXI, 593-94.

Praz, Mario. *The Hero in Eclipse in Victorian Fiction.* . . . See VB 1957, 400.
Rev. by W. D. Templeman in *Personalist,* XXXIX, 314-15; by Kathleen Tillotson in *RES,* n.s. IX, 103-4.

Pucelle, Jean. *L'Idéalisme en Angleterre, de Coleridge à Bradley: Etre et Penser.* Neuchâtel: La Baconnière, 1955. Pp. 295.
Rev. by Albert Laffay in *Études anglaises,* XI, 176-77.

Pursell, G. "Unity in the Thought of Alfred Marshall." *Quart. Jour. Econ.,* LXXII, 588-600.

Quinton, Anthony. "The Neglect of Victorian Philosophy." *VS,* I, 245-54.
Mill is berated by contemporary analytic philosophers, while other Victorian philosophers are ignored by contemporary idealists. Mr. Quinton also suggests why the Scottish common-sense school (on which Mill drew) and the English Machians warrant rescue from neglect.

Race, Sydney. "J. O. Halliwell and Simon Forman." *N & Q,* n.s. V, 315-20.

Raleigh, John Henry. "Victorian Morals and the Modern Novel." *ParR,* XXV, 241-64.
As Mayhew's work showed, the lower classes of London never accepted middle-class prudery. Butler and Hardy mark the resurgence of lower class, "natural" morality in literature, Butler leading forward to the kinetic fiction of Forster and Lawrence, Hardy to the static fiction of Woolf and Joyce. This is an important article.—F. G. T.

Reeves, James (ed.). *The Idiom of the People: English Traditional Verse.* London: Heinemann. Pp. xii + 244.
Rev. favorably by Christopher Logue in *NS,* 10 May, pp. 608-9. A collection of one hundred fifteen rural songs taken from Cecil Sharp's MSS. This late Victorian collector had fourteen handwritten volumes of English song, in all 2,356 pages, expurgated but not eviscerated.

Rendall, Vernon. " 'Athenaeum' and Other Memories." *LR,* XVI, 302-5.
Personal reminiscences of some Victorian literary figures.

Richards, James Maude. *The Functional Tradition in Early Industrial Buildings.* London: Architectural Pr. Pp. 200.
Rev. by Reyner Banham in *NS,* 27 Dec., pp. 913-14.

Roll-Hansen, Diderik. *The Academy, 1869-1879.* . . . See VB 1957, 401.
Rev. by A. Dwight Culler in *JEGP,* LVII, 153-55; by J. D. Jump in *RES,* n.s. IX, 336-38.

Roppen, Georg. *Evolution and Poetic Belief.* . . . See VB 1957, 401.
Rev. by R. L. Brett in *RES*, n.s. IX, 347.

Rowell, George. *The Victorian Theatre: A Survey.* . . . See VB 1957, 401.
Rev. favorably by A. J. Farmer in *Études anglaises*, XI, 167-68.

Ryals, Clyde de L. "Towards a Definition of *Decadent* as Applied to British Literature of the Nineteenth Century." *JAA*, XVII, 85-92.
Concludes that "decadence" (grotesqueness, lack of moral restraint) is a condition inherent in romanticism, and comes to the fore when the romantic impulse is not held in check.

Seat, William Robert, III. "Harriet Martineau in America." *DA*, XVIII, 224.
Includes study of contemporary periodicals, biographies, journals, memoirs, and unpublished letters consulted in twenty-five American libraries.

Shattuck, Charles H. (ed.). *Bulwer and Macready: A Chronicle of the Early Victorian Theatre.* Urbana, Ill.: Univ. of Illinois Pr. Pp. 278.
Rev. by Frank W. Wadsworth in *NCF*, XIII, 173-74; in *TLS*, 14 Nov., p. 652.

Shklar, Judith N. *After Utopia: The Decline of Political Faith.* Princeton: Princeton Univ. Pr., 1957. Pp. 309.
Rev. by W. M. Simon in *AHR*, LXIII, 639; by W. H. Chapman in *Amer. Scholar*, XXVII, 242; by W. S. Fiser in *Ethics*, LXVIII, 217; by Raymond English in *YR*, n.s. XLVII, 273. "Traces the decline of political philosophy from the hope and enthusiasm of the Enlightenment to the fatalism of the present."

Sims, L. G. A. "The History of the Determination of the Ohm." *Ann. Sci. (Bull. of the British Soc. for the History of Science*, Vol. II) XIII (1957), 57-61.
The development of the theoretical concept on which the international unit of resistance is based.

Smith, John Warren. "Emerson's *English Traits*: A Critical and Annotated Study." *DA*, XVIII, 584.
Includes a statement "which orients the book to the large body of travel literature of the early nineteenth century." Considers Basil Hall's *Travels in North America* (1829), Frances Trollope's *Manners of the Americans* (1832), Harriet Martineau's *Society in America* (1839), and Dickens' *American Notes* (1842) as representatives of the English side of the Eng-

lish-American culture controversy.

Stang, Richard. "The Theory of the Novel in England, 1850-1870." *DA*, XIX, 330.
Treats critical comments by numerous novelists and critics, among them Bulwer-Lytton, Thackeray, C. Brontë, Dickens, Reade, Trollope, G. Eliot, Meredith, W. C. Roscoe, R. H. Hutton, Bagehot, Lewes, L. Stephen, G. Brimley, etc.

Steegman, John. "Aaron Penley: A Forgotten Water-Colourist." *Apollo*, LXVII, 14-17.

Sutherland, James. *English Satire.* London: Cambridge Univ. Pr. Pp. 174.
Rev. briefly in *NCF*, XIII, 78. Includes discussion of Dickens, Butler, Thackeray, and other novelists.

Sutherland, James R. *On English Prose.* The Alexander Lectures, 1956-57. Toronto: Univ. of Toronto Pr., 1957. Pp. 123.
Rev. by L. A. Duchemin in *Dalhousie Rev.*, XXXVIII, 377-79; includes treatment of Carlyle, Arnold, Macaulay, etc.

Swarthout, Glendon F. "The Creative Crisis." *DA*, XIX, 816.
Includes treatment of Conrad and Samuel Butler.

Taylor, Robert H. *Authors at Work: An Address Delivered by Robert H. Taylor at the Opening of an Exhibition of Literary Manuscripts at the Grolier Club: Together with a Catalogue of the Exhibition by Herman W. Liebert, and Facsimiles of Many of the Exhibits.* New York: Grolier Club, 1957. Pp. 52.
Rev. by John T. Winterich in *BSP*, LII, 67-68; by E. M. Forster in *Library*, XIII, 142-43. Contains anecdotes pertaining to Carlyle, Mill, and others.

Thearle, Beatrice June. "Malory in the Nineteenth Century." *DA*, XIX, 133.
Rediscovery of Malory early in the nineteenth century led to an Arthurian revival that has been not merely a resurrection of the old stories.

Thomson, Patricia. *The Victorian Heroine.* . . . See VB 1957, 401.
Rev. by Edgar F. Shannon, Jr., in *MLN*, LXXII, 371-72; by Joseph H. Dugas in *VNL*, No. 13 (Spring), pp. 17-18.

Tillyard, E. M. W. *The Epic Strain in the English Novel.* London: Chatto & Windus. Pp. 208.
Rev. by John Bayley in *NER*, CL, 252-53; in *TLS*, 2 May, p. 242 (see also 9 May, p. 255).

Tillyard, E. M. W. *The Muse Unchained:*

An Intimate Account of the Revolution in English Studies at Cambridge. London: Bowes & Bowes. Pp. 142.
Rev. by Raymond Williams in *NS*, 1 Nov., p. 604.

Torchiana, Donald T. "Victorian and Modern Fiction: A Rejoinder." *CE*, XX, 140-43.
Rejoinder to Wayne Burns, "The Genuine and Counterfeit: A Study in Victorian and Modern Fiction" (see *VB* 1956, 244).

Trifilo, Samuel Santo. "Argentina as Seen by British Travelers: 1810-1860." *DA*, XVIII, 1440-41.

Tylecote, Mabel. *The Mechanics' Institutes of Lancashire and Yorkshire.* . . . See *VB* 1957, 401.
Rev. briefly in *TLS*, 24 Jan., p. 50; by J. F. C. Harrison in *VS*, I, 372-74.

Vandekieft, Ruth Marguerite. "The Nineteenth Century Reputation of Sir Thomas Browne." *DA*, XVIII, 2151.
Browne's reputation in England and America; includes mention of Bulwer-Lytton, Leslie Stephen, Walter Pater, John Addington Symonds.

Warburg, Jeremy (ed.). *The Industrial Muse: The Industrial Revolution in English Poetry.* London: Oxford Univ. Pr. Pp. xxv + 174.
Rev. by Norman Nicholson in *NS*, 4 Oct., pp. 458-60; in *TLS*, 26 Sept., p. 547.

Warburg, Jeremy. "Poetry and Industrialism: Some Refractory Material in Nineteenth-Century and Later English Verse." *MLR*, LIII, 161-70.
Images of steam-power as developed from 1830 to the present.

Warren, Robert Penn. *Selected Essays.* New York: Random House. Pp. 305.
Rev. by Sam Hynes in *Commonweal*, 3 Oct., p. 27; in *HTB*, 31 Aug., p. 10; briefly by P. C. Wermuth in *LJ*, LXXXIII, 2318; by B. R. Redman in *SR*, 19 July, p. 28.

West, Anthony. *Principles and Persuasions.* London: Eyre & Spottiswoode. Pp. viii + 214.
Rev. by Richard Mayne in *NS*, 22 Feb., pp. 243-44. Contains essays on Dickens and Eliot.

West, Paul. "A Note on the 1890's." *English*, XII, 54-57.
On the separation of the artist from the public as a phenomenon of the 1890's.

West, Rebecca. *The Court and the Castle.* . . . See *VB* 1957, 402.
Rev. by Jacob Korg in *N*, 4 Jan., p. 15; briefly in *NCF*, XII, 332-33; by Eric Gil-

lett in *NER*, CLI, 119-20; by John Raymond in *NS*, 26 July, pp. 117-18 ("a dazzling and provocative succession of opinions").

White, Alan. *G. E. Moore: A Critical Exposition.* Oxford: Blackwell. Pp. 226.
Rev. in *TLS*, 31 Oct., p. 629.

Willey, Basil. *More Nineteenth-Century Studies.* . . . See *VB* 1957, 402.
Rev. briefly by John Edwards in *BA*, XXXII, 193; by David Owen in *Canadian Historical Rev.*, XXXIX, 327-30; by Carl R. Woodring in *MLN*, LXXIII, 223-25.

Williams, Raymond. *Culture and Society, 1780-1950.* London: Chatto & Windus. Pp. xx + 363.
Rev. by John Jones in *NS*, 27 Sept., pp. 422-23; by D. W. Harding in *S*, 10 Oct., p. 495; in *TLS*, 26 Sept., p. 548. Evaluations of the social commentary of many Victorians, among them Dickens, Eliot, Kingsley, Mrs. Gaskell, Disraeli, Carlyle and Arnold.

Wimsatt, William K., and Brooks, Cleanth. *Literary Criticism: A Short History.* . . . See *VB* 1957, 402.
Rev. by William Bysshe Stein in *CE*, XIX, 236; by Kenneth Burke in *Poetry*, XCI, 320-28; in *TLS*, 11 Apr., p. 194.

Winters, Yvor. *The Function of Criticism: Problems and Exercises.* Denver: Alan Swallow, 1957. Pp. 200.
Rev. by Don Stanford in *Poetry*, XCI, 393-95. Contains criticism of Hopkins.

Wood, Margaret. "Lord Macaulay, Parliamentary Speaker: His Leading Ideas." The British Orators, V. *QJS*, XLIV, 375-84.

Wright, Herbert G. *Boccaccio in England.* . . . See *VB* 1957, 402.
Rev. by V. De S. Pinto in *N & Q*, n.s. V, 275-76; by Joseph A. Mazzeo in *RoR*, XLIX, 209-10.

Zabel, Morton D. *Craft and Character in Modern Fiction.* . . . See *VB* 1957, 402.
Rev. by Jacques Vallette in *Mercure de France*, CCCXXXIII, 134-35.

IV. INDIVIDUAL AUTHORS

Allingham. Freeman, Ronald Edward. "William Allingham: The Irish Years, 1824-1863." *DA*, XVIII, 587.
Based on hundreds of unpublished letters, some of them Allingham's own, but most of them letters written to him.

Arnold, Matthew (see also I, Wing; III,

Buckler, Foakes, Ford, Sutherland, Williams).

Allott, Kenneth. "A Birthday Exercise by Matthew Arnold." *N & Q,* n.s. V, 225.

A Latin verse written at the age of twelve for his sister Frances.

Allott, Kenneth. "Matthew Arnold's Original Version of 'The River'." *TLS,* 28 Mar., p. 172.

Six quatrains, hitherto unpublished, in the first poem of the "Faded Leaves" sequence.

Allott, Kenneth. "Matthew Arnold's 'Stagirius' and Saint-Marc Girardin." *RES,* n.s. IX, 286-90.

Arnold's debt to a secondary source.

Baum, Paull Franklin. *Ten Studies in the Poetry of Matthew Arnold.* Durham, N. C.: Duke Univ. Pr. Pp. 139.

Rev. by Ralph Lawrence in *English,* XII, 106-7; in *TLS,* 22 Aug., p. 472; by Frederic E. Faverty in *VNL,* No. 14 (Fall), pp. 11-14; by William A. Madden in *VS,* II, 173-75.

Brooks, Roger L. "Matthew Arnold's Testimonial Letters for Candidates for the Greek Chair of the University of Edinburgh." *N & Q,* n.s. V, 161-63.

Buckler, William E. "Matthew Arnold in America: The 'Reason'." *AL,* XXIX, 464-70.

Arnold undertook his American lecture tour to pay "a debt, not of money, but of spirit—a debt to Emerson."

Buckler, William E. *Matthew Arnold's Books: Toward a Publishing Diary.* Genève: Librarie E. Droz. Pp. 182.

Rev. in *TLS,* 22 Aug., p. 472; by Frederic E. Faverty in *VNL,* No. 14 (Fall), pp. 11-14; by William A. Madden in *VS,* II, 173-74. Arranges chronologically by title "passages from Arnold's letters and (where available) from the letters of his correspondents which pertain to specific Arnold publications."

Buckler, William E. "Studies in Three Arnold Problems." *PMLA,* LXXIII, 260-69.

On *Culture and Anarchy,* "A Guide to Greek Poetry," and *Essays in Criticism.*

Butts, Denis. "Newman's Influence on Matthew Arnold's Theory of Poetry." *N & Q,* n.s. V, 254-55.

Carnall, Geoffrey. "Matthew Arnold's 'Great Critical Effort'." *EC,* VIII, 256-58.

Gérard, Albert. "L'Exemple de Matthew Arnold." *Révue Nouvelle,* XXIII (1956), 360-70.

Considers *Empedocles on Etna* and Arnold's subsequent practice as a critic as reflecting his attempt to define his role as a man of his time.

Gollin, Richard M. "Gladstone's Mistaken Praise of Matthew Arnold: An Old Irony and a New Letter." *Western Humanities Rev.,* XII, 277-80.

"Gladstone, reading carelessly, took Arnold's masterfully ironic criticism of Butler for genuine praise. . . ."

Greenwood, E. B. "Matthew Arnold: Thoughts on a Centenary." *TC,* CLXII (1957), 469-79.

An appraisal of Arnold's achievement in criticism.

Hoctor, Sister Thomas Marion. "Matthew Arnold's *Essays in Criticism:* A Critical Edition." *DA,* XIX, 1382.

This dissertation attempts to establish the text of the first series of *Essays in Criticism,* and to present a correct version of that text, which in subsequent editions has become surprisingly corrupt; shows that the Miles and Smith ed. (1918) does not warrant reprinting as a standard edition; makes use of E. K. Brown's chapter in his *Studies in the Text of Matthew Arnold's Prose Works* as an outline, but corrects and completes Brown's assertation; gives explanatory notes that explore the background of the essays; and, finally, gives a brief bibliographical list of items specifically concerned with *Essays in Criticism,* first series. This is unusually noteworthy for the study of Arnold.—W. D. T.

Houghton, Walter E. "Arnold's 'Empedocles on Etna'." *VS,* I, 311-36.

Jamison, William Alexander. *Arnold and the Romantics.* Anglistica, Vol. X. Copenhagen: Rosenkilde and Bagger. Pp. 167.

Rev. in *TLS,* 21 Mar., p. 154; by Frederic E. Faverty in *VNL,* No. 14 (Fall), pp. 11-14; by William A. Madden in *VS,* II, 173-74.

Madden, William A. "The Divided Tradition of English Criticism." *PMLA,* LXXIII, 69-80.

The critical inheritance from Arnold, as seen in Pater, Yeats, Hulme, I. A. Richards, Herbert Read, and T. S. Eliot.

Raleigh, John Henry. *Matthew Arnold and American Culture.* . . . See VB 1957, 403.

Rev. by William E. Buckler in *AL,* XXX, 253-55; by Kenneth Allott in *MLR,* LIII, 575-77; by Frederic E. Faverty in *VNL,* No. 14 (Fall), pp. 11-14; by Robert A. Donovan in *VNL,* No. 13 (Spring), pp. 14-15.

133

Seturanam, V. S. *"The Scholar Gipsy* and Oriental Wisdom." *RES*, n.s. IX, 411-13.
Amplifying and correcting Dyson's "The Last Enchantments" (see VB 1957, 402), Seturanam concludes that *The Scholar Gipsy* is neither an escapist poem nor a stalemate, but an "integrated vision."

Tobias, Richard Clark. "Matthew Arnold and Edmund Burke." *DA*, XVIII, 1041-42.

Aytoun. Schweik, Robert C. "Selected Reviews of William Edmondstoune Aytoun." *DA*, XIX, 532-33.
The bibliography includes a list of all of Aytoun's unsigned contributions to Blackwood, including some poems not printed in the Page edition of his poetry.

Bagehot (see also Mill: Greenberg).

Halsted, John B. "Walter Bagehot on Toleration." *JHI*, XIX, 119-28.

Barham. Lane, William G. "The Primitive Muse of Thomas Ingoldsby." *HLB*, XII, 47-83, 220-41.
Lane's work is of first-rank importance for its biographical, critical, and bibliographical contributions, and its treatment of the history of the reputation of Barham's work; includes use of unpublished letters, etc.—W. D. T.

Baring-Gould. Purcell, William. *Onward Christian Soldier.* . . . See VB 1957, 403.
Rev. by William D. Templeman, *VS*, I, 300-301.

Barrie (see also **Pinero:** Pearson). Brockett, Lenyth and O. G. "J. M. Barrie and the Journalist at His Elbow." *QJS*, XLIV, 413.
The lasting influence of Barrie's journalistic experience.

Beardsley. "Additions to the Beardsley Collection." *PLC*, XIX, 104-5.

Beerbohm. *Mainly on the Air.* . . . See VB 1957, 403.
Rev. by Edward Weeks in *AM*, CCI, 82; by Carlyle Morgan in *Christian Science Monitor*, 10 July, p. 7; by George Freedley in *LJ*, LXXXIII, 1458; by Cecil Sprigge in *Manchester Guardian*, 7 Jan., p. 4; by Frank Swinnerton in *SR*, 2 Aug., p. 13.

Selected Essays. Ed. N. L. Clay. London: Heinemann. Pp. xviii + 141.

Max's Nineties: Drawings, 1892-1899. Ed. Osbert Lancaster. London: Hart-Davis. Pp. 10.
Rev. by Cyril Ray in *S*, 21 Nov., p. 710; in *TLS*, 21 Nov., p. 668. Caricatures, several hitherto unpublished, including the remarkable series on Mr. Gladstone in Heaven.

Bentham. Cranston, Maurice. "On Writing a 'Life' of Jeremy Bentham." *Listener*, 2 Oct., pp. 503-5.

Blunt. Going, William T. "Oscar Wilde and Wilfrid Blunt: Ironic Notes on Prison, Prose, and Poetry." *VNL*, No. 13 (Spring), pp. 27-28.

Borrow (see also I, Wing).

Fréchet, René. *George Borrow.* . . . See VB 1956, 250.
Rev. favorably by Herbert G. Wright in *Études anglaises*, XI, 63-65; by Henry Gifford in *RES*, n.s. IX, 104-5; in *TLS*, 19 Sept., p. 530.

Lightbown, R. W. "Transylvanian Gypsies, as Seen by a Victorian Traveller (With an Anecdote about Borrow)." *Jour. of the Gypsy Lore Society*, 3rd ser. XXXVII, 121-26.
Appreciation of Charles Boner's *Transylvania* (1865).

Bosanquet (see III, Pucelle).

Bowles. Woolf, Cecil. "Some Uncollected Authors: William Lisle Bowles, 1762-1850." *Book Collector*, VII, 286-94, 407-16.

Bradley, F. H. (see III, Pucelle).

Brontës (See also I, Clark; III, Ford, Stang).

Adams, Ruth M. "Wuthering Heights: the Land East of Eden." *NCF*, XIII, 58-62.
Like Cain's land of retreat, Wuthering Heights is a place where conventional morality does not prevail.

Allott, Miriam. "*Wuthering Heights:* The Rejection of Heathcliff?" *EC*, VIII, 27-47.

Blondel, Jacques. "Emily Brontë: Récentes Explorations." *Études anglaises*, XI, 323-30.

Brontë Society, Transactions and Other Publications of.
Vol. XIII, No. 3 (Part 68) has items: Briggs, Asa, "Private and Social Themes in *Shirley*" (pp. 203-19); Arnold, Helen H., "The Reminiscences of Emma Huidekoper Cortazzo: a Friend of Ellen Nussey" (pp. 220-31); Nixon, Ingeborg, "The Brontë Portraits: Some Old Problems and a New Discovery" (pp. 232-38); Brooke, Susan, "Anne Brontë at Blake Hall" [account of difficulties encountered by Anne in her first position as governess] (pp. 239-50); Holgate, Ivy, "The Key to Caroline: Branwell Brontë and the Hollins" [the "Caroline" of Branwell's poems is Caroline Anne Dearden] (pp. 251-59); "The 64th Annual Meeting" (pp. 278-87); "The Brontë Parsonage Museum" [report

for 1957; lists additions to museum and library] (pp. 288-89).

Christian, Mildred G. "The Brontës." *VNL*, No. 13 (Spring), p. 19.

Fréchet, René. "Emily Brontë et son élan mystique." *Foi Education*, XXVII (1957), 95-103.

Discussion of Jacques Blondel's *Emily Brontë: Expérience spirituelle et création poétique* (1956).

Hafley, James. "The Villain in *Wuthering Heights*." *NCF*, XIII, 199-215.

Nelly Dean is seen as the villain.

Hopkins, Annette Brown. *The Father of the Brontës*. Baltimore: Johns Hopkins Pr. Pp. xi + 179.

Rev. by Phyllis Bentley in *Listener*, 4 Dec., pp. 952-53.

Paden, William Doremus. *An Investigation of Gondal*. New York: Bookman Associates. Pp. 85.

Visick, Mary. *The Genesis of "Wuthering Heights."* Introd. Edmund Blunden. Hong Kong: Hong Kong Univ. Pr. Pp. xiii + 88.

Rev. by Phyllis Bentley in *Brontë Society Transactions*, XIII, 266-68; in *TLS*, 5 Sept., p. 498.

Worth, George J. "Emily Brontë's Mr. Lockwood." *NCF*, XII, 315-20.

Brougham. Hawes, Frances. *Henry Brougham.* . . . See VB 1957, 404.

Rev. by E. G. Collieu in *EHR*, LXXIII, 370-71; by Raymond Carr in *NER*, CXLIX (1957), 83-84.

Brown. Mizer, Raymond Everett. "A Critical Survey of the Poetry of Thomas Edward Brown (1830-1897)." *DA*, XVIII, 1435-38.

Brownings (see also III, Foakes, Ford, Pucelle; *Rossetti:* Adrian). Landis, Paul, and Freeman, Ronald E. (eds.). *Letters of the Brownings to George Barrett.* Urbana, Ill.: Univ. of Illinois Pr. Pp. 392.

Rev. by Fraser Neiman in *Amer. Scholar*, XXVIII, 116; by S. C. Chew in *HTB*, 6 July, p. 5; by E. F. Walbridge in *LJ*, LXXXIII, 1530; by Sheila M. Smith in *N & Q*, n.s. V, 497-98; by Frances Winwar in *NYTBR*, 6 July, p. 4; in *TLS*, 16 May, p. 270; by William Irvine in *VS*, II, 85-87.

Baker, Joseph E. "Religious Implications in Browning's Poetry." *PQ*, XXXVI (1957), 436-52.

A valuable synthesis of Browning criticism on the poet's religious position: his "unorthodox views and attitudes" were expressed in a "theological vocabulary that is inappropriate for his meanings."—O. M.

Corrigan, Beatrice (trans. and ed.). *Curious Annals.* . . . See VB 1957, 404.

Rev. by James K. Robinson in *Italica*, XXXIV (1957), 188-91.

Cutts, John P. "Browning's 'Soliloquy of the Spanish Cloister'." *N & Q*, n.s. V, 17-18.

A different source for Browning's "great text in Galatians."

DeVane, William C. "Robert Browning." *VNL*, No. 13 (Spring), p. 22.

Erdman, David V. "Browning's Industrial Nightmare." *PQ*, XXXVI (1957), 417-35.

"Childe Roland" as a symbolic protest against the dehumanizing tendencies of the age.

Goldstein, Melvin. "Elizabeth Barrett Browning's *Sonnets from the Portuguese* in the Light of the Petrarchan Tradition." *DA*, XIX, 1371.

Herring, Jack W. "Critical Attitudes toward Browning since His Death." *DA*, XIX, 798.

Johnson, Agnes Boswell. "The Faust Motif in Browning's *Paracelsus*." *DA*, XIX, 319.

King, Roma A., Jr. *The Bow and the Lyre.* . . . See VB 1957, 405.

Rev. by Patrick J. McCarthy in *ArQ*, XIV, 72-73; briefly by Stewart C. Wilcox in *BA*, XXXII, 189-90; by Thomas P. Harrison in *CE*, XX, 59; by Robert Langbaum in *VNL*, No. 13 (Spring), pp. 12-13; by G. Robert Stange in *VS*, I, 289-90.

Litzinger, Boyd A. "Browning on Immortality." *N & Q*, n.s. V, 446-47.

A conversation reported by Henry Adams.

McCrory, Thomas E. "Browning and Dante." *DA*, XIX, 813.

Marks, Emerson R. "Browning's 'Abt Vogler', 43-56." *Ex*, XVI, Item 29.

Morse, J. Mitchell. "Browning's Grammarian, Warts and All." *CEA Critic*, XX, No. 1, 1, 5.

Page, David. "Split in Wain." *EC*, VIII, 447-50.

Page defends Browning against Wain's treatment of him in *Preliminary Essays* (see VB 1957, 401).

Patterson, Rebecca. "Elizabeth Browning and Emily Dickinson." *Educational Leader* (Kansas State Teachers College), XX (1956), 21-48.

Contends not only for the influence of Mrs. Browning, but also that Emily's appropriation of her was "subtle and complicated."

Po*r*ter, Katherine H. *Through a Glass Darkly: Spiritualism in the Browning Circle.* Lawrence, Kans.: Univ. of Kansas Pr. Pp. 160.

Rev. by A. L. Bader in *VS*, II, 183-84.

Tanzy, C. E. "Browning, Emerson, and Bishop Blougram." *VS*, I, 255-66.

Discusses significant and illuminating parallels between "Bishop Blougram" and Emerson's "Montaigne."

Taplin, Gardner B. "Elizabeth Barrett Browning." *VNL*, No. 13 (Spring), pp. 20-21.

Watkins, Charlotte Crawford. "Browning's 'Fame Within These Four Years'." *MLR*, LIII, 492-500.

On the "revaluation" of Browning's work by reviewers in the 'sixties: a valuable chapter in the history of Browning's literary career and fame.

Watkins, Charlotte Crawford. "Browning's *Men and Women* and the Spasmodic School." *JEGP*, LVII, 57-59.

The reviewers' ascription of "spasmodic" characteristics played a significant part in the unfavorable reception of the book.

Zamwalt, Eugene E. "Christian Symbolism in 'My Last Duchess'." *N & Q*, n.s. V, 446.

Buckle. St. Aubyn, Giles. *A Victorian Eminence: The Life and Works of Henry Thomas Buckle.* London: Barrie. Pp. ix + 229.

Rev. briefly by John Pick in *BA*, XXXII, 326; by Kenneth Rose in *NER*, CL, 117-18; favorably by Raymond Postgate in *NS*, 1 Mar., p. 279 ("a well-written, scholarly and valuable book"); by Geoffrey Barraclough in *S*, 14 Mar., p. 338; in *TLS*, 28 Feb., p. 111; by George Nadel in *VS*, II, 84-85.

Bulwer-Lytton (see also III, Shattuck, Stang, Vandekieft).

Liljegren, S. B. *Bulwer-Lytton's Novels and "Isis Unveiled."* . . . See VB 1957, 405.

Rev. by A. L. Bader in *VS*, II, 183-84.

Butler (see also III, Raleigh, Sutherland, Swarthout).

Silver, Arnold Jacques. "The Way of Samuel Butler: The Early Phase." *DA*, XIX, 320-21.

Carlyle (see also I, Clark; II, Kegel; III, Buckler, *English Libraries,* Ford, Lindley, Pankhurst, Pennington, Pucelle, Sutherland, Taylor, Williams; **Trollope:** Gragg).

Fraser, Russell A. "Shooting Niagara in the Novels of Thackeray and Trollope." *MLQ*, XIX, 141-46.

Carlyle's scepticism about democracy as a clue to the decline of the hero in fiction.

Rollins, Hyder E. "Charles Eliot Norton and Froude." *JEGP*, LVII, 651-64.

Norton vs. Froude and Ruskin in the controversy over Froude's editorial and biographical work on Carlyle. Based in part on unpublished letters.

Sanders, Charles Richard. "Carlyle's Letters to Ruskin: A Finding List with Some Unpublished Letters and Comments." *Bull. John Rylands Libr.*, XLI, 208-38.

Examines Carlyle's letters to Ruskin, and looks at Ruskin as if by Carlyle's eyes; deals with thirty-six letters, nineteen of which are published for the first time (eighteen of these written by Carlyle, one by his wife). This is fascinating material, and the article is of first-rate importance. —W. D. T.

Shine, Hill. "Thomas Carlyle." *VNL*, No. 13 (Spring), p. 22.

Slater, Joseph. "Goethe, Carlyle and the Open Secret." *Anglia*, LXXVI, 422-26.

Welsh, Alexander. "A Melville Debt to Carlyle." *MLN*, LXXII, 489-91.

An image in "The Funeral" (*Moby Dick*, chap. 69) traced to Carlyle's essay on Boswell's *Johnson.*

Carpenter. Vanson, Frederick. "Edward Carpenter: The English Whitman." *CR*, CXCIII, 314-16.

Carroll (see also I, Clark, Wing).

Godman, Stanley. "Lewis Carroll's Sister: Henrietta Dodgson." *N & Q*, n.s. V, 38-39. Henrietta's refutations of two stories about Lewis.

Thody, Philip. "Lewis Carroll and the Surrealists." *TC*, CLXIII, 427-34.

Louis Aragon's attempt, in *Le Surréalisme au service de la révolution,* to read Carrol as a surrealist and a revolutionary.

Church. Smith, Basil Alec. *Dean Church: The Anglican Response to Newman.* London: Oxford Univ. Pr. Pp. xiii + 334.

Rev. by Alec Vidler in *S*, 30 May, p. 706; in *TLS*, 4 July, p. 379; by R. W. Greaves in *VS*, II, 165-66. A biography of R. W. Church, an early disciple of Newman, historian of the Oxford Movement, and Dean of St. Paul's from 1871 to 1890.

Clarke. Elliott, Brian. *Marcus Clarke.* Oxford: Clarendon Pr. Pp. xvi + 281.

Rev. in *TLS*, 7 Mar., p. 129. Biography of major nineteenth-century Australian novelist.

Clough. Mulhauser, Frederick L. (ed.). *The Correspondence of Arthur Hugh Clough.* . . . See VB 1957, 406.

Rev. with detailed care and general appreciation and approval (somewhat qualified) by Kenneth Allott in *EC*, VIII, 438-46; by Michael Timko in *JEGP*, LVII, 825-29; by A. O. J. Cockshut in *Manchester Guardian*, 10 Dec., 1957, p. 4; by S. K. Winther in *MLQ*, XIX, 271-72; by Lawrence Thompson in *NYTBR*, 26 Jan., p. 4; by Thomas Parkinson in *VS*, I, 367-69.

Gollin, Richard M. "Sandford's Bid for the Edinburgh Professorship and Arthur Hugh Clough's Expectations." *N & Q*, n.s. V, 470-72.

Veyriras, Paul. "Un Regain d'Interêt pour Arthur Hugh Clough." *Études anglaises*, XI, 226-28.

A summary of recent Clough studies.

Collins (see I, Clark, Wing).

Conrad (see also I, Wing; III, Swarthout, Warren).

Letters to William Blackwood and David S. Meldrum. Ed. William Blackburn. Durham, N. C.: Duke Univ. Pr. Pp. 209.

Rev. briefly by Charles W. Mann, Jr. in *LJ*, LXXXIII, 3138; by Harry T. Moore in *NYTBR*, 30 Nov., p. 62. Letters concerning Conrad's relationship with *Blackwood's Magazine*.

Allen, Jerry. *The Thunder and the Sunshine: A Biography of Joseph Conrad.* New York: Putnam. Pp. 256.

Rev. by Phoebe Adams in *AM*, CCI, 86; by Edward Wagenknecht in *Chicago Sunday Tribune*, 18 May, p. 4; by Morton Zabel in *HTB*, 17 Aug., pp. 1, 9; briefly by Charles Mann in *LJ*, LXXXIII, 2163-64; by Ian Watt in *NCF*, XIII, 258-59; by DeLancey Ferguson in *NYTBR*, 4 May, p. 5; by Ben Ray Redman in *SR*, 16 Aug., pp. 31-32; by Marvin Mudrick in *VQR*, XXXIV, 630-33.

Bantock, G. H. "Conrad and Politics." *ELH*, XXV, 122-36. On *Nostromo, The Secret Agent*, and *Under Western Eyes*.

Bayley, John. "White Man's Freedom." *NER*, CL, 72-73.

Ostensibly a review of books by Thomas Moser (see VB 1957, 407) and Richard Curle (see below), this article is really concerned with setting Conrad and Kipling against James and Forester.

Bradbrook, Frank W. "Samuel Richardson and Joseph Conrad." *N & Q*, n.s. V, 119. Reminiscences of Richardson in *Victory*.

Cook, Albert. "Conrad's Void." *NCF*, XII, 326-30.

At the heart of almost all of Conrad's plots the protagonist is faced with the recognition of a void.

Curle, Richard. *Joseph Conrad and His Characters.* . . . See VB 1957, 407.

Rev. by Phoebe Adams in *AM*, CCI, 86; by Edward Wagenknecht in *Chicago Sunday Tribune*, 18 May, p. 4; briefly by Charles Mann in *LJ*, LXXXIII, 2163-64; briefly in *NCF*, XIII, 79; by John Bayley in *NER*, CL, 72-73; by David Daiches in *NYTBR*, 17 Aug., p. 4; by Ben Ray Redman in *SR*, 16 Aug., pp. 31-32; by Marvin Mudrick in *VQR*, XXXIV, 630-33; by Dorothy Van Ghent in *YR*, 153-56.

Davis, Harold E. "Conrad's Revisions of *The Secret Agent*: A Study in Literary Impressionism." *MLQ*, XIX, 244-54.

Comparison of serial and book reveals important stylistic changes.

Gleckner, Robert F. "Conrad's "The Lagoon'." *Ex*, XVI, Item 33.

Guerard, Albert Joseph. *Conrad the Novelist.* Cambridge, Mass.: Harvard Univ. Pr. Pp. xiv + 322.

Rev. by Leo Gurko in *Amer. Scholar*, XXVIII, 120; in *Booklist*, LV, 1 Sept., p. 16; by Edward Wagenknecht in *Chicago Sunday Tribune*, 31 Aug., p. 2; by R. C. Blackman in *Christian Science Monitor*, 11 Sept., p. 7; by DeLancey Ferguson in *HTB*, 17 Aug., pp. 1, 8; briefly by Charles Mann in *LJ*, LXXXIII, 2163-64; by David Daiches in *NYTBR*, 17 Aug., p. 4; by Marvin Mudrick in *VQR*, XXXIV, 630-33; by Dorothy Van Ghent in *YR*, XLVIII, 153-56.

Gurko, Leo. "Joseph Conrad at the Crossroads." *Univ. of Kansas City Rev.*, XXV, 97-100.

Haugh, Robert F. *Joseph Conrad: Discovery in Design.* . . . See VB 1957, 407.

Rev. briefly by Melvin J. Friedman in *BA*, XXXII, 189; briefly in *NCF*, XII, 335.

Jean-Aubry, Gérard. *The Sea Dreamer.* . . . See VB 1957, 407.

Rev. by Joseph L. Blotner in *CE*, XX, 54-55; by Bruce Harkness in *JEGP*, LVII, 157-58; by Hans J. Gottlieb in *VNL*, No. 13 (Spring), pp. 15-17.

Kimpel, Ben, and Eaves, T. C. Duncan. "The Geography and History in *Nostromo*." *MP*, LVI, 45-54.

Knopf, Alfred A. "Joseph Conrad: A Footnote to Publishing History." *AM*, CCI, 63-67.

Includes unpublished letters from Conrad.

Leavis, F. R. "Joseph Conrad." *SeR*, LXVI, 179-200.

Includes a provocative analysis of *The Shadow-Line*.

Levin, Gerald H. "An Allusion to Tasso in Conrad's *Chance*." *NCF*, XIII, 145-51.

Lohf, Kenneth A., and Sheehy, Eugene Paul (eds.). *Joseph Conrad at Mid-Century*. . . . See VB 1957, 407.

Rev. by William White in *BB*, XXII, 78; briefly by Joseph L. Blotner in *CE*, XX, 54-55; by L. B. in *Études anglaises*, XI, 355-56; by Bruce Harkness in *JEGP*, LVII, 567-68; by J. Hillis Miller in *MLN*, LXXIII, 131-32.

Macshane, Frank. "Conrad on Melville." *AL*, XXIX, 463-64.

Conrad refused to write a preface to *Moby Dick*.

Moser, Thomas. *Joseph Conrad: Achievement and Decline*. . . . See VB 1957, 407.

Rev. by Richard M. Ludwig in *CE*, XIX, 281; by Bruce Harkness in *JEGP*, LVII, 358-64; by John Bayley in *NER*, CL, 72-73; by W. M. Blackburn in *SAQ*, LVII, 141-42; by Vernon Young in *Southwest Rev.*, XLIII, 80-81.

Owen, Guy, Jr. "Crane's 'The Open Boat' and Conrad's 'Youth'." *MLN*, LXXIII, 100-2.

Owen, R. J. "Joseph Conrad: Two Books." *N & Q*, n.s. V, 260.

An incident which may have suggested *Heart of Darkness*.

Poznar, Walter P. "The Two Worlds of Joseph Conrad." *DA*, XIX, 532.

Spector, Robert D. "Irony as Theme: Conrad's 'Secret Agent'." *NCF*, XIII, 69-71.

Stevens, Arthur Wilber. "George Orwell and Contemporary British Fiction of Burma: The Problem of 'Place'." *DA*, XVIII, 1799-1800.

Makes considerable use of Conrad.

Van Baaren, Betty Bishop. "Character and Background in Conrad." *DA*, XIX, 1392.

Van Slooten, Henry. "The Reception of the Writings of Joseph Conrad in England and the United States from 1895 through 1915." *Univ. of Southern Calif. Abstracts of Diss.* . . . 1957, pp. 103-5.

Watt, Ian. "Conrad Criticism and *The Nigger of the 'Narcissus'*." *NCF*, XII, 257-83.

Zellar, Leonard Eugene. "Conrad's Use of Extra-Narrative Devices to Extend Theme." *DA*, XIX, 1075.

Darwin (see also III, Ellegård).

Barlow, Nora (ed.). *The Autobiography of Charles Darwin, 1809-1882, with Original Omissions Restored*. London: Collins. Pp. 253.

Rev. by J. Z. Young in *NS*, 15 Mar., pp. 337-38; by Magnus Pyke in *S*, 11 Apr., p. 463; in *TLS*, 4 Apr., p. 179; by C. C. Gillispie in *VS*, II, 166-69. Contains about 6,000 words, some concerning Darwin's religious beliefs, omitted from previous editions.

Barnett, Samuel Anthony (ed.). *A Century of Darwin*. London: Heinemann. Pp. xvi + 376.

Rev. by Stephen Toulmin in *Manchester Guardian*, 22 July, p. 4; by N. W. Pirie in *NS*, 28 June, pp. 842-43; in *TLS*, 18 July, p. 403; by Cyril Bibby in *Universities Quart.*, XIII, 83-86. Essays by fifteen biologists and naturalists on Darwin's central ideas and their present validity.

De Beer, Sir Gavin. *Charles Darwin: Lecture on a Master Mind*. Master Mind Lectures, Henrietta Hertz Trust Series—1958. London: Oxford Univ. Pr. Pp. 23.

Rev. in *TLS*, 18 July, p. 403.

Eiseley, Loren. *Darwin's Century: Evolution and the Men Who Discovered It*. Garden City, N. Y.: Doubleday. Pp. 378.

Rev. by Paul B. Sears in *Amer. Scholar*, XXVIII, 108; by David Owen in *Canadian Historical Rev.*, XXXIX, 327-30; by R. C. Cowen in *Christian Science Monitor*, 10 July, p. 7; by Paul Pickrel in *Harper's*, CCXV (July), 90-91; by Gerald Wendt in *HTB*, 29 June, p. 4; briefly by A. F. Fessler in *LJ*, LXXXIII, 1918; by William Irvine in *NYTBR*, 29 June, p. 4.

Huxley, Julian S., *et al*. *A Book That Shook the World: Anniversary Essays on Charles Darwin's Origin of Species*. Pittsburgh: Univ. of Pittsburgh Pr. Pp. vii + 60.

Huxley, Julian, and Fisher, James (eds.). *The Living Thoughts of Darwin*. New rev. ed. London: Cassell. Pp. viii + 156.

Rev. in *TLS*, 18 July, p. 403. Previous edition published 1939.

Mandelbaum, Maurice. "Darwin's Religious Views." *JHI*, XIX, 363-78.

Dickens (see also I, Clark, Dickson; II, Mitchell; III, Cary, Clive, Ford, Pennington, Smith, Stang, Sutherland, Williams).

"Charles Dickens Looks at the News Trade." *LJ*, LXXXIII, 1151-52.

Reprinted with permission from National News Agent, Bookseller, Stationer (London), 14 Dec., 1957.

Adrian, Arthur A. *Georgina Hogarth and the Dickens Circle*. . . . See VB 1957, 408.

Rev. favorably by R. D. McMaster in *Dalhousie Rev.*, XXXVIII, 95-96; favorably by Sylvère Monod in *Études anglaises*, XI, 259; by K. J. Fielding in VS, I, 379; by Joan Bennett in YR, XLVII, 448.

Bredsdorff, Elias. *Hans Andersen and Charles Dickens.* . . . See VB 1957, 408.

Rev. by John Butt in *RES*, n.s. IX, 331-32; by Karl Litzenberg in VS, I, 302.

Broderick, James H., and Grant, John E. "The Identity of Esther Summerson." *MP*, LV, 252-58.

The structure of *Bleak House* defined in terms of Esther's successful quest for a place in the society depicted by the novel.

Butt, John, and Tillotson, Kathleen. *Dickens at Work.* . . . See VB 1957, 408.

Rev. by Henry Gifford in *DUJ*, L, 85-88; by Sylvère Monod in *Études anglaises*, XI, 166-67; briefly by Earle F. Walbridge in *LJ*, LXXXIII, 1078-79; by Geoffrey Carnall in *MLR*, LIII, 574-75; by De-Lancey Ferguson in *NYTBR*, 27 Apr., p. 14; by Edgar Johnson in *SR*, 29 Mar., p. 19; by Monroe Engel in VS, I, 288-89.

Cox, C. B. "In Defence of Dickens." *Essays and Studies*, 1958, n.s. XI (for the English Assoc.), 86-100.

Crompton, Louis. "Satire and Symbolism in *Bleak House*." *NCF*, XII, 284-303.

Dickensian (quarterly), Vol. LIII (1957) (Nos. 321-23). . . . See VB 1932, 422.

Items as follows: Addison, W., and Kirk-Smith, H., "Two Conference Tributes: A Toast and a Sermon" (pp. 163-69); Anderson, R. G., "Mrs. Goodman's and 'The Red Lion' at Highgate" (pp. 16-19); Auberon, F., "Dickens *versus* Gissing: *In re* Varden: Mr. Justice Stareleigh's Summing-up" (pp. 82-84); Carlton, W. J., "Captain Morgan — *Alias* Jorgan" (pp. 75-82); Carlton, W. J., "Fanny Dickens, Pianist and Vocalist" (pp. 133-43); Carlton, W. J., "John Dickens, Journalist" (pp. 5-11); Dickins, L. G., "The Friendship of Dickens and Carlyle" (pp. 98-106); Fielding, K. J., "Dickens at Work [rev. of book by J. Butt and K. Tillotson]" (pp. 160-62); Finlay, I. F., "Dickens's Influence on Dutch Literature" (pp. 40-42); Gibson, F. A., "Dogs in Dickens" (pp. 145-52); Gibson, F. A., "A 17th Century Kit Nubbles" (pp. 12-15); Greaves, J., "Alphington" (pp. 170-71); Hill, T. W., "Notes on *Barnaby Rudge* [concluded]" (pp. 52-57); Hill, T. W., "Notes to *Great Expectations*" (pp. 119-26; 184-86); Hunter, R. A., and Macalpine, I., "A Note on Dickens's Psychiatric Reading" (pp. 49-51); Johnson, E., "Immortal Memory [A Toast at the Dinner in Celebration of the 145th Anniver-

sary of the Birth of Charles Dickens]" (pp. 70-74); Jones-Evans, E., "Playing Dickens in Schools" (pp. 107-09); Mason, L., "Dickens and Dostoevsky [rev. of article by M. H. Futrell]" (pp. 114-16); Morley, M., "Stage Solutions to the Mystery [of Edwin Drood]" (pp. 46-48; 93-97; 180-84); Peyrouton, N. C. (ed.), "Dickens Breakfasts with Longfellow [Vignette by H. W. L. Dana]" (pp. 85-92); Peyrouton, N. C., "Dickens, Dolby and Dolliver: An American Note" (pp. 153-59); Piper, W. J., "New Light on the Old Tipper: A Beverage Report" (p. 39); Rigby, S., "Olfactory Gleanings" (pp. 36-38); Shusterman, D., "Peter Cunningham, Friend of Dickens" (pp. 20-35); Staples, L. C., "Belzoni [rev. of W. Disher, *Pharaoh's Fool*]" (p. 118); Staples, L. C., "Hans Christian Andersen [rev. of E. Bredsdorff, *Hans Andersen and Charles Dickens*]" (pp. 117-18); Staples, L. C., "The Honeymoon Cottage of Chalk" (pp. 110-11); Staples, L. C., "The *Mrs. Gamp* Reading [rev. of facsimile reprint of the author's prompt copy]" (p. 117); Staples, L. C., "*Phiz* [rev. of A. Johannsen, *Phiz: Illustrations from the Novels of Charles Dickens*]" (p. 116); Stone, H., "Dickens and Wilkie Collins [rev. of N. P. Davis, *The Life of Wilkie Collins*]" (pp. 112-14); Stone, H., "Dickens's Knowledge of Thackeray's Writings" (pp. 42-45).

Dickensian (quarterly), Vol. LIV (1958) (Nos. 324-26). . . . See VB 1932, 422.

Items as follows: Bomans, G., "The Immortal Memory of Charles Dickens" (pp. 173-78); Bowkett, Rev. C. E. V., "Dickens Commemoration Sermon" (pp. 182-84); Bowkett, Rev. C. E. V., "Sermon at the Dickens Commemoration Service" (pp. 44-46); Carlton, W. J., "Captain Morgan Again" (pp. 88-93); Carlton, W. J., "Dickens's 'Old Stage-Coaching House'" (pp. 13-20); Carlton, W. J., "Who Wrote 'Mr. Robert Bolton'?" (pp. 178-81); Colburn, W. E., "Dickens and the 'Life-Illusion'" (pp. 110-18); "Dinner with Dickens [a menu written by Georgina Hogarth]" (p. 94); "Dummy Books at Gad's Hill Place" (pp. 46-47); Fielding, K. J., "The Monthly Serialisation of Dickens's Novels" (pp. 4-11); Fielding, K. J., "The Weekly Serialisation of Dickens's Novels" (pp. 134-41); Finlay, I. F., "Dickens in the Cinema" (pp. 106-09); G., J., "A Victorian Canvas [rev. of N. Wallis (ed.), *The Memoirs of W. P. Frith, R.A.*]" (p. 53); Gibson, F. A., "The Love Interest in *Barnaby Rudge*" (pp. 21-23); Goodheart, E., "Dickens Method of Characterisation" (pp. 35-37); Greaves, J., "Report of Council, 1957-1958" (pp. 166-72); Lane, M., "The Immortal Memory of Charles Dickens" (pp. 69-73); Morley, M., "The Theatrical Ternans" (pp. 38-43; 95-106;

155-64); Murdock, M., "Jip" (p. 37); Ollé, J. G., "Dickens and Dolby" (pp. 27-35); "Operas from Dickens" (p. 43); Pakenham, P., "Dickens's 'Old Stage-Coaching House' " (pp. 121-22), answered by W. J. Carlton (p. 122); Pakenham, P., "Georgina Hogarth [rev. of A. A. Adrian, *Georgina Hogarth and the Dickens Circle*]" (pp. 23-26); Parker, C., "Success to Dickens on the Screen" (pp. 73-76); Peyrouton, N. C., "The Gurney Photographs" (pp. 145-55); Postlethwaite, A., "Poor Sir John!" (pp. 83-87); Seawin, G., "A Newly Discovered Dickens Fragment" (pp. 48-49); Seyler, A., "Athene Seyler Replies" (pp. 76-78); Staples, L. C., "Farewell to Devonshire Terrace" (pp. 79-80); Staples, L. C., "The New Film Version of *A Tale of Two Cities*" (pp. 119-20); Staples, L. C., "St. James's, Theatre of Distinction" (p. 109); Stevenson, Lionel, "Thackeray [rev. of G. N. Ray, *Thackeray: The Age of Wisdom*]" (pp. 143-44); Stone, H., "Dickens and Melville Go to Chapel" (pp. 50-52); Tillotson, Kathleen, "Seymour Illustrating Dickens in 1834" (pp. 11-12); Ziegler, A. U., "A *Barnaby Rudge* Source" (pp. 80-82).

Edminson, Mary. "The Date of the Action in *Great Expectations*." NCF, XIII, 22-35.
Interior evidence sets the action of the novel within 1807-10 to 1823-26.

Fielding, Kenneth Joshua. *Charles Dickens: A Critical Introduction*. London: Longmans. Pp. v + 218.
Rev. by Hesketh Pearson in *Listener*, 18 Dec., pp. 1045-46; in *TLS*, 7 Nov., p. 642.

Fielding, K. J. "Charles Dickens." VNL, No. 14 (Fall), pp. 22-23.

Gimbel, Richard. "The Earliest State of the First Edition of Charles Dickens' *A Christmas Carol*." PLC, XIX, 82-86.

Gordan, John Dozier. *Reading for Profit: The Other Career of Charles Dickens*. New York: New York Public Library. Pp. 28. Reprinted from *Bull. New York Pub. Libr.*, LXII, 425-42, 515-22. Description of an exhibition from the Berg Collection.

Gottshall, James K. "Dickens' Rhythmic Imagery: Its Development from *Sketches by Boz* through *Bleak House*." DA, XIX, 797-98.
"Rhythmic imagery" refers to those metaphors and details of action and description which by their repetition within the novel become either atmospheric or symbolic.

Graham, W. H. "Notes on Barnaby Rudge." CR, CXCIV, 90-92.
On the Gordon Riots and the historical background of the novel.

Humphrey, Harold Edward. "The Background of *Hard Times*." DA, XIX, 318.

Lane, Lauriat, Jr. "Dickens' Archetypal Jew." PMLA, LXXIII, 94-100.
Dickens's portraits of the Jew in his fiction.

McMaster, R. D. "Dickens and the Horrific." Dalhousie Rev., XXXVIII, 18-28.
Speaks of three of the primary elements of Dickens's work as a whole: horror, the child's viewpoint, and fairy tale.

Miller, Joseph Hillis. *Charles Dickens: The World of His Novels*. Cambridge, Mass.: Harvard Univ. Pr. Pp. 346.
Rev. briefly by Earle F. Walbridge in LJ, LXXXIII, 2170; by David Daiches in NYTBR, 28 Sept., p. 49; by Edgar Johnson in SR, 30 Aug., pp. 17-18; by Julian L. Moynahan in VS, II, 170-72.

Monod, Sylvère. "Une Amitié Française de Charles Dickens: Lettres Inédites à Philoclès Régnier." Part I: *Études anglaises*, XI, 119-35; Part II: *Études anglaises*, XI, 210-25.
Monod has edited twenty-two letters from Dickens to the noted French actor, Philoclès Régnier. The originals are in the library of the Comédie-Française. Of these letters, fifteen are hitherto unpublished, and the published versions of the other seven are mutilated.

Raleigh, John Henry. "Dickens and the Sense of Time." NCF, XIII, 127-37.
Dickens's statements about time in his fiction and his use of time in his plots and in the rhythm of remembrance of his narrators.

Reinhold, Heinz. "Kritik an den Religiösen und Moralischen Anschauungen in Dickens' Werken im 19. Jahrhundert." Anglia, LXXVI, 145-76.

Sharples, Sister Marian. "Dickens' Use of Imagery: A Study of Narrative Technique in Four Novels." Univ. of Southern Calif. Abstr. of Diss. . . . 1957, pp. 100-2.
Evaluates the figurative language in *Martin Chuzzlewit*, *David Copperfield*, *Bleak House*, and *Great Expectations*; finds great improvement in Dickens's handling of imagery from 1844 to 1860.

Steadman, John M. "Dickens' Typography, and the Dragon's Teeth." N & Q, n.s. V, 256-57.
The origin of a Dickens metaphor.

Stone, Harry. "Dickens's Tragic Universe: 'George Silverman's Explanation'." SP, LV, 86-97.
A study of the artistry and compression

of Dickens's last completed serious story. In the tragic life of George Silverman, good is invariably translated into evil by the selfishness and hypocrisy of the world.

Weintraub, Stanley. "Ibsen's 'Doll's House' Metaphor Foreshadowed in Victorian Fiction." *NCF*, XIII, 67-69.
Both Dickens, in *Our Mutual Friend*, and Shaw, in *The Irrational Knot*, had used the metaphor in a context similar to Ibsen's.

Woodall, Robert. "The Dickens Readings." *CR*, CXCIV, 248-51.

Digby. Hill, A. G. "A Medieval Victorian." *TLS*, 5 Sept., p. 504.
On the life and work of Kenelm Henry Digby, 1796-1880: medievalist, Roman Catholic convert, and author of *The Broad Stone of Honour*.

Dilke. Garrett, William. "Charles Wentworth Dilke as a Literary Critic." *DA*, XIX, 1078.

Disraeli (see also III, Williams).

Dahl, Curtis. "Baroni in Disraeli's *Tancred*." *N & Q*, n.s. V, 152.
Originals of Disraeli characters.

Doyle.
Baylen, Joseph O. "A Letter from Conan Doyle on the 'Novelist-Journalist'." *NCF*, XII, 321-23.
A letter to W. T. Stead concerning a new type of serialized novel.

Harrison, Michael. *In the Footsteps of Sherlock Holmes*. London: Cassell. Pp. xii + 292.
Rev. briefly in *TLS*, 21 Nov., p. 679. Sidelights on the late Victorian and Edwardian world.

Egerton. White, Terence de Vere (ed.). *A Leaf from the "Yellow Book": The Correspondence of George Egerton*. London: Richards Pr. Pp. 184.
Rev. by Brian Inglis in *S*, 14 Nov., p. 660; in *TLS*, 31 Oct., p. 626. Diaries and correspondence of and to (including letters from Wilde, Shaw, and John Lane) Chavelita Dunne.

Eliot (see also I, Clark; III, Ford, Raleigh, Stang, Williams).

Beaty, Jerome. "The Forgotten Past of Will Ladislaw." *NCF*, XIII, 159-63.
Suggests that George Eliot may have intended to show her interest in the Jewish people before *Daniel Deronda*.

Currey, R. N. "Joseph Liggins: A Slight Case of Literary Identity." *TLS*, 26 Dec., p. 753.

On the "passive impostor" who let people suppose he had written *Scenes from Clerical Life* and *Adam Bede*.

Haight, Gordon S. "George Eliot." *VNL*, No. 13 (Spring), p. 23.

Harvey, W. J. "George Eliot and the Omniscient Author Convention." *NCF*, XIII, 81-108.
A defense of George Eliot's use of author intrusions.

Harvey, W. J. "The Treatment of Time in *Adam Bede*." *Anglia*, LXXV (1957), 429-40.

Huzzard, John A. "The Treatment of Florence and Florentine Characters in George Eliot's *Romola*." *Italica*, XXXIV, 158-65.

Owens, R. J. "The Effect of George Eliot's Linguistic Interests on Her Art." *N & Q*, n.s. V, 311-13.

Thale, Jerome. "George Eliot's Fable for Her Times." *CE*, XIX, 141-46.
In *Silas Marner*, two visions of the world, that of aspiration and that of realism, are given side by side in one artistic piece.

Walters, Gerald. "A Memory of George Eliot." *Listener*, 2 Jan., p. 20.
George Eliot's use of Spring Farm and Kirk Hallam in her early fiction.

FitzGerald. Weber, Carl J. (ed.). *FitzGerald's Rubáiyát. Centennial Edition*. Waterville, Me.: Colby College Pr., 1959. Pp. 158.
This attractive and scholarly work is far more than just another edition of the *Rubáiyát*. Carl J. Weber has given us the original text of the poem as first printed in London in 1859 and a record of all the many changes of that text made by Fitz-Gerald as well as a gathering of pertinent critical comment on the poem. The Introduction tells the fascinating and little-known true story of the poem's discovery and propagation. A census is given of the eighteen copies of the 1859 edition now in American libraries, and a useful checklist of the 215 editions of the *Rubáiyát* in the Colby College Library collection, compiled by James Humphry III. A real boon to scholars and admirers of Fitz-Gerald.—R. C. S.

Ford, Ford Madox. Meixner, John Albert. "The Novels of Ford Madox Ford: A Critical Study." *DA*, XVIII, 1047-48.

Ford, Richard. Hoskins, W. G. " 'The Finest Travel-Book in English'." *Listener*, 4 Sept., pp. 337-39.
On Richard Ford, contributor to the

Quarterly Review and author of *Handbook for Travellers in Spain*, 1845.

Gaskell, Mrs. (see I, Clark; III, Williams).

Gilbert. Hall, Robert A., Jr. "The Satire of *The Yeomen of the Guard.*" *MLN*, LXXIII, 492-97.

A valuable analysis, showing that in this libretto Gilbert is satirizing his own form of "topsy-turvy" humor.—O. M.

Pearson, Hesketh. *Gilbert: His Life and Strife.* . . . See VB 1957, 410.

Rev. by Melville Cane in *Amer. Scholar*, XXVII, 398; by DeLancey Ferguson in *HTB*, 9 Feb., p. 3; briefly by George Freedley in *LJ*, LXXXIII, 599; by George Dangerfield in *N*, 26 Apr., p. 359; by J. W. Krutch in *NYTBR*, 9 Feb., p. 16; by Gerald Fay in *S*, 3 Jan., p. 24; by W. W. Appleton in *SR*, 8 Mar., p. 20; by Reginald Allen in *Theatre Notebook*, XIII, 31-32; by Elizabeth Sewell in *VS*, II, 87-88.

Gissing (See also I, Wing).

Amis, Kingsley. "The Hateful Profession." *S*, 4 July, p. 19.

On Gissing, and Morley Roberts's portrait of him as Henry Maitland.

Maurois, André. "George Gissing." *Rev. de Paris*, LXV (February), 3-13.

Roberts, Morley. *The Private Life of Henry Maitland: A Portrait of George Gissing.* Ed. Morchard Bishop. London: Richards Pr. Pp. 256.

Rev. by V. S. Pritchett in *NS*, 14 June, pp. 781-82; in *TLS*, 5 Sept., p. 491. New edition of fictionalized life identifies each character, corrects dates, etc.

Young, Arthur C. "George Gissing's Friendship with Eduard Bertz." *NCF*, XIII, 227-37.

An account of Gissing's enduring relationship with the German friend who encouraged him to complete *Workers in the Dawn.*

Young, Arthur C. "A Note on George Gissing." *Jour. Rutgers Univ. Libr.*, XXII, 23-24.

Gladstone (see also Arnold: Gollin). Austen, Albert A. "Gladstone's Characteristics as a Speaker. The British Orators, IV." *QJS*, XLIV, 244-54.

Conacher, J. B. (ed.). "A Visit to the Gladstones in 1894." *VS*, II, 155-60.

Memorandum by Ishbel Majoribanks of a visit to Gladstone shortly after his retirement.

Gosse (see **Moore:** Burkhart). Matthiesen, Paul F. "An Account of Queen Victoria."

Jour. Rutgers Univ. Libr., XXI (December, 1957), 7-32.

Prints previously unpublished letters from Lady Ponsonby to Gosse, showing her to be a collaborator in an article in the *Quarterly Rev.* for April, 1901, that put a halt to "the spirit of uncritical adulation" of the Queen.

Young, Arthur C. "Edmund Gosse Visits Robert Louis Stevenson." *Jour. Rutgers Univ. Libr.*, XX (June, 1957), 8-32.

Green. Richter, Melvin. "T. H. Green and His Audience: Liberalism as a Surrogate Faith." *Rev. of Politics*, XVIII (1956), 444-72.

Haggard. Cohen, Morton N. "H. Rider Haggard — His Life and Works." *DA*, XIX, 324-25.

States that with the aid of new material we can trace Haggard's friendships with Andrew Lang, W. E. Henley, Kipling, Gosse, and others. Material not before published indicates, furthermore, the extent to which Haggard helped Lang and Kipling; and to which he relied on acquaintances for assistance and advice.

Hardy (see also I, Clark, Weber, Wing; III, Cary, Ford, Raleigh).

Bailey, James Osler. *Thomas Hardy and the Cosmic Mind.* . . . See VB 1957, 411.

Rev. by S. Sebaoun in *Études anglaises*, XI, 169-70; by Philip Larkin in *MLR*, LIII, 116; by G. W. Sherman in *Sci. & Soc.*, XXII, 77-80.

Church, Richard. "Thomas Hardy as Revealed in *The Dynasts.*" *Essays by Divers Hands: Being the Transactions of the Royal Society of Literature*, n.s. XXIX, 1-17.

Rev. in *TLS*, 10 Oct., p. 578.

Hardy, Evelyn. "Thomas Hardy: Plots for Five Unpublished Stories." *London Mag.*, V, 33-45.

Hyde, William J. "Hardy's View of Realism: A Key to the Rustic Characters." *VS*, II, 45-59.

O'Connor, William Van. "Cosmic Irony in Hardy's 'The Three Strangers'." *EJ*, XLVII, 248-54.

Rouse, Blair (ed.). *Letters of Ellen Glasgow.* New York: Harcourt, Brace & Co. Pp. 384.

Ellen Glasgow describes two visits to Hardy, in 1914 and 1927.

Shirreff, A. G. "The 'Eve of St. Agnes' & *A Pair of Blue Eyes.*" *N & Q*, n.s. V, 252.

Hardy, Scott, Keats, and Goethe on light through stained glass windows.

Short, Clarice. "In Defense of *Ethelberta*." *NCF*, XIII, 48-57.

Stedmond, J. M. "Hardy's *Dynasts* and the 'Mythical Method'." *English*, XII, 1-4.
Hardy's myth contrasted (by implication) with the Aeschylean.

Weber, Carl J. "An Important Hardy Manuscript." *Colby Libr. Quart.*, IV, 303-4.
The original autograph of "The Two Tall Men" — the poem later expanded to become "The Three Tall Men" as printed in the London *Daily Telegraph*, August 9, 1928.

Weber, Carl J. "Honeysuckles at Princeton: A Sororicidal Investigation." *PLC*, XIX, 69-81.
On a supposedly "unique" copy of a first edition of *Tess*.

Hobson. Cole, G. D. H. "J. A. Hobson." *NS*, 5 July, p. 12.
Cole commemorates the centenary of Hobson's birth by recalling the debt economics owes to Ruskin's disciple, who anticipated so much of Keynes and current orthodoxy.

Nemmers, Erwin Esser. *Hobson and Under-consumption*. Amsterdam: North-Holland Publishing Co., 1956. Pp. xii + 152.
Rev. by T. W. Hutchison in *Economica*, n.s. XXV, 76-77.

Hopkins (see also III, Bogan, Melchiori, Winters).

Reliquiae par G. M. Hopkins. Trans. Pierre Leyris. Paris: Editions du Seuil. Pp. 173.
Rev. by Jacques Vallette in *Mercure de France*, CCCXXXI, 696 ("Ses équivalences sont à peine plus étrangères au français que le langage de Hopkins à l'anglais . . . première fidelité"); by Henri Thomas in *Nouvelle revue française*. n.s. VI, 122-25; in *TLS*, 4 Apr., p. 184.

Abbott, Claude Colleer (ed.). *Further Letters of Gerard Manley Hopkins*. . . . See VB 1957, 411.
Rev. by Louis Allen in *DUJ*, XLIX (1957), 136-37; by Rosalie Moore in *Poetry*, XCII, 113-15; by John A. M. Rillie in *RES*, n.s. IX, 334-36.

Bischoff, A. "Gerard Manley Hopkins." *VNL*, No. 13 (Spring), pp. 23-24.

Britton, John. " 'Pied Beauty' and the Glory of God." *Renascence*, XI, 72-75.

Gibson, Walker. "Sound and Sense in G. M. Hopkins." *MLN*, LXXIII, 95-100.

Heuser, Alan. *The Shaping Vision of Gerard Manley Hopkins*. London: Oxford Univ. Pr. Pp. viii + 128.

Rev in *TLS*, 17 Oct., p. 594.

Kelly, John C. "Gerard Manley Hopkins: Piety versus Poetry." *StI*, XLVII, 421-30.

Kissane, James. "Classical Echoes in Hopkins' 'Heaven-Haven'." *MLN*, LXXIII, 491-92.
Homer's description of the Elysian Fields (*Odyssey*, Book IV) as source of imagery.

Schneider, Elizabeth. "Hopkins' 'The Wreck of the Deutschland', Stanza 33." *Ex*, XVI, Item 46.

Storey, Graham. "The Notebooks and Papers of Gerard Manley Hopkins: A New Edition." *Month*, CCVI, 273-81.
Two new volumes of Hopkins announced for January, 1959 (Oxford Univ. Pr.): *Journals and Papers*, ed. by Humphry House and completed by Graham Story; and *Sermons and Devotional Writings*, ed. by Christopher Devlin, S.J.

Housman. Fletcher, G. B. A. "On Housman Lucretiana." *Class. Jour.*, LIV, 171.

Haber, Tom Burns. "A. E. Housman's Poetry in Book-Titles, II." *BSP*, LII, 62-64.
Eleven more book titles chosen from Housman's poems; additions to an earlier list published in *BSP*, XLIX.

Hawkins, Maude M. *A. E. Housman: Man behind a Mask*. Chicago: H. Regnery Co. Pp. 292.
Rev. by Horace Gregory in *NYTBR*, 4 May, p. 5; see letter by William White in *TLS*, 1 Aug., p. 435.

"Housman's 'The Deserter'." *N & Q*, n.s. V, 258-60.
Influence of two ballads on Housman's poem.

Marlow, Norman. *A. E. Housman: Scholar and Poet*. Minneapolis: Univ. of Minnesota Pr. Pp. 192.
Rev. briefly by Burton A. Robie in *LJ*, LXXXIII, 2306-7; by Andrew Wordsworth in *NS*, 26 Apr., p. 540; unfavorably by Anthony Thwaite in *S*, 25 Apr., p. 537; in *TLS*, 21 Mar., p. 150.

Marshall, George O. "A Miltonic Echo in Housman." *N & Q*, n.s. V, 258.

Stevenson, John W. "The Martyr as Innocent: Housman's Lonely Lad." *SAQ*, LVII, 69-85.
An examination of Housman's poetic persona.

Watson, George L. *A. E. Housman: A Divided Life*. . . . See VB 1957, 412.
Rev. by William White in *MLN*, LXXIII, 225-27.

White, William. "Housman's Sydney Address." *BSP*, LII, 138-39.
An address in Latin for the jubilee celebration of the University of Sydney in 1902, believed to have been written by Housman.

White, William. "Misprints in Housman." *BB*, XXII, 82.
Seven errors in the Penguin Edition, *Collected Poems*.

White, William. "A Note on Scholarship: Willa Cather on A. E. Housman." *VNL*, No. 13 (Spring), pp. 26-27.
Biographers of Willa Cather insist on quoting her article in the *Nebraska State Journal*, in which she wrote: "I went to Shrewsbury chiefly to get information about Housman, and saw the old files of the little country paper where many of his lyrics first appeared as free contributions and signed 'A Shropshire Lad'."
Housman did not publish any of his poems in such a newspaper in such a fashion; the fact has been pointed out in *N & Q*, yet the story persists.

White, William. "Published Letters of A. E. Housman: A Survey." *BB*, XXII, 80-82.

Hudson (see III, McGehee).

Hunt. Green, David Bonnell. "Some New Leigh Hunt Letters." *N & Q*, n.s. V, 355-58.
Six hitherto unpublished letters to Roden, Talfourd, Moxon, and Ollier.

Huxley (see also III, Armstrong, Buckler).

Bibby, Cyril. "Thomas Henry Huxley and University Development." *VS*, II, 97-116.
Argues that Huxley, working largely through various commissions and committees, exercised a major influence on university education.

Jowett. Faber, Sir Geoffrey. *Jowett: A Portrait with Background.* . . . See VB 1957, 413.
Rev. by Rhys Carpenter in *AHR*, LXIV, 153-54; by B. C. Plowright in *CR*, CXCIII, 220; by John F. Glaser in *JMH*, XXX, 290-91; by Cecil Woodham-Smith in *NYTBR*, 12 Jan., p. 6; by Paull F. Baum in *SAQ*, LVII, 392-94; by W. H. G. Armytage in *Universities Rev.*, XXX, 66-68; by James E. Suiter in *VNL*, No. 14 (Fall), pp. 16-18; by Noel Annan in *VS*, I, 282-84.

Kingsley (see also I, Clark; III, Williams).

American Notes: Letters from a Lecture Tour, 1874. Ed. Robert Bernard Martin. Princeton: Princeton Univ. Libr. Pp. 62.
Twenty-four letters presented here complete for the first time including the unflattering remarks on America withheld by his wife from publication; noticed in *PLC*, XX, 40-41.

Kipling (see also **Conrad**: Bayley).

Fussell, Paul, Jr. "Irony, Freemasonry, and Humane Ethics in Kipling's 'The Man Who Would Be King'." *ELH*, XXV, 216-33.

Kipling Journal.
March issue has items: Kipling, "The Battle of Rupert Square," pp. 5-7; Elwell, T. E., "Sorting the Night Mail," pp. 7-8; Carrington, Charles, "Some Conjectures about 'The Light That Failed'," pp. 9-14; The Earl of Scarborough, "The Unfading Genius of Rudyard Kipling," pp. 14-15. June issue has item: Kipling, "Proofs of Holy Writ," pp. 5-13. September issue has items: Kipling, "Shakespeare and *The Tempest*, a letter to the 'Spectator'," pp. 5-7; Lewis, C. S., "Kipling's World," pp. 8-16; Purefoy, A. E. Bagwell, "'All in a Garden Fair'," pp. 17-19; Stanford, J. D., "'Dark Bungalows'," pp. 20-21.

Millet, Stanton. "Rudyard Kipling: A Study of His Thought and Social Criticism." *DA*, XIX, 524-25.
Analysis of Kipling's thought and social criticism leads to redefinition of "Tory" and "imperialism" with reference to his writings. His imperialism was not exploitation but the establishment of "the Law," the order necessary for true progress.

Landor. Elwin, Malcolm. *Landor: A Replevin.* London: Macdonald. Pp. xii + 502.
Rev. by Eric Gillett in *NER*, CLI, 73; by Betty Miller in *NS*, 12 July, pp. 53-54; by Anthony Thwaite in *S*, 11 July, p. 65; in *TLS*, 25 July, p. 422.

Lecky. Auchmuty, J. J. "The Lecky-Lea Correspondence in the Henry Charles Lea Library of the University of Pennsylvania." *Hermathena*, XCII, 45-61.

Mulvey, Helen. "The Historian Lecky: Opponent of Irish Home Rule." *VS*, I, 337-51.

Le Fanu. Pritchett, V. S. "Aristophanes and Le Fanu." *NS*, 4 Jan., p. 12.
Account of a performance of *Green Tea*.

Lewes. Brett, R. L. "George Henry Lewes: Dramatist, Novelist and Critic." *Essays and Studies*, 1958, n.s. XI (for the English Assoc.), 101-20.

Livingstone. Farwell, Byron. *The Man Who Presumed.* . . . See VB 1957, 413.

Rev. by Paul Johnson in *NS*, 26 July, p. 122; in *TLS*, 27 June, p. 354.

Gelfand, Michael. *Livingstone the Doctor.* . . . See VB 1957, 413.

Rev. briefly in *TLS*, 14 Mar., p. 143; by L. Gray Cowan in *VS*, II, 80-82.

Maurice, Albert (ed.). *H. M. Stanley: Unpublished Letters.* . . . See VB 1957, 413.

Rev. by H. S. Wilson in *JMH*, XXX, 281-82.

Seaver, George. *David Livingstone.* . . . See VB 1957, 413.

Rev. by P. J. Searles in *HTB*, 5 Jan., p. 6; by Geoffrey Bruun in *SR*, 15 Feb., pp. 43-44; by L. Gray Cowan in *VS*, II, 80-82.

Macaulay (see also III, Buckler, Sutherland).

Morgan, H. A. "Boswell to Macaulay." *CR*, CXCIII, 27-29.

Maitland. Cam, Helen M. (ed.). *Selected Historical Essays.* . . . See VB 1957, 413.

Rev. by F. M. Powicke in *Jour. of Ecclesiastical History*, IX, 246.

Malthus (see II, Corry, Keller, Würgler).

Mansel. Matthews, Walter Robert. *The Religious Philosophy of Dean Mansel.* London: Oxford Univ. Pr., 1956. Pp. 23.

Rev. by Thomas MacPherson in *Philosophy*, XXXIII, 375. A lecture on Mansel's *Limits of Religious Thought*, 1858.

Marshall (see II, Hague, Macfie, Majumdar, T.).

Martineau (see also III, Seat, Smith).

Wheatley, Vera. *The Life and Work of Harriet Martineau.* . . . See VB 1957, 414.

Rev. by Wendell Calkins in *JMH*, XXX, 256-57; briefly in *NCF*, XII, 331-32; by Joan Bennett in *YR*, XLVII, 445-49.

Maurice (see also III, Williams). *The Kingdom of Christ: Or, Hints to a Quaker Respecting the Principles, Constitution and Ordinances of the Catholic Church.* Ed. Alec R. Vidler. 2 vols. London: S. C. M. Pr. Pp. 288, 371.

Rev. in *TLS*, 21 Nov., p. 678. This is a new edition of a book long out of print. The text is based on the 2nd edition of 1842.

Meredith (see also I, Clark, Wing; III, Friedman, Stang, Sutherland).

Bartlett, Phyllis. "George Meredith's Lost 'Cleopatra'." *Yale Univ. Libr. Gazette*, XXXIII, 57-62.

Introductory account of the poem, and transcript of the MS, now at Yale.

Coburn, Alvin Langdon. "Photographing

George Meredith." *Listener*, 1 May, pp. 731-32.

Haight, Gordon S. "George Meredith and the *Westminster Review*." *MLR*, LIII, 1-16.

A notable article identifying Meredith's contributions to the "Belles Lettres" section of the *Westminster*, 1857-58: articles on Kingsley, Ruskin, Trollope, Reade, Flaubert, and on his own *Farina*.

Ketcham, Carl H. "Meredith's 'Modern Love,'" XXXI, 7-11." *Ex*, XVII, Item 7.

Stevenson, Lionel. "George Meredith." *VNL*, No. 13 (Spring), p. 24.

Stevenson, Lionel. "Meredith and the Problem of Style in the Novel." *Zeitschrift für Anglistik und Amerikanistik*, VI, 181-89.

Wright, Elizabeth Cox. "The Significance of the Image Patterns in Meredith's *Modern Love*." *VNL*, No. 13 (Spring), pp. 1-9.

Merrick. Holcombe, Warne Conwell. "The Novels of Leonard Merrick." *DA*, XIX, 531.

Merriman. Cox, Homer T. "Henry Seton Merriman: A Critical Survey." *DA*, XIX, 808.

On the life and work of the Victorian novelist Hugh Stowell Scott (1862-1903), who wrote under the pseudonym of Henry Seton Merriman. He was a pioneer in the use of the sympathetically portrayed secret agent as a focal point in novels interpreting international politics.

Mill (see also II, Corry, Keller, Myint; III, Buckler, Clive, Lindley, Pankhurst, Quinton, Taylor, Williams).

Cranston, Maurice. *John Stuart Mill.* ("British Book News: Bibliographical Ser. of Supplements," No. 99.) London: Longmans. Pp. 34.

Rev. briefly in *TLS*, 12 Sept., p. 519.

Cranston, Maurice. "J. S. Mill as a Political Philosopher." *History Today*, VIII, 38-46.

Mill was ideally a socialist and a democrat, but his immediate political program was capitalistic and reflected a distrust of the uneducated masses. See comments by J. H. Burn (*History Today*, VIII, 283-84) and J. T. Mattison (*History Today*, VIII, 431).

Greenberg, R. A. "Mill on Bagehot and Reform." *N & Q*, n.s. V, 83-84.

Suggests a possible source for a proposal Mill condemns in *Representative Government*.

Rudman, Harry. "Mill on Perpetual Endowments." *History of Ideas News Letter*, III (1957), 70-72.

Scanlan, James P. "J. S. Mill and the Definition of Freedom." *Ethics*, LXVIII, 194-206.

Monckton Milnes (see III, Clive).

Moore (see also I, Taylor, Wing; III, Friedman, Howarth).

Burkhart, Charles Joseph. "The Letters of George Moore to Edmund Gosse, W. B. Yeats, R. I. Best, Miss Nancy Cunard, and Mrs. Mary Hutchinson." *DA*, XIX, 131.

Collet, Georges-Paul. *George Moore et la France.* Thèse présentées à la Faculté des Lettres de l'Université de Genève. Genève: Librarie E. Droz, 1957. Pp. 231.
Rev. briefly by George A. Cevasco in *BA*, XXXII, 139-40; favorably by A. J. Farmer in *Études anglaises*, XI, 355; by Henri Peyre in *MLR*, LIII, 572-74; by Ruth Z. Temple in *RoR*, XLIX, 226-28.

Noël, Jean. "George Moore et Mallarmé." *Rev. de litt. comp.*, XXXII, 363-76.

Small, Ray. "A Critical Edition of *Diarmuid and Grania,* by William Butler Yeats and George Moore." *DA*, XIX, 1073-74.

Morley. Moore, Dwain E. "John Morley: Critic of Public Address." *QJS*, XLIV, 161-65.

Stelzner, Hermann Georg. "Ethical Qualities in John Morley's Speaking on Irish Home Rule, 1885-1921." *DA*, XVIII, 699.

Morris (see also II, Kegel; III, Williams).

Catalogue of the Morris Collection. Walthamstow: William Morris Gallery. Pp. viii + 53.
Descriptive catalog of collection of designs for stained glass, textiles, wallpapers; also of manuscripts, books and pictures in Water House at Walthamstow.

Kegel, Charles H. "William Morris and the Religion of Fellowship." *Western Humanities Rev.*, XII, 233-40.

Patrick, John M. "Morris and Froissart: 'Geffray Teste Noire' and 'The Haystack in the Floods'." *N & Q*, n.s. V, 425-27.

Victoria and Albert Museum. *William Morris.* Small Picture Books, No. 43. London: H. M. S. O. Pp. 5.
Contains twenty-seven plates.

The Works of Geoffrey Chaucer: A Facsimile of the William Morris Kelmscott Chaucer, with the original 87 illustrations by Edward Burne-Jones. Ed. John T. Winterich. Cleveland: World Publishing Co. Pp. xix + 554.

Nesbit. Streatfeild, Noel. *Magic and the Magician: E. Nesbit and her Children's Books.* London: Benn. Pp. 160.
Rev. by Naomi Lewis in *Listener*, 11 Dec., p. 1003; by Jean Howard in *S*, 28 Nov., p. 770; in *TLS*, 24 Oct., p. 603.

Newman (see also III, Buckler; Arnold: Butts, Church: Smith). *Autobiographical Writings.* . . . See VB 1957, 415.
Rev. by R. W. Greaves in *EHR*, LXXIII, 169-70.

Spark, Muriel, and Stanford, Derek (eds.). *The Letters of John Henry Newman.* . . . See VB 1957, 415.
Rev. by H. Francis Davis in *Blackfriars*, XXXIX, 39-41.

Bouyer, Louis. *Newman: His Life and Spirituality.* Trans. J. Lewis May. London: Burns & Oates. Pp. xvi + 391.
Rev. by Luke A. Carroll in *CWd*, CLXXXVII, 395-96; by Eric Gillett in *NER*, CL, 81; by Rose Macaulay in *S*, 31 Jan., p. 137; in *StI*, XLVII, 98; in *TLS*, 23 May, supp. pp. i-ii; by Martin J. Svaglic in *VS*, II, 162-65.

Cardinal Newman Studien. Ed. Heinrich Fries and Werner Becker. Vol. I. Nurnberg: Glock and Lutz, 1948. Pp. 348. (Two subsequent volumes have been published.)

Vol. I has items: Simon, Paul, "Newman und der englische Katholizismus" (pp. 13-28); Fries, Heinrich, "Newman und Döllinger" (pp. 29-76); Przywara, Erich, "Kierkegaard-Newman" (pp. 77-101); Dennerlein, Hans, "Newman als Dichter" [includes twelve of Newman's poems, translated] (pp. 105-38); Reade, Francis Vincent, "Der Mythus von 'sentimentalen' Newman" (pp. 139-56); Breucha, Hermann, "Newman als Prediger" (pp. 157-77); Fries, Heinrich, "Newmans Bedeutung für die Theologie" (pp. 181-98); Laros, Matthias, "Das Wagnis des Glaubens bei Newman" (pp. 199-235); Becker, Werner, "Newman und die Kirche" (pp. 236-47); Becker, Werner, "Der Überschritt von Kierkegaard zu Newman in der Lebensentscheidung Theodors Kaeckers" (pp. 251-70); Karrer, Otto, "Die geistige Krise des Abendlandes nach Newman" (pp. 271-84); Läpple, Alfred, "Chronologie der Schriften Newmans" (pp. 287-94); Becker, Werner, "Chronologie von Übersetzungen der Werke Newmans" (pp. 295-300); Becker, Werner, and Fries, Heinrich, "Werke über Newman" (pp. 301-17); Becker, Werner, and Fries, Heinrich, "Zeitschriftenaufsätze" (pp. 318-26).

ter of Robert Bridges to Coventry Patmore." *MP*, LV, 198-99.

Oliver, Edward James. *Coventry Patmore.* . . . See VB 1957, 416.

Rev. briefly by Fred Beharriell in *BA*, XXXII, 191; by Pierre Danchin in *Études anglaises*, XI, 168.

Reid, John Cowie. *The Mind and Art of Coventry Patmore.* . . . See VB 1957, 416.

Rev. by Valerie Pitt in *EC*, VIII, 103-6; by Kenneth Allott in *RES*, n.s. IX, 332-34.

Pattison. Green, Vivian Hubert Howard. *Oxford Common Room.* . . . See VB 1957, 416.

Rev. by E. F. Walbridge in *LJ*, LXXXIII, 838; by Roger Fulford in *Manchester Guardian*, 24 Dec., 1957, p. 2; by Eric Gillett in *NER*, CL, 31-32; by John Raymond in *NS*, 18 Jan., pp. 74-75; by Robert Blake in *S*, 7 Feb., pp. 167-68; by Max Beloff in *TC*, CLXIII, 282-84; by W. H. G. Armytage in *Universities Rev.*, XXX, 65-66; by H. W. Garrod in *VS*, I, 382.

Payne. Ryan, Mariana. "John Payne et Mallarmé: Une Longue Amitié." *Rev. de litt. comp.*, XXXII, 377-89.

Pinero. Pearson, Hesketh. "Pinero and Barrie." *Theatre Arts*, XLII (July), 56-59.

Reade (see also Meredith: Haight).

Burns, Wayne. "*Hard Cash*: 'Uncomparably My Best Production'." *Literature and Psychology*, VIII, 34-43.

Martin, Robert B. "Manuscripts and Correspondence of Charles Reade." *PLC*, XIX, 102-4.

Acquisition of some five hundred items.

Smith, Sheila M. "Realism in the Drama of Charles Reade." *English*, XII, 94-100.

On Reade's stage versions of *It Is Never Too Late to Mend* (1865), *Foul Play* (1868), and *Free Labour* (1870).

Ricardo (see also II, Corry, Macfie, Rasmussen).

Blaug, Mark. *Ricardian Economics: A Historical Study.* Yale Studies in Economics, No. 8. New Haven: Yale Univ. Pr. Pp. x + 269.

Rev. briefly by Harold C. Whitford in *LJ*, LXXXIII, 1774; by George Hilton in *VS*, II, 70-72.

Rolfe. *Nicholas Crabbe: Or, the One and the Many.* Ed. Cecil Woolf. London: Chatto & Windus. Pp. vii + 246.

First publication of one of Rolfe's autobiographical novels.

Rossetti. Adrian, Arthur A. "The Browning-Rossetti Friendship: Some Unpublished

Letters." *PMLA*, LXXIII, 538-44.

A group of Rossetti letters in the Huntington Library.

Packer, Lona Mosk. "Symbol and Reality in Christina Rossetti's *Goblin Market*." *PMLA*, LXXIII, 375-85.

Concludes that this poem "has both chronological significance and emotional relevance in the order of her creative productions."

Paden, W. D. "*La Pia de' Tolomei* by Dante Gabriel Rossetti." *The Register of the Museum of Art, The University of Kansas*, II, 1-48.

Paden's fine study occupies the entire number, which was apparently issued in connection with a loan exhibition of paintings, drawings, and decorative objects by the Pre-Raphaelites, held at the University of Kansas, Nov. 4 to Dec. 15, 1958. *La Pia de' Tolomei* has recently been acquired by the Museum of Art, the University of Kansas.

"Rossetti and a Poe Image." *N & Q*, n.s. V, 257-58.

Poe's 1831 "To Helen" may have influenced a poem of Rossetti's.

Ruskin (see also I, Clark, Weber; II, Blow, Kegel, Mongan; III, Ford, Williams; Carlyle, Rollins, Sanders; Hobson: Cole; Meredith: Haight).

Bradley, John Lewis. "An Unpublished Ruskin Letter." *Burlington Mag.*, C, 25-26.

Letter to Mrs. John Simon, dated by Bradley 20 July 1858, criticizing panel of a triptych by Augustus Egg.

Evans, Joan, and Whitehouse, J. H. (eds.). *The Diaries of John Ruskin.* Vol. II; *1848-1873.* London: Oxford Univ. Pr. Pp. x + 405.

Vol. I (see VB 1957, 416) rev. by C. H. Salter in *RES*, n.s. IX, 228-31; Vol. II rev. by Montague Weekley in *Apollo*, LXVII, 250; by T. S. R. Boase in *Burlington Mag.*, C, 294; by J. F. in *Connoisseur*, CXLII, 184-85; by Jacques Vallette in *Mercure de France*, CCCXXXIII, 346; by Oliver Van Oss in *NER*, CL, 153-56; by Peter Quennell in *S*, 28 Feb., p. 267; by Betty Miller in *TC*, CLXIII, 276-77; in *TLS*, 14 Mar., p. 138; by John L. Bradley in *VS*, II, 88-89.

Bush-Brown, Albert. "'Get an Honest Bricklayer!': The Scientist's Answer to Ruskin." *JAA*, XVI, 348-56.

Huxley, Gilman, and Charles W. Eliot challenge Ruskin's architectural views.

Dougherty, Charles T. "John Ruskin." *VNL*, No. 14 (Fall), pp. 23-24.

Fain, John Tyree. *Ruskin and the Economists.*
. . . See VB 1957, 416.
Rev. by Asa Briggs in *Econ. Jour.*, LXVIII,
391-92; in *Economist*, CLXXXII (1957),
905-6; by Francis G. Townsend in *JEGP*,
LVII, 155-56; by W. H. G. Armytage in
MLR, LIII, 115-16; by Merle M. Beving-
ton in *SAQ*, LVI (1957), 523-24; by Har-
ris Chewning in *South Atlantic Bulletin*,
XXIII (1957), 18-19; by Alfred Chalk in
Southern Economic Jour., XXIV (1957),
94-95.

Squire, Sir John. "The Notebooks of Ruskin
in His Prime." *Illustrated London News*,
CCXXXII (March 15), 423.

Shaw (see also III, Groshong; Egerton:
White). *Bernard Shaw's Letters to Gran-
ville Barker.* Ed. C. B. Purdom. . . . See
VB 1957, 417.
Rev. by A. J. Farmer in *Études anglaises*,
X (1957), 304-9.

An Unfinished Novel. Ed. Stanley Weintraub.
New York: Dodd, Mead.
Rev. by H. F. Rubinstein in *TC*, CLXIII,
583-84; in *TLS*, 2 May, p. 242. Novel
about medicine whose situation anticipates
that of *Candide*.

Altrincham, Lord. "Reflections on *The Apple
Cart.*" *NER*, CLI, 18-23.

Blissett, William. "Bernard Shaw: Imperfect
Wagnerite." *TQ*, XXVII, 185-99.

Hyams, Edward. "Bernard Shaw's Barber."
NS, 28 June, pp. 831-32.
Shaw's favorite topic for barber chair
talk was the weather.

Kaye, Julian Bertram. *Bernard Shaw and the
Nineteenth-Century Tradition.* Norman:
Univ. of Oklahoma Pr. Pp. 222.
Rev. by Hesketh Pearson in *SR*, 11 Oct.,
p. 47.

Maulnier, Thierry. "*Heartbreak House* (La
maison des Coeurs brisés)." *Rev. de Paris*,
LXV (March), 142.

Moffett, John. "When Shaw to Savage Spoke."
NER, CXLIX (1957), 27-29.
Shaw's 1934 visit to New Zealand.

"On Printed Plays" (an excerpt from *Shaw
on Theatre*). *Theatre Arts*, XLII (August),
14.

Park, Bruce R. "A Mote in the Critic's Eye:
Bernard Shaw and Comedy." *Univ. of
Texas Studies in English*, XXXVII, 195-
210.

Reichart, Walter A. "Gerhart Hauptmann,
War Propaganda, and George Bernard
Shaw." *Germanic Rev.*, XXXIII, 176-80.

Though Hauptmann was deceived by
some propaganda during World War I,
Shaw never was.

Shaw Bulletin—
Vol. II, No. 4 (January, 1958), has items:
Lupis-Vukic, J. F., "Shaw's 1929 Program
For Easing World Tensions—and How It
Originated" (pp. 1-2); "A Statement writ-
ten by Mr. G. Bernard Shaw while in Split,
Jugoslavia in May 1929" (pp. 3-4);
O'Donnell, Norbert F., "Harmony and Dis-
cord in *Good King Charles*" (pp. 5-8);
Kornbluth, Martin L., "Shaw and Resto-
ration Comedy" (pp. 9-17); Ozy, "The
Dramatist's Dilemma: an Interpretation
of *Major Barbara*" (pp. 18-24); Arlen,
Sara, "The Fabric of Memory," a review
of Eleanor Robson Belmont's *The Fabric
of Memory* (pp. 25-26); "Shavian News
Notes" (pp. 26-27); "A Continuing
Check-list of Shaviana" (pp. 28-29).
No. 5 (May, 1958) has items: Evans, T.
F., "Granville Barker: Shavian Disciple"
(pp. 1-19); "More on Barbara and Under-
shaft," two rebuttals of the article by Ozy
in No. 4: Nethercot, Arthur H., "Major
Barbara: Rebuttal and Addendum" (pp.
20-21); and Weintraub, Stanley, " 'Shaw's
Divine Comedy': Addendum" (pp. 21-
22); "Shavian Dead Letter File" (pp. 23-
24); "Shavian News Notes" (pp. 24 and
29); Seabrook, Alexander, "Colin Wilson:
Neo-Shavian," a review of Colin Wilson's
Religion and the Rebel (pp. 25-26);
Greenfield, Joseph D., "A Telescoped
Methuselah," a review of the 1958 Theatre
Guild production of an abridged *Back to
Methuselah* (pp. 26-27); "A Continuing
Check-list of Shaviana" (p. 28).
No. 6 (September, 1958) has items: Rud-
man, Harry W., "Shaw's *Saint Joan* and
Motion Picture Censorship" (pp. 1-4);
"Ideas and the Theatre: A G.B.S. Sym-
posium" (pp. 15-20); McDowell, Fred-
erick P. W., "Shaw and the Novel, Vic-
torian and Modern," a review of '*An Un-
finished Novel*' *by Bernard Shaw* edited
by Stanley Weintraub (pp. 21-23); Phil-
brick, Norman, "Shaw on Theatre," a review of *Shaw on Theatre* edited by E. J.
West (pp. 23-24); "A Continuing Check-
list of Shaviana," compiled and edited by
Charles A. Carpenter, Jr. (pp. 25-29);
"Shavian News Notes" (p. 29).

Shenfield, M. "Shaw as a Music Critic." *M
& L*, XXXIX, 378-84.

Simon, Louis. *Shaw on Education.* New York:
Columbia Univ. Pr. Pp. 290.

Spencer, Terence James. "The Dramatic
Principles of George Bernard Shaw." *DA*,
XVIII, 594.

Weales, Gerald Clifford. "Religion in Modern
English Drama." *DA*, XIX, 142.

Includes treatment of plays by Shaw and by Wilde.

Webster, Margaret. "Methuselah Shaw." *Theatre Arts*, XLII (April), 11-12.
Memories of Shaw and comment on *Back to Methuselah*.

West, E. J. (ed.). *Shaw on Theatre*. New York: Hill and Wang. Pp. 306.
Rev. by E. F. Melvin in *Christian Science Monitor*, 10 July, p. 7; by George Freedley in *LJ*, LXXXIII, 2066. Fifty pieces, the majority of which have never before appeared in book form.

Winsten, Stephen. *Jesting Apostle*. . . . See VB 1957, 419.
Rev. by Eleazer Lecky in *Personalist*, XXXIX, 322-23.

Shorthouse. Bishop, Morchard. "*John Inglesant* and Its Author." *Essays by Divers Hands: Being the Transactions of the Royal Society of Literature*, n.s. XXIX, 73-86.

Sidgwick (see II, Keller).

Smiles. *Self-Help, with Illustrations of Conduct & Perseverance*. Ed. Asa Briggs. London: John Murray. Pp. 386.
Rev. in *TLS*, 26 Dec., p. 750. A centenary edition.

Smiles, Aileen. *Samuel Smiles and His Surroundings*. . . . See VB 1957, 419.
Rev. by D. K. Bestor in *JEGP*, LVII, 355-56.

Smith. Wallace, Elisabeth. *Goldwin Smith: Victorian Liberal*. . . . See VB 1957, 395.
Rev. briefly in *APSR*, LII, 883; by David Owen in *Canadian Historical Rev.*, XXXIX, 74-76; by Gordon L. Goodman in *JMH*, XXX, 84; by J. M. Beck in *QQ*, LXV, 327-28; by Francis E. Mineka in *VNL*, No. 14 (Fall), pp. 15-16; by Herman Ausubel in *VS*, I, 380-81.

Spencer. Burrow, J. W. "Herbert Spencer, The Philosopher of Evolution." *History Today*, VIII, 676-83.

Stephen, Fitzjames. Radzinowicz, Leon. *Sir James Fitzjames Stephen, 1829-1894, and His Contribution to the Development of Criminal Law*. Selden Society: Annual Lectures, 1957. London: Quaritch. Pp. 70.
Rev. in *TLS*, 26 Sept., p. 540. A lecture on Stephen as a master of criminal law, with a bibliographical appendix.

Stephen, Leslie (see III, Clive).

Stevenson (see also Trollope: Knox).

Aldington, Richard. *Portrait of a Rebel: The Life and Work of Robert Louis Stevenson*. . . . See VB 1957, 419-20.

Rev. by Bradford A. Booth in *NCF*, XIII, 75-77; by David Daiches in *VS*, I, 371-72.

LaGuardia, Eric. "The Sire de Maletroit's Door." *Amer. Imago*, XV, 411-23.
The whole thing is an erotic dream of Denis de Beaulieu.

McKay, George Leslie. *Some Notes on Bobert Louis Stevenson, His Finances, and His Agents and Publishers*. New Haven: Yale Univ. Libr. Pp. 43.
Rev. briefly in *TLS*, 7 Nov., p. 648.

Marshall, George. "R. L. Stevenson and the Lepers." *Blackfriars*, XXXIX, 327-32.

Surtees. Ray, Cyril. "A Master of Life." *S*, 31 Oct., pp. 573-74.
On Surtees, Jorrocks, and *Handley Cross*.

Swinburne. Baum, Paull F. "Swinburne's 'A Nympholept'." *SAQ*, LVII, 58-68.

Henry, Anne W. "A Reconstructed Swinburne Ballad." *HLB*, XII, 354-62.

Tennyson (see also III, Foakes, Ford). Assad, Thomas J. "Analogy in Tennyson's 'Crossing the Bar'." *Tulane Studies in English*, VIII, 153-64.
Assad's close reading of an oft misread poem is a welcome whiff of common sense. It has taken an enormous amount of ingenuity to find confusion in this poem. Assad dispels the fog.—F. G. T.

B., A. D. "Extant Copies of Tennyson's *Timbuctoo*." *Book Collector*, VII, 296.
Lists six copies of separate pamphlet issue.

Dahl, Curtis. "A Double Frame for Tennyson's Demeter?" *VS*, I, 356-62.
Interpretation of the poem as "a perhaps unconscious reply to Swinburne's 'Hymn to Proserpine'."

Elliott, Philip L., Jr. "Another Manuscript Version of 'To the Queen'." *N & Q*, n.s. V, 82-83.
Notes on a holograph poem of Tennyson.

Gibson, Walker. "Behind the Veil: A Distinction between Poetic and Scientific Language in Tennyson, Lyell, and Darwin." *VS*, II, 60-68.
A provocative consideration of how a poet's "angle" of vision is manifested in his syntax.

Gullason, Thomas Arthur. "Tennyson's Influence on Stephen Crane." *N & Q*, n.s. V, 164-65.
Crane's reaction against "The Charge of the Light Brigade."

Johnson, E. D. H. *"In Memoriam*: The Way of a Poet." VS, II, 139-48.
Traces through the poem a statement on the nature of poetry.

Killham, John. *Tennyson and "The Princess": Reflections of an Age*. London: Athlone Pr. Pp. x + 299.
Rev. in TLS, 5 Dec., p. 699.

Killham, John. "Tennyson and the Sinful Queen—A Corrected Impression." N & Q, n.s. V, 507-11.
A rebuttal to the conclusions arrived at by Betty Miller in an article, "Tennyson and the Sinful Queen," in TC, Oct. 1955.

Korg, Jacob. "The Pattern of Fatality in Tennyson's Poetry." VNL, No. 14 (Fall), pp. 8-11.
Tennyson seemed to feel that fulfillment preceded disaster, if we may judge from the unforeseen, inexplicable catastrophe which so often befalls his heroes at the moment of highest success. In Korg's words, "Tennyson could not rid himself of the profound conviction that somehow ill would be the final goal of good."

Lewis, Naomi. "Whose Arthur?" NS, 12 July, pp. 50-51.
Reflections on Tennyson's poem in the course of a review-article on a modern version of the story, T. H. White's *The Once and Future King*.

MacEachen, Dougald B. "Tennyson and the Sonnet." VNL, No. 14 (Fall), pp. 1-8.

Miller, Betty. "Camelot at Cambridge." TC, CLXIII, 133-47.
Tennyson's associations at Cambridge, with Hallam and others of the "Apostles," provided a model of the male society of the Round Table. "*In Memoriam* . . . appears as an elegy, not for . . . Hallam alone, but for the whole group of the poet's friends and contemporaries; an elegy not only for promise unfulfilled, or for aspiration quenched in death, but . . . for high hopes cut short by life itself, suffocated by the slow pressure of the unproductive years."

Preyer, Robert. "Tennyson as an Oracular Poet." MP, LV, 239-51.
An illuminating analysis of the "visionary mode" of Tennyson's early poems; its nature and origin, and the reasons for its abandonment.

Thackeray (see also I, Clark, Dickson; III, Ford, Stang, Sutherland).

Fielding, K. J. "Thackeray and the 'Dignity of Literature'." TLS, 19 and 26 Sept., pp. 536, 552.
A review of Thackeray's controversy with Forster and Dickens on the social status of authorship, and an account, based on unpublished letters, of his resignation from the Royal Literary Fund.

Ray, Gordon N. *Thackeray: The Age of Wisdom (1847-1863)*. London: Oxford Univ. Pr. Pp. xv + 525.
Rev. by Edward Weeks in AM, CCI, 86; by Robert Maurer in Antioch Rev., XVIII, 125-28; by Edward Wagenknecht in Chicago Sunday Tribune, 19 Jan., p. 1; by Francis Russell in Christian Science Monitor, 9 Jan., p. 5; by T. F. Curley in Commonweal, LXVII, 465; by R. D. McMaster in Dalhousie Rev., XXXVIII, 391-93; by Gilbert Thomas in English, XII, 108; by DeLancey Ferguson in HTB, 12 Jan., p. 6; by J. H. Buckley in JEGP, LVII, 823-25; by J. R. Willingham in LJ, LXXXIII, 2925; by A. O. J. Cockshut in Manchester Guardian, 25 Apr., p. 8; by Jacob Korg in N, 26 Apr., p. 358; by Kathleen Tillotson in NCF, XIII, 164-67; by Eric Gillett in NER, CL, 254; by William Allen in NS, 19 Apr., p. 506; by Edgar Johnson in NYTBR, 12 Jan., p. 6; by Frank Kermode in S, 9 May, p. 597; by William Irvine in SR, 11 Jan., p. 17; by Betty Miller in TC, CLXIII, 582-83; in TLS, 18 Apr., p. 210; by Austin Wright in VQR, XXXIV, 314-17; by Lionel Stevenson in VS, I, 369-71.

Swenson, Paul B. "Thackeray Drawings in the Print Department." BPLQ, X, 101-5.
Boston Public Library has twelve drawings and two short notes to Lady Elton. Collection also includes drawings by Rowlandson and Cruikshank.

Thompson. Pope, Myrtle Pihlman. "A Critical Bibliography of Works by and about Francis Thompson." *Bull. New York Pub. Libr.*, LXII, 571-76 (apparently to be continued).

Thomson (see III, Foakes).

Torrens. Robbins, Lionel. *Robert Torrens and the Evolution of Classical Economics*. London: Macmillan. Pp. xiii + 367.
Rev. by Frank Whitson Fetter in Economica, n.s. XXV, 345-48; in TLS, 11 Apr., p. 198; by George Hilton in VS, II, 70-72.

Trollope, Frances (see III, Ford, Smith).

Trollope, Anthony (see also I, Clark, Dickson; II, Fortescue; III Stang; **Meredith:** Haight).

Booth, Bradford A. "Anthony Trollope." VNL, No. 13 (Spring), pp. 24-25.

Booth, Bradford A. *Anthony Trollope: Aspects of His Life and Art*. Bloomington: Indiana Univ. Pr. Pp. xi + 258.

Rev. by Donald Smalley in *NCF*, XIII, 254-57; by H. C. Webster in *SR*, 19 July, pp. 28-29; by A. O. J. Cockshut in *VS*, II, 169-70.

Gragg, Wilson B. "Trollope and Carlyle." *NCF*, XIII, 266-70.

Though Trollope disliked Carlyle's vehemence, he was influenced by the prophet.

Hagan, John H. "*The Duke's Children*: Trollope's Psychological Masterpiece." *NCF*, XIII, 1-21.

Knox, Ronald A. *Literary Distractions*. London: Sheed & Ward.

Essays on Trollope, Stevenson, and others.

Maxwell, J. C. "Cockshut on 'Dr. Wortle's School'." *NCF*, XIII, 153-59.

Questions Cockshut's interpretation of the novel.

Watts-Dunton. Truss, Tom James. "Theodore Watts-Dunton as Critic." *DA*, XVIII, 1049-50.

Attempts to supply in detail the exact contours of Watts's literary criticism and to outline its relationship to the aims and to the art primarily, of Tennyson, Browning, D. G. Rossetti, William Morris, and Swinburne; gives brief statements of his criticism of Dickens, George Eliot, the Brontës, Arnold, Ruskin, Whitman, and Wilde.

Webbe. Green, David Bonnell. "Four Letters of Cornelius Webbe." *N & Q*, n.s. V, 40-41.

These hitherto unpublished letters by the Cockney poet, an acquaintance of Keats and Hunt, were written in 1845.

White. Stock, Irvin. *William Hale White.* . . . See VB 1956, 268.

Rev. by James H. Durbin, Jr., in *Personalist*, XXXIX, 97.

Wilberforce (see III, Armstrong).

Wilde (see also I, Taylor, Wing; **Blunt:** Going, **Egerton:** White, **Shaw:** Weales).

The Portrait of Mr. W. H. Ed. Vyvyan Holland. London: Methuen. Pp. xviii + 90.

Rev. by Hilary Corke in *Listener*, 4 Dec., p. 950; in *TLS*, 21 Nov., p. 668 (and see letter by H. Montgomery Hyde, 5 Dec., p. 705). This complete edition of Wilde's speculations on the subject of Shakespeare's sonnets has hitherto been published only in a limited edition.

Ganz, Arthur F. "The Dandiacal Drama: A Study of the Plays of Oscar Wilde." *DA*, XVIII, 1429.

Ojala, Aatos. *Aestheticism and Oscar Wilde.* . . . Pt. I, see VB 1955, 272; Pt. II, see VB 1957, 421.

Rev. by A. J. Farmer in *Études anglaises*, XI, 170; by R. L. Peters in *JAA*, XVII, 135-36.

Sims, George. "Who Wrote *For Love of the King?*" *Book Collector*, VII, 269-77.

Sims seems to suspect Mrs. Chan Toon of the authorship of this play (published in *Hutchinson's Magazine* in 1921 and there attributed to Wilde), but he leaves the question open.

Wyndham, Horace. "'Edited by Oscar Wilde'." *TC*, CLXIII, 435-40.

Oscar Wilde's editorship of the short-lived *Woman's World*.

Yü, Margaret Man Sang. *Two Masters of Irony: Annotations on Three Essays by Oscar Wilde and Lytton Strachey, with Special Reference to Their Manner of Writing*. Hong Kong: Hong Kong Univ. Pr. Pp. 42.

Rev. briefly in *TLS*, 24 Jan., p. 50.

Wiseman. Dougherty, Charles T., and Welch, Homer C. (eds.). "Wiseman on the Oxford Movement: An Early Report to the Vatican." *VS*, II, 149-54.

Translation of a letter from Wiseman to Secretary of the Propaganda in Rome.

Yeats (see also I, Clark, Wing; III, Alvarez, Bogan, Kenner; **Arnold:** Madden, **Moore:** Burkhart, Small).

The Variorum Edition of the Poems of W. B. Yeats. . . . See VB 1957, 422.

Rev. briefly in *CE*, XIX, 273; by M. L. Rosenthal in *N*, 5 Apr., pp. 298-99; by Andrew G. Hoover in *QJS*, XLIV, 90-91; by Curtis Bradford in *SeR*, LXVI, 668-78; in *TLS*, 7 Mar., p. 126 (and see note by R. W. Chapman, 28 Mar., p. 169); by Iain Fletcher, *VS*, II, 72-75.

Alvarez, A. "Eliot and Yeats: Orthodoxy and Tradition." *TC*, CLXII (1957), 149-63, 224-34.

Engelberg, Edward. "The Herald of Art: A Study of W. B. Yeats' Criticism and Aesthetic." *DA*, XVIII, 2140.

Gross, Martha. "Yeats' 'I Am of Ireland'." *Ex*, XVII, Item 15.

Howarth, Herbert. "Yeats' 'In the Seven Woods', 6." *Ex*, XVII, Item 14.

Kiernan, T. J. "Lady Gregory and W. B. Yeats." *Dalhousie Rev.*, XXXVIII, 295-306.

Based in part on personal memories of both Yeats and Lady Gregory.

Martin, C. G. "W. B. Yeats: An Unpublished Letter." *N & Q*, n.s. V, 260-61.

A brief note on prosody written in 1906.

Melchiori, Giorgio. "Yeats' 'Beast' and the Unicorn." *DUJ*, LI, 10-23.

The unicorn as a symbol of violent rebirth.

Newton, Norman. "Yeats as Dramatist: *The Player Queen*." *EC*, VIII, 269-84.

Raine, Kathleen. "A Little Song about a Rose." *NS*, 8 Feb., p. 170.

In replying to Helen Gardner's review, Raine asks why the greatest English poetry has insisted on regarding symbols as symbols of something and not as technical devices. See also F. A. C. Wilson, "Symbolic Equations," *NS*, 1 Mar., p. 273, in which he defends Porphyry as the source of the honey-bee symbol in "The Stare's Nest by My Window." See also Helen Gardner's reply, "Symbolic Equations," *NS*, 8 Mar., p. 305.

Reid, B. L. "Yeats and Tragedy." *Hudson Rev.*, XI, 391-410.

Rose, Phyllis Hoge. "Yeats and the Dramatic Lyric." *DA*, XVIII, 2130.

Saul, George Brandon. *Prolegomena to the Study of Yeats's Poems*. Philadelphia: Pennsylvania Univ. Pr., 1957. Pp. 196.

Rev. briefly by F. L. Gwynn in *CE*, XX, 58.

Schmalenbeck, Hildegard. "The Early Career of W. B. Yeats." *DA*, XVIII, 593.

Shanley, J. Lyndon. "Thoreau's Geese and Yeats's Swans." *AL*, XXX, 361-64.

Thwaite, Anthony. "Yeats and the Noh." *TC*, CLXII (1957), 235-42.

Wade, Allan. *A Bibliography of the Writings of W. B. Yeats*. 2nd ed. rev. London: Hart-Davis. Pp. 449.

Rev. by Gerald D. McDonald in *BSP*, LII, 322-26; in *TLS*, 7 Mar., p. 126. Previous edition, 1951; see VB 1952, 268.

Watson, Thomas Lee. "A Critical Edition of Selected Lyrics of William Butler Yeats." *DA*, XIX, 1080.

The main body of the dissertation consists of some one hundred selected lyrics with notes and annotations to the text of the poems.

Wilson, Francis Alexander Charles. *W. B. Yeats and Tradition*. London: Gollancz. Pp. 286.

Rev. by Christopher Busby in *Dublin Rev.*, CCXXXII, 178-81; by R. F. Rattray in *HJ*, LVI, 311-12; by Helen Gardner in *NS*, 1 Feb., pp. 141-42; by Thomas Hogan in *S*, 17 Jan., p. 78; by Thomas Parkinson in *SeR*, LXVI, 678-85; by G. F. Hudson in *TC*, CLXIII, 482-83; in *TLS*, 24 Jan., p. 43.

VICTORIAN  IBLIOGRAPHY FOR 1959

Robert C. Slack, editor

THIS BIBLIOGRAPHY has been prepared by a committee of the Victorian Literature Group of the Modern Language Association of America: Robert C. Slack, chairman, Carnegie Institute of Technology; Oscar Maurer, University of Texas; Robert A. Donovan, Cornell University; Charles T. Dougherty, St. Louis University; Donald J. Gray, Indiana University; Richard C. Tobias, University of Pittsburgh; and Ronald E. Freeman, University of Southern California. It attempts to list the noteworthy publications of 1959 (including reviews of these and earlier items) that have a bearing on the Victorian period, as well as similar publications of earlier date that have been inadvertently omitted from the preceding Victorian bibliographies. Unless otherwise stated, the date of publication is 1959. Reference to a page in the bibliography for 1958, in *Victorian Studies,* June, 1959, is made by the following form: See VB 1958, 263. Some cross-references are given, though not all that are possible. For certain continuing bibliographical works the reader should consult VB 1941, the last annual bibliography in which such works are listed in full. Bibliographical entries are made to conform as closely as possible with the British National Bibliography for books first published in

Great Britain, and with the Library of Congress Catalog for books first published in the United States.

The editor wishes to thank his predecessor, Professor Francis G. Townsend of Florida State University, as well as Professor Carl J. Weber of Colby College and Professor Austin Wright of Carnegie Institute of Technology, for special assistance.

KEY TO ABBREVIATIONS

AHR = American Historical Review
AL = American Literature
AM = Atlantic Monthly
APSR = American Political Science Review
APSS = Annals of the American Academy of Political and Social Science
ArQ = Arizona Quarterly
BA = Books Abroad
BB = Bulletin of Bibliography
BLR = Bodleian Library Record
BPLQ = Boston Public Library Quarterly
BSP = Papers of the Bibliographical Society of America
CE = College English
CHJ = Historical Journal (formerly *Cambridge Historical Journal*)

CJ = *Cambridge Journal*
CR = *Contemporary Review*
CWd = *Catholic World*
DA = *Dissertation Abstracts*
DUJ = *Durham University Journal*
EC = *Essays in Criticism*
EHR = *English Historical Review*
EJ = *English Journal*
ELH = *Journal of English Literary History*
ESt = *English Studies*
Ex = *Explicator*
HJ = *Hibbert Journal*
HLB = *Harvard Library Bulletin*
HLQ = *Huntington Library Quarterly*
HTB = *New York Herald Tribune Book Review*
JAA = *Journal of Aesthetics and Art Criticism*
JEGP = *Journal of English and Germanic Philology*
JEH = *Journal of Economic History*
JHI = *Journal of the History of Ideas*
JMH = *Journal of Modern History*
JP = *Journal of Philosophy*
JPE = *Journal of Political Economy*
KR = *Kenyon Review*
LJ = *Library Journal*
LQ = *Library Quarterly*
LQHR = *London Quarterly and Holborn Review*
LR = *Library Review*
M & L = *Music and Letters*
MLJ = *Modern Language Journal*
MLN = *Modern Language Notes*
MLQ = *Modern Language Quarterly*
MLR = *Modern Language Review*
MP = *Modern Philology*
N = *Nation*
N & Q = *Notes and Queries*
NCF = *Nineteenth-Century Fiction*
NEQ = *New England Quarterly*
NER = *National and English Review*
New R = *New Republic*
NS = *New Statesman*
NYTBR = *New York Times Book Review*
PAPS = *Proceedings of the American Philological Society*
ParR = *Partisan Review*
PLC = *Princeton University Library Chronicle*
PMLA = *Publications of the Modern Language Association of America*
PQ = *Philological Quarterly*
PSQ = *Political Science Quarterly*

QJS = *Quarterly Journal of Speech*
QQ = *Queen's Quarterly*
QR = *Quarterly Review*
RES = *Review of English Studies*
RoR = *Romanic Review*
S = *Spectator*
SAQ = *South Atlantic Quarterly*
SeR = *Sewanee Review*
SP = *Studies in Philology*
SR = *Saturday Review*
StI = *Studies: An Irish Quarterly Review*
TC = *Twentieth Century*
TLS = *Times Literary Supplement*
TQ = *University of Toronto Quarterly*
VNL = *Victorian News Letter*
VQR = *Virginia Quarterly Review*
VS = *Victorian Studies*
YR = *Yale Review*

I. BIBLIOGRAPHICAL MATERIAL

Altick, Richard D. "Another Victorian First." *VNL*, No. 16 (Fall), pp. 34-36.
A preview of the forthcoming *Guide to Doctoral Dissertations in Victorian Literature, 1886-1958.*

"Annual Bibliography for 1958." *PMLA*, LXXIV, No. 2, 141-60; "English Language and Literature: IX. Nineteenth Century, X. Twentieth Century," ed. Charles C. Mish, Harrison T. Meserole, Robert M. Pierson, and Gordon Ross Smith, with the help of James Walt.

Bell, Inglis Freeman, and Baird, Donald (eds.). *The English Novel, 1578-1956: A Checklist of Twentieth-Century Criticisms.* Denver: Alan Swallow. Pp. xii + 169.
Rev. by E. S. in *College and Research Libr.*, XX, 294; by Alan M. Cohn in *LJ*, LXXXIV, 1520.

Bell, Martha S. "Special Women's Collections in United States Libraries." *College and Research Libr.*, XX, 235-42.
Contains brief description of the Browning Collection at Scripps College Library, Claremont, California; of the Florence Nightingale Collection at the Presbyterian Hospital, Columbia-Presbyterian Medical Center, New York.

A *Bibliography of Parliamentary Debates of Great Britain.* . . . See VB 1957, 384.
Rev. by J. B. C. in *APSR*, LIII, 863-64.

Bowers, Fredson (ed.). *Studies in Bibliogra-*

phy: Papers of the Bibliographical Society of the University of Virginia. Vol. 12. Charlottesville: The Society. Pp. 260.

Rev. by L. F. Peck in *CE,* XX, 330; by Betty Rosenberg in *LJ,* LXXXIV, 1438-39. Contains Richard D. Altick's "From Aldine to Everyman," a survey of cheap reprints of English classics between 1830 and 1906 (see VB 1958, 365).

Cohen, I. Bernard, *et al.* (eds.). "Eighty-fourth Critical Bibliography of the History of Science and Its Cultural Influences (to 1 January 1959)." *Isis,* L, 289-407.

Dickson, Sarah Augusta. *The Arents Collection of Books in Parts and Associated Literature.* . . . See VB 1958, 352.

Rev. by Donald F. Bond in *LQ,* XXIX, 61-62.

Faverty, Frederic E. (ed.). *The Victorian Poets: A Guide to Research.* . . . See VB 1958, 353.

Rev. by J. G. Ritz in *Études anglaises,* XII, 71-72.

Gordan, John D. "New in the Berg Collection: 1957-1958." *Bull. New York Pub. Libr.,* LXIII, 134-47; 205-15.

Represented are Barrie, Charlotte and Branwell Brontë, Carroll, Conrad, Eliot, Hardy, Moore, Newman, Pater, Shaw, Stevenson, Swinburne, Yeats, and others.

Houghton, Walter E. "British Periodicals of the Victorian Age: Bibliographies and Indexes." *Library Trends,* April, pp. 554-65.

Houghton, Walter E. "Report from *The Wellesley Index.*" *VNL,* No. 15 (Spring), pp. 30-31. Also "Victorian Periodicals." *TLS,* 6 Mar., p. 133.

Descriptions of the projected *Wellesley Index to Victorian Periodicals, 1824-1900.*

Leary, Lewis (ed.). *Contemporary Literary Scholarship.* . . . See VB 1958, 353.

Rev. by Garland Greever in *Personalist,* XL, 435-36; by Haskell M. Block in *Comparative Lit.,* XI, 270-75; in *TLS,* 17 July, p. 424; Ch. 8, "The Victorian Period" by Lionel Stevenson rev. by Austin Wright in *CE,* XX, 198.

Lindsay, Jean (ed.). *Annual Bulletin of Historical Literature, No. XLIII.* London: The Historical Association. Pp. 57.

Guide to "more substantial" historical studies published in 1957. Briefly rev. in *TLS,* 22 May, p. 310.

Lynskey, Winifred. "A Survey of Reprint Texts of Twentieth-Century British Novels." *CE,* XXI, 183-89.

Includes a survey of recent editions of Conrad novels.

McLean, Ruari. *Modern Book Design from William Morris to the Present Day.* . . . See VB 1958, 353.

Rev. by Ellsworth Mason in *BB,* XXII, 199-200; by M. M. in *Connoisseur,* CXLIV, 50-51; by Charles H. Morris in *LR,* XVII, 56-57; by James Shand in *NS,* LVI, 860; briefly in *SR,* 21 Mar., p. 24.

Maurer, Oscar (ed.). "Recent Publications: A Selected List." *VNL,* No. 15 (Spring), pp. 33-38; No. 16 (Fall), pp. 38-40.

Nicoll, Allardyce. *A History of English Drama, 1600-1900.* Vol. VI: *A Short-Title Alphabetical Catalogue of Plays Produced or Printed in England from 1660 to 1900.* New York: Cambridge U. Pr. Pp. xii + 565.

Rev. by Claude E. Jones in *BB,* XXII, 200; in *TLS,* 26 June, p. 380.

Pettit, Henry, and Macdonald, Angus (eds.). *Annual Bibliography of English Language and Literature.* Vol. XXX: *1950-1952.* London: Cambridge Univ. Pr. Pp. xv + 752.

Rev. in *TLS,* 10 Apr., p. 216.

Pick, John. "Victorian Anthologies." *CE,* XX, 374-78.

A review of important current anthologies.

Ransom, H. H. "The Hanley Library." *Library Chronicle of the Univ. of Texas,* VI, 33-35.

A notable collection, now at TxU, includes Shaw, Browning, Yeats, Wilde material.

St. John, Judith. *The Osborne Collection of Early Children's Books 1566-1910: A Catalogue.* Toronto: Toronto Pub. Libr., 1958. Pp. xxiv + 561.

Rev. by Earle F. Walbridge in *BSP,* LIII, 351-54; by A. M. M. in *The Library,* 5th Ser. XIV, 302-04.

Stamm, Rudolf. *Englische Literatur.* Bern: Francke, 1957. Pp. 422.

Rev. by Arno Esch in *Anglia,* LXXVII, 76-77; by Albrecht B. Strauss in *BA,* XXXIII, 185. A survey of scholarship in the field of English literature (1500-1900), published 1935-1955.

Stange, G. Robert. "Reprints of Nineteenth-Century British Fiction." *CE,* XXI, 178-83.

A survey of more than eighty volumes reprinted in the last ten years.

Topsfield, L. T., *et al.* (eds.). *The Year's*

Work in Modern Language Studies. Vol.
XIX (1957). London: Cambridge Univ.
Pr., 1958. Pp. ix + 701.
Rev. in *TLS*, 24 Apr., p. 242.
Townsend, Francis G. (ed.). "Victorian Bib-
liography for 1958." *VS*, II, 351-92.
Watson, George (ed.). *The Cambridge Bib-
liography of English Literature.* Vol. V:
Supplement. . . . See VB 1958, 353.
Rev. by Dieter Riesner in *Anglia*,
LXXVII, 209-15; by Gwin Kolb in *MP*,
LVI, 197-203 (this review contains a
useful list of errata).
Watson, George (ed.). *The Concise Cam-
bridge Bibliography of English Litera-
ture, 600-1950.* Cambridge: Cambridge
Univ. Pr., 1958. Pp. xii + 272.
Rev. by Dieter Riesner in *Anglia*,
LXXVII, 209-15; by William White in
BB, XXII, 175; by E. F. in *Canadian
Forum*, XXXVIII, 237; in *CE*, XXI, 112;
by C. J. Rawson in *DUJ*, LII (n.s. XXI),
39-41; by V. de S. Pinto in *N & Q*, n.s.
VI, 121; by Helen M. Focke in *LJ*,
LXXXIV, 688; in *TLS*, 9 Jan., p. 24; in
Wisconsin Libr. Bulletin, LV, 247.
Wright, Esmond. "Historical Periodicals in
Britain and the United States." *LR*, XVII,
106-10.
A useful description of some of the lead-
ing journals published in Britain and the
U. S.

II. ECONOMIC, POLITICAL,
RELIGIOUS, AND SOCIAL
ENVIRONMENT

Adams, W. S. *Edwardian Portraits.* . . . See
VB 1957, 385.
Rev. by Pierre Weil-Nordon in *Études
anglaises*, XII, 266.
Addis, John P. *The Crawshay Dynasty.* . . .
See VB 1958, 354.
Rev. by A. H. John in *EHR*, LXXIV,
507-09.
"Adult Education in Barnsley, 1831-1848."
N & Q, n. s. VI, 27-32.
Albrecht-Carrié, Rene. *A Diplomatic History
of Europe since the Congress of Vienna.*
London: Methuen. Pp. 736.
Rev. in *Canadian Hist. Rev.*, XL, 77; in
TLS, 30 Jan., p. 56.
Allchin, Arthur Macdonald. *The Silent Rebel-
lion: Anglican Religious Communities,
1845-1900.* . . . See VB 1958, 354.
Rev. in *QR*, CCXCVII, 364.

Appleman, Philip, Madden, William A., and
Wolff, Michael (eds.). *1859: Entering an
Age of Crisis.* Bloomington, Ind.: Indi-
ana Univ. Pr. Pp. 320.
Rev. favorably by Crane Brinton in *HTB*,
20 Dec., p. 7. Essays on science, religion,
diplomacy, trade and economics, domes-
tic politics, poetry, the novel, criticism,
and popular journalism in mid-Victorian
England. Among the writers and works
discussed are Darwin's *Origin*, Mill's *On
Liberty*, Tennyson's *Idylls*, Pater, Ruskin,
Arnold, Meredith, and Eliot.
Archer, Mildred. "India and Natural History:
The Role of the East India Company,
1785-1858." *History Today*, IX, 736-43.
Baylen, Joseph O. "W. T. Stead and the Boer
War: The Irony of Idealism." *Canadian
Hist. Rev.*, XL, 304-14.
Sees Stead's dilemma, his open disagree-
ment with policies and men (Rhodes, Mil-
ner, Garrett) he had publicly sponsored
and encouraged, as that of nonconform-
ist liberalism struggling to reconcile im-
perialism and conscience.
Bealey, Frank, and Pelling, Henry. *Labour
and Politics, 1900-1906.* . . . See VB 1958,
354.
Rev. by J. H. S. Reid in *Canadian Hist.
Rev.*, XL, 248-49; by John P. Mackintosh
in *EHR*, LXXIV, 373-74; by G. D. H.
Cole in *VS*, II, 331-34.
Beard, Geoffrey W. *Nineteenth-Century
Cameo Glass.* Newport, Eng.: Ceramic
Book Co., 1956. Pp. xiv + 149.
Rev. by R. J. C. in *Connoisseur*, CXLIV,
117.
Beckett, James Camlin, and Moody, Theo-
dore William. *Queen's Belfast, 1845-1949:
The History of a University.* London:
Faber. 2 vols. Pp. lxvii + 451 and xv
+ 532.
Rev. in *TLS*, 31 July, p. 445.
Bellerby, J. R. "National and Agricultural In-
come: 1851." *Econ. Jour.*, LXIX, 95-104.
Benians, E. A., Butler, Sir James, and Car-
rington, C. E. (eds.). *The Cambridge
History of the British Empire.* Vol. III:
The Empire-Commonwealth, 1870-1919.
London: Cambridge Univ. Pr. Pp. xxi +
948.
Rev. by Paul Knaplund in *AHR*, LXIV,
935; by Walter P. Hall in *APSS*,
CCCXXIV, 171-72; by A. L. Burt in *JMH*,
XXXI, 137-38; by J. D. B. Miller in *His-
tory*, XLIV, 287-89; by F. E. Hirsch in
LJ, LXXXIV, 849; by Asa Briggs in *TC*,
CLXV, 432-38; by Neal Ascherson in *S*,

30 Jan., p. 164; in *TLS*, 27 Feb., p. 108 ("a work of great and lasting value"); by Preston Slosson in *VS*, II, 340-42.

Bernstein, Aline. *Masterpieces of Women's Costume of the 18th and 19th Centuries.* New York: Crown. Pp. xxii + 83.

Blackie, Agnes A. C. *Blackie and Son, 1809-1959.* Edinburgh: Blackie. Pp. 64.
Rev. in *TLS*, 25 Dec., p. 760.

Bligh, N. M. "The Royal Kent Theatre, Kensington." *Theatre Notebook*, XIII, 124-28.
A history of the Royal Kent Theatre, 1831-50.

Bradford, Ernle D. S. *English Victorian Jewellry.* New York: McBride. Pp. 141.
Rev. by C. C. Oman in *Apollo*, LXIX, 154; by Paul von Khrum in *LJ*, LXXXIV, in *TLS*, 12 June, p. 358.

Briggs, Asa. *The Age of Improvement, 1783-1867.* London: Longmans. Pp. 547.
Rev. by David Owen in *AHR*, LXV, 108-09; by W. D. Handcock in *History*, XLIV, 273-74; by Maurice Ashley in *Listener*, 19 Feb., p. 343; by George Basalla in *LJ*, LXXXIV, 1508; by E. J. Hobsbawm in *NS*, LVIII, 226; by Neal Ascherson in *S*, 20 Feb., p. 268; by Hiram M. Stout in *Science*, n. s. CXXIX, 1735; in *TLS*, 27 Mar., p. 174; by W. L. Burn in *VS*, III, 208-09.

Briggs, Asa (ed.). *Chartist Studies.* London: Macmillan. Pp. viii + 423.
Rev. by E. P. Thompson in *Listener*, 10 Dec., pp. 1030-31; by E. J. Hobsbawm in *NS*, LVIII, 594-95; by Neal Ascherson in *S*, 13 Nov., pp. 676-77; in *TLS*, 18 Dec., p. 738.

Brittain, Vera. "An Oxford Anniversary." *NER*, CLIII, 115-18.
The opening, in 1879, of two "halls" for women, Lady Margaret Hall and Somerville College.

Brose, Olive J. *Church and Parliament: The Reshaping of the Church of England, 1828-1860.* Stanford, Calif.: Stanford Univ. Pr. Pp. vi + 239.
Rev. briefly by Robert Henderson in *LJ*, LXXXIV, 2188.

Brown, Lucy. *The Board of Trade and the Free Trade Movement, 1830-42.* . . . See VB 1958, 355.
Rev. by Albert H. Imlah in *AHR*, LXIV, 696; by W. Ashworth in *Economica*, n.s. XXVI, 279-80; in *Econ. Jour.*, LXIX, 205; by Arthur Radford in *History*, XLIV, 279-80; by Roger Prouty in *VS*, II, 348-49.

Carpenter, Spencer Cecil. *Church and Peo-*

ple, 1778-1889. London: S. P. C. K. 3 vols. Pp. 181, 188, 202.

Churchill, Winston S. *A History of the English-Speaking Peoples.* Vol. IV. . . . See VB 1958, 355.
Rev. by H. C. Allen in *EHR*, LXXIV, 305-11.

Clarke, William Kemp Lowther. *A History of the S. P. C. K.* London: S. P. C. K. Pp. ix + 244.
Rev. in *TLS*, 10 Apr., p. 213. Founded in 1699, the Society for the Promotion of Christian Knowledge has been an important publisher of books and periodicals.

Cockshut, Anthony Oliver John. *Anglican Attitudes: A Study of Victorian Religious Controversies.* London: Collins. Pp. 128.
Rev. by Robin Deniston in *NER*, CLII, 187-88; by Alec Vidler in *S*, 20 Mar., p. 412; by F. A. Lea in *TC*, CLXVI, 120-21; in *TLS*, 3 Apr., p. 197. A study of three significant Victorian church controversies: the Gorham Judgment, the publication of *Essays and Reviews*, and the Colenso affair.

Coleman, Donald Cuthbert. *The British Paper Industry, 1495-1860: A Study in Industrial Growth.* . . . See VB 1958, 355.
Rev. by Rondo E. Cameron in *AHR*, LXIV, 426-27; by Peter Mathias in *Economica*, n.s. XXVI, 268-69; by A. Beacham in *Econ. Jour.*, LXIX, 149-50; by W. H. B. Court in *EHR*, LXXIV, 526-27; by Frank Meissner in *JPE*, LXVII, 536-37; by Rupert Jarvis in *The Library*, 5th Ser., XIV, 66-67; by J. C. D. Sinclair in *N & Q*, n.s. VI, 43-44; in *TLS*, 9 Jan., p. 24; by Arthur J. Taylor in *VS*, II, 277-79.

Cooper, Leonard. *Radical Jack: The Life of the First Earl of Durham.* London: Cresset. Pp. x + 309.
Rev. by R. H. S. Crossman in *NS*, LVIII, 252-53; by Brian Inglis in *S*, 24 July, p. 111.

Cope, Sir Zachary. *Florence Nightingale and the Doctors.* . . . See VB, 1958, 356.
Rev. by F. G. Young, *VS*, II, 283-84.

Cowherd, Raymond G. *The Politics of English Dissent.* . . . See VB 1958, 356.
Rev. by E. J. Hobsbawm in *NS*, LVIII, 199.

Coxe, Antony Hippisley. "The Lesser-Known Circuses of London." *Theatre Notebook*, XIII, 89-100.
Chiefly on the circus of the 19th century.

Cramp, A. B. "Horsley Palmer on Bank Rate."

Economica, n.s. XXVI, 341-49.
A strong force in British banking between 1827-48.

Cruise O'Brien, Conor. *Parnell and His Party*. . . . See VB 1958, 356.
Rev. by C. H. D. Howard in *EHR*, LXXIV, 139-41; by Elisabeth Wallace in *QQ*, LXV, 706-07.

Cunnington, Cecil Willett, and Cunnington, Phillis. *Handbook of English Costume in the 19th Century*. London: Faber. Pp. 606.
Rev. by J. L. in *Connoisseur*, CXLIV, 115; by Paul von Khrum in *LJ*, LXXXIV, 2647; in *TLS*, 25 Dec., p. 758.

Curry, George. "The Sovereign's Private Secretary." *History Today*, IX, 122-31.
Includes estimate of influence on Victoria of those men who served as her advisers and secretaries.

Dalton, George. "Robert Owen and Karl Polanyi as Socio-Economic Critics and Reformers of Industrial Capitalism." *DA*, XX, 1634-35.

Darley, Lionel Seabrook. *Bookbinding Now and Then: A Survey of the First 178 Years of James Burn and Co.* London: Faber. Pp. 127.

Darton, Frederick Joseph Harvey. *Children's Books in England: Five Centuries of Social Life*. Second Edition with an Introduction by Kathleen Lines. Cambridge: Cambridge Univ. Pr. Pp. xviii + 367.
Rev. by Earle F. Walbridge in *BSP*, LIII, 351-54.

DeTocqueville, Alexis. *Journeys to England and Ireland*. . . . See VB 1958, 356.
Rev. by J. P. T. Bury in *EHR*, LXXIV, 362-63; by J. A. Lukacs in *JMH*, XXXI, 57-59; by J. T. Winterich in *SR*, 6 Dec., 1958, p. 24; in *TLS*, 8 Aug., 1958, p. 442.

Edwardes, Michael. *The Necessary Hell: John and Henry Lawrence and the Indian Empire*. . . . See VB 1958, 356.
Rev. by F. J. L. Young in *QQ*, LXVI, 171-72.

Edwards, Ralph, and Ramsey, L. G. G. (eds.). *The "Connoisseur" Period Guides . . . The Early Victorian Period, 1830-1860*. . . . See VB 1958, 357.
Rev. briefly in *HTB*, 22 Mar., p. 11; in *N & Q*, n.s. VI, 123-24; in *TLS*, 28 Aug., p. 492; by John Steegman in *VS*, II, 328-29.

Elletson, D. H. *Maryannery*. London: Murray. Pp. 164.
Rev. by Paul Johnson in *NS*, LVIII, 282-

83; by Ronald Bryden in *S*, 4 Sept., p. 308; in *TLS*, 18 Sept., p. 532. Studies of Mary Ann Lincoln and Mary Ann Disraeli.

Ellis, C. Hamilton. *British Railway History, 1877-1947*. London: Allen and Unwin. Pp. xii + 429.
Rev. in *TLS*, 25 Dec., p. 759. Vol. II of the author's history of British railways.

Engels, Friedrich. *The Condition of the Working Class in England*. . . . See VB 1958, 357.
Rev. by G. D. H. Cole in *EHR*, LXXIV, 178-79; by Henry R. Winkler in *JMH*, XXXI, 60-61.

Erickson, Arvel B. *Edward T. Cardwell: Peelite*. Philadelphia: Transactions of the Am. Philosophical Soc., n.s. XLIX, Pt. 2. Pp. 107.

Evans, Eric Wyn. *Mabon: A Study in Trade Union Leadership*. Cardiff: Univ. of Wales Pr. Pp. xii + 115.
Biography of William Abraham, 1842-1922, trade unionist among coal miners of South Wales.

Eyck, Frank. *The Prince Consort: A Political Biography*. London: Chatto & Windus. Pp. 269.
Rev. by David Owen in *Canadian Hist. Rev.*, XL, 340-41; by G. P. Gooch in *CR*, CXCV, 281-84; by Ralph Partridge in *NS*, LVII, 420-21; by Geoffrey Bruun in *HTB*, 30 Aug., p. 5; by William B. Willcox in *NYTBR*, 30 Aug., p. 7; in *QR*, CCXCVII, 361-62; by Neal Ascherson in *S*, 27 Mar., p. 445; in *TLS*, 27 Mar., p. 178.

Fay, Gerald. *The Abbey Theatre: Cradle of Genius*. . . . See VB 1958, 357.
Rev. by George Freedley in *LJ*, LXXXIV, 532; by E. B. Pettet in *QJS*, XLV, 212-13; by Brian Inglis in *S*, 7 Nov., 1958, p. 622; by B. Iden Payne in *Theatre Notebook*, XIII, 68-69.

Ferguson, Thomas. *Scottish Social Welfare, 1864-1914*. . . . See VB 1958, 357.
Rev. by David Roberts in *Isis*, L, 286-87; by R. H. Campbell in *VS*, III, 218.

Feuchtwanger, E. J. "The Conservative Party under the Impact of the Second Reform Act." *VS*, II, 289-304.

Fitton, Robert Sucksmith, and Wadsworth, A. P. *The Strutts and the Arkwrights, 1758-1830*. Manchester: Manchester Univ. Pr. Pp. xii + 361.
Rev. by J. F. C. Harrison in *NS*, LVII, 265-66; in *TLS*, 13 Mar., p. 143.

Fleming, Peter. *The Siege at Peking.* London: Hart-Davis. Pp. 273.
Rev. by Henry McAleavy in *History Today,* IX, 629-30. Account of Boxer Uprising.

Fletcher, Max E. "The Suez Canal and World Shipping, 1869-1914." *JEH,* XVIII, 556-73.

Fox, Alan. *A History of the National Union of Boot and Shoe Operatives, 1874-1957.* . . . See VB 1958, p. 357.
Rev. by H. W. McCready in *VS,* II, 334-37.

Freeman, T. W. *Pre-Famine Ireland.* . . . See VB 1958, 357.
Rev. by R. B. McDowell in *EHR,* LXXIV, 541-42; by G. L. Davies in *Irish Hist. Studies,* XI, 363-64.

Galbraith, John S. *The Hudson's Bay Company as an Imperial Factor, 1821-1869.* . . . See VB 1958, 357.
Rev. by E. E. Rich in *Canadian Hist. Rev.,* XL, 67-69.

Gernsheim, Helmut, and Gernsheim, Alison. *Queen Victoria: A Biography in Word and Picture.* London: Longmans, Green. Pp. 307.
Rev. by Robert R. Rea in *LJ,* LXXXIV, 3554; by Ellen H. Smith in *HTB,* 8 Nov., p. 4; by Anne Fremantle in *NYTBR,* 1 Nov., p. 7; in *TLS,* 11 Dec., p. 722. A pictorial biography, illustrated with over 400 photographs and engravings.

Godden, Geoffrey. "Victorian Ceramic Artists." *Apollo,* LXIX, 76, 145, 183; LXX, 29, 51, 90-91, 185.

Gooch, G. P. *Under Six Reigns.* . . . See VB 1958, 357.
Rev. by A. Cobban in *CR,* CXCV, 49; in *TLS,* 9 Jan., p. 14.

Goodman, Gordon L. "Liberal Unionism: The Revolt of the Whigs." *VS,* III, 173-89.

Gopal, S. "Governors-General of India: II, Dalhousie." *History Today,* IX, 186-94.
Because of his development of communication systems, his efforts to integrate Indian states, and his interest in Indian culture, Dalhousie is remembered as "one of the architects of modern India."

Graham, Andrew. "A National Gallery Controversy of a Century Ago." *Connoisseur,* June, pp. 14-17.
How the National Gallery fumbled Turner's bequest of a great collection of his work.

Greenleaf, W. H. "Biography and the 'Amateur' Historian: Mrs. Woodham-Smith's 'Florence Nightingale.'" *VS,* III, 190-202.

Grierson, Edward. *Storm Bird: The Strange Life of Georgina Weldon.* London: Chatto and Windus, Pp. 287.
Rev. by D. J. Enright in *S,* 27 Nov., p. 778 ("A minor Victorian — complex, heroic, and vulnerable"); in *TLS,* 11 Dec., p. 720.

Guest, Ivor. *Adeline Genée, A Lifetime of Ballet under Six Reigns.* . . . See VB 1958, 358.
Rev. by J. B. Booth in *Theatre Notebook,* XIII, 74-75.

Habakkuk, H. J. "The Economic History of Modern Britain." *JEH,* XVIII, 486-501.
A study of the relationship between population pressures and economic history.

Haber, L. F. *The Chemical Industry During the Nineteenth Century.* . . . See VB 1958, 358.
Rev. by Aaron Ihde in *Isis,* L, 183-84; by D. W. F. Hardie in *JEH,* XIX, 291-94; by W. Woodruff in *JMH,* XXXI, 76.

Hanham, Harold John. *Elections and Party Management: Politics in the Time of Disraeli and Gladstone.* London: Longmans. Pp. xvii + 468.
Rev. by Raymond Postgate in *NS,* LVIII, 448; in *TLS,* 2 Oct., p. 566.

Harris, Abram L. *Economics and Social Reform.* New York: Harper & Bros., 1958. Pp. xvi + 357.
Rev. by Peter Alt in *Science and Society,* XXIII, 88-90. Includes a chapter on John Stuart Mill.

Harrison, Royden. "E. S. Beesly and Karl Marx." *International Rev. of Social History,* IV, 22-58, 208-38.
Beesly, who held the chair of history at University College, London, was an early Positivist who chaired the inaugural meeting of the First International and conducted a long and full correspondence with Marx. This is a long and valuable article containing many extracts from the Marx-Beesly correspondence and a useful assessment of the influence of Positivists on radical and socialist opinion in the 1860's and 1870's — D. J. G.

Hartwell, R. M. "Interpretations of the Industrial Revolution in England: A Methodological Inquiry." *JEH,* XIX, 229-49.

Harwood, Thomas Franklin. "Great Britain and American Antislavery." *DA,* XX, 2251-52.

Havard, William C. *Henry Sidgwick and*

Late Utilitarian Political Philosophy. Gainesville: Univ. of Florida Pr. Pp. viii + 197.

Henley, Dorothy. *Rosalind Howard, Countess of Carlisle.* Introduction by Bertrand Russell. London: Hogarth, 1958. Pp. 147. Rev. in *TLS,* 2 Jan., p. 3. Memoir of a late Victorian peeress by her daughter.

Hewitt, Margaret. *Wives and Mothers in Victorian Industry.* . . . See VB 1958, 358. Rev. by M. S. in *NS,* LVII, 23; in *TLS,* 16 Jan., p. 31; by S. G. Checkland in *VS,* III, 211-12.

Hobsbawm, Eric John. *Primitive Rebels.* Manchester: Manchester Univ. Pr. Pp. vii + 208. Rev. by Christopher Hill in *History Today,* IX, 502-03; in *TLS,* 10 July, p. 413. Includes a discussion of 19th-century Primitive Methodists in his study of non-political movements of social protest.

Hodge, Francis. "Yankee in England: James Henry Hackett and the Debut of American Comedy." *QJS,* XLV, 381-90. American actor in England in 1832.

Hoffman, Walther Gustav. *The Growth of Industrial Economics.* Tr. by W. O. Henderson and W. H. Chaloner. Manchester: Manchester Univ. Pr. Pp. xiii + 183.

Holt, Edgar. *The Boer War.* . . . See VB 1958, 358. Rev. by Ronald V. Sires in *JMH,* XXXI, 378-79.

Hough, Richard. *Admirals in Collision.* London: Hamilton. Pp. 174. Rev. in *TLS,* 23 Oct., p. 611. Account of collision of *Victoria* and *Camperdown* in 1893.

Hurst, P. G. *The Age of Jean de Reszke: Forty Years of Opera, 1874-1914.* London: Christopher Johnson, 1958. Pp. 256. Rev. unfavorably by Harold Rosenthal in *M & L,* XL, 85-86. A record of opera performances in London.

Imlah, Albert Henry. *Economic Elements in the Pax Britannica: Studies in British Foreign Trade in the Nineteenth Century.* . . . See VB 1958, 358. Rev. by Sidney Ratner in *AHR,* LXIV, 939-40; by Ida Greaves in *APSS,* CCCXXIV, 179-80; by Phyllis Deane in *Econ. Jour.,* LXIX, 562-63; by Sydney H. Zebel in *JMH,* XXXI, 344-45.

James, Robert Rhodes. "Gladstone and the Greenwich Seat: The Dissolution of January 26th, 1874." *History Today,* IX, 344-51.

James, Robert Rhodes, *Lord Randolph Churchill.* London: Weidenfeld and Nicolson. Pp. 384. Rev. by H. W. McCready in *Canadian Hist. Rev.,* XL, 342-43; by Kenneth Young in *History Today,* IX, 359-61; by Kenneth Rose in *NER,* CLII, 186-87; by Robert Blake in *S,* 20 Mar., p. 411; by Betty Miller in *TC,* CLXVI, 118-19; in *TLS,* 29 May, p. 323 ("a biography of great distinction").

Jenkins, Roy. *Sir Charles Dilke.* . . . See VB 1958, 359. Rev. by M. A. Fitzsimons in *VS,* III, 215-16.

John, Arthur Henry. *A Liverpool Merchant House.* London: Allen and Unwin. Pp. 198. Briefly rev. in *TLS,* 3 July, p. 404. History of nineteenth-century firm of Alfred Booth and Co. and of radical, dissenting social group to which family belonged.

Johnson, Leonard George. *The Social Evolution of Industrial Britain.* Liverpool: Liverpool Univ. Pr. Pp. ix + 178. Rev. in *TLS,* 30 Oct., p. 628 ("a muddled book"). Considers how a sense of community is achieved in 19th- and 20th-century industrial society.

Jones, Wilbur Devereux. *Lord Derby and Victorian Conservatism.* . . . See VB 1958, 359. Rev. by G. M. Craig in *Canadian Hist. Rev.,* XL, 72-73; by C. H. Stuart in *History,* XLIV, 173-74; by Michael Kraus in *VS,* II, 337-40.

Kennedy, W. F. *Humanist Versus Economist: The Economic Thought of Samuel Taylor Coleridge.* University of California Publications in Economics, Vol. 17. Berkeley and Los Angeles: Univ. of Cal. Pr., 1958. Pp. 96. Rev. in *Econ. Jour.,* LXIX, 215-16. "The conflict in the writings of later economists between the clear but narrow Benthamite philosophy and the humanistic ideas represented by Coleridge is . . . traced out, with special reference to Mill, Marshall and Keynes."

Kirk-Smith, Harold. *William Thompson, Archbishop of York.* . . . See VB 1958, 359. Rev. by E. H. Eckel in *Hist. Mag. of Protestant Episcopal Church,* XXVIII, 203-04; by Claude Jenkins in *Journal of Eccl. History,* X, 119-21.

Kruger, Rayne. *Good-Bye Dolly Gray.* London: Cassell. Pp. 539.

Rev. by Neal Ascherson in S, 18 Dec., p. 913; in TLS, 4 Dec., p. 703. A history of the Boer War.

Lamb, Geoffrey Frederick. *The Happiest Days*. London: Michael Joseph. Pp. 252. Rev. in TLS, Nov. 20, p. 675. History of brutal behavior of public school boys during last two centuries.

Latourette, Kenneth Scott. *Christianity in a Revolutionary Age*.

Vol. I: *The Nineteenth Century in Europe: Background and the Roman Catholic Phase*. New York: Harper, 1958. Pp. 486. Rev. by Paul Ramsey in NYTBR, 23 Nov., 1958, p. 4; by D. M. Smith in S, 17 Apr., p. 558; in TLS, 20 Mar. (Religious Suppl.), p. xii.

Vol. II: *The Nineteenth Century in Europe: The Protestant and Eastern Churches*. New York: Harper. Pp. 540. Noticed by Nash K. Burger in NYTBR, 8 Nov., p. 68.

Legge, J. D. *Britain in Fiji, 1858-1880*. London: Macmillan. Pp. xi + 307. Rev. by W. P. Morrell in EHR, LXXIV, 747-48.

Leighton-Boyce, J. A. S. L. *Smiths the Bankers, 1658-1958*. London: National Provincial Bank, Ltd., 1958. Pp. xiv + 337. Rev. by J. K. Horsefield in *Economica*, n.s. XXVI, 279-80; noted in *Econ. Jour.*, LXIX, 207-08; in TLS, 27 Feb., p. 119. The family reached its apogee in the 19th century.

Link, Robert G. *English Theories of Economic Fluctuations, 1815-1848*. New York: Columbia Univ. Pr. Pp. viii + 232. Noted in *Econ. Jour.*, LXIX, 634; rev. by Harold C. Whitford in LJ, LXXXIV, 1128-29; by Ronald L. Meek in *Science and Society*, XXIII, 271-73.

Lochhead, Marion. *Young Victorians*. London: Murray. Pp. xii + 240. Rev. by Mary Scrutton in NS, LVIII, 203; in TLS, 15 May, p. 287. A sequel to *Their First Ten Years* (see VB 1956, 240), this deals with Victorian adolescents.

London Univ., School of Librarianship and Archives. *English Libraries, 1800-1850*. London: H. K. Lewis, 1958. Pp. 78. Rev. by Sidney Forman in *College and Research Libraries*, XX, 500; by David C. Mearns in LQ, XXIX, 145-46. Three lectures, delivered by C. B. Oldman, W. A. Munford, and Simon Nowell-Smith.

Lunt, James. "Lady Sale in Kapul, 1842." *History Today*, IX, 653-63.

Account of the adventures of an English officer's wife during the siege of and withdrawal from Kapul in the Afghan War.

McCord, Norman. *The Anti-Corn Law League, 1838-1846*. . . . See VB 1958, 360. Rev. by Asa Briggs in DUJ, LI (n.s. XX), 140-42; by G. D. H. Cole in EHR, LXXIV, 542-43.

McCord, N., and Wood, P. A. "The Sunderland Election of 1845." DUJ, LII (n.s. XXI), 11-21.

McCormick, Donald. *The Identity of Jack the Ripper*. London: Jarrolds. Pp. 192. Rev. by R. P. in NS, LVIII, 554; in TLS, 16 Oct., 598.

McDowell, Robert Brendon. *British Conservatism 1832-1914*. London: Faber. Pp. 194.

Maclagen, Michael. "Governors-General of India: III, 'Clemency Canning.'" *History Today*, IX, 233-42. Treatment of Indian mutineers earned Canning his nickname and temporary unpopularity in England, but it also helped to allay the unfortunate consequences of the Mutiny.

McMenemey, William Henry. *The Story of Sir Charles Hastings*. London: Livingstone: Pp. xii + 516. Biography of one of the founders of the British Medical Association.

Magnus, Sir Philip. *Kitchener: Portrait of an Imperialist*. . . . See VB 1958, 360. Rev. by Edward Weeks in AM, Apr., p. 130; by Walter Millis in HTB, 25 Jan., p. 1; by R. R. Rea in LJ, LXXXIV, 750; by Leon Wolff in NYTBR, 25 Jan., p. 3; by J. D. Hill in SR, 31 Jan., pp. 20-21; by D. W. Brogan in S, 31 Oct., 1958, p. 589; by M. R. D. Foot in VS, III, 209-11.

Mallalieu, J. P. W. *Extraordinary Seaman*. New York: Macmillan, 1958. Pp. ix + 179. Rev. by Alan K. Manchester in SAQ, LVIII, 318. A biography of Captain Lord Cochrane, tenth Earl of Dundonald.

Mander, Raymond and Mitchenson, Joe. *A Picture History of the British Theatre*. . . . See VB 1958, 360. Rev. by E. K. Bristow in QJS, XLV, 222.

Marsh, David Charles. *The Changing Social Structure of England and Wales, 1871-1951*. . . . See VB 1958, 360. Rev. in TLS, 16 Jan., p. 31.

Marshall, J. D. *Furness and the Industrial Revolution: An Economic History of Fur-*

ness *(1711-1900) and the Town of Barrow (1757-1897).* Barrow-in-Furness: Barrow-in-Furness Library and Museum Committee, 1958. Pp. xiii + 438.
Rev. by W. A. Cole in *Economic Jour.,* LXIX, 794-96; in *TLS,* 30 Jan., p. 63.

Martin, E. W. *Where London Ends: English Provincial Life after 1750.* Fair Lawn, N. J.: Essential Books, 1958. Pp. 312.
Rev. by Charles F. Mullett in *JMH,* XXXI, 277.

Medlicott, W. N. *Bismarck, Gladstone, and the Concert of Europe.* . . . See VB 1957, 391.
Rev. by M. R. D. Foot in *EHR,* LXXIV, 138-39.

Mitchell, Rosamund Joscelyne and Leys, Mary Dorothy Rose. *A History of London Life.* . . . See VB 1958, 361.
Rev. by Charles F. Mullett in *JMH,* XXXI, 277.

Mondini, Luigi. "Una Legione Anglo-Italiana per la Guerra di Crimea." *Nuova Antologia,* CCCCLXXVI, 81-92.

Moore, David C. "Politics of Deference: A Study of the Political Structure, Leadership, and Organization of English County Constituencies in the Nineteenth Century." *DA,* XX, 730.

Morris, John Henry, and Williams, Lawrence John. *The South Wales Coal Industry, 1841-1875.* . . . See VB 1958, 361.
Rev. by A. H. John in *History,* XLIV, 280-81.

Morton, A. L. and Tate, George. *The British Labor Movement, 1770-1920: A Political History.* New York: International Pub., 1957. Pp. 313.
Rev. by Morton H. Cowden in *APSR,* LII, 1195.

Mosse, Werner Eugen. *The European Powers and the German Question, 1848-1871: With Special Reference to England and Russia.* London: Cambridge Univ. Pr., 1958. Pp. ix + 409.
Rev. by T. S. Hamerow in *AHR,* LXIV, 355; by F. H. Soward in *Canadian Hist. Rev.,* XL, 152; by Charles K. Webster in *History,* XLIV, 82-83; by D. M. Smith in *S,* 1 Aug., 1958, p. 174; by Frederic B. M. Hollyday in *SAQ,* LVIII, 321-22; in *TLS,* 26 Sept., 1958, p. 539.

Murdoch, Iris. "A House of Theory." *ParR,* XXVI, 17-31.
Origin of British Socialist thinking in 19th century.

Murphy, James. *The Religious Problem in English Education.* Liverpool: Liverpool Univ. Pr. Pp. 287.
Rev. by P. J. Dowling in *Dublin Review,* CCXXXIII, 281-83; by William Walsh in *NS,* LVIII, 553-54; in *TLS,* 31 July, p. 450. A study of the Liverpool Corporation School's attempt to meet church education requirements in a non-sectarian school, December 1835-December 1841.

Musson, A. E. "The Great Depression in Britain, 1873-1896: A Reappraisal." *JEH,* XIX, 199-228.

Neill, Thomas P. *1859 in Review.* Westminster, Md.: Newman Press. Pp. xxx + 203.

Newsome, David. *A History of Wellington College, 1859-1959.* London: Murray. Pp. xii + 414.
Rev. in *TLS,* 29 May, p. 325.

North, Douglass. "Ocean Freight Rates and Economic Development 1750-1913." *JEH,* XVIII, 537-55.

Oldham, J. B. "Shrewsbury School Library," *The Library,* 5th Ser., XIV, 81-99.
The library owns letters of Darwin, two important Samuel Butler manuscripts, a map with Darwin's doodles.

Oliver, Roland. *Sir Harry Johnston and the Scramble for Africa.* . . . See VB 1958, 361.
Rev. by H. William Rodemann in *JMH,* XXXI, 377-78.

Olson, Mancur Lloyd, Jr., and Harris, C. C., Jr. "Free Trade in 'Corn': A Statistical Study of the Prices and Production of Wheat in Great Britain from 1873 to 1914." *Quarterly Jour. of Econ.,* LXXIII, 145-68.

Parsons, Coleman O. "The Wintry Duel: A Victorian Import." *VS,* II, 317-322.
Two paintings, one by Thomas Couture and one by Jean Léon Gérome, of an actual duel fought by duelists in masquerade costume inspired a series of theatrical representations in London.

Pelling, Henry. "The Labour Church Movement." *International Rev. of Social Hist.,* IV, 111-12.
A critique of K. S. Inglis' article on this subject (see VB 1958, 358). See also K. S. Inglis, "Reply to Mr. Pelling," *International Rev. of Social Hist.,* IV, 112-13.

Perham, Margery and Bull, Mary (eds.). *The Diaries of Lord Lugard. East Africa, 1889-1892.* London: Faber. 3 vols. Pp. 432, 481, 454.
Rev. by Thomas Hodgkin in *NS,* LVIII,

437-38; by Neal Ascherson in *S*, 9 Oct., p. 492; in *TLS*, 30 Oct., p. 622.

Poirier, Philip Patrick. *The Advent of the British Labour Party*. . . . See VB 1958, 362.

Rev. by C. F. Brand in *APSS*, CCCXXI, 167; by John P. Mackintosh in *EHR*, LXXIV, 373-74; by D. K. Oko in *LJ*, LXXXIII, 2771; by G. D. H. Cole in *VS*, II, 331-34.

Pollard, Sidney. *A History of Labour in Sheffield, 1850-1939*. Liverpool: Liverpool Univ. Pr. Pp. xix + 372.

Ponsonby, Doris Almon. *The Lost Duchess: The Story of the Prince Consort's Mother*. . . . See VB 1958, 362.

Rev. by Betty Miller in *TC*, CLXV, 94-96.

Pope-Hennessy, James. *Queen Mary, 1867-1953*. London: Allen and Unwin. Pp. 685.

Rev. by Oliver Warner in *History Today*, IX, 773; by Kenneth Rose in *NER*, CLIII, 159-61; by Christopher Sykes in *S*, 30 Oct., pp. 600-02; in *TLS*, 16 Oct., pp. 585-86.

Pope-Hennessy, James (ed.). *Queen Victoria at Windsor and Balmoral: Letters from her Grand-daughter Princess Victoria of Prussia, June, 1889*. London: Allen and Unwin. Pp. 103.

Rev. by Grace Banyard in *CR*, CXCV, 255; in *QR*, CCXCVII, 471; by Neal Ascherson in *S*, 27 March, p. 445; in *TLS* 10 Apr., p. 206.

Pound, Reginald, and Harmsworth, Geoffrey. *Northcliffe*. London: Cassell. Pp. 936.

Rev. by Anthony Hartley in *S*, 26 June, p. 917; in *TLS*, 26 June, pp. 377-78.

Pritchett, V. S. "Improvers and Infidels." *NS*, LVIII, 166-67.

". . . the conflict between the moralists and the fairy tale tellers" in the early nineteenth-century children's literature.

Pumphrey, Ralph E. "The Introduction of Industrialists into the British Peerage: A Study in Adaptation of a Social Institution." *AHR*, LXV, 1-16.

Pumphry, Richard J. "The Forgotten Man: Sir John Lubbock." *Science*, n.s. CXXIX, 1087-92.

Randall, Sir Alec. "A British Agent at the Vatican." *Dublin Review*, CCXXXIII, 37-57.

A study of the English diplomatist, Mr. Odo Russell, a semi-official agent of the English government in Rome, 1858-1870.

Randall, Sir Alec. "British Diplomacy and

the Holy See, 1555-1925." *Dublin Review*, CCXXXIII, 291-303.

Almost half of the article surveys nineteenth-century relations.

Raymond, John. "Rosebery." *History Today*, IX, 75-82, 176-84.

Rice, Nicholas Talbot. "Nineteenth Century Tartan Keepsakes." *Connoisseur*, CXLII, 242-45.

Ridley, Viscountess (ed.). *Cecilia: The Life and Letters of Cecilia Ridley, 1819-1845*. . . . See VB 1958, 362.

Rev. by Betty Miller in *TC*, CLXV, 94-96.

Rippy, J. Fred. *British Investments in Latin America, 1822-1949: A Case Study in the Operations of Private Enterprise in Retarded Regions*. Minneapolis: Univ. of Minnesota Pr. Pp. xii + 249.

Rev. in *APSR*, LIII, 1196-97.

Roberts, Benjamin Charles. *The Trades Union Congress, 1868-1921*. . . . See VB 1958, 362.

Rev. by Henry Pelling in *Economica*, n.s. XXVI, 89-90; by H. W. McCready in *VS*, II, 334-37.

Roberts, David. "Bentham and the Administrative State." *VS*, II, 193-210.

Roberts, Michael (ed.). *Historical Studies II*. London: Bowes and Bowes. Pp. 95.

Rev. briefly in *TLS*, 28 Aug., p. 499. This collection of papers read before the third Conference of Irish Historians includes studies of Parnell's economic ideas, a reassessment of the nature of Chartism, and an analysis of the personnel of the Cape Parliament, 1854-1910.

Roe, Frederic Gordon. *The Victorian Child*. London: Phoenix. Pp. 144.

Rev. by Mary Scrutton in *NS*, LVIII, 203; in *TLS*, 29 May, suppl. p. xi.

Rolt, L. T. C. *Isambard Kingdom Brunel: A Biography*. New York: St. Martin's Pr. Pp. 345.

Rev. by Robin Le Sueur in *LJ*, LXXXIV, 2487. The engineer who designed the *Great Eastern* steamship.

Römer, Klaus. *England und die Europäischen Mächte im Jahre 1887*. Aarau: H. R. Sauerländer, 1957. Pp. 153.

Rev. by Hajo Holborn in *AHR*, LXIV, 696-97.

Rosenfeld, Sybil. "An Ipswich Theatre Book." *Theatre Notebook*, XIII, 129-33.

The way a circuit theatre was run in the 18th and 19th centuries.

Rosenthal, Harold. *Two Centuries of Opera at Covent Garden*. . . . See VB 1958, 363.

Rev. by Catharine K. Miller in *LJ*, LXXXIV, 1516-17.

Routh, Guy. "The Relation between Unemployment and the Rate of Change of Money Wage Rates: A Comment." *Economica*, n.s. XXVI, 299-315. Attacks earlier article on this subject by A. W. Phillips (see VB 1958, 362).

St. John, Christopher Marie. *Ethel Smyth.* Additional chapters by V. Sackville-West and Kathleen Dale. London: Longmans. Pp. xx + 316.
Rev. by C. K. Miller in *LJ*, LXXXIV, 1256; by S. Bayliss in *M&L*, XL, 286-88; by Eric Gillett in *NER*, CLII, 190; by William Plomer in *NS*, LVII, p. 338; by Stevie Smith in *S*, 13 Mar., p. 377; in *TLS*, 6 Mar., p. 126. A biography of Dame Ethel, the British composer.

Schoyen, Albert Robert. *The Chartist Challenge: A Portrait of George Julian Harney.* . . . See VB 1958, 363.
Rev. by W. O. Aydelotte in *AHR*, LXIV, 431; by S. Maccoby in *History*, XLIV, 76-77; in *TLS*, 16 Jan., pp. 25-26; see also *TLS*, 23 Jan., p. 47.

Schrier, Arnold. *Ireland and the American Emigration, 1850-1900.* . . . See VB 1958, 363.
Rev. by Frank H. Hankins in *APSS*, CCCXXII, 189-90; by E. R. R. Green in *Irish Hist. Studies*, XI, 345-47; by Mildred Campbell in *JEH*, XIX, 320-21; by Lawrence J. McCaffrey in *JMH*, XXXI, 374; by Emmet Larkin in *VS*, III, 216-18.

Shryock, Richard Harrison. *The History of Nursing.* Philadelphia: Saunders. Pp. 330.

Sigsworth, Eric M. *Black Dyke Mills: A History, with Introductory Chapters on the Development of the Worsted Industry in the Nineteenth Century.* Liverpool: Liverpool Univ. Pr., 1958. Pp. xvii + 385.
Rev. by T. C. Barker in *Economica*, n.s. XXVI, 377-78; by Lesley Cook in *Econ. Jour.*, LXIX, 571-72; by William Ashworth in *JPE*, LXVII, 537-38; briefly in *TLS*, 13 Feb., p. 87.

Simmons, Jack. *New University.* Leicester, Eng.: Leicester Univ. Pr., 1958. Pp. 233.
Rev. by H. Hale Bellot in *EHR*, LXXIV, 757-58.

Singer, Charles, et al. (eds.). *A History of Technology.* Vol. V: *The Late Nineteenth Century.* . . . See VB 1958, 363.
Rev. by Asa Briggs in *NS*, LVII, 306; in *TLS*, 9 Jan., p. 16; by T. C. Barker in *VS*, III, 204-06; by Raymond Williams in *VS*, III, 206-08.

Smith, Colin Leonard. *The Embassy of Sir William White.* . . . See VB 1958, 363.
Rev. by F. V. Parsons in *EHR*, LXXIV, 184-85.

Spearman, Diana. *Democracy in England.* . . . See VB 1958, 363.
Rev. by G. Kitson Clark in *VS*, II, 347-48.

Spence, Clark C. *British Investments and the American Mining Frontier, 1860-1901.* Ithaca: Cornell Univ. Pr. Pp. xii + 288.
Rev. by William S. Greever in *The Mississippi Valley Hist. Rev.*, XLVI, 327-28.

Stark, Werner. *Social Theory and Christian Thought.* London: R. & K. Paul. Pp. 250.
Rev. by Alasdair MacIntyre in *NS*, LVII, 197; in *TLS*, 20 Mar. (Religious Suppl.), p. vii. "A turgidly written collection of essays on Pascal, Kierkegaard, Newman."

Steinberg, S. H. *Five Hundred Years of Printing.* London: Faber. Pp. 286.
Rev. by M. H. Black in *The Library*, 5th Ser., XIV, 300-02; in *TLS*, 25 Sept., p. 552 (see also letter by David Bland in *TLS*, 30 Oct., p. 632).

Stern, Gladys Bronwyn. *And Did He Stop and Speak to You?* New York: Regnery, 1958. Pp. 202.
Rev. by Mary Brody in *CWd*, Dec., 1958, p. 257; by Aleen Pippett in *NYTBR*, 21 Sept., 1958, p. 12. Includes reminiscences about Max Beerbohm.

Stevenson, Lionel. "1859: Year of Fulfillment." *The Centennial Review*, III, 337-56.
Concerns Darwin, Eliot, FitzGerald, Meredith, Mill, Smiles, Tennyson.

Stieb, Ernst Walter. "Controlling Drug Adulteration in England (1820-1906)." *DA*, XX, 1748-49.

Stokes, Eric. *The English Utilitarians and India.* Oxford: Clarendon Pr. Pp. xvi + 350.
Rev. by Holden Furber in *AHR*, LXV, 112-13; in *APSR*, LIII, 1144; by John Raymond in *NS*, LVII, 303-04; in *TLS*, 4 Dec., p. 712.

Sykes, John. *The Quakers.* London: Wingate. Pp. 280.
Rev. by Asa Briggs in *NS*, LVII, 80; in *TLS*, 20 Mar. (Religious Suppl.), xii. "He contrives . . . to illuminate the tangled relationship between Quakerism and Evangelicalism on both sides of the Atlantic in the nineteenth century."

Symonds, John. *Madame Blavatsky.* London: Odhams. Pp. 254.
Rev. by Maurice Richardson in *NS*, LVIII, 447-48; by Anthony Thwaite in *S*, 18 Sept., p. 382; in *TLS*, 25 Sept., p. 543.

Taine, Hippolyte Adolphe. *Notes on England.*
. . . See VB 1958, 364.
Rev. by Henri Peyre in *VS*, II, 275-77.
Taylor, A. J. P. *The Trouble Makers: Dissent over Foreign Policy, 1792-1939.* . . . See VB 1958, 364.
Rev. by J. A. S. Grenville in *EHR*, LXXIV, 126-30; by David Owen in *JMH*, XXXI, 347-48; by René Albrecht-Carrié in *PSQ*, LXXIV, 441-43.
Taylor, Frank Sherwood. *A History of Industrial Chemistry.* . . . See VB 1958, 364.
Rev. by A. R. Hall in *EHR*, LXXIV, 700-01.
Tennyson, Sir Charles. "They Taught the World to Play." *VS*, II, 211-22.
Survey of development and popularity of games in Victorian England.
Terrot, Charles. *The Maiden Tribute.* London: Muller. Pp. 230.
Briefly rev. in *TLS*, Oct. 16, p. 598. White slavery in 19th-century England.
Thompson, F. M. L. "Whigs and Liberals in West Riding, 1830-1860." *EHR*, LXXIV, 214-39.
By 1859 a solid coalition between Whigs and Liberals had been built in this borough, between 1832 and 1865 the largest Parliamentary constituency in Britain.
Thomson, Arthur Alexander, and Middleton, Dorothy. *Lugard in Africa.* London: Hale. Pp. 189.
Rev. in *TLS*, Sept. 18, p. 533.
Thornley, David. "The Irish Conservatives and Home Rule, 1869-1873." *Irish Hist. Studies*, XI, 200-22.
Discusses idea that Isaac Butts' Home Rule League owed much of its strength to protestant nationalism.
Thornton, A. P. *The Imperial Idea and Its Enemies: A Study in British Power.* London: Macmillan. Pp. xiv + 370.
Rev. by Vernon J. Puryear in *APSS*, CCCXXV, 152; by J. D. Hargreaves in *History Today*, IX, 213-15; by Lord Altrincham in *NER*, CLII, 65-66; by John Raymond in *NS*, LVII, 303-04; by M. R. D. Foot in *VS*, III, 209-11.
Treves, Guiliana Artom. *The Golden Ring: The Anglo-Florentines, 1847-1862.* . . . See VB 1956, 242.
Rev. by M. Parent in *Études anglaises*, XII, 73.
Turberville, Arthur Stanley. *The House of Lords in the Age of Reform, 1784-1837.* . . . See VB 1958, 364.
Rev. by Paul Knaplund in *AHR*, LXIV,

430-31; in *APSR*, LIII, 860; by Norman Gash in *EHR*, LXXIV, 303-05; by Madeline R. Robinton in *JMH*, XXXI, 150-51; by M. G. Brock, in *VS*, II, 280-82.
Underhill, Frank H. *The British Commonwealth: An Experiment in Co-operation among Nations.* Durham: Duke U. Pr., 1956. Pp. xxiii + 127.
Rev. by Philip W. Buck in *APSR*, LII, 1188.
Vernon, Anne. *A Quaker Business Man: The Life of Joseph Rowntree, 1836-1925.* . . . See VB 1958, 364.
Rev. by Asa Briggs in *NS*, LVII, 80; in *TLS*, 23 Jan., p. 44.
Viner, Jacob. *The Long View and the Short: Studies in Economic Theory and Policy.* Glencoe, Ill.: Free Press, 1958. Pp. 462.
Rev. by T. W. Hutchison in *Am. Economic Rev.*, XLVIII, 994; in *APSR*, LIII, 265; by Charles Hoffman in *APSS*, CCCXX, 183; by Roy Harrod in *Economica*, n.s. XXVI, 260-62; by D. H. Robertson in *Econ. Jour.*, LXIX, 543-44; by Howard S. Ellis in *JPE*, LXVII, 87-88. ". . . full length accounts of the thought of Adam Smith, Bentham, J. S. Mill, and Marshall."
Ward, John M. "The Retirement of a Titan: James Stephen, 1847-50." *JMH*, XXXI, 189-205.
Watt, F. W. "The National Policy, the Workingman, and Proletarian Ideas in Victorian Canada." *Canadian Hist. Rev.*, XL, 1-26.
Includes discussion of influence of ideas of English radicals and reformers.
Wearmouth, Robert Featherstone. *Methodism and the Trade Unions.* London: Epworth Pr. Pp. 78.
Briefly rev. in *TLS*, 7 Aug., p. 463.
Weber, Carl J. *The Rise and Fall of James Ripley Osgood.* Waterville: Colby College Pr. Pp. 283.
The biography of an influential but almost forgotten Victorian publisher. Osgood's career is rich with literary associations — with Hardy, Dickens, and Kipling among many others. Gives us an interesting insight into the nineteenth-century publishing world. — R. C. S.
Whyte, J. H. "Daniel O'Connell and the Repeal Party." *Irish Hist. Studies*, XI, 297-315.
Investigates and qualifies opinions that repeal party was subservient to O'Connell and that it was ineffective because of inadequate members in rank and file.

Whyte, John Henry. *The Independent Irish Party, 1850-1859.* . . . See VB 1958, 365.
Rev. by J. C. Beckett in *History*, XLIV, 174-75; by D. J. McDougall in *JMH*, XXXI, 370-71.

Wilkins, M. S. "The Non-Socialist Origins of England's First Important Socialist Organization." *International Rev. of Social Hist.*, IV, 199-207.
The Social Democratic Federation was radical but not socialistic at its inception.

Williams, Richmond Dean. "The Policy of Lord Salisbury Toward France, 1886-1892." *DA*, XX, 1760-61.

Wilson, Charles, and Reader, William. *Men and Machines: A History of D. Napier & Son, Engineers, Ltd., 1808-1958.* . . . See VB 1958, 365.
Rev. in *TLS*, 13 Mar., p. 150; by Arthur J. Taylor in *VS*, II, 277-79.

Wingfield-Stratford, Esme. *The Lords of Cobham Hall.* London: Cassell. Pp. xii + 451.
Rev. in *QR*, CCXCVII, 362-63; in *TLS*, 8 May, p. 267. History from 1713 of country home of Earls of Darnley.

Woodcock, George. "'Radical Jack', John George Lambton, First Earl of Durham." *History Today*, IX, 3-12.

Woodruff, William. *The Rise of the British Rubber Industry during the Nineteenth Century.* . . . See VB 1958, 365.
Rev. by T. C. Barker in *Economica*, n.s. XXVI, 377-78; by Arthur J. Taylor in *VS*, II, 277-79.

Wrench, Sir John Evelyn. *Alfred Lord Milner.* . . . See VB 1958, 365.
Rev. by M. R. D. Foot in *VS*, III, 209-11.

Wright, Noel. *Quest for Franklin.* London: Heinemann. Pp. xii + 258.
Rev. in *TLS*, 5 June, p. 334. The disappearance of Sir John Franklin's Arctic expedition.

Young, Howard V., Jr. "The Evangelical Clergy in the Church of England, 1790-1850." *DA*, XIX, 1734.
A study of social and political influence as well as ecclesiastical reform.

III. MOVEMENTS OF IDEAS AND LITERARY FORMS

Abrams, M. H. (ed.). *Literature and Belief.* New York: Columbia Univ. Pr., 1958. Pp. xvi + 184.

Rev. by Spire Pitou in *BA*, XXXIII, 223.

Albee, Ernest. *A History of English Utilitarianism:* London: Macmillan. Pp. xx + 427.
Rev. by William D. Templeman in *Personalist*, XL, 191.

Allott, Miriam (ed.). *Novelists on the Novel.* London: Routledge and K. Paul. Pp. xv + 330.
Rev. by V. S. Pritchett in *NS*, LVIII, 851-52; by Bernard Bergonzi in *TC*, CLXVI, 513-16; in *TLS*, 20 Nov., p. 678.

Altick, Richard D. *The English Common Reader.* . . . See VB 1958, 365.
Rev. by Helen MacGill Hughes in *Amer. Jour. of Sociology*, LXIV, 425-26; by R. L. MacDougall in *QQ*, LXVI, 178-79.

Altick, Richard D. "English Lives and American Scholars." *N*, CLXXXVIII, 73-74.
A review article including references to Edgar Johnson's *Charles Dickens*, Gordon Ray's *Thackeray*, and Helen Viljoen's *Ruskin's Scottish Heritage*.

Andrews, John S. "*Immensee* and Victorian Letters." *MLR*, LIV, 406-10.
The reputation in England of Theodor Storm's novella.

Beckson, Karl E. "The Rhymers' Club." *DA*, XX, 1021-22.
Organization and history of the literary group that attempted to give form to the *fin de siècle* aesthetic movement.

Belvin, Betty J. M. "Expanding Themes in the Novels of E. M. Forster." *DA*, XIX, 2610-11.
Holds that Forster was influenced by the ideas of Carlyle, Arnold, and Ruskin among the Victorians.

Bland, David. *History of Book Illustration: The Illuminated Manuscript and the Printed Book.* Cleveland: World Publishing Co., 1958. Pp. 448.
Rev. by John P. Harthan in *Apollo*, LXIX, 52; by R. McL. in *Connoisseur*, CLXIII, 47; in *HTB*, 25 Jan., p. 13; by Philip Hofer in *LJ*, LXXXIV, 175; by L. F. Perusse in *LQ*, XXIX, 137; by James Shand in *NS*, 13 Dec., 1958.

Boase, T. S. R. *English Art, 1800-1870.* (Vol. X in *The Oxford History of English Art.*) Oxford: Clarendon Pr. Pp. xxiv + 352.
Rev. by Mary Woodall in *Apollo*, LXX, 196; by Karl Nyren in *LJ*, LXXXIV, 3024; by Eric Newton in *Manchester Guardian Weekly*, 25 June, p. 11; by Jacques Vallette in *Mercure de France*,

CCCXXXVII, 321-22; by Basil Taylor in *NS*, LVIII, 138-39; by Alan Bowness in *S*, 31 July, p. 147; in *TLS*, 24 July, pp. 429-30.

Bøe, Alf. *From Gothic Revival to Functional Form*. . . . See VB 1958, 366.

Rev. by Ruari McLean in *TC*, CLXV, 301-02; by John Steegman in *VS*, II, 328-29.

Brennan, Neil Francis. "The Aesthetic Tradition in the English Comic Novel." *DA*, XX, 1780-81.

The modern comic novel as an art form from Wilde and echoes of past writers.

Brinton, Crane. *A History of Western Morals*. New York: Harcourt, Brace. Pp. 502.

Rev. by R. M. Malone in *LJ*, LXXXIV, 1259; by Marvin Lowenthal in *HTB*, 19 Apr., p. 6; by Hans Meyerhoff in *N*, 15 Aug., p. 74; by T. V. Smith in *NYTBR*, 28 June, p. 12; by Ward Madden in *SR*, 2 May, p. 22.

Buckley, Vincent. *Poetry and Morality*. Intro. by Basil Willey. London: Chatto & Windus. Pp. 239.

Rev. by Howard Sergeant in *CR*, CXCVI, 127; by Jacques Vallette in *Mercure de France*, CCCXXXVI, 337; by John Bayley in *NER*, CLII, 185-86; by Raymond Williams in *NS*, LVII, 410; in *QR*, CCXCVII, 364; by Frank Kermode in *S*, 13 Mar., pp. 375-76; in *TLS*, 27 Mar., p. 175. ". . . examines the critical procedures of Arnold, Eliot and Leavis, with the question of 'moral judgment' in mind."

Clarke, Martin Lowther. *Classical Education in Britain 1500-1900*. London: Cambridge Univ. Pr. Pp. 233.

Rev. by E. M. Jenkinson in *N & Q*, n.s. VI, 236-37; in *QR*, CCXCVII, 476; in *TLS*, 13 Mar., p. 148.

Cohen, Victor. "Auguste Comte." *CR*, CXCV, 360-63.

Includes an account of Comte's English disciples.

Cotgrove, Stephen Frederick. *Technical Education and Social Change*. . . . See VB 1958, 366.

Rev. by T. C. Barker in *VS*, II, 279-80.

Coveney, Peter. *Poor Monkey: The Child in Literature* . . . See VB 1958, 366.

Rev. by L. F. Bonnerot in *Études anglaises*, XII, 274.

Dalziel, Margaret. *Popular Fiction 100 Years Ago*. . . . See VB 1958, 366.

Rev. by E. F. Walbridge in *LJ*, LXXXIV, 519; by Edgar Johnson in *NYTBR*, 22 Feb., p. 4.

DeMaria, Robert. "From Bulwer-Lytton to

George Orwell; the Utopian Novel in England, 1870-1950." *DA*, XX, 667.

Digeon, Aurélien. *The English School of Painting*. New York: Universe Books. Pp. 137.

Rev. by Marchal E. Landgren in *LJ*, LXXXIV, 3849. ". . . a general survey with emphasis on the 'golden age' . . . from Hogarth to Turner and Constable."

Donagan, Alan and Steinmann, Martin, Jr. "Art and Counterfeit Art." *CE*, XX, 252-54.

Comment on critical theory advanced by Wayne Burns in "The Genuine and Counterfeit: A Study in Victorian and Modern Fiction." (See VB 1956, 244.)

Donoghue, Denis. *The Third Voice: Modern British and American Verse Drama*. Princeton, N. J.: Princeton Univ. Pr. Pp. 286.

Includes study of Yeats' verse plays.

Duncan, Joseph E. *The Revival of Metaphysical Poetry: The History of a Style, 1800 to the Present*. Minneapolis: Univ. of Minnesota Pr. Pp. 227.

Rev. by Melvin W. Askew in *BA*, XXXIII, 460; by John R. Willingham in *LJ*, LXXXIV, 1892.

Ellegård, Alvar. "The Readership of the Periodical Press in Mid-Victorian Britain." . . . See VB 1958, 367.

Rev. by Heinz Reinhold in *Anglia*, LXXVII, 113; by John Butt in *MLR*, LIV, 455.

Fairchild, Hoxie Neale. *Religious Trends in English Poetry*. Vol. IV. . . . See VB 1958, 367.

Rev. by Francis G. Townsend in *MLN*, LXXVI, 267-70; by B. R. McElderry, Jr., in *Personalist*, XL, 99-100; by Kenneth Allott in *RES*, n.s. X, 97-98.

Flanagan, Thomas J. B. *The Irish Novelists, 1800-1850*. New York: Columbia Univ. Pr. Pp. 362.

Rev. by Patrick R. Penland in *LJ*, LXXXIV, 3039. Literary and biographical studies of Maria Edgeworth, Lady Morgan, John Banim, Gerald Griffin, and William Carleton.

Foakes, Reginald Anthony. *The Romantic Assertion: A Study in the Language of Nineteenth Century Poetry*. . . . See VB 1958, 367.

Rev. by Melvin W. Askew in *BA*, XXXIII, 217; by Kenneth Allott in *DUJ*, LI (n.s. XX), 90-92; by John Holloway in *MLR*, LIV, 99-100; in *QR*, CCXCVII, 118; by

Donald Davie in VS, III, 212-14.

Ford, Boris (ed.). *From Dickens to Hardy.*
. . . See VB 1958, 367.

Rev. briefly in *CE*, XXI, 112; by Sylvère
Monod in *Études anglaises*, XII, 174-75.

Foster, Richard Jackson. "Modern Critics and
Romantic Sensibility: A Study of the New
Romanticism of the New Criticism." *DA*,
XIX, 1755-56.

Attention is given to Arnold's critical doctrines as basic to the concept of the twentieth-century movement.

Frankl, Paul. *The Gothic: Literary Sources
and Interpretations through Eight Centuries.* Princeton, N. J.: Princeton Univ. Pr.
Pp. 873.

Fraser, G. S. *Vision and Rhetoric.* London:
Faber. Pp. 285.

Rev. in *TLS*, 10 Apr., p. 210. Includes
essay on Yeats.

Goldberg, Gerald Jay. "The Artist as Hero in
British Fiction, 1890 to 1930." *DA*, XX,
2289.

Greene, John C. *Death of Adam: Evolution
and Its Impact on Western Thought.*
Ames, Iowa: Iowa State Univ. Pr. Pp.
388.

Gregory, Horace. *The World of James Mc-
Neill Whistler.* New York: Thomas Nelson. Pp. 255.

Rev. by DeLancey Ferguson in *HTB*, 27
Dec., p. 7.

Haber, Francis C. *The Age of the World:
Moses to Darwin.* Baltimore: Johns Hopkins Pr. Pp. xi + 303.

Hinton, R. W. K. "History Yesterday: Five
Points about Whig History." *History Today*, IX, 720-28.

Considers assumptions (history was not
only development but a fortunate development), excellences (primarily literary),
and deficiencies of the constitutional history of Hallam, Macaulay, Stubbs, and
Gardiner.

Hitchcock, Henry Russell. *Architecture: Nineteenth and Twentieth Centuries.* . . . See
VB 1958, 367.

Rev. by Edward D. Mills in *Apollo*,
LXIX, 153; by Reyner Banham in *Bur-
lington Mag.*, CI, 354-57; by M. E. Land-
gren in *LJ*, LXXXIII, 3527; by Colin St.
John Wilson in *S*, 23 Jan., pp. 125-26; by
Vincent Scully in *VS*, II, 329-31.

Hoblitzelle, Harrison. "The War against War
in the Nineteenth Century: A Study of
the Western Backgrounds of Gandhian
Thought." *DA*, XX, 1016.

Traces indebtedness of Gandhi to Ruskin,
Tolstoy, Emerson, Thoreau, Carlyle and
to theories of non-violence.

Houghton, Walter. *The Victorian Frame of
Mind.* . . . See VB 1958, 368.

Rev. by Asa Briggs in *EHR*, LXXIV, 135-
37.

Howarth, Herbert. *The Irish Writers, 1880-
1940.* . . . See VB 1958, 368.

Rev. by René Fréchet in *Études anglaises*,
XII, 338-44; by John Hewitt in *MLR*,
LIV, 631; in *QR*, CCXCVII, 236; by G.
S. Fraser in *TC*, CLXV, 524-27; in *TLS*,
6 Feb., p. 72.

Howes, Alan B. *Yorick and the Critics.* . . .
See VB 1958, 368.

Rev. in *TLS*, 16 Jan., p. 39.

Inglis, Brian. "The Thunderer." *S*, 10 July,
pp. 23-24.

Attempts to explode the myth of Delane's
greatness as editor by contending that he
prostituted *The Times* in following Palmerston's line.

Jones, Howard Mumford. "The Generation of
1830." *HLB*, XIII, 401-414.

The generation of 1830, born in 1809—
Poe, Holmes, Tennyson, Gladstone, Darwin, FitzGerald, Lincoln—are characterized as writers with a common style, a
resonance which permits the individual to
melt into the great and the lasting. Being
thus in harmony with their age, they dem-
onstrate a "style of responsibility," a concern for tradition, "a concern that the patterns of English speech shall not die out
with them." This is a significant approach
to an often-neglected aspect of writers.—
R. E. F.

Joseph, Bertram Leon. *The Tragic Actor.*
London: Routledge and Paul. Pp. 415.

Rev. by Arthur Colby Sprague in *Theatre
Notebook*, XIV, 23-24; in *TLS*, 8 May, p.
276. Tragic acting in England from Elizabethan to modern times.

Keith, Sara. "Nineteenth-Century Anonyma:
Some Identifications." *N & Q*, n.s. VI,
210-12.

Kelly, Doris Borrup. "The Decline of Rome
in Nineteenth Century English Fiction."
DA, XX, 1767.

Kenner, Hugh. *Gnomon.* . . . See VB 1958,
368.

Rev. in *StI*, XLVIII, 106.

Kermode, Frank. *Romantic Image.* . . . See
VB 1958, 368.

Rev. by Hazard Adams in *The American
Scholar*, XXVIII, 226-28; by Hazard
Adams in *JAA*, XVII, 529-30; by Robert

Louis Peters in *MLQ*, XX, 289.

Kildahl, Phillip A. "British and American Reactions to Layard's Discoveries in Assyria (1845-1860)." *DA*, XX, 1749-50.

Traces the emotional shock caused by the explorations and discoveries of the literary prototypes of the Old Testament.

Knox, Ronald Arbuthnott. *Literary Distractions*. London: Sheed, 1958. Pp. 232.

Rev. by Ashley Pettis in *CWd*, CLXXXVIII, 517; by B. R. Redman in *SR*, 15 Nov., 1958, p. 13; by Evelyn Waugh in *S*, 17 Oct., 1958, p. 523. Contains comments on Trollope and Stevenson.

Krook, Dorothea. *Three Traditions of Moral Thought*. London: Cambridge Univ. Pr. Pp. 355.

Rev. by Raymond Williams in *NS*, LVIII, 588-90; in *TLS*, 18 Dec., p. 740. Contains comment on Mill, Arnold, Bradley.

Langbaum, Robert. *The Poetry of Experience....* See VB 1958, 368.

Rev. by Ben W. Fuson in *CE*, XX, 259-60; by William H. Rueckert in *JEGP*, LVIII, 518-20; by Phyllis Bartlett in *Ex*, XVII, Review 4; by Robert L. Peters in *JAA*, XVII, 530.

Little, Tenison. "Young Ireland Poets." *CR*, CXCVI, 115-18.

Thomas Davis, John O'Hagan, and other poets and patriots of the 1840's.

Lyons, Edward. *"The Fortnightly Review* and France: Politics and Literature, 1865-1882." *DA*, XX, 1017-18.

McCall, Joseph Darryl, Jr. "Factors Affecting the Literary Canon." *DA*, XIX, 1744.

"The description of the process through which a book may go from the time it is published until the time it becomes a 'classic'" is the purpose of this study, which uses the careers of Tennyson and Arnold, among others from earlier and later periods, for illustration.

McDonald, Hugh Dermot. *Ideas of Revelation: An Historical Study A. D. 1700 to A. D. 1860*. London: Macmillan. pp. xi + 300.

Mackerness, Eric David. *The Heeded Voice: Studies in the Literary Status of the Anglican Sermon, 1830-1900*. London: Heffer. Pp. xvi + 158.

McPherson, Robert G. *Theory of Higher Education in Nineteenth-Century England*. Athens, Ga.: Univ. of Georgia Pr. Pp. 127.

Marshall, James F. "Alfred de Vigny and William Charles Macready." *PMLA*, LXXIV, 98-101.

Concern over Bulwer-Lytton's *Richelieu*.

Martin, Harold C. (ed.). *Style in Prose Fiction*. English Institute Essays 1958. New York: Columbia Univ. Pr. Pp. xi + 209.

Includes an essay by G. Armour Craig on the style of *Vanity Fair*, and an essay by S. F. Johnson on Hardy and Burke's idea of the sublime.

Millhauser, Milton. *Just before Darwin: Robert Chambers and Vestiges*. Middletown, Conn.: Wesleyan Univ. Pr. Pp. lx + 246.

Rev. by Bert James Loewenberg in *The American Scholar*, XXIX, 120-22; by Marston Bates in *NYTBR*, 16 Aug., p. 6; by Philip Appleman in *VS*, III, 115-25.

Moir, Esther. "The Industrial Revolution: A Romantic View." *History Today*, IX, 589-97.

Müller-Schwefe, Gerhard. "Fortschrittsglaube und Dichtung im Victorianischen England." *Anglia*, LXXVII, 145-72.

In attempting to deal with the theme of progress the Victorian poets were limited by the fact that they understood and treated it literally, not as a metaphor for a transcendant reality.

Murch, Alma Elizabeth. *The Development of the Detective Novel*. London: Peter Owen, 1958. Pp. 272.

Rev. unfavorably by Pierre Weil-Nordon in *Études anglaises*, XII, 176; by C. E. Kilpatrick in *LJ*, LXXXIII; briefly in *NCF*, XIII, 368; unfavorably by Anthony Boucher in *NYTBR*, 14 Dec., 1958, p. 20; favorably by Sergeant Cuff in *SR*, 17 Jan., p. 64; in *TLS*, 26 Sept., 1958, p. 542.

Nicoll, Allardyce. *A History of English Drama 1660-1900*. Vol. V: *Late Nineteenth Century Drama, 1850-1900*. London: Cambridge Univ. Pr. Pp. vi + 901. (For Vol. VI, see I, Nicoll.)

Rev. by M. M. Aneny in *LJ*, LXXXIV, 3583-84; by William Angus in *QQ*, LXVI, 501-03; by George Rowell in *Theatre Notebook*, XIV, 32-33; in *TLS*, 26 June, p. 380. A new edition, with supplementary bibliographical notes and 75 pages of addenda to the Hand-List of Plays, 1850-1900.

O'Sullivan, Vincent. *Opinions*. With an Introduction by Alan Anderson. London: Unicorn Pr. Pp. 204.

Rev. by Frank Kermode in *S*, 7 Aug., p. 170; in *TLS*, 14 Aug., p. 473. A selection of O'Sullivan's sketches and biographical reminiscences of Wilde, Moore, Rolfe, Gissing, Harris, and others.

Pascal, Roy. "The Autobiographical Novel and the Autobiography." *EC*, IX, 134-150.

With three examples — *Villette, Sons and Lovers*, and *A Portrait of the Artist as a Young Man* — Pascal suggests the "obvious advantages of the novel-form over the straight autobiographical narrative."

Passmore, John Arthur. *A Hundred Years of Philosophy.* . . . See VB 1957, 400.

Rev. by Willis Doney in *Philosophical Rev.*, LXVIII, 256-60; by J. N. Findlay in *Philosophy*, XXXIV, 166-68.

Peters, Robert L. "Toward an 'Un-Definition' of Decadent as Applied to British Literature of the Nineteenth Century." *JAA*, XVIII, 258-64.

An attack on Ryals (see VB 1958, 370), whose definition of "decadent" is, according to Peters, oversimplified and insufficiently documented.

Proctor, Mortimer R. *The English University Novel.* . . . See VB 1957, 400.

Rev. by Arnold Kettle in *MLR*, LIV, 301.

Pruvost, René. "Boccace en Angleterre." *Études anglaises*, XII, 124-34.

Pryme, Eileen E. "Zola's Plays in England, 1870-1900." *French Studies*, XIII, 28-38.

Rathburn, Robert C. and Steinmann, Martin, Jr. (eds.). *From Jane Austen to Joseph Conrad: Essays Collected in Memory of James T. Hillhouse.* Minneapolis: Univ. of Minnesota Pr., 1958. Pp. xii + 326.

Rev. by Marvin Fisher in *CE*, XXI, 112; by Arthur Collins in *NCF*, XIV, 83-86; by John Stedmond in *QQ*, LXVI, 346-47; by Bruce McCullough in *SAQ*, LVIII, 625-26; by Vincent Miller in *Southwest Rev.*, XLIV, 184; in *TLS*, 14 Aug., p. 468. Essays on: Austen, Brontës, Bulwer-Lytton, Butler, Conrad, Dickens, Eliot, Gaskell, Gissing, Hardy, Meredith, Reade, Thackeray, Trollope.

Richards, James Maude. *The Functional Tradition in Early Industrial Buildings.* . . . See VB 1958, 369.

Rev. in *TLS*, 6 Feb., p. 68.

Roach, J. P. C. "Victorian Universities and the National Intelligensia." *VS*, III, 131-50.

Roll-Hansen, Diderik. *The Academy, 1869-1879.* . . . See VB 1958, 369.

Rev. by Leslie A. Marchand in *MLQ*, XX, 101-02.

Rosenberg, Edgar. "Jewish Stereotypes in English Fiction: 1795-1895." *DA*, XIX, 2617-18.

Rowell, George. *The Victorian Theatre.* . . . See VB 1958, 370.

Rev. by J. F. Arnott in *RES*, n.s. X, 108.

Ryals, Clyde de L. "The Nineteenth-Century Cult of Inaction." *Tennessee Studies in Literature*, IV, 51-60.

Asserts that a commercial society's emphasis on practical values caused the artists to retreat into idealism and inaction. A striking article. — R. C. S.

Rycenga, John Arthur. "Theories and Forms in English Biography, 1836-1899." *DA*, XX, 2302-03.

Scott, Wilson. "The Significance of 'Hard Bodies' in the History of Scientific Thought." *Isis*, L, 199-210.

"This paper deals with eighteenth- and nineteenth-century scientific discussions on mechanical impact of hard bodies, a subject directly related to assumptions in both the atomic theory and the nineteenth-century law of conservation of energy."

Shattuck, Charles H. (ed.). *Bulwer and Macready: A Chronicle of the Early Victorian Theatre.* . . . See VB 1958, 370.

Rev. by George Rowell in *JEGP*, LVIII, 311-13; by Curtis Dahl in *MLN*, LXXIV, 649-51; by Phyllis Hartnoll in *N & Q*, n.s. VI, 462; by Pat M. Ryan, Jr. in *QJS*, XLV, 447-48; by William Angus in *QQ*, LXVI, 349-50; by R. C. Churchill in *S*, 18 Dec,. p. 915; by Merle M. Bevington in *SAQ*, LVIII, 483-84; by St. Vincent Troubridge in *Theatre Notebook*, XIII, 72-73; in *TLS*, 20 Nov., p. 678; by Alan S. Downer in *VS*, II, 344-46.

Smidt, Kristian. "The Intellectual Quest of the Victorian Poets." *ESt*, XL, 90-102.

The primary object of the quest was intellectual certainty, but the Victorian poets chose verse rather than the philosopher's systematic prose as a medium of expression "because their intellectual dilemma was also an *emotional* one."

Solomon, Eric. "Prophetic War Novels." *N & Q*, n.s. VI, 36-37.

Late 19th-century propaganda novels to persuade the English people to avoid the complacent belief that all wars are ended.

Souffrin, Eileen. " 'Gringoire' en Angleterre a l' Époque Victorienne." *Revue de Littérature Comparée*, XXXIII, 26-39.

History of French "seasons" at the Gaiety Theater in London, particularly the greatest hit, the historical play by Banville, *Gringoire*.

Stang, Richard. *The Theory of the Novel in England, 1850-1870.* New York: Columbia Univ. Pr. Pp. xii + 251 (See VB 1958, 370).

Rev. by V. S. Pritchett in *NS*, LVIII, 851-

52; by Bernard Bergonzi in *TC*, CLXVI, 513-16; in *TLS*, 20 Nov., p. 678.

Sutherland, James. *English Satire.* . . . See VB 1958, 370.
Rev. by Helmut Papajewski in *Anglia*, LXXVII, 78-79; by Norman Knox in *SAQ*, LVIII, 138-39.

Thistlethwaite, Frank. *The Anglo-American Connection in the Early Nineteenth Century.* Philadelphia: Univ. of Pennsylvania Pr., 1958. Pp. 222.
Rev. by Ruth Miller Elson in *The Mississippi Valley Hist. Rev.*, XLVI, 307-08; in *TLS*, 1 May, p. 258; by Michael Kraus in *VS*, II, 337-40.

Tillyard, E. M. W. *The Epic Strain in the English Novel.* . . . See VB 1958, 370.
Rev. by A. J. Farmer in *Études anglaises*, XII, 82; briefly in *NCF*, XIII, 367; by Richard Ries in *TC*, CLXV, 299-301.

The Times. "Enough of Blood." *TLS*, 4 Dec., suppl. pp. i-ii.
On early sensational serials for young people, fore-runners of children's magazines.

The Times. "Seriously . . ." *TLS*, 23 Jan., p. 47.
A "leading article" on *VNL* and Victorian scholarship, noting the need of information as to whereabouts of letters, MSS., etc.

Tindall, William York. *The Literary Symbol.* . . . See VB 1956, 248.
Rev. by F. L. McCurdy in *QJS*, XLV, 338.

Underwood, V. P. *Verlaine et l'Angleterre.* . . . See VB 1957, 401.
Rev. in *TLS*, 2 Jan., pp. 1-2.

Walsh, William Henry. *The Use of Imagination: Educational Thought and the Literary Mind.* London: Chatto & Windus. Pp. 252.
Rev. by Raymond Williams in *NS*, LVII, 410; in *TLS*, 10 Apr., p. 212. Contains material on Arnold, Hopkins, Lewis.

Warburg, Jeremy (ed.). *The Industrial Muse: The Industrial Revolution in English Poetry.* . . . See VB 1958, 371.
Rev. by Helmut Papajewski in *Anglia*, LXXVII, 249-50; by P. A. Larkin in *MLR*, LIV, 300.

Weinstein, Leo. *The Metamorphoses of Don Juan.* Stanford Studies in Languages and Literature, XVIII. Stanford: Stanford Univ. Pr. Pp. 223.
Rev. briefly by Burton A. Robie in *LJ*, LXXXIV, 2187.

Willey, Basil. *More Nineteenth Century Studies.* . . . See VB 1958, 371.

Rev. by William D. Templeman in *Personalist*, XL, 95-96.

Williams, Raymond. *Culture and Society, 1780-1950.* . . . See VB 1958, 371.
Rev. by John Clive in *AHR*, LXIV, 934-35; by Edward F. Jost in *America*, CI, 676-77; by J. J. Hecht in *Am. Sociological Rev.*, XXIV, 746; by Arthur Lerner in *BA*, XXXIII, 471-72; by Walter E. Houghton in *Canadian Hist. Rev.*, XL, 147; by Richard Hoggart in *EC*, IX, 171-79 (see also rejoinders in *EC*, IX, by Ian Gregor, 425-30; by Malcolm Pittock, 430-32; and reply by Raymond Williams, 432-37); by Harold Rosenberg in *N*, 7 Feb., pp. 121-22; by Irving Howe in *NewR*, 2 Feb., pp. 17-19, and 9 Feb., pp. 23-24; by Richard Ries in *TC*, CLXV, 182-84.

Wimsatt, William K. and Brooks, Cleanth. *Literary Criticism: A Short History.* . . . See VB 1958, 371.
Rev. by Hazard Adams in *The American Scholar*, XXVIII, 226-32; by P. LeBrun in *EC*, IX, 323-33; by Frederick J. Hoffman in *WR*, XXIII, 187-92.

Woolf, Virginia. *Granite and Rainbow: Essays.* London: Hogarth Pr., 1958. Pp. 239.
Rev. by Leo Lerman in *The American Scholar*, XXVIII, 246. Includes material on Dickens, Eliot, Stevenson.

Wright, Herbert G. *Boccaccio in England.* . . . See VB 1958, 371.
Rev. by James Kinsley in *RES*, n.s. X, 78-80.

Zabel, Morton D. *Craft and Character in Modern Fiction.* . . . See VB 1958, 371.
Rev. by Hazard Adams in *The American Scholar*, XXVIII, 238; by P. A. W. Collins in *Dickensian*, LV, 34-35; by J. Loiseau in *Études anglaises*, XII, 82-83.

IV. INDIVIDUAL AUTHORS.

ARNOLD, MATTHEW (see also II, Appleman; III, Belvin, Buckley, Foster, Krook, McCall, Ryals, Smidt, Walsh, Williams; **HOUSMAN**: Walde).

Allott, Kenneth. "Matthew Arnold's Reading-Lists in Three Early Diaries." *VS*, II, 254-66.

Baum, Paull Franklin. *Ten Studies in the Poetry of Matthew Arnold.* . . . See VB 1958, 372.
Rev. by A. Dwight Culler in *JEGP*, LVIII, 142-43.

Brooks, Roger L. "Matthew Arnold and His Contemporaries: A Check List of Unpublished and Published Letters." *SP,* LVI, 647-53.

Supplements Motter's list: *SP,* XXXI (1934), 600-05.

Brooks, Roger L. "A Matthew Arnold Letter to James Russell Lowell: The Reason for the American Lecture Tour." *AL,* XXXI, 336-37.
Arnold undertook the tour to pay his son's debts.

Buckler, William E. *Matthew Arnold's Books: Toward A Publishing Diary.* . . . See VB 1958, 372.
Rev. by A. Dwight Culler in *JEGP,* LVIII, 140-42; by Kenneth Allott in *MLR,* LIV, 267-68; by Fraser Neiman in *MP,* LVI, 215-16.

Curgenven, J. P. " 'The Scholar Gipsy': A Study of the Growth, Meaning, and Integration of a Poem." *Litera,* II, 41-58; III, 1-13.

Curgenven, J. P. " 'Thyrsis,' " *Litera,* IV, 27-39; V, 7-16.

Delasanta, Rodney. "Arnold's 'Dover Beach.' " *Ex,* XVIII, Item 7.

Gottfried, Leon Albert. "Matthew Arnold and the Romantics." *DA,* XIX, 2600.
Arnold as influenced by the Romantics and serving as a bridge between his and later generations through his interpretation of the Romantics.

Guthrie, William Bell. "Matthew Arnold's Diaries; the Unpublished Items: A Transcription and Commentary." *DA,* XX, 1541.
Transcription of the forty-four diaries Arnold kept from 1852 through 1888. Notes relate the entries to his letters and works. Besides personal, financial, and literary subjects, Arnold noted observations and problems in the pursuit of his educational duties. This study supplements all other studies of Arnold. "Access to the full diary entries, here first transcribed, would seem to be essential to any future biographer of Arnold or to any student of Arnold's life in relation to his works." This study of 2313 pages is of vast importance, and it is hoped it will be published soon.—R. E. F.

Jamison, William A. *Arnold and the Romantics.* . . . See VB 1958, 372.
Rev. by William E. Buckler in *MLN,* LXXIV, 77-79; by G. D. Klingopoulos in *MLR,* LIV, 105; by A. Dwight Culler in *JEGP,* LVIII, 144.

Lowe, Robert Liddell. "A Further Note on Arnold in America." *AL,* XXX, 530-33.
Vigorous defense of his earlier conjecture

that A. undertook an American lecture tour to pay his son's debts.

Montague, Gene. "Arnold's 'Dover Beach' and 'The Scholar Gipsy.' " *Ex,* XVIII, Item 15.
Parallel structure in the two poems.

Mordell, Albert (ed.). *Literary Reviews and Essays by Henry James.* New York: Twayne, 1957. Pp. 400.
Rev. with comments on affinities between Arnold and James by Marius Bewley in *S,* 24 July, pp. 114-15. The book includes James's essay on Arnold (1884).

Neiman, Fraser. "Matthew Arnold's Review of the *Lettres et opuscules inédits* by Joseph de Maistre." *MLN,* LXXIV, 492-94.
Evidence for Arnold's authorship of a substantial article in the *Quarterly Review,* October, 1879.

Parrish, Stephen Maxfield. *Concordance to the Poems of Matthew Arnold.* Ithaca, N. Y.: Cornell Univ. Pr. Pp. xxi + 965.

Raleigh, John Henry. *Matthew Arnold and American Culture.* . . . See VB 1958, 372.
Rev. by Lynn Altenbernd in *MLR,* LIII, 575-77.

Robbins, William. *The Ethical Idealism of Matthew Arnold: A Study of the Nature and Sources of His Moral Ideas.* London: Heinemann. Pp. xi + 258.
Rev. by John Holloway in *Listener,* 26 Nov., pp. 944-45; by Raymond Williams in *NS,* LVIII, 588-90; by R. C. Churchill in *S,* 13 Nov., p. 679.

Stevenson, Lionel. "Matthew Arnold's Poetry: A Modern Appraisal." *Tennessee Studies in Literature,* IV, 31-41.
In his poetry, Arnold "brings our own suppressed anxieties into the open and refrains from offering any easy panaceas or confident solutions."

Super, R. H. "Arnold's Notebooks and Arnold Bibliography." *MP,* LVI, 268-69.
Supplements Fraser Neiman's "Some Newly Attributed Contributions of Matthew Arnold to the *Pall Mall Gazette*" (see VB 1957, 403).

Tillotson, Kathleen. "Matthew Arnold and Carlyle." . . . See VB 1957, 403.
Rev. by J. P. Curgenven in *RES,* n.s.X, 108.

Waller, John O. "The Arnolds and Particular Truth." *N & Q,* n.s. VI, 163-64.

Westlake, Neda. "Matthew Arnold at the University." *The Library Chronicle* (Univ. of Pennsylvania), XXV, 43-44.

Whitridge, Arnold. "The Gaiety of Matthew

Arnold." *The Library Chronicle* (Univ. of Pennsylvania), XXV, 45-49.

Wilkins, Charles T. "The English Reputation of Matthew Arnold, 1840-1877." *DA*, XX, 293-94.

Arnold relied upon critical reception to decide his course in publishing essays and books, often answering the criticism with another essay or preface.

Zigerell, James. "MacLeish's ' "Dover Beach" — A Note to That Poem.' " *Ex*, XVII, Item 38.

ARNOLD, THOMAS (see also **CLOUGH:** Gollin).

Smith, Leslie. "The Doctor's Dictionary." *Classical Jour.*, LIV, 352-54.

Thomas Arnold's "services to the Classics."

BAGEHOT (see also **TENNYSON:** Tener).

Buchan, Alastair. *The Spare Chancellor: The Life of Walter Bagehot.* London: Chatto and Windus. Pp. 287.

Rev. in *Economic Jour.*, LXIX, 850; by R. H. S. Crossman in *NS*, LVIII, 548-49; by James Joll in *S*, 6 Nov., pp. 636-37; in *TLS*, 16 Oct., p. 594.

St. John-Stevas, Norman. *Walter Bagehot: A Study of His Life and Thought together with a Selection from His Political Writings.* Bloomington: Indiana Univ. Pr. Pp. xvi + 485.

Rev. by Jacques Barzun in *AHR*, LXV, 110; favorably in *APSR*, LIII, 1145; by Thomas I. Cook in *APSS*, CCCXXVI, 170; by P. Baratier in *Études anglaises*, XII, 263-64; by Herbert Read in *Listener*, 12 Feb., p. 297; by Angus Macintyre in *NER*, CLII, 149-50; by E. V. Walter in *New R*, 29 June, p. 18; by R. H. S. Crossman in *NS*, LVII, 419-20; by Richard Wollheim in *S*, 20 Feb., p. 267; by J. W. Krutch in *SR*, 14 Mar., p. 63; by Betty Miller in *TC*, CLXV, 302-04; in *TLS*, 27 Feb., p. 112; by Robert A. Greenberg in *VNL*, No. 15 (Spring), pp. 21-23; by A. Dwight Culler in *YR*, XLVIII, 584-87.

BARRIE (see also I, Gordan).

McGraw, William R., Jr. "The Theatricality of James M. Barrie: An Analysis of His Plays to Determine the Source of Their Effectiveness in the Theater." *DA*, XIX, 2188.

BEERBOHM (see also II, Stern).

Max's Nineties: Drawings, 1892-1899. . . . See VB 1958, 373.

Rev. by John T. Winterich in *HTB*, 12 Apr., p. 3; by Jacques Vallette in *Mercure de France*, CCCXXXVI, 335; in *NS*, 20

Dec., 1958, p. 891; by Jerome H. Buckley in *VS*, II, 343-44.

BENTHAM (see II, Roberts, Viner).

BORROW. Fréchet, René. *George Borrow (1803-1881): Vagabond Polyglotte, Agent Biblique, Écrivain.* Paris: Didier, 1956. Pp. x + 378.

Rev. by Geoffrey Tillotson in *MLR*, LIV, 266-67.

BRADLEY (see also III, Krook).

Wollheim, Richard. *F. H. Bradley.* London: Penguin. Pp. 288.

Rev. by Alasdair MacIntyre in *NS*, LVIII, 886-87.

BRIDGES. Sparrow, John (ed.). *Robert Bridges: Poetry and Prose.* . . . See VB 1955, 252.

Rev. by J. G. Ritz in *Études anglaises*, XII, 72-3.

BRONTËS (see also I, Gordan; III, Pascal, Rathburn).

Brick, Allan R. "*Wuthering Heights*: Narrators, Audience, and Message." *CE*, XXI, 80-86.

Brontë Society, Transactions and Other Publications of.

Vol. XIII, No. 4 (Part 69) has items: Holgate, Ivy, "The Brontës at Thornton: 1815-1820" (pp. 323-41); Curtis, Dame Myra, "The 'Profile' Portrait" (pp. 342-46); Duthie, E. L., "Charlotte Brontë's Translation: The First Canto of Voltaire's 'Henriade' " (pp. 347-51); Visick, Mary, "Anne Brontë's Last Poem" (pp. 352-56); Stollard, Mary L., "The Brontës in Leeds" (pp. 360-62); Cunliffe, W. R., "Emily Brontë: A Clue to Her Appearance" (p. 363); "The 65th Annual Meeting" (pp. 367-70); "The Brontë Parsonage Museum" report for 1958-59 (pp. 375-76).

Brooks, Roger L. "Unrecorded Newspaper Reviews of Charlotte Brontë's *Shirley* and *Villette*." *PBS*, LIII, 270-71.

Crandall, Norma. *Emily Brontë: A Psychological Portrait.* . . . See VB 1957, 404.

Rev. briefly in *NCF*, XIV, 92.

Ewbank, Jane M. *The Life and Works of William Carus Wilson, 1791-1859.* Kendal: Titus Wilson. Pp. 30.

Rev. in *TLS*, 21 Aug., p. 484. Wilson founded the Cowan Bridge Clergy Daughter's School, portrayed by Charlotte Brontë in *Jane Eyre*.

Gérin, Winifred. *Anne Brontë.* London: Nelson. Pp. xv + 368.

Rev. by Grace Banyard in *CR*, CXCVI, 63; by Gilbert Thomas in *English*, XII,

232-33; by J. Blondel in *Études anglaises*, XII, 255-56; by DeLancey Ferguson in *HTB*, 6 Dec., p. 4; by Beatrice B. Libaire in LJ, LXXXIV, 3466; by Jacques Vallette in *Mercure de France*, CCCXXXVII, 144-45; by Arthur Boyars in S, 17 July, p. 82; in *TLS*, 29 May, p. 318.

Goldstone, Herbert. "Wuthering Heights Revisited." *EJ*, XLVIII, 175-85.

Harrison, Ada, and Stanford, Derek. *Anne Brontë: Her Life and Work*. London: Methuen. Pp. 252.
  Rev. by Howard Sergeant in *CR*, CXCVI, 127-28; by J. Blondel in *Études anglaises*, XII, 256-57; by Eric Gillett in *NER*, CLII, 189-90; by Arthur Boyars in S, 17 July, p. 82; by Frank Davison in *TC*, CLXVI, 211-12; in *TLS*, 3 Apr., p. 195. Biographical sketch by Ada Harrison; study of the poems and of *The Tenant of Wildfell Hall* by Stanford.

Hopkins, Annette Brown. *The Father of the Brontës.* . . . See VB 1958, 374.
  Rev. by Fanny E. Ratchford in *MLN*, LXXIV, 647-49; briefly in *NCF*, XIII, 367-68; in *TLS*, 16 Jan., p. 35.

Paden, William Doremus. *An Investigation of Gondal.* . . . See VB 1958, 374.
  Rev. by Mary Visick in *NCF*, XIV, 87-89; in *TLS*, 27 March, p. 178; see letter from Phyllis Bentley and reviewer's reply, *TLS*, 3 April, p. 193.

Prescott, Joseph. "*Jane Eyre* di Charlotte Brontë." (Tr. anon.) *Idee* (Rome), XV, 330-35 and 405-07.

Shannon, Edgar F., Jr. "Lockwood's Dreams and the Exegesis of *Wuthering Heights*." *NCF*, XIV, 95-109.

Solomon, Eric. "The Incest Theme in *Wuthering Heights*." *NCF*, XIV, 80-83.

Visick, Mary. *The Genesis of "Wuthering Heights*." . . . See VB 1958, 374.
  Rev. by Werner Habicht in *Anglia*, LXXVII, 111-12; by Miriam Allott in *EC*, IX, 179-87; by Arnold Kettle in *MLR*, LIV, 300-01; by Allan R. Brick in *NCF*, XIII, 358-60.

BROWNINGS (see also I, Bell, M., Ransom; III, Smidt). Landis, Paul, and Freeman, Ronald E. (eds.) *Letters of the Brownings to George Barrett.* . . . See VB 1958, 374.
  Rev. by Edward C. McAleer in *CE*, XX, 378; by R. H. Super in *JEGP*, LVIII, 138-40; by Charles T. Dougherty in *Manuscripts*, III, 182-83; by K. L. Knickerbocker in *MLN*, LXXIV, 113-15; by Walter M. Crittenden in *Personalist*, XL, 431.

Altick, Richard D. "Browning's 'Transcen-

dentalism.'" *JEGP*, LVIII, 24-28.
  Suggests that Browning is "replying" to Carlyle, who had urged writers to speak in prose.

Bevan, Bryan. "Poet's Novel." *Poetry Rev.*, L, 29-31. On *Aurora Leigh*.

Britton, John. "Browning's 'Bishop Blougram's Apology,'" 702-709." *Ex*, XVII, Item 50.

Bryson, John. *Browning*. (Writers and Their Work, No. 106.) London: Longmans. Pp. 44.
  Rev. by Jacques Vallette in *Mercure de France*, CCCXXXV, 152. ("Il semble que de nos jours il retrouve moins la faveur que les autres grands poètes victoriens, à cause de son obscurité et de ses défauts de style.")

Cundiff, Paul A. "Robert Browning: 'Our Human Speech.'" *VNL*, No. 15 (Spring), pp. 1-9.
  The meaning of "truth" in *The Ring and the Book*.

Goldsmith, Richard Weinberg. "The Relation of Browning's Poetry to Religious Controversy 1833-1868." *DA*, XIX, 2612.

Honan, Park. "Browning's Poetic Laboratory: The Uses of *Sordello*." *MP*, LVI, 162-66.
  This interesting article considers *Sordello*, not as the "*product* of Browning's linguistic and prosodic experiments," but as the "experiments themselves—a considerable laboratory of them."—R. A. D.

Hughes, R. E. "Browning's *Childe Roland* and the Broken Taboo." *Lit. and Psychology*, IX, 18-19.
  "Read from the standpoint of fantasy and symbol, 'Childe Roland' stands revealed . . . as a complex account of a strong emotional drive and consequent guilt feelings." The drive is carnality; the resolution of the guilt is retribution through castration, i.e., success through failure.

Johnson, Charles E., Jr. "The Dramatic Career of Robert Browning: A Survey and Analysis." *DA*, XIX, 2601.

King, Roma A., Jr. *The Bow and the Lyre.* . . . See VB 1958, 374.
  Rev. by Walter M. Crittenden in *Personalist*, XL, 223-24.

Knickerbocker, Kenneth L. "Robert Browning: A Modern Appraisal." *Tennessee Studies in Literature*, IV, 1-11.

Lindberg, John. "Grail-Themes in Browning's 'Childe Roland.'" *VNL*, No. 16 (Fall), pp. 27-30.

Litzinger, Boyd. "Browning's Reputation as a

Thinker, 1889-1900." *Tennessee Studies in Literature*, IV, 43-50.

Maxwell, J. C. "Browning and Christopher Smart." *N & Q*, n.s. VI, 449.

Perrine, Laurence. "Browning's Shrewd Duke." *PMLA*, LXXIV, 157-59. Rejoinder to B. R. Jerman's "Browning's Witless Duke" (see VB 1957, 405).

Pettitt, Kenneth J. "By Elizabeth Barrett Browning." *The Yale University Library Gazette*, XXXIV, 34-37. Describes contents of the Adrian Van Sindern presentation to Yale of six volumes of manuscripts. "Casa Guidi Windows," "Last Poems," "Poems and Sonnets," "The Runaway Slave at Pilgrim's Point," and a notebook. Also presentation copy to Miss Ridley of *The Battle of Marathon* (1820).

Porter, Katherine H. *Through a Glass Darkly: Spiritualism in the Browning Circle. . . .* See VB 1958, 375. Rev. by Edward C. McAleer in *CE*, XX, 270-71.

Preyer, Robert. "Robert Browning: A Reading of the Early Narratives." *ELH*, XXVI, 531-48. An account of Browning's shift from the subjective to the dramatic after *Pauline*.

Raymond, W. O. "Browning's 'The Statue and the Bust.'" *TQ*, XXVIII, 233-49. Suggests that in this poem Browning himself is directly involved and speaks in his own person, recognizing the criticism he foresees the poem will evoke. Raymond then analyzes the poem from the standpoint of dramatic action and moral, ethical, and religious positions. He concludes that "despite the approach to casuistry and the confusion of thought in which Browning is frequently befogged through his nescient theory of knowledge and distrust of reason, there is no real ground for the assertion that he is indifferent to ethical ends, or that for him 'the exercise of energy is the absolute good, irrespective of motives or of circumstances.'" This is a significant piece of interpretation by a solid Browning scholar.—R. E. F.

Rivers, Charles Leo. "Browning's Theory of the Poet, 1833-1841." *Abstracts of Diss.*, Univ. of So. Calif., 1958, 52-53.

Smalley, Donald. "Browning's View of Fact in *The Ring and the Book*." *VNL*, No. 16 (Fall), pp. 1-9. Largely a reply to Paul Cundiff's "Robert Browning: 'Our Human Speech.'" (See above).

Stange, G. Robert. "Browning's 'James Lee's Wife.'" *Ex*, XVII, Item 32. "Beside the Drawing Board" as the climactic section of the poem.

Trawick, Buckner. "The Moon Metaphor in Browning's 'One Word More.'" *N & Q*, n.s. VI, 448.

Vanson, Frederic. "Robert Browning — Christian Optimist." *LQHR*, CLXXXIV (Ser. 6, XXVIII), 331-35. This is hardly a new idea, and the treatment is cursory and shallow.—R. A. D.

Watkins, Charlotte Crawford. "The 'Abstruser Themes' of Browning's *Fifine at the Fair*." *PMLA*, LXXIV, 426-37.

BUCKLE. St. Aubyn, Giles. *A Victorian Eminence: The Life and Works of Henry Thomas Buckle. . . .* See VB 1958, 375. Rev. by Duncan Forbes in *EHR*, LXXIV, 174-75; by Geoffrey Barraclough in *History*, XLIV, 78-79.

BULWER (see III, DeMaria, Marshall, Rathburn, Shattuck).

BUTLER (see also II, Oldham; III, Rathburn).

Black, Laurence Norman. "Samuel Butler (1835-1902) as Satirist." *DA*, XX, 2283.

Jones, Joseph Jay. *The Cradle of Erewhon: Samuel Butler in New Zealand*. Austin: Univ. of Texas Pr. Pp. xii + 224.

CARLYLE (see also III, Belvin, Hoblitzelle, Williams; ARNOLD: Tillotson; BROWNINGS: Altick; TENNYSON: Marshall).

Symons, Julian (ed.). *Carlyle: Selected Works, Reminiscences, and Letters. . . .* See VB 1957, 405. Rev. by L. C. B. in *Études anglaises*, XII, 71.

Sartor Resartus. Préface et traduction par Louis Cazamian. Collection bilingue. Paris: Aubier, 1958. Pp. 486. Rev. by A. Carey Taylor in *Études anglaises*, XII, 257-58.

Hughes, A. M. D. (ed.). *Thomas Carlyle, Selections*, with Appreciations by Edward Caird, Joseph Mazzini, Matthew Arnold, George Saintsbury and others. Oxford: Clarendon Pr., 1957. Pp. xxxiv + 127. Rev. by L. C. B. in *Études anglaises*, XII, 71.

Calder, Grace J. "Erasmus A. Darwin, Friend of Thomas and Jane Carlyle." *MLQ*, XX, 36-48. Unpublished letters from Erasmus Darwin to Mrs. Wedgwood.

Ericson, Eston Everett. "An American Indebtedness to Carlyle." *N & Q*, n.s. VI, 456-57.

Mendel, Sydney. "Carlyle's 'Sartor Resartus,' II, ix." *Ex*, XVII, Item 65.

Peters, Robert Louis. "Some Illustrations of Carlyle's Symbolist Imagery." *VNL*, No. 16 (Fall), pp. 31-34.

Saunders, Beatrice. *Portraits of Genius*. London: Murray. Pp. viii + 214. Includes essay on Carlyle.

Taylor, A. Carey. "Carlyle interprète de Dante." *Études anglaises*, XII, 293-305. Traces Carlyle's references to Dante before "Hero as Poet" and analyzes how Dante fits into Carlyle's concept of the hero.

Witte, William. *Schiller and Burns and Other Essays*. Oxford: Blackwell. Pp. ix + 118. Includes essay on influence of Schiller on Carlyle.

CARROLL (see also I, Gordan).

Berol, Alfred C. "Lanrick: A Game for Two Players, by Lewis Carroll," *BSP*, LIII, 74.

Black, Duncan. *The Theory of Committees and Elections*. London: Cambridge Univ. Pr., 1958. Pp. xiii + 242. Rev. by Alan Stuart in *Economica*, n.s. XXVI, 275-76; by Anthony Downs in *JPE*, LXVII, 211-12. Prints "three scarce pamphlets" on voting theories by Rev. C. L. Dodgson.

Holmes, Roger W. "The Philosopher's Alice in Wonderland." *Antioch Rev.*, XIX, 133-49.

CHURCH. Smith, Basil Alec. *Dean Church: The Anglican Response to Newman.* . . . See VB 1958, 375. Rev. by Howard R. Murphy in *AHR*, LXIV, 432; in *Canadian Hist. Rev.*, XL, 175; by E. R. Hardy in *Church History*, XXVIII, 444-45; by J. F. Burnet in *EHR*, LXXIV, 545-46; by E. H. Eckel in *Hist. Mag. of Protestant Episcopal Church*, XXVIII, 207-09; by T. M. Parker in *History*, XLIV, 79; by K. C. Turpin in *Jour. of Eccl. Hist.*, X, 118-19.

CLOUGH (see also III, Smidt; ARNOLD: Curgenven).

Mulhauser, Frederick L. (ed.). *The Correspondence of Arthur Hugh Clough.* . . . See VB 1958, 375. Rev. by Gordon S. Haight in *MLR*, LIV, 103-04; by R. H. Super in *MP*, LVI, 213-15; by James Bertram in *RES*, n.s. X, 313-16.

Gollin, Richard M. "Arthur Hugh Clough's

Formative Years: 1819-1841." *DA*, XX, 2276. Influence of the Oxford Movement and Dr. Thomas Arnold in particular on Clough's developing moral sensibility.

Polhemus, George W. "A Clough Epitaph." *N & Q*, n.s. VI, 65-66.

Timko, Michael. "Arthur Hugh Clough: A Portrait Retouched." *VNL*, No. 15 (Spring), p. 24. Claims Clough was not a failure nor a weakling.

CONRAD (see also I, Gordan, Lynskey; III, Rathburn).

Letters to William Blackwood and David S. Meldrum. Ed. William Blackburn. . . . See VB 1958, 376. Rev. by Albert J. Guerard in *The American Scholar*, XXVIII, 244-46; by Jocelyn Baines in *Book Collector*, VIII, 441-43; in *CE*, XXI, 111; by Morton D. Zabel in *HTB*, 8 Feb., p. 4; briefly in *NCF*, XIV, 93; by J. A. S. in *NS*, LVIII, 369-70; by G. D. Klingopulos in *S*, 17 July, p. 85; in *TLS*, 24 Apr., p. 242.

Andreas, Osborn. *Joseph Conrad: A Study in Nonconformity*. New York: Philosophical Library. Pp. 212. Rev. by Walter F. Wright in *NCF*, XIV, 278-80.

Cox, Roger L. "Conrad's Nostromo as Boatswain." *MLN*, LXXIV, 303-06.

Curle, Richard. "Joseph Conrad as I Remember Him." *CR*, CXCVI, 25-31.

Guerard, Albert J. *Conrad the Novelist.* . . . See VB 1958, 376. Rev. by Adam Gillon in *Dalhousie Rev.*, XXXVIII, 533-39; by C. J. Rawson in *N & Q*, n.s. VI, 298-300; by Richard Mayne in *NS*, LVII, 264; by John Stedmond in *QQ*, LXVI, 346-47; in *TLS*, 24 Apr., p. 242.

Gurko, Leo. "Conrad's First Battleground." *Univ. of Kansas City Rev.*, XXV, 189-94. On *Almayer's Folly* as Conrad's apprenticeship.

Halverson, John, and Watt, Ian. "The Original Nostromo: Conrad's Source." *RES*, n.s. X, 45-52. Conrad's debt to *On Many Seas: The Life and Exploits of a Yankee Sailor*.

Haugh, Robert F. *Joseph Conrad: Discovery in Design.* . . . See VB 1958, 376. Rev. by John Stedmond in *QQ*, LXVI, 347; by M. C. Bradbrook in *RES*, n.s. X, 209-11.

Karl, Frederick R. "The Rise and Fall of *Un-*

der *Western Eyes.*" *NCF*, XIII, 313-27.

Kreiger, Murray. "Conrad's *Youth:* A Naive Opening to Art and Life." *CE*, XX 275-80.

Point of view and theme.

Kwartanik Neofilologiczny. V (June, 1958), Nos. 1 and 2. Warsaw.

Rev. by C. L. Barber in *MLR*, LIV, 455-56. A Conrad centenary number of this Polish quarterly.

Lohf, Kenneth A., and Sheehy, Eugene Paul (eds.). *Joseph Conrad at Mid-Century.* . . . See VB 1958, 377.

Rev. by Adam Gillon in *Dalhousie Rev.*, XXXVIII, 533-39.

McCann, Charles J. "Conrad's 'The Lagoon.'" *Ex*, XVIII, Item 3.

Moser, Thomas. *Joseph Conrad.* . . . See VB 1958, 377.

Rev. by Adam Gillon in *Dalhousie Rev.*, XXXVIII, 533-39; by Charles Barber in *MLR*, LIV, 301-02; by M. C. Bradbrook in *RES*, n.s. X, 209-11.

Mudrick, Marvin. "The Originality of Conrad." *Hudson Review*, XI, 545-53.

Conrad's innovation—his fictional technique—is the double-plot, "a developing order of actions . . . lucidly symbolic of a developing state of spirit. . . ." Illustration restricted to *Heart of Darkness.*

Napier, James. "Conrad's Praise of Joseph Hergesheimer." *N & Q*, n.s. VI, 210.

Rawson, C. J. "Conrad's 'Heart of Darkness.'" *N & Q*, n.s. VI, 110-11.

On the original of Kurtz.

Stallman, Robert Wooster. "Conrad Criticism Today." *SeR*, LXVII, 135-45.

A review of recent studies, with emphasis on Guerard and Moser.

DARWIN (see also II, Appleman, Oldham, Stevenson; III, Greene, Haber, Jones, Millhauser; HUXLEY: Bibby; KINGSLEY: Johnston).

Evolution and Natural Selection. Ed. with an introd. essay by Bert James Loewenberg. Boston: Beacon Pr. Pp. 438.

Rev. by Stanley Marion Garn in *Antioch Rev.*, XIX, 112; by George Basalla in *LJ*, LXXXIV, 1146; in *SR*, 18 Apr., p. 27; by E. W. Sinnott in *YR*, XLVIII, 578. Contains "an autobiographical sketch, some personal correspondence, descriptions of the famous Beagle voyage, and selections from his major scientific works . . . Thomas Huxley's essay on The Origin of Species is also included."

The Origin of Species: A Variorum Text. Ed.

Morse Peckham. Philadelphia: Univ. of Pennsylvania Pr. Pp. 816.

Rev. briefly by George Basalla in *LJ*, LXXXIV, 765-66; by Loren Eiseley in *Science*, n.s. CXXIX, 1121-22.

Barlow, Nora (ed.). *The Autobiography of Charles Darwin.* . . . See VB 1958, 377.

Rev. by Stanley Marion Garn in *Antioch Rev.*, XIX, 111; by Joseph Wood Krutch in *HTB*, 1 Feb., p. 3; by George Basalla in *LJ*, LXXXIV, 590; by Marston Bates in *NYTBR*, 1 Feb., p. 7; by Loren Eiseley in *Science*, n.s. CXXIX, 1121-22; by E. W. Sinnott in *YR*, XLVIII, 578-83.

Barnett, Samuel Anthony (ed.). *A Century of Darwin.* . . . See VB 1958, 377.

Rev. by Stanley Marion Garn in *Antioch Rev.*, XIX, 113-14; by A. D. Ritchie in *EHR*, LXXIV, 366; by Conway Zirkle in *Isis*, L, 282-85.

Bell, Peter Robert (ed.). *Darwin's Biological Work: Some Aspects Reconsidered.* London: Cambridge Univ. Pr. Pp. xiv + 342.

Blair, W. Frank. "Ecology and Evolution." *Antioch Rev.*, XIX, 47-55.

Blau, Joseph L. "The Influence of Darwin on American Philosophy." *Bucknell Rev.*, VIII, 141-53.

Collins, James. "Darwin's Impact on Philosophy." *Thought*, XXXIV, 185-248.

"There are no living sciences, human attitudes, or institutional powers which remain unaffected by the ideas that were catalytically released by Darwin's work . . ." A massive survey; an outstanding article.—C. T. D.

Darlington, Cyril Dean. *Darwin's Place in History.* Oxford: Blackwell. Pp. ix + 101.

Darlington, Philip J., Jr. "Darwin and Zoogeography." *PAPS*, CIII, 307-19.

Darwin, Charles Galton. "Some Episodes in the Life of Charles Darwin." *PAPS*, CIII, 609-15.

Episodes include Darwin's attitude toward Eyre case, and reminiscences of Captain Fitzroy of the *Beagle*.

Darwin, Francis (ed.). *The Life and Letters of Charles Darwin.* New York: Basic Books. 2 vols. Pp. xxii + 558 and 562.

Rev. by Loren C. Eiseley in *HTB*, 14 June, p. 1; by George Basalla in *LJ*, LXXXIV, 1521-22; by Philip Appleman in *VS*, III, 115-25.

De Beer, Sir Gavin. "Charles Darwin." *Proceedings of the British Academy*, XLIV, 163-83.

Traces the sources of Darwin's theories and evaluates the genius and importance of the scientist in a succinct, readable account.—R. E. F.

Dobzhansky, Theodosius. "Variation and Evolution." *PAPS*, CIII, 252-63.
Review of theories about origin of hereditary variations.

Dougherty, Charles T. "Darwin in the Ozarks." *VNL*, No. 15 (Spring), p. 28.

Dupree, A. Hunter. *Asa Gray.* Cambridge, Mass.: Harvard Univ. Pr. Pp. x + 505.
Biography of American botanist, friend and collaborator of Darwin.

Eiseley, Loren C. "Charles Darwin, Edward Blyth, and the Theory of Natural Selection." *PAPS*, CIII, 94-158.
Argues that Darwin got the idea of natural selection from Blyth (who saw natural selection operating as a conserving and not as a creative principle), and that Darwin did not acknowledge Blyth's contributions to his theory because he wanted to launch evolution as a new idea, owing nothing to those natural historians like Blyth who had used the concept of selection for different purposes. An ingenious and instructive essay.—D. J. G.

Eiseley, Loren C. *Darwin's Century.* . . . See VB 1958, 377.
Rev. by Stanley Marion Garn in *Antioch Rev.*, XIX, 113; by Conway Zirkle in *Isis*, L, 282-85; by Jonathan Miller in S, 30 Jan., p. 167; in *TLS*, 6 Feb., p. 74; by Sydney Smith in VS, III, 109-14.

Ellegård, Alvar. *Darwin and the General Reader: The Reception of Darwin's Theory of Evolution in the British Periodical Press, 1859-1872.* Gothenburg Studies in English, VIII, 1958. Publ. by the Univ. of Göteborg, 1958; distributed by Almqvist and Wiskell, Stockholm. Pp. 394.
Rev. by John Roach in *History*, XLIV, 281-84; in *TLS*, 1 May, p. 261.

Ewing, J. Franklin. "Darwin up to Date." *CWd*, CLXXXIX, 344-49.

Fitch, Robert E. "Darwinism and Christianity." *Antioch Rev.*, XIX, 20-32.

Fitch, Robert E. "Darwin's Gift of Positive Thinking." *NewR*, 9 Feb., pp. 12-14.
The author of *The Origin of Species* was a "kindly and gentle conservative" who believed in the Moral Law and the Happy Ending.

Fleming, Donald. "The Centenary of the *Origin of Species*." *JHI*, XX, 437-46.
This review is especially valuable for listing the studies published in recent years. —R. E. F.

Fulton, James Street. "Philosophical Adventures of the Idea of Evolution: 1859-1959." *Rice Institute Pamphlet*, XLVI, 1-31.

Girvetz, Harry K. "Philosophical Implications of Darwinism." *Antioch Rev.*, XIX, 9-19.

Glass, Hiram Bentley, *et al.* (eds.). *Forerunners of Darwin, 1745-1859.* Baltimore: Johns Hopkins Pr. Pp. 471.
Rev. by Loren Eiseley in *Science*, n.s. CXXIX, 1121-22; by Philip Appleman in VS, III, 115-25.

Gleason, Robert W. "A Note on Theology and Evolution." *Thought*, XXXIV, 249-58.

Goldman, Irving. "Evolution and Anthropology," VS, III, 55-75.

Greene, John C. "Darwin and Religion." *PAPS*, CIII, 716-25.

Himmelfarb, Gertrude. *Darwin and the Darwinian Revolution.* New York: Doubleday. Pp. 480.
Rev. by Joshua C. Gregory in *CR*, CXCVI, 313-14; by John Roach in *History*, XLIV, 281-84; by J. W. Burrow in *History Today*, IX, 575-76; by I. Bernard Cohen in *HTB*, 10 May, pt. 2, p. 6; by George Basalla in *LJ*, LXXXIV; unfavorably by Gavin de Beer in *Nature*, CLXXXIV, 385-88; unfavorably by Anthony West in *New Yorker*, 10 Oct., p. 188; by Anthony Barnett in *NS*, 1 Aug., p. 139; by Loren Eiseley in *NYTBR*, 26 Apr., p. 5; by Joseph Wood Krutch in *Reporter*, 28 May, pp. 40-42; by D. W. Harding in S, 14 Aug., p. 200; by Michael Polanyi in *TC*, CLXVI, 196-99; favorably in *TLS*, 17 July, p. 417; unfavorably by Philip Appleman in VS, III, 115-25; by E. W. Sinnott in *YR*, XLVIII, 578-83.

Hopkins, Vincent C. "Darwinism and America." *Thought*, XXXIV, 259-68.

Huxley, Francis. "Charles Darwin: Life and Habit." *The American Scholar*, Part I, XXVIII, 489-99; Part II, XXIX, 85-93.
A reappraisal of Darwin's essential personality.

Huxley, Julian. "Darwin and the Idea of Evolution." *HJ*, LVIII, 1-12.
A chapter from *A Book that Shook the World* (see VB 1958, 377), which also includes Theodosius Dobzhansky, "The Causes of Evolution"; Reinhold Niebuhr, "Christianity and Darwin's Revolution"; Oliver L. Reiser, "The Concept of Evolution in Philosophy"; Swami Nikhilananda, "Hinduism and the Idea of Evolution."

Hyman, Stanley Edgar. "The 'Origin' as Scripture." *VQR*, XXXV, 540-52.

179

Irvine, William. "The Influence of Darwin on Literature." *PAPS*, CIII, 616-28.

Lerner, I. Michael. "The Concept of Natural Selection: A Centennial View." *PAPS*, CIII, 173-82.

Loewenberg, Bert James. "Darwin Scholarship in the Darwin Year." *American Quart.*, XI, 526-33.

Loewenberg, Bert James. *Darwin, Wallace and the Theory of Natural Selection: Including the Linnean Society Papers.* Cambridge: Arlington Books. Pp. viii + 97.
Rev. by Stanley Marion Garn in *Antioch Rev.*, XIX, 112; in *The Mississippi Valley Hist. Rev.*, XLVI, 169; by E. W. Sinnott in *YR*, XLVIII, 578-83.

Loewenberg, Bert James. "The Mosaic of Darwinian Thought." *VS*, III, 3-18.

London Quarterly and Holborn Review, October.
A centennial symposium on Darwin, with articles as follows: Coulson, C. A., "The Changing Relationship of Science and Religion," pp. 280-83; Heathcote, A. W., "Science and Religion Today," pp. 284-88; Fothergill, P. C., "Darwinian Theory and Its Effects," pp. 289-94; Raven, C. E., "The Struggle for Existence," pp. 295-98; Smith, D. S., "Inheritance," pp. 299-305; Howarth, F., "Evolution or Special Creation," pp. 306-309; Grensted, L. W., "Determinism in Psychology," pp. 310-14.

Lurie, Edward. "Louis Agassiz and the Idea of Evolution." *VS*, III, 87-108.

Mayr, Ernst. "Agassiz, Darwin, and Evolution." *HLB*, XIII, 165-94.

Müntzing, Arne. "Darwin's Views on Variation under Domestication in the Light of Present-Day Knowledge." *PAPS*, CIII, 190-220.

Passmore, John. "Darwin's Impact on British Metaphysics." *VS*, III, 41-54.

Peckham, Morse. "Darwinism and Darwinisticism," *VS*, III, 19-40.
Darwinism is a set of propositions and assumptions which may properly be ascribed to a source in the *Origin*; Darwinisticism is a set of propositions and assumptions (such as the belief that evolution works toward some distant good or that Darwin revealed immanent laws of nature) improperly ascribed to Darwin by those who do not fully understand the scientific character of his investigation and conclusions. The influence of Darwinisticism, it is argued, is often confused with that of Darwinism.

Rattray, R. F. "Neodarwinism Challenged." *QR*, CCXCVII, 393-99.

Raven, Charles E. "Charles Darwin: The Man and His Work." *SAQ*, LVIII, 421-26.

Rohmann, Paul H. "The Origin of Species—100 Years Later." *Antioch Rev.*, XIX, 5-8.

Simpson, George Eaton. "Darwin and 'Social Darwinism.'" *Antioch Review*, XIX, 33-45.

Simpson, George Gaylord. "Anatomy and Morphology: Classification and Evolution: 1859 and 1959." *PAPS*, CIII, 286-306.

Spencer, T. J. B. *From Gibbon to Darwin.* Birmingham: Univ. of Birmingham Pr. Pp. 19.
Rev. in *TLS*, 20 Nov., p. 682.

T., J. D. "Proœmium de Anno Mirabili." *Rice Institute Pamphlet*, XLVI, v-x.
The introductory article for a number devoted to the effects of "Darwinism in philosophy and literature as well as in biology and paleontology."

Thomas, J. D. "The Supernatural Naturalism of Dreiser's Novels." *Rice Institute Pamphlet*, XLVI, 53-69.
Influence of Darwin in the American's novels.

Tsanoff, Radoslav A. "Evolution, Teleology, and History." *Rice Institute Pamphlet*, XLVI, 32-52.

Wolsky, Alexander. "A Hundred Years of Darwinism in Biology." *Thought*, XXXIV, 165-84.

Wyllie, Irvin G. "Social Darwinism and the Businessman." *PAPS*, CIII, 629-35.

Wynn-Tyson, Esme. "Darwinism and Spiritual Evolution." *CR*, CXCVI, 234-36.
Origen's heresy as analogous to the doctrine of evolution.

Zimmerman, Paul (ed.). *Darwin, Evolution and Creation.* St. Louis: Concordia. Pp. xii + 231.

DAVIDSON. Macleod, Robert (ed.). *Poems and Ballads.* London: Unicorn Pr. Pp. 226.
Rev. in *TLS*, 27 Mar., p. 175.

DICKENS (see also II, Weber; III, Altick, Ford, Rathburn, Williams, Woolf).

Adrian, Arthur A. *Georgina Hogarth and the Dickens Circle.* . . . See VB 1958, 377.
Rev. by Wolfgang Schmidt-Hidding in *Anglia*, LXXVII, 110-11; by John L.

Bradley in *MLR*, LIV, 102-03; by Morton Dauwen Zabel in *NCF*, XIII, 363-66; by William D. Templeman in *Personalist*, XL, 430-31; by John Butt in *RES*, n.s. X, 207-09.

Aylmer, Felix. *Dickens Incognito*. London: Hart-Davis. Pp. 95.

Rev. by Ralph Partridge in *NS*, LVIII, 810-11; by R. C. Churchill in *S*, 11 Dec., p. 881; in *TLS*, 27 Nov., p. 694. Argues that Ellen Ternan gave birth to a son by Dickens in 1867.

Aylmer, Felix. "Dickens's Hidden Life." *The Sunday Times* (London), 22 Nov., pp. 5, 33.

Extracts from Aylmer's *Dickens Incognito*. (See below, Graham Storey.)

Bishop, Jonathan. "The Hero-Villain of *Oliver Twist*." *VNL*, No. 15 (Spring), pp. 14-16.

Butt, John, and Tillotson, Kathleen. *Dickens at Work*. . . . See VB 1958, 378.

Rev. by Daniel F. Howard in *KR*, XXI, 309-20; by Lauriat Lane, Jr., in *MLN*, LXXIV, 543-46; by J. D. Jump in *RES*, n.s. X, 98-100; by Charles J. McCann in *Thought*, XXXIV, 313-14.

Butt, John. "The Topicality of *Little Dorritt*." *TQ*, XXIX, 1-11.

Cahoon, Herbert. "News and Notes." *BSP*, LIII, 78, 274.

Two notes on copies of a broadside written by Dickens entitled "The Great International Walking-Match."

Cox, Charles B. "Comic Viewpoints in *Sketches by Boz*." *English*, XII, 132-38.

Faith in individual goodness prevents Dickens's humor from ever becoming cynical.

Dickensian (quarterly), Vol. LV (Nos. 327-29). . . . See VB 1932, 422.

Items as follows: Baetzhold, H. G., "What Place Was the Model for Martin Chuzzlewit's 'Eden'? A Last Word on the 'Cairo Legend' " (pp. 169-75); Carlton, W. J., "Dickens's Debut in America" (pp. 55-56); Carlton, W. J., "The Dickens Diaries" (pp. 134-39); Carlton, W. J., "A Five-Year-Old Critic of *Nicholas Nickleby*" (pp. 89-93); Collins, P. A. W., "Dickens and the Ragged Schools" (pp. 94-109); Dolmetsch, C. R., "Dickens and *The Dead Heart*" (pp. 179-87); Greaves, J., "Hail Columbia!" (pp. 123-26); Greenhalgh, M., "*Edwin Drood*: The Twilight of a God" (pp. 68-75); Hill, T. W., "Notes on *Great Expectations*" (pp. 57-59); Lane, L., Jr., "Dickens and the Double" (pp. 47-55); Major, G., "No Thoroughfare" (pp. 175-78); Morley, M.,

"The Theatrical Ternans" (pp. 36-44, 109-117, 159-68); Peyrouton, N. C., "The Eytinge Portrait" (pp. 9-11); Peyrouton, N. C., "Rapping the Rappers: More Grist for the Biographers' Mill" (pp. 19-30, 75-89); Reed, J., "The Fulfilment of Pip's Expectations" (pp. 12-18); Staples, L. C., "48 Doughty Street: Dickens Negotiates" (pp. 5-9); Verkoren, L., "Dickens in Holland" (pp. 44-46).

Engel, Monroe. *The Maturity of Dickens*. Cambridge, Mass.: Harvard Univ. Pr. Pp. 202.

Rev. by N. C. Peyrouton in *Dickensian*, LV, 155-56; in *Lit, and Psych.*, IX, 23; by Earle F. Walbridge in *LJ*, LXXXIV, 1892; by Edgar Johnson in *NCF*, XIV, 182-84; by R. C. Churchill in *S*, 20 Nov., p. 679; in *TLS*, 27 Nov., p. 678.

Fielding, Kenneth Joshua. *Charles Dickens: A Critical Introduction*. . . . See VB 1958, 379.

Rev. by Pansy Pakenham in *Dickensian*, LV, 31-32; by Sylvère Monod in *Études anglaises*, XII 169; by Earle F. Walbridge in *LJ*, LXXXIV, 1124; by J. Hillis Miller in *NCF*, XIV, 178-82.

Folland, Harold F. "The Doer and the Deed: Theme and Pattern in *Barnaby Rudge*." *PMLA*, LXXIV, 406-17.

Lane, Lauriat, Jr. "Mr. Pickwick and *The Dance of Death*." NCF, XIV, 171-72.

Manning, John. *Dickens on Education*. Toronto: Univ. of Toronto Pr. Pp. 251.

Miller, Joseph Hillis. *Charles Dickens: The World of His Novels*. . . . See VB 1958, 379.

Rev. by G. Robert Stange in *CE*, XX, 379; by R. D. McMaster in *Dalhousie Rev.*, XXXVIII, 512-16; by N. C. Peyrouton in *Dickensian*, LV, 32-33; by Marvin Rosenberg in *JEGP*, LVIII, 544-45; by Daniel F. Howard in *KR*, XXI, 309-20; by Hesketh Pearson in *Listener*, 26 Feb., p. 388; by Bradford A. Booth in *MP*, LVII, 69-71 ("one of the most important Dickens studies of our time"); by Sheila M. Smith in *N & Q*, n.s. VI, 294-95; by Sylvère Monod in *NCF*, XIII, 360-63; by Gabriel Pearson in *NS*, LVII, 306-07; by D. J. Dooley in *QQ*, LXVI, 349; by Lionel Stevenson in *SAQ*, LVIII, 478-79; in *TLS*, 16 Jan., p. 30.

Monod, Sylvère. *Charles Dickens*. Paris: Editions Seghers, 1958. Pp. 224.

Rev. by R. Cazes in *Études anglaises*, XII, 259 (". . . un modèle du genre par sa valeur sa condensation"); by Jacques Vallette in *Mercure de France*, CCCXXXVI, 528.

Moritz, Harold Kennett. "Visual Organization

in Dickens." *DA*, XX, 1026-27.

Nelson, Harland Stanley. "Evangelicalism in the Novels of Charles Dickens." *DA*, XX, 2295-96.

Nisbet, Ada. "The Autobiographical Matrix of *Great Expectations*." *VNL*, No. 15 (Spring), pp. 10-13.

Pakenham, Pansy. "Dickens and the Class Question." *VNL*, No. 16 (Fall), p. 30.

Spilka, Mark. "Kafka and Dickens: The Country Sweetheart." *Amer. Imago*, XVI, 367-78.
Suggests parallel themes in *David Copperfield* and *Amerika*.

Stone, Harry. "Dickens and Interior Monologue." *PQ*, XXXVIII, 52-65.
A study of Dickens's experiments with this form, especially in *Household Words* sketches.

Stone, Harry. "Dickens and the Jews," *VS*, II, 223-53.

Storey, Graham. " 'Dickens Incognito': New Evidence." *The Sunday Times* (London), 13 Dec., p. 6.
As co-editor of the Pilgrim Edition of Dickens's letters, Storey investigated Aylmer's hypothesis and finds evidence to refute it. The same article contains a reply from Aylmer apologizing for his "error" and suggesting possible theories about the child of Ellen Ternan and Dickens.

Tillotson, Kathleen. "Oliver Twist." *Essays and Studies by Members of the English Association*, XII, 87-105.
Undertakes to trace the plan and development of the novel as a slow and long process in which Dickens explores his own childhood and early youth.

Wright, James A. "The Comic Imagination of the Young Dickens." *DA*, XX, 294.
The study, based on six early novels, forms a definition of imagination based on Taine's, Bagehot's, and Van Ghent's, adding "precision" as a necessary element.

DISRAELI (see also II, Elletson, Hanham; III, Williams).

Edelman, Maurice. "A Political Novel: Disraeli Sets a Lively Pace." *TLS*, 7 Aug., suppl., pp. vi-vii.
A Member of Parliament on *Coningsby* as "one of the seminal books of the nineteenth century."

DOYLE. Carr, John Dickson (ed.). *Great Stories by Sir Arthur Conan Doyle*. A centenary volume. London: Murray. Pp. 256.
Rev. briefly in *TLS*, 18 Dec., p. 746.

Carr, John Dickson. *La Vie de Sir Arthur Conan Doyle*; Traduit de l'anglais par André Algarron. Paris: Robert Laffont, 1958. Pp. 468.
Rev. by P. Weil-Nordon in *Études anglaises*, XII, 369-70.

Harrison, Michael. *In the Footsteps of Sherlock Holmes*. . . . See VB 1958, 380.
Rev. by P. W. N. in *Études anglaises*, XII, 264.

Holroyd, James Edward. *Baker Street By-Ways*. London: Allen and Unwin. Pp. 158.
Rev. by Pierre Weil-Nordon in *Études anglaises*, XII, 264-65; by Anthony Boucher in *NYTBR*, 5 July, p. 12; in *TLS*, 22 May, p. 311.

Leaves from the Copper Beeches. Narbeth, Pa.: Livingstone Pub. Co. Pp. viii + 134.
Essays by members of the Sons of the Copper Beeches, scion society of the Baker Street Irregulars.

Loesch, Katherine. "A Dangerous Criminal Still at Large." *N & Q*, n.s. VI, 8-9.
On "the undoubted identity of Professor Moriarty and Mr. T. S. Eliot's *Macavity: The Mystery Cat*."

Preston, Priscilla. "A Note on T. S. Eliot and Sherlock Holmes." *MLR*, LIV, 397-99.

Weil-Nordon, Pierre, "George Meredith Vu par Sir Arthur Conan Doyle." *Études anglaises*, XII, 231-36.

ELIOT (see also I, Gordan; II, Appleman, Stevenson; III, Rathburn, Williams, Woolf).

Barry, James D. "The Literary Reputation of George Eliot's Fiction: A Supplementary Bibliography." *BB*, XXII, 176-82.

Beaty, Jerome. "*Daniel Deronda* and the Question of Unity in Fiction." *VNL*, No. 15 (Spring), pp. 16-20.

Carroll, D. R. "The Unity of 'Daniel Deronda.' " *EC*, IX, 369-80.
Argues against F. R. Leavis for the organic unity of the novel.

Carroll, David R. "Unity Through Analogy: An Interpretation of 'Middlemarch.' " *VS*, II, 305-16.

Casson, Allan. " 'Thee' and 'you' in 'Adam Bede.' " *N & Q*, n.s. VI, 451.

Deneau, Daniel P. "From 'Amos Barton' to *Daniel Deronda*: Studies in the Imagery of George Eliot's Fiction." *DA*, XX, 1783.

Deneau, Daniel P. "Inconsistencies and Inaccuracies in *Adam Bede*." *NCF*, XIV, 71-75.

Deneau, Daniel P. "A Note on George Eliot's 'Amos Barton'–Reticence and Chronology." *N & Q*, n.s. VI, 450-51.

Haight, Gordon S. "George Eliot: The Moralist as Artist." *VNL*, No. 16 (Fall), pp. 25-27.

Hardy, Barbara. *The Novels of George Eliot: A Study in Form.* London: Athlone. Pp. xii + 242.

Rev. by Gilbert Thomas in *English*, XII, 232-33; by Jacques Vallette in *Mercure de France*, CCCXXXVI, 338-39; by Graham Handley in *N & Q*, n.s. VI, 198; by Gordon S. Haight in *NCF*, XIV, 272-76; by John Jones in *NS*, LVII, 698-99; in *TLS*, 24 Apr., p. 239.

Maheu, Placide-Gustave. *La Pensée religieuse et morale de George Eliot.* Paris: Didier. Pp. 135.

Rev. by Irène Simon in *Études anglaises*, XII, 261-63.

Monod, Sylvère. "George Eliot et les personnages de *Middlemarch.*" *Études anglaises*, XII, 306-14.

Peterson, Virgil A. "Forgotten Bastards: A Note on *Daniel Deronda.*" *VNL*, No. 15 (Spring), p. 29.

Stump, Reva. *Movement and Vision in George Eliot's Novels.* Seattle, Wash.: Univ. of Washington Pr. Pp. xi + 232.

Rev. by R. G. Baldwin in *Dalhousie Rev.*, XXXIX, 245-47; by Jerome Thale in *NCF*, XIV, 276-78; by Ben Ray Redman in *SR*, 18 July, pp. 32-33; in *TLS*, 11 Sept., p. 520.

Thale, Jerome. *The Novels of George Eliot.* New York: Columbia Univ. Pr. Pp. 175.

Rev. by B. B. Libaire in *LJ*, LXXXIV, 1893; by Ben Ray Redman in *SR*, 18 July, pp, 32-33; in *TLS*, 6 Nov., p. 638.

Thomson, Fred C. "The Genesis of *Felix Holt.*" *PMLA*, LXXIV, 576-84.

Doubts that *Felix Holt* was conceived as a political novel.

Tosello, Maria. *Le Fonti Italiane della "Romola" di George Eliot.* Torino: Giappichelli, 1956. Pp. 144.

Rev. by John A. Huzzard in *MLQ*, XX, 289-91.

Welsh, Alexander. "George Eliot and the Romance." *NCF*, XIV, 241-54.

George Eliot's use of characteristics of the romance.

Wolff, Michael. "Marian Evans to George Eliot: the Moral and Intellectual Foundations of Her Career." *DA*, XIX, 2350.

"The primary material of this study is the body of book reviews, written by Marian Evans between 1855 and 1857. . . . This study aims to conduct the reader from Marian Evans' most basic assumptions through the logic of her ideas and up to the threshold of her artistic career."

ELLIS. Calder-Marshall, Arthur. *Havelock Ellis.* London: Hart-Davis. Pp. 292.

Rev. by Herbert Read in *Listener*, 29 Jan., p. 218; by Eric Gillett in *NER*, CLII, 110; by D. W. Harding in *S*, 6 Feb., p. 198; in *TLS*, 6 Feb., pp. 65-66.

Collis, John Stewart. *Havelock Ellis: Artist of Life: A Study of His Life and Work.* London: Cassell. Pp. vii + 245.

Rev. by Joseph Wood Krutch in *HTB*, 29 Mar., p. 3; by Herbert Read in *Listener*, 29 Jan., p. 218; by Harold Lancour in *LJ*, LXXXIV, 748; by Eric Gillett in *NER*, CLII, 111; by Peter Quennell in *NYTBR*, 22 Mar., p. 7; by D. W. Harding in *S*, 6 Feb., p. 198; by E. M. L. Burchard in *SR*, 11 Apr., p. 42; in *TLS*, 6 Feb., p. 65.

FITZGERALD (see also II, Stevenson; III, Jones).

Arberry, Arthur John. *The Romance of the Rubáiyát.* London: Allen and Unwin. Pp. 244.

Rev. by Grace Banyard in *CR*, CXCV, 320; by André Guimbrétière in *Études anglaises*, XII, 259-60; in *HTB*, 2 Aug., p. 11; by Paul C. Wermuth in *LJ*, LXXXIV, 1514; in *TLS*, 27 Mar., p. 179 (see also letters on the Omar Khayyám Club, founded in 1892, by Derek Hudson and Alan Thomas in *TLS*, 3 Apr., p. 193).

Barth, Max. "Jubiläum eines Buches." *Deutsches Rundschau*, LXXXV, 1017-24.

Includes German translations of several of FitzGerald's quatrains.

Emden, Cecil Stuart. *Poets in Their Letters.* New York: Oxford Univ. Pr. Pp. xii + 232.

Rev. in *QR*, CCXCVII, 475-76; unfavorably in *TLS*, 17 Apr., p. 226. Includes character-sketch of FitzGerald, related to his correspondence.

Piddington, R. A. "FitzGerald's Indian Colonel." *N & Q*, n.s. VI, 449-50.

Quinlan, John. "The Centenary of the Rubáiyát." *CR*, CXCV, 180-81.

Weber, Carl J. (ed.). *FitzGerald's Rubáiyát.* . . . See VB 1958, 380.

Rev. by Edward Weeks in *AM*, CCIV, 79; in *TLS*, 27 Mar., p. 179 (see also the letter by Reginald Horrox, "The Rubáiyát after One Hundred Years," *TLS*, 10 Apr., p. 209); by Jerome H. Buckley in *VNL*, No. 15 (Spring), pp. 20-21.

Weber, Carl J. "Preparing for the Centenary of FitzGerald's *Rubáiyát.*" *Colby Libr. Quart.,* V, 5-14.

Correction of errors about the publication date and the "discovery" of the *Rubáiyát.*

GASKELL (see also III, Rathburn, Williams).

Altick, Richard D. "Dion Boucicault Stages *Mary Barton.*" *NCF,* XIV, 129-41.

The transformation of Mrs. Gaskell's novel of social criticism into a successful stage melodrama.

GILBERT. Vandiver, Edward P., Jr. "The Significance of *The Yeomen of the Guard.*" *Furman Studies, Furman Univ. Bulletin,* VII, 1-5.

GISSING (see also III, O'Sullivan, Rathburn).

Murry, J. Middleton. *Katherine Mansfield and Other Literary Studies.* London: Constable. Pp. xiii + 162.

Rev. in *TLS,* 1 May, p. 254. Includes essay on Gissing.

Ward, Alfred Charles. *Gissing.* (Writers and Their Work.) London: Longmans. Pp. 43.

Rev. by Jacques Vallette in *Mercure de France,* CCCXXXVII, 145; noted in *TLS,* 4 Sept., p. 511.

GLADSTONE (see II, Hanham, James, Medlicott; III, Jones).

GOSSE (see also **SWINBURNE:** Bissell).

Brugmans, Linette F. (ed.). *The Correspondence of André Gide and Edmund Gosse, 1904-1928.* New York: New York Univ. Pr. Pp. ix + 220.

Harper, George Graham, Jr. "A Study of the Prose Works of Sir Edmund Gosse, 1872-1907." *DA,* XX, 2290-91.

Kirk, Clara and Rudolf. "Letters to an 'Enchanted Ghost': W. D. Howells to Edmund Gosse." *Journal of the Rutgers University Library,* XXII (June, 1959), 1-25.

Five unpublished letters of Howell to Gosse in Houghton Library, Harvard, augment a discussion of the relationship of the two men.

Mattheisen, Paul F. "Edmund Gosse: A Literary Record." *DA,* XX, 299.

Shuman, R. Baird. "A New Edmund Gosse Letter." *N & Q,* n.s. VI, 33 (see also letter from George Graham Harper, *N & Q,* n.s. VI, 196).

GRAHAME. Braybrooke, Neville. "Kenneth Grahame Centenary." *CR,* CXCV, 236-38.

Green, Peter. *Kenneth Grahame.* London: Murray. Pp. xvi + 400.

Rev. by Ralph Lawrence in *English,* XII, 233-34; by L. F. Bonnerot in *Études anglaises,* XII, 265; by Alan Pryce-Jones in *HTB,* 7 June, p. 1; by Earle F. Walbridge in *LJ,* LXXXIV, 1124; by Eric Gillett in *NER,* CLII, 188-89; by James Reeves in *NS,* 21 Mar., p. 408; by Peter Quennell in *NYTBR,* 24 May, p. 4; by G. D. Klingopulos in *S,* 13 Mar., p. 378; by Walter Teller in *SR,* 30 May, p. 18; in *TLS,* 13 Mar., p. 144.

"The Kenneth Grahame Centenary," *Publishers' Weekly,* 16 Feb., pp. 76-78.

HALLAM. Nowell-Smith, Simon. "A. H. Hallam's *Poems,* 1830." *Book Collector,* VIII, 430-31.

Describes two forms in which the book is found.

HARDY (see also I, Gordan; II, Weber; III, Ford, Martin, Rathburn).

"The Dorsetshire Labourer." (First printed in 1883; now reprinted in) *The Countryman,* Oxfordshire, England, LVI, 497-502.

Bailey, J. O. "Hardy's Visions of the Self." *SP,* LVI, 74-101.

Hardy's use of apparitions to reveal to the characters in his novels their own inner nature and to bring them to accept responsibility for disasters they had blamed on circumstances.

Block, Haskell M. "James Joyce and Thomas Hardy." *MLQ,* XIX, 337-42.

A letter by Joyce refusing to contribute to an issue of the *Nouvelle Revue* dedicated to Hardy's memory.

Calhoun, Philo. "An Old Architect's Last Draft." *Colby Libr. Quart.,* V, 61-66.

A marble tablet in the Dorchester Post-office designed by Hardy in his eighty-first year.

[Cary, Richard.] "Weber and the Wessex Giant." *Colby Libr. Quart.,* V, 34-35.

Brief review of a distinguished career of Hardy scholarship.

Clifford, Emma. "Thomas Hardy and the Historians." *SP,* LVI, 654-68.

Another look at the sources of *The Dynasts.* Suggests that Hardy may have been more interested in the historians' interpretations of facts than has generally been supposed.

Green, David Bonnell. "A New Thomas Hardy Letter." *N & Q,* n.s. VI, 34-35.

Herman, William R. "Hardy's 'Tess of the D'Urbervilles.'" *Ex,* XVIII, Item 16.

Hogan, Donald Joseph. "Structural Design in Thomas Hardy's Poetry." *DA*, XX, 2291.
Hardy's "ordering of experience was instinctively analytical." He sees the world through his own metaphors of pattern.

Hurley, Robert. "A Note on Some Emendations in *Jude the Obscure*." *VNL*, No. 15 (Spring), pp. 29-30.

Hynes, Sam. "Hardy and Barnes: Notes on Literary Influence." *SAQ*, LVIII, 44-54.
The form of Hardy's poems was influenced by the Dorsetshire poet, William Barnes.

Lowe, Robert Liddell. "Three New Hardy Letters." *MLR*, LIV, 396-97.
Letters to the editor of the *Contemporary Review*.

Maxwell, J. C. "Hardy's 'Our Exploits at West Poley': A Correction." *N & Q*, n.s. VI, 113.

Paterson, John. "'The Mayor of Casterbridge' as Tragedy." *VS*, III, 151-72.

Paterson, John. "*The Return of the Native* as Antichristian Document." *NCF*, XIV, 111-27.
The pagan and demoniacal elements in the novel which appear to be a denunciation of the Christian outlook.

Perkins, David. "Hardy and the Poetry of Isolation." *ELH*, XXVI, 253-70.

Purdum, Richard. "A Year and a Day in 'The Return of the Native.'" *N & Q*, n.s. VI, 40.

Slack, Robert C. "Some Characteristics of Hardy's Novels," pp. 41-52 in *Six Novelists*. Carnegie Series in English, No. 5. Pittsburgh: Carnegie Institute of Technology Pr. Pp. 81.

Weber, Carl J. (ed.). Introduction, Notes, Glossary and a Map for *Far from the Madding Crowd*. New York: Rinehart. Pp. xxvi + 388.

Wheeler, Otis B. "Four Versions of *The Return of the Native*." *NCF*, XIV, 27-44.
A study of the textual revisions that Hardy made in various editions of the novel; they involve significant changes in plot and character.

HARRIS (see also III, O'Sullivan; WILDE: Harris).

Brome, Vincent. *Frank Harris*. London: Cassell. Pp. ix + 246.
Rev. by Hesketh Pearson in *Listener*, 5 Feb., p. 257; by Eric Gillett in *NER*, CLII, 149-50; by Evelyn Waugh in *S*,

20 Feb., p. 268 (an attack on Harris; see a letter by Michael Foot, 27 Feb., pp. 297-98); in *TLS*, 20 Feb., p. 91.

HARRISON. Ricks, C. B. "Frederic Harrison and Bergson." *N & Q*, n.s. VI, 175-78.
Harrison's comments on Bergson's *Introduction to Metaphysics*.

Salmon, Martha. "Frederic Harrison: The Evolution of an English Positivist, 1831-1881." *DA*, XX, 1356.

HOPKINS (see also III, Walsh; ROSSETTI: Mellown).

The Journals and Papers of Gerard Manley Hopkins. Edited by Humphry House, completed by Graham Storey. London: Oxford Univ. Pr. Pp. xxxii + 579.
Rev. by B. A. Park in *BA*, XXXIII, 461; by C. Busby in *Dublin Rev.*, CCXXXIII, 183-90; by John Wain in *HTB*, 15 Mar., p. 8; by Burton A. Robie in *LJ*, LXXXIV, 1133-34; by Jacques Vallette in *Mercure de France*, CCCXXXVI, 337; by Eric Gillett in *NER*, CLII, 150; by John Jones in *NS*, LVII, 338-39; by Samuel French Morse in *NYTBR*, 5 Apr., p. 4; by W. W. Robson in *S*, 27 Feb., p. 300; in *StI*, XLVIII, 226; in *TLS*, 25 Sept., p. 544.

The Sermons and Devotional Writings of Gerard Manley Hopkins. Ed. with an Introduction by Christopher Devlin, S.J. London: Oxford Univ. Pr. Pp. xiv + 370.
Rev. by C. Busby in *Dublin Rev.*, CCXXXIII, 183-90; by John Pick in *MP*, LVII, 137-38; by John Jones in *NS*, LVII, 338-39; by Samuel French Morse in *NYTBR*, 5 Apr., p. 4; by W. W. Robson in *S*, 27 Feb., p. 300; in *StI*, XLVIII, 226; in *TLS*, 25 Sept., p. 544.

Abraham, John August. "Hopkins and Scotus: An Analogy between Inscape and Individuation." *DA*, XX, 2281-82.

Allison, Alexander. "Hopkins' 'I Wake and Feel the Fell of Dark.'" *Ex*, XVII, Item 54.

Baum, Paull F. "Sprung Rhythm." *PMLA*, LXXIV, 418-25.
Presents Sprung Rhythm as not a modification of conventional verse, but a new creation.

Goodin, George. "Man and Nature in Hopkins' 'Ribblesdale.'" *N & Q*, n.s. VI, 453-54.

Heuser, Alan. *The Shaping of Vision of Gerard Manley Hopkins.* . . . See VB 1958, 382.
Rev. by B. A. Park in *BA*, XXXIII, 351; briefly in *CE*, XXI, 113; by Thomas P. McDonnell in *CWd*, CLXXXIX, 174-75;

by Derek Stanford in *English*, XII, 146; by W. H. Gardner in *MLR*, LIV, 424-25; by John Pick in *MP*, LVI, 282-83; by W. C. Lougheed in *QQ*, LXVI, 173-74; by John Edward Hardy in *YR*, XLVIII, 410-13.

Howarth, R. G. "An Unconscious Prophet of Hopkins." *N & Q*, n.s. VI, 443-44.
On Edwin Guest, author of *A History of English Rhythms*, 1838.

Johnson, W. Stacy. "The Imagery of Gerard Manley Hopkins: Fire, Light, and the Incarnation." *VNL*, No. 16 (Fall), pp. 18-23.

Litzinger, Boyd. "Hopkins' 'The Wreck of the Deutschland,' Stanza 33." *Ex*, XVIII, Item 19.
(A reply to Scheve; see below.)

Mellown, Elgin W. "Gerard Manley Hopkins and His Public, 1889-1918." *MP*, LVII, 94-99.
Hopkins had a limited, but receptive audience before Bridges published the *Poems*.

Pearson, W. H. "G. M. Hopkins and 'Gifted Hopkins.' " *N & Q*, n.s. VI, 452-53.

Scheve, Adalbert. "Hopkins' 'The Wreck of the Deutschland,' Stanza 33." *Ex*, XVII, Item 60.

Schoeck, R. J. "Peine Forte et Dure and Hopkins' 'Margaret Clitheroe.' " *MLN*, LXXIV, 220-24.
Hopkins' use of John Morris, *The Troubles of Our Catholic Forefathers*, 1877.

Stillinger, Jack. "Hopkins' 'Skate's Heel' in 'The Windhover.' " *N & Q*, n.s. VI, 215-16.

Sister Therese, S. N. D. "Hopkins' 'Spelt from Sibyl's Leaves.' " *Ex*, XVII, Item 45.

HOUSMAN. *Complete Poems of A. E. Housman*, edited by Tom Burns Haber with an introduction by Basil Davenport. Centennial Edition. New York: Holt. Pp. 268.
Rev. by William White in *BB*, XXII, 199; by DeLancey Ferguson in *HTB*, 29 Mar., p. 1; by Ivor Brown in *NYTBR*, 29 Mar., p. 1. On the text, see letter by John Carter in *TLS*, 29 May, p. 321; reply by Haber, 24 July, p. 435; rejoinder by Carter, 14 Aug., p. 471.

"A. E. Housman Centenary." *Publishers' Weekly*, 9 Mar., pp. 26-28.

Hawkins, Maude M. *A. E. Housman: Man behind a Mask*. . . . See VB 1958, 382.
Rev. by Tom Burns Haber in *JEGP*, LVIII, 147-49; by John W. Stevenson in *SAQ*, LVIII, 130-32.

Marlow, Norman. *A. E. Housman: Scholar and Poet*. . . . See VB 1958, 382.
Rev. briefly by B. A. Park in *BA*, XXXIII, 89; briefly in *CE*, XXI, 113; by Tom Burns Haber in *JEGP*, LVIII, 149-51; by William White in *MLN*, LXXIV, 652-54; by John W. Stevenson in *SAQ*, LVIII, 130-32.

Sparrow, John. "A Housman 'Reminiscence.' " *RES*, n.s. X, 183-85.

The Times. "A. E. Housman: A Centenary Exhibition." *TLS*, 4 Sept., p. 512.
An exhibition held at University College, London, with a catalogue by John Carter.

Walde, E. H. S. and Dorsch, T. S. "A. E. Housman and Matthew Arnold." *Boston University Studies in English*, IV, 22-39.
Suggests through parallel passages and reminiscences Housman's poetic indebtedness to Arnold.

Watson, George L. *A. E. Housman: A Divided Life*. . . . See VB 1958, 382.
Rev. by John Pick in *BA*, XXXIII, 229; by William White in *BB*, XII, 175; by DeLancey Ferguson in *HTB*, 29 Mar., p. 1; by John Edmund Hardy in *YR*, XLVIII, 411.

HUDSON. Dewar, David R. "W. H. Hudson's First Days in England." *N & Q*, n.s. VI, 57-58.

HUXLEY. Bibby, Cyril. "Huxley and the Reception of the 'Origin.' " *VS*, III, 76-86.

Bibby, Cyril. *T. H. Huxley: Scientist, Humanist, and Educator*. London: Watts. Pp. xxi + 330.
Rev. by John Roach in *History*, XLIV, 281-84; by J. W. Burrow in *History Today*, IX, 433-35; by Raymond Williams in *NS*, LVII, 584; by D. W. Harding in *S*, 1 May, pp. 628-29; by Paul Bloomfield in *TC*, CLXV, 611-15; in *TLS*, 1 May, p. 255.

JOWETT. Faber, Sir Geoffrey. *Jowett: A Portrait with Background*. . . . See VB 1958, 383.
Rev. by W. L. Burn in *History*, XLIV, 79-82; by H. W. McCready in *QQ*, LXV, 708-09.

KINGSLEY (see also III, Williams).

American Notes: Letters from a Lecture Tour, 1874. Ed. Robert Bernard Martin. . . . See VB 1958, 383.
Rev. in *TLS*, 12 June, p. 354.

Campbell, Olwen. *Mary Kingsley: A Victorian in the Jungle*. . . . See VB, 1957, 413.
Rev. by Léonie Villard in *Études anglaises*, XII, 358-59.

Johnston, Arthur. *"The Water Babies:* Kingsley's Debt to Darwin." *English,* XII, 215-19.

Wolff, Robert Lee. "Henry Kingsley." *HLB,* XIII, 195-226.

Writing with an obvious fondness for his subject, this collector of Kingsley's novels reviews the state of scholarship on Kingsley and presents a personal sketch.

KIPLING (see also II, Weber).

"Lettres de Guerre à André Chevrillon." Trans. by B. Hovelaque. *Revues des Deux Mondes,* No. 18 (15 Sept.), 195-211.

Kaplan, Israel. "Kipling's First Visit to America." *Dalhousie Review,* XXXIX, 153-65.

Léaud, F. "La Bibliothèque de Rudyard Kipling." *Études anglaises,* XII, 315-23.

Léaud, Francis. *La Poetique de Rudyard Kipling.* Collection des Études anglaises No. 5. Paris: Didier. Pp. 563.

Rev. by Bonamy Dobrée in *Études anglaises,* XII, 75-76.

Tompkins, J. M. S. *The Art of Rudyard Kipling.* London: Methuen. Pp. xiv + 277.

Rev. by V. S. Pritchett in *NS,* LVIII, 801-02; by Ronald Bryden in *S,* 11 Dec., pp. 879-80.

LANDOR. Elwin, Malcolm. *Landor. . . .* See VB, 1958, 383.

Rev. by Edgar Johnson in *VS,* III, 214-15.

LE FANU. Eenhoorn, Michael. (ed.). *Sheridan Le Fanu: The Diabolical Genius.* New York: Juniper.

Rev. by Anthony Boucher, in *NYTBR,* 21 June, p. 19. Includes short stories and a condensation of *Uncle Silas.*

Maxwell, J. C. "J. S. Le Fanu's 'The Cock and Anchor': Notes for D. E. D." *N & Q,* n.s. VI, 284-85.

LIVINGSTONE.

Schapera, I. (ed.). *David Livingstone: Family Letters, 1841-1856.* London: Chatto and Windus. 2 vols. Pp. 266 and 320.

Rev. by J. D. Hargreaves in *History Today,* IX, 776-77; by V. S. Pritchett in *NS,* LVIII, 515-16; by Neal Ascherson in *S,* 9 Oct., p. 492; in *TLS,* 23 Oct., p. 603.

LOCKER-LAMPSON. Bates, Madison C. " 'That Delightful Man': A Study of Frederick Locker." *HLB,* XIII, (in three parts) 92-113; 265-91; 444-70.

An enthusiastic account of Locker's life, writings, library, personality, and friendships. Some of the new information regarding Locker's second marriage and the

clash of temperaments is based on 80 unpublished letters of Locker to Austin Dobson now in the Harvard Library. A final portion on personality and his precarious health deals with his literary friendships, particularly those with Kate Greenaway, O. W. Holmes, and George Eliot. A supplement lists unpublished Locker materials.—R. E. F.

MACAULAY (see also III, Hinton).

Hartley, Anthony. "Lord Macaulay, 1800-1859." *Manchester Guardian Weekly,* 31 Dec., p. 11.

"It looks as though Macaulay were in for a revival. His life and his work are part of that nineteenth-century tradition of liberal thought to which we are increasingly turning."

Thomson, Mark Alméras. *Macaulay.* London: Published for Historical Association by Routledge and K. Paul. Pp. 28.

Briefly rev. in *TLS,* 2 Oct., p. 567.

MALLOCK. Yarker, P. M. "W. H. Mallock's Other Novels." *NCF,* XIV, 189-205.

An evaluation of Mallock's total output.

MARTINEAU. Seat, William R., Jr. "Harriet Martineau in America." *N & Q,* n.s. VI, 207-08.

MEREDITH (see also II, Appleman, Stevenson; III, Rathburn, Smidt; DOYLE; Weil-Nordon).

Bartlett, Phyllis. "Richard Feverel, Knight-Errant." *Bull. of the New York Public Library,* LXIII, 329-40.

Green, David Bonnell. "George Meredith's 'Austrian Poets': A Newly Identified Review Essay with Translations." *MLR,* LIV, 321-26.

Meredith on Grillparzer, Lenau, and others, in *Fraser's Magazine,* August, 1852.

Peterson, Virgil A. "The Entitlement of Meredith's 'Love in the Valley.' " *VNL,* No. 15 (Spring), pp. 28-29.

MILL (see also II, Appleman, Harris, Kennedy, Stevenson, Viner; III, Krook).

Considerations on Representative Government. Ed. with an intro. by Currin V. Shields. New York: Liberal Arts Pr., 1958. Pp. xliv + 275.

Rev. by William D. Templeman in *Personalist,* XL, 191.

Prefaces to Liberty: Selected Writings of John Stuart Mill. Ed. Bernard Wishy. Boston: Beacon Pr. Pp. 240.

Rev. by Eli M. Oboler in *LJ,* LXXXIV, 3580.

Balassa, Bela A. "John Stuart Mill and the

Law of Markets." *Quart. Jour. of Economics,* LXXIII, 263-74.

Burns, J. H. "J. S. Mill and the Term 'Social Science.'" *JHI,* XX, 431-32.

Earlier use of term by Mill than that suggested by Peter R. Senn, *JHI,* XIX (Oct. 1958) 568-70. (See also Iggers, below.)

Clark, George A. "Mill's 'Notorious Analogy.'" *JP,* LVI, 652-56.

A defence of Mill's analogy between "visible" and "desirable" in *Utilitarianism.*

Harris, Abram L. "J. S. Mill on Monopoly and Socialism: A Note." *JPE,* LXVII, 604-11.

Iggers, Georg G. "Further Remarks about Early Uses of the Term 'Social Science.'" *JHI,* XX, 433-36.

Carries the discussion back to various 18th century French uses of the term before Comte and Mill.

Lennard, R. V. "Mill — and Others — on Liberty." *HJ,* LVII, 342-48.

A centenary essay examining Mill's essay in the light of more recent theories.

Levi, Albert William. "The Value of Freedom: Mill's *Liberty* (1859-1959)." *Ethics,* LXX, 37-46.

Powers, Richard H. "John Stuart Mill: Morality and Inequality." *SAQ,* LVIII, 206-12.

The applicability of Mill's arguments for equality between the sexes to present problems of inequality.

Ward, John William. "Mill, Marx, and Modern Individualism." *VQR,* XXXV, 527-39.

Wellman, Carl. "A Reinterpretation of Mill's Proof." *Ethics,* LXIX, 268-76.

Mill's "desire as proof of desirability" is inconclusive but provocative.

MOORE (see also I, Gordan; III, Howarth, O'Sullivan).

Brown, Calvin S. "Balzac as a Source of George Moore's *Sister Teresa.*" *CL,* XI, 124-30.

Collet, Georges-Paul. *George Moore et la France.* . . . See VB 1958, 385.

Rev. by Jacqueline S. de La Harpe in *Contemp. Lit.,* XI, 174-76; by C. M. Bowra in *Franch Studies,* XIII, 372-74.

Hart-Davis, Rupert (ed.). *George Moore. Letters to Lady Cunard, 1895-1933.* New York: Macmillan, 1958. Pp. 208.

Rev. by Richard Harris in *QJS,* XLV, 96.

MORLEY Stelzner, Herman G. "The British Orators, VII: John Morley's Speechmaking." *QJS,* XLV, 171-81.

MORRIS (see also I, McLean; **TENNYSON:** Henderson).

Canning, George Rolland, Jr. "William Morris: Man and Literary Artist." *DA,* XIX, 1753.

DuPont, V. (ed.). *Nouvelles de Nulle Part* [*News from Nowhere*]. Paris: Editions Montaigne, F. Aubier, 1957. Pp. 519.

Rev. by Joan Rees in *Études anglaises,* XII, 260. Bilingual text.

Patrick, John M. "Morris and Froissart Again: 'Sir Peter Harpdon's End.'" *N & Q,* n.s. VI, 331-33.

The Works of Geoffrey Chaucer: A Facsimile of the William Morris Kelmscott Chaucer. . . . See VB 1958, 385.

Rev. by Paul C. Wermuth in *LJ,* CXXXIV, 96.

NEWMAN (see also I, Gordan; II Stark; **CHURCH:** Smith).

The Abbot of Downside. "The Significance of Newman Today." *Dublin Review,* CCXXXIII, 337-46.

Gill, John M. "Newman's Dialectic in *The Idea of a University:* 'He can ask a question pertinently.'" *QJS,* XLV, 415-18.

Hong, Theodore Norman. "Cardinal Newman as a Literary Critic." *DA,* XIX, 2089-90.

Kenney, Terence. *The Political Thought of John Henry Newman.* . . . See VB 1958, 386.

Rev. by Ulrich S. Allers in *APSR,* 1144-45; by A. Dwight Culler in *YR,* XLVIII, 584-87.

Renz, W. *Newmans Idee einer Universität:* Probleme hoeherer Bildung. Studia Friburgensia, Neue Folge, 19. Pp. xxii + 338.

Rev. in *StI,* XLVIII, 234.

Reynolds, Ernest Edwin. *Three Cardinals: Newman — Wiseman — Manning.* . . . See VB 1958, 386.

Rev. by Rev. Paul R. Rust in *CWd,* CLXXXVIII, 344-45; by Josef L. Altholz in *JMH,* XXXI, 373-74; in *StI,* XLVIII, 245; by J. M. Cameron in *VS,* II, 282-83.

NIGHTINGALE (see I, Bell, M.; II, Cope, Greenleaf).

OUIDA. Tappe, E. D. "Ouida's 'Idalia': The Source of Its Moldavian Scenes." *N & Q,* n.s. VI, 285-86.

PATER (see also I, Gordan; II, Appleman; III, Ryals).

Baker, Joseph E. "Ivory Tower as Laboratory:

Pater and Proust." *Accent,* XIX, 204-16.
"Pater and Proust may detach themselves
from moral action, but they do not . . .
repudiate Truth as a main concern of the
artist"; their withdrawal from actuality is
a strategy by which reality may be discovered and defined.

Chandler, Edmund. *Pater on Style.* . . . See
VB 1958, 386.
Rev. extensively by Iain Fletcher in *EC,*
IX, 411-18; by G. J. d'Hangest in *Étude
anglaises,* XII, 169-70.

Fletcher, Iain. *Walter Pater.* (Writers and
Their Work, No. 114.) London: Long-
mans, Green. Pp. 44.
Noted in *TLS,* 23 Oct., p. 614.

Sudrann, Jean. "Victorian Compromise and
Modern Revolution." *ELH,* XXVI, 425-
44.
On *Marius* as significant in the development of the novel.

PATMORE. Guyard, Marius-François. "De
Patmore à Claudel." *Revue de Littérature
Comparée,* XXXIII, 500-17.
Patmore's *Unknown Eros* was a major in-
fluence on Claudel's early investigations
of the ode as a lyric form.

PATTISON. Green, Vivian Hubert Howard.
*Oxford Common Room: A Study of Lin-
coln College and Mark Pattison.* . . . See
VB 1958, 387.
Rev. by W. L. Burn in *History,* XLIV,
79-82.

PINERO. Carb, Nathan R. E., Jr. "The Social
Plays of Sir Arthur Wing Pinero: An Old
Answer to a New Question." *DA,* XX,
1781.
Sees Pinero as opposed to Ibsen on standards for feminine conduct and the validity of restrictive social codes.

READE (see also III, Rathburn).

Shuman, R. Baird. "Charles Reade's Con-
tract with Fields, Osgood and Co."
N & Q, n.s. VI, 212.

RICARDO. Barkai, H. "Ricardo on Factor
Prices and Income Distribution in a Growing Economy." *Economica,* n.s. XXVI,
240-50.

Blaug, Mark. *Ricardian Economics: A Historical Study.* . . . See VB 1958, 387.
Rev. by W. D. Grampp in *American Economic Rev.,* XLIX, 419; by H. W. Spiegel
in *APSS,* CCCXXI, 197; by George J.
Stigler in *JPE,* LXVII, 641; by Maurice
Dobb in *Science and Society,* XXIII, 263-
66.

ROLFE. Woolf, Cecil (ed.). *Letters to*

C. H. C. Pirie-Gordon. London: Nicholas
Vane. Pp. 146.
Rev. in *TLS,* Sept. 4, p. 508.

ROSSETTIS. (see also TENNYSON: Henderson).

Doughty, Oswald (ed.). *The Poems of Dante
Gabriel Rossetti.* . . . See VB 1957, 416.
Rev. by L. C. B. in *Études anglaises,* XII,
72.

Holberg, Stanley Marquis. "Image and Symbol in the Poetry and Prose of Dante
Gabriel Rossetti." *DA,* XX, 1016-17.
"Rossetti's system of symbolic expression
called for the creation of a literature of
dream—a literature that exploits the proposition that intense feeling has the power
to abstract the mind in some degree from
its normal conscious activities. . . . These
unconscious demands appear to have
been organized around a necessity to
withhold some part of himself from active
participation in life."

Mellown, Elgin W. "Hopkins, Hall Caine,
and D. G. Rossetti." *N & Q* n.s. VI, 109-
110.
Rossetti advised rejection of Hopkin's
sonnet in 1881.

Packer, Lona Mosk. "Christina Rossetti and
Alice Boyd of Penkill Castle." *TLS,* 26
June, p. 389.
Hitherto unpublished letters.

Packer, Lona Mosk. "Christina Rossetti's
Correspondence with Her Nephew: Some
Unpublished Letters." *N & Q,* n.s. VI,
425-32.

Packer, Lona Mosk. "The Protestant Existen-
tialism of Christina Rossetti." *N & Q,* n.s.
VI, 213-15.

The Times. "Not All Roses in the Victorian
Nursery." *TLS,* 29 May, suppl. p. xi.
On Christina Rossetti's *Speaking Like-
nesses,* 1874. (See letter on this subject
by Lona Mosk Packer, *TLS,* 5 June, p.
337.)

RUSKIN (see also II, Appleman; III, Altick,
Belvin, Hoblitzelle).

Evans, Joan, and Whitehouse, John Howard
(eds.). *The Diaries of John Ruskin.*
Vol. II: *1848-1873* (see VB 1958, 387).
Rev. by John Tyree Fain in *MLN,* LXXIV,
458-59.
Vol. III: *1874-1889.* London: Oxford
Univ. Pr. Pp. 439.
Rev. by C. M. Weekley in *Apollo,* LXX,
199; by Herbert Read in *Listener,* 10
Dec., p. 1045; by Peter Quennell in *S,* 20
Nov., p. 726; in *TLS,* 4 Dec., p. 702.

Evans, Joan (ed.). *The Lamp of Beauty: Writings on Art by John Ruskin*. London: Phaidon Pr. Pp. 344.
Rev. by Michael Kitson in *S*, 18 Dec., p. 914; in *TLS*, 4 Dec., p. 702.

Brown, Samuel E. "The Unpublished Passages in the Manuscript of Ruskin's Autobiography." *VNL*, No. 16 (Fall), pp. 10-18.

Burd, Van Akin. "Background to *Modern Painters*: The Tradition and the Turner Controversy." *PMLA*, LXXIV, 254-67.

Burd, Van Akin. "Ruskin's Defense of Turner: The Imitative Phase." *PQ*, XXXVII, 465-83.

Edwards, Ralph. "Ruskin on English Contemporary Artists." *Connoisseur*, CXLIV, 91-95.

Neville, Sister Mary E. "The Function of the Concept of Organic Unity in the Writings of John Ruskin between 1857 and 1870." *DA*, XX, 291.
"Ruskin's repudiation of the social philosophy of his age in 1860 . . . was part of the continuous development of his concept of organic unity."

Spence, Margaret E. "Ruskin's Correspondence with Miss Blanche Atkinson." *Bull. of the John Rylands Libr.*, XLII, 194-219.
An unusually personal correspondence between Ruskin and an avid reader of the *Fors Clavigera* essays.

RUSSELL. *My Indian Mutiny Diary*. . . . See VB 1957, 417.
Rev. by F. J. L. Young in *QQ*, LXVI, 171-72.

SHAW (see also I, Gordan, Ransom).

Alexander, Doris M. "Captain Brant and Captain Brassbound: The Origin of an O'Neill Character." *MLN*, LXXIV, 306-10.

Bond, George Robert. "The Method of Iconoclasm in George Bernard Shaw." *DA*, XX, 1780.

Dickson, Ronald J. "The Diabolonian Character in Shaw's Plays." *Univ. of Kansas City Rev.*, XXVI, 145-51.
On Dudgeon, Don Juan and Undershaft; ". . . given a religious context and the paradoxical nature of Shavian invention, the diabolonian character . . . is inevitable."

Ervine, St. John Greer. *Bernard Shaw*. . . . See VB 1957, 418.
Rev. by H. Lüdeke in *ESt*, XL, 328-30.

Evans, Maurice. "Some Reminiscences of Shaw." *Theatre Arts*, XLIII (November), 17-19.

Holroyd, Stuart. "Ambassador Extraordinary: The Ubiquity of Bernard Shaw." *TLS*, 7 August, suppl. pp. xxii-xxiii.

Kaye, Julian Bertram. *Bernard Shaw and the Nineteenth-Century Tradition*. . . . See VB 1958, 388.
Rev. by Marvin Magalaner in *BA*, XXXIII, 218; by Richard P. Benton in *CE*, XXI, 65; by George Freedley in *LJ*, LXXXIII, 3453; by Carlyle King in *QQ*, LXV, 707-08; in *Theatre Arts*, Dec., 1958, p. 68; by Melvin Richter in *VS*, II, 346-47.

King, Carlyle. "G. B. S. on Literature: The Author as Critic." *QQ*, LXVI, 135-45.

Kozelka, Paul. *Glossary to the Plays of Bernard Shaw*. New York: Bureau of Publications, Teachers College, Columbia Univ. Pp. 55.
Rev. briefly by George Freedley in *LJ*, LXXXIV, 1531.

Leary, Daniel James. "The Superman and Structure in George Bernard Shaw's Plays: A Study in Dialectic Action." *DA*, XIX, 2081.

Lowe, Robert Liddell. "Two Shaw Letters." *MLR*, LIII, 548-50.

McKee, Irving. "Bernard Shaw's Beginnings on the London Stage." *PMLA*, LXXIV, 470-81.

Nickson, Joseph Richard. "The Art and Politics of the Later Plays of Bernard Shaw." *Abst. of Diss. Univ. of So. Calif.*, 1958, 49-51.

Pearson, Hesketh. "Music to Shaw's Ears?" *Theatre Arts*, XLIII (Jan.) 54-56.
Shaw's attitude toward musical versions of his work.

Rankin, H. D. "Plato and Bernard Shaw, Their Ideal Communities." *Hermathena*, XCIII, 71-76.
Discusses correspondences between *Republic* and fifth play of *Back to Methuselah*.

The Shaw Review (continuing *The Shaw Bulletin*).
Vol. II, No. 7 (January, 1959), has items: O'Donnell, Norbert F., "Doctor Ridgeon's Deceptive Dilemma" (pp. 1-5); Reed, Robert R., "Boss Mangan, Peer Gynt and *Heartbreak House*" (pp. 6-12); Weisert, John J., "Bahr Describes GBS on the Platform" (pp. 13-15); "Shavian Dead Letter File" (pp. 16-18); Stokes, E. E., Jr., a review of Julian B. Kaye's

Bernard Shaw and the Nineteenth-Century Tradition (pp. 19-21); McKiernan, John, a review of Louis Simon's *Shaw on Education* (p. 21); Bennett, Mark, "Magnus and Orinthia on Wax," a review of the Caedmon recording *The Apple Cart: Interlude between Acts One and Two* (pp. 21-22); Ozy, a review of the Metro-Goldwyn Mayer film *The Doctor's Dilemma* (pp. 22-23); "A Continuing Check-list of Shaviana," compiled and edited by Charles A. Carpenter, Jr. (pp. 24-26); "Shavian News Notes" (pp. 27-29).

No. 8 (May, 1959) has items: O'Neill, Michael J., "Some Shavian Links with Dublin as Recorded in the Holloway Diaries" (pp. 2-7); Wellwarth, George E., "Mrs. Warren Comes to America, or the Blue-Noses, the Politicians and the Procurers" (pp. 8-16); "The Complimentary Dinner to Mr. J. E. Vedrenne and Mr. H. Granville Barker: a transcript of the proceedings" (pp. 17-34); "A Continuing Check-list of Shaviana," compiled and edited by Charles A. Carpenter, Jr. (pp. 35-36); [Carpenter, Charles A., Jr.] and [Bosworth, Raymond F.], two reviews of Paul Kozelka's *A Glossary to the Plays of Bernard Shaw* (pp. 37-38); "News and Queries" (pp. 39-40).

No. 9 (September, 1959) has items: Corrigan, Robert W., "*Heartbreak House*: Shaw's Elegy for Europe" (pp. 2-6); Hummert, Paul A., "Bernard Shaw's Marxist Utopias" (pp. 7-26); McDowell, Frederick P. W. "The 'Pentecostal Flame' and the 'Lower Centers': *Too True to Be Good*" (pp. 27-38); Nickson, Richard, "The World Betterer: Shav versus Shav" (pp. 39-44); Spencer, T. J., "An Annotated Check-List of the post-*Saint Joan* Plays" (pp. 45-48); Watson, Barbara, "Off-Broadway Shaw Festival," reviews of the New York Provincetown Playhouse productions of *Overruled* and *Buoyant Billions* (pp. 49-50); "News and Queries" (pp. 50-51).

Shields, Jean Louise. "Shaw's Women Characters: An Analysis and a Survey of Influences from Life." *DA*, XIX, 2347-48.

Simon, Louis. *Shaw on Education.* . . . See VB 1958, 388.
  Rev. by Arthur Heilman in *BA*, XXXIII, 230; by E. M. Oboler in *LJ*, LXXXIII, 2435; in *Theatre Arts*, Dec., 1958, p. 69; in *TLS*, 24 Apr., p. 247.

Stigler, George J. "Bernard Shaw, Sidney Webb, and the Theory of Fabian Socialism." *PAPS*, CIII, 469-75.

Turner, Ethel. *The Child of the Children.* Introduction by J. B. Wright. London: Ward, Lock. Pp. 31.

Noticed in *TLS*, 2 Oct., p. 567 (see also letters on "Eliza's Prototypes," *TLS*, 13 Nov., p. 668; 20 Nov., p. 677; 11 Dec., p. 725). Re-issue of a magazine story of 1897 which may have suggested the idea of *Pygmalion*.

SMILES (see also II, Stevenson).

Self-Help. . . . See VB 1958, 389.
  Rev. by Geoffrey Barraclough in *S*, 6 Feb., p. 198.

Bradley, John L. "Samuel Smiles' *Self-Help*: Forgotten Centenary." *VNL*, No. 16 (Fall), pp. 23-25.
  Another look at the "primer of the self-made man."

STEPHEN, JAMES (see II, Ward; TENNYSON: Bevington).

STEVENSON (see also I, Gordan; III, Knox, Woolf; THOMPSON: Connolly).

Aldington, Richard. *Portrait of a Rebel: The Life and Work of Robert Louis Stevenson.* . . . See VB 1958, 389.
  Rev. by G. Miallon in *Études anglaises*, XII, 360.

Bramley, J. A. "The Courage of Robert Louis Stevenson." *HJ*, LVII, 171-76.
  On Stevenson's place in literature.

McKay, George L. (comp.). *A Stevenson Library: Catalogue of a Collection of Writings by and about Robert Louis Stevenson formed by Edwin J. Beinecke.* Vol. IV: *Letters to and about Robert Louis Stevenson.* New Haven, Conn.: Yale Univ. Libr. (For Vol. I see VB 1951, 270; Vol. II see VB 1953, 262; Vol. III see VB 1957, 420). Pp. 506.
  Rev. by T. J. Brown in *Book Collector*, VIII, 95; in *TLS*, 5 June, p. 344.

Riggs, Roy A. "The Vogue of Robert Louis Stevenson in America, 1880-1900." *DA*, XX, 304-05.
  Traces Stevenson's reputation and technique of fiction, utilizing unpublished letters between Stevenson and Charles Baxter, his legal advisor and literary agent.

SURTEES. Bovill, E. W. *The England of Nimrod and Surtees, 1815-1854.* London: Oxford Univ. Pr. Pp. 188.

SWINBURNE (see also I, Gordon; III, Ryals, Smidt).

Lang, Cecil Y. (ed.). *Swinburne Letters.* New Haven, Conn.: Yale Univ. Pr. Vol. I: *1854-1869.* Vol. II: *1869-1875.* Pp. l + 315 and vi + 378.

Rev. by J. R. Willingham in *LJ*, LXXXIV, 3775.

Adams, Donald K. "Swinburne and Hazlitt." *N & Q*, n.s. VI, 451-52.

Baum, Paull F. "The Fitzwilliam Manuscript of Swinburne's 'Atalanta,' Verses 1038-1204. *MLR*, LIV, 161-78.
Frequent and extensive revisions in the third stasimon of *Atalanta* show Swinburne's strenuous workmanship.

Bissell, E. E. "Gosse, Wise and Swinburne." *Book Collector*, VIII, 297-99.
Argues that Wise has been unjustly accused of initiating idea that certain poems printed in *Fraser's* in the 1840's were written by Swinburne.

Hively, Robert William. "Algernon Charles Swinburne as a Literary Critic." *DA*, XIX, 1740-41.
Analysis of the biographical, social, political, original, and stylistic forces that produced Swinburne's critical theories.

Kerr, Lowell. "Swinburne and Correggio." *TLS*, 31 July, p. 447.
An unpublished letter apparently establishes the fact that Landor gave Swinburne a "Correggio" painting.

Lang, Cecil Yelverton. "Swinburne's Lost Love." *PMLA*, LXXIV, 123-30.
Contends Swinburne was in love with his cousin Mary Gordon.

Maxwell, J. C. "Swinburne and 'The Cult of the Calamus.' " *N & Q*, n.s. VI, 452.

Paden, William Doremus. "Footnote to a Footnote." *TLS*, 23 Oct., p. 616.
More light on the publication of "A Word for the Navy," 1886-1887.

Tener, Robert H. "Swinburne as Reviewer." *TLS*, 25 Dec., p. 755.
On Swinburne's contributions to the *Spectator*.

TENNYSON (see also II, Appleman, Stevenson; III, Jones, McCall, Ryals, Smidt).

Bevington, Merle M. "Tennyson and Sir James Stephen on 'The Last Great Englishman.' " *N & Q*, n.s. VI, 445-46.
Both men came on the same phrase to describe the Duke of Wellington.

Duncan, Edgar Hill. "Tennyson: A Modern Appraisal." *Tennessee Studies in Literature*, IV, 13-30.
Surveys modern critical positions regarding Tennyson, concluding that the more recent students have concentrated on the "ways he made poetic symbols the vehicle of his private sensibilities." Utilizing ele-

ments of "pure" criticism heavily buttressed by historical-biographical criticism, the author illustrates his point with a close reading of "Ulysses," emphasizing the psychic subjective nature of the poem. This study is impressive for the review and bibliography of modern views and for the new reading of a significant poem. —R. E. F.

Elliott, Philip L., Jr. "Tennyson's 'To Virgil.' " *N & Q*, n.s. VI, 147-48.
Original publication of Tennyson's poem in Italy and an Italian translation.

Forker, Charles R. "Tennyson's 'Tithonus' and Marston's 'Antonio's Revenge.' " *N & Q*, n.s. VI, 445.

Gossman, Ann and Whiting, George W. "King Arthur's Farewell to Guinevere." *N & Q*, n.s. VI, 446-48.

Hartman, Joan E. "The Manuscript of Tennyson's 'Gareth and Lynette.' " *HLB*, XIII, 239-64.
From notebooks in Harvard College Library, the writer traces the developing concept of this idyll through the various drafts, noting changes in style, "translation" from Tennyson's prose summaries to verse, and relating the development to Tennyson's ideas, biography, and other works. This is a significant article for students of poetic creation and of Tennyson in particular.—R. E. F.

Henderson, Stephen E. "A Study of Visualized Detail in the Poetry of Tennyson, Rossetti, and Morris." *DA*, XX, 1015.

Hess, M. Whitcomb. "Tennyson: 1809-1959." *CR*, CXCVI, 183-85.

Killham, John. *Tennyson and "The Princess": Reflections of an Age. . . .* See VB 1958, 390.
Rev. by Douglas Bush in *MLR*, LIV, 422-23; by Betty Miller in *TC*, CLXV, 192-93.

Lawry, J. S. "Tennyson's 'The Epic': A Gesture of Recovered Faith." *MLN*, LXXIV, 400-03.
"Morte d'Arthur" and its introduction as affirmation of faith in Christ and in human greatness.

Marshall, George O., Jr. "An Incident from Carlyle in Tennyson's 'Maud.' " *N & Q*, n.s. VI, 77-78.

Marshall, George O., Jr. "Textual Changes in a Presentation Copy of Tennyson's *Poems* (1833)." *Library Chronicle of the Univ. of Texas*, VI, 16-19.

Roppen, Georg. " 'Ulysses' and Tennyson's Sea Quest." *ESt*, XL, 77-90.
"Tennyson achieves a powerful . . . syn-

thesis of the chaotic feelings of 'The Two Voices,' and integrates the two worlds which Ulysses explores, that of heroic action and that of spiritual possibility," A perceptive and judicious reading.— R. A. D.

Rosenberg, John D. "The Two Kingdoms of *In Memoriam.*" *JEGP*, LVIII, 228-40.
A valuable and perceptive analysis of the symbolic structure of the poem.—O. M.

Ryals, Clyde de L. "The 'Fatal Woman' Symbol in Tennyson." *PMLA*, LXXIV, 438-43.
The many appearances in Tennyson's earlier poetry of the Fatal Woman, inspired by Keats' *La Belle Dame.*

Shannon, Edgar F., Jr. "Alfred Tennyson's Admission to Cambridge." *TLS*, 6 March, p. 136.
New letters revealing the chaotic state of affairs at Somersby which led to Tennyson's "escape" to the University.

Shannon, Edgar F., Jr. " 'Locksley Hall' and 'Ivanhoe.' " *N & Q*, n.s. VI, 216-17.

Sonn, Carl Robinson. "Poetic Vision and Religious Certainty in Tennyson's Earlier Poetry." *MP*, LVII, 83-93.
The religious impulse in Tennyson is not antagonistic to the aesthetic impulse, but identical with it.

Tener, Robert H. "Bagehot and Tennyson." *TLS*, 21 Aug., p. 483. Convincing evidence that Bagehot was author of the *National Review* article on Tennyson's *Idylls*, October, 1859.

Tennyson, Charles. "Tennyson's Conversation." *TC*, CLXV, 34-44.

Wilson, Charles. "Mirror of a Shire: Tennyson's Dialect Poems." *DUJ*, LII (n.s. XXI), 22-28.

THACKERAY (see also III, Altick, Martin, Rathburn).

Brander, Laurence. *Thackeray.* (Writers and Their Work, No. 110.) London: Longmans. Pp. 52.
Rev. by Jacques Vallette in *Mercure de France,* CCCXXXVI, 722; noticed in *TLS,* 4 Sept., p. 511.

Preus, Ove Jacob Hjort. "Anne Thackeray Ritchie and the Victorian Literary Aristocracy." *DA,* XIX, 2082.
A study of Thackeray's daughter and her relationship to Victorian and early twentieth century writers, particularly her aunt, Virginia Woolf.

Ray, Gordon N. *Thackeray: The Age of Wisdom (1847-1863).* . . . See VB 1958, 390.

Rev. by L. L. Schücking in *Anglia,* LXXVII, 109-10; by E. D. H. Johnson in *MLN,* LXXIV, 455-57; by K. J. Fielding in *MLR,* LIV, 268-69.

Tilford, John E., Jr. "The Degradation of Becky Sharp." *SAQ,* LVIII, 603-08.
Thackeray wanted to portray Becky as a very bad woman, and her degradation in the later chapters of *Vanity Fair* is therefore consistent with his purpose.

THOMPSON. Connolly, Terence L. (ed.). *The Real Robert Louis Stevenson and Other Critical Essays by Francis Thompson.* New York: University Publishers. Pp. xiii + 409.
Rev. by Herbert Burke in *LJ,* LXXXIV, 3858.

Meynell, Sir Francis. "Francis Thompson, My Godfather; Part I." *Poetry Review,* L, 80-83.

Pope, Myrtle Pihlman. "A Critical Bibliography of Works by and about Francis Thompson." *Bull. New York Public Libr.,* LXIII, 40-49; 155-161; 195-204. (See VB 1958, 390.)

Pope, Myrtle Pihlman. *A Critical Bibliography of Works by and about Francis Thompson.* New York: N. Y. Public Libr. Pp. 37.
Noted in *CE,* XXI, 70.

Quinlan, John. "The Centenary of Francis Thompson." *CR,* CXCVI, 306-08.

Reid, John Cowie. *Francis Thompson: Man and Poet.* London: Routledge and K. Paul. Pp. xi + 232.

TORRENS. Robbins, Lionel. *Robert Torrens and the Evolution of Classical Economics.* . . . See VB 1958, 390.
Rev. by Manuel Gottlieb in *Science and Society,* XXIII, 282-87.

TROLLOPE (see also III, Knox, Rathburn).

Booth, Bradford A. *Anthony Trollope: Aspects of His Life and Art.* . . . See VB 1958, 390.
Rev. by William Coyle in *CE,* XX, 268; by Robert A. Colby in *MP,* LVI, 210; by Arthur Mizener in *NS,* 4 Apr., p. 481; in *QR,* CCXCVII, 474-75; by Boris Ford in *S,* 10 Apr., p. 517; by Lionel Stevenson in *SAQ,* LVIII, 324-26; in *TLS,* 3 Apr., p. 195.

Hagan, John. "The Divided Mind of Anthony Trollope." *NCF,* XIV, 1-26.

WHITE. Michie, James A. "The Wisdom of Mark Rutherford." *LQHR,* CLXXXIV (Ser. 6, XXVIII), 124-28.

WILDE (see also I, Ransom; III, Brennan, O'Sullivan, Ryals).

The Importance of Being Earnest: The Original Four-Act Version with an explanatory foreword by Vyvyan Holland. London: Methuen, 1957. Pp. 114.

Rev. by A. J. Farmer in *Études anglaises*, XII, 364.

Gide, André. "The Last Days of Oscar Wilde." *SR*, 13 June, pp. 10-12, 56-57.

From an essay written in 1901, "adapted from the translation by Jeffrey J. Carre."

Powers, Lyall. "Mr. James's Aesthetic Mr. Nash — Again." *NCF*, XIII, 341-49.

Denies Oscar Cargill's contention that Mr. Nash was modeled on Oscar Wilde (*NCF*, XII, 177-87).

Ryals, Clyde De L. "Oscar Wilde's 'Salome.' " *N & Q*, n.s. VI, 56-57.

On the manuscripts of the play.

Souffrin, Eileen. "La Rencontre de Wilde et de Mallarmé." *Revue de Littérature Comparée*, XXXIII, 529-35.

Wilde and Mallarmé did not meet until 1891, and their interest in one another was never very acute.

YEATS (see also I, Gordan, Ransom; III Donoghue, Fraser, Howarth).

Mythologies. New York: Macmillan. Pp. 269.

Rev. by Babette Deutsch in *HTB*, 23 Aug., p. 8; by Burton A. Robie in *LJ*, LXXXIV, 2065; by T. R. Henn in *NS*, LVII, 518-19; by Padraic Colum in *SR*, 1 Aug., pp. 16-17.

The Variorum Edition of the Poems of W. B. Yeats. . . . See VB 1958, 391.

Rev. by W. J. Harvey in *EC*, IX, 287-99; by James Reany in *TQ*, XXVIII, 203-04.

Adams, Hazard. *Blake and Yeats.* . . . See VB 1957, 422.

Rev. by William D. Templeton in *Personalist*, XL, 86-87.

Cohen, Joseph. "In Memory of W. B. Yeats — and Wilfred Owen." *JEGP*, LVIII, 637-49.

On Yeats' exclusion of Wilfred Owen and other war poets from the *Oxford Book of Modern Verse*, 1936.

Donoghue, Denis. "The Vigour of Its Blood." *KR*, XXI, 376-87.

"Words for Music Perhaps" is Yeats's interpretation of the human condition under its bodily aspect.

Fay, William P. "Le Theatre National Irlandais ou les Débuts de l'Abbey Theatre." *Revue des Deux Mondes*, (No. 17: 1 Sept.), 93-103.

Fixler, Michael. "The Affinities between J.-K. Huysmans and the 'Rosicrucian' Stories of W. B. Yeats." *PMLA*, LXXIV, 464-69.

Gibbon, Monk. *The Masterpiece and the Man: Yeats as I Knew Him.* London: Hart-Davis. Pp. 226.

Rev. by Donald Davie in *NS*, LVII, 695; by Donat O'Donnell in *S*, 22 May, p. 736; in *TLS*, 8 May, p. 274.

Häusermann, H. W. "W. B. Yeats and W. J. Turner, 1935-1937." *ESt*, XL, 233-41.

Contains unpublished letters.

Moore, Virginia. *The Unicorn: William Butler Yeats' Search for Reality.* . . . See VB 1956, 269.

Rev. by René Fréchet in *Études anglaises*, XII, 365-66.

Notopoulos, James A. "Byzantine Platonism in Yeats." *The Classical Jour.*, LIV, 315-21.

Saul, George Brandon. *Prolegomena to the Study of Yeats's Poems.* . . . See VB 1958, 392.

Rev. by Sarah Youngblood in *BA*, XXXIII, 219-20; briefly by George Freedley in *LJ*, LXXXIV, 1621; by Denis Donoghue in *StI*, XLVIII, 106-08; in *TLS*, 24 Apr., p. 239.

Seng, Peter J. "Yeats' 'The Folly of Being Comforted.' " *Ex*, XVII, Item 48.

Snow, Wilbert. "A Yeats-Longfellow Parallel." *MLN*, LXXIV, 302-03.

"When you are old . . ." and a prose passage in Longfellow's *Outre-Mer*.

Unterecker, John. *A Reader's Guide to William Butler Yeats.* New York: Noonday Pr. Pp. 310.

Rev. by Paul C. Wermuth in *LJ*, LXXXIV, 2643.

Whitaker, Thomas R. "The Dialectic of Yeats's Vision of History." *MP*, LVII, 100-12.

Wilson, Francis Alexander Charles. *W. B. Yeats and Tradition.* . . . See VB 1958, 392.

Rev. by Thomas P. McDonnell in *CWd*, Mar., p. 520; by Babette Deutsch in *HTB*, 17 May, p. 5; by Harold Orel in *Prairie Schooner*, XXXIII, 283-84; by A. Norman Jeffares in *MLR*, LIV, 271-73; by Andrew G. Hoover in *QJS*, XLVI, 95-96; by Hazard Adams in *SAQ*, LVIII, 479-80; in *Theatre Arts*, Oct., 1958, p. 70; by John Edward Hardy in *YR*, XLVIII, 412.

Youngblood, Sarah Helen. "William Butler Yeats: The Mature Style." *DA*, XIX, 1764.

VICTORIAN  IBLIOGRAPHY FOR 1960

Robert C. Slack, editor

THIS BIBLIOGRAPHY has been prepared by a committee of the Victorian Literature Group of the Modern Language Association of America: Robert C. Slack, chairman, Carnegie Institute of Technology; Oscar Maurer, University of Texas; Robert A. Donovan, Cornell University; Charles T. Dougherty, St. Louis University; Donald J. Gray, Indiana University; Richard C. Tobias, University of Pittsburgh; and Ronald E. Freeman, University of Southern California. It attempts to list the noteworthy publications of 1960 (including reviews of these and earlier items) that have a bearing on the Victorian period, as well as similar publications of earlier date that have been inadvertently omitted from the preceding Victorian bibliographies. Unless otherwise stated, the date of publication is 1960. Reference to a page in the bibliography for 1959, in *Victorian Studies,* June 1960, is made by the following form: See VB 1959, 423. Some cross-references are given, though not all that are possible. For certain continuing bibliographical works the reader should consult VB 1941, the last annual bibliography in which such works are listed in full. Bibliographical entries are made to conform as closely as possible with the British National Bibliography for books first published in Great Britain, and with the Library of Congress Catalog for books first published in the United States.

The editor wishes to thank Professor Carl J. Weber for his helpful assistance with the Hardy section of the bibliography.

KEY TO ABBREVIATIONS

AHR = American Historical Review
AL = American Literature
AM = Atlantic Monthly
APSR = American Political Science Review
APSS = Annals of the American Academy of Political and Social Science
ArQ = Arizona Quarterly
BA = Books Abroad
BB = Bulletin of Bibliography and Magazine Notes
BLR = Bodleian Library Record
BPLQ = Boston Public Library Quarterly
BSP = Papers of the Bibliographical Society of America
CE = College English
CHJ = Historical Journal (formerly *Cambridge Historical Journal*)
CR = Contemporary Review
CWd = Catholic World
DA = Dissertation Abstracts
DUJ = Durham University Journal
EC = Essays in Criticism
EHR = English Historical Review
EJ = English Journal
ELH = Journal of English Literary History
ESt = English Studies
Ex = Explicator
HJ = Hibbert Journal
HLB = Harvard Library Bulletin
HLQ = Huntington Library Quarterly
HTB = New York Herald Tribune Book Review

JAA = Journal of Aesthetics and Art Criticism
JEGP = Journal of English and Germanic Philology
JEH = Journal of Economic History
JHI = Journal of the History of Ideas
JMH = Journal of Modern History
JP = Journal of Philosophy
JPE = Journal of Political Economy
KR = Kenyon Review
LJ = Library Journal
LQ = Library Quarterly
LQHR = London Quarterly and Holborn Review
LR = Library Review
M & L = Music and Letters
MLJ = Modern Language Journal
MLN = Modern Language Notes
MLQ = Modern Language Quarterly
MLR = Modern Language Review
MP = Modern Philology
N = Nation
N & Q = Notes and Queries
NCF = Nineteenth-Century Fiction
NEQ = New England Quarterly
NER = National and English Review
New R = New Republic
NS = New Statesman
NYTBR = New York Times Book Review
PAPS = Proceedings of the American Philosophical Society
ParR = Partisan Review
PLC = Princeton University Library Chronicle
PMLA = Publications of the Modern Language Association of America
PQ = Philological Quarterly
PSQ = Political Science Quarterly
QJS = Quarterly Journal of Speech
QQ = Queen's Quarterly
QR = Quarterly Review
RES = Review of English Studies
RoR = Romanic Review
S = Spectator
SAQ = South Atlantic Quarterly
SeR = Sewanee Review
SP = Studies in Philology
SR = Saturday Review
StI = Studies: An Irish Quarterly Review
TC = Twentieth Century
TLS = Times Literary Supplement
TQ = University of Toronto Quarterly
VNL = Victorian News Letter

VQR = Virginia Quarterly Review
VS = Victorian Studies
YR = Yale Review

I. BIBLIOGRAPHICAL MATERIAL

(For bibliographies pertaining to individuals, see – CLOUGH; Houghton; DARWIN: *Handlist;* DICKENS: *Dickens;* DOBSON: Dobson; GISSING: Malbone, Wolf; HARDY: *Modern Fiction Studies;* HOUSMAN: Carter; KIPLING: Stewart; MOORE: Gerber).

Allentuck, Marcia. "Morgan and Hohlfeld's 'Bibliography' and the Füssils." *N & Q,* n.s. VII, 99.
Two corrections to their *German Literature in British Magazines: 1750-1860.*

Altick, Richard Daniel, and Matthews, William R. (comps.). *Guide to Doctoral Dissertations in Victorian Literature, 1886-1958.* Urbana: Univ of Illinois Pr. Pp. vii + 119.
Rev. by William D. Templeman in *VNL,* No. 18 (Fall), p. 27.

Altick, Richard D., and Wright, Andrew. *Selective Bibliography for the Study of English and American Literature.* New York: Macmillan. Pp. 138.
Rev. by William White in *BB,* XXIII, 54.

"Annual Bibliography for 1959." *PMLA,* LXXV, No. 2, 218-39; "English Language and Literature: IX. Nineteenth Century, X. Twentieth Century," ed. Charles C. Mish, Harrison T. Meserole, Robert M. Pierson, and Gordon Ross Smith, with the help of Sherod M. Cooper and Charles W. Mann.

Arnold, Armin. *Heine in England and America. A Bibliographical Check-List.* London: Linden Pr., 1959. Pp. 80.
Rev. by Sol Liptzin in *The German Quarterly,* XXXIII, 395-96.

Barbar, W. H. (ed.). *The Year's Work in Modern Language Studies.* Vol. XX (1958). Cambridge: Cambridge Univ. Pr. Pp. ix + 716.

Bell, Inglis F., and Baird, Donald. *The English Novel, 1578-1956.* . . . See VB 1959, 410.
Rev. briefly by Frederick L. Gwynn in *CE,* XXI, 233.

Bowers, Fredson (ed.). *Studies in Bibliog-*

*raphy: Papers of the Bibliographical So-
ciety of the University of Virginia.* Vol.
XIII. Charlottesville: The Society. Pp.
290.

Rev. by William White in *BB,* XXIII, 8.
Contains a study of Tennyson's *Ode on
the Death of the Duke of Wellington* by
Edgar F. Shannon, Jr.

Carter, John, Pollard, Graham, and Todd,
William B. (eds.). *Thomas J. Wise: Cen-
tenary Studies.* Austin: Univ. of Texas Pr.
Pp. 128.

Rev. by Roland Baughman in *Book Collector,* IX, 232-36; by Edwin Wolf, 2nd,
in *BSP,* LIV, 211-12; by A. N. L. Munby
in *NS,* LX, 621.

De Ricci, Seymour. *English Collectors of
Books & Manuscripts (1530-1930) and
Their Marks of Ownership.* Bloomington:
Indiana Univ. Pr. Pp. 203.

Rev. by H. Cahoon in *LJ,* LXXXV, 2805.

Glaister, Geoffrey Ashall. *An Encyclopedia
of the Book: Terms Used in Papermaking,
Printing, Bookbinding, and Publishing,
with Notes on Illuminated Manuscripts,
Bibliophiles, Private Presses, and Printing
Societies.* Cleveland: World. Pp. 484.

Rev. by L. W. Griffin in *LJ,* LXXXV,
3995.

Greenberg, Robert A. (ed.). "Recent Publications: A Selected List: March, 1960-
August, 1960." *VNL,* No. 18 (Fall), pp.
28-32.

Houghton, Walter. "British Periodicals of the
Victorian Age: Bibliographies and Indexes" in *Library Trends,* VII (1959), 554-
565.

Rev. by Lee Ash in *LJ,* LXXXV, 74-76.

Juchhoff, Rudolf (comp.). *Sammelkatalog
der biographischen und literarkritischen
Werke zu englischen Schriftstellern des
19. und 20. Jahrhunderts (1830-1958);
Verzeichnis der Bestände in deutschen
Bibliotheken.* Krefeld: Scherpe Verlag,
1959. Pp. 272.

Rev. briefly in *PBS,* LIV, 143. ". . . students of English literature everywhere
may neglect it at their peril. Particularly
important is the listing of manuscript dissertations in German university libraries."

Kennedy, Arthur G., and Sands, Donald B.
*A Concise Bibliography for Students of
English.* Stanford, Calif.: Stanford Univ.
Pr. Pp. 467.

Rev. by William White in *BB,* XXIII, 56.

Maurer, Oscar (ed.). "Recent Publications:

A Selected List: September, 1959-Feb-
ruary, 1960." *VNL,* No. 17 (Spring), 41-
44.

Milne, Alexander Taylor (comp.). *Writings
on British History: 1940-45.* 2 vols. London: Cape. Pp. 475, 540.

Rodenberg, Julius. *Grösse und Grenzen der
Typographie; Betrachtungen über typo-
graphische Grundfragen, wie sie sich in
der Buchkunst der letzten siebenzig Jahre
widerspiegeln.* Stuttgart: Poeschel. Pp.
204.

Rev. by Antje B. Lemke in *BSP,* LIV, 210-
11. "The greatness and the limitations of
typography, as illustrated in the last sev-
enty years of bookmaking." Three introductory chapters outline "the basic principles of typography and the developments since William Morris."

Sawin, Lewis, *et al.* (eds.). *Annual Bibliography of English Language and Literature.* Vol. XXXVI (1953-54). Cambridge:
Cambridge Univ. Pr. Pp. xvi + 534.

Rev. briefly in *TLS,* 27 May, p. 342.

Slack, Robert C. (ed.). "Victorian Bibliography for 1959." *VS,* III, 409-49.

Strout, Alan Lang. *A Bibliography of Articles
in Blackwood's Magazine, 1817-1825.*
Lubbock: Texas Technological College,
1959. Pp. x + 201.

Rev. by Edith C. Batho in *MLR,* LV,
626-27; by Derek Roper in *N & Q,* n.s.
VII, 116-17. Includes an appendix, "The
Authorship of Articles in Blackwood's
Contributors Book, 1825-1870."

Thurston, Harvis, Emerson, O. B., Hartman,
Carl, and Wright, Elizabeth V. *Short Fiction Criticism, a Checklist of Interpretation since 1925 of Stories and Novelettes
(American, British, Continental, 1800-
1958).* Denver: Alan Swallow. Pp. 265.

Rev. briefly in *PBS,* LIV, 145; by E. F.
Walbridge in *LJ,* LXXXV, 1594.

Walsh, Donna (ed.). "1960 Research in Progress in the Modern Languages and Literatures." *PMLA,* LXXV, No. 2; "English—
IX. Nineteenth Century," pp. 102-06.

White, Beatrice, and Dorsch, T. S. (eds.).
The Year's Work in English Studies. Vol.
XXVIII (1957). London: Oxford Univ.
Pr. Pp. 274.

Williams, McDonald. "*Blackwood's Magazine:* A Selective and Critical Bibliography
of Reviews (With an Introductory Essay), 1850-1880." *DA,* XX, 2815-17.

Besides the obviously useful list of reviews, the study contains evaluations of categories of literature reviewed and judgment of the treatment of some individual authors, works, and genre.

Woolf, Harry, and Bosson, Phyllis Brooks (eds). "Eighty-fifth Critical Bibliography of the History of Science and Its Cultural Influences (to 1 January 1960)." *Isis*, LI, 371-484.

II. ECONOMIC, POLITICAL, RELIGIOUS, AND SOCIAL ENVIRONMENT

Allen, Harry Cranbrook. *The Anglo-American Relationship since 1783*. London: A. and C. Black, 1959. Pp. 247.
    Rev. by R. R. Rea in *LJ*, LXXXV, 1582; in *TLS*, 15 Apr., p. 234. A revised edition, with an additional chapter.

Allen, Walter Gore. *King William IV*. London: Cresset Pr. Pp. ix + 225.
    Rev. by Geoffrey Barraclough in S, 18 Nov., p. 790; in *TLS*, 4 Nov., p. 707.

Altholz, Josef L. "The Liberal Catholic Movement in England." *DA*, XXI, 601. The mid-Victorian movement associated with the *Rambler*.

Anderson, Olive. "The Russian Loan of 1855: An example of Economic Liberalism?" *Economica*, XXVII, 368-71.

Anson, Peter Frederick. *Fashions in Church Furnishings, 1840-1940*. London: Faith Pr. Pp. 383.
    Rev. by Evelyn Waugh in S, 22 Apr., p. 581; in *TLS*, 27 May, p. 332.

Appleman, Philip, Madden, William A., and Wolff, Michael (eds.). *1859: Entering an Age of Crisis*. . . . See VB 1959, 412.
    Rev. by Herman Ausubel in *AHR*, LXV, 888-89; by Priscilla Robertson in *American Scholar*, XXIX, 252-54; by Frank U. Underhill in *Canadian Hist. Rev.*, XLI, 353; by William Bleifuss in *CE*, XXII, 205-06; by R. L. Brett in *Critical Quart.*, II, 187-88; by J. A. Clarke in *LJ*, LXXXIV, 3562; by George Dangerfield in *N*, 13 Feb., p. 148; briefly in *NCF*, XV, 90; in *TLS*, 22 Apr., p. 257; by H. B. Parkes in *VNL*, No. 17 (Spring), 38-40; by John Henry Raleigh in *VS*, III, 302-05.

Armstrong, William A. "The Nineteenth-Century Matinee." *Theatre Notebook*, XIV, 56-59.

Ashworth, William. *An Economic History of England, 1870-1939*. London: Methuen. Pp. ix + 438.

Final volume in series edited by T. S. Ashton.

Ausubel, Herman. *In Hard Times: Reformers among the Late Victorians*. New York: Columbia Univ. Pr. Pp. 403.
    Rev. by R. W. Henderson in *LJ*, LXXXV, 4463; by Hans Kohn in *NYTBR*, 25 Dec., p. 4. Deals with reform movements, 1873-96.

Backstrom, Philip N., Jr. "John Malcolm Forbes Ludlow, A Little Known Contributor to the Cause of the British Working Man in the 19th Century." *DA*, XXI, 859-60.

Baker, Theodore Cardwell. *The Pilkington Brothers and the Glass Industry*. London: Allen and Unwin. Pp. 296.
    Rev. by D. E. C. Eversley in *Economica*, XXVII, 384-85.

Baldwin, Arthur Windham. *The Macdonald Sisters*. London: P. Davies. Pp. 238.
    Rev. by F. Léaud in *Études anglaises*, XIII, 387-88; by Ralph Partridge in *NS*, LVIX, 564-65; by Marghanita Laski in S, 29 Apr., p. 633; by Betty Miller in *TC*, CLXVIII, 279-80 ("Of the eleven children born to George Macdonald and his wife, Hannah Jones, Alice became the mother of Rudyard Kipling; Georgiana married Ned Burne-Jones; Agnes married a President of the Royal Academy; and Louisa gave birth to Stanley Baldwin, Prime Minister of England."); in *TLS*, 24 June, p. 398.

Barnaby, Kenneth Cloves. *The Institution of Naval Architects, 1860-1960*. London: Allen and Unwin. Pp. 645.
    Briefly rev. in *TLS*, 22 July, p. 470.

Bédarida, François. "La crise de 1886 et le Home Rule." *Revue des sciences-politiques* (1958), pp. 277-310.
    Rev. by Louis Trénard in *Revue du nord*, XLII, 162-63.

Bédarida, François. "L'Histoire sociale de Londres au XIXe siècle: sources et problèmes." *Annales: économies, sociétés, civilisations*, XV, 949-62.
    A valuable survey stressing the "dimensions inhumains de la documentation" for this immense subject.

Benians, E. A., Butler, Sir James, and Carrington, C. E. (eds.). *The Cambridge History of the British Empire*. Vol. III: *The Empire-Commonwealth, 1870-1919*. . . . See VB 1959, 412-13.
    Rev. by Wilfrid F. Knapp in *APSR*, LIV, 579; by John Conway in *Canadian Hist. Rev.*, XLI, 224-31; by Vincent Harlow in

EHR, LXXV, 502-05; by S. B. Saul in *JEH*, XX, 98-100.

Best, G. F. A. "The Whigs and the Church Establishment in the Age of Grey and Holland." *History*, XLV, 103-18.
A discussion of the "liberalism" which provoked Keble's Assize Sermon of 1833.

Beveridge, Janet. *An Epic of Clare Market.* London: Bell. Pp. xiii + 98.
Account of association of Beatrice Potter and Sidney Webb to found London School of Economics.

Black, R. D. Collison. *Economic Thought and the Irish Question, 1817-1870.* Cambridge: Cambridge Univ. Pr. Pp. xiv + 299.

Black, R. D. Collison. "Jevons and Cairnes." *Economica*, XXVII, 214-32.
Letters between Mill's opponent, William Stanley Jevons, and J. E. Cairnes, 1863-74.

Blackall, Henry. "O'Connell and the Repeal Party." *Irish Hist. Studies*, XII, 139-43.
Disputes J. H. Whyte's claim (see *VB* 1959, 421) that members of repeal party were of lower social origin than that of other Irish MP's. Includes reply by Mr. Whyte.

Blake, Clagette. *Charles Elliott R. N., 1801-1875: A Servant of Britain Overseas.* London: Cleaver-Hume Pr. Pp. xv + 130.
Briefly rev. in *TLS*, 16 Dec., p. 818. Biography of naval officer who fulfilled assignments ranging from China to Texas and who was Governer successively of Bermuda, Trinidad, and St. Helena.

Bobbitt, Mary Reed. *With Dearest Love to All: The Life and Letters of Lady Jebb.* Chicago: Regnery. Pp. 277.
Rev. by Ellen Hart Smith in *HTB*, 11 Sept., p. 8; by K. T. Willis in *LJ*, LXXXV, 3434; by D. W. Brogan in *S*, 15 July, pp. 108-09; in *TLS*, 8 July, p. 431. Biography of a 19th-century American, wife of a Civil War general, who later married a British M.P. and classical scholar.

Bonham-Carter, Victor. *In a Liberal Tradition.* London: Constable. Pp. xiii + 255.
Rev. by Asa Briggs in *NS*, LVIX, 197-98; in *TLS*, 13 May, p. 303. History of a family, 1700-1950, and especially of Harry Bonham-Carter, the author's Victorian grandfather.

Bradfield, Nancy Margetts. *Historical Costumes of England, from the Eleventh to the Twentieth Century.* London: Harrap, 1958. Pp. 183.
Rev. by A. G. Hassall in *N & Q*, n.s. VII, 358-59.

Briggs, Asa. *The Age of Improvement, 1783-*

1867. ... See *VB* 1959, 413.
Rev. by Norman Gash in *EHR*, LXXV, 173-74.

Briggs, Asa (ed.). *Chartist Studies.* ... See *VB* 1959, 413.
Rev. by Madeline R. Robinton in *AHR*, LXVI, 140-41; by A. Temple Patterson in *History*, XLV, 165; by W. H. Chaloner in *History Today*, X, 65-66; by G. Basalla in *LJ*, LXXXV, 2426; by A. R. Schoyen in *VS*, IV, 67-69.

Briggs, Asa, and Saville, John (eds.). *Essays in Labour History.* London: Macmillan. Pp. vii + 364.
Rev. by W. Ashworth in *History*, XLV, 279; by Dorothy Kuhn Oko in *LJ*, LXXXV, 1794; by Kingsley Martin in *NS*, LIX, 224; by Geoffrey Barraclough in *S*, 11 Mar., p. 363; by J. E. Williams in *VS*, IV, 180-82. Essays in memory of G. D. H. Cole. Aspects of working-class history (mainly in England) in the 19th century.

Brittain, Vera Mary. *The Women at Oxford: A Fragment of History.* London: Harrap. Pp. 272.
Rev. by S. S. Smith in *LJ*, LXXXV, 758; by J. A. Smith in *NS*, LIX, 198; by Penelope Gilliatt in *S*, 26 Feb., p. 294; in *TLS*, 19 Feb., p. 107; by Mary Warnock in *Universities Quart.*, XIV, 312-15.

Bromley, J. *The Man of Ten Talents: A Portrait of Richard Chenevix Trench, 1807-1886: Philologist, Poet, Theologian, Archbishop.* London: S.P.C.K., 1959. Pp. 253.
Rev. by N. Masterman in *History*, XLV, 67; in *TLS*, 20 Mar. 1959, suppl. p. v.

Brose, Olive J. *Church and Parliament: The Reshaping of the Church of England, 1828-1860.* ... See *VB* 1959, 413.
Rev. by Donald O. Wagner in *AHR*, LXV, 413-14; in *Canadian Hist. Rev.*, XL, 352; by John T. McNeill in *Church History*, XXIX, 368-69; by Terence Penelhum in *Ethics*, LXX, 83; by R. W. Greaves in *History*, XLV, 275-76; by Dudley W. R. Bahlman in *JMH*, XXXII, 170-71; by Owen Chadwick in *Jour. Eccl. Hist.*, XI, 255-56; by Geddes MacGregor in *Personalist*, XLI, 397-98; in *TLS*, 15 Apr., suppl. p. vi; by A. R. Vidler in *VS*, IV, 81-82.

Brown, Lucy. *The Board of Trade and the Free Trade Movement, 1830-1842.* ...
See *VB* 1959, 413.
Rev. by Asa Briggs in *EHR*, LXXV, 361-62; by J. R. T. Hughes in *JEH*, XIX, 429-30; by Henry Parris in *JMH*, XXXII, 76.

Bullock, Alan. *The Life and Times of Ernest Bevin.* Vol. I: *Trade Union Leader, 1881-1940.* London: Heinemann. Pp. xv + 672.

Bury, J. P. T. (ed.). *The New Cambridge Modern History.* Vol. X: *The Zenith of European Power, 1830-1870.* Cambridge: Cambridge Univ. Pr. Pp. xxii + 766.

Rev. by F. E. Hirsch in *LJ*, LXXXV, 3656-57; by John Roberts in *S*, 26 Aug., pp. 315-16; in *TLS*, 7 Oct., p. 642.

Cannon, Walter F. "The Uniformitarian-Catastrophist Debate." *Isis*, LI, 38-55.

Carpenter, James. *Gore: A Study in Liberal Catholic Thought.* London: Faith Pr. Pp. 307.

Rev. in *TLS*, 26 Aug., p. 539.

Chadwick, Owen. *Victorian Miniature.* London: Hodder and Stoughton. Pp. 189.

Rev. by Lord Altrincham in *S*, 9 Dec., p. 962; in *TLS*, 9 Dec., p. 794. Study of relations between squire and parson in a Norfolk village in the Victorian period.

Chandler, George. *Liverpool Shipping: A Short History.* London: Phoenix. Pp. xiii + 256.

Cholmondeley, Essex. *The Story of Charlotte Mason.* London: Dent. Pp. xiv + 306.

Biography of nineteenth-century educator, founder of P. N. E. U.

Churchill, Randolph. *Lord Derby, King of Lancashire: The Official Life of Edward, Seventeenth Earl of Derby, 1865-1948.* London: Heinemann. Pp. xii + 641.

Rev. by Paul Johnson in *NS*, LIX, 563-64; by Roy Jenkins in *S*, 15 Apr., p. 547; in *TLS*, 15 Apr., pp. 233-34. The seventeenth earl entered Parliament in 1886.

Clarke, William Kemp Lowther. *A History of the S. P. C. K.* . . . See VB 1959, 413.

Rev. by E. H. Eckel in *Hist. Mag. of Protestant Episcopal Church*, XXIX, 358-59; by L. W. Cowie in *Jour. Eccl. Hist.*, XI, 274-75.

Cockshut, Anthony Oliver John. *Anglican Attitudes.* . . . See VB 1959, 413.

Rev. by A. G. Hill in *VS*, III, 404-05.

Cohen, J. M. *The Life of Ludwig Mond.* . . . See VB 1956, 238.

Rev. by François Crouzet in *Annales: économies, sociétés, civilisations,* XV, 805-06.

Coleman, Donald Cuthbert. *The British Paper Industry, 1495-1860.* . . . See VB 1959, 413.

Rev. by W. E. Minchinton in *JEH*, XIX, 432-34.

Coleman, D. C. "The New Age of Technology, 1750-1900." *Economica*, XXVII, 162-71.

A long review article on volumes IV and

V of Singer, Charles, *A History of Technology* (See VB 1958, 363).

Colum, Padraic. *Ourselves Alone: The Story of Arthur Griffith and the Origin of the Irish Free State.* New York: Crown Publ., 1959. Pp. 400.

Rev. by J. F. Moran in *LJ*, LXXXV, 1442.

Conhaim, Louis H. "The Background of the Home Rule Crisis." *DA*, XXI, 856.

The Home Rule bill of 1886.

Cope, Zachary. *The Royal College of Surgeons of England.* London: Anthony Blond. Pp. xii + 360.

Rev. in *TLS*, 18 Mar., p. 180.

Cowherd, Raymond G. "The Humanitarian Reform of the English Poor Laws from 1782 to 1815." *PAPS*, CIV, 328-42.

Claims that reforms of the Poor Laws were more extensive and effective than 19th- and 20th-century defenders of the 1834 Poor Law have allowed.

Cowherd, Raymond G. *The Politics of English Dissent.* . . . See VB 1959, 413.

Rev. by Roger Thomas in *HJ*, LVIII, 206; in *TLS*, 8 Apr., p. 230.

Cunnington, Cecil Willett, *et al.* *A Dictionary of English Costume, 900-1900 A.D.* London: A. and C. Black. Pp. vii + 281.

Rev. by I. K. F. in *Theatre Notebook*, XIV, 137-38.

Cunnington, Cecil Willett, and Cunnington, Phillis. *A Picture History of English Costume.* London: Vista. Pp. 160.

Rev. by P. von Khrum in *LJ*, LXXXV, 3974.

Curtis, Stanley James, and Boultwood, Myrtle E. A. *An Introductory History of English Education since 1800.* London: University Tutorial Pr. Pp. vii + 382.

Rev. in *TLS*, 19 Aug., p. 534.

Dalzell, Robert F. *American Participation in the Great Exhibition of 1851.* Amherst, Mass.: Amherst College Pr. Pp. 64.

Darley, Lionel S. *Bookbinding Then and Now.* . . . See VB 1959, 414 (where title is incorrectly listed as *Bookbinding Now and Then* . . .).

Rev. in *TLS*, 22 Apr., p. 264.

Davis, Robert E. "The Characteristic Parliamentary Practices of the Fourth Party." *DA*, XX, 3427-28.

Attempts to oppose Gladstone's government in 1880.

Dawson, Lionel. *Squires and Sepoys, 1857-1958.* London: Hollis and Carter. Pp. vii + 98.

Rev. in *TLS*, 26 Aug., p. 543. Contrasts life of 19th-century English squire with that of subaltern in India.

Derry, Thomas Kingston, and Williams, Trevor Illytd. *A Short History of Technology from the Earliest Times to A. D. 1900*. Oxford: Clarendon Pr. Pp. xviii + 782.
Rev. in *TLS*, 30 Dec., p. 842.

Dibner, Bern. *The Atlantic Cable*. Norwalk: Burndy Library, 1959. Pp. 95.
Rev. by John W. Oliver in *Isis*, LI, 367-69.

Durham, John. *Telegraphs in Victorian London*. Cambridge: Golden Head Pr. Pp. 31.
Noticed in *TLS*, 4 Mar., p. 150.

Edwards, Tudor. "Charles Barry and the Palace of Westminster." *History Today*, X, 302-12.

Eliot, Lady Elizabeth. *They All Married Well*. London: Cassell. Pp. 293.
Rev. by Cleveland Amory in NYTBR, 7 Feb., p. 18; in *TLS*, 25 Nov., p. 764. Marriages, 1870-1909, between wealthy Americans and titled Europeans.

[Eliot, Emily M.] "A Visit to Oxford in 1880 by an American Girl." *BLR*, VI, 551-58. Diary of mother of Prof. S. E. Morison of Harvard.

Ellis, C. Hamilton. *British Railway History, 1877-1947*.... See VB 1959, 414.
Rev. in *QR*, CCXCVIII, 116-17; by H. J. Dyos in *VS*, III, 395-97.

Ellis, C. Hamilton. *The London, Brighton and South Coast Railway*. London: I. Allen. Pp. 271.

Elwin, Verrier (ed.). *India's North-East Frontier in the Nineteenth Century*. London: Oxford Univ. Pr., 1959. Pp. 473.
Rev. in *TLS*, 11 Mar., p. 159.

Epton, Nina. *Love and the English*. London: Cassell. Pp. xiv + 390.
Rev. in *TLS*, 25 Nov., p. 764.

Erickson, Arvel B. *Edward T. Cardwell: Peelite*.... See VB 1959, 414.
Rev. by J. B. Conacher in *Canadian Hist. Rev.*, XLI, 169-70; by J. Alun Thomas in *History*, XLV, 166-67; by Norman Gash in *JMH*, XXXII, 78-79.

Erickson, Charlotte. *British Industrialists: Steel and Hosiery, 1850-1950*. Cambridge: Cambridge Univ. Pr., 1959. Pp. xxi + 276.
Rev. by A. G. Pool in *Economica*, XXVII, 385-86.

Escott, Harry. *A History of Scottish Congre-*

gationalism. Glasgow: Congregational Union of Scotland. Pp. 400.
Rev. by James Porter in *HJ*, LIX, 98-99.

Evans, Eric Wyn. *Mabon*.... See VB 1959, 414.
Rev. in *TLS*, 5 Feb., p. 83.

Eversley, David Edward Charles. *Social Theories of Fertility and the Malthusian Debate*. Oxford: Clarendon Pr., 1959. Pp. 313.
Rev. by D. H. Wrong in *American Sociological Rev.*, XXV, 294; by S. G. Checkland in *Economica*, XXVII, 194-96; by Charles Madge in *NS*, LVIII, 514.

Eyck, Frank. *The Prince Consort*.... See VB 1959, 414.
Rev. by Norman Gash in *History*, XLV, 67-68; by Maurice Edelman in *SR*, 5 Sept. 1959, p. 25.

Eyre, J. Vargas. *Henry Edward Armstrong, 1848-1937*.... See VB 1958, 357.
Rev. by Aaron Ihde in *JEH*, XX, 117-18.

Eyton, John. "Eyton's 'Antiquities': A Shropshire Landmark." *N & Q*, n.s. VII, 444-46.
On the Rev. Robert William Eyton (1815-81), antiquarian.

Fabunmi, L. A. *The Sudan in Anglo-Egyptian Relations*. London: Longmans. Pp. xvii + 466.

Feiling, Sir Keith. *In Christ Church Hall*. London: Macmillan. Pp. xiii + 209.
Rev. in *TLS*, 25 Nov., p. 754. On 21 alumni, including Ruskin, Pusey, and Stanley Weyman.

Ferguson, Henry, "The Birmingham Political Union and the Government, 1831-32." *VS*, III, 261-76.
Estimates effectiveness of popular agitation on legislative action.

Fernandez, Thomas L. "The Speeches of Sir Robert Peel on the Repeal of the Corn Laws." *DA*, XXI, 1661.

Ferns, Henry Stanley. *Britain and Argentina in the Nineteenth Century*. Oxford: Clarendon Pr. Pp. xiv + 517.

Fisher, John (ed.). *Eye-Witness*. London: Cassell. Pp. 284.
Rev. in *TLS*, 18 Nov., p. 738. An anthology of 150 years of British reporting.

Fitton, Robert Sucksmith, and Wadsworth, A.P. *The Strutts and the Arkwrights, 1758-1830*.... See VB 1959, 414.
Rev. by A. H. John in *Economica*, XXVII, 83-85; by T. C. Barker in *JEH*, XX, 119-20.

Flint, John E. *Sir George Goldie and the*

Making of Nigeria. London: Oxford Univ. Pr. Pp. xiv + 340.
Rev. in *TLS*, 23 Dec., pp. 821-22.

Fox, Adam. *Dean Inge.* London: John Murray. Pp. xv + 295.
Rev. by Leonard Woolf in *NS*, LX, 96; in *TLS*, 8 July, p. 431.

Fraser, Peter. "The Growth of Ministerial Control in the Nineteenth-Century House of Commons." *EHR*, LXXV, 444-63.

Freeman, T. W. *Pre-Famine Ireland....* See VB 1959, 415.
Rev. by R. Dudley Edwards in *History*, XLV, 65-67; by Emmet Larkin in *JEH*, XIX, 634-35.

Fremantle, Anne. *This Little Band of Prophets: The Story of the Gentle Fabians.* London: Allen and Unwin. Pp. 256.
Rev. by Keith Hutchison in *N*, 17 Sept., pp. 163-64; by Daniel M. Friedenberg in *NewR*, 29 Feb., pp. 16-18; by John Kenneth Galbraith in *NYTBR*, 6 Mar., p. 34; in *TLS*, 29 July, p. 478; by Mary Peter Mack in *VS*, IV, 69-71.

Fulford, Roger. *Hanover to Windsor: British Monarchs from 1830 to 1936.* London: Batsford. Pp. 208.
Rev. in *Blackwood's Mag.*, CCLXXXVII, 558-60; by R. R. Rea in *LJ*, LXXXV, 2157; by Christopher Sykes in *S*, 17 June, pp. 887-88; in *TLS*, 6 May, p. 287.

Furneaux, Rupert. *The Breakfast War.* New York: Crowell. Pp. 240.
Rev. by Ray R. Suput in *LJ*, LXXXV, 1112. British intervention in Russo-Turkish war 1877-78.

Galbraith, John S. *The Hudson's Bay Company as an Imperial Factor, 1821-1869.* ... See VB 1959, 415.
Rev. by Paul Knaplund in *JMH*, XXXII, 74-75.

Garnett, Laidlaw Eskew. *Cradle of Ships: A History of the Bath Iron Works.* Intro. by Samuel Eliot Morison. New York: Putnam, 1958. Pp. 279.
Rev. by Roger Burlingame in *Isis*, LI, 102.

Gartner, Lloyd P. *The Jewish Immigrant in England, 1870-1914.* London: Allen and Unwin. Pp. 320.
Rev. in *TLS*, 15 July, p. 452.

Gernsheim, Helmut, and Gernsheim, Alison (comps.). *Historic Events, 1839-1939.* London: Longmans, Pp. ix + 254.
Rev. in *TLS*, 11 Nov., p. 728. Photographs of historic occasions and importance in the century preceding the Second World War.

Gernsheim, Helmut, and Gernsheim, Alison. *Queen Victoria: A Biography in Word and Picture....* See VB 1959, 415.
Rev. by Lincoln Kirstein in *N*, 12 Dec., 1959, p. 451.

Gettmann, Royal A. *A Victorian Publisher: A Study of the Bentley Papers.* Cambridge: Cambridge Univ. Pr. Pp. xi + 272.
Rev. by Conrad Tanzy in *VS*, IV, 175-76.

Gibbs, Mary Ann. *The Years of the Nannies.* London: Hutchinson. Pp. 191.
Rev. in *TLS*, 20 May, p. 326. Anecdotes of governesses of great, rich families in the 19th century.

Gibbs, Peter. *Crimean Blunder.* London: Muller. Pp. 297.
Rev. by G. A. Craig in *HTB*, 19 June, p. 10; by Joseph Ruef in *LJ*, LXXXV, 1112; in *TLS*, 29 Jan., p. 62.

Gibbs-Smith, Charles Harvard. *The Fashionable Lady in the 19th Century.* London: H. M. Stationery Office. Pp. 184.
Rev. by Paul von Khrum in *LJ*, LXXXV, 4135; in *TLS*, 30 Sept., p. 634.

Gill, John Clifford. *The Ten Hours Parson: Christian Social Action in the Eighteen-Thirties.* London: S. P. C. K., 1959. Pp. xiv + 210.
Rev. by N. Masterman in *History*, XLV, 64-65; by K. S. Inglis in *VS*, III, 390-91. On the work of the Rev. George Bull, a Tory Radical.

Gilliard, D. R. "Salisbury's African Policy and the Heligoland Offer of 1890." *EHR*, LXXV, 631-53.

Glaser, Hugo. *The Road to Modern Surgery: The Advances in Medicine and Surgery during the Past Hundred Years.* Tr. by Maurice Michael. London: Lutterworth. Pp. 224.

Glaser, John F. "Parnell's Fall and the Nonconformist Conscience." *Irish Hist. Studies*, XII, 119-38.

Glover, Janet Reaveley. *The Story of Scotland.* New York: Roy. Pp. 399.
Rev. by Gerald D. McDonald in *LJ*, LXXXV, 2935.

Goldworth, Amnon. "The Utilitarianism of Jeremy Bentham as a Social Decision Method." *DA*, XXI, 925.

Gooch, G. P. *Under Six Reigns....* See VB 1959, 415.
Rev. by David Owen in *JMH*, XXXII, 84.

Grampp, William Dyer. *The Manchester School of Economics.* Stanford, Calif.: Stanford Univ. Pr. Pp. xi + 155.

Rev. by Rendigs Fels in *APSR*, LIV, 1013; by Donald Thompson in *LJ*, LXXXV, 1898.

Greaves, Rose Louise. *Persia and the Defense of India 1844-1892: A Study in the Foreign Policy of the Third Marquis of Salisbury.* Fair Lawn, N.J.: Essential Books, 1959. Pp. 301.
Rev. by Gilbert M. Hull in *JMH*, XXXII, 184.

Gruber, Jacob W. *A Conscience in Conflict: The Life of St. George Jackson Mivart.* New York: Columbia Univ. Pr. for Temple Univ. Publications. Pp. x + 266.

Guthrie, Douglas, *et al. The Royal Edinburgh Hospital for Sick Children, 1860-1960.* Edinburgh, London: Livingstone. Pp. xii + 75.

Hales, E. E. Y. *Revolution and Papacy, 1769-1846.* Garden City, N.Y.: Hanover House. Pp. 320.
Rev. by Gerard Culkin in *Dublin Rev.*, CCXXXIV, 378-83; by H. R. Trevor-Roper in *NS*, LX, 1041-42.

Handover, P. M. *Printing in London: From 1476 to Modern Times.* Cambridge, Mass.: Harvard Univ Pr. Pp. 224.
Rev. by L. W. Griffin in *LJ*, LXXXV, 3078.

Hanham, H. J. *Elections and Party Management: Politics in the Time of Disraeli and Gladstone.* . . . See VB 1959, 415.
Rev. by William O. Aydelotte in *AHR*, LXV, 889-90; by J. Alun Thomas in *History*, XLV, 167-68; by David Owen in *JMH*, XXXII, 302-03; by D. C. Moore in *VS*, III, 393-94.

Hanham, H. J. "The Sale of Honours in Late Victorian England." *VS*, III, 277-89.

Harrison, Royden. "The British Working Class and the General Election of 1868." *International Review of Social History*, V, 424-55.
Negotiations between labor leaders and Gladstone's whips. First part of an article to be concluded in a later issue.

Hassing, Per Schioldborg. "The Christian Missions and the British Expansion in Southern Rhodesia, 1888-1923." *DA*, XXI, 605.

Havard, William C. *Henry Sidgwick and Later Utilitarian Philosophy.* . . . See VB 1959, 415-16.
Rev. by Mary Peter Mack in *VS*, IV, 69-71.

Henriques, Robert. *Marcus Samuel: The First Viscount Bearsted and Founder of*

the "Shell" Transport and Trading Company, 1853-1927.* London: Barrie and Rockliff. Pp. xi + 676.
Rev. by M. R. Brown in *LJ*, LXXXV, 3978; by J. D. Scott in *NS*, LX, 704-05; in *TLS*, 4 Nov., p. 706.

Hill, Alwyn S. "The Group Struggle over the Education of the Poor in England and Wales — 1800-1870." *DA*, XXI, 661-62.

Hill, Gilbert M. "British Socialism and British Foreign Affairs, 1880-1900." *DA*, XXI, 606-07.

Hollis, Christopher. *Eton.* London: Hollis and Carter. Pp. x + 332.
Rev. by Francis Huxley in *NS*, LX, 938; in *TLS*, 18 Nov., p. 745. Surveys entire history of the school.

Hough, Richard. *Admirals in Collision.* . . . See VB 1959, 416.
Rev. by F. J. Dempsey in *LJ*, LXXXV, 115; by H. W. Baehr in *HTB*, 6 Dec. 1959, p. 13; by C. N. Parkinson in *NYTBR*, 13 Dec. 1959, p. 10; by Geoffrey Nicholson in *S*, 13 Nov. 1959.

Howey, R. S. *The Rise of the Marginal Utility School, 1870-1889.* Lawrence: Univ. of Kansas Pr. Pp. 271.

Hudson, Derek. *Arthur Rackham: His Life and Work.* London: Heinemann. Pp. 181.
Rev. in *TLS*, 25 Nov., p. 752.

Hughes, George Bernard. *Victorian Pottery and Porcelain.* London: Country Life, 1959. Pp. 184.
Rev. by G. G. in *Connoisseur*, CXLV, 263-64.

Hughes, J. R. T. *Fluctuations in Trade, Industry and Finance: A Study of British Economic Development, 1850-1860.* Oxford: Clarendon Pr. Pp. xviii + 344.
Rev. by W. Ashworth in *Economica*, XXVII, 288-89; by W. H. Chaloner in *VS*, IV, 71-73.

Hyde, Harford Montgomery. *Sir Patrick Hastings: His Life and Cases.* London: Heinemann. Pp. xv + 416.
Biography of late-19th-century lawyer.

Imlah, Albert Henry. *Economic Elements in the Pax Britannica: Studies in British Foreign Trade in the Nineteenth Century.* . . . See VB 1959, 416.
Rev. by S. B. Saul in *JEH*, XIX, 452-53; by W. H. Chaloner in *VS*, IV, 71-73.

Inglis, K. S. "Patterns of Religious Worship in 1851." *Jour. of Eccl. Hist.*, XI, 74-86.

James, Robert Rhodes. *Lord Randolph*

Churchill. . . . See VB 1959, 416.
Rev. by R. R. Rea in *LJ,* LXXXV, 4139;
by Lindsay Rogers in *NYTBR,* 25 Dec.,
p. 16; by Maurice Shock in *VS,* III, 394-
95.

Jamieson, John. *The History of the Royal
Belfast Academical Institution, 1810-
1960.* Belfast: Wm. Mullan, for the Institution. Pp. xvi + 300.
Briefly rev. in *TLS,* 29 Jan., p. 70.

Johnson, Franklyn Arthur. *Defence by Committee: The British Committee of Imperial Defence 1885-1959.* London: Oxford
Univ. Pr. Pp. 416.
Rev. by A. J. P. Taylor in *NS,* LX, 898-
99; in *TLS,* 16 Dec., pp. 805-06.

Johnson, Leonard George. *The Social Evolution of Industrial Britain.* . . . See VB
1959, 416.
Rev. by Richard W. Lyman in *JMH,*
XXXII, 167.

Kaye, Barrington. *The Development of the
Architectural Profession in Britain.* London: Allen and Unwin. Pp. 224.

Kennedy, Michael. *The Hallé Tradition.*
Manchester: Manchester Univ. Pr. Pp.
xiv + 424.
Rev. in *TLS,* 4 Nov., p. 704.

Kerr, James Lennox. *The Unfortunate Ship.*
London: Harrap. Pp. 190.
History of H. M. S. *Birkenhead,* the
British Navy's first iron ship, and an in-
vestigation of its sinking in 1852.

Kirk-Smith, Harold. *William Thompson,
Archbishop of York.* . . . See VB 1959,
416.
Rev. by Asa Briggs in *EHR,* LXXV, 547-
48; by G. F. A. Best in *History,* XLV,
166.

Klemm, Friedrich. *A History of Western
Technology.* Tr. by Dorothea Waley.
New York: Scribner's, 1959. Pp. 401.
Rev. by R. J. Forbes in *Isis,* LI, 228-29.

Krause, John T. "Some Neglected Factors
in the English Industrial Revolution."
JEH, XIX, 528-40.
Argues that Western Europe on the eve
of industrialization differed more sharply
in its level of living from the currently
less developed countries than is allowed
by the present theory of demographic
transition.

Kruger, Rayne. *Good-Bye Dolly Gray.* . . .
See VB 1959, 416.
Rev. by H. W. Baehr in *HTB,* 11 Sept.,
p. 3; by R. R. Rea in *LJ,* LXXXV, 2428;
by Gordon Harrison in *NYTBR,* 11 Sept.,

p. 34; by T. R. Adam in *SR,* 17 Sept., p.
37.

Lamb, G. F. *The Happiest Days.* . . . See VB
1959, 417.
Rev. by G. H. Bantock in *VS,* IV, 167-70.

Lane, Nicholas. "The Bank of England in
the Nineteenth Century." *History Today,*
X, 535-41.

Lane, Nicholas. "The City of London in the
Nineteenth Century: The Growth of Insurance." *History Today,* X, 788-94.

Laski, Marghanita. "The Letters of Cecilia
Ridley (1819-1845) and O. E. D."
N & Q, n.s. VII, 184-85.

Latourette, Kenneth Scott. *Christianity in a
Revolutionary Age.* Vol. II: *The Nineteenth Century in Europe: The Protestant
and Eastern Churches.* . . . See VB 1959,
417.
Rev. by F. A. Norwood in *Church History,* XXIV, 221-23; by Owen Chadwick
in *S,* 9 Dec., p. 955; in *TLS,* 13 May,
p. 308.

Legge, J. D. *Britain in Fiji, 1858-1880.* . . .
See VB 1959, 417.
Rev. by F. J. West in *History,* XLV, 283-
84.

Lewis, Clyde J. "The Disintegration of the
Tory-Anglican Alliance in the Struggle
for Catholic Emancipation." *Church History,* XXIX, 25-43.

Lewis, M. J. T. *The Pentewan Railway,
1829-1918.* Truro: D. B. Barton. Pp.
58.

Liebman, Marcel. "Fabianisme et Communisme: Les Webb et l'Union Soviétique."
International Rev. of Social Hist., V,
400-23.

Link, R. G. *English Theories of Economic
Fluctuations, 1815-1848.* . . . See VB
1959, 417.
Rev. by Mark Blaug in *VS,* IV, 73-74.

Lipsey, Richard G. "The Relation between
Unemployment and the Rate of Change
of Money Wage Rates in the United
Kingdom, 1862-1957: A Further Analysis." *Economica,* XXVII, 1-31. (See VB
1958, 362, Phillips.)

Lochhead, Marion. *The Young Victorians.*
. . . See VB 1959, 417.
Rev. by Naomi Lewis, in *VS,* IV, 170-73.

Lowndes, G. A. N. *Margaret McMillan: 'The
Children's Champion.'* London: Museum
Pr. Pp. 110.
Rev. by Letitia Fairfield in *NS,* LX, 130-
131. Biography of a late Victorian social

and educational reformer.

Lumby, E. W. R. "Lord Elgin and the Burning of the Summer Palace." *History Today*, X, 479-87.

Lynch, Patrick, and Vaizey, John. *Guinness's Brewery in the Irish Economy 1759-1876*. Cambridge: Cambridge Univ. Pr. Pp. viii + 278.

Lyons, F. S. L. *The Fall of Parnell, 1890-91*. London: Routledge and K. Paul. Pp. xii + 363.
Rev. by R. E. Burns in *Canadian Hist. Rev.*, XLI, 354-55; by J. A. Thomas in *History*, XLV, 280-81; by Robert Rhodes James in *History Today*, X, 431-33; by Conor Cruise O'Brien in *S*, 29 Apr., pp. 633-34; by Philip Toynbee in *TC*, CLXVII, 575-77; in *TLS*, 22 Apr., p. 260; by Philip M. Williams in *VS*, IV, 178-79.

Machin, Frank. *The Yorkshire Miners: A History*. Barnsley: National Union of Mineworkers, 1958. Pp. xi + 496.
Rev. by George W. Hilton in *JEH*, XX, 130-31.

Martin, Briton. "The Viceroyalty of Lord Dufferin." *History Today*, X, 821-30.

Mather, F. C. *Public Order in the Age of the Chartists*. Manchester: Manchester Univ. Pr., 1959. Pp. ix + 260.
Rev. by J. B. Conacher in *AHR*, LXVI, 141-43; by R. A. Lewis in *History*, XLV, 276-77; by Asa Briggs in *NS*, LIX, 45-46; in *TLS*, 8 Apr., p. 222; by A. R. Schoyen in *VS*, IV, 67-69.

Mathias, Peter. *The Brewing Industry in England, 1700-1830*. Cambridge: Cambridge Univ Pr., 1959. Pp. xxviii + 595.
Rev. by S. Pollard in *JEH*, XX, 339-40.

Matthews, Joseph J. "The First Harvard-Oxford Boat Race." *NEQ*, XXXIII, 74-82.
A sensational international event, London, 1869.

Maynard, Douglas H. "The World's Anti-Slavery Convention of 1840." *Miss. Valley Hist. Rev.*, XLVII, 452-71.

McClatchey, Diana. *Oxfordshire Clergy, 1777-1869*. Oxford: Clarendon Pr. Pp. vi + 252.

McCord, Norman. *The Anti-Corn Law League, 1838-1846*.... See VB 1959, 417.
Rev. by Christopher Howard in *H* XLV, 65.

McDowell, Robert Brendon. *British Conservatism 1832-1914*.... See VB 1959, 417.
Rev. by Francis H. Herrick in *AHR*,
LXV, 956-57; in *QR*, CCXCVIII, 235-36.

McGee, Earl W. "The Anglican Church and Social Reform, 1830-1850." *DA*, XX, 3710-11.
The church in 1830, "lethargic and insensitive to the needs of society," opposed utilitarianism and materlialism. But by 1850 in order to realize its mission and relieve social ills, it was in the van of the movement for social reform.

McMenemey, W. H. *The Story of Sir Charles Hastings*.... See VB 1959, 417.
Rev. by J. A. Banks in *VS*, III, 391-93.

Mechie, Stewart. *The Church and Scottish Social Development, 1780-1870*. London: Oxford Univ. Pr. Pp. xi + 181.

Miller, T. B. "The Egyptian Question and British Foreign Policy, 1892-1894." *JMH*, XXXII, 1-15.

Moers, Ellen. *The Dandy: Brummell to Beerbohm*. New York: Viking Pr. Pp. 372.
Rev. by Calvin D. Linton in *American Scholar*, XXIX, 576; by DeLancey Ferguson in *HTB*, 24 Apr., p. 11; by B. A. Robie in *LJ*, LXXXV, 772; by V. S. Pritchett in *NS*, LIX, 297; by Frances Winwar in *NYTBR*, 24 Apr., p. 20; by Hesketh Pearson in *SR*, 21 May, p. 24; by Mark Boxer in *S*, 4 Mar., p. 329; in *TLS*, 15 Apr., p. 240.

Moncure, James A. "James Wilson and the *Economist*, 1805-1860." *DA*, XX, 4642-43.

Moody, Theodore W., and Beckett, J. C. *Queen's, Belfast, 1845-1949: The History of a University*. London: Faber, 1959. 2 vols. Pp. lxvii + 983.
Rev. by J. W. Blake in *Univ. Rev.*, XXXII, 65-66.

Moore, Jerrold N. "Sir Edward Elgar as a University Professor." *Univ. of Rochester Libr. Bull.*, XV, 29-39.

Moorehead, Alan. *The White Nile*. New York: Harper. Pp. 385.
Rev. by Peter Duval Smith in *S*, 9 Dec., pp. 951-52; in *TLS*, 30 Dec., p. 839. 19th-century exploration and conquest in central Africa, from Livingstone and Burton to Gordon and Kitchener.

Morley, Malcolm. "More about the Royal Kent Theatre." *Theatre Notebook*, XIV, 43-44. (See VB 1959, 413, Bligh.)

Morris, John Henry, and Williams, Lawrence John. *The South Wales Coal Industry, 1841-1875*.... See VB 1959, 418.
Rev. by W. H. B. Court in *EHR*, LXXV, 542; by George W. Hilton in *JEH*, XX, 130-31.

Mosley, Leonard Oswald. *The Glorious Fault: The Life of Lord Curzon.* New York: Harcourt, Brace. Pp. 334.

Rev. by H. W. Baehr in *HTB*, 29 May, p. 10; by R. R. Rea in *LJ*, LXXXV, 1574; by Horace Gregory in *N*, 28 May, p. 475; by Paul Johnson in *NS*, LX, 614-15; by D. W. Brogan in *NYTBR*, 15 May, p. 6; by Roy Jenkins in *S*, 28 Oct., pp. 659-60; by Aubrey Menen in *SR*, 28 May, p. 22; in *TLS*, 28 Oct., p. 692.

Mosse, W. E. "England, Russia and the Rumanian Revolution of 1866." *Slavonic and East European Rev.*, XXXIX, 73-94.

Mosse, Werner Eugen. *The European Powers and the German Question, 1848-1871.* . . . See VB 1959, 418.

Rev. by Agatha Ramm in *EHR*, LXXV, 363-64.

Munford, William Arthur. *William Ewart, M. P., 1798-1869.* London: Grafton. Pp. xvi + 208.

Rev. by Betty Kemp in *History*, XLV, 276; in *TLS*, 29 Apr., p. 271.

Murphy, James. *The Religious Problem in English Education.* . . . See VB 1959, 418.

Rev. by Neville Masterman in *History*, XLV, 277-78; by G. H. Bantock in *VS*, 167-70.

Murray, John. "Britain and Argentina in the Nineteenth Century." *StI*, XLIX, 420-36.

Neill, Thomas P. *1859 in Review.* . . . See VB 1959, 418.

Rev. by R. H. Heimanson in *LJ*, LXXXV, 761.

Newman, Peter. "The Erosion of Marshall's Theory of Value." *Quart. Journ. of Econ.*, LXXIV, 587-601.

Newsome, David. *A History of Wellington College, 1859-1959.* . . . See VB 1959, 418.

Rev. by W. H. G. Armytage in *EHR*, LXXV, 366.

Nicoloff, Philip L. "Emerson's Thought in *English Traits*." *DA*, XX, 3748.

Examines the influence of Victorian writers on Emerson's ideas.

O'Brien, Conor Cruise (ed.). *The Shaping of Modern Ireland.* London: Routledge and K. Paul. Pp. vi + 201.

Rev. by William Hughes in *NS*, LX, 398; in *TLS*, 12 Aug., p. 518. Assessment of Irish leaders between Parnell and 1916 Rising.

Oliver, Ronald. *Sir Henry Johnston and the Scramble for Africa.* . . . See VB 1959, 418.

Rev. by M. D. Hemphill in *AHR*, LXIV, 994.

Ollard, Richard. "New Year, 1860." *NER*, CLIV, 13-18.

Pakenham, Elizabeth. *Jameson's Raid.* London: Weidenfeld and Nicolson. Pp. 366.

Rev. by Edgar Holt in *History Today*, X, 213; by Geoffrey Barraclough in *S*, 26 Feb., p. 295; in *TLS*, 5 Feb., p. 75; by Richard H. Wilde in *VS*, IV, 179-80.

Parkinson, Cyril Northcote. *British Intervention in Malaya, 1867-1877.* Singapore: Univ. of Malaya Pr.; distr. by Oxford Univ. Pr. Pp. xx + 384.

Payne, Ernest A. *The Baptist Union — A Short History.* London: Carey Kingsgate Pr., 1959. Pp. 317.

Baptist history in Great Britain, 1812-13 to date.

Payne, Pierre Stephen Robert. *The White Rajahs of Sarawak.* London: Hale. Pp. 274.

Rev. by S. L. Hopkinson in *LJ*, LXXXV, 1585-86; by James Leasor in *NYTBR*, 24 Apr., p. 6; by Ronald Bryden in *S*, 30 Sept., p. 493; in *TLS*, 7 Oct., pp. 637-38.

Pelling, Henry. *Modern Britain, 1885-1955.* London: Nelson. Pp. xii + 212. Vol. VIII of *A History of Britain*, edited by Christopher Brooke and D. Mack Smith.

Briefly rev. in *TLS*, 2 Dec., p. 786.

Perham, Margery. *Lugard: The Years of Authority, 1898-1945.* London: Collins. Pp. xx + 748.

Rev. in *TLS*, 23 Dec., pp. 821-22. Second and final volume of Margery Perham's biography. For first volume, see VB 1957, 392.

Petrie, Sir Charles. *The Victorians.* London: Eyre and Spottiswoode. Pp. 271.

Rev. in *Blackwood's Mag.*, CCLXXXVII, 558; briefly in *NS*, LIX, 870; in *QR*, CCXCVIII, 365-66; in *TLS*, 3 June, p. 351; by C. L. Mowat in *VS*, IV, 182.

Pierson, Stanley, "John Trevor and the Labor Church Movement in England, 1891-1900." *Church History*, XXIX, 463-78.

Pollard, Sidney. *A History of Labour in Sheffield.* . . . See VB 1959, 419.

Rev. by Harry Townsend in *Economica*, XXVII, 293-94; by J. E. Williams in *VS*, IV, 180-82.

Pope-Hennessy, James. *Queen Mary, 1867-1953.* . . . See VB 1959, 419.

Rev. by Grace Banyard in *CR*, CXCVII, 63; by Geoffrey Bruun in *HTB*, 14 Feb., p. 1; by R. R. Rea in *LJ*, LXXXV, 269; by J. A. Smith in *NS*, LVIII, 512; by

Peter Quennell in *NYTBR*, 14 Feb., p. 1; by Walter Starkie in *SR*, 13 Feb., p. 23.
Potter, George W. *To the Golden Door: The Story of the Irish in Ireland and America*. Boston: Little, Brown. Pp. viii + 631.
Rev. in *Current Hist.*, XXXVIII, 292; by William Miller in *HTB*, 24 Apr., p. 6; by Oscar Handlin in *NYTBR*, 3 Apr., p. 6.
Pound, Reginald, and Harmsworth, Geoffrey. *Northcliffe.* . . . See VB 1959, 419.
Rev. by D. W. Brogan in *NYTBR*, 30 Oct., p. 36.
Pressnell, Leslie Sedden (ed.). *Studies in the Industrial Revolution*. London: Athlone Pr. Pp. 350.
Prest, John Michael. *The Industrial Revolution in Coventry*. London: Oxford Univ. Pr. Pp. xi + 152.
Raymond, John. "Cromer: The Proconsul." *History Today*, X, 180-86; 240-46.
Presents "The Maker of Modern Egypt" as the archetypal British Consul.
Redman, Alvin. *The House of Hanover*. London: Alvin Redman. Pp. 471.
Rev. in *TLS*, 19 Aug., p. 527.
Reeves, George H. "Great Britain and the Unification of Italy." *DA*, XX, 3712-13.
Rich, Edwin Ernest. *The History of the Hudson's Bay Company, 1670-1870*. Vol. II: *1763-1870*. London: Hudson's Bay Record Society, 1959. Pp. 975.
Richardson, Philip John Sampley. *Social Dances of the Nineteenth Century in England*. London: Jenkins. Pp. 152.
Briefly rev. in *TLS*, 21 Oct., p. 682.
Rimmer, William Gordon. *Marshalls of Leeds, Flax-Spinners, 1788-1886*. Cambridge: Cambridge Univ. Pr. Pp. xiii + 342.
Rippy, J. Fred. *British Investments in Latin America, 1822-1949*. . . . See VB 1959, 419.
Rev. by J. L. Stein in *Amer. Econ. Rev.*, L, 230; by R. R. Hill in *APSS*, CCCXXVII, 167; by Dorothy R. Adler in *Econ. Jour.*, LXX, 148-49; by Bailey W. Diffie in *JEH*, XX, 140-41; by Harold Eugene Davis in *JMH*, XXXII, 170; by Joseph Boromé in *LJ*, LXXXIV, 1506.
Ritt, Lawrence. "The Victorian Conscience in Action: The National Association for the Promotion of Social Science, 1857-1886." *DA*, XX, 3713-14.
Roberts, David. *Victorian Origins of the*

British Welfare State. New Haven, Conn.: Yale Univ. Pr. Pp. xiii + 369.
Rev. by H. H. Folkler in *LJ*, LXXXV, 1814.
Roe, Frederic Gordon. *The Victorian Child*. . . . See VB 1959, 419.
Rev. by Naomi Lewis in *VS*, IV, 170-73.
Rolt, Lionel Thomas Caswell. *George and Robert Stephenson: The Railway Revolution*. London: Longmans. Pp. xix + 356.
Rev. by W. H. Chaloner in *History Today*, X, 803-04; by T. L. Cottrell in *NS*, LX, 133; in *TLS*, 15 July, p. 446.
Rothstein, Morton. "America in the International Rivalry for the British Wheat Market, 1860-1914." *Miss. Valley Hist. Rev.*, XLVII, 401-18.
Runciman, Sir Steven. *The White Rajahs: A History of Sarawak, 1841-1946*. Cambridge: Cambridge Univ. Pr. Pp. xii + 320.
Rev. by Harold Nicolson in *NYTBR*, 16 Oct., p. 3; by Ronald Bryden in *S*, 30 Sept., p. 493; in *TLS*, 7 Oct., pp. 637-38.
Rygh, Andrew R. "English Periodicals and the Democratic Movement: 1865-85." *DA*, XXI, 1547.
The idea of democracy among English governing classes as seen in the literary and political periodicals — the *Quarterly Review*, *Edinburgh Review*, and *Fortnightly Review*.
Saul, Samuel Berrick. *Studies in British Overseas Trade, 1870-1914*. Liverpool: Liverpool Univ. Pr. Pp. ix + 246.
Rev. by W. Ashworth in *History*, XLV, 286-87.
Sayers, R. S. "Monetary Thought and Monetary Policy in England." *Econ Jour.*, LXX, 710-24.
A review of "certain basic notions that have underlain English monetary policy during the 19th and 20th centuries."
Schoyen, Albert Robert. *The Chartist Challenge: A Portrait of George Julian Harney*. . . . See VB 1959, 420.
Rev. by Earl A. Reitan in *JEH*, XX, 345-46; by Corinne Weston in *JMH*, XXXII, 77-78.
Schrier, Arnold. *Ireland and the American Emigration, 1850-1900*. . . . See VB 1959, 420.
Rev. by H. L. Calkin in *AHR*, LXIV, 996; by Arthur Mann in *American Sociological Rev.*, XXIV, 602; by J. F. Moran in *LJ*, LXXXIII, 2174.
Schuyler, Robert Livingstone (ed.). *Freder-*

ick *William Maitland, Historian.* Berkeley: Univ. of California Pr. Pp. vi + 261.

Seymer, Lucy Ridgely. *Florence Nightingale's Nurses: The Nightingale Training School, 1860-1960.* London: Pitman. Pp. xi + 169.

Seznec, Jean. "Michelet à Oxford." *French Studies,* XIV, 149-52.

Sideman, Belle Becker, and Friedman, Lillian (eds.). *Europe Looks at the Civil War.* New York: Orion Pr. Pp. xx + 323.

Sigsworth, Eric M. *Black Dyke Mills: A History.* . . . See VB 1959, 420.
Rev. by E. A. Beever in *JMH,* XXXII, 167-68.

Simey, T. S., and Simey, Margaret Bayne. *Charles Booth: Social Scientist.* London: Oxford Univ. Pr. Pp. x + 282.

Simon, Brian. *Studies in the History of Education, 1780-1870.* London: Lawrence and Wishart. Pp. 375.
Rev. by W. H. G. Armytage in *History,* XLV, 277; by William Walsh in *NS,* LIX, 600: in *TLS,* 15 Apr., p. 242; by W. H. G. Armytage in *Universities Quart.,* XIV, 320-22; by G. H. Bantock in *VS,* IV, 167-70.

Singer, Charles, *et al.* (eds.). *A History of Technology.* Vol. V: *The Late Nineteenth Century.* . . . See VB 1959, 420.
Rev. by Herbert Heaton in *AHR,* LXIV, 626; in *Chemical and Engineering News,* XXXVII, 108; by Cyril Stanley Smith in *Isis,* LI, 354-56; by David S. Landers in *JEH,* XIX, 473-75; by I. B. Cohen in *NYTBR,* 1 Feb., 1959; in *TLS,* 9 Jan., p. 16.

Smith, Gordon C. "The Oratory of Lord Brougham." *DA,* XX, 3434.
Influence of Brougham's oratory on British history.

Sommer, Dudley. *Haldane of Cloan: His Life and Times, 1856-1928.* London: Allen and Unwin. Pp. 448.

Spence, Clark C. *British Investments and the American Mining Frontier, 1860-1901.* . . . See VB 1959, 420.
Rev. by Earl Pomeroy in *JEH,* XIX, 475.

Spence, Clark C. *God Speed the Plow: The Coming of Steam Cultivation to Great Britain.* Urbana: Univ. of Illinois Pr. Pp. 183.
Rev. by W. T. Johnson in *LJ,* LXXXV, 4145.

Spring, David. "Some Reflections on Social History in the Nineteenth Century." *VS,* IV, 55-64.

In this discussion of several memoirs and social histories of late-Victorian life Spring suggests the necessity for a reconsideration of the role of the aristocracy in Victorian society.

Sterling, Thomas. *Stanley's Way: A Sentimental Journey through Central Africa.* London: Hart-Davis. Pp. 258.
Rev. by John Barkham in *NYTBR,* 20 Nov., p. 36; in *TLS,* 21 Oct., p. 670. An account of the journey to find Livingstone, based on a retracing of Stanley's route.

Stewart, William. *Characters of Bygone London.* London: Harrap. Pp. 143.
Descriptions and illustrations of oyster-stall men, cabbies, and other picturesque characters of (especially 19th-century) London streets.

Stokes, Eric. *The English Utilitarians and India.* . . . See VB 1959, 420.
Rev. by B. A. Corry in *Economica,* XXVII, 85-86; by Maurice Cowling in *EHR,* LXXV, 532; by J. H. Burns in *History,* XLV, 165-65; by Morris David Morris in *JPE,* LXVIII, 86-87; by Geoffrey Barraclough in *S,* 2 Jan. 1959, p. 20; by H. S. Gordon in *VS,* III, 389-90.

Stokes, Eric. "Great Britain and Africa: The Myth of Imperialism." *History Today,* X, 554-63.
A revaluation of the thesis that the motives of expansion changed after 1870.

Swift, David E. "Charles Simeon and J. J. Gurney: A Chapter in Anglican-Quaker Relations." *Church Hist.,* XXIX, 167-86.

Tappe, E. D. "Meat Canning in Rumania for the British Navy." *Slavonic and East European Rev.,* XXXIX, 214-15.
"At least three factories seem to have been set up in the Rumanian principalities in the mid-19th century to preserve meat for the British navy."

Tappe, E. D. "Rumania after the Union as Seen by Two English Journalists." *Slavonic and East European Rev.,* XXXIX, 198-214.
Travel articles by Lawrence Oliphant and William Beatty-Kingston.

Taylor, A. J. "Progress and Poverty in Britain, 1780-1850: A Reappraisal." *History,* XLV, 16-31.

Terrot, Charles. *The Maiden Tribute.* . . . See VB 1959, 421.
Rev. by Christopher Pym in *S,* 9 Oct. 1959, p. 494.

Thierry, Adrien. "Au temps de Paul Cambon." *Revue des deux mondes* (no. 14, 15 July), 289-99.

Diplomatic history of relations between England and France from 1843 (Victoria's visit) to 1904.

Thirsk, Joan (ed.). *Suffolk Farming in the Nineteenth Century.* Ipswich: Suffolk Records Society. 1958. Pp. 178. Rev. by Barbara M. H. Strang in *N & Q*, n.s. VII, 195-96.

Thomas, David St. John (ed.). *A Regional History of the Railways of Great Britain.* Vol. I: *The West Country.* London: Phoenix. Pp. x + 212. Rev. briefly in *NS*, LIX, 507; noticed in *TLS*, 29 Apr., p. 279.

Thornley, David. "The Home Rule Party and Obstruction." *Irish Hist. Studies*, XII, 38-57.

Thornton, A. P. *The Imperial Idea and Its Enemies: A Study in British Power....* See VB 1959, 421. Rev. by John S. Galbraith in *AHR*, LXV, 596-97; by John Conway in *Canadian Hist. Rev.*, XLI, 224-31; in *Current Hist.*, XXXVII, 51; in *Foreign Affairs*, XXXVII, 695; by Paul Knaplund in *JMH*, XXXII, 184-85; by A. L. Burt in *PSQ*, LXXIV, 624.

Tibble, Anne. *With Gordon in the Sudan.* London: Muller. Pp. 144.

Tucker, G. S. L. *Progress and Profits in British Economic Thought, 1650-1850.* Cambridge: Cambridge Univ. Pr. Pp. viii + 206. Rev. in *TLS*, 25 Nov., p. 761; by Mark Blaug in *VS*, IV, 73-74.

Turberville, Arthur Stanley. *The House of Lords in the Age of Reform....* See VB 1959, 421. Rev. by David Thomson in *History*, XLV, 270-71.

Vane-Tempest-Stewart, Edith, Marchioness of Londonderry. *Frances Anne: ... Marchioness of Londonderry, and Her Husband....* See VB 1958, 364. Rev. by David Spring in *JMH*, XXXIII, 75-76.

Wainwright, David. *Liverpool Gentlemen: A History of Liverpool College, An Independent Day School, from 1840.* London: Faber. Pp. 342. Rev. in *TLS*, 18 Nov., p. 745.

Wallace, Elisabeth. "The Political Ideas of the Manchester School." *TQ*, XXIX, 122-38.

"Technically Liberals, in temperament and practice the Manchester group were independents, with a deep-seated distrust of parties."

Weber, Carl J. *The Rise and Fall of James Ripley Osgood....* See VB 1959, 421. Rev. by William Charvat in *AL*, XXXII, 225-26; by Earle F. Walbridge in *LJ*, LXXXV, 648; by Rollo G. Silver in *NEQ*, Sept., 407-09; by J. O. Bailey in *SAQ*; by Daniel Melcher in *SR*, 30 July, p. 21; in *TLS*, 29 Jan., p. 70; by Clarence Gohdes in *VNL*, No. 17 (Spring), 36-37.

White, James Floyd. "The Cambridge Camden Society and the Medieval Revival in the Church of England during the Nineteenth Century." *Church History*, XXIX, 207.

Whitely, William H. "The Social Composition of the House of Commons, 1868-1885." *DA*, XX, 4646-47.

Whittington-Egan, Richard, and Smerdon, Geoffrey. *The Quest of the Golden Boy: The Life and Letters of Richard LeGallienne.* London: Unicorn Pr. Pp. 580. Rev. by Frank Kermode in *S*, 25 Nov., pp. 850-51; in *TLS*, 11 Nov., p. 726.

Whyte, John Henry. *The Independent Irish Party, 1850-1859....* See VB 1959, 422. Rev. by R. B. McDowell in *Irish Hist. Studies*, XII, 76-78.

Williams, L. Pearce. "Michael Faraday's Education in Science." *Isis*, LI, 515-30.

Wood, Anthony C. *Nineteenth-Century Britain, 1815-1914.* London: Longmans. Pp. xiii + 476. Briefly rev. in *TLS*, 11 Mar., p. 166.

Woodruff, William. *The Rise of the British Rubber Industry during the Nineteenth Century....* See VB 1959, 422. Rev. by Barry Supple in *JEH*, XIX, 477-79.

Wright, Lawrence. *Clean and Decent: The Fascinating History of the Bathroom and the Water Closet.* London: Routledge and K. Paul. Pp. xii + 282. Rev. by R. M. Malone in *LJ*, LXXXV, 1612; in *TLS*, 11 Mar., p. 164.

III. MOVEMENTS OF IDEAS AND LITERARY FORMS

Abercrombie, Nigel. *The Life and Work of Edmund Bishop.* London: Longmans, 1959. Pp. xv + 539. Rev. by Stephen J. Tonsor in *AHR*, LXV, 957; by Eric John in *Dublin Rev.*, CCXXXIV, 52-67; in *TLS*, 15 July, p. 448; by R. J. Schoeck in *VS*, IV, 79-81.

Bishop helped to found the study of the development of liturgy.

Allen, Louis. "The Oxford Movement and the Vatican." *VS*, III, 458-59.

Comment on Charles Dougherty's note on this subject (*VS*, II, 149-54).

Allott, Miriam (ed.). *Novelists on the Novel.* . . . See VB 1959, 422.

Rev. by A. O. J. Cockshut in *EC*, X, 473-75; briefly in *NCF*, XIV, 372; by G. Armour Craig in *VS*, IV, 173-75.

Arberry, Arthur John. *Oriental Essays: Portraits of Seven Scholars.* London: Allen and Unwin. Pp. 262.

Rev. in *TLS*, 8 July, p. 437. Includes essays on E. W. Lane (1801-76), student of Egypt and translator of first accurate version in English of the Arabian Nights; and E. H. Palmer (1840-82), professor of Arabic at Cambridge.

Baumer, Franklin L. *Religion and the Rise of Scepticism.* New York: Harcourt, Brace. Pp. 308.

Rev. by Harold Lancour in *LJ*, LXXXV, 2941.

Becker, Eugene M. "Whistler and the Aesthetic Movement." *DA*, XX, 2744.

Analysis of the doctrines of art from Pre-Raphaelitism to the 'nineties.

Bell, Vereen M. "Character and Point of View in Representative Victorian Novels." *DA*, XX, 3741-42.

Treats the subjective analysis of characters in the novels of Dickens, Thackeray, Emily Brontë, George Eliot, Meredith, and James.

Bentwich, Norman. "A Public School's Boys-of-Letters." *CR*, CXCVIII, 434-36.

On literary activity at St. Paul's School, London, in the 'nineties.

Betsky, Seymour. "Toward a New Definition of Culture." *Chicago Review*, XIV, 31-58.

An extended discussion of Raymond Williams' *Culture and Society* (see VB 1958, 371) which offers its own definition of culture and suggests methods by which the culture of 19th-century England can be profitably studied. A thoughtful and useful contribution.

Blake, Ralph M., Ducasse, Curt J., and Madden, Edward H. *Theories of Scientific Method: The Renaissance through the Nineteenth Century.* Seattle: Univ. of Washington Pr. Pp. iv + 346.

Briefly rev. in *TLS*, 26 Aug., p. 551.

Boase, T. S. R. *English Art, 1800-1870.* (Vol. X in *The Oxford History of English Art.*) . . . . See VB 1959, 422.

Rev. by Kenneth Garlick in *Burlington*

Mag., CII, 267; in *HTB*, 6 Dec. 1959, p. 15; by Cyril Barrett in *StI*, XLIX, 82-83; by John Alford in *VS*, III, 397-400; by A. C. Ritchie in *YR*, XLIX, 464.

Brose, Olive. "F. D. Maurice and the Victorian Crisis of Belief." *VS*, III, 227-48.

Browse, Lillian. *Sickert.* London: Hart-Davis. Pp. 124.

Rev. in *TLS*, 27 May, p. 336.

Bruce, Donald. "Vamp's Progress." *Cornhill Mag.*, No. 1025 (Autumn), 353-59.

La femme fatale from Poe to Beerbohm.

Burton, Ernest James. *The British Theatre, Its Repertory and Practice, 1100-1900.* London: Jenkins. Pp. 271.

Rev. in *TLS*, 16 Dec., p. 814.

Cannon, Walter. "The Problem of Miracles in the 1830's." *VS*, IV, 5-32.

The problem of miracles involved explanations of how the cosmos was created and how it moved. "With their stubborn insistence on the historical nature of the cosmos" men like William Whewell "forced speculation away from Lyell's unprogressive position and kept a developmental view of the world alive."

Cazamian, Madeleine L. *Le Roman et les Idées en Angleterre, 1860-1914.* Vol. III: *Les Doctrines d'Action et d'Aventure, 1880-1914.* . . . See VB 1958, 366.

Rev. by J. G. Riewald in *ESt*, XLI, 34-40.

Clarke, Martin Lowther. *Classical Education in Britain, 1500-1900.* . . . See VB 1959, 423.

Rev. by Peter D. Arnott in *Classical Jour.*, LV, 284-85; by Richard T. Bruiere in *Classical Philology*, LV, 143-44; by D. C. C. Young in *Classical Rev.*, X, 166-67; by Charles Garton in *DUJ*, LIII (n.s. XXII), 33-37; by P. G. Walsh in *Irish Hist. Studies*, XII, 87-88; by G. H. Bantock in *VS*, IV, 167-70.

Clive, Geoffrey. *The Romantic Enlightenment: Ambiguity and Paradox in the Western Mind, 1750-1920.* New York: Meridian. Pp. 219.

Rev. by Mary Barrett in *LJ*, LXXXV, 764-65.

Colby, Reginald. "Whistler and 'Miss Cissie.'" *QR*, CCXCVIII, 309-20.

Crompton, Donald W. "The New Criticism: A Caveat." *EC*, X, 359-64.

Comments on theme and symbol in recent criticism of Victorian novels, particularly *Jane Eyre* and Moynahan's article on *Great Expectations* (see below DICKENS: Moynahan).

Daiches, David. *A Critical History of English Literature.* 2 vols. London: Secker and Warburg. Pp. viii + 534; iii + 635.

Rev. by Raymond Williams in *Guardian,* 23 Sept., p. 8; by J. R. Willingham in *LJ,* LXXXV, 2938; by William Walsh in *NS,* LX, 533-34.

Daniel-Rops, H. "Le Mouvement d'Oxford." *Revue des deux mondes,* (no. 5, 1 Mar.), 3-17.

Davies, Robertson. *A Voice from the Attic.* New York: Knopf. Pp. 400.

Rev. by E. Moon in *LJ,* LXXXV, 3446. A series of essays by a Canadian bookman. Comment on Samuel Smiles, Havelock Ellis, and forgotten Victorian fiction.

Dobzhansky, Theodosius. "Evolutionism and Man's Hope." *SeR,* LXVIII, 274-88.

Donoghue, Denis. *The Third Voice.* . . . See VB 1959, 423.

Rev. in *TLS,* 22 Jan., p. 50.

Duncan, Joseph E. *The Revival of Metaphysical Poetry.* . . . See VB 1959, 423.

Rev. by Joseph H. Summers in *MLN,* LXXV, 517-19.

Edwards, Oliver. *Talking of Books.* London: Heinemann, 1957. Pp. 306.

Rev. by J. Loiseau in *Études anglaises,* XIII, 72. A selection of articles which first appeared in *The Times.* Many Victorian writers included in this collection of essays.

Elliott, Robert C. *The Power of Satire: Magic, Ritual, Art.* Princeton, N.J.: Princeton Univ. Pr. Pp. 300.

Rev. by Patrick Penland in *LJ,* LXXXV, 1912; by Stephen Potter in *SR,* 4 June, p. 15.

Ellmann, Richard (ed.). *Edwardians and Late Victorians.* New York: Columbia Univ. Pr. Pp. x + 245.

Rev. by R. H. Donahugh in *LJ,* LXXXV, 2790; briefly in *NCF,* XV, 279. The English Institute Essays: Includes essays by Graham Hough on George Moore, Ruth Z. Temple on late-19th-century literary criticism, Helmut E. Gerber on "The Nineties: Beginning, End, or Transition?", Thomas R. Whitaker on Yeats, Gordon N. Ray on Wells, and Gerald Weales on Shaw and the Edwardian theatre.

Entwisle, Eric Arthur. *A Literary History of Wallpaper.* London: Batsford. Pp. 211.

Rev. in *TLS,* 9 Sept., 580.

Fairlie, Henry. "Oratory in Political Life." *History Today,* X, 3-13.

Includes remarks on oratorical style and effect of Gladstone and Disraeli.

Fay, William P. "Dublin, capitale littéraire." *Revue des deux mondes,* (No. 23, 1 Dec.), 403-16.

A literary history from Swift to Yeats and Joyce.

Flanagan, Thomas J. B. *The Irish Novelists,* 1800-1850. . . . See VB 1959, 423.

Rev. by Emmet Larkin in *CE,* XXII, 61; by Lionel Stevenson in *NCF,* XV, 86-89; by Vivian Mercier in *NYTBR,* 20 Dec. 1959, p. 5; in *TLS,* 18 Mar., p. 176; by David H. Greene in *VNL,* No. 17 (Spring), 37-38.

Foakes, Reginald Anthony. *The Romantic Assertion: A Study of the Languages of Nineteenth Century Poetry.* . . . See VB 1959, 423.

Rev. by Leon A. Gottfried in *JEGP,* LIX, 299-304; by Marshall McLuhan in *MP,* LVII, 279-80; by Edwin Morgan in *RES,* n.s. XI, 105-07.

Fraser, George Sutherland. *Vision and Rhetoric: Studies in Modern Poetry.* New York: Barnes and Noble. Pp. 285.

Rev. by H. Burke in *LJ,* LXXXV, 2431. Discusses Yeats.

Fredeman, William E. "Pre-Raphaelite Caricature: 'The Choice of Paris: An Idyll,' by Florence Caxton." *Burlington Mag.,* CII, 523-29.

Gibson, William M. "Mark Twain and the Victorians." *VNL,* No. 18 (Fall), p. 26.

A review of Walter Blair's *Mark Twain and Huck Finn.* Stresses the influence of several English Victorians on Twain.

Gilkes, Lillian. *Cora Crane: A Biography of Mrs. Stephen Crane.* Bloomington: Indiana Univ. Pr. Pp. 416.

Rev. by B. A. Robie in *LJ,* LXXXV, 3436; by Maxwell Geismar in *NYTBR,* 20 Nov., p. 74. The relations of Crane and his wife in the 'nineties with Conrad, James, Wells, and others.

Gillispie, Charles Coulston. *The Edge of Objectivity: An Essay in the History of Scientific Ideas.* Princeton, N.J.: Princeton Univ. Pr. Pp. 562.

Rev. by William G. Pollard in *American Scholar,* XXX, 140.

Gloag, John. *The English Tradition in Design.* London: A. and C. Black. New enlarged and revised ed. Pp. x + 89.

Rev. by Paul von Khrum in *LJ,* LXXXV, 1100. Considers continuity of English design, which the author believes was interrupted twice: in the 16th century by the "italianate fashion," and in the 19th century by the confusion which is Victorian style.

Greene, John C. *Death of Adam: Evolution and Its Impact on Western Thought.* . . . See VB 1959, 424.

Rev. in *TLS*, 4 Mar., p. 149.

Gregory, Horace. *The World of James McNeill Whistler.* . . . See VB 1959, 424.

Rev. by Karl Nyren in *LJ*, LXXXIV, 3764; by Anne Fremantle in *NYTBR*, 14 Feb., p. 6.

Griffin, Ernest G. "The Dramatic Chorus in English Literary Theory and Practice." *DA*, XX, 3726-27.

Uses Arnold's *Merope*, Swinburne's *Atalanta in Calydon* and *Erechtheus*, and Hardy's *The Dynasts* for the Victorian portion.

Haber, Francis C. *The Age of the World: Moses to Darwin.* . . . See VB 1959, 424.

Rev. by Walter F. Cannon in *Isis*, LI, 213-14; by George Basalla in *LJ*, LXXXIV, 3114.

Harkness, Bruce. "Bibliography and the Novelistic Fallacy." *Studies in Bibliography*, XII, 59-73.

Comments on texts of novels by Conrad, Hardy, and Dickens, among others.

Hart, Francis R. "Boswell and the Romantics: A Chapter in the History of Biographical Theory." *ELH*, XXVII, 44-65.

The "romantics" are Carlyle, Macaulay, and Lockhart, whose reviews of Croker's Boswell are the basis of this study.

Hawkes, Jacquetta. "Archaeology and the Concept of Progress." *History Today*, X, 73-82.

Highet, Gilbert. *The Powers of Poetry.* New York: Oxford Univ. Pr. Pp. 356.

Rev. by R. D. Spector in *HTB*, 12 June, p. 4; by J. R. Willingham in *LJ*, LXXXV, 2171; by F. J. Warnke in *NewR*, 11 July, p. 27; by F. C. Baxter in *NYTBR*, 29 May, p. 5; by John Ciardi in *SR*, 7 May, p. 66.

Holman-Hunt, Diana. *My Grandmothers and I.* London: Hamish Hamilton. Pp. 208.

Rev. by Evelyn Waugh in *S*, 14 Oct., p. 567. Waugh's review, entitled "The Only Pre-Raphaelite," deals mainly with Holman Hunt and his deceased wife's sister who became the second Mrs. Hunt.

Hopley, I. B. "Clerk Maxwell's Apparatus for the Measurement of Surface Tension." *Annals of Science*, XIII, 180-87.

Hopley, I. B. "Maxwell's Work on Electrical Resistance." *Annals of Science*, XIII, 265-72; XIV, 197-210.

Hough, Graham. *Image and Experience: Studies in a Literary Revolution.* London: Duckworth. Pp. 228.

Rev. by Hermann Peschmann in *English*, XIII, 106; by Richard Hoggart in *NS*, LX, 166; by Frank Kermode in *S*, 1 July, p. 25; in *TLS*, 24 June, p. 404. Includes essays on Moore and Conrad.

Houghton, Walter E. *The Victorian Frame of Mind.* . . . See VB 1959, 424.

Rev. by Lionel Stevenson in *MLQ*, XXI, 273-75.

Howarth, Herbert. *The Irish Writers, 1880-1940.* . . . See VB 1959, 424.

Rev. by Howard Sergeant in *English*, XIII, 26; by J. T. Winterich in *HTB*, 8 Nov. 1959, p. 9; by Vivian Mercier in *NYTBR*, 20 Dec. 1959, p. 5.

Hudson, Derek. *The Forgotten King.* London: Constable. Pp. 287.

Rev. in *TLS*, 13 May, p. 306. Includes essays on William IV, Theodore Hook, the Pre-Raphaelites, and Eliza Cook.

Hughes, Gervase. *The Music of Arthur Sullivan.* London: Macmillan. Pp. viii + 180.

Rev. by C. K. Miller in *LJ*, LXXXV, 2793-94; in *TLS*, 6 May, p. 284.

Johnson, Robert Clyde. *Authority in Protestant Theology.* Philadelphia: Westminster Pr., 1959. Pp. 224.

Rev. by J. A. Clarke in *LJ*, LXXXIV, 3139.

Jones, Alun Richard. *The Life and Opinions of T. E. Hulme.* London: Gollancz. Pp. 233.

Rev. by J. C. Pine in *LJ*, LXXXV, 3150; by Alasdair Macintyre in *NS*, LIX, 761-62; in *TLS*, 24 June, p. 400.

Kirk, Rudolf, and Main, C. F. (eds.). *Essays in Literary History.* Presented to J. Milton French. New Brunswick, N.J.: Rutgers Univ. Pr. Pp. 270.

Contains essays on two Victorians: "A Reading of *Tess of the D'Urbervilles*" by Horace E. Hamilton and "The Death of Gissing: A Fourth Report" by Arthur C. Young.

Krook, Dorothea. *Three Traditions of Moral Thought.* . . . See VB 1959, 425.

Rev. by R. G. Lunt in *HJ*, LVIII, 297; by W. A. Christian in *Jour. of Religion*, XL, 216; by Robert Taubman in *S*, 6 Nov. 1959, p. 637; by W. I. Carr in *Universities Quart.*, XIV, 206-14; by John Passmore in *VS*, IV, 78-79; by D. C. Berggren in *YR*, XLIX, 458.

Langbaum, Robert. *The Poetry of Experience.* . . . See VB 1959, 425.
Rev. by R. A. Foakes in *EC*, X, 104-08; by J.-G. Ritz in *Études anglaises*, XIII, 492-93.

Laski, Audrey L. "Myths of Character: An Aspect of the Novel." *NCF*, XIV, 333-43.
Basic types of character in the novel; one type as revealed in Trollope's two Dukes of Omnium.

Lewis, Clive Staples. *Studies in Words.* Cambridge: Cambridge Univ. Pr. Pp. vii + 240.
Rev. in *TLS*, 30 Sept., p. 627. Considers meanings of *nature, sad, wit, free, sense, simple, conscious,* and *conscience* at different periods of English history.

Lodge, David. "An Earlier Foxglove Saga: The First English Catholic Novel?" *Dublin Rev.*, CCXXXIV, 365-71.
Argues that *Poverty, and the Baronet's Family* (1845) by Henry Digby Best is the first English Catholic novel.

MacInnes, Colin. "Wherefore Does He Why?" *S*, 23 Dec., p. 1020.
A centenary tribute to the great Dan Leno, singer and comedian of the London "Halls" in the 'eighties and 'nineties.

Mackerness, Eric David. *The Heeded Voice: Studies in the Literary Status of the Anglican Sermon, 1830-1900.* . . . See VB 1959, 425.
Rev. by A. R. Vidler in *Jour. Eccl. Hist.*, XI, 257; by Malcolm Ross in *QQ*, LXVII, 132-34; in *TLS*, 6 May, p. 292; by Kenneth Allott in *VS*, IV, 82-84.

Maddison, Carol. *Apollo and the Nine: A History of the Ode.* Baltimore: Johns Hopkins Univ. Pr. Pp. 427.
Rev. by J. R. Willingham in *LJ*, LXXXV, 1913.

Maurer, Oscar. " 'My Squeamish Public': Some Problems of Victorian Magazine Publishers and Editors." *Studies in Bibliography*, XII, 21-40.

Maurer, Oscar. "*Punch* and the Opera War, 1847-1867." *Texas Studies in Literature and Language*, I, 139-70.
An interesting survey of *Punch's* coverage of operatic and musical events between 1847-67, illustrating dominant modes and stars' rivalries as they are reflected by advertisement and comment in the magazine.

May, Derwent. "The Novelist as Moralist and the Moralist as Critic." *EC*, X, 320-28.

Utilizes Dickens, Conrad, Hardy among others for examples of his approach.

McPherson, Robert G. *The Theory of Higher Education in Nineteenth-Century England.* . . . See VB 1959, 425.
Rev. by Robert M. Gutchen in *JMH*, XXXII, 68-69; by W. H. G. Armytage in *Universities Rev.*, XXXII, 65; by G. H. Bantock in *VS*, IV, 167-70.

Miles, Josephine. *Eras and Modes in English Poetry.* . . . See VB 1958, 368.
Rev. by B. R. McElderry, Jr. in *Personalist*, XLI, 114-15.

Millhauser, Milton. *Just Before Darwin: Robert Chambers and Vestiges.* . . . See VB 1959, 425.
Rev. by John C. Greene in *Isis*, LI, 116-17.

Mix, Katherine Lyon. *A Study in Yellow: The "Yellow Book" and Its Contributors.* Lawrence: Univ. of Kansas Pr. Pp. 325.
Rev. by Mary A. Reilly in *CE*, XXII, 206-07; by Earle Walbridge in *LJ*, LXXXV, 1119-20; by Ben Ray Redman in *NYTBR*, 8 Apr., p. 7; by Frank Kermode in *S*, 14 Oct., p. 568; by Hesketh Pearson in *SR*, 21 May, pp. 24-25; in *TLS*, 14 Oct., p. 662.

Nicoll, Allardyce. *A History of English Drama, 1660-1900.* Vol. VI: *Alphabetical Catalogue of Plays, 1660-1900.* Cambridge: Cambridge Univ. Pr. Pp. xii + 565.
Rev. by Thomas B. Stroup, *PBS*, LIV, 139-40.

Phelps, Gilbert. "The Early Phases of British Interest in Russian Literature." *Slavonic and East European Rev.*, XXXVIII, 415-30.

Pope, Willard B. (ed.). *The Diary of Benjamin Robert Haydon.* 2 vols. London: Oxford Univ. Pr. Pp. 495-553.
Rev. by Phoebe Adams in *AM*, May, pp. 110-12; by M. E. Landgren in *LJ*, LXXXV, 1573; by Peter Quennell in *NYTBR*, 3 July, p. 5; by F. W. Bateson in *S*, 1 July, pp. 27-28; in *TLS*, 1 July, p. 415; by Leslie A. Marchand in *VQR*, XXXVI, 476-79; by A. Dwight Culler in *YR*, XLIX, 604-07.

Porter, John F. "The Place of Christ in the Thought of F. D. Maurice." *DA*, XX, 3869-70.

Priestley, John Boynton. *Literature and Western Man.* London: Heinemann. Pp. 512.
Rev. by Phoebe Adams in *AM*, Apr., p. 114; by C. B. Cox in *Critical Quart.*,

II, 279-80; by J. W. Krutch in *HTB*, 13 Mar., p. 3; by E. M. Oboler in *LJ*, LXXXV, 763; by John Raymond in *NS*, LIX, 257; by H. M. Jones in *NYTBR*, 13 Mar., p. 5; by Houston Peterson in *SR*, 23 Apr., p. 46; by Donat O'Donnell in *S*, 26 Feb., p. 296; in *TLS*, 26 Feb., p. 128.

Rathburn, Robert C., and Steinmann, Martin, Jr. (eds.). *From Jane Austen to Joseph Conrad....* See VB 1959, 426.
Rev. by Joan Bennett in *MLR*, LV, 272-73; by J. C. Maxwell in *N & Q*, n.s. VII, 156-57; by Frank O'Connor in *VS*, III, 308-09.

Reardon, B. M. G. "A Centenary of Liberal Anglicanism." *QR*, CCXCVIII, 301-08.
The centenary of *Essays and Reviews*.

Rosenberg, Edgar. *From Shylock to Svengali: Jewish Stereotypes in English Fiction.* Stanford, Calif.: Stanford Univ. Pr. Pp. viii + 388.
Rev. by Samuel Simon in *LJ*, LXXXV, 1796.

Roy, G. Ross. "A Bibliography of French Symbolism in English-Language Publications to 1910." *Revue de littérature comparée*, XXIV, 645-59.
Lists articles about French symbolist poets, reviews of their work, and translations and original works by Rimbaud, Verlaine, and Mallarmé.

Semmel, Bernard. *Imperialism and Social Reform: English Social-Imperial Thought 1895-1914.* London: Allen and Unwin. Pp. 287.
Rev. in *TLS*, 30 Sept., pp. 621-22.

Sewell, Elizabeth. *The Orphic Voice: Poetry and Natural History.* New Haven, Conn.: Yale Univ. Pr. Pp. 463.
Rev. by H. Burke in *LJ*, LXXXV, 2594-95.

Shapiro, Charles (ed.). *Twelve Original Essays on Great English Novels.* Detroit: Wayne State Univ. Pr. Pp. 281.
Includes essays on *Great Expectations, Jane Eyre,* and *Victory.*

Shapley, Harlow (ed.). *Science Ponders Religion.* New York: Appleton-Century-Crofts. Pp. 308.
Includes essays by Alfred E. Emerson, "The Impact of the Theory of Evolution on Religion," and by John C. Greene, "Darwin and Religion."

Shattuck, Charles H. (ed.). *Bulwer and Macready: A Chronicle of the Early Victorian Theatre....* See VB 1959, 426.
Rev. by James W. Hall in *MLQ*, XXI, 87;

by Sybil Rosenfield in *MLR*, LV, 142.

Shelley, Philip Allison, with Lewis, Arthur O., Jr., and Betts, William W. (eds.). *Anglo-German and American-German Cross-Currents.* University of North Carolina Studies in Comparative Literature, No. 19. Chapel Hill: Univ. of North Carolina Pr. Pp. 303.
Rev. by Karl J. R. Arndt in *JEGP*, LIX, 378-79. Includes essays on Mangan and Meredith.

Smith, Bernard. *European Vision and the South Pacific, 1768-1850.* Oxford: Clarendon Pr. Pp. xix + 287.
Through a study of the work of artists attached to scientific expeditions, Smith considers the relationship of contemporary ideas about art and science and the evolution of a form of landscape art which introduced to western Europe the world beyond it.

Stang, Richard. *The Theory of the Novel in England, 1850-1870....* See VB 1959, 426.
Rev. by Donald T. Torchiana in *CE*, XXII, 60; briefly in *NCF*, XIV, 372; by G. D. Klingopulos in *Universities Quart.*, XIV, 189-92; by G. Armour Craig in *VS*, IV, 173-75.

Starkie, Enid. *From Gautier to Eliot: The Influence of France on English Literature, 1851-1939.* London: Hutchinson. Pp. 236.
Rev. by Paul West in *English*, XIII, 71-72; by Jacques Vallette in *Mercure de France*, CCCXXXIX, 540; by Donald Davie in *NS*. LIX, 532-33; by Frank Kermode in *S*, 1 Apr., pp. 447-48; in *TLS*, 8 Apr., p. 224.

Stevenson, Lionel. *The English Novel: A Panorama.* Boston: Houghton Mifflin. Pp. 539.
Rev. by R. G. Baldwin in *Dalhousie Rev.*, XL, 262-63; briefly in *NCF*, XV, 280.

Sutherland, James. *English Satire....* See VB 1959, 427.
Rev. by A. Demadre in *Études anglaises*, XIII, 70-71.

Sypher, Wylie. *Rococo to Cubism in Art and Literature.* New York: Random House. Pp. 353.
Includes discussion of Pre-Raphaelitism.

Talmon, Jacob Leib. *Political Messianism: The Romantic Phase.* London: Secker and Warburg. Pp. 607.
Rev. by Charles Taylor in *NS*, LX, 1013-14. ". . . the early nineteenth century up to 1848."

Tave, Stuart M. *The Amiable Humorist: A Study in the Comic Theory and Criticism of the Eighteenth and Early Nineteenth Centuries.* Chicago: Univ. of Chicago Pr. Pp. 304.

Rev. by J. R. Willingham in *LJ*, LXXXV, 1594; by Stephen Potter in *SR*, 4 June, p. 15.

Tener, Robert H. "R. H. Hutton's 'Essays Theological and Literary': A Bibliographical Note." *N & Q*, n.s. VII, 185-87.

Tener, Robert H. "The Spectator Records, 1874-1897." *VNL*, No. 17 (Spring), 33-36.

Identification of contributors.

Thistlethwaite, Frank. *The Anglo-American Connection in the Early Nineteenth Century.* . . . See VB 1959, 427.

Rev. by Richard Lowitt in *JEH*, XX, 148.

Trewin, J. C. *Benson and the Bensonians.* London: Barrie and Rockliff. Pp. xv + 320.

Rev. in *TLS*, 28 Oct., p. 688. Biography of a veteran actor whose career began with Irving and Terry at the Lyceum.

Troughton, Marion. "Schools in Literature." *CR*, CXCVII, 338-40.

Treatment of this theme in 19th- and 20th-century fiction.

Victoriana, An Exhibition of the Arts of the Victorian Era in America. Brooklyn: Brooklyn Museum. Unpaged.

Walbank, Alan. "Railway Reading." *Book Collector*, IX, 285-91.

Description of some mid-Victorian railway novels collected by Mr. Walbank.

Willey, Basil. *Darwin and Butler: Two Versions of Evolution.* New York: Harcourt, Brace. Pp. 115.

Rev. by Mary Barrett in *LJ*, LXXXV, 4380.

Williams, Raymond. *Culture and Society, 1780-1950.* . . . See VB 1959, 427.

Rev. by Madeleine L. Cazamain in *Études anglaises*, XIII, 491; by Richard Chase in *ParR*, XXVII, 148-54; by M. S. Wilkins in *PSQ*, LXXV, 302-03; by Seymour Betsky in *VS*, III, 298-301.

Wood, Violet. *Victoriana: A Collector's Guide.* London: Bell. Pp. 175.

Briefly rev. in *TLS*, 9 Sept., p. 582.

Woolf, Leonard Sidney. *Sowing: An Autobiography of the Years 1880-1904.* London: Hogarth Pr. Pp. 205.

Rev. by Arnold de Montmorency in *CR*,

CXCVIII, 645-46; by Lloyd W. Griffin in *LJ*, LXXXV, 2932; by Kingsley Martin in *NS*, LX, 391-92; by Walter Allen in *NYTBR*, 2 Oct., p. 5; by Frank Kermode in *S*, 9 Sept., pp. 377-78; in *TLS*, 9 Sept., pp. 571-73.

Wright, Austin (ed.). *Victorian Literature: Modern Essays in Criticism.* New York: Oxford Univ. Pr., 1961. Pp. vi + 377.

A judicious selection of twenty-eight essays — most of them on individual Victorian writers — produced by modern scholars in the past three decades. A sparkling collection. R. C. S.

IV. INDIVIDUAL AUTHORS

ARNOLD, MATTHEW (see also III, Griffin).

Baum, Paull Franklin. *Ten Studies in the Poetry of Matthew Arnold.* . . . See VB 1959, 427.

Rev. by J. G. Curgenven in *EC*, X, 345-48; by Kenneth Allott in *RES*, n.s. XI, 112-13.

Brick, Allan. "Equilibrium in the Poetry of Matthew Arnold." *TQ*, XXX, 45-56.

Emphasizes that the search for self-knowledge as a theme in Victorian poetry often leads Tennyson and Browning to a glimpse of ultimate truth, while in Arnold the search leads to further doubt of ever understanding the whole self, the nature of man.

Brooks, Roger L. "A Census of Matthew Arnold's 'Poems' (1853)." *BSP*, LIV, 184-86.

Brooks, Roger L. "Matthew Arnold's Poetry 1849-1855: An Account of the Contemporary Criticism and Its Influence." *DA*, XX, 4107.

Study indicates Arnold's early poetry was more favorably received than hitherto believed and that he suppressed and revised poems according to the criticism of readers and reviewers. (See also VB 1959, 429, Wilkins, Charles T. "The English Reputation of Matthew Arnold, 1840-1877.")

Brooks, Roger L. " 'A Septuagenarian Poet': An Addition to the Matthew Arnold Bibliography." *MP*, LVII, 262-63.

Gottfried, Leon A. "Matthew Arnold's 'The Strayed Reveller.' " *RES*, n.s. XI, 403-09.

The reveller's search for sensation as an ironic allegory of the Keatsian "multitudinousness."

Holloway, John. *The Charted Mirror: Literary and Critical Essays.* London: Routledge and K. Paul, Pp. 226.

Rev. in *TLS*, 10 June, p. 367. Includes an essay on Arnold.

Jamison, William A. *Arnold and the Romantics*. . . . See VB 1959, 428.

Rev. by J. P. Curgenven in *RES*, n.s. XI, 226-27.

Johnson, Wendell Stacey. "Matthew Arnold's Dialogue." *Univ. of Kansas City Rev.*, XXVII, 109-16.

"It is precisely the dialogue of the mind with itself that produces his finest work . . . but one that is never neatly concluded. . . . A. . . . is peculiarly conscious . . . of the effort to represent if not to reconcile the several voices . . . [with which] most intelligent Victorians, and fragmented modern men as well, must speak." A perceptive article.

Kenosian, Charles K. "The Position of Matthew Arnold in the Religious Dilemma of His Time." *DA*, XXI, 897-98.

Arnold feared extremes and therefore attempted to temper the scientific approach with the humanistic.

Neiman, Fraser (ed.). *Essays, Letters, and Reviews by Matthew Arnold*. Cambridge, Mass.: Harvard Univ. Pr. Pp. xv + 398.

Rev. by John M. Robson in *Dalhousie Rev.*, XL, 397-99; by Earle F. Walbridge in *LJ*, LXXXV, 1117; in *TLS*, 16 Sept., pp. 585-86. Contains a number of pieces hitherto uncollected or out of print.

Neiman, Fraser. " 'My Dear Summer': Three Letters from Matthew Arnold." *VNL*, No. 17 (Spring), 28-30.

Identification of the addressee.

Parrish, Stephen Maxfield. *Concordance to the Poems of Matthew Arnold*. . . . See VB 1959, 428.

Rev. briefly by Frederick L. Gwynn in *CE*, XXI, 359; by E. S. in *College and Research Libr.*, XXI, 282; by A. Dwight Culler in *JEGP*, LIX, 589-92; by Kenneth Allott in *MLR*, LV, 598-99.

Robbins, William. *The Ethical Idealism of Matthew Arnold*. . . . See VB 1959, 428.

Rev. by Louis Crompton in *CE*, XXII, 206; by John M. Robson in *Dalhousie Rev.*, XL, 397-99; by Gilbert Thomas in *English*, XIII, 24; by Edgar Hill Ducan in *Ethics*, LXXI, 60-62; by Joan Harding in *HJ*, LVIII, 194-96; by G. Robert Stange in *MP*, LVII, 280-82; by Malcolm Ross in *QQ*, LXVII, 132-34; by Fraser Neiman in *VS*, III, 402-04.

Salerno, Nicholas A. "Shakespeare and Arnold's "Dover Beach." *Shakespeare Quarterly*, XI, 495-96.

Suggests a source in *Antony and Cleopatra* for the last image in "Dover Beach."

Super, R. H. (ed.). "Matthew Arnold and Tennyson." *TLS*, 28 Oct., p. 693.

Based on "unpublished" letters, one of which had already been printed in the Ashley Library Catalogue, vol. X.

Super, R. H. (ed.). *On the Classical Tradition*. Vol. I of *The Complete Prose Works of Matthew Arnold*. Ann Arbor: Univ. of Michigan Pr. Pp. viii + 271.

Rev. by J. R. Willingham in *LJ*, LXXXV, 2593; in *TLS*, 16 Sept., pp. 585-86. An annotated edition, first volume of a collected edition of Arnold's prose. This volume contains "On the Modern Element in Literature," the Preface to *Merope*, the Homeric lectures, and "England and the Italian Question."

Williamson, Eugene L., Jr. "Matthew Arnold's 'Eternal Not Ourselves . . .' " *MLN*, LXXV, 309-12.

Sources in Dr. Arnold and Jacob Abbott for Arnold's early rejection of anthropomorphism.

Williamson, Eugene L., Jr. "Matthew Arnold's Reading." *VS*, III, 317-18.

A comment on Kenneth Allott's note on Arnold's reading from 1845 to 1847 (*VS*, II, 254-66). See also Mr. Allott's reply (*VS*, III, 318-20), and Mr. Williamson's rejoinder (*VS*, III, 460-61).

ARNOLD, THOMAS. Bamford, T. W. *Thomas Arnold*. London: Cresset Pr. Pp. 232.

Rev. by William Walsh in *NS*, LX, 193; by William Golding in *S*, 12 Aug., p. 252; in *TLS*, 5 Aug., p. 491.

Williamson, Eugene L. "The Religious and Political Ideas of Thomas Arnold." *DA*, XXI, 346.

BAGEHOT. Buchan, Alastair. *The Spare Chancellor*. . . . See VB 1959, 429.

Rev. by David Spring in *Canadian Hist. Rev.*, XLI, 241; by Florence O'Donoghue in *CR*, CXCVII, 121-22; by Asa Briggs in *Econ. Jour.*, LXX, 606-07; by Asa Briggs in *VS*, IV, 75-77.

Greenberg, Robert A. "Walter Bagehot: Victorian Critic." *DA*, XX 3706-07.

Study of Bagehot's ideas and thought rather than individual works.

Rudman, Harry W. "Walter Bagehot — 'The Greatest Victorian?' " *The History of Ideas News Letter*, V, 75-77.

St. John-Stevas, Norman. *Walter Bagehot*. . . . See VB 1959, 429.

Rev. by Duncan Forbes in *EHR*, LXXV, 740; by W. L. Burn in *History*, XLV, 168-69; by Asa Briggs in *VS*, IV, 75-77.

BARING-GOULD. Hyde, William J. "The Stature of Baring-Gould as a Novelist." *NCF*, XV, 1-16.

Reeves, James (ed.). *The Everlasting Circle*. London: Heinemann. Pp. xv + 303.

Rev. by Margaret Dean-Smith in *M & L*, XLI, 370-74; by Charles Causley in *NS*, LVIX, 798-99. Collection of folk-songs and ballads which draws on the Baring-Gould manuscripts.

BARRIE. Duffin, Henry Charles. "J. M. Barrie." *CR*, CXCVII, 264-66.

Barrie as a "Scotch, introspective Dickens."

Green, Roger Lancelyn. *J. M. Barrie*. London: Bodley Head. Pp. 64.

Short study and bibliography of Barrie's works for children.

BEERBOHM (see also II, Moers; HARRIS: Brome).

Behrman, Samuel Nathaniel. *Portrait of Max.* New York: Random House. Pp. 317. Publ. in England as *Conversation with Max.* London: Hamish Hamilton.

Rev. by Edward Weeks in *AM*, Oct., p. 116; by Alan Pryce-Jones in *HTB*, 2 Oct., p. 1; by E. F. Walbridge in *LJ*, LXXXV, 4138; by Walter Allen in *NS*, LX, 702; by Peter Quennell in *NYTBR*, 2 Oct., p. 1; by Kingsley Amis in *S*, 25 Nov., p. 845 (a solemn attack on Beerbohm, who had "nothing to say"); in *TLS*, 18 Nov., p. 742.

BENTHAM. Lomer, Gerhard R. "Jeremy Bentham." *QQ*, LXVII, 28-40.

On the renovation of Bentham's clothed skeleton preserved at University College, London. Announces the preparation by the College of a new and definitive edition of Bentham's works including hitherto unpublished material.

Preyer, Robert. *Bentham, Coleridge, and the Science of History.* "Beiträge zur englischen Philologie," ed. by Edgar Mertner, No. 41. Bochum-Langendreer: Verlag Heinrich Pöppinghaus, 1958. Pp. v + 105.

Rev. by D. Forbes in *JMH*, XXXII, 49-50.

BESANT, ANNIE. Nethercot, Arthur Hobart. *The First Five Lives of Annie Besant.* Chicago: Univ. of Chicago Pr. Pp. xii + 418.

Rev. by Joseph Bram in *LJ*, LXXXV, 1897; by Ben Ray Redman in *NYTBR*,

21 Aug., p. 3. The first volume of a two-volume biography.

BLACKMORE. Budd, Kenneth. *The Last Victorian: R. D. Blackmore and His Novels.* London: Centaur Pr. Pp. 125.

Rev. in *TLS*, 18 Mar., p. 178.

BORROW. *The Bible in Spain.* Edited, with an introduction and notes by Peter Quennell. London: Macdonald, 1959. Pp. 586.

Rev. by René Frechet in *Études anglaises*, XIII, 480.

BRADLEY. Wollheim, Richard. *F. H. Bradley.* . . . See VB 1959, 429.

Rev. by Gilbert Ryle in *S*, 15 Jan., p. 81; in *TLS*, 4 Mar., p. 148; by John Passmore in *VS*, IV, 78-79.

BRIDGES (see also TENNYSON: Altick).

Ritz, Jean-Georges. *Robert Bridges and Gerard Manley Hopkins, 1863-1889.* London: Oxford Univ. Pr. Pp. xvii + 182.

Rev. by V. deS. Pinto in *Critical Quart.*, II, 281-82; by James Reeves in *NS*, LIX, 724; in *TLS*, 6 May, p. 288; by J. C. Reid in *VS*, IV, 182-83.

BRONTËS (see also III, Bell).

Brammer, M. M. "The Manuscript of *The Professor.*" *RES*, n.s. XI, 157-70.

Revisions by Charlotte Brontë and bowdlerizing by the Rev. Mr. Nicholls, in a fair copy now at the Morgan Library.

Brick, Allan R. "Lewes's Review of *Wuthering Heights.*" *NCF*, XIV, 355-59.

Brontë Society, Transactions . . . Part 69 (See VB 1959, 429).

Rev. in *TLS*, 5 Feb., p. 88.

Brontë Society, Transactions and Other Publications of.

Vol. XIII, No. 5 (Part 70) has items: Curtis, Myra, "Charlotte Brontë in Her Letters" (pp. 411-24); Holgate, Ivy, "The Branwells at Penzance" (p. 425-32); Beckwith, Frank, "Letters of the Rev. Patrick Brontë to *The Leeds Intelligencer*" (pp. 433-36); Dodds, M. Hope, "The Howitts' Review of *Jane Eyre*" (pp. 438-39); "The 66th Annual Meeting" (pp. 442-46); "The Brontë Parsonage Museum: Report of the Curatorship Committee" [lists additions to museum and library] (pp. 451-52).

Colby, Robert A. "*Villette* and the Life of the Mind." *PMLA*, LXXV, 410-19.

Day, Martin S. "Central Concepts of *Jane Eyre*." *Personalist*, XLI, 495.

Suggests that romantic patterns are governed by love and marriage. The writer suggests that a maternalistic love emerges victorious.

Dean, Christopher. "Joseph's Speech in

'Wuthering Heights'." *N & Q*, n.s. VII, 73-76.

Du Maurier, Daphne. *The Infernal World of Branwell Brontë*. London: Gollancz. Pp. 260.
Rev. by L. P. Hartley in *NS*, LX, 752-53; in *TLS*, 18 Nov., p. 734.

Dunbar, Georgia S. "Proper Names in *Villette*." *NCF*, XV, 77-80.

Gérin, Winifred. *Anne Brontë: A Biography* ... See VB 1959, 429.
Rev. by Fannie Ratchford in *NCF*, XIV, 363; by J. M. S. Tompkins in *RES*, n.s. XI, 339-40.

Harrison, Ada, and Stanford, Derek. *Anne Brontë: Her Life and Work*. ... See VB 1959, 430.
Rev. by Margaret Heideman in *Canadian Forum*, XXXIX, 166; by Gilbert Thomas in *English*, XIII, 24; by J. R. Willingham in *LJ*, LXXXV, 108; by Fannie Ratchford in *NCF*, XIV, 363; by De-Lancey Ferguson in *NYTBR*, 7 Feb., p. 16; by J. M. S. Tompkins in *RES*, n.s. XI, 339-40.

Heilman, Robert B. "Charlotte Brontë, Reason, and the Moon." *NCF*, XIV, 283-302.
The competing claims of the rational and the non-rational.

Justus, James. "Beyond Gothicism: *Wuthering Heights* and an American Tradition." *Tennessee Univ. Studies in Literature*, V, 25-33.
Compares the "intensity of private visions and individual wills" of *Wuthering Heights* with an American tradition of Melville and Hawthorne in which the tragic heroes are more boldly motivated by the spirit of "mental place" than the English Victorian tradition of social structure.

McKibben, Robert C. "The Image of the Book in *Wuthering Heights*." *NCF*, XV, 159-69.

Prescott, Joseph. "*Jane Eyre*: A Romantic Exemplum with a Difference," in *Twelve Original Essays on Great English Novels*, ed. by Charles Shapiro, pp. 87-102. Detroit: Wayne State Univ. Pr. Pp. 281.
Reprinted in *Studies in Eng. Lit.* (Tokyo), XXXVI, 1-13; in *Letterature Moderne* (Bologna), IX, 719-28. See also VB 1959, 430 for Italian translation.

Quertermous, Harry M. "The Byronic Hero in the Writings of the Brontës." *DA*, XXI, 191-92.
From Angria to Heathcliff, the changing concepts of the Byronic hero.

Randall, David A. "The First American Edi-

tion of the Brontës' Poems." *Book Collector*, IX, 199-201.

Spark, Muriel, and Stanford, Derek. *Emily Brontë: Her Life and Work*. New York: British Book Centre. Pp. 271.
Rev. by H. Burke in *LJ*, LXXXV, 2792.

BROWNINGS (see also CARLYLE: Sanders).

Assad, Thomas J. "Browning's 'My Last Duchess.'" *Tulane Studies in English*, X, 117-28.

Barbery, Y. "La critique moderne face à Elizabeth et Robert Browning." *Études anglaises*, XIII, 444-51.
Review of recent biographical studies of Elizabeth Barrett Browning.

Barnett, Howard A. "Robert Browning and the Drama. Browning's Plays Viewed in the Context of the Victorian Theatre: 1830-1850." *DA*, XX, 4097.

Bevington, Merle M. "Three Letters of Robert Browning to the Editor of the *Pall Mall Gazette*." *MLN*, LXXV, 304-09.
Browning defends his notion that Masaccio was Fra Lippo Lippi's pupil.

Brown, T. J. "English Literary Autographs XXXV: Elizabeth Barrett Browning, 1806-1861, and Robert Browning, 1812-1889." *Book Collector*, IX, 317.

Corrigan, Beatrice. "Vernon Lee and the Old Yellow Book." *Colby Libr. Quart.*, V, 116-22.

Cundiff, Paul A. "Robert Browning: 'Indisputably Fact.'" *VNL*, No. 17 (Spring), pp. 7-11.
Further comment on Browning's use of fact in *The Ring and the Book* (See VB 1959, Cundiff, 430, and Smalley, 431; see also Langbaum below.)

Dougherty, Charles T. "Browning Letters in the Vatican Library." *Manuscripta*, IV, 164-69.
The Vatican Library contains two letters from E. B. and four from R. B. One from each is published with notes.

Garriott, Harold M. "Characterization through Metaphor in *The Ring and the Book*, with Special Reference to the Guido Monologues." *DA*, XXI, 892-93.

Honan, Park. "Browning's *Pauline*: The Artistic Safety Device." *VNL*, No. 18 (Fall), pp. 23-24.

Kendall, J. L. "Lippo's Vision." *VNL*, No. 18 (Fall), pp. 18-21.

Landis, Paul, and Freeman, Ronald E. (eds.). *Letters of the Brownings to George Bar-*

rett. . . . See VB 1959, 430.

Rev. by Kenneth Allott in *RES*, n.s. XI, 109-11.

Langbaum, Robert. "The Importance of Fact in 'The Ring and the Book.'" *VNL*, No. 17 (Spring), pp. 11-17.

Conclusion of a symposium on the subject. (See Cundiff above.)

Litzinger, Boyd. "Did Cardinal Wiseman Review *Men and Women*?" *VNL*, No. 18 (Fall), pp. 22-23.

Millet, Stanton. "Art and Reality in 'My Last Duchess.'" *VNL*, No. 17 (Spring), 25-27.

Palmer, Rupert E., Jr. "The Uses of Character in 'Bishop Blougram's Apology.'" *MP*, LVIII, 108-18.

"Contradictory interpretations of Blougram's character have arisen because the poem actually makes no judgment of that character and . . . the poem's central meaning is not dependent upon such a judgment."

Pipes, B. N., Jr. "The Portrait of 'My Last Duchess.'" *VS*, III, 381-86.

Porter, Jenny Lind. "Physical Locale in *The Ring and the Book*." *Personalist*, XLI, 48-59.

An ingeniously suggestive article pointing up symbolism, contrasts, and incongruities in Browning's use of locale and place-names. A significant article for students of Browning. — R. E. F.

Poston, Lawrence, III. "Ritual in 'The Bishop Orders His Tomb.'" *VNL*, No. 17 (Spring), 27-28.

Reed, Joseph W. "Browning and Macready: The Final Quarrel." *PMLA*, LXXV, 597-603.

Starkman, Miriam K. "The Manichee in the Cloister: A Reading of Browning's 'Soliloquy of the Spanish Cloister.'" *MLN*, LXXV, 399-405.

See the central irony of the poem in the fact that the speaker is himself a Manichaean heretic.

Stevenson, Lionel. "'My Last Duchess' and *Parisina*." *MLN*, LXXIV, 489-92.

Taplin, Gardner B. *The Life of Elizabeth Barrett Browning*. . . . See VB 1957, 405.

Rev. by Ronald E. Freeman in *Personalist*, XLI, 406-08.

Waters, D. Douglas, Jr. "Does Browning's 'Great Text in Galatians' Entail 'Twenty-nine Distinct Damnations'?" *MLR*, LV, 243-44.

Considers twenty "works of the flesh"

and nine "fruits of the spirit" in Gal. V. 16-26.

Wilkinson, D. C. "The Need for Disbelief: A Comment on *Pippa Passes*." *TQ*, XXIX, 139-51.

Taking issue with four recent interpretive studies of Browning's poetry, especially as they pertain to *Pippa Passes*, the writer consistently charges overstatement in evaluation and too much reliance upon Browning's intention. He argues for a serious, realistic, critical evaluation. "I believe it is still left to someone to prove its merit — but on the level of fairy tale." Some of his charges are just, but the interpretive evidence to refute the estimates of other critics remains hazy and incomplete. — R. E. F.

Willoughby, John W. "Browning's Familiarity with the Bible." *N & Q*, n.s. VII, 459.

BULWER (see also II, Moers).

Ganzel, Dewey. "Bulwer and His *Lady*." *MP*, LVIII, 41-52.

An account of Bulwer's adaptation of Helen Maria Williams' *Perouron* into *The Lady of Lyons*, "the most popular play of the nineteenth century."

BUTLER (see also DARWIN: Willey).

Howard, Daniel F. "The Critical Significance of Autobiography in *The Way of All Flesh*." *VNL*, No. 17 (Spring), pp. 1-4.

Jones, Joseph Jay. *The Cradle of Erewhon*. . . . See VB 1959, 431.

Rev. briefly in *NCF*, XIV, 373; by Daniel F. Howard in *VS*, IV, 77-78.

Taylor, C. R. H. "Samuel Butler Centenary." *TLS*, 6 May, p. 289.

Announces a commemorative exhibition in the Alexander Turnbull Library, Wellington, in honor of the centenary of Butler's arrival in New Zealand.

CARLYLE (see also II, Moers; III, Hart; MILL: Pankhurst).

Deneau, Daniel P. "Relationship of Style and Device in *Sartor Resartus*." *VNL*, No. 17 (Spring), pp. 17-20. (See Lindberg below.)

Jones, Joseph. "Carlyle, Whitman, and the Democratic Dilemma." *English Studies in Africa*, Sept., pp. 179-97.

Democratic Vistas as in part a reply to "Shooting Niagara."

Lindberg, John. "The Artistic Unity of *Sartor Resartus*." *VNL*, No. 17 (Spring), pp. 20-23. (See Deneau above.)

Lochhead, Marion. "Jane Welsh Carlyle." *QR*, CCXCVIII, 321-32.

Sanders, Charles Richard. "Carlyle, Browning, and the Nature of a Poet." *Emory*

Univ. Quart., XVI, 197-209.

CARROLL. Gardner, Martin (ed.). *The Annotated Alice: Alice's Adventures in Wonderland and Through the Looking Glass.* New York: Clarkson N. Potter. Pp. 351. Rev. by Alan Pryce-Jones in *HTB*, 17 July, p. 1; by Earle F. Walbridge in *LJ*, LXXXV, 1794-95; by Joseph Carroll in *N*, 25 June, pp. 556-58; by Naomi Lewis in *VS*, IV, 170-73.

CLOUGH. Houghton, Walter E. "The Prose Works of Arthur Hugh Clough: A Checklist and Calendar, with Some Unpublished Passages." *Bull. New York Pub. Libr.*, LXIV, 377-94.

Tener, Robert H. "Clough, Hutton, and University Hall." *N & Q*, n.s. VII, 456-57.

Timko, Michael. "The 'True Creed' of Arthur Hugh Clough." *MLQ*, XXI, 208-22. Contends that Clough had a positive faith in the essence of Christianity.

CONRAD (see also III: Harkness, Hough, May, Shapiro).

Letters to William Blackwood and David S. Meldrum. Ed. William Blackburn. . . . See VB 1959, 432. Rev. by Thomas Moser in *MLN*, LXXV, 363-66; by C. L. Barber in *MLR*, LV, 275-76.

Andreas, Osborn. *Joseph Conrad: A Study in Nonconformity.* . . . See VB 1959, 432. Rev. by Carl H. Ketcham in *ArQ*, XVI, 192; briefly by Frederick L. Gwynn in *CE*, XXI, 235; by Kellog W. Hunt in *EJ*, XLVIII, 556-57; by Zdzislaw Najder in *JAA*, XVIII, 534-35; by Robert D. Spector in *MLQ*, XXI, 275-76; by William Blackburn in *SAQ*, LIX, 122-23.

Baines, Jocelyn. *Joseph Conrad: A Critical Biography.* London: Weidenfeld and Nicolson. Pp. 507. Rev. by Leo Gurko in *American Scholar*, XXIX, 574; by Adam Gillon in *Dalhousie Rev.*, XL, 415-19; by A. J. Guerard in *HTB*, 3 Apr., p. 4; by C. W. Mann in *LJ*, LXXXV, 1783; by Jacques Vallette in *Mercure de France*, CCCXL, 340-42; by Thomas Moser in *N*, 30 Apr., p. 386; by Michael Straight in *New R*, 18 Apr., p. 15; by V. S. Pritchett in *NS*, LIX, 157; by David Daiches in *NYTBR*, 3 Apr., p. 5; by Frank Kermode in *S*, 5 Feb., p. 189; by Richard Ress in *TC*, CLXVIII, 87-89; in *TLS*, 5 Feb., p. 73 (see also letter by Baines, 19 Feb., p. 189); by G. D. Klingopulos in *Universities Quart.*, XIV, 307-11; by A. M. Hollingsworth in *VS*, IV, 65-67.

Brennan, Joseph X., and Gross, Seymour L. "The Problem of Moral Values in Conrad and Faulkner." *Personalist*, XLI, 60-70. Showing the contrasting worlds of the two novelists while delineating Conrad's moral values.

Cook, Albert Spaulding. *The Meaning of Fiction.* Detroit: Wayne State Univ. Pr. Pp. xi + 317. Includes discussion of Conrad's novels.

Dowden, Wilfred S. "The 'Illuminating Quality': Imagery and Theme in *The Secret Agent.*" *Rice Institute Pamphlet*, XLVII (October), 17-33.

Gillon, Adam. "Conrad and Sartre." *Dalhousie Rev.*, XL, 61-71. Conrad the individualist compared with Sartre the existentialist.

Gillon, Adam. *The Eternal Solitary: A Study of Joseph Conrad.* New York: Bookman Associates. Pp. 191.

Gose, Elliott B., Jr. " 'Cruel Devourer of the World's Light': *The Secret Agent.*" *NCF*, XV, 39-51.

Greenberg, Robert A. "The Presence of Mr. Wang." *Boston Univ. Studies in English*, IV, 129-37. Function of Wang in *Victory*.

Guerard, Albert J. *Conrad the Novelist.* . . . See VB 1959, 432. Rev. by C. L. Barber in *MLR*, LV, 275-76.

Gurko, Leo. "*Under Western Eyes*: Conrad and the Question of 'Where To?' " *CE*, XXI, 445-52.

Guetti, James L., Jr. *The Rhetoric of Joseph Conrad.* Amherst, Mass.: Amherst College Pr. Pp. 47.

Harkness, Bruce (ed.). *Conrad's "Heart of Darkness" and the Critics.* San Francisco: Wadsworth. Pp. 176. Rev. by A. L. Soens in *CE*, XXII, 68.

Herndon, Richard. "The Genesis of Conrad's *Amy Foster.*" *SP*, LVII, 549-66.

Hunt, Kellogg W. "*Lord Jim* and *The Return of the Native*: A Contrast." *EJ*, XLIX, 447-56.

Karl, Frederick Robert, and Magalaner, Marvin. *Reader's Guide to Great Twentieth-Century English Novels.* New York: Noonday Pr. Pp. 293. Rev. by M. L. Barrett in *LJ*, LXXXIV, 3858; briefly in *SR*, 13 Feb., p. 31; in *TLS*, 20 May, p. 324.

Karl, Frederick Robert. *A Reader's Guide to Joseph Conrad.* New York: Noonday Pr. Pp. 308.

Rev. by Charles W. Mann in *LJ*, LXXXV, 2594; in *TLS*, 21 Oct., p. 678.

M. Martin, Sister. "Conrad's 'Typhoon.'" *Ex*, XVIII, Item 57.

Morey, John H. "Joseph Conrad and Ford Madox Ford. A Study in Collaboration." *DA*, XXI, 1568.

Examination of *The Inheritors* (1901), *Romance* (1903), and *The Nature of a Crime* (1924) together with the claims and counter-claims of each writer concerning the participation in the writing of the other's novels.

Moser, Thomas. *Joseph Conrad*. . . . See *VB* 1959, 433.

Rev. by Madeleine L. Cazamian in *Études anglaises*, XIII, 66-67.

Moser, Thomas. "The Pleasure of Creative Surprise." *N*, 30 Apr., pp. 386-88.

A review article surveying ten recent books on Conrad.

Owen, Guy. "Conrad's 'The Lagoon.'" *Ex*, XVIII, Item 47.

Maintains that the story attacks the illusion that love is worth all.

Robinson, E. Arthur. "Conrad's 'The Secret Sharer.'" *Ex*, XVIII, Item 28.

Stallman, Robert Wooster (ed.). *The Art of Joseph Conrad: A Critical Symposium.* East Lansing: Michigan State Univ. Pr. Pp. xxix + 354.

Rev. by C. W. Mann in *LJ*, LXXXV, 2172.

Stallman, R. W. "Time and *The Secret Agent.*" *Texas Studies in Literature and Language*, I, 101-22.

Exploring themes, structure, and characterization, the writer sustains his theory that "Time-Now is the Unpredictable, life in all its irrational particulars, including X the unknown event. Wherefore I conclude that it is Time the Unpredictable — agent of life and death — that Conrad's novel cryptographically intends as *the* Secret Agent."

Watt, Ian. "Story and Idea in Conrad's 'The Shadow-Line.'" *Critical Quart.*, II, 133-48.

Wright, Elizabeth Cox. "The Defining Function of Vocabulary in Conrad's *The Rover.*" *SAQ*, LIX, 265-77.

DARWIN (see also III, Greene, Haber, Millhauser, Shapley).

Evolution and Natural Selection. Ed. with an introd. essay by Bert James Loewenberg. . . . See *VB* 1959, 433.

Rev. by A. Hunter Dupree in *Isis*, LI, 217.

Handlist of Darwin Papers at the University Library, Cambridge. Cambridge: Cambridge Univ. Pr. Pp. 72.

Briefly rev. in *TLS*, 16 Dec., p. 818.

The Origin of Species: A Variorum Text. Ed. Morse Peckham. . . . See *VB* 1959, 433.

Rev. by Melville H. Hatch in *Isis*, LI, 211-12; in *TLS*, 1 Jan., p. 9.

Barnett, Samuel Anthony (ed). *A Century of Darwin*. . . . See *VB* 1959, 433.

Rev. by Harry Grundfest in *Science and Society*, XXIV, 150-57.

Bell, Peter Robert (ed.). *Darwin's Biological Work*. . . . See *VB* 1959, 433.

Rev. by George Basalla in *LJ*, LXXXV, 974; in *TLS*, 1 Jan., p. 9; by Conway Zirkle in *VS*, III, 405-06.

Boller, Paul F., Jr. "Darwin's American Champion." *Southwest Rev.*, XLV, 156-64.

Darwin's relations with Asa Gray.

Brett, Raymond L. "The Influence of Darwin upon His Contemporaries." *SAQ*, LIX, 69-81.

Burnaby, John. *Darwin and the Human Situation.* Cambridge: Heffer. Pp. iii + 30.

Darlington, Cyril Dean. *Darwin's Place in History*. . . . See *VB* 1959, 433.

Rev. in *TLS*, 1 Jan., p. 9.

De Beer, Sir Gavin (ed.). "Further Unpublished Letters of Charles Darwin." *Annals of Science*, XIV, 83-115.

De Beer, Sir Gavin (ed.). *Notebooks on Transmutation of Species, Parts 1-4.* London: H. M. Stationary Office. Pp. 48; 43; 31; 32.

Dupree, A. Hunter. *Asa Gray*. . . . See *VB* 1959, 434.

Rev. by Edward Lurie in *Miss. Valley Hist. Rev.*, XLVII, 150-52; in *TLS*, 27 May, p. 341.

Eiseley, Loren C. *Darwin's Century*. . . . See *VB* 1959, 434.

Rev. by Allan Shields in *Personalist*, XLI, 259-60; by D. R. Newth in *Science and Society*, XXIV, 278-80.

Ellegård, Alvar. *Darwin and the General Reader*. . . . See *VB* 1959, 434.

Rev. by Bert James Loewenberg in *AHR*, LXV, 414; by Duncan Forbes in *EHR*, LXXV, 544-45; by Walter F. Cannon in *Isis*, LI, 213-15; by Henry R. Winkler in *JMH*, XXXII, 180; by John C. Greene in *MLN*, LXXV, 519-24; by George Roppen in *Studia Neophilologica*, XXI, 260-61.

Glass, Hiram Bentley, *et al.* (eds.). *Forerunners of Darwin, 1745-1859.* . . . See VB 1959, 434.
Rev. by Helmut de Terra in *Isis,* LI, 206; by George Basalla in *LJ,* LXXXIV, 857; in *TLS,* 26 Feb., p. 134; by Allan Shields in *Personalist,* XLI, 258-59.

Hardin, Garrett James. *Nature and Man's Fate.* London: Cape. Pp. xv + 375.
Rev. by Paul A. Zahl in *American Scholar,* XXIX, 258-60; by J. F. Ewing in *CWd,* CXC, 255; by B. B. Libaire in *LJ,* LXXXIV, 2656; by J. W. Krutch in *HTB,* 20 Sept. 1959, p. 7; by John Greenway in *SR,* 26 Dec. 1959, p. 15. A history of evolutionary opinions, containing material on Darwin.

Himmelfarb, Gertrude. *Darwin and the Darwinian Revolution.* . . . See VB 1959, 434.
Rev. by Francis G. Townsend in *EJ,* XLVIII, 554; by Charles C. Gillispie in *Isis,* LI, 216; by Charles F. Mullett in *JMH,* XXXII, 179-80.

Kimball, Solon T. "Darwin and the Future of Education." *Educational Forum,* XXV, 59-72.

Loewenberg, Bert James. *Darwin, Wallace and the Theory of Natural Selection.* . . . See VB 1959, 435.
Rev. by F. C. Haber in *AHR,* LXV, 155; by A. Hunter Dupree in *Isis,* LI, 216-17.

Mason, Philip (comp.). *Man, Race, and Darwin.* London: Oxford Univ. Pr. Pp. 151.
Rev. by Edmund Leach in *S,* 2 Dec., p. 912. A collection of papers read to a conference organized by the Royal Anthropological Institute and the Institute of Race Relations.

Ong, Walter J. (ed.). *Darwin's Vision and Christian Perspectives.* New York: Macmillan. Pp. 154.

Osborne, E. A. "The First Edition of *On the Origin of Species.*" *Book Collector,* IX, 77-78.
See also William B. Todd, "Variant Issues of *On the Origin of Species.*" *Book Collector,* IX, 78.

Spencer, T. J. B. *From Gibbon to Darwin.* . . . See VB 1959, 435.
Rev. briefly in *N & Q,* n.s. VII, 122.

Stauffer, Robert Clinton. "Ecology in the Long Manuscript Version of Darwin's *Origin of Species* and Linnaeus' *Oeconomy of Nature,*" *PAPS,* CIV, 235-41.
The fundamental ideas of what was to be called ecology "appear in primitive form in Linnaeus, reappear in Lyell, and then are transmuted by Darwin into vital elements of his theory of evolution."

Stevenson, Lionel. "Darwin and the Novel." *NCF,* XV, 29-38.
Concepts leading toward Darwin's theory appeared in fiction between 1855-1859.

Tax, Sol (ed.). *Evolution after Darwin.* 3 vols. Chicago: Univ. of Chicago Pr. Pp. viii + 629; viii + 473; viii + 310.
Papers and proceedings of Darwin Centennial celebration at University of Chicago. Vol. III edited by Sol Tax and Charles Callender.

Willey, Basil. *Darwin and Butler: Two Versions of Evolution.* London: Chatto and Windus. Pp. viii + 116.
Rev. by R. L. Brett in *Critical Quart.,* II, 288; by Cyril Bibby in *Universities Quart.,* XV, 87-89; in *TLS,* 9 Sept., p. 573. The Hibbert Lectures for 1959.

DICKENS (see also II, Weber; III, Bell, Harkness, May, Shapiro; NIGHTINGALE: Rees).

Adrian, Arthur A. "Charles Dickens as Verse Editor." *MP,* LVIII, 99-107.

Aylmer, Felix. *Dickens Incognito.* . . . See VB 1959, 436.
Rev. by Sylvère Monod in *Études Anglaises,* XIII, 387; by K. J. Fielding in *MLR,* LV, 436-37.

Bodelsen, C. A. "Some Notes on Dickens' Symbolism." *ESt,* XL, 420-31.

Cahoon, Herbert. "News and Note." *BSP,* LIV, 299.
A note on the progress of an edition of Dickens' letters.

Carlton, William J. "Mr. and Mrs. Dickens: The Thomas-Stark Letter." *N & Q,* n.s. VII, 145-47.

Collins, P. A. W. "*Bleak House* and Dickens' *Household Narrative.*" *NCF,* XIV, 345-49.

Coolidge, Archibald C., Jr. "Dickens's Humor." *VNL,* No. 18 (Fall), pp. 8-15.

Cooperman, Stanley. "Dickens and the Secular Blasphemy: Social Criticism in *Hard Times, Little Dorrit* and *Bleak House.*" *CE,* XXII, 156-60.

Cox, C. B. "A Dickens Landscape." *Critical Quart.,* II, 58-60.

De Leeuw, Margaret L. "The Significance of Humor in the Early Works of Charles Dickens." *DA,* XXI, 872-73.

Dickens. An Excerpt from "The General Catalogue of Printed Books" in the British Museum. London: British Museum. Pp. 75.
Rev. in *TLS,* 21 Oct., p. 680 (and see leading article, "Beyond the Rotunda," p. 677). Includes all material published up to 1955.

Dickensian (quarterly), Vol. LVI (Nos. 330-32).... See VB 1932, 422.

Items as follows: Adrian, A. A., "Dickens Faces a Libel Suit" (pp. 114-16); Bowkett, C. E., "Charles Dickens Commemoration Sermon [St. George's, Southwark, 8 May 1960]" (pp. 182-84); Butt, J., "Education [rev. of John Manning, *Dickens on Education*]" (pp. 98-99); Capon, R. L., "Gamaliel Bradford and Charles Dickens" (pp. 34-40); Cardwell, Margaret, "Rosa Dartle and Mrs. Brown" (pp. 29-33); Carlton, W. J., "Charles Dickens, Dramatic Critic" (pp. 11-27); Carlton, W. J., "The Strange Story of Thomas Mitton" (pp. 141-52); Collins, P. A. W., "Dickens and the Maimed Boy [records of an 1877 anecdote by the Rev. C. J. Whitmore]" (pp. 185-86); Collins, P. A. W., "Dickens as Editor: Some Uncollected Fragments" (pp. 85-96); Dunstan, J. L., "The Ministers in Dickens" (pp. 103-13); Edminson, Mary, "Charles Dickens and *The Man in the Moon*" (pp. 50-59); Fielding, K. J., "Dickens and the Novel" (pp. 160-64); Fielding, K. J., "*Les Grandes Espérances* [a translation of *Great Expectations* by Sylvère Monod]" (pp. 97-98); Fielding, K. J., "Two Prologues for the Amateur Players" (pp. 100-102); Gibson, F. A., "Mysteries in Dickens" (pp. 176-78); Hill, T. W., "Notes on *Great Expectations* [concluded]" (pp. 121-26); Lane, Margaret, "Presidential Address [Staple Inn Hall, 7 Oct. 1959]" (pp. 4-10); Lane, Margaret, "The Speeches of Charles Dickens [rev. of K. J. Fielding (ed.), *The Speeches of Charles Dickens*]" (pp. 69-70); Lascalles, T. S., "The Signalman's Story" (p. 84); Monod, S., "*Great Expectations* a Hundred Years After" (pp. 133-40); Morley, M., "The Theatrical Ternans [continued]" (pp. 41-46; 76-83; 153-57); "Peggotty's Boat: Fact and Fiction" (pp. 117-19); Peyrouton, N. C., "A Children's *Life of Dickens* [rev. of Catherine Owens Peare. *Charles Dickens, His Life*]" (pp. 46-47); Peyrouton, N. C., "A Postscript on Pirates" (pp. 179-81); Staples, L. C., "The Dickens Fellowship Players in *Dombey and Son*" (p. 187); Staples, L. C., "Ellen Ternan [rev. of Felix Aylmer, *Dickens Incognito*]" (pp. 28-29); Staples, L. C., "*Oliver!* Dickens to Music [a London musical version of *Oliver Twist*]" (pp. 174-75); Staples, L. C. "Tavistock House Theatricals" (pp. 158-59); Stewart, D. H., "Dickens's Contribution, Then and Now" (pp. 71-75); Stone, H., "Dickens and the Naming of Sam Weller" (pp. 47-49).

Dupee, F. W. "The Other Dickens." *ParR*, XXVII, 111-22.

The introduction to *The Selected Letters of Charles Dickens*.

Dupee, F. W. (ed.). *Selected Letters of Charles Dickens.* New York: Farrar, Strauss, and Cudahy. Pp. xxiv + 293.

Rev. by Earle F. Walbridge in *LJ*, LXXXV, 1118; by Leon Edel in *SR*, 23 Apr., p. 48.

Engel, Monroe. *The Maturity of Dickens....* See VB 1959, 436.

Rev. by Gilbert Thomas in *English*, XIII, 24; by Lionel Stevenson in *JEGP*, LIX, 308-10; by Kathleen Tillotson in *MLR*, LV, 597-98; by John Butt in *RES*, n.s. XI, 440-43; by Augustine Martin in *StI*, XLIX, 205-08; by Ada Nisbet in *VS*, III, 311-13.

Fielding, Kenneth Joshua. *Charles Dickens: A Critical Introduction....* See VB 1959, 436.

Rev. by Daniel B. Risdon in *CE*, XXII, 60; by J. D. Jump in *RES*, n.s. XI, 223-25; by Ada Nisbet in *VS*, III, 311-13.

Fielding, Kenneth Joshua (ed.). *The Speeches of Charles Dickens.* Oxford: Clarendon Pr. Pp. xxiv + 456.

Rev. by Heinz Reinhold in *Anglia*, LXXVIII, 254-57; by R. D. McMaster in *Dalhousie Rev.*, XL, 412-13; by Edgar Johnson in *NCF*, XV, 271-74; by Asa Briggs in *NS*, LIX, 258-60; by Melvin H. Miller in *QJS*, XLVI, 320-21; in *TLS*, 12 Feb., p. 98; by Kenneth Allott in *VS*, IV, 82-84.

Manning, John. *Dickens on Education....* See VB 1959, 436.

Rev. by Paul Stoakes in *EJ*, XLVIII, 556; by Sylvère Monod in *Études anglaises*, XIII, 386-87; by Robert A. Donovan in *JMH*, XXXII, 173; by Ada B. Nisbet in *NCF*, XV, 89-90; by Wilhelmina Gordon in *QQ*, LXVII, 316; in *TLS*, 4 Mar., p. 146; by G. H. Bantock in *VS*, IV, 167-70.

Marshall, William H. "The Image of Steerforth and the Structure of David Copperfield." *Tennessee Studies in Literature*, V, 57-65.

The reader should see the image of Steerforth as David presents him in his memoirs in order to understand the process of revelation and growth inherent in Dickens' technique. The article examines the place of Steerforth in the structure, rejecting the heavily moralistic judgment of Steerforth intended by Dickens and given in the novel by Agnes.

McMaster, R. D. "Birds of Prey: A Study of *Our Mutual Friend*." *Dalhousie Rev.*, XL, 372-81.

Through examination of character, the writer holds that the novel is Dickens' composite statement of the havoc and rapacity of an acquisitive business society in which the only regenerative hope is through individual character, though Dickens furnishes no plan or formula.

Miller, Joseph Hillis. *Charles Dickens: The World of His Novels.* . . . See VB 1959, 436.

Rev. by Kathleen Tillotson in *MLN,* LXXV, 439-42; by Barbara Hardy in *MLR,* LV, 433-36; by Augustine Martin in *StI,* XLIX, 205-08.

Moynahan, Julian. "The Hero's Guilt: The Case of *Great Expectations.*" *EC,* X, 60-79.

A persuasive reading of the novel in relation to the themes of Pip's great expectations, his sinning and being sinned against, and his frequent fears of guilt. A significant portion of the article explores Pip's relationship with Magwitch and Orlick, concluding, ingeniously, that Orlick is Pip's *alter ego* and hence fulfills one of Dickens' purposes in characterizing his hero. This article should stimulate discussion of Pip's character and Dickens' purpose in *Great Expectations.*

Quirk, Randolph. *Charles Dickens and Appropriate Language.* Durham: Univ. of Durham, 1959. Pp. 26.

Rev. by Susie I. Tucker and Henry Gifford in *DUJ,* LIII (n.s. XXII), 47-48; by R. W. Zandvoort in *N & Q,* n.s. VII, 159. Inaugural lecture of the Professor of English Language in the Durham Colleges.

Rosenberg, Marvin. "The Dramatist in Dickens." *JEGP,* LIX, 1-12.

On Dicken's early farce, *The Lamplighter;* his last play, *No Thoroughfare;* and the novels as "storyteller's theatre."

Schmidt-Hidding, Wolfgang. *Sieben Meister des literarischen Humors in England und Amerika.* Heidelberg: Quelle and Meyer, 1959. Pp. 168.

Rev. by Werner Habicht in *Anglia,* LXXVIII, 119-20.

Sørensen, Knud. "Subjective Narration in *Bleak House.*" *ESt,* XL, 431-39.

A not remarkably lucid or cogent attempt to maintain an important distinction between "indirect speech" and "represented speech." — R.A.D.

Spilka, Mark. "Little Nell Revisited." *Papers of the Michigan Academy of Science, Arts, and Letters,* XLV, 427-37.

An extremely tenuous and speculative attempt to account on psychological grounds for the bathos with which little Nell is presented. Nell, in Spilka's analysis, is simply a mechanism by which Dickens rids himself of his incestuous

longing for his sister Fanny and his wife's sister, Mary Hogarth. Her death is a "delicious atonement" for his own guilty longing. — R.A.D.

Stone, Harry. "Dickens and the Jews." *VS,* III, 459-60.

Rejoinder to Lauriat Lane's comment (*VS,* III, 222-23) on Mr. Stone's article on this subject (see VB 1959, 431).

Suter, Rufus. "Galileo and Dickens." (A letter to the Editor.) *Isis,* LI, 206.

Dickens' only reference to Galileo.

Tillotson, Kathleen. "A Letter from Mary Hogarth." *TLS,* 23 Dec., p. 833.

Dickens' much loved and lamented sister-in-law writes about his early married life.

Tillotson, Kathleen. " 'Pickwick' and Edward Jesse." *TLS,* 1 Apr., p. 214.

On Jesse's *Gleanings in Natural History* (1832-35), to which Dickens referred in a footnote.

Wagenknecht, Edward. "Mrs. Hawthorne on Dickens." *BPLQ,* XII, 120-21.

Two letters from Hawthorne's widow about Dickens, written after she heard him read in Boston.

Waller, John O. "Charles Dickens and the American Civil War." *SP,* LVII, 535-48.

The editorial sympathies of *All the Year Round* shifted abruptly from the North to the South in the late winter of 1861. Waller attributes the change to the influence of James Spence's *The American Union.*

Webb, Howard W., Jr. "A Further Note on the Dickens-Poe Relationship." *NCF,* XV, 80-82.

Wilson, Angus. "Charles Dickens: A Haunting." *Critical Quart.,* II, 101-08.

DISRAELI (see also II, Moers).

Frietzshe, Arthur H. *"The Monstrous Clever Young Man": The Novelist Disraeli and His Heroes.* Logan: Utah State Univ. Pr., 1959. Pp. 60.

Jerman, B. R. *The Young Disraeli.* Princeton, N.J.: Princeton Univ. Pr. Pp. xiv + 327.

Rev. by DeLancey Ferguson in *HTB,* 28 Aug., p. 6; by Joseph Ruef in *LJ,* LXXXV, 2930; by C. L. Cline in *NCF,* XV, 265-68; by Paul Johnson in *NS,* LX, 975-76; by Ronald Bryden in *S,* 30 Dec., p. 1050; in *TLS,* 23 Dec., p. 823; by Stephen R. Graubard in *VS,* IV, 177-78.

Maxwell, J. C. " 'Jingler,' 'Man John': Two Words from Disraeli." *N & Q,* n.s. VII, 389.

Painting, David E. " 'Juvenile Delinquency' and 'Banausic'; Young England Coinage?" *N & Q,* v.s. VII, 456.

Stewart, R. W. "The Publication and Reception of Disraeli's *Vivian Grey*." *QR*, CCXCVIII, 409-17.

DOBSON. Dobson, Alban T. A. (comp.). *Catalogue of the Collection of the Works of Austin Dobson*. London: London Univ. Libr. Pp. 62.

Rev. by Margaret Canney in *Book Collector*, IX, 478-81; by C. J. Rawson in *N & Q*, n.s. VII, 443.

DOYLE. Carr, John Dickson (ed.). *Great Stories by Sir Arthur Conan Doyle....* See VB 1959, 437.

Rev. by Anthony Boucher in *NYTBR*, 17 Jan., p. 22.

Harrison, Michael. *In the Footsteps of Sherlock Holmes....* See VB 1959, 437.

Rev. by E. F. Walbridge in *LJ*, LXXXV, 2593-94.

Sir Arthur Conan Doyle Centenary, 1859-1959. London: John Murray, 1959. Pp. 137.

Rev. in *TLS*, 26 Feb., p. 133. Photographs and documents from "Doyle Archives," with a preface by P. Weil-Nordon.

Starrett, Vincent. *The Private Life of Sherlock Holmes*. Revised and enlarged ed. Chicago: Univ. of Chicago Pr. Pp. 155.

Rev. by James Sandoe in *HTB*, 1 May, p. 11; by E. F. Walbridge in *LJ*, LXXXV, 1796; by Rex Stout in *New R*, 9 May, p. 15; by Anthony Boucher in *NYTBR*, 4 Sept., p. 13; by Sergeant Cuff in *SR*, 13 Aug., p. 34.

Van Liere, Edward J. *A Doctor Enjoys Sherlock Holmes*. New York: Vantage Pr. Pp. 141.

Rev. by Anthony Boucher in *NYTBR*, 17 Jan., p. 22.

ELIOT (see also III, Bell).

Beaty, Jerome. *Middlemarch from Notebook to Novel: A Study of George Eliot's Creative Method*. Illinois Studies in Language and Literature. Vol. XLVII. Urbana: Univ. of Illinois Pr. Pp. ix + 134.

Rev. briefly in *NCF*, XV, 278; in *TLS*, 11 Nov., p. 726.

Carroll, D. R. "An Image of Disenchantment in the Novels of George Eliot." *RES*, n.s. XI, 29-41.

A recurring pattern — illusion to disenchantment to regeneration — in the novels, and the symbols used to project it.

Casson, Allan. "*The Mill on the Floss* and Keller's *Romeo und Julia auf dem Dorfe*." *MLN*, LXXV, 20-22.

Similarities in plot and situation suggest influence of Keller's novelle (1856) on Eliot's novel.

Crompton, Margaret. *George Eliot: The Woman*. London: Cassell. Pp. x + 214.

Rev. by Penelope Gilliatt in *S*, 16 Sept., p. 411; in *TLS*, 21 Oct., p. 678.

Diamond, Naomi J. "Vision and the Role of the Past in the Novels of George Eliot." *DA*, XX, 2782-83.

Handley, Graham. "A Note on 'Daniel Deronda.'" *N & Q*, n.s. VII, 147-48.

Hardy, Barbara. *The Novels of George Eliot.* ...See VB 1959, 438.

Rev. by A. O. J. Cockshut in *EC*, X, 211-15; by Bernard J. Paris in *MLN*, LXXV, 442-49; by Gordon Haight in *MP*, LVIII, 140-42; by John Holloway in *RES*, n.s. XI, 443-44; by Olov W. Fryckstedt in *Studia Neophilologica*, XXI, 255-60; by Jerome Beaty in *VS*, III, 310-11.

Levine, George L. "Determinism in the Novels of George Eliot." *DA*, XX, 4112.

A thorough analysis of the reasons for George Eliot's beliefs and the importance of them in construction, characterization, and theme in her novels.

Maheu, Placide-Gustave. *La pensée religieuse et morale de George Eliot....* See VB 1959, 438.

Rev. by Bernard J. Paris in *MLN*, LXXV, 442-49.

Preyer, Robert. "Beyond the Liberal Imagination: Vision and Unreality in *Daniel Deronda*." *VS*, IV, 33-54.

Proposes that in *Daniel Deronda* Eliot considered not only how environment shapes response but how "our receptivity (or lack of it) to signs and portents helps us to break free from the tyranny of habitual responses."

Stang, Richard (ed.). *Discussions of George Eliot*. Boston: Heath. Pp. 104.

Collection of essays on Eliot's fiction.

Stump, Reva. *Movement and Vision in George Eliot's Novels....* See VB 1959, 438.

Rev. by R. Schieder in *Canadian Forum*, XL, 16; by Bernard J. Paris in *MLN*, LXXV, 442-49; by Miriam Allott in *MLR*, LV, 273-74; by Gordon Haight in *MP*, LVIII, 140-42; by Graham Handley in *N & Q*, n.s. VII, 157-59; by Jerome Beaty in *VS*, III, 310-11.

Thale, Jerome. *Novels of George Eliot....* See VB 1959, 438.

Rev. by R. Schieder in *Canadian Forum*, XL, 16; by Bernard J. Paris in *MLN*, LXXV, 442-49; by Gordon Haight in *MP*, LVIII, 140-42; by Graham Handley in *N & Q*, n.s. VII, 157-59; by Robert

B. Heilman in *NCF*, XV, 83-86; by
Jerome Beaty in *VS*, III, 310-11.

ELLIS (see III, Davies).

Calder-Marshall, Arthur. *Havelock Ellis....*
See VB 1959, 438.

Rev. by Kermit Lansner in *HTB*, 27
Mar., p. 11; by George Adelman in *LJ*,
LXXXV, 754; by John Dollard in
NYTBR, 17 Jan., p. 6; by Leo Katcher
in *SR*, 13 Feb., p. 24.

FALKNER. Pollard, Graham. "Some Uncollected Authors XXV: John Meade
Falkner, 1858-1932." *Book Collector*, IX,
318-25.

FITZGERALD. *Letters of Edward Fitz-
Gerald.* Ed. by J. M. Cohen. London:
Centaur Pr. Pp. 275.

Rev. by Stephen Graham in *Poetry Rev.*,
LI, 228; by Bernard Bergonzi in *S*, 19
Aug., pp. 289-90; in *TLS*, 17 June, p.
390.

Arberry, Arthur John. *The Romance of the
Rubáiyát....* See VB 1959, 438.

Rev. by Richard P. Benton in *CE*, XXI,
238; by William D. Templeman in *Personalist*, XLI, 247-48; by A. McKinley
Terhune in *VS*, III, 313-14.

Richardson, Joanna. *Edward FitzGerald.*
Writers and Their Work. London: Longmans. Pp. 42.

Noticed in *TLS*, 16 Dec., p. 818.

Weber, Carl J. (ed.). *FitzGerald's Rubáiyát.*
... See VB 1959, 439.

Rev. by J. D. Jump in *RES*, n.s. XI, 234;
by A. McKinley Terhune in *VS*, III, 313-
14.

Wolff, Michael. The *Rubáiyát's* Neglected
Reviewer: A Centennial Recovery." *VNL*,
No. 17 (Spring), pp. 4-6.

FORD (see CONRAD: Morey).

GASKELL. Allott, Miriam. *Elizabeth Gaskell.* Writers and Their Work. London:
Longmans. Pp. 46.

Briefly rev. in *TLS*, 19 Aug., p. 534.

GISSING (see also III, Kirk; HARDY:
Hodgins).

Boll, T. E. M. "A Forgotten Poem of George
Gissing." *N & Q*, n.s. VII, 465.

Francis, C. J. "Gissing and Schopenhauer."
NCF, XV, 53-63.

The ideas of Schopenhauer pervaded
Gissing's work.

Malbone, Raymond G. "George Gissing: Novelist." *DA*, XX, 4113.

Critical examination of Gissing's novels
to establish an evaluation of Gissing as
novelist. An extensive bibliography "cor-

rects errors in previous bibliographies and
is more nearly complete than any which
has been published."

Murry, J. Middleton. *Katherine Mansfield and
Other Literary Studies....* See VB 1959,
439.

Rev. by G. D. McDonald in *LJ*, LXXXV,
1120; by Raymond Williams in *NS*, LVII,
662; by Karl Miller in *S*, 1 May, p. 626.

Preble, Harry E. "Gissing's Contributions to
Vyestnik Evropy." *DA*, XXI, 1571.

Gissing wrote eight articles in 1881-82
for this Russian journal which were translated into Russian. The articles reveal
Gissing's views on socialism and other
aspects of "radicalism."

Roberts, Morley. *The Private Life of Henry
Maitland: A Portrait of George Gissing.*
... See VB 1958, 381.

Rev. by Madeleine L. Cazamian in *Études
anglaises*, XIII, 65-66.

Wolf, Joseph J. "George Gissing: An Anno-
tated Bibliography of Writings about
Him: Supplement." *English Fiction in
Transition*, III, 3-33.

Same issue has a supplement to George
Moore Bibliography in 1959. Rev. briefly
in *BSP*, LIV, 217-18.

GLADSTONE (see also III, Fairlie).

Bahlman, Dudley W. R. "The Queen, Mr.
Gladstone, and Church Patronage." *VS*,
III, 349-80.

A thorough account, documented from
unpublished official correspondence, of
the many contests which arose between
Gladstone and his queen concerning
church appointments.

Kelley, Robert. "Midlothian: A Study in
Politics and Ideas." *VS*, IV, 119-40.

Myres, Sir John L. "Gladstone's View of
Homer," in *Homer and His Critics*. Ed.
by Dorothea Gray. London: Routledge
and K. Paul, 1958. Pp. xii + 302.

Rev. by J. A. Davison in *Class. Jour.*, X,
108-09; by Frederick M. Combellack in
Classical Philology, LV, 273-74. "... provides information about the views of English readers of Homer in the middle of
the nineteenth century which is not easily
available in such compass elsewhere."

GOSSE (see also MOORE: Burkhart).

Brugmans, Linette F. (ed.). *The Correspondence of André Gide and Edmund Gosse,
1904-1928....* See VB 1959, 439.

Rev. by V. S. Pritchett in *NS*, LIX, 598;
by Peter Quennell in *SR*, 23 Jan., p. 34.

GRAHAME. Green, Peter. *Kenneth Grahame.*
... See VB 1959, 439.

Rev. by Naomi Lewis in *VS*, IV, 170-73.

HAGGARD (see also KIPLING: Cohen).
Cohen, Morton. *Rider Haggard: His Life and Works.* London: Hutchinson. Pp. 327.
Rev. by V. S. Pritchett in *NS*, LX, 277-78 (see also letter by Graham Greene in *NS*, LX, 310); by Neal Ascherson in *S*, 26 Aug., p. 312; in *TLS*, 30 Sept., p. 630.

HALLAM. Mathews, Elkin. "A. H. Hallam's *Poems*, 1830." *Book Collector*, IX, 64-65.

HARDY (see also II, Weber; III, Griffin, Harkness, Kirk, May; CONRAD: Hunt).
Allen, Don Cameron (ed.). *Four Poets on Poetry.* Baltimore: Johns Hopkins Univ. Pr. Pp. 111.
Rev. by Robert Gajdusek in *American Scholar*, XXIX, 264-66; by B. A. Robie in *LJ*, LXXXIV, 2642; by Kathleen Valmai Richardson in *Poetry Rev.*, LI, 170. Contains an essay on Hardy by Mark Van Doren.
Bradley, John Lewis. "An Echo of Tess." *TLS*, 9 Sept., p. 577.
An incident from *Tess*, later used in *Satires of Circumstance*, and based on a scene Hardy had observed in 1878-81. See also a letter by Sir Sidney Cockerell, 23 Sept., p. 611.
Bradley, John L. "A Footnote to Hardy's 'Channel Firing.'" *N & Q*, n.s. VII, 188-89.
Crompton, Louis. "The Sunburnt God: Ritual and Tragic Myth in *The Return of the Native*." *Boston Univ. Studies in English*, IV, 229-40.
Tracing the heroic and legendary prototypes for characters in the novel to classical and mythic sources, the writer illustrates the thematic-symbolic bases for the novel.
Deen, Leonard W. "Heroism and Pathos in Hardy's *Return of the Native*." *NCF*, XV, 207-19.
Denniston, Robin. "The World of Thomas Hardy." *Time and Tide*, XLI, 27 Aug. pp. 1010-11.
Green, David Bonnell. "The First Publication of 'The Spectre of the Real.'" *The Library*, 5th Ser., XV, 60-61.
The problem of newspaper serialization of a Hardy story.
Hodgins, James R. "A Study of the Periodical Reception of the Novels of Thomas Hardy, George Gissing, and George Moore." *DA*, XXI, 196-97.
"What they held in common was their belief in man's weakness and his inability to overcome internal and external forces."

To nineteenth century reviewers, who did not define their terms, the pessimism and despair illustrated in the novels signified naturalism."
Marcus, Mordecai, and Marcus, Erin. "Hardy's 'During Wind and Rain.'" *Ex*, XIX, Item 4.
On the dramatic structure of the poem.
Marshall, George O., Jr. "Hardy's *Tess* and Ellen Glasgow's *Barren Ground*." *Texas Studies in Lit. and Language*, I, 517-21.
Influences of Hardy's novel on Glasgow's, in theme, tone, and detail.
Modern Fiction Studies, VI, No. 3 (Fall).
Thomas Hardy Special Number.
Contains following items: Karl, Frederick R., " 'The Mayor of Casterbridge': A New Fiction Defined" (pp. 195-213); Paterson, John. "The 'Poetics' of 'The Return of the Native' " (pp. 214-22); Carpenter, Richard C., "Hardy's 'Gurgoyles' " (pp. 223-32); McDowell, Frederick P. W., "Hardy's 'Seemings or Personal Impressions': The Symbolic Use of Image and Contrast in 'Jude the Obscure' " (pp. 233-50); Drake, Robert Y., Jr., " 'The Woodlanders' as Traditional Pastoral" (pp. 251-57); Beebe, Maurice, Culotta, Bonnie, and Marcus, Erin, "Criticism of Thomas Hardy: A Selected Checklist" (pp. 258-79).
Paterson, John. "The Genesis of *Jude the Obscure*." *SP*, LVII, 87-98.
MS revisions suggest how Hardy's intention changed during composition.
Paterson, John. *The Making of "The Return of the Native."* Berkeley: Univ. of Calif. Pr. Pp. 168.
A study of Hardy's significant changes in theme and characterization, in manuscript, serial, and book.
Purdy, R. L. "Authorship of Hardy's Biography." *TLS*, 30 Dec., p. 845.
Claims Cyril Clemens' *My Chat with Thomas Hardy* is a pastiche of published sources.
Ransom, John Crowe. "Thomas Hardy's Poems." *KR*, XXII, 169-93.
Sanders, E. N. "Authorship of Hardy's Biography." *TLS*, 18 Nov., p. 741.
Schneider, Franz K. "The Concept of Realism in the Novel: A Re-Examination." *DA*, XX, 2785-86.
Hardy's *Return of the Native* included.
Scott, James F. "The Gothic Element in the Fiction of Thomas Hardy." *DA*, XXI, 1556.
Use of the "Gothic" tradition for Hardy's "sensationalism."

Six Novelists. Carnegie Series in English, No. 5. . . . See VB 1959, 440.
Rev. briefly by S. Sébaoun in *Études anglaises*, XIII, 404.

Weber, Carl J. (ed.). Introduction to *Tess of the D'Urbervilles.* New York: Dodd, Mead. Pp. 446.

Webster, Harvey Curtis. "*The Mayor of Casterbridge* as Tragedy," *VS*, IV, 90-93.
A comment on John Paterson's article on the same subject: see VB 1959, 440.

HARRIS. Brome, Vincent. *Frank Harris.* . . . See VB 1959, 440.
Rev. by P. R. Penland in *LJ*, LXXXV, 1421; by H. T. Moore in *NYTBR*, 8 May, p. 7.

HARRISON. Marandon, S. "Frederic Harrison (1831-1923)." *Études anglaises*, XIII, 415-26.
Review of the various social, political, and literary contributions of Frederic Harrison.

HOPKINS (see also BRIDGES: Ritz; TENNYSON: Altick).
The Journals and Papers of Gerard Manley Hopkins. . . . See VB 1959, 440.
Rev. by A. G. Hill in *EC*, X, 215-19; by J. A. Westrup in *M & L*, XLI, 74-75; by Peter Ure in *RES*, n.s. XI, 445-47; by Walter J. Ong in *VS*, III, 305-08.
The Sermons and Devotional Writings of Gerard Manley Hopkins. . . . See VB 1959, 440.
Rev. by A. G. Hill in *EC*, X, 215-19; by Peter Ure in *RES*, n.s. XI, 445-47; by Walter J. Ong in *VS*, III, 305-08.

Assad, Thomas J. "A Closer Look at Hopkins' '(Carrion Comfort).' " *Tulane Studies in English*, IX, 91-102.
Intensive reading to bring out the spiritual meaning through the literal meaning of the "overthought," and Hopkins' intimacy with Ignatius' *Spiritual Exercises.*

Downes, David A. *Gerard Manley Hopkins: A Study of his Ignatian Spirit.* New York: Bookman Associates. Pp. 195.
Rev. by Alan Heuser in *QQ*, LXVII, 492.

Heuser, Alan. *The Shaping Vision of Gerard Manley Hopkins.* . . . See VB 1959, 440.
Rev. by Carlisle Moore in *Comp. Lit.*, XII, 172-75; by Walter J. Ong in *VS*, III, 305-08.

Jennings, Elizabeth. "The Unity of Incarnation: A Study of Gerard Manley Hopkins." *Dublin Rev.*, CCXXXIV, 170-84.

Litzinger, Boyd. "The Genesis of Hopkins'

'Heaven-Haven.' " *VNL*, No. 17 (Spring), 31-33.

Mooney, Stephen. "Hopkins and Counterpoint." *VNL*, No. 18 (Fall), pp. 21-22.

Schneider, Elisabeth. "Hopkins' 'The Windhover.' " *Ex*, XVIII, Item 22.
A plea against assigning a "mechanical, dictionary-flowered ambiguity" to the crucial word "buckle."

Wain, John. "Gerard Manley Hopkins: An Idiom of Desperation." *Proceedings of the British Academy*, XLV, 173-97.
Hopkins' "idiom of desperation" arises from his loneliness, his monastic life, and his isolation from the idiom and events of the 19th century. His "new" poetry and idiom is more vigorous and 20th-century in mode and temper.

HOUSMAN. Carter, John, and Scott, Joseph W. *A. E. Housman: Catalogue of an Exhibition on the Centenary of His Birth.* London: University College, 1959. Pp. 35.
Rev. by William White in *BB*, XXIII, 7.

Lucas, Frank Lawrence. *The Greatest Problem, and Other Essays.* London: Cassell. Pp. xi + 335.
Rev. in *TLS*, 1 July, p. 420. Includes essay on Housman.

Randall, David A. "*A Shropshire Lad* with a Variant Title Page." *The Book Collector*, IX, 458.

Rudd, Nial. "Patterns in Horatian Lyric." *American Jour. of Philology*, LXXXI, 373-92.
Brief comment on pp. 388-89 on the affinity between Horatian Ode and Housman's 'On Wenlock Edge.'

Skutsch, Otto. *Alfred Edward Housman, 1859-1936.* London: Athlone Pr. Pp. 14.
Briefly rev. in *TLS*, 29 Apr., p. 278. An address delivered at University College, London.

Sparrow, John. "A Housman Reminiscence." *RES*, n.s. XI, 190-91.
Echoes of a Spanish ballad in Housman's "The Land of Biscay."

White, William. "A Checklist of A. E. Housman's Writings in Latin." *BSP*, LIV, 188-90.

White, William. "Housman in Sudbury, Ontario." *BSP*, LIV, 295.

HUDSON. Dewar, David R. "W. H. Hudson's Visit to Ireland." *N & Q*, n.s. VII, 188.

HUGHES. Winn, William E. "*Tom Brown's School Days* and the Development of

'Muscular Christianity.' " *Church History*, XXIX, 64-73.

Also speaks of influences of Kingsley and Thomas Arnold on Hughes and on the movement.

HUXLEY. Bibby, Cyril. *T. H. Huxley: Scientist, Humanist, and Educator.* . . . See VB 1959, 441.

Rev. by Caryl P. Haskins in *HTB*, 26 June, p. 5; by A. Hunter Dupree in *Isis*, LI, 607-08; by J. K. Lucker in *LJ*, LXXXV, 2156; by Frank Greenaway in *N*, 7 May, p. 406; by Gertrude Himmelfarb in *New R*, 16 May, p. 20; by William Irvine in *NYTBR*, 24 Apr., p. 30; by J. H. Rush in *SR*, 23 Apr., p. 21; by Charles S. Blinderman in *VS*, III, 406-07.

Crowe, M. B. "Huxley and Humanism." *StI*, XLIX, 249-60.

A discussion of scientific humanism which springs from and returns to the "great debate."

Irvine, William. *Thomas Henry Huxley*. Writers and Their Work. London: Longmans. Pp. 40.

Noticed in *TLS*, 15 Apr., p. 238.

Jensen, John V. "The Rhetoric of Thomas H. Huxley and Robert G. Ingersoll in Relation to the Conflict between Science and Theology." *DA*, XX, 4215-16.

KINGSLEY. *American Notes: Letters from a Lecture Tour, 1874.* . . . See VB 1959, 441.

Rev. briefly in *NCF*, XIV, 371.

Martin, Robert Bernard. *The Dust of Combat: A Life of Charles Kingsley*. London: Faber. Pp. 308.

Rev. by David Daiches in *HTB*, 3 July, p. 5; by R. R. Rea in *LJ*, LXXXV, 2581; by Walter E. Houghton in *NCF*, XV, 274-75; by John Raymond in *NS*, LIX, 492-93; by Ronald Bryden in *S*, 8 Apr., p. 512 (see also letter by Margaret Cole, 22 Apr., p. 571); in *TLS*, 29 Apr., p. 271; by Neville C. Masterman in *VS*, IV, 176-77.

KIPLING (see also II, Baldwin, Weber).

Annan, Noel. "Kipling's Place in the History of Ideas." *VS*, III, 323-48.

Sees Kipling as one of the first Englishmen to perceive how a code of behavior proceeds from the demands of a culture; maintains that he "is almost the sole analogue in England at the turn of the century to Durkheim and Weber and the German and Italian thinkers . . . who were in revolt against mid-nineteenth-century constructs of the individual and society."

Cohen, Morton N. "Rudyard Kipling and Rider Haggard." *Dalhousie Rev.*, XL,

297-322.

Based mainly on letters and diaries, this study traces the development of the friendship between Kipling and Haggard.

Goodwin, John Hanchard. "Song of the Old Guard." *TLS*, 5 Feb., p. 81.

On Kipling's apparent use, in *Traffics and Discoveries*, of a 17th-century ballad. See a further letter by John Horder, 26 Feb., p. 129.

Haber, Tom Burns. "The War Memorial at Sudbury, Ontario." *BSP*, LIV, 186-88.

On a quatrain Kipling wrote for the memorial.

Stewart, James McG. *Rudyard Kipling: A Bibliographical Catalogue*, ed. by A. W. Yeats. Toronto: Dalhousie Univ. Pr. and Univ. of Toronto Pr., 1959. Pp. xv + 673.

Rev. by Bonamy Dobrée in *Critical Quart.*, II, 286; by Stanton Millet in *JEGP*, LIX, 741-43; by H. P. Gundy in *QQ*, LXXVII, 494-95; in *TLS*, 2 Sept., p. 568.

Sutcliff, Rosemary. *Rudyard Kipling*. London: Bodley Head. Pp. 61.

Short study and bibliography of Kipling's books which are written for children.

Tompkins, J. M. S. *The Art of Rudyard Kipling*. . . . See VB 1959, 442.

Rev. by F. Léaud in *Études anglaises*, XIII, 481-83; by C. A. Bodelsen in *EST*, XLI, 277-80; by Stanton Millet in *JEGP*, LIX, 594-95; by Jacques Vallette in *Mercure de France*, CCCXL, 706-08; by C. J. Sisson in *MLR*, LV, 437-38; by Stephen Graham in *Poetry Rev.*, LI, 42; in *QR*, CCXCVIII, 117-18; by V. de S. Pinto in *RES*, n.s. XI, 447-48; by Betty Miller in *TC*, CLXVIII, 279-80; in TLS, 15 Jan., pp. 25-26.

LANDOR. Zall, P. M. "Landor's Marginalia on a Volume of Cowper's Poems." *Bull. New York Pub. Libr.*, LXIX, 55-57.

LIVINGSTONE (see also II; Moorehead).

Schapera, I. (ed.). *David Livingstone: Family Letters, 1841-1856.* . . . See VB 1959, 442.

Rev. by R. W. Henderson in *LJ*, LXXXV, 1423; by Stuart Cloete in *NYTBR*, 18 Sept., p. 58; by Godfrey Lienhardt in *Universities Quart.*, XIV, 214-16.

Schapera, I. (ed.). *Livingstone's Private Journals, 1851-1853*. London: Chatto and Windus. Pp. xxv + 341.

Rev. by Neal Ascherson in *S*, 30 Dec., p. 1053; in *TLS*, 25 Nov., p. 751.

Chadwick, Owen. *Mackenzie's Grave*. London: Hodder and Stoughton, 1959. Pp. 254.

Rev. by M. Mortimer in *CR,* CXCVII, 344-45; by Colin Leys in *NS,* LIX, 18. On Livingstone's 1861 Zambesi expedition and its tragedy.

Harlow, Vincent. "David Livingstone and Central Africa To-day." *HJ,* LVIII, 329-37.

MACAULAY (see also III, Hart).

Hudson, Derek. "Macaulay: A Footnote to the Centenary." *N & Q,* n.s. VII, 202. On W. M. Praed and on Macaulay's father's disapproval of his son's publications in *Knight's Quarterly.*

Knowles, David. *Lord Macaulay, 1800-1859.* Cambridge: Cambridge Univ. Pr. Pp. 31. Rev. in *TLS,* 15 Apr., p. 238. A lecture.

Potter, George Reuben. *Macaulay.* Writers and Their Work. London: Longmans, 1959. Pp. 40.

MARRYAT. Zanger, Jules (ed.). *Diary in America.* Bloomington: Indiana Univ. Pr. Pp. 342. Rev. by R. Woodward in *LJ,* LXXXV, 3656; in *TLS,* 30 Dec., p. 843.

MARTINEAU. Webb, Robert Kiefer. *Harriet Martineau: A Radical Victorian.* New York: Columbia Univ. Pr. Pp. xiii + 385. Rev. by Alan P. Grimes in *APSR,* LIV, 1010; by Adele M. Fasick in *LJ,* LXXXV, 2424; by Penelope Gilliatt in *S,* 15 Apr., p. 548; in *TLS,* 6 May, p. 286; by C. R. Fay in *VS,* IV, 74-75.

MEREDITH (see also III, Bell, Shelley).

Bartlett, Phyllis. "Meredith's 'The Old Chartist.' " *Ex,* XVIII, Item 56. On the symbolism of the "dandy rat."

Baylen, Joseph O. "George Meredith and W. T. Stead: Three Unpublished Letters." *HLQ,* XXIV, 47-57.

Hardy, Barbara. " 'A Way to Your Hearts through Fire or Water': The Structure of Imagery in *Harry Richmond.*" *EC,* X, 163-80.

Kelvin, Norman. "Nature and Society in the Works of George Meredith." *DA,* XX, 4655.

Marshall, William H. "Richard Feverel, 'The Original Man.' " *VNL,* No. 18 (Fall), pp. 15-18.

Tompkins, J. M. S. "Meredith's *Periander.*" *RES,* n.s. XI, 286-95. Autobiographical implications in Meredith's treatment of a tragic episode from Herodotus.

MILL. Cooney, Séamus. "Mill, Poets, and Other Men." *VNL,* No. 17 (Spring), pp. 23-25.

DeSelincourt, Aubrey. *Six Great Thinkers.* London: Hamish Hamilton, 1958. Pp. 180. Rev. by J. Loiseau in *Études anglaises,* XIII, 71-72. J. S. Mill is included.

Mill, Anna Jean (ed.). *John Mill's Boyhood Visit to France: Being a Journal and Notebook Written by John Stuart Mill in France, 1820-21.* Toronto: Univ. of Toronto Pr. Pp. xxxi + 133.

Hunter, Laurence C. "Mill and the Law of Markets: Comment." *Quart. Journ. of Econ.,* LXXIV, 158-62. (See Bela Balassa, VB 1959, 442-43.)

Kemp, Murray C. "The Mill-Bastable Infant-Industry Dogma." *JPE,* LXVIII, 65-67. A criticism of Mill's argument for protection.

Mueller, Iris W. *John Stuart Mill and French Thought.* . . . See VB 1957, 414. Rev. by Irving Louis Horowitz in *Philosophy,* XXXV, 181-83.

Pankhurst, Richard K. P. *The Saint Simonians, Mill and Carlyle: A Preface to Modern Thought.* . . . See VB 1958, 369. Rev. by L. Robbins in *Economica,* XXVII, 278-79.

Robson, John M. "J. S. Mill's Theory of Poetry." *TQ,* XXIX, 420-38.

Russell, Bertrand. "John Stuart Mill." . . . See VB 1956, 260. Rev. by Karl Britton in *Philosophy,* XXXV, 62-65.

Stillinger, Jack. "The Text of John Stuart Mill's *Autobiography.*" *Bulletin of the John Rylands Library,* XLIII, 220-42. With the press copy of the *Autobiography,* the third known MS now in the John Rylands Library, the writer establishes convincing evidence for dating, collating, and editing an authoritative text, closer to the plan and words of Mill. He lists variants among the MSS and suggests the problems of a new edition. The University of Toronto Press is planning a new edition of Mill's works. This article is of first importance for students of Mill and Victorian prose. — R.E.F.

MOORE (see also III, Ellman, Hough; HARDY: Hodgins).

Burkhart, Charles. "George Moore and *Father and Son.*" *NCF,* XV, 71-77.

Collet, Georges-Paul. *George Moore et la France.* . . . See VB 1959, 443. Rev. by Jean Noel in *Revue de littérature comparée,* XXXIV, 627-30.

Gerber, Helmut E. *George Moore: An Anno-*

tated Bibliography of Writings about Him. English Fiction in Transition, II, No. 2. Lafayette, Indiana, 1959. Pp. 91. Rev. briefly in BSP, LIV, 143.

Heywood, C. "Flaubert, Miss Braddon, and George Moore." Comp. Lit., XII, 151-58. Attempts to illustrate by parallels that Moore in A Mummer's Wife used Miss Braddon's French heroine in The Doctor's Wife (1864) as a model, representing "the earliest borrowing from Flaubert in English literature and . . . a major source of A Mummer's Wife."

MORRIS. William Morris and the Kelmscott Press: An Exhibition Held in the Library of Brown University, Providence, Rhode Island, from October 9 to December 31, 1959. Providence, R.I.: Brown Univ. Lib. Pp. iii + 48. Catalogue is prefaced by an address by Philip C. Duschnes.

"News and Notes." BSP, LIV, 129-30. On Morris as a printer. Mentions a speech by Robert F. Metzdorf, editor of BSP, "Victorian Book Decoration," at Yale University Library, which discussed Morris' contemporary printers and gives them credit for innovations commonly granted to Morris.

NEWMAN. Blehl, Vincent F. "Newman's Delation: Some Hitherto Unpublished Letters." Dublin Rev., CCXXXIV, 296-305.

Bokenkotter, Thomas S. Cardinal Newman as an Historian. Louvain: Bibliothèque de l'Université, Bureaux de Recueil, 1959. Pp. ix + 156. Rev. by Meriol Trevor in Dublin Rev., CCXXXIV, 190-92.

Cameron, J. M. "The Night Battle: Newman and Empiricism." VS, IV, 99-117. Argues that "the philosophical affinities of Newman are peculiarly with one philosopher in the British empiricist tradition, namely, David Hume; and . . . Newman's cast of mind and intellectual sympathies are, in philosophical matters, always with the empiricist school."

Dessain, Charles Stephen. "Cardinal Newman's Papers: A Complete Edition of His Letters." Dublin Rev., CCXXXIV, 291-96.

Houghton, Walter E. " 'New' Articles by Cardinal Newman." TLS, 15 Apr., p. 241. Seven articles in the British Critic, 1836-40, identified from MS sources in the Oratory at Birmingham. See also letter by C. Stephen Dessain, 22 Apr., p. 257.

Shook, Laurence K. "Newman and the Dialogue." The Basilian Teacher, V, 49-52. The present Catholic-Protestant dialogue has created a suitable climate for the study of what the Protestant Newman had to say about Protestantism.

Shook, Laurence K. "Newman's Correspondence with Two Canadians." Dublin Rev., CCXXXIV, 205-21. Letters to and from Newman 1839-43.

Walgrave, J. H. Newman the Theologian. New York: Sheed and Ward. Pp. 378. Tr. by A. V. Littledale; first published in Paris in 1957.

Whyte, J. H. "Newman in Dublin: Fresh Light from the Archives of Propaganda." Dublin Rev., CCXXXIV, 31-39.

NIGHTINGALE. Rees, Richard. For Love or Money: Studies in Personality and Essence. London: Secker and Warburg. Pp. 191. To support his case that modern civilization overemphasizes specialized skills which earn material rewards and neglects the wisdom which proceeds from deeper psychic levels, Rees draws on the careers of Florence Nightingale and Dickens, and on Nightingale's book of meditations, Suggestions.

PATER (see also SYMONS: Garbáty).

Chandler, Edmund. Pater on Style. . . . See VB 1959, 444. Rev. by Richard Gerber in Anglia, LXXVIII, 257-58; by John Leje in Studia Neophilologica, XXI, 262-63.

Duffey, Bernard. "The Religion of Pater's Marius." Texas Studies in Lit. and Language, II, 103-14.

Turner, Paul. "Pater and Apuleius," VS, III, 290-96.

PATMORE. Thomas A. "Coventry Patmore's 'Signatures.' " N & Q, n.s. VII, 266.

PEACOCK. Read, Bill. The Critical Reputation of Thomas Love Peacock. Ann Arbor, Mich.: Univ. Microfilms. 1959. Pp. 285. Available in microfilm or Xerox from Dept. of English, Boston Univ. College of General Education, Boston, Mass. Survey of Peacock's reputation and bibliography of his works and of published criticism about his works to June 1958.

ROLFE. Woolf, Cecil (ed.). The Centenary Edition of the Letters of Frederick William Rolfe. Vol. II: Letters to Leonard Moore. London: Nicholas Vane. Pp. 76. Rev. in TLS, 9 Sept., p. 573.

ROSSETTIS (see also III, Hudson, Sypher).

Doughty, Oswald. *A Victorian Romantic: Dante Gabriel Rossetti.* London: Oxford Univ. Pr. Pp. 712.
Rev. by Frank Kermode in *S*, 25 Nov., p. 850 (and see letter by R. Glynn Grylls, 2 Dec., pp. 896-97); in *TLS*, 23 Dec., p. 826. A new edition with corrections and additions.
Johnston, Robert D. "Imagery in Rossetti's *House of Life*." *DA*, XX, 2783-84.
Ricks, Christopher: "'O Where Are You Going?': W. H. Auden and Christina Rossetti." *N & Q*, n.s. VII, 472.
Swann, Thomas Burnett. *Wonder and Whimsey: The Fantastic World of Christina Rosetti.* Francestown, N.H.: Marshall Jones. Pp. 111.
Todd, William B. "D. C. Rossetti's *Early Italian Poets*, 1861." *Book Collector*, IX, 329-31.
Description of a variant edition.
RUSKIN (see also II, Feiling).
Evans, Joan, and Whitehouse, John Howard (eds.). *The Diaries of John Ruskin....* See VB 1959, 444.
Rev. by T. S. R. Boase in *Burlington Mag.*, CII, 173; by A. G. Hill in *EC*, X, 342-45; by Bertram Morris in *JAA*, XVIII, 398-99; by Jacques Vallette in *Mercure de France*, CCCXXXIX, 135-38; by John Lewis Bradley in *VS*, III, 401-02.
Evans, Joan (ed.). *The Lamp of Beauty....* See VB 1959, 445.
Rev. by Henri Lemaitre in *Études anglaises*, XIII, 386; by Francis Steegmuller in *NYTBR*, 27 Mar., p. 32.
Fontaney, Pierre. "Ruskin d'après des Livres Nouveaux." *Études anglaises*, XIII, 32-37. Critical summary of recent studies of Ruskin.
Kimbrough, Robert. "Calm Between Crises: Pattern and Direction in Ruskin's Mature Thought," *Transactions of the Wisconsin Academy of Sciences, Arts and Letters*, XLIX, 219-27.
Spence, Margaret E. "Ruskin's Friendship with Mrs. Fanny Talbot." *Bulletin of the John Rylands Library*, XLII, 453-80. Utilizing 365 letters written between 1875-89, the author traces and records Ruskin's friendly attachment to the "motherly" Mrs. Talbot.
Walton, Paul H. "Seven Ruskin Drawings in the Fogg Art Museum." *HLB*, XIV, 265-82.
SHAW (see also II, Fremantle; III, Ellmann; HARRIS: Brome).

Adler, Jacob H. "Ibsen, Shaw, and *Candida*." *JEGP*, LIX, 50-58.
Parallels between *Candida* and *The Wild Duck*.
Allen, Don Cameron (ed.). *Studies in Honor of T. W. Baldwin.* Urbana: Univ. of Illinois Pr. Pp. 276.
Rev. by G. R. Hibbard in *N & Q*, n.s. VII, 38. Contains an essay on "Shaw's long flirtation with *Cymbeline*."
Austin, Don D. "The Comic Structure in Five Plays of Bernard Shaw." *DA*, XX, 4658.
Caesar and Cleopatra, Man and Superman, Major Barbara, Pygmalion, and *Saint Joan*.
Brooks, Harold F. "'Pygmalion' and 'When We Dead Awaken.'" *N & Q*, n.s. VII, 469.
Clarke, Arthur C. "Shaw and the Sound Barrier." *VQR*, XXXVI, 72-77.
A correspondence showing Shaw's interest in high-speed flight.
Dunlap, Joseph R. "The Typographical Shaw: GBS and the Revival of Printing." *Bull. New York Pub. Libr.*, LXIV, 534-47.
Farmer, H. G. *Bernard Shaw's Sister and Her Friends.* London: Barmerlea.
Rev. by J. A. Westrup in *M & L*, XLI, 369-70; in *QR*, CCXCVIII, 361-62; in *TLS*, 20 May, p. 316. A defense of Lucy Carr Shaw.
Kaye, Julian B. *Bernard Shaw and the Nineteenth-Century Tradition....* See VB 1959, 445.
Rev. by David Wiley in *QJS*, XLVI, 315-16.
Keough, Lawrence C. "George Bernard Shaw, 1946-1955: A Bibliography." *BB*, XXIII, 20-24; 36-41.
Kozelka, Paul. *Glossary to the Plays of Bernard Shaw....* See VB 1959, 445.
Rev. briefly by George E. Nichols, III, in *CE*, XXI, 237.
Matthews, John F. (ed.). *Shaw's Dramatic Criticism (1895-98).* New York: Hill and Wang, 1959. Pp. 306.
Rev. briefly by George E. Nichols, III, in *CE*, XXI, 237.
Morgan, Margery M. "'Back to Methuselah': The Poet and the City." *Essays and Studies by Members of the English Association*, XIII, 82-98.
Attempts to show the relationship of form and style as an outgrowth of shifts in Shaw's ideas and philosophy and therefore carefully planned for in the drama.

The Shaw Review (containing *The Shaw Bulletin*). Vol. III, No. 1 (January, 1960), has items: Smith, Warren S., "The Bishop, the Dancer, and Bernard Shaw" (pp. 2-10); Couchman, Gordon W., "Comic Catharsis in *Caesar and Cleopatra*" (pp. 11-14); Whiting, George W., "The Cleopatra Rug Scene: Another Source" (pp. 15-17); Weisert, John J., "Oh, Bottom, Thou Art Translated!" (pp. 18-20); "St. Pancras Manifesto" (pp. 21-31); "A Continuing Check-List of Shaviana," compiled and edited by Charles A. Carpenter, Jr. (pp. 32-37); Kozelka, Paul, "*Heartbreak House* Revived," a review of the Billy Rose Theatre production (pp. 38-39); Steinhardt, Maxwell, "*The Devil's Disciple* on the Screen," a review (pp. 39-41); "News and Queries" (pp. 42-44).

No. 2 (May, 1960) has items: Nethercot, Arthur H., "What Shaw Really Thought of Americans" (pp. 2-8); "British Museum Acquires Shaw MSS. from Estate" (p. 8); Matlaw, Myron, "Bernard Shaw and *The Interlude at the Playhouse*" (pp. 9-17); Lewis, Arthur O., Jr., and Weintraub, Stanley, "Bernard Shaw — Aspects and Problems of Research" (pp. 18-26); Johnson, Maurice, "Charles Surface and Shaw's Heroines" (pp. 27-28); "A Continuing Check-List of Shaviana," compiled and edited by Charles A. Carpenter, Jr. (pp. 29-32); Kaye, Julian B., a review of Anne Fremantle's *This Little Band of Prophets* (pp. 33-34); Mann, Charles W., Jr., a review of Upton Sinclair's *My Lifetime in Letters* (pp. 34-35); Rayvis, Harold I., " 'Dear Liar' on Tour," a review (pp. 36-37); Klein, Helene, "Franklyn Barnabas at Home" (pp. 37-38); "News and Queries" (pp. 39-40).

No. 3 (September, 1960) has items: Phillpotts, Eden, "From the Angle of Ninety-Eight" (pp. 2-5); Quartermaine, Leon, "Talking about Actors and Acting" (pp. 6-13); Lauter, Paul, " 'Candida' and 'Pygmalion': Shaw's Subversion of Stereotypes" (pp. 14-19); Laurence, Dan H., "G. B. S. and the *Gazette*: A Bibliographical Study" (pp. 20-26); "Reviews and Essays Contributed by Shaw to *The Pall Mall Gazette*" (pp. 27-31); "A Continuing Check-List of Shaviana," compiled and edited by Charles A. Carpenter, Jr. (pp. 32-35); Rosset, B. C., a review of Arthur Nethercot's *The First Five Lives of Annie Besant* (p. 36); "News and Queries" (pp. 37-38); "Index" Vol. III, 1-3 (pp. 39-40).

"Shaw's Manuscripts Go to British Museum." *LJ*, LXXXV, 2142.

Simon, Louis. *Shaw on Education.* . . . See VB 1958, 388.
Rev. by G. H. Bantock in VS, IV, 167-70.

Weintraub, Stanley. "Bernard Shaw, Actor." *Theatre Arts*, Oct., pp. 66-67.

Weintraub, Stanley. "The Embryo Playwright in Bernard Shaw's Early Novels." *Texas Studies in Literature and Language*, I, 327-55.

West, E. J. (ed.). *Shaw on Theatre.* . . . See VB 1958, 389.
Rev. briefly by George E. Nichols, III, in *CE*, XXI, 237; by Ronald Hayman in *NS*, LX, 222; by Penelope Gilliatt in S, 5 Aug., pp. 623-24; in *TLS*, 5 Aug., p. 499.

SMILES. *Self-Help.* . . . See VB 1959, 446.
Rev. by L. Bonnerot in *Études anglaises*, XIII, 481.

SPENCER. Molloy, John I. "Spencer's Impact on American Conservatism, 1870-1912." *DA*, XX, 4430.

Munro, Thomas. "Evolution and Progress in the Arts: A Reappraisal of Herbert Spencer's Theory." *JAA*, XVIII, 294-318.
Spencer's theory in evolution in art retains some valid and suggestive ideas.

Simon, Walter M. "Herbert Spencer and the 'Social Organism.' " *JHI*, XXI, 294-99.
Explains the dichotomy in Spencer's thought concerning "Social Darwinism" and his views on collectivism and social science.

STEVENSON (see also THOMPSON: Connolly).

Aring, Charles D. "The Case Becomes Less Strange." *American Scholar*, XXX, 67-78.
Of dreams and Jekyll and Hyde.

Balfour, Michael. "How the Biography of Robert Louis Stevenson Came to be Written." *TLS*, 15 Jan., p. 37; 22 Jan., p. 52. See also letters by Ernest J. Nehew, 12 Feb., p. 97; by Alan Osbourne, 25 Mar., p. 193; and a further letter by Michael Balfour, 29 July, p. 481. On Graham Balfour and the "authorized" biography.

Bevington, Merle M. "Locke and Stevenson on Comparative Morality." *N & Q*, n.s. VII, 73.

Caldwell, Elsie Noble. *Last Witness for Robert Louis Stevenson.* Norman: Univ. of Oklahoma Pr. Pp. xiv + 384.
Rev. by David Daiches in *HTB*, 24 Apr., p. 8; by E. F. Walbridge in *LJ*, LXXXV, 754; in *TLS*, 13 May, p. 306; by J. C. Furnas in *VS*, IV, 183-84. Based on reminiscences of stepdaughter, Isobel Osbourne Field.

SURTEES. Bovill, E. W. *The England of*

Nimrod and Surtees. . . . See VB 1959, 446.

Rev. by J. Golliet in *Études anglaises*, XIII, 478-79; by T. R. Henn in *MLR*, LV, 432-33; in *QR*, CCXCVIII, 263-67; in *TLS*, 26 Feb., p. 130.

SWINBURNE (see also III, Griffin; TEN-NYSON: Altick).

Lang, Cecil Y. (ed.). *Swinburne Letters.* . . . See VB 1959, 446.

Rev. by DeLancey Ferguson in *American Scholar*, XXIX, 406; by S. C. Chew in *HTB*, 10 Jan., p. 3; by John Willingham in *LJ*, LXXXV, 2939; by Ralph Partridge in *NS*, LIX, 722; by Gordon N. Ray in *NYTBR*, 24 Jan., p. 22 and 25 Dec., p. 10; by W. W. Robson in *S*, 3 June, p. 808; by Merle M. Bevington in *SAQ*, LIX, 436-38; in *TLS*, 3 June, p. 352 (see also the letter to the Editor by Robert H. Tener, "Swinburne as Reviewer," *TLS*, 25 Dec. 1959); by James E. Suiter in *VNL*, No. 18 (Fall), pp. 24-26; by Hazard Adams in *VS*, IV, 84.

Maxwell, J. C. "The Swinburne Letters and O. E. D." *N & Q*, n.s. VII, 346-47.

Sitwell, Edith (ed.). *Swinburne: A Selection.* London: Weidenfeld and Nicolson; New York: Harcourt, Brace. Pp. 286.

Rev. by J. R. Willingham in *LJ*, LXXXV, 4477; by Horace Gregory in *NYTBR*, 27 Nov., p. 4; by G. D. Klingopulos in *S*, 21 Oct., pp. 610-11; in *TLS*, 14 Oct., p. 662.

Souffrin, Eileen. "Swinburne et *Les Misér-ables*." *Revue de littérature comparée*, XXXIV, 578-84.

Gosse attributed to Swinburne five articles in the *Spectator* (1862) on *Les Miséra-bles*. The writer attempts to show that two were clearly not by Swinburne and further suggests that the other three were probably not Swinburne's.

Todd, William B. "Swinburne Manuscripts at Texas." *Texas Quarterly*, II, 152-63.

Werner, Alfred. "The Sad Ballad of Simeon Solomon." *KR*, XXII, 392-407.

Sympathetic account of the alcoholic, de-praved friend of Swinburne.

SYMONS (see also YEATS: Witt).

Garbáty, Thomas Jay. "An Appraisal of Ar-thur Symons by Pater and Mallarmé." *N & Q*, n.s. VII, 187-88.

TENNYSON (See I, Bowers; ARNOLD: Su-per; TURNER, CHARLES TENNY-SON).

Altick, Richard D. "Four Victorian Poets and an Exploding Island." *VS*, III, 249-60.

The island is Krakatoa, a volcanic island which erupted in 1883; the poets are Ten-nyson, Bridges, Swinburne, and Hopkins, each of whom described the effects of the explosion in England's sky.

B., C. "Tennyson in Lincolnshire." *English*, XIII, 22.

On the celebration of the sesquicenten-nial of Tennyson's birth.

Brashear, William R. "The Concept of the 'Living Will' as an Interpretive Key to Tennyson's Poetry." *DA*, XX, 4652.

Buckley, Jerome Hamilton. *Tennyson: The Growth of a Poet.* Cambridge, Mass.: Harvard Univ. Pr. Pp. xii + 298.

Rev. by J. R. Willingham in *LJ*, LXXXV, 4374.

Green, David Bonnell. "Leigh Hunt's Hand in Samuel Carter Hall's *Book of Gems*." *Keats-Shelley Jour.*, VIII, 103-17.

Hunt believed in Tennyson's future great-ness.

Killham, John (ed.). *Critical Essays on the Poetry of Tennyson.* London: Routledge and K. Paul. Pp. viii + 263.

Rev. by Jacques Vallette in *Mercure de France*, CCCXXXIX, 342-44; by John Jones in *NS*, LIX, 196-97; by F. W. Bateson in *S*, 29 Jan., p. 141; in *TLS*, 11 Mar., p. 162.

Killham, John. *Tennyson and "The Princess": Reflections of an Age.* . . . See VB 1959, 447.

Rev. by F. Basch in *Études anglaises*, VIII, 479-80; by Jerome H. Buckley in *JEGP*, LIX, 164-65; by Kenneth Allott in *RES*, n.s. XI, 225-26; by E. D. Pendry in *Studia Neophilologica*, XXI, 251-55.

Miller, Betty. "Tennyson: The Early Years." *TC*, CLXVII, 520-29.

Nowell-Smith, Simon. "Tennyson's *In Me-moriam* 1850." *Book Collector*, IX, 76-77.

Cites some changes from first to subse-quent editions.

P., L. "Tennyson's 'The Palace of Art.'" *Ex*, XVIII, Query 2.

Schweik, Robert C. "The 'Peace or War' Passages in Tennyson's 'Maud.'" *N & Q*, n.s. VII, 457-58.

Source in *Blackwood's Magazine*, Novem-ber 1854.

THACKERAY (see also II, Moers; III, Bell).

Ray, Gordon N. *Thackeray: The Age of Wis-dom* (1847-1863). . . . See VB 1959, 448.

Rev. by Henry Gifford in *RES*, n.s. XI, 107-09.

"*La Rose et l'Anneau*. Présentation et traduc-tion de Jean Queval." *Mercure de France*, CCCXL, 582-608.

A *"transcription libre"* of chapters from Thackeray's Christmas pantomime. In his preface M. Queval suggests that in this book Thackeray anticipated the "Ubu Roi" of Alfred Jarry.

Taube, Myron. "The Character of Amelia in the Meaning of *Vanity Fair." VNL*, No. 18 (Fall), pp. 1-8.

Taube, Myron. "*Vanity Fair:* A Study of Background, Composition, and Meaning." *DA*, XX, 3311.

Taylor, A. Carey. "Balzac et Thackeray." *Revue de littérature comparée*, XXXIV, 354-369.
Suggests the influence of *La Cousine Bette* on *Vanity Fair.*

THOMPSON. Connolly, Terence L. "Francis Thompson's 'Chatter.'" *TLS*, 9 Sept., p. 577.
On an alleged misprint in "The Hound of Heaven."

Connolly, Terence L. (ed.). *The Real Robert Louis Stevenson and Other Critical Essays by Francis Thompson. . . .* See VB 1959, 448.
Rev. briefly in *NCF*, XIV, 374; in *TLS*, 8 Jan., p. 20.

Danchin, Pierre. *Francis Thompson: La vie et l'oeuvre d'un poète.* Paris: A.-G. Nizet, 1959. Pp. 554.
Rev. by Sir Francis Meynell in *Études anglaises*, XIII, 484.

Danchin, Pierre. "Francis Thompson (1859-1907): À propos d'un centenaire." *Études anglaises*, XIII, 427-43.
Review of Thompson's views on poetry and religion, partially based on unpublished letters.

Dingle, Reginald J. "Francis Thompson's Centenary: The Fashionable Reaction." *Dublin Rev.*, CCXXXIV, 74-83.

Francis Thompson Centenary, 1859-1959: Catalogue of Manuscripts, Letters and Books in the Harris Public Library, Preston. Preston: Public Libr. Pp. 77.
Rev. in *TLS*, 8 Jan., p. 20 (and see correspondence, 15 Jan., p. 33).

Lees, F. N. "Francis Thompson: 1859-1907." *Bulletin of the John Rylands Library*, XLII, 378-94.
Biographical and literary survey.

Reid, John Cowie. *Francis Thompson: Man and Poet. . . .* See VB 1959, 448.
Rev. by Philip Larkin in *S*, 5 Feb., p. 188; in *TLS*, 8 Jan., p. 20.

THOMSON. Brown, Calvin S. "James Thom-

son and D'Annunzio on Dürer's *Melancolia." JAA*, XIX, 31-35.
Thomson in "The City of Dreadful Night" and D'Annunzio in *Il Fuoco* read themselves into Dürer's picture.

TREVELYAN. Hart, Jennifer. "Sir Charles Trevelyan at the Treasury." *EHR*, LXXV, 92-110.

TROLLOPES (see also III, Laski).

Chaloner, W. H. "Mrs. Trollope and the Early Factory System." *VS*, IV, 159-66.
Description of genesis and reception of Mrs. Trollope's *Michael Armstrong*, a novel about the conditions of factory labor.

Davies, Hugh Sykes. *Trollope.* Writers and Their Work. London: Longmans. Pp. 40.
Noticed in *TLS*, 15 Apr., p. 238.

Jones, Iva G. "A Study of the Literary Reputation of Anthony Trollope, 1847-1953." *DA*, XX, 2803-04.

Mahoney, John L. "Thomas A. Trollope: Victorian Man of Letters," *Univ. of Rochester Libr. Bull.*, XV, 25-28.
Discusses a letter of T. A. Trollope in library of Univ. of Rochester.

Shrewsbury, James B., Jr. "Trollope's Concept of a Gentleman." *DA*, XX, 3308-10.

Thale, Jerome. "The Problem of Structure in Trollope." *NCF*, XV, 147-57.

TURNER, CHARLES TENNYSON. *A Hundred Sonnets.* Ed. by John Betjeman and Sir Charles Tennyson. London: Hart-Davis. Pp. 135.
Rev. in *TLS*, 23 Dec., p. 830. Poems by Alfred's brother, Charles.

WARD. Knoepflmacher, U. C. "The Rival Ladies: Mrs. Ward's 'Lady Connie' and Lawrence's 'Lady Chatterley's Lover.'" *VS*, IV, 141-58.

WHITE. *L'Autobiographie de Mark Rutherford.* Trad. de P. Leyris. Paris: Fasquelle, 1957. Pp. 248.
Rev. by O. Lutaud in *Études anglaises*, XIII, 64-65.

WILDE (see also HARRIS: Brome).

Gide, André. *Pretexts: Reflections on Literature and Morality.* Ed. by Justin O'Brien. New York: Meridian, 1959. Pp. 352.
Rev. by Henri Peyre in *American Scholar*, XXIX, 266. Contains material on Wilde.

Holland, Vyvyan. *Oscar Wilde: A Pictorial Biography.* London: Thames and Hudson. Pp. 144.

James, Norman. "Oscar Wilde's Dramaturgy." *DA*, XX, 3744.

Spivey, Ted R. "Damnation and Salvation in *The Picture of Dorian Gray.*" *Boston Univ. Studies in English,* IV, 162-70.

YEATS (see also III, Ellmann).

The Variorum Edition of the Poems of W. B. Yeats. . . . See VB 1959, 449.
Rev. by Peter Ure in *ESt,* XLI, 281-83.

Allen, James L., Jr. "Bird Symbolism in the Work of William Butler Yeats." *DA,* XX, 3288.

Allen, James L., Jr. "Yeats' 'Her Vision in the Wood.'" *Ex,* XVIII, Item 45.
Symbolizes physical decay by identifying Adonis with the boar that destroys him.

Bradford, Curtis. "Yeats's Byzantium Poems: A Study of Their Development." *PMLA,* LXXV, 110-25.

Cosman, Madeleine Pelner. "Mannered Passion: W. B. Yeats and the Ossianic Myths." *Western Humanities Rev.,* XIV, 163-71.

Gibbon, Monk. *The Masterpiece and the Man: Yeats as I Knew Him.* . . . See VB 1959, 449.
Rev. by DeLancey Ferguson in *HTB,* 4 Sept., p. 6; by L. W. Griffin in *LJ,* LXXXV, 1422; by Jacques Vallette in *Mercure de France,* CCCXXXVIII, 738-39; by Frank O'Connor in *N,* 27 Feb., p. 190; by John Unterecker in *NYTBR,* 17 Apr., p. 20.

Hausermann, H. W. "W. B. Yeats and W. J. Turner, 1935-1937" (Concluded. See VB 1959, 449). *ESt,* XLI, 241-53.

Keith, W. J. "Yeats's Arthurian Black Tower." *MLN,* LXXV, 119-23.

MacLeish, Archibald. *Poetry and Experience.* Boston: Houghton Mifflin. Pp. 204.
Includes essay on poetry of Yeats.

Parks, Lloyd C. "The Influence of Villiers De L'Isle-Adam on W. B. Yeats." *DA,* XX, 2784-5.

Pearce, Donald R. (ed.). *The Senate Speeches of W. B. Yeats.* Bloomington: Indiana Univ. Pr. Pp. 183.
Rev. by L. W. Griffin in *LJ,* LXXXV, 3988.

Rosenthal, M. L. "On Yeats and the Cultural Symbolism of Modern Poetry." *YR,* XLIX, 573-83.

Saul, George Brandon. *Prolegomena to the Study of Yeats's Poems.* . . . See VB 1959, 449.
Rev. by Peter Ure in *RES,* n.s. XI, 113-14; by Thomas Parkinson in *SeR,* LXVIII, 143-49.

Saul, George Brandon. "W. B. Yeats: Corrigenda." *N & Q,* n.s. VII, 302-03.
See VB 1958, 392.

Saul, George Brandon. "Yeats's Verse Before Responsibilities." *ArQ,* XVI, 158-67.

Schanzer, Ernest. " 'Sailing to Byzantium,' Keats, and Andersen." *ESt,* XLI, 376-80.
Andersen's "The Emperor's Nightingale" and Keats's Ode as possible sources of the imagery of Yeats's poem.

Senior, John. *The Way Down and Out: The Occult in Symbolist Literature.* Ithaca, N.Y.: Cornell Univ. Pr., 1959, Pp. 217.
Rev. by Hazard Adams in *CE,* XXI, 357.
Contains material on Yeats.

Unterecker, John. *A Reader's Guide to William Butler Yeats.* . . . See VB 1959, 449.
Rev. briefly in *HTB,* 8 Nov., 1959, p. 15; by Stephen Graham in *Poetry Rev.,* LI, 42; by Wallace A. Bacon in *QJS,* LXXIV, 102; by Thomas Parkinson in *SeR,* LXVIII, 143-49.

Ure, Peter. "Yeats's Christian Mystery Plays." *RES,* n.s. XI, 171-82.
A study of *Calvary* and *The Resurrection.*

Watson, Thomas L. "The French Reputation of W. B. Yeats." *Comp Lit.,* XII, 256-62.
Yeats was known in France, until recently, principally by his nineteenth-century poetry.

Wilson, F. A. C. *W. B. Yeats and Tradition.* . . . See VB 1959, 449.
Rev. by Aerol Arnold in *Personalist,* XLI, 115-16.

Whitaker, Thomas R. "The Early Yeats and the Pattern of History." *PMLA,* LXXV, 320-28.

Whitaker, Thomas R. "Yeats's Alembic." *SeR,* LXVIII, 576-94.

Wilson, Francis Alexander Charles. *Yeats's Iconography.* London: Gollancz. Pp. 349.
Rev. by G. S. Fraser in *NS,* LX, 280; by Frank Kermode in *S,* 5 Aug., p. 220; in *TLS,* 19 Aug., p. 531.

Winters, Yvor. *The Poetry of W. B. Yeats.* Denver: Alan Swallow. Pp. 24.

Witt, Marion. "A Note on Yeats and Symons." *N & Q,* n.s. VII, 467-69.

Zwerdling, Alex. "W. B. Yeats: Variations on the Visionary Quest." *TQ,* XXX, 72-85.
A complex interpretative article attempting to show both the unity of Yeats's quest for the real and visionary in early and later poetry and establishing the various stages in the dichotomy between the two "quests." This interpretive argument must be read with specific poems for its full significance. — R.E.F.

VICTORIAN BLIOGRAPHY FOR 1961

Robert C. Slack, editor

THIS BIBLIOGRAPHY has been prepared by a committee of the Victorian Literature Group of the Modern Language Association of America: Robert C. Slack, chairman, Carnegie Institute of Technology; Oscar Maurer, University of Texas; Robert A. Donovan, Cornell University, Charles T. Dougherty, St. Louis University; Donald J. Gray, Indiana University; Richard C. Tobias, University of Pittsburgh; Ronald E. Freeman, University of Southern California; and Michael Timko, Queens College. It attempts to list the noteworthy publications of 1961 (including reviews of these and earlier items) that have a bearing on the Victorian period, as well as similar publications of earlier date that have been inadvertently omitted from the preceding Victorian bibliographies. Unless otherwise stated, the date of publication is 1961. Reference to a page in the bibliography for 1960, in *Victorian Studies,* June, 1961, is made by the following form: See VB 1960, 392. Some cross-references are given, though not all that are possible. Annotations to items are made at the discretion of committee members and the editor; some are intended to indicate content, others to emphasize important contributions; every annotation containing a judgment is initialed by the committee member responsible. For certain continuing bibliographical works the reader should consult VB 1941, the last annual bibliography in which such works are listed in full. Bibliographical entries are made to conform as closely as possible with the British National Bibliography for books first published in Great Britain, and with the Library of Congress Catalog for books first published in the United States.

The editor wishes to thank Professor Carl J. Weber for his helpful assistance with the Hardy section of the bibliography.

MLQ = *Modern Language Quarterly*
MLR = *Modern Language Review*
MP = *Modern Philology*
N = *Nation*
N & Q = *Notes and Queries*
NCF = *Nineteenth-Century Fiction*
NEQ = *New England Quarterly*
NER = *National and English Review*
New R = *New Republic*
NS = *New Statesman*
NYTBR = *New York Times Book Review*
PAPS = *Proceedings of the American Philosophical Society*
ParR = *Partisan Review*
PLC = *Princeton University Library Chronicle*
PMLA = *Publications of the Modern Language Association of America*
PQ = *Philological Quarterly*
PSQ = *Political Science Quarterly*
QJS = *Quarterly Journal of Speech*
QQ = *Queen's Quarterly*
QR = *Quarterly Review*
RES = *Review of English Studies*
RoR = *Romanic Review*
S = *Spectator*
SAQ = *South Atlantic Quarterly*
SeR = *Sewanee Review*
SP = *Studies in Philology*
SR = *Saturday Review*
StI = *Studies: An Irish Quarterly Review*
TC = *Twentieth Century*
TLS = *Times Literary Supplement*
TQ = *University of Toronto Quarterly*
VNL = *Victorian News Letter*
VQR = *Virginia Quarterly Review*
VS = *Victorian Studies*
YR = *Yale Review*

I. BIBLIOGRAPHICAL MATERIAL

(For bibliographies pertaining to individuals, see — DARWIN: Bailey; DICKENS: Carr; KIPLING: Gerber, Stewart; STEVENSON: McKay; TENNYSON: *The Tennyson Collection*).

Altick, Richard Daniel, and Matthews, William R. (comps.). *Guide to Doctoral Dissertations in Victorian Literature.* . . . See VB 1960, 368.
Rev. by Malcolm Ross in *QQ*, LXVIII, 517-18.
"Annual Bibliography for 1960." *PMLA*,

LXXVI, No. 2, 176-95; "English Language and Literature: IX. Nineteenth Century, X. Twentieth Century," ed. Charles C. Mish, Joan Corbett, Robert M. Pierson, and Gordon Ross Smith, with the help of Sherod M. Cooper and Mervyn R. Lowe.
Bandy, W. T. "Baudelaire in English: A Check List." *BB*, XXIII, 106-09.
Barber, Giles. "Galignani's and the Publication of English Books in France from 1800 to 1852." *The Library*, 5th Ser., XVI, 267-86.
Barton, Mary N. "Rare Books and Other Bibliographical Resources in Baltimore Libraries." *BSP*, LV, 1-16.
Hutzler collection of economic classics at Johns Hopkins; five volumes of correspondence of John Stuart Mill. College of Notre Dame Library has a Hopkins collection.
Berol, Alfred C. "The Daniel Press." *BSP*, LV, 40.
Block, Andrew. *The English Novel, 1740-1850: A Catalogue Including Prose Romances, Short Stories and Translations of Foreign Fiction.* New and rev. ed. London: Dawsons of Pall Mall. Pp. xv + 349. Rev. by John Hayward in *Book Collector*, X, 216-19; in *TLS*, 21 Apr., p. 256.
British Books on India. London: The British Council. Pp. 142. Briefly noted in *TLS*, 10 Nov., p. 810.
Casson, L. F. "The Manuscripts of the Grey Collection in Cape Town." *Book Collector X*, 147-55.
Books and manuscripts collected by Sir George Grey, governer of Cape Colony, 1853-61.
Chapman, R. W., *et al. Annals of English Literature, 1475-1950.* 2nd ed. London: Oxford Univ. Pr. Pp. 400.
Foxon, D. F. and Todd, W. B. "Thomas J. Wise and the Pre-Restoration Drama: A Supplement." *The Library*, 5th Ser., XVI, 287-93.
Glaister, Geoffrey Ashall. *An Encyclopedia of the Book.* . . . See VB 1960, 369.
Rev. by Lee Ash in *Special Libraries*, LII, 272.
Greenberg, Robert A. (ed.). "Recent Publications: A Selected List." *VNL*, No. 19 (Spring), pp. 30-32; No. 20 (Fall), pp. 30-32.

Father Hugh. *Nineteenth-Century Pamphlets at Pusey House*. London: Faith Pr. Pp. 98. Noticed in *TLS*, 21 Apr., p. 254; in *VS*, IV, 410-411. Index to a collection of 18,-500 pamphlets on Tractarianism and other church affairs of the Victorian age.

Irwin, Raymond and Staveley, Ronald (eds.). *The Libraries of London*. 2nd Rev. Ed. London: The Library Assoc. Pp. 332. Rev. by J. Clement Harrison in *LJ*, LXXXVI, 3266-67.

Juchhoff, Rudolf (comp.). *Sammelkatalog der biographischen und literarkritischen Werke zu englishchen Schriftstellern des 19. und 20. Jahrhunderts (1830-1958); Verzeichnis der Bestände in deutschen Bibliotheken.* . . . See VB 1960, 369. Rev. by Horst Oppel in *Anglia*, LXXVIII (1960), 510-11.

Lombard, C. M. "Lamartine in America and England (1820-1876): A Check List." *BB*, XXIII, 103-06.

Mitchell, Philip Marshall. *A Bibliography of British Imprints of Denmark through 1900*. Lawrence: Univ. of Kansas Pr., 1960. Pp. 85. Rev. by B. G. Madsen in *Scandinavian Studies*, XXXIII, 259.

Moran, James. "William Blades." *The Library*, 5th Ser., XVI, 251-66. The man whom Pollard called "The first bibliographer England ever had."

Nilon, Charles, Macdonald, Angus, and White, William (eds.). *The Annual Bibliography of English Language and Literature*. Vol. XXXII, 1955-56. Cambridge: Cambridge Univ. Pr., in association with Univ. of Colorado Pr. Pp. xvi + 631.

Reeves, D. D. *Resources for the Study of Economic History: A Preliminary Guide to Pre-Twentieth Century Printed Material Located in Certain American and British Libraries.* Cambridge, Mass.: Harvard Grad. School of Bus. Admin. Pp. ix + 61. Noted briefly in *Econ. Journ.*, LXXI, 900.

Slack, Robert C. (ed.). "Victorian Bibliography for 1960." *VS*, IV, 367-406.

Truss, Tom J., Jr. "Theodore Watts-Dunton: A Primary Bibliography." *BB*, XXIII, 114-17.

White, Beatrice and Dorsch, T. S. (eds.). *The Year's Work in English Studies.* Vol. XXXIX (1958). London: Oxford Univ. Pr. Pp. 319. The Nineteenth Century section is annotated by P. M. Yarker, pp. 229-65.

White, Beatrice and Dorsch, T. S. (eds.). *The Year's Work in English Studies.* Vol. XL (1959). London: Oxford Univ. Pr. Pp. 307. The Nineteenth Century section is annotated by P. M. Yarker and Sheila Smith, pp. 217-51.

Woolf, Harry, Bosson, Phyllis Brooks, and Hewitt, Carol B. "Eighty-sixth Critical Bibliography of the History of Science and Its Cultural Influences (to 1 January 1961)." *Isis*, LII, 445-526.

"Writings on Irish History, 1960." *Irish Historical Studies* XII, 345-65.

II. ECONOMIC, POLITICAL, RELIGIOUS, AND SOCIAL ENVIRONMENT

Abrash, Merritt G. "Personalities behind Policies: Studies of Seven Leading Figures in Anglo-Russian Relations, 1855-1895." *DA*, XXII, 1135.

Adburgham, Alison. *A "Punch" History of Manners and Modes, 1841-1940*. London: Hutchinson. Pp. 368. Rev. by William Plomer in *Listener*, 9 March, p. 448; by Asa Briggs in *NS*, LXI, 513-14; in *TLS*, 24 Feb., p. 123.

Ambirajan, S. *Malthus and Classical Economics*. Bombay, India: Popular Book Depot, 1959. Pp. ix + 212. Noted briefly in *Econ. Jour.*, LXXI, 891.

Antonelli, E. *Nouvelles études d' économie humaniste: Le capitalisme du XIXème siècle de 1814 à 1914 et le monde économique présent de 1914 à 1957*. Montpellier: La Licorne, 1959. Pp. 470. Rev. by E. A. J. Johnson in *JPE*, LXIX, 84-85.

Appleman, Philip, Madden, William A., and Wolff, Michael (eds.). *1859: Entering an Age of Crisis.* . . . See VB 1960, 370. Rev. by J. A. Altholz in *JMH*, XXXIII, 77-78; by Malcolm Ross in *QQ*, LXVIII, 516-17.

Armytage, W. H. G. *Heavens Below: Utopian Experiments in England, 1560-1960*. London: Routledge and Kegan Paul. Pp. viii + 458.

Armytage, W. H. G. *A Social History of Engineering.* London: Faber. Pp. 378.
Rev. in *TLS,* 26 May, p. 322.

Arnold, J. C. "The Rise and Progress of Joint Stock Companies." *QR,* CCIC, 263-74.

Arnold, Ralph. *The Whiston Matter.* London: Hart-Davis. Pp. 213.
Rev. by Hugh Lloyd-Jones in *Listener,* 14 Sept., p. 396; by A. Howard in *NS,* LXII, 356; by Raymond Postgate in *S,* 1 Sept., p. 296; in *TLS,* 8 Sept., p. 591. One of the cases which suggested to Trollope the Hiram's Hospital controversy in *The Warden.*

Ashby, Mabel K. *Joseph Ashby of Tysoe, 1859-1919.* Cambridge: Cambridge Univ. Pr. Pp. xiv + 303.
Rev. by W. G. Hoskins in *Listener,* 25 May, p. 935; by V. S. Pritchett in *NS,* LXI, 792; in *TLS,* 2 June, p. 342.

Ashworth, William. *An Economic History of England, 1870-1939.* . . . See VB 1960, 370.
Rev. by Sydney H. Zebel in *AHR,* LXVI, 1023-24; by J. B. Conacher in *Canadian Hist. Rev.,* XLII, 246-49; by H. J. Dyos in *Economica,* XXVIII, 449-51; by A. J. Youngson in *Econ. Jour.,* LXXI, 628-29; by W. H. Chaloner in *History Today,* XI, 221; by Donald E. Thompson in *LJ,* LXXXVI, 994; in *TLS,* 31 Mar., p. 204; by David Owen in *VS,* V, 163-65.

Ausubel, Herman. *In Hard Times: Reformers among the Late Victorians.* . . . See VB 1960, 370.
Rev. by John Clive in *AHR,* LXVI, 1021-23; by R. G Cowherd in *APSS,* CCC-XXXV, 206; by R. J. Lambert in *Econ. Jour.,* LXXI, 814-16; by W. Ashworth in *History,* XLVI, 272; by Ellen Hart Smith in *HTB,* 14 May, p. 29; by J. F. Glaser in *JMH,* XXXIII, 455-56; by Samuel Clyde McCulloch in *PSQ,* LXXVI, 446-47; in *QR,* CCIC, 475; in *TLS,* 1 Sept., p. 574; by Ruth Emery in *VS,* IV, 360-61.

Balston, Thomas. *Staffordshire Portrait Figures of the Victorian Age.* New York: Charles T. Branford, 1960. Pp. 93.
Rev. by P. von Khrum in *LJ,* LXXXVI, 87.

Banton, Michael (ed.). *Darwinism and the Study of Society.* London: Tavistock. Pp. xx + 191.
Rev. by G. Basalla in *LJ,* LXXXVI, 3294; in *TLS,* 6 Oct., p. 661.

Barrington, Charles George. "Political Recollections: II." *History Today,* XI, 572-80.

Barrington, Charles George. "Recollections of Lord Palmerston." *History Today,* XI, 182-90.

Extract from papers of Palmerston's private secretary from 1856-1865.

Bartle, G. F. "Sir John Bowring and the *Arrow* War in China." *Bull. of the John Rylands Library,* XLIII, 293-316.

Beales, Derek Edward Dawson. *England and Italy, 1859-1860.* London: Nelson. Pp. xii + 196.
Rev. by Alec Randall in *Listener,* 28 Sept., pp. 477-78.

Beames, John. *Memoirs of a Bengal Civilian.* London: Chatto and Windus. Pp. 312.
Rev. by R. Taubman in *NS,* LXII, 250; in *TLS,* 11 Aug., p. 519.

Bearce, George Donham. *British Attitudes Towards India, 1784-1858.* London: Oxford Univ. Pr. Pp. viii + 315.
Rev. in *TLS,* 29 Dec., p. 931.

Benians, E. A., Butler, Sir James, and Carrington, C. E. (eds.). *The Cambridge History of the British Empire.* Vol. III: *The Empire-Commonwealth, 1870-1919.* . . . See VB 1960, 370.
Rev. by D. G. Creighton in *CHJ,* III (1960), 96-98.

Bennett, James R. "Francis W. Newman and Religious Liberalism in Nineteenth Century England." *DA,* XXI, 3233.

Bergonzi, Bernard. "'The Battle of Dorking.'" *N & Q,* n.s. VIII, 346-47.

Best, G.F.A. "The Road to Hiram's Hospital: A Byway of Early Victorian History." *VS,* V, 135-50.

Birkett, Lord. "Sir Charles Russell." *Listener,* 15 June, pp. 1037-39.

Black, R. D. Collison. *Economic Thought and the Irish Question, 1817-1870.* . . . See VB 1960, 371.
Rev. by Lawrence J. McCaffrey in *AHR,* LXVI, 436-37; by G. A. Duncan in *Econ. Jour.,* LXXI, 812-14; by S. G. Checkland in *History,* XLVI, 269-71; by George W. Hilton in *JEH,* XXI, 233-34; by Emmet Larkin in *JMH,* XXXIII, 333-34; by Robert Lekachman in *PSQ,* LXXVI, 598-600; by E. R. R. Green in *VS,* IV, 358-59.

Blackie, A. A. C. *Blackie & Son: 1809-1959.* . . . See VB 1959, 413.
Rev. by R. D. Macleod in *LR,* XVII (1960), 341-42.

Blagden, Cyprian. *The Stationers' Company: A History 1403-1959.* Harvard Univ. Pr., 1960. Pp. 321.
Rev. by Frances L. S. Dugan in *BSP,* LV, 247-48; briefly in *Economica,* XXVIII, 343-44; by A. E. Musson in *The Library,* 5th Ser., XVI, 151-53.

Blake, Clagette. *Charles Elliott, R.N.* . . . See VB 1960, 371.
Rev. by Grace Fox in *AHR*, LXVII, 188.

Bloomfield, Paul. *Edward Gibbon Wakefield.* London: Longmans. Pp. xii + 378.
Rev. by Brian Inglis in *S*, 14 July, pp. 55-56; in *TLS*, 11 Aug., p. 514 (and see letters by Bloomfield and reviewer's replies, 25 Aug., p. 565, and 1 Sept., p. 581).

Bobbitt, Mary Reed. *With Dearest Love to All: The Life and Letters of Lady Jebb.* . . . See VB 1960, 371.
Rev. by Robert Halsband in *SR*, 24 Sept., 1960, p. 20.

Bond, Brian. "The Late-Victorian Army." *History Today*, XI, 616-24.
Characterizes the army between the Crimean and South African wars.

Bonham-Carter, Victor. *In a Liberal Tradition.* . . . See VB 1960, 371.
Rev. by John F. Glaser in *VS*, IV, 355-57.

Bourne, Kenneth. "British Preparations for War with the North, 1861-1862." *EHR*, LXXVI, 600-32.

Bourne, Kenneth. "The Clayton-Bulwer Treaty and the Decline of British Opposition to the Territorial Expansion of the United States, 1857-60." *JMH*, XXXIII, 287-91.

Bowditch, John, and Ramsland, Clement (eds.). *Voices of the Industrial Revolution: Selected Readings from the Liberal Economists and Their Critics.* Ann Arbor: Univ. of Michigan Pr. Pp. 187.

Bradlow, Edna. "A South African Year of Crisis, 1899." *History Today*, XI, 712-19.

Breeze, Lawerence E. "British Opinion of Russian Foreign Policy, 1841-1871." *DA*, XXI, 3074.

Briggs, Asa (ed.). *Chartist Studies.* . . . See VB 1959, 413.
Rev. by Norman Gash in *EHR*, LXXVI, 170-71.

Briggs, Asa. "The Escape Hatch." *NS*, LXII, 60.
Review article on Paul Bloomfield's *Edward Gibbon Wakefield* (see above).

Briggs, Asa. "The Factory King." *Listener*, 9 Nov., pp. 761-62.
A tribute to Richard Oastler.

Briggs, Asa (ed.). *They Saw It Happen: An Anthology of Eyewitness Accounts of Events in British History, 1897-1940.* London: Blackwell, 1960. Pp. 512.

Rev. by A. J. P. Taylor in *NS*, LXI, 52-53.

Briggs, Asa, and Saville, John (eds.). *Essays in Labour History.* . . . See VB 1960, 371.
Rev. by James L. Godfrey in *JMH*, XXXIII, 424-25.

Briggs, F. Allen. "The Sunday-School Library in the Nineteenth Century." *LQ*, XXXI, 166-77.

Bromley, John. *The Armorial Bearings of the Guilds of London.* New York: Frederick Warne. Pp. 282.
Rev. by G. D. McDonald in *LJ*, LXXXVI, 2457.

Brose, Olive J. *Church and Parliament: The Reshaping of the Church of England, 1828-1860.* . . . See VB 1960, 371.
Rev. by F. C. Mather in *EHR*, LXXVI, 741-42; by E. R. Hardy in *JR*, XL, 322-23.

Brown, Ford K. *Fathers of the Victorians: The Age of Wilberforce.* Cambridge: Cambridge Univ. Pr. Pp. 569.
Rev. by Beryl Gaster in *CR*, CC, 662-663; by A. O. J. Cockshut in *Manchester Guardian Weekly*, 28 Dec., p. 10; by Simon Raven in *S*, 15 Dec., p. 905. A study of William Wilberforce and his evangelical associates.

Brunschwig, Henri. *Mythes et réalitiés de l'imperialisme colonial 1871-1914.* Paris: Armand Colin, 1960, Pp. 204.
Rev. by Georges Joyaux in *French Rev.*, XXXV, 216-17.

Buck, Anne M. *Victorian Costume and Costume Accessories.* London: Jenkins. Pp. 215.
Noticed in *TLS*, 26 May, p. 330.

Burleigh, John H. S. *Church History of Scotland.* London and New York: Oxford Univ. Pr., 1960. Pp. 456.
Rev. by Norman V. Hope in *JR*, XLI, 150.

Bury, J. P. T. (ed.). *The New Cambridge Modern History.* Vol. X: *The Zenith of European Power, 1830-1870.* . . . See VB 1960, 372.
Rev. by Mildred Campbell in *APSS*, CCCXXXV, 206-07; by David Owen in *History*, XLVI, 266-67.

Cadogan, Sir Edward. *Before the Deluge: Memories and Reflections, 1880-1914.* London: Murray. Pp. viii + 232.
Rev. in *TLS*, 10 Nov., p. 803.

Cameron, James Reese. *Frederick William Maitland and the History of English Law.* Norman: Univ. of Oklahoma Pr. Pp. xvi + 214.

Campbell, A. E. *Great Britain and the United States, 1895-1903*. London: Longmans. Pp. 216.

Rev. by Norman Pellington in *Canadian Hist. Rev.*, XLII, 361-62; by Brian Farrell in *History Today*, XI, 435-36; in *TLS*, 24 Feb., p. 116.

Campbell, Ray Hutcheson. *Carron Company*. Edinburgh: Oliver and Boyd. Pp. xii + 346.

History of a Scottish ironworks, 1759-1959.

Chamberlin, Edward H. "The Origin and Early Development of Monopolistic Competition Theory." *Quart. Jour. of Econ.*, LXXV, 515-43.

Includes critique of Alfred Marshall.

Chambers, J. D. *The Workshop of the World: British Economic History from 1820 to 1880*. London: Oxford Univ. Pr. Pp. viii + 239.

Rev. by W. H. Chaloner in *History Today*, XI, 724-25; by David Owen in *VS*, V, 163-65.

Chandler, Alice K. "The New Feudalism: The Middle Ages as a Social and Political Ideal in Early Nineteenth-Century English Literature." *DA*, XXI, 1938.

Carlyle and Disraeli figure in this study.

Chapman, Ronald. *Father Faber*. London: Burns and Oates. Pp. x + 374.

Rev. by Philip Hengist in *NS*, LXI, 306-07; in *TLS*, 3 March, p. 134; by R. W. Greaves in *VS*, V, 82-83; by E. E. Reynolds in *Wiseman Rev.*, CCXXXV, 89-91.

Chastenet, Jacques. "L'Irlande au milieu du XIXᵉ siècle." *Revue des deux mondes* (No. 3, 1 Feb.), 396-408.

Chastenet, Jacques. *La Vie quotidienne en Angleterre au début du regne de Victoria (1837-1851)*. Paris: Hachette. Pp. 300.

Rev. by Jean Ruer in *Études anglaises*, XIV, 249-51; in *Revue des deux mondes* (No. 10, 15 May), 381.

Chastenet, Jacques. "Voyages et Villégiatures en Angleterre au Milieu du XIXᵉ Siècle." *La Revue de Paris*, Mar., 49-60.

Chesney, Kellow (ed.). *Crimean War Reader*. London: Muller. Pp. xii + 254.

Rev. by Cyril Ray in *S*, 6 Jan., p. 20; in *TLS*, 17 Feb., p. 103. A series of excerpts from contemporary sources, with explanatory comments.

Christian, Garth (ed.). *A Victorian Poacher: James Hawker's Journal*. London: Oxford Univ. Pr. Pp. xii + 114.

Rev. by C. Henry Warren in *Listener*, 28 Dec., p. 1129; by Raleigh Trevelyan in *S*, 10 Nov., pp. 674-75; in *TLS*, 10 Nov., p. 802.

Churchill, Randolph S. *Lord Derby, King of Lancashire: The Official Life of Edward, Seventeenth Earl of Derby, 1865-1948*. New York: Putnam. Pp. 642.

Rev. by R. R. Rea in *LJ*, LXXXVI, 1837.

Clark, E. A. G. *The Ports of the Exe Estuary: 1660-1860*. Exeter: The University of Exeter, 1960. Pp. 247.

Rev. by Norman J. G. Pounds in *JEH*, XXI, 395-96.

Clark, G. Kitson. "The Making of Victorian England." *Listener*, 16, 23, 30 March, pp. 479-81; 521-23; 560-62.

Various industrial, moral, and political changes and their effect on Victorian England. Clark's conclusion is pertinent. The religiosity, taboos, and conventions of the time became the conventional objects of satire in the twentieth century, and it is from these that we often receive a distorted picture of the period.

Coates, A. W. "Alfred Marshall and Richard T. Ely: Some Unpublished Letters." *Economica*, XXVIII, 191-94.

Cole, Margaret. *The Story of Fabian Socialism*. London: Heinemann. Pp. xv + 366.

Rev. by Raymond Williams in *Listener*, 30 Nov., pp. 933-34; by Malcolm Muggeridge in *NS*, LXII, 707-08 (see also Mrs. Cole's letter, *NS*, LXII, 743-44); in *TLS*, 17 Nov., p. 828.

Connell, Brian (ed.). *Regina vs. Palmerston: The Correspondence between Queen Victoria and her Foreign and Prime Minister, 1837-1865*. New York: Doubleday. Pp. 408.

Rev. by Geoffrey Bruun in *HTB*, 1 Oct., p. 10; by K. T. Willis in *LJ*, LXXXVI, 2651; by J. H. Plumb in *NYTBR*, 17 Sept., p. 30; by Morse Peckham in *SR*, 2 Sept., pp. 20-21.

Conway, Alan (ed.). *The Welsh in America: Letters from the Immigrants*. Minneapolis: Univ. of Minnesota Pr. Pp. 341.

Cope, Sir Zachary. *Sir John Tomes: A Pioneer of British Dentistry*. London: Dawsons. Pp. xi + 108.

Cope, Sir Zachary. *Six Disciples of Florence Nightingale*. London: Pitman. Pp. xii + 76.

Corfe, T. H. "The Phoenix Park Murders." *History Today*, XI, 828-35.

Cowan, C. D. *Nineteenth-Century Malaya: The Origins of British Control*. London:

Oxford Univ. Pr. Pp. 286.
Rev. in *TLS*, 11 Aug., p. 519.

Cowan, Helen I. *British Emigration to British North America: The First Hundred Years.* Toronto: Univ. of Toronto Pr. Revised ed. Pp. xiv + 321.
Rev. by Paul Knaplund in *Miss. Valley Hist. Rev.*, XLVIII, 507-08.

Cowling, Maurice. "Lytton, the Cabinet, and the Russians, August to November 1878." *EHR*, LXXVI, 59-82.

Cox, David. "The Labour Party in Leicester: A Study in Branch Development," *International Rev. of Social Hist.*, VI, 197-211.

Cramer, Richard S. "The British Magazines and the United States, 1815-1848." *DA*, XXI, 3075-76.

Cumpston, Mary. "Some Early Indian Nationalists and Their Allies in the British Parliament. 1851-1906." *EHR*, LXXVI, 279-97.

Dainton, Courtney. *The Story of England's Hospitals.* London: Museum Pr. Pp. 184.

Daniels, Elizabeth A. "Collaboration of Mazzini on an Article in the Westminster Review." *Bull. New York Pub. Libr.*, LXV, 577.

Davies, C. S. (ed.). *A History of Macclesfield.* Manchester: Manchester Univ. Pr. Pp. xiv + 404.

Davies, Horton. *Worship and Theology in England.* Vol. III: *From Watts and Wesley to Maurice, 1690-1850.* Princeton: Princeton Univ. Pr. Pp. xiv + 355.
Rev. unfavorably by Richard Schlatter in *AHR*, LXVII, 110-11; by John J. Murray in *APSS*, CCCXXXVIII, 165-66; by E. E. White in *QJS*, XLVII, 315-16; by Kenneth Scott Latourette in *VS*, V, 80-82.

Davies, R. E. "Parliamentary Practices of the Fourth Party." *QJS*, XLVII, 275.

Dent, Alan. *Mrs. Patrick Campbell.* London: Museum Pr. Pp. 334.
Rev. by John Barton in *NS*, LXI, 798-99; by John Mortimer in *S*, 28 Apr., pp. 617-18; in *TLS*, 21 Apr., p. 251.

Derry, Thomas Kingston, and Williams, Trevor Illytd. *A Short History of Technology from the Earliest Times to A.D. 1900.* . . . See VB 1960, 373.
Rev. by Melvin Kranzberg in *AHR*, LXVII, 81-82; by D. C. Coleman in *Economica*, XXVIII, 332-33.

Dickson, P. G. M. *The Sun Insurance Office, 1710-1960: The History of Two and a*

Half Centuries of British Insurance. London: Oxford Univ. Pr., 1960. Pp. xiv + 324.
Rev. by A. H. John in *Economica*, XXVIII, 330-31; by Morton Keller in *JEH*, XXI, 398-99; by Shepard B. Clough in *JMH*, XXXIII, 439-40.

Donaghy, Brother Lewis. "Operational History of the Liverpool and Manchester Railway, 1831-1845." *DA*, XXI, 3758.

Dwyer, F. J. "R. A. Cross and the Eastern Crisis of 1875-8." *Slavonic and East European Rev.*, XXXIX, 440-58.

Dyos, H. J. *Victorian Suburb: A Study of the Growth of Camberwell.* Leicester: Leicester Univ. Pr. Pp. 240.
Rev. by W. G. Hoskins in *Listener*, 29 June, pp. 1143-44; by Mervyn Jones in *NS*, LXI, 926.

Elsas, Madeleine (ed.). *Iron in the Making: Dowlais Iron Company Letters, 1782-1860.* Cardiff: Glamorgan County Records Committee, 1960. Pp. xix + 247.
Rev. by W. E. Minchinton in *JEH*, XXI, 98-99; by R. G. Cowherd in *JMH*, XXXIII, 325.

Elton, Lord (ed.). *General Gordon's Khartoum Journal.* London: Kimber. Pp. 224.
Rev. by N. Ascherson in *NS*, LXII, 893; by Philip Magnus in *S*, 24 Nov., p. 776.

Erickson, Charlotte. *British Industrialists: Steel and Hosiery, 1850-1950.* . . . See VB 1960, 373.
Rev. by Elinor G. Barber in *Amer. Jour. of Sociology*, LXVII, 238; by Sidney Pollard in *JEH*, XX, 465-66; by Sydney H. Zebel in *JMH*, XXXIII, 75; by Hugh G. J. Aitken in *JPE*, LXIX, 512-13.

Evans, Eric Wyn. *The Miners of South Wales.* Cardiff: Univ. of Wales Pr. Pp. x + 274.

Eyck, Frank. *The Prince Consort.* . . . See VB 1959, 414.
Rev. by M. R. D. Foot in *EHR*, LXXVI, 171-72.

Eyton, John. "Sir Thomas Phillipps, Bart., of Middle Hill: Some Unpublished Letters." *N & Q*, n.s. VIII, 322-26.

Fabunmi, L. A. *The Sudan in Anglo-Egyptian Relations.* . . . See VB 1960, 373.
Rev. in *TLS*, 31 March, p. 203.

Feinstein, C. H. "Income and Investment in the United Kingdom, 1856-1914." *Econ. Jour.* LXXI, 367-85; 856-59.

Ferns, Henry Stanley. *Britain and Argentina in the Nineteenth Century.* . . . See VB 1960, 373.

Rev. by Arthur P. Whitaker in *AHR*, LXVI, 998-99; by Thomas F. McGann in *Canadian Hist. Rev.*, XLII, 170; in *TLS*, 14 Apr., p. 231.

Fetter, Frank Whitson. "The Russian Loan of 1855: A Postscript." *Economica*, XXVIII, 421-26.
(See VB 1960, 370, Anderson.)

Fifoot, C. H. S. *Judge and Jurist in the Reign of Victoria.* London: Stevens, 1959.
Rev. by W. L. Burn in *EHR*, LXXVI, 749-50.

Finberg, Alexander Joseph. *The Life of J. M. W. Turner, R. A.* Revised and with a Supplement by Hilda F. Finberg. Oxford: Clarendon Pr. Pp. xvi + 543.

Fishlow, Albert. "The Trustee Savings Banks, 1817-1861." *JEH*, XXI, 26-40.

Fleming, Peter, *The Seige at Peking.* . . . See VB 1959, 415.
Rev. by C. L. Wayper in VS, IV, 263-64.

Flint, John E. *Sir George Goldie and the Making of Nigeria.* . . . See VB 1960, 373.
Rev. by J. D. Hargreaves in *History Today*, XI, 70-72.

Foster, Charles I. *An Errand of Mercy: The Evangelical United Front, 1790-1837.* Chapel Hill: Univ. of North Carolina Pr., 1960. Pp. 320.
Rev. by Winthrop S. Hudson in *JR*, XL, 320-21.

Fowler, William Stewart. *A Study in Radicalism and Dissent: The Life and Times of Henry Joseph Wilson, 1833-1914.* London: Epworth Pr. Pp. 192.

Fulford, Roger. *Hanover to Windsor: British Monarchs from 1830 to 1936.* . . . See VB 1960, 374.
Rev. by J. H. Plumb in *SR*, 27 Aug., 1960, p. 19; by Betty Kemp in VS, V, 71-74.

Fuller, J. F. C. *The Conduct of War, 1789-1961.* London: Eyre and Spottiswoode. Pp. 352.
Rev. in *TLS*, 17 Nov., p. 820.

Fulweiler, Howard W. "Heaven versus Utopia: A Study of the *Tracts For the Times*, 1833-1841." *DA*, XXI, 1939-40.

Galbraith, John S. "Myths of the 'Little England' Era." *AHR*, LXVII, 34-48.

Garlick, Kenneth. "Landseer in the Diploma Galleries." *Burlington Mag.*, CIII, 143-44.

Garnett, Emmeline. *Florence Nightingale's Nuns.* New York: Farrar, Straus and Cudahy, Pp. 185.

Gartner, Lloyd P. *The Jewish Immigrant in England, 1870-1914.* . . . See VB 1960, 374.
Rev. by Joseph O. Baylen in *AHR*, LXVI, 788-89; by Bernard D. Weinryb in *APSS*, CCCXXXV, 204-06; by Charlotte Erickson in *JEH*, XXI, 249; by R. Newton Flew in *LQHR*, CLXXXVI (6th ser. XXX), 66-67; by Sol Liptzin in VS, IV, 279-80.

Gash, Norman. *Mr. Secretary Peel: the Life of Sir Robert Peel to 1830.* London: Longmans. Pp. 693.
Rev. by E. N. MacConomy in *APSR*, LV, 957-58; by Asa Briggs in *Listener*, 25 May, pp. 935-36; by R. C. Woodward in *LJ*, LXXXVI, 2940; by John Owens in *NS*, LXI, 713-14; by Robert Blake in *S*, 2 June, p. 804; in *TLS*, 16 June, pp. 365-66.

Gelfand, Michael. *Northern Rhodesia in the Days of the Charter: A Medical and Social Study, 1878-1924.* Oxford: Blackwell. Pp. xvii + 291.
Briefly rev. in *TLS*, 31 Mar., p. 206.

Gettman, Royal A. *A Victorian Publisher: A Study of the Bentley Papers.* . . . See VB 1960, 374.
Rev. by Cyprian Blagden in *Book Collector*, X, 94-97; by D. B. Green in *BSP*, LV, 253-54; by Louis Dudek in *Dalhousie Rev.*, XLI, 348-49; by Jean Ruer in *Études anglaises*, XIV, 251-52; by Gordon S. Haight in *JEGP*, LX, 558-60; by Richard D. Altick in *LQ*, XXXI, 192-93; by Joanna Richardson in *Listener*, 5 Jan., pp. 40, 43; by Jacques Vallette in *Mercure de France*, CCCXLI, 318; by Katherine Tillotson in *MLR*, LVI, 597-98; by Oscar Maurer in *MP*, LIX, 147-49; briefly in *NCF*, XV, 372; in *QR*, CCIC, 233-34; by Rayner Unwin in *RES*, n.s. XII, 432-34; in *TLS*, 17 Feb., p. 112.

Ghose, Dilip Kumar. *England and Afghanistan: A Phase in Their Relations.* Calcutta: World Press Private Ltd., 1960. Pp. xxi + 230.
Rev. by Paul L. Hanna in *AHR*, LXVI, 787; by Gilbert M. Hill in *JMH*, XXXIII, 459.

Gibbs, Peter. *Crimean Blunder.* . . . See VB 1960, 374.
Rev. by Theodore Ropp in *SAQ*, LX, 108-09; by Arvel B. Erickson in VS, IV, 268-70.

Gibbs-Smith, Charles H. *The Fashionable Lady in the Nineteenth Century.* . . . See VB 1960, 374.
Rev. by R. E. in *Connoisseur*, CLXVII, 45; by Winslow Ames in VS, V, 151-62.

Gloag, John. *Victorian Comfort: A Social History of Design from 1830-1900.* London: A. and C. Black. Pp. xvi + 252.

Rev. by W. H. Chaloner in *History To-day*, XI, 511; by Paul von Khrum in *LJ*, LXXXVI, 2647; in *TLS*, 21 Apr., p. 246; by Winslow Ames in *VS*, V, 151-62.

Glover, Janet Reaveley. *The Story of Scotland.* . . . See VB 1960, 374.

Rev. by C. S. Bennett in *NS*, LIX, 680; in *TLS*, 15 Apr., 1960, p. 242.

Godden, Geoffrey Arthur. *Victorian Porcelain.* London: Herbert Jenkins. Pp. 222.

Noticed in *TLS*, 26 May, p. 330. A volume in the "Victorian Collector Series."

Gooch, Brison D. *The New Bonapartist Generals in the Crimean War: Distrust and Decision-Making in the Anglo-French Alliance.* The Hague: Nijhoff, 1959.

Rev. by T. H. McGuffie in *History*, XLVI, 70-71.

Gosden, Peter Henry John Heather. *The Friendly Societies in England, 1815-1875.* Manchester: Manchester Univ. Pr. Pp. x + 262.

Rev. in *TLS*, 8 Sept., p. 595.

Graham, A. H. "The Lichfield House Compact 1835." *Irish Historical Studies*, XII, 209-25.

Grampp, William Dyer. *The Manchester School of Economics.* . . . See VB 1960, 374.

Rev. by J. S. Prybyla in *AHR*, LXVI, 200; by G. W. Hilton in *Amer. Econ. Rev.*, L, 742; by W. H. Chaloner in *History*, XLVI, 157; by R. G. Cowherd in *JMH*, XXXIII, 204-05; by Simon Rottenberg in *JPE*, LXIX, 104; by Wendell N. Calkins in *VS*, IV, 270-71.

Gray, Richard. *A History of the Southern Sudan, 1839-1889.* London: Oxford Univ. Pr. Pp. xi + 219.

Rev. in *TLS*, 22 Dec., p. 914.

Greaves, C. Desmond. *The Life and Times of James Connolly.* London: Lawrence and Wishart. Pp. 363.

Rev. in *TLS*, 5 May, p. 274. Biography of Irish revolutionary and labor unionist executed after 1916 rebellion.

Greaves, Rose Louise. *Persia and the Defense of India, 1844-1892.* . . . See VB 1960, 375.

Rev. by V. G. Kiernan in *CHJ*, III, 201-03.

Grubel, Herbert G. "Ricardo and Thornton on the Transfer Mechanism." *Quart. Jour. of Econ.*, LXXV, 292-301.

Gruber, Jacob W. *A Conscience in Conflict: The Life of St. George Jackson Mivart.* . . . See VB 1960, 375.

Rev. by Alexander Sandow in *VNL*, No. 19 (Spring), pp. 29-30; by Joseph Allan Panuska, S. J. in *VS*, IV, 363-64.

Guillebaud, C. W. (ed.). *A. Marshall's Principles of Economics, Variorum Edition.* London and New York: Macmillan. 2 Vols. Pp. xxxiv + 858 and x + 886.

Guillebaud, C. W. "The Variorum Edition of Alfred Marshall's *Principles of Economics.*" *Econ. Jour.*, LXXI, 677-90.

Gutchen, Robert M. "Local Improvements and Centralization in Nineteenth-century England." *CHJ*, IV, 85-96.

Haldane, Louisa Kathleen. *Friends and Kindred.* London: Faber. Pp. 248.

Rev. by Margaret Lane in *NS*, LXI, 635-36; in *TLS*, 12 May, p. 298.

Hales, E. E. Y. *Revolution and Papacy, 1769-1846.* . . . See VB 1960, 375.

Rev. by Derek Beales in *CHJ*, IV, 234-36.

Handover, P. M. *Printing in London: From 1476 to Modern Times.* . . . See VB 1960, 375.

Rev. by W. M. Thompkins in *AHR*, LXVI, 778; by Ruari McLean in *Guardian*, 24 June, 1960, p. 7.

Hanford, James H. "Victorian Literary Autographs." *PLC*, XXII, 42-43.

New acquisitions including the files of the publisher William Isbister and an extensive correspondence of Trollope.

Harrison, John Fletcher Clews. *Learning and Living, 1790-1960: A Study in the History of the English Adult Education Movement.* London: Routledge and K. Paul. Pp. xvi + 404.

Harrison, John F. C. "The Society for the Study of Labour History." *VS*, V, 68-69.

Harrison, Royden. "British Labor and American Slavery." *Science & Society*, XXV, 291-319.

Effect of the Civil War upon the British labor movement.

Harrison, Royden. "The British Working Class and the General Election of 1868." *International Rev. of Social Hist.*, VI, 74-109.

Conclusion of an article (see VB 1960, 375) which documents agreement between the Liberal Party and leaders of labor movement.

Harvey, Van A. "D. F. Strauss' *Life of Jesus* Revisited." *Church History*, XXX, 191-211.

Havard, William C. *Henry Sidgwick and*

Later Utilitarian Philosophy. . . . See VB
1960, 375.
Rev. in *Dalhousie Rev.*, XLI, 131; by S. R.
Graubard in *JMH*, XXXIII, 79; by Henry
M. Oliver, Jr. in *JPE*, LXIX, 102.

Heath, Frederick B. "The Grenvilles in the
Nineteenth Century: The Emergence of
Commercial Affiliations." *HLQ*, XXV, 29-
49.

Henderson, W. O. and Chaloner, W. H.
(eds.). *Engels as Military Critic.* Manchester Univ. Pr., 1959. Pp. 146.
Rev. by M. R. D. Foot in *EHR*, LXXVI,
174-75.

Hendy, Philip. *The National Gallery, London.*
New York: Abrams, 1960. Pp. 318.
Rev. by Paul von Khrum in *LJ*, LXXXV,
2416; by Stuart Preston in *NYTBR*, 19
June, 1960, p. 7.

Hibbert, Christopher. *The Destruction of
Lord Raglan.* London: Longmans. Pp.
xxi + 338.
Rev. by S. W. Jackman in *Canadian Hist.
Rev.*, XLII, 358-59; by F. D. Fawcett in
History Today, XI, 438-40; by W. Baring
Pemberton in *Listener*, 30 Mar., p. 577;
by Nigel Nicolson in *NS*, LXI, 431-32; by
Cyril Ray in *S*, 31 March, p. 450; in *TLS*,
24 Mar., p. 183; by Giles St. Aubyn in
VS, V, 177.

Hobsbawn, E. J. "The British Secret." *NS*,
LXI, 548-49.

Hopley, I. B. "Maxwell's Determination of
the Number of Electrostatic Units in One
Electromagnetic Unit of Electricity." *Annals of Science*, XV, 91-108.

Hopley, I. B. "Maxwell's Work on Electrical
Resistance III. Improvement on Mance's
Method for the Measurement of Battery
Resistance." *Annals of Science*, XV, 51-55.

Howey, Richard S. *The Rise of the Marginal
Utility School.* . . . See VB 1960, 375.
Rev. by C. W. Guillebaud in *Econ. Jour.*,
LXXI, 606-07; by Ross M. Robertson in
VS, IV, 359-60.

Hughes, G. Bernard. *English and Scottish
Earthenware, 1660-1860.* London: Lutterworth. Pp. 238.
Rev. by P. von Khrum in *LJ*, LXXXVI,
990.

Hughes, J. R. T. *Fluctuations in Trade, In-
dustry, and Finance: A Study of British
Economic Development, 1850-1860.* . . .
See VB 1960, 375.
Rev. by E. Victor Morgan in *Econ. Jour.*,
LXXI, 153-54; by Peter Mathias in *EHR*,

LXXVI, 693-94; by P. K. Chaudhuri in
JEH, XXI, 254-56; by W. W. Roston in
JMH, XXXIII, 451-52; by George Mace-
sich in *JPE*, LXIX, 87-88.

Hughes, Therle. *English Domestic Needle-
work, 1660-1860.* London: Lutterworth.
Pp. 255.
Rev. by K. T. Willis in *LJ*, LXXXVI,
3468; in *TLS*, 29 Sept., p. 561.

James, Robert Rhodes. *Lord Randolph
Churchill.* . . . See VB 1960, 375.
Rev. by Paul Johnson in *NS*, LVII, 449;
by J. H. Plumb in *SR*, 7 Jan., p. 27.

Jameson, Storm. *Morley Roberts, The Last
Eminent Victorian.* London: Unicorn Pr.
Pp. 64.
Rev. in *TLS*, 27 Oct., p. 767.

Jeffreys, Alan E. (comp.). *Michael Faraday:
A List of his Lectures and Published
Writings.* London: Chapman and Hall.
Pp. xxviii + 86.
Rev. in *TLS*, 28 July, p. 472.

Jenkins, Romilly. *The Dilessi Murders.* London: Longmans. Pp. xiii + 190.
Rev. by J. Morgan in *NS*, LXII, 125; by
Francis Noel-Baker in *S*, 16 June, p. 887;
in *TLS*, 26 May, p. 322. English travellers
murdered by Greek brigands: an international incident of the 1870's.

Johnson, Franklyn Arthur. *Defence by Committee: The British Committee of Imperial Defence, 1885-1959.* . . . See VB 1960,
376.
Rev. by Walter Millis in *APSS*,
CCCXXXV, 204; by Robin D. S. Higham
in *JMH*, XXXIII, 459-60.

Johnson, Leonard George. *The Social Evolution of Industrial Britain.* . . . See VB
1960, 376.
Rev. by Asa Briggs in *EHR*, LXXVI,
746-47; by Sidney Pollard in *JEH*, XXI,
409-10.

Jones, I. G. "The Election of 1868 in Merthyr
Tydfil: A Study in the Politics of an In-
dustrial Borough in the Mid-Nineteenth
Century." *JMH*, XXXIII, 270-86.
An analysis of the effects of the Second
Reform Act on a highly industrialized
constituency.

Kahl, William F. *The Development of Lon-
don Livery Companies: An Historical Es-
say and a Select Bibliography.* Boston:
Harvard Grad. School of Bus. Admin.,
1960. Pp. viii + 104.
Rev. by Walter Stern in *Economica*,
XXVIII, 342-43; by Walter M. Stern in
The Library, 5th Ser., XVI, 73.

Kane, Peter E. "Richard Whately in the

United States." *BB*, XXIII, 87-88.

Kardiner, Abram and Preble, Edward. *They Studied Man.* Cleveland: World. Pp. 288. Rev. by Collin Clark in *LJ*, LXXXVI, 1605. Includes Charles Darwin and Herbert Spencer in "an evaluation of social anthropology in the light of, and with special pleading for, psychodynamics."

Kegel, Charles H. "Lord John Manners and the Young England Movement: Romanticism in Politics." *Western Political Quart.*, XIV, 691-97.

Kemble, Frances Ann. *Journal of a Residence on a Georgian Plantation in 1838-39.* Ed. by John A. Scott. London: Jonathan Cape. Pp. 416. Rev. by D. W. Brogan in *Listener*, 21 Dec., pp. 1083-84; by J. D. Marshall in *LJ*, LXXXVI, 1773-74; by John Bowen in *NS*, LXII, 995; in *TLS*, 8 Dec., p. 878.

Kennedy, Michael. *The Hallé Tradition.* . . . See VB 1960, 376. Rev. by W. L. Webb in *M & L*, XLII, 60-62; by John H. Mueller in *VS*, IV, 361-63.

Kruger, Rayne. *Good-bye Dolly Gray.* . . . See VB 1960, 376. Rev. by Arvel B. Erickson in *VS*, IV, 268-70.

Larkin, Emmet. "The Roman Catholic Hierarchy and the Fall of Parnell." *VS*, IV, 315-36.

Latourette, Kenneth Scott. *Christianity in a Revolutionary Age.* Vol. II: *The Nineteenth Century in Europe: The Protestant and Eastern Churches.* . . . See VB 1960, 376. Rev. by Reinhold Niebuhr in *AHR*, LXVI, 126; by J. F. Maclear in *Jour. of Religion*, XL, 225.

Latourette, Kenneth Scott. *Christianity in a Revolutionary Age.* Vol III: *The Nineteenth Century outside Europe.* New York: Harper. Pp. 527. Rev. by Horton Davies in *NYTBR*, 26 March, p. 7; by Ronald Bryden in *S*, 8 Dec., pp. 875-76; in *TLS*, 26 May, p. 327.

Lawrance, Alan H. "The Influence of British Ideas in the British North American Revolution." *DA*, XXI, 3078-79.

Lawson-Tancred, Mary. "The Anti-League and the Corn Law Crisis of 1846." *CHJ*, III, 162-83.

Lean, Garth, *Brave Men Choose.* London: Blandford Pr. Pp. 208. Rev. in *TLS*, 10 March, p. 150. Biographies of nineteenth-century figures, including Wilberforce, Shaftesbury, Manning, and Prince Albert.

Leigh-Smith, Philip. *Record of An Ascent: A Memoir of Sir Richmond Thackeray Ritchie.* London: Dillon's Univ. Bookshop. Pp. 41. Rev. in *TLS*, 14 July, p. 430 (and see letters from E. B. and Roger Bernard, 8 Sept., p. 597); noticed in *VS*, V, 83-84. A brief account of Thackeray's son-in-law.

Leslie, Sir Shane. "St. George Mivart: An Angry Victorian." *Wiseman Rev.*, CCXXXV, 48-55.

Levi, Peter, S. J. *Beaumont, 1861-1961.* London: Deutsch. Pp. 76. Rev. by David Lodge in *S*, 22 Sept., p. 393.

Liebman, Marcel. "Fabianisme et Communisme: Les Webb et l'Union Sovietique." *International Rev. of Social Hist.*, VI, 49-73. Conclusion of article (see VB 1960, 376).

Lipman, Vivian Davied (ed.). *Three Centuries of Anglo-Jewish History.* London: Heffer. Pp. xi + 201.

Lochhead, Marion. *Elizabeth Rigby, Lady Eastlake.* London: Murray. Pp. ix + 162. Rev. by Robert H. Hill in *Blackwood's*, CCLXXXIX, 562-64; by F. Basch in *Études anglaises*, XIV, 255; in *TLS*, 9 June, p. 355; by Mark Roskill in *VS*, V, 177-78.

Lührs, Wilhelm, *Die freie Hansestadt Bremen und England in der Ziet des deutschen Bundes 1815-1867.* Bremen: Water Dorn Verlag, 1958. Rev. by W. O. Henderson in *EHR*, LXXVI, 167-68.

Lutyens, Mary (ed.). *Lady Lytton's Court Diary, 1895-1899.* London: Hart-Davis. Pp. 192. Rev. by Lord Altrincham in *S*, 13 Jan., pp. 48-49; in *TLS*, 6 Jan., p. 7. Diary of a Lady-in-Waiting to Victoria.

Lynch, Patrick, and Vaizey, John. *Guinness's Brewery in the Irish Economy, 1759-1876.* . . . See VB 1960, 377. Rev. by G. A. Duncan in *Econ. Jour.*, LXXI, 810-12; by Max E. Fletcher in *JPE*, LXIX, 511-12; by Peter Mathias in *S*, 13 Jan., p. 53; in *TLS*, 6 Jan., p. 6.

Lyons, F. S. L. *The Fall of Parnell, 1890-91.* . . . See VB 1960, 377. Rev. by Nicholas Mansergh in *CHJ*, IV, 113-14; by Arthur Garratt Dorland in *Dalhousie Rev.*, XLI, 102-03; by Christopher Howard in *Irish Hist. Studies*, XII, 276-77.

Lytton, Noel Anthony Scawen. *Wilfred Scawen Blunt: A Memoir By His Grandson, the Earl of Lytton.* London: Macdonald. Pp. x + 368.
Rev. by Roger Fulford in *Listener*, 29 June, p. 1144; by Donald Davie in *NS*, LXI, 1047-48; in *TLS*, 30 June, p. 395.

Manning, Helen Taft, and Galbraith, John S. "The Appointment of Francis Bond Head: A New Insight." *Canadian Hist. Rev.*, XLII, 50-52.

Marriner, Sheila. *Rathbones of Liverpool, 1845-1873.* Liverpool: Univ. Pr. Pp. xiii + 246.
Rev. in *TLS*, 21 July, p. 451.

Martin, Brittan, Jr. "The Viceroyalty of Lord Dufferin." *History Today*, XI, 56-64.

Masani, Sir Rustom Pestonji. *Britain in India.* London: Oxford Univ. Pr. Pp. xv + 278.
Rev. by Francis Watson in *NS*, LXI, 225-26; in *TLS*, 10 Mar., p. 151.

Masur, Gerhard. *Prophets of Yesterday.* New York: Macmillan. Pp. 496.
Rev. by F. M. Wasserman in *LJ*, LXXXVI, 2467. Includes material on Darwin and Shaw.

Mather, F. C. *Public Order in the Age of the Chartists.* . . . See VB 1960, 377.
Rev. by Norman Gash in *EHR*, LXXVI, 169-70.

Mathias, Peter. *The Brewing Industry in England.* . . . See VB 1960, 377.
Rev. by D. C. Coleman in *EHR*, LXXVI, 108-10; by W. E. Minchinton in *JPE*, LXIX, 85-86.

McAree, James G. "The Passage of the Government of India Bill of 1858." *DA*, XXII, 556.

McClatchey, Diana. *Oxfordshire Clergy, 1777-1869.* . . . See VB 1960, 377.
Rev. by Charles F. Mullett in *AHR*, LXVI, 783; by Neville Masterman in *History*, XLVI, 155-56; in *TLS*, 13 Jan., p. 29; by G. F. A. Best in *VS*, IV, 357-58.

McDowell, R. B. *British Conservatism, 1832-1914.* . . . See VB 1960, 377.
Rev. by W. L. Burn in *EHR*, LXXVI, 742-43; by John F. Glaser in *VS*, IV, 355-57.

McLeod, A. L. "Rajah Sir Charles J. Brooke: An Unpublished Letter." *N & Q*, n.s. VIII, 230-31.

Mechie, Stewart, *The Church and Scottish Social Development, 1780-1870.* . . . See VB 1960, 377.
Rev. by N. V. Hope in *Church Hist.*, XXX, 491-92; by Gordon Donaldson in *Jour. of Eccl. Hist.*, XII, 133-34; by H. G. Alexander in *N & Q*, n.s. VIII, 33-34; by G.F.A. Best in *VS*, IV, 357-58.

Megson, Barbara, and Lindsay, Jean. *Girton College, 1869-1959: An Informal History.* London: Heffer. Pp. x + 71.

Metcalf, Thomas R. "The Influence of the Mutiny of 1857 on Land Policy in India." *CHJ*, IV, 152-63.

Moers, Ellen. *The Dandy: Brummell to Beerbohm.* . . . See VB 1960, 377.
Rev. by Ian Fletcher in *VS*, IV, 345.

Moore, D. C. "The Other Face of Reform." *VS*, V, 7-34.
Considers the effect of three issues — a deflationary fiscal policy, the relaxation of the Corn Laws, and Catholic emancipation — which turned many members of the aristocracy, gentry, and urban magnate classes against the Government and prompted them to return pro-Reform Bill members to Parliament in 1830 and 1831.

Moorehead, Alan. *The White Nile.* . . . See VB 1960, 377.
Rev. by W. O. Douglas in *HTB*, 15 Jan., p. 27; by M. D. Herrick in *LJ*, LXXXVI, 96; by V. S. Pritchett in *NS*, LXI, 20; by James Duffy in *NYTBR*, 15 Jan., p. 3; by G. M. Carter in *SR*, 25 Feb., p. 42.

Moss, Arthur William. *Valiant Crusade: The History of the R. S. P. C. A.* London: Cassell. Pp. 221.
History of the 150 years of the Royal Society for the Prevention of Cruelty to Animals.

Mosse, W. E. "The End of the Crimean System: England, Russia and the Neutrality of the Black Sea, 1870-1." *CHJ*, IV, 164-90.

Mowat, Charles Loch. *The Charity Organisation Society, 1869-1913.* London: Methuen. Pp. xii + 188.
Rev. by Richard Titmuss in *NS*, LXI, 962.

Munby, A. N. L. "Sir Frederic Madden at Cambridge." *Book Collector*, X, 156-63.

Munford, William Arthur. *William Ewart, M. P., 1798-1869.* . . . See VB 1960, 378.
Rev. by John F. Glaser in *VS*, IV, 355-57.

Murphy, James. *The Religious Problem in English Education.* . . . See VB 1960, 378.
Rev. by W. H. G. Armytage in *EHR*, LXXVI, 369-70.

Nock, Oswald Stevens. *British Steam Railways.* London: A. and C. Black. Pp. xv + 326.
Briefly rev. in *TLS*, 7 July, p. 423.

Nock, Oswald Stevens. *Scottish Railways.* Rev. ed. London: A. and C. Black. Pp. xv + 326.

O'Higgins, Rachel. "Irish Trade Unions and Politics, 1830-50." *CHJ*, IV, 208-17.

Owsley, Harriet C. "Henry Shelton Sanford and Federal Surveillance Abroad, 1861-1865." *Miss. Valley Hist. Rev.*, XLVIII, 211-28.
An espionage network established in England.

Paget, George Henry Charles Victor. *One-Leg: The Life and Letters of William Paget, 1st Marquess of Anglesay, K. G., 1768-1854.* London: Cape. Pp. 428.
Rev. by Antony Brett-James in *History Today*, XI, 581-83; by R. K. Webb in *HTB*, 31 Dec., pp. 6-7; by Anne Fremantle in *NYTBR*, 31 Dec., p. 5; by Cyril Ray in *S*, 2 June, p. 805; in *TLS*, 26 May, pp. 317-18.

Paglin, M. *Malthus and Lauderdale: The Anti-Ricardian Tradition.* New York: Augustus Kelly. Pp. 184.
Noted briefly in *Econ. Jour.*, LXXI, 672.

Pakenham, Elizabeth. *Jameson's Raid.* . . . See VB 1960, 378.
Rev. by S. W. Jackman in *Canadian Hist. Rev.*, XLII, 73-75.

Pantazzi, Sybille. "Four Designers of English Publishers' Bindings, 1850-1880, and Their Signatures." *BSP*, LV, 88-99.

Parkinson, Cyril Northcote. *British Intervention in Malaya, 1867-1877.* . . . See VB 1960, 378.
Rev. by J. Norman Parmer in *AHR*, LXVI, 788; by Victor Purcell in *CHJ*, IV, 111-13; by Thomas E. Ennis in *JMH*, XXXIII, 339-40; by Emily Sadka in *VS*, IV, 264-66.

Parris, Henry. "The Nineteenth-century Revolution in Government: A Reappraisal Reappraised." *CHJ*, III, 17-37.
A reply to Oliver MacDonagh, "The Nineteenth-century Revolution in Government: A Reappraisal," *CHJ*, I (1958), 52-67 (See VB 1958, 368).

Payne, P. L. *Rubber and Railways in the Nineteenth Century.* Liverpool: Univ. Pr. Pp. xiv + 246.
Briefly noted in *Econ. Jour.*, LXXI, 667.

Payne, Pierre Stephen Robert. *The White Rajahs of Sarawak.* . . . See VB 1960, 378.
Rev. by Jonathan Bishop in *VS*, IV, 266-67.

Pearl, Cyril. *Always Morning: The Life of Richard Henry "Orion" Horne.* London: Angus and Robertson. Pp. 276.
Rev. in *TLS*, 22 Dec., p. 910.

Pearson, Hesketh. *The Marrying Americans.* New York: Coward-McCann. Pp. 313.
Rev. by Katharine Whitehorn in *S*, 25 Aug., p. 265; in *TLS*, 25 Aug., p. 563. Marriages of American heiresses to English aristocrats.

Pelling, Henry. *Modern Britain.* . . . See VB 1960, 378.
Rev. by Carl F. Brand in *AHR*, LXVII, 188-89; by F. M. L. Thompson in *History*, XLVI, 166.

Pelling, Henry. *A Short History of the Labour Party.* London: Macmillan. Pp. vii + 135.
Rev. by J. B. Conacher in *Canadian Hist. Rev.*, XLII, 246-49.

Perham, Margery. *Lugard: The Years of Authority, 1898-1945.* . . . See VB 1960, 378.
Rev. by J. D. Hargreaves in *History Today*, XI, 70-72.

Perham, Margery and Bull, Mary (eds.). *The Diaries of Lord Lugard.* . . . See VB 1959, 418.
Rev. by P. D. Curtin in *AHR*, LXV, 661.

Petrie, Sir Charles. *The Modern British Monarchy.* London: Eyre and Spottiswoode. Pp. 228.
Rev. in *TLS*, 8 Sept., p. 591.

Petrie, Sir Charles. *The Victorians.* . . . See VB 1960, 378.
Rev. by Jean Ruer in *Études angliases*, XIV, 162-63; by L. B. Saunders in *LJ*, LXXXVI, 4294; briefly in *NCF*, XVI, 281.

Pfeifer, Edward Justin. "The Reception of Darwinism in the United States, 1859-1880." *Church History*, XXX, 109-10.
Abstract of dissertation reprinted from *DA*.

Pollard, Sidney. *A History of Labour in Sheffield.* . . . See VB 1960, 378.
Rev. by Asa Briggs in *Econ. Jour.*, LXXI, 160-62; by D. C. Coleman in *EHR*, LXXVI, 374-75; by E. M. Sigsworth in *JEH*, XXI, 413-15; by William H. Maehl, Jr. in *JMH*, XXXIII, 74-75.

Pressnell, Leslie Sedden (ed.). *Studies in the Industrial Revolution.* . . . See VB 1960, 379.
Rev. by Frank Fetter in *Economica*, XXVIII, 220-21; by Barry E. Supple in *JEH*, XXI, 264-66; by Morris David Morris in *JPE*, LXIX, 509-10.

Prest, John Michael. *The Industrial Revolution in Coventry.* . . . See VB 1960, 379.

Rev. by Charles W. Coolidge in *AHR*, LXVI, 1097-98; by D. E. C. Eversley in *Econ. Jour.*, LXXI, 808-10; in *TLS*, 24 Feb., p. 123; by Sidney Pollard in *VS*, V, 75-77.

Pritchard, John Laurence. *Sir George Cayley, The Inventor of the Aeroplane*. London: Max Parrish, Pp. xxii + 277.
Cayley (1773-1857) in 1849 put the first man-carrying glider into flight.

Pritchett, V. S. "The Mean Time." *NS*, LXI, 478-79.
An essay occasioned by the publication of *John Davidson: A Selection of His Poems*. Ed. Maurice Lindsay. London: Hutchinson.

Rauner, Robert M. *Samuel Bailey and the Classical Theory of Value*. Cambridge, Mass.: Harvard Univ. Pr. Pp. 162.

Read, Donald. *Press and People, 1790-1850: Opinion in Three English Cities*. London: Edward Arnold. Pp. ix + 227.
Rev. by W. D. Handcock in *History*, XLVI, 261; by Harold Perkin in *History* LXXXI, 2485-86; by Brian Inglis in *S*, 21 Apr., p. 648; in *TLS*, 21 Apr., p. 252. The development of a dozen weekly *Today*, XI, 431-32; by Eric Moon in *LJ*, newspapers in Manchester, Leeds, and Sheffield during the first half of the nineteenth century.

Read, Donald. "Fergus O'Connor, Irishman and Chartist." *History Today*, XI, 165-74.

Read, Donald, and Glasgow, Eric. *Feargus O'Connor: Irishman and Chartist*. London: Edward Arnold. Pp. 160.
Rev. by H. W. McCready in *Canadian Hist. Rev.*, XLII, 359; by F. C. Mather in *History*, XLVI, 263-64; by J. F. Moran in *LJ*, LXXXVI, 2662; by Asa Briggs in *NS*, LXI, 710-11; in *TLS*, 5 May, p. 274.

Redman, Alvin. *The House of Hanover. . . .* See VB 1960, 375.
Rev. unfavorably by W. C. Allen in *LJ*, LXXXVI, 1141-42; by Betty Kemp in *VS*, V, 71-74.

Reynolds, E. E. "Cardinal Bourne: A Centenary Tribute." *Wiseman Rev.*. CCXXXV, 4-14.

Rich, Edwin Ernest. *The History of the Hudson's Bay Company, 1763-1870. . . .* See VB 1960, 379.
Rev. by W. Kaye Lamb in *Canadian Hist. Rev.*, XLII, 145-47; by W. T. Easterbrook in *Econ. Jour.*, LXXI, 631-33; by H. S. Ferns in *EHR*, LXXVI, 690-92; by Mason Wade in *NYTBR*, 4 June, p. 6; in *TLS*, 31 Mar., p. 200.

Richards, Denis, and Quick, Anthony. *Britain,*

1714-1851. London: Longmans. Pp. x + 406.

Richardson, Joanna. *My Dearest Uncle: A Life of Leopold, First King of the Belgians*. London: Cape. Pp. 232.
Rev. in *TLS*, 8 Sept., p. 591. Relations between Queen Victoria and her uncle Leopold I.

Richmond, Sir Arthur. *Twenty-Six Years: 1879-1905*. London: Bles. Pp. 260.
Rev. by A. Howard in *NS*, LXII, 661-62; in *TLS*, 24 Nov., p. 848. Memoirs of son of portrait-painter, member of Milner's staff in South Africa.

Rimmer, William Gordon. *Marshalls of Leeds, Flax Spinners, 1788-1886. . . .* See VB 1960, 379.
Rev. by T. C. Barker in *Economica*, XXVIII, 332; by E. M. Sigsworth in *Econ. Jour.*, LXXI, 807-08; by C. P. Wright in *JEH*, XXI, 217-18.

Ritchie, William A. "Henry Sidgwick and the Received Liberal-Utilitarian Tradition." *DA*, XXI, 2349-50.

Roberts, David. *Victorian Origins of the British Welfare State. . . .* See VB 1960, 379.
Rev. by William O. Aydelotte in *AHR*, LXVI, 1020-21; by John J. Murray in *APSS*, CCCXXXIII, 190-91; by Stanley Pierson in *Canadian Hist. Rev.*, XLII, 79-80; by R. A. Lewis in *History*, XLVI, 271-72; by C. F. Mullett in *JMH*, XXXIII, 203-04; by Robert Lekachman in *PSQ*, LXXVI, 311-13; by S. E. Finer in *VS*, IV, 259-61.

Robinson, Ronald, Gallagher, John, and Denny, Alice. *Africa and the Victorians*. London: Macmillan. Pp. xii + 491.
Rev. by C. E. Carrington in *Listener*, 10 Aug., p. 214; by Asa Briggs in *NS*, LXII, 279-80; by Sir Philip Magnus in *S*, 4 Aug., pp. 176-77; in *TLS*, 11 Aug., p. 494.

Robson, Maureen M. "The *Alabama* Claims and the Anglo-American Reconciliation, 1865-71." *Canadian Hist. Rev.*, XLII, 1-22.

Robson, Maureen M. "Lord Clarendon and the Cretan Question, 1868-9." *CHJ*, III, 38-55.

Rogers, P. G. *Battle in Bossenden Wood: The Strange Story of Sir William Courtenay*. London: Oxford Univ. Pr. Pp. xi + 241.
Rev. by W. Baring Pemberton in *Listener*, 6 July, p. 31; by J. Morgan in *NS*, LXII, 125.

Rothstein, Morton. "American Wheat and the

British Market, 1860-1905." *DA*, XXI, 2261.

Routley, Erik. *English Religious Dissent*. New York: Cambridge Univ. Pr., 1960, Pp. 214.
Rev. by Horton Davies in *Church Hist.*, XXX, 247-48; by Winthrop S. Hudson in *JR*, XLI, 215-16.

Runciman, Sir Steven. *The White Rajahs: A History of Sarawak, 1841-1946.* . . . See VB 1960, 379.
Rev. by P. Harnetty in *Canadian Hist. Rev.*, XLII, 244-45; by Hugh Tinker in *History*, XLV, 289; by Burton Stein in *JMH*, XXXIII, 336-37; by Jonathan Bishop in *VS*, IV, 266-67.

Rutherford, James. *Sir George Grey, K. C. B. 1812-1898*. London: Cassell, Pp. xvii + 709.
Rev. in *TLS*, 17 Mar., p. 166.

Salt, John. "Trade Union Farms in Sheffield." *N & Q*, n.s. VIII, 82-83.

Sarkissian, A. O. (ed.). *Studies in Diplomatic History and Historiography in Honour of G. P. Gooch*. London: Longmans, Green. Pp. 304.
Rev. by Deryck Abel in *CR*, CC, 658-69; in *TLS*, 6 Oct., p. 664. Includes an essay on Lord Acton by Herbert Butterfield and a list of Gooch's publications.

Saul, Samuel Berrick. *Studies in British Overseas Trade, 1870-1914.* . . . See VB 1960, 379.
Rev. by Ida Greaves in *APSS*, CCCXXX-VII, 207-08; by Max E. Fletcher in *JEH*, XXI, 127-28; by Albert H. Imlah in *JMH*, XXXIII, 457-58.

Savage, D. C. "The Origins of the Ulster Unionist Party, 1885-6." *Irish Hist. Studies*, XII, 185-208.

Schalck, Harry G. "The London Newspapers and British Politics: A Period of Transition, 1880-1895." *DA*, XXI, 1932-33.

Schrier, Arnold. *Ireland and the American Emigration, 1850-1900.* . . . See VB 1960, 379.
Rev. by T. W. Moody in *History*, XLVI, 68-69; by John Tracy Ellis in *JR*, XL, 318-19.

Scott-Elliot, A. H. "The Etchings by Queen Victoria and Prince Albert." *Bull. New York Pub. Libr.*, LXV, 139-53.

Segal, Harvey H., and Simon, Matthew. "British Foreign Capital Issues, 1865-1894." *JEH*, XXI, 566-81.

Shaffer, Harry G. "The Economic Functions of Government in Early English Classical Economic Thought." *DA*, XXII, 463.
Includes John Stuart Mill.

Sheridan, Richard B. "The West India Sugar Crisis and British Slave Emancipation, 1830-1833." *JEH*, XXI, 539-51.

Shoup, Carl S. *Ricardo on Taxation*. New York: Columbia Univ. Pr., 1960. Pp. 285.
Rev. by Lord Robbins in *Economica*, XXVIII, 326-28; by Luigi L. Pasinetti in *Econ. Jour.*, LXXI, 388-90; by D. G. Barnes in *JMH*, XXXIII, 203.

Simey, T. S., and Simey, Margaret Bayne. *Charles Booth: Social Scientist*. . . . See VB 1960, 380.
Rev. by W. J. H. Sprott in *Listener*, 23 Feb., p. 362; by Karl de Schweinitz in *AHR*, LXVII, 189-90; by T. H. Marshall in *Econ. Jour.*, LXXI, 421-22; by Michael Young in *S*, 10 Feb., pp. 191-92; in *TLS*, 13 Jan., p. 22.

Simmons, Jack. *The Railways of Britain: An Historical Introduction*. London: Routledge and K. Paul. Pp. 264.
Briefly rev. in *TLS*, 31 Mar., p. 207.

Simon, Brian. *Studies in the History of Education, 1780-1870.* . . . See VB 1960, 380.
Rev. by David Owen in *AHR*, LXVI, 783-84; by W. H. G. Armytage in *EHR*, LXXVI, 738.

Singer, Charles, *et al.* (ed.). *A History of Technology*. Vol V: *The Late Nineteenth Century.* . . . See VB 1960, 380.
Rev. by Rondo E. Cameron in *JMH*, XXXIII, 72-74.

Smelser, Neil J. *Social Change in the Industrial Revolution: An Application of Theory to the Lancashire Cotton Industry, 1770-1840*. London: Routledge & Kegan Paul, 1959. Pp. xii + 440.
Rev. by Ronald L. Meek in *APSS*, CCCXXXVII, 207; by A. E. Musson in *JEH*, XX, 497-99; by R. B. Eckles in *JMH*, XXXIII, 323-24; by Karl Polanyi in *JPE*, LXIX, 88-89.

Smith, Edwin G. "The Establishment of the British Commission of 1867-69 to Investigate Trade Unionism." *DA*, XXI, 3082.

Smyth, Sir John. *Sandhurst*. London: Weidenfeld and Nicolson. Pp. 310.
Rev. by David Rees in *S*, 24 Nov., pp. 784-85.

Spence, Clark C. *God Speed the Plow: The Coming of Steam Cultivation to Great Britain.* . . . See VB 1960, 380.
Rev. by Ronald M. Wik in *AHR*, LXVI,

785; by Clarence H. Danhof in *JEH*, XXI, 271-73.

Spencer, Herbert. *London's Canal*. London: Putnam. Pp. 103.
History of Regent's Canal.

Spring, David. "The Clapham Sect: Some Social and Political Aspects." *VS*, V, 35-48.

Stafford, Ann. *A Match to Fire the Thames*. London: Hodder and Stoughton. Pp. 219.
Account of London dock strike of 1889.

Stanley, Richard, and Neame, Alan (eds.). *The Exploration Diaries of H. M. Stanley*. London: Kimber, Pp. xxiv + 208.
Rev. by N. Ascherson in *NS*, LXII, 893; by Andrew Sinclair in *S*, 24 Nov., p. 778; in *TLS*, 20 Oct., p. 757.

Stewart, William. *Characters of Bygone London*. . . . See VB 1960, 380.
Rev. in *TLS*, 21 Apr., p. 247.

Symons, Julian. "Buller in South Africa, 1899." *History Today*, XI, 770-78.

Taylor, O. H. *A History of Economic Thought: Social Ideals and Economic Theories from Quesnay to Keynes*. New York: McGraw-Hill, 1960. Pp. xix + 524.
Rev. in J. F. Bell in *JMH*, XXXIII, 199-200.

Tholfsen, Trygve R. "The Transition to Democracy in Victorian England." *International Rev. of Social Hist.*, VI, 226-48.
Surveys the institutions and attitudes created or strengthened by the necessity for the working and middle classes to co-operate in towns after the Chartist agitation.

Thomas, Hugh. *The Story of Sandhurst*. London: Hutchinson. Pp. 244.
Rev. by John Freeman in *NS*, LXII, 484; by David Rees in *S*, 24 Nov., pp. 784-85.

Tibawi, Abdul Latif. *British Interests in Palestine, 1800-1901: A Study of Religious and Educational Enterprise*. London: Oxford Univ. Pr. Pp. ix + 280.

Tisdall, Evelyn Ernest Percy. *Queen Victoria's Private Life, 1837-1901*. London: Jarrolds. Pp. 224.
Rev. by Norman St. John-Stevas in *Listener*, 31 Aug., p. 323; by Jacques Vallette in *Mercure de France*, CCCXLI, 530; by V. S. Pritchett in *NS*, LXII, 346-47; by Christopher Sykes in *S*, 18 Aug., p. 235; in *TLS*, 8 Sept., p. 591.

Tsuzuki, Chushichi. *H. M. Hyndman and British Socialism*. Ed. by Henry Pelling. London: Oxford Univ. Pr. Pp. x + 304.

Rev. by John S. Harris in *APSR*, LV, 958-59; by Daniel F. Calhoun in *JMH*, XXXIII, 461-62; by A. J. P. Taylor in *NS*, LXI, 674-75; in *TLS*, 2 June, p. 334; by Royden Harrison in *VS*, V, 165-67.

Tucker, G. S. L. *Progress and Profits in British Economic Thought, 1650-1850*. . . . See VB 1960, 381.
Rev. by Eric E. Lampard in *APSS*, CCCXXXVII, 209-11; by G. A. Petch in *DUJ*, LIII (n.s. XXII), 139-40; by B. A. Corry in *Economica*, XXVIII, 203-11; by Barry E. Supple in *JEH*, XXI, 132-33.

Tucker, G. S. L. "Ricardo and Marx." *Economica*, XXVIII, 252-69.

Turner, Frank L. "The Movement to Provide Improved Working-Class Housing in England, 1840-1860." *DA*, XXI, 1933-34.

Tuttle, Elizabeth O. *The Crusade against Capital Punishment in Great Britain*. London: Stevens & Sons. Pp. xii + 177.
Rev. by Adam C. Breckenridge in *APSR*, LV, 959-60.

Victoria, Queen. *Leaves from a Journal: A Record of the Visit of the Emperor and Empress of the French to the Queen and the Visit of the Queen and H.R.H. the Prince Consort to the Emperor of the French, 1855*. Intro. by Raymond Mortimer. London: André Deutch. Pp. 160.
Rev. by Jane Hodge in *History Today*, XI, 722-24; by Norman St. John-Stevas in *Listener*, 31 Aug., p. 323; by K. T. Willis in *LJ*, LXXXVI, 4297; by V. S. Pritchett in *NS*, LXII, 346-47; by Anne Fremantle in *NYTBR*, 19 Nov., p. 7; by Christopher Sykes in *S*, 18 Aug., p. 235; in *TLS*, 8 Sept., p. 591.

Wakefield, Hugh. *Nineteenth-Century British Glass*. London: Faber. Pp. 64.

Welch, P. J. "Blomfield and Peel: A Study in Co-operation between Church and State, 1841-1846." *Jour. of Eccl. Hist.*, XII, 71-84.

Wescott, Roger W. "Darwinism and Utopia." *University College Quart.*, VII, 7-12.

Wexler, P. J. "The Great Nomenclator: Whewell's Contributions to Scientific Terminology." *N & Q*, n.s. VIII, 27-29, 32.

Wheeler-Bennett, Sir John. "The Trent Affair: How the Prince Consort Saved the United States." *History Today*, XI, 805-16.

White, H. P. *A Regional History of the Railways*. Vol. II: *Southern England*. London:

Phoenix House. Pp. ix + 214.
Rev. in *TLS*, 20 Oct., p.758.

Willis, Frederich. "Poles Apart." *Listener*, 14 Sept., pp. 379-80.
Brief discussion of workhouses in Victorian England.

Wood, Anthony C. *Nineteenth-Century Britain, 1815-1914....* See VB 1960, 381.
Rev. by David Roberts in *AHR*, 723-24.

Wood, Violet. *Victoriana: A Collector's Guide.* New York: Macmillan. Pp. 169.
Rev. by Paul von Khrum in *LJ*, LXXXVI, 4174.

III. MOVEMENTS OF IDEAS AND LITERARY FORMS

Aarsleff, Hans C. "The Study of Language in England 1780-1860." *DA*, XXI, 1944-45.

Abercrombie, Nigel. *The Life and Work of Edmund Bishop.* . . . See VB 1960, 381.
Rev. by C. H. Talbot in *EHR*, LXXVI, 175-76.

Adams, Donald K. "A Certain 4to 'Elegy.'" *BSP*, LV, 229-31.
Concerns a letter from Thomas Wise to Sir Edmund Gosse.

Allott, Miriam (ed.). *Novelists on the Novel.* . . . See VB 1960, 382.
Rev. by L. A. Leclaire in *Études anglaises*, XIV, 377-78.

Andrews, John S. "The Reception of Fritz Reuter in Victorian England." *MLR*, LVI. 54-61.

Auchincloss, Louis. *Reflections of a Jacobite.* Boston: Houghton, Mifflin. Pp. 220.
Rev. by Charles Rolo in *AM*, May, p. 102; by M. E. Chase in *HTBLA*, 23 Apr., p.29; by B. B. Libaire in *LJ*, LXXXVI, 1595; by D. L. Stevenson in *NYTBR*, 14 May, p. 4; by James Gray in *SR*, 3 June, p. 38. Contains material on Eliot, Meredith, Thackeray, and Trollope.

Baylen, Joseph O., and Holland, Robert B. "Whitman, W. T. Stead, and the *Pall Mall Gazette*: 1886-1887." *AL*, XXXIII, 68-72.

Bill, Alfred Hoyt. "Long Ago and Far Away." *PLC*, XXII, 157-62.
Conversations with Wilfrid Meynell concerning some Victorian writers.

Bligh, N. M. "Mirror Curtains." *Theatre Notebook*, XV, 56.

Blorent, Paul G. "The Reputation of George

Sand in Victorian England (1832-1886)." *DA*, XXII, 1974-75.

Boase, T. S. R. *English Art, 1800-1870.* . . . See VB 1960, 382.
Rev. by Seymour Howard in *JAA*, XX, 486-87.

Brion, Mercel. *Romantic Art.* New York: Mc-Graw-Hill, 1960. Pp. 240.
Rev. by Emily Genauer in *HTB*, 27 Nov., 1960, p. 28; by Paul von Khrum in *LJ*, LXXXVI, p. 790; by John Canaday in *NYTBR*, 22 Jan., p. 22; in *TLS*, 27 Jan., p. 52.

Buckler, William E. (ed.). *Novels in the Making.* Boston: Houghton, Mifflin. Pp. 266.
Rev. by Jerome Beaty in *CE*, XXIII, 241-42.

Cannon, Walter F. "The Impact of Uniformitarianism: Two Letters from John Herschel to Charles Lyell, 1836-1837." *PAPS*, CV, 301-14.

Cannon, Walter F. "The Uniformitarian-Catastrophist Debate." *Isis*, LI, 38-55.

Chadwick, Owen (ed.). *The Mind of the Oxford Movement.* London: A. and C. Black, 1960. Pp. 239.
Rev. by E. R. Hardy in *Church Hist.*, XXX, 370; by H. Keith Markell in *JR*, XLI, 306; by J. A. Clarke in *LJ*, LXXXVI, 1002; by Geddes MacGregor in *The Personalist*, XLII, 604-05; by Alec Vidler in *S*, 9 Dec., 1960, pp. 959-60; in *TLS*, 17 Feb., supp., p. xi; by Kenneth Scott Latourette in *VS*, V, 80-82.

Charensol, G. "Whistler au centre culturel Américain." *Revue des deux mondes* (No. 10, 15 May), 354-57.

Clapp, Edwin R. "The Victorian Mettle: Three Words More." *Western Humanities Rev.*, XV, 11-22.

Daiches, David. *A Critical History of English Literature.* . . . See VB 1960, 383.
Rev. by R. G. Baldwin in *Dalhousie Rev.*, XL, 3556-58.

Davie, George Elder. *The Democratic Intellect: Scotland and Her Universities in the Nineteenth Century.* Edinburgh: Univ. Pr. Pp. xx + 352.
Rev. by C. P. Snow in *NS*, LXII, 186-87; by David Daiches in *S*, 18 Aug., p. 236; in *TLS*, 29 Sept., p. 644; by Donald J. Withrington in *Universities Quart.*, XVI, 94-98; by Brian Simon in *VS*, V, 168-69.

Davies, Robertson. *A Voice from the Attic.* . . . See VB 1960, 383.

Rev. by Robert Molloy in *HTB*, 15 Jan., p. 33; by Carlos Baker in *NYTBR*, 20 Nov., 1960, p. 54.

Davis, Paul B. "Industrial Fiction, 1827-1850." *DA*, XXII, 1995.

Duncan, Joseph E. *The Revival of Metaphysical Poetry: The History of a Style, 1800 to Present.* . . . See VB 1960, 383.
Rev. by Robert Ellrodt in *Études anglaises*, XIV, 152-53.

Eddleman, Floyd E. "Dostoevsky and *The Brothers Karamazov* in English, 1879-1959." *DA*, XXII, 1172-73.

Ellmann, Richard (ed.). *Edwardians and Late Victorians.* . . . See VB 1960, 383.
Rev. in *TLS*, 7 Apr., p. 217; by Ian Fletcher in *VS*, IV, 345-54.

Estey, George F. "The Constituted Scene in Certain English Novels: 1817-1872." *DA*, XXI, 3097.
Includes discussion of *Pendennis*, *David Copperfield*, and *Middlemarch*.

Falk, Doris V. "Mary Cowden Clarke and Her East End Injun." *Jour. of the Rutgers Univ. Libr.*, XXIV, 85-99.
On an amusing parody of *Hiawatha*.

Field, G. W. "Herman Hesse as Critic of English and American Literature." *Monatschefte*, LIII, 147-58.
Gives some brief excerpts from Hesse's reviews, including material on Dickens and Meredith.

Flanagan, Thomas J. B. *The Irish Novelists, 1800-1850.* . . . See VB 1960, 383.
Rev. by André Boué in *Études anglaises*, XIV, 278-79; by D. M. Davin in *RES*, n.s. XII, 330.

Fowler, W. S. "The Influence of Idealism upon State Provision of Education." *VS*, IV, 337-44.

Gray, Donald J. "Arthur, Roland, Empedocles, Sigurd, and the Despair of Heroes in Victorian Poetry." *Boston Univ. Studies in English*, V, 1-17.
Recognizing the Victorian passion for the hero who will establish order and fulfill the destiny of change for the future, the writer analyzes the personal failure of four heroes' of poetry to accomplish their goals. This article is an effective analysis of the importance of hope, change, and progress in Victorian England. — R.E.F.

Gregory, Horace. *The World of James McNeill Whistler.* . . . See VB 1960, 384.
Rev. by Frank Kermode in *NS*, LXII, 928; in *TLS*, 29 Dec., p. 924.

Harris, Wendell V. "Transitional Short Fiction in England during the 1890's." *DA*, XXII, 1176.

Heilburn, Carolyn G. *The Garnett Family.* New York: Macmillan. Pp. 214.
Rev. by Charles W. Mann in *LJ*, LXXXVI, 93; by Richard Hoggart in *NS*, LXII, 22; by Robert Halsband in *NYTBR*, 8 Oct., p. 6; by Francis Hope in *S*, 14 July, p. 66; in *TLS*, 7 July, p. 414.

Hofmann, Werner. *The Earthly Paradise: Art in the Nineteenth Century.* New York: George Braziller. Pp. 436. Tr. from the German by Brian Battershaw.
Rev. by P. von Khrum in *LJ*, LXXXVI, 4280-81.

Hollingsworth, Joseph K. "The Newgate Novel, 1830-1847: Bulwer, Ainsworth, Dickens, and Thackeray." *DA*, XXI, 1948.

Holman-Hunt, Diana. *My Grandmothers and I.* . . . See VB 1960, 384.
Rev. by Alan Pryce-Jones in *HTB*, 12 Feb., p. 27; by Robert Kenedy in *LJ*, LXXXVI, 91; by Anne Fremantle in *NYTBR*, 12 Mar., p. 4; in *TLS*, 23 Sept., p. 612.

Hough, Graham. *Reflections on a Literary Revolution.* Washington: Catholic Univ. Pr., 1960. Pp. vi + 127.
Rev. by Kenneth Allott in *N & Q*, n.s. VIII, 114-15. This book is the first essay in the previously reported *Image and Experience: Studies in a Literary Revolution.* . . . See VB 1960, 384.

Houghton, Walter E. *The Victorian Frame of Mind.* . . . See VB 1960, 384.
Rev. by John Bicknell in *Science & Society*, XXV, 75-77; by Frederick P. W. McDowell in *PQ*, XXXIX, 254.

Houghton, Walter E. and Stange, G. Robert. *Victorian Poetry and Poetics.* Boston: Houghton, Mifflin. Pp. xxiv + 854.
Rev. by P. Veyriras in *Études anglaises*, XIV, 252.

Howarth, Herbert. *The Irish Writers, 1880-1940: Literature under Parnell's Star.* . . . See VB 1960, 384.
Rev. by J. Mitchell Morse in *Comparative Lit.*, XII, 374-76.

Hudson, Derek. *The Forgotten King.* . . . See VB 1960, 384.
Rev. by J. Loiseau in *Études anglaises*, XIV, 170; by W. S. Mitchell in *N & Q*, n.s. VIII, 355-56.

Hyman, Stanley Edgar. *Poetry and Criticism: Four Revolutions in Literary Taste.* New York: Atheneum. Pp. 178.

Rev. by B. A. Robie in *LJ*, LXXXVI, 1596.

Krook, Dorothea. *Three Traditions of Moral Thought*. . . . See VB 1960, 384.

Rev. by Stuart M. Brown, Jr., in *Philosophical Rev.*, LXX, 126-28; by Karl Britton in *Philosophy*, XXXVI, 224-27.

Laski, Marghanita. "The Life Beautiful." *N & Q*, n.s. VIII, 341-43.

On Victorian medieval utopianism.

Lauterbach, Edward Stewart. "*Fun* and Its Contributors: The Literary History of a Victorian Humor Magazine." *DA*, XXII, 565.

Lelyveld, Toby. *Shylock on the Stage*. London: Routledge & Kegan Paul. Pp. 149.

Rev. by G. Freedley in *LJ*, LXXXVI, 3803; by D. G. Schaal in *QJS*, XLVII, 436; in *TLS*, 22 Dec., p. 916.

Lombard, C. "Portrait of Lamartine in the English Periodical." *MLR*, LVI, 335-38.

Loth, David. *The Erotic in Literature*. New York: Messner. Pp. 256.

Includes a chapter on Victorian pornography.

Mackerness, Eric David. *The Heeded Voice: Studies in the Literary Status of the Anglican Sermon, 1830-1900*. . . . See VB 1960, 385.

Rev. by John M. Robson, in *Dalhousie Rev.*, XLI, 95-96.

Maison, Margaret M. "Adulteresses in Agony." *Listener*, 19 Jan., pp. 133-134.

Matthews, William R. "Late Victorian Journalistic Criticism: A Study of Gosse, Lang, Saintsbury, and Churton Collins." *DA*, XXII, 574-75.

McCleary, G. F. *On Detective Fiction and Other Things: Including Pickwick, Cambridge, Infant Mortality, Slums, Stevenson, Motherhood and Incentives*. London: Hollis & Carter, 1960. Pp. 161.

Rev. by Weil-Norden in *Études anglaises*, XIV, 273-74.

Mix, Katherine Lyon. *A Study in Yellow: The "Yellow Book" and Its Contributors*. . . . See VB 1960, 385.

Rev. by A. J. Farmer in *Études anglaises*, XIV, 258-59; by Ian Fletcher in *VS*, IV, 345-54.

Murphree, Idus L. "The Evolutionary Anthropologists: The Progress of Mankind: The Concepts of Progress and Culture in the Thought of John Lubbock, Edward B. Tylor, and Lewis H. Morgan." *PAPS*, CV, 265-300.

Myres, Sir John L. *Homer and His Critics*. Ed. by Dorothea Gray. London: Routledge & Kegan Paul, 1958. Pp. xii + 302.

Rev. by L. A. MacKay in *American Jour. of Philology*, LXXXII, 215-16.

Nelson, James G. "The Sublime Puritan: Studies in the Victorian Attitude Toward Milton." *DA*, XXII, 1160.

Newsome, David. *Godliness and Good Learning*. London: Murray. Pp. xii + 291.

Rev. by O. A. J. Cockshut in *Manchester Guardian*, 28 Dec., p. 10; in *TLS*, 24 Nov., p. 842 (and see letters, 8 Dec., p. 881, and 15 Dec., p. 897). Effects of their education on four of Thomas Arnold's pupils.

Nowell-Smith, Simon. "Some Uncollected Authors XXIX: Richard Watson Dixon 1833-1900." *Book Collector*, X, 322-28.

Ody, Herman Joseph. *Begegnung zwischen Deutschland, England und Frankreich in höheren Schulwesen seit Beginn des 19 Jahrhunderts*. Saarbrücken, 1959.

Rev. by W. H. G. Armytage in *EHR*, LXXVI, 537-38.

Pizer, Donald. "Evolutionary Ideas in Late Nineteenth-Century English and American Criticism." *JAA*, XX, 305-15.

Preyer, Robert. "Sydney Dobell and the Victorian Epic." *TQ*, XXX, 163-79.

An analysis of Dobell's 1857 address, published in 1876, "The Nature of Poetry."

Randall, John H., Jr. "The Changing Impact of Darwin on Philosophy." *JHI*, XXII, 435-61.

Rathbun, Robert C., and Steinmann, Martin, Jr. (eds.). *From Jane Austen to Joseph Conrad*. . . . See VB 1960, 386.

Rev. by Alex Page in *Criticism*, III, 65-67.

Rees, Richard. *For Love or Money: Studies in Personality and Essence*. London: Secker & Warburg, 1960. Pp. 191.

Rev. by J. Loiseau in *Études anglaises*, XIV, 272-73; by L. W. Griffin in *LJ*, LXXXVI, 2316-17. Studies of Florence Nightingale, Dickens, Henry James, and Conrad.

Reitlinger, Gerald. *The Economics of Taste, The Rise and Fall of Picture Prices, 1760-1960*. London: Barrie and Rockcliff. Pp. xvi + 518.

Rev. in *TLS*, 8 Dec., p. 880.

Roll-Hansen, Diderik. *The Academy, 1869-1879*. . . . See VB 1959, 426.

Rev. by Neil Nilsson in *MLR*, LVI, 110-11.

Rosenbaum, Robert A. *Earnest Victorians.* New York: Hawthorn Books. Pp. 383.
 Rev. by R. R. Rea in *LJ*, LXXXVI, 1001; by Gordon N. Ray in *NYTBR*, 26 March, p. 5; noticed in *VS*, IV,365-66. Darwin, Shaftesbury, Mrs. Browning, Rossetti, Gordon and Newman "portrayed in their own words and those of their contemporaries."

Rosenberg, Edgar. *From Shylock to Svengali: Jewish Stereotypes in English Fiction.* . . . See VB 1960, 386.
 Rev. by Leon O. Barron in *CE*, XXIII, 165-66; by Harry Stone in *NCF*, XV, 369-71; in *TLS*, 31 Mar., p. 199; by Sol Liptzinin, *VS*, IV, 279-80.

Semmel, Bernard. *Imperialism and Social Reform.* . . . See VB 1960, 386.
 Rev. by Leonidas Dodson in *APSS*, CCCXXXIII, 191-92; by A. P. Thornton in *EHR*, LXXVI, 752-53; by A. P. Thornton in *VS*, IV, 261-63.

Sewell, Elizabeth. *The Orphic Voice.* . . . See VB 1960, 386.
 Rev. by C. Brooke-Rose in *NS*, LXI, 518; by Robert Beum in *Southwest Rev.*, XLVI, (Spring) X.

Shapiro, Charles (ed.). *Twelve Original Essays on Great English Novels.* . . . See VB 1960, 386.
 Rev. by Patrick J. McCarthy in *Ariz. Q.*, XVII, 180-81; unfavorably by Marvin Mudrick in *NCF*, XV, 361-64.

Shapley, Harlow (ed.). *Science Ponders Religion.* . . . See VB 1960, 386.
 Rev. by Rabbi Norman Gerstenfeld in *American Scholar*, XXX, 271-272.

Shattuck, Charles H. "Macready Prompt-Books." *Theatre Notebook*, XVI, 7-10.

Slack, Robert C. "Victorian Literature as It Appears to Contemporary Students." *CE*, XXII, 344-47.

Smith, David R. "Origins of the International Novel: Studies in Transatlantic Fiction — 1812 to 1865." *DA*, XXI, 3101.

Smith, Timothy D'Arch. "Some Uncollected Authors XXX: Edward Cracroft Lefroy 1855-1891." *Book Collector* X, 442-45.

Stallman, R. W. *The Houses That James Built and Other Literary Studies.* Ann Arbor: Michigan Univ. Pr. Pp. 268.
 Rev. by Fred H. Higginson in *CE*, XXIII, 240. Contains essays on Hardy and Conrad.

Stang, Richard. *The Theory of the Novel in England, 1850-1870.* . . . See VB 1960, 386.
 Rev. by Irene Simon in *MP*, LVIII, 62; by Eleazor Lecky in *The Personalist*, XLII, 123-24; by Katherine Tillotson in *RES*, n.s. XII, 95-98.

Stange, G. Robert. "Recent Studies in Nineteenth-Century Literature." *Studies in English Literature*, I, 149-66.
 A useful and discriminating survey in which Mr. Stange remarks, among other tendencies, the increasing habits of applying neo-existential theology to romantic poetry and of taking Victorian novelists such as Dickens and Eliot as highly sophisticated practitioners of their form.

Stansky, Peter, and Abrahams, William. "Looking for a Laureate." *History Today*, XI, 683-92.
 Difficulties of three successive governments — those of Gladstone, Rosebery, and Salisbury — in finding a successor to Tennyson as laureate.

Starkie, Enid. *From Gautier to Eliot: The Influence of France on English Literature, 1851-1939.* . . . See VB 1960, 386.
 Rev. by A. J. Farmer in *Études anglaises*, XIV, 268-69; by Francis Scarfe in *French Studies*, XV, 85-88; by Peter Ure in *RES*, n.s. XII, 318-19.

Talmon, Jacob Leib. *Political Messianism: The Romantic Phase.* . . . See VB 1960, 386.
 Rev. by David Williams in *History*, XLVI, 156-57.

Temperley, Nicholas. "Mozart's Influence on English Music." *M & L*, XLII, 307-18.

Thaler, Alwin and Davis, Richard Beale (eds.). *Tennessee Studies in Literature.* Knoxville: U. of Tennessee, 1960. Pp. 120.
 Rev. by Arthur Fenner, Jr. in *CE*, XXII, 445.

Thistlethwaite, Frank. *The Anglo-American Connection in the Early Nineteenth Century.* . . . See VB 1960, 387.
 Rev. by J. A. Hawgood in *EHR*, LXXVI, 745-96; by Marvin Fisher in *Western Humanities Rev.*, XV, 88-89.

Townsend, Francis G. "The Teaching of Victorian Literature." *CE*, XXII, 347-50.

Turnell, Martin. *Modern Literature and the Christian Faith.* London: Darton, Longman, and Todd. Pp. 69.
 Rev. by Bernard Bergonzi in *S*, 18 Aug., p. 238. Includes discussions of Patmore and Hopkins.

Tuveson, Ernest Lee. *The Imagination as a Means of Grace*. Berkeley: U. of Calif. Pr. Pp. 218.
Rev. by Joseph H. Summers in *CE*, XXII, 443.

Van Arsdel, Rosemary T. "The *Westminster Review*, 1824-1857: with Special Emphasis on Literary Attitudes." *DA*, XXII, 251.

Walsh, William. *The Use of Imagination*. . . . See VB 1959, 429.
Rev. by J. R. Willingham in *LJ*, LXXXVI, 1772.

Weinstein, Leo. *The Metamorphoses of Don Juan*. . . . See VB 1959, 427.
Rev. by J. Voisine in *Études anglaises*, XIV, 171-72; by Armand E. Singer in *Hispanic Rev.*, XXIX, 153-56; by Albert J. George in *Symposium*, XV, 67-69.

White, Terence de Vere. *A Leaf from "The Yellow Book," the Correspondence of George Egerton*. London: The Richards Pr. Pp. 184.
Rev. by A. J. Farmer in *Études anglaises*, XIV, 257-58.

Williamson, Henry. "Some Nature Writers and Civilization." *Essays by Divers Hands: Transactions of the Royal Society of Literature*. Vol. XXX, 1-18.
A nostalgic account of the life of Richard Jeffries.

Woolf, Leonard Sidney. *Sowing: An Autobiography of the Years 1880-1904*. . . . See VB 1960, 387.
Rev. by Alan Pryce-Jones in *HTB*, 6 Nov., 1960, p. 10; by Frank Swinnerton in *SR*, 19 Nov., 1960, p. 49.

Worth, George J. " 'Popular Culture' and the Seminal Books of 1859." *VNL*, No. 19 (Spring), pp. 24-27.

Wright, Austin (ed.). *Victorian Literature: Modern Essays in Criticism*. . . . See VB 1960, 387.
Rev. briefly in *CE*, XXIII, 72; noticed in *VS*, V, 84.

IV. INDIVIDUAL AUTHORS

ARNOLD, MATTHEW (see also III, Hyman, Newsome).

Brooks, Roger L. "Matthew Arnold and the *London Review*." *PMLA*, LXXVI, 622-23.

Brooks, Roger L. "Matthew Arnold and the National Eisteddfod." *N & Q*, n.s. VIII, 343-44.

Brooks, Roger L. "Matthew Arnold and the *Pall Mall Gazette*." *MP*, LVIII, 202-03.

Brooks, Roger L. "A Neglected Edition of Matthew Arnold's Poetry and a Bibliographical Correction." *BSP*, LV, 140-41.

Brooks, Roger L. "An Unrecorded American Edition of the Selected Poems of Matthew Arnold." *The Library*, 5th Ser. XVI, 213-14.

Buckler, William E. *Matthew Arnold's Books: Toward a Publishing Diary*. . . . See VB 1959, 428.
Rev. by William D. Templeman in *The Personalist*, XLII, 251-54.

Coulling, Sidney M. B. "Matthew Arnold and the *Daily Telegraph*." *RES*, n.s. XII, 173-79.

DeLaura, David J. "Matthew Arnold's Religious and Historical Vision." *DA*, XXI, 3088.

Francis, Nelle T. "The Critical Reception of Arnold's Poetry: the Religious Issue." *DA*, XXII, 259.

Holloway, John. *The Charted Mirror: Literary and Critical Essays*. . . . See VB 1960, 387.
Rev. by David Pole in *TC*, CLXIX, 88-89.

James, David Gwilym. *Matthew Arnold and the Decline of English Romanticism*. London: Oxford Univ. Pr. Pp. viii + 110.
Rev. by John Holloway in *Listener*, 23 March, pp. 537-38; by William Walsh in *NS*, LXI, 353; in *TLS*, 14 Apr., p. 235; by Arthur J. Carr in *VS*, V, 77-79.

Johnson, Wendell Stacy. *The Voices of Matthew Arnold: An Essay in Criticism*. New Haven: Yale Univ. Pr. Pp. 146.
Rev. by Robert Preyer in *CE*, XXIII, 166-67; by G. A. Cevasco in *LJ*, LXXXVI, 1887.

Lott, John B. "Matthew Arnold as Satirist." *DA*, XXII, 248-49.

Lubell, Albert J. "Matthew Arnold: Between Two Worlds." *MLQ*, XXII, 248-63.

Müller-Schwefe, Gerhard. *Das persönliche Menschenbild Matthew Arnolds in der dichterischen Gestaltung*. . . . See VB 1957, 403.
Rev. by Paul Turner in *ESt*, XLII, 178-80.

Nagarajan, S. "Arnold and the *Bhagavad Gita*: A Re-interpretation of *Empedocles on Etna*." *Comparative Literature*, XII, 335-47.

Neiman, Fraser (ed.). *Essays, Letters, and Reviews by Matthew Arnold*. . . . See VB 1960, 388.

Rev. by Roger L. Brooks in *Comparative Lit.*, XIII, 183-84; by A. Dwight Culler in *JEGP*, LX, 336-38; by R. H. Super in *MLQ*, XXII, 307-08; by Kenneth Allott in *MLR*, LVI, 416-17; by Malcolm Ross in *QQ*, LXVIII, 517-18.

Parrish, Stephen Maxfield. *Concordance to the Poems of Matthew Arnold*. . . . See VB 1960, 388.

Rev. by J. P. Curgenven in *RES*, n.s. XII, 315-16.

Robbins, William. *The Ethical Idealism of Matthew Arnold*. . . . See VB 1960, 388.

Rev. by S. K. Winther in *MLQ*, XXII, 94-95; by William D. Templeman in *The Personalist*, XLII, 251-54; by J. P. Curgenven in *RES*, n.s. XII, 99-100.

Robinson, James K. "The First Published American Text of Arnold's 'Literature and Science.'" *VNL*, No. 19 (Spring), pp. 19-21.

Shafer, Robert L. "The Concept of Culture in the Works of Matthew Arnold." *DA*, XXI, 2299.

Timko, Michael. "Corydon Had a Rival." *VNL*, No. 19 (Spring), pp. 5-11.

Stresses the important influence that Clough as a critic and poet had upon Arnold.

Super, R. H. (ed.). *On the Classical Tradition*. . . . See VB 1960, 388.

Rev. by J. C. Maxwell in *N & Q*, n.s. VIII, 235-36, 355; by William D. Templeman in *The Personalist*, XLII, 251-54; by Kenneth Allott in *VS*, IV, 280-281.

Super, R. H. "The First Publication of 'Thyrsis.'" *N & Q*, n.s. VIII, 229.

Super, R. H. (ed.). *Democratic Education*. Ann Arbor: Univ. of Michigan Pr. Pp. 422.

Second volume in Prof. Super's edition of Arnold's complete prose works.

Trilling, Lionel. "On The Modern Element in Modern Literature." *ParR*, XXVIII, 9-35.

Trilling discusses his course on modern literature. He begins with a graceful reference to Arnold's essay and invokes the spirit of the Arnoldian method. Then he summarizes the essay and contrasts Arnold's position with his own. — R.C.T.

Truss, Tom J., Jr. "Arnold's 'Shakespeare.'" *Ex*, XIX, Item 56.

Wallace, John M. "Landscape and 'The General Law': the Poetry of Matthew Arnold." *Boston Univ. Studies in English*, V, 91-106.

Williamson, Eugene L., Jr. "Significant Points of Comparison between the Biblical Criticism of Thomas and Matthew Arnold." *PMLA*, LXXVI, 539-43.

ARNOLD, THOMAS. Allott, Kenneth. "Thomas Arnold the Younger, New Zealand, and the 'Old Democratic Fervour.'" *Landfall* (Sept., 1961), 208-25.

Williamson, E. L. "Dr. Arnold as a Literary Critic: Two Uncollected Essays." *N & Q*, n.s. VIII, 465-66.

BAGEHOT. Buchan, Alastair. *The Spare Chancellor*. . . . See VB 1960, 388.

Rev. by Thomas I. Cook in *APSS*, CCCXXXIV, 167-68; by Oliver MacDonagh in *EHR*, LXXVI, 538.

Tener, Robert H. "Bagehot, Jeffrey, and Renan." *TLS*, 11 Aug., p. 515.

On two hitherto unidentified articles by Bagehot.

BARNES. Levy, William Turner. *William Barnes: The Man and the Poems*. Dorchester: Longmans. Pp. 195.

Rev. in *TLS*, 20 Jan., p. 44.

BEERBOHM (see also II, Moers).

Behrman, Samuel Nathaniel. *Portrait of Max*. . . . See VB 1960, 389.

Rev. by Stanley Weintraub in *Shaw Rev.*, IV, No. 1, pp. 36-39; by B. R. Redman in *SR*, 8 Oct., 1960, p. 25; by George Freedley in *Theatre Arts*, May, p. 67; in *YR*, L, vi.

Riewald, Jacobus Gerhardus. *Sir Max Beerbohm, Man and Writer*. Brattleboro, Vt.: Stephen Greene Pr. Pp. xxxii + 369.

Roberts, Sir Sydney. "Max Beerbohm" *Essays by Divers Hands: Transactions of the Royal Society of Literature*. XXX, 115-30.

BESANT, ANNIE. Nethercot, Arthur Hobart. *The First Five Lives of Annie Besant*. . . . See VB 1960, 389.

Rev. by A. L. Bader in *JEGP*, LX, 338-39; by Trygve R. Tholfsen in *JMH*, XXXIII, 211-12; by R. D. Altick in *MP*, LVIII, 220; by V. S. Pritchett in *NS*, LXI, 348; by Lord Altrincham in *S*, 10 Mar., pp. 337-38; by Ranjee Shahani in *SR*, 30 July, 1960, p. 20; in *TLS*, 10 Mar., p. 150.

BLACKMORE. Budd, Kenneth. *The Last Victorian*. . . . See VB 1960, 389.

Rev. by John Greaves in *Dickensian*, LVII, 54-55.

BORROW. Todd, William B. "Borrow's *Lavengro* and *Faustus*." *Book Collector*, X, 70.

Wolf, Donald A. "The Scholar Gypsy: George Borrow as Lavengro (1803-1844)." *DA*, XXII, 1164-65.

BRADLEY. Wolheim, Richard. *F. H. Bradley.* . . . See VB 1960, 389.
Rev. by Arthur E. Murphy in *Philosophical Rev.*, LXX, 254-56; by Brand Blanshard in *Philosophy*, XXXVI, 372-74.

BRIDGES. Ritz, Jean-Georges. *Robert Bridges and Gerard Manley Hopkins, 1863-1889.* . . . See VB 1960, 389.
Rev. by Peter Ure in *RES*, n.s. XII, 317-18.

BRONTËS. Beard, Geoffrey. "The Brontë Society." *TLS*, 28 July, p. 465.
A letter announcing that the Society is approaching a membership of 1000.

Bronte Society, Transactions and Other Publications of. Vol. XIV, No. 1 has items: Holgate, Ivy, "A Pilgrim at Haworth—1879" (pp. 29-37); Hopkins, A. B., "Biographer's Postscript" (pp. 8-12); Timings, E. K. , "A Great Fancy for Arms" (pp. 13-17); Tompkins, J. M. S., "Caroline Helstone's Eyes" (pp. 18-28); Treacy, Ven. Eric, "Centenary of the Death of the Rev. Patrick Brontë, A.B." (pp. 3-7); Announcements and Reports.

Burkhart, Charles. "Another Key Word for *Jane Eyre*." *NCF*, XVI, 177-79.

DuMaurier, Daphne. *The Infernal World of Branwell Brontë.* . . . See VB 1960, 390.
Rev. by A. L. Bader in *Antioch Rev.*, XXI, 525-27; by R. D. Spector in *HTB*, 19 Mar., p. 39; by E. F. Walbridge in *LJ*, LXXXVI, 992; by Mildred G. Christian in *NCF*, XVI, 185-86; by Ivor Brown in *NYTBR*, 12 Mar., p. 4; by Phyllis Bentley in *SR*, 11 Mar., p. 27; by M. Curtin in *Trans. of Br. Soc.*, XIV, 38-41.

Gérin, Winifred. *Branwell Brontë.* London: Nelson. Pp. xiii + 338.
Rev. by De Lancey Ferguson in *HTB*, 15 Oct., p. 9; by Jacques Vallette in *Mercure de France*, CCCXLIII, 533; by Naomi Lewis in *NS*, LXII, 128; by Stevie Smith in *S*, 4 Aug., pp. 179-80; in *TLS*, 28 July, p. 462; by M. Curtin in *Trans. of Br. Soc.*, XIV, 38-41.

Odom, Keith C. "The Brontës and Romantic Views of Personality." *DA*, XXII, 2004-05.

BROUGHAM (see also II, Barrington).

New, Chester William. *The Life of Henry Brougham to 1830.* Oxford: Clarendon Pr. Pp. xi + 458.
Rev. by Paul Johnson in *NS*, LXII, 959-60; in *TLS*, 10 Nov., p. 802. The first vol. of a biography which the author did not live to complete.

BROWNINGS (see also III, Rosenbaum).

Assad, Thomas J. "Browning's 'My Last Duchess.'" *Tulane Studies in English*, X, 117-28.
A close reading of the poem taking issue with several customary interpretations.

Austin, James C. "The Hawthorne and Browning Acquaintance: Including an Unpublished Browning Letter." *VNL*, No. 20 (Fall), pp. 13-18.

Bevington, Merle M. "Browning and Wordsworth: The Argument for Immortality in 'Saul.'" *VNL*, No. 20 (Fall), pp. 19-21.

Blair, Carolyn L. "Robert Browning as a Literary Critic." *DA*, XXII, 1974.

Buhl, Paulina E. "A Historical and Critical Study of Browning's *Asolando* Volume." *DA*, XXII, 562.

Chiarenza, Frank J. "Browning's 'The Bishop Orders His Tomb at St. Praxed's Church,' 73-79; 99-100." *Ex*, XIX, Item 22.

"E. B. B." *TLS*, 2 June, p. 348.
Account of an exhibition of Mrs. Browning's works and memorabilia in honor of the centenary of her death.

Green, David Bonnell. "Elizabeth Barrett to Hugh Stuart Boyd: An Additional Letter." *PMLA*, LXXVI, 154-55.

Harper, James W. "Browning and the Evangelical Tradition." *DA*, XXI, 3089-90.

Harrison, Thomas P. "Browning's *Childe Roland* and Wordsworth." *Tennessee Studies in Literature*, VI, 119-23.

Honan, Park. *Browning's Characters: A Study in Poetic Technique.* New Haven, Conn.: Yale Univ. Pr. Pp. 327.

Johnson, E. D. H. "Robert Browning's Pluralistic Universe." *TQ*, XXXI, 20-41.
William James's pluralistic speculations are remarkably similar to Browning's characteristic assumptions in *The Ring and the Book*, relying on Browning's "sense of indeterminacy of the human condition" and his idea that the "individual engenders truths on the world. . ."

Kelley, Lachlan Phil. "Robert Browning and

George Smith." *QR*, CCC, 323-35.

Kilburn, Patrick E. "Browning's 'My Last Duchess.'" *Ex*, XIX, Item 31.

King, Roma A., Jr. "Browning: 'Mage' and 'Maker'—A Study in Poetic Purpose and Method." *VNL*, No. 20 (Fall), pp. 22-25. A careful analysis of "Cleon" provides an example.

Lewis, Naomi. "The Genius of Elizabeth Barrett Browning." *Listener*, 20 July, pp. 91-92.

Litzinger, Boyd. "Incident as Microcosm: The Prior's Niece in 'Fra Lippo Lippi.'" *CE*, XXII, 409-10.

Litzinger, Boyd A. "A Note on Browning's Defense of Chatterton." *VNL*, No. 19 (Spring), pp. 17-19.

Litzinger, Boyd A. "The Prior's Niece in 'Fra Lippo Lippi.'" *N & Q*, n.s. VIII, 344-45.

McAleer, Edward C. "Browning's 'Nationality in Drinks.'" *Ex*, XX, Item 34.

McNally, James J., Jr. "The Political Thought of Robert Browning." *DA*, XXII, 1629.

Mendl, R. W. S. "Robert Browning, the Poet-Musician." *M & L*, XLII, 142-50.

Nathanson, Leonard. "Browning's 'My Last Duchess.'" *Ex*, XIX, Item 68.

Poisson, Jean. "Georges Connes: le livre et l'anneau de Browning, 1959." *Études anglaises*, XIV, 354-55.
On the French version of *The Ring and the Book*.

Rivers, Charles. *Three Essays on Robert Browning's Theory of the Poet*. Northwest Missouri State College Studies, Vol. XXV, No. 3. Maryville, Missouri: Northwest Missouri State College. Pp. 40.
Contains "God's Puppet," "*An Essay on Shelley*: The Function of the Poet," and "Robert Browning's Existential Humanism."

Schweik, Robert C. "The Structure of 'A Grammarian's Funeral.'" *CE*, XXII, 411-12.

Shanks, Edward (ed.). *Poems of Robert Browning*. London: Macmillan. Pp. 326. Noticed in *TLS*, 14 July, p. 438.

Wasserman, George R. "The Meaning of Browning's Ring-Figure." *MLN*, LXXVI, 420-26.

BULWER (see also III, Hollingsworth).

Barr, D. J. "A Misquotation in Lytton." *N & Q*, n.s. VIII, 466.

Fradin, Joseph I. "'The Absorbing Tyranny of Every-day Life': Bulwer-Lytton's *A Strange Story*." *NCF*, XVI, 1-16. Implications in Bulwer's use of the occult.

Ganzel, Dewey. "Patent Wrongs and Patent Theatres: Drama and the Law in the Early Nineteenth Century." *PMLA*, LXXVI, 384-96. Findings of the Select Committee on Dramatic Literature chaired by Bulwer.

BUTLER. Cole, George Douglas Howard. *Samuel Butler*. Rev. ed. London: Longmans. Pp. 52. Writers and Their Work series.

Jones, Joseph Jay. *The Cradle of Erewhon*. . . . See VB 1960, 391.
Rev. by Frank Gees Black in *Comparative Lit.*, XIII, 78-79; by Joan Stevens in *N & Q*, n.s. VIII, 38-39; by James Bertram in *RES*, n.s. XII, 217-18.

Simpson, George Gaylord. "Lamarck, Darwin and Butler." *American Scholar*, XXX, 238-49.
A reappraisal of the ideas and influence of the three evolutionists; Butler's methods are harshly criticized.

CARLYLE. Malin, James C. "Carlyle's Philosophy of Clothes and Swedenborg's." *Scandinavian Studies*, XXXIII, 155-68.

Sanders, Charles Richard. "Retracing Carlyle's Journey of 1849 through Ireland." *Studies: An Irish Quarterly Rev.*, L, 38-50.

Smeed, J. W. "Carlyles Jean-Paul Übersetzungen." *Deutsche Vierteljahrsschrift für Literaturwissenschaft und Geistesgeschichte*, XXXV, 262-79. Influence of Richter on Carlyle's style.

CARROLL. Green, R. Lancelyn. *Lewis Carroll*. London: Bodley Head, 1960. Pp. 83. Rev. by L. C. Bonnerot in *Études anglaises*, XIV, 382.

CLOUGH (see also ARNOLD: Timko).

Green, David Bonnell. "Arthur Hugh Clough and Francis H. Underwood." *VNL*, No. 19 (Spring), pp. 15-17.

Houghton, Walter E. "Arthur Hugh Clough: A Hundred Years of Disparagement." *Studies in English Lit., 1500-1900*, I, 35-61.

Mulhauser, Frederick L. (ed.). *The Correspondence of Arthur Hugh Clough*. . . . See VB 1959, 432.
Rev. by Gerhard Müller-Schwefe in *Anglia*, LXXVIII, 383-86.

Rudman, Harry W. "Clough and Graham Greene's *The Quiet American*." *VNL*, No. 19 (Spring), pp. 14-15.

CONRAD (see also III, Heilbrun, Rees, Stallman).

Baines, Jocelyn. *Joseph Conrad: A Critical Biography*. . . . See VB 1960, 392.
Rev. by Walter F. Wright in *NCF*, XV, 367-69; by Robert M. Adams in *ParR*, XXVIII, 124-30.

Letters to William Blackwood and David S. Meldrum. Ed. William Blackburn. . . . See VB 1960, 392.
Rev. by M. L. Cazamian in *Études anglaises*, XIV, 75.

Cox, Roger L. "Master and Man: A Study of Conrad's *Nostromo*." *DA*, XXII, 255.

Evans, Robert O. "Dramatization of Conrad's 'Victory': and a New Letter." *N & Q*, n.s. VIII, 108-10.

Foulke, Robert D. "Conrad's Sea World: the Voyage Fiction and the British Merchant Service, 1875-95." *DA*, XXII, 1173.

Gillon, Adam. *The Eternal Solitary: A Study of Joseph Conrad*. . . . See VB 1960, 392.
Rev. by A. E. Sawyer in *QQ*, LXVIII, 190-91.

Gossman, Ann M. and Whiting, George W. "The Essential Jim." *NCF*, XVI, 75-80.

Gross, Seymour L. "The Devil in Samburan: Jones and Ricardo in *Victory*." *NCF*, XVI, 81-85.

Guerard, Albert Joseph. *Conrad the Novelist*. . . . See VB 1960, 392.
Rev. by A. C. Kettle in *RES*, n.s. XII, 100-102.

Gurko, Leo. "Death Journey in *The Nigger of the 'Narcissus.'*" *NCF*, XV, 301-11.
Considers the symbolic meaning of the work.

Harkness, Bruce (ed.). *Conrad's "Heart of Darkness" and the Critics*. . . . See VB 1960, 392.
Rev. by Matthew J. Bruccoli in *JEGP*, LX, 185-86.

Hay, Eloise K. "Lord Jim: From Sketch to Novel." *Comparative Lit.*, XII, 289-309.
Traces the origin of the novel to Conrad's twenty-eight page pencilled MS of "Tuan Jim: A Sketch" in the Harvard Library.

Herndon, Richard J. "The Collaboration of Joseph Conrad with Ford Madox Ford." *DA*, XXI, 3098.

Karl, Frederick R. *A Reader's Guide to Joseph Conrad*. . . . See VB 1960, 392.
Rev. by Charles Kaplan in *CE*, XXIII, 167; by Adam Gillon in *Dalhousie Rev.*, XLI, 255-56; by Jacques Vallette in *Mercure de France*, CCCXLI, 143.

Lordi, R. J. "The Three Emissaries of Evil: Their Psychological Relationship in Conrad's *Victory*." *CE*, XXIII, 136-40.

Masback, Frederic J. "Conrad's Jonahs." *CE*, XXII, 328-33.

Michel, Lois A. "The Absurd Predicament in Conrad's Political Novels." *CE*, XXIII, 131-36.

Wills, John Howard. "Conrad's 'The Secret Sharer.'" *Univ. of Kansas City Rev.*, XXVIII, 115-26.

COLLINS. Corrigan, Beatrice. "Antonio Fogazzaro and Wilkie Collins." *Comparative Lit.*, XIII, 39-51.

DARWIN (see also II, Banton, Kardiner; III, Rosenbaum; BUTLER: Simpson; SPENCER: Plochmann).

Bailey, R. V. C. and Gosse, J. S. *The Handlist of Darwin Papers at the University Library, Cambridge*. Cambridge: Cambridge Univ. Pr. Pp. 72.
Rev. briefly in *BSP*, LV, 179.

Bell, Peter Robert. (ed.). *Darwin's Biological Work: Some Aspects Reconsidered*. . . . See VB 1960, 433.
Rev. by Ernst Mayr in *Isis*, LII, 433-35.

Cannon, Walter F. "The Bases of Darwin's Achievement: A Revaluation." *VS*, V, 109-34.
"The ecological mechanisms of natural selection are not Christian, but they operate in a universe already accepted and defined by the natural theologians."

Comfort, Alex. *Darwin and the Naked Lady*. London: Routledge and Kegan Paul. Pp. vi + 170.
Rev. by Geoffrey Gorer in *Listener*, 14 Sept., p. 395.

Fleming, Donald. "Charles Darwin, The Anaesthetic Man." *VS*, IV, 219-36.

Glass, Hiram Bentley, *et al.* (eds.). *Forerunners of Darwin*. . . . See VB 1960, 394.
Rev. by Edward Lurie in *AHR*, LXVII, 84-85.

Greene, John C. *Darwin and the Modern World View*. Baton Rouge: Louisiana State Univ. Pr. Pp. 141.
Modern religious views on Darwinism.

Gruber, Howard E. "Darwin and *Das Kapital.*" *Isis*, LII, 582-83.
Darwin's refusal of the dedication of the English edition of *Das Kapital.*

Himmelfarb, Gertrude. *Darwin and the Darwinian Revolution.* . . . See VB 1960, 394.
Rev. by J. F. Burnet in *EHR*, LXXVI, 173-74.

Ong, Walter J. (ed.). *Darwin's Vision and Christian Perspectives.* . . . See VB 1960, 394.
Rev. by Rev. J. Edgar Bruns in *CWd*, CXCII, 314-15; by Paul L. Homer in *SR*, 1 Apr., p. 14.

Osborne, E. A. "The First Edition of *On the Origin of Species.*" *Book Collector*, X, 446.

Shideler, Emerson W. "Darwin and the Doctrine of Man." *JR*, XL, 198-211.

Stauffer, Robert C. " 'On the Origin of Species': An Unpublished Version." *Science*, CXXX, 1449-52.
The MS in the University Library, Cambridge, contains a wealth of material, of which the published version is, in Darwin's own term, an abstract.

Tax, Sol (ed.). *Evolution after Darwin.* . . . See VB 1960, 394.
Rev. by Gertrude Himmelfarb in *N*, CXCII, 14-15.

Tax, Sol (ed.). *Evolution After Darwin.* 3 vols. Vol. 1: *The Evolution of Life*; vol. 2: *The Evolution of Man*; vol. 3: *Issues in Evolution*. Chicago: Univ. of Chicago Pr., 1960. Pp. 629, 473, 310.
Rev. by G. Basalla in *LJ*, LXXXVI, 588. Record of the Darwin Centennial celebration at the University of Chicago.

Wichler, Gerhard. *Charles Darwin: The Founder of the Theory of Evolution and Natural Selection*. Oxford: Pergamon Pr. Pp. xvii + 228.
Rev. by Ernst Mayr in *Science*, CXXXIV, 607.

Willey, Basil. *Darwin and Butler: Two Versions of Evolution.* . . . See VB 1960, 394.
Rev. by D. Lack in *HJ*, LIX, 201-02.

DAVIDSON. Townsend, J. Benjamin. *John Davidson: Poet of Armageddon*. Yale Studies in English. New Haven: Yale Univ. Pr. Pp. 555.
Rev. by B. W. Fuson in *LJ*, LXXXVI, 3285.

DICKENS (see also III, Field, Hollingsworth, Rees).

Atthill, Robin. "Dickens and the Railway." *English*, XIII, 130-35.

Bevington, David M. "Seasonal Relevance in *The Pickwick Papers.*" *NCF*, XVI, 219-30.
Dickens gradually came to relate the time of the story to the month in which a number was published.

Bloom, Ursula. *The Romance of Charles Dickens*. London: Robert Hale, 1960. Pp. 185.
Rev. by Pansy Pakenham in *Dickensian*, LVII, 53-54.

Carr, Sister Mary Callista (ed.). *Catalogue of the Dickens Collection at the University of Texas*. Austin: Univ. of Texas Humanities Research Center. Pp. ix + 195.
Rev. by E. A. Osborne in *Book Collector*, X, 231-35; briefly in *BSP*, LV, 408; in *TLS*, 31 March, p. 208.

Clark, William Ross (ed.). *Discussions of Charles Dickens*. Boston: Heath. Pp. viii + 115.

Cockshut, A. O. J. *The Imagination of Charles Dickens*. London: Collins. Pp. 192.
Rev. by Robert H. Hill in *Blackwood's*, CCXC, 578-80; by Pamela Hansford Johnson in *Listener*, 14 Sept., p. 395; by Steven Marcus in *NS*, LXII, 278-79; by John Bayley in *S*, 8 Sept., pp. 328-29; in *TLS*, 15 Sept., p. 615; by J. Hillis Miller in *VS*, V, 174-76.

Collins, P. A. W. "The Middlesex Magistrate in 'David Copperfield.' " *N & Q*, n.s. VIII, 86-91.

Coolidge, Archibald C., Jr. "Dickens and the Heart as the Hope for Heaven: A Study of the Philosophic Basis of Sensational Literary Technique." *VNL*, No. 20 (Fall), pp. 6-11.

Coolidge, Archibald C., Jr. "Dickens and the Philosophic Basis of Melodrama." *VNL*, No. 20 (Fall), 1-6.

Dickensian (quarterly), Vol. LVII (Nos. 333-35). . . . See VB 1932, 422. Items as follows: "A Great Bookseller [rev. of E. Wolf and J. Fleming, *Rosenbach, A Biography*]" (pp. 120-23); Carlton, W. J., " 'Captain Holland' Identified" (pp. 69-77); Carlton, W. J., "More about the Dickens Ancestry" (pp. 5-10); Clinton-Baddeley, V. C., "Snevellicci" (pp. 43-52); Clinton-Baddeley, V. C., "Wopsle" (pp. 150-59); Collins, I., "The Immortal Memory of Charles Dickens" (pp. 146-49); Collins, P. A. W., "Dickens and the Prison Governer George Laval Chesterton" (pp. 11-26); Collins, P. A. W., "Dickens on the Education of Girls" (pp. 86-96); Coolidge, A. C., Jr., "Dickens' Complex Plots" (pp. 174-82); Drayton, W. H., "The Uncommercial Traveller and the Royal Commercial Travellers' Schools" (p. 118-20); Fielding, K. J., "Dickens and Miss Burdett-Coutts: The Last Phase" (pp. 97-105); Fielding, K. J., "International Copyright [rev. of A. J. Clark, *The Movement for International Copyright in Nineteenth Century America*]" (p. 55); Gibson, F. A., "A Note on George Gordon" (pp. 81-85); Gibson, F. A., "A Note on George Gordon" (pp. 81-85); Gibson, F. A., "On Not Reading Dickens" (pp. 26-28); Gilenson, B., "Dickens in Russia" (pp. 56-58); Green, R. L., "Andrew Lang — Real Reader of Dickens" (pp. 124-27); Kelty, J. M., "The Modern Tone of Charles Dickens" (pp. 160-65); Marshall, W. H., "The Method of *A Tale of Two Cities*" (pp. 183-89); Monod, S., "The Immortal Memory of Charles Dickens" (pp. 112-16); Morley, M., "Messrs. Four, Two and One [identity of characters in a recently discovered Dickens fragment]" (pp. 78-81); Morley, M., "The Theatrical Ternans, Part X" (pp. 29-35); Peyrouton, N. C., "Dickens and the Other Hughes" (pp. 36-42); Peyrouton, N . C., "When the Wine Merchant Wrote to Dickens: The Dickens-Ellis Correspondence" (pp. 105-11); Tillotson, K., "A Letter from Mary Hogarth" (pp. 133-37); Walbank, A., "With a Blush Retire [the Victorians' enjoyment of death and its ritual]" (pp. 166-73).

Du Cann, Charles Garfield Lott. *The Love-Lives of Charles Dickens.* London: Muller. Pp. 288.
Rev. in *TLS*, 8 Dec., p. 883.

Fielding, Kenneth Joshua (ed.). *The Speeches of Charles Dickens.* . . . See VB 1960, 395.
Rev. by Sylvère Monod in *Études anglaises*, XIV, 73-75; by P. A. W. Collins in *RES*, n.s. XII, 312-14.

Ford, George Harry, and Lane, Lauriat (eds.). *The Dickens Critics.* Ithaca, N.Y.: Cornell Univ. Pr. Pp. 417.

Forker, Charles R. "The Language of Hands in *Great Expectations*." *Texas Studies in Lit. and Lang.*, III, 281-93.

Hands as a unifying symbol of plot and theme in the novel.

Glenn, Robert B. "Linguistic Class-Indicators in the Speech of Dickens' Characters." *DA*, XXII, 569.
A descriptive analysis of the language of the lower classes found in Dickens' novels.

Gottshall, James K. "Devils Abroad: The Unity and Significance of *Barnaby Rudge*." *NCF*, XVI, 133-46.

Hardy, Barbara. "The Change of Heart in Dickens' Novels." *VS*, V, 49-67.

Hoff, Rhoda. *Why They Wrote: Dickens, Thoreau, Flaubert, Clemens, Stevenson.* New York: Walck. Pp. 147.

House, Madeline, Collins, Philip, and Storey, Graham. "Dickens's Letters." *TLS*, 21 July, p. 449.
Announcing the publication in 1962 of the first vol. of *The Pilgrim Edition of the Letters of Charles Dickens.*

Hunter, Richard A., and Macalpine, Ida. "Dickens and Conolly: An Embarrassed Editor's Disclaimer." *TLS*, 11 Aug., pp. 534-35. (See letter by Philip Collins, 18 Aug., p. 549.)

Irwin, Edward E. "Dickens and Thackeray: The Reciprocal Influences. *DA*, XXII, 247.

Kieft, Ruth M. Vande. "Patterns of Communication in *Great Expectations*." *NCF*, XV, 325-34.

Lindberg, John. "Individual Conscience and Social Injustice in *Great Expectations*." *CE*, XXIII, 118-22.

Manning, John. *Dickens on Education.* . . . See VB 1960, 395.
Rev. by P. A. W. Collins in *RES*, n.s. XII, 312-14.

McCelvey, George. " 'A Tale of Two Cities' and Gin-drinking." *N & Q*, n.s. VIII, 96-97.

Miller, Melvin. "Charles Dickens at the English Charity Dinner." *QJS*, XLVII, 143-49.

Monod, Sylvère. "Un curiosité dans l'histoire de la traduction; le neveu de ma tante, d'Amédée Pichot." *Études anglaises*, XIV, 353.
A French adaptation of *David Copperfield.*

Moynahan, Julian. "Dickens Criticism." *EC*, XI, 239-41.
A defense of his psychological interpretation of character in *Great Expectations.* See VB 1960, 396.

Nelson, Harland S. "Dickens' Plots: 'The Ways of Providence' or the Influence of Collins?" *VNL*, No. 19 (Spring), pp. 11-14.
Asserts that Dickens' plotting was influenced more by evangelical influences than by Collins.

Partlow, Robert B., Jr. "The Moving I: A Study of the Point of View in *Great Expectations*." *CE*, XXIII, 122-31.

Priestley, John Boynton. *Charles Dickens: A Pictorial Biography*. London: Thames and Hudson. Pp. 144.
Rev. in *TLS*, 1 Dec., p. 858.

Review of English Literature, Vol. II, no. 3. A Dickens number, ed. by John Butt. Includes articles by Arnold Kettle on *David Copperfield*, by K. J. Fielding on *Great Expectations*, by Robert Bernard on *Our Mutual Friend*, and by P. A. W. Collins on *Household Words* and *All the Year Round*. Rev. in *TLS*, 15 Sept., p. 615.

Sharp, Sr. M. Corona. "The Archetypal Feminine." *Univ. of Kansas City Rev.*, XXVII, 307-11; XXVIII, 74-80.
Two-part study of the river image in *Our Mutual Friend*.

Shea, Francis X. "The Text of *Our Mutual Friend*: A Study of the Variations between the Copy Text and the First Printed Edition." *DA*, XXII, 2007.

Todd, William B. "Dickens's *Christmas Carol*." *Book Collector*, X, 449-54.
Justifies description in the catalogue of the Texas collection. See above.

Tartella, Vincent Paul. "Charles Dickens's *Oliver Twist*: Moral Realism and the Uses of Style." *DA*, XXII, 1616-17.

Worth, George J. "The Genesis of Jo the Crossing-Sweeper." *JEGP*, LX, 44-47.

DISRAELI (See also II, Kegel; THACKERAY: Green).

Bloomfield, Paul. *Disraeli*. London: Longmans. Pp. 39. Writers and Their Work series. Rev. in *TLS*, 27 Oct., p. 768.

Faber, Richard. *Beaconsfield and Bolingbroke*. London: Faber. Pp. 107.
Rev. by Ian R. Christie in *Listener*, 2 Nov., p. 739; by J. Owen in *NS*, LXII, 521; in *TLS*, 27 Oct., p. 768.

Frietzsche, Arthur H. *Disraeli's Religion: The Treatment of Religion in Disraeli's Novels*. Logan: Utah State Univ. Pr. Pp. 46.

Graubard, Stephen R. *Burke, Disraeli, and Churchill: The Politics of Perseverance*. Cambridge, Mass.: Harvard Univ. Pr. Pp. 262.
Rev. by C. L. Mowat in *AHR*, LXVII, 186; by Leonidas Dodson in *APSS*, CCCXXXVIII, 164-65; by Albert V. Tucker in *Canadian Hist. Rev.*, XLII, 242; by B. R. Jerman in *N*, CXCII, 398; in *QR*, CCIC, 479; by Howard R. Murphy in *VS*, V, 74-75.

Jerman, B. R. *The Young Disraeli*. . . . See VB 1960, 396.
Rev. by Giovanni Costigan in *AHR*, LXVI, 785; by A. F. Havighurst in *APSS*, CCCXXXIII, 189; by Robert Blake in *History Today*, XI, 362-63; by John Clive in *JMH*, XXXVIII, 206-07.

Levine, Richard A. "Disraeli and the Middle Ages: The Influence of Medievalism in The Nineteenth Century." *DA*, XXII, 1611-12.

Lewis, Clyde Joseph. "Disraeli's Conservatism." *DA*, XXI, 2692.

Lewis, Clyde J. "Theory and Expediency in the Policy of Disraeli." *VS*, IV, 237-58.

Maxwell, J. C. "Words from 'Popanilla.'" *N & Q*, n.s. VIII, 330.

Maxwell, J. C. "Words from 'Vivian Grey.'" *N & Q*, n.s. VIII, 225-26.

DOWSON. Goldfarb, Russell M. "Ernest Dowson, A Study of the Romantic Elements in His Poetry and Prose." *DA*, XXII, 1977.

DOYLE. Holroyd, James Edward. "'Our Client's Foot upon the Stair.'" *Cornhill*, Winter, 239-50.
Delightful illustrated study of Paget's illustrations of Holmes and Watson. — C.T.D.

Lejeune, Anthony. "Age of the Great Detective." *TLS*, 23 June, supp. p. vii.
On Sherlock Holmes and his successors.

Pearson, Hesketh, *Conan Doyle*. New York: Walker. Pp. 256.

Starrett, Vincent. *The Private Life of Sherlock Holmes*. . . . See VB 1960, 397.
Rev. by Jacques Vallette in *Mercure de France*, CCCXLI, 346; in *TLS*, 1 Sept., p. 586.

du MAURIER. Stevenson, Lionel. "George du Maurier and the Romantic Novel." *Essays by Divers Hands: Transactions of the Royal Society of Literature*. Vol. XXX, 36-54.
An unusually full and vivid account of du

Maurier's career as realistic caricaturist, satirist, and romantic novelist. This is impressive scholarship. — R.E.F.

ELIOT (see also III, Auchincloss).

Allott, Miriam. "George Eliot in the 1860's." *VS*, V, 93-108.

Beaty, Jerome. *Middlemarch from Notebook to Novel.* . . . See VB 1960, 397.
Rev. by Walter F. Wright in *CE*, XXII, 291; by Bernard J. Paris in *MLN*, LXXVI, 657-59; by Kathleen Tillotson in *MP*, LVIII, 288-90; by J. C. Maxwell in *N & Q*, n.s. VIII, 476-77.

Casson, Allan. "*The Scarlet Letter* and *Adam Bede.*" *VNL*, No. 20 (Fall), pp. 18-19.

Crompton, Margaret. *George Eliot: The Woman.* . . . See VB 1960, 397.
Rev. briefly in *NCF*, XVI, 187.

Greenberg, Robert A. "The Heritage of Will Ladislaw." *NCF*, XV, 355-58.

Hagan, John. "*Middlemarch:* Narrative Unity in the Story of Dorothea Brooke." *NCF*, XVI, 17-31.

Haight, Gordon S. "The George Eliot and George Henry Lewes Collection." *Yale Univ. Library Gazette*, XXXV, 170-71.
An account of the important collection of diaries, letters, and manuscripts of George Eliot at Yale.

Handley, Graham. "A Missing Month in 'Daniel Deronda.' " *TLS*, 3 Feb., p. 73.

Hardy, Barbara. *The Novels of George Eliot.* . . . See VB 1960, 397.
Rev. by R. Schieder in *Canadian Forum*, XL, 16; by Miriam Allott in *MLR*, LV, 111-12; by John Jones in *NS*, LVII, 698.

Harvey, W. J. *The Art of George Eliot.* London: Chatto and Windus. Pp. 254.
Rev. by Robert H. Hill in *Blackwood's*, CCXC, 580-82; by Lettice Cooper in *Listener*, 21 Dec., p. 1084; by Frank Kermode in *NS*, LXII, 796; by David Lodge in *S*, 1 Dec., pp. 828-29; in *TLS*, 24 Nov., p. 846.

Knoepflmacher, U. C. "*Daniel Deronda* and William Shakespeare." *VNL*, No. 19 (Spring), pp. 27-28.

Lyons, Richard S. "A Study of *Middlemarch.*" *DA*, XXI, 2276-77.

McKenzie, Keith Alexander. *Edith Simcox and George Eliot.* London: Oxford Univ. Pr. Pp. xix + 146.
Rev. by Norman St. John-Stevas in *Listener*, 22 June, pp. 1102-05; by Jacques Vallette in *Mercure de France*, CCCXLI, 344; by Karl Miller in *NS*, LXI, 926; by Margaret Drabble in *S*, 30 June, p. 959;

in *TLS*, 9 June, p. 351.

Selig, Robert L. "The Red Haired Lady Orator: Parallel Passages in *The Bostonians* and *Adam Bede.*" *NCF*, XVI, 164-69.

Simon, Irène. "Innocence in the Novels of George Eliot." *English Studies Today*, Second Series. Berne: Francke Verlag.
Rev. in *TLS*, 14 July, p. 434.

Steinhoff, William R. "The Metaphorical Texture of *Daniel Deronda.*" *BA*, XXXV, 220-24.
Like a good many modern critics of fiction Steinhoff attempts to derive the deepest meaning of the novel from the patterns of its imagery.

Thale, Jerome. *Novels of George Eliot.* . . . See VB 1960, 397.
Rev. by Walter F. Wright in *CE*, XXII, 290; by Miriam Allott in *MLR*, LV, 274-75; by William D. Templeman in *The Personalist*, XLII, 415-17; by Irène Simon in *RES*, n.s. XII, 98-99.

Thomson, Fred C. "*Felix Holt* as Classic Tragedy." *NCF*, XVI, 47-58.

Tucker, Houston C. "George Eliot's Ideal Self: A Study of Subjective Influences in Her Prose Fiction." *DA*, XXI, 2723.

Stump, Reva. *Movement and Vision in George Eliot's Novels.* . . . See VB 1960, 397.
Rev. by Walter F. Wright in *CE*, XXII, 291; by William D. Templeman in *The Personalist*, XLII, 415-17.

GLADSTONE (see II, Barrington; III, Myres).

FITZGERALD. Ahmad, S. N. "FitzGerald's 'The Rubaiyat of Omar Khayyam,' L." *Ex*, XX, Item 15.

FORD. Ludwig, Richard M. "The Reputation of Ford Madox Ford." *PMLA*, LXXVI, 544-51.

FROUDE. Bennett, Raymond M. "Letters of James Anthony Froude." (Part 3). *Jour. of the Rutgers Univ. Libr.*, XXV, 10-23.

Dunn, Waldo H. *James Anthony Froude, 1818-1856: A Biography.* Vol. I. Oxford: Clarendon Pr. Pp. xiv + 261.
Rev. by J. W. Burrow in *History Today*, XI, 796-97; by Basil Willey in *Listener*, 5 Oct., p. 524; by Anthony Hartley in *Manchester Guardian Weekly*, 7 Sept., p. 11; by R. H. S. Crossman in *NS*, LXII, 850-51; by Ronald Bryden in *S*, 29 Sept., pp. 432-33; in *TLS*, 13 Oct., p. 687.

GASKELL. Allott, Miriam. "Mrs. Gaskell's

'The Old Nurse's Story': A Link between 'Wuthering Heights' and 'The Turn of the Screw.'" *N & Q*, n.s. VIII, 101-02.

Laski, Marghanita. "Words from Mrs. Gaskell." *N & Q*, n.s. VIII, 339-41; 468-69.

Pollard, Arthur. "The Novels of Mrs. Gaskell." *Bull. of the John Rylands Libr.*, XLIII, 403-23.

GILBERT. Allen, Reginald. "William Schwenck Gilbert: An Anniversary Survey." *Theatre Notebook*, XV, 118-28.
A useful summary of Gilbert's works, containing a list of first performance dates and theaters and printed editions. See corrections to these lists in *Theatre Notebook*, XVI, 30-31.

GISSING. Gettmann, Royal A. (ed.). *George Gissing and H. G. Wells: Their Friendship and Correspondence.* Urbana: Univ. of Illinois Pr. Pp. 285.
Rev. in *TLS*, 7 July, p. 416; by A. G. Hill in *CQ*, III, 373-75; by Hilary Corke in *Listener*, 25 May, p. 939; by E. F. Walbridge in *LJ*, LXXXVI, 3483; by V. S. Pritchett in *NS*, LXI, 841; by Martin Shuttleworth in *S*, 23 June, pp. 926-28; in *TLS*, 7 July, p. 416 (and see letters by Anthony Curtis, 28 July, p. 465, and J. R. Hammond, Secretary of the H. G. Wells Society, 4 Aug., p. 481).

Korg, Jacob. "George Gissing's Commonplace Book: A Manuscript from the Berg Collection of the New York Public Library." *Bull. New York Pub. Libr.*, LXV, 417-34; 534-46; 588-614.

Young, Arthur C. (ed.). *The Letters of George Gissing to Eduard Bertz: 1887-1903.* New Brunswick, N. J.: Rutgers Univ. Pr. Pp. 337.

GOSSE. Berol, Alfred C. "Gosse and Henry Patmore's *Poems.*" *Book Collector*, X, 71-72.

Bredsdorff, Elias (ed.). *Sir Edmund Gosse's Correspondence with Scandinavian Writers.* Copenhagen: Glydendal; London: Heinemann.
Rev. in *TLS*, 17 Feb., p. 106.

LADY GREGORY. Coxhead, Elizabeth. *Lady Gregory: A Literary Portrait.* London: Macmillan. Pp. xii + 241.
Rev. by W. R. Rodgers in *Listener*, 2 March, p. 401; by Mary H. Zipprich in *LJ*, LXXXVI, 92; by Walter Allen in *NS*, LXI, 186; by Anne O'Neil-Barna in *NYTBR*, 24 Sept., p. 6; by Harry T. Moore in *SR*, 23 Sept., p. 20; in *TLS*, 17 Feb., pp. 97-98.

HAGGARD. Cohen, Morton. *Rider Haggard: His Life and Works.* . . . See VB 1960, 399.
Rev. by Carl F. Keppler in *Ariz. Q.*, XVII, 272-75; by DeLancey Ferguson in *HTB*, 9 Apr., p. 28; by E. F. Walbridge in *LJ*, LXXXVI, 1450; by Benjamin DeMott in *N*, CXCII, 442-43; briefly in *NCF*, XVI, 186; by Ivor Brown in *NYTBR*, 26 Mar., p. 5; in *YR*, L (Summer, 1961), viii-xii.

Haggard, Lilian Rider. "A Born Story-Teller." *Listener*, 22 June, p. 1078.
Excerpts from a talk on Rider Haggard by the daughter of the author.

HARDY (see also III, Stallman).

Selected Poems of Thomas Hardy. Ed. John Crowe Ransom. New York: Macmillan. Pp. 192.
Rev. by B. A. Robie in *LJ*, LXXXVI, 1468.

Beatty, C. J. P. "Two Rare Birds in Hardy's 'The Return of the Native.'" *N & Q*, n.s. VIII, 98-99.

Carpenter, Richard C. "Thomas Hardy and the Old Masters." *Boston Univ. Studies in English*, V, 18-28.

Cecil, Lord David. "Hardy's Unhappy First Marriage." *Sunday Times*, London, 22 Oct.

Clifford, Emma. "The Impressionistic View of History in *The Dynasts.*" *MLQ*, XXII, 21-31.

Dale, T. R. " 'The Dynasts' and Eduard von Hartman." *N & Q*, n.s. VIII, 100-01.

Fayer, George S., Jr. "Hardy's *The Woodlanders*: Inwardness and Memory." *Studies in English Literature*, I, 81-100.

Hagan, John. "A Note on the Significance of Diggory Venn." *NCF*, XVI, 147-55.

Hardy, Evelyn, and Gittings, Robert (eds.). *Some Recollections by Emma Hardy with Some Relevant Poems by Thomas Hardy.* London: Oxford Univ. Pr. Pp. 91.
Lengthy comment in *The Bookseller*, London, 16 Sept., pp. 1468-1470; rev. by Henry Reed in *Listener*, 26 Oct., p. 678; by Donald Davie in *NS*, LXII, 560-61; by P. N. Furbank in *S*, 3 Nov., pp. 632-33; in *TLS*, 27 Oct., p. 773.

Houghton, R. E. C. "Hardy and Shakespeare." *N & Q*, n.s. VIII, 98.

Hyde, William J. "Hardy's Response to the Critics of *Jude.*" *VNL*, No. 19 (Spring), pp. 1-4.

Hynes, Samuel Lynn. *The Pattern of Hardy's Poetry.* Chapel Hill: Univ. of North Carolina Pr. Pp. 193.

Rev. by John B. Carr, Jr., in *Ariz. Q.*, XVII, 279-81; by J. H. Prynne in *VS*, V, 176.

Lewis, C. Day. "A Half-Open Door." *Listener*, 23 Feb., pp. 358-59.

An appreciative discussion of Hardy, inspired by Lewis's visit to the museum at Dorchester.

Lowe, Robert Liddell. "Two Letters of Thomas Hardy to P. W. Bunting." *N & Q*, n.s. VIII, 99-100.

Paterson, John. "Hardy, Faulkner, and the Prosaics of Tragedy." *Centennial Rev.*, V, 156-75.

Paterson, John. *The Making of "The Return of the Native."* . . . See VB 1960, 399.

Rev. by Carl J. Weber in *JEGP*, LX, 339-42; by Lionel Stevenson in *MLR*, LVI, 601; by Robert C. Slack in *NCF*, XVI, 88-90; by R. W. King in *RES*, n.s. XII, 436-37.

Patton, John. "An Unpublished Hardy Letter to Millay." *Colby Libr. Quart.*, V, 284-85.

Scott, Nathan A., Jr. "The Literary Imagination and the Victorian Crisis of Faith: The Example of Thomas Hardy." *JR*, XL, 267-81.

Hardy's response to the "Victorian crisis of faith" was, in Arnoldian phrase, "of the center." He is to be aligned, not with the "self-assured, complacent secularian" of the stamp of Meredith, Shaw, or Wells, but with the more representative, and more modern, figure (like Tennyson, Clough, or Arnold), torn by conflict and anxiety. In this view *The Return of the Native* becomes central in Hardy's work, because it formulates most fully and cogently a spiritual, a "religious," problem, even though it does not offer a "religious" solution. A sensitive, though sometimes annoyingly deliberate, essay. — R.A.D.

Six Novelists. Carnegie Series in English, No. 5. . . . See VB 1960, 400.

Rev. by Clifford Leech in *DUJ*, LIII (n.s. XXII), 88-89.

Smart, Alastair. "Pictorial Imagery in the Novels of Thomas Hardy." *RES*, n.s. XII, 262-80.

Spring, Howard. "Hardy's Secret Inspiration." *Country Life*, London, CXXX, 1029.

Van Doren, Mark. *The Happy Critic and Other Essays.* New York: Hill and Wang. Pp. 177.

Rev. by B. B. Libaire in *LJ*, LXXXVI, 2946-47.

HOPKINS (see also I, Barton).

The Journals and Papers of Gerard Manley Hopkins. . . . See VB 1960, 400.

Rev. by Boyd Litzinger in *Cithara*, I, 48-50.

The Sermons and Devotional Writings of Gerard Manley Hopkins. . . . See VB 1960, 400.

Rev. by Boyd Litzinger in *Cithara*, I, 48-50.

Assad, Thomas J. "Hopkins' 'The Windhover.'" *Tulane Studies in English*, XI, 87-95.

Boyle, Robert Richard. *Metaphor in Hopkins.* Chapel Hill: Univ. of North Carolina Pr. Pp. xxiv + 231.

Rev. by Burton A. Robie in *LJ*, LXXXVI, 2945.

Brown, T. J. "English Literary Autographs XXXIX: Gerard Manley Hopkins, 1844-1889." *Book Collector*, X, 321.

Litzinger, Boyd A. "Hopkins' 'Pied Beauty' Once More." *Renascence*, XIII, 136-38.

Litzinger, Boyd. "Hopkins' 'The Wreck of the Deutschland,' Stanza 19." *Ex*, XX, Item 7.

Miller, J. Hillis. "'Orion' in 'The Wreck of the Deutschland.'" *MLN*, LXXVI, 509-14.

Nist, John. "Gerard Manley Hopkins and Textural Intensity: A Linguistic Analysis." *CE*, XXII, 497-500.

See also comment on this article by Walter J. Ong, S.J. in *CE*, XXIII, 60.

Nowell-Smith, Simon. "Bridge's Debt to Hopkins." *TLS*, 12 May, p. 293.

On Bridges's acknowledgment in 1873 of his debt to Hopkin's prosody. See further letters by J. G. Ritz and Geoffrey Tillotson, 30 June, p. 408; by W. H. Gardner, 18 Aug., p. 549; by Norman Mackenzie, 1 Sept., p. 588.

O'Brien, A. P. "Structure Complex of Hopkins' Words," *The Indian Journal of English Studies*, I (1960), 48-56.

Parker, Dorothy E. H. "Gerard Manley Hopkins and the Critics." *DA*, XXII, 263.

Sutherland, Donald. "Hopkins Again." *Prairie Schooner*, XXXV, 197-242.

The title is ironic. The point that H. is a baroque poet is made successfully, but this is no ordinary academic contribution. In the tradition of Pound, Lewis, and Lawrence, it is erudite, dazzling, witty, smart-alec, ignorant, offensive, and out of date. Sutherland, a classics professor by trade, should be read as one reads his predecessors in this tradition — for delight and stimulation. — C.T.D.

Thomas, J. D. "Hopkins' 'The Windhover.'" *Ex*, XX, Item 31.

HOUSMAN. Carter, John (ed.). *A. E. Housman: Selected Prose*. Cambridge: Cambridge Univ. Pr. Pp. xv + 204.

Rev. by M. I. Finley in *NS*, LXII, 926.

Haber, Tom Burns. "A. E. Housman's Poetry in Book-Titles: III." *BSP*, LV, 239-41.

Lucas, Frank Lawrence. *The Greatest Problem, and Other Essays*. . . . See VB 1960, 400.

Rev. by B. B. Libaire in *LJ*, LXXXVI, 1144-45; by Carlos Baker in *NYTBR*, 19 March, p. 4; by Howard Mumford Jones in *SR*, 11 Mar., pp. 31-32.

HUXLEY (see also KINGSLEY: Blinderman).

Bibby, Cyril. *T. H. Huxley, Scientist, Humanist, and Educator*. . . . See VB 1960, 401.

Rev. by Bentley Glass in *Science*, CXXXIII, 1122-23.

KINGSLEY (see also NEWMAN: Pett).

Blinderman, Charles S. "Huxley and Kingsley." *VNL*, No. 20 (Fall), pp. 25-28.

Martin, Robert Bernard. *The Dust of Combat: A Life of Charles Kingsley*. . . . See VB 1960, 401.

Rev. by Malcolm Ross in *QQ*, LXVIII, 516-18.

KIPLING. Birkenhead, Earl of. "Kipling and the Vermont Feud." *Essays by Divers Hands: Transactions of the Royal Society of Literature*. Vol. XXX, 85-101.

An absorbing biographical account of Kipling's life in Vermont harassed by his wife's brother and the effect on his character and last years. — R.E.F.

Gerber, Helmut and Edward S. Lauterbach. *English Fiction in Transition*, III (1960). Pp. 148.

Rev. briefly in *BSP*, LV, 178. "Part Two of the annotated bibliography of writings about Rudyard Kipling."

Rice, Howard C., Jr. " 'Into the hold of Remembrance': Notes on the Kipling Material in the Doubleday Collection." *PLC*, XXII, 105-17.

Stewart, James McG. *Rudyard Kipling, a Bibliographical Catalogue*. Ed. A. W. Yeats. Toronto: Dalhousie Univ. Pr. and Univ. of Toronto Pr., 1959. Pp. xv + 673.

Rev. by Carl T. Naumburg in *BSP*, LV, 64-65; by I. Angus in *The Library*, 5th Ser., XVI, 63-65.

Tompkins, J. M. S. *The Art of Rudyard Kipling*. . . . See VB 1960, 401.

Rev. by Edgar Mertner in *Anglia*, LXXVIII, 389-91; by James R. Thrane in *MP*, LVIII, 222-24; briefly in *NCF*, XVI, 92.

LANDOR (see also TENNYSON: Paden).

Owens, R. J. "Palgrave's Marginalia on Landor's Works." *N & Q*, n.s. VIII, 227-28.

Warren, John W. "Walter Savage Landor's Views of English Life and Literature: A Critical Study of His English *Imaginary Conversations*." *DA*, XXII, 2009.

LEE. Pantazzi, Sybille. "Eugene Lee-Hamilton." *BSP*, LV, 231-32.

LIVINGSTONE. Schapera, I. (ed.). *Livingstone's Missionary Correspondence, 1841-1856*. London: Chatto and Windus. Pp. xxvi + 342.

Rev. by Max Gluckman in *Listener*, 11 May, p. 842; by N. Ascherson in *NS*, LXII, 893; by Ronald Bryden in S, 8 Dec., pp. 875-76.

MACDONALD. Wolff, Robert Lee. *The Golden Key: A Study of the Fiction of George MacDonald*. New Haven: Yale Univ. Pr. Pp. 425.

Rev. by William Kean Seymour in *CR*, CC, 553-55; by E. F. Walbridge in *LJ*, LXXXVI, 1598; by R. H. Reis in *NCF*, XVI, 182-85; by Naomi Lewis in *NS*, LXII, 693-94; by Barbara Hardy in *VS*, V, 171-72.

MARRYAT. Zanger, Jules (ed.). *Diary in America*. . . . See VB 1960, 402.

Rev. by S. W. Jackman in *AHR*, LXVI, 819; by De Lancey Ferguson in *HTBLA*, 18 Dec. 1960, p. 35; briefly in *NCF*, XV, 373; by John Phillips in *SR*, 24 Dec. 1960, p. 23.

MARTINEAU. Webb, Robert Kiefer. *Harriet Martineau: A Radical Victorian*. . . . See VB 1960, 402.

Rev. by Chester Kirby in *AHR*, LXVI, 511; by Frank Thistlethwaite in *CHJ*, III, 199-201; by F. Basch in *Études anglaises*, XIV, 253-54; briefly by Garrett Mattingly in *Harper's*, Feb., p. 104; by J. H. Burns in *History*, XLVI, 69-70; by D. Owen in *JMH*, XXXIII, 205-06; by Marie H. Nichols in *QJS*, XLVII, 204-05.

MAURICE. Ranson, Guy H. "The Kingdom of God as the Design of Society: An Important Aspect of F. D. Maurice's Theology." *Church History,* XXX, 458-72.

MEREDITH (see also III, Auchincloss, Field).

Buchen, Irving H. "The Importance of Minor Characters in *The Ordeal of Richard Feverel." Boston Univ. Studies in English,* V, 154-66.

Cline, C. L. "The Betrothal of George Meredith to Marie Vulliamy." *NCF,* XVI, 231-43.

Karl, Frederick R. "*Beauchamp's Career:* An English Ordeal." *NCF,* XVI, 117-31.

Kelvin, Norman. *A Troubled Eden: Nature and Society in the Works of George Meredith.* Stanford: Stanford Univ. Pr. Pp. 250.
Rev. by Carl H. Ketcham in *Ariz. Q.,* XVII, 178-80; unfavorably by Harvey Kerpneck in *Dalhousie Rev.,* XLI, 250-51; by R. R. McClarren in *LJ,* LXXXVI, 1463; by Robert D. Spector in *MLQ,* XXII, 309; unfavorably by Bernard A. Brunner in *MP,* LIX, 146-47; by Lionel Stevenson in *NCF,* XVI, 179-82; by Robert W. Watson in *VS,* IV, 364-65.

Smith, Carolyn Herbert. "Journey, Ordeal, Recovery: Metaphoric Patterns in Meredith's Early Prose and Poetry, 1849-1859." *DA,* XXI, 2299-3000.

Thompson, Fred C. "Stylistic Revisions of *One of Our Conquerers." Yale University Library Gazette,* XXXVI, 62-74.

Sturges, Irene M. "George Meredith: A Study in Theory and Practice." *DA,* XXI, 2706.

MILL (see also I, Barton).

Prefaces to Liberty: Selected Writings of John Stuart Mill. Ed. Bernard Wishy. . . . See VB 1959, 442.
Rev. by A. L. Harris in *JMH,* XXXIII, 69-70; by Laurence C. Hunter in *JPE,* LXIX, 102-03.

Berlin, Isaiah. *John Stuart Mill and the Ends of Life.* London: Council of Christians and Jews.
Noticed in *TLS,* 10 March, p. 153.

Hacker, A. *Political Theory: Philosophy, Ideology, Science.* New York and London: Macmillan. Pp. xiv + 609.
Rev. by David Thomson in *Econ. Jour.,* LXXI, 843-44.

Holloway, Harry A. "Mill's Liberty, 1859-1959." *Ethics,* LXXI, 130-32.

Lakeman, Enid. "Centennial — Mill: Representative Government." *CR,* CXCIX, 204-07.

Mill, Anna Jean (ed.). *John Mill's Boyhood Visit to France.* . . . Cee VB 1960, 402.
Rev. by Francis H. Herrick in *AHR,* LXVI, 785; by Jessie Macpherson in *Dalhousie Rev.,* XLI, 99-100; by F. A. Hayek in *JPE,* LXIX, 103-04; by J. Robson in *QQ,* LXVIII, 194-95; in *TLS,* 30 June, p. 406.

Miller, Kenneth E. "John Stuart Mill's Theory of International Relations." *JHI,* XXII, 493-514.
The role of Mill as "philosopher for English Liberalism" and his understanding of the need for international harmony, beyond commercial enterprise, fortified by nationalism and self-determination. A realistic and cautionary Mill adaptable to the vicissitudes of a changing world.

Pappe, H. O. *John Stuart Mill and the Harriet Taylor Myth.* London: Cambridge Univ. Pr. Pp. ix + 51.
Rev. in *TLS,* 17 Feb., p. 102.

Spiegelberg, Herbert. " 'Accident of Birth': A Non-Utilitarian Motif in Mill's Philosophy." *JHI,* XXII, 475-92.

Stillinger, Jack (ed.). *The Early Draft of John Stuart Mill's "Autobiography."* Urbana: Univ. of Illinois Pr. Pp. 218.

Thomas, Powell Stackhouse. "John Stuart Mill's Problem: The Unsuccessful Reconciliation of the Individual to Society." *DA,* XXII, 1163.

"The Wood and the Trees." *TLS,* 10 March, p. 153.
A leading article on recent interpretations of Mill's *Liberty.*

Woods, Thomas. *Poetry and Philosophy: A Study in the Thought of John Stuart Mill.* London: Hutchinson. Pp. 207.
Rev. by Maurice Cranston in *Listener,* 23 Feb., p. 361; by William Walsh in *NS,* LXI, 226; by John Holloway in *S,* 3 Feb., p. 155; by G. Ingli James in *VS,* V, 170-71.

MOORE. Adams, Mildred D. "The Apprenticeship of George Moore: His Response to Cultural Influences." *DA,* XXI, 1935.

Blissett, William F. "George Moore and Literary Wagnerism." *Comparative Lit.,* XIII, 52-71.

MORRIS. *William Morris Society, Journal of.* Vol. I, no. 1 (Winter, 1961) has items: Fairbank, Alfred, "Morris and Calligraphy" (pp. 5-6); Bushell, Hugh, "News from Iceland" (pp. 7-12); Stokes, E. E., Jr., "Morris and Bernard Shaw" (pp. 13-

18); Sewter, A. C., "Notes on Morris and Co's. Domestic Stained Glass" (pp. 22-28); "Morris and Trafalgar Square" (pp. 28-31).

Bellas, Ralph A. "William Morris' Treatment of Sources in *The Earthly Paradise*." *DA*, XXII, 857-58.

Gordon, Walter K. "A Critical Selected Edition of William Morris's *Oxford and Cambridge Magazine* (1856)." *DA*, XXI, 3781-82.
Emphasizes the Pre-Raphaelite qualities of the magazine.

Graham, Hugh. "Morris and Co." *S*, 21 Apr., pp. 559-60.
Exhibitions at the Victoria and Albert Museum and at the Geffrye Museum celebrate the centennial of the founding of Morris's firm.

"Morris & Co." *New Yorker*, 25 Nov., pp. 43-44.
On a centennial exhibit arranged by the New York members of the William Morris Society at the Avery Architectural Library, Columbia University.

Russell, (Sir) Gordon. "Design as a Social Problem." *Listener*, 15 June, p. 1033.
Comments made on an exhibition illustrating the work of William Morris and his collaborators, including Edward Burne-Jones and D. G. Rossetti.

NEWMAN (see also I, Fr. Hugh; III, Chadwick, Rosenbaum). Bokenkotter, Thomas S. *Cardinal Newman as an Historian.* . . . See VB 1960, 403.
Rev. by Owen Chadwick in *EHR*, LXXVI, 172-73; by Josef L. Altholz in *VS*, IV, 278-79.

Collins, James (ed.). *Philosophical Readings in Cardinal Newman*. Chicago: Regnery. Pp. 436.
Rev. by C. G. Gros in *LJ*, LXXXVI, 105.

Dessain, Charles Stephen (ed.). *Letters and Diaries of John Henry Newman*. Vol. XI, *Littlemore to Rome, Oct. 1845 to Dec. 1846*. London: Nelson. Pp. xxviii + 363.
Rev. by Philip Mairet in *NS*, LXII, 930-31; by Bernard Bergonzi in *S*, 8 Dec., pp. 868-69.

Dessain, Father Stephen. "A Poem Wrongly Ascribed to Newman." *BLR*, VI, 583-86.

Hollis, Christopher. "Cardinal Newman's Letters." *Wiseman Rev.*, CCXXXV, 318-29.
Article based on *The Letters and Diaries of John Henry Newman* (see above).

Kenny, Terence. *The Political Thought of*

John Henry Newman. . . . See VB 1959, 443.
Rev. by Kenneth Lewalski in *Church History*, XXX, 119-21.

Mulcahy, Daniel J. "Source of an 'Inspiration': Francis Newman's Influence on the Form of 'The Dream of Gerontius.'" *VNL*, No. 19 (Spring), pp. 21-24.

Pett, Douglas E. "The Newman-Kingsley Dispute Continues." *TLS*, 17 Feb., supp. p. xvi.
Newman's arguments, and some of his facts, called into question. The dispute continued: see letters by C. Stephen Dessain, 24 Feb., p. 121; by Douglas E. Pett, 3 March, p. 137; by Edward E. Kelly, S.J., 10 March, p. 153; by Douglas E. Pett, 17 March, p. 161.

Walgrave, J. H. *Newman the Theologian.* . . . See VB 1960, 403.
Rev. article by H. Francis Davis in *Blackfriars*, XLII, 150-56; by Kenneth F. Lewalski in *JR*, XLI, 233-34; by W. Charles Heiser in *LJ*, LXXXVI, 801-02; in *TLS*, 20 Jan., p. 45; by Vincent F. Blehl in *Wiseman Rev.*, CCXXXV, 77-80.

NIGHTINGALE (see III, Rees).

OLIPHANT. Lochhead, Marion. "Margaret Oliphant, A Half-Forgotten Victorian." *QR*, CCIC, 300-10.

PATER. Iser, Wolfgang. *Walter Pater: Die Autonomie des Ästhetischen*. Tübingen: Niemeyer, 1960.
Rev. by Gustav Mueller in *JAA*, XX, 216-17. A study of Pater's aesthetics, especially in relation to Hegel.

Johnson, R. V. *Walter Pater*. Melbourne: Melbourne Univ. Pr. Pp. viii + 55.
Rev. briefly by D.M.S. in *English*, XIII, 243.

Lenaghan, R. T. "Pattern in Walter Pater's Fiction." *SP*, LVIII, 69-91.
The pattern is the Hegelian dialectic, and its elements are the Apollonian and Dionysian forces. An excellent article. — R.A.D.

PATMORE. Thomas, A. "Coventry Patmore's Literary Criticism: Attribution of Articles." *N & Q*, n.s. VIII, 229.

READE. Burns, Wayne. *Charles Reade: A Story in Victorian Authorship*. New York: Bookman Associates, Pp. 360.
Rev. by Francis Grierson in *CR*, CC, 496-98; by Thomas D. Clareson in *VS*, V, 172-74.

ROLFE. Gawsworth, John, *et al. Frederick Rolfe and Others*. Aylesford: St. Albert's

Pr. Pp. 39.
Briefly rev. in *TLS*, 6 Oct., p. 670. Essays on Rolfe and the recent Corvo Exhibition, John Gray, and Andre Raffalovich.
Woolf, Cecil, and Sewell, Brocard. (eds.). *Corvo, 1860-1960*. Aylesford: St. Albert's Pr. Pp. xiv + 156.
Rev. by R. Mayne in *NS*, LXII, 222-23; in *TLS*, 18 Aug., p. 550. Collection of eleven essays on Rolfe's life and work.
ROSSETTIS (see also III, Rosenbaum; MORRIS: Russell).
Doughty, Oswald. *A Victorian Romantic: Dante Gabriel Rossetti.* . . . See VB 1960, 404.
Rev. by Joan Rees in *MLR*, LVI, 633-34.
Fredeman, William E. "D. G. Rosetti's *Early Itilian Poets.*" *Book Collector*, X, 193-98.
Fredeman, William E. "D. G. Rossetti and T. J. Wise." *TLS*, 19 May, p. 309.
Peterson, Carl A. "The Poetry and Painting of Dante Gabriel Rossetti." *DA*, XXI, 3460.
Putt, S. Gorley. "Christina Rossetti, Almsgiver." *English*, XIII, 222-23.
Letters to a persistent and accomplished writer of begging letters.
Sambrook, A. J. "D. G. Rossetti and R. W. Dixon." *Études anglaises*, XIV, 331-38.
RUSKIN. Evans, Joan, and Whitehouse, John Howard (eds.). *The Diaries of John Ruskin.* . . . See VB 1960, 404.
Vols. II and III rev. by C. H. Salter in *RES*, n.s. XII, 108.
Autret, Jean. *L'Influence de Ruskin sur la vie les idées et l'oeuvre de Marcel Proust.* . . . See VB 1957, 416.
Rev. by Gérard Tougas in *Revue de litt. Comparee*, XXXV, 315-16.
Bradley, John Lewis. "Ruskin's Advice to an Amateur Artist: Some New Letters to Louisa, Marchioness of Waterford." *Studies in English Literature*, I, 101-22.
Brown, T. J. "English Literary Autographs XXXVIII: John Ruskin, 1819-1900." *Book Collector*, X, 185.
Forbes-Robertson, Beatrice. "Glimpses of the Great." *Listener*, 6 July, p. 9.
Mentions Ruskin and Shaw.
Rosenberg, John D. *The Darkening Glass: A Portrait of Ruskin's Genius*. New York: Columbia Univ. Pr. Pp. 274.
Rev. briefly by Katherine Gauss Jackson in *Harper's*, Dec., p. 108; by J. R. Willingham in *LJ*, LXXXVI, 3957.

Spence, Margaret E. "Ruskin's Correspondence with His God — Daughter Constance Oldham." *Bull. of the John Rylands Library*, XLIII, 520-37.
Thomas, J. D. "Poetic Truth and the Pathetic Fallacy." *Texas Studies in Literature and Language*, III, 342-47.
A defense of Ruskin's criteria of psychological and dramatic truth.
SHAW (see also II, Dent; RUSKIN: Forbes-Robertson).
Laurence, Dan H. (ed.). *How to Become a Musical Critic*. New York: Hill and Wang. Pp. 358.
Rev. by Herbert Kupferberg in *HTB*, 4 June, p. 29; by Alec Robertson in *Listener*, 9 Mar., pp. 454-55; by C. K. Miller in *LJ*, LXXXVI, 2108; by J. A. Westrup in *M & L*, XLII, 269-70; by Alfred Frankenstein in *NYTBR*, 19 March, pp. 4-5; by David Cairns in *S*, 12 May, pp. 687-88; in *TLS*, 24 March, p. 180. A collection of articles written for *The Hornet*.
Laurence, Dan H. (ed.). *Platform and Pulpit*. New York: Hill and Wang. Pp. xvii + 301.
Texts of over thirty lectures and speeches by Shaw.
Tompkins, Peter (ed.). *To a Young Actress: The Letters of Bernard Shaw to Molly Tompkins*. London: Constable. Pp. 192.
Rev. by Alan Pryce-Jones in *HTB*, 8 Jan., pp. 23, 33; by Roy Walker in *Listener*, 30 Mar., p. 577; by Brooks Atkinson in *NYTBR*, 29 Jan., p. 10; by B. F. Dukore in *QJS*, XLVII, 311-12; by David Cairns in *S*, 12 May, pp. 687-88; in *TLS*, 21 Apr., p. 251.
Wilson, Edwin (ed.). *Shaw on Shakespeare: An Anthology of Bernard Shaw's Writings on the Plays and Productions of Shakespeare*. New York: Dutton. Pp. xxii + 284.
Rev. by Bernard F. Dukore in *QJS*, XLVII, 311-12.
Behrman, S. N. "The Paddy Vein." *Prairie Schooner*, XXXV, 10-13.
An appreciation of *You Never Can Tell*.
Bissell, Claude "The Butlerian Inheritance of G. B. Shaw." *Dalhousie Rev.*, XLI, 159-73.
Chappelow, Allan (ed.). *Shaw the Villager and Human Being*. London: Charles Skilton. Pp. 354.
Rev. in *TLS*, 22 Dec., p. 916. Reminiscences of Shaw by his neighbors in Ayot St. Lawrence.
Dupler, Dorothy. "An Analytical Study of the Use of Rhetorical Devices in Three Se-

lected Plays of George Bernard Shaw: *Saint Joan, Androcles and the Lion,* and *Candida.*" *DA,* XXII, 359.

Foster, Brian. "A Shavian Allusion." *N & Q,* n.s. VIII, 106-07.
A nickname from Kipling's *Jungle Book.* See also C.J.P. Beatty's letter, 232-33.

Gellert, Roger. "Religion and Sex." *NS,* LXII, 529-30. Review article on productions of *Androcles* and *Blanco Posnet.*

Hogan, Patrick G., Jr., and Boylen, Joseph O. "G. Bernard Shaw and W. T. Stead: An Unexplored Relationship." *Studies in English Literature,* I, 123-47.

Kaye, Julian B. *Bernard Shaw and the Nineteenth-Century Tradition.* . . . See VB 1960, 404.
Rev. by E. J. Hobsbawm in *Science & Society,* XXV, 92-95.

Krutch, Joseph Wood "G.B.S. and Intimations of Immortality." *Theatre Arts,* Feb., pp. 65-67, 77.

McDowell, Frederick P. W. "Another Look at Bernard Shaw: A Reassessment of His Dramatic Theory, His Practice and His Achievement." *Drama Survey,* I, 34-53.

McDowell, Frederick P. W. "Crisis and Unreason: Shaw's *On the Rocks.*" *Educational Theatre Jour.,* XIII, 192-200.

McDowell, Frederick P. W. "Spiritual and Political Reality: Shaw's *Simpleton of the Unexpected Isles.*" *Modern Drama,* III, 196-210.

Meisel, Martin. "Shaw and the Nineteenth-Century Theater." *DA,* XXI, 3788.

Morgan, Margery M. " 'Back to Methuselah': The Poet and the City." *Essays and Studies.* . . . See VB 1960, 404.
Rev. briefly by L.C.B. in *Études anglaises,* LIV, 97.

Paxson, Omar Martin. "Bernard Shaw's Stage Directons." *DA,* XXI, 2827.

Pearson, Hesketh. *Bernard Shaw: His Life and Personality.* London: Methuen. Pp. 480.
Rev. by Roy Walker in *Listener,* 30 Mar., p. 577; by John Coleman in *S,* 3 Feb., p. 156. First complete edition of a biography published in part in 1942. Also included in this edition is a Postscript published separately in 1952.

Rankin, H. D. "Plato and Bernard Shaw, Their Ideal Communities." *Hermathena,* XCIII, 71-77.
Briefly rev. in *Classical Jour.,* LVI, 214.

Rodger, Ian. "The Lost Tradition in the Theatre." *Listener,* 9 March, pp. 432-33. Contains some remarks on Shaw's attitude towards the theater of his time.

Rypins, Stanley and McKee, Irving. "Influential Women in Bernard Shaw's Life." *PMLA,* LXXVI, 156-57.

The Shaw Review. Vol IV, No. 1 (January, 1961), has items: Max Beerbohm, Aylmer Maude, Bernard Shaw, "Translating Drama: a *Saturday Review* Debate" (pp. 2-10); Geduld, H. M., "Bernard Shaw and Adolf Hitler" (pp. 11-20); Henson, Janice, "Bernard Shaw's Contribution to the Wagner Controversy in England" (pp. 21-26); Pallette, Drew B., "An Early Shaw Article on Actors" (pp. 27-29); "Weisert, John J., "Clothes Make the Man" (pp. 30-31); "A Continuing Check-List of Shaviana," compiled and edited by Charles A. Carpenter, Jr. (pp. 32-35); Weintraub, Stanley, a review of Richard Ellmann, ed., *Edwardians and Late Victorians,* Harris Wilson's *Arnold Bennett and H. G. Wells,* S. N. Behrman's *Portrait of Max* (pp.36-39); Miles, Nadine, a review of Lawrence Langner's *The Play's the Thing* (p. 39); "News and Queries" (p. 40).

No. 2 (May 1961) has items: Dietrich, Richard Farr, "Shaw and the Passionate Mind" (pp. 2-11); Leary, Daniel and Richard Foster, "Adam and Eve: Evolving Archetypes in *Back to Methuselah*" (pp. 12-24); Zeltmann, William, "Shaw, Farleigh and a Collection" (pp. 25-28); "Bernard Shaw — Ten Years After (1950-1960); a Transcript of the Second MLA Conference of Scholars on Shaw," edited by Arthur O. Lewis, Jr., and Stanley Weintraub (pp. 29-32); "A Continuing Check-List of Shaviana," compiled and edited by Charles A. Carpenter, Jr. (pp. 33-35); Bosworth, P. F., a review of the screen version of *The Millionairess* (p. 36); Shyre, Paul, a review of Robert Hogan's *The Experiments of Sean O'Casey* (p. 37); Weintraub, Stanley, "G.B.S.'s Musical Criticism: the Canon Expands" (pp. 38-39); "News and Queries" (pp. 39-40).

No. 3 (September, 1961) has items: Dukore, Bernard F., "Shaw and a Chicago Art Theatre" (pp. 2-6); Ayling, Ronald

F., "Charwoman of the Abbey" (pp. 7-15); Webster, Grant, "Smollett and Shaw: a Note on a Source for *Heartbreak House*" (pp. 16-17); Northwood, Eric, "Mr. Shaw's 'Romeo and Juliet'" (pp. 18-22); Smith, Warren S., " 'Bernard Shaw and the Human Bond'; An ANTA Panel on Dramatic Literature" (pp. 23-24); "A Continuing Check-List of Shaviana," compiled and edited by Charles A. Carpenter, Jr. (pp. 25-28); Bowman, Thomas D., a review of *Shaw on Shakespeare*, ed. Edwin Wilson (pp. 29-30); Weintraub, Stanley, a review of the Frank Jones translation of Brecht's *Saint Joan of the Stockyards* in the Grove edition of *Seven Plays by Bertolt Brecht*, ed. by Eric Bentley (pp. 30-31); Cornell, Katherine, a review of Sir Cedric Hardwicke's *A Victorian in Orbit* (p. 32); "News and Queries" (pp. 33-34); "Index to *The Shaw Review*," (pp. 35-36).

Stanton, Stephen S. "Shaw's Debt to Scribe." *PMLA*, LXXVI, 575-85.
Claims that Shaw, though he openly scorned Scribe and the well-made play, was directly influenced by both.

SPENCER (see also II, Kardiner).

Plochmann, George Kimball. "Darwin or Spencer?" *Science*, CXXX, 1452-56.
Spencer's scientific reputation has declined while Darwin's has grown, not because of any lack of "biological expertness," but because of "confusions in terminology, subject matter, and scientific method."

STEVENSON (see also DICKENS: Hoff).

Caldwell, Elsie Noble. *Last Witness for Robert Louis Stevenson.* . . . See VB 1960, 405.
Rev. by Roger Lancelyn Green in *RES*, n.s. XII, 316-17.

McKay, George L. (comp.). *A Stevenson Library: Catalogue of a Collection of Writings By and About Robert Louis Stevenson. Vol. 5: Manuscripts by Robert Louis Stevenson and Others.* New Haven, Conn.: Yale Univ. Library. Pp. 508.

SURTEES. Bovill, E. W. *The England of Nimrod and Surtees.* . . . See VB 1960, 405.
Rev. by Edgar Mertner in *Anglia*, LXXVIII, 512-13.

SWINBURNE. Dobrée, Bonamy (ed.). *Poems of Algernon Charles Swinburne.*

London: Penguin. Pp. 252.
Rev. in *TLS*, 14 Apr., p. 235. Selections, with a critical introduction.

Lang, Cecil Y. (ed.). *Swinburne Letters.* . . . See VB 1960, 406.
Vols. I-II rev. by A. G. Hill in *EC*, XI, 353-58; by Charles T. Dougherty in *Manuscripta*, V, 112-13. Vol. III rev. by De Lancey Ferguson in *HTB*, 15 Jan., p. 34. Vols. III-IV rev. by De Lancey Ferguson in *Am. Scholar*, XXX, 278; by William Plomer in *Listener*, 25 May, p. 935; by Merle M. Bevington in *SAQ*, LX, 348-49; in *TLS*, 9 June, p. 358; by Hazard Adams in *VS*, IV, 277-78. Vols. I-IV rev. by Gordon S. Haight in *MLR*, LVI, 599-600.

Sitwell, Edith (ed.). *Swinburne: A Selection* . . . See VB 1960, 406.
Rev. by A. G. Hill in *EC*, XI, 353-58; by De Lancey Ferguson in *HTB*, 15 Jan., p. 34.

Boswell, Grace H. "Swinburne's Mary, Queen of Scots, and the Historical Mary." *DA*, XXI, 1937.

Brown, T. J. "English Literary Autographs, XXXVII: Algernon Charles Swinburne, 1837-1909." *Book Collector*, X, 57.

Hargreaves, H. A. "Swinburne's Greek Plays and God, 'The Supreme Evil.'" *MLN*, LXXVI, 607-16.
Biblical background for anti-God passages in *Atalanta* and *Erectheus*.

Maxwell, J. C. "The Swinburne Letters and D. E. D." *N & Q*, n.s. VIII, 345-46. See VB 1960, **406.**

Paden, W. D. "A Few Annotations by Swinburne." *N & Q*, n.s. VIII, 469-70.

TENNYSON. Barker, George. "The Face behind the Poem." *Poetry*, XCVII, 310-15.
The author's foreword to the Signet edition of Tennyson's poetry.

Britton, John. "Tennyson's 'The Palace of Art,' 1-16." *Ex*, XX, Item 17.

Buckley, Jerome Hamilton. *Tennyson: The Growth of a Poet.* . . . See VB 1960, 406.
Rev. by R. D. McMaster in *Dalhousie Rev.*, XL, 400-02; by De Lancey Ferguson in *HTB*, 8 Jan., p. 32; by Graham Hough in *Listener*, 1 June, p. 787; by E. D. H. Johnson in *MP*, LIX, 143-44 ("the most authoritative study of Tennyson's poetry which has yet apeared"); by Gordon N. Ray in *NYTBR*, 1 Jan., p. 5; by Malcolm Ross in *QQ*, LXVIII, 516-17; by G. D. Klingopoulos in *S*, 21 Apr., pp. 567-68; by T. H. Johnson in *SR*, 28 Jan., p. 23; by P. F. Baum in *SAQ*, LX, 349; in *TLS*,

11 Aug., p. 535; by Carl R. Woodring in
VQR, XXXVII, 157-60; by Donald J.
Gray in *VS,* IV, 274-76.

Collins, Rowland L. "Clara Tennyson-D'Eyn-
court's Copy of 'Poems, Chiefly Lyrical':
New Facts and New Queries." *N & Q,* n.s.
VIII, 466-68.

Halio, Jay L. " 'Prothalamion,' 'Ulysses,' and
Intention in Poetry." *CE,* XXII, 390-94.

Kendall, J. L. "A Neglected Theme in Tennyson's *In Memoriam.*" *MLN,* LXXVI, 414-
20.

The theme of failure and defeat as crucial
to the pattern of the poem.

Killham, John (ed.). *Critical Essays on the
Poetry of Tennyson.* . . . See VB 1960,
406.

Rev. by R. D. McMaster in *Dalhousie
Rev.,* XLI, 400-02; by Donald J. Gray in
VS, IV, 274-76.

MacLaren, Malcolm. "Tennyson's Epicurean
Lotos-Eaters." *Classical Journal,* LVI,
259-67.

Paden, W. D. "Twenty New Poems Attributed to Tennyson, Praed, and Landor."
VS, IV, 195-218, 291-314.

In Part I of his study Mr. Paden prints
eleven poems he attributes to Tennyson;
in the concluding part he prints eight
poems he attributes to Praed and one he
attributes to Landor. See also the remarks on the attribution to Landor by
R. H. Super, *VS,* IV, 409-10.

Sanders, Charles Richard. "Carlyle and Tennyson." *PMLA,* LXXVI, 82-97.

A detailed account of their friendship.

*The Tennyson Collection Presented to the
University of Virginia in Honor of Edgar
Finley Shannon, Jr.* Charlottesville: Univ.
of Virginia Pr. Pp. 52.

Briefly noted in *BSP,* LV, 409.

THACKERAY (see also III, Auchincloss,
Hollingsworth; DICKENS: Irwin). *Aus
den Tagebüchern des Charles J. Yellow-
plush ehem. Lakai vornehmer Herrschaft.*
Bremen: Carl Schünemann.

Rev. in *Deutsche Rundschau,* LXXXVII,
988. The unnamed translator is praised
for his rendering of the Jamesian dialect.

Davies, Phillips George. "The Miscegenation
Theme in the Works of Thackeray."
MLN, LXXVI, 326-31.

Traces the recurrence of the theme in the
novels to Thackeray's concern over his
illegitimate Eurasian half-sister in India.

Dickins, Bruce. "The Story of 'Washington
Square.'" *TLS,* 13 Oct., p. 690.

The unhappy affair between Henry Kemble and Mary Ann Thackeray, used by
Henry James as basis for his novel.

Green, D. J. "Becky Sharp and Lord Steyne
— Thackeray or Disraeli?" *NCF,* XVI,
157-64.

Hagan, John. "A Note on the Napoleonic
Background of *Vanity Fair.*" *NCF,* XV,
358-61.

Johnson, E. D. H. "*Vanity Fair and Amelia:*
Thackeray in the Perspective of the
Eighteenth Century." *MP,* LIX, 100-13.

An elaborate scholarly apparatus (46
footnotes) is made to take the place of
rigorous scholarship in this comparison of
the two novels. There are some acute
critical observations in all this, if one has
the patience to quarry them out. — R.A.D.

McCarthy, Helen L. "Thackeray and Serialization." *DA,* XXII, 1612-13.

Worth, George J. "The Unity of *Henry Esmond.*" *NCF,* XV, 345-53.

THOMPSON. Danchin, Pierre. *Francis
Thompson: La vie et l'oeuvre d'un poete.*
. . . See VB 1960, 407.

Rev. by Georg Roppen in *ESt,* XLII, 180-
81; by Myrtle Pihlman Pope in *JEGP,*
LX, 344-48; by Miriam Allott in *MLR,*
LVI, 419-20.

Reid, John Cowie. *Francis Thompson: Man
and Poet.* . . . See VB 1960, 407.

Rev. by Pierre Danchin in *Études anglaises,* XIV, 255-57; by V. de S. Pinto in
RES, n.s. XII, 219-20.

Rieman, Donald H. "Shelley, De Vere, and
Thompson's 'Hound of Heaven.'" *VNL,*
No. 19 (Spring), pp. 18-19.

Thomson, Paul van Kuykendall. *Francis
Thompson: A Critical Biography.* New
York: Nelson. Pp. 280.

Rev. in *TLS,* 17 Nov., p. 825; by Paul
West in *VS,* V, 79-80.

THOMSON. Paolucci, Henry. "James Thom-
son's *The City of Dreadful Night.* A
Study of the Cultural Resources of Its
Author and a Reappraisal of the Poem."
DA, XXII, 1185.

A sound reading relies on understanding
of Dante and the pessimistic thought and
poetry of Leopardi.

TROLLOPE (see also II, Arnold; III, Auchincloss).

Booth, Bradford A. *Anthony Trollope.* . . . See
VB 1958, 390.

Rev. by William Bleifuss in *CE,* XXIII,
167.

Cadbury, William Edward III. "Varieties of Form in the Novels of Anthony Trollope." *DA*, XXII, 867.

Carter, John. "Trollope's *La Vendée*, London, Colbourn, 1850." *Book Collector*, X, 69-70.

Greenberg, Clement. *Art and Culture: Critical Essays*. Boston: Beacon Pr. Pp. 278.
Rev. by J. L. Dewton in *LJ*, LXXXVI, 2089. Contains an essay on Trollope.

Lundeen, Thomas B. "Trollope and the Mid-Victorian Episcopate." *Historical Magazine of the Protestant Episcopal Church*, XXX, 56-63.

Mohan, Ramesh. "Trollope's Political Novels." *The Indian Journal of English Studies*, I, 57-69.

"News from the Field." *College and Research Libr.*, XXII, 293.
Cites the acquisition of a "fine collection" of Anthony Trollope by the library of Michigan State University.

MRS. HUMPHRY WARD. Laski, Marghanita. "Words from 'Robert Elsmere.'" *N & Q*, n.s. VIII, 229-30.

WILDE. Walker, R. A. (tr. and ed.). *Salome*. Illus. by Aubrey Beardsley. London: Heinemann, 1957. Pp. 108.
Rev. by Robert L. Peters in *JAA*, XX, 489. The first edition of the play to include all of Beardsley's drawings, unexpurgated.

Birkett, Lord. "A Master of Persuasion." *Listener*, 11 May, pp. 818-20. A tribute to Sir Edward Clarke, counsel for Wilde.

Dyson, A. E. "The Socialist Aesthete." *Listener*, 24 Aug., pp. 273-74. Wilde's ideas have been misunderstood, as well as his laughter.

Holland, Vyvyan. *Oscar Wilde: A Pictorial Biography*. . . . See VB 1960, 407.
Rev. by William Plomer in *Listener*, 5 Jan., p. 40; by G. Freedley in *LJ*, LXXXVI, 992; briefly in *NCF*, XVI, 92; in *TLS*, 6 Jan., p. 4.

Julian, Philippe. "Un Conteur fin de siècle." *Revue des deux mondes* (no. 15, 1 August), 361-72.

Long, Richard A. and Jones, Iva G. "Towards a Definition of the 'Decadent Novel.'" *CE*, XXII, 245-49.
Includes discussion of *The Picture of Dorian Gray*.

Ojala, Aatos. *Aestheticism and Oscar Wilde*, Part II: *Literary Style*. . . . See VB 1958, 391.

Rev. by Gerhard Muller-Schwefe in *Anglia*, LXXVIII, 386-89.

Pearson, Hesketh. "Oscar Wilde and His Actors." *Theatre Arts*, Feb., pp. 62-64; 75.

YEATS. *Essays and Introductions.* New York: Macmillan. Pp. xi + 530.
Rev. by Babette Deutsch in *HTB*, 6 Aug., p. 4; by Herbert Read in *Listener*, 9 March, p. 459; by L. W. Griffin in *LJ*, LXXXVI, 3285; by Jacques Vallette in *Mercure de France*, CCCXLI, 530; by Richard Ellmann in *NS*, LXI, 1011-12; by Frank O'Connor in *NYTBR*, 2 July, p. 4; by Charles Tomlinson in *Poetry*, XCVIII, 263-66; by Frank Kermode in *S*, 31 March, pp. 448-49; in *TLS*, 17 Feb., pp. 97-98. Two previously unpublished essays conclude the volume.

Adams, Hazard. "Yeats Scholarship and Criticism: A Review of Research." *Texas Studies in Lit. and Lang.*, III, 439-51.
Annotated compilation of significant scholarship.

Beum, Robert. "Yeats's Octaves." *Texas Studies in Literature and Language*, III, 89-96.
On the development of a more complex stanza in Yeats's later work.

Bierman, Robert. "Yeats' 'The Gyres.'" *Ex*, XIX, Item 44.

Blackburn, Thomas. *The Price of an Eye.* New York: Morrow. Pp. 170.
Rev. by Burton A. Robie in *LJ*, LXXXVI, 98. A chapter on the dream world of Yeats.

Bradford, Curtis. "The Order of Yeats's *Last Poems*." *MLN*, LXXVI, 515-16.
Based on Yeats's MS. table of contents.

Bradford, Curtis. "Yeats and Maud Gonne." *Texas Studies in Lit. and Lang.*, III, 452-74.

Diskin, Patrick. "A Source for Yeats's 'The Black Tower.'" *N & Q*, n.s. VIII, 107-08.

Dunseath, T. K. "Yeats and the Genesis of Supernatural Song." *ELH*, XXVIII, 399-416.
A study of "Ribh at the Tomb of Baile and Aillinn."

Ellmann, Richard. *Yeats: The Man and the Masks*. . . . See VB 1949, 282.
Rev. by Brian Inglis in *S*, 30 June. p. 956.

Fraser, G. S. "Images of Yeats." *NS*, LXI, 763.
Comment on exhibit: see catalogue by D. J. Gordon, *et al.*

Fraser, George Sutherland. *Vision and Rhetoric: Studies in Modern Poetry.* New York: Barnes and Noble, 1960. Pp. 285.

Rev. by Herbert Burke in *LJ,* LXXXV, 2431; by Richard Hoggart in *NS,* LVII, 374; by Frank Kermode in *S,* 20 Mar., 1959, p. 413; in *TLS,* 10 Apr., 1959, p. 210. Contains an essay on Yeats.

Fréchet, René. "L'Étude de Yeats: textes, jugements et éclairissements." *Études anglaises,* XIV, 36-47.

Gibbon, Monk. *The Masterpiece and the Man: Yeats as I Knew Him.* . . . See VB 1960, 408.

Rev. by Aerol Arnold in *The Personalist,* XLII, 254-55.

Gordon, D. J., Fletcher, Ian, Kermode, Frank and Skelton, Robin (eds.). *W. B. Yeats: Images of a Poet.* Manchester: Manchester Univ. Pr. Pp. 150.

Rev. by Richard Ellmann in *NS,* LXII, 887-88.

Hahn, Sister M. Norma. "Yeats' 'The Wild Swans at Coole': Meaning and Structure." *CE,* XXII, 419-21.

MacLeish, Archibald. *Poetry and Experience.* . . . See VB 1960, 408

Rev. by Paul Engle in *HTBLA,* 5 Feb., p. 33; by G. D. McDonald in *LJ,* LXXXV, 4473; by Richard Eberhart in *N,* 8 Apr., p. 308; by Edward Lucie-Smith in *NS,* LXII, 395-96; by G. W. Allen in *NYTBR,* 8 Jan., p. 6; by Joseph Slater in *SR,* 6 May, p. 29.

Martin, Graham. "Fine Manners, Liberal Speech: A Note on the Public Poetry of W. B. Yeats." *EC,* XI, 40-59.

Melchiori, Giorgio. *The Whole Mystery of Art.* London: Routledge, 1960, Pp. xiv + 306.

Rev. by Burton A. Robie in *LJ,* LXXXVI, 1001; by T. R. Henn in *NS,* LXI, 60; by A. Norman Jeffares in *RES,* n.s. XII, 437-39; in *TLS,* 17 Feb., pp. 97-98. A study of Yeats's symbolism.

Mendel, Sydney. "Yeats' 'Lapis Lazuli.'" *Ex,* XIX, Item 64.

Moore, John R. "Yeats as a Last Romantic." *VQR,* XXXVII, 432-49.

Pearce, Donald R. (ed.). *The Senate Speeches of W. B. Yeats.* . . . See VB 1960, 408.

Rev. by Richard Ellmann in *NS,* LXII, 887-88 (see also a letter by William Empson, *NS,* LXII, 989); by T. R. Henn in *Listener,* 21 Dec., p. 1084; by A. Norman

Jeffares in *Poetry,* XCVIII, 253-63; by Joseph O'Rourke in *QJS,* XLVII, 318; in *TLS,* 22 Dec., p. 916.

Reid, Benjamin Lawrence. *William Butler Yeats: The Lyric of Tragedy.* Norman: Univ. of Oklahoma Pr. Pp. 280.

Senior, John. *The Way Down and Out: The Occult in Symbolist Literature.* . . . See VB 1960, 408.

Rev. by D. T. Torchiana in *MP,* LVII, 286; by Frank Kermode in *S,* 1 Apr., 1960, p. 477.

Staub, August W. "The 'Unpopular Theatre' of W. B. Yeats." *QJS,* XLVII, 363-71.

Stock, Amy Geraldine. *W. B. Yeats: His Poetry and Thought.* Cambridge Univ. Pr. Pp. xii + 255.

Rev. by Derek Stanford in *English,* XIII, 237; by Brian Inglis in *S,* 30 June, p. 956; in *TLS,* 4 Aug., p. 480.

Terwilliger, Patricia J. "A Re-interpretation of Stanzas VII and VIII of W. B. Yeats's *Among School Children.*" *Boston Univ. Studies in English,* V, 29-34.

Unterecker, John. *A Reader's Guide to William Butler Yeats.* . . . See VB 1960, 408.

Rev. by Martin Steinmann, Jr. in *CE,* XXII, 443-44.

Ure, Peter. "Yeats's 'Deirdre.'" *ESt,* XLII, 218-30.

Ure, Peter, "Yeats's Hero-Fool in *The Herne's Egg.*" *HLQ,* XXIV, 125-36.

Watkins, Vernon. "W. B. Yeats — The Religious Poet." *Texas Studies in Lit. and Lang.,* III, 475-88.

Analysis of Yeats's development as poet and his increasing reliance on religion for his poetic themes and vision.

Whitaker, Thomas R. "Yeats's 'Dove or Swan.'" *PMLA,* LXXVI, 121-32.

Wilson, Francis A. C. *Yeats's Iconography.* . . . See VB 1960, 408.

Rev. by B. A. Robie in *LJ,* LXXXVI, 1463.

Winters, Yvor. *The Poetry of W. B. Yeats.* . . . See VB 1960, 408.

Rev. by Denis Donoghue in *SeR,* LXIX, 476-84.

Wright, George T. *The Poet and the Poem: The Personae of Eliot, Yeats, and Pound.* Berkeley: Univ. of California Pr.; Cambridge, Cambridge Univ. Pr., 1960.

Rev. by A. R. Jones in *MLR,* LVI, 601-02.

Zwerdling, Alex. "Yeats and the Heroic Ideal." *DA,* XXI, 2301.

VICTORIAN  BIBLIOGRAPHY FOR 1962

Robert C. Slack, editor

THIS BIBLIOGRAPHY has been prepared by a committee of the Victorian Literature Group of the Modern Language Association of America: Robert C. Slack, chairman, Carnegie Institute of Technology; Oscar Maurer, University of Texas; Robert A. Donovan, State University of New York; Charles T. Dougherty, St. Louis University; Donald J. Gray, Indiana University; Richard C. Tobias, University of Pittsburgh; Ronald E. Free-· man, University of Southern California; and Michael Timko, Queens College. It attempts to list the noteworthy publications of 1962 (including reviews of these and earlier items) that have a bearing on the Victorian period, as well as similar publications of earlier date that have been inadvertently omitted from the preceding Victorian bibliographies. Unless otherwise stated, the date of publication is 1962. References to a page in the bibliography for 1961, in *Victorian Studies,* June 1962, is made by the following form: See VB 1961, 371. Some cross-references are given, though not all that are possible. Annotations to items are made at the discretion of committee members and the editor; some are intended to indicate content, others to emphasize important contributions; every annotation containing a judgment is initialed by the committee member responsible. For certain continuing bibliographical works the reader should consult VB 1941, the last annual bibliography in which such works are listed in full. Bibliographical entries are made to conform as closely as possible with the British National Bibliography for books first published in Great Britain, and with the Library of Congress Catalog for books first published in the United States.

The editor wishes to thank Professor Carl J. Weber for his helpful assistance with the Hardy section of the bibliography. Also, he wishes to thank John Filor of Indiana University for special assistance.

KEY TO ABBREVIATIONS

AHR = American Historical Review
AL = American Literature
AM = Atlantic Monthly
APSR = American Political Science Review
APSS = Annals of the American Academy of Political and Social Science
ArQ = Arizona Quarterly
BA = Books Abroad
BB = Bulletin of Bibliography and Magazine Notes
BLR = Bodleian Library Record
BSP = Papers of the Bibliographical Society of America
CE = College English
CHJ = Historical Journal (formerly *Cambridge Historical Journal*)
CR = Contemporary Review
CWd = Catholic World
DA = Dissertation Abstracts
DUJ = Durham University Journal
EC = Essays in Criticism
EHR = English Historical Review
EJ = English Journal
ELH = Journal of English Literary History
ESt = English Studies
Ex = Explicator
HJ = Hibbert Journal
HLB = Harvard Library Bulletin
HLQ = Huntington Library Quarterly
HTB = New York Herald Tribune Book Review
JAA = Journal of Aesthetics and Art Criticism
JEGP = Journal of English and Germanic Philology
JEH = Journal of Economic History
JHI = Journal of the History of Ideas
JMH = Journal of Modern History

JP = Journal of Philosophy
JPE = Journal of Political Economy
KR = Kenyon Review
LJ = Library Journal
LQ = Library Quarterly
LQHR = London Quarterly and Holborn Review
LR = Library Review
M & L = Music and Letters
MLJ = Modern Language Journal
MLN = Modern Language Notes
MLQ = Modern Language Quarterly
MLR = Modern Language Review
MP = Modern Philology
N = Nation
N & Q = Notes and Queries
NCF = Nineteenth-Century Fiction
NEQ = New England Quarterly
NER = National and English Review
New R = New Republic
NS = New Statesman
NYTBR = New York Times Book Review
PAPS = Proceedings of the American Philosophical Society
ParR = Partisan Review
PLC = Princeton University Library Chronicle
PMLA = Publications of the Modern Language Association of America
PQ = Philological Quarterly
PSQ = Political Science Quarterly
QJS = Quarterly Journal of Speech
QQ = Queen's Quarterly
QR = Quarterly Review
RES = Review of English Studies
RoR = Romanic Review
S = Spectator
SAQ = South Atlantic Quarterly
SeR = Sewanee Review
SP = Studies in Philology
SR = Saturday Review
StI = Studies: An Irish Quarterly Review
TC = Twentieth Century
TLS = Times Literary Supplement
TQ = University of Toronto Quarterly
VNL = Victorian News Letter
VQR = Virginia Quarterly Review
VS = Victorian Studies
YR = Yale Review

I. BIBLIOGRAPHICAL MATERIAL

(For bibliographies pertaining to individuals listed in IV, see – ARNOLD: Brooks;

DICKENS: Carr, Gimbel; FARADAY: Jeffreys; HARDY: Bowden; KIPLING: Stewart; SULLIVAN: Poladian).

Altholz, Josef L. "Bibliographical Note on the 'Rambler.'" *BSP,* LVI, 113-14.

"Annual Bibliography for 1961." *PMLA,* LXXVII, No. 2, 193-212; "English Language and Literature: IX. Nineteenth Century, X. Twentieth Century," ed. Paul A. Brown, Charles C. Mish, Mervin R. Lowe, Robert M. Pierson, and Gordon Ross Smith, with the help of Sherod M. Cooper and Earl L. Dachslager.

"Bibliography" [of recent books and pamphlets on social and political history]. *International Rev. of Social Hist.,* VII, 105-62; 291-349.

Block, Andrew. *The English Novel, 1740-1850.* . . . See VB 1961, 358.
Rev. by F. Wezeman in *LJ,* LXXXVII, 1883; by Robert A. Colby in *NCF,* XVI, 354-59.

Canney, Margaret B. C. (comp.). *Robert Owen, 1771-1858: Catalogue of an Exhibition of Printed Books Held in the Library of the University of London, October-December 1958.* London: Chiswick Pr., 1959. Pp. viii + 40.
Noted in *Economica,* XXVIII (1961), 106.

Clarke, Ignatius Frederick (comp.). *The Tale of the Future from the Beginning to the Present Day: A Checklist.* London: The Library Assoc., 1961. Pp. 165.
Rev. by Hal Draper in *LJ,* LXXXVII, 956.

Crick, Bernard R., and Alman, Miriam (eds.). *A Guide to Manuscripts Relating to America in Great Britain and Ireland.* London: Oxford Univ. Pr., 1961. Pp. xxxvi + 667.
Noted in *Church Hist.,* XXXI, 381; rev. by S. B. Baxter in *JMH,* XXXIV, 317-18.

Faverty, Frederick. *The Victorian Poets: A Guide to Research.* . . . See VB 1959, 411.
Rev. by E. N. W. Mottram in *ESt,* XLIII, 518-20.

Gherity, James A. "The History of Economic Thought: A Check List of English Language Books." *BB,* XXIII, 185-87.

Greenberg, Robert A. (ed.). "Recent Publications: A Selected List." *VNL,* No. 21 (Spring), pp. 24-29; No. 22 (Fall), pp. 27-31.

Irwin, Raymond, and Staveley, Ronald (eds.). *The Libraries of London.* 2nd Rev. Ed.

. . . See VB 1961, 359.
Rev. by Ralph T. Esterquest in *LQ*, XXXII, 179-80.

Jerman, B. R. "Nineteenth-Century Holdings at the Folger." *VNL*, No. 22 (Fall), p. 23.

Jones, Claude E. "*Vanity Fair* Portraits, 1868-1881: A Selected Check List." *BB*, XXIII, 159-62.
Contains the names of most of the major literary and political figures of the period.

Macleod, R. D. "Some Scottish Publishers." *LR*, XVIII, 435-40; 515-20; 597-603.

Munby, Alan Noel Latimer. *The Cult of the Autograph Letter in England*. London: Athlone Pr.; New York: Oxford Univ. Pr. Pp. viii + 117.
Rev. by P. J. Croft in *Book Collector*, XI, 380-84; by P. L. Heyworth in *N & Q*, n.s. IX, 473-74; in *TLS*, 15 June, p. 448.
Includes account of Victorian collections and collecting methods.

Nilon, Charles, *et al*. (eds.). *Annual Bibliography of English Language and Literature*. Vol. XXXIII, 1957-58. Vol. XXXIV, 1958-59. Cambridge: Cambridge Univ. Pr. Pp. xv + 628; xv + 379.

Peterson, Annamarie. "Israel Zangwill (1864-1926): A Selected Bibliography." *BB*, XXIII (Sept.-Dec., 1961), 136-40.

Slack, Robert C. (ed.) "Victorian Bibliography for 1961." *VS*, V, 357-96.

Stewart, James D., with Hammond, Muriel E., and Saenger, Erwin (eds.). *British Union-Catalogue of Periodicals*. . . . See VB 1955, 241.
Rev. in *TLS*, 27 July, p. 548.
A supplement now brings this indispensable catalogue to 1960.

Stillinger, Jack. "Recent Studies in Nineteenth-Century Literature." *Studies in English Literature*, II, 509-28.
Discusses about forty books published in the past year or so.

Stratman, Carl J. *A Bibliography of British Dramatic Periodicals 1720-1960*. New York: New York Public Libr. Pp. 58.
Mentioned briefly in *Bull. New York Pub. Libr.*, LXVI, 279 (see also Stratman, Carl J. "Preparing a Bibliography of British Dramatic Periodicals 1720-1960." *Bull. New York Pub. Libr.*, LXVI, 405-08).

Stratman, Carl J. "Unpublished Dissertations in the History and Theory of Tragedy, 1899-1957 — Addenda." Part II. *BB*,

XXIII, 187-92.
Contains a section on the nineteenth century.

"Theatrical Material in the British Museum." *Theatre Notebook*, XVII, 10-11.
Entries from the *British Museum Quarterly*, among which are listed items pertaining to Gilbert, Dickens, and Shaw.

Walbank, Alan. "Contemporary Collectors XXXII: Gothic Romances and Yellowbacks." *Book Collector*, XI, 313-22.

"Writings on Irish History, 1960." *Irish Historical Studies*, XII, 345-65.

II. ECONOMIC, POLITICAL, RELIGIOUS, AND SOCIAL ENVIRONMENT

Abell, Sir Wescott. *The Shipwright's Trade*. New York: Caravan Bk. Serv. Pp. 218.
Rev. by V. D. Tate in *LJ*, LXXXVII, 3671.

Allaway, Albert John. *Vaughan College, Leicester, 1862-1962*. Leicester: Leicester Univ. Pr. Pp. viii + 136.

Allen, Cecil John. *Great Western*. London: Ian Allen; New Rochelle, N. Y.: Sportshelf. Pp. 72.

Altholz, Josef L. *The Liberal Catholic Movement in England: The "Rambler" and its Contributors, 1848-1864*. London: Burns and Oates. Pp. x + 251.
Rev. in *TLS*, 24 Aug., p. 644.

Altholz, Josef Lewis. "The Liberal Catholic Movement in England." *Church Hist.*, XXI, 100-01.
Reprints abstract of Columbia University dissertation from *DA*.

Anstey, R. T. *Britain and the Congo in the Nineteenth Century*. Oxford: Clarendon Pr.; New York: Oxford Univ. Pr. Pp. xiii + 260.

Appleman, Philip, Madden, William A., and Wolff, Michael (eds.). *1859: Entering an Age of Crisis*. . . . See VB 1960, 370.
Rev. by Asa Briggs in *EHR*, LXXVII, 576-78.

Archer, Mildred. "India and Archaeology: The Role of the East India Company, 1785-1858." *History Today*, XII, 272-79.

Armstrong, Warren. *Atlantic Highway*. London: Harrap, 1961. Pp. 239.
Atlantic shipping from 1840 to the present.

Armytage, W. H. G. *Heavens Below: Uto-*

pian Experiments in England, 1560-1960.
. . . See VB 1961, 359.

Rev. by Charles F. Mullett in *AHR*, LXVII, 1092-93; by James Winter in *Canadian Hist. Rev.*, LXIII, 243-45; by John Roach in *History*, XLVII, 315-17; by I. D. Lloyd-Jones in *History Today*, XII, 363-65; by D. F. Calhoun in *JMH*, XXXIV, 435-36; by Maurice Cranston in *Listener*, 18 Jan., p. 139; by John F. C. Harrison in *PSQ*, LXXVII, 442-43; by Christopher Hill in *S*, 5 Jan. pp. 19-20; in *TLS*, 16 Mar., p. 184.

Arnstein, Walter L. "The Bradlaugh Case: A Study in Late Victorian Opinion and Politics." *DA*, XXII, 2769-70.

Ashby, Mabel K. *Joseph Ashby of Tysoe, 1859-1919.* . . . See VB 1961, 360.

Rev. by A. Robinson in *Econ. Jour.*, LXXII, 223-24; by Dorothy Greene Johnson in *JMH*, XXXIV, 211-12.

Ashworth, William. *An Economic History of England, 1870-1939.* . . . See VB 1961, 360.

Rev. by David Wightman in *EHR*, LXXVII, 405-06; by Arthur J. Taylor in *History*, XLVII, 331; by Albert H. Imlah in *JEH*, XXII, 82; by Roy Church in *JPE*, LXX, 97-99.

Aslin, Elizabeth. *Nineteenth-Century English Furniture.* London: Faber and Faber. Pp. 96.

Rev. by Evelyn Waugh in *S*, 19 Oct., pp. 599-600; in *TLS*, 6 July, p. 488.

Ausubel, Herman. *In Hard Times: Reformers among the Late Victorians.* . . . See VB 1961, 360.

Rev. by C. L. Mowat in *EHR*, LXXVII, 802-03.

Bailey, Sir Edward. *Charles Lyell.* London: Nelson; Garden City, N.Y.: Doubleday. Pp. x + 214.

Banton, Michael (ed.). *Darwinism and the Study of Society.* . . . See VB 1961, 360.

Rev. by Bernard Barber in *Amer. Jour. of Sociology*, LXVIII, 145-46; by Theodore Abel in *APSS*, CCCXL, 180-81; by Martin Jarrett-Kerr in *Manchester Guardian*, 2 June, 1961, p. 9.

Barker, T. C. *Pilkington Brothers and the Glass Industry.* London: George Allen & Unwin, 1960. Pp. 296.

Rev. by Frank Thistlethwaite in *EHR*, LXXVII, 181-82; by J. M. Price in *JMH*, XXXIV, 99-100.

Bates, Hazel, and Wells, Anne Arabella Macdonald. *A History of Shrewsbury High School, 1855-1960.* Shrewsbury: Wilding. Pp. 39.

Bateson, Gregory (ed.). *Perceval's Narra-*

tive. London: Hogarth; Stanford: Stanford Univ. Pr. Pp. xxii + 331.

Rev. by S. Coates in *NS*, LXIV, 205. The account of a Victorian's psychosis, written by himself.

Baylen, Joseph O. (ed.). "Sumner and Lord Wharncliffe: Some Unpublished Letters." *NEQ*, XXXV, 390-95.

Beales, Derek Edward Dawson. *England and Italy, 1859-1860.* . . . See VB 1961, 360.

Rev. by Albert H. Imlah in *AHR*, LXVII, 775; by J. B. Conacher in *Canadian Hist. Rev.*, LXIII, 165-66; by Agatha Ramm in *History*, XLVII, 328-29; by Raymond Grew in *JMH*, XXXIV, 210-11; in *TLS*, 16 Mar., p. 182; by H. Hearder in *VS*, V, 274-75.

Bearce, George Donham. *British Attitudes towards India.* . . . See VB 1961, 360.

Rev. by Robert I. Crane in *AHR*, LXVII, 1019-20.

Bell, Enid. *Josephine Butler: Flame of Fire.* London: Constable. Pp. 268.

Biography of opponent of Contagious Diseases Act.

Bennett, George (ed.). *The Concept of Empire: Burke to Attlee 1774-1947.* 2nd ed. London: A. and C. Black. Pp. xix + 434.

Second edition revised and bibliographies brought up to date.

Berkeley, Humphry. "Catholics in English Politics." *Wiseman Rev.*, CCXXXVI (No. 494), 300-08.

Betjeman, John. "Sir Henry Newbolt after a Hundred Years." *Listener*, 28 June, pp. 1114-15.

Bishop, John J. "The Role of the Circus and Crescent in 18th and 19th Century British Town Planning." *DA*, XXIII, 1317.

Black, R. D. Collison. *Economic Thought and the Irish Question, 1817-1870.* . . . See VB 1961, 360.

Rev. by Oliver MacDonagh in *CHJ*, V, 208-10; by A. W. Coats in *Economica*, XXVII, 89-91; by Christopher Howard in *EHR*, LXXVII, 176-77; by Patrick Lynch in *Irish Hist. Studies*, XIII, 59-61.

Blake, Clagette. *Charles Elliott, R.N.* . . . See VB 1961, 361.

Rev. by D. R. Gillard in *EHR*, LXXVII, 392-93.

Blakemore, H. "John Thomas North, the Nitrate King." *History Today*, XII, 467-75.

Blakiston, Noel (ed.). *The Roman Question: Extracts from the Despatches of Odo Russell from Rome, 1858-1870.* London: Chapman and Hall. Pp. 474.

Rev. in *TLS*, 26 Oct., p. 828.

Bond, Brian. "Recruiting the Victorian Army, 1870-92." *VS*, V, 331-38.

Brett-James, Anthony. "Disaster in Manipur: An Imperial Episode." *History Today*, XII, 48-55.
Internal trouble in Manipur in 1891.

Briant, Keith. *Passionate Paradox: The Life of Marie Stopes*. New York: Norton; London: Hogarth. Pp. 285.
Rev. by E. T. Smith in *LJ*, LXXXVII, 4531; by Maurice Richardson in *NS*, LXIII, 865-66.
A friend of Shaw and Lord Alfred Douglas.

Briggs, Asa. *The Age of Improvement.* . . . See VB 1960, 371.
Rev. by James L. Godfrey in *JMH*, XXXIV, 95.

Brockett, Allan. *Nonconformity in Exeter, 1650-1875*. Manchester: Manchester Univ. Pr., for Exeter Univ. Pp. vii + 252.
Rev. by Maurice Ashley in *Listener*, 19 July, p. 111; in *TLS* 7 Sept., p. 677.

Brogan, D. W. "The Remote Revolution—A British View." *PAPS*, CVI, 1-9.

Brown, Ford K. *Fathers of the Victorians: The Age of Wilberforce.* . . . See VB 1961, 361.
Rev. by Herman Ausubel in *AHR*, LXVII, 772; by David Spring in *Canadian Hist. Rev.*, XLIII, 245-46; by John Kent in *Jour. of Eccl. Hist.*, XIII, 254-55; by Jerome H. Buckley in *JEGP*, LXI, 935-37; by John Clive in *JMH*, XXXIV, 337-38; by Norman St. John-Stevas in *Listener*, 15 Mar., pp. 481-82; by Jacques Vallette in *Mercure de France*, CCCXLV, 549-51; by G. R. Kelly in *LJ*, LXXXVII, 978; by Carl B. Cone in *QJS*, XLVIII, 204; by Merle M. Bevington in *SAQ*, LXI, 550-52; in *TLS*, 5 Jan., p. 11; by Standish Meachem in *VS*, V, 340-42; by J. B. Schneewind in *YR*, LI, 475-77.

Bruce, Maurice, *The Coming of the Welfare State*. London: Batsford, 1961. Pp. xii + 253.
Rev. by H. J. Dyos in *VS*, VI, 189-91.

Buck, Anne. *Victorian Costume and Costume Accessories*. New York: Nelson. Pp. 215.
Rev. by P. von Khrum in *LJ*, LXXXVII, 1779.

Bury, J. P. T. (ed.). *The New Cambridge Modern History*. Vol. X: *The Zenith of European Power, 1830-1870*. . . . See VB 1961, 361.
Rev. by Asa Briggs in *CHJ*, V, 210-13; by M. Loup in *Études anglaises*, XV, 307-08; by T. S. Hamerow in *JMH*, XXXIV, 100-01.

Bury, Shirley. "The Prince Consort and the Royal Plate Collections." *Burlington Mag.*, CIV, 352-54.

Butler, Edward Cuthbert. *The Vatican Council, 1869-1870, Based on Bishop Ullathorne's Letters*. London: Collins, with Harvill Pr. Pp. 510.
Rev. by Bernard Bergonzi in *S*, 7 Dec., p. 908; in *TLS*, 26 Oct., p. 828.

Butlin, Martin (ed.). *Turner Watercolours*. London: Barrie and Rockliff. Pp. 84.

Calder-Marshall, Arthur. *The Enthusiast*. London: Faber. Pp. 304.
Rev. by Robert Harbinson in *Listener*, 28 June, pp. 1125-26; by Dom Sylvester Hovédard in *Wiseman Rev.*, CCXXXVII (No. 494), 364-68.
Study of a Victorian evangelical preacher, the Rev. Joseph Leycester Lyne, alias Father Ignatius of Llanthony.

Campanella, Anthony P. "Ammiratori di Garibaldi in Inghilterra." *Nuova Antologia*, CCCCLXXXVI, 83-90.

Campbell, A. E. *Great Britain and the United States, 1895-1903*. . . . See VB 1961, 362.
Rev. by Zara Steiner in *AHR*, LXVII, 380; by J. A. S. Grenville in *EHR*, LXXVII, 583-85.

Campbell, Ray H. *Carron Company*. . . . See VB 1961, 362.
Rev. by D. C. Coleman in *Economica*, XXIX, 324-25.

Carpenter, James. *Gore: A Study in Liberal Catholic Thought*. . . . See VB 1960, 372.
Rev. by Charles Smyth in *VS*, V, 261-63.

Carr, J. C., and Taplin, W. *A History of the British Steel Industry*. Oxford: Blackwell; Cambridge, Mass.: Harvard Univ. Pr. Pp. 623.

Carter, Harry. *Orlando Jewitt*. London: Oxford Univ. Pr. Pp. 50.
Biography of wood-engraver who specialized in Gothic architecture.

Carter, John. "T. J. Wise and the Technique of Promotion." *Book Collector*, XI, 480-82.

Carter, Mark Bonham (ed.). *The Autobiography of Margot Asquith*. London: Eyre and Spottiswoode. Pp. xxxvii + 342.
Rev. by John Gross in *NS*, LXIV, 572.

Chadwick, George F. *The Works of Sir Joseph Paxton, 1803-1865*. London: Architectural Pr., 1961. Pp. 275.
Rev. by Reyner Banham in *NS*, LXIII, 61-62; by John Betjeman in *S*, 19 Jan., pp. 77-78; in *TLS*, 20 April, p. 260.
On the designer of the Crystal Palace.

Chadwick, Owen. *Victorian Miniature.* . . .
See VB 1960, 372.
Rev. by F. C. Mather in *EHR*, LXXVII,
399-400.

Chambers, J. D. *The Workshop of the World.*
. . . See VB 1961, 362.
Rev. by W. H. B. Court in *Economica*,
XXIX, 107-09; by A. J. Youngson in *EHR*,
LXXVII, 796-97; by A. R. Schoyen in
JEH, XXII, 265; by Jacob M. Price in
JMH, XXXIV, 450-51.

Chapman, Ronald. *Father Faber.* . . . See VB
1961, 362.
Rev. by N. K. Burger in *NYTBR*, 23 July,
1961, p. 25.

Chilston, Eric Alexander Akers-Douglas, 3rd
Viscount. *Chief Whip*. London: Rout-
ledge and K. Paul, 1961. Pp. xiii + 370.
Rev. by James Cornford in *S*, 5 Jan., p.
21.
A biography of Aretas Akers-Douglas,
Conservative Whip, 1886-1892.

Christensen, Torben. *Origin and History of
Christian Socialism, 1848-1854*. Copenhagen: Universitetsforlaget I Aarhus. Pp.
364.
Noticed in *TLS*, 22 June, p. 466.

Clapp, B. W. "A Manchester Merchant and
His Schedules of Supply and Demand."
Economica, XXIX, 185-87.

Clark, G. Kitson. *The Making of Victorian
England*. London: Methuen; Cambridge:
Harvard Univ. Pr. Pp. xiii + 312.
Rev. by F. R. Salter in *CR*, CCII, 105;
by C. Gordon Bolam in *HJ*, LXI, 52; by
Asa Briggs in *NS*, LXIV, 18; by Robert
Blake in *S*, 22 June, p. 830; in *TLS*, 20
July, p. 524; by E. J. Hobsbawm in *VS*,
VI, 178-80.

Cole, Margaret. *The Story of Fabian Socialism.* . . . See VB 1961, 362.
Rev. by Richard W. Lyman in *AHR*,
LXVIII, 116-17; by Lewis A. Coser in
Amer. Jour. of Sociology, LXVIII, 377;
by Mary E. Murphy in *APSS*, CCCXLII,
174-75; by H. A. Marquand in *Econ.
Jour.*, XXIX, 447-48; by S. R. Graubard
in *JMH*, XXXIV, 348-49; by Keith
Hutchison in *N*, 31 Mar., pp. 286-87; by
Herman Ausubel in *NYTBR*, 8 Apr., p.
7; by Philip P. Poirier in *PSQ*, LXXVII,
440-42.

Collins, Robert O. *The Southern Sudan,
1883-1898: A Struggle for Control*. New
Haven: Yale Univ. Pr. Pp. viii + 212.
Rev. by Gwendolen M. Carter in *APSS*,
CCCXLIV, 176-77; in *TLS*, 10 Aug., p.
574.

Connell, Brian (ed.). *Regina vs. Palmerston.*
. . . See VB 1961, 362.

Rev. by Tresham Lever in *History Today*,
XII, 519-20; by E. G. Collieu in *Listener*,
17 May, p. 875; by Paul Johnson in *NS*,
LXIII, 833-34; by Robert Blake in *S*, 25
May, p. 687; in *TLS*, 22 June, pp. 453-
54.

Conway, Alan (ed.). *The Welsh in America:
Letters from the Immigrants.* . . . See VB
1961, 362.
Rev. by Oscar Handlin in *JEH*, XXII, 90.

Cook, Charles T. (ed.). *Sermons on the Sec-
ond Coming of Christ*. Grand Rapids,
Mich.: Zondervan. Pp. 256.
Vol. 18 in a library of the sermons of
Charles Haddon Spurgeon.

Cope, Zachary. *The Royal College of Surgeons of England.* . . . See VB 1960, 372.
Rev. by F. N. L. Poynter in *Isis*, LIII,
241-42.

Corry, B. A. *Money, Saving, and Invest-
ment*. London: Macmillan; New York:
St. Martin's Pr. Pp. 188.
Rev. by C. H. Feinstein in *Econ. Jour.*,
LXXII, 959-60.
Study of theory of money and saving
from Hume to John Stuart Mill.

Course, Edwina. *London Railways*. London:
Batsford. Pp. 280.
Rev. in *TLS*, 21 Sept., p. 748.

Cowan, C. D. *Nineteenth-Century Malaya.*
. . . See VB 1961, 362.
Rev. by B. Harrison in *EHR*, LXXVII,
806; by David McIntyre in *VS*, V, 275-
76.

Cowan, Helen I. *British Emigration to British
North America: The First Hundred Years.*
. . . See VB 1961, 363.
Rev. by John S. Galbraith in *JMH*,
XXXIV, 94-95.

Cramp, Alfred Bernard. *Opinion on Bank
Rate, 1822-60*. London: Bell. Pp. xi +
118.
Rev. by J. K. Horsefield in *Economica*,
XXIX, 427-29.

Curate, Federico (ed.). *Le Relazioni Diplo-
matiche Fra La Gran Bretagna E Il
Regno Di Sardegna.*
Rev. by Lynn M. Case in *AHR*, LXVII,
691-93.

Dainton, Courtney. *The Story of England's
Hospitals.* . . . See VB 1961, 363.
Rev. in *TLS*, 19 Jan., p. 46.

Davies, Horton. *Worship and Theology in
England*. Vol. III: *From Watts and Wesley to Maurice, 1690-1850.* . . . See VB
1961, 363.
Rev. by C. A. Holbrook in *Christian Century*, LXXVIII, 1053; by Leonard W.

Cowie in *History*, XLVII, 319; by Erik
Routley in *Jour. of Eccl. Hist.*, XIII, 247-
49; by M. H. Shepherd in *Jour. of Religion*, XLII, 141; in *TLS*, 9 Mar., p. 174.

Davies, Horton. *Worship and Theology in
England: Vol. IV: From Newman to
Martineau, 1850-1900.* Princeton, N. J.:
Princeton Univ. Pr.; London: Oxford
Univ. Pr. Pp. 390.
Rev. by E. E. White in *QJS*, XLVIII, 321;
in *TLS*, 5 Oct., p. 780; by Olive Brose in
VS, VI, 187-88.

Davis, David B. "The Emergence of Im-
mediatism in British and American Anti-
slavery Thought." *Miss. Valley Hist.
Rev.*, XLIX, 209-30.

Deane, Phyllis, and Cole, W. A. *British Economic Growth, 1688-1959.* New York
and Cambridge: Cambridge Univ. Pr.
Pp. xvi + 348.

Derry, Thomas Kingston, and Williams, Tre-
vor Illytd. *A Short History of Technology
from the Earliest Times to A.D. 1900.*
. . . See VB 1961, 363.
Rev. by D. E. Eichholz in *The Classical
Rev.*, XI, 282-83; by M. M. Knight in
JEH, XXII, 99.

Dickins, Molly. "Marianne North." *Cornhill*
(Spring), 319-29.

Draper, Frederick William Marsden. *Four
Centuries of Merchant Taylors' School,
1561-1961.* London and New York: Oxford Univ. Pr. Pp. 260.
Briefly rev. in *TLS*, 29 June, p. 482.

Duffy, A. E. P. "Differing Policies and Personal Rivalries in the Origins of the Independent Labour Party." *VS*, VI, 43-65.
Policies and rivalries are those of and
between Tom Mann, H. H. Champion,
Keir Hardie, Shaw, Blatchford, and
others.

Duncan, Bingham. "A Letter on the Fur Seal
in Canadian-American Diplomacy." *Canadian Hist. Rev.*, XLIII, 42-47.

Dyos, H. J. *Victorian Suburb: A Study of
the Growth of Camberwell.* . . . See VB
1961, 363.
Rev. by T. C. Barker in *Economica*, XXIX,
445-46; in *TLS*, 27 Apr., p. 278; by
Christopher Tunnard in *VS*, V, 272-74.

Eagly, Robert V. "Sir James Steuart and the
'Aspiration Effect.'" *Economica*, XXVIII,
53-61.

Edmonds, E. L. *The School Inspector.* London: Routledge and Kegan Paul. Pp.
xi + 202.
Rev. in *TLS*, 2 Nov., p. 839.

Edwardes, Michael. "The Viceroyalty of Lord
Curzon." *History Today*, XII, 833-44.

Edwards, Harold Raymond. *Competition and
Monopoly in the British Soap Industry.*
New York: Oxford Univ. Pr.; Oxford:
Clarendon Pr. Pp. 270.
Rev. in *TLS*, 3 Aug., p. 563.

Elliott, Blanche Beatrice. *A History of English Advertising.* London: Batsford. Pp.
xvi + 231.
Rev. in *TLS*, 5 Oct., p. 775.

Elton, Lord (ed.). *General Gordon's Khartoum Journal.* . . . See VB 1961, 363.
Rev. in *TLS*, 19 Jan., p. 39.

Engel, Claire-Elaine. *La Reine Victoria.*
Paris: Ed. du Seuil. Pp. 186.
Rev. in *Revue des deux mondes* (No. 7:
1 April), 478.

Evans, Eric Wyn. *The Miners of South
Wales.* . . . See VB 1961, 363.
Rev. by W. E. Minchinton in *VS*, V, 346-
47.

Fabunmi, L. A. *The Sudan in Anglo-Egyptian
Relations.* . . . See VB 1961, 363.
Rev. by Helen A. B. Rivlin in *JMH*,
XXXIV, 341-42.

Ferguson, William Thompson, and Immel-
man, René Frederick Malan (comps.).
*Sir John Herschel and Education at the
Cape, 1834-1840.* London: Oxford Univ.
Pr., 1961. Pp. xii + 94.

Fetter, Frank W. "Economic Articles in the
Westminster Review and Their Authors,
1824-51." *JPE*, LXX, 570-96.

Fetter, Frank W. "Robert Torrens: Colonel
of Marines and Political Economist."
Economica, XXIX, 152-65.

Fletcher, Geoffrey S. *Popular Art in England.*
London: Harrap. Pp. 80.

Foran, William Robert. *The Kenya Police,
1887-1960.* London: Robert Hale. Pp.
xvi + 237.

Forbes, Thomas R. "William Yarrell, British
Naturalist." *Proceedings of American
Philosophical Society*, CVI, 505-15.

Ford, Alec George. *The Gold Standard 1880-
1914: Britain and Argentina.* Oxford:
Clarendon Pr.; New York: Oxford Univ.
Pr. Pp. 200.

Ford, Percy and Grace (eds.). *Luke Graves
Hansard; His Diary, 1814-1841. A Case
Study in the Reform of Patronage.* Ox-
ford: Basil Blackwell. Pp. liv + 225.
Rev. by J. B. Childs in *BSP*, LVI, 505.

Fothergill, Brian. "Wiseman: The Man and

His Mission." *Wiseman Rev.* CCXXXVII (No. 493), 236-46.

Fox, Adam. *Dean Inge.* . . . See VB 1960, 374.
Rev. by Charles Smyth in *VS*, V, 261-63.

Fraser, P. "The Liberal Unionist Alliance: Chamberlain, Hartington, and the Conservatives, 1886-1904." *EHR*, LXXVII, 53-78.

Fyfe, Christopher. *A History of Sierra Leone.* Oxford: Clarendon Pr.; New York: Oxford Univ. Pr. Pp. vii + 773.
Rev. in *TLS*, 10 Aug., p. 574.

Gash, Norman. *Mr. Secretary Peel: The Life of Sir Robert Peel to 1830.* . . . See VB 1961, 364.
Rev. by David Roberts in *AHR*, LXVII, 392-93; by R. W. Lyman in *APSS*, CCCXXXIX, 185-86; by J. B. Conacher in *Canadian Hist. Rev.*, XLIII, 59-61; by E. G. Collieu in *History*, XLVII, 86-88; by Galen Broeker in *JMH*, XXXIV, 338-39; by P. H. Noyes in *PSQ*, LXXVI, 624; by R. J. White in *VS*, VI, 84-88.

Gavin, R. J. "The Bartle Frere Mission to Zanzibar, 1873." *CHJ*, V, 122-48.

Gernsheim, Helmut. *Creative Photography: Aesthetic Trends, 1839-1960.* London: Faber. Pp. 258.
Rev. in *TLS*, 17 Aug., p. 620.

Gettman, Royal A. *A Victorian Publisher.* . . . See VB 1961, 364.
Rev. by John Butt in *N & Q*, n.s. IX, 116-17.

Ghose, Dilip Kumar. *England and Afghanistan.* . . . See VB 1961, 364.
Rev. by Maurice Cowling in *EHR*, LXXVII, 804-05.

Gibbs-Smith, Charles Harvard. *Sir George Cayley's Aeronautics, 1796-1855.* London: H. M. S. O. Pp. xxiii + 269.
Rev. in *TLS*, 5 Oct., p. 779.

Gloag, John. *Victorian Taste: Some Social Aspects of Architecture and Industrial Design from 1820-1900.* New York: Macmillan; London: A. & C. Black. Pp. xvi + 175.
Rev. by William Plomer in *Listener*, 17 May, p. 868; by Paul von Khrum in *LJ*, LXXXVII, 2886; in *TLS*, 11 May, p. 332.

Godden, Geoffrey Arthur. *Victorian Porcelain.* . . . See VB 1961, 365.
Rev. by P. von Khrum in *LJ*, LXXXVII, 1779.

Gosden, Peter H. J. H. *The Friendly Societies in England, 1815-1875.* . . . See VB 1961, 365.
Rev. by David Owen in *AHR*, LXVII,

772-73; by Raymond G. Cowherd in *APSS*, CCCXL, 142-43; by F. C. Mather in *EHR*, LXXVII, 794-95; by W. H. Chaloner in *History*, XLVII, 84-85; by Bernard Semmel in *JEH*, XXII, 271-72; by John F. C. Harrison in *VS*, V, 267-68.

Graham, Thomas R. "The British Impact on Brazil, 1850-1918." *DA*, XXII, 3628-29.

Grampp, William Dyer. *The Manchester School of Economics.* . . . See VB 1961, 365.
Rev. by Peter Mathias in *EHR*, LXXVII, 337-38; by David Roberts in *JEH*, XXII, 109-10.

Gregory, Theodore. *Ernest Oppenheimer and the Economic Development of South Africa.* London: Oxford Univ. Pr. Pp. xx + 637.
Rev. in *TLS*, 14 Dec., p. 970.

Grimble, Ian. *The Trial of Patrick Sellars: The Tragedy of Highland Evictions.* London: Routledge and Kegan Paul. Pp. xviii + 166.

Guillebaud, C. W. (ed.). *A Marshall's Principles of Economics, Variorum Edition.* . . . See VB 1961, 365.
Rev. by D. H. Robertson in *Econ. Jour.*, XXIX, 677-84; by George J. Stigler in *JPE*, LXX, 282-86.

Gwyn, William Brent. *Democracy and the Cost of Politics in Britain.* London: Athlone Pr.; New York: Oxford Univ. Pr. Pp. vii + 256.
Rev. by A. Howard in *NS*, LXIII, 681; in *TLS*, 1 June, p. 382; by E. J. Feuchtwanger in *VS*, VI, 191-92.

Habakkuk, H. J. *American and British Technology in the Nineteenth Century: The Search for Labour-Saving Inventions.* Cambridge: Cambridge Univ. Pr. Pp. 222.
Rev. by T. C. Cochran in *AHR*, LXVIII, 172; by Leo Marx in *American Quart.*, XIV, 633; by Jacob M. Price in *JMH*, XXXIV, 450-51; by N. Rosenberg in *JPE*, LXX, 615-16; by George Basalla in *LJ*, LXXXVII, 2370; in *TLS*, 27 July, p. 539.

Habakkuk, H. J. "Fluctuations in House-Building in Britain and the United States in the Nineteenth Century." *JEH*, XXII, 198-230.

Haig, Charles Aneurin. *John Angell James (1785-1859).* London: Independent Pr. Pp. 23.
An early Victorian preacher.

Hall, Peter Geoffrey. *The Industries of London Since 1861.* London: Hutchinson.

Pp. 192.

Hall, Trevor Henry. *The Spiritualists: The Story of Florence Cook and William Crookes*. London: Duckworth. Pp. xix + 188.

Rev. by Arthur Calder-Marshall in *Listener*, 26 July, p. 147.

Hancock, Sir Keith. *Smuts, the Official Biography*. Vol. I: *The Sanguine Years, 1870-1919*. London and New York: Cambridge Univ. Pr. Pp. 618.

Rev. by David Lytton in *Listener*, 25 Oct., p. 681; by Asa Briggs in *NS*, LXIV, 672; by Nicholas Mansergh in *S*, 30 Nov., pp. 860-61.

Hargreaves, J. H. "Victorians in Africa." *VS*, VI, 75-80.

Harhetty, P. "The Indian Cotton Duties Controversy, 1894-1896." *EHR*, LXXVII, 684-702.

Harris, Alan. *The Rural Landscape of the East Riding of Yorkshire, 1700-1850*. University of Hull Publication, Oxford Univ. Pr., 1961, Pp. xvi + 136.

Rev. by J. W. House in *N & Q*, n.s. IX, 440.

Harrison, John Fletcher Clews. *Learning and Living, 1790-1960: A Study in the History of the English Adult Education Movement*. . . . See VB 1961, 365.

Rev. by David E. Wilder in *Amer. Jour. of Sociology*, LXVIII, 393-94; by James Winter in *Canadian Hist. Rev.*, LXIII, 243-45; by John Roach in *History*, XLVII, 315-17; by Paul B. Johnson in *JMH*, XXXIV, 448-49; by Raymond Williams in *NS*, LXIII, 21-22; by John Vaizey in *S*, 16 Feb., pp. 213-14; in *TLS*, 26 Jan., p. 59.

Harrison, Michael. *Painful Details: Twelve Victorian Scandals*. London: Max Parrish. Pp. 200.

Noticed in *TLS*, 11 May, p. 345.

Hayden, Eric W. *Spurgeon on Revival*. Grand Rapids, Mich.: Zondervan. Pp. 144.

Heasman, Kathleen. *Evangelicals in Action*. London: Bles. Pp. ix + 310.

Noticed in *TLS*, 9 Nov., p. 860.

Helm, Robert M. *The Gloomy Dean: The Thought of William Ralph Inge*. Winston-Salem: Blair. Pp. 310.

Hibbert, Christopher. *The Destruction of Lord Raglan*. . . . See VB 1961, 366.

Rev. by Raymond Postgate in *N*, 25 Aug., pp. 75-76; by Drew Middleton in *NYTBR*, 12 Aug., p. 21; by C. Northcote Parkinson in *SR*, 6 Oct., pp. 48-49.

Hilton, George W. *The Truck System: Including a History of the British Truck Acts, 1465-1960*. London: Heffer & Sons. Pp. ix + 166.

Rev. by T. C. Barker in *Economica*, XXIX, 444-45.

Hinchliff, Peter. "John William Colenso: A Fresh Appraisal." *Jour. of Eccl. Hist.*, XIII, 203-16.

Sympathetic and intelligent examination of Colenso as a missionary and a controversialist.

Hinsley, F. H. (ed.). *The New Cambridge Modern History*. Vol. XI. *Material Progress and Worldwide Problems, 1870-1898*. Cambridge and New York: Cambridge Univ. Pr. Pp. xi + 744.

Rev. by F. R. Salter in *CR*, CCII, 271-72; by Asa Briggs in *Listener*, 25 Oct., p. 677; by Geoffrey Barraclough in *S*, 21 Sept., pp. 405-06; in *TLS*, 7 Dec., pp. 945-46.

Hobsbawm, E. J. *The Age of Revolution (1789-1848)*. London: Weidenfeld and Nicolson. Pp. xvi + 356.

Rev. by A. J. P. Taylor in *NS*, LXIV, 780; by Desmond Williams in *S*, 28 Dec., p. 995.

A history from the Marxist point of view.

Holcombe, Lee. "Middle-Class Working Women in England, 1850-1914." *DA*, XXIII, 1004-05.

Holt, Edgar. *The Strangest War: The Story of the Maori Wars, 1860-1872*. London: Putnam. Pp. 280.

Rev. by Asa Briggs in *NS*, LXIV, 825; in *TLS*, 21 Dec., p. 985.

Hoskins, W. G. "Richard Thornton, 1776-1865: A Victorian Millionaire." *History Today*, XII, 574-79.

Howard, C. H. D. "Select Documents, XXI. Joseph Chamberlain, W. H. O'Shea, and Parnell, 1884-1891-2." *Irish Hist. Studies*, XIII, 33-38.

Howard, Christopher. "'Splendid Isolation.'" *History*, XLVII, 32-41.

Hufford, Roger A. "The Place of Ambiguity in Political Speaking." *DA*, XXIII, 746.

Focuses on Gladstone's speeches in the Irish home rule debates of 1866.

Humphreys, R. A. *The Diplomatic History of British Honduras, 1638-1901*. London: Oxford Univ. Pr., 1961. Pp. x + 196.

Rev. by Paul S. Lietz in *JMH*, XXXIV, 438-39.

Hunter, Jack W. "Some Research Problems in a Study of *The Corsican Brothers*."

The OSU Theatre Collection Bull., No. 9, pp. 6-22.

The production of Dion Boucicault's English version.

Huttenback, Robert A. *British Relations with Sind, 1799-1843: An Anatomy of Imperialism.* Berkeley: Univ. of California Pr.; Cambridge: Cambridge Univ. Pr. Pp. 161.

Jameson, Storm. *Morley Roberts: The Last Eminent Victorian.* . . . See VB 1961, 366.
Rev. by P. Coustillas in *Études anglaises*, XV, 197-98.

Jennings, Sir Ivor. *Party Politics.* Vol. III: *The Stuff of Politics.* New York and London: Cambridge Univ. Pr. Pp. ix + 492.
Rev. in *TLS*, 26 Jan., p. 51; by H. J. Hanham in *VS*, VI, 81-84.

Johnson, Franklyn Arthur. *Defence by Committee: The British Committee of Imperial Defence, 1885-1959.* . . . See VB 1961, 366.
Rev. by W. N. Medlicott in *EHR*, LXXVII, 580-81.

Jordan, R. Furneaux. "Pugin's Clients." *Cornhill* (Autumn), 26-42.

Jullian, Philippe. "Le Prince de Galles en France." *Revue de deux mondes* (No. 10: 15 May), 190-203.

Kardiner, Abram, and Preble, Edward. *They Studied Man.* . . . See VB 1961, 367.
Rev. by Collin Clark in *LJ*, LXXXVI, 1605; by Ashley Montagu in *NYTBR*, 13 Aug., 1961, p. 6; in *TLS*, 21 Sept., p. 745.

Keir, David Edwin. *The Bowring Story.* London: Bodley Head. Pp. 448.
History of a British shipping line.

Kellas, James G. "The Crofters' War, 1882-1888." *History Today*, XII, 281-88.
Establishment of Crofters' Commission to fix rents and secure tenure.

Kelly, Thomas. *A History of Adult Education in Great Britain.* Liverpool: Liverpool Univ. Pr. Pp. xii + 352.
Rev. in *TLS*, 24 Aug., p. 639.

Kemp, Betty. "Reflections on the Repeal of the Corn Laws." *VS*, V, 189-204.
Peel's tactics were to make repeal the work of Parliament and not the product of extra-Parliamentary influence.

Kennedy, S. D. "Victorian Ambassadress in Three Capitals." *QR*, Apr., 175-86.
Life of Lady Bloomfield, diplomat's wife.

Kidson, Peter, and Murray, Peter. *A History of English Architecture.* London: Harrap. Pp. 256.

Rev. in *TLS*, 10 Aug., p. 605.

Kurtz, Henry I. "The Undeclared War between Britain and America." *History Today*, XII, 777-83; 872-80.
Border disputes and American support of Canadian rebels between 1837 and 1842.

Lambert, R. J. "A Victorian National Health Service: State Vaccination, 1855-71." *CHJ*, V, 1-18.

Lambert, Royston. "Central and Local Relations in mid-Victorian England: The Local Government Act Office, 1858-71." *VS*, VI, 121-50.
The activities and development of the L.G.A.O., created in 1858 to give to localities the powers and responsibilities formerly centralized in the General Board of Health.

Lane, Margaret. "A Light-Hearted Explorer." *Listener*, 12 April, pp. 629-30.
Mary Kingsley (1862-1900), niece of Charles Kingsley.

Larkin, Emmet. "Church and State in Ireland in the Nineteenth Century." *Church Hist.*, XXI, 294-306.

Larsen, Egon. *The Cavendish Laboratory.* London: Edmund Ward. Pp. 95.
Rev. by G. Basalla in *LJ*, LXXXVII, 4032; in *TLS*, 9 Nov., p. 859. One of the early university laboratories in England, opened in 1873.

Latourette, Kenneth Scott. *Christianity in a Revolutionary Age.* Vol. III: *The Nineteenth Century outside Europe.* . . . See VB 1961, 367.
Rev. by Anne Pannell in *AHR*, LXVI, 999; by J. F. Maclear in *Jour. of Religion*, XLI, 305; by R. W. Schwarz in *LJ*, LXXXVI, 2109.

Lehmann, John. *Ancestors and Friends.* London: Eyre and Spottiswoode. Pp. 287.
Rev. by John Daniel in *Manchester Guardian Weekly*, 1 Nov., p. 10; by E. Lucie-Smith in *NS*, LXIV, 906-07; in *TLS*, 9 Nov., p. 855.
Records of a family whose acquaintances included many eminent Victorians.

Leigh, Denis. *The Historical Development of British Psychiatry.* Vol. I: *18th and 19th Century.* London: Pergamon Pr., 1961. Pp. xiv + 277.
Rev. in *TLS*, 27 Apr., p. 278.

Lipman, Vivian David (ed.). *Three Centuries of Anglo-Jewish History.* . . . See VB 1961, 367.
Rev. by A. S. Comyns-Carr in *CR*, CCII, 220-21; by Arthur J. Taylor in *History*, XLVII, 318-19.

Liu, Kwang-Ching. *Anglo-American Steamship Rivalry in China, 1862-1874*. London: Oxford Univ. Pr.; Cambridge, Mass.: Harvard Univ. Pr. Pp. xvii + 218.

Longford, Elizabeth. "Queen Victoria's Religious Life." *Wiseman Rev.*, CCXXXVI (No. 492), 107-26.

Luard, D. E. T. *Britain and China*. Baltimore: Johns Hopkins Pr.; London: Chatto and Windus. Pp. 256.
Rev. in *TLS*, 20 Apr., p. 259.

Lubbock, Eric. "Bank Holidays and Sir John Lubbock." *CR*, CCII, 322-24.

Lynch, Patrick, and Vaizey, John. *Guinness's Brewery in the Irish Economy, 1759-1876*. . . . See VB 1961, 367.
Rev. by D. C. Coleman in *JEH*, XXII, 279-80.

Lyons, F. S. L. *The Fall of Parnell*. . . . See VB 1961, 367.
Rev. by W. L. Burn in *EHR*, LXXVII, 197-98.

MacDonagh, Oliver. *A Pattern of Government Growth, 1800-60*.
London: MacGibbon and Kee, 1961. Pp. 368.
Rev. in *TLS*, 2 Feb., p. 71; by H. J. Dyos in *VS*, VI, 189-91.
Studies conditions of transport available to emigrants from Liverpool and practices worked out by the government to rectify worst abuses and regulate the enterprise.

Mackintosh, John P. *The British Cabinet*. London: Stevens & Sons Limited. Pp. xi + 546.
Rev. by Roland Young in *APSR*, LVI, 986-87.

Maclagan, Michael. *"Clemency" Canning*. London: Macmillan. Pp. xvi + 420.
Rev. by Francis Watson in *Listener*, 15 Nov., p. 823; in *TLS*, 7 Dec., p. 950.
A biography of the first Earl Canning, Governor-General of India during the Mutiny.

MacRae, Donald Gunn. *Ideology and Society*. New York: Free Press. Pp. 231.

Mannix, Daniel P. in collab. with Cowley, Malcolm. *Black Cargoes: A History of the Atlantic Slave Trade, 1518-1865*. New York: Viking. Pp. 306.
Unfavorably rev. by R. F. Kugler in *LJ*, LXXXVII, 4539.

Manson-Bahr, Sir Philip. *Patrick Manson, the Father of Tropical Medicine*. London: Nelson. Pp. viii + 192.

Marais, J. S. *The Fall of Kruger's Republic*. New York: Oxford Univ. Pr., 1961. Pp. xiv + 366.

Rev. by C. W. de Kiewiet in *JMH*, XXXIV, 106-07.

Marriner, Sheila. *Rathbones of Liverpool, 1845-1873*. . . . See VB 1961, 368.
Rev. by M. Greenberg in *Econ. Jour.*, LXXII, 212-14; by Margaret G. Myers in *JEH*, XXII, 120-21.

Martin, Robert Bernard. *Enter Rumour: Four Early Victorian Scandals*. London: Faber; New York: Norton. Pp. 258.
Rev. in *TLS*, 26 Oct., p. 822.

Martin, Kingsley. *The Magic of the British Monarchy*. Boston: Little, Brown. Pp. 192.
Rev. by R. R. Rea in *LJ*, LXXXVII, 3054; by Malcolm Muggeridge in *NS*, LXIII, 799; in *TLS*, 1 June, p. 383.

Masur, Gerhard. *Prophets of Yesterday*. . . . See VB 1961, 368.
Rev. by Harold T. Parker in *SAQ*, LXI, 278-79; by J. S. Shapiro in *SR*, 9 Dec., 1961, p. 23.

McBriar, A. M. *Fabian Socialism and English Politics, 1884-1918*. Cambridge and New York: Cambridge Univ. Pr. Pp. x + 387.
Rev. by Eugene P. Chase in *VQR*, XXXVIII, 693-96.

McClatchey, Diana. *Oxfordshire Clergy, 1777-1869*. . . . See VB 1961, 368.
Rev. by F. C. Mather in *EHR*, LXXVII, 385; by F. Bussby in *Jour. of Eccl. Hist.*, XIII, 129-30; by J. F. A. Mason in *N & Q*, n.s. IX, 191-92.

McClelland, Vincent Alan. *Cardinal Manning: His Public Life and Influence 1865-1892*. London: Oxford Univ. Pr. Pp. 256.
Rev. by C. Colleer Abbott in *Listener*, 18 Oct., pp. 625-26; by G. F. A. Best in *NS*, LXIV, 522; by David Lodge in *S*, 21 Dec., p. 967; in *TLS*, 28 Sept., p. 764.

McCormick, Donald. *Blood on the Sea*. London: Muller. Pp. 158.
Rev. by G. W. Stonier in *NS*, LXIV, 420. A case of cannibalism at sea that startled Victorian England.

McCormick, Donald. *The Temple of Love*. London: Jarrolds. Pp. 222.
Rev. by A. Howard in *NS*, LXIV, 260.
The Spaxton harem in Somerset.

McDowell, R. B. *British Conservatism, 1832-1914*. . . . See VB 1961, 368.
Rev. by James L. Godfrey in *SAQ*, LXI, 272-73.

McGill, Barry. "Francis Schnadhorst and the Liberal Party Organization." *JMH*, XXXIV, 19-39.

McIntyre, W. D. "British Policy in West

Africa: The Ashanti Expedition of 1873-4." *CHJ*, V, 19-46.

McKee, Alexander. *The Golden Wreck: the True Story of a Great Maritime Disaster.* New York: Morrow. Pp. 224.
Rev. by F. K. Cylke in *LJ*, LXXXVII, 2137.

Mechie, Stewart. *The Church and Scottish Social Development, 1780-1870.* . . . See VB 1961, 368.
Rev. by Alexander Law in *EHR*, LXXVII, 389-90.

Metcalf, Thomas R. "The British and the Moneylender in Nineteenth-Century India." *JMH*, XXXIV, 390-97.
The effect of British policy on rural Indian society.

Metcalfe, C. E. *Maclean of the Gold Coast: The Life and Times of George Maclean, 1801-1847.* New York and London: Oxford Univ. Pr. Pp. 344.
Rev. in *TLS*, 20 July, p. 522.

Milburn, D. "Impressions of an English Bishop at the First Vatican Council: Letters of Bishop Chadwick of Hexham and Newcastle to the President of Ushaw." *Wiseman Rev.*, CCXXXVII (No. 493), 217-35.

Moorehead, Alan. *The Blue Nile.* New York: Harper; London: Hamish Hamilton. Pp. 308.
Rev. by Edward Weeks in *AM*, CCX, 136; by Elspeth Huxley in *Listener*, 19 July, p. 107; by C. Haycraft in *NS*, LXIV, 371; by Basil Davidson in *NYTBR*, 12 Aug., p. 1; by Peter Fleming in *S*, 13 July, p. 58; in *TLS*, 13 July, p. 503.

Morgan, Edward Victor, and Thomas, W. A. *The Stock Exchange: Its History and Functions.* London: Elek. Pp. 293.

Morrell, W. P. *Britain in the Pacific Islands.* New York: Oxford Univ. Pr., 1960. Pp. ix + 454.
Rev. by S. C. McCulloch in *JMH*, XXXIV, 92-93.

Morris, Barbara. *Victorian Embroidery.* London: Herbert Jenkins; New York: Nelson. Pp. 238.
Rev. in *TLS*, 16 Nov., p. 868.

Mortimer, Roger. *The History of the Derby Stakes.* London: Cassell. Pp. xv + 695.
Rev. in *TLS*, 8 June, p. 431.

Morton, A. L. *The Life and Ideas of Robert Owen.* London: Lawrence and Wishart. Pp. 187.
Noticed in *TLS*, 26 Oct., p. 830.

Morton, Frederic. *The Rothschilds.* New

York: Atheneum; London: Secker and Warburg. Pp. 305.
Rev. by C. Georgi in *LJ*, LXXXVII, 552; in *TLS*, 21 Sept., p. 714.

Mowat, Charles Loch. *The Charity Organisation Society, 1869-1913.* . . . See VB 1961, 368.
Rev. by Ralph E. Pumphrey in *AHR*, LXVII, 774; by W. H. Chaloner in *History*, XLVII, 84-85; by Mary E. Seldon in *JMH*, XXXIV, 345.

Munford, William Arthur. *William Ewart, M.P., 1798-1869.* . . . See VB 1961, 368.
Rev. by L. F. MacRae in *LQ*, XXXII, 172-73.

Myers, Sydney. R. W. *Dale (1829-1895).* London: Independent Pr. Pp. 23.

Nicholls, David. "Positive Liberty, 1880-1914." *APSR*, LVI, 114-28.
An examination of the clash between "negative" and "positive" liberals in the period 1880-1914.

Nock, Oswald Stevens. *The Caledonian Railway.* London: I. Allan; New Rochelle, N. Y.: Sportshelf. Pp. 190.

Nock, Oswald Stevens. *The Great Western Railway in the Nineteenth Century.* London: I. Allan. Pp. 200.

Nock, Oswald Stevens. *Locomotives of the North Eastern Railway.* London: I. Allan; New Rochelle, N. Y.: Sportshelf. Pp. viii + 200.

Northcott, Cecil. *Robert Moffatt: Pioneer in Africa, 1817-1870.* New York: Harper; London: Lutterworth. Pp. 357.
Rev. by W. C. Harr in *Church Hist.*, XXXI, 373-74; by Neal Ascherson in *NS*, LXII, 893; in *TLS*, 5 Jan., p. 11.
Biography of David Livingstone's father-in-law.

Nugent, Elinor R. "The Relationship of Fashion in Women's Dress to Selected Aspects of Social Change from 1850 to 1950." *DA*, XXIII, 1112.

O'Brien, Conor Cruise (ed.). *The Shaping of Modern Ireland.* . . . See VB 1960, 378.
Rev. by C. L. Mowat in *Irish Hist. Studies*, XIII, 61-62.

O'Leary, Cornelius. *The Elimination of Corrupt Practices in British Elections, 1868-1911.* Oxford: Clarendon Pr.; New York: Oxford. Pp. 253.
Rev. by Asa Briggs in *Listener*, 10 May, p. 825; by A. Howard in *NS*, LXIII, 681; by E. J. Feuchtwanger in *VS*, VI, 191-92.

Paget, George Charles Henry Victor. *One-Leg: The Life and Letters of William*

Paget. . . . See VB 1961, 369.

Rev. by R. R. Rea in *LJ*, LXXXVII, 216; by Asa Briggs in *NS*, LXI, 922.

Palmer, A. W. *A Dictionary of Modern History, 1789-1945*. London: Cresset Pr. Pp. 314.

Noticed in *TLS*, 19 Oct., p. 814.

Parkinson, Cyril Northcote. *British Intervention in Malaya, 1867-1877*. . . . See VB 1961, 369.

Rev. by D. G. E. Hall in *EHR*, LXXVII, 193-94.

Payne, P. L. *Rubber and Railways in the Nineteenth Century*. . . .See VB 1961, 369.

Rev. by T. C. Barker in *Economica*, XXIX, 323-24.

Pearce, Gordon James Martin. *Charles Haddon Spurgeon (1834-1892)*. London: Independent Pr. Pp. 16.

Pearson, Hesketh. *The Marrying Americans*. . . . See VB 1961, 369.

Rev. by Phoebe Adams in *AM*, Sept. (1961), p. 104; by E. H. Smith in *HTB*, 3 Sept., 1961, p. 3; by K. T. Willis in *LJ*, LXXXVI, 2463; by R. R. James in *NS*, LXII, 251; by Cleveland Amory in *NYTBR*, 16 July, 1961, p. 12.

Pelling, Henry. *A Short History of the Labour Party*. . . . See VB 1961, 369.

Rev. by Donald Read in *History*, XLVII, 90.

Pemberton, William Baring. *Battles of the Crimean War*. London: Batsford; New York: Macmillan. Pp. 239.

Rev. by T. H. McGuffie in *History*, XLVII, 327-28; by David Rees in *S*, 27 Apr., p. 557; in *TLS*, 13 July, p. 507.

Peterson, Owen. "The Role of Public Speaking in the Early Years of the British Labour Party." *QJS*, XLVIII, 254-60.

Petrie, Sir Charles. *The Victorians*. . . . See VB 1961, 369.

Rev. by Chester Kirby in *AHR*, LXVII, 773; by Geoffrey Bruun in *HTB*, 21 Jan., p. 4.

Pinhorn, Malcolm. "Leonard Charles Smithers." *TLS*, 12 Oct., p. 800.

On the unhappy death of a publisher of the 'nineties. See also a letter by Martin Secker, *TLS*, 19 Oct., p. 809.

Pressnell, Leslie S. (ed.). *Studies in the Industrial Revolution*. . . . See VB 1961, 369.

Rev. by Eric Lampard in *AHR*, LXVII, 1018-19.

Prest, John. *The Industrial Revolution in Coventry*. . . . See VB 1961, 369.

Rev. by A. H. John in *Economica*, XXIX,

110-12; by W. H. Chaloner in *EHR*, LXXVII, 797-98; by J. D. Chambers in *History*, XLVII, 204.

Primrose, J. B. "The Pitsligo Press of George Hay Forbes." *Edinburgh Bibliographical Society Trans.*, IV, pt. 2 (Session 1956-57), 53-89.

A private press in Scotland, publishing between 1852 and 1883.

Pryde, George Smith. *Scotland from 1603 to the Present Day*. London: Nelson. Pp. viii + 359.

Rev. by G. D. McDonald in *LJ*, LXXXVII, 2746; by A. J. P. Taylor in *NS*, LXIII, 236; in *TLS*, 18 May, p. 355; in *YR*, LII, 120.

Ravner, Robert M. *Samuel Bailey and the Classical Theory of Value*. . . . See VB 1961, 370.

Rev. by M. Bowley in *Economica*, XXIX, 210-11.

Read, Donald. *Press and People, 1790-1850*. . . . See VB 1961, 370.

Rev. by E. R. Black in *Canadian Forum*, XLI, 187.

Read, Donald and Glasgow, Eric. *Feargus O'Connor, Irishman and Chartist*. . . . See VB 1961, 370.

Rev. by F. S. L. Lyons in *EHR*, LXXVII, 801-02; by Henry Pelling in *Irish Hist. Studies*, XIII, 93; by L. J. McCaffrey in *JMH*, XXXIV, 209; by R. K. Webb in *VS*, V, 266-67.

Reardon, Bernard M. G. (ed.). *Henry Scott Holland: A Selection from his Writings*. London: S.P.C.K. Pp. vii + 216.

Noticed in *TLS*, 7 Dec., p. 962.

A prominent late-Victorian clergyman.

Reeder, D. A. "The Politics of Urban Leaseholds in Late Victorian England." *International Rev. of Social Hist.*, VI, 413-30.

Reitlinger, Gerald. *The Economics of Taste, The Rise and Fall of Picture Prices, 1760-1960*. . . . See VB 1961, 375.

Rev. by Denys Sutton in *Burlington Mag.*, CIV, 437-38 (see also Reitlinger's reply, 543-44); by David Loshak in *VS*, V, 348-49.

Rennell, Lord. *Valley on the March: A History of a Group of Manors on the Herefordshire March of Wales*. Oxford: Oxford Univ. Pr., 1958. Pp. xv + 297.

Rev. by Edmund B. Fryde in *JEH*, XXII, 132-34.

Richard, Margaret and others (eds.). *Some Bedfordshire Diaries*.

Bedfordshire Historical Record Society,

Vol. XL, 1960. Pp. vi + 256.
Rev. by F. W. Steer in *N & Q*, n.s. IX, 199-200.
Includes several 19th Century diaries.

Richards, Rev. G. C. *An Oxonian Looks Back (1885-1945)*. New York: Columbia Univ. Pr., 1960.
Printed for Private Circulation by J. F. C. Richards. The memoirs of an Oxford classical scholar, including "a vivid picture of Rugby School" between 1875-1885.

Rimmer, William Gordon. *Marshalls of Leeds*. . . . See VB 1961, 370.
Rev. by R. K. Webb in *AHR*, LXVI, 1096; by William Woodruff in *JMH*, XXXIV, 445-46; in *TLS*, 30 June, 1961, p. 398.

Robbins, Richard Michael. *The Railway Age*. London: Routledge and Kegan Paul. Pp. x + 227.
Rev. by Jeremy Tunstall in *S*, 15 June, pp. 798-99; noticed in *TLS*, 29 June, p. 482.

Roberts, Charles. *The Radical Countess: The History of the Life of Rosalind Countess of Carlisle*. Carlisle: Steel Brothers. Pp. xii + 198.
Rev. in *TLS*, 20 July, p. 524.

Roberts, David. *Victorian Origins of the British Welfare State*. . . . See VB 1961, 370.
Rev. by W. H. Chaloner in *EHR*, LXXVII, 184-85.

Robinson, Ronald, Gallagher, John, and Denny, Alice. *Africa and the Victorians*. . . . See VB 1961, 370.
Rev. by Margaret Bates in *AHR*, LXVII, 1020-21; by Trevor Lloyd in *Canadian Hist. Rev.*, LXIII, 62-63; by Christopher Fyfe in *Irish Hist. Studies*, XIII, 93-94; by L. Barron in *LJ*, LXXXVII, 222; by Robert G. Gregory in *SAQ*, LXI, 411-12; by J. D. Hargreaves in *VS*, VI, 75-80; by Harry Rudin in *YR*, LI, 319-21.

Robson, John M. "Victorian Liberals." *TQ*, XXXI, 242-45.
Reviews recent books on Victorian thought, Mill, Arnold, and Harriet Martineau.

Rogers, P. G. *Battle in Bossenden Wood*. . . . See VB 1961, 370.
Rev. by F. C. Mather in *EHR*, LXXVII, 800-01; by Alan Everitt in *N & Q*, n.s. IX, 430-31.

Rolt, Lionel Thomas Caswell. *George and Robert Stephenson: The Railway Revolution*. . . . See VB 1960, 379.
Rev. by R. C. Black in *AHR*, LXVIII, 196; by R. R. McClarren in *LJ*, LXXXVII, 1891.

Roscoe, Theodora. "The Tinted Venus." *CR*, CCII, 33-36.
On John Gibson.

Rose, Saul. *Britain and South-East Asia*. London: Chatto and Windus. Pp. 208.

Roth, Cecil. *Essays and Portraits in Anglo-Jewish History*. Philadelphia: Jewish Publishing Society of America. Pp. xii + 318.

Routley, Erik. *English Religious Dissent*. . . . See VB 1961, 371.
Rev. by L. H. Carlson in *AHR*, LXVII, 185; by Anne Whitman in *History*, XLVII, 105-06; in *TLS*, 17 Feb., 1961, p. x.

Rutherford, James. *Sir George Grey, K.C.B. 1812-1898*. . . . See VB 1961, 371.
Rev. by W. P. Morrell in *EHR*, LXXVII, 545-48; by J. D. Hargreaves in *VS*, VI, 75-80.

Saul, Samuel Berrick, *Studies in British Overseas Trade, 1870-1914*. . . . See VB 1961, 371.
Rev. by H. H. Liesner in *Econ. Jour.*, LXXII, 947-49; by David Landes in *VS*, V, 344-46.

Semmel, Bernard. *The Governor Eyre Controversy*. London: MacGibbon and Kee. Pp. 189.
Rev. by Brian Chapman in *Manchester Guardian Weekly*, 6 Dec., p. 10; in *TLS*, 28 Dec., p. 998.

Semmel, Bernard. *Imperialism and Social Reform: English Social-Imperial Thought, 1895-1914*. Cambridge, Mass.: Harvard Univ. Pr., 1960. Pp. 283.
Rev. by G. L. Goodman in *JMH*, XXXIV, 107-08.

Sewter, A. C. "The Place of Charles Winston in the Victorian Revival of the Art of Stained Glass." *Journal of the Archaeological Association*, 3rd ser., XXIV (1961), 80-91.

Shattuck, Charles H. (ed.). *William Charles Macready's "King John."* Urbana: Univ. of Illinois Pr. Pp. 75.
Facsimile of Macready's promptbook.

Short, H. L. "Priestley and Martineau." *HJ*, LX, 211-19.

Simey, T. S., and Simey, Margaret Bayne. *Charles Booth: Social Scientist*. . . . See VB 1961, 371.
Rev. by Everett C. Hughes in *VS*, V, 268-69.

Simmons, Jack. *The Railways of Britain: An Historical Introduction*. . . . See VB 1961, 371.
Rev. by W. H. Chaloner in *History*, XLVII, 89.

Simpson, F. A. "England and the Italian War of 1859." *CHJ*, V, 111-21.

Singer, George C. "T. J. Wise and the Technique of Promotion." *Book Collector*, XI, 347-48.

Sitwell, Osbert. *Tales My Father Taught Me.* Hutchinson. Pp. 206.
Rev. by William Plomer in *Listener*, 8 March, pp. 428, 431.

Smellie, K. B. *Great Britain Since 1688.* Ann Arbor: Univ. of Michigan Pr. Pp. 462.
Rev. by R. R. Rea in *LJ*, LXXXVII, 4435.

Smith, Corinna Lindon. *Interesting People: Eighty Years with the Great and Near-great.* Norman: Univ. of Okla. Pr. Pp. 456.
Rev. by B. B. Libaire in *LJ*, LXXXVII, 2534; by R. P. Corsin in *NYTBR*, 24 June, p. 10.

Smyth, Sir John. *Sandhurst.* . . . See VB 1961, 371.
Rev. by Brian Bond in *Listener*, 25 Jan., p. 191.

Snyder, Louis Leo (ed.). *The Imperialism Reader.* Princeton, N. J.: Van Nostrand. Pp. 619.

Southgate, Donald. *The Passing of the Whigs, 1832-1886.* London: Macmillan; New York: St. Martin's Pr. Pp. 488.
Rev. by Paul Johnson in *NS*, LXIV, 201-02; by Robert Blake in *S*, 10 Aug., p. 191; in *TLS*, 24 Aug., p. 638.

Sparrow, Gerald. *Gordon: Mandarin and Pasha.* London: Jarrold's. Pp. 187.
Noticed in *TLS*, 28 Dec., p. 1010.

Spence, Clark C. *God Speed the Plow: The Coming of Steam Cultivation to Great Britain.* . . . See VB 1961, 371.
Rev. by G. E. Fussell in *EHR*, LXXVII, 186-87.

Spencer, Herbert. *London's Canal.* . . . See VB 1961, 372.
Rev. in *TLS*, 26 Jan., p. 62.

St. John-Stevas, Norman. "The Victorian Conscience: An Assessment and Explanation." *Wiseman Rev.*, CCXXXVII (No. 493), 247-59.

Stafford, Ann. *A Match to Fire the Thames.* . . . See VB 1961, 372.
Rev. by Margaret Cole in *Listener*, 4 Jan., p. 524; in *TLS*, 12 Jan., p. 23; by A. E. Musson in *VS*, V, 347-48.

Stanford, John Keith (ed.). *Ladies in the Sun: The Memsahibs' India, 1790-1860.* London: Galley Pr. Pp. xii + 145.
Rev. by Cyril Ray in *S*, 20 April, pp. 517-18; noticed in *TLS*, 27 April, p. 286.

Stanley, Richard and Neame, Alan (eds.). *The Exploration Diaries of Henry Morton Stanley.* New York: Vanguard. Pp. 208.
Rev. by L. Barron in *LJ*, LXXXVII, 3057.

Stansky, Peter. "Lyttelton and Thring: A Study in Nineteenth-Century Education." *VS*, V, 205-23.

Stasny, John F. "W. Winwood Reade's *The Martyrdom of Man*: A Darwinian History." *Philological Papers* (W. Va. U.), XIII, 37-49.

Steen, Marguerite. " 'Only Me,' An Appreciation of Mary Kingsley." *Listener*, 11 Oct., pp. 561-62.

Steen, Marguerite. *A Pride of Terrys.* London: Longmans, Green. Pp. xvi + 412.
Rev. in *TLS*, 16 March, p. 183.
On Kate, Ellen, Fred, and others of the great theatrical family.

Stern, Walter M. *Britain Yesterday and Today: An Outline Economic History from the Middle of the Eighteenth Century.* London: Longmans, Green. Pp. 294.
Rev. by C. Ehrlich in *Economica*, XXIX, 432-33.

Stern, Walter M. *The Porters of London.* London: Longmans, 1960. Pp. xvi + 346.
Rev. by H. J. Dyos in *Economica*, XXVIII, 104-05; by Wallace T. MacCaffrey in *JEH*, XXII, 140.

Stokes, Eric. "Milnerism." *CHJ*, V, 47-60.
The Boer War was not the spontaneous expression of popular imperialism or jingoism it has sometimes been thought, but the calculated policy of Lord Milner.

Strang, Lord. *Britain in World Affairs: A Survey of the Fluctuations in British Power and Influence, Henry VIII to Elizabeth II.* New York: Frederick A. Praeger, 1961. Pp. 426.
Rev. by P. H. Hardacre in *AHR*, LXVII, 389-90; by Austen Albu in *APSS*, CCCXXXIX, 186-87; by H. R. Winkler in *JMH*, XXXIV, 189-90.

Swart, Koenraad W. " 'Individualism' in the Mid-Nineteenth Century." *JHI*, XXIII, 77-90.
Definition and use of *individualism* by philosophers and political writers in mid-nineteenth century Europe, including in England Mill and Carlyle.

Symonds, Robert W., and Whineray, Bruce Blundell. *Victorian Furniture.* London: Country Life. Pp. 232.
Rev. by Evelyn Waugh in *S*, 19 Oct., pp. 599-600; in *TLS*, 16 Nov., p. 868.

Taylor, O. H. *A History of Economic Thought.* . . . See VB 1961, 372.

Rev. by B. Corry in *Economica*, XXIX, 102-03.
Telling, Marjorie Beach. *Over My Shoulder.* London: Hogarth Pr. Pp. 111.
Rev. in *TLS*, 3 Aug., p. 554.
Reminiscences of late-Victorian rectory life.
Temperley, Nicholas. "Mendelssohn's Influence on English Music." *M & L*, XLIII, 224-33.
Thomas, Hugh. *The Story of Sandhurst.* . . . See VB 1961, 372.
Rev. by Brian Bond in *Listener*, 25 Jan., p. 191.
Thomas, W. E. S. "Francis Place and Working Class History." *CHJ*, V, 61-70.
Thompson, Brooks. "A Letter of Roger Casement (1888) in the Sanford Collection." *EHR*, LXXVII, 98-102.
Tibawi, Abdul Latif. *British Interests in Palestine, 1800-1901.* . . . See VB 1961, 372.
Rev. by Edward Every in *Jour. of Eccl. Hist.*, XIII, 271; in *TLS* 12 Jan., p. 29.
Tilleux, Geneva F. M. "The Paintings of James McNeill Whistler." *DA*, XXIII, 1318.
Tischendorf, Alfred. *Great Britain and Mexico in the Era of Porfirio Diaz.* Durham: Duke Univ. Pr., 1961. Pp. xii + 197.
Rev. by Howard F. Cline in *APSS*, CCCXXXIX, 183; by J. Fred Rippy in *JMH*, XXXIV, 104-05.
Tisdall, Evelyn Ernest Percy. *Queen Victoria's Private Life, 1837-1901.* . . . See VB 1961, 372.
Rev. by E. H. S. in *HTB*, 25 Mar., p. 9; by D. W. Brogan in *NYTBR*, 18 Feb., p. 7.
Todd, John Murray. *African Mission.* London: Burnes and Oates. Pp. 230.
History of Society of African Missions.
Toller, Jane. *Papier-Maché in Great Britain and America.* London: G. Bell. Pp. 126.
Noticed in *TLS*, 23 Nov., p. 296, as "a particularly useful contribution to Victorian studies."
Tomasson, Katherine, and Buist, Francis. *Battles of the '45.* London: Batsford; New York: Macmillan. Pp. 216.
Rev. by Joanna Richardson in *Listener*, 18 Oct., p. 629.
Tsuzuki, Chushichi. *H. M. Hyndman and British Socialism.* . . . See VB 1961, 372.
Rev. by S. R. Graubard in *AHR*, LXVII, 190; by Margaret Cole in *APSS*, CCCXXXIX, 187-88; by P. P. Poirier in *PSQ*, LXXVII, 138.

Tucker, G. S. L. *Progress and Profits in British Economic Thought, 1650-1850.* . . . See VB 1961, 372.
Rev. by Lionel Robbins in *Econ. Jour.*, LXXII, 374-76.
Turner, Ernest Sackville. *What the Butler Saw: Two Hundred and Fifty Years of the Servant Problem.* London: Michael Joseph. Pp. 304.
Rev. by William Plomer in *Listener*, 4 Oct., pp. 530-31; by M. Muggeridge in *NS*, LXIV, 674; in *TLS*, 5 Oct., p. 779.
Tute, Warren. *Atlantic Conquest.* London: Cassell; Boston: Little, Brown. Pp. 247.
Rev. briefly in *TLS*, 18 May, p. 362.
Transatlantic shipping 1816 to the present.
Unruh, Fred P. "A Historical Study of Robert Vaughan and His Views on Politics, Education, Religion and History as Reflected in the *British Quarterly Review.*" *DA*, XXIII, 1005-06.
Conservative dissenters, 1845-65.
Van Trump, James D., and Ziegler, Arthur P., Jr. "Thomas Bird Mosher, Publisher and Pirate." *Book Collector*, XI, 295-312.
American publisher of elegantly designed collections of the work of late-century writers infrequently published in America.
Victoria, Queen. *Leaves from a Journal.* . . . See VB 1961, 372.
Rev. by E. H. Smith in *HTB*, 11 Feb., p. 15.
Waite, P. B. "Edward Cardwell and Confederation." *Canadian Hist. Rev.*, XLIII, 17-41.
Wakefield, Hugh. *Nineteenth-Century British Glass.* . . . See VB 1961, p. 372.
Rev. in *TLS*, 5 Jan., p. 4.
Wakefield, Hugh. *Victorian Pottery.* London: Herbert Jenkins. Pp. 208.
Rev. in *TLS*, 9 Nov., p. 852.
Waller, John O. "Edward Dicey and the American Negro in 1862: An English Working Journalist's View." *Bull. New York Pub. Libr.*, LXVI, 31-45.
Ward, John Trevor. *The Factory Movement, 1830-1855.* London: Macmillan. Pp. xi + 515.
Waterhouse, Rachel Elizabeth. *Children in Hospital: A Hundred Years of Child Care in Birmingham.* London: Hutchinson. Pp. 136.
White, James F. *The Cambridge Movement: The Ecclesiologists and the Gothic*

Revival. Cambridge: Cambridge Univ. Pr. Pp. xii + 272.
Rev. by Wm. H. Baar in *Church Hist.,* XXI, 371-72.

Whiteside, Thomas. *The Tunnel under the Channel.* New York: Simon and Schuster; London: Hart-Davis. Pp. 133.
Rev. by J. E. Rivers in *S,* 23 Nov., p. 827.

Whitridge, Arnold. "British Liberals and the American Civil War." *History Today,* XII, 688-95.
See also remonstrance by R. F. Betteridge, 863, and Mr. Whitridge's reply, 863, 881.

Wickenden, Thomas Douglas. *William Ellis School, 1862-1962.* London: William Ellis School. Pp. 305.
Briefly rev. in *TLS,* 23 Mar., p. 206.

Williams, James Eccles. *The Derbyshire Miners: A Study in Industrial and Social History.* London: Allen and Unwin. Pp. 936.
Rev. by John Saville in *VS,* VI, 192-94.

Williamson, Jeffrey G. "The Long Swing: Comparisons and Interactions between British and American Balance of Payments, 1820-1913." *JEH,* XXII, 21-46.

Winstone, Reece. *Bristol in the 1880's.* Bristol: The Author (23 Hyland Grove, Henbury Hill, Bristol 9). Pp. 104.
Noticed in *TLS,* 21 Sept., p. 748.
200 photographs with commentary.

Woodcock, George. "The Army of the Pure." *History Today,* XII, 603-13.
Military exploits of the Sikhs, under British and Indian rulers.

Woodham-Smith, Cecil. *The Great Hunger: Ireland 1845-1849.* London: Hamilton. Pp. xiv + 385.
Rev. by Joanna Richardson in *Listener,* 22 Nov., p. 871; by A. J. P. Taylor in *NS,* LXIV, 741-42; by D. W. Brogan in *S,* 23 Nov., pp. 830-31; in *TLS,* 16 Nov., p. 872.

Woodham-Smith, Cecil. "Victorian Comfort." *Listener,* 22 Nov., p. 851.

Woodhowe, C. M. "The Missing Telegrams and the Jameson Raid." *History Today,* XII, 395-404; 506-14.
The committee which investigated the Raid saw various textual versions of the telegrams.

Woodward, Ernest Llewellyn. *The Age of Reform, 1815-1870.* 2nd ed. London and New York: Oxford Univ. Pr. Pp. xix + 681.
Rev. by A. J. P. Taylor in *NS,* LXIII, 832-33; in *TLS,* 20 July, p. 524.

Woodward, John. "Wilkie's Portrait of Esdaile." *Burlington Mag.,* CIV, 117.
Describes rediscovered portrait painted in 1836.

Young, G. M. *Victorian Essays.* New York and London: Oxford Univ. Pr. Pp. 216.

III. MOVEMENTS OF IDEAS AND LITERARY FORMS

Aarsleff, Hans. "The Early History of the Oxford English Dictionary." *Bull. New York Pub. Libr.,* LXVI, 417-39.

Altick, Richard D. "The Sociology of Authorship: The Social Origins, Education, and Occupations of 1,100 British Writers, 1800-1935." *Bull. New York Pub. Libr.,* LXVI, 389-404.

Barber, R. W. *Arthur of Albion: An Introduction to the Arthurian Literature and Legends of England.* London: Barrie and Rockliff, 1961. Pp. 218.
Rev. by R. T. Davies in *RES,* n.s. XIII, 399-400.
Includes "reasons for Arthur's dramatic reappearance in the 12th and 19th centuries."

Basden, E. B. "Job Lousley and Letters to James Hardy on Provincialisms." *N & Q,* n.s. IX, 83-85.

Bicknell, John W. "On a Certain Deficiency in Victorian Anthologies." *VNL,* No. 22 (Fall), pp. 23-26.
Utilitarian and rationalist writers (*e.g.,* Mill, Huxley, Harrison, Stephen) are inadequately represented in Victorian anthologies.

Billingsley, Bruce A. " 'Take Her Up Tenderly': A Study of the Fallen Woman in the Nineteenth-Century English Novel." *DA,* XXIII, 1661-62.
Includes Thackeray, Dickens, Gaskell, Eliot, Meredith, Trollope, Hardy.

Booth, Wayne C. *The Rhetoric of Fiction.* Chicago: Univ. of Chicago Pr., 1961. Pp. xiv + 456.
Rev. by Mark Roberts in *EC,* XII, 322-34; by Donald H. Reiman in *SAQ,* XLI, 427; noticed in *VS,* V, 276.

Bowman, Sylvia (ed.). *Edward Bellamy Abroad.* New York: Twayne. Pp. 543.
Includes chapter on Bellamy's influence in England.

Brower, Reuben A. and Poirier, Richard (eds.). *In Defense of Reading: A Reader's*

Approach to Literary Criticism. New York: Dutton. Pp. 311.
Rev. by Rosemary Neiswender in *LJ*, LXXXVII, 1904.
Contains material on Arnold and Yeats.

Bryant, Donald C. (ed.). "After Goodrich: New Resources in British Public Address: A Symposium." *QJS*, XLVIII, 1-14.
On the use of Goodrich's *Select British Eloquence*, 1852.

Buckley, Jerome H. "The Fourth Dimension of Victorianism." *VNL*, No. 21 (Spring), pp. 1-4.
"The significance of time as a motif in Victorian culture."

Cassou, Jean, Langui, Emil, and Pevsner, Nikolaus. *Gateway to the Twentieth Century: Art and Culture in a Changing World.* New York: McGraw-Hill. Pp. 362.
Rev. by John Canaday in *NYTBR*, 24 June, p. 7.
Art nouveau and other developments at the end of the nineteenth century.

Coleman, William. "Lyell and the 'Reality' of Species: 1830-1833." *Isis*, LIII, 325-38.

Courthion, Pierre. *Romanticism.* Tr. Stuart Gilbert. Cleveland: World. Pp. 137.
Rev. by P. von Khrum in *LJ*, LXXXVII, 214.
Relationship between Delacroix and Constable.

Davie, George Elder. *The Democratic Intellect.* . . . See VB 1961, 373.
Rev. by Maurice Lee, Jr. in *AHR*, LXVII, 1096.

Davies, Hugh Sykes (ed.). *The Poets and their Critics:* Vol. II: *Blake to Browning.* London: Hutchinson. Pp. 351.
Rev. by Philip Hobsbaum in *Listener*, 19 July, p. 111; by G. M. Matthews in *S*, 27 July, p. 123; in *TLS*, 13 July, p. 510.

Duerksen, Roland A. "Shelleyan Ideas in Victorian Literature." *DA*, XXII, 3199.

Duncan, Joseph E. *The Revival of Metaphysical Poetry: The History of a Style, 1800 to Present.* . . . See VB 1961, 374.
Rev. by William D. Templeman in *The Personalist*, XLIII, 130-31.

Earle, Peter G. *Unamuno and English Literature.* New York: Hispanic Institute in the United States, 1960. Pp. 160.
Rev. by J. M. Alberich in *Hispanic Review*, XXX, 59-62.
The reviewer dislikes the treatment of Unamuno and Carlyle, Tennyson, and Browning.

Ellmann, Richard (ed.). *Edwardians and Late Victorians.* . . . See VB 1961, 374.

Rev. by Joan Rees in *MLR*, LVII, 309-10; by Lionel Stevenson in *RES*, n.s. XIII, 88-89.

Fairchild, Hoxie Neal. *Religious Trends in English Poetry.* Vol. V: *1880-1920, Gods of a Changing Poetry.* New York: Columbia University Pr. Pp. 663.
Rev. by J. R. Willingham in *LJ*, LXXXVII, 4018.
Includes discussions of Hopkins, Hardy, Housman, and Yeats.

Fletcher, Ifan Kyrle. "The Royal Marylebone Theatre." *Theatre Notebook,* XVII, 7-9.

Fletcher, Richard M. "English Romantic Drama: 1795-1843. A Critical and Historical Study." *DA*, XXIII, 1364.
Includes discussion of Bulwer, Horne, and Browning.

Foakes, Reginald A. *The Romantic Assertion: A Story in the Language of Nineteenth Century Poetry.* . . . See VB 1958, 367.
Rev. by A. Durandeau in *Études anglaises,* XXV, 83-84.

Frankl, Paul. *The Gothic: Literary Sources and Interpretations through Eight Centuries.* Princeton Univ. Pr., 1960. Pp. x + 916.
Rev. by Nathan Edelman and Phoebe Stanton in *MLN*, LXXVII, 541-47.
Includes discussions of Ruskin, Pugin, Gilbert Scott, and others.

Fulweiler, Howard W. "Tractarians and Philistines: The *Tracts for the Times* Versus Victorian Middle-Class Values." *Historical Mag. of the Protestant Episcopal Church,* XXXI, 36-53.
Tracts antagonistic to both middle-class protestant religious opinion and to secular spirit of "common-sense materialism."

Goldfarb, Russell M. "Late Victorian Decadence." *JAA*, XX, 369-73.
An essay in definition (cf. Ryals, VB 1958, 370, and Peters, VB 1959, 426) based on a survey of critical reactions to decadence, 1890 to the present.

Golding, Alfred S. "The Theory and Practice of Presentational Acting in the Serious Drama of France, England and Germany during the Eighteenth and Nineteenth Centuries." *DA*, XXIII, 745-46.

Gilmour, J. S. L. "Contemporary Collectors, XXXI: A Freethought Collection and Its Predecessors." *Book Collector*, XI, 184-96.
Collection includes George Eliot's translation of Strauss' *Leben Jesu*, all the numbers of George Jacob Holyoake's *The

Oracle of Reason, James Anthony Froude's *Shadows of the Clouds,* Francis Newman's *Phases of Faith,* and a copy of a children's story by William Kingdon Clifford.

Gossman, Norbert J. "Republicanism in Nineteenth Century England." *International Rev. of Social History,* VII, 47-60.

Gray, Donald J. "Humor as Poetry in Nineteenth-Century Criticism." *JEGP,* LXI, 249-57.

Green, Roger L. "The Golden Age of Children's Books." *Essays and Studies by Members of the English Assoc.,* XV, 59-87.
Many Victorian authors included in this appraisal.

Gregor, Ian, and Nicholas, Brian. *The Moral and the Story.* London: Faber. Pp. 275.
Rev. by Martin Turnell in *Listener,* 22 Feb., p. 349; by John Gross in NS, LXIII, 236-37.
Includes treatment of Eliot, Hardy, George Moore.

Gregory, Horace. *The World of James McNeill Whistler.* . . . See VB 1961, 374.
Rev. by Michael Jaffe in S, 23 Feb., pp. 248-49.

Harris, Wendell. "Innocent Decadence: The Poetry of the *Savoy.*" *PMLA,* LXXVII, 629-36.

Heilbrun, Carolyn G. *The Garnett Family.* . . . See VB 1961, 374.
Rev. by Aileen Pippett in *SR,* 14 Oct., 1961, p. 37.

Hetherington, Hugh W. *Melville's Reviewers, British and American, 1846-1891.* Chapel Hill: Univ. of North Carolina Pr., 1961. Pp. x + 304.
Rev. by William Braswell in *AL,* XXXIII, 538-39; by M. L. Allen in *MLR,* LVII, 598; by Richard H. Fogle in *NEQ,* XXXV, 264-66.

Hofmann, Werner. *The Earthly Paradise: Art in the Nineteenth Century.* . . . See VB 1961, 374.
Rev. by Jacques Vallette in *Mercure de France,* CCCXLV, 721-22; by A. Brookner in *NS,* LXIV, 206-07; in *TLS,* 21 Sept., p. 718.

Honig, Edwin. *Dark Conceit: The Making of Allegory.* Evanston: Northwestern Univ. Pr., 1959. Pp. ix + 210.
Rev. by Joseph N. Riddel in *SAQ,* LXI, 115-16.

Hough, Graham. "The Muse and Her Chains." *Listener,* 3 May, 763-65; 10 May, 803-05; 17 May, 843-45.

Much attention is given to Arnold's claims for the power of poetry.

Hulin, J.-P. "Exotisme et littérature sociale au debut de l'ère victorienne." *Études anglaises,* XV, 411-12.

Huntley, John. "Aline and Henry Harland, Aubrey Beardsley, and 'The Yellow Book': A Verification of Some Evidence." *N & Q,* n.s. IX, 107-08.

Jacobi, Erwin R. *Die Entwicklung der Musiktheorie in England Nach der Zeit von Jean-Phillippe Rameau.* (Sammlung Musikwisserschaftlichen Abhandlungen, Vols. 35, 39, 39a.) Strasbourg: P. H. Heitz, 1957, 1960. Pp. 10, 39; 6, 186; 5, 149.
Rev. by Wm. J. Mitchell in *Musical Quart.,* XLVIII, 254-60.
English theorists of the Nineteenth Century.

Johnson, Wendell Stacy. "Victorian Self-Consciousness." *VNL,* No. 21 (Spring), pp. 4-7.
The Victorians' attempts to capture their own elusive identity.

Kissane, James. "Victorian Mythology." *VS,* VI, 5-28.
Discusses the Nineteenth-Century "aesthetic" conception of mythology as a treatment of ethical or psychological truth.

Kneale, William and Martha. *The Development of Logic.* London: Oxford Univ. Pr. Pp. 761.
Rev. by A. J. Ayer in *NS,* LXIII, 650.

Kreisel, Henry. "Recent Criticism of the Novel." *TQ,* XXXI, 246-50.
Omnibus review, including recent books on George Eliot and Dickens.

Laski, Marghanita. *Ecstasy: A Study of Some Secular and Religious Experiences.* London: Cresset Pr., 1961. Pp. xiv + 544.
Rev. by D. Hudson in *N & Q,* n.s. IX, 432.
Analyzes texts by Tennyson and the Brontës.

Laski, Marghanita, and Offord, M. Y. "Words from Lady Charlotte Schreiber's Journals." *N & Q,* n.s. IX, 89-92; 147-50; 167-71.

Lewis, Naomi. "Palgrave and his 'Golden Treasury'." *Listener,* 4 Jan., pp. 23, 26.
(See also "Victorian Parnassus," p. 10.)

Lochhead, Marion. "Victorian Rooms in Fiction." *QR,* July, pp. 318-28.

Lukács, Georg. *The Historical Novel.* London: Merlin Pr. Pp. 363.
Rev. by Raymond Williams in *Listener,* 8 March, pp. 436-37.

Maison, Margaret M. *The Victorian Vision: Studies in the Religious Novel.* New York: Sheed and Ward. Pp. 360.
Published in England in 1961 by the same publisher under the title, *Search Your Soul, Eustace.* Rev. in *TLS,* 9 Mar., p. 154; by Horton Davies in *VS,* VI, 90-91.

Marshall, William H. "Some English Verses of Sir John Taylor Coleridge." *Libr. Chronicle, Univ. of Penna.,* XXVIII, 1-13.

Mercier, Vivian. *The Irish Comic Tradition.* Oxford: Clarendon Pr. Pp. xx + 258.

Milne, Alan John Mitchell. *The Social Philosophy of English Idealism.* London: Allen and Unwin. Pp. 320.
Rev. by W. M. Simon in *VS,* VI, 194-95. Study of philosophy of Bradley, Green, Bosanquet, and Royce.

Morgan, Estelle. "Bourgeois and Philistine." *MLR,* LVII, 69-72.
European sources for the epithet.

Muir, Edwin. *The Estate of Poetry.* Foreword by Archibald MacLeish. Cambridge: Harvard Univ. Pr. Pp. 118.
Rev. by J. R. Willingham in *LJ,* LXXXVII, 1136; by Geoffrey Grigson in *NS,* LXIV, 330; by Horace Gregory in *NYTBR,* 11 Mar., p. 5; by D. G. Hoffman in *SR,* 30 June, p. 20.
Contains an essay on Yeats.

Munby, A. N. L. *The Dispersal of the Phillipps Library.* Phillipps Studies No. 5. Cambridge Univ. Pr., 1960. Pp. xi + 204.
Rev. by Louis B. Wright in *BSP,* LVI, 140-42.
The library of a Victorian book collector.

Newsome, David. *Goodliness and Good Learning.* . . . See VB 1961, 375.
Rev. by John Kent in *VS,* VI, 188-89.

Orel, Harold, and Worth, George J. (eds.). *Six Studies in Nineteenth-Century English Literature and Thought.* Lawrence: Univ. of Kansas Publications, Humanistic Studies, No. 35. Pp. 122.
Contains essays on "Browning's Use of Historical Sources in *Stafford,*" by Harold Orel; "Liberalism in the Political Philosophy of Thomas Hill Green," by Walter E. Sandelius; "The Intruder-Motif in George Eliot's Fiction," by George J. Worth; "Evidence and Testimony: Philip Henry Gosse and the *Omphalos* Theory," by Peter Cows; and "Swinburne, the *Spectator* in 1862, and Walter Bagehot," by W. D. Paden.

Parker, W. M. "Lady Davy in Her Letters." *QR,* Jan., 79-89.
Letters of a literary lady, cousin of Scott

and friend of Lockhart, written 1806-55.

Payne, Ernest A. "The Period of Establishment, 1828-1910." *LQHR,* CLXXXVII (6th ser., XXXI), 193-97.
One of a series on the history of Protestant Dissent in England from 1662 to the present.

Pearson, Hesketh. *Lives of the Wits.* London: Heinemann; New York: Harper & Row. Pp. 334.
Rev. by M. Muggeridge in *NS,* LXIV, 82. Includes Chesterton, Sydney Smith, Disraeli, W. S. Gilbert, Beerbohm Tree, Wilde, and Shaw.

Peckham, Morse. *Beyond the Tragic Vision: The Quest for Identity in the Nineteenth Century.* New York: George Braziller. Pp. 380.
Rev. by T. M. Bogie in *LJ,* LXXXVII, 1131; by George Steiner in *NYTBR,* 1 July, p. 5; by Oliver Warner in *SR,* 2 June, p. 38; by Mark Spilka in *VS,* VI, 92-93; by Wm. C. DeVane in *YR,* LII, 112-18.

Pritchett, V. S. "Saints and Rogues." *Listener,* 6 Dec., pp. 957-59.

Rees, Richard. *For Love or Money.* . . . See VB 1961, 375.
Rev. by H. G. Porteus in *S,* 12 Aug., 1960, p. 255.

Richardson, J. "Pan & Co." *NS,* LXIV, 657-58.

Rosenbaum, Robert A. *Earnest Victorians.* . . . See VB 1961, 376.
Rev. in *TLS,* 2 Feb., p. 70.

Rosenberg, Edgar. *From Shylock to Svengali: Jewish Stereotypes in English Fiction.* . . . See VB 1961, 376.
Rev. by Ronald Bryden in *S,* 21 Apr., 1961, p. 568.

Salerno, Nicholas A. "Romantic Love in Victorian Poetry." *DA,* XXII, 4354-55.

Smith, Bernard. *European Vision and the South Pacific, 1768-1850.* Oxford Univ. Pr. Pp. 287.
Rev. in *TLS,* 21 Sept., p. 730.
Impact of the South Pacific on European thought, from Captain Cook to Darwin and Huxley.

Speaight, Robert. *William Rothenstein: The Portrait of an Artist in his Time.* London: Eyre and Spottiswoode. Pp. 443.
Rev. in *TLS,* 7 Dec., p. 947.

Starkie, Enid. *From Gautier to Eliot.* . . . See VB 1961, 376.
Rev. by Henri Fluchère in *MLR,* LVII, 97-98.

Symons, Julian. *The Detective Story in Britain.* London: Longmans. Pp. 48.

Rev. by G. W. Stoner in *NS*, LXIII, 805.

Talmon, Jacob Leib. *Political Messianism: The Romantic Phase.* . . . See VB 1961, 376.
Rev. by W. H. McNeill in *JMH*, XXXIV, 97-98.

Tanzy, Conrad E. "Publishing the Victorian Novel: A Study of the Economic Relationships of Novelists and Publishers in England, 1830-1880." *DA*, XXII, 2387-88.

Thorslev, Peter L., Jr. *The Byronic Hero: Types and Prototypes.* Minneapolis: Univ. of Minnesota Pr. Pp. 240.
Rev. by John R. Willingham in *LJ*, LXXXVII, 2381-82.

Tillyard, E. M. W. *Essays Literary and Educational.* London: Chatto; New York: Barnes & Noble. Pp. 223.
Rev. by J. B. Beer in *NS*, LXIV, 235-36.

Watson, George. *The Literary Critics: A Study of English Descriptive Criticism.* Harmondsworth and Baltimore: Penguin. Pp. 249.
Rev. by D. J. Enright in *NS*, LXIII, 761-62; in *TLS*, 8 June, p. 430.

Weales, Gerald. *Religion in Modern English Drama.* Philadelphia: Univ. of Pennsylvania Pr., 1961. Pp. xiv + 317.
Rev. by Nelvin Vos in *JR*, XLII, 147-48.
Contains material on Henry Arthur Jones.

Wells, Stanley. "Burlesques of Charles Kean's *Winter's Tale.*" *Theatre Notebook*, XVI, 78-83.

Zink, David D., II. "The Beauty of the Alps: A Study of the Victorian Mountain Aesthetic." *DA*, XXIII, 2123.

IV. INDIVIDUAL AUTHORS

ACTON (see also NEWMAN: MacDougall).
Acton, Harold. "Lord Acton." *Chicago Review*, XV, 31-44.

ARNOLD (see also III, Brower, Watson).
Allott, Kenneth. "Arnold's 'Empedocles on Etna' and Byron's 'Manfred.'" *N & Q*, n.s. IX, 300-02.

Atkin, John R. "An Unpublished Report on Roman Catholic Schools by Matthew Arnold." *N & Q*, n.s. IX, 94-95.

Balliet, Conrad A. "The Verse Technique of Matthew Arnold." *DA*, XXII, 2382-83.

Berger, Harold L. "Recognition of Nonconformity." *Humanist*, XXII, 68-69.

Brooks, Roger L. "A Danish 'Balder Dead.'" *BSP*, LVI, 253-54.

Brooks, Roger L. "Matthew Arnold's Correspondence." *MP*, LIX, 273-75.
A further supplement to Motter's check list (see *SP*, XXXI [1934], 600-05).

Brooks, Roger L. "The Publication of Matthew Arnold's Early Volumes of Poetry." *VNL*, No. 22 (Fall), p. 22.

DeLaura, David J. "Four Arnold Letters." *Texas Studies in Lit. and Lang.*, IV, 276-84.

Davis, Arthur Kyle, Jr. "Matthew Arnold's Letters: A Progress Report on a Descriptive Checklist." *VNL*, No. 21 (Spring), pp. 7-8.

Duffin, Henry Charles. *Arnold the Poet.* London: Bowes and Bowes. Pp. 158.
Rev. by William Kean Seymour in *CR*, CCII, 108; in *TLS*, 3 Aug., p. 555.

Fairclough, G. T. "*A Fugitive and Gracious Light*": *The Relation of Joseph Joubert to Matthew Arnold's Thought.* Lincoln: Univ. of Nebraska Pr., 1961. Pp. 79.
Rev. by Kenneth Allott in *MLR*, LVII, 308-09.

Fairclough, G. Thomas. "The Sestet of Arnold's 'Religious Isolation.'" *N & Q*, n.s. IX, 302-03.

Feltes, N. N. "Matthew Arnold and the Modern Spirit: A Reassessment." *TQ*, XXXII, 27-36.

Hipple, Walter J., Jr. "Matthew Arnold, Dialectician." *TQ*, XXXII, 1-26.
An informative analysis of Arnold's purpose, method, and philosophy stemming from Arnold's "single principle" — "expansion, conduct, the humanisation of man in society." This article demands close study for its illuminating analysis of both style and philosophy. — R.E.F.

Holloway, John. *The Charted Mirror: Literary and Critical Essays.* . . . See VB 1961, 377.
Rev. by Graham Martin in *NS*, LIX, 830; by Frank Kermode in *S*, 27 May, 1960, p. 774.

James, David Gwilym. *Matthew Arnold and the Decline of English Romanticism.* . . . See VB 1961, 377.
Rev. by J. Hillis Miller in *CE*, XXIV, 71; by Donald H. Reiman in *JEGP*, LXI, 190-92; by Kenneth Allott in *MLR*, LVII, 93-94; by William D. Templeman in *The Personalist*, XLIII, 423; by A. G. Hill in *RES*, n.s. XIII, 318-20.

Jamison, William A. *Arnold and the Romantics.* . . . See VB 1960, 388.

Rev. by Paul Turner in *ESt*, XLIII, 67-68.

Marks, Emerson R. "Pragmatic Poetics: Dryden to Valery." *Bucknell Rev.*, X, 213-23.
Includes discussion of Arnold's preface to *Poems* of 1853.

Neiman, Fraser (ed.). *Essays, Letters, and Reviews by Matthew Arnold.* . . . See VB 1961, 378.
Rev. by J. P. Curgenven in *RES*, n.s. XIII, 83-86.

Owen, H. P. "The Theology of Coleridge." *Critical Quart.*, IV, 59-67.
Arnold's attitude towards the Bible is unfavorably contrasted to that of Coleridge.

Polhemus, George W. "An Additional Variation in Arnold's 'The Terrace at Berne.'" *N & Q*, n.s. IX, 299.

Roper, Alan H. "The Moral Landscape of Arnold's Poetry." *PMLA*, LXXVII, 289-96.

Shumaker, Wayne. "Matthew Arnold's Humanism: Literature as a Criticism of Life." *Studies in English Lit.*, II, 387-402.

Super, R. H (ed.). *On the Classical Tradition.* . . . See VB 1961, 378.
Rev. by G. D. Klingopoulos in *MLR*, LVII, 429; by J. P. Curgenven in *RES*, n.s. XIII, 83-86; by Arthur Kyle Davis, Jr., in *VQR*, XXXVIII, 335-38.

Super, R. H. (ed.). *Democratic Education.* . . . See VB 1961, 378.
Rev. by William D. Templeman in *The Personalist*, XLIII, 570-71; in *TLS*, 9 March, p. 156; by Arthur Kyle Davis, Jr., in *VQR*, XXXVIII, 335-38; by Kenneth Allott in *VS*, V, 349-50.

Super, R. H. (ed.). *Lectures and Essays in Criticism.* Ann Arbor: Univ. of Michigan Pr. Pp. 578. Vol. III of *The Complete Prose Works of Matthew Arnold*.
Rev. by R. E. Wagenknecht in *LJ*, LXXXVII, 4546.

Vogeler, Martha Salmon. "Matthew Arnold and Frederic Harrison: the Prophet of Culture and the Prophet of Positivism." *Studies in English Lit.*, II, 441-62.

Waller, John O. "Matthew Arnold and the American Civil War." *VNL*, No. 22 (Fall), pp. 1-5.

Wilkins, Charles T. "Matthew Arnold's 'Ineffectual Angel.'" *N & Q*, n.s. IX, 92-94.

ARNOLD, THOMAS.

Jackson, M. J., and Rogan, J., (eds.). *Principles of Church Reform.* London: S.P.C.K. Pp. v + 174.
Annotated edition of Thomas Arnold's essay.

BAGEHOT.

Lombard Street. With a New Introduction by Frank C. Genovese. Homewood, Illinois: R. D. Irwin. Pp. 176.
Rev. by R. S. Sayers in *Economica*, XXIX, 448-49.

Buchan, Alastair. *The Spare Chancellor.* . . . See VB 1961, 378.
Rev. by R. S. Sayers in *Economica*, XXIX, 94-95.

St. John-Stevas, Norman. *Walter Bagehot.* . . . See VB 1960, 388.
Rev. by R. S. Sayers in *Economica*, XXIX, 94-95.

BAILEY.

Birley, Robert. *Sunk Without Trace: Some Forgotten Masterpieces Reconsidered.* New York: Harcourt Brace; London: Hart-Davis. Pp. 208.
Rev. by C. Ricks in *NS*, LXIII, 942-43.
Among the forgotten masterpieces is Bailey's *Festus*.

BARNES.

Jones, Bernard (ed.). *The Poems of William Barnes.* London: Centaur Pr.; Carbondale: So. Illinois Univ. Pr. Pp. 960.
Rev. by Philip Larkin in *Listener*, 16 Aug., p. 257; by G. Grigson in *NS*, LXIV, 202 (see also Jones' letter, *NS*, LXIV, 286); by Charles Causley in *S*, 10 Aug., p. 194; in *TLS*, 3 Aug., p. 558.
The first collected edition of Barnes's poetry.

BEERBOHM.

Hill, Draper. "The Urge of Caricature." *Listener*, 12 July, pp. 57-59.
On Beerbohm's philosophy of caricature.

BLACKMORE.

Carter, John Archer. "Supplement to Blackmore Bibliography." *N & Q*, n.s. IX, 305.

BRIDGES.

Nowell-Smith, Simon. "Mosher and Bridges." *Book Collector*, XI, 482-83.

Ritz, J. G. *Robert Bridges and Gerard Hopkins, 1863-1889.* . . . See VB 1961, 379.
Rev. by F. Scarfe in *Études anglaises*, XV, 85-86; by M. C. Bradbrook in *MLR*, LVII, 254-55.

BRONTËS.

Bell, Vereen M. "*Wuthering Heights* and the Unforgivable Sin." *NCF*, XVII, 188-91.

Brontë Society. *The Brontë Parsonage Museum.* Haworth: The Council of the Brontë Society. Pp. 40.
Noticed in *TLS*, 25 May, p. 378. See also "Home of the Brontës," *TLS*, 17 Aug.-12 Oct., correspondence on the alterations

made by the Brontë Society in the Parsonage at Haworth.

Brontë Society Transactions. Vol. XIV, No. 2 has items: Dodds, M. H., "George Hudson and the Brontës" (pp. 56-57); "Further Thoughts on Branwell Brontë's Story: A Discussion" (pp. 3-16); Holgate, Ivy, "The Structure of 'Shirley'" (pp. 27-35); Isenberg, D. R., "A Gondal Fragment" (pp. 24-26); Stanley, B. E., "Patrick Brontë's Notebook" (pp. 17-19); "The 'Taste' of Charlotte Brontë" (pp. 20-24); Announcements and Reports.

Burkhart, Charles. "Brontë's *Villette.*" *Ex,* XXI, Item 8.
   On the use of moon images.

DuMaurier, Daphne. *The Infernal World of Branwell Brontë.* . . . See VB 1961, 379.
   Rev. by Fannie Ratchford in *Southwest Rev.,* XLVII, 101-04.

DuMaurier, Daphne. *Le Monde Infernal de Branwell Brontë.* Trans. Jane Fillon. Paris: Ed. Albin Michel. Pp. 288.
   Rev. by G. d'Houville in *Revue des deux mondes* (No. 10: 15 May), 276-77.

Gérin, Winifred. *Branwell Brontë.* . . . See VB 1961, 379.
   Rev. by Gilbert Thomas in *English,* XIV, 27-28; briefly in *NCF,* XVI, 373; by Stephen Graham in *Poetry Rev.,* LIII, 40-41; by J. M. S. Tompkins in *RES,* n.s. XIII, 315-17.

Livermore, Ann Lapraik. "Byron and Emily Brontë." *QR,* July, pp. 337-44.

Marshall, William H. "Hareton Earnshaw: Natural Theology on the Moors." *VNL,* No. 21 (Spring), pp. 14-15.
   A parallel with Browning's Caliban.

Moser, Thomas. "What Is the Matter with Emily Jane? Conflicting Impulses in *Wuthering Heights.*" *NCF,* XVII, 1-19.
   Asserts that the latter half of the novel loses force because Emily Brontë abandoned her true subject.

BROUGHAM.

Kennedy, William F. "Lord Brougham, Charles Knight, and *The Rights of Industry.*" *Economica,* XXIX, 58-71.
   Study of an economist, publisher, and writer who not only wrote the book in the title which is usually credited to Brougham but also contributed to Dickens' *Household Words.*

New, Chester W. *The Life of Henry Brougham to 1830.* . . . See VB 1961, 379.
   Rev. by David Spring in *AHR,* LXVII, 771-72; by David Owen in *Canadian*

Hist. Rev., LXIII, 164-65; by W. H. Chaloner in *History Today,* XII, 219-20; by R. K. Webb in *JMH,* XXXIV, 447-48; by Asa Briggs in *Listener,* 1 Feb., pp. 226-27; by John Clive in *VS,* V, 264-66.

BROWN.

Nowell-Smith, Simon. "Some Uncollected Authors XXXIII: Thomas Edward Brown, 1830-1897." *Book Collector,* XI, 338-44.

BROWNINGS (see also III, Fletcher).

L'Anneau et le livre. Traduction de Georges Connes. Avantpropos de René Lalou. Paris: Gallimard, 1959.
   Rev. by Jean Poisson in *Études anglaises,* XIV, 354-55; by John Bryson in *RES,* n.s. XIII, 208-09.

Bowers, Fredson (ed.). *Studies in Bibliography. Papers of the Bibliographical Society of the University of Virginia.* Vol. XIV, 1961. Charlottesville, Virginia, 1961. Pp. vi + 291.
   Rev. by K. Povey in *The Library,* 5th Ser., XVII, 171-72. Includes two letters from Mrs. Browning.

Curran, E. M. "Browning: Tallow and Brown Sugar?" *Colby Libr. Quart.,* VI, 169-75.

Davies, Hugh Sykes. *Browning and the Modern Novel.* Hull Univ. Pr. Pp. 28.
   Briefly rev. in *TLS,* 23 Nov., p. 926. Lecture given at St. John's College, Cambridge.

DeLaura, David J. "The Religious Imagery in Browning's 'The Patriot.'" *VNL,* No. 21 (Spring), pp. 16-18.

Docherty, Helen A. "Browning's Use of History: Its Effect on Meaning and Structure in His Poetry." *DA,* XXII, 3659.

Dougherty, Charles T. "Three Browning Letters to His Son." *Manuscripta,* VI, 98-103.
   Letters in the Vatican library.

Hayter, Alethea. *Mrs. Browning: A Poet's Work and Its Setting.* London: Faber and Faber. Pp. 261.
   Rev. by Elizabeth Jennings in *Listener,* 13 Sept., p. 400; by Naomi Lewis in *NS,* LXIV, 364-66; in *TLS,* 28 Sept., p. 762.

Honan, Park. *Browning's Characters.* . . . See VB 1961, 379.
   Rev. by Robert Langbaum in *VS,* V, 269-71.

Kemper, Frances C. "Irony and Browning's 'Fifine at the Fair.'" *DA,* XXIII, 1351-52.

Kendall, J. L. "Browning's *Fifine at the Fair:* Meaning and Method." *VNL,* No. 22 (Fall), pp. 16-18.

Kendall, Lyle H., Jr. "A New Browning Letter." *N & Q,* n.s. IX, 298-99.

Kenmare, Dallas. *An End to Darkness: A New Approach to Robert Browning and His Work.* London: Peter Owen. Pp. 220.
Rev. by Jacques Vallette in *Mercure de France,* CCCXLV, 728; in *TLS,* 27 July, p. 536.

"Letters from the Brownings." *Listener,* 17 May, p. 842.
An excerpt from an interview by Angus McDermid of Philip Kelley, who is collecting and hopes to collate "all the letters and material he can find written by Robert Browning, his wife, and their families." He began his search two-and-a-half years ago, hoped to find about 4,000 letters, to date has found some 10,000. The most important manuscript is a diary of Elizabeth's covering a ten-month period when she was twenty-five.

Phillipson, John S. " 'How Do I Love Thee?' — an Echo of St. Paul." *VNL,* No. 22 (Fall), p. 22.

Pietch, Frances. "The Relationship between Music and Literature in the Victorian Period: Studies in Browning, Hardy and Shaw." *DA,* XXII, 2386-87.

Puckett, Brother Walter E. "The Nineteenth-Century Foundations of the Robert Browning-Ezra Pound Bridge to Modernity in Poetry." *DA,* XXII, 3205.

Raymond, William O. "Browning and the Harriet Westbrook Shelley Letters." *TQ,* XXXII, 184-92.
Reaffirms that Browning read the Harriet Westbrook Shelley letters in 1858.

Seturaman, V. S. "Browning's 'By the Fireside': The Path Grey Heads Abhor.' " *N & Q,* n.s. IX, 297-98.

Stevenson, Lionel. "The Hawthorne and Browning Acquaintance: An Addendum." *VNL,* No. 21 (Spring), p. 16.
See James C. Austin, "The Hawthorne and Browning Acquaintance." *VNL,* No. 20 (Fall, 1961), pp. 13-18.

Tompkins, J. M. S. *Aurora Leigh.* The Fawcett Lecture, 1961-62. London: Bedford College. Pp. 21.

Willoughby, John W. "Browning's 'Johannes Agricola in Meditation.' " *Ex,* XXI, Item 5.

BULWER (see III, Fletcher).

BURTON.

Bercovici, Alfred. *That Blackguard Burton!: The Life of Richard Burton.* Indianapolis, Ind.: Bobbs-Merrill. Pp. 284.
Rev. by D. L. F. in *HTB,* 12 Aug., p. 8; by E. L. Yonge in *LJ,* LXXXVII, 1598.

BUTLER (see also ELIOT: Knoepflmacher).

Currie, A. W. "Samuel Butler's Canadian Investment." *TQ,* XXXII, 109-25.
Careful analysis of Butler's investments and business experience.

Davin, Dan. "Samuel Butler in New Zealand." *Listener,* 22 March, pp. 501-02.

Dyson, A. E. "The Honest Sceptic." *Listener,* 13 Sept., pp. 383-84.
Samuel Butler as a satirist.

Howard, Daniel F. (ed.). *Correspondence of Samuel Butler with His Sister May.* Berkeley: Univ. of California Pr.; Cambridge: Cambridge Univ. Pr. Pp. xx + 265.
Rev. by Burton A. Robie in *LJ,* LXXXVII, 3452.
153 letters, mostly hitherto unpublished.

Marshall, William H. "*The Way of All Flesh:* The Dual Function of Edward Overton." *Univ. of Tex. Studies in Lit. and Lang.,* IV, 583-90.

Montague, Gene. "A Nowhere That Goes Somewhere." *Jour. of Conference on College Comp. and Communication,* XIII, 18-22.

Silver, Arnold (ed.). *The Family Letters of Samuel Butler, 1841-1886.* Palo Alto: Stanford Univ. Pr.; London: Cape. Pp. 295.
Rev. by P. N. Furbank in *Listener,* 31 May, p. 999; by Newton Arvin in *N,* 1 Sept., p. 98; by Malcolm Muggeridge in *NS,* LXIII, 864-65; by Bernard Bergonzi in *S,* 15 June, p. 798; in *TLS,* 8 June, p. 422.
Two-thirds of these letters have never before been printed.

CARLYLE (see also II, Swart; TENNYSON: Ryals).

Sanders, Charles Richard. "Carlyle, Poetry, and the Music of Humanity." *Western Humanities Rev.,* XVI, 53-66.
Carlyle joins Browning as an influence on modern poets with his concern for the significance of sound. An important article based on many unpublished letters. — C. T. D.

CARROLL.

Gardner, Martin. *The Annotated Snark: Full Text of Lewis Carroll's Great Nonsense Epic "The Hunting of the Snark" and the Original Illustrations by Henry Holiday.* New York: Simon and Shuster. Pp. 111.
Rev. by Burton A. Robie in *LJ,* LXXXVII, 3457.

Williams, Sidney Herbert and Madan, Falconer. *The Lewis Carroll Handbook.* Oxford Univ. Pr. Originally published in

1931 as *Handbook of the Literature of the Rev. C. L. Dodgson,* now revised, augmented, and brought to the year 1960 by Roger Lancelyn Green. New York and London: Oxford Univ. Pr. Pp. xv + 307.

Rev. by John Hayward in *Book Collector,* XI, 372-76; in *TLS,* 17 July, p. 516 (see letter by Green, 20 July, p. 525).

CLOUGH.

Armstrong, Isobel. *Arthur Hugh Clough.* Writers and Their Work Series. London: Longmans, Green. Pp. 48.

Chorley, Katharine. *Arthur Hugh Clough: The Uncommitted Mind,* New York: Oxford Univ. Pr.; Oxford: Clarendon Pr. Pp. xi + 372.

Rev. by Richard M. Gollin in *EC,* XII, 426-35; by Paul Veyriras in *Études anglaises,* XV, 191-92; by Michael Timko in *JEGP,* LXI, 937-40; by Basil Willey in *Listener,* 8 Feb., pp. 261-62; by Kenneth Allott in *MLR,* LVII, 428-29; by A. Alvarez in *NS,* LXIII, 163-64; by David Lodge in *S,* 16 Feb., p. 214; in *TLS* ("Dipsychus Unmasked"), 2 Feb., p. 72; by Walter Houghton in *VS,* VI, 91-92; by C. Hollis in *Wiseman Rev.,* CCXXXVI, 271-72.

Gollin, Richard M. "The 1951 Edition of Clough's *Poems:* A Critical Re-examination." *MP,* LX, 120-27.

A belated but nonetheless important review article on the Oxford edition of Clough's poems. Gollin concludes that the text is not complete or "impeccable." – R. A. D.

Timko, Michael. "The Poetic Theory of Arthur Hugh Clough." *ESt,* XLIII, 240-47.

COLLINS (see II, Lehmann).

CONRAD.

Allen, Jerry. "Conrad's River." *Columbia Univ. Forum,* V, 29-33.

Brady, Marion B. "Conrad's Whited Sepulcher." *CE,* XXIV, 24-29.

Fleischmann, Wolfgang B. "Conrad's *Chance* and Bergson's *Laughter.*" *Renascence,* XIV, 66-71.

Freeman, Rosemary. "Conrad's *Nostromo:* A Source and Its Use." *Mod. Fict. Studies,* VII, 317-26.

Graver, Lawrence. " 'Typhoon': A Profusion of Similes." *CE,* XXIV, 62-64.

Gurko, Leo. *Joseph Conrad: Giant in Exile.* New York: Macmillan Pp. 258.

Rev. by R. D. Spector in *HTB,* 7 Oct., p. 10; by J. R. Willingham in *LJ,* LXXXVII,

1888; by Carlo Beuf in *NYTBR,* 22 July, p. 5.

Hertz, Robert N. "The Scene of Mr. Verloc's Murder in *The Secret Agent:* A Study of Conrad's Narrative and Dramatic Method." *Personalist,* XLIII, 214-25.

Hodges, Robert. "The Death of Stefan Bobrowski: A Conrad Discovery." *N & Q,* n.s. IX, 109-10.

Hoffman, Charles G. "Point of View in 'The Secret Sharer.' " *CE,* XXIII, 651-54.

Rosenfield, Claire. "An Archetypal Analysis of Conrad's *Nostromo.*" *Texas Studies in Lit. and Lang.,* III, 510-34.

Smith, David R. "*Nostromo* and the Three Sisters." *Studies in English Literature,* II, 497-508.

Tanner, Tony. "Nightmare and Complacency; Razumov and the Western Eye." *Critical Quart.,* IV, 197-214.

An analysis of *Under Western Eyes,* which reveals "a man unwillingly made intimate with the nightmare which hovers forever just under the complacencies of civilized existence."

DARWIN (see also II, Banton; III, Coleman).

Comfort, Alex. *Darwin and the Naked Lady.* . . . See VB 1961, 361.

Rev. by D. W. Harding in *NS,* LXII, 350; by J. B. Broadbent in *S,* 25 May, p. 690; in *TLS,* 15 Dec., 1961, p. 894.

Darlington, C. D. *Darwin's Place in History.* . . . See VB 1960, 393.

Rev. by Bert J. Loewenberg in *AHR,* LXVII, 1085-86.

De Beer, Sir Gavin. "Darwin's Evolution – I and II." *Listener,* 6 Sept., pp. 347-48; 13 Sept., 387-88.

A lucid discussion of the origins of Darwin's ideas on evolution and natural selection.

Dodson, E. O. "Some Problems of Evolution and Religion. A Darwin Centennial Address." *Revue de l'université d'Ottowa.* 1961.

Listed in *Revista de filologia,* XX (1961), 255.

Ellegård, Alvar. *Darwin and the General Reader.* . . . See VB 1960, 393.

Rev. by Georg Roppen in *ESt,* XLIII, 132-33.

Greene, John C. *Darwin and the Modern World View.* . . . See VB 1961, 381.

Rev. by Richard S. Westfall in *AHR,* LXVII, 1086; by Bernard Barber in *Am. Jour. of Soc.,* LXVIII, 145-46.

Gruber, Howard E., and Gruber, Valmai. "The Eye of Reason: Darwin's Development during the *Beagle* Voyage." *Isis,* LIII, 186-200.

Hyman, Stanley Edgar. *The Tangled Bank: Darwin, Marx, Frazer and Freud as Imaginative Writers.* New York: Atheneum Pr. Pp. 492.
Rev. by Paul Pickerel in *Harper's,* Apr., pp. 90-91; by Perry Miller in *HTB,* 22 Apr., p. 4; by B. W. Fuson in *LJ,* LXXXVII, 1466; by Hans Meyerhoff in *N,* 28 July, pp. 36-39; By Harold Rosenberg in *NYTBR,* 22 Apr., p. 6; by James Gray in *SR,* 26 May, p. 33; by Morse Peckham in *VS,* VI, 180-82.

Loewenberg, Bert James. "Darwin and the Tragic Vision." *American Quart.,* XIV, 618-22.

Ong, Walter J. (ed.). *Darwin's Vision and Christian Perspectives.* . . . See VB 1961, 382.
Rev. by Conway Zirkle in *Isis,* LIII, 396-97.

Plaine, Henry L. (ed.). *Darwin, Marx, and Wagner: A Symposium.* Columbus: Ohio State Univ. Pr. Pp. viii + 165.

Reid, Leslie. "Something Curious and Hitherto Unknown." *QR,* Apr., 206-17.
The work of A. R. Wallace compared with that of Darwin.

Rezneck, Samuel. "Notes on a Correspondence between Charles Darwin and James Dwight Dana, 1861-1863." *Yale Univ. Library Gazette,* XXXVI, 176-83.

Stevenson, Robert Scott. *Famous Illlnesses in History.* London: Eyre and Spottiswoode. Pp. 239.
Includes chapter on Darwin's illness.

Symoens, J.-J., Laurent, R., Bouillon, J., and Rasmont, R. *Actualité de Darwin.* Brussels: Les Naturalistes Belges, 1960. Pp. 140.
Rev. by Albert De Lorme in *Revue de synthèse,* LXXXII, 297-98.

Wanstall, P. J. (ed.). *A Darwin Centenary: The Report of the Conference Held by the Botanical Society of the British Isles in 1959 to Mark the Centenary of the Publication of "The Origin of Species."* London: The Botanical Society of the British Isles, 1961. Pp. 140.
Contains an introductory essay by Lady Barlow and six papers on contemporary theories about the mechanism of plant evolution.

Zimmerman, Paul Albert (ed.). *Darwin, Evolution, and Creation.* St. Louis: Concordia Pr. Pp. xii + 231.

DAVIDSON.

Lindsay, Maurice (ed.). *John Davidson: A Selection of his Poems.* Preface by T. S. Eliot, with an Essay by Hugh McDiarmid. London: Hutchinson, 1961. Pp. 220.
Rev. by Ian Fletcher in *EC,* XII, 435-41; by M. Levy in *Études anglaises,* XV, 392-93; by Edwin Morgan in *RES,* n.s. XIII, 210-11

Macleod, R. D. *John Davidson: A Study in Personality.* . . . See VB 1957, 407.
Rev. by Edwin Morgan in *RES,* n.s. XIII, 210-11.

Macleod, R. D. (ed.). *Poems and Ballads by John Davidson.* . . . See VB 1959, 435.
Rev. by Edwin Morgan in *RES,* n.s. XIII, 210-11.

Townsend, J. Benjamin. *John Davidson: Poet of Armageddon.* . . . See VB 1961, 382.
Noticed unfavorably in *TLS,* 26 Jan., p. 63; rev. by J. B. Schneewind in *YR,* LI, 479; by R. D. Macleod in *VS,* V, 353-54.

DICKENS (see also I, "Theatrical Material"; II Lehmann; III, Billingsley, Kreisel, Rees).

Axton, William F. "Dramatic Style in Dickens' Novels." *DA,* XXII, 2788-89.

Brain, Russel. *Some Reflections on Genius and Other Essays.* London: Pitman Medical Publishing Co., 1960. Pp. vii + 192.
Rev. by L. F. Bonnerot in *Études anglaises,* XV, 195.
An essay on Dickens' "eye of the expert clinician."

Barrett, Edwin B. "Charles Dickens: the Essential Fable. Character, Idea, Form, and Diction in Four Novels of His Maturity." *DA,* XXII, 2789.
David Copperfield, Bleak House, Little Dorritt, Great Expectations

Birkett, Lord. "The Versatility of Charles Dickens." *Listener,* 15 Feb., p. 282.

Blount, Trevor. "A Revised Image in the Opening Chapter of Dickens's 'Bleak House.'" *N & Q,* n.s. IX, 303-04.

Bort, Barry D. "A Study of Dickens' Heroes From Oliver Twist to Jasper." *DA,* XXIII, 1666-67.

Butt, John. "Dickens's Manuscripts." *Yale Univ. Library Gazette,* XXXVI, 149-61.
Opening of Dickens exhibition at Yale University Library.

Calhoun, Philo. "Charles Dickens in Maine." *Colby Libr. Quart.,* VI, 137-48.

Carr, Sister Mary Callista (ed.). *Catalogue of the Dickens Collection at the Uni-*

versity of Texas. . . . See VB 1961, 382.
Rev. by Simon Nowell-Smith in *The Library*, 5th Ser., XVII, 173-75.
Cockshut, A. O. J. *The Imagination of Charles Dickens.* . . . See VB 1961, 382.
Rev. by Sylvère Monod in *Études anglaises*, XV, 84; by B. W. Fuson in *LJ*, LXXXVII, 4546; by Harry Stone in *NCF*, 89-91; by R. D. McMaster in *QQ*, LXIX, 483-84.
Collins, Philip Arthur William. *Dickens and Adult Education.* Leicester: Vaughan College Papers No. 7. Pp. ii + 34.
Collins, Philip. *Dickens and Crime.* London: Macmillan; New York: St. Martin's Pr. Pp. 371.
Rev. by John D. Jump in *Critical Quart.*, IV, 371-72; by Pamela Hansford Johnson in *Listener*, 9 Aug., p. 218; by Malcolm Bradbury in *Manchester Guardian Weekly*, 6 Dec., p. 12; by J. Gross in *NS*, LXIV, 234; by Colin MacInnes in *S*, 24 Aug., pp. 277-78; in *TLS*, 17 Aug., p. 627.
Collins, Philip. "Dickens and the Trained Schoolmaster." *Univ. of Leeds Institute of Education Researches and Studies*, XXII (1961), 1-13.
Collins, Philip. "John Forster's Diary." *TLS*, 30 Nov., p. 937.
Collins, Philip. "Mr. Pardiggle in 'Bleak House.'" *N & Q*, n.s. IX, 150-51.
Coolidge, Archibald C., Jr. "Dickens' Use of Character as Novelty." *SAQ*, LXI, 405-10.
Dickensian, Vol. LVIII (Nos. 336-38). . . . See VB 1932, 422. Items as follows: "A Dickens Review [rev. of the Dickens Number of *A Review of English Literature*, ed. John Butt]" (p. 57); Broadbent, C. R., "Dickens, You Say?" (pp. 54-57); Brogunier, Joseph, "The Dreams of Montague Tigg and Jonas Chuzzlewit" (pp. 165-70); Carlton, W. J., "'Boz' and the Beards" (pp. 9-21); Carlton, W. J., "Postscripts to Forster" (pp. 87-92); Carter, J. A., "The World of Squeers and the World of Crummles" (pp. 50-53); Collins, Philip, "Dickens and the Whiston Case" (pp. 47-49); Coolidge, A. C., Jr., "Charles Dickens and Mrs. Radcliffe: A Farewell to Wilkie Collins" (pp. 112-16); Cox, A. J., "The Morals of *Edwin Drood*" (pp. 32-42); F[ielding], K. J., "Comprehensive Education" (p. 119); Fielding, K. J., "Dickens and the Critics" (pp. 150-51); Fielding, K. J., "The Imagination of Charles Dickens" (pp. 21-22); Fleissner, R. F., "'Fancy's

Knell'" (pp. 125-27); G., J., "Dickens for the Younger Reader" (p. 141); Gibson, F. A., "Nature's Possible: A Reconsideration of *The Battle of Life*" (pp. 43-46); Gibson, F. A., "A Trifle on Titles" (pp. 117-19); Lascelles, T. S., "Transport in the Dickensian Era" (pp. 75-86; 152-60); Morley, Malcolm, "Dickens Contributions to *Sweeney Todd*" (pp. 92-95); Morley, Malcolm, "Fiction or Fact" (pp. 180-81); Morley, Malcolm, "Where Crummles Played" (pp. 23-29); Pakenham, Pansy, "C.G.L. DuCann on the 'Love Lives' of Dickens [rev. of DuCann, *The Love Lives of Charles Dickens*]" (pp. 29-31); Peyrouton, N. C., "Boz — Town Conference" (pp. 7-8); Peyrouton, N. C., "Charles Dickens and the Christian Socialists: The Kingsley-Dickens Myth" (pp. 96-109); S[taples], L. C., "Priestley's Pictorial Dickens [rev. of J. B. Priestley, *Charles Dickens: A Pictorial Biography*]" (p. 31); Stedman, J. W., "Boz and Bab" (pp. 171-78); van Voss-Moeton, J.F.G.H., "Tears in Literature: Particularly in Dickens" (pp. 182-87); Wagenknecht, Edward, "'Immortal Memory'" (pp. 133-41); Wiley, Elizabeth, "Four Strange Cases" (pp. 120-25); Ziegler, Rev. A. F., "The Haunted Man" (pp. 145-48).
Donovan, Robert A. "Structure and Idea in *Bleak House*." *ELH*, XXIX, 175-201.
The solving of mysteries as a pattern for Dickens's revelations of social injustice.
Dupee, F. W. (ed.). *The Selected Letters of Charles Dickens.* New York: Farrar, Straus, 1960. Pp. 293.
Rev. by R. D. McMaster in *QQ*, LXIX, 483-84.
Fielding, K. J. "Dickens and International Copyright." *Bulletin of the British Association for American Studies*, n.s. No. 4, pp. 29-35.
Ford, George Harry, and Lane, Lauriat (eds.). *The Dickens Critics.* . . . See VB 1961, 383.
Rev. by Louis Crompton in *CE*, XXIV, 70; by John D. Jump in *Critical Quart.*, IV, 371-72; by R. D. McMaster in *Dalhousie Rev.*, XLII, 392-93; by Malcolm Bradbury in *Manchester Guardian Weekly*, 6 Dec., p. 12; by Matthew Hodgart in *NS*, LXIV, 744-45; by Walter M. Crittenden in *The Personalist*, XLIII, 571; by R. D. McMaster in *QQ*, LXIX, 483-84.

Gimbel, Richard. "An Exhibition of 150 Manuscripts, Illustrations, and First Editions of Charles Dickens." *Yale Univ. Libr. Gazette,* XXXVII, 46-93.
Noted in "News and Notes," *BSP,* LVI, 118-19.
Catalogue of the Yale Dickens exhibit.

Goldfarb, Russell M. "The Menu of *Great Expectations.*" *VNL,* No. 21 (Spring), pp. 18-19.

Gross, John, and Pearson, Gabriel (eds.). *Dickens and the Twentieth Century.* London: Routledge; Toronto: Univ. of Toronto Pr. Pp. xxiv + 244.
Rev. by Pamela Hansford Johnson in *Listener,* 15 Nov., p. 823; by Malcolm Bradbury in *Manchester Guardian Weekly,* 6 Dec., p. 12; by M. Hodgart in *NS,* LXIV, 744-45.

Johnson, Edgar. "Dickens and His Critics." *SR,* 10 Feb., pp. 31, 69.

Lazenby, Walter S., Jr. "Stage Versions of Dickens's Novels in America to 1900." *DA,* XXIII, 2250.

Leavis, F. R. "Dombey and Son." *SeR,* LXX, 177-201.
"There is a greater Dickens than the traditional cult has tended to realize."

McMaster, R. D. "Man into Beast in Dickensian Caricature." *TQ,* XXXI, 354-61.

Monod, Sylvère. "Une Curiosité dans L'Histoire de la Traduction: *Le Neveu de ma tante, D'Amédée Pichot.*" *Études anglaises,* XIV, 353.
Translation of *David Copperfield* in 1851.

Priestley, John Boynton. *Charles Dickens: A Pictorial Biography.* . . . See VB 1961, 384.
Rev. by J. K. Hutchens in *HTB,* 11 Feb., p. 7; by Edgar Johnson in *NYTBR,* 11 Feb., p. 5; in *SR,* 10 Feb., p. 30.

Stone, Harry. "Dickens' Artistry and *The Haunted Man.*" *SAQ,* LXI, 492-505.

Stone, Harry. "Fire, Hand, and Gate: Dickens' *Great Expectations.*" *KR,* XXIV, 662-91.

Vann, J. Don. "The Death of Dora Spenlow in *David Copperfield.*" *VNL,* No. 22 (Fall), pp. 19-20.

Viebrock, Helmut. "The Knocker: Physiognomical Aspects of a Motif in Hoffman and Dickens." *ESt,* XLIII, 396-402.
A thoughtful and provocative essay on the imaginative affinities of Dickens and Hoffman. – R. A. D.

Wexler, Alexandra. "Dickens und Dosto-jewski." *Deutsche Rundschau,* LXXXVIII, 732-40.
Similarities show Dostoevski borrowing from and enriching Dickens's themes and characters.

Yanko, Ann E. "Technique and Vision in *Bleak House, Little Dorritt,* and *Our Mutual Friend.*" *DA,* XXIII, 2143.

DISRAELI.

Faber, Richard. *Beaconsfield and Bolingbroke.* . . . See VB 1961, 384.
Rev. by P. Baratier in *Études anglaises,* XV, 78-80; by S. R. Graubard in *JMH,* XXXIV, 329.

Graubard, Stephen R. *Burke, Disraeli, and Churchill.* . . . See VB 1961, 384.
Rev. by Richard W. Lyman in *JMH,* XXXIV, 445.

Jerman, B. R. *The Young Disraeli.* . . . See VB 1961, 384.
Rev. by Norman Gash in *EHR,* LXXVII, 397-98; by S. M. Smith in *MLR,* LVII, 308.

McCabe, Bernard. "From *Vivian Grey* to *Tancred:* A Critical Study of Disraeli's Development as a Novelist." *DA,* XXII, 4351-52.

Smith, Sheila M. "Willenhall and Wodgate: Disraeli's Use of Blue Book Evidence." *RES,* n.s. XIII, 368-84.
Sources for *Sybil* in reports of the Children's Employment Commission, 1841-42.

DIXON.

Sambrook, James. *A Poet Hidden: The Life of Richard Watson Dixon, 1833-1900.* London: Athlone Press. Pp. ix + 134.
Rev. by C. Colleer Abbott in *Listener,* 5 Apr., pp. 609, 611; by Kenneth Allott in *MLR,* LVII, 430-31; in *TLS,* 23 March, p. 203 (also see letter by Geoffrey Soden, 30 March, p. 223); by J. G. Ritz in *VS,* VI, 185-86.

DOWSON.

Fletcher, Ian. "Some Unpublished Letters of Ernest Dowson to Herbert Horne." *N & Q,* n.s. IX, 100-05.

DOYLE.

Hardwick, John Michael and Mollie. *The Sherlock Holmes Companion.* London: John Murray. Pp. xi + 232.
Rev. by G. W. Stonier in *NS,* LXIV, 420; by Rosalie Packard in *S,* 12 Oct., p. 569; in *TLS,* 26 Oct., p. 829.

Holroyd, James E. "Baedeker and Baker Street." *Cornhill* (Winter), 139-45.

Pearson, Hesketh. *Conan Doyle.* . . . See VB 1961, 384.

Rev. briefly in *NCF*, XVI, 373; by J. T. Winterich in *SR*, 28 Oct., 1961, p. 24.

ELIOT (see also III, Billingsley, Kreisel; HARDY: Yuill).

Adam, I. W. "Restoration through Feeling in George Eliot's Fiction: A New Look at Hetty Sorrel." *VNL*, No. 22 (Fall), pp. 9-12.

Beaty, Jerome. *Middlemarch from Notebook to Novel.* . . . See VB 1961, 385.
Rev. by Daniel P. Deneau in *JEGP*, LXI, 192-94; by Barbara Hardy in *MLR*, LVII, 94-95; by Irene Simon in *RES*, n.s. XIII, 317-18; by George Levine in *VS*, V, 342-44.

Collins, Rowland L. "The Present Past: The Origin and Exposition of Theme in the Prose Fiction of George Eliot." *DA*, XXII, 3657.
Use of man's past to influence his present in terms of inseparability of man and his environment, the irrevocability of man's deeds, and the need for sympathy for other human beings.

Crompton, Margaret. *George Eliot: The Woman.* . . . See VB 1961, 385.
Rev. by George Levine in *VS*, V, 342-44.

Daiches, David. "The Return of George Eliot." *N*, 9 June, pp. 518-19.

Harvey, W. J. *The Art of George Eliot.* . . . See VB 1961, 385.
Rev. by Mary E. Knapp in *BA*, XXXVI, 429; by Jerome Thale in *CE*, XXIV, 70; by Gilbert Thomas in *English*, XIV, 27-28; by Jacques Vallette in *Mercure de France*, CCCXLVI, 734; by Miriam Allott in *MLR*, LVII, 427; by Gordon S. Haight in *NCF*, XVII, 84-87; by George Levine in *VS*, V, 342-44.

Hester, Waverly E. "George Eliot's Technique as a Novelist." *DA*, XXII, 2396-97.

Hoggart, Richard. "A Victorian Masterpiece." *Listener*, 8 Mar., pp. 407-08.
On *Middlemarch*.

Knoepflmacher, U. C. "The Victorian Novel of Religious Humanism: A Study of George Eliot, Walter Pater, and Samuel Butler." *DA*, XXII, 2794-95.
Examines *Middlemarch, Daniel Deronda, Marius the Epicurean,* and *The Way of All Flesh* for religious humanism, a fusion of science, morality, and historicism.

Laing, Robert C., Jr. "Humor in George Eliot's Novels." *DA*, XXII, 3667.

Lainoff, Seymour. "James and Eliot: The Two Gwendolens." *VNL*, No. 21 (Spring), pp. 23-24.

Gwendolen Erme ("The Figure in the Carpet") derives from Gwendolen Harleth (*Daniel Deronda*).

Laski, Marghanita. "Some Words from George Eliot's 'Scenes of Clerical Life.'" *N & Q*, n.s. IX, 304-05.

Levine, George, "Determinism and Responsibility in the Works of George Eliot." *PMLA*, LXXVII, 268-79.

Masters, Donald C. "George Eliot and the Evangelicals." *Dalhousie Rev.*, XLI, 505-12.

McKenzie, Keith Alexander. *Edith Simcox and George Eliot.* . . . See VB 1961, 385.
Rev. by Miriam Allott in *MLR*, LVII, 95-96; by George Levine in *VS*, V, 342-44.

McMahon, Catherine R. "George Eliot and the Feminist Movement in Nineteenth Century England." *DA*, XXII, 3649-50.

Paris, Bernard J. "George Eliot's Religion of Humanity." *ELH*, XXIX, 418-43.
Defends the thesis that Eliot's characters are not automata but responsible individuals.

Pinney, Thomas. "Another Note on the Forgotten Past of Will Ladislaw." *NCF*, XVII, 69-73.

Robinson, Carole. "Romola: A Reading of the Novel," *VS*, VI, 29-42.

Rubinstein, Elliot L. "A Forgotten Tale by George Eliot." *NCF*, XVII, 175-83. "The Lifted Veil."

Ryals, Clyde De L. "The Thorn Imagery in *Adam Bede*." *VNL*, No. 22 (Fall), pp. 12-13.

Simon, Irène. "Innocence in the Novels of George Eliot." *English Studies Today*. . . . See VB 1961, 385.
Rev. by Pierre Janelle in *Études anglaises*, XV, 93-96.

FARADAY.

Jeffreys, Alan E. *Michael Faraday, a List of his Lectures and Published Writings.* Foreward by Sir Lawrence Bragg. London: Published on behalf of The Royal Institution of Great Britain by Chapman & Hall, 1960. Pp. xxviii + 86.
Rev. by Bern Dibner in *BSP*, LVI, 135-37.

FITZGERALD.

Gittelman, Sol. "Edward FitzGerald's 'Rubaiyat of Omar Khayyam' in Germany." *N & Q*, n.s. IX, 95-96.

Gittelman, Sol. "The Reception of Edward FitzGerald's *Rubaiyat of Omar Khayyam* in England and Germany." *DA*, XXII, 2384.

Kermode, Frank. "Allusions to Omar." *NS*,

LXIV, 146-47.
An article reviewing Joanna Richard-
son's *Selected Works of FitzGerald* (see
below).
Parrinder, E. G. "Omar Khayyam – Cynic or
Mystic." *LQHR*, CLXXXVII (6th ser.,
XXXI), 222-26.
Richardson, Joanna (ed.). *FitzGerald: Se-
lected Works*. London: Hart-Davis. Pp.
775.
Rev. in *TLS*, 3 Aug., p. 555.

FORD.
Cassell, Richard A. *Ford Madox Ford: A
Study of His Novels*. Baltimore: Johns
Hopkins Pr., 1961. Pp. 307.
Rev. by James W. Gargano in *CE*, XXIV,
71; by Patricia Hutchins in *Listener*, 21
June, p. 1083; by E. J. Gaines in *LJ*,
LXXXVII, 1904; by V. S. Pritchett in
NS, LXIII, 906; by Granville Hicks in
SR, 23 June, p. 26; by Bernard Bergonzi
in *S*, 11 May, p. 624; in *TLS*, 15 June, p.
437.
Cassell, Richard A. "The Two Sorrells of
Ford Maddox Ford." *MP*, LXIX, 114-21.
Cox, James Trammell. "Ford's Passion for
Provence." *ELH*, XXVIII, 383-98.
Gordon, Ambrose, Jr. "A Diamond of Pat-
tern: The War of F. Madox Ford." *SeR*,
LXX, 464-83.
Lid, R. W. "Ford Madox Ford and His Com-
munity of Letters." *Prairie Schooner*,
XXXV, 132-36.

FROUDE.
Bennett, Raymond M. "Letters of James An-
thony Froude." *Rutgers Univ. Libr. Jour.*,
XXVI, 14-22.
Fourth and last of a series of letters to
Theodore Stanton written between 1888-
1894.
Dunn, Waldo Hilary. *James Anthony Froude,
1818-1856*. . . . See VB 1961, 385.
Rev. by Archibald S. Foord in *AHR*,
LXVII, 699-700; by John Johnston in
MLR, LVII, 425-26; by Paul Veyriras in
Études anglaises, XV, 192; by Joel Hurst-
field in *History*, XLVII, 88-89; by J. P.
Schneewind in *YR*, LI, 475-77.

GASKELL (see also III, Billingsley).
Laski, Marghanita. "Words from Mrs. Gaskell." *N & Q*, n.s. IX, 27-28, 30 (com-
pletion of entry noted in VB 1961, 386).

GILBERT (see also I, "Theatrical Material").
The Savoy Operas. Vol. I. Intro. by Lord
David Cecil. (World's Classics) Oxford
Univ. Pr. Pp. 396.
Rev. in *TLS*, 2 Nov., p. 836.
Guthrie, Sir Tyrone. "Yeomen, Pirates, and
All." *Listener*, 8 Feb., p. 245.

Mander, Raymond, and Mitchenson, Joe
(eds.). *A Picture History of Gilbert and
Sullivan*. London: Vista. Pp. 160.
Rev. in *TLS*, 21 Dec., p. 991.
Moore, Frank Ledlie (ed.). *The Handbook
of Gilbert and Sullivan*. London: Barker;
New York: Crowell. Pp. 264.
Rev. in *TLS*, 21 Dec., p. 991.
Parker, Ralph. "The Mikado in Moscow."
NS, LXIV, 44-46. Stanislovsky's pro-
duction in 1887.
Rollins, Cyril, and Witts, R. John (eds.). *The
D'Oyly Carte Opera Company in Gil-
bert and Sullivan Operas. A Record of
Productions, 1875-1961*. London: Michael
Joseph. Pp. 186.
Rev. by Roger Gellert in *NS*, LXIII, 310;
in *TLS*, 9 March, p. 156.

GISSING.
Coustillas, P. "Les femmes dans l'oeuvre de
George Gissing." *Études anglaises*, XV,
412-13.
Coustillas, Pierre. "Une lettre inédite de Ga-
brielle Fleury a Clara Collet." *Études
anglaises*, XV, 167-71.
Gettmann, Royal A. (ed.). *George Gissing
and H. G. Wells*. . . . See VB 1961, 386.
Rev. at length by Pierre Coustillas in
Études anglaises, XV, 156-66; by Ber-
nard Bergonzi in *EC*, XII, 314-21; by
Arthur C. Young in *NCF*, XVI, 369-72;
by Ruth M. Adams in *VS*, V, 271-72.
Korg, Jacob (ed.). *George Gissing's Com-
monplace Book*. . . . See VB 1961, 386.
Rev. in *TLS*, 13 April, p. 250.
Young, Arthur C. (ed.). *The Letters of
George Gissing to Eduard Bertz: 1887-
1903*. . . . See VB 1961, 386.
Rev. briefly in *NCF*, XVII, 93; by V. S.
Pritchett in *NS*, LXIII, 164-65; by Ber-
nard Bergonzi in *S*, 26 Jan., pp. 115-16; in
TLS, 12 Jan., p. 27; by Ruth M. Adams
in *VS*, V, 271-72.

GLADSTONE (see NEWMAN: Ryan).
Arnstein, Walter. "Gladstone and the Brad-
laugh Case." *VS*, V, 303-30.
Gladstone's handling of Charles Brad-
laugh's repeated attempts to take his seat
in the House of Commons.
Beckett, J. C. "Select Documents, XXII.
Gladstone, Queen Victoria, and the Dis-
establishment of the Irish Church, 1868-
9." *Irish Historical Studies*, 38-47.
Jones, J. R. "The Conservatives and Glad-
stone in 1855." *EHR*, LXXVII, 95-98.
Knaplund, Paul (ed.). *Gladstone-Gordon
Correspondence, 1851-1896: Selections*

from the Private Correspondence of a British Prime Minister and a Colonial Governor. Philadelphia: American Philosophical Society, 1961. Pp. 116.
Rev. by Glyndwr Williams in *History,* XLVII, 207.

Ramm, Agatha (ed.). *The Political Correspondence of Mr. Gladstone and Lord Granville, 1876-1886.* Oxford: Clarendon Pr.; New York: Oxford Univ. Pr. Two vols.: Pp. xlviii + 482; 509.
Rev. by Paul Knaplund in *AHR,* LXVII, 1096-97; by Harold Kurtz in *History Today,* XII, 515; by E. G. Collieu in *Listener,* 22 Feb., p. 350, 353; by Asa Briggs in *NS,* LXIII, 197; in *TLS,* 6 Apr., pp. 225-26; by M. R. D. Foot in *VS,* V, 339-40.

GOSSE.

Bredsdorff, Elias (ed.). *Sir Edmund Gosse's Correspondence with Scandinavian Writers.* . . . See VB 1961, 386.
Rev. by W. Glyn Jones in *MLR,* LVII, 145-46.

GREEN.

Pucelle, Jean. *La Nature et l'esprit dans la philosophie de T. H. Green: La Renaissance de l'idealisme en Angleterre au XIXe siècle.* Louvain: Editions Nauwelaerts, 1961. Pp. 326.
Rev. by G. R. C. Mure in *Philosophy,* XXXVII, 279-80

LADY GREGORY.

Coxhead, Elizabeth. *Lady Gregory: A Literary Portrait.* . . . See VB 1961, 386.
Rev. by John B. Carr, Jr. in *Ariz. Q.,* XVIII, 284-85; by R. Fréchet in *Études anglaises,* XV, 311; by M. H. Zipprich in *LJ,* LXXXVII, 92; by Kevin Sullivan in *N,* 14 Oct., 1961, p. 253; by Frank Kermode in *S,* 31 Mar., 1961, p. 449.

HAGGARD.

Cohen, Morton N. *Rider Haggard: His Life and Works.* . . . See VB 1961, 386.
Rev. by Lionel Stevenson in *SAQ,* LXI, 280-82.

HARDY (see also III, Billingsley, Fairchild; ARNOLD: Holloway; BROWNING: Pietch; TENNYSON: Grigson, Young).

Bailey, J. O. "Temperament as Motive in *The Return of the Native.*" *Eng. Fiction in Transition,* V, 21-29.

Beatty, C. J. P. "Emma Hardy's Recollections." *TLS,* 1 June, p. 420.
Strictures on the editing by Evelyn Hardy and Robert Gittings of *Some Recollections by Emma Hardy* (see VB 1961, 386). See reply by Robert Gittings, 8 June, p. 429.

Bowden, Ann. "The Thomas Hardy Collection." *TxU,* VII, 7-14.
Description of important holdings at Univ. of Texas, illustrated.

Brick, Allan. "Paradise and Consciousness in Hardy's *Tess.*" *NCF,* XVII, 115-34.
An extended comparison of the novel with *Paradise Lost.*

Brown, Douglas. *Thomas Hardy: The Mayor of Casterbridge.* London: Arnold. Pp. 64.
Close critical analysis of Hardy's novel.

Bugler, Gertrude. *Personal Recollections of Thomas Hardy.* Dorchester: Dorset Natural History and Archaeological Society. Pp. 10.

Danby, John F. "Under the Greenwood Tree." *CQ,* I, 5.

Deacon, Lois. *Tryphena and Thomas Hardy,* introduction by Richard Curle. Beaminster, Dorset: The Toucan Pr. Pp. 30.

Fischler, Alexander. "Thomas Hardy's Short Stories: Their Relation to Major Trends and Interests in the Criticism of His Works." *DA,* XXII, 3199-200.

Hardy, Evelyn. "Emma Hardy's Diaries: Some Foreshadowings of *The Dynasts.*" *English,* XIV, 9-12.

Hardy, Evelyn, and Gittings, Robert (eds.). *Some Recollections by Emma Hardy with Some Relevant Poems by Thomas Hardy.* . . . See VB 1961, 386.
Rev. by Phoebe Adams in *AM,* CCIX, 99; by Philip Larkin in *Critical Quarterly,* IV, 75-79; by S. Sebaoun in *Études anglaises,* XV, 290-91; by DeLancey Ferguson in *HTB,* 7 Jan., p. 6; by Miriam Allott in *MLR,* LVII, 433-34; by C. J. Beatty in *N & Q,* n.s., IX, 313-17; briefly in *NCF,* XVI, 374.

Hardy, Florence Emily. *The Life of Thomas Hardy, 1840-1928.* London: Macmillan; New York: St. Martin's Pr. Pp. 470.
Rev. by Robert Gittings in *Listener,* 26 April, pp. 739-40; in *TLS,* 6 Apr., p. 234. *The Early Life* and *The Later Years* reissued as one volume.

Hellstrom, Ward. "A Study of *Jude the Obscure.*" *DA,* XXII, 3645.
The novel as Hardy's final statement of the tragic hero.

Hynes, Samuel Lynn. *The Pattern of Hardy's Poetry.* . . . See VB 1961, 386.
Rev. by W. D. Snodgrass in *CE,* XXIII, 322-23; by John M. Robson in *Dalhousie Rev.,* XLI, 552-53; by S. Sebaoun in *Études anglaises,* XV, 291-92; by Robert L. Peters in *JAA,* XXI, 103; by Miriam Allott in *MLR,* LVII, 433-34; by David Perkins in *MP,* LIX, 295-97; by Kenneth

Allott in *RES*, n.s. XIII, 422-23; by P. N. Furbank in *S*, 12 Jan., pp. 47-48; by George W. Sherman in *Science & Society*, XXVI, 456-59; by Bruce E. Teets in *SAQ*, LXI, 120; by Charles T. Dougherty in *Thought*, XXXVII, 143-44; in *TLS*, 12 Jan., p. 26.

King, R. W. "Verse and Prose Parallels in the Work of Thomas Hardy." *RES*, n.s. XIII, 52-61.

McCormick, Benedict, O.F.M. "Thomas Hardy: A Vision and a Prelude." *Renascence*, XIV, 155-59.

Morrell, Roy. "Hardy in the Tropics." *Rev. of Eng. Lit.*, III, 7-21.

Paterson, John. *The Making of "The Return of the Native."* . . . See VB 1961, 387.
Rev. by Jerome Beaty in *CE*, XXIV, 70; by S. Sebaoun in *Études anglaises*, XV, 291.

Roberts, James L. "Legend and Symbol in Hardy's 'The Three Strangers.'" *NCF*, XVII, 191-94.

Schweik, Robert C. "Moral Perspective in *Tess of the D'Urbervilles*." *CE*, XXIV, 14-18.

Schweik, Robert C. "Theme, Character, and Perspective in Hardy's *The Return of the Native*." *PQ*, XLI, 757-67.
As a result of his tragedy, Clym Yeobright has new insight but remains the victim of delusion.

Selna, Barbara. "Hardy's *Tess of the D'Urbervilles*." *Ex*, XX, Item 47.
On the imagery of cards and card-playing.

Thomson, George H. "The Trumpet-Major Chronicle." *NCF*, XVIII, 45-56.

Toliver, Harold E. "The Dance under the Greenwood Tree: Hardy's Bucolics." *NCF*, XVII, 57-68.
The desire to escape bucolic life is a recurring situation in Hardy's fiction.

Weber, Carl J. *Hardy of Wessex*. Hamden, Conn.: Archon Books. Pp. 304. Pp. 303-04 give "Addenda and Corrigenda" for Weber's 1940 centennial biography.

Wing, George. "Tess and the Romantic Milkmaid." *Rev. of Eng. Lit.*, III, 22-30.

Yamamoto, Bunnosuke. *Bibliography of Thomas Hardy in Japan*. With a list of reference books in England and America. Tokyo: Shinozaki Shorin. Pp. 530.
An inclusive compilation sponsored by The Thomas Hardy Society of Japan.

Yuill, W. E. " 'Character is Fate': A Note on Thomas Hardy, George Eliot, and Novalis." *MLR*, LVII, 401-02.

Hardy took the aphorism from *The Mill on the Floss*.

HARRISON (see ARNOLD: Vogeler).

HOPKINS (see also III, Fairchild).

The Journals and Papers of Gerard Manley Hopkins. . . . See VB 1961, 387.
Rev. by E. E. Duncan-Jones in *MLR*, LVII, 445-47.

The Sermons and Devotional Writings of Gerard Manley Hopkins. . . . VB 1961, 387.
Rev. by E. E. Duncan-Jones in *MLR*, LVII, 431-33.

Bernad, Miguel A. "Hopkins' Pied Beauty: A Note on its Ignatian Inspiration." *EC*, XII, 217-20.

Boyle, Robert Richard. *Metaphor in Hopkins*. . . . See VB 1961, 387.
Rev. by George Hemphill in *CE*, XXIII, 514; by W. H. Gardner in *MLR*, LVII, 600-01; by Alan Heuser in *QQ*, XLIX, 323; by Newton P. Stallknecht in *YR*, LI, 637-42; by Walker Gibson in *VS*, V, 353.

Gavin, Sister Rosemarie Julie. "Hopkins' 'The Candle Indoors.'" *Ex*, XX, Item 50.

Greiner, Francis J. "Hopkins' 'The Habit of Perfection.'" *Ex*, XXI, Item 19.

McNamee, M. B. "Mastery and Mercy in *The Wreck of the Deutschland*." *CE*, XXIII, 267-76.

Myers, John A., Jr. "Intimations of Mortality: An Analysis of Hopkins' 'Spring and Fall.'" *EJ*, LI, 585-87.

Stempel, Daniel. "A Reading of 'The Windhover.'" *CE*, XXIII, 305-07.

Templeman, William D. "Ruskin's Ploughshare and Hopkins' 'The Windhover.'" *ESt*, XLIII, 103-06.
Suggests that the plow image of "The Windhover" may derive from a passage in Ruskin's "Ad Valorem."

Wain, John. *Gerard Manley Hopkins: An Idiom of Desperation*. London: Pub. for the British Acad. by Oxford Univ. Pr. Pp. 24.
Rev. by E. E. Duncan-Jones in *MLR*, LVII, 431-33.
Chatterton Lecture on an English Poet, British Acad., 1959.

Winters, Yvor. *The Function of Criticism*. London: Routledge. Pp. 200.
Rev. by Frank Kermode in *NS*, LXIII, 382.
Contains an essay on Hopkins.

Wooton, Carl. "The Terrible Fire of Gerard Manley Hopkins." *Texas Studies in Lit. and Lang.*, IV, 367-75.

Use of fire as image and symbol in Hopkins' poetry.

HORNE.

Pearl, Cyril. *Always Morning: The Life of Richard Henry "Orion" Horne.* . . . See VB 1961, 369.

Rev. by Ronald E. Freeman in *VS,* VI, 93-94.

HOUSMAN (see also III, Fairchild).

Allen, Don Cameron (ed.). *The Moment of Poetry.* Baltimore: Johns Hopkins Pr. Pp. 144.

Rev. by Herbert Burke in *LJ,* LXXXVII, 1610.

Includes Richard Wilbur's explication of Housman's "Epitaph of an Army of Mercenaries."

Carter, John (ed.). *A. E. Housman: Selected Prose.* . . . See VB 1961, 388.

Rev. by Tom Burns Haber in *Classical Jour.,* LVII, 371-73; by A. S. F. Gow in *Classical Rev.,* XII, 161-62; by Maurice Pollet in *Études anglaises,* XV, 196-97; by DeLancey Ferguson in *HTB,* 14 Jan., p. 8; by Tom Burns Haber in *JEGP,* LXI, 436-38; in *TLS,* 26 Jan., p. 58.

Carter, John. "Housmaniana." *Book Collector,* XI, 84.

Report of existence of a third copy of first edition of *Shropshire Lad* with presentation inscription in the author's hand.

Carter, John. "Missing Housman MSS." *TLS,* 7 Dec., p. 964.

Five poems are missing from the fair copies of *A Shropshire Lad* and *Last Poems* at Cambridge.

Dean-Smith, Margaret. "Housman's 'The Deserter.'" *N & Q,* n.s. IX, 275-76.

Haber, Tom Burns. "A. E. Housman and *Ye Rounde Table.*" *JEGP,* LXI, 797-809.

White, William, "Housman in French and Music." *BSP,* LVI, 257-59.

HUXLEY.

Blinderman, Charles S. "Semantic Aspects of T. H. Huxley's Literary Style." *Jour. of Communication,* XII, 171-78.

Blinderman, Charles S. "T. H. Huxley's Theory of Aesthetics: Unity in Diversity." *JAA,* XXI, 49-55.

JONES (see III, Weales).

KINGSLEY.

Martin, Roger B. "Manuscript Sermons of Charles Kingsley." *Princeton Univ. Library Chronicle,* XXIII, 181.

KIPLING.

Gilbert, Elliot L. "What Happens in 'Mrs. Bathurst.'" *PMLA,* LXXVII, 450-58.

Lewis, C. S. *They Asked For a Paper.* London: Geoffrey Bles. Pp. viii + 211.

Rev. by F. W. Bateson in *NS,* LXIII, 376; in *TLS,* 30 Mar., p. 219.

Includes an essay on Kipling.

Rowse, A. L. "Kipling's Enduring Reputation." *Listener,* 25 Oct., pp. 652-53; 55.

Solomon, Eric. *"The Light That Failed* as a War Novel." *Eng. Fiction in Transition,* V, 30-34.

Stewart, James McG. *Rudyard Kipling: A Bibliographical Catalogue.* . . . See VB 1961, 388.

Rev. by Roger Lancelyn Green in *RES,* n.s. XIII, 102-03.

LANG.

Green, Roger Lancelyn. *Andrew Lang.* London: Bodley Head. Pp. 84.

Rev. in *TLS,* 1 June, p. 408.

Short biography discussing Lang as a children's author.

LEE-HAMILTON.

MacBeth, George. "Lee-Hamilton and the Romantic Agony." *Critical Quart.,* IV, 141-50.

The illness of this neglected Victorian poet, called an essential link in the chain of nineteenth-century pessimism, is seen as the key to his poetry and the "batteries" of its power. The author's sympathetic insight into and understanding of the poet's thoughts and his perceptive analysis of a number of the poems make this article a significant one. — M. T.

LIVINGSTONE.

Schapera, I. (ed.). *Livingstone's Missionary Correspondence.* . . . See VB 1961, 388.

Rev. by M. D. Herrick in *LJ,* LXXXVII, 1614-15; in *TLS,* 2 Mar., p. 134.

MACAULAY.

Zall, Paul M. "Selina Macaulay's Diary." *Bull. New York Pub. Libr.,* LXVI, 440-43.

MALLOCK.

Nickerson, Charles C. "W. H. Mallock's Contributions to 'The Miscellany.'" *VS,* VI, 169-77.

Tucker, Albert V. "W. H. Mallock and Late Victorian Conservatism." *TQ,* XXXI, 223-41.

Concerned principally with Mallock's essays on conservatism published in the *National Review,* 1883-1889.

MARRYAT.

Jackman, Sydney (ed.). *A Diary in America.* New York: Knopf. Pp. xxvi + 487.

Rev. by Phoebe Adams in *AM,* CCIX, 128-29; by R. C. Woodward in *LJ,* LXXXVII, 977.

MARTINEAU.

Webb, Robert K. *Harriet Martineau: A Radical Victorian.* . . . See VB 1961, 388.

Rev. by Asa Briggs in *EHR*, LXXVII, 395-96.

MAURICE.

Dring, Tom. "The Philosophy of Frederick Denison Maurice." *LQHR*, CLXXXVII (6th ser., XXXI), 276-84.

MEREDITH (see also III, Billingsley).

Selected Poems. Edited with an introduction by Graham Hough. London: Oxford Univ. Pr. Pp. 95.

Rev. by Madeline L. Cazamian in *Études anglaises*, XV, 289-90.

Baylen, Joseph O. "George Meredith and W. T. Stead: Two Unpublished Letters." *Texas Studies in Lit. and Lang.*, IV, 21-23.

Buchen, Irving H. "*The Ordeal of Richard Feverel:* Science versus Nature." *ELH*, XXIX, 47-66.

Sir Austin's "system" represents mechanistic science in conflict with nature.

Fanger, Donald. "George Meredith as Novelist." *NCF*, XVI, 317-28.

Kelvin, Norman. *A Troubled Eden: Nature and Society in the Works of George Meredith.* . . . VB 1961, 389.

Rev. by A. G. Hill in *Critical Quart.*, IV, 286-87; by Walter F. Wright in *JEGP*, LXI, 194-95; by Andrew Wright in *SAQ*, LXI, 555-56; in *TLS*, 12 Jan., p. 30.

Kerpneck, Harvey. "A Shorn Shagpat." *Book Collector*, XI, 80-83.

Smith, John H. "Similarities of Imagery and Diction Between *The Ordeal of Richard Feverel* and *Modern Love.*" *DA*, XXII, 3209.

Stewart, Donald C. "Dramatic Power and Technique in the Novels of George Meredith." *DA*, XXIII, 2122.

Thomson, Fred C. "The Design of *One of Our Conquerors.*" *Studies in English Literature*, II, 463-80.

MILL (see also II, Corry, Swart).

Carr, Robert. "The Religious Thought of John Stuart Mill: A Study in Reluctant Scepticism." *JHI*, XXIII, 475-95.

Like other Victorian writers, Mill found reason no sure guide in religious matters.

Cooney, Seamus. " 'The Heart of That Mystery': A Note on John Stuart Mill's Theory of Poetry." *VNL*, No. 21 (Spring), pp. 20-23.

Himmelfarb, Gertrude (ed.). *Essays on*

Politics and Culture. New York: Doubleday. Pp. xxxi + 494.

Rev. by T. M. Bogie in *LJ*, LXXXVII, 4449.

Hoffman, Robert. "A Note on Mill's Method of Residues." *JP*, LIX, 495-97.

Mill, Anna Jean (ed.). *John Mill's Boyhood Visit to France.* . . . See VB 1961, 389.

Rev. by Geoffrey Carnall in *MLR*, LVII, 307-08.

Stillinger, Jack (ed.). *The Early Draft of John Stuart Mill's "Autobiography".* . . . See VB 1961, 389.

Rev. by Lionel Robbins in *Economica*, XXIX, 202-04; by Walter E. Houghton in *JMH*, XXXIV, 453; by Geoffrey Carnall in *MLR*, LVII, 424-25; by Harold T. Parker in *SAQ*, LXI, 552-53.

Waller, John O. "John Stuart Mill and the American Civil War." *Bull. New York Pub. Libr.*, LXVI, 505-18.

MORRIS.

Faulkner, Peter. *William Morris and William Butler Yeats.* Oxford Univ. Pr. Pp. 31.

Grierson, Janet. *Isabella Gilmore, Sister to William Morris.* London: S.P.C.K. Pp. xii + 243.

Rev. in *TLS*, 14 Dec., p. 970.

Thompson, Edward Palmer. *William Morris, Romantic to Revolutionary.* New York: Monthly Rev. Pr. Pp. 908.

Rev. by Jack VanDerhoof in *LJ*, LXXXVII, 1602.

NEWMAN (see also II, Altholz, Davies; III, Fulweiler).

Barmann, Lawrence F. (ed.). *Newman at St. Mary's.* Westminster, Md.: Newman Pr. Pp. 211.

Selections from sermons.

Boekraad, Adrian J., and Tristam, Henry. *The Argument from Conscience to the Existence of God, According to J. H. Newman.* Louvain: Editions Nauwelaerts. Pp. 205.

Rev. in *TLS*, Mar. 9, p. 158.

Presents and annotates a previously unpublished essay of Newman's.

Cameron, James Munro. *The Night Battle.* London: Burns and Oates. Pp. xii + 243.

Rev. by P. Mairet in *NS*, LXIV, 905. Includes an essay on Newman and empiricism.

Collins, James (ed.). *Philosophical Readings in Cardinal Newman.* . . . See VB 1961, 390.

Rev. by C. G. Gross in *LJ*, LXXXVII, 105.

Coulson, John (ed.). *On Consulting the Faithful in Matters of Doctrine.* London: Geoffrey Chapman. Pp. 118.
A new critical edition.

Deen, Leonard W. "The Rhetoric of Newman's Apologia." *ELH*, XXIX, 224-38.
Devices of narrative, confessional, factual, and imaginative rhetoric in Newman's book.

Dessain, Charles Stephen (ed.). *Letters and Diaries of John Henry Newman.* Vol. XI, *Littlemore to Rome, Oct. 1845 to Dec. 1846.* . . . See VB 1961, 390.
Rev. by Arthur T. Leone in *CWd*, CXCV, 374-76; by Douglas E. Pett in *Jour. of Eccl. Hist.*, XIII, 255-56; by A. O. J. Cockshut in *Manchester Guardian Weekly*, 15 Mar., p. 10; by Fergal McGrath in *StI*, L, 322-24; in *TLS*, 26 Jan., p. 56; by Martin J. Svaglic in *VS*, VI, 88-90.
Vol. XII: *Rome to Birmingham, 1 January 1847 to 31 December 1848.* London: Nelson. Pp. 441.
Rev. by Marghanita Laski in *Manchester Guardian Weekly*, 20 Dec., p. 10; by P. Mairet in *NS*, LXIV, 905; by David Lodge in *S*, 21 Dec., p. 967.

Hollis, Christopher. "Newman the Man: Freedom and Love." *Wiseman Rev.*, CCXXXVII (No. 492), 182-90.

MacDougall, Hugh A. *The Acton-Newman Relations.* N.Y.: Fordham Univ. Pr. Pp. xi + 199.

Mozley, Dorothea (ed.). *Newman Family Letters.* London: S.P.C.K. Pp. xx + 219.
Rev. by David Lodge in *S*, 21 Dec., p. 967; noted in *Wiseman Rev.*, CCXXXVII, 358.
Letters of Newman's two sisters, Harriet and Jemima.

Ryan, Alvan S. (ed.). *Newman and Gladstone: The Vatican Decrees.* Notre Dame, Ind.: Notre Dame Univ. Pp. xxii + 228.
Contain's Gladstone's *The Vatican Decrees in their Bearing on Civil Allegiance* and Newman's *A Letter Addressed to His Grace the Duke of Norfolk.*

Trevor, Meriol. *Newman: The Pillar of the Cloud.* London: Macmillan; New York: Doubleday. Pp. 649.
Rev. by W. C. Heiser in *LJ*, LXXXVII, 4549; by A. O. J. Cockshut in *Manchester Guardian Weekly*, 15 Mar., p. 10; by Stuart Hampshire in *NS*, LXIII, 371-72; by David Lodge in *S*, 13 Apr., pp. 484-85; by Fergal McGrath in *StI*, L, 320-22; in *TLS*, 9 Mar., p. 158.
First volume of a two-part biography.

Trevor, Meriol. *Newman: Light in Winter.* London: Macmillan. Pp. xiv + 659.

Rev. by Marghanita Laski in *Manchester Guardian Weekly*, 20 Dec., p. 10; by P. Mariet in *NS*, LXIV, 905; by David Lodge in *S*, 21 Dec., p. 967.
The second volume of a two-part biography.

Walgrave, J. H. *Newman the Theologian.* . . . See VB 1961, 390.
Rev. by W. Norman Pittenger in *VS*, V, 263-64.

Zale, Eric M. "The Defenses of John Henry Newman." *DA*, XXIII, 637.
Examination of Newman's defensive attitudes in religion and thought.

NIGHTINGALE (see III, Rees).

OLIPHANT.

Colby, Robert and Vineta. "A Beleaguered City: A Fable for the Victorian Age." *NCF*, XVI, 283-301.
An analysis of Mrs. Oliphant's "finest story."

PATER (see also III, Kissane, Watson; ELIOT: Knoepflmacher; YEATS: Nathan).

Cierpial, Leo J. "Degeneration and the Religion of Beauty: A Traditional Pattern in Coleridge's *The Rime of the Ancient Mariner*, Pater's *The Renaissance*, Maugham's *Of Human Bondage*, and Joyce's *Ulysses*." *DA*, XXIII, 1361-62.

d'Hangest, Germain. *Walter Pater: L'homme et l'oeuvre.* Paris: Didier. 2 vols. Pp. 372, 404.
Rev. by Flory Turot in *Revue des deux mondes* (No. 18: 15 Sept.), 292; in *TLS*, 20 July, p. 526.

Inman, Billie Andrew. "The Organic Structure of *Marius the Epicurean*." *PQ*, XLI, 475-91.

Inman, Billie Jo Andrew. "Pater's Idea of Man." *DA*, XXII, 3665.

Iser, Wolfgang. *Walter Pater: Die Autonomie des Aesthetischen.* . . . See VB 1961, 390.
Rev. by Lawrence Evans in *VS*, V, 350-51.

Johnson, R. V. *Walter Pater: A Study of His Critical Outlook.* . . . See VB 1961, 390.
Rev. by J. P. Curgenven in *RES*, XIII, 327.

Knoepflmacher, U. C. "Pater's Religion of Sanity: 'Plato and Platonism' as a Document of Victorian Unbelief." *VS*, VI, 151-68.

PATMORE (see ARNOLD: Holloway).

PINERO.

Davies, Cecil W. "Pinero: The Drama of Reputation." *English*, XIV, 13-17.

READE.

Burns, Wayne. *Charles Reade: A Study in Victorian Authorship.* . . . See VB 1961, 390.

Rev. by E. G. Sutcliff in *Lit. and Psych.,* XII, 25-27; by Royal A. Gettmann in *NCF,* XVI, 363-66; by Edwin R. Clapp in *Western Humanities Rev.,* XVI, 89-90.

ROLFE.

Woolf, Cecil (ed.). *Letters to R. M. Dawkins.* London: Vane. Pp. 180.

Vol. III of edition of Corvo's letters.

ROSSETTIS.

Lindberg, John. "Rossetti's Cumaean Oracle." *VNL,* No. 22 (Fall), pp. 20-21.

Packer, Lona Mosk. "Christina Rosetti's 'Songs in a Cornfield': A Misprint Uncorrected." *N & Q,* n.s. IX, 97-100.

Packer, Lona Mosk. "F. S. Ellis and the Rossettis: A Publishing Venture and Misadventure, 1870." *Western Humanities Rev.,* XVI, 243-53.

Robillard, Douglas J. "Rossetti's 'Willowwood' Sonnets and the Structure of *The House of Life.*" *VNL,* No. 22 (Fall), pp. 5-9.

Sambrook, A. J. "D. G. Rossetti and R. W. Dixon." *Études anglaises,* XIV, 331-38.

Savarit, Jacques. *Tendances mystiques et esoteriques chez Dante-Gabriel Rossetti.* Paris: Didier, 1961.

Rev. by Joan Rees in *MLR,* LVII, 429-30.

RUSKIN (see also III, Frankl, Kissane; HOPKINS: Templeman).

Curtin, Frank D. "Ruskin in French Criticism: A Possible Reappraisal." *PMLA,* LXXVII, 102-08.

Rosenberg, John D. *The Darkening Glass: A Portrait of Ruskin's Genius.* . . . See VB 1961, 391.

Rev. by Phoebe Adams in *AM,* CCIX, 122; by Paul Walton in *Burlington Mag.,* CIV, 502; by Bertram Morris in *JAA,* XX, 446-47; by Francis Steegmuller in *NYTBR,* 21 Jan., p. 19; by Gaylord Le Roy in *VS,* V, 351-53; by Clarence Short in *Western Humanities Rev.,* XVI, 286-87; by J. B. Schneewind in *YR,* LI, 477-78.

Walton, Paul. "A Water-colour by John Ruskin." *Burlington Mag.,* CIV, 21-25.

Description of view of Amalfi.

SHAW (see also I, "Theatrical Material"; II, Cole, Duffy; BROWNING: Pietch).

Laurence, Dan H. and Greene, David H. (eds.). *The Matter with Ireland.* New York: Hill and Wang; London: Hart-Davis. Pp. xviii + 308.

Rev. by Martin Tucker in *Commonweal,* LXXV, 668; by H. K. in *HTB,* 18 Mar., p. 8; by Gerald Weales in *New R,* 23 Apr., p. 35; by J. V. Kelleher in *SR,* 17 Mar., p. 24; in *TLS,* 13 Apr., p. 250. Further previously uncollected Shaw writings.

Laurence, Dan H. (ed.). *Platform and Pulpit.* . . . See VB 1961, 391.

Rev. by Donald Emerson in *Christian Century,* LXXIX, 231; by Eric J. Batson in *English,* XIV, 97-100; by Herbert Kupferberg in *HTB,* 24 Dec., 1961, p. 4; by Roy Walker in *Listener,* 8 Feb., p. 262; by D. J. Enright in *NS,* LXIII, 196; by M. H. Nichols in *QJS,* XLVIII, 204-05; by Alan Brien in *S,* 16 Feb., p. 211; in *TLS,* 9 Feb., p. 88.

Bennett, Kenneth C., Jr., "George Bernard Shaw's Philosophy of Art." *DA,* XXII, 3197.

Bullough, Geoffrey. "Literary Relations of Shaw's Mrs. Warren." *PQ,* XLI, 339-58.

The relationship of Shaw's play with Maupassant's *Yvette* and Janet Achurch's *Mrs. Daintree's Daughter.*

Chappelow, Allan (ed.). *Shaw the Villager and Human Being.* . . . See VB 1961, 391.

Rev. by Eric J. Batson in *English,* XIV, 97-100; by Kingsley Martin in *NS,* LXIII, 58-59; by Brooks Atkinson in *NYTBR,* 25 Nov., p. 5; by Alan Brien in *S,* 16 Feb., p. 212.

Cherry, D. R. "The Fabianism of Shaw." *QQ,* LXIX, 83-93.

Dietrich, Margaret. "Die Rebellion gegen das Ueberlebte in der Dramatik des 20. Jahrhunderts — von Shaw bis Ionesco." *Universitas,* XVI, 955-65.

Gassner, John. "Bernard Shaw and the Making of the Modern Mind." *CE,* XXIII, 517-25.

Lewis, Allan. *The Contemporary Theatre: The Significant Playwrights of Our Time.* New York: Crown. Pp. 312.

Rev. by H. M. Miller in *LJ,* LXXXVII, 1805.

Mills, John A. "Language and Laughter: A Study of Comic Diction in the Plays of Bernard Shaw." *DA,* XXII, 4017-18.

Ohmann, Richard M. *Shaw: The Style and the Man.* Middletown, Conn.: Wesleyan Univ. Pr. Pp. xv + 200.

Rev. by J. R. Willingham in *LJ,* LXXXVII, 4440.

Pilecki, Gerard A. "Shaw's *Geneva:* A Critical Study of the Evolution of the Text in Relation to Shaw's Political Thought and Dramatic Practice." *DA,* XXII, 2399.

Shenfield, Margaret. *Bernard Shaw: A Pic-*

torial Biography. London: Thames and Hudson; New York: Viking. Pp. 144.
Rev. by Robert Greacen in *Listener*, 24 May, p. 920; by J. F. Moran in *LJ*, LXXXVII, 2741; in *TLS*, 13 Apr., p. 250.
The Shaw Review. Vol. V, No. 1 (January, 1962), has items: Gelb, Arthur and Barbara, "O'Neill and Shaw: Excerpts from O'Neill" (pp. 2-4); Beerbohm, Max, "Mr. Shaw's Profession" (pp. 5-9); Huss, Roy, "Max the 'Incomparable' on G.B.S. the 'Irrepressible'" (pp. 10-20); Calvin, Judith S., "The GBSsence of Giraudoux" (pp. 21-35); "A Continuing Check-list of Shaviana," compiled and edited by the editor (pp. 36-37); Smith, Warren S., a review of Dan H. Laurence's *Platform and Pulpit* (pp. 38-40); "Queries" (p. 40).
No. 2 (May, 1962) has items: Leary, Daniel H., "The Moral Dialectic in *Caesar and Cleopatra*" (pp. 42-53); Geduld, H. M., "The Textual Problem in Shaw" (pp. 54-60); Torn, Jessie, "A Figleaf in Her Bonnet: A Scene and a Preface" (pp. 61-68); "A Continuing Check-list of Shaviana," compiled and edited by Charles A. Carpenter, Jr. (pp. 69-71); Charters, John, a review of *Shaw the Villager and Human Being*, narrated and edited by Allan Chappelow (pp. 72-75); McKiernan, John, a review of *The Matter with Ireland*, edited with an introduction by Dan H. Laurence and David H. Greene (pp. 75-78); Weintraub, Stanley, a review of *Shaw and Molly Tompkins: In Their Own Words*, edited by Peter Tompkins (pp. 79-80).
No. 3 (September, 1962) has items: Sister M. Corona Sharp, O.S.U., "The Theme of Masks in *Geneva*" (pp. 82-91); Solomon, Stanley J., "Theme and Structure in *Getting Married*" (pp. 92-96); James, Eugene Nelson, "The Critic as Dramatist: Bernard Shaw, 1895-1898" (pp. 97-108); Stokes, E. E., "Sydney Carlyle Cockerell: 1867-1962" (pp. 109-111); "A Continuing Check-list of Shaviana," compiled and edited by Stephen S. Stanton (pp. 112-114); Rudman, Harry W., a review of A. M. McBriar's *Fabian Socialism and English Politics 1884-1918* (p. 118); "Index to The Shaw Review" (pp. 119-120).
Tompkins, Peter (ed.). *Shaw and Molly Tompkins.* New York: Clarkson H. Pot-

ter; London: Anthony Blond. Pp. 288.
Rev. by George Cloyne in *HTB*, 29 Apr., p. 10; by Stanley Weintraub in *NYTBR*, 1 Apr., p. 16; by Victor Chapin in *SR*, 17 Mar., p. 25; in *TLS*, 3 Nov., 1961, p. 794.
Wilson, Edwin (ed.). *Shaw on Shakespeare.* . . . See VB 1961, 391.
Rev. by Roy Walker in *Listener*, 8 Feb., p. 262; by D. J. Enright in *NS*, LXIII, 196; by Alan Brien in *S*, 16 Feb., p. 211; in *TLS*, 9 Feb., p. 88.

STEPHEN.
Bicknell, John W. "Leslie Stephen's 'English Thought in the Eighteenth Century': A Tract for the Times." *VS*, VI, 103-20.
Stephen used his *English Thought* both to expose the arguments of the orthodox and to warn his generation of the failure of eighteenth-century rationalism when it ignored the hopes and fears exploited by Methodism and Evangelicanism.

STEVENSON.
Gossmann, Ann. "On the Knocking at the Gate in 'Markheim.'" *NCF*, XVII, 73-76.
McKay, George L. "Note on R. L. Stevenson's 'Requiem.'" *Yale Univ. Libr. Gazette*, XXXVI, 122-25.
McKay, George L. (comp.). *A Stevenson Library.* Vol. V: *Manuscripts by Robert Louis Stevenson and Others.* . . . See VB 1961, 393.
Rev. by P. J. Croft in *Book Collector*, XI, 105-06; by Lionel Stevenson in *BSP*, LVI, 137-38; in *TLS*, 2 Mar., p. 144.

SULLIVAN.
Poladian, Sirvart (comp.). *Sir Arthur Sullivan: An Index to the Texts of His Vocal Works.* Detroit, Mich.: Information Serv., Inc. Pp. 91.
Rev. briefly by C. K. Miller in *LJ*, LXXXVII, 1448.

SWINBURNE.
Dobrée, Bonamy (ed.). *Poems of Algernon Charles Swinburne.* . . . See VB 1961, 393.
Rev. by Robert Creeley in *Poetry*, C, 324-28.
Lang, Cecil Y. (ed.). *Swinburne Letters.* . . . See VB 1961, 393.
Vols. V-VI rev. by De L. Ferguson in *HTB*, 13 May, p. 9; by William Plomer in *Listener*, 2 Aug., p. 183; by J. R. Willingham in *LJ*, LXXXVII, 2381; by Christopher Ricks in *NS*, LXIV, 176; by G. N. Ray in *NYTBR*, 13 May, p. 4; in *TLS*, 10 Aug., p. 593; by Hazard Adams in *VS*, VI, 182-85.
Sitwell, Edith (ed.). *Swinburne: A Selection.* . . . See VB 1961, 393.

Rev. by Robert Creeley in *Poetry*, C, 324-28; unfavorably by Robert L. Peters in *Prairie Schooner*, XXXVI, 87-88.

de Graaf, Daniel A. "L'influence de Swinburne sur Verlaine et Rimbaud." *Revue des sciences humaines,* n.s. No. 97 (1960), 87-92.

Lang, Cecil Y. "Atalanta in Manuscript." *Yale Univ. Libr. Gazette*, XXXVII, 19-24. Account of the surviving portions of the MS.

Peters, Robert L. "Algernon Charles Swinburne and the Use of Integral Detail." *VS*, V, 289-302.

Wilson, Edmund. "Swinburne of Capheaton and Eton." *New Yorker*, 6 Oct., pp. 165-200.
A review article based on Lang's *Swinburne Letters* (see above).

SYMONS.

Lhombreaud, Roger. *Arthur Symons: His Life and Letters*. London: Unicorn Pr.

TENNYSON (see also II, Lehman).

Berry, Francis. *Poetry and the Physical Voice*. New York and London: Oxford Univ. Pr. Pp. 205.
Includes discussion of Tennyson's intonations and rhythms.

Bishop, Jonathan. "The Unity of 'In Memoriam.'" *VNL* No. 21 (Spring), pp. 9-14.

Blunden, Edmund. (ed.). *Selected Poems of Tennyson*. New York: Macmillan Co., 1960. Pp. 162.
Rev. by William D. Templeman in *The Personalist*, XLIII, 132-33.

Buckley, Jerome Hamilton. *Tennyson: The Growth of a Poet*. . . . See VB 1961, 393.
Rev. by Timothy Rogers in *English*, XIV, 26-27; by Donald Smalley in *JEGP*, LXI, 349-57; by John Killham in *MLR*, LVII, 144-45; by R. W. King in *RES*, n.s. XIII, 439; by F. E. L. Priestley in *TQ*, XXXII, 102-06.

Danzig, Allan. "The Contraries: A Central Concept in Tennyson's Poetry." *PMLA*, LXXVII, 577-85.

DeMott, Benjamin. *Hells and Benefits: A Report on American Minds, Matters, and Possibilities*. New York: Basic Books. Pp. 264.
Rev. by C. M. Brown in *LJ*, LXXXVII, 3463.
Includes a provocative essay on Tennyson's "The Lotus-Eaters."

Gridley, Roy. "Confusion of the Seasons in Tennyson's 'The Last Tournament'." *VNL*, No. 22 (Fall), pp. 14-16.

Grant, Stephen Allen. "The Mystical Implications of *In Memoriam*." *Studies in English Lit.*, II, 481-95.

Grigson, Geoffrey. *Poets in Their Pride*. London: Phoenix House. Pp. 151.
Rev. in *TLS*, 7 Dec., p. 956.
Includes chapters on Tennyson and Hardy.

Nowell-Smith, Simon. "Tennyson, A. C. and F. *Poems by Two Brothers*, 1827." *Book Collector*, XI, 80.
Omission by Wise in description of original issue.

Pitt, Valerie. *Tennyson Laureate*. London: Barrie and Rockliff. Pp. xi + 289.
Rev. by Christopher Ricks in *Listener*, 25 Oct., p. 678 (see also "Great Reputations," p. 648); by John Gross in *Manchester Guardian Weekly*, 1 Nov., p. 11; by R. Mayne in *NS*, LXIV, 782; by Roy Fuller in *S*, 2 Nov., p. 688.

Rader, Ralph Wilson. "The Composition of Tennyson's *Maud*." *MP*, LIX, 265-69.
"Tennyson's own involvement in the production of his poem was much more complex than his note or de Vere's account implies."

Rader, Ralph W. "Tennyson and Rosa Baring." *VS*, V, 224-60.
Tennyson's love for Rosa.

Rader, Ralph Wilson. "Tennyson in the Year of Hallam's Death." *PMLA*, LXXVII, 419-24.

Richardson, Joanna. *The Pre-Eminent Victorian*. London: Cape. Pp. 313.
Rev. by Christopher Ricks in *Listener*, 25 Oct., p. 678 (see also "Great Reputations," p. 648); by Richard Mayne in *NS*, LXIV, 782; by Roy Fuller in *S*, 2 Nov., p. 688.

Ricks, Christopher. " 'Peace and War' and 'Maud.' " *N & Q*, n.s. IX, 230.

Ryals, Clyde De L. "The 'Heavenly Friend': The 'New Mythus' of *In Memoriam*." *The Personalist*, XLIII, 383-402.
Relates Tennyson's spiritual struggle to Carlyle's and suggests that for Tennyson the "new mythus" was Hallam as his "heavenly friend."

Ryals, Clyde De L. "The 'Weird Seizures' in *The Princess*." *Texas Studies in Lit. and Lang.*, IV, 268-75.

Smalley, Donald. "A New Look at Tennyson — and Especially the *Idylls*." *JEGP*, LXI, 349-57.

Smith, Elton E. " 'The Two Voices': A Tennyson Study." *DA*, XXIII, 239.

Svaglic, Martin J. "A Framework for Tennyson's *In Memoriam*." *JEGP*, LXI, 810-25.
Suggests nine natural divisions in the poem.

Turner, Paul. "Some Ancient Light on Tennyson's *Oenone*." *JEGP*, LXI, 52-72.
A study of the classical literary sources of the poem.

Young, Andrew. *The Poet and the Landscape*. London: Hart-Davis. Pp. 167.
Rev. in *TLS*, 10 Aug., p. 605.
Pastoral poetry in English, including that of Tennyson and Hardy.

THACKERAY (see also III, Billingsley).

Baker, Joseph E. "Thackeray's Recantation." *PMLA*, LXXVII, 586-94.
Concerned chiefly with the novel *Philip*.

Mudge, Isadore Gilbert, and Sears, M. Earl (eds.). *A Thackeray Dictionary: The Characters and Scenes of the Novels and Short Stories Alphabetically Arranged*. New York: Humanities Pr. Pp. xlv + 304.

Sharp, Sister M. Corona. "Sympathetic Mockery: A Study of the Narrator's Character in *Vanity Fair*." *ELH*, XXIX, 324-36.

Talon, Henri-A. "Time and Memory in Thackeray's *Henry Esmond*." *RES*, n.s. XIII, 147-56.

THOMPSON.

Butter, Peter H. *Francis Thompson*. Writers and Their Work Series. London: Longmans, Green. 1961. Pp. 38.

Danchin, Pierre. *Francis Thompson: La vei et l'oeuvre d'un poete*. . . . See VB 1961, 394.
Rev. by J. C. Reid in *RES*, n.s. XIII, 86-87.

THOMSON.

Forsyth, R. A. "Evolutionism and the Pessimism of James Thomson (B.V.)." *EC*, XII, 148-66.

Schaefer, William D. "James Thomson: A Study in Intellectual Development." *DA*, XXIII, 2139.

Schaefer, William D. "The Two Cities of Dreadful Night." *PMLA*, LXXVII, 609-15.

TREVELYAN.

McRae, Malcolm. "Sir Charles Trevelyan's Indian Letters, 1859-1865." *EHR*, LXXVII, 706-12.
Survey of 1500 letters at the Bodleian.

TROLLOPE (see also III, Billingsley).

Booth, Bradford A. *Anthony Trollope: Aspects of His Life and Work*. . . . See VB 1961, 394.
Rev. by Jacques Surel in *Études anglaises*, XV, 192-94.

Darbishire, Helen. *Somerville College Chapel Addresses*. Privately printed; distributed by Blackwell, Oxford. Pp. xiv + 139.
Rev. in *TLS*, 31 Aug., p. 658.
Includes address on Trollope.

Davies, Hugh Sykes. *Trollope*. . . . See VB 1960, 407.
Rev. by Jacques Surel in *Études anglaises*, XV, 192-94.

Dustin, John E. "Thematic Alternation in Trollope." *PMLA*, LXXVII, 280-87.

Hawkins, Sherman. "Mr. Harding's Church Music." *ELH*, XXIX, 202-33.
Mr. Harding's life as an imitation of Christ, his music as a symbol of harmony. Hawkins's article is brilliantly perceptive, showing the rewards for a close study of Trollope in discovery of more levels of meaning and richer complexity of characterization. — O. M.

"Trollope in the West Indies." *Listener*, 15 Mar., p. 461.

WILDE.

Barnett, J. H. "My Own Dear Boy." *CR*, CCII, 146-50.

Harrod, Roy. "Oscar Wilde." *TLS*, 27 July, p. 541.
Reminiscences of Wilde by a daughter of Forbes-Robertson. (See also letter by Lindsay M. Jopling, 7 Sept., p. 673.)

Hart-Davis, Rupert (ed.). *The Letters of Oscar Wilde*. London: Rupert Hart-Davis; New York: Harcourt Brace. Pp. xxv + 958.
Rev. by George Cloyne in *HTB*, 28 Oct., p. 5; by Gerald Weales in *Hudson Rev.*, XV, 620-22; by William Plomer in *Listener*, 28 June, p. 1125; by R. E. Wagenknecht in *LJ*, LXXXVII, 4548; by Richard Ellmann in *Manchester Guardian Weekly*, 5 July, p. 11; by Ronald Bryden in *N*, 3 Nov., pp. 290-91; by Stuart Hampshire in *NS*, LXIII, 941-42; by Peter Quennell in *NYTBR*, 28 Oct., p. 1; by H. Montgomery Hyde in *QR*, July, pp. 279-90; by Constantine Fitzgibbon in *S*, 29 June, p. 861; by Harry T. Moore, in *SR*, 20 Oct., p. 26; in *TLS*, 29 June, pp. 469-71.

Lucie-Smith, Edward. "For Herod." *NS*, LXIII, 728.

Wadleigh, Paul C. "Form in Oscar Wilde's Comedies: A Structural Analysis." *DA*, XXIII, 2257.

YEATS (see also III: Brower, Fairchild, Muir; MORRIS: Faulkner).
Essays and Introductions. . . . See VB 1961, 395.
Rev. by Robert Langbaum in *American Scholar*, XXXI, 454-60.

Explorations. Selected by Mrs. W. B. Yeats.

London: Macmillan. Pp. 453.

Rev. by F. Kermode in *NS*, LXIV, 366; by Micheál Mac Liammóir in *S*, 21 Sept., p. 403; in *TLS*, 5 Oct., p. 778.

Berkelman, Robert. "The Poet, the Swan, and the Woman." *Univ. of Kansas City Rev.*, XXVIII, 229-30.

Blackburn, Thomas. *The Price of an Eye.* . . . See VB 1961, 395.

Rev. by Richard Hoggart in *Manchester Guardian*, 8 Sept., 1961, p. 6; by Edward Lucie-Smith in *NS*, LXII, 396; in *TLS*, 8 Sept., 1961, p. 598.

Dean-Smith. "Celtic Twilight." *N & Q*, n.s. IX, 30.

Engelberg, Edward. "Passionate Reverie: W. B. Yeats's Tragic Correlative." *TQ*, XXXI, 201-22.

An essay in definition and analysis indicating the "tragic correlative" leads to Yeats's "Unity of Being."

Gordon, D. J., Fletcher, Ian, Kermode, Frank, and Skelton, Robin (eds.). *W. B. Yeats: Images of a Poet.* . . . See VB 1961, 396.

Rev. by Margaret Willy in *English*, XIV, 29-30.

Gullans, Charles B. "Leda and the Swan." *TLS*, 9 Nov., p. 864. (See also letter by Charles Madge, 16 Nov., p. 873.)

Hardy, John Edward. *The Curious Frame: Seven Poems in Text and Context.* Univ. of Notre-Dame Pr. Pp. xiv + 196.

Rev. by P. Janelle in *Études anglaises*, XV, 397-98.

Yeats's "Prayer for My Daughter" is one of the seven.

Jeffares, A. Norman. *W. B. Yeats: The Poems.* London: Edward Arnold, 1961. Pp. 64.

Rev. by L. C. Bonnerot in *Études anglaises*, XV, 296.

Kain, Richard M. *Dublin in the Age of William Butler Yeats and James Joyce.* Norman: Univ. of Oklahoma Pr. Pp. 216.

Rev. by J. F. Moran in *LJ*, LXXXVII, 4433-34; by Denis Donoghue in *N*, 6 Oct., pp. 203-04.

Leach, Elsie. "Yeats's 'A Friend's Illness' and Herbert's 'Vertue.'" *N & Q*, n.s. IX, 215.

Madge, Charles. "Leda and the Swan." *TLS*, 20 July, p. 532.

Nathan, Leonard P. "W. B. Yeats's Experi-

ments with an Influence." *VS*, VI, 66-74.

By testing, adapting, and going beyond Pater's ideas, Yeats escaped the sterility and ruin into which aestheticism led many of his contemporaries.

Nist, John. "In Defense of Yeats." *ArQ*, XVIII, 58-65. Reply to Yvor Winter's attack on Yeats (see VB 1960, 408).

Parish, John E. "The Tone of Yeats' *After Long Silence*." *Western Humanities Rev.*, XVI, 377-79.

Polletta, Gregory T. "The Progress of W. B. Yeats's Theories of Poetry." *DA*, XXII, 2399-2400.

Reid, Benjamin Lawrence. *William Butler Yeats: The Lyric of Tragedy.* . . . See VB 1961, 396.

Rev. by Francis Murphy in *BA*, XXXVI, 319-20; by L. W. Griffin in *LJ*, LXXXVII, 560.

Seiden, Morton Irving. *William Butler Yeats: The Poet as Mythmaker, 1865-1939.* East Lansing: Michigan State Univ. Pr. Pp. xiv + 397.

Sidnell, M. J. "Manuscript Versions of Yeats's *The Countess Cathleen*." *BSP*, LVI, 79-103.

Spanos, William V. "Sacramental Imagery in the Middle and Late Poetry of W. B. Yeats." *Texas Studies in Lit. and Lang.*, IV, 214-27.

Stock, Amy Geraldine. *W. B. Yeats: His Poetry and Thought.* . . . See VB 1961, 396.

Rev. by G. B. Saul in *ArQ*, XVIII, 95-96; by John Unterecker in *CE*, XXIII, 605; by John Fraser in *Dalhousie Rev.*, XLII, 99-100; by Hazard Adams in *JEGP*, LXI, 439-40; by V. L. O. Chittick in *MLQ*, XXIII, 272-73; by A. Norman Jeffares in *MLR*, LVII, 255-56; by Aerol Arnold in *The Personalist*, XLIII, 278-79; by Jon Stallworthy in *RES*, n.s. XIII, 425-27.

Unger, Leonard. "Yeats and Milton." *SAQ*, LXI, 197-212.

Miltonic echoes in Yeats.

Wilson, Francis A. C. *Yeats's Iconography.* . . . See VB 1961, 396.

Rev. by Aerol Arnold in *The Personalist*, XLIII, 278-79.

Wright, George T. *The Poet in the Poem: The Personae of Eliot, Yeats, and Pound.* . . . See VB 1961, 396.

Rev. by Peter Ure in *RES*, n.s. XIII, 214-15.

VICTORIAN IBLIOGRAPHY FOR 1963

Robert C. Slack, editor

THIS BIBLIOGRAPHY has been prepared by a committee of the Victorian Literature Group of the Modern Language Association of America: Robert C. Slack, chairman, Carnegie Institute of Technology; Oscar Maurer, University of Texas; Robert A. Donovan, State University of New York; Charles T. Dougherty, St. Louis University; Donald J. Gray, Indiana University; Richard C. Tobias, University of Pittsburgh; Ronald E. Freeman, University of Southern California; and Michael Timko, Queens College. It attempts to list the noteworthy publications of 1963 (including reviews of these and earlier items) that have a bearing on the Victorian period, as well as similar publications of earlier date that have been inadvertently omitted from the preceding Victorian bibliographies. Unless otherwise stated, the date of publication is 1963. Reference to a page in the bibliography for 1962, in *Victorian Studies,* June, 1963, is made by the following form: See VB 1962, 395. Some cross-references are given, though not all that are possible. Annotations to items are made at the discretion of committee members and the editor; some are intended to indicate content, others to emphasize important contributions; every annotation containing a judgment is initialed by the committee member responsible. For certain continuing bibliographical works the reader should consult VB 1941, the last annual bibliography in which such works are listed in full. Bibliographical entries are made to conform as closely as possible with the British National Bibliography for books first published in Great Britain, and with the Library of Congress Catalog for books first published in the United States.

The editor wishes to thank Professor Carl J. Weber for his helpful assistance with the Hardy section of the bibliography.

ABBREVIATIONS OF TITLES USED FREQUENTLY

AHR = American Historical Review
AL = American Literature
AM = Atlantic Monthly

APSR = American Political Science Review
APSS = Annals of the American Academy of Political and Social Science
ArQ = Arizona Quarterly
BA = Books Abroad
BB = Bulletin of Bibliography and Magazine Notes
BLR = Bodleian Library Record
BSP = Papers of the Bibliographical Society of America
CE = College English
CHJ = Historical Journal (formerly Cambridge Historical Journal)
CR = Contemporary Review
CWd = Catholic World
DA = Dissertation Abstracts
DUJ = Durham University Journal
EC = Essays in Criticism
EHR = English Historical Review
EJ = English Journal
ELH = English Literary History
ESt = English Studies
Ex = Explicator
HJ = Hibbert Journal
HLB = Harvard Library Bulletin
HLQ = Huntington Library Quarterly
HTB = New York Herald Tribune
JAA = Journal of Aesthetics and Art Criticism
JEGP = Journal of English and Germanic Philology
JEH = Journal of Economic History
JHI = Journal of the History of Ideas
JMH = Journal of Modern History
JP = Journal of Philosophy
JPE = Journal of Political Economy
KR = Kenyon Review
LJ = Library Journal
LQ = Library Quarterly
LQHR = London Quarterly and Holborn Review
LR = Library Review
M & L = Music and Letters
MLJ = Modern Language Journal
MLN = Modern Language Notes
MLQ = Modern Language Quarterly
MLR = Modern Language Review
MP = Modern Philology
N = Nation

N & Q = *Notes and Queries*
NCF = *Nineteenth-Century Fiction*
NEQ = *New England Quarterly*
New R = *New Republic*
NS = *New Statesman*
NYTBR = *New York Times Book Review*
PAPS = *Proceedings of the American Philosophical Society*
ParR = *Partisan Review*
PLC = *Princeton University Library Chronicle*
PMLA = *Publications of the Modern Language Association of America*
PQ = *Philological Quarterly*
PSQ = *Political Science Quarterly*
QJS = *Quarterly Journal of Speech*
QQ = *Queen's Quarterly*
QR = *Quarterly Review*
RES = *Review of English Studies*
RoR = *Romanic Review*
S = *Spectator*
SAQ = *South Atlantic Quarterly*
SeR = *Sewanee Review*
SP = *Studies in Philology*
SR = *Saturday Review*
StI = *Studies: An Irish Quarterly Review*
TC = *Twentieth Century*
TLS = *Times Literary Supplement*
TQ = *University of Toronto Quarterly*
VNL = *Victorian News Letter*
VQR = *Virginia Quarterly Review*
VS = *Victorian Studies*
YR = *Yale Review*

I. BIBLIOGRAPHICAL MATERIAL

(For bibliographies pertaining to individuals listed in Section IV, see – BROWNINGS: Barnes; CARLYLE: Tennyson; FORD: Harvey; TENNYSON: Collins).

Adams, Ruth A. and Winkler, Henry R. "An Inter-Departmental Course on Victorian England." *VS*, VII, 100-02.

"Annual Bibliography for 1962." *PMLA*, LXXVIII, No. 2, 155-73. "English Language and Literature: IX. Nineteenth Century, X. Twentieth Century," ed. Charles C. Mish, *et al.*

"Bibliography [of recent books and monographs in social history]." *International Rev. of Social History*, VIII, 109-76; 286-350.

"Bibliography in the Lecture Hall. I – Three Great Victorian Collectors." *TLS*, 29 March, p. 224.
Oxford lectures by A. N. Munby on the collections of Lord Ashburnham, Lord Zouche, and the Rev. Walter Sneyd.

Briggs, Asa, and Daiches, David. "Interdisciplinary Studies at the University of Sussex." *VS*, VII, 98-99.

Collins, Philip. "The University of Leicester Victorian Studies Group." *VS*, VI, 281-82.

Conisbee, L. R. *A Bedfordshire Bibliography.* Bedfordshire Historical Society, 1962. Pp. 333.
Rev. by J. F. A. Mason in *N&Q*, n.s. X, 389-90.

Davies, H. M. P. "The King's School, Canterbury." *Études anglaises*, XVI, 59-62.
Manuscripts in the school library. Includes many manuscripts of 19th-century writers.

Duncan, George Sang. *Bibliography of Glass (from the Earliest Records to 1940).* London: Dawson's of Pall Mall for the Society of Glass Technology, Sheffield, 1960. Pp. 544.
Rev. in *BSP*, LVII, 258-59.

French, Warren (ed.). "Current Bibliography." *Twentieth Cent. Lit.*, IX, 22-53; 101-24; 158-70.

Gerstenberger, Donna, and Hendrick, George. "1962 Supplement to *Directory of Periodicals.*" *Twentieth Cent. Lit.*, IX, 89-92.

Gordan, John. "New in the Berg Collection: 1959-1961." *Bull. New York Pub. Libr.*, LXVII, 625-38.
Includes Dickens, Wilkie Collins, Shaw.

Greenberg, Robert A. (ed.). "Recent Publications: A Selected List." *VNL*, No. 23 (Spring), pp. 29-32; No. 24 (Fall), pp. 28-32.

Guide to the Contents of the Public Record Office. 2 vols. London: H.M.S.O. Pp. vi + 249; vii + 410.
Revised from edition published in 1960 and edited by M. S. Giuseppi.

Houghton, Walter E. "Reflections on Indexing Victorian Periodicals." *VS*, VII, 192-96.

Houghton, Walter E. "Wellesley Index." *TLS*, 2 Aug., p. 599.
Announcing the publication in 1965 of

Vol. I of *The Wellesley Index to Victorian Periodicals 1824-1900.*

Jones, Robert Huhn. "The American Civil War in the British Sessional Papers: Catalogue and Commentary." *PAPS,* CVII, 415-26.

Kruse, Paul. "Piracy and the *Britannica:* Unauthorized Reprintings of the Ninth Edition." *LQ,* XXXIII, 313-28.

Osborne, John W. "Recent Acquisitions of the William Cobbett Collection in the Rutgers University Library." *Jour. of the Rutgers Univ. Libr.,* XXVI, 60-64.

Peckham, Morse. "Recent Studies in Nineteenth-Century English Literature." *SEL,* III, 595-611.

Rave, Paul Ortwin. *Kunstgeschichte in Festschriften: Allgemeine Bibliographie Kunstwissenschaftlicher Abhandlung in den bis 1960 Erscheinen Festschriften.* Berlin: Verlag Gebrüder Mann, 1962. Pp. 314.
Briefly mentioned in *BSP,* LVII, 476.

"Research on Irish History in Irish Universities, 1962-3." *Irish Hist. Studies,* XIII, 254-57.

Rigby, Margery, and Nilon, Charles (eds.). *Annual Bibliography of English Language and Literature.* Vol. XXXV, 1960. London and New York: Cambridge Univ. Pr. Pp. xvi + 376.

Rush, N. Orivin. "Special Collections." *College and Research Libr.,* XXIV, 113-18.
Mentions important items by Arnold (a first edition of *The Strayed Reveller*) and Tennyson (five distinct issues of *The Princess*).

Slack, Robert C. (ed.). "Victorian Bibliography for 1962." *VS,* VI, 383-424.

Stratman, Carl J. "The New York Stage: A Checklist of Unpublished Dissertations and Theses." *BB,* XXIV, 41-44.
Covers the years 1915-1961; contains some items of interest to Victorians: Dickens, Pinero, Wilde.

Tobias, R. C. "The Year's Work in Victorian Poetry: 1962." *Vict. Poetry,* I, 223-30.

White, Beatrice, and Dorsch, T. S. (eds.). *The Year's Work in English Studies.* Vols. XLI and XLII: 1960 and 1961. London and New York: Oxford Univ. Pr. Pp. 321 and 318.

"Writings on Irish History, 1961." *Irish Hist. Studies,* XIII, 153-72.

Zwicky, Laurie Bowman (ed.). "Relations of Literature and Science: Selected Bibliography for 1962. V. Nineteenth and Twentieth Centuries." *Symposium,* XVII, 315-17.

II. ECONOMIC, POLITICAL, RELIGIOUS, AND SOCIAL ENVIRONMENT

Altholz, Josef L. *The Liberal Catholic Movement in England....* See VB 1962, 385.
Rev. by J. H. Whyte in *St I,* LII, 102-04; by Stephen J. Tonsor in *VS,* VII, 197-200.

Anstey, R. T. *Britain and the Congo in the Nineteenth Century....* See VB 1962, 385. Rev. by A. J. Hanna in *History,* XLVIII, 414; by Paul Knaplund in *JMH,* XXXV, 437-38.

Anstruther, Ian. *The Knight and the Umbrella: An Account of the Eglinton Tournament, 1839.* London: Geoffrey Bles. Pp. xvii + 270.
Rev. in *CR,* CCIII, 333; by Joanna Richardson in *Listener,* 16 May, p. 839; in *TLS,* 14 June, p. 418; by Harold Perkin in *VS,* VII, 216-17.

Archer, Mildred. "Mission to Burma 1855." *History Today,* XIII, 691-99.

Armytage, W. H. G. *Heavens Below: Utopian Experiments in England, 1560-1960....* See VB, 1961, 359.
Rev. by Kenneth E. Bock in *VS,* VI, 372-74.

Armytage, W. H. G. *A Social History of Engineering....* See VB 1961, 360.
Rev. by Melvin Kranzberg in *VS,* VI, 293-94.

Arnstein, Walter L. "Parnell and the Bradlaugh Case." *Irish Hist. Studies,* XIII, 212-35.

Ashworth, William. *An Economic History of England, 1870-1939....* See VB 1962, 386.
Rev. by Douglas F. Dowd in *Science & Society,* XXVII, 244-46.

Aziz, K. K. *Britain and Muslim India.* London: Heinemann. Pp. 278.
Rev. in *TLS,* 12 Dec., p. 1035.

Backstrom, Philip N., Jr. "The Practical Side of Christian Socialism in Victorian England." *VS,* VI, 305-24.

Bagwell, Philip Sidney. *The Railwaymen: The History of the National Union of Railwaymen.* London: Allen and Unwin. Pp. 725.

Rev. by H. A. Clegg in *Econ. Jour.*, LXXIII, 753-54; in *TLS*, 17 May, p. 351.

Bailey, Sir Edward. *Charles Lyell.* . . . See VB 1962, 386.
Rev. by R. J. Haulik in *LJ*, LXXXVIII, 94; by A. O. Woodford in *Science*, CXXXIX, 821-22; in *TLS*, 8 Feb., p. 91.

Baker, Samuel White. *The Albert N'Yanza: Great Basin of the Nile and Explorations of the Nile Sources.* London: Sidgwick and Jackson. Pp. 569.
Rev. in *TLS*, 11 Jan., p. 28.
A centennial edition of a Victorian classic, with preface by Alan Moorehead.

Ball, Nancy. *Her Majesty's Inspectorate, 1839-1849.* Edinburgh: Oliver and Boyd. Pp. viii + 268.

Barker, T. C. "The Centenary of London's Underground." *History Today*, XIII, 115-22.

Bartle, G. F. "The Decimal Coinage Agitation of the Eighteen-Fifties." *CR*, CCIII, 36-39.

Bartlett, Christopher John. *Great Britain and Sea Power, 1815-1853.* Oxford: Clarendon Pr. Pp. xviii + 364.
Rev. by Arthur Marder in *AHR*, LXIX, 114; by John Terraine in *History Today*, XIII, 433-35; by Michael Lewis in *Listener*, 21 Feb., p. 346; in *TLS*, 17 May, p. 359; by Kenneth Bourne in *VS*, VII, 118-19.

Beales, Derek. *England and Italy 1859-1860.* . . . See VB 1962, 386.
Rev. by John M. Roberts in *EHR*, LXXVIII, 810-11.

Bearce, George Donham. *British Attitudes towards India.* . . . See VB 1962, 386.
Rev. by A. P. Thornton in *JMH*, XXXV, 80-82; by Eric Stokes in *History*, XLVIII, 113-14; by D. A. Low in *VS*, VI, 285-86.

Bell, Enid. *Josephine Butler.* . . . See VB 1962, 386.
Rev. by Lois Mitchison in *Listener*, 7 Mar., p. 433; by Marghanita Laski in *Manchester Guardian Weekly*, 24 Jan., p. 11; by L. Fairfield in *NS*, LXV, 278; in *TLS*, 25 Jan., p. 54.

Bell, Quentin. *The Schools of Design.* London: Routledge and Kegan Paul. Pp. x + 290.
Rev. in *TLS*, 1 Nov., p. 880.
Government-aided schools of design in early-Victorian England.

Bernstein, Henry T. "J. Clerk Maxwell on the History of the Kinetic Theory of Gases, 1871." *Isis*, LIV, 206-16.

Binns, C. T. *The Last Zulu King.* London: Longmans. Pp. xv + 240.
Rev. by Lucy Mair in *Listener*, 18 Apr., p. 684; in *TLS*, 12 April, p. 246.
On Cetshwayo and the Zulu War of 1879.

Birch, Alan. "Sydney: A Colonial Capitol." *History Today*, XIII, 407-15.

Black, Matthew W., and Miller, William E. "Some Letters from Actors and Actresses to Dr. Horace Howard Furness: Part I." *Libr. Chronicle, Univ. of Penna.* XXIX, 105-15.
Letters from Fanny Kemble and Ellen Terry.

Blakiston, Noel (ed.). *The Roman Question.* . . . See VB 1962, 386.
Rev. by C.E.E. in *Revue des deux mondes* (no. 8, 15 Apr.), 637; by J. H. Whyte in *St I*, LII, 102-04.

Booth, Harry F. "The Knowledge of God and the Practice of Society in Frederick Denison Maurice." *DA*, XXIV, 863.

Bouch, C. M. L., and Jones, G. P. *A Short Economic and Social History of the Lake Counties.* Manchester: Manchester Univ. Pr., 1961. Pp. 371.
Rev. by Mildred Campbell in *JEH*, XXIII, 90-91.

Bramley, T. A. "Australian Explorers." *CR*, CCIII, 200-03.
On nineteenth-century explorers who opened up the continent.

Briggs, Asa. *Victorian Cities.* London: Oldhams. Pp. 416.
Rev. by W. G. Hoskins in *Listener*, 10 Oct., p. 573; by A. J. P. Taylor in *Manchester Guardian Weekly*, 26 Sept., p. 10; by E. J. Hobsbawm in *NS*, LXVI, 365; by Paul Thompson in *S*, 25 Oct., pp. 536-37; in *TLS*, 14 Nov., p. 925.

Brightfield, Myron F. "The Medical Profession in Early Victorian England, as Depicted in the Novels of the Period (1840-1870)." *Bull. Hist. Med.*, XXXV, 238-56.

Brissenden, Alan, and Higham, Charles (eds.). *They Came to Australia.* London: Angus and Robertson. Pp. 171.
Rev. by Asa Briggs in *NS*, LXV, 907-08.

Brittain, Vera. *Pethick-Lawrence.* London: Allen and Unwin. Pp. 232.
Rev. by Margaret Cole in *Listener*, 11 July, pp. 63-64.

Brockett, Allan. *Nonconformity in Exeter, 1650-1875.* . . . See VB 1962, 387.
Rev. by Geoffrey F. Nuttall in *Jour. of Eccl. Hist.*, XIV, 239-41.

Brown, Ford K. *Fathers of the Victorians: The Age of Wilberforce.* . . . See VB 1962, 387.
Rev. by G. F. A. Best in *EHR*, LXXVIII, 741-44.

Bruce, Maurice. *The Coming of the Welfare State.* . . . See VB 1962, 387.
Rev. by A. F. Havighurst in *JMH*, XXXV, 71-72.

Bünger, Siegfried. *Friedrich Engels und die Britische Sozialistische Bewegung, 1881-1895.* Berlin: Rütten & Loening. Pp. 242.
Rev. by Daniel F. Calhoun in *AHR*, LXVIII, 789-90.

Burrow, J. W. "Evolution and Anthropology in the 1860's: The Anthropological Society of London, 1863-71." *VS*, VII, 137-54.

Butlin, Martin. *Turner Watercolours.* London: Barrie and Rockliff. Pp. 96; 32 col. plates.
Rev. in *TLS*, 12 July, pp. 501-02.

Caine, Sir Sydney. *The History of the Foundation of the London School of Economics and Political Science.* London: G. Bell. Pp. viii + 103.
Rev. by Margaret Cole in *Econ. Jour.*, LXXIII, 762-64.

Campbell, Ray Hutcheson. *Carron Company.* . . . See VB 1962, 387.
Rev. by Barry E. Supple in *JEH*, XXIII, 94-95.

Canady, Charles E. "A Comparative Study of the Piety of George Herbert and John Keble." *DA*, XXIV, 1262-63.

Carr, J. C., and Taplin, W. *A History of the British Steel Industry.* . . . See VB 1962, 387.
Rev. by R. J. Alexander in *Am. Econ. Rev.*, LIII, 235; by T. A. Wertime in *AHR*, LXVIII, 433; by Robert Dean in *Econ. Jour.*, LXXIII, 136-38; by Donald A. Fink in *JEH*, XXIII, 237.

Carter, Harry. *Orlando Jewitt.* London: Oxford Univ. Pr. Pp. 48.
Rev. in *TLS*, 8 March, p. 164.
An important wood engraver of the Gothic revival.

Carter, John. "T. J. Wise and the Technique of Promotion." *Book Collector*, XII, 202.

Carus-Wilson, E. M. (ed.). *Essays in Economic History.* Vol. III. New York: St. Martin's Press, 1962. Pp. viii + 393.
Rev. by Ian M. Drummond in *JPE*, LXXI, 608.

Case, Lynn M. "A Duel of Giants in Old

Stambul, Stratford Versus Thouvenel." *JMH*, XXXV, 262-67.

Chadwick, George F. *The Works of Sir Joseph Paxton, 1803-1865.* London: Architectural Pr., 1961. Pp. 275.
Rev. by Denys Hinton in *VS*, VI, 292-93.

Chadwick, Owen. *Westcott and the University.* Cambridge: Cambridge Univ. Pr. Pp. 39.
Bishop Westcott Memorial Lecture for 1962.

Christensen, Torben. *Origin and History of Christian Socialism, 1848-1854.* . . . See VB 1962, 388.
Rev. by Charles F. Mullett in *AHR*, LXIX, 201; by Neville Masterman in *History*, XLVIII, 97-98; in *TLS*, 22 Feb., p. 117; by Gordon K. Lewis in *VS*, VII, 202-04.

Christian, Garth (ed.). *A Victorian Poacher: James Hawker's Journal.* . . . See VB 1961, 362.
Rev. by J. Loiseau in *Études anglaises*, XVI, 295-96; by W. L. Burn in *N & Q*, n.s. X, 34.

Cirker, Blanche. *1,800 Woodcuts by Thomas Bewick and His School.* New York: Dover, 1962. Pp. 247.
Briefly noted in *BSP*, LVII, 477.

Clark, G. Kitson. *The Making of Victorian England.* . . . See VB 1962, 388.
Rev. by Josef L. Altholz in *AHR*, LXVIII, 434-35; by Alfred F. Havighurst in *APSS*, CCCXLV, 147; by Norman Gash in *History*, XLVIII, 91-93; by David Owen in *JMH*, XXXV, 194-95; by Raymond English in *VQR*, XXXIX, 330-34.

Cole, Margaret. *The Story of Fabian Socialism.* . . . See VB 1962, 388.
Rev. by Madeleine Rebérioux in *Annales: économies, sociétés, civilisations*, XVII, 1021-22; briefly by Henry Pelling in *EHR*, LXXVIII, 816; by George J. Stigler in *VS*, VI, 374-75.

Cole, Phillip A. "The British Image of the French Third Republic, 1870-1882." *DA*, XXIV, 1993.

Collier, Richard. *The Sound of Fury: The Great Indian Mutiny.* London: Collins. Pp. 384.
Rev. in *TLS*, 14 Nov., p. 930.

Collins, Robert O. *The Southern Sudan, 1883-1898: A Struggle for Control.* . . . See VB 1962, 388.
Rev. by Richard Hill in *VS*, VII, 210-12.

Cominos, Peter. "Late Victorian Sexual Respectability and the Social System." *In-*

ternational Rev. of Social History, VIII, 18-48; 216-50.

Mr. Cominos tries to fit late nineteenth-century ideas about sexuality into the framework of late-nineteenth-century ideas about men and society.

Coombs, Douglas. *The Gold Coast, Britain and the Netherlands, 1850-1874.* London and New York: Oxford University Press. Pp. xiii + 160.

Cooper, Leonard. *The Life and Times of the Duke of Wellington, 1769-1852.* New York: Dodd, Mead. Pp. xi + 308.

Rev. by Lawrence J. McCaffrey in *HTB,* 24 Nov., p. 12.

Cornford, James. "The Transformation of Conservatism in the Late Nineteenth Century." *VS,* VII, 35-66.

An instructive essay, not only for its careful but suggestive conclusions, but also for its methods of analysis.—D.J.G.

Corry, B. A. *Money, Saving, and Investment in English Economics, 1800-1850.* . . . See VB 1962, 388.

Rev. by Dudley Dillard in *Amer. Econ. Rev.,* LII, 1156; by J. K. Horsefeld in *Economica,* XXX, 198-99; by Elmus R. Wicker in *JEH,* XXIII, 238-40; by L. C. Hunter in *JPE,* LXXI, 195.

Cox-Johnson, Ann. "A Gentleman's Servant's Journal." *History Today,* XIII, 102-07.

Cramp, Alfred Bernard. *Opinion on Bank Rate, 1822-60.* . . . See VB 1962, 388.

Rev. by R. C. O. Matthews in *Econ. Jour.,* LXXIII, 309-11; by W. H. B. Court in *History,* XLVIII, 95-96; by S. F. Forter in *JEH,* XXIII, 95-96.

Cropper, Margaret Beatrice. *Shining Lights — Six Anglican Saints of the Nineteenth Century.* London: Darton, Longman, and Todd. Pp. xi + 192.

Short biographies of Shaftesbury, Patteson, Christina Rossetti, Edward King, Mother Cecile, and Mary Brown.

Crow, Duncan. *Henry Wickoff: The American Chevalier.* London: Macgibbon and Kee. Pp. 236.

Rev. by Leon Edel in *NS,* LXVI, 882-83. An American who, among other things, was once an agent in Palmerston's employ.

Cruickshank, Marjorie. *Church and State in English Education: 1870 to the Present Day.* London: Macmillan. Pp. xvi + 200.

Rev. by R. W. Henderson in *LJ,* LXXXVIII, 3073; in *TLS,* 14 June, p. 448.

Curtis, Lewis Perry, Jr. *Coercion and Con-ciliation in Ireland 1880-1892.* Princeton, New Jersey: Princeton. Pp. xiii + 460.

Rev. by John Moran in *LJ,* LXXXVIII, 3841.

Dare, Reginald Arthur. *A History of Owen's School.* Wallington, Carwal. Pp. 192.

Davies, Horton. *Worship and Theology in England:* Vol. IV: *From Newman to Martineau, 1850-1900.* . . . See VB 1962, 389.

Rev. by J. L. Altholz in *AHR,* LXVIII, 197; by Owen Chadwick in *EHR,* LXXVIII, 790-91; by L. W. Cowie in *History,* XLVIII, 99; by Erik Routley in *Jour. Eccl. Hist.,* XIV, 131-32; by R. M. Brown in *SR,* 21 Apr., 1962, p. 24; in *YR,* LI, viii.

Davis, Frank. *Victorian Patrons of the Arts.* London: Country Life. Pp. 158.

Rev. in *TLS,* 5 Dec., p. 1004.

Davis, Henry William Carless. *A History of Balliol College.* Revised by R. H. C. Davis and Richard Hunt, and supplemented by Harold Hartley and others. Oxford: Blackwell. Pp. xii + 329. First appeared in 1889; includes chapters on Jowett and other Victorians.

Rev. in *TLS,* 5 July, p. 496.

Day, John Robert. *The Story of London's Underground.* London: London Transport Bd. Pp. v + 153.

Deane, Phyllis and Cole, W. A. *British Economic Growth, 1688-1959.* . . . See VB 1962, 389.

Rev. by Rondo Cameron in *American Econ. Rev.,* LIII, 475; in *Economist,* CCVI, 513; in *TLS,* 5 July, p. 495.

Derry, John Wesley. *Reaction and Reform, 1793-1868.* New York: New American Libr. *England in the Early Nineteenth Century.* London: Blandford. Pp. viii + 232.

Derry, Thomas Kingston, and Williams, Trevor Illytd. *A Short History of Technology.* . . . See VB 1962, 389.

Rev. by Thomas P. Hughes in *Isis,* LIV, 417-18.

Domb, C. (ed.). *Clerk Maxwell and Modern Science.* London: Athlone Pr. Pp. ix + 118.

Six eminent contemporary scientists on Clerk Maxwell's electromagnetic theory of light.

Draper, F. W. M. *Four Centuries of the Merchant Taylors' School.* . . . See VB 1962, 389.

Rev. by Donald J. Olsen in *AHR*, LXVIII, 505.

Dunbabin, J. P. D. "The Politics of the Establishment of County Councils." *CHJ*, VI, 226-52.

Dunning, E. G. "Football in Its Early Stages." *History Today*, XIII, 838-47.
History of football from twelfth century to the 1840's.

Dury, George Harry. *The East Midlands and the Peak*. Part II: *1800-1900*. London: Nelson. Pp. xii + 299.

Edwardes, Michael. *Battles of the Indian Mutiny*. London: Batsford. Pp. 216.
Rev. in *TLS*, 21 Nov., p. 949.

Elton, Lord (ed.). *General Gordon's Khartoum Journal*. . . . See VB 1962, 389.
Rev. by Lewis Gannett in *HTB*, 1 Sept., p. 5; by R. R. Rea in *LJ*, LXXXVIII, 2001-02; by Richard Hill in *VS*, VII, 210-12.

English Nineteenth Century Cameo Glass. Corning, New York: Corning Museum. Pp. 43.

Erwood, Peter Malcolm Elliston (ed.). *Woolwich in 1846*. Sidcup: Lambarde Pr. Pp. 27.

Eshag, Eprime. *From Marshall to Keynes*. Oxford: Basil Blackwell. Pp. xx + 144.

L'Europe du XIXe et du XXe Siecle (1870-1914): Problèmes et Interprétations Historiques. Milan: Marzorati; Oxford: Parker. 2 vols., pp. 1152.
Rev. in *TLS*, 1 Feb., p. 75.

Ferriday, Peter (ed.). *Victorian Architecture*. London: Cape. Pp. 306.
Rev. in *TLS*, 5 Dec., p. 1004.

Finberg, Alexander Joseph *The Life of J. M. W. Turner, R. A.* . . . See VB 1961, 364.
Rev. in *TLS*, 12 July, pp. 501-02.

Fisher, Marvin. "Richard Cobden and the Protestant Ethic." *SAC*, LXII, 43-50.

Fleck, George M. "Atomism in Late Nineteenth-Century Physical Chemistry." *JHI*, XXIV, 106-14.

Flinn, M. W. *Men of Iron: The Crowleys in the Early Iron Industry*. Edinburgh: Nelson & Sons for the Edinburgh Univ. Pr., 1962. Pp. x + 270.
Rev. by C. Erickson in *Econ. Jour.*, LXXIII, 325-27.

Florescu, Radu R. "Stratford Canning, Palmerston, and the Wallachian Revolution of 1848." *JMH*, XXXV, 227-44.

Footprints on the Sands of Time, 1863-1963: *The Story of the House of Livingstone*. Edinburgh: E. and S. Livingstone. Pp. 71.
Rev. in *TLS*, 16 Aug., p. 632.
Centennial history of an important firm of medical publishers.

Ford, Alec George. *The Gold Standard 1880-1914.* . . . See VB 1962, 389.
Rev. by Arthur I. Bloomfield in *Economica*, XXX, 200-02; by C. P. Kindleberger in *JEH*, XXIII, 243-44; by D. J. Coppock in *JPE*, LXXI, 609-11.

Ford, Percy and Grace (eds.). *Luke Graves Hansard*. . . . See VB 1962, 389.
Rev. by Gordon L. Goodman in *AHR*, LXVIII, 510-11; by R. S. Sayers in *Economica*, XXX, 434-35.

Forsyth, R. A. "The Victorian Self-Image and the Emergent City Sensibility." *TQ*, XXXIII, 61-77.

Fothergill, Brian. *Nicholas Wiseman*. London: Faber and Faber. Pp. 303.
Rev. by Msgr. Florence Cohalan in *CWd*, CXCVIII, 190; by Robert Harbinson in *Listener*, 11 Apr., 642; by C. G. Gros in *LJ*, LXXXVIII, 3068; in *TLS*, 5 April, p. 236.

Fox, Daniel M. "Artists in the Modern State: The Nineteenth-Century Background." *JAA*, XXII, 135-48.
An able survey of relations between artists and their patrons, public and private.

Freeman, John. *Literature and Locality*. London: Cassell. Pp. xiii + 402.
Includes descriptions of physical settings used by Victorian writers.

Fryer, Peter. *Mrs. Grundy: Studies in English Prudery*. London: Dobson. Pp. 368.

Furneaux, Rupert. *The Zulu War*. London: Weidenfeld & Nicolson. Philadelphia: Lippincott. Pp. 210.
Rev. by John Owen in *NS*, LXVI, 170; by Richard Glover in *VS*, VII, 208-10.

Galbraith, John S. *Reluctant Empire: British Policy on the South African Frontier, 1834-1854*. Berkeley: Univ. of California Pr. Pp. 293.
Rev. by C. R. Lovell in *AHR*, LXIX, 141; by H. J. Spiro in *APSS*, CCCV, 174; by Louis Barron in *LJ*, LXXXVIII, 2899; in *VQR*, XXXIX, cxliii.

Gash, Norman. *Mr. Secretary Peel*. . . . See VB 1962, 390.
Rev. by R. W. Greaves in *EHR*, LXXVIII, 738-39.

Gathorne-Hardy, Robert (ed.). *Ottoline: The Early Memoirs of Lady Ottoline Morrell, 1873-1915*. London: Faber. Pp. 308.

Rev. by William Plomer in *Listener*, 7 Nov., p. 750; by Richard Mayne in *NS*, LXVI, 654-55.
She recalls Conrad and Eliot.

Gernsheim, Alison. *Fashion and Reality, 1840-1914*. London: Faber and Faber. Pp. 104.
Rev. by Alison Adburgham in *Manchester Guardian Weekly*, 5 Dec., p. 11; by Marghanita Laski in *NS*, LXVI, 944.

Ghosh, R. N. "Malthus on Emigration and Colonization: Letters to Wilmot-Horton." *Economica*, XXX, 45-62; 415.
Twenty letters from Malthus dating February, 1823 to May, 1831.

Gibbs, Charles Robert Vernon. *British Passenger Liners of the Five Oceans: A Record of the British Passenger Lines and Their Liners from 1838 to the Present Day*. London: Putnam. Pp. 559.

Gibbs, Peter. *The Battle of the Alma*. London: Weidenfeld and Nicolson; Philadelphia: Lippincott. Pp. xii + 194.
Rev. in *TLS*, 5 Dec., p. 1013; by Richard Glover in *VS*, VII, 208-10.

Gibson, James A. "The Duke of Newcastle and British North American Affairs, 1859-64." *Canadian Hist. Rev.*, XLIV, 142-56.

Giles, Frank. *A Prince of Journalists: The Life and Times of De Blowitz*. London: Faber and Faber, 1962. Pp. 228.
Rev. by E. W. Edwards in *History*, XLVIII, 237.

Gill, John Clifford. *Parson Bull of Byerley*. London: S.P.C.K. Pp. xii + 163.

Gloag, John. *The English Tradition in Architecture*. London: Adam and Charles Black; New York: Barnes and Noble. Pp. xvi + 258.
Rev. in *TLS*, 31 May, p. 384.

Gloag, John. *Victorian Taste*. . . . See VB 1962, 390.
Rev. by Paul Zucker in *JAA*, XXI, 490-91; by Clifford Musgrave in *Burl. Mag.*, CV, 570-71.

Gokhale, B. G. "Indians and the British: A Study in Attitudes." *History Today*, XIII, 230-38.

Gollan, Robin. *The Coalminers of New South Wales: A History of the Union, 1860-1960*. Melbourne: Melbourne Univ. Pr.; Cambridge: Cambridge Univ. Pr. Pp. xii + 249.

Gooch, G. P. "Dr. Barnardo, Father of the Fatherless." *CR*, CCIII, 24-26.

Gopal, Ram. *British Rule in India: An Assessment*. London: Asia Pub. House. Pp. xi + 364.

Grampp, William Dyer. *The Manchester School of Economics*. . . . See VB 1962, 390.
Rev. by François Crouzet in *Annales: économies, sociétés, civilisations*, XVII, 1200-01.

Grattan, Clinton Hartley. *The Southwest Pacific to 1900*. Ann Arbor: Univ. of Michigan Pr. Pp. 558.
Rev. by S. Hopkinson in *LJ*, LXXXVIII, 1878.

Greenslade, S. L. *The Cambridge History of the Bible: The West from the Reformation to the Present Day*. Cambridge: Cambridge Univ. Pr. Pp. 598.
Rev. by S. Johnson in *LJ*, LXXXVIII, 4766.

Grenville, J. A. S. *Lord Salisbury and Foreign Policy*. London: Athlone Pr. Pp. xi + 451.

Greville, Charles Cavendish Fulke. *The Great World: Portraits and Scenes from Greville's Memoirs* (1814-1860). Ed. by Louis Kronenberger. New York: Doubleday. Pp. 354.
Rev. by K. G. Jackson in *Harper's*, May, p. 113; by R. C. Woodward in *LJ*, LXXXVIII, 217; by J. H. Plumb in *NYTBR*, 7 Apr., p. 42; by Robert Halsband in *SR*, 26 Jan., p. 45.

Grimble, Ian. *The Trial of Patrick Sellar: The Tragedy of Highland Evictions*. . . . See VB 1962, 390.
Rev. by R. J. Adam in *History*, XLVIII, 233.

Gupta, Prantul Chandra. *Nana Sahib and the Rising at Cawnpore*. Oxford: Clarendon Pr.; New York: Oxford Univ. Pr. Pp. xii + 227.
Rev. by C. Collin Davies in *History*, XLVIII, 408-09; by Jon Manchip White in *History Today*, XIII, 429-31; by George D. Bearce in *JMH*, XXXV, 428; in *TLS*, 12 Apr., p. 246; by Mark Naidis in *VS*, VII, 212-13.

Guttsman, Wilhelm Leo. *The British Political Élite, 1832-1935*. London: Macgibbon & Kee. Pp. 398.
Rev. in *TLS*, 6 Sept., p. 667; by Donald Southgate in *VS*, VII, 204-06.

Gwyn, William Brent. *Democracy and the Cost of Politics in Britain*. . . . See VB 1962, 390.
Rev. by G. A. Cahill in *AHR*, LXVIII,

511; by J. B. Shannon in *APSR*, LVI, 1018.

Habakkuk, H. J. *American and British Technology in the Nineteenth Century.* . . . See VB 1962, 390.
Rev. by D. C. Coleman in *Economica*, LXXIII, 215-17; by W. Ashworth in *History*, XLVIII, 90-91; by W. Paul Strassmann in *JEH*, XXIII, 104-06

Hall, Peter Geoffrey. *The Industries of London since 1861.* . . . See VB 1962, 390.
Rev. briefly by Charles W. Coolidge in *AHR*, LXVIII, 789.

Hancock, Sir Keith. *Smuts, the Official Biography.* Vol. I: *The Sanguine Years, 1870-1919.* . . . See VB 1962, 391.
Rev. by Leo Kuper in *APSR*, LVII, 491; by G. P. Gooch in *CR*, CCIII, 49-51; by J. L. McCracken in *History*, XLVIII, 255-56; by P. D. Curtin in *JMH*, XXXV, 88-89; by Donald Wasson in *LJ*, LXXXVIII, 772; by G. M. Carter in *SR*, 2 Mar., p. 43; in *TLS*, 2 Nov., 1962, p. 833.

Handover, P. M. "Some Uncollected Authors XXXV. Talbot Baines Reed, 1852-1893." *Book Collector*, XII, 62-67.

Hargreaves, John Desmond. *Prelude to the Partition of West Africa.* London: Macmillan; New York: St. Martin's Pr. Pp. xi + 383.
European interests in Africa between 1860 and 1885.

Harrison, Brian. "Drunkards and Reformers: Early Victorian Temperance Tracts." *History Today*, XIII, 178-85.

Harrison, John Fletcher Clews. *Learning and Living, 1790-1960: A Study in the History of the English Adult Education Movement.* . . . See VB 1962, 391.
Rev. by J. R. Kidd in *QQ*, LXX, 151-52; by Eric Ashby in *VS*, VI, 290-92.

Harrison, Michael. *London by Gaslight, 1861-1911.* London: Peter Davies. Pp. vi + 250. Noticed in *TLS*, 7 Nov., p. 914.

Harrison, Michael. *Painful Details: Twelve Victorian Scandals.* . . . See VB 1962, 391.
Rev. by Harold Perkin in *VS*, VII, 216-17.

Harrison, Royden. " 'The Free Inheritance of Us All': Beesly's Speech in St. James' Hall, London, March 26, 1863." *Science & Society*, XXVII, 465-73.

Harrison, Royden. "The 10th April of Spencer Walpole: The Problem of Revolution in Relation to Reform, 1865-1867." *International Rev. of Social History*, VII (1962), 351-99.

Considers the events and motives preceding and following the Hyde Park disturbances in 1865.

Harthan, John P. *Bookbindings.* Victoria and Albert Museum, Illustrated Booklet No. 2. Second (revised) edition. London: H.M.S.O., 1961. Pp. 73.
Rev. by Giles Barber in *The Library*, 5th Ser., XVIII, 76-77.

Hartley, Harold. *Balliol Men.* Oxford: Blackwell. Pp. 36.
Rev. in *TLS*, 5 July, p. 496.
On some contributions to English life made by Balliol men of the past 100 years.

Heasman, Kathleen. *Evangelicals in Action.* . . . See VB 1962, 391.
Rev. by W. L. Burn in *CHJ*, VI, 314-15; by C. Gordon Bolam in *HJ*, LXI, 154; by John H. S. Kent in *LQHR*, CLXXXVIII (6th ser., XXXII), 247-48; by D. V. Donnison in *VS*, VII, 106-08.

Helm, Robert M. *The Gloomy Dean: The Thought of William Ralph Inge.* . . . See VB 1962, 391.
Rev. by J. F. Maclear in *Church Hist.*, XXXII, 105-06.

Henderson, W. O. *The Industrial Revolution in Europe, 1815-1914.* Chicago: Quadrangle Books, 1962. Pp. ix + 288.
Rev. by Roy A. Church in *JEH*, XXIII, 106-08; by William N. Parker in *JPE*, LXXI, 522.

Hennock, E. P. "Finance and Politics in Urban Local Government in England, 1835-1900." *CHJ*, XI, 212-25.

Herrmann, Luke. *J. M. W. Turner.* London: Methuen. Pp. 41.
Rev. in *TLS*, 12 July, pp. 501-02.

Heussler, Robert. *Yesterday's Rulers: The Making of the British Colonial Service.* Syracuse: Syracuse Univ. Pr. Pp. xxvi + 260.
Rev. by Philip Mason in *APSS*, CCCXLIX, 199-200.

Hibbert, Christopher. *The Destruction of Lord Raglan.* . . . See VB 1962, 391.
Rev. by Henry R. Winkler in *AHR*, LXVIII, 513-14.

Hilton, William Samuel. *Foes to Tyranny: A History of the Amalgamated Union of Building Trade Workers.* London: Amalgamated Union of Building Trade Workers. Pp. vi + 301.

Hinsley, F. H. (ed.). *The New Cambridge Modern History.* Vol. XI. *Material Progress and Worldwide Problems, 1870-1898.* . . . See VB 1962, 391.

Rev. by Preston Slosson in *JMH*, XXXV, 306-08.

Hobsbawm, E. J. *The Age of Revolution (1789-1848).* . . . See VB 1962, 391.

Rev. by F. E. Hirsch in *LJ*, LXXXVII, 4433; by Hans Kohn in *NYTBR*, 7 Apr., p. 42; in *TLS*, 11 Jan., p. 22.

Hobsbawm, E. J. "En Angleterre: Révolution industrielle et vie matérielle des classes populaires." *Annales: économies, sociétés, civilisations*, XVII, 1047-61.

Holt, Edgar. *The Strangest War: The Story of the Maori Wars, 1860-1872.* . . . See VB 1962, 391.

Rev. by D. K. Fieldhouse in *History*, XLVIII, 233-34; by Keith Sinclair in *VS*, VI, 297.

Hookham, H. "An Englishman at the Court of the Taiping Kingdom." *History Today*, XIII, 556-63.

Howard, D. L. *John Howard: Prison Reformer.* New York: Archer House. Pp. 186.

Rev. by J. L. Andrews in *LJ*, LXXXVIII, 4363.

Hunter, Richard Alfred, and MacAlpine, Ida (eds.). *Three Hundred Years of Psychiatry, 1535-1860.* London and New York: Oxford Univ. Pr. Pp. xxvi + 1107.

Rev. by J. A. C. Brown in *NS*, LXV, 281; in *TLS*, 5 April, p. 225.

Hurst, M. C. *Joseph Chamberlain and West Midland Politics, 1886-1895.* Stratford-upon-Avon: Dugdale Society. Pp. 72.

Rev. in *TLS*, 8 March, p. 163.

Huttenback, Robert A. *British Relations with Sind, 1799-1843.* . . . See VB 1962, 392.

Rev. by R. E. Frykenberg in *AHR*, LXVIII, 510; by Kenneth Ballhatchet in *APSS*, CCCXLVIII, 217; by A. P. Thornton in *JMH*, XXXV, 80-82; by D. A. Low in *VS*, VI, 285-86.

Inglis, Kenneth Stanley. *Churches and the Working Classes in Victorian England.* London: Routledge & Kegan Paul. Pp. viii + 350.

Rev. by E. G. Collieu in *Listener*, 1 Aug., p. 176; by Christopher Driver in *Manchester Guardian Weekly*, 27 June, p. 12; by Angus MacIntyre in *S*, 28 June, p. 842; in *TLS*, 19 July, p. 527.

Jackson, John Archer. *The Irish in Britain.* London: Routledge and Kegan Paul; Cleveland: Western Reserve Univ. Pr. Pp. xvi + 208.

Rev. in *TLS*, 21 Nov., p. 943.

James, Robert Rhodes. *Rosebery: A Biography of Archibald Philip, Fifth Earl of Rosebery.* London: Weidenfeld and Nicolson. Pp. 534.

Rev. by G. P. Gooch in *CR*, CCIII, 308-11; in *Economist*, CCVI, 1125; by Christopher Howard in *History*, XLVIII, 395-96; by Max Beloff in *Listener*, 14 Mar., p. 471; by Shane Leslie in *Nat. Rev.*, XV, III; by Paul Johnson in *NS*, LXV, 307; in *TLS*, 15 Feb., p. 103; by A. H. Gollin in *VS*, VII, 117-18.

James, Walter. *The Christian in Politics.* London: Oxford Univ. Pr., 1962. Pp. x + 216. Briefly noted in *Church Hist.*, XXXII, 374.

Jarman, Thomas Leckie. *Democracy and World Conflict, 1868-1962: A History of Modern Britain.* London: Blandford; New York: New American Library. Pp. ix + 206.

Jennings, Sir Ivor. *Party Politics.* . . . See VB 1962, 392.

Rev. by J. B. Conacher in *Canadian Hist. Rev.*, XLIV, 176-79; by William O. Aydelotte in *JMH*, XXXV, 413-14.

Jones, J. R. "The Qualities Needed in a Governor-General of India." *N & Q*, n.s. X, 22-23.

Karminski, Sir Seymour Edward. *Some Aspects of the Development of English Personal Law in the Last Century.* London: Oxford Univ. Pr. Pp. 40.

Kelly, Thomas. *A History of Adult Education in Great Britain.* . . . See VB 1962, 392.

Rev. by J. R. Kidd in *QQ*, LXX, 151-52; by Eric Ashby in *VS*, VI, 290-92.

Kennedy, Brian A. "Select Documents. XXIII. Sharman Crawford on Ulster Tenant Right, 1846." *Irish Hist. Studies*, XIII, 246-53.

How Crawford, the "father of tenant right," treated his own tenants.

Kent, John. *Elizabeth Fry.* London: Batsford, 1962. Pp. 144.

Rev. by J.-P. Hulin in *Études anglaises*, XVI, 401-02.

Kerr, Eleanor. *Hunting Parson: The Life and Times of the Rev. John Russell.* London: Herbert Jenkins. Pp. 192.

Noticed in *TLS*, 19 Dec., as a "curious piece of minor Victoriana."

King-Hele, Desmond. *Erasmus Darwin.* London: Macmillan. Pp. 183.

Rev. in *TLS*, 19 Dec., p. 1039.

Kirwan, Daniel Joseph. *Palace and Hovel.*

London: Abelard-Schumann. Pp. 219.
Rev. by D. A. N. Jones in NS, LXVI, 580-81; in TLS, 28 Nov., p. 963. Reissue of contemporary account of mid-Victorian London.

Kitson Clark, G. *The Making of Victorian England.* See VB 1962, 388.
Rev. by J. L. Altholz in AHR, LXVIII, 434; by Harold Perkin in APSR, LVII, 204.

Krutch, Joseph Wood. "If You Don't Mind My Saying So. . . ." *American Scholar,* XXXII, 275-76; 278; 280.
Possible "design" in evolution, with references to Wallace, the Darwins, Huxley.

Lambert, Royston. *Sir John Simon, 1816-1904, and English Social Administration.* London: MacGibbon & Kee. Pp. 669.
Rev. by G. Best in NS, LXVI, 658; by Paul Thompson in S, 25 Oct., pp. 536-37; in TLS, 7 Nov., p. 902.

Lampe, David. *The Tunnel.* London: Harrap. Pp. 224.
A history of the Thames tunnel, built 1824-42.

Langer, William L. "Europe's Initial Population Explosion." AHR, LXIX, 1-17.

Lee, John Michael. *Social Leaders and Public Persons: A Study of County Government in Cheshire since 1888.* London: Oxford Univ. Pr. Pp. xi + 261.

Leigh, Denis. *The Historical Development of British Psychiatry:* Vol. I: *Eighteenth and Nineteenth Century.* London: Pergamon Pr., 1961. Pp. xiv + 277.
Rev. by Phyllis Greenacre in VS, VII, 111-12.

Liu, Kwang-Ching. *Anglo-American Steamship Rivalry in China, 1862-1874.* . . . See VB 1962, 393.
Rev. by Jack Gerson in *Canadian Hist. Rev.,* XLIV, 77-78; by Max E. Fletcher in JEH, XXIII, 116-17; by Robert Hartwell in JMH, XXXV, 433-34; by Victor Purcell in VS, VI, 364-65.

Lloyd, Christopher, and Coulter, Jack L. S. *Medicine and the Navy, 1200-1900.* Vol. IV: *1815-1900.* Edinburgh: E. and S. Livingstone. Pp. xi + 300.
Rev. in TLS, 2 Aug., p. 591.

Lockhart, John Gilbert, and Woodhouse, Christopher Montague. *Rhodes: The Colossus of Southern Africa.* London: Hodder and Stoughton; New York: Macmillan. Pp. 525.
Rev. by William Plomer in *Listener,* 19

Sept., p. 435; by Asa Briggs in NS, LXVI, 362-63; by Herman Ausubel in NYTBR, 19 May, p. 6; by David Watt in S, 18 Oct., p. 501; by J. H. Plumb in SR, 3 Aug., p. 29; in TLS, 20 Sept., p. 699.

Loshak, David. "G. F. Watts and Ellen Terry." *Burl. Mag.,* CV, 476-85.

Lowenthal, Leo and Lawson, Ina. "The Debate on Cultural Standards in Nineteenth Century England." *Social Research,* XXX, 417-33.

Lundeen, Thomas B. "The Bench of Bishops: A Study of the Secular Activities of the Bishops of the Church of England and of Ireland, 1801-1871." DA, XXII, 2447-48.

MacDonagh, Oliver. *A Pattern of Government Growth, 1800-60.* . . . See VB 1962, 393.
Rev. by W. L. Burn in CHJ, VI, 140-43.

MacInnes, Colin. "A Pre-Raphaelite Memory." S, 11 Oct., pp. 453-55.
On Burne-Jones's daughter, Mrs. Mackail.

Mackenzie, Compton. *My Life and Times: Octave One, 1883-1891.* London: Chatto and Windus. Pp. 255.
Rev. by William Kean Seymour in CR, CCII, 218-20; by Ronald Bryden in S, 8 Feb., pp. 170-71; in TLS, 18 Jan., p. 35.

Mackenzie, Compton. *My Life and Times: Octave Two, 1891-1900.* London: Chatto and Windus. Pp. 327.
Rev. in TLS, 11 Oct., p. 802.

Mackintosh, John P. *The British Cabinet.* . . . See VB 1962, 393.
Rev. by Richard W. Lyman in APSS, CCCXLV, 145-46.

Maclagan, Michael. *"Clemency" Canning.* . . . See VB 1962, 393.
Rev. by G. D. Bearce in AHR, LXVIII, 1119; by R. R. Rea in LJ, LXXXVIII, 1519; by Mark Naidis in VS, VII, 212-13.

Mannix, Daniel P., in collaboration with Malcolm Cowley. *Black Cargoes: A History of the Atlantic Slave Trade, 1518-1865.* New York: Viking. Pp. 306.
Rev. by Paul Pickrel in *Harper's,* Feb., p. 102; by D. W. Bogan in *Listener,* 3 Oct., p. 519; by R. F. Kugler in LJ, LXXXVII, 4539; by J. C. Furnas in NYTBR, 4 Nov., 1962, p. 3; by Saunders Redding in SR, 29 June, p. 26.

Marston, Thomas. *Britain's Imperial Role in the Red Sea Area 1800-1878.* Hamden, Conn.: Shoe String Pr., 1961. Pp. 550.
Rev. by W. N. Medlicott in *The Slavonic*

and East European Rev., XLI, 564-65.

Martin, Robert B. *Enter Rumor: Four Early Victorian Scandals.* . . . See VB 1962, 393.
Rev. briefly in *NCF*, XVIII, 101; by Harold Perkin in *VS*, VII, 216-17.

Masterman, N. C. *John Malcolm Ludlow, the Builder of Christian Socialism.* Cambridge: Cambridge Univ. Pr. Pp. 299.
Rev. by G. P. Gooch in *CR*, CCIV, 160-62; by C. L. Mowat in *Listener*, 26 Sept., p. 478; by Eric Hobsbawm in *NS*, LXVI, 323; in *TLS*, 13 Sept., p. 686.

Matthews, Leslie G. *History of Pharmacy in Britain.* Edinburgh: E. and S. Livingstone, 1962; Baltimore: Williams and Wilkins. Pp. xiv + 427.
Rev. in *TLS*, 2 Aug., p. 591.

Maynard, Douglas. "Reform and the Origin of the International Organization Movement," *PAPS*, CVII, 220-31.
Account of eleven international congresses convened in the 1840's.

McBriar, A. M. *Fabian Socialism and English Politics, 1884-1918.* . . . See VB 1962, 393.
Rev. by S. R. Graubard in *AHR*, LXIX, 116; by O. H. K. Spate in *APSS*, CCCXLIX, 198; in *Economist*, CCVI, 123; by Richard W. Lyman in *JMH*, XXXV, 91-92; by Margaret Cole in *NS*, LXV, 125; in *TLS*, 11 Jan., p. 22; by George J. Stigler in *VS*, VI, 374-75.

McCaffrey, Lawrence J. *Irish Federalism in the 1870's: A Study in Conservative Nationalism. Transactions of the American Philosophical Society*, n.s. LII, Part 6, 1962. Pp. 58.
Rev. by Hereward Senior in *Canadian Hist. Rev.*, XLIV, 358-59.

McCallum, Ronald Buchanan. *The Liberal Party from Earl Grey to Asquith.* London: Gollancz. Pp. 192.
Rev. by G. P. Gooch in *CR*, CCIII, 325-27; in *TLS*, 3 May, p. 327.

McClelland, Vincent Alan. *Cardinal Manning: His Public Life and Influence, 1865-1892.* . . . See VB, 1962, 393.
Rev. by J. T. Ellis in *Church Hist.*, XXXII, 220-21; by David Newsome in *History*, XLVIII, 98-99; by J. H. Whyte in *StI*, LII, 102-04; by Walter L. Arnstein in *VS*, VI, 365-66.

McKeown, T. and Record, R. G. "Reasons for the Decline of Mortality in England and Wales during the Nineteenth Century." *Population Studies*, XVI (November 1962).

McLean, Ruari. *Victorian Book Design and Colour Printing.* New York: Oxford Univ. Pr. Pp. xvi + 182.
Rev. by P. H. Muir in *Book Collector*, XII, 231; by David Kaser in *College and Research Libr.*, XXIV, 522; in *Economist*, CCVII, 55; by Douglas Cleverdon in *Listener*, 21 Mar., p. 522; by Bill Katz in *LJ*, LXXXVIII, 2680; by Christopher Salvesen in *NS*, LXV, 430; by John Betjeman in *S*, 3 May, p. 579; in *TLS*, 26 Apr., p. 284.

Medlicott, W. N. (ed.). *From Metternich to Hitler: Aspects of British and Foreign History, 1814-1939.* London: Routledge. Pp. 267.
Rev. by David Thomson in *Listener*, 25 July, p. 138; in *TLS*, 5 Dec., p. 1009.

Meisel, Martin. "Perspectives on Victorian Acting: The Actor's Last Call, or, No Curtain Like the Shroud." *VS*, VI, 355-60.

Melitz, J. "Sidgwick's Theory of International Values." *Econ. Jour.*, LXXIII, 431-41.

Metcalfe, George Edgar. *Maclean of the Gold Coast: The Life and Times of George Maclean 1801-1847.* . . . See VB 1962, 394 (there listed erroneously under Metcalfe, C. E.).
Rev. by Martin Kilson in *AHR*, LXIX, 224; by J. E. Flint in *History*, XLVIII, 253; by Paul Knaplund in *JMH*, XXXV, 310.

Middlemas, Robert Keith. *The Master Builders.* London: Hutchinson. Pp. 328.
Rev. in *TLS*, 25 Oct., p. 863.
Four major contractors between 1830 and 1930.

Milliken, Ernest Kenneth. *The Victorian Era, 1820-1901.* London: Harrap. Pp. 263.

Milne, A. J. M. *The Social Philosophy of English Idealism.* London: Allen and Unwin, 1962. Pp. 320.
Rev. by Frederick A. Olafson in *Philosophical Rev.*, LXXII, 390-91.

Minney, R. J. *No. 10 Downing Street: A House in History.* Boston: Little. Pp. 483.
Rev. by R. R. Rea in *LJ*, LXXXVIII, 2693.

Mitchell, B. R. *Abstract of British Historical Statistics.* With the collaboration of Phyllis Deane. London: Cambridge Univ. Pr., 1962. Pp. 513.
Rev. by D. J. Olsen in *AHR*, LXIX, 109; by J. N. W. in *College and Research Libr.*, XXIV, 318; by R. G. D. Allen in *Economica*, XXX, 433-34.

Moir, Esther. "The Architecture of Dissent." *History Today*, XIII, 383-89.

Montgomery, John. *Toll for the Brave.* Lon-

don: Max Parrish. Pp. 189.
Biography of Hector Macdonald, general in Boer War.

Morgan, Bryan (ed.). *The Railway-Lover's Companion*. London: Eyre and Spottiswoode, Pp. 556.
Writings about 19th- and 20th-century British railways.

Morgan, Kenneth Owen. *Wales in British Politics, 1868-1922*. Cardiff: Univ. of Wales Pr. Pp. xii + 354.
Rev. by D. Marquand in *NS*, LXVI, 326-27; by Gwyn A. Williams in *S*, 15 Nov., pp. 632-33; in *TLS*, 7 Nov., p. 904.

Morrah, Patrick. *Alfred Mynn and the Cricketers of His Time*. London: Eyre and Spottiswoode. Pp. 224.
Rev. by Maurice Latey in *History Today*, XIII, 801-03.

Mosse, W. E. "Public Opinion and Foreign Policy: The British Public and the War-scare of November 1870." *CHJ*, VI, 38-58.

Mosse, W. E. "Queen Victoria and Her Ministers in the Schleswig-Holstein Crisis 1863-1864." *EHR*, LXXVIII, 263-83.

Mosse, Werner Eugen. *The Rise and Fall of the Crimean System, 1855-1871; The Story of a Peace Settlement*. London: Macmillan; New York: St. Martin's Pr. Pp. 213.

Mowat, Charles Loch. *The Charity Organisation Society, 1869-1913*. . . . See VB 1961, 368.
Rev. by D. V. Donnison in *VS*, VII, 106-08.

Muir, Edwin. *The Estate of Poetry*. . . . See VB 1962, 402.
Rev. by Kathleen Raine in *Poetry*, CI, 272-74.

Munby, A. N. L. *The Cult of the Autograph Letter in England*. London: Univer. of London, The Athlone Press, 1962. Pp. viii + 117.
Rev. by W. A. Myers in *BSB*, LVII, 246-49; by Andrew G. Watson in *The Library*, 5th Ser., XVIII, 75-76.

Munford, William Arthur. *Edward Edwards, 1812-86: Portrait of a Librarian*. London: Library Assn. Pp. 240.

Murray, Margaret. *My First Hundred Years*. London: William Kimber. Pp. 208.
Rev. by N. Mitchison in *NS*, LXVI, 85; in *TLS*, 16 Aug., p. 627.
Includes reminiscences of Sir Flinders Petrie and early studies in archeology.

Naidis, Mark. "British Attitudes toward the Anglo-Indians." *SAQ*, LXII, 407-22.

New Horizons: A Hundred Years of Women's Migration. London: H. M. S. O. Pp. xi + 181.
Rev. in *TLS*, 26 Dec., p. 1069.

Newsome, David. "How Soapy Was Sam? A Study of Samuel Wilberforce." *History Today*, XIII, 624-32.
After retailing the adroitness that probably earned Wilberforce his sobriquet, Newsome observes that his life also contained disappointments and solid achievements.

Nicholas, Herbert George. *Britain and the United States*. London: Chatto and Windus; Baltimore: Johns Hopkins Univ. Pr. Pp. 192.

Nutall, Barbara H. *A History of Thornhill: West Riding Village*. 14 Red Hall Ave., Leeds: Author, Pp. 52.

Norris, David. "Cardinal Wiseman: The Diocesan Bishop." *Wiseman Rev.*, CCXXXVII, 158-67.

O'Leary, Cornelius. *The Elimination of Corrupt Practices in British Elections, 1868-1911*. . . . See VB 1962, 394.
Rev. by Madeline R. Robinton in *AHR*, LXIX, 202-03; by H. J. Hanham in *EHR*, LXXVIII, 814; by David Spring in *JMH*, XXXV, 88; by Anthony Howard in *NS*, LXIII, 681; by William B. Gwyn in *PSQ*, LXXVIII, 151-53.

Olorenshaw, Arthur. *Broadwell: The Story of Nonconformity in a Warwickshire Village*. Broadwell Methodist Chapel, Broadwell, War. Pp. 88.

O'Neill, James E. "The Authorship of the 1872 'Memorial on Government Insurance.'" *N&Q*, n.s. X, 458-59.

Paar, H. W. *A History of the Railways of the Forest of Dean*. Vol. I: *The Severn and Wye Railway*. London: Macdonald. Pp. 173.
Briefly rev. in *TLS*, 20 Sept., p. 710.

Parry, Ann. *Parry of the Arctic: The Life Story of Admiral Sir Edward Parry, 1790-1855*. London: Chatto and Windus. Pp. 240.
Rev. in *TLS*, 12 Dec., p. 1033.

Patterson, A. Temple. *The University of Southampton: A Centenary History*. Southampton: Univ. of Southampton. 1962. Pp. 245.
Rev. by John Roach in *CHJ*, VI, 143-45; by Dorothy Greene Johnson in *JMH*, XXXV, 86.

Peaston, A. Elliott. *The Prayer Book Revisions of the Victorian Evangelicals.* Dublin: Assoc. for Promoting Christian Knowledge. Rev. in *HJ*, LXII, 54.

Pelling, Henry. *A History of British Trade Unionism.* London: Macmillan. Pp. xi + 287.
 Rev. by Margaret Cole in *Listener*, 10 Oct., pp. 579-80; in *TLS*, 7 Nov., p. 905.

Pemberton, William Baring. *Battles of the Crimean War.* . . . See VB 1962, 395.
 Rev. by Vernon J. Puryear in *JMH*, XXXV, 195; by Richard Glover in *VS*, VII, 208-10.

Perham, Margery, and Bull, Mary (eds.). *The Diaries of Lord Lugard.* Vol. IV: *Nigeria 1894/5 and 1898.* London: Faber; Evanston, Ill.: Northwestern Univ. Pr. Pp. 444.
 Rev. in *TLS*, 26 April, p. 297.

Philips, C. H. *The Evolution of India and Pakistan, 1858-1947. Select Documents on the History of India and Pakistan.* Vol. IV. London: Oxford Univ. Pr., 1962. Pp. xxi + 786.
 Rev. by Thomas R. Metcalf in *JMH*, XXXV, 303-04; in *TLS*, 16 Aug., p. 622.

Pike, Royston. *Pioneers of Social Change.* London: Barrie and Rockliff. Pp. vi + 218.
 Chapters on Chadwick, Shaftesbury, Mill, and Barbara Bodichon, agitator for women's emancipation.

Platt, D. C. M. "The Role of the British Consular Service in Overseas Trade, 1825-1914." *Economic History Rev.*, XV (April, 1963), 494-512.

Plumb, J. H. *Men and Places.* London: Cresset Pr.; Boston: Houghton Mifflin. Pp. 294.
 Rev. by Robert Halsband in *NYTBR*, 24 Nov., p. 3; by Jon Manchip White in *S*, 15 Feb., p. 206.
 Includes essays on Macaulay and Cecil Rhodes.

Pollock, John Charles. *Moody Without Sankey.* London: Hodder and Stoughton; New York: Macmillan. Pp. xiv + 288.
 Rev. in *TLS*, 9 Aug., p. 607.

Pope, Walter Bissell (ed.). *The Diary of Benjamin Robert Haydon.* Vols. III, IV, and V: *1825-1846.* Cambridge, Mass.: Harvard Univ. Pr. Pp. 660, 664, 688.
 Rev. by M. Dodsworth in *NS*, LXVI, 913-14; in *TLS*, 5 Dec., p. 1012.

Porter, McKenzie. *Overture to Victoria.* London: Alvin Redman. Pp. 204.

Rev. in *TLS*, 1 Feb., p. 74.
 On the Duke of Kent, Victoria's father, and his French mistress, Mme. de St. Laurent.

Prebble, John. *The Highland Clearances.* London: Secker and Warburg. Pp. 352.
 Rev. by Ian MacLennan in *S*, 18 Oct., pp. 503-03; in *TLS*, 7 Nov., p. 804.
 On the removal of Highland tenants by landlords, 1800-1850.

Pritchard, D. G. *Education and the Handicapped, 1760-1960.* London: Routledge. Pp. 250.
 Rev. in *TLS*, 15 Feb., p. 112.

Purcell, Victor. *The Boxer Uprising.* Cambridge and New York: Cambridge Univ. Pr. Pp. xiv + 349.
 Rev. by Henry McAleavy in *History Today*, XIII, 355-56.

Qanungo, Bhupen. "Lord Canning's Administration and the Modernization of India, 1856-62." *DA*, XXIII, 2508.

Rawley, James A. "Joseph John Gurney's Mission to America, 1837-1840." *Miss. Valley Hist. Rev.*, XLIX, 653-74.

Read, Donald. *Press and People.* . . . See VB 1962, 395.
 Rev. by Norman Gash in *EHR*, LXXVIII, 191-92.

Reitlinger, Gerald. *The Economics of Taste.* Vol. II: *The Rise and Fall of Objets d'Art Prices since 1750.* London: Barrie and Rockliff. Pp. xvi + 708.
 Rev. in *TLS*, 14 Nov., p. 920.

Reynolds, Adam, and Charlton, William. *Arthur Machen.* John Baker, for Richards Press.
 Rev. by Ian Fletcher in *Listener*, 17 Oct., p. 625.

Rimmer, W. G. *Marshall's of Leeds.* . . . See VB 1962, 396.
 Rev. by Peter Mathias in *EHR*, LXXVIII, 801-03.

Robbins, Michael, and Barker, T. C. *A History of London Transport.* Vol. I: *The Nineteenth Century.* London: Allen and Unwin. Pp. xxxii + 412.
 Rev. by C. Foster in *NS*, LXVI, 747-48.

Roberts, David. "How Cruel Was the Victorian Poor Law?" *CHJ*, VI, 97-107.

Robinson, J. A. (ed.). *The Ames Correspondence: Letters to Mary, 1837-1847.* Norwich: Norfolk Record Society. Pp. 99.
 Noticed in *TLS*, 17 May, p. 362.

Robinson, Ronald, Gallagher, John, and

Denny, Alice. *Africa and the Victorians.* . . . See VB 1962, 396.
Rev. by George Shepperson in *EHR,* LXXVIII, 345-47; by W. L. Burn in *History,* XLVIII, 249-52; by Holden Furber in *JMH,* XXXV, 199-201; by L. Gray Cowan in *PSQ,* LXXVIII, 158-59; by K. A. MacKirdy in *QQ,* LXX, 149-50.

Roger-Marx, Claude. *Graphic Art of the Nineteenth Century.* London: Thames and Hudson. Pp. 254.
Rev. in *TLS,* 29 March, p. 212.

Rogers, Philip George. *The Sixth Trumpeter: The Story of Jezreel and His Tower.* London and New York: Oxford Univ. Pr. Pp. xii + 154.
Rev. by C. Heywood in *N & Q,* n.s. X, 277-78; by C. Driver in *NS,* LXV, 278-79; by John Kent in *VS,* VII, 217-19.

Rolt, Lionel Thomas Caswell. *George and Robert Stephenson: The Railway Revolution.* . . . See VB 1962, 396.
Rev. by E. F. Jost in *America,* CVII, 251-52.

Sanderson, G. N. "The Anglo-German Agreement of 1890 and the Upper Nile." *EHR,* LXXVIII, 49-72.

Saul, Samuel Berrick. *Studies in British Overseas Trade.* . . . See VB 1962, 396.
Rev. by A. H. John in *EHR,* LXXVIII, 142-44.

Scott, John Dick. *Vickers: A History.* London: Weidenfeld and Nicholson. Pp. xxiii + 416.
Rev. in *TLS,* 9 Aug., pp. 601-02.

Sellers, Ian. "Unitarians and Social Change." Part 1: "Varieties of Radicalism, 1795-1815." *HJ,* LXI, 16-22. Part 2: "Benthamism and Liberty, 1815-40." LXI, 76-80. Part 3: "The English Transcendentalists, 1840-1850." LXI, 122-27. Part 4: "Dissentient Voices, 1850-1900." LXI, 177-80.

Semmel, Bernard. *The Governor Eyre Controversy.* . . . See VB 1962, 396.
Rev. by David Owen in *YR,* LIII, 279.

Shannon, R. T. *Gladstone and the Bulgarian Agitation 1876.* London: Nelson, Pp. xxviii + 308.

Shattuck, Charles H. (ed.). *William Charles Macready's "King John."* . . . See VB 1962, 396.
Rev. by Phyllis Hartnoll in *N & Q,* n.s. X, 356-57; by Muriel St. Clare Byrne in *Theatre Notebook,* XVII, 136-40; in *TLS,* 25 Jan., p. 60.

Shull, Thelma. *Victorian Antiques.* Rutland, Vt.: Tuttle. Pp. 421.

Simon, Walter G. "The Bishops and Reform." *Hist. Mag, of the Protestant Episcopal Church,* XXXII, 367-70.

Simpson, William Douglas (ed.). *The Fusion of 1860: A Record of the Centenary Celebrations and a History of the University of Aberdeen, 1860-1960.* Edinburgh: Oliver and Boyd, for the University of Aberdeen. Pp. viii + 331.

Singh, Hira Lal. *Problems and Policies of the British in India, 1885-1898.* London: Asia Publ. House; New York: Taplinger. Pp. xi + 284.

Singh, Khushwant. *Ranjit Singh, Maharajah of the Punjab.* London: Allen and Unwin, 1962. Pp. 237.
Rev. by Francis Watson in *Listener,* 29 Aug., pp. 320-21.

Smellie, K. B. *Great Britain Since 1688.* . . . See VB 1962, 397.
Rev. by Ann Beck in *AHR,* LXVIII, 727; by Asa Briggs in *NS,* LXV, 309; by Lindsay Rogers in *NYTBR,* 7 Apr., p. 43; in *TLS,* 17 May, p. 359.

Smythe, Sir John. *The Story of the Victoria Cross, 1856-1963.* London: Muller. Pp. 496.

Southgate, Donald. *The Passing of the Whigs, 1832-1886.* . . . See VB 1962, 397.
Rev. by F. H. Herrick in *AHR,* LXVIII, 731; by C. H. Kirby in *APSS,* CCCXLVII, 157; by H. J. Hanham in *History,* XLVIII, 96-97; by J. B. Conacher in *VS,* VI, 289-90.

Spring, David. "Aristocracy, Social Structure, and Religion in the Early Victorian Period." *VS,* VI, 263-80.

Spring, David. *The English Landed Estate in the Nineteenth Century: Its Administration.* Baltimore, Md.: Johns Hopkins Pr. Pp. 216.
Rev. by H. L. Beales in *VS,* VII, 206-07.

St. Aubyn, Giles. *The Royal George, 1819-1904: The Life of H. R. H. Prince George, Duke of Cambridge.* London: Constable. Pp. xi + 380.
Rev. by E. G. Collieu in *Listener,* 3 Oct., p. 515; by A. J. P. Taylor in *NS,* LXVI, 490-91; in *TLS,* 27 Sept., p. 736 (also see letter by Brian Bond, 11 Oct., p. 812); by Angus MacIntyre in *S,* 11 Oct., p. 466 (also see letter by E. D. Murfet, 18 Oct., p. 492).

Steen, Ivan D. "The British Traveler and the

American City, 1850-1860." *DA*, XXIV, 2005.

Steer, Francis William. *The Chichester Literary and Philosophical Society and Mechanic's Institute, 1831-1924.* Chichester: Chichester City Council. Pp. 24.

The Story of London's Underground. London: London Transport. Pp. 150.
Noticed in *CR*, CCIV, 56.
A centennial history of London subways, 1863-1963.

Symons, Julian. *Buller's Campaign.* London: Cresset Pr. Pp. xvi + 312.
Rev. by John Owen in *NS*, LXVI, 170; by Howard Enzenberger in *S*, 26 July, pp. 112-13; in *TLS*, 5 July, p. 490.

Tappe, E. D. "E. E. and J. A. Crowe and Rumanian Union: Some Unpublished Letters of 1857."
The Slavonic and East European Review, XLI, 135-43.

Taylor, A. J. P. "Lord Palmerston." *Listener*, 20 June, pp. 1033-35.

Taylor, Don. *The British in Africa.* London: Hale, 1962. Pp. 192.
Rev. by M. Mortimer in *CR*, CCIII, 331-32.

Thérèse, Mother Marie. *Cornelia Connelly.* London: Burns and Oates. Pp. 326.
Rev. in *TLS*, 11 Oct., p. 814.

Thomas, David St. John. *A Regional History of the Railways of Great Britain.* Vol. I: *The West Country.* Rev. ed., London: Phoenix. Pp. x + 214.

Thompson, Edward Palmer. *The Making of the English Working Class.* London: Gollancz. Pp. 848.
Rev. by Raymond Williams in *Listener*, 5 Dec., pp. 939-41; by E. J. Hobsbawm in *NS*, LXVI, 787-88; by Henry Pelling in *S*, 13 Dec., p. 796; in *TLS*, 12 Dec., pp. 1021-23.

Thompson, Francis Michael Longstreth. *English Landed Society in the Nineteenth Century.* London: Routledge and Kegan Paul. Pp. xiii + 374.
Rev. by Arthur L. Stinchcombe in *Am. Jour. of Sociology*, LXIX, 299; by Llewellyn Woodward in *Listener*, 6 June, pp. 972-73; by Hugh Trevor-Roper in *NS*, LXV, 795-96; by Angus MacIntyre in *S*, 28 June, p. 842; in *TLS*, June 21, p. 458; by H. L. Beales in *VS*, VII, 206-07.

Tibawi, Abdul Latif. *British Interests in Palestine, 1800-1901.* . . . See VB, 1962, 398.
Rev. by J. B. Kelly in *VS*, VI, 361-64.

The Times, London. Red and Black. The Duty and Postage Stamps Impressed on Newspapers 1812-1870, and on The Times or Its Postal Wrappers from 1785-1962. London: *The Times* Publishing Co. Pp. 22.
Rev. in *TLS*, 14 Nov., p. 936 (and see letter by R. M. Wiles, 19 Dec., p. 1054).

Tisdall, Evelyn Ernest Percy. *Mrs. Duberly's Campaigns.* London: Jarrolds. Pp. 224.
Rev. by D. A. N. Jones in *NS*, LXV, 277; in *TLS*, 15 Feb., p. 103.
A Victorian officer's wife in the Crimea and India.

Tryon, W. S. *Parnassus Corner: A Life of James T. Fields, Publisher to the Victorians.* Boston: Houghton Mifflin. Pp. xiv + 445.
Rev. by Henry Steele Commager in *NYTBR*, 6 Oct., p. 7; by John T. Winterich in *Publisher's Weekly*, 29 July, pp. 26-30.

Turner, Ernest Sackville. *What the Butler Saw.* . . . See VB 1962, 398.
Rev. by Shirley W. Lerner in *Economica*, XXX, 428-29; by Jessica Mitford in *NYTBR*, 21 Apr., p. 42; by Iola Haverstick in *SR*, 23 Mar., p. 35.

Turner, H. A. *Trade Union Growth, Structure, and Policy: A Comparative Study of the Cotton Unions.* London: Allen and Unwin, 1962. Pp. 412.
Rev. by D. F. MacDonald in *History*, XLVIII, 237; by Wilfred Altman in *CR*, CCIII, 105-06.

Unstead, Robert John. *A Century of Change, 1837-Today.* London: Adam and Charles Black. Pp. 232.

Vallance, Hugh Aymer. *The Highland Railway.* Rev. ed. London: Macdonald. Pp. 182.

Victorian Furniture. London: H. M. S. O. Pp. 5 + 27 plates.

Ward, David. *King of the Lags: The Story of Charles Peace.* London: Elek Books. Pp. 176.
Noticed in *TLS*, 14 June, p. 450.
A mid-Victorian criminal.

Ward, John Trevor. *The Factory Movement, 1830-1855.* . . . See VB 1962, 398.
Rev. by R. A. Church in *AHR*, LXIX, 115; by David Owen in *Canadian Hist. Rev.*, XLIV, 252-53; by Deryck Abel in *CR*, CCIII, 272-73; in *Economist*, CCVI, 808; by Donald Read in *History*, XLVIII, 388; by Philip Rappaport in *LJ*,

LXXXVIII, 2250; in *TLS*, 21 June, p. 458; by Royden Harrison in *VS*, VII, 108-10.

Wardle, Patricia. *Victorian Silver and Silver-Plate*. London: Herbert Jenkins; New York: Nelson. Pp. 238.

Wakefield, Hugh. *Victorian Pottery*. . . . See VB 1962, 398.
Rev. by P. von Khrum in *LJ*, LXXXVIII, 1151.

Waterfield, Gordon. *Layard of Nineveh*. London: Murray. Pp. x + 535.
Rev. by Elizabeth Wiskeman in *History Today*, XIII, 721-23; by Edward Lucie-Smith in *Listener*, 26 Sept., p. 478; by M. I. Finley in *NS*, LXVI, 325; by Robert Rhodes James in *S*, 20 Sept., p. 358; in *TLS*, 13 Sept., p. 686.
Biography of Sir Austen Henry Layard, archaeologist and diplomat.

Weasmer, Charles B. "The Politics of the Disruption: A Study of the Relationship between Church and State in Scotland, 1834-1843." *DA*, XXIV, 2549-50.

Webb, Beatrice. *Beatrice Webb's American Diary, 1898*. Ed. by David A. Shannon. Madison: Univ. of Wisconsin Pr. Pp. 181.
Rev. by Paul Pickerel in *Harper's*, June, p. 106; by E. P. Stickney in *LJ*, LXXXVIII, 2527; by J. R. Hollingsworth in *Miss. Valley Hist. Rev.*, L, 323-24; by Stanley Kauffmann in *New R*, 22 June, p. 28; by Norman MacKenzie in *NS*, LXV, 979; in *TLS*, 5 July, p. 485.

Webb, Sidney and Webb, Beatrice. *English Local Government*. 11 vols. With new Introductions by B. Keith Lucas, G. J. Ponsby, L. Radzinowicz, and W. A. Robinson. London: Frank Cass.
Rev. by Asa Briggs in *NS*, LXVI, 200.

Weber, Frank G. "Palmerston and Prussian Liberalism." *JMH*, XXXV, 125-36.
A sympathetic analysis of Palmerston's refusal to help the Prussian liberals in 1848.

Welcome, John. *Cheating at Cards: Three Nineteenth-Century Court Cases*. London: Faber. Pp. 235.
Rev. in *TLS*, 19 July, p. 527.

Whetham, E. H. "Prices and Production in Scottish Farming, 1850-1870." *Scottish Journal of Political Economy*, IX (November, 1962).

White, Henry Patrick. *A Regional History of the Railways of Great Britain*. Vol. III: *Greater London*. London: Phoenix. Pp. xii + 227.

Noticed in *CR*, CCIV, 278.

White, James F. *The Cambridge Movement: The Ecclesiologists and the Gothic Revival*. . . . See VB 1962, 398.
Rev. by R. W. Greaves in *History*, XLVIII, 386-87; by Horton Davies in *Jour. of Religion*, XLIII, 334; by Alan B. Wilkinson in *LQHR*, CLXXXVIII (6th ser., XXXII), 340-41; in *TLS*, 22 Feb., p. 124 (also see letter by M. V. Taylor, 8 Mar., p. 169).

Whiteside, Thomas. *The Tunnel under the Channel*. . . . Seee VB 1962, 399.
Rev. in *TLS*, 8 March, p. 171.

Wilkinson, John T. *1662 and After: Three Centuries of English Nonconformity*. London: Epworth. Pp. 269.
Rev. by John Foster in *LQHR*, CLXXXVIII (6th ser., XXXII), 245-47.

Wilkinson, R. "Political Leadership in the Late Victorian Public School." *British Journal of Sociology*, XIII (December, 1962).

Williams, W. M. *A West Country Village: Ashworthy*. London: Routledge. Pp. xxii + 229.
Rev. by C. Madge in *NS*, LXV, 382-83.

Willy, Todd G. "The Agitation in Parliament and England over Charles George 'Chinese' Gordon and His Mission to the Soudan; January, 1884 to February, 1885." *DA*, XXIII, 4023-24.

Winch, D. N. "Classical Economics and the Case for Colonization." *Economica*, XXX, 387-99.

Woodham-Smith, Cecil. *The Great Hunger: Ireland 1845-1849*. . . . See VB 1962, 399.
Rev. by Edward Weeks in *AM*, July, p. 127; by William Ready in *Critic*, Apr., p. 73; by André Boué in *Études anglaises*, XVI, 411-12; by K. G. Jackson in *Harper's*, May, p. 112; by E. T. Smith in *LJ*, LXXXVIII, 220; by Sean O'Faolain in *N*, 30 Mar., p. 269; by F. D. Cohalan in *National Rev.*, XIV, p. 499; by A. L. Rowse in *HTB*, 7 Apr., p. 6; by D. W. Brogan in *NYTBR*, 14 Apr., p. 7; by Constantine Fitzgibbon in *SR*, 23 Mar., p. 34; by Francis Finegan in *StI*, LII, 326-31; by R. Dudley Edwards in *VS*, VII, 110-11.

Woodward. Ernest Llewellyn. *The Age of Reform, 1815-1870*. . . . See VB 1962, 399.
Rev. by W. D. Handcock in *History*, XLVIII, 94; by Giovanni Costigan in *JMH*, XXXV, 190-91.

Wyndham, Violet. *The Sphinx and Her Circle: A Biographical Sketch of Ada Lever-

son, *1862-1933.* London: Andre Deutsch.
Pp. 128.
Rev. by William Plomer in *Listener,* 2
May, p. 761; by Bernard Bergonzi in *S,*
12 July, p. 63; in *TLS,* 3 May, p. 326.
Young, Kenneth. *Arthur James Balfour: The
Happy Life of the Politician, Prime Minister, Statesmen, and Philosopher.* London: G. Bell. Pp. 516.
Rev. by Christopher Howard in *History,*
XLVIII, 395-96; by Philip Magnus in *Listener,* 7 Mar., p. 431; by A. J. P. Taylor
in *NS,* LXV, 390-91; by Nicholas Mansergh in *S,* 29 March, pp. 401-02; in *TLS,*
8 Mar., p. 163.

III. MOVEMENTS OF IDEAS
AND LITERARY FORMS

Aitken, David Jared. "The Victorian Idea of
Realism: A Study of the Aims and Methods of the English Novel Between 1860
and 1875." *DA,* XXIII, 2910.
Bennett, Mary. "A Check List of Pre-Raphael-
ite Pictures Exhibited at Liverpool 1846-
67, and Some of their Northern Collec-
tors." *Burl. Mag.,* CV, 486-95.
Benziger, James. *Images of Eternity: Studies
in the Poetry of Religious Vision from
Wordsworth to T. S. Eliot.* Carbondale:
Univ. of Southern Illinois Pr., 1962.
Rev. by Max F. Schulz in *JEGP,* LXII,
810-13.
Includes chapters on Tennyson, Brown-
ing, and Arnold.
Billiar, Donald E. "The Philosophic Romance
in Nineteenth-Century England." *DA,*
XXIV, 2472-73.
Concerning Morris, MacDonald, Conrad.
Bloom, Lynn M. Z. "How Literary Biograph-
ers Use Their Subjects' Works: A Study of
Biographical Method, 1865-1962." *DA,*
XXIV, 2458. Dickens and Shaw included.
Booth, Wayne C. *The Rhetoric of Fiction.* . . .
See VB 1962, 399.
Rev. by Earl Rovit in *BA,* XXXVII, 73:
by Alan D. McKillop in *MP,* LX, 295-98;
by B. R. McElderry, Jr. in *The Personal-
ist,* XLIV, 263-64.
Burns, C. A. "Zola in Exile. Notes on an Un-
published Diary of 1898." *French Studies,*
XVII, 14-26.
Davie, George Elder. *The Democratic Intel-
lect.* . . . See VB 1962, 400.
Rev. by Jacques Voisine in *Études an-
glaises,* XVI, 409-10; by D. M. Tulloch in
Philosophy, XXXVIII, 373-74.

Davis, Frank. *Victorian Patrons of the Arts:
Twelve Famous Collectors and Their
Owners.* London: Country Life. Pp. 158.
Rev. in *TLS,* 5 Dec., p. 1004.
Davis, Kenneth W. "Letters of William Henry
Smith to the Blackwoods, 1836-1862."
DA, XXIV, 282-83.
De Michelis, Euralio. "Un Poeta d'Autunno."
Nuova Antologia, CDLXXXVII, 323-34.
On d'Annunzio and the Pre-Raphaelites.
Dowse, Robert E. and Palmer, David. " 'Drac-
ula': the Book of Blood." *Listener,* 7
March, pp. 428-29.
Fairchild, Hoxie Neal. *Religious Trends in
English Poetry.* Vol. V: *1880-1920, Gods
of a Changing Poetry.* . . . See VB 1962,
400.
Rev. by Max F. Schulz in *JEGP,* LXII,
813-16; by Geddes MacGregor in *The
Personalist,* XLIV, 275-76; by Geoffrey
Bullough in *VS,* VII, 121-22.
Foerster, Donald M. *The Fortunes of Epic
Poetry.* Washington: Catholic Univ. of
America Pr., 1962. Pp. ix + 250.
Rev. by J. Golliet in *Études anglaises,*
XVI, 197-98.
Covers 1750-1950.
Gere, J. A. "Alexander Munro's 'Paolo and
Francesca'." *Burl. Mag.,* CV, 509-10.
Green, David Bonnell. "Two Popular Novel-
ists of the 'Fifties and Their Publisher:
Letters from G. J. White-Melville and
Charlotte M. Yonge to John William
Parker, Jr." *N & Q,* n.s. X, 450-54.
Handley-Read, C. "Notes on William Burges's
Painted Furniture." *Burl. Mag.,* CV, 496-
508.
Harden, Edgar F. "The American Girl in
British Fiction, 1860-1880." *HLQ,* XXVI,
263-85.
Three types: The Quadroon, the Ingenue,
and the Title-Seeker.
Harding, Denys Wyatt. *Experience into
Words.* London: Chatto and Windus. Pp.
199.
Essays on poets from Blake to Eliot.
Harris, Arthur J. "William Poel's Elizabethan
Stage: The First Experiment." *Theatre
Notebook,* XVII, 111-14.
Hollingsworth, Keith. *The Newgate Novel
1830-1847.* Detroit: Wayne State Univ.
Pr. Pp. 279.
Rev. by William Kean Seymour in *CR,*
CCIV, 273-76; briefly in *NCF,* XVIII,
305; in *TLS,* 28 Nov., p. 964; by Mar-

garet Dalziel in *VS*, VII, 215-16.

Hulin, Jean-Paul. "Exotisme et littérature sociale an début de l'ère Victorienne." *Études anglaises*, XVI, 23-37.

James, Louis, *Fiction for the Working Man, 1830-1870*. London: Oxford Univ. Pr. Pp. xiv + 226.
Rev. in *Bookseller*, 7 Sept., pp. 1318-20; by Pamela Hansford Johnson in *Listener*, 10 Oct., p. 570; by John Gross in *NS*, LXVI, 574-75; by Geoffrey Tillotson in *S*, 13 Sept., p. 321; in *TLS*, 28 Nov., p. 964.

Kopp, Karl C. "The Origin and Characteristics of 'Decadence' in British Literature of the 1890's." *DA*, XXIV, 1604.
Principally Wilde, Beardsley, and Dowson.

Land, Myrick. *The Fine Art of Literary Mayhem: A Lively Account of Famous Writers and Their Feuds*. New York: Holt. Pp. 242.
Rev. by R. E. Wagenknecht in *LJ*, LXXXVIII, 217; by W. F. Gavin in *SR*, 5 Jan., p. 85.
Includes material on Dickens, Thackeray, and Shaw.

Le Chevalier, Charles. *Ethique et idéalisme, le courant neo-hegelien en Angleterre, Bernard Bosanquet et ses amis*. Paris: Vrin. Pp. 190.
Rev. by A.-L. Leroy in *Études anglaises*, XVI, 420.
A survey of the ideas in Ruskin, Coleridge, T. H. Green, and F. H. Bradley. The connection with Bradley is the most important in the study.

Lough, Arthur Geoffrey. *The Influence of John Mason Neale*. London: S. P. C. K. 1962. Pp. ii + 282.
Rev. by G. W. O. Addleshaw in *Jour. Eccl. Hist.*, XIV, 113-15; by Phoebe B. Stanton in *VS*, VI, 369-71.

Lukács, Georg. *The Historical Novel*. . . .See VB 1962, 401.
Rev. by Alexander Welsh in *New R.*, 2 Mar., pp. 30-34.

Madden, William A. "The Victorian Sensibility." *VS*, VII, 67-97.
Considers the characteristic way in which experience was organized and evaluated as it is expressed in the most important literature of the period.

Maison, Margaret. *The Victorian Vision: Studies in the Religious Novel.* . . . See VB 1962, 402.
Rev. by J. P. Hulin in *Études anglaises*, XVI, 191-92; by Norman T. Weyand in *Rev. for Religions*, XXII, 247.

Mercier, Vivian. *The Irish Comic Tradition*. . . . See VB 1962, 402.
Rev. in *Critic*, XXI, 82; by André Boué in *Études anglaises*, XVI, 412-13; by Denis Johnston in *N*, 18 May, p. 425; by Austin Clarke in *Poetry*, CII, 185-87; in *TLS*, 11 Jan., p. 26.

Merivale, Patricia. "The 'Death of Pan' in Victorian Literature." *VNL*, No. 23 (Spring), pp. 1-3.

Metzdorf, Robert F. "Victorian Book Decoration." *Princeton Univ. Libr. Chronicle*, XXIV, 91-100.

Miller, Joseph Hillis. *The Disappearance of God: Five Nineteenth-Century Writers*. Cambridge, Mass.: Harvard Univ. Pr. Pp. ix + 367.
Rev. by R. L. Perkins in *LJ*, LXXXVIII, 4222.
Includes DeQuincey, Robert Browning, Arnold, Emily Brontë, and Hopkins.

Miller, J. Hillis. "The Theme of the Disappearance of God in Victorian Poetry." *VS*, VI, 207-27.
Arnold, Browning, Tennyson, and Hopkins "tried, each in his own way, to bring God back to earth as a benign power inherent in self, in nature, and in the human community. . . ."

Moers, Ellen. "Literary Economics in the 1890's: Golden Boys for Sale." *VS*, VII, 185-91.

Morley, Malcolm. *The Royal West London Theatre*. London: The St. Marylebone Society Publications Group, 1962. Pp. 48.
Rev. by Phyllis Hartnoll in *N & Q*, n.s. X, 273-74; by George Speaight in *Theatre Notebook*, XVII, 101-02.

Mosse, George L. *The Culture of Western Europe: The Nineteenth and Twentieth Centuries*. Chicago: Rand McNally, 1961. Pp. 439.
Rev. by Peter Fison in *S*, 3 May, pp. 571-72.

Nelson, James G. *The Sublime Puritan: Milton and the Victorians*. Madison: Univ. of Wisconsin Pr. Pp. 209.
Rev. by E. Saillens in *Études anglaises*, XVI, 395; by Bernard Groom in *VS*, VII, 219.

Newsome, David. *Godliness and Good Learning*. . . . See VB, 1962, 402.
Rev. by W. H. G. Armytage in *EHR*, LXXVIII, 570-71.

Omans, Glen A. "Medieval French Poetic Forms in Victorian Poetry." *DA*, XXIV, 1173-74.

Patridge, Monica. "Slavonic Themes in English Poetry of the 19th Century." *The Slavonic and East European Review*, XLI, 420-41.
The extinction of Poland, the defeat of Napoleon, and the Crimean War made English poets conscious of Russia.

Pearson, Hesketh. *Lives of the Wits*. . . . See VB 1962, 402.
Rev. by Phoebe Adams in *AM*, Nov., 1962, p. 140; by DeLancey Ferguson in *HTB*, 4 Nov., 1962, p. 7; in *LJ*, LXXXVIII, 358; by Burling Lowrey in *SR*, 19 Jan., p. 54; in *TLS*, 27 July, 1962, p. 536.

Peckham, Morse. *Beyond the Tragic Vision*. . . . See VB 1962, 402.
Rev. by Frank E. Manuel in *AHR*, LXVIII, 415-16; by Maurice Beebe in *SAQ*, LXII, 150-52.

Pitts, Gordon. "Lord de Tabley: Poet of Frustration." *West Virginia University Philological Papers*, XIV, 57-73.
He is "perhaps [the] most persistent voice" of the wasteland theme in Victorian poetry.

Preyer, Robert. "Victorian Wisdom in Literature: Fragments and Maxims." *VS*, VI, 245-62.

Prynne, J. H. "The Elegiac World in Victorian Poetry." *Listener*, 14 Feb., pp. 290-91.

Raleigh, John Henry. "What Scott Meant to the Victorians." *VS*, VII, 7-34.
An acute and wide-ranging essay. – D.J.G.

Roskill, Mark. "Holman Hunt's Differing Versions of the 'Light of the World'." *VS*, VI, 229-44.

Schorer, Mark (ed.). *Modern British Fiction: Essays in Criticism*. New York: Oxford Univ. Pr., 1961. Pp. x + 438.
Rev. by Miriam Allott in *MLR*, LVIII, 113-14.
Essays on Hardy, Conrad, and Ford.

Simon, Walter Michael. *European Positivism in the Nineteenth Century*. Ithaca, New York: Cornell. Pp. xi + 384.
Includes chapters on Mill, Frederic Harrison, and English positivists.

Slater, Michael. "The Victorians." *S*, 9 Aug., p. 175.
On revivals of plays by Jerrold, Boucicault, Robertson and others. (See letter by W. M. Tydeman, 23 Aug., p. 228; by Michael Slater, 30 Aug., p. 257.)

Smith, D. J. "Music in the Victorian Novel." *KR*, XXV, 517-32.
Brief general comment upon Victorian music meshed with chatter on the subject

selected from major novelists. – C.T.D.

Spitzer, Leo. *Essays on English and American Literature*. Ed. by Anna Hatcher. Princeton: Princeton Univ. Pr. Pp. 290.
Rev. by G. W. Dunleavy in *MLJ*, XLVII, 178; by *VQR*, XXXIX, lvi.
Contains material on Tennyson and Yeats.

Staley, Allen. "William Dyce and Outdoor Naturalism." *Burl. Mag.*, CV, 470-75.

Stewart, John James Mackintosh. *Eight Modern Writers*. Oxford: Clarendon Pr.; New York: Oxford Univ. Pr. Pp. ix + 704.
Rev. by Graham Hough in *Listener*, 25 July, p. 137; by Frank Kermode in *NS*, LXVI, 142.
Volume XII in Oxford History of English Literature; includes discussion of Hardy, Shaw, Conrad, Kipling, Yeats.

Sutton, Denys. *Nocturne: The Art of James McNeill Whistler*. Country Life. Pp. 153.
Rev. by Edward Lucie-Smith in *Listener*, 26 Dec., p. 1075.

Tiemersma, Richard R. "Fiction in the *Cornhill Magazine*, January 1860 – March 1871." *DA*, XXIII, 3358.

Voll, Dieter. *Catholic Evangelicalism: The Acceptance of Evangelical Traditions by the Oxford Movement during the Second Half of the Nineteenth Century*. London: Faith Pr. Pp. 150.
Originally published in German in 1960; translated by Veronica Ruffer.

Wain, John. *Essays on Literature and Ideas*. London: Macmillan. Pp. xi + 270.
Rev. by Peter Levi in *S*, 1 Nov., p. 566; in *TLS*, 11 Oct., p. 799.
Includes essays on *Little Dorrit* and on G. M. Hopkins.

Walsh, Chad. *From Utopia to Nightmare*. New York: Harper. Pp. 190.
Rev. by Brand Blanshard in *NYTBR*, 7 April, pp. 46-48.
Includes discussions of Morris's *News from Nowhere* and Butler's *Erewhon*.

White, James F. *The Cambridge Movement*. . . . See VB 1962, 398.
Rev. by P. E. Clarke in *Burl. Mag.*, CV, 569-70; by G. W. O. Addleshow in *Jour. Eccl. Hist.*, XIV, 113-15; in *TLS*, 22 Feb., pp. 124-25; by Phoebe B. Stanton in *VS*, VI, 369-71.

Wilson, Angus. "Evil in the English Novel." *Listener*, 3 Jan., pp. 15-16; 17 Jan., pp. 63-65; 17 Jan., pp. 115-17.
These three of four talks on the "Third Programme" contain many references to Victorian novelists, especially Dickens, Eliot, Thackeray.

IV. INDIVIDUAL AUTHORS

ACTON (See II, Altholz; NEWMAN: MacDougall).

AINSWORTH (see III, Hollingsworth).

ARNOLD (see also III, Benziger; BROWNING: Balliet; CARLYLE: Ludwig).

Allott, Kenneth. "Arnold's 'Tyrian Trader'." *TLS*, 18 Oct., p. 826.

Allott, Kenneth. "Matthew Arnold's 'The New Sirens' and George Sand." *Vict. Poetry*, I, 156-58.

Brooks, Roger L. "The Genesis of Matthew Arnold's 'Thyrsis'." *RES*, n.s. XIV, 172-74.

Brooks, Roger L. "A New Source for Matthew Arnold's 'Sohrab and Rustum'." *PQ*, XLII, 129-31.

Brooks, Roger L. "The Strayed Reveller Myth." *The Library*, 5th Ser., XVIII, 57-60.

Brown, T. J. "English Literary Autographs XLVI. Matthew Arnold, 1822-28." *Book Collector*, XII, 195.

Buckler, William E. (ed.). *Passages from the Prose Writings of Matthew Arnold. Selected by the Author.* New York: New York Univ. Pr. Pp. xx + 235.
Noticed in *TLS*, 25 Oct., p. 873.
Selections made by Arnold for Macmillan in 1880.

Coulling, Sidney M. B. "The Background of 'The Function of Criticism at the Present Time'." *PQ*, XLII, 36-54.
The Colenso controversy as background for Arnold's essay.

Coulling, Sidney M. B. "The Evolution of *Culture and Anarchy*." *SP*, LX, 637-68.

Duffin, Henry Charles. *Arnold the Poet.* . . .
See VB 1962, 403.
Rev. by Gilbert Harding in *English*, XIV, 155-56; by Kenneth Allott in *MLR*, LVIII, 109-10.

Ebel, Henry. "Matthew Arnold and Marcus Aurelius." *SEL*, III, 555-66.

Fulweiler, Howard W. "Mathew Arnold: The Metamorphosis of a Merman." *Vict. Poetry*, I, 208-22.

Gottfried, Leon. *Matthew Arnold and the Romantics.* London: Routledge & Kegan Paul; Lincoln: Univ. of Nebraska Pr. Pp. x + 277.
Rev. by Basil Willey in *Critical Quart.*, V, 274-75; by Kenneth Allott in *Listener*, 14 Mar., p. 469; by J. R. Willingham in *LJ*, LXXXVIII, 3209; in *TLS*, 24 May, p. 372.

Greenberg, Robert A. "Matthew Arnold's Mournful Rhymes: A Study of "The World and the Quietist'." *Vict. Poetry*, I, 284-90.

Honan, Park. "Matthew Arnold and Cacophony." *Vict. Poetry*, I, 115-22.

James, David Gwilym. *Matthew Arnold and the Decline of English Romanticism.* . . .
See VB 1962, 403.
Rev. by Robert Langbaum in *MP*, LX, 298-300.

Kendall, J. L. "The Unity of Arnold's *Tristram and Iseult*." *Vict. Poetry*, I, 140-45.

Kermode, Frank. "Grand Objects of Concern." *NS*, LXV, 159-60.

Knoepflmacher, U. C. "Dover Revisited: The Wordsworthian Matrix in the Poetry of Matthew Arnold." *Vict. Poetry*, I, 17-26.

LeRoy, Gaylord C. "Arnold and Aselegia." *Bull., New York Pub. Libr.*, LXVII, 301-06.
On Arnold's shifting political and social attitudes.

Mattheisen, Paul F., and Young, Arthur C. (eds.). "Some Letters of Matthew Arnold." *VNL*, No. 24 (Fall), pp. 17-20.

Mazzaro, Jerome L. "Corydon in Matthew Arnold's 'Thyrsis'." *Vict. Poetry*, I, 304-06.

McCarthy, Patrick J. "Matthew Arnold and the Three Classes." *DA*, XXIV, 301-02.

Monjian, Mercedes C. "Matthew Arnold's Criticism: The Mythic Strain." *DA*, XXIV, 2017-18.

Monteiro, George. "Matthew Arnold and John Hay: Three Unpublished Letters." *N & Q*, n.s. X, 461-63.

Osborne, David G., Jr. "Matthew Arnold, 1843-1849: A Study of the Yale Manuscript." *DA*, XXIV, 2018.
Arnold's thoughts in prose and poetry contained in a notebook written between 1843 and 1849.

Stevens, Earl E. "Arnold's Tyrian Trader." *VNL*, No. 24 (Fall), pp. 24-26.

Stocking, George W., Jr. "Matthew Arnold, E. B. Tylor, and the Uses of Invention." *American Anthropologist*, LXV, 783-99.

Sundell, M. G. "The Intellectual Background and Structure of Arnold's *Tristram and Iseult*." *Vict. Poetry*, I, 272-83.

Super, R. H. (ed.). *Democratic Education.*

... see VB 1962, 404.

Rev. by Roger L. Brooks in *MP*, LXI, 141-42.

Super, R. H. "Documents in the Matthew Arnold — Sainte-Beuve Relationship." *MP*, LX, 206-10.
A chronological list.

Super, R. H. (ed.). *Lectures and Essays in Criticism.* . . . See VB 1962, 404.

Rev. by Louis Crompton in *CE*, XXIV, 663; by A. R. Rolfs in *Christian Sci. Monitor*, 6 Dec., 1962, p. 25; in *Economist*, CCVII, 1392; by Kenneth Allott in *Listener*, 14 Mar., p. 469; in *TLS*, 24 May, p. 372.

Super, R. H. (ed.). *On the Classical Tradition.* . . . See VB 1962, 404.

Rev. by R. L. Brooks in *Comparative Literature*, XV, 377-79.

Williamson, Eugene L., Jr. "Matthew Arnold and the Archbishops." *MLQ*, XXIV, 245-52.

BAGEHOT (see TENNYSON: St. John-Stevas).

St. John-Stevas, Norman. *Walter Bagehot.* Writers and Their Work Series. London: Longman. Pp. 42.

St. John-Stevas, Norman. "Walter Bagehot as a Writer." *Wiseman Rev.*, CCXXXVII, 38-65.

Tener, Robert H., and St. John-Stevas, Norman. "Bagehot and Bailey." *TLS*, 8 Feb., p. 93.
Bagehot's authorship of a review of Bailey's *Festus.*

BAILEY (see BAGEHOT: Tener).

Birley, Robert. *Sunk without Trace: Some Forgotten Masterpieces Reconsidered.* . . . See VB 1962, 404.

Rev. by J. R. Willingham in *LJ*, LXXXVIII, 103; by Marya Zaturenska in *NYTBR*, 21 Oct., 1962, p. 52; in *TLS*, 15 June, 1962, p. 442.

BARNES.

Forsyth, R. A. "The Conserving Myth of William Barnes." *VS*, VI, 325-54.
Barnes was creating a myth which both conserved the qualities of the past and country life and presented them as a criticism of the industrial, urban, progressing present.

BEERBOHM.

Riewald, J. G. (ed.). *Max in Verse: Rhymes and Parodies by Max Beerbohm.* Foreword by S. N. Behrman. Brattleboro: Stephen Greene Pr. Pp. 167.

Rev. by David McCord in *NYTBR*, 27 Oct., pp. 12-14.

BESANT.

Nethercot, Arthur Hobart. *The Last Four Lives of Annie Besant.* London: Rupert Hart-Davis. Pp. 483.

Rev. by Norman St. John-Stevas in *Listener*, 5 Dec., p. 947; in *TLS*, 7 Nov., p. 912.
Concludes a two-part biography (see VB 1960, 389).

BORROW.

Bartle, G. F. "George Borrow's 'Old Radical'." *N & Q*, n.s. X, 242-47.

BRADLEY.

Assaad, Fawzeia Mikhail. "L'autre et l'absolu dans la philosophie de F. H. Bradley." *Revue de metaphysique et de morale,* LXVII, (1962), 273-90.

Bollier, E. P. "T. S. Eliot and F. H. Bradley: A Question of Influence." *Tulane Studies in English,* XII (1962), 87-111.
A study of Bradley's *Ethical Studies* (1876) and *Appearance and Reality* (1893) to show the extent of Bradley's influence on Eliot's development.

BRONTËS (see also III, Miller).

Bell, Vereen. "*Wuthering Heights* as Epos." *CE*, XXV, 199-208.

"The Brontë Society." Correspondence by Phyllis Bentley, Winifred Gérin, Sir Linton Andrews and others in controversy over the management of the Brontë Parsonage Museum. *TLS*, 8 March — 3 May.

Ekebald, Inga-Stina. "'The Tenant of Wildfell Hall' and 'Women Beware Women'." *N & Q*, n.s. X, 449-50.

Howard, Margaret A. "Charlotte Brontë's Novels: An Analysis of Their Thematic and Structural Patterns." *DA*, XXIV, 728.

Moser, Thomas (ed.). *Wuthering Heights: Text, Sources, Criticism.* New York: Harcourt, Brace, 1962. Pp. 229.

Rev. by Ted E. Boyle in *CE*, XXV, 160.

Sharps, J. G. "Charlotte Brontë and the Mysterious 'Miss H': A Detail in Mrs. Gaskell's *Life*." *English*, XIV, 236.
A textual change by Mrs. Gaskell in a letter of Charlotte Brontë.

Solomon, Eric. "*Jane Eyre*: Fire and Water." *CE*, XXV, 215-17.

Thompson, Wade. "Infanticide and Sadism in *Wuthering Heights*." *PMLA*, LXXVIII, 69-74.
Emphasizes the novel's preoccupation

with these two characteristics to the point of being "a perverse book."

Todd, William B. "An Early State of Charlotte Brontë's *Shirley*, 1849." *Book Collector*, XII, 355-56.

BROUGHAM.

New, Chester W. *The Life of Henry Brougham to 1830.* . . . See VB 1962, 405.
Rev. by Norman Gash in *EHR*, LXXVIII, 739-41.

BROWNINGS (see also III, Benziger, Miller; CARLYLE: Sanders).

Altick, Richard D. " 'A Grammarian's Funeral': Browning's Praise of Folly?" *SEL*, III, 449-60.
Proposes that the poem is a mock-encomium.

Altick, Richard D. "Memo to the Next Annotator of Browning." *Vict. Poetry*, I, 61-68.

Balliet, Conrad A. " 'Growing Old' along with 'Rabbi Ben Ezra'." *Vict. Poetry*, I, 300-01.

Barnes, Warner. "The Browning Collection." *Libr. Chronicle of the Univ. of Texas*, VII, 12-13.
Brief description of what must be the richest holdings on E.B.B. in America, and one of the richest on R.B. — C.T.D.

Cary, Richard. "Robinson on Browning." *VNL*, No. 23 (Spring), pp. 19-21.

Columbus, Robert R. "A Critical Explication of Robert Browning's *Parleyings with Certain People of Importance in Their Day*." *DA*, XXIII, 3370.

Drew, Philip. "Browning's *Essay on Shelley*." *Vict. Poetry*, I, 1-6.

Fleisher, David. " 'Rabbi Ben Ezra,' 49-72: A New Key to an Old Crux." *Vict. Poetry*, I, 46-52.

Fryxell, Lucy Dickinson, and Adair, Virginia H. "Browning's 'Soliloquy of the Spanish Cloister'." *Ex*, XXII, Item 24.

Gainer, Patrick W. " 'Hy, Zy, Hine'." *Vict. Poetry*, I, 158-60.

Guerin, Wilfred L. "Irony and Tension in Browning's 'Karshish'." *Vict. Poetry*, I, 132-39.

Hayter, Alethea. *Mrs. Browning: A Poet's Work and Its Setting.* . . . See VB 1962, 405.
Rev. by Ian Fletcher in *Critical Quart.*, V, 181-83; by Gilbert Thomas in *English*, XIV, 155-56; by Elizabeth Muller in *LJ*, LXXXVIII, 2009; by Kenneth Allott in *RES*, n.s. XIV, 422-23; by Morse Peckham in *SR*, 7 Sept., p. 34; by Gardner B. Taplin in *VS*, VII, 123.

Holloway, Sister Marcella M. "A Further Reading of 'Count Gismond'." *SP*, LX, 549-53.
A supplementary note to Tilton and Tuttle (see below), arguing that Count Gismond is not the chivalrous protector of his wife. An original and perceptive paper. — R.A.D.

Honan, Park. *Browning's Characters.* . . . See VB 1962, 405.
Rev. by John Killham in *MLR*, LVIII, 110-11; by W. O. Raymond in *MP*, LX, 231-33.

Howard, John. "Caliban's Mind." *Vict. Poetry*, I, 249-57.

Johnson, Wendell Stacy. "Browning's Music." *JAA*, XXII, 203-07.

Kelley, Philip and Hudson, Ronald. "The Letters of the Brownings." *Vict. Poetry*, I, 238-39.
Kelley and Hudson announce that they will co-edit a 20-volume "definitive edition of the letters."

Kenmare, Dallas. *An End to Darkness: A New Approach to Robert Browning and His Work.* . . . See VB 1962, 406.
Rev. by Gilbert Thomas in *English*, XIV, 155-56.

Kishler, Thomas C. "A Note on Browning's 'Soliloquy of the Spanish Cloister'." *Vict. Poetry*, I, 70-71.

Litzinger, Boyd. *Robert Browning and the Babylonian Woman*. Baylor Browning Interests, No. 19. Waco, Tex.: Baylor Univ., 1962. Pp. 35.
A thorough catalogue of Browning's use of Roman Catholic speakers and Browning's attitude toward the Roman Catholic Church.

Martin, Hugh. *The Faith of Robert Browning.* London: S. C. M. Pr. Pp. 128.
Rev. in *Methodist Recorder*, 19 Dec., p. 6.

Maxwell, J. C. "Browning's Concept of the Poet: A Revision in *Pauline*." *Vict. Poetry*, I, 237-38.

Monteiro, George. "Browning's 'My Last Duchess'." *Vict. Poetry*, I, 234-37.

Page, David. "And So Is Browning." *EC*, XIII, 146-54.
A weak attempt to resurrect the "good" poems, those generally not revealing the optimist but dealing with "realities." — R.E.F.

Ridenour, George M. "Browning's Music Poems: Fancy and Fact." *PMLA*, LXX-

VIII, 369-77.

Ryan, William M. "The Classification of Browning's 'Difficult' Vocabulary." *SP*, LX, 542-48.

Slakey, Roger I. "Browning's 'Soliloquy of the Spanish Cloister.' " *Ex*, XXI, Item 42.

Stevens, Lewis R. "Robert Browning as a Myth-Maker in *The Ring and the Book*." *DA*, XXIV, 1164.

Tilton, John W., and Tuttle, R. Dale. "A New Reading of 'Count Gismond'." *SP*, LIX (1962), 83-95.

This essay, together with the one by Sister Marcella M. Holloway (see above), offers a conjectural, but persuasive new reading of the poem — that the Countess is by no means the persecuted innocent of earlier commentary.

Tompkins, J. M. S. *Aurora Leigh*. . . . See VB 1962, 406 [Fawcett Lecture, not Fawcell].

Rev. by Kenneth Allott in *MLR*, LVIII, 625-26.

Whitla, William. *The Central Truth: The Incarnation in Browning's Poetry*. Toronto: Univ. of Toronto Pr. Pp. vii + 161.

Willoughboy, John W. "Browning's 'Childe Roland to the Dark Tower Came'." *Vict. Poetry*, I, 291-99.

BULWER (see III, Hollingsworth).

BURTON.

Burton, Richard (tr.). *The Perfumed Garden of the Shaykh Nefzawi*. London: Neville Spearman. Pp. 271.

Translation of Persian text originally published in late 19th-century for private circulation only.

Brodie, Fawn M. (ed.). *The City of the Saints*. New York: Knopf. Pp. xlii + 654.

Rev. by Phoebe Adams in *AM*, Aug., p. 125.

Burton's journal of a visit to Salt Lake City in 1860.

Edwardes, Allen. *Death Rides A Camel: A Biography of Sir Richard Burton*. New York: Julian Pr. Pp. 422.

Unfavorably rev. by E. T. Smith in *LJ*, LXXXVIII, 2505-06.

Farwell, Byron. *Burton*. New York: Holt, Rinehart, and Winston; London: Longmans. Pp. xv + 431.

Rev. by Hugh Gordon Porteus in *Listener*, 31 Oct., p. 707; by V. S. Pritchett in *NS*, LXVI, 743-44; by Robert Rhodes James in *S*, 22 Nov., p. 672; in *TLS*, 25 Oct., p. 864.

BUTLER (see also III, Walsh; **DARWIN:** Greenacre).

Howard, Daniel F. (ed.). *Correspondence of Samuel Butler with His Sister May*. . . . See VB 1962, 406.

Rev. by C. T. Houpt in *Christian Science Monitor*, 30 Aug., 1962, p. 11; by Margaret Willy in *English*, XIV, 154-55; in *TLS*, 11 Jan., p. 26; by John Henry Raleigh in *VS*, VI, 375-76; by A. D. Culler in *YR*, LII, 289.

Marshall, William H. "*The Way of All Flesh*: The Dual Function of Edward Overton." *Texas Studies in Lit. and Lang.*, IV, 583-90.

Shoenberg, Robert E. "The Conservatism of Samuel Butler (1835-1902)." *DA*, XXIII, 3387.

Silver, Arnold (ed.). *The Family Letters of Samuel Butler, 1841-1886*. . . . See VB 1962, 406.

Rev. by Walter F. Wright in *CE*, XXIV, 330; by J. B. Fort in *Études anglaises*, XVI, 90-91; by Laurence N. Black in *JEGP*, LXII, 413-16; by Jacques Vallette in *Mercure de France*, CCCLXXXVI, 510-12; by Walter M. Crittenden in *The Personalist*, XLIV, 126-27; by Bernard Bergonzi in *S*, 15 June, p. 798; by Royal A. Gettmann in *SAQ*, LXII, 442-43; in *TLS*, 8 June, p. 422; by Claude T. Bissell in *TQ*, XXXII, 294-95; by John Henry Raleigh in *VS*, VI, 375-76; by A. Dwight Culler in *YR*, LII, 283-90.

CARLYLE.

Brown, T. J. "English Literary Autographs XLVII. Thomas Carlyle, 1795-1881." *Book Collector*, XII, 339.

Cobban, Alfred. "Carlyle's French Revolution." *History*, XLVIII, 306-16.

Deen, Leonard W. "Irrational Form in *Sartor Resartus*." *Texas Studies in Lit. and Lang.*, V, 438-51.

Garrison, Joseph M., Jr. "John Burroughs as a Literary Critic: A Study Emphasizing His Treatment of Emerson, Whitman, Thoreau, Carlyle, and Arnold." *DA*, XXIII, 3372-73.

Ludwig, Hans-Werner. *Die Self-Komposita bei Thomas Carlyle, Matthew Arnold und Gerard Manley Hopkins*. Tubingen: Max Niemeyer.

Ryan, Alvin S. "The Attitude toward the Reader in Carlyle's *Sartor Resartus*." *VNL*, No. 23 (Spring) pp. 15-16.

Sanders, Charles Richard. (ed.). "Some Lost and Unpublished Carlyle-Browning Correspondence." *JEGP*, LXII, 323-35.

Four hitherto unpublished Carlyle letters

throw light on his friendship with Browning.

Tener, Robert H. "Sources of Hutton's 'Modern Guides' Essay on Carlyle." *N & Q*, n.s. X, 463-64.

Tennyson, G. B. "Carlyle's Poetry to 1840: A Checklist and Discussion, A New Attribution, and Six Unpublished Poems." *Vict. Poetry*, I, 161-81.

CARROLL.

Gardner, Martin (ed.). *The Annotated Snark.* . . . See VB 1962, 406.
Rev. by W. J. Smith in *NYTBR*, 18 Nov., 1962, p. 26; in *SR*, 6 Oct., 1962, p. 41; in *TLS*, 15 Feb., p. 111.

Kirk, Daniel F. *Charles Dodgson, Semeiotician.* Univ. of Florida Monographs, Humanities, No. 11, Fall 1962. Gainesville: Univ. of Florida Pr., 1962. Pp. 78.
Unfavorably rev. by P. T. Geach in *N & Q*, n.s. X, 473.

O'Brien, Hugh. " 'Alice in Wonderland' — 'The French Lesson Book'." *N & Q*, n.s. X, 461.

Williams, Sidney Herbert, and Madan, Falconer. *The Lewis Carroll Handbook.* . . . See VB 1962, 406.
Rev. by W. H. Bond in *JEGP*, LXII, 411-12; by Stanley Godman in *N & Q*, n.s. X, 476-78.

CLOUGH.

Chorley, Katharine. *Arthur Hugh Clough: The Uncommitted Mind.* . . . See VB 1962, 407.
Rev. by Patrick McCarthy in *ArQ*, XIX, 177-80; by John Clive in *JMH*, XXXV, 423-24.

Houghton, Walter E. *The Poetry of Clough.* New Haven, Conn.: Yale Univ. Pr. Pp. xii + 236.
Rev. by J. R. Willingham in *LJ*, LXXXVIII, 2701.

Green, David Bonnell. "Arthur Hugh Clough and the Parkers." *N & Q*, n.s. X, 24-26.

Ryals, Clyde de L. "An Interpretation of Clough's *Dipsychus*." *Vict. Poetry*, I, 182-88.

Timko, Michael. "The Satiric Poetry of Arthur Hugh Clough." *Vict. Poetry*, I, 104-14.

COLLINS.

Lawson, Lewis A. "Wilkie Collins and *The Moonstone*." *American Imago*, XX, 61-79.
The main thesis is that underlying the detective plot of the novel is a sexual schema involving four persons. The author's extreme Freudian position leads him

to some rather strange conclusions. — M.T.

CONRAD (see also III, Billiar, Schorer, Stewart).

Beebe, Maurice. "The Masks of Conrad." *Bucknell Rev.*, XI, 35-53.
A Conrad with a "creative spirit that functions like a Holy Ghost in joining the creator with the creation." Close attention paid to the *Heart of Darkness* and *Victory*.

Bennett, Carl D. "A Choice of Nightmares: A Study of Conrad's Ethocal Vision." *DA*, XXIV, 293-94.

Boyle, Ted E. "Symbol and Meaning in the Writings of Joseph Conrad." *DA*, XXIII, 3894.

Burgess, C. F. "Conrad's Pesky Russian." *NCF*, XVIII, 189-93.

Dale, Patricia. "Conrad: A Borrowing from Hazlitt's Father." *N & Q*, n.s. X, 146.

Graver, Lawrence. "Conrad's 'The Lagoon.' " *Ex*, XXI, Item 70.

Gross, Seymour L. "Conrad's Revision of 'Amy Foster'." *N & Q*, n.s. X, 144-46.

Gurko, Leo. *Joseph Conrad: Giant in Exile.* . . . See VB 1962, 407.
Rev. by Ted E. Boyle in *CE*, XXIV, 664; by Frederick R. Karl in *SeR*, LXXI, 680-83; by William Blackburn in *SAQ*, LXII, 444-45; by Ian Watt in *VS*, VI, 376-78.

Hay, Eloise Knapp. *The Political Novels of Joseph Conrad.* Chicago: Univ. of Chicago Pr. Pp. 350.
Rev. by Lawrence Graver in *NCF*, XVIII, 302-05; by C. W. Mann, Jr. in *LJ*, LXXXVIII, 3846-47; by Frederick R. Karl in *SeR*, LXXI, 680-83.

Hodges, Robert R. "Joseph Conrad's Dual Heritage." *DA*, XXIV, 1160-61.

Hoffman, Stanton de Voren. "Comedy and Form in the Fiction of Joseph Conrad." *DA*, XXIII, 3898-99.

Johnson, Bruce M. "Conrad's 'Karain' and *Lord Jim*." *MLQ*, XXIV, 13-20.

Johnson, Bruce. "Joseph Conrad and Crane's *Red Badge of Courage*." *Papers of the Michigan Academy of Science, Arts, and Letters*, XLVIII, 649-55.

Lee, Robert Francis. "Conrad's Colonialism." *DA*, XXIV, 1172.

Mackenzie, Manfred. "Fenimore Cooper and Conrad's 'Suspense.' " *N & Q*, n.s. X, 373-75. (See also letter from D. C. Cross, *N & Q*, n.s. X, 467).

Maxwell, J. C. "Conrad and Turgenev: A

Minor Source for 'Victory'." *N & Q*, n.s. X, 372-73.

Mitchell, Sidney H. "Conrad and His Critics: 1895-1914." *DA*, XXIII, 2917.

Moore, Carlisle. "Conrad and the Novel as Ordeal." *PQ*, XLII, 55-74.

Ordonez, Elmer A. "The Early Development of Joseph Conrad: Revisions and Style." *DA*, XXIII, 4362.
Revisions from manuscript to print (serial or book) and from serial to first edition.

Palmer, John Alfred. "Joseph Conrad's Fiction." *DA*, XXIII, 3383.

Ridley, Florence H. "The Ultimate Meaning of 'Heart of Darkness'." *NCF*, XVIII, 43-53.

Saveson, J. E. "Masterman as a Source of 'Nostromo'." *N & Q*, n.s. X, 368-70.

Sherry, Norman. "Conrad and the S. S. *Vidar*." *RES*, n.s. XIV, 157-63.

Sherry, Norman. "Conrad's 'Otago': A Case of Mistaken Identity." *N & Q*, n.s. X, 370-72.

Sherwin, Jane K. "The Literary Epiphany in Some Early Fiction of Flaubert, Conrad, Proust, and Joyce." *DA*, XXIII, 3902.

Tanner, Tony. *Conrad: Lord Jim*. Studies in English Literature, No. 12. London: Edward Arnold. Pp. 62.
Rev. by Mark Roberts in *EC*, XIII, 403-15; by W. J. Harvey in *MLR*, LVIII, 568-69.

Tick, Stanley. "Heart of Darkness." *Explicator*, XXI, No. 67.

Tomlinson, Maggie. "Conrad's Integrity: *Typhoon, Nostromo, The Shadow-Line*." *The Melbourne Critical Rev.*, No. 5, 1962, pp. 40-53.

Wills, John Howard. "A Neglected Masterpiece: Conrad's *Youth*." *Texas Studies in Lit. and Lang.*, IV, 591-601.

Yelton, Donald C. "Symbol and Metaphor in Conrad's Fiction." *DA*, XXIV, 752-53.

Zuckerman, Jerome. "The Theme of Rule in Joseph Conrad." *DA*, XXIII, 4367.

DARWIN.

Barlow, Nora (ed.). *Ornithological Notes*. British Museum Historical Series Bulletin, Vol. II, No. 7. London: H. M. S. O. Pp. 77.

De Beer, Sir Gavin. *Charles Darwin: Evolution by Natural Selection*. London: Nelson. Pp. xi + 290.
Rev. in *TLS*, 28 Nov., p. 996.

Gates, Eunice Joiner. "Charles Darwin and Benito Lynch's *El Inglés de los güesos*." *Hispania*, XLIV, 250-53.

Gray, Asa. *Darwiniana: Essays and Reviews Pertaining to Darwinism*. Ed. by A. Hunter Dupree. Cambridge, Mass.: Belknap Pr. Pp. 327.

Greenacre, Phyllis. *The Quest for the Father: A Study of the Darwin-Butler Controversy, as a Contribution to the Understanding of the Creative Individual*. New York: International Univ. Pr. Pp. 128.
Rev. by L. DeRosis in *LJ*, LXXXVIII, 2918.

Greene, John C. *Darwin and the Modern World View*. . . . See VB 1962, 407.
Rev. by Allan Shields in *The Personalist*, XLIV, 141; by Garrett Hardin in *VS*, VI, 296-97.

Hyman, Stanley Edgar (ed.). *Darwin for Today: The Essence of His Works*. New York: Viking. Pp. viii + 435.
Rev. by G. Basalla in *LJ*, LXXXVIII, 3216.

Hyman, Stanley Edgar. *The Tangled Bank*. . . . See VB 1962, 408.
Rev. unfavorably by Ronald S. Berman in *KR*, XXV, 161.

Nursall, J. R. "The Consequences of Darwinism." *Dalhousie Rev.*, XLII, 472-80.

Plaine, Henry L. (ed.). *Darwin, Marx, and Wagner: A Symposium*. . . . See VB 1962, 408.
Rev. by Leonard Krieger in *JMH*, XXXV, 426-28; by Garrett Hardin in *VS*, VII, 112-15.

Vorzimmer, Peter. "Charles Darwin and Blending Inheritance." *Isis*, LIV, 371-90.

DAVIDSON.

Peterson, Carroll V. "John Davidson: The Development of His Ideas." *DA*, XXIV, 2464-65.

Townsend, J. Benjamin. *John Davidson: Poet of Armageddon*. . . . See VB 1962, 408.
Rev. by Robert O. Preyer in *CE*, XXIV, 588-89; by M. Levy in *Études anglaises*, 296-97; by Walter E. Swayze in *QQ*, LXX, 454-55.

DICKENS (see also III, Aitken, Bloom, Hollingsworth, Land, Wain, Wilson).

Axton, William. "Tonal Unity in *Dombey and Son*." *PMLA*, LXXVIII, 341-48.
Asserts the tonal unity of the novel's symbolic structure.

Blount, Trevor. "The Graveyard Satire of *Bleak House* in the Context of 1850."

RES, n.s. XIV, 370-78.
Current agitation about the problem of overcrowded London cemeteries.

Brown, Ivor. *Dickens in His Time*. London: Nelson. Pp. 248.

Clipper, Lawrence J. "Crime and Criminals in the Novels of Charles Dickens." *DA*, XXIV, 2474-75.

Cockshut, A. O. J. *The Imagination of Charles Dickens*. . . . See VB 1962, 409.
Rev. by H. P. Collins in *EC*, XIII, 177-80.

Collins, Philip. *Dickens and Crime*. . . . See VB 1962, 409.
Rev. by John Butt in *Dickensian*, LIX, 44-45; by Sylvère Monod in *Études anglaises*, XVI, 190-91; by F. C. Mather in *History*, XLVIII, 95; by D. W. Elliott in *N & Q*, n.s. X, 271-72; by K. J. Fielding in *RES*, n.s. XIV, 308-09; by Sergeant Cuff in *SR*, 26 Jan., p. 48; in *VQR*, XXXIX, lviii.

Collins, Philip. *Dickens and Education*. London: Macmillan. Pp. ix + 258.
Rev. by Christopher Ricks in *Listener*, 7 Nov., p. 756; in *TLS*, 12 Dec., p. 1034; by Monroe Engel in *VS*, VII, 105-06.

Collins, Philip. "Dickens and the *Edinburgh Review*." *RES*, n.s. XIV, 167-72.

Cross, Barbara M. "Comedy and Drama in Dickens." *Western Humanities Rev.*, XVII, 143-49.

Davis, Earle. *The Flint and the Flame: The Artistry of Charles Dickens*. Columbia: Univ. of Missouri Pr. Pp. 333.

Dickensian, Vol. LIX (Nos. 339-41). . . . See VB 1932, 422. Items as follows: Brooks, Harold F., and Jean R., "Dickens in Shaw" (pp. 93-99); Butt, John, Review of P. Collins, *Dickens and Crime* (pp. 44-45); Carlton, William J., "Dickens Studies French" (pp. 21-27); Carlton, William J., "George Hogarth – a Link with Scott and Dickens" (pp. 78-89); Carlton, William J., "'Old Nick' at Devonshire Terrace: Dickens through French Eyes in 1843" (pp. 138-44); Collins, Philip, "Dickens in Conversation" (pp. 145-55); Collins, Philip, "Dickens on Chatham: An Uncollected Piece" (pp. 69-73); Collins, Philip, "Dickens on Ghosts: An Uncollected Article" (pp. 5-14); Collins, Philip, "The Immortal Memory" (pp. 133-37); Coolidge, Archibald C., Jr., "Dickens and Latitudinarian Christianity" (pp. 57-60); Dettelbach, Cynthia, "Bird Imagery in

Bleak House" (pp. 177-81); Fielding, K. J. "Dickens Criticism: A Symposium [rev. of *Dickens Criticism: Past, Present and Future Directions. A Symposium*]" (pp. 73-77); Fielding, K. J., Review of J. Gross and W. Pearson, *Dickens and the Twentieth Century* (pp. 45-47); Gibson, Frank A., "Hard on the Lawyers?" (pp. 160-64); Gibson, Frank S., "Why Those 'Papers'?" (pp. 99-101); Lovett, Robert W., "Mr. Spectator in *Bleak House*" (p. 124); Morley, Malcolm, "Dickens Goes to the Theatre" (pp. 165-71); Morley, Malcolm, "More about Crummles" (pp. 51-56); Morley, Malcolm, "Private Theatres and Boz" (pp. 119-23); Pakenham, Pansy, "Hebe Elsna's Defence of Mrs. Charles Dickens [rev. of Hebe Elsna, *Unwanted Wife: A Defence of Mrs. Charles Dickens*]" (pp. 125-28); Peyrouton, N. C., "George Gissing [rev. of Jacob Korg, *George Gissing: A Critical Biography*]" (pp. 175-76); Peyrouton, N. C., "The Life of Our Lord: Some Notes of Explication" (pp. 102-12); Peyrouton, N. C., "Mr. 'Q': Dickens's American Secretary" (pp. 156-59); Peyrouton, N. C., Review of Victoria Lincoln, *Charles, A Novel Inspired by Certain Events in the Life of Mr. Charles Dickens*" (pp. 47-48); Phillips, George L., "Dickens and the Chimney-Sweepers" (pp. 28-44); Phillips, George L. "The Poor Chimney Sweep of Windsor': A Philanthropist without a Name" (pp. 91-92); Reffold, A. E., "Dr. Manette in Soho: Some New Notes and Suggestions" (pp. 172-74); S[taples], L. C., "The 150th Birthday at the Birthplace" (pp. 15-19); S[taples], L. C., Review of John Lehmann, *Ancestors and Friends* (pp. 48-49); S[taples], L. C. Review of R. B. Martin, *Enter Rumour* (p. 50); S[taples], L. C., Review of Ian Norrie (ed.), *The Heathside Book* (pp. 49-50); Stedman, Jane W., "Child-Wives of Dickens" (pp. 112-18); Valentine, Marian G., "A Contemporary View of the Dexter Bust" (pp. 90-91).

Elsna, Hebe. *Unwanted Wife: A Defense of Mrs. Charles Dickens*. London: Jarrolds. Pp. 239.

Ford, George Harry, and Lane, Lauriat, Jr. (eds.). *The Dickens Critics*. . . . See VB 1962, 409.

Rev. in *TLS*, 15 Feb., p. 108.

Gross, John, and Pearson, Gabriel (eds.), *Dickens and the Twentieth Century.* . . . See VB 1962, 410.

Rev. by Sylvère Monod in *Études anglaises*, XVI, 289-90; by Lauriat Lang, Jr., in *NCF*, XVIII, 200-02; in *TLS*, 15 Feb., p. 108.

Hardy, Barbara. "The Food and Ceremony in *Great Expectations.*" *EC*, XIII, 351-63.

Hosbaum, Philip. "The Critics and *Our Mutual Friend.*" *EC*, XIII, 231-40.

Hynes, Joseph A. "Image and Symbol in *Great Expectations.*" *ELH*, XXX, 258-92. "Illusion vs. reality" as the central pattern of symbolic imagery in the novel.

Lanham, Richard A. "Our Mutual Friend: The Birds of Prey." *VNL*, No. 24 (Fall), pp. 6-12.

Leavis, F. R. "Dickens and the Critics," *S*, 4 Jan., p. 15.
A letter asserting that Dr. Leavis *does* like Dickens.

Levine, George. "Communication in *Great Expectations.*" *NCF*, XVIII, 175-81.

Marshall, William H. "The Conclusion of *Great Expectations* as the Fulfillment of Myth." *The Personalist*, XLIV, 337-47.

Noland, Richard W. "A Letter from Basil Hall to Charles Dickens." *Journal of Rutgers Univ. Libr.*, XXVII, 19-23.

Peyrouton, Noel C. (ed.). *Dickens Criticism, Past, Present, and Future Directions: A Symposium with George H. Ford and Others.* Cambridge, Mass.: Charles Dickens Reference Center Pp. x + 64.
Rev. briefly in *NCF*, XVIII, 202.

Playfair, Lyon. "Dear Gentle Little Fellow." *Listener*, 25 Apr., pp. 716-17.

Seehase, Georg. *Charles Dickens: Zu einer Besonderheit seines Realismus.* Halle: Max Niemeyer, 1961. Pp. 176.
Rev. by George J. Worth in *JEGP*, LXII, 405-07.

Spilka, Mark. *Dickens and Kafka.* Bloomington: Indiana University Press. Pp. 315.
Rev. by B. W. Fuson in *LJ*, LXXXVIII, 1015-16; by Joseph P. Bauke in *SR*, 13 July, p. 31; by Paul West in *VS*, VII, 214-15.

Stone, Harry. "Dark Corners of the Mind: Dickens' Childhood Reading." *The Horn Book Mag.*, June.

Stone, Harry. "Dickens and Leitmotif: Music-Staircase Imagery in *Dombey and Son.*" *CE*, XXV, 217-20.

Ward, W. A. "Language and Charles Dickens." *Listener*, 23 May, pp. 870-71, 874.

Winters, Warrington. "Charles Dickens: The Pursuers and Pursued." *VNL*, No. 23 (Spring), pp. 23-24.

DISRAELI.

Faber, Richard. *Beaconsfield and Bolingbroke.* . . . See VB 1962, 410.
Rev. by R. V. Sampson in *VS*, VI, 288-89.

Graubard, Stephen R. *Burke, Disraeli, and Churchill: The Politics of Perseverance.* . . . See VB 1962, 410.
Rev. by Donald C. Bryant in *QJS*, LXIX, 90.

DIXON.

Sambrook, James. *A Poet Hidden: The Life of Richard Watson Dixon, 1833-1900.* . . . See VB 1962, 410.
Rev. by J. G. Ritz in *Études anglaises*, XVI, 400-01; by Derek Hudson in *N & Q*, n.s. X, 276-77.

DOUGLAS.

Berkovitz, Miriam J. "Notes Toward a Chapter of Biography: Lord Alfred Douglas and Ronald Firbank." *Bull., New York Pub. Libr.*, LXVII (143-51).

Croft-Cooke, Rupert. *Bosie.* London: W. H. Allen. Pp. 414.
An attempted defense of Lord Alfred Douglas.
Rev. by John Gross in *NS*, LXV, 901; by Julian Symons in *S*, 24 May, p. 674; in *TLS*, 7 June, p. 402.

DOWSON.

Longaker, Mark (ed.). *The Poems of Ernest Dowson.* Philadelphia: Univ. of Pennsylvania Pr.; London: Oxford Univ. Pr. Pp. 263.
Rev. by Ian Fletcher in *Listener*, 16 May, p. 840; by B. A. Robie in *LJ*, LXXXVIII, 1889; in *TLS*, 14 June, p. 446.

Kermode, Frank. "Amateur of Grief." *NS*, LXV, 865-66.

DOYLE.

Klinefelter, Walter. *Sherlock Holmes in Portrait and Profile.* Syracuse, New York: Syracuse Univ. Pr. Pp. ix + 104.

ELIOT (see also III, Aitken, Wilson).

Buchen, Irving H. "Arthur Donnithorne and *Zeluco*: Characterization via Literary Allusion in *Adam Bede.*" *VNL*, No. 23 (Spring), pp. 18-19.

Cate, Hollis L. "The Literary Reception of

George Eliot's Novels in America (1858-1882)." *DA*, XXIII, 3885-86.

Cox, Charles Brian. *The Free Spirit: A Study of Liberal Humanism in the Novels of George Eliot, Henry James, E. M. Forster, Virginia Wolfe, Angus Wilson.* London: Oxford Univ. Pr. Pp. 195.

Rev. by Jean Guiguet in *Études anglaises*, XVI, 403-04; by Raymond Williams in *Listener*, 30 May, p. 927; by P. N. Furbank in *NS*, LXVI, 175; in *TLS*, 12 July, p. 511 (see also letter by Cox, 26 July, p. 559); by Bernard Bergonzi in *S*, 31 May, pp. 710-11; in *Va. Quart. Rev.*, XXXIX, cxxvii.

Daiches, David. *George Eliot: Middlemarch.* Studies in English Literature, No. 11. London: Edward Arnold. Pp. 72.

Rev. by Mark Roberts in *EC*, XIII, 403-15; by W. J. Harvey in *MLR*, LVIII, 568-69.

Elsbree, Langdon. "The Breaking Chain: A Study of the Dance in the Novels of Jane Austen, George Eliot, Thomas Hardy, and D. H. Lawrence." *DA*, XXIV, 2476.

Ferguson, Suzanne C. "Mme. Laure and Operative Irony in *Middlemarch*: A Structural Analogy." *SEL*, III, 509-16.

Hampshire, Stuart. "The Horses on the Common." *NS*, LXVI, 783.

A discussion of the moral basis of Eliot's criticism.

Harvey, W. J. *The Art of George Eliot. . . .* See VB 1962, 411.

Rev. by James S. Wheatley in *JEGP*, LXII, 405-11; by Graham Handley in *N & Q*, n.s. X, 36.

Isaacs, Neil D. "*Middlemarch*: Crescendo of Obligatory Drama." *NCF*, XVIII, 21-34. Identifies the "structural principle" of the novel.

Levine, George. "Isabel, Gwendolen, and Dorothea." *ELH*, XXX, 244-57.

Heroines of *Middlemarch* and *Daniel Deronda* as models for Isabel Archer in *Portrait of a Lady.*

McKenzie, Keith Alexander. *Edith Simcox and George Eliot. . . .* See VB 1962, 411.

Rev. by John Hagan in *MP*, LXI, 64-66.

Pinney, Thomas (ed.). *Essays of George Eliot.* London: Routledge and Kegan Paul. Pp. xii + 476.

Rev. in *TLS*, 25 Oct., p. 859; by John Daniel in *S*, 1 Nov., p. 563.

Twenty-nine articles from *Westminster Rev., Fortnightly*, and *Leader*, 1847-1868, of which eleven are reprinted for the first time.

Pinney, Thomas. "George Eliot's Reading of Wordsworth: The Record." *VNL*, No. 24 (Fall), pp. 20-22.

Sambrook, A. J. "The Natural Historian of Our Social Classes." *English*, XIV, 130-34.

Santangelo, Gennaro A. "The Background of George Eliot's *Romola*." *DA*, XXIV, 2485-86.

Thomson, Patricia. "The Three Georges." *NCF*, XVIII, 137-50.

Centers on the influence of George Sand on George Eliot.

Wade, Rosalind. "George Eliot and Her Poetry." *CR*, CCIV, 38-42.

FITZGERALD.

Gittleman, Sol. "An Early Reference to Fitz-Gerald's 'Rubaiyat of Omar Khayyam' in Germany." *N & Q*, n.s. X, 269.

Gittleman, Sol. "John Hay as a Critic of *The Rubaiyat of Omar Khayyam*." *VNL*, No. 24 (Fall), pp. 26-27.

Weber, Carl J. "The 'Discovery' of Fitz-Gerald's *Rubaiyat*." *Libr. Chronicle of the Univ. of Texas*, VII, 3-11.

The discoverer was Whitley Stokes. Here is gentle wit, civilized dialogue, subdued drama, and a rap on the wrist for those authorities who have the facts wrong. — C.T.D.

FORD (see also III, Schorer).

Cassell, Richard A. *Ford Madox Ford: A Study of His Novels. . . .* See VB 1962, 412.

Rev. by C. B. Cox in *RES*, n.s. XIV, 423-24.

Gordon, Caroline. *A Good Soldier: A Key to the Novels of Ford Madox Ford.* Berkeley: Univ. of California Pr. Pp. 31.

Noticed in *TLS*, 4 Oct., p. 794.

Harvey, David Dow. *Ford Madox Ford, 1873-1939: A Bibliography of Works and Criticism.* Princeton: Princeton Univ. Pr., 1962. Pp. 633.

Rev. by John A. Meixner in *CE*, XXV, 156.

Hill, A. C. "The Literary Career of Ford Madox Ford." *Critical Quart.*, V, 369-79.

A review-article with comments on *The Bodley Head Ford Madox Ford*, ed. and intro. Graham Greene; Cassell, Richard A., *Ford Madox Ford. A Study of His Novels*; Harvey, David Dow, *Ford Madox Ford, 1873-1939. A Bibliography of Works & Criticism*; Meixner, John A.,

Ford Madox Ford's Novels. A Critical Study.

Lehan, Richard. "Ford Madox Ford and the Absurd: *The Good Soldier.*" *Texas Studies in Lit. and Lang.*, V, 219-31.

Lid, R. W. "Ford Madox Ford, Flaubert, and the English Novel." *Spectrum*, VI, 10-19.

Meixner, John A. *Ford Madox Ford's Novels.* London: Oxford. Pp. 303.
Rev. by Vernon Scannell in *Listener*, 21 March, p. 518; by Samuel Hynes in *KR*, XXV, 352-56.

Moser, Thomas. "Towards *The Good Soldier:* Discovery of a Sexual Theme." *Daedalus*, XCII, 312-25.

Wiley, Paul L. *Ford Madox Ford: Novelist of Three Worlds.* Syracuse: Syracuse Univ. Pr. Pp. 321.
Rev. by Jeremy Brooks in *S*, 11 Jan., p. 49.

FROUDE.

Dunn, Waldo Hilary. *James Anthony Froude, 1818-1856.* . . . See VB 1962, 412.
Rev. by Owen Chadwick in *EHR*, LXXVIII, 195-96; by John Clive in *JMH*, XXXV, 191-92.

Dunn, Waldo Hilary. *James Anthony Froude: A Biography.* Vol. II: *1857-1894.* Oxford: Clarendon Pr. Pp. xvii + 390.

GASKELL.

Dodsworth, Martin. "Women without Men in Cranford." *EC*, XIII, 132-45.

GILBERT.

The Savoy Operas. Vol. II. Intro. by Bridget D'Oyly Carte and notes on the operas by Derek Hudson. (World's Classics) Oxford Univ. Pr. Pp. 423.
Rev. in *TLS*, 12 April, p. 244.

GISSING.

Coustillas, Pierre. "George Gissing à Manchester." *Études anglaises*, XVI, 255-61.

Gettmann, Royal A. *George Gissing and H. G. Wells.* . . . See VB 1962, 412.
Rev. by Joseph J. Wolff in *JEGP*, LXII, 816-17; by Jacob Korg in *MLQ*, XXIV, 112-14; by Robert A. Colby in *MP*, LXI, 66-68.

Korg, Jacob (ed.). *George Gissing's Commonplace Book.* . . . See VB 1962, 412.
Rev. by P. Coustillas in *Études anglaises*, XVI, 89-90.

Korg, Jacob. *George Gissing: A Critical Biography.* Seattle: Univ. of Washington Pr. Pp. 311.
Rev. by Morton N. Cohen in *NYTBR*, 24 Nov., p. 26; by Malcolm Bradbury in *S*,

19 July, p. 88; in *TLS*, 5 July, p. 494; by Richard Stang in *VS*, VII, 122; by Gordon S. Haight in *YR*, LIII, 107-09.

Koike, Shigerv. "Gissing in Japan." *Bull. New York Pub. Libr.*, LXVII, 565-73.

Preble, Harry E. "Gissing's Articles for *Vyestnik Evropy.*" *VNL*, No. 23 (Spring), pp. 12-15.

Sherif, Nur. "The Friendship between George Gissing and Edward Bertz as Revealed in Gissing's Letters." *Cairo Studies in English*, II (1961-62).

Young, Arthur C. (ed.). *The Letters of George Gissing to Eduard Bertz: 1887-1903.* . . . See VB 1962, 412.
Rev. by P. Coustillas in *Études anglaises*, XVI, 88-89; by Jacob Korg in *MLQ*, XXIV, 112-14.

GLADSTONE.

Ramm, Agatha (ed.). *The Political Correspondence of Mr. Gladstone and Lord Granville, 1876-1886.* . . . See VB 1962, 413.
Rev. by James Winter in *Canadian Hist. Rev.*, XLIV, 64-65; by J. A. S. Grenville in *History*, XLVIII, 234-35; by Francis H. Herrick in *JMH*, XXXV, 197-98.

GOSSE.

Brugmans, Linette F. (ed.). *The Correspondence of André Gide and Edmund Gosse, 1904-1928.* . . . See VB 1960, 398.
Rev. by Georges I. Brachfeld in *RoR*, LIV, 308-10.

Mattheisen, Paul F. "More on Gosse and Gide." *N & Q*, n.s. X, 377-79.

GRAY.

Sewell, Brocard (ed.). *Two Friends: John Gray and André Raffalovich.* Aylesford: St. Albert's Pr. Pp. xiv + 193.
Rev. by Timothy d'Arch Smith in *Book Collector*, XII, 379-80; by Geoffrey Grigson in *NS*, LXV, 644; in *TLS*, 31 May, p. 387 (see also letter by Sewell, 7 June, p. 405).

Stuart, Alice V. "David Gray, 1838-1861: A Study of MS. Material." *Poetry Rev.*, LIV, 10-16.

GROTE.

Clarke, M. L. *George Grote.* London: Athlone Pr., 1962. Pp. x + 196.
Rev. by G. P. Gooch in *CR*, CCII, 96-101; by J. H. Burns in *History*, XLVIII, 222-23; by P. N. Furbank in *S*, 6 July, 1962, p. 31; in *TLS*, 27 July, 1962, p. 536; by H. O. Pappe in *VS*, VII, 119-20.

HARDY (see also III, Schorer, Stewart; ELIOT: Elsbree).

Atkins, N. J. *Hardy, Tess and Myself.* Beaminster: Toucan Pr. Pp. 23.

Babb, Howard. "Setting and Theme in *Far From the Madding Crowd.*" *ELH*, XXX, 147-61.

Bailey, J. O. "Evolutionary Meliorism in the Poetry of Thomas Hardy." *SP*, LX, 569-87.

Beatty, C. J. P. "The Tranter's Cottage in 'Under the Greenwood Tree'." *N & Q*, n.s. X, 26.

Beckman, Richard. "A Character Typology for Hardy's Novels." *ELH*, XXX, 70-87.
On dynamic balance of human types, as a structural and philosophical gambit.

Berry, Minta Sue. "Creation's Groan: Late Nineteenth-Century Thought as Reflected in the Works of Thomas Hardy." *DA*, XXIV, 280-81.

Bowden, Ann. "The Thomas Hardy Collection." . . . See VB 1962, 413.
Rev. by C. J. P. Beatty in *N & Q*, n.s. X, 122-23.

Deacon, Lois and Cox, J. S. *Tryphena and Thomas Hardy.* Beaminster: Toucan Pr. Pp. 30.

Duffin, Henry Charles. *Thomas Hardy: A Study of the Wessex Novels.* Manchester: Manchester Univ. Pr. Pp. 356.
Rev. by Ralph Lawrence in *English*, XIV, 160-61.
A revised edition.

Gose, Elliott B., Jr. "Psychic Evolution: Darwinism and Initiation in *Tess of the d'Urbervilles.*" *NCF*, XVIII, 261-72.

Griffin, Ernest G. "Hardy and the Growing Consciousness of the Immanent Will." *Cairo Studies in English*, II (1961-62).

Guerard, Albert Joseph (ed.). *Hardy: A Collection of Critical Essays.* Englewood Cliffs, N. J.: Prentice Hall. Pp. 180.

Hardy, Evelyn, and Gittings, Robert (eds.). *Some Recollections by Emma Hardy with Some Relevant Poems by Thomas Hardy.* . . . See VB 1962, 413.
Rev. by Edward McCourt in *QQ*, LXX, 290-91; by R. W. King in *RES*, n.s. XIV, 220.

Hardy, Florence Emily. *The Life of Thomas Hardy, 1840-1928.* . . . See VB 1962, 413.
Rev. by Phoebe Adams in *AM*, Sept., 1962, p. 124; in *VQR*; XXXIX, xxiv.

Hazen, James F. "The Imagery and Symbolism of Thomas Hardy's Major Novels." *DA*, XXIV, 1616.

Heilman, Robert B. "Hardy's 'Mayor' and the Problem of Intention." *Criticism*, V, 199-213.
As illustrated in the *Mayor*, a writer's stated intention may be contradicted when the imaginative vision takes over.

Heywood, C. "*The Return of the Native* and Miss Braddon's *The Doctor's Wife:* A Probable Source." *NCF*, XVIII, 91-94.

Hynes, Samuel. *The Pattern of Hardy's Poetry.* . . . See VB 1962, 413.
Rev. by D. H. Burden in *EC*, XIII, 277-82; by J. Hillis Miller in *SeR*, LXXI, 107-09.

Kramer, Dale. "A Query Concerning the Handwriting in Hardy's Manuscripts." *BSP*, LVII, 357-60.

Kramer, Dale. "Repetition of Imagery in Thomas Hardy." *VNL*, No. 23 (Spring), pp. 26-27.

Marshall, William H. "Motivation in 'Tess of the D'Urbervilles'." *Revue des langues vivants*, XXIX, 224-31.

Meech, Dorothy M. *Memories of Mr. and Mrs. Thomas Hardy.* Beaminster: Toucan Pr. Pp. 14.

Mills, William George, as told to J. Stevens Cox. *Thomas Hardy at the Barbers.* Beaminster: Toucan Pr. Pp. 8.

Mitchell, Charles. "Hardy's 'Afterwards'." *Vict. Poetry*, I, 68-70.

Morcos, Louis. "The Overworld: A Projection of Hardy's Personality." *Cairo Studies in English*, II (1961-62).

Morrell, Roy. "'The Dynasts' Reconsidered." *MLR*, LVIII, 161-71.

Orel, Harold. *Thomas Hardy's Epic-Drama.* Lawrence: University of Kansas Pr. Pp. 122.

Parker, W. M. "Hardy's Letters to Sir George Douglas." *English*, XIV, 218-25.
Excerpts from hitherto unpublished letters, 1887-1924.

Riesner, Dieter. "Zur Textgeschichte von Hardy's Romanen." *Archiv*, CXCIX, 398-404.

Scott, James F. "Thomas Hardy's Use of the Gothic: An Examination of Five Representative Works." *NCF*, XVII, 363-80.
A perceptive essay which examines Hardy's Gothic materials in certain minor works and suggests how such material enriched his major fiction. — R.C.S.

Stephens, Bertie Norman. *Thomas Hardy in His Garden.* Beaminster: Toucan Pr. Pp. 18.

Titterington, Ellen E., as told to J. Stevens Cox. *The Domestic Life of Thomas Hardy, 1921-1928*. Beaminster: Toucan Pr. Pp. 20.
Rev. in *TLS*, 26 July, p. 555.

Voss, Harold Lionel. *Motoring with Thomas Hardy*. Beaminster: Toucan Pr. Pp. 15.

Wade, Rosalind. "Thomas Hardy: The Sources of His Inspiration." *CR*, CCIV, 248-53.

Weber, Carl J. (ed.). *"Dearest Emmie": Thomas Hardy's Letters to His First Wife*. London: Macmillan; New York: St. Martin's Pr. Pp. xvi + 112.
Rev. by Robert Gittings in *Listener*, 27 June, pp. 1083-84; by C. Ricks in *NS*, LXVI, 198-99; by W. M. Parker in *The Scotsman*, Edinburgh, 20 July; in *Time*, 27 Dec., p. 64; in *TLS*, 26 July, p. 555; by Bonamy Dobree in *Yorkshire Post*, 11 July.
Seventy-four letters, 1885-1911, with notes, an Introduction, and an Editorial Epilogue which provide a rounded biographical setting.

Weber, Carl J. (ed.). *Hardy's Love Poems*. London: Macmillan; New York: St. Martin's Pr. Pp. xvii + 253.
Rev. by David Dewar in *Glasgow Herald*, 9 Nov.; by John Bayley in *Manchester Guardian*, 15 Nov.; in *TLS*, 26 Dec., p. 1063.
In a fully developed introductory essay, the editor recreates the charm of Hardy's romance and the varied atmosphere of the married years. Professor Weber magically relates the love poems to the tissue of life from which they emerged and in so doing enhances the reader's awareness of their inner authenticity. A convincing demonstration that literature does arise from life. — R.C.S.

Weber, Carl J. "He [Thomas Hardy] Came from Dorset." *Viewpoint Mag.* No. 1 (Feb.), pp. 14-15.

Wing, George Douglas. *Hardy*. Writers and Critics Series. Edinburgh: Oliver and Boyd; New York: Grove Pr. Pp. 119.
Rev. by Mark Roberts in *EC*, XIII, 403; by C. Ricks in *NS*, LXVI, 198-99; noticed in *TLS*, 12 July, p. 511.

HENLEY.

Herman, George. "Henley's 'Space and Dread and the Dark'." *Ex*, XXII, Item 14.

HOPKINS (see also III, Miller, Wain; CARLYLE: Ludwig).

August, Eugene R. "Hopkins' Dangerous Fire." *Vict. Poetry*, I, 72-74.

Bender, Todd K. "Hopkins' 'God's Grandeur'." *Ex*, XXI, Item 55.

Bender, Todd K. "Some Derivative Elements in the Poetry of Gerard Manley Hopkins." *DA*, XXIII, 4352.

Boyle, Robert Richard. *Metaphor in Hopkins*. . . . See VB 1962, 414.
Rev. by James R. Kreuzer in *Criticism*, V, 191-92; by E. J. Rose in *Dalhousie Rev.*, XLIII, 110-11; by John E. Keating in *JEGP*, LXII, 413.

Campbell, Sister M. Mary Hugh. "The Silent Sonnet: Hopkins' 'Shepherd's Brow'." *Renascence*, XV, 133-42.

Chamberlain, Robert L. "George MacDonald's 'A Manchester Poem' and Hopkins's 'God's Grandeur'." *The Personalist*, XLIV, 518-27.

Graves, William L. "Gerard Manley Hopkins as Composer: An Interpretive Postscript." *Vict. Poetry*, I, 146-55.

Grennen, Joseph E. "Grammar as Thaumaturgy: Hopkins' 'Heraclitean Fire'." *Renascence*, XV, 208-11.

Keating, John Edward. *The Wreck of the Deutschland: An Essay and a Commentary*. Kent, Ohio: Kent State Univ. Pr. Pp. 110.

Louise, Sister Robert. "Hopkins' 'Spring and Fall'." *Ex*, XXI, Item 65.

McQueen, William A. " 'The Windhover' and 'St. Alphonsus Rodriguez'." *VNL*, No. 23 (Spring), pp. 25-26.

Montag, George E. "Hopkins' 'God's Grandeur' and 'The Ooze of Oil Crushed'." *Vict. Poetry*, I, 302-03.

Norris, Carolyn B. " 'Fused Images' in the Sermons of Gerard Manley Hopkins." *Tennessee Studies in Lit.*, VII, 127-33.

Norris, Carolyn Brimley. "Gerard Manly Hopkins in His Sermons and His Poetry." *N & Q*, n.s. X, 27.

Stevens, Sister Mary Dominic. "Hopkins' 'That Nature is a Heraclitean Fire'." *Ex*, XXII, Item 18.

HOUSMAN.

Allen, Don Cameron (ed.). *The Moment of Poetry*. . . . See VB 1962, 415.
Rev. by Allen Austin in *CE*, XXIV, 586.

Carter, John. "Housman, Shelley, and Swinburne." *TLS*, 6 Sept., p. 680 (see also a letter by Carter, 13 Sept., p. 689).

Franklin, Ralph. "Housman's Shropshire." *MLQ*, XXIV, 164-71.

Haber, Tom Burns. "Housman and Lucretius." *Classical Jour.*, LVIII, 173-82.

Haber, Tom Burns. "Three Unreported Letters of A. E. Housman." *BSP*, LVII, 230-33.
From an album kept by Theodore Spicer-Simpson.

Spender, Stephen. *The Making of a Poem.* New York: Norton. Pp. 205.
Rev. by Benjamin DeMott in *Harper's*, Jan., p. 93; by John Berryman in *NewR*, 29 June, p. 19; by M. L. Rosenthal in *NYTBR*, 28 Apr., p. 18.
Contains an essay on Housman.

Spivey, Edward. "Housman's 'The Oracles'." *Ex*, XXI, Item 44.

HUXLEY.

Randel, William. "A Letter from Harold Frederic to T. H. Huxley." *VNL*, No. 23 (Spring), pp. 27-28.

KEBLE.

Battiscombe, Georgina. *John Keble: A Study in Limitations.* London: Constable. Pp. xix + 395.
Rev. by C. Colleer Abbot in *Listener*, 28 Nov., p. 891; by G. Best in *NS*, LXVI, 883-84; by Meriol Trevor in *S*, 6 Dec., p. 761; in *TLS*, 5 Dec., pp. 1001-02.

KINGSLEY.

Jones, D. A. N. "Do Right." *NS*, LXV, 759-60.

Waller, John O. "Charles Kingsley and the American Civil War." *SP*, LX, 554-68.

KIPLING (see also III, Stewart).

Bodelsen, C. A. *Aspects of Kipling's Art.* Manchester: Manchester Univ. Pr. Pp. 169.

Deutsch, Karl W., and Wiener, Norbert. "The Lonely Nationalism of Rudyard Kipling." *YR*, LII, 499-17.
Kipling distorted the facts in "A Ballad of East and West."

Gilbert, Elliot L. "A Case for Kipling." *DA*, XXIV, 2031.
Critical analysis of six short stories.

Lewis C. S. *They Asked for a Paper.* . . . See VB 1962, 415.
Rev. by J. Loiseau in *Études anglaises*, XVI, 413-14.

LANDOR.

Brumbaugh, Thomas B. "A Landor Letter." *N & Q*, n.s. X, 18-19.

Grigson, Geoffrey. "I Strove with None." *Listener*, 30 May, pp. 911-12.

Lohrli, Anne. "The First Publication of Landor's 'Diana de Poictiers'." *N & Q*, n.s. X, 19-20.

LE FANU.

Edens, Walter E. "Joseph Sheridan Le Fanu: A Minor Victorian and His Publisher." *DA*, XXIV, 725-26.

Lewis, Naomi. "Le Fanu." *NS*, LXVI, 663-64.

LE GALLIENNE.

Whittington-Egan, Richard, and Smerdon, Geoffrey. *The Quest of the Golden Boy: The Life and Letters of Richard Le Gallienne.* Barre, Mass.: Barre Publishing Company. Pp. xxiii + 580.
Rev. by Ellen Moers in *VS*, VII, 185-91.

LIVINGSTONE.

Butt, John. "David Livingstone and the Idea of African Evolution." *History Today*, XIII, 376-82.

Schapera, I. (ed.). *Livingstone's African Journal, 1853-1856.* London: Chatto and Windus; Berkeley: Univ. of Cal. Pr. Vol. I, pp. xxiii + 235; Vol. II. pp. vii + 258.
Rev. in *Economist*, CCVIII, 147; by Harold Lancour in *LJ*, LXXXVIII, 3616; by G. W. Stonier in *NS*, LXVI, 323; by G. H. T. Kimble in *NYTBR*, 15 Sept., p. 3; in *TLS*, 2 Aug., p. 595.

MACAULAY.

Bruni, Bruno. "Un' amica irlandese del Carducci: Louisa Grace Bartolini." *Nuova Antologia*, XCVIII, 541-46.
On the Italian translation of *Lays of Ancient Rome.*

Lowenthal, David. "Macaulay and the Freedom of the Press." *APSR*, LVII, 661-64.

MACREADY.

Shattuck, Charles H. (ed.). *Mr. Macready Produces As You Like It.* Urbana, Illinois: Beta Phi Mu. Pp. 20.

Shattuck, Charles H. (ed.). *William Charles Macready's "King John".* . . . See VB 1962, 396.
Rev. in *TLS*, 25 Jan., p. 60; by Martin Meisel in *VS*, VI, 355-60.

MARTINEAU.

Dewey, Robert E., and Loftsgordon, Donald. "Dante and Martineau: A Report on Changing Values." *Ethics*, LXXII, 41-45.

"The Living Tradition. 4: Worship and Poetry — James Martineau." *HJ*, LXI, 195-97.

"Martineau Studies: 1. His Prayers. 2. His Christology." *HJ*, LXI, 146-49.

MAYHEW.

Bradley, John L. "Henry Mayhew: Farce Writer of the 1830's." *VNL*, No. 23 (Spring), pp. 21-23.

2013; in *TLS*, 5 Apr., p. 237.

Dessain, Charles Stephen (ed.). *The Letters and Diaries of John Henry Newman.*
Vol. XI: *Littlemore to Rome, Oct., 1845 to Dec., 1846.* . . . See VB 1962, 417.
Rev. by Owen Chadwick in *EHR*, LXXVIII, 745-46; by A. Dwight Culler in *YR*, LII, 283-90.
Vol. XII, *Rome to Birmingham, 1 January 1847 to 31 December 1848.* . . . See VB 1962, 417.
Rev. by Gerard J. Aylward in *CWd*, CXCVII, 73-74; by Douglas E. Pott in *Jour. of Eccl. Hist.*, LXIV, 243-44; by Fergal McGrath in *StI*, LII, 109-12; in *TLS*, 22 Feb., p. 133; by A. Dwight Culler in *VS*, VI, 367-68.
Vol XIII: *Birmingham and London, January 1849 to June 1850.* London: Nelson. Pp. xiv + 520.
Rev. by F. X. Connolly in *America*, CIX, 391; in *TLS*, 21 June, p. 464.

Dessain, Charles Stephen. "Newman and Oxford." *The Wiseman Rev.*, CCXXXVII, 295-302.

Hollis, Christopher. "Cardinal Newman: The Life Completed." *Wiseman Rev.*, CCXXXVII, 78-86.

Jost, Edward F. "Newman and Liberalism: The Later Phase." *VNL*, No. 24 (Fall), pp. 1-6.

Lenz, Sister Mary Baylon. "A Rhetorical Analysis of Cardinal Newman's *Apologia Pro Vita Sua.*" *DA*, XXIII, 2518.

MacDougall, Hugh A. *The Acton-Newman Relations.* . . . See VB 1962, 417.
Rev. by H. Butterfield in *AHR*, LXIX, 201-02; by Brian Heeney in *Dalhousie Rev.*, XLIII, 420-21; by W. C. Heiser in *LJ*, LXXXVIII, 224; by Stephen J. Tonsor in *VS*, VII, 197-200.

McGrath, Fergal. *The Consecration of Learning: Lectures on Newman's "Idea of a University."* New York: Fordham Univ. Pr.; Dublin: Gill. Pp. 341.
Rev. by Peter Kasteel in *StI*, LII, 321-23; in *TLS*, 21 June, p. 464; in *YR*, LII, x.

Mozley, Dorothea (ed.). *Newman Family Letters.* . . . See VB 1962, 417.
Rev. in *TLS*, 22 Feb., p. 133.

Sillem, Edward A. "Cardinal Newman: A New Discovery." *Wiseman Rev.*, CCXXXVII, 66-77.

Trevor, Meriol. *Newman: The Pillar of the Cloud.* . . . See VB 1962, 417.
Rev. by A. M. Melville in *Critic*, XXI,

79; by Msgr. Florence D. Cohalan in *CWd*, CXCVI, 259-61; by Edmund Fuller in *NYTBR*, 30 Sept., 1962, p. 22; by J. M. Cameron in *VS*, VII, 200-02; by A. D. Culler in *YR*, LII, 283-90.

Trevor, Meriol. *Newman: Light in Winter.* . . .
See VB 1962, 417.
Rev. by A. M. Melville in *Critic*, XXI, 69; by Msgr. Florence Cohalan in *CWd*, CXCVII, 326-27; by W. C. Heiser in *LJ*, LXXXVIII, 1665; by Edmund Fuller in *NYTBR*, 24 Nov., p. 28; by Fergal McGrath in *StI*, LII, 323-25; by *TLS*, 22 Feb., p. 133; by J. M. Cameron in *VS*, VII, 200-02.

PATER.

André, Robert. "Walter Pater et Marcel Proust." *Nrf*, N.S. Année 11, 1082-89.

d'Hangest, Germain. *Walter Pater: L'homme et l'oeuvre.* . . . See VB 1962, 417.
Rev. by Ian Fletcher in *MLR*, LVIII, 415-17.

Rosenblatt, Louise M. "The Genesis of Pater's *Marius the Epicurean.*" *Comparative Lit.*, XIV, 242-60.
Traces not only possible sources, but also the significance of the intellectual and philosophic milieu of Renan and Arnold.

West, Paul. "Pater's Cordial Canon." *English*, XIV, 185-88.

PEACOCK.

Manning, Olivia. "Peacock's Private Eye." *S*, 6 Sept., p. 293.

Stewart, John Innes Mackintosh. *Thomas Love Peacock.* Writers and Their Work Series. London: Longmans. Pp. 36.

ROLFE.

Don Renato. London: Chatto and Windus. Pp. 344.
Rolfe's last novel, previously unpublished.

Woolf, Cecil (ed.). *Letters to R. M. Dawkins.* . . . See VB 1962, 418.
Rev. in *TLS*, 18 Jan., p. 35.

ROSSETTIS (see also II, Cropper; FITZ-GERALD: Weber; SWINBURNE: Packer).

Adrian, Arthur A. "The Genesis of Rossetti's 'Found'," *Texas Studies in Lit. and Lang.*, V, 79-82.

Bracker, Jon. "Notes on the Texts of Two Poems by Dante Gabriel Rossetti." *Libr. Chronicle of the Univ. of Texas*, VII, 14-16.

Fredeman, William E. "Rossetti's Impromptu Portraits of Tennyson Reading 'Maud'." *Burl. Mag.*, CV, 117-18, 413.

Hyder, Clyde K. "Rossetti's *Rose Mary:* A

Study in the Occult." *Vict. Poetry*, I, 197-207.

Packer, Lona Mosk. *Christina Rossetti.* Berkeley: Univ. of California Pr. Pp. 459.
Rev. by Peter Quennell in *NYTBR*, 15 Dec., p. 4; by Morse Peckham in *SR*, Dec. 28, p. 41.

Packer, Lona Mosk. (ed.). *The Rossetti-Macmillan Letters.* Berkeley: University of Calif. Pr. Pp. xxi + 166.
Rev. by Peter Quennell in *NYTBR*, 15 Dec., p. 4.

Packer, Lona Mosk. "William Michael Rossetti and the Quilter Controversy: 'The Gospel of Intensity'." *VS*, VII, 170-83.

Savarit, Jacques. *Tendances mystiques et esoteriques chez Dante Gabriel Rossetti.* . . . See VB 1962, 418.
Rev. by Joan Rees in *Études anglaises*, XVI, 192-93.

Vogel, Joseph F. "Rossetti's 'The House of Life.' LXXVIII." *Ex*, XXI, Item 64.

RUSKIN (see also III, LeChevalier).

Arthos, John. "Ruskin and Tolstoy: 'The Dignity of Man'." *Dalhousie Review*, XLIII, 5-15.

Bell, Quentin. *Ruskin.* Writers and Critics Series. Edinburgh: Oliver and Boyd. Pp. 120.

Boas, George. *The Heaven of Invention.* Baltimore, Md.: Johns Hopkins Pr. Pp. 420.
Rev. by F. D. Lazenby in *LJ*, LXXXVIII, 105.
Includes resume of the *Seven Lamps.*

Coulling, Sidney M. B. "Two Unpublished Letters of John Ruskin to Edward Clayton." *HLQ*, XXVII, 87-92.

Dougherty, Charles T. "Of Ruskin's Gardens." In Northrop Frye, L. C. Knights, and others, *Myth and Symbol.* Lincoln: Univ. of Nebraska Pr. Pp. 196.
A reading of *Modern Painters* V and *Sesame and Lilies.*

Fishman, Solomon. *The Interpretation of Art: Essays on the Art Criticism of John Ruskin, Walter Pater, Clive Bell, Roger Fry, Herbert Read.* Berkeley: University of Calif. Pr. Pp. 195. Rev. by G. A. Cebasco in *LJ*, LXXXVIII, 4202.

Le Breton, Georges. "La folie de Ruskin." *Mercure de France*, CCCLXXXIX, 615-19.

Rosenberg, John D. *The Darkening Glass: A Portrait of Ruskin's Genius.* . . . See VB 1962, 418.

Rev. by W. Stacy Johnson in *Criticism*, V, 91-93; by Graham Hough in *Listener*, 30 May, p. 921; unfavorably by D. Donaghue in *NS*, LXV, 868; by John Daniel in *S*, 14 June, p. 786; in *TLS*, 14 June, p. 446.

Rosenberg, John D. "The Genuis of John Ruskin." *VNL*, No. 23 (Spring), pp. 4-6.

Williams, R. E. T. "Three Ruskin Letters." *N & Q*, n.s. X, 23-34.

RUTHERFORD.

Merton, Stephen. "Mark Rutherford: The World of His Novels." *Bull. New York Pub.Libr.,LXVII*, 470-78.

SHAW (see also III, Bloom, Land, Stewart).

Baylen, Joseph O. "George Bernard Shaw and the Socialist League. Some Unpublished Letters," *International Rev. of Social History,VII* (1962), 426-40.

Bernd, Daniel W. "The Dramatic Theory of George Bernard Shaw." *DA*, XXIII, 2910-11.

Carpenter, Charles A., Jr. "Bernard Shaw's Development as a Dramatic Artist, 1884-1889." *DA*, XXIV, 295.

Cherry, D. R. "Shaw's Novels." *Dalhousie Rev.*, XLII, 459-71.

Crompton, Louis. "Shaw's Challenge to Liberalism." *Prairie Schooner*, XXXVII, 229-44.
A study of *Major Barbara.*

Demaray, John G. "Bernard Shaw and C. E. M. Joad: The Adventures of Two Puritans in Their Search for God." *PMLA*, LXXVIII, 262-70.

DuCann, C. G. L. *The Loves of George Bernard Shaw.* New York: Funk and Wagnalls; London: Arthur Barker. Pp. 300.
Rev. by K. T. Willis in *LJ*, LXXXVIII, 4624; by Brooks Atkinson in *NYTBR*, 3 Nov., p. 52; by Roger B. Dooley in *SR*, 23 Nov., pp. 47-49; in *TLS*, 19 Dec., p. 1044.

Duerksen, Roland A. "Shelley and Shaw." *PMLA*, LXXVIII, 114-27.
A detailed treatment of the poet's influence on Shaw.

Dunbar, Janet. *Mrs. G. B. S.: A Biographical Portrait of Charlotte Shaw.* London: Harrap; New York: Harper. Pp. 326.
Rev. by Paul Pickrel in *Harper's*, June, pp. 104-05; by Alan Pryce-Jones in *HTB*, 9 June, p. 3; by M. McAneny in *LJ*, LXXXVIII, 3605; by Kingsley Martin in *NS*, LXV, 979; by Gene Baro in *NYTBR*, 16 June, p. 1; by Stanley Weintraub in

SR, 8 June, p. 33; in *TLS*, 7 June, p. 402; by Stanley Rypins in *VQR*, XXXIX, 514-18.

Gerould, Daniel G. "George Bernard Shaw's Criticism of Ibsen." *Comparative Lit.*, XV, 130-45.

Hogan, Patrick G., Jr., and Baylen, Joseph O. "An Unpublished Letter from Shaw to Archer." *N & Q*, n.s. X, 267-68.

The Independent Shavian. Vol. I, No. 3 (April, 1963), has items: Barzun, Jacques, "Shaw against the Alphabet" (pp. 1, 3-5); Cordell, Richard A., a review of Allan Chappelow's *Shaw the Villager and Human Being* (pp. 5-6); Goldstein, Malcolm, a review of Stephen S. Stanton's *A Casebook on Candida* (pp. 6-7).

Vol. II, No. 1 (Fall, 1963) has items: Gassner, John, "Shaw on Shakespeare, Part I" (pp. 1, 3-5); Matlaw, Myron, a theater review of *Too True to Be Good* (p. 5); Whitman, Wanda, "Shaw and Shakespeare on Saint Joan" (p. 6); Batson, Edic J., a review of C. B. Purdom's *A Guide to the Plays of Bernard Shaw* and some comments on London productions of Shaw's plays (pp. 7-8); Masumoto, Masahiko, "A Report from Japan" (p. 9); Scriabine, Vera, a review of Stanley Weintraub's *Private Shaw and Public Shaw* (p. 10).

Vol. II, No. 2 (Winter, 1963/64) has items: Gassner, John, "Shaw on Shakespeare, Part II" (pp. 13, 15, 23-24); Pettet, Carolyn, a review of Janet Dunbar's *Mrs. G.B.S.: A Portrait* (p. 16); Batson, Eric J., "Our London Correspondent" (pp. 18-19); Dunlap, Joseph R., "A Note on Shaw's 'Formula' and Pre-Kelmscott Printing" (p. 20); Leary, Daniel J., a theater review of *Caesar and Cleopatra* at Stratford, Conn. (p. 21).

Lagner, Lawrence. *G.B.S. and the Lunatic: Reminiscences of the Long, Lively and Affectionate Friendship between George Bernard Shaw and the Author.* New York: Atheneum Pr. Pp. 313.

Rev. by Joseph Papp in *Book Week*, 22 Dec., p. 9; by Joseph Papp in *HTB*, 22 Dec., p. 9; by J. F. Moran in *LJ*, LXXXVIII, 4391; by Brooks Atkinson in *NYTBR*, 3 Nov., p. 52; by R. B. Dooley in *SR*, 23 Nov., p. 47.

Meisel, Martin. *Shaw and the Nineteenth-Century Theater.* Princeton: Princeton Univ. Pr.; London: Oxford Univ. Pr. Pp. 477.

Rev. in *TLS*, 19 Dec., p. 1044; by Stanley Rypins in *VQR*, XXXIX, 514-518.

Ohmann, Richard M. *Shaw: The Style and the Man.* . . . See VB 1962, 418.

Rev. by Harry W. Rudman in *BA*, XXXVII, 202; by R. L. Scott in *QJS*, LXIX, 331; by Martin Meisel in *SAQ*, LXII, 448-49.

Purdom, Charles Benjamin. *A Guide to the Plays of Bernard Shaw.* London: Methuen. Pp. 344.

Rev. in *TLS*, 19 April, p. 266.

Quinn, Michael. "Form and Intention: A Negative View of *Arms and the Man*." *Critical Quart.*, V, 148-54.

The Shaw Review, Vol. VI, No. 1 (January, 1963), has items: Lausch, Anne N., "The Road to Rome by Way of Alexandria and Tavazzano." (pp. 2-12); "An English Academy of Letters: A Correspondence of 1897" (pp. 13-26); Black, Matthew W., "Shaw to Arliss" (pp. 28-29); "A Continuing Checklist of Shaviana," compiled and edited by Stephen S. Stanton (pp. 30-33); Smith, Warren S., a review of *The Shaw Alphabet Edition of "Androcles and the Lion"* (pp. 34-36); Holt, Charles Loyd, a review of Stephen S. Stanton's *A Casebook on Candida* (pp. 37-38); Pettet, Edwin Burr, a review of Richard M. Ohmann's *Shaw, The Style and The Man* (pp. 38-40).

No. 2 (May, 1963) has items: Lausch, Anne N., Robert Sherwood's 'Heartbreak Houses' " (pp. 42-50); Auchincloss, Katharine L., "Shaw and the Commisssars: The Lenin Years, 1917-1924" (pp. 51-59); Hogan, Patrick G., and Baylen, Joseph O., "Shaw, W. T. Stead, and the 'International Peace Crusade,' 1898-1899" (pp. 60-61); Dukore, Bernard F., "Toward an Interpretation of 'Major Barbara' " (pp. 62-70); Chapman, Robert H., a review of *Private Shaw and Public Shaw* (pp. 71-72); a drama review by Richard L. Coe of *Too True to Be Good* "Minor Shaw is Major Joy" (pp. 73-74); "A Continuing Checklist of Shaviana," compiled and edited by Stephen S. Stanton (pp. 75-80).

No. 3 (September, 1963) has items: Spink, Judith B., "The Image of the Artist in the Plays of Bernard Shaw" (pp. 82-88); Mendelsohn, Michael J., "The Heartbreak Houses of Shaw and Chekhov" (pp. 89-95); Harris, Harold J., "Shaw, Chekhov, and Two Great Ladies of the Theater" (pp. 96-99); Mix, Katharine Lyon, "Max on Shaw" (pp. 100-104); "A Continuing Checklist of Shaviana," compiled and edited by Stephen S. Stanton (pp. 105-110); Rosset, B. C., a review of Janet Dunbar's *Mrs. G.B.S.: A Portrait* (pp. 111-119); "Shavian News and Notes" (p. 120).

Tauber, Abraham (ed.). *George Bernard Shaw on Language.* New York: Philosophical Library. Pp. 205.

Weintraub, Stanley. *Private Shaw and Public Shaw: A Dual Portrait of Lawrence of Arabia and G.B.S.* London: Cape. Pp. 302.

Rev. by Russell Shaw in *Critic*, XXI, 70; by Paul Pickrel in *Harper's*, June, p. 105; by Alan Pryce-Jones in *HTB*, 5 May, p. 7; by L. W. Griffin in *LJ*, LXXXVIII, 565; by William Irvine in *NYTBR*, 7 Apr., p. 25; by H. T. Moore in *SR*, 2 Mar., p. 23; in *TLS*, 25 Oct., p. 853; by Stanley Rypins in *VQR*, XXXIX, 514-18.

Williamson, Audrey. *Bernard Shaw: Man and Writer.* London: Macmillan. Pp. 224.

Rev. in *TLS*, 19 Dec., p. 1044.

Woodbridge, Homer Edwards. *George Bernard Shaw.* Carbondale, Illinois: Southern Illinois Univ. Pr. Pp. xii + 181.

Rev. by Roger B. Dooley in *SR*, 23 Nov., pp. 47-49.

SPURGEON.

Spurgeon, Charles Haddon. *The Early Years, 1834-1859.* London: Banner of Truth. Pp. xviii + 562.

Revised and shortened edition of first two volumes of Spurgeon's autobiography.

Spurgeon, Charles Haddon. *The New Park Street Pulpit.* 2 vols. London: Banner of Truth. Pp. 410, 424.

Sermons preached by Spurgeon in 1855-56.

Spurgeon, Charles Haddon. *The Soul Winner.* Edited by Helmut Thielicke. Grand Rapids, Mich.: Eerdmans. Pp. 319.

Thielicke, Helmut. *Encounter with Spurgeon.* Tr. from German by John W. Boberstein, Philadelphia: Fortress Press. Pp. 283.

STEPHEN.

Bateson, F. W. "God-Killer." *NS*, LXV, 945-56.

STEVENSON.

Eigner, Edwin M. "The Double in the Fiction of R. L. Stevenson." *DA*, XXIV, 741-42.

Fiedler, Leslie. *No! in Thunder.* London: Eyre & Spottiswoode. Pp. 336.

Rev. by John Gross in *NS*, LXVI, 288-89.

Grundy, J. Owen. "R.L.S. in Greenwich Village." *Bull., New York Pub. Libr.,* LXVII (152-55).

Nakajima, Atsushi. *Light, Wind, and Dreams: An Interpretation of the Life and Mind of Robert Louis Stevenson.* Tokyo: Hokuseido Pr. 1962. Pp. xxiv + 183.

Ricklefs, Roger. (ed.). *The Mind of Robert Louis Stevenson.* New York: Yoseloff. Pp. 127.

Rev. by R. E. Wagenknecht in *LJ*, LXXXVIII, 4762.

SWINBURNE (see also FITZGERALD: Weber; HOUSMAN: Carter).

The Novels of A. C. Swinburne: Love's Cross-currents [and] *Lesbia Brandon.* Intro. by Edmund Wilson. New York: Farrar, Straus. Pp. 377.

Rev. by Phoebe Adams in *AM*, Mar., p. 164; by W. J. Igoe in *Critic*, XXI, 79; by J. R. Willingham in *LJ*, LXXXVIII, 238; by I. R. Buchen in *SR*, 29 Dec., 1962, p. 36.

Ehrenpreis, Anne Henry. "Swinburne's Edition of Popular Ballads." *PMLA*, LXXVIII, 559-71.

An examination of the MS of the anthology.

Grosskurth. P. M. "Swinburne and Symonds: An Uneasy Literary Relationship." *RES*, n.s. XIV, 257-68.

Lang, Cecil Y. (ed.). *Swinburne Letters.* . . . See VB 1962, 419.

Vols. V-VI rev. by Merle M. Bevington in *SAQ*, LXII, 119-21.

Packer, Lona Mosk. "Swinburne and Christina Rossetti: Atheist and Anglican." *TQ*, XXXIII, 30-42.

Peters, Robert L. "Swinburne's Idea of Form." *Criticism*, V, 45-63.

SYMONDS.

Peters, Robert L. "Athens and Troy: Notes on John Addington Symond's Aestheticism." *Eng. Fiction in Transition*, V, 14-26.

Schueller, Herbert M. "John Addington Symonds as a Theoretical and as a Practical

Critic." *DA*, XXIV, 2041-42.

SYMONS.

Goldfarb, Russell M. "Arthur Symons' Decadent Poetry." *Vict. Poetry*, I, 231-34.

Lhombreaud, Roger. *Arthur Symons: His Life and Letters.* . . . See VB 1962, 420.
Rev. by Ian Fletcher in *Listener*, 20 June, p. 1045; by John Gross in *NS*, LXV, 901; by Francis Watson in *S*, 12 July, p. 61; in *TLS*, 7 June, p. 402.

Munro, John M. "Arthur Symons: A Critical Survey of His Major Writings, with Special Reference to Their Significance as Documents in the History of the Development of the English Literary Tradition." *DA*, XXIV, 1619-20.

TENNYSON (seee also III, Benziger, Miller, Spitzer; **ROSSETTI:** Fredeman).

Ancaster, Lord, and Tennyson, Sir Charles. "The Tennyson Society." *TLS*, 14 June, p. 451.
On the plans for publication of manuscripts and other material collected by the society.

Assad, Thomas J. "Tennyson's 'Break, Break, Break'." *Tulane Studies in English*, XII, 71-80.

Ball, Patricia M. "Tennyson and the Romantics." *Vict. Poetry*, I, 7-16.
Centers on relationships between Tennyson's work and *The Prelude*.

Berry, Francis. *Poetry and the Physical Voice.* . . . See VB 1962, 420.
Rev. by Charles Tomlinson in *Poetry*, CII, 343; in *TLS*, 16 Feb., 1962, p. 104.

Blunden, Edmund. *Selected Poems of Tennyson.* . . . See VB 1962, 420.
Rev. by Louis Bonnerot in *Études anglaises*, XVI, 294.

Brown, T. J. "English Literary Autographs XLV. Lord Tennyson, 1809-1892." *Book Collector*, XII, 61.

Collins, Rowland L. "How Rare Are Montagu Butler's Translations of Tennyson?" *Book Collector*, XII, 72-73.

Collins, Rowland L. "The Frederick Tennyson Collection." *Publications of the Tennyson Society*, published as a supplement (pp. 57-76) to VS, VII.
Catalog of manuscripts and memorabilia in collection at the Lilly Library, Indiana University.

Collins, Rowland L. "Tennyson's Original Issue of Poems, Reviews, etc., 1842-1886."

Princeton Univ. Libr. Chronicle, XXIV, 39-50.
Record of the holdings of Tennyson's published works in Princeton Library.

Elliott, Philip L., Jr. " 'The Charge of the Light Brigade.' " *N & Q*, n.s. X, 263-64. (See also letter from C. Ricks, *N & Q*, X, 385).

Elliott, Philip L., Jr. "A Textual Study of *In Memoriam*." *DA*, XXIV, 2462.
Study of MSS and various editions.

Fulweiler, Howard. "Mermen and Mermaids: A Note on an 'Alien Vision' in the Poetry of Tennyson, Arnold, and Hopkins." *VNL*, No. 23 (Spring), pp. 16-17.

Goldberg, J. Philip. "Two Tennysonian Allusions to a Poem of Andrew Marvell." *N & Q*, n.s. X, 264-65. (See also letter from C. Ricks, *N & Q*, n.s. X, 385).

Huxter, E. W. "Tennyson and Juvenal." *N & Q*, n.s. X, 448-49.

Kauffman, Corinne E. "Spenser and Tennyson: A Comparative Study." *DA*, XXIV, 729.

Lally, Sister Mary Aquin. "A Comparative Study of Five Plays on the Becket Story: By Tennyson, Binyon, Eliot, Anouilh, and Fry." *DA*, XXIV, 2479.

Litzinger, Boyd. "The Structure of Tennyson's 'The Last Tournament'." *Vict. Poetry*, I, 53-60.

Marshall, George O., Jr. *A Tennyson Handbook.* New York: Twayne. Pp. 291.

Marshall, George O., Jr. "Tennyson's 'Oh! That 'twere Possible': A Link between *In Memoriam* and *Maud*." *PMLA*, LXXVIII, 225-29.

Marshall, George O., Jr. "Tennyson's 'Ulysses,' 33-43." *Ex*, XXI, Item 50.

Metzger, Lore. "The Eternal Process: Some Parallels between Goethe's *Faust* and Tennyson's *In Memoriam*." *Vict. Poetry*, I, 189-96.

Moore, Carlisle. "Faith, Doubt, and Mystical Experience in 'In Memoriam'." *VS*, VII, 155-69.

Pettigrew, John. "Tennyson's 'Ulysses': A Reconciliation of Opposites." *Vict. Poetry*, I, 27-45.
Explores the complexity of the poem.

Pipes, B. N., Jr. "A Slight Meteorological Disturbance: The Last Two Stanzas of Tennyson's 'The Poet'." *Vict. Poetry*, I, 74-76.

Pitt, Valerie. *Tennyson Laureate*. . . . See VB 1962, 420.

Briefly noted by Louis James in *Critical Quart.*, V, 277; by A. H. Qureski in *Dalhousie Rev.*, XLIII, 409-11; by Gilbert Thomas in *English*, XV, 155-56; by Louis Bonnerot in *Études anglaises*, XVI, 291-93; in *TLS*, 15 Feb., p. 108; by Clyde de L. Ryals in *VS*, VII, 115-17.

Rader, Ralph Wilson. "Tennyson's 'Strange' Father: The Comments of a Lincolnshire Neighbour." *N & Q*, n.s. X, 447-48.

Rehak, Louise R. "On the Use of Martyrs: Tennyson and Eliot on Thomas Becket." *TQ*, XXXIII, 43-60.

Richardson, Joanna. *The Pre-Eminent Victorian*. . . . See VB 1962, 420.

Rev. by L. Bonnerot in *Études anglaises*, XVI, 293; in *TLS*, 15 Feb., p. 108; by Clyde de L. Ryals in *VS*, VII, 115-17.

Ricks, Christopher. "Tennyson and Gray." *TLS*, 21 June, p. 468.

Ricks, Christopher. "The Variants of *In Memoriam*." *The Library*, 5th Ser., XVIII, 64.

Ryals, Clyde de L. "The Moral Paradox of the Hero in *Idylls of the King*." *ELH*, XXX, 53-69.

Arthur's defeat is that of a tragic hero.

Ryals, Clyde de L. "Percivale, Ambrosius, and the Method of Narration in 'The Holy Grail.' " *Die Neueren Sprachen*, XII, 533-43.

Ryals, Clyde de L. "The Poet as Critic: Appraisals of Tennyson by His Contemporaries." *Tenn. Studies in Lit.*, VII, 113-25.

Ryals, Clyde de L. "Point of View in Tennyson's *Ulysses*." *Archiv.*, Band 199, Heft 4, pp. 232-34.

Ryals, Clyde de L. "Tennyson's *Maud*." *Connotation*, I, 12-32.

Solomon, Stanley J. "Tennyson's Paradoxical King." *Vict. Poetry*, I, 258-71.

Contends that the *Idylls* deliberately contain major paradoxes, most of them involving the portrayal of Arthur.

St. John-Stevas, Norman. "Bagehot on Tennyson." *TLS*, 26 April, p. 314.

Taaffe, James G. "Circle Imagery in Tennyson's *In Memoriam*." *Vict. Poetry*, I, 123-31.

Templeman, William Darby. "A Consideration of the Fame of 'Locksley Hall.' " *Vict. Poetry*, I, 81-103.

A record of 120 years of criticism of this notable poem.

Tennyson, Charles. "The Somersby Tennysons." *Publications of the Tennyson Society*, published as a supplement (pp. 7-55) to *VS*, VII.

Vandiver, Edward P., Jr. "Tennyson's 'Tears, Idle Tears.' " *Ex*, XXI, Item 53.

THACKERAY (see also III, Hollingsworth, Land, Wilson).

Vanity Fair. Edited with an Introduction and Notes by Geoffrey and Kathleeen Tillotson. London: Methuen. Pp. 680.

Rev. in *TLS*, 28 Nov., p. 961 (see letters on Thackeray's illustrations by Joan Evans, 5 Dec., p. 1011; Joan Bryant, 12 Dec., p. 1031; Reynolds Stone and Simon Nowell-Smith, 19 Dec., p. 1054).

Mathison, John K. "The German Sections of *Vanity Fair*." *NCF*, XVIII, 235-46.

The Rhine passages contain satire of Thackeray's fellow-countrymen.

Solomon, Eric. "Thackeray on War." *VNL*, No. 23 (Spring), pp. 6-11.

Stewart, David H. "Thackeray's Modern Detractors." *Papers of the Michigan Academy of Science, Arts, and Letters.* XLVIII, 629-38.

Stewart, D. H. "*Vanity Fair*: Life in the Void." *CE*, XXV, 209-14.

Summerfield, Henry (ed.). "*Letters from a Club Arm-Chair*: William Makepeace Thackeray." *NCF*, XVIII, 205-33.

Six articles by Thackeray in the form of letters by "SQUAB" which appeared in the *Calcutta Star* between 1844 and 1845; introductory statements by the editor.

Taube, Myron. "Contrast as a Principle of Structure in Vanity Fair." *NCF*, XVIII, 119-35.

Contrasts or variations on a theme, appearing in each monthly number, gave the novel a "formal principle of structure."

Taube, Myron. "Thackeray and the Reminiscential Vision." *NCF*, XVIII, 247-59.

Taube, Myron. "Thackeray at Work: The Significance of Two Deletions from *Vanity Fair*." *NCF*, XVIII, 273-79.

Taube, Myron. "The Race for the Money in the Structure of *Vanity Fair*." *VNL*, No. 24 (Fall), pp. 12-17.

Von Hendy, Andrew. "Misunderstandings about Becky's Characterization in *Vanity Fair*." *NCF*, XVIII, 279-83.

Williamson, Karina. "A Note on the Function of Castlewood in *Henry Esmond*." *NCF*, XVIII, 71-77.

Davis, E. *Yeats's Early Contacts with French Poetry.* Pretoria: Communications of the Univ. of South Africa, 1961. Pp. 63.
Negatively reviewed by P. Ure in *N & Q*, n.s. x, 400.

Duryee, Mary Ballard. *Words Alone Are Certain Good. William Butler Yeats: Himself: The Poet: His Ghost.* Dublin: Dolmen Pr.; London: Oxford Univ. Pr. Pp. 43.
Noticed in *TLS*, 5 July, pp. 498-99.

Linebarger, James M. "Yeats's 'Among School Children' and Shelley's 'Defence of Poetry.'" *N & Q*, n.s. X, 375-77.

Farag, Fahmy Fawzy. "W. B. Yeats's Daimon." *Cairo Studies in English*, II (1961-62).

Faulkner, Peter, "Yeats, Ireland, and Ezra Pound." *Threshold*, No. 18, 58-68.

Gallagher, Patrick (ed.). *The Yeats Country.* Compiled by Sheelah Kirby. Dublin: Dolmen Pr.; London: Oxford Univ. Pr. Pp. 47.
Rev. by Denis Donoghue in *Manchester Guardian Weekly*, 24 Jan., p. 11; by T. R. Henn in *MLR*, LVIII, 627; in *TLS*, 25 Jan., p. 62.

Goldman, Michael P. "The Point of Drama: The Concept of Reverie in the Plays of William Butler Yeats." *DA*, XXIII, 3373-74.

Guha, Naresh. "W. B. Yeats: An Indian Approach." *DA*, XXIII, 4684.

Jumper, Will C. "Form *versus* Structure in a Poem of W. B. Yeats." *Iowa Eng. Yearbook*, No. 7, pp. 41-44.

Kirby, Sheelah (comp.). *The Yeats Country: A Guide to Places in the West of Ireland Associated with the Life and Writings of William Butler Yeats.* Ed. by Patrick Gallagher. Oxford: Oxford Univ. Pr. Pp. 47.
Rev. by Charles Tomlinson in *Poetry*, CII, 345; in *TLS*, 25 Jan., p. 62.

Lucas, Frank Lawrence. *The Drama of Chekhov, Synge, Yeats, and Pirandello.* London: Cassell. Pp. xii + 452.

Mayhew, George. "A Corrected Typescript of Yeats's 'Easter 1916'." *HLQ*, XXVII, 53-71.

McHugh, Roger. "Yeats and Irish Politics." *Texas Quart.*, V, 90-100.

Parks, L. C. "The Hidden Aspect of 'Sailing to Byzantium'." *Études anglaises*, XVI, 333-44.

Parrish, Stephen Maxfield. *A Concordance to the Poems of W. B. Yeats.* Ithaca, New York: Cornell Univ. Pr. Pp. xxxvii + 967.

Phillips, Robert S. "Yeats' 'Sailing to Byzantium,' 25-32." *Ex*, XXII, Item 11.

Quinn, C. C. W. "W. B. Yeats and Irish Tradition." *Hermathena*, XCVII, 3-19.

Rosenthal, M. L. (ed.). *Selected Poems of William Butler Yeats.* New York: Macmillan, 1962.
Rev. by John R. Moore in *SeR*, LXXI, 123-33.

Seiden, Morton Irving. *William Butler Yeats: The Poet as Mythmaker, 1865-1939. . . .* See VB 1962, 422.
Rev. by Austin Clarke in *Poetry*, CII, 185-87; in *TLS*, 29 March, p. 218; by John Unterecker in *YR*, LII, 585-88.

Stallworthy, Jon. *Between the Lines: Yeats's Poetry in the Making.* Oxford: Clarendon Pr. Pp. 261.
Rev. in *Economist*, CCVII, 54; by Howard Sergeant in *English*, XIV, 203-05; by Louis MacNeice in *Listener*, 21 Mar., p. 521; by Robert Conquest in *S*, 3 May, pp. 577-78; in *TLS*, 29 Mar., p. 218.

Torchiana, Donald T. "W. B. Yeats, Jonathan Swift, and Liberty." *MP*, LXI, 26-39.

Unterecker, John. "The Putting Together of William Butler Yeats." *Columbia Univ. Forum.* VI, 41-44.

Ure, Peter. *Yeats.* Writers and Critics Series. Edinburgh: Oliver and Boyd. Pp. 129.

Ure, Peter. *Yeats the Playwright: A Commentary on Character and Design in the Major Plays.* London: Routledge and Kegan Paul; New York: Barnes and Noble. Pp. viii + 182.
Rev. by G. S. Fraser in *Listener*, 16 May, p. 843; by Keith Harrison in *S*, 22 Feb., p. 237; in *TLS*, 1 Feb., p. 78.

Vendler, Helen Henessy. *Yeats's Vision and the Later Plays.* London: Oxford Univ. Pr.; Cambridge, Mass.: Harvard Univ. Pr. Pp. xiii + 286.
Rev. by Howard Sergeant in *English*, XIV, 243-44; by L. W. Griffin in *LJ*, LXXXVIII, 1167; by John Unterecker in *YR*, LII, 586; by E. L. Mayo in *SR*, 15 June, p. 43; by Austin Clarke in *Poetry*, CII, 185-87; in *TLS*, 21 Nov., p. 945 (also see letter by Peter Ure, 5 Dec., p. 1020).

Watson-Williams, Helen. "All the Olympians: W. B. Yeats and His Friends." *English*, XIV, 178-84.

Youngblood, Sarah. "The Structure of Yeats's Long Poems." *Criticism*, V, 323-35.

VICTORIAN  IBLIOGRAPHY FOR 1964

Robert C. Slack, editor

The editor wishes to thank Professor Carl J. Weber for his helpful assistance with the Hardy section of the bibliography.

The editor of the Victorian Bibliography for 1965 will be Ronald E. Freeman.

THIS BIBLIOGRAPHY has been prepared by a committee of the Victorian Literature Group of the Modern Language Association of America: Robert C. Slack, chairman, Carnegie Institute of Technology; Oscar Maurer, University of Texas; Charles T. Dougherty, St. Louis University; Donald J. Gray, Indiana University; Richard C. Tobias, University of Pittsburgh; Ronald E. Freeman, University of Southern California; and Michael Timko, Queens College. It attempts to list the noteworthy publications of 1964 (including reviews of these and earlier items) that have a bearing on the Victorian period, as well as similar publications of earlier date that have been inadvertently omitted from the preceding Victorian bibliographies. Unless otherwise indicated, the date of publication is 1964. Reference to a page in the bibliography for 1963, in *Victorian Studies*, June 1964, is made by the following form: See VB 1963, 430. Some cross-references are given, though not all that are possible. Annotations to items are made at the discretion of committee members and the editor; some are intended to indicate content, others to emphasize important contributions; every annotation containing a judgment is initialed by the committee member responsible. Bibliographical entries are made to conform as closely as possible with the British National Bibliography for books first published in Great Britain, and with the Library of Congress Catalog for books first published in the United States.

ABBREVIATIONS OF TITLES USED FREQUENTLY

AHR = American Historical Review
AL = American Literature
AM = Atlantic Monthly
APSR = American Political Science Review
APSS = Annals of the American Academy of Political and Social Science
ArQ = Arizona Quarterly
BA = Books Abroad
BB = Bulletin of Bibliography and Magazine Notes
BLR = Bodleian Library Record
BSP = Papers of the Bibliographical Society of America
CE = College English
CR = Contemporary Review
CWd = Catholic World
DA = Dissertation Abstracts
DUJ = Durham University Journal
EC = Essays in Criticism
EHR = English Historical Review
EJ = English Journal
ELH = English Literary History
ELN = English Language Notes (formerly *Modern Language Notes*)
ESt = English Studies
Ex = Explicator
HJ = Hibbert Journal
HLQ = Huntington Library Quarterly
JAA = Journal of Aesthetics and Art Criticism
JEGP = Journal of English and Germanic Philology
JEH = Journal of Economic History

JHI = *Journal of the History of Ideas*
JMH = *Journal of Modern History*
JP = *Journal of Philosophy*
JPE = *Journal of Political Economy*
KR = *Kenyon Review*
LJ = *Library Journal*
LQ = *Library Quarterly*
LQHR = *London Quarterly and Holborn Review*
LR = *Library Review*
M & L = *Music and Letters*
MLJ = *Modern Language Journal*
MLQ = *Modern Language Quarterly*
MLR = *Modern Language Review*
MP = *Modern Philology*
N = *Nation*
N&Q = *Notes and Queries*
NCF = *Nineteenth-Century Fiction*
NEQ = *New England Quarterly*
New R = *New Republic*
NS = *New Statesman*
NYTBR = *New York Times Book Review*
PAPS = *Proceedings of the American Philosophical Society*
ParR = *Partisan Review*
PLC = *Princeton University Library Chronicle*
PMLA = *Publications of the Modern Language Association of America*
PQ = *Philological Quarterly*
PSQ = *Political Science Quarterly*
QJS = *Quarterly Journal of Speech*
QQ = *Queen's Quarterly*
QR = *Quarterly Review*
RES = *Review of English Studies*
RoR = *Romanic Review*
S = *Spectator*
SAQ = *South Atlantic Quarterly*
SeR = *Sewanee Review*
SP = *Studies in Philology*
SR = *Saturday Review*
StI = *Studies: An Irish Quarterly Review*
TC = *Twentieth Century*
TLS = *Times Literary Supplement*
TQ = *University of Toronto Quarterly*
VNL = *Victorian News Letter*
VQR = *Virginia Quarterly Review*
VS = *Victorian Studies*
YR = *Yale Review*

I. BIBLIOGRAPHICAL MATERIAL

(For bibliographies pertaining to individuals listed in Section IV, see — FORD: Harvey; GILBERT: Allen; RUSKIN: Wise;

STEVENSON: McKay; SHAW: *The Shaw Review;* TROLLOPE: Sadlier.)

"Annual Bibliography for 1963." *PMLA,* LXXIX, No. 2, 169-86. "English Language and Literature: IX. Nineteenth Century, X. Twentieth Century," ed. Charles C. Mish, *et al.*

Gilbert, Judson Bennett. *Disease and Destiny: A Bibliography of Medical References to the Famous.* London: Dawsons of Pall Mall, 1962. Pp. 535.
Rev. by W. LeFanu in *The Library*, 5th Ser., XVIII (1963), 157-58.

Gordon, John D. "Doctors as Men of Letters: English and American Writers of Medical Background: An Exhibition in the Berg Collection." *Bull. New York Pub. Libr.,* LXVIII, 574-601.
A catalogue of the display of works by eighty authors who had received at least some medical training. Also published separately.

Gordon, John D. *New in the Berg Collection, 1959-1961.* An exhibition. New York: New York Public Libr. Pp. 36.
Rev. by P. Coustillas in *Études anglaises,* XVII, 209.

Gordan, John D. "New in the Berg Collection: 1959-1961." *Bull. New York Pub. Libr.,* LXVIII, 6-12; 73-82.
Gissing, Charlotte Mew, Lord and Lady Alfred Douglas, Beerbohm, Maurice Baring, and other writers.

Greenberg, Robert A. (ed.). "Recent Publications: A Selected List." *VNL,* No. 25 (Spring), pp. 29-32.

Heyl, Edgar. *A Contribution to Conjuring Bibliography, English Language, 1580 to 1850.* Baltimore: The Author, 11 West Chase St., 1962. Pp. 62.
Rev. briefly in *BSP,* LVIII, 74; by R. B. Jackson in *LJ,* LXXXIX, 94.

Mynors, R. A. B. *Catalogue of the Manuscripts at Balliol College, Oxford.* Oxford: Clarendon, 1963. Pp. 404.
Rev. briefly in *BSP,* LVIII, 82.
Records Mss. of Browning, Arnold, Eliot, and others.

O'Neil, Perry. "The Arents Collection of Books in Parts and Associated Literature: A Supplement to the Checklist, 1957-1963." *Bull. New York Pub. Libr.,* LXVIII, 141-52; 259-69. See VB 1957, 384, Dickson for original checklist.

Plesner, K. F. *Bøger og Bogsamlere: Biblio-*

filiens Histoirie. Copenhagen: Rosenkilde og Bagger, 1962. Pp. 242.

Rev. by Bent Juel-Jensen in *The Library*, 5th Ser. XVIII (1963), 151-52.

Its discussion of English collectors is a "synthesis of Elton, W. Y. Fletcher, de Ricci, and John Carter."

Ray, Gordon N. "Contemporary Collectors XXXVII: A 19th-Century Collection." *Book Collector*, XIII, 33-44; 171-84.

"Research on Irish History in Irish Universities." *Irish Hist. Studies*, XIV, 61-64.

Rigby, Margery, and Nilon, Charles (eds.). *Annual Bibliography of English Language and Literature.* Volume XXXVI, 1961. New York: Cambridge Univ. Pr. Pp. xvi + 401.

Slack, Robert C. (ed.). "Victorian Bibliography for 1963." *VS*, VII, 413-54.

Standley, Fred L. "Stopford Augustus Brooke (1832-1916): A Primary Bibliography." *BB*, XXIV, 79-82.

Stevenson, Lionel (ed.). *Victorian Fiction: A Guide to Research.* Cambridge, Mass.: Harvard Univ. Pr. Pp. vi + 440.

Rev. by B. W. Fuson in *LJ*, LXXXIX, 3754.

Super, R. H. "Recent Studies in Nineteenth-Century English Literature." *St. in English Lit.*, IV, 663-85.

Discusses books published in 1963.

Tobias, R. C. "The Year's Work in Victorian Poetry: 1963." *Vict. Poetry*, II, 187-202.

White, Beatrice and Dorsch, T. S. (eds.). *The Year's Work in English Studies.* Vol. XLIII (1962). London: John Murray. Pp. 348.

The Nineteenth-Century section is annotated by P. M. Yarker and Brian Lee, pp. 225-52.

Wood, Frederick T. "Current Literature, 1963: I. Prose, Poetry and Drama; II. Criticism and Biography." *ESt*, XLV, 259-69; 335-50.

Review article which comments on several books dealing with Victorians.

II. ECONOMIC, POLITICAL, RELIGIOUS, AND SOCIAL ENVIRONMENT

Abel-Smith, Brian. *The Hospitals, 1800-1948: A Study in Social Administration in England and Wales.* Cambridge, Mass.: Harvard Univ. Pr. Pp. xiii + 514.

Rev. by Asa Briggs in *NS*, LXVIII, 792.

Abu-Lughod, Ibrahim A. *Arab Rediscovery of Europe: A Study in Cultural Encounters.* Princeton: Princeton Univ. Pr. Pp. 188.

Rev. by Daniel Lerner in *Am. Jour. of Sociology*, XLIX, 564; by S. D. Goitein in *APSS*, CCCLII, 211.

Adburgham, Alison. *Shops and Shopping, 1800-1914.* London: Allen and Unwin. Pp. xx + 304.

Rev. by Stevie Smith in *Manchester Guardian Weekly*, 17 Dec., p. 10; in *TLS*, 3 Dec., p. 1104.

Alder, G. J. *British India's Northern Frontier, 1865-95: A Study in Imperial Policy.* London: Longmans, 1963. Pp. ix + 392.

Allen, V. L. "The Origins of Industrial Conciliation and Arbitration." *International Rev. of Social History*, IX, 237-54.

Studies methods by which disputes were settled in the nineteenth century in England and Scotland.

Altholz, Josef L. *The Liberal Catholic Movement in England.* . . . See VB 1963, 415.

Rev. by Emmet Larkin in *AHR*, LXX, 126-27

Anderson, Olive. "Cabinet Government and the Crimean War. *EHR*, LXXIX, 548-51.

Anderson, Olive. "Great Britain and the Beginnings of the Ottoman Public Debt, 1854-55." *Hist. Jour.*, VII, 47-63.

Anson, Peter F. *Bishops at Large.* London: Faber and Faber. Pp. 593.

Rev. by Archdale A. King in *Wiseman Rev.*, CCXXXVIII, 262-64.

Anstey, R. T. *Britain and the Congo in the Nineteenth Century.* . . . See VB 1963, 415.

Rev. by J. D. Fage in *AHR*, LXX, 234; briefly by J. D. Hargreaves in *EHR*, LXXIX, 870; by Richard J. Hammond in *JEH*, XXIV, 247.

Argles, Michael. *South Kensington to Robbins: An Account of English Technical and Scientific Education since 1851.* London: Longmans, Pp. xiii + 178.

Badger, Kingsbury. "Christianity and Victorian Religious Confessions." *MLQ*, XXV, 86-109.

Liberalism *vs.* orthodoxy in Victorian spiritual autobiographies.

[Baker, Wyndham.] "An Artillery Officer in China, 1840-1842." *Blackwood's*, CCXCVI, 73-86; 150-66.

Letters written home by Baker.

Banks, J. A. and Olive. *Feminism and Family*

Planning in Victorian England. Liverpool: Univ. of Liverpool Pr. Pp. xi + 142.
Rev. by N. MacKenzie in *NS*, LXVIII, 251-52; in *TLS*, 9 July, p. 586.

Banno, Masataka. *China and the West, 1858-1861: The Origins of the Tsungli Yamen.* London: Oxford Univ. Pr.; Cambridge, Mass.: Harvard Univ. Pr. Pp. xi + 369.

Barbier, Carl Paul (ed.). *Correspondence: Mallarmé-Whistler.* Paris: A. G. Nizet. Pp. 307.
Rev. in *TLS*, 8 Oct., p. 920.

Barnes, James J. *Free Trade in Books: A Study of the London Book Trade since 1800.* Oxford: Clarendon Pr. Pp. 198.
Rev. by Simon Nowell-Smith in *Book Collector*, XIII, 254-58; by A. Robinson in *Econ. Jour.*, LXXIV, 702-04; by J. C. Harrison in *LJ*, LXXXIX, 1720; by Asa Briggs in *NS*, LXVII, 336-37; in *TLS*, 20 Feb., p. 156.

Barker, T. C. and Robbins, Michael. *A History of London Transport. Vol. I: The Nineteenth Century.* London: George Allen and Unwin, 1963. Pp. xxxii + 412.
Rev. by Kent T. Healy in *JEH*, XXIV, 251.

Bartle, G. F. "Bowring and the Near Eastern Crisis of 1838-1840." *EHR*, LXXIX, 761-74.

Bartlett, Christopher John. *Great Britain and Sea Power, 1815-1853.* . . . See VB, 1963, 416.
Rev. by Christopher Lloyd in *History*, XLIX, 94-95; by Albert H. Imlah in *JMH*, XXXVI, 84-85.

Baylen, Joseph O. "A Victorian's 'Crusade' in Chicago, 1893-1894." *Journal of American History* (formerly *Mississippi Valley Hist. Rev.*), LI, 418-34.
The Victorian is W. T. Stead.

Berghaus, Erwin. *The History of Railways.* London: Barrie & Rockliff. Pp. xi + 215.

Best, Geoffrey Francis Andrew. *Shaftesbury.* London: Batsford; New York: Arco. Pp. 139.
Rev. in *TLS*, 1 Oct., p. 896.
A study of the seventh Earl.

Best, Geoffrey Francis Andrew. *Temporal Pillars: Queen Anne's Bounty, the Ecclesiastical Commissioners, and the Church of England.* New York: Cambridge Univ. Pr. Pp. xv + 582.
Rev. by W. R. Ward in *Jour. Eccl. Hist.*, XV, 266-67; in *TLS*, 14 May, p. 419 ("important reading for church historian, social historian, and student of Trol-

lope"); by Dudley W. R. Bahlman in *VS*, VIII, 186-88.

Bird, Anthony. *Early Victorian Furniture.* London: Hamish Hamilton. Pp. 64.
Noticed in *TLS*, 17 Dec., p. 1149.

Bishop, Edward. *Blood and Fire!: The Story of General William Booth and the Salvation Army.* London: Longmans. Pp. 114.

Black, Matthew W. and Miller, W. E. "Some Letters from Actors and Actresses to Dr. Horace Howard Furness: Part II." *Libr. Chronicle, Univ. of Pa.*, XXX, 10-22. See VB 1963, 416.

Blakiston, Noel. *The Roman Question.* . . . See VB 1963, 416.
Rev. briefly by Derek Beales in *EHR*, LXXIX, 876.

Blaug, Mark. *Economic Theory in Retrospect.* London: Heinemann; Homewood, Ill.: Irwin. Pp. xvi + 633.

Blaug, Mark. "The Poor Law Report Reexamined." *JEH*, XXIV, 229-45.

Blunt, Wilfred. *Cockerell: Sydney Carlyle Cockerell, Friend of Ruskin and William Morris and Director of the Fitzwilliam Museum.* London: Hamish Hamilton. Pp. 385.
Rev. by Douglas Cleverdon in *Listener*, 10 Sept., p. 398; by Naomi Lewis in *NS*, LXVIII, 579-80; in *TLS*, 10 Sept., p. 843.

Boahen, Albert Adu. *Britain, the Sahara, and the Western Sudan, 1788-1881.* New York: Oxford Univ. Pr. Pp. ix + 268.
Rev. by Andrew Roberts in *NS*, LXVIII, 662-63.

Bolitho, Hector. *Albert: Prince Consort.* London: Max Parrish. Pp. xiv + 250.
Rev. in *TLS*, 31 Dec., p. 1179.

Bond, W. H. "Henry Hallam, *The Times* Newspaper, and the Halliwell Case." *The Library*, 5th Ser., XVIII (1963), 133-40.

Booth, Michael (ed.). *Hiss the Villain.* London: Eyre and Spottiswoode. Pp. 390.
Noticed in *TLS*, 24 Dec., p. 1169.
An edition, with commentary, of six popular nineteenth-century melodramas.

Brand, Carl Fremont. *The British Labour Party: A Short History.* Stanford: Stanford Univ. Pr. Pp. 340.

Briggs, Asa. "Religion and Capitalism." *Listener*, 27 Feb., pp. 339-41.

Briggs, Asa. *Victorian Cities.* . . . See VB 1963, 416.
Rev. by Jean-Paul Hulin in *Études anglaises*, XVII, 195-97; by S. G. Checkland in *History*, XLIX, 246-48.

Burn, William Laurence. *The Age of Equipoise: A Study of the Mid-Victorian Generation.* London: Allen and Unwin. Pp. 340.

Rev. in *HJ*, LXII, 160; by John Roach in *History*, XLIX, 378-80; in *Economist*, CCX, 806; by R. R. Rea in *LJ*, LXXXIX, 2084; by A. J. P. Taylor in *NS*, LXVII, 129; in *TLS*, 30 Jan., p. 83.

Concentrates on the generation of 1852-1867.

Burnett, John. "Plenty and Want: The Social History of English Diet." *History Today*, XIV, 222-33.

Bury, John B. *History of the Papacy in the Nineteenth Century: Liberty and Authority in the Catholic Church.* New York: Schocken. Pp. xxxiv + 217.

A new edition, with Introduction, Epilogue and Notes by Frederick C. Grant.

Butlin, Noel G. *Investment in Australian Economic Growth, 1861-1900.* New York and Cambridge: Cambridge Univ. Pr. Pp. xv + 477.

Buxton, Ellen E. *Family Sketchbook: A Hundred Years Ago.* London: Bles. Pp. 96.

Noticed in *TLS*, 12 Nov., p. 1025.

Drawings of family life by a sixteen-year-old Victorian girl.

Campbell, James W. "The Influences of the Revolutions of 1848 on Great Britain." *DA*, XXV, 1167.

Carleton, William G. "Hawthorne Discovers the English." *YR*, LIII, 395-414.

On *Our Old Home* (1863) and *English Notebooks* (1870).

Carr, J. C. and Taplin, W. *A History of the British Steel Industry.* . . . See VB 1963, 417.

Rev. by N. Rosenberg in *JPE*, LXXII, 103.

Cathcart, Helen. *Sandringham.* London: W. H. Allen. Pp. 224.

Noticed in *TLS*, 17 Dec., p. 1149.

History of a royal country house, 1864 to the present.

Causley, Charles. "The Stone Man." *Listener*, 2 Jan., pp. 15-16.

On the nineteenth-century sculptor Neville Northey Burnard.

Cecil, Robert. "The Cession of the Ionian Islands." *History Today*, XIV, 616-26.

Chapman, J. K. *The Career of Arthur Hamilton Gordon, First Lord Stanmore, 1829-1912.* Toronto: Univ. of Toronto Pr. Pp. vii + 387.

On a notable colonial governor.

Charles, Conrad, C. P. "The Origins of the Parish Mission in England and the Early Passionist Apostolate, 1840-1850." *Journal Eccl. Hist.*, XV, 60.

Checkland, S. G. *The Rise of Industrial Society in England, 1815-1885.* London: Longmans. Pp. xiv + 471.

Clacy, Mrs. Charles. *A Lady's Visit to the Gold Diggings of Australia in 1852-53.* Ed. by Patricia Thompson. London: Angus and Robertson. Pp. 160.

Rev. in *TLS*, 2 Jan., p. 14.

Clark, George N. *A History of the Royal College of Physicians of London.* Vol. I: *To 1858.* London: Oxford Univ. Pr. Pp. xxiii + 425.

Clarke, M. L. *George Grote: A Biography* . . . See VB 1963, 442.

Rev. by S. I. Oost in *Classical Philology*, LIX, 116-17.

Clegg, Hugh Armstrong, Fox, Alan, and Thompson, A. F. *A History of British Trade Unions since 1889.* Vol. I: *1889-1910.* Oxford: Clarendon Pr. Pp. xi + 514.

Rev. by Margaret Cole in *Listener*, 23 July, p. 136; by Asa Briggs in *NS*, LXVIII, 187-88; by Henry Pelling in *S*, 19 June, pp. 826-27; in *TLS*, 18 June, p. 528.

Cole, Margaret. *The Story of Fabian Socialism.* . . . See VB 1963, 417.

Rev. by N. McCord in *DUJ*, XXV, 132.

Collier, Richard. *The Sound of Fury: The Great Indian Mutiny.* . . . See VB 1963, 417.

Rev. by Eric Britter in *Herald Tribune*, 12 Apr., p. 11; by P. W. Filby in *LJ*, LXXXIX, 1084; by John Masters in *NYTBR*, 16 Feb., p. 4.

Collins, Irene. *The Age of Progress: A Survey of European History from 1789-1870.* London: Edward Arnold. Pp. 467.

Rev. in *TLS*, 4 June, p. 474.

Collins, Robert O. *The Southern Sudan, 1883-1898: A Struggle for Control.* . . . See VB 1963, 417.

Rev. by T. B. Miller in *JMH*, XXXVI, 95.

Colvin, Howard Montagu (ed.). *A Catalogue of Architectural Drawings of the 18th and 19th Centuries in the Library of Worcester College, Oxford.* Oxford: Clarendon Pr. Pp. xxvi + 71.

Cooke, Raymond M. "British Evangelicals, Native Peoples and the Concept of Empire, 1837-1852." *DA*, XXIV, 4644-45.

Coombs, Douglas. *The Gold Coast, Britain*

and the Netherlands, 1850-1874. . . . See VB 1963, 418.
Rev. by John S. Galbraith in *JMH*, XXXVI, 210.

Cooper, F. Renad. *Nothing Extenuate: The Life of Frederick Fox Cooper.* London: Barrie and Rockliff. Pp. 259.
Rev. by Derek Hudson in *N&Q*, n.s. XI, 240.
Dramatist, theatrical manager, and journalist: 1806-1879.

Cooper, Leonard. *The Age of Wellington, 1769-1852.* London: Macmillan. Pp. 308.
Rev. by Christopher Hibbert in *S*, 25 Sept., p. 407.

Corfe, T. H. "The Troubles of Captain Boycott." *History Today*, XIV, 758-64; 854-62.

Crombie, A. C. and Hoskin, M. A. (ed.). *History of Science: An Annual Review of Literature, Research, and Teaching.* Vol. III. Cambridge: Heffer. Pp. 155.
Rev. in *TLS*, 17 Sept., p. 863.
Includes items: Walter F. Cannon, "History in Depth: the Early Victorian Period"; Everett Mendelssohn, "The Biological Sciences in the Nineteenth Century: Some Problems and Sources."

Cruickshank, Marjorie. *Church and State in English Education: 1870 to the Present Day.* . . . See VB 1963, 418.
Rev. by G. A. Cahill in *AHR*, LXIX, 1127; by John Roach in *Hist. Jour.*, VII, 181-82.

Curtin, Philip D. *The Image of Africa: British Ideas and Action, 1780-1850.* Madison: Univ. of Wis. Pr. Pp. 526.
Rev. by R. I. Rotberg in *AHR*, LXX, 165; by Louis Barron in *LJ*, LXXXIX, 862.

Curtis, Lewis Perry, Jr. *Coercion and Conciliation in Ireland 1880-1892.* . . . See VB 1963, 418.
Rev. by S. P. Ryan in *America*, CIX, 360; in *Economist*, CCXI, 282; by A. J. P. Taylor in *NS*, LXVII, 296; by Robert Rhodes James in *S*, 7 Aug., p. 187; by A. L. Morton in *Science & Society*, XXVIII, 379; in *TLS*, 5 Mar., p. 190; by David Owen in *YR*, LIII, 279-82.

Davies, Horton. *Worship and Theology in England.* Vol. IV. *From Newman to Martineau, 1850-1900.* . . . See VB 1963, 418.
Rev. by R. H. Bainton in *Church Hist.*, XXXIII, 107-08.

Deane, Phyllis, and Cole, W. A. *British Economic Growth, 1688-1959.* . . . See VB 1963, 418.

Rev. by T. C. Barker in *Economica*, XXXI, 449-52.

De Iongh, Peter. "Nigeria: Two Imperialists and their Creation." *History Today*, XIV, 835-43.
The imperialists are Lugard and Sir George Goldie.

Derry, John W. *A Short History of Nineteenth-Century England.* N. Y.: New American Library, 1963. Pp. 239.
Rev. briefly by John H. Gleason in *AHR*, LXIX, 433-34.

Dorfman, Joseph. "Wicksteed's Recantation of the Marginal Productivity Theory." *Economica*, XXXI, 294-95.

Doughty, Oswald. *Early Diamond Days.* London: Longmans, 1963. Pp. 237.
Rev. by David Watt in *S*, 18 Oct., 1963, p. 501; in *TLS*, 9 Jan., p. 32.
On life in the diamond fields of South Africa in the 1870's and 1880's.

Duhamel, Jean. "Le prince impérial en Angleterre." *Revue de deux mondes* (No. 8: 15 Apr.), 564-71.

Duncan, Barry. *The St. James's Theatre: Its Strange & Complete History, 1835-1957.* London: Barrie and Rockliff. Pp. xxiii + 407.

Easton, Stewart C. *The Rise and Fall of Western Colonialism: A Historical Survey from the Early Nineteenth Century to the Present.* New York: Praeger; London: Pall Mall. Pp. 402.
Rev. by Erwin K. Welsch in *LJ*, LXXXIX, 1605; by Brian Crozier in *S*, 4 Dec., pp. 786-87.

Edwards, Michael. *Battles of the Indian Mutiny.* . . . See VB 1963, 419.
Rev. in *Economist*, CCVIII, 1130; by P. W. Filby in *LJ*, LXXXIX, 1084; by Stephen Hugh Jones in *NS*, LXVI, 747.

Eshag, Eprime. *From Marshall to Keynes: An Essay on the Monetary Theory of the Cambridge School.* . . . See VB 1963, 419.
Rev. by R. Hawtrey in *Economica*, XXXI, 93-94.

Fairweather, Eugene R. (ed.). *The Oxford Movement.* London: Oxford Univ. Pr. Pp. 400.
Rev. by G. R. Kelly in *LJ*, LXXXIX, 3166; in *TLS*, 15 Oct., p. 943.
An anthology of documents (tracts, letters, sermons, essays).

Fallows, W. G. *Mandell Creighton and the English Church.* London: Oxford Univ. Pr. Pp. 127.
Rev. by Neville Masterman in *History*,

XLIX, 394-95; in *TLS*, 9 July, p. 586.

Fenton, E. W. *A Portfolio of Railway Notices, 1825-1892.* London: Holland Pr. Pp. 16.
Noticed in *TLS*, 13 Aug., p. 734.

Fenton, William. *Nineteenth Century Locomotive Engravings.* London: Hugh Evelyn.
Noticed in *TLS*, 17 Sept., p. 865.
Twenty plates, with contemporary descriptions.

Ferriday, Peter (ed.). *Victorian Architecture....* See VB 1963, 419.
Rev. by P. von Khrum in *LJ*, LXXXIX, 4515.

Fontane, Theodor. *Aus England und Schottland.* Ed. by Charlotte Jolles. (Vol. XVII of Fontane's *Sämtliche Werke*). Munich: Nymphenburger Verlagsbuchhandlung. Pp. 695.
Rev. in *TLS*, 16 Jan., p. 43 (and see note, 12 March, p. 218.)
Reminiscences of a German novelist's visits to Britain, 1844-1859.

Ford, Alec George. *The Gold Standard 1880-1914....* See VB 1962, 389.
Rev. by C. A. E. Goodhart in *Econ. Jour.*, LXXIV, 670; by S. B. Saul in *VS*, VII, 326-27.

Fothergill, Brian. *Nicholas Wiseman....* See VB 1963, 419.
Rev. by J. H. Whyte in *Irish Hist. Studies*, XIV, 93; by Edward I. Watkin in *VS*, VIII, 189-90.

Fulford, Roger (ed.). *Dearest Child: Letters between Queen Victoria and the Princess Royal, 1858-1861.* London: Evans Brothers. Pp. x + 401.
Rev. by Joanna Richardson in *Listener*, 2 July, p. 25; by Anne Duchene in *Manchester Guardian Weekly*, 24 Sept., p. 10; by D. A. N. Jones in *NS*, LXVIII, 58-59; by Christopher Sykes in *S*, 3 July, p. 18; in *TLS*, 9 July, p. 586.

Furneaux, Rupert. *What Happened on the 'Mary Celeste.'* London: Max Parrish. Pp. 171.
Account of accident at sea in 1872.

Galbraith, John S. *Reluctant Empire: British Policy on the South African Frontier, 1834-1854....* See VB 1963, 419.
Rev. by A. P. Thornton in *JMH*, XXXVI, 344-45; by Leonard M. Thompson in *VS*, VII, 323-24.

Gathorne-Hardy, Robert (ed.). *Ottoline: The Early Memoirs of Lady Ottoline Morrell, 1873-1915....* See VB 1963, 419.
Rev. by Alan Pryce-Jones in *Book Week*, 5 July, p. 2; in *Economist*, CCIX, 918; by

Bernard Bergonzi in *Encounter*, XXI, 86; by K. T. Willis in *LJ*, LXXXIX, 2079; by Walter Allen in *New R*, 13 June, p. 27; by Noel Annan in *NY Rev. of Books*, 9 July, p. 13; by Anne Fremantle in *NYTBR*, 14 June, p. 6; by Leon Edel in *SR*, 20 June, p. 37; in *TLS*, 1 Nov., 1963, p. 883.

Gelfand, Michael. *Lakeside Pioneers: Socio-Medical Study of Nyasaland (1875-1920).* Oxford: Blackwell. Pp. x + 330.
Rev. in *TLS*, 18 June, p. 535.

George, Wilma. *Biologist Philosopher: A Study of the Life and Writings of Alfred Russel Wallace.* London: Abelard Schuman. Pp. 320.
Rev. in *TLS*, 26 March, p. 253.

Ghosh, R. N. "The Colonization Controversy: R. J. Wilmot-Horton and the Classical Economists." *Economica*, XXXI, 385-400.

Gibbs, Peter. *The Battle of the Alma....* See VB 1963, 420.
Rev. by John Shelton Curtis in *Slavic Rev.*, XXIII, 141.

Gill, John Clifford. *Parson Bull of Byerley....* See VB 1963, 420.
Rev. by R. W. Greaves in *Jour. Eccl. Hist.*, XV, 274; in *TLS*, 9 Jan., p. 31; by D. E. H. Mole in *VS*, VIII, 192-93.

Giordan, Marion (ed.). *The Victorian Book of Dreams.* London: Hugh Evelyn. Pp 84.
Rev. by Fiona MacCarthy in *Manchester Guardian Weekly*, 29 Oct., p. 11.
Popular interpretation of dreams, compiled from various nineteenth-century "dream-books."

Gloag, John. *Victorian Taste....* See VB 1962, 390.
Rev. by Kenneth Garlick in *VS*, VII, 311-12.

Godden, Geoffrey A. *British Pottery and Porcelain, 1780-1850.* London: Arthur Barker. Pp. 199.
Rev. by P. von Khrum in *LJ*, LXXXIX, 4328; in *TLS*, 27 Aug., p. 760.

Gollin, Alfred M. *Proconsul in Politics: A Study of Lord Milner in Opposition and in Power, 1854-1905.* New York: Macmillan; London: Blond. Pp. xi + 627.
Rev. by Terence O'Brien in *History Today*, XIV, 585-86; by R. R. Rea in *LJ*, LXXXIX, 3005; by Paul Johnson in *NS*, LXVII, 214-16.

Gopal, Ram. *British Rule in India: An Assessment....* See VB 1963, 420.
Rev. by B. P. Lamb in *APSS*, CCCLIV, 186; by Hyman Kublin in *LJ*, LXXXVIII, 4753.

Graham, Gerald S. "By Steam to India." _History Today_, XIV, 301-12.

Graves, Charles. _Leather Armchairs: The Book of London Clubs._ New York: Coward-McCann. Pp. xxv + 194.
Rev. by P. W. Filby in _LJ_, LXXXIX, 4348.

The Great Exhibition of 1851. London: H.M.S.O. Pp. 142.

Grenville, J. A. S. _Lord Salisbury and Foreign Policy._ . . . See VB 1963, 420.
Rev. by H. R. Winkler in _AHR_, LXX, 127; by G. P. Gooch in _CR_, CCV, 185-92; by Zara Steiner in _Historical Jour._, VII, 340-44; by E. W. Edwards in _History_, XLIX, 396-98; by Harold Kurts in _History Today_, XIV, 427; by E. G. Collieu in _Listener_, 5 March, p. 402; by A. J. P. Taylor in _NS_, LXVII, 296; in _TLS_, 13 Feb., p. 125.

Guttsman, Wilhelm Leo. _The British Political Elite, 1832-1935._ . . . See VB 1963, 420.
Rev. by Richard Rose in _APSR_, LVIII, 408; by Jo Grimond in _Book Week_, 10 May, p. 4; in _Economist_, CCVIII, 1130; by David Marquand in _NS_, LXVI, 110; in _TLS_, 6 Sept., p. 667.

Gwyn, William Brent. _Democracy and the Cost of Politics in Britain._ . . . See VB 1963, 420.
Rev. by H. J. Hanham in _EHR_, LXXIX, 195-96.

Hall, Peter Geoffrey. _The Industries of London since 1861._ . . . See VB 1963, 421.
Rev. by Leroy Dunn in _JMH_, XXXVI, 90-91.

Hall, Trevor H. _The Strange Case of Edmund Gurney._ London: Duckworth. Pp. xi + 219.
Account of life and mysterious death of late-century spiritualist.

Hambly, G. R. G. "Richard Temple and the Punjab Tenancy Act of 1868." _EHR_, LXXIX, 47-66.

Hamburger, Joseph. _James Mill and the Art of Revolution._ New Haven, Conn. and London: Yale Univ. Pr., 1963. Pp. xiii + 289.

Hamilton, Gerald. _Blood Royal._ London: Gibbs & Phillips. Pp. 178.
Rev. by A. Howard in _NS_, LXVII, 334-35 (see also letters, 451).
On haemophilia in the Royal Household.

Hammond, Rolt. _The Forth Bridge and Its Builders._ London: Eyre and Spottiswoode. Pp. 226.

Hargreaves, John Desmond. _Prelude to the Partition of West Africa._ . . . See VB 1963, 421.
Rev. article by Ronald Hyam in _Historical Jour._, VII, 154-69.

Hearnshaw, Leslie Spencer. _A Short History of British Psychology 1840-1940._ New York: Barnes and Noble. Pp. xi + 331.
Rev. by D. W. Harding in _NS_, LXVIII, 122.

Heasman, Kathleen. _Evangelicals in Action._ . . . See VB 1963, 421.
Rev. by F. R. Salter in _EHR_, LXXIX, 873-74.

Heasman, Kathleen J. "The Medical Mission and the Care of the Sick Poor in Nineteenth-Century England." _Historical Jour._, VII, 230-45.

Hernon, Joseph M., Jr. "The Use of the American Civil War in the Debate over Irish Home Rule." _AHR_, LXIX, 1022-26.

Heuston, R. F. V. _Lives of the Lord Chancellors, 1885-1940._ Oxford. Pp. xxiii + 632.
Rev. by E. G. Collieu in _Listener_, 21 May, pp. 841-42.

Hibbert, Christopher. _The Court at Windsor._ London: Longmans. Pp. xx + 347.
Rev. by D. A. N. Jones in _NS_, LXVIII, 58-59; by Christopher Sykes in _S_, 3 July, p. 18.
Includes a chapter on Queen Victoria and her family.

Higham, Norman. _A Very Scientific Gentleman: The Major Achievements of Henry Clifton Sorby._ Foreword by Cyril Stanley Smith. London: Pergamon Pr. Pp. 160.
Rev. in _TLS_, 19 March, p. 236.
On a notable Victorian geologist.

Hillcourt, William, and Baden-Powell, Olave. _Baden-Powell: The Two Lives of a Hero._ London: Heinemann. Pp. x + 457.
Rev. by J. Buechler in _LJ_, LXXXIX, 4337; in _TLS_, 24 Sept., p. 878.
Soldier, founder of Boy Scouts (1857-1941).

Hinchliff, Peter. _John William Colenso, Bishop of Natal._ London: Nelson. Pp. x + 199.

Hinsley, F. H. (ed.). _The New Cambridge Modern History._ Vol. XI. _Material Progress and Worldwide Problems, 1870-1898._ . . . See VB 1963, 421.
Rev. by Arno J. Mayer in _AHR_, LXIX, 717-20; by V. G. Kiernan in _History_, XLIX, 388-91.

Hobsbawm, E. J. _The Age of Revolution (1789-1848)._ . . . See VB 1963, 422.
Rev. by George Rudé in _Science & Society_, XXVIII, 242.

Hobsbawm, E. J. *Labouring Men: Studies in the History of Labour.* London: Weidenfeld and Nicolson. Pp. viii + 401.
Rev. by A. J. P. Taylor in *NS*, LXVIII, 832.

Holloway, S. W. F. "Medical Education in England, 1830-1858." *History*, XLIX, 299-324.
Cites Thackeray, Gaskell, Trollope; throws much light on the problems of Lydgate in *Middlemarch*.

Hurst, M. C. *Joseph Chamberlain and West Midland Politics.* Dugdale Society Occasional Papers, No. 15, 1962. Pp. 72.
Rev. by N. McCord in *N&Q*, n.s. XI, 240.

Hurst, M. C. "Joseph Chamberlain, the Conservatives and the Succession to John Bright, 1886-89." *Historical Jour.*, VII, 64-93.

Huxley, Elspeth. *Back Street New Worlds: A Look at Immigrants in Britain.* London: Chatto and Windus, in association with *Punch*. Pp. 168.
Rev. in *TLS*, 3 Dec., p. 1104.

Inglis, Kenneth Stanley. *Churches and the Working Classes in Victorian England.* . . . See VB 1963, 422.
Rev. by David Owen in *AHR*, LXIX, 436-38; by James Winter in *Canadian Hist. Rev.*, XLV, 329; by W. S. Hudson in *Church Hist.*, XXXIII, 368-69; in *HJ*, LXII, 159; by I. G. Jones in *History*, XLIX, 245-46; by R. K. Webb in *JMH*, XXXVI, 210; by Stanley Pierson in *VS*, VIII, 83-85.

Jackson, John Archer. *The Irish in Britain.* . . . See VB 1963, 422.
Rev. by Herman Ausubel in *AHR*, LXIX, 1124; by E. R. R. Green in *History Today*, XIV, 291; by Julian Moynahan in *NS*, LXVI, 880.

James, Robert Rhodes. *Rosebery: A Biography.* . . . See VB 1963, 422.
Rev. by P. W. Filby in *LJ*, LXXXIX, 2078; by John Clive in *NY Rev. of Books*, 25 June, p. 15; by Lindsay Rogers in *NYTBR*, 22 March, pp. 6-7.

Jenks, Leland. *The Migration of British Capital to 1875.* London: Nelson. Pp. 442.
Rev. by G. D. N. Worswick in *NS*, LXVII, 811-12.

Jenkins, Roy. *Asquith.* London: Collins. Pp. 572.
Rev. by D. Marquand in *NS*, LXVIII, 737-38; also see letter by Margaret Cole in *NS*, LXVIII, 788.

Jenkins, Roy. "From Gladstone to Asquith: The Late Victorian Pattern of Liberal

Leadership." *History Today*, XIV, 445-52.
Estimates of character and capacities of Gladstone, Asquith, Hartington, Rosebery, Harcourt, and Campbell-Bannerman.

Jones, Howard Mumford, and Cohen, I. Bernard, with the assistance of Everett Mendelssohn (ed.). *Science Before Darwin: A Nineteenth-Century Anthology.* London: Andre Deutsch. Pp. 372.
Rev. in *TLS*, 19 March, p. 236.

Joslin, D. *A Century of Banking in Latin America.* London: Oxford Univ. Pr., 1963. Pp. xi + 307.
Rev. by A. G. Ford in *Econ. Jour.*, LXXIV, 672-74.
On the Bank of London and South America.

Kellas, James G. "The Liberal Party and the Scottish Church Disestablishment Crisis." *EHR*, LXXIX, 31-46.

Kindleberger, Charles P. *Economic Growth in France and Britain, 1851-1950.* Cambridge: Harvard Univ. Pr. Pp. viii + 378.
Rev. by P. S. Florence in *APSS*, CCCLVI, 196; in *Economist*, CCXII, 929; by H. H. Bernt in *LJ*, LXXXIX, 3003; by E. J. Hobsbawm in *NY Rev. of Books*, 25 June, p. 18.

King, A. Hyatt. *Some British Collectors of Music, c. 1600-1900.* (The Sandars lecture for 1961). London: Cambridge Univ. Pr. Pp. 177.
Rev. by P. W. Filby in *LJ*, LXXXIX, 3297-98.

King, Anthony. "George Godwin and the Art Union of London 1837-1911." *VS*, VIII, 101-30.
Godwin (1813-1888) was an architect, editor of *The Builder*, reformer and journalist as well as a tireless promoter of art.

Kingsford, P. W. "Radical Dandy: Thomas Slingsby Duncombe 1796-1861." *History Today*, XIV, 399-407.

Kitson-Clark, G. *The Making of Victorian England.* . . . See VB 1963, 423.
Rev. by David Spring in *Canadian Hist. Rev.*, XLV, 61-63; by Torben Christensen in *Jour. Eccl. Hist.*, XV, 124-25.

Knorr, K. E. *British Colonial Theories 1570-1850.* London: Frank Cass & Co., 1963. Pp. xix + 429.
Rev. by S. G. Checkland in *Econ. Jour.*, LXXIV, 708-10; by Asa Briggs in *NS*, LXVII, 218-19.

Koebner, Richard, and Schmidt, Helmut Dan. *Imperialism: The Story and Significance*

of a Political Word, 1840-1960. Cambridge Univ. Pr. Pp. xxv + 432.
Rev. by Asa Briggs in *NS*, LXVIII, 56-57; by F. H. Hinsley in *S*, 15 May, p. 666.

Krantz, Charles K. "The British Secularist Movement: A Study in Militant Dissent." *DA*, XXIV, 2946-47.

Kubie, Nora Benjamin. *Road to Nineveh: The Adventures and Excavations of Sir Austen Henry Layard.* New York: Doubleday. Pp. 324.
Rev. by Lee Ash in *LJ*, LXXXIX, 858; by C. W. Ceram in *NYTBR*, 9 Feb., p. 6; by Leonard Cottrell in *SR*, 7 Mar., p. 34.

Lambert, Royston. *Sir John Simon, 1816-1904, and English Social Administration.* . . . See VB 1963, 423.
Rev. by R. A. Lewis in *History*, XLIX, 249; by Robert M. Gutchen in *VS*, VIII, 82-83.

Lee, John Michael. *Social Leaders and Public Persons.* . . . See VB 1963, 423.
Rev. by D. C. Moore in *AHR*, LXIX, 1127-28; by B. Keith-Lucas in *VS*, VIII, 193-94.

Leetham, Claude. "Gentili's Reports to Rome." *Wiseman Rev.*, CCXXXVII, 395-415.

Lehmann, Joseph H. *All Sir Garnet. A Life of Field-Marshal Lord Wolseley.* London: Cape; Boston: Houghton-Mifflin (as *The Modern Major-General*). Pp. 415.
Rev. by John Raymond in *History Today*, XIV, 590-91; by E. G. Collieu in *Listener*, 9 July, p. 64; by V. S. Pritchett in *NS*, LXVII, 952.

Lelievre, F. J. *Cory's Lucretilis.* Cambridge: Rampant Lions Pr. Pp. 13.
Discussion of William (Johnson) Cory's book of exercises in Latin verse, published in 1871.

Levy-Leboyer, Maurice. "Quatre generations de maitres de forge gallois: les Crawshy." *Revue du nord*, XLVI, 27-50.

Lewis, Paul. *Queen of the Plaza: A Biography of Adah Isaacs Menken.* New York: Funk and Wagnalls. Pp. 307.
Rev. by G. Freedley in *LJ*, LXXXIX, 3950; by Gerald Carson in *NYTBR*, 4 Oct., p. 12.

Little, Bryan. *English Historic Architecture.* London: Batsford; New York: Hastings House. Pp. 256.
Particular emphasis on Victorian and Edwardian buildings.

Lloyd, Alan. *The Drums of Kumasi.* London: Longmans. Pp. 208.

Rev. by E. G. Collieu in *Listener*, 9 July, p. 64; by V. S. Pritchett in *NS*, LXVII, 952.

Lloyd, Christopher, and Coulter, Jack L. *Medicine and the Navy, 1200-1900.* Vol. IV:*1815-1900.* . . . See VB 1963, 423.
Rev. by T. F. Reddaway in *History*, XLIX, 400-01.

Lochhead, Marion. *The Victorian Household.* London: John Murray. Pp. x + 230.
Rev. by D. A. N. Jones in *NS*, LXVIII, 58-59.

Longford, Elizabeth. *Victoria R. I.* London: Weidenfeld and Nicholson. Pp. 635.
Rev. by Felix Markham in *History Today*, XIV, 799; by Roger Fulford in *Listener*, 1 Oct., pp. 513-14; by Anne Duchene in *Manchester Guardian Weekly*, 24 Sept., p. 10; by Paul Johnson in *NS*, LXVII, 359; by Robert Rhodes James in *S*, 2 Oct., p. 442; in *TLS*, 1 Oct., p. 898 (see also letter by Roger F. Betteridge, 29 Oct., p. 986).

Lorantas, Raymond M. "Lord Cowley's Mission to Paris, 1852-1856." *DA*, XXV, 436.

Lunt, James. " 'Bokhara' Burnes." *History Today*, XIV, 665-77.

Lunt, James. *Scarlet Lancer.* London: Hart-Davis. Pp. 223.
Rev. by Joanna Richardson in *Listener*, 18 June, pp. 1002; 05.

Mackenzie, Compton. *My Life and Times: Octave Two, 1891-1900.* . . . See VB 1963, 423.
Rev. by W. K. Seymour in *CR*, CCV, 51-52.

Magnus, Sir Philip. *King Edward the Seventh.* London: John Murray; New York: Dutton. Pp. 528.
Rev. by John Raymond in *History Today*, XIV, 260; by Lir Llewellyn Woodward in *Listener*, 19 Mar., pp. 479-80; by Neal Ascherson in *NY Rev. of Books*, 11 June, p. 10; by D. W. Brogan in *NYTBR*, 17 May, p. 1; by Paul Johnson in *NS*, LXVII, 458-60; in *TLS*, 19 Mar., p. 234.

Marshall, Aubrey. *Fishbones into Butterflies.* London: Chatto and Windus. Pp. 221.
Reminiscences of late-nineteenth-century touring theatrical company managed by the author's parents.

Masterman, N. C. *John Malcolm Ludlow, the Builder of Christian Socialism.* . . . See VB 1963, 424.
Rev. by Josef L. Altholz in *AHR*, LXIX, 508; by S. Moos in *DUJ*, XXV, 133; by Jenifer Hart in *History*, XLIX, 381-83; by David Owen in *JMH*, XXXVI, 345-46; by W. R. Ward in *Jour. Eccl. Hist.*, XV, 123-

24; by C. Torben Christensen in *VS*, VII, 320-21.

Maude, Pamela. *Worlds Away*. London: John Baker. Pp. 196.
Noticed in *TLS*, 5 Nov., p. 1005.
Reminiscences of the Victorian stage by the daughter of Cyril Maude.

McCallum, Ronald Buchanan. *The Liberal Party from Earl Grey to Asquith*. . . . See VB 1963, 424.
Rev. by Peter Fraser in *History*, XLIX, 248-49.

McClelland, Vincent Alan. *Cardinal Manning*. . . . See VB 1963, 424.
Rev. by A. Chapeau in *EHR*, LXXIX, 880-81; by Christopher Howard in *Jour. Eccl. Hist.*, XV, 267-68.

McClelland, Vincent Alan. "The Protestant Alliance and Roman Catholic Schools, 1872-74." *VS*, VIII, 173-82.

McDowell, R. B. *The Irish Administration, 1801-1914*. Toronto: Univ. of Toronto Pr.; London: Routledge and Kegan Paul. Pp. xi + 329.
Rev. by A. J. P. Taylor in *NS*, LXVIII, 90; by Robert Rhodes James in *S*, 7 Aug., p. 187; in *TLS*, 1 Oct., p. 902.

McLean, Ruari. *Victorian Book Design and Colour Printing*. . . . See VB 1963, 424.
Rev. by Joseph R. Dunlap in *VS*, VII, 314.

Medlicott, William Norton (ed.). *From Metternich to Hitler: Aspects of British and Foreign History, 1814-1939*. . . . See VB 1963, 424.
Rev. by H. M. Ehrmann in *AHR*, LXX, 100; in *Economist*, CCIX, 1344; by C. W. Crawley in *History*, XLIX, 95-96; by A. J. P. Taylor in *NS*, LXVI, 118.

Meinertzhagen, R. *Diary of a Black Sheep*. Preface by Malcolm Muggeridge. London: Oliver and Boyd. Pp. 364.
Rev. by Dan Jacobson in *NS*, LXVII, 412-13; by Patrick Anderson in *S*, 20 March, p. 388; in *TLS*, 18 June, p. 533.
Reminiscences of Spencer, Huxley, Darwin, Florence Nightingale, Burton, Rhodes, and others.

Merli, Frank J., and Green, Thomas W. "Great Britain and the Confederate Navy, 1861-1865." *History Today*, XIV, 687-95.

Middlemas, Robert. *The Master-Builders*. London: Hutchinson. Pp. 328.
Rev. by Reyner Banham in *NS*, LXVII, 216.
Four Victorian contractors: includes Thomas Brassey and Sir John Norton-Griffiths.

Millman, Richard. "British Foreign Policy and the Coming of the Franco-Prussian War." *DA*, XXV, 1163.

Milne, A. J. M. *The Social Philosophy of English Idealism*. . . . See VB 1963, 424.
Rev. by George L. Kline in *Ethics*, LXXIV, 226-27.

Mitchell, B. R. "The Coming of the Railway and United Kingdom Economic Growth." *JEH*, XXIV, 315-36.

Moore, R. J. "The Abolition of Patronage in the Indian Civil Service and the Closure of Haileybury College." *Historical Jour.*, VII, 246-57.

Morgan, Kenneth Owen. *Wales in British Politics, 1868-1922*. . . . See VB 1963, 425.
Rev. by H. J. Hanham in *History*, XLIX, 103-04.

Morison, Stanley. *The Typographical Book, 1450-1935 : A Study of Fine Typography through Five Centuries*. London: Ernest Benn, 1963; Chicago: Univ. of Chicago Pr. Pp. 98.
Rev. by F. S. Shine in *BSP*, LVIII, 490-93; by B. Katz in *LJ*, LXXXIX, 2076.

Morton, A. L. *The Life and Ideas of Robert Owen*. New York: Monthly Review Pr., 1963. Pp. 187.
Rev. by Henry Collins in *Science & Society*, XXVIII, 369.

Moseley, Maboth. *Irascible Genius: A Life of Charles Babbage, Inventor*. London: Hutchinson. Pp. 288.

Mosse, Werner Eugen. *The Rise and Fall of the Crimean System, 1855-1871*. . . . See VB 1963, 425.
Rev. by D. E. Lee in *AHR*, LXIX, 1132; in *Economist*, CCX, 1007; by Harold Kurtz in *History Today*, XIV, 427; by Barbara Jelavich in *Slavic Rev.*, XXIII, 747; in *TLS*, 12 Mar., p. 212; by Agatha Ramm in *VS*, VIII, 87-88.

Munford, William Arthur. *Edward Edwards, 1812-1886: Portrait of a Librarian*. . . . See VB 1963, 425.
Rev. in *TLS*, 9 Apr., p. 293.

Neill, Stephen. *The Interpretation of the New Testament, 1861-1961*. London: Oxford Univ. Pr. Pp. 358.
Rev. by S. Johnson in *LJ*, LXXXIX, 3164; in *TLS*, 4 June, p. 492.

Nelson, Walter D. "British Rational Secularism: Unbelief from Bradlaugh to the Mid-Twentieth Century." *DA*, XXIV, 4659-60.

New Horizons: A Hundred Years of Women's Migration. . . . See VB 1963, 425.

Rev. by Helen F. Mulvey in *AHR*, LXX, 236-37; by J. A. Banks in *VS*, VIII, 88-89.

Northcott, Cecil. "Countryman Cleric: James Morton of Holbeach." *CR*, CCV, 599-601.

Excerpts from the MS. diaries of a Victorian clergyman, 1837-1850.

O'Brien, Terence H. "Lord Milner's Irish Journal 1886." *History Today*, XIV, 43-51

Milner's doubts about Home Rule and his hopes for Land Purchase.

O'Neill, James E. "Finding a Policy for the Sick Poor." *VS*, VII, 265-84.

Various attempts from 1834 to 1860's to care for the sick poor.

Oram, R. B. "The Great Strike of 1889: The Fight for the 'Dockers' Tanner.'" *History Today*, XIV, 532-41.

Orwin, Christabel Susan, and Whetham, Edith Holt. *A History of British Agriculture, 1846-1914.* London: Longmans. Pp. xx + 411.

Rev. in *TLS*, 29 Oct., p. 983.

Parker, Wyman W. *Henry Stevens of Vermont: American Rare Book Dealer in London, 1845-1886.* Amsterdam: N. Israel, 1963, Pp. 348.

Rev. by John Alden in *NEQ*, XXXVII, 424-26.

Parnaby, Owen W. *Britain and the Labor Trade in the Southwest Pacific.* Durham: Univ. of North Carolina Pr. Pp. xviii + 234.

Pelling, Henry. *A History of British Trade Unionism.* . . . See VB 1963, 426.

Rev. by H. W. McCready in *AHR*, LXIX, 1046-47; by Sidney Pollard in *History*, XLIX, 100-01; by Philip Rappaport in *LJ*, LXXXIX, 258; by Asa Briggs in *NS*, LXVI, 620.

Pemberton, William Baring. *Battles of the Boer War.* London: Batsford. Pp. 216.

Rev. by R. Taubman in *NS*, LXVII, 958; by Robert Kee in *S*, 17 July, pp. 88-89; in *TLS*, 4 June, p. 676.

Pence, James W. "The Rhetoric of British Civil Service Reform: 1848-1870." *DA*, XXIV, 3882.

Perham, Margery, and Bull, Mary (eds.). *The Diaries of Lord Lugard.* Vol. IV: *Nigeria 1894-5 and 1898.* . . . See VB 1963, 426.

Rev. by Arthur N. Cook in *JMH*, XXXVI, 96-97.

Perham, Margery and Simmons, J. (eds.). *African Discovery: An Anthology of Exploration.* Evanston, Ill.: Northwestern

Univ. Pr., 1963. Pp. 280.

Rev. by L. Barron in *LJ*, LXXXIX, 863.

An anthology of excerpts from the writings of ten British explorers of Africa, 1769-1873.

Pollock, John Charles. *Moody without Sankey.* . . . See VB 1963, 426.

Rev. by F. E. Luchs in *Christian Century*, LXXX, 1550; by R. W. Schwarz in *LJ*, LXXXVIII, 774; by C. W. Ferguson in *NYTBR*, 14 Apr., p. 30.

Pool, Phoebe. *John Constable.* New York: Barnes and Noble; London: Blandford. Pp. 90.

Pope-Hennessy, James. *Verandah: Some Episodes in the Crown Colonies, 1867-1889.* New York: Knopf; London: Allen and Unwin. Pp. 313.

Rev. by Harry A. Gailey, Jr. in *AHR*, LXX, 237; by Eric Britter in *Book Week*, 12 Apr., p. 23; in *Economist*, CCXI, 847; by Roger Fulford in *Listener*, 30 Jan., p. 203; by R. R. Rea in *LJ*, LXXXIX, 1599; by D. A. N. Jones in *NS*, LXVII, 135; by Patrick Anderson in *S*, 21 Feb., p. 256; in *TLS*, 30 Jan., p. 84.

Pulling, Christopher. *Mr. Punch and the Police.* Foreword by A. P. Herbert. London: Butterworth.

The police as seen by *Punch* cartoonists over the past 120 years.

Punnett, R. M. "The Parliamentary and Personal Backgrounds of British Prime Ministers, 1812 to 1963." *QR* (Jul.), pp. 254-66.

Includes useful tables.

Raymond, John (ed.). *The Reminiscences and Recollections of Captain Gronow, being Anecdotes of the Camp, the Court, the Clubs and Society from 1810-1860.* London: Bodley Head. Pp. 384.

Rev. by V. S. Pritchett in *NS*, LXVIII, 324; by Patrick Anderson in *S*, 21 Aug., p. 248; in *TLS*, 10 Sept., p. 836.

Read, Donald. *The English Provinces, c. 1760-1960: A Study in Influence.* London: Edward Arnold, Pp. xi + 319.

Rev. by Anthony Howard in *Listener*, p. 97; by Geoffrey Moorhouse in *Manchester Guardian Weekly*, 30 July, p. 10; in *TLS*, 30 July, pp. 657-58.

Reader, W. J. *Life in Victorian England.* London: Batsford. Pp. xv + 176.

Rev. by D. A. N. Jones in *NS*, LXVIII, 58-59; noticed favorably in *TLS*, 9 July, p. 618.

Reed, John R. *Old School Ties: The Public Schools in British Literature.* Syracuse, N.

Y.: Syracuse Univ. Pr. Pp. xiv + 330.

Reid, James M. *James Lithgow, Master of Work*. London: Hutchinson. Pp. 255.
Rev. by R. Banham in *NS*, LXVII, 216.

Roads, Christopher Herbert. *The British Soldier's Firearm, 1850-1864*. London: Herbert Jenkins, Pp. 332.

Robin, A. de Q. "Bishop Perry and Lay Representation in Colonial Synods." *Jour. Eccl. Hist.*, XV, 51-59.

Robinson, Howard. *Carrying British Mails Overseas*. New York: New York Univ. Pr. Pp. 327.

Robinson, Ronald, Gallagher, John, and Denny, Alice. *Africa and the Victorians*. . . . See VB 1963, 426.
Rev. article by Ronald Hyam in *Historical Jour.*, VII, 154-69.

Rodríguez, Mario. "The 'Prometheus' and the Clayton-Bulwer Treaty." *JMH*, XXXVI, 260-78.

Ross, Angus. *New Zealand Aspirations in the Pacific in the Nineteenth Century*. Oxford: Clarendon Pr. Pp. xi + 332.
Rev. in *TLS*, 26 Nov., p. 1055.

Rothenstein, John, and Butlin, Martin. *Turner*. London: Heinemann. Pp. 94.
Rev. by Nevile Wallis in *S*, 20 Nov., p. 680.

Sanderson, G. N. "England, Italy, the Nile Valley and the European Balance, 1890-91." *Historical Jour.*, VII, 94-119.

Saunders, John Whiteside. *The Profession of English Letters*. London: Routledge and Kegan Paul; Toronto: Univ. of Toronto Pr. Pp. viii + 239.

Scherer, Paul H. "British Policy with Respect to the Unification of Germany, 1848-1871." *DA*, XXIV, 5366-67.

Schmutzler, Robert. *Art Nouveau*. Tr. by Edouard Roditi. London: Thames and Hudson. Pp. 322.
Rev. in *TLS*, 15 Oct., pp. 929-31.

Schoonderwoerd, N. H. G. *J. T. Grein: Ambassador of the Theatre, 1862-1935: A Study in Anglo-Continental Relations*. Assen: Van Gorcum, 1963. Pp. vi + 356.
Rev. by G. W. Brandt in *MLR*, LIX, 653-54; by Marjorie Thompson in *Theatre Notebook*, XVIII, 69-71.

Semmel, Bernard. *The Governor Eyre Controversy*. . . . See VB 1962, 396. (Published in U.S. as *Jamaican Blood and Victorian Conscience;* Boston: Houghton, Mifflin.)

Rev. in *VQR*, XL, xxxviii; by W. L. Burn in *VS*, VII, 406-07; by David Owen in *YR*, LIII, 279-82.

Shannon, R. T. *Gladstone and the Bulgarian Agitation, 1876*. . . . See VB 1963, 427.
Rev. by A. J. P. Taylor in *NS*, LXVII, 296-98; by M. R. D. Foot in *VS*, VII, 405-06.

Singh, Hira Lal. *Problems and Policies of the British in India, 1885-1898*. . . . See VB 1963, 427.
Rev. by M. D. Lewis in *AHR*, LXIX, 537; by C. Collin Davies in *History*, XLIX, 277-78; by A. T. Embree in *PSQ*, LXXIX, 319.

Southgate, Donald. *The Passing of the Whigs, 1832-1886*. . . . See VB 1963, 427.
Rev. by James Winter in *Canadian Historical Rev.*, XLV, 60-61.

Spinner, Thomas J., Jr. "George Joachim Goschen 1831-1907: British Statesman and Politician." *DA*, XXV, 2954-55.

Spring, David. *The English Landed Estate in the Nineteenth Century*. . . . See VB 1963, 427.
Rev. by David Roberts in *AHR*, LXIX, 507-08; by F. M. L. Thompson in *History*, XLIX, 383-84; by R. K. Webb in *JMH*, XXXVI, 81-82.

Spry, Irene M. *The Palliser Expedition: An Account of John Palliser's British North American Expedition 1857-1860*. New York: St. Martins. Pp. 310.
Rev. by L. G. Thomas in *AHR*, LXX, 236; in *TLS*, 28 May, p. 459.

Stacey, Colonel C. P. *Canada and the British Army, 1846-1871*. Toronto: Univ. of Toronto Pr., 1963. Pp. xiv + 293.
Rev. by D. J. Goodspeed in *Dalhousie Rev.*, XLIV, 249-53.

Staff, Frank. *The Penny Post, 1680-1918*. London: Lutterworth Pr. Pp. 219.
Rev. in *TLS*, 14 May, p. 411.

Stafford, Ann. *The Age of Consent*. London: Hodder and Stoughton. Pp. 256.
Rev. by Perrott Phillips in *CR*, CCV, 388; by N. MacKenzie in *NS*, LXVIII, 251-52. On the trial of W. T. Stead, 1885.

Stansky, Peter. *Ambitions and Strategies: The Struggle for the Leadership of the Liberal Party in the 1890's*. New York: Oxford Univ. Pr. Pp. xvi + 312.
Rev. by D. Marquand in *NS*, LXVIII, 737-38.

St. Aubyn, Giles. *The Royal George, 1819-1904: The Life of H. R. H. Prince George, Duke of Cambridge*. . . . See VB 1963,

427.
Rev. by K. T. Willis in *LJ*, LXXXIX, 3738-39.

Starkie, Walter. *Scholars and Gypsies: An Autobiography*. Univ. of California Pr., 1963. Pp. 324.
Rev. by L. W. Griffin in *LJ*, LXXXIX, **624**.
Includes vignettes on Yeats and other late 19th-century figures.

Steen, Marguerite. *A Pride of Terrys*. . . . See VB 1962, 397.
Rev. by Jean-Claude Amalric in *Études anglaises*, XVII, 201-02.

Tabler, Edward C. (ed.). *The Zambèsi Papers of Richard Thornton, 1858-1863*. London: Chatto and Windus. Pp. xxii + 360.
Rev. by David Wright in *Listener*, 23 Apr., p. 691; in *TLS*, 12 March, p. 211.
Papers of a member of Livingstone's expedition.

Tawney, R. H. *The Radical Tradition: Twelve Essays on Politics, Education, and Literature*. Ed. by Rita Hinden. London: Allen and Unwin. Pp. 214.
Rev. by Margaret Cole in *Listener*, 5 Mar., p. 401; by Ralph Miliband in *S*, 27 Mar., p. 422; in *TLS*, 27 Feb., p. 159.
Includes essays on Owen, Ruskin, and William Lovett.

Thompson, Edward Palmer. *The Making of the English Working Class*. . . . See VB 1963, 428.
Rev. by John Gross in *NY Rev. of Books*, 16 Apr., p. 8; by Herman Ausubel in *NYTBR*, 26 Apr., p. 44; by David V. Erdman in *VS*, VIII, 183-85.

Thompson, Francis Michael Longstreth. *English Landed Society in the Nineteenth Century*. . . . See VB 1963, 428.
Rev. by Mildred Campbell in *AHR*, LXIX, 747-48; by H. W. McCready in *Canadian Hist. Rev.*, XLV, 341-43; by J. D. Chambers in *Economica*, XXXI, 330-31; by S. Pollard in *Econ. Jour.*, LXXIV, 211-13; by W. L. Burn in *History*, XLIX, 243-45; by David Owen in *JMH*, XXXVI, 343-44; by John Clive in *JPE*, LXXII, 421-22.

Thompson, Paul. "The Victorian Society." *VS*, VII, 387-92.
Account of founding (in 1958) and purposes of a society concerned with study of Victorian culture, especially architecture.

Thomson, Sir George. *J. J. Thomson and the Cavendish Laboratory in His Day*. London: Nelson. Pp. xi + 186.

Thornley, David. *Isaac Butt and Home Rule*. London: MacGibbon and Kee. Pp. 413.

Rev. by Robert Rhodes James in *S*, 7 Aug., p. 187; by E. G. Collieu in *History*, XLIX, 393; in *TLS*, 16 July, p. 629.

Tracy, M. *Agriculture in Western Europe: Crises and Adaptation Since 1880*. London: Jonathan Cape. Pp. 415.
Rev. by H. Frankel in *Econ. Jour.*, LXXIV, 990-92.

Tryon, W. S. *Parnassus Corner: A Life of James T. Fields, Publisher to the Victorians*. . . . See VB 1963, 428.
Rev. by Edward Weeks in *AM*, CCXIV, No. 7, 131-32; by G. Thomas Tanselle in *BB*, XXIV, 60; by Conrad Tanzy in *Journal of American History*, LI, 313-14; by Paul C. Wermuth in *NEQ*, XXXVII, 106-08.

Turner, H. A. *Trade Union Growth, Structure, and Policy*. . . . See VB 1963, 428.
Rev. by Irving Bernstein in *JEH*, XXIV, **117**.

Turrill, W. B. *Joseph Dalton Hooker: Botanist, Explorer, and Administrator*. London: Nelson. Pp. xi + 228.
Rev. in *TLS*, 26 Mar., p. 253.

Tyler, Warwick P. N. "Sir Frederic Rogers, Permanent Under-Secretary at the Colonial Office, 1860-1871." *DA*, XXIV, 4167.

Vidler, A. R. *A Century of Social Catholicism, 1820-1920*. London: S.P.C.K. Pp. xii + 171.
Rev. by Neville Masterman in *History*, XLIX, 378.

Wagenknecht, Edward. *Seven Daughters of the Theatre*. Norman: Oklahoma Univ. Pr. Pp. 264.
Includes chapters on Jenny Lind and Ellen Terry.

Wakefield, Hugh. *Victorian Pottery*. . . . See VB 1963, 429.
Rev. by Kenneth Garlick in *VS*, VII, 311-12.

Ward, David. *The Shortest Route to Paradise: The Story of the Master Criminal, Charles Peace*. New York: Horizon. Pp. 176.
Rev. by M. K. Grant in *LJ*, LXXXIX, 3002.

Ward, John Trevor. *The Factory Movement, 1830-1855*. . . . See VB 1963, 428.
Rev. by John Roach in *EHR*, LXXIX, 623-24; by W. L. Burn in *Historical Jour.*, VII, 179-80; by George W. Hilton in *JEH*, XXIV, 286.

Ward, Stephen G. P. *Wellington*. London: Batsford, 1963, Pp. 152.
Rev. by C. S. Bennett in *NS*, LXVII, 17.

Wardle, Patricia. *Victorian Silver and Silver-Plate.* . . . See VB 1963, 429.
Rev. by Paul von Khrum in *LJ*, LXXXIX, 855; in *TLS*, 23 Jan., p. 60.

Watt, E. D. "Ethics and Politics: the Example of Lord Acton." *TQ*, XXXIII, 279-90.

Watson, William. "The Namamugi Incident, 1862." *History Today*, XIV, 318-25.

Webb, Beatrice. *Beatrice Webb's American Diary, 1898.* . . . See VB 1963, 429.
Rev. in *Economica*, XXXI, 224.

Welcome, John. *Cheating at Cards.* . . . See VB 1963, 429.
Rev. by Anthony Boucher in *NYTBR*, 12 July, p. 12.

Wiggins, Arch R. *The History of the Salvation Army.* Vol. IV: *1886-1904*. London: Nelson. Pp. xvi + 410.
Rev. in *TLS*, 14 May, p. 411; by Howard R. Murphy in *VS*, VIII, 185-86.
Continuation of a history begun by Robert Sandall in 1947.

Wilkinson, Rupert. *Gentlemanly Power: British Leadership and the Public School Tradition: A Comparative Study in the Making of Rulers.* New York: Oxford Univ. Pr. Pp. xv + 243.
Rev. by John Clive in *AHR*, LXIX, 1045-46; by C. L. Mowat in *APSS*, CCCLVI, 172; by A. H. Halsey in *Manchester Guardian Weekly*, 6 Feb., p. 10; by Francis Williams in *NYTBR*, 15 Mar., p. 10; in *TLS*, 6 Feb., p. 109; by Noel Annan in *VS*, VIII, 194-95; by Raymond English in *YR*, LIII, 114-17.

Winther, Oscar O. "English Migration to the American West 1865-1900." *HLQ*, XXVII, 159-73.

Wise, Dorothy and Cox-Johnson, Ann. *Diary of William Taylor, Footman, 1837.* The St. Marlybone Soc. Pub. Group, Pub. No. 7, 1962. Pp. 63.
Rev. by Derek Hudson in *N&Q*, n.s. XI, 39-40.

Wolff, Michael. "Victorian Study: An interdisciplinary Essay." *VS*, VIII, 59-70.

Woodham-Smith, Cecil. *The Great Hunger: Ireland 1845-1849.* . . . See VB 1963, 429.
Rev. by F. S. L. Lyons in *Irish Hist. Studies*, XIV, 77-79; by E. A. J. Johnson in *JEH*, XXIV, 120.

Wyndham, Violet. *The Sphinx and Her Circle: A Biographical Sketch of Ada Leverson, 1862-1933.* New York: Vanguard. Pp. 128.
Rev. by K. T. Willis in *LJ*, LXXXIX, 3741;

by John Gross in *NS*, LXV, 901; by H. T. Moore in *SR*, 24 Oct., p. 74; in *TLS*, 3 May, 1963, p. 326.

III. MOVEMENTS OF IDEAS AND LITERARY FORMS

Ball, Patricia M. "Sincerity: the Rise and Fall of a Critical Term." *MLR*, LIX, 1-11.
Carlyle's criterion traced through its gradual debasement in the twentieth century.

Barker, Kathleen M. D. "The Theatre Proprietors' Story." *Theatre Notebook*, XVIII, 79-91.
An account of the Theatre Royal, Bristol, from its inception in 1764, based on recovered documents and related accounts.

Barron, Diana. "The Royal West London Theatre." *Theatre Notebook*, XVIII, 126.
Some additions to Malcolm Morley's history; see *VB*, 1963, 431.

Beebe, Maurice. *Ivory Towers and Sacred Founts: The Artist as Hero in Fiction from Goethe to Joyce.* New York: N.Y. Univ. Pr. Pp. x + 323.
Rev. by L. W. Griffin in *LJ*, LXXXIX, 3314; by R. M. Adams in *NY Rev. of Books*, 22 Oct., p. 19; in *TLS*, 1 Oct., p. 900.
Includes material on Dickens, Wilde, and Conrad.

Bentley, Eric. *The Life of the Drama.* New York: Atheneum Pr. Pp. 371.
Rev. by Richard Gilman in *Book Week*, 4 Oct., p. 14; by H. A. Zeiger in *Harper's*, Oct., p. 134; by Clancy Sigal in *NewR*, 26 Sept., p. 20; by John Gassner in *NYTBR*, 11 Oct., p. 6; by Norris Houghton in *SR*, 10 Oct., p. 64.
Contains material on Shaw.

Benziger, James. *Images of Eternity: Studies in the Poetry of Religious Vision from Wordsworth to T. S. Eliot.* . . . See VB 1963, 430.
Rev. by Edward E. Bostetter in *SeR*, LXXII, 545-48.

Booth, Michael R. "The Drunkard's Progress: Nineteenth-Century Temperance Drama." *Dalhousie Rev.*, XLIV, 205-12.

Bose, Amalendu. *Chroniclers of Life.* Bombay: Orient Longmans, 1962. Pp. xiii + 313.
Essays on *Pauline*, the verse of the English annuals, the Victorian verse-novel, *In Memoriam*, and socially conscious poetry.

Brustein, Robert. *The Theater of Revolt: An Approach to the Modern Drama.* Boston:

Little, Pp. 435.
Rev. by Richard Gilman in *Book Week*, 4 Oct., p. 5; by C. A. Raines in *LJ*, LXXXIX, 3768; by Nigel Dennis in *NY Rev. of Books*, 22 Oct., p. 10; by Alex Szogyi in *NYTBR*, 11 Oct., p. 6; by Norris Houghton in *SR*, 10 Oct., p. 64.
Contains material on Shaw.

Cockshut, A. O. J. *The Unbelievers: English Agnostic Thought, 1840-1890.* London: Collins. Pp. 192.
Rev. by Basil Willey in *Critical Quart.*, VI, 279-80; by Raymond Williams in *Manchester Guardian Weekly*, 16 July, p. 11; by John Gross in *NS*, LXVIII, 88-89; by Robin Denniston in *S*, 24 July, p. 115; in *TLS*, 15 Oct., p. 932.

Cooke, Deryck. "Delius the Unknown." In *Proceedings of the Royal Musical Association*: 89th Session, 1962-63. London: Royal Musical Assoc., 1963. Pp. 124.
Rev. by M. Tilmouth in *M&L*, XLV, 160-63.

Davies, Hugh Sykes. *The English Mind: Studies in the English Moralists Presented to Basil Willey.* New York: Cambridge Univ. Pr. Pp. viii + 302.
Rev. by C. Ricks in *NS*, LXVIII, 663.
Contains "Coleridge and the Victorians," by Graham Hough, pp. 175-92; "Newman and the Romantic Sensibility," by John Beer, pp. 193-218; "John Stuart Mill," by Noel Annan, pp. 219-39; "Matthew Arnold and the Continental Idea," by Heinrich Straumann, pp. 240-56; and "Joseph Conrad: Alienation and Commitment," by Ian Watt, pp. 257-78.

Davis, Frank. *Victorian Patrons of the Arts.* London: Country Life, 1963. Pp. 158.
Rev. by M. Levey in *NS*, LXVII, 52-53.

Day, Martin Steele. *History of English Literature 1837 to the Present.* Garden City, N. Y.: Doubleday. Pp. 442.

Dobrée, Bonamy (ed.). *British Writers and Their Work.* Vol. II. Lincoln: Univ. of Nebraska Pr. Pp. 120.
Rev. by Marlies K. Danziger in *CE*, XXVI, 245.
Includes Maurice Cranston, "John Stuart Mill"; Kenneth Allott, "Matthew Arnold"; William Irvine, "Thomas Henry Huxley."

Drew, Elizabeth. *The Literature of Gossip: Nine English Letterwriters.* New York: Norton. Pp. 256.
Rev. by B. W. Fuson in *LJ*, LXXXIX, 4537.
Among the nine are Jane Carlyle and Edward FitzGerald.

Drew, Elizabeth. *The Novel: A Modern Guide to Fifteen English Masterpieces.*

New York: Norton. Pp. 287.
Rev. by Melvin Maddocks in *Christian Science Monitor*, 13 Feb., p. 5.
Contains essays on *Vanity Fair, The Mill on the Floss, Far from the Madding Crowd, Lord Jim, Wuthering Heights,* and *Great Expectations.*

Fairchild, Hoxie Neal. *Religious Trends in English Poetry.* Vol. V: *1880-1920, Gods of a Changing Poetry.* . . . See VB 1963, 430.
Rev. by E. D. Mackerness in *MLR*, LIX, 470-71; by Frederick P. W. McDowell in *PQ*, XLIII, 567-73; by Kenneth Allott in *RES*, n.s. XV, 106-07.

Forsyth, R. A. "The Myth of Nature and the Victorian Compromise of the Imagination." *ELH*, XXXI, 213-40.

Gressman, Malcolm G. "The Career of John Baldwin Buckstone." *DA*, XXIV, 4862-63.
Popular 19th-century comedian.

Gross, Harvey. *Sound and Form in Modern Poetry: A Study of Prosody from Thomas Hardy to Robert Lowell.* Ann Arbor: Univ. of Michigan Pr. Pp. 346.
Rev. by Ben W. Fuson in *LJ*, LXXXIX, 4807-08.

Hayward, John (ed.). *The Oxford Book of Nineteenth-Century English Verse.* Oxford: Clarendon Pr.; New York: Oxford Univ. Pr. Pp. xxxv + 969.
Rev. by Aileen Ward in *NYTBR*, 16 Aug., p. 1; by Graham Hough in *S*, 10 July, pp. 53-54; in *TLS*, 25 June, p. 550.

Hardy, Barbara. *The Appropriate Form: An Essay on the Novel.* . . . London: Athlone Pr. Pp. 218.
Rev. in *TLS*, 31 Dec., p. 1177.
Includes discussions of Charlotte Brontë, Eliot, Meredith, and Hardy.

Harris, Katharine S. "The New Woman in the Literature of the 1890's: Four Critical Approaches." *DA*, XXIV, 4678-79.

Henry, Donald R. "The American Theatre as Viewed by 19th-Century British Travellers, 1860-1900." *DA*, XXIV, 4313.

Hollingsworth, Keith. *The Newgate Novel, 1830-1847.* . . . See VB 1963, 430.
Rev. by Arthur C. Young in *Criticism*, VI, 192; by John L. Bradley in *JEGP*, LXIII, 816-18; by Victor Brombert in *YR*, LIII, 443-47.

James, Louis. *Fiction for the Working Man, 1830-1870.* . . . See VB 1963, 431.
Rev. by J.-P. Hulin in *Études anglaises*, XVIII, 85; by Richard D. Altick in *JEGP*, LXIII, 529-31; by Angela Hookham in *MLR*, LIX, 282-83; review article by

Robert A. Colby in *NCF*, XIX, 91-95; rev. by Vereen M. Bell in *Studies in Short Fiction*, I, 295-99.

Jewett, Iran Banu Hassani. "Kinglake and the English Travelogue of the Nineteenth Century." *DA*, XXV, 2961-62.

King, A. Hyatt. *Some British Collectors of Music*. London: Cambridge Univ. Pr., 1963. Pp. xvi + 178.
Rev. by A. Rosenthal in *M&L*, XLV, 258-60.

Kohn, Hans. *Reflections on Modern History: The Historian and Human Responsibility*. Princeton, N.J.: Van Nostrand, 1963. Pp. 360.
Rev. by W. J. Dannhauser in *Commentary*, XXXVII, 92.
Contains an essay on Bagehot.

Levy, F. J. "The Founding of the Camden Society." *VS*, VII, 295-305.

Lombard, C. M. "Anglo-American Protestantism and Lamartine." *Revue de littérature comparée*, XXXVII (1963), 540-49.

Ludwig, Hans-Werner. *Die Self-Komposita bei Thomas Carlyle, Matthew Arnold, und Gerard Manley Hopkins: Untersuchungen zum geistigen Gehalt einer sprachlichen Form*. Tübingen: Max Niemeyer Verlag, 1963. Pp. xvi + 244.

Mackerness, E. D. "Edward Holmes (1797-1859)." *M&L*, XLV, 213-27.
A music critic whose best book is on Mozart.

MacLure, Millar, and Watt, F. W. (eds.). *Essays in English Literature from the Renaissance to the Victorian Age, Presented to A. S. P. Woodhouse*. Univ. of Toronto Pr.; London: Oxford Univ. Pr. Pp. 339.
Rev. in *TLS*, 17 Dec., p. 1146.

Mandel, Oscar (ed.). *The Theatre of Don Juan: A Collection of Plays and Views, 1630-1963*. Lincoln: Univ. of Nebraska Pr., 1963. Pp. x + 731.
Rev. by W. I. Oliver in *QJS*, L, 329-30.

Marcus, Steven. "Mr. Acton of Queen Anne Street, or, the Wisdom of Our Ancestors." *Par R*. XXXI, 201-30.
Part of a study of writings about sex and sexuality in mid-nineteenth-century England.

Meiss, Millard, et al. (eds.). *Studies in Western Art: Acts of the Twentieth International Congress of the History of Art*. Vol. IV. *Problems of the 19th and 20th Centuries*. Princeton: Princeton Univ. Pr. Pp.

218.

Miller, Joseph Hillis. *The Disappearance of God: Five Nineteenth-Century Writers*.
. . . See VB 1963, 431.
Rev. by Louis Crompton in *CE*, XXV, 634; by Sydney Mendel in *Dalhousie Rev.*, XLIV, 107-09; by Boyd Litzinger in *JEGP*, LXIII, 818-20; by Basil Willey in *MLR*, LIX, 467-68; by Paul de Man in *ParR*, XXI, 640; by Griffin Taylor in *SeR*, LXXII, 698-09; in *TLS*, 27 Feb., p. 168; in *VQR*, XL, xvii; by Sybil Oldfield in *VS*, VIII, 195-96; by A. Dwight Culler in *YR*, LIII, 440-43.

Mizener, Arthur. *The Sense of Life in the Modern Novel*. Boston: Houghton, 1962. Pp. 291.
Rev. by Richard Poirier in *Book Week*, 2 Feb., p. 4; by R. C. LeClair in *Christian Science Monitor*, 30 Jan., p. 5; by Benjamin DeMott in *Harper's*, Feb., p. 114; by B. W. Fuson in *LJ*, LXXXVIII, 4645; by Marvin Mudrick in *NY Rev. of Books*, 23 Jan., p. 5; by Walter Allen in *NYTBR*, 2 Feb., p. 4; by Granville Hicks in *SR*, 18 Jan., p. 29.
Includes discussion of Trollope and Hardy.

Morley, Malcolm. "The First Strand Theatre." *Theatre Notebook*, XVIII, 100-02.

Morley, Malcolm and Speaight, George. "The Minor Theatre in Catherine Street." *Theatre Notebook*, XVIII, 117-20; XIX, 29.
A brief history of one of London's private theatres.

Munro, Thomas. *Evolution in the Arts and Other Theories of Culture History*. Cleveland: The Cleveland Museum of Art, 1963. Pp. xxxi + 562.
Rev. by Herbert M. Schueller in *Criticism*, VI, 178-80.
Contains a treatment of Spencer.

Ogilvie, R. M. *Latin and Greek: A History of the Influence of the Classics on English Life from 1600 to 1918*. Routledge and Kegan Paul. Pp. 189.
Rev. by Hugh Lloyd-Jones in *Listener*, 25 June, p. 1041.

Peck, Kenneth M. "The Oxford Controversy in America: 1839." *Historical Magazine of the Protestant Episcopal Church*, XXXIII, 49-63.

Peckham, Morse. *Beyond the Tragic Vision*.
. . . See VB 1963, 432.
Rev. by Earl Rovit in *Books Abroad*, XXXVIII, 189; by Raymond Immerwahr in *The German Quart.*, XXXVII, 75-78; by Richard Tobias in *Vict. Poetry*, II, 211-13.

Pelles, Geraldine. *Art, Artists, and Society: Origins of a Modern Dilemma: Painting in England and France, 1750-1850.* Englewood Cliffs: Prentice-Hall, 1963. Pp. 180.
Rev. by Delores McColm in *LJ*, LXXXIX, 1075; by Francis Haskell in *NY Rev. of Books*, 11 June, p. 17.

Pitts, Gordon. "Lord de Tabley: Poet of Frustration." *W. Va. Univ. Bull. Philological Papers*, XIV, 57-73.

Priestley, J. B. *Margin Released.* London: Heinemann, 1963. Pp. 236.
Rev. by G. Nigot in *Études anglaises*, XVII, 303-04.

Pritchett, V. S. *The Living Novel and Later Appreciations.* New York: Random House. Pp. 467.
Rev. by John Gross in *Book Week*, 5 July, p. 4; by Leon Edel in *NewR*, 8 Aug., p. 26; by Steven Marcus in *NY Rev. of Books*, 8 Oct., p. 12; by R. W. B. Lewis in *NYTBR*, 5 July, p. 6; by Granville Hicks in *SR*, 27 June, p. 23.

San Juan, E., Jr. "Toward a Definition of Victorian Activism." *St. in English Lit.*, IV, 583-600.

Shelley, Phillip Allison, with Lewis, Arthur O., Jr. (eds.). *Anglo-German and American-German Crosscurrents.* Vol. II. Chapel Hill: Univ. of North Carolina Pr., 1962. Pp. 312.
Rev. by Karl J. R. Arndt in *JEGP*, LXII, 821-22; by Harry Tucker, Jr., in *MLN*, LXXIX, 472-73; by Ann C. Weaver in *MLR*, LVIII, 288.
Includes articles on Borrow and Shaw.

Simon, W. M. "Auguste Comte's English Disciples." *VS*, VIII, 161-72.
Among the disciples: Richard Congreve, E. S. Beesly, and Frederic Harrison.

Simon, Walter Michael. *European Positivism in the Nineteenth Century.* . . . See VB 1963, 432.
Rev. by W. W. Wagar in *AHR*, LXIX, 739; by F. N. House in *APSS*, CCCLIV, 194; by Jack Lively in *History*, XLIX, 377-78; by George L. Mosse in *JMH*, XXXVI, 346-47; by Royden Harrison in *VS*, 397-99.

Sontag, Susan. "Notes on 'Camp.'" *ParR.*, XXXI, 515-30.
An art movement with some basis in art nouveau and Oscar Wilde.

Sowder, William J. "Emerson's Rationalist Champions: A Study in British Periodicals." *NEQ*, XXXVII, 147-70.
Defense of Emerson in the secularist and theosophical press.

Stevenson, Lionel (ed.). *Victorian Fiction: A Guide to Research.* Cambridge: Harvard Univ. Pr. Pp. 440.
Rev. by Lawrence Poston, III in *CE*, XXVI, 244.

Stewart, John James Mackintosh. *Eight Modern Writers.* . . . See VB 1963, 432.
Rev. in *Economist*, CCVIII, 593; by Hermann Paschmann in *English*, XV, 26; by Edward H. Davidson in *JEGP*, LXIII, 825; by M. J. Friedman in *Mod. Lang. Jour.*, XLVIII, 116; by John Simon in *ParR*, XXI, 632; by J. O. Bailey in *SAQ*, LXIII, 440-42; in *TLS*, 30 Aug., 1963, p. 649; in *VQR*, XL, xxi.

St. John-Stevas, Norman. "Science and Faith." *Wiseman Rev.*, CCXXXVIII, 138-46.

Stone, George Winchester. "The British Theatre Museum." *Theatre Notebook*, XVIII, 49-51.
Brief description of holdings, which fall into two main categories: documents and properties.

Sutton, Denys. *Nocturne: The Art of James McNeill Whistler.* . . . See VB 1963, 432.
Rev. by Francis Haskell in *NY Rev. of Books*, 3 Dec., p. 29; by M. Levey in *NS*, LXVII, 52-53.

Tener, Robert H. "Spectatorial Strachey." *TLS*, 31 Dec., p. 1181.
Dramatic criticism in the *Spectator* during R. H. Hutton's editorship.

Thomas, Alfred, " 'The Month' — Attribution of Articles." *N&Q*, n.s. XI, 235.

Thomson, Arthur. "The Philosophy of J. F. Ferrier." *Philosophy*, XXXIX, 46-62.

Thwaite, M. F. *From Primer to Pleasure: An Introduction to the History of Children's Books in England from the Invention of Printing to 1900.* London: Library Association, 1963. Pp. x + 318.
Rev. by Harriet G. Long in *LQ*, XXXIV, 216-17.

"Victoriana: Living? Or Laid Up in Lavender." *TLS*, 9 July, p. 600.
On the children's stories of Juliana Horatia Ewing.

Wain, John. *Essays on Literature and Ideas.* . . . See VB 1963, 432.
Rev. by Paul Pickrel in *Book Week*, 26 Apr., p. 15, by Timothy Rogers in *English*, XV, 27; by J. Loiseau in *Études anglaises*, XVII, 300; by Robert Dumas in *LJ*, LXXXIX, iii; by Francis Hope in *NS*, LXVI, 616; by Lionel Stevenson in *SAQ*, LXIII, 447-48; by Granville Hicks in *SR*, 14 Dec., 1963, p. 39; by Martin Price in *YR*, LIII, 597.

Weintraub, Stanley (ed.). *The Yellow Book: Quintessence of the Nineties.* New York: Doubleday-Anchor. Pp. 373.
Rev. by A. L. Fessler in *LJ*, LXXXIX, 4539; by Frank Kermode in *NYTBR*, 25 Oct., p. 22.

White, James F. *The Cambridge Movement.* . . . See VB 1963, 432.
Rev. by Leland H. Carlson in *AHR*, LXX, 235-36.

Wright, David (ed.). *Seven Victorian Poets.* London: Heinemann. Pp. 183.
Rev. by C. Ricks in *NS*, LXVIII, 18; in *TLS*, 20 Aug., p. 745.
An anthology, with introduction and commentary: Arnold, Barnes, Clough, Patmore, Christina and Dante Rossetti, and Swinburne.

Wyatt, Sibyl W. "Nineteenth Century English Novel and Austrian Censorship." *DA*, XXIV, 3328.

IV. INDIVIDUAL AUTHORS

ACTON

Conzemius, Victor (ed.). *Ignaz von Döllinger: Briefwechsel, 1820-1890. Vol. I: Briefwechsel mit Lord Acton, 1850-1869.* Munich: C. H. Beck, 1963. Pp. 580.
Rev. by Frank Eyck in *CR*, CCV, 554-55; in *TLS*, 31 Dec., p. 1183; by Josef L. Altholz in *VS*, VIII, 191-92.
Döllinger's correspondence with Acton will be completed in three volumes.

AINSWORTH (see III, Hollingsworth).

ARNOLD (see also III, Cockshut, Davies, Dobrée, Ludwig, Miller, Wright).

Selected Essays. Chosen and with an Introduction by Noel Annan. London: Oxford Univ. Pr. Pp. 392.
Rev. in *TLS*, 29 Oct., p. 975.

Allott, Kenneth. "The Date of 'Thyrsis.'" *RES*, n.s. XV, 304-05.
A proposed amendment to R. L. Brooks's "The Genesis of Matthew Arnold's 'Thyrsis'" (see VB 1963, 433).

Allott, Kenneth. "Matthew Arnold's 'The Neckan': The Real Issues." *Vict. Poetry, II*, 60-63.

Allott, Kenneth. "The Motto of Matthew Arnold's 'Thyrsis.'" *N&Q*, n.s. XI, 228.

Bittner, William. "On the Study of Celtic Literature — A Century Later." *The Lock Haven Review*, No. 6, 1-13.

Brooks, Roger L. "Matthew Arnold and Ticknor & Fields." *AL*, XXXV, 514-19.

Brooks, Roger L. "Matthew Arnold's Revision of *Tristram and Iseult*: Some Instances of Clough's Influence." *Vict. Poetry, II*, 57-60.

Brooks, Roger L. "The Story Manuscript of Matthew Arnold's 'New Rome.'" *BSP*, LVIII, 295-97.
Discovery of the text of the poem.

Coulling, Sidney M. B. "Matthew Arnold's 1853 Preface: Its Origin and Aftermath." *VS*, VII, 233-63.

Coursen, Herbert R., Jr. "'The Moon Lies Fair': The Poetry of Matthew Arnold." *St. in English Lit.*, IV, 569-81.
Arnold's attempt to recapture in his poetry characteristic Wordsworthian scenes and to find in them the transcendental significance such scenes held for Wordsworth usually issued in themes of disillusion or alienation.

Day, Paul W. "Matthew Arnold and the Philosophy of Vico." *Bulletin 70, English Series 12.* Auckland: Univ. of Auckland Pr. Pp. 46.

DeLaura, David J. "Arnold and Carlyle." *PMLA*, LXXIX, 104-29.
Carlyle's ambivalent influence on Arnold's critical writings.

Fulweiler, Howard W. "The Real Issues in Arnold's 'The Neckan.'" *Vict. Poetry, II*, 205-08.

Gottfried, Leon. *Matthew Arnold and the Romantics.* . . . See VB 1963, 433.
Rev. by Nicholas A. Salerno in *CE*, XXV, 475; by Donald H. Reimann in *JEGP*, LXIII, 532-34; by Joseph E. Baker in *PQ*, XLIII, 575; by Clyde de L. Ryals in *SAQ*, LXIII, 248; by W. Stacy Johnson in *Western Humanities Rev.*, XVIII, 280-81.

Greenberg, Robert A. "Matthew Arnold's Refuge of Art: 'Tristram and Iseult.'" *VNL*, No. 25 (Spring), pp. 1-4.

Harding, F. J. W. *Matthew Arnold the Critic and France.* Geneva: Droz. Pp. 203.
Rev. in *TLS*, 29 Oct., p. 975.

Howell, P. A. *Thomas Arnold the Younger in Van Diemen's Land.* Hobart: Tasmanian Historical Research Assoc. Pp. 60.
Noticed in *TLS*, 24 Dec., p. 1169.
On the activities of Matthew Arnold's brother as school inspector in Tasmania in the 1850's.

James, David Gwilym. *Matthew Arnold and the Decline of English Romanticism.* . . . See VB 1963, 433.
Rev. by Karl Britton in *Philosophy*, XXXIX, 90-91.

Kerpneck, Harvey. "The Road to Rugby Chapel." *TQ*, XXXIV, 178-96.
Examines Arnold's concern for his father,

letters to his mother, and imagery of the poem to refute theory that Arnold wrote "Rugby Chapel" only after a violent attack on his father by Fitzjames Stephen in 1858.

Lefcowitz, Allan B. "Matthew Arnold's Other Countrymen: The Reputation of Matthew Arnold in America from 1853 to 1870." *DA*, XXV, 2963.

Lieblich, Hyman. "Matthew Arnold as Prose Stylist." *DA*, XXV, 453.

McCarthy, Patrick Joseph. *Matthew Arnold and the Three Classes*. New York: Columbia Univ. Pr. Pp. xiii + 257.
Rev. by Dwight N. Lindley in *ArizQ*, XX, 370-72; by J. R. Willingham in *LJ*, LXXXIX, 1965; in *TLS*, 27 Aug., p. 766; by Wendell Stacy Johnson in *Vict. Poetry*, II, 290-92.

Moews, Daniel D. "Humanism and Ideology: A Study of Matthew Arnold's Ideas on Man and Society." *DA*, XXIV, 3753-54.

Peterson, William S. "The Landscapes of 'Rugby Chapel.'" *VNL*, No. 25 (Spring), pp. 22-23.

Plotinsky, Melvin L. "Help for Pain: The Narrative Verse of Matthew Arnold." *Vict. Poetry*, II, 165-77.
Finds alienation in the imagery of Arnold's narratives.

Super, R. H. (ed.). *Schools and Universities on the Continent*. Ann Arbor: Univ. of Michigan Pr.; London: Cresset Pr. Pp. viii + 437. Vol. IV of *The Complete Prose Works of Matthew Arnold*.
Rev. in *TLS*, 29 Oct., p. 975.

Trilling, Lionel. *Matthew Arnold*. Second edition. London: Allen and Unwin, 1963. Pp. xviii + 465.
Rev. by Kenneth Allott in *MLR*, LIX, 468-69.

Wright, Charles D. "Matthew Arnold's Response to German Culture." *DA*, XXIV, 4706-07.

ARNOLD, THOMAS.

Henderson-Howat, G. M. D. "Thomas Arnold and the Teaching of History." *QR*, (Apr.), pp. 213-21.

Williamson, Eugene L., Jr. *The Liberalism of Thomas Arnold, A Study of His Religious and Political Writings*. University: Univ. of Alabama Pr. Pp. 261.

AYTOUN.

Frykman, Erik. *Aytoun, Pioneer Professor of English at Edinburgh: A Study of his Literary Opinions and His Contribution to the Development of English as an Academic Discipline*. Göteborg: Acta Universitatis Gothoburgensis, 1963; New York: Almquist and Wiksell, 1963. Pp. 139.

Renwick, W. L. (ed.). *Stories and Verse*. Chicago: Aldine. Pp. 374.
Rev. by E. H. Walden in *LJ*, LXXXIX, 3332; by N. MacCaig in *NS*, LXVIII, 188.

BAGEHOT (see III, Kohn).

BARNES (see also III, Wright).

Jones, Bernard (ed.). *The Poems of William Barnes*. . . . See VB 1962, 404.
Rev. by William H. Marshall in *MP*, LXII, 81.

BEERBOHM (see also SHAW: Gollin).

Cecil, Lord David. *Max: A Biography*. London: Constable. Pp. xiv + 507.
Rev. by Naomi Lewis in *NS*, LXVII, 789-90; by Philip Hope-Wallace in *Manchester Guardian Weekly*, 5 Nov., p. 10; by Patrick Anderson in *S*, 6 Nov., pp. 610-11; in *TLS*, 26 Nov., p. 1056.
The authorized life of Beerbohm.

Hart-Davis, Rupert (ed.). *Letters to Reggie Turner*. London: Hart-Davis. Pp. 312.
Rev. by Naomi Lewis in *NS*, LXVIII, 789-90; by Patrick Anderson in *S*, 6 Nov., p. 611; in *TLS*, 26 Nov., p. 1056 (and see letter by Stanley Weintraub, 10 Dec., p. 1127).

Riewald, J. G. (ed.). *Max in Verse: Rhymes and Parodies by Max Beerbohm*. . . . See VB 1963, 434.
Rev. by James D. Merritt in *Books Abroad*, XXXVIII, 314; by Melvin Maddocks in *Christian Science Monitor*, 30 Jan., p. 5; by Robert Nye in *Manchester Guardian Weekly*, 19 Mar., p. 11; by Patrick Anderson in *S*, 6 Nov., p. 611; in *TLS*, 12 Mar., p. 216.

BESANT.

Nethercot, Arthur Hobart. *The Last Four Lives of Annie Besant*. Chicago: Univ. of Chicago Pr. Pp. 483.

BLUNT (see BURTON: Assad).

Going, William T. "Wilfrid Scawen Blunt, Victorian Sonneteer." *Vict. Poetry*, II, 67-85.
Delineates the content of Blunt's six sonnet sequences.

BOUCICAULT.

Faulkner, Seldon. "The Great Train Scene Robbery." *QJS*, L, 24-28.
On Boucicault's adaptation of a scene in a play by the American Gus Daly.

BRADLEY.

Eliot, Thomas Stearns. *Knowledge and Experience in the Philosophy of F. H.*

Bradley. London: Faber; New York: Farrar, Straus. Pp. 216.

Rev. by H. B. Acton in *Listener*, 20 Feb., p. 325; by W. S. Debenham in *LJ*, LXXXIX, 1614; by Richard Wollheim in *NS*, LXVII, 401; by E. P. Bollier in *SAQ*, LXIII, 588; in *TLS*, 7 May, p. 394; by J. B. Schneewind in *VS*, VIII, 198. Eliot's doctoral dissertation, written in 1916.

BRONTËS (see also III, Drew, Hardy, Miller). *Brontë Society Transactions*. Vol. XIV, No. 5 (1963) has items: Butterfield, Herbert, "Charlotte Brontë and her Sisters in the Crucial Year [1845]" (pp. 3-17); Cooper, Dorothy, "Dr. Blondel Writes Again on Emily Brontë" [review of an article] (pp. 21-22); Grayson, Laura, " 'Shirley' Charlotte Brontë's Own Evidence" (p. 31); Hutton, Joanna, "Items from the Museum's Cuttings Book" (pp. 26-30); Lemon, Charles, "Sickness and Health in 'Wuthering Heights' " (pp. 23-25); W., E. M. "The Hegers and a Yorkshire Family" (p. 32); Willis, Irene Cooper, "Looking for a Key to 'Wuthering Heights' " [a review of Thomas C. Moser (ed.) "*Wuthering Heights*: Text, Sources, Criticism"] (pp. 18-20); Letters, Announcements, and Reports.

Cott, Jeremy. "Structures of Sound: The Last Sentence of *Wuthering Heights*." *Texas Studies in Lit. & Lang.*, VI, 280-89. Linguistic analysis.

Drew, Philip. "Charlotte Bronte as a Critic of *Wuthering Heights*." *NCF*, XVIII, 365-81.

Hughes, R. E. "*Jane Eyre*: The Unbaptized Dionysos." *NCF*, XVIII, 347-64.

Marks, William S., III. "The Novel as Puritan Romance: A Comparative Study of Samuel Richardson, the Brontës, Thomas Hardy, and D. H. Lawrence." *DA*, XXV, 1214.

Monod, Sylvère. "L'Imprécision dans *Jane Eyre*." *Études anglaises*, XVII, 21-29. Tracing sources for some passages and garbled quotations in *Jane Eyre*.

BROWNINGS (see also III, Bose, Miller; RUSKIN: Poston).

Armstrong, Isobel. "Browning's *Mr. Sludge, 'The Medium.*' " *Vict. Poetry*, II, 1-9.

Bachem, Rose M. "Musset's and Browning's *Andrea del Sarto*." *Revue de litt. comparée*, XXXVIII, 248-54. Comparison of Musset's drama (1833)

and Browning's poem (1852) revealing contrasting literary temperaments.

Bonner, Francis W. "Browning's 'The Bishop Orders His Tomb at St. Praxed's Church.' " *Ex*, XXII, Item 57.

Cadbury, William. "Lyric and Anti-Lyric Forms: A Method for Judging Browning." *TQ*, XXXIV, 49-67. An ingenious attempt to "bypass the perpetual argument about the nature of the dramatic monologue" by considering poetic intention as lyric or anti-lyric and then examining structure, character, and the essential rhetoric for either form. Although not a clearly persuasive method, it is significant for the insights and analyses of several poems. – R.E.F.

Collins, Thomas J. "Browning's *Essay on Shelley*: In Context." *Vict. Poetry*, II, 119-24.

Columbus, Robert R. and Kemper, Claudette. "Sordello and the Speaker: A Problem in Identity." *Vict. Poetry*, II, 251-67.

Crowell, Norton B. *The Triple Soul: Browning's Theory of Knowledge*. Albuquerque: Univ. of New Mexico Pr., 1963. Pp. xiv + 235. Rev. by John Pick in *Books Abroad*, XXXVIII, 424; in *TLS*, 13 Feb., p. 128.

Drew, Philip. "Henry Jones on Browning's Optimism." *Vict. Poetry*, II, 29-41. Questions Jones' account of the philosophical implications of Browning's poetry and advances a refutation.

Friend, Joseph H. "Euripides Browningized: The Meaning of *Balaustion's Adventure*." *Vict. Poetry*, II, 179-86.

Hayter, Alethea. *Mrs. Browning: A Poet's Work and Its Setting*. . . . See VB 1963, 435. Rev. by M. Barbery in *Études anglaises*, XVII, 202-03.

Honan, Park. "Belial Upon Setebos." *Tennessee Studies in Lit.*, IX, 87-98. Browning's use of Milton's Belial in developing character and ideas in "Caliban Upon Setebos."

Hope-Wallace, Philip. "Song and Dance in Wimpole Street." *Manchester Guardian Weekly*, 29 Oct., p. 10. On "Robert and Elizabeth," a musical-comedy version of Besier's *The Barretts of Wimpole Street*.

Irvine, William. "Four Monologues in Browning's *Men and Women*." *Vict. Poetry*, II, 155-64.

Kramer, Dale. "Character and Theme in *Pippa*

Passes." Vict. Poetry, II, 241-49.

Litzinger, Boyd. *Time's Revenges: Browning's Reputation as a Thinker, 1889-1962.* Knoxville: Univ. of Tennessee Pr. Pp. xv + 192.

Martin, Hugh. *The Faith of Robert Browning.* . . . See VB 1963, 435.
Noticed in *TLS*, 20 Feb., p. 154.

Mendel, Sydney. "Browning's 'Andrea del Sarto.'" *Ex*, XXII, Item 77.

Nelson, Charles E. "Creative Consciousness in *The Ring and the Book*." *DA*, XXIV, 4179.

Perrine, Laurence. "Browning's 'Caliban Upon Setebos': A Reply." *Vict. Poetry*, II, 124-27.

Priestley, F. E. L. "The Ironic Pattern of Browning's *Paracelsus*." *TQ*, XXXIV, 68-81.

Rivers, Charles. *The Twin Revealment: Subjective-Objective Polarity in the Poetry of Robert Browning.* Northwest Missouri State College Studies. Vol. XXVIII, No. 1. Pp. 31.

Shaw, W. David. "The Analogical Argument of Browning's 'Saul.'" *Vict. Poetry*, II, 277-82.

Shaw, W. David. "Character and Philosophy in 'Fra Lippo Lippi.'" *Vict. Poetry*, II, 127-32.

Sullivan, Mary Rose. "Browning's Voices: A Study of the Speaker-Environment Relationship as a Primary Means of Control in the Dramatic Monologues of *The Ring and the Book*." *DA*, XXV, 2989.

Tamagnan, Jean. "Fenêtre ouverte sur Browning." *Études anglaises*, XVII, 163-70.
Review of Georges Connes's translation into French of *The Ring and the Book*. (Paris: Gallimard, 1959; pp. 705.)

Tillotson, Geoffrey. "A Word for Browning." *SeR*, LXXII, 389-97.
An enlightening article, based on Tillotson's discussions of Browning with his students.

Watkins, Charlotte Crawford. "Browning's 'Red Cotton Night-Cap Country' and Carlyle." *VS*, VII, 359-74.

Whitla, William. *The Central Truth: The Incarnation in Robert Browning's Poetry.* Toronto: Univ. of Toronto Pr.; London: Oxford Univ. Pr. Pp. vii + 161.
Rev. by W. O. Raymon in *TQ*, XXXIII, 422-24; in *TLS*, 20 Aug., p. 748; by Park Honan in *Vict. Poetry*, II, 214.

BULWER (see also III, Hollingsworth).

Usrey, Malcolm O. "The Letters of Sir Edward Bulwer-Lytton to the Editors of *Blackwood's Magazine*, 1840-1873, in the National Library of Scotland [with] Volume II." *DA*, XXIV, 5392.

BURTON.

Assad, Thomas J. *Three Victorian Travellers: Burton, Blunt, Doughty.* London: Routledge and Kegan Paul. Pp. x + 154.
Rev. by D. A. N. Jones in *NS*, LXVII, 259; in *TLS*, 6 Feb., p. 105.

Brodie, Fawn M. (ed.). *The City of the Saints*. . . . See VB 1963, 436.
Rev. by M. E. Bradford in *SeR*, LXXII, 720-24; in *TLS*, 20 Feb., p. 143.

Edwardes, Allen. *Death Rides a Camel: A Biography of Sir Richard Burton*. . . . See VB 1963, 436.
Rev. by H. T. Moore in *SR*, 29 Feb., p. 31.

Farwell, Byron. *Burton*. . . . See VB 1963, 436.
Rev. in *Economist*, CCIX, 1274; by Paul Pickrel in *Harper's*, Mar., p. 118; by Eric Britter in *Herald Trib.*, 12 Apr., p. 11; by Louis Barron in *LJ*, LXXXIX, 238; by F. W. Dupee in *NY Rev. of Books*, 16 Apr., p. 3; by Peter Quennell in *NYTBR*, 12 Apr., p. 7; by M. E. Bradford in *SeR*, LXXII, 720-24; by H. T. Moore in *SR*, 29 Feb., p. 31.

Walker, Kenneth (ed.). *Love, War, and Fancy: The Customs and Manners of the East from Writings on the Arabian Nights.* London: William Kimber. Pp. 288.
Rev. in *NS*, LXVII, 953-54; in *TLS*, 11 June, p. 508.

BUTLER (see also III, Cockshut; DARWIN: Greenacre).

Holt, Lee. *Samuel Butler.* New York: Twayne. Pp. 183.

Shoenberg, Robert E. "The Literal-Mindedness of Samuel Butler." *St. in English Lit.*, IV, 601-16.

CARLYLE (see also III, Ludwig; ARNOLD: DeLaura; BROWNING: Watkins).

Earle, Peter G. "Unamuno and the Theme of History." *Hispanic Review*, XXXII, 319-39.
Carlyle had some influence on the theme.

Grenberg, Bruce L. "Thomas Carlyle and Herman Melville: Parallels, Obliques, and Perpendiculars." *DA*, XXIV, 3323.

Hertz, Robert N. "Victory and the Consciousness of Battle: Emerson and Carlyle." *The Personalist*, XLV, 60-71.
Comparative study of the writers' views of

individualism and self-knowledge with consideration of tone, form, and language in their presentation.

Lea, F. A. "Carlyle and the French Revolution." *Listener*, 17 Sept., pp. 421-23.

Levine, Richard A. "Carlyle as Poet: The Phoenix Image in 'Organic Filaments.'" *VNL*, No. 25 (Spring), pp. 18-20.

Levine, George. "'Sartor Resartus' and the Balance of Fiction." *VS*, VIII, 131-60.

Pouilliart, Raymond. "Maurice Maeterlinck et Carlyle." *Revue de litt. comparée*, XXXVIII, 337-58.
Relationship of Maeterlinck's reading of Carlyle in 1888 to his more symbolic and mystical works.

Sanders, Charles Richard. "The Byron Closed in *Sartor Resartus.*" *Studies in Romanticism*, III, 77-108.

Sanders, Charles Richard. "Carlyle as Editor and Critic of Literary Letters." *The Emory Univ. Quart.*, XX, 108-20.

Sanders, Charles Richard. "The Correspondence and Friendship of Thomas Carlyle and Leigh Hunt: The Early Years." *Bull. of the John Rylands Library*, XLV, 439-85.
Publication of both sides of the correspondence from 1832-1837.

Sanders, Charles Richard. "The Correspondence and Friendship of Thomas Carlyle and Leigh Hunt: The Later Years." *Bull. of the John Rylands Library*, XLVI, 179-216.
Covers years after 1838.

Sanders, Charles Richard. *The Correspondence and Friendship of Thomas Carlyle and Leigh Hunt*. Manchester: The John Rylands Library, 1963. Pp. 85.
Reprinted from two issues of the *Bulletin of the John Rylands Library* (XLV, March, 1963 and XLVI, September, 1963).

Sharples, Edward, Jr. "Carlyle and His Readers: The Froude Controversy Once Again." *DA*, XXV, 2987-88.

Slater, Joseph (ed.). *The Correspondence of Emerson and Carlyle*. New York: Columbia Univ. Pr. Pp. viii + 622.
Rev. by Morse Peckham in *SR*, 19 Dec., p. 34.

Smeed, J. W. "Thomas Carlyle and Jean Paul Richter." *Comparative Literature*, XVI, 226-53.
Study of influence of Jean Paul on Carlyle's ideas as well as style.

Tennyson, Georg B. "*Sartor* Called *Resartus*: A Study of the Genesis, Style, and Struc-

ture of Thomas Carlyle's *Sartor Resartus.*" *DA*, XXIV, 4201.

CARROLL.

Carruthers, Clive Harcourt (tr.). *Alicia in Terra Mirabili*. London: Macmillan. Pp. 117.
Noticed in *TLS*, 8 Oct., p. 925.

Gardner, Martin (ed.). *The Annotated Alice*. London: Anthony Blond. Pp. 352.
Rev. in *TLS*, 24 Dec., p. 1164.
Supersedes an earlier annotated edition.

Hiscock, W. G. "The Lost Christ Church 'Alice.'" *TLS*, 7 May, p. 402.
On the copy of the suppressed 1865 *Alice*, presented and inscribed by Carroll to Christ Church Senior Common Room, and lost or stolen before 1928.

Leach, Elsie. "'Alice in Wonderland' in Perspective." *VNL*, No. 25 (Spring), pp. 9-11.

Pryce-Jones, Alan. "To Alice, with Love, from Dairyland." *HTB*, 2 Aug., p. 2.
Essay on Warren Weaver's *Alice in Many Tongues*.

Rackin, Donald. "The Critical Interpretations of *Alice in Wonderland*: A Survey and Suggested Reading." *DA*, XXV, 1217.

Weaver, Warren. *Alice in Many Tongues:·The Translations of Alice in Wonderland*. Madison: Univ. of Wisconsin Pr. Pp. 147.
Noticed in *TLS*, 20 Aug., p. 753.

CLOUGH (see also III, Cockshut, Wright; ARNOLD: Brooks).

Barish, Evelyn. "A New Clough Manuscript." *RES*, n.s. XV, 168-74.
Four additional stanzas to "Solvitur Acris Hiems."

Chorley, Katharine. *Arthur Hugh Clough: The Uncommitted Mind. . . .* See VB 1963, 437.
Rev. by A. G. Hill in *RES*, n.s. XV, 332-34.

Houghton, Walter E. *The Poetry of Clough.* . . . See VB 1963, 437.
Rev. by Kenneth Allott in *EC*, XIV, 409-16; by Jerome H. Buckley in *JEGP*, LXIII, 378-80; by Michael Timko in *MLQ*, XXV, 226-27; in *TLS*, 9 Jan., p. 22; by Richard Tobias in *Vict. Poetry*, II, 209-11; by Patrick McCarthy in *VS*, VIII, 316-17; by A. Dwight Culler in *YR*, LIII, 440.

Peattie, Roger W. "William Michael Rossetti." *TLS*, 30 July, p. 665.
A letter from Clough thanking W. M. Rossetti for his review of *The Bothie* in *The Germ*.

CONRAD (See also III, Beebe, Davies, Drew, Stewart).

Boyle, Ted E. "Marlow's 'Lie' in 'Heart of Darkness.'" *Studies in Short Fiction*, I, 159-63.

Bruffee, Kenneth A. "The Lesser Nightmare: Marlowe's Lie in *Heart of Darkness*." *MLQ*, XXV, 322-29.

Day, Robert A. "The Rebirth of Leggatt." *Lit. and Psychology*, XII, 74-81.

Farmer, Norman, Jr. "Conrad's 'Heart of Darkness.'" *Ex*, XXII, Item 51.

Gose, Elliott B., Jr. "Pure Exercise of Imagination: Archetypal Symbolism in *Lord Jim*." *PMLA*, LXXIX, 137-47.

Harper, George M. "Conrad's Knitters and Homer's Cave of the Nymphs." *ELN*, I, 53-57.

Hay, Eloise Knapp. *The Political Novels of Joseph Conrad*. . . . See VB 1963, 437.
Rev. by David Cowden in *MLQ*, XXV, 227-28; by Elizabeth Martell in *QQ*, LXXI, 138-39; by W. S. Dowden in *SAQ*, LXIII, 255; in *TLS*, 9 Jan., p. 28; by Avrom Fleishman in *VS*, VII, 404-05.

Heimer, Jackson W. "Patterns of Betrayal in the Novels of Joseph Conrad." *DA*, XXIV, 5408-09.

Hicks, John H. "Conrad's *Almayer's Folly*: Structure, Theme, and Critics." *NCF*, XIX, 17-31.
Claims there is a coherence and meaning in the novel which many modern critics have overlooked.

Hodges, Robert R. "The Four Fathers of Lord Jim." *University Rev.*, XXXI, 103-10.

Levine, Paul. "Joseph Conrad's Blackness." *SAQ*, LXIII, 198-206.

Levy, Milton A. "Conrad's 'The Lagoon.'" *Ex*, XXIII, Item 35.

Lodge, David. "Conrad's 'Victory' and 'The Tempest': An Amplification." *MLR*, LIX, 195-99.
Heyst, Lena, and Pedro as Prospero, Miranda, and Caliban.

Martin, W. R. "The Captain of the *Narcissus*." *English Studies in Africa*, VI, 191-97.

McIntyre, Allan O. "Conrad on Conscience and the Passions." *University Rev.*, XXXI, 69-74.

McIntyre, Allen O. "Conrad on the Functions of the Mind." *MLQ*, XXV, 187-97.
Conscience, facts, memory, tradition are valued above ideas, reason, logic, books, reflection.

Najder, Zdzislaw (ed.). *Conrad's Polish Background: Letters to and from Polish Friends*. Translated by Halina Carroll.

London: Oxford Univ. Pr. Pp. vii + 313.
Rev. by Richard Curle in *CR*, CCV, 552; by V. S. Pritchett in *NS*, LXVII, 846; by Tony Tanner in *S*, 8 May, p. 636; in *TLS*, 4 June, p. 488.

Nelson, Harland S. "Eden and Golgotha: Conrad's Use of the Bible in *The Nigger of the Narcissus*." *Iowa English Yearbook*, No. 8 (Fall, 1963), pp. 63-67.

Pilecki, G. A. "Conrad's 'Victory.'" *Ex*, XXIII, Item 26.

Sherry, Norman. "Conrad's Source for 'Lord Jim.'" *MLR*, LIX, 545-57.
A. P. Williams, first mate of the "Jeddah," as original for Jim.

Sherry, Norman. "'Exact Biography' and *The Shadow-Line*." *PMLA*, LXXIX, 620-25.

Sherry, Norman. "'Rajah Laut' — A Quest for Conrad's Source." *MP*, LXII, 22-41.

Smith, J. Oates. "The Existential Comedy of Conrad's 'Youth.'" *Renascence*, XVI, 22-28.

Sullivan, Sister Mary Petrus. "The Descriptive Style of Joseph Conrad." *DA*, XXV, 486-87.

Tanner, Jimmie E. "The Twentieth Century Impressionistic Novel: Conrad and Faulkner." *DA*, XXV, 1927-28.

Tanner, Tony. "Butterflies and Beetles — Conrad's Two Truths." *Chicago Rev.*, XVI, 123-40.

Williams, George Walton. "Conrad's 'The Lagoon.'" *Ex*, XXIII, Item 1.

Williams, Porter, Jr. "The Matter of Conscience in Conrad's *The Secret Sharer*." *PMLA*, LXXIX, 626-30.

Wright, Walter F. (ed.). *Joseph Conrad on Fiction*. Lincoln: Univ. of Nebraska Pr. Pp. 236.

Yates, Norris W. "Social Comment in *The Nigger of the 'Narcissus*.'" *PMLA*, LXXIX, 183-85.

Zuckerman, Jerome. "'A Smile of Fortune': Conrad's Interesting Failure." *Studies in Short Fiction*, I, 99-102.

DARWIN.

On the Origin of Species. A Facsimile of the First Edition with an Introduction by Ernst Mayr. Cambridge: Harvard Univ. Pr.; London: Oxford Univ. Pr. Pp. 502.
Noticed in *TLS*, 29 Oct., p. 985.

DeBeer, Sir Gavin. *Charles Darwin: Evolution by Natural Selection*. . . . See VB 1963, 438.
Rev. by George Basalla in *LJ*, LXXXIX,

1597; by A. R. Hall in *NS*, LXVII, 300; by Leonard Engel in *NYTBR*, 12 Apr., p. 7; by Conway Zirkle in *Science*, CXLIV, 724; by E. W. Sinnott in *YR*, LIII, 586.

Gray, Asa. *Darwiniana: Essays and Reviews Pertaining to Darwinism.* . . . See VB 1963, 438.

Rev. by Conway Zirkle in *Science*, CXLIV, 725; in *TLS*, 16 Jan., p. 50.

Greenacre, Phyllis. *The Quest for the Father: A Study of the Darwin-Butler Controversy.* . . . See VB 1963, 438.

Rev. by P. B. Medawar in *NS*, LXVII, 527; by Howard E. Gruber in *VS*, VIII, 79-81.

Hyman, Stanley Edgar. *The Tangled Bank.* . . . See VB 1963, 438.

Rev. by Griffin Taylor in *SeR*, LXXII, 698-709.

Medawar, P. B. "Darwin's Illness." *NS*, LXVII, 527-28; 561.

Mellersh, H. E. L. *Charles Darwin.* London: Arthur Barker. Pp. 124.

Rev. in *TLS*, 9 April, p. 297.

DICKENS (see also III, Beebe, Drew, Hollingsworth).

Axton, William. "Dombey and Son: From Stereotype to Archetype." *ELH*, XXXI, 301-17.

Dickens's debt to Victorian melodrama.

Aylmer, Felix. *The Drood Case.* London: Hart-Davis. Pp. x + 218.

Rev. in *TLS*, 5 Nov., p. 1000 (and see letter by Aylmer, 12 Nov., p. 1026; by reviewer, 19 Nov., p. 1039).

Blount, Trevor. "The Chadbands and Dickens' View of Dissenters." *MLQ*, XXV, 295-307.

Brook, G. L. "The Language of Dickens." *Bull. of the John Rylands Library*, XLVII, 32-48.

Dickens's use of regional, occupational, and class dialects as well as "special languages" for specific Dickensian characters.

Brown, Ivor. *Dickens in His Time.* . . . See VB 1963, 439.

Rev. by E. R. Rizzo in *LJ*, LXXXIX, 1866; by Harry Stone in *NCF*, XIX, 308-09; by Kathryn Montgomery in *NYTBR*, 26 Apr., p. 39; in *TLS*, 16 Jan., p. 48.

Carnall, Geoffrey. "Dickens, Mrs. Gaskell, and the Preston Strike." *VS*, VIII, 31-48.

Collins, Philip. *Dickens and Crime.* . . . See VB 1963, 439.

Rev. by R. D. McMaster in *QQ*, LXXI, 278-79.

Collins, Philip. *Dickens and Education.* . . . See VB 1963, 439.

Rev. by Gilbert Thomas in *English*, XV, 64-65; by Sylvère Monod in *Études anglaises*, XVII, 197-98; by R. D. McMaster in *NCF*, XIX, 306-08; in *VQR*, XL, lxvi.

Davis, Earle. *The Flint and the Flame: The Artistry of Charles Dickens.* . . . See VB 1963, 439.

Rev. by Gilbert Thomas in *English*, XV, 64-65; by J. Hillis Miller in *JEGP*, LXIII, 534-36; by John Butt in *NCF*, XIX, 88-91; by J. R. Willingham in *LJ*, LXXXIX, 259; in *TLS*, 16 Jan., p. 48; in *VQR*, XL, xx.

Dickensian, Vol. LX (Nos. 342-44). . . . See VB 1932, 422. Items as follows: Bart, Barry D., " 'George Silverman's Explanation' " (pp. 48-51); Brain, Lord, *et al.*, "152d Anniversary of the Birth of Charles Dickens" (pp. 91-96); Brown, F. J., "Those Dickens Christmases" (pp. 17-19); Carlton, William J., "In the Blacking Warehouse" (pp. 11-16); Carlton, William J., " 'Who Was the Lady?' Mrs. Christian's Reminiscences of Dickens" (pp. 68-77); Collins, Philip, "Dickens on Keeley the Comedian: An Uncollected Piece, with Introduction and Notes" (pp. 5-10); Collins, Philip, "Dickens's Reading" (pp. 136-51); Collins, Philip, "Inspector Bucket Visits the Princess Puffer" (pp. 88-90); Deneau, Daniel P. "The Brother-Sister Relationship in *Hard Times*" (pp. 173-77); Deneau, Daniel P. "Pip's Age and Other Notes on *Great Expectations*" (pp. 27-29); Easson, Angus, "Dickens, *Household Words*, and a Double Standard" (pp. 104-14); Fielding, K. J., "Dickens and Education" (pp. 38-39); Gibson, Frank A., "The Saddest Book [*A Tale of Two Cities*]" (pp. 30-32); Gibson, John W., "*The Old Curiosity Shop*: The Critical Allegory" (pp. 178-83); Gordon, D. L., "Dickens and America through Italian Eyes" (p. 135); Heldring, E., "Some European Reactions to Dickens" (pp. 55-56); Jeffares, A. N., "Immortal Memory: Toast at the Dickens Fellowship Conference Dinner" (pp. 133-35); Morley, Malcolm, "Pickwick on Horseback" (pp. 33-38); Morley, Malcolm, "Revelry by Night" (pp. 97-101); Pederson, Winnifred J., "Jo in *Bleak House*" (pp. 162-67); Perkins, George, "Death by Spontaneous Combustion in Marryat, Melville, Dickens, Zola, and Others" (pp. 57-63); Peyrouton, N. C., "Dickens and the Chartists" (pp. 78-88; 152-61); Peyrouton,

N. C., "Ergo: The Dickens Tinder Box" (pp. 40-42); Peyrouton, N. C., A Review of Edgar and Eleanor Johnson, *The Dickens Theatrical Reader* (p. 177); Peyrouton, N., A Review of Keith Hollingsworth, *The Newgate Novel*, 1830-1847 (pp. 102-03); Peyrouton, N. C., A Review of Mark Spilka, *Dickens and Kafka, A Mutual Interpretation* (pp. 115-16); Peyrouton, N. C., "Some Boston Abolitionists on Boz: A Lost American Note" (pp. 20-26); Roulet, Ann, "A Comparative Study of *Nicholas Nickleby* and *Bleak House* (pp. 117-24); Smith, Timothy d'Arch, "The Penny Dreadful" (pp. 44-46); Staples, Leslie C., 'The Back-Cloth" (p. 47); Staples, L. C., A Review of *Nothing Extenuate, the Life of Frederick Fox Cooper* (p. 96); Stowell, Gordon, "The Pickwick Club of New Zealand, 1840" (p. 77); Thompson, Leslie M., "The Masks of Pride in *Our Mutual Friend*" (pp. 124-28); Vasta, Edward, "*Great Expectations* and *The Great Gatsby*" (pp. 167-72); Warner, John R., "Dickens Looks at Homer" (pp. 52-54); Woodings, R. B., "A Cancelled Passage in *Hard Times*" (pp. 42-43).

Fielding, K. J. "'American Notes' and Some English Reviewers." *MLR*, LIX, 527-37.
On reviews by Warren, Croker, and Spedding.

Fleissner, Robert F. "Lear's 'Poor Fool' and Dickens." *EC*, XIV, 425.

Gard, Roger. "The 'Poor Fool.'" *EC*, XIV, 209.
Refers to Fleissner's article, *EC*, XIII, 425. (see above).

Garis, Robert. "Dickens Criticism." *VS*, VII, 375-86.
A review-article in which Mr. Garis discusses, among other books, *The Dickens Critics*, ed. by George H. Ford and Lauriat Lane, Jr. (See VB 1963, 439), and *Dickens and the Twentieth Century*, ed. by John Gross and Gabriel Pearson (see below).

Grob, Shirley, "Dickens and Some Motifs of the Fairy Tale." *Texas Studies in Lit. and Lang.*, V, 567-79.

Gross, John and Pearson, Gabriel (eds.). *Dickens and the Twentieth Century.* . . .
See VB 1963, 440.
Rev. by R. D. McMaster in *Dalhousie Rev.*, XLIII, 552-54; by Robert Garis in *EC*, XIV, 197-208; by R. George Thomas in *RES*, n.s. XV, 212-14; by G. D. Klingo-

pulos in *Universities Quart.*, XVIII, 321-28.

Grylls, R. Glynn. "Dickens and Holman Hunt." *Texas Studies in Lit. and Lang.*, VI, 76-79.
Dickens' replies to Hunt, who believed he was caricatured in "Calmuck" in *Household Words* (April 3, 1858).

Hirsch, David H. "'Hard Times' and F. R. Leavis." *Criticism*, VI, 1-16.

Johnson, Edgar and Eleanor (eds.). *The Dickens Theatrical Reader*. Boston: Little. Pp. 370.
Rev. by Paul Pickrel in *Harper's*, Jan., p. 105; by W. H. Matthews in *LJ*, LXXXIX, 1620; in *TLS*, 24 Sept., p. 880.

Johnson, Paul. "Garrick at War." *NS*, LXVII, 595-96.
On the Dickens-Thackeray feud.

Lohrli, Anne. "*Household Words* and Its 'Office Book.'" *Princeton Univ. Libr. Chronicle*, XXVI, 27-47.
A significant account of the "Office Book," listing contributors, dates, titles, amounts paid. The "Office Book" is in the Morris L. Parrish Collection at Princeton. — R. E. F.

Marcus, Mordecai. "The Pattern of Self-Alienation in 'Great Expectations.'" *VNL*, No. 26 (Fall), pp. 9-12.

Marcus, Steven. "Dickens from Pickwick to Dombey." *DA*, XXV, 1195.

Mistler, Jean. "Un grand éditeur et ses auteurs." *Revue des deux mondes* (No. 14: 15 July), 192-207.
Translates two letters from Dickens to his Parisian publisher, Louis Hachette, and prints a letter Dickens wrote in French.

Miyoshi Masao. "Resolution of Identity in 'Our Mutual Friend.'" *VNL*, No. 26 (Fall), pp. 5-9.

Morsiani, Yamile. *Dickens e l'America*. Bologna: Ricardo Pàtron. Pp. 154.
Noticed in *TLS*, 15 Oct., p. 945.

Priestley, J. B. *Dickens*. Trans. into French by Anne Rousseau. Paris: Hachette.
Rev. in *Revue de deux mondes*, No. 10 (15 May), 318.

Prins, Albert J. "The Fabulous Art: Myth, Metaphor, and Moral Vision in Dickens' *Bleak House*." *DA*, XXV, 1896.

Reid, J. C. *The Hidden World of Charles Dickens*. Auckland: The University, 1962. Pp. 48.
Rev. by K. J. Fielding in *RES*, n.s. XV, 104-06.

Røstvig, Maren-Sofie, Løsnes, Arvid, Reinert, Otto, Roll-Hansen, Diderik. *The Hidden*

Sense and Other Essays. Norwegian Studies in English (formerly *Oslo Studies in English*), No. 9. Oslo: Univeritetsforlaget, 1963. Pp. 226.
Rev. by P. Legouis in *Études anglaises*, XVII, 191-92.
Contains Roll-Hansen's essay "Characters and Contrasts in *Great Expectations*."

Smith, Sheila M. "An Unpublished Letter from Dickens to Disraeli." *N&Q*, n.s. xi, 233.

Spilka, Mark. *Dickens and Kafka*. . . . See VB 1963, 440.
Rev. by Mim Ann Houk in *Lit. and Psychology*, XIV, 37-39; by J. Hillis Miller in *NCF*, XVIII, 404-07; in *TLS*, 16 Jan., p. 48.

Steig, Michael. "Erotic Themes in Dickens' Novels." *DA*, XXIV, 4704-05.

Stone, Harry. "Fairy Tales and Ogres: Dickens' Imagination and 'David Copperfield.' " *Criticism*, VI, 324-30.

Tillotson, Kathleen. "*Oliver Twist* in Three Volumes." *The Library*, 5th Ser., XVIII, (1963), 113-32.

Ward, J. A. "Dining with the Novelists." *The Personalist*, XLV, 399-411.
Uses of dining scenes by various novelists, including Dickens and Thackeray.

Wilde, Alan. "Mr. F's Aunt and the Analogical Structure of *Little Dorrit*." *NCF*, XIX, 33-44.

Williams, Raymond. "Social Criticism in Dickens: Some Problems of Method and Approach." *Critical Quart.*, VI, 214-27.

DISRAELI (see also THACKERAY: Painting).
Duerksen, Roland A. "Disraeli's Use of Shelley." *VNL*, No. 26 (Fall), pp. 19-22.

Jerman, B. R. "The Production of Disraeli's Trilogy." *BSP*, LVIII, 239-51.

Maxwell, J. C. "Words from 'The Young Duke.' " *N&Q*, n.s. xi, 29.

Merritt, James D. "The Novels of Benjamin Disraeli: A Study." *DA*, XXIV, 4702.

DOUGLAS.
Croft-Cooke, Rupert. *Bosie: Lord Alfred Douglas, His Friends and Enemies*. . . . See VB 1963, 440.
Rev. by L. W. Griffin in *LJ*, LXXXIX, 2781-82; by Richard Ellmann in *NY Rev. of Books*, 30 Apr., p. 6; by Carolyn Heilbrun in *NYTBR*, 24 May, p. 7; by H. T. Moore in *SR*, 16 May, p. 48; by Thomas J. Garbáty in *VS*, VII, 401-04.

DOWDEN.
Ludwigson, Kathryn M. "Transcendalism

in Edward Dowden." *DA*, XXV, 479-80.

DOWSON.
Goldfarb, Russell M. "The Dowson Legend Today." *St. in English Lit.*, IV, 653-62.

Longaker, Mark (ed.). *The Poems of Ernest Dowson*. . . . See VB 1963, 440.
Rev. by W. K. Seymour in *CR*, CCV, 51-52; by Ian Fletcher in *MLR*, LIX, 122-23.

Munro, John M. "A Previously Unpublished Letter from Ernest Dowson to Arthur Symons." *Études anglaises*, XVII, 284-87.

DOYLE.
Hardwick, Michael and Mollie. *Four Sherlock Holmes Plays*. London: John Murray. Pp. 129.
Noticed in *TLS*, 24 Dec., p. 1169.
Adaptations for the stage of "The Blue Carbuncle," "Charles Augustus Milverton," "The Mazarin Stone," and "The Speckled Band."

Hardwick, Michael and Mollie. *The Man Who Was Sherlock Holmes*. London: John Murray. Pp. 92.
Noticed in *TLS*, 12 March, p. 222.
On Doyle as the original of his own character.

Kissane, James and John M. "Sherlock Holmes and the Ritual of Reason." *NCF*, XVII, 353-62.
Inadvertently omitted from VB 1963.

Klinefelter, Walter. *Sherlock Holmes in Portrait and Profile*. . . . See VB 1963, 440.
Noticed (as "the definitive iconography") in *TLS*, 20 Feb., p. 154.

ELIOT (see also III, Cockshut, Drew, Hardy; RUSKIN: Poston).
Adam, Ian. "A Huxley Echo in 'Middlemarch.' " *N&Q*, n.s. XI, 227.

Allen, Walter Ernest. *George Eliot*. New York: Macmillan. Pp. 192.
Rev. by Carlos Baker in *NYTBR*, 13 Dec., p. 4.

Anderson, Roland F. "Formative Influences on George Eliot, with Special Reference to George Henry Lewes." *DA*, XXV, 1205-06.

Bedient, Calvin B. "The Fate of the Self: Self and Society in the Novels of George Eliot, D. H. Lawrence, and E. M. Forster." *DA*, XXV, 1187.

Bennett, Joan. *George Eliot: Her Mind and Her Art*. Cambridge: Cambridge Univ. Pr., 1962, Pp. 203.
Rev. (in German) by Ludwig Borinski in *Anglia*, LXXXII, 129.

Brown, Keith. "The Ending of 'The Mill on

the Floss.' " *N&Q*, n.s. XI, 226.

Burns, John S. "The Wider Life: A Study of the Writings of George Eliot." *DA*, XXV, 1903-04.

Chandler, Jagdish. "Religious and Moral Ideas in the Novels of George Eliot." *DA*, XXIV, 2905.

Cox, Charles Brian. *The Free Spirit: A Study of Liberal Humanism in the Novels of George Eliot.* . . . See VB 1963, 441.
Rev. by Miriam Allott in *MLR*, LIX, 136-37.

Feltes, N. N. "George Eliot and the Unified Sensibility." *PMLA*, LXXIX, 130-36.

Gillespie, H. R. "George Eliot's Tertius Lydgate and Charles Kingsley's Tom Thurnall." *N&Q*, n.s. XI, 226-27.

Goldfarb, Russell M. "Caleb Garth of 'Middlemarch.' " *VNL*, No. 26 (Fall), pp. 14-19.

Greene, Philip L. "Henry James and George Eliot." *DA*, XXIV, 4188-89.

Knoepflmacher, U. C. "George Eliot, Feuerbach, and the Question of Criticism." *VS*, VII, 306-09.

Ledger, Marshall. "George Eliot and Nathaniel Hawthorne." *N&Q*, n.s. XI, 225-26.

Luecke, Sister Jane Marie. "Ladislaw and the *Middlemarch* Vision." *NCF*, XIX, 55-64.

Merton, Stephen. "George Eliot and William Hale White." *VNL*, No. 25 (Spring), pp. 13-15.

Pinney, Thomas (ed.). *Essays of George Eliot.* . . . See VB 1963, 441.
Rev. by Nicholas A. Salerno in *CE*, XXVI, 63; by J. W. Fuller in *Christian Science Monitor*, 17 Apr., p. 9; by Miriam Allott in *Critical Quart.*, VI, 92-94; by Laurence Lerner in *MLR*, LIX, 283-84; in *NCF*, XIX, 100; by David R. Carroll in *VS*, VIII, 77-79.

Poston, Lawrence, III. " 'Romola' and Thomas Trollope's 'Filippo Strozzi.' " *VNL*, No. 25 (Spring), pp. 20-22.

Robinson, Carole. "The Severe Angel: A Study of *Daniel Deronda.*" *ELH*, XXXI, 278-300.

Templin, Lawrence H. "George Eliot: A Study of the Omniscient Point of View in Her Fiction." *DA*, XXV, 2967-68.

FITZGERALD.

Draper, John W. "FitzGerald's Persian Local Color." *W. Va. Univ. Bull. Philological Papers*, XIV, 26-56.

FORD.

Baumwoll, Dennis. "The Fiction of Ford Madox Ford: Theory and Practice." *DA*, XXIV, 5404-05.

Cassell, Richard A. *Ford Madox Ford: A Study of His Novels.* . . . See VB 1963, 441.
Rev. by J. A. Bryant, Jr., in *SeR*, LXXII, 495-500; by Margaret Lowery in *Western Humanities Rev.*, XVIII, 83-84.

Gordon, Ambrose, Jr. "*Parade's End:* Where War Was Fairy Tale." *Texas Studies in Lit. and Lang.*, VI, 25-41.

Harvey, David Dow. *Ford Madox Ford, 1873-1939: A Bibliography of Works and Criticism.* . . . See VB 1963, 441.
Rev. by N. Rougier-Lenoir in *Études anglaises*, XVII, 87-88; by Miriam Allott in *MLR*, LIX, 123-24; by J. A. Bryant, Jr., in *SeR*, LXXII, 495-500.

Lid, R. W. *Ford Madox Ford: The Essence of His Art.* Berkeley: Univ. of California Pr. Pp. 192.
Rev. by J. R. Willingham in *LJ*, LXXXIX, 4538.

Meixner, John. *Ford Madox Ford's Novels.* . . . See VB 1963, 442.
Rev. by Elliott B. Gose in *Criticism*, VI, 99; by N. Rougier-Lenoir in *Études anglaises*, XVII, 88-89; by Miriam Allott in *MLR*, LIX, 123-24; by C. B. Cox in *RES*, n.s. XV, 335-36; by J. A. Bryant, Jr., in *SeR*, LXXII, 495-500.

Ohmann, Carol. *Ford Madox Ford: From Apprentice to Craftsman.* Middletown: Wesleyan Univ. Pr., Pp. 185.
Rev. by Bill Katz in *LJ*, LXXXIX, 1965; by Granville Hicks in *SR*, 16 May, p. 37.

Wiley, Paul L. *Ford Madox Ford: Novelist of Three Worlds.* . . . See VB 1963, 442.
Rev. by Elliott B. Gose in *Criticism*, VI, 99.

FROUDE.

Dunn, Waldo Hilary. *James Anthony Froude: A Biography.* Vol. I: *1818-1856;* Vol. II: *1857-1894.* . . . See VB 1963, 442.
Rev. in *Economist*, CCX, 116; by John Clive in *JMH*, XXXVI, 466-67; by E. G. Collieu in *Listener*, 6 Feb., p. 242; by R. H. S. Crossman in *NS*, LXVII, 81; by Gertrude Himmelfarb in *NY Rev. of Books*, 25 June, p. 9; by Herman Ausubel in *NYTBR*, 15 Mar., p. 14.

O'Connor, Peter. "An Unpublished Letter from J. A. Froude to Ruskin." *N&Q*, n.s. XI, 233-35.

GASKELL (see also II, Holloway; DICKENS: Carnall).

Hulin, Jean-Paul. "Les débuts littéraires de

Mrs. Gaskell: réflexions sur un poeme oublié." *Études anglaises*, XVII, 128-39. The poem is "Rich and Poor."

GILBERT.

Allen, Reginald. *W. S. Gilbert: An Anniversary Survey and Exhibition Checklist.* Charlottesville: Bibl. Soc. of the Univ. of Virginia. Pp. 82.

Rev. by P. L. Miller in *LJ*, LXXXIX, 4327; by P. H. Muir in *Theatre Notebook*, XVIII, 137-39; in *TLS*, 19 March, p. 244.

Ellis, James D. "The Comic Vision of W. S. Gilbert." *DA*, XXV, 1207-08.

Hammond, John W. "Gilbert's 'Trial by Jury.'" *Ex*, XXIII, Item 34.

GISSING.

Coustillas, Pierre. "The Letters of George Gissing to Gabrielle Fleury." *Bull. New York Pub. Libr.*, LXVIII, 433-61; 525-48; 602 ff.

A selection from the complete series of one hundred letters.

Coustillas, Pierre (ed.). *The Letters of George Gissing to Gabrielle Fleury.* New York: New York Public Libr., Pp. 194.

Haight, Gordon S. "Gissing: Some Biographical Details." *N&Q*, n.s. XI, 235-36.

Korg, Jacob. *George Gissing: A Critical Biography.* . . . See VB 1963, 442.

Rev. by R. F. Anderson in *Dalhousie Rev.*, XLIV, 103-04; by Pierre Coustillas in *Études anglaises*, XVII, 86-87; by H. A. Smith in *MLR*, LIX, 652; by Arthur C. Young in *NCF*, XVIII, 399-402; by Ruth M. Adams in *SAQ*, LXIII, 254; by Norman Kelvin in *Western Humanities Rev.*, XVIII, 184-85.

GLADSTONE (see also II, Jenkins).

Shannon, R. T. *Gladstone and the Bulgarian Agitation, 1876.* . . . See VB 1963, 427.

Rev. by E. G. Collieu in *History*, XLIX, 255-56; in *TLS*, 5 March, p. 190.

GREEN.

Richter, Melvin. *The Politics of Conscience: T. H. Green and His Age.* Cambridge, Mass.: Harvard Univ. Pr.; London: Weidenfeld and Nicholson. Pp. 415.

Rev. by H. B. Acton in *Listener*, 20 Aug., p. 279; by Stuart Hampshire in *NS*, LXVIII, 184; by Maurice Cowling in *S*, 25 Sept., p. 405; in *TLS*, 15 Oct., p. 932.

HARDY (see also III, Drew, Gross, Hardy, Mizener; Stewart; BRONTËS: Marks).

Blunt, Wilfrid. "Thomas and Florence Hardy." (Pp. 212-23 in *Cockerell*. See Section II above.)

Bugler, Gertrude. *Personal Recollections of*

Thomas Hardy. Dorchester: Dorset Natural History and Archaeological Society.

Carpenter, Richard C. "The Mirror and the Sword: Imagery in *Far from the Madding Crowd.*" *NCF*, XVIII, 331-45.

Dawson, E. W. "Two 'Flat' Characters in *Jude the Obscure.*" *The Lock Haven Review*, No. 6, 36-44.

On little Father Time and Physician Vilbert.

Deacon, Lois, and Cox, J. S. *Tryphena and Thomas Hardy.* . . . See VB 1963, 443.

Rev. by C. J. P. Beatty in *N&Q*, n.s. XI, 80.

Gerber, Helmut E. "Hardy's *The Well-Beloved* as a Comment on the Well-Despised." *ELN*, I, 48-53.

Griffith, Philip Mahone. "The Image of the Trapped Animal in Hardy's *Tess of the D'Urbervilles,*" *Tulane Studies in English*, XIII, 85-94.

Guerard, Albert J. "The Illusion of Simplicity: The Shorter Poems of Thomas Hardy." *SeR*, LXXII, 363-89.

Hardy, Evelyn. "Hardy's Romance." *TLS*, 20 Feb., p. 153.

Heilman, Robert B. "Hardy's *Mayor:* Notes on Style." *NCF*, XVIII, 307-29.

Illustrates weaknesses and strengths of Hardy's style with examples from the one novel.

Hellstrom, Ward. "Hardy's Use of Setting and 'Jude the Obscure.'" *VNL*, No. 25 (Spring), pp. 11-13.

Heywood, C. "Miss Braddon's *The Doctor's Wife.*" *Revue de littérature comparée*, XXXVIII, 255-61.

Hoffman, Russell. "The Idea of the Unconscious in the Novels of Thomas Hardy." *DA*, XXIV, 4190.

Homer, Christine Wood. *Thomas Hardy and His Two Wives.* Beaminster: Toucan Pr. Pp. 16.

Horne, Lewis B. "Fawley's Quests: A Reading of *Jude the Obscure.*" *Tennessee Studies in Literature*, IX, 117-27.

Following Northrop Frye's three stages of the romance-quest.

McDowell, Frederick P. W. "In Defense of Arabella A Note on *Jude the Obscure.*" *ELN*, I, 274-80.

Oliver, Constance Muriel. *Thomas Hardy Proposes to Mary Waight.* Beaminster: Toucan Pr. Pp. 14.

Orel, Harold. *Thomas Hardy's Epic-Drama.* . . . See VB 1963, 443.

Rev. by Walter F. Wright in *CE*, XXV, 634; by J. O. Bailey in *JEGP*, LXIII, 380-83.

Parish, John E. "Thomas Hardy on the Evidence of Things Unseen." *Vict. Poetry*, II, 203-05.

Posey, Horace G., Jr. "*The Dynasts*: Unity in Irony (A Critical Study)." *DA*, XXIV, 4682.

Riesner, Dieter. "Kunstprosa in der Werkstatt: Hardy's *The Mayor of Casterbridge*." Pp. 267-326 in *Festschrift fur Walter Hübner*; Berlin: Erich Schmidt. "An excellent, detailed study of Hardy's manuscript, with seven reproductions of the novelist's autograph; thorough-going, authoritative." – Carl J. Weber.

Scudamore, Joyce. *Florence and Thomas Hardy: A Retrospect.* Beaminster: Toucan Pr. Pp. 14.

Spradley, John D. "The Contrast of Old and New in the Novels of Thomas Hardy." *DA*, XXV, 456.

Urwin, George G. *The Mayor of Casterbridge: Notes on English Literature.* New York: Barnes and Noble. Pp. 82.

Weber, Carl J. (ed.). "*Dearest Emmie*": *Thomas Hardy's Letters to His First Wife.* . . . See VB 1963, 444.
Rev. by K. T. Willis in *LJ*, LXXXIX, 110; in *New Yorker*, 18 Jan., p. 117.

Weber, Carl J. "Hardy's Comet." *ELN*, I, 215-18.

Weber, Carl J. (ed.). *Hardy's Love Poems.* . . . See VB 1963, 444.
Rev. by H. C. Burke in *LJ*, LXXXIX, 2351; by William Kean Seymour in *Poetry Rev.*, LV, 106-09.

Wessex Redivivus: *The Return of "Wessex,"* with an Introduction by Richard Curle. Beaminster: Toucan Pr.

Wing, George Douglas. *Hardy.* . . . See VB 1963, 444.
Rev. by Carl J. Weber in *NCF*, XVIII, 402-04.

HENLEY (see also III, San Juan).

San Juan, Epifanio. "The Question of Values in Victorian Activism." *The Personalist*, XLV, 41-59.
Activist philosophies of Henley, Kipling, Stevenson as manifested in their works.

HENTY.

Naidis, Mark. "G. A. Henty's Idea of India." *VS*, VIII, 49-58.

HOPKINS (see also III, Ludwig, Miller; RUSKIN: Fike).

Andreach, Robert J. "The Spiritual Life in Hopkins, Joyce, Eliot, and Hart Crane." *DA*, XXV, 467.

Bates, Ronald. " 'The Windhover.' " *Vict. Poetry*, II, 63-64.

Colson, Ted D. "An Analysis of Selected Poems of Gerard Manley Hopkins for Oral Interpretation and a Study of His Poetic Theories." *DA*, XXIV, 5604.

Doherty, Francis. "A Note on Spelt from Sibyl's Leaves." *EC*, XIV, 428-32.
Refers to article by Gomme (below).

Gomme, Ander. "A Note on Two Hopkins Sonnets." *EC*, XIV, 327-31.
Reinterprets two passages in *Spelt from Sibyl's Leaves* explicated by Leavis.

Hafley, James. "Hopkins: 'A Little Sickness in the Air.' " *Ariz. Q.*, XX, 215-22.

Hines, Leo. "Pindaric Imagery in G. M. Hopkins." *Month*, CCXV (1963), 294-307.

Huntley, John F. "Hopkins' 'The Windhover' as a Prayer of Request." *Renascence*, XV, 154-62.

Keating, John Edward. "*The Wreck of the Deutschland*": *An Essay and a Commentary.* . . . See VB 1963, 444.
Rev. by Robert Boyle in *JEGP*, LXIII, 536-38.

Kopper, Edward A., Jr. "Hopkins' 'The Windhover.' " *Ex*, XXII, Item 54.

Litzinger, Boyd. "The Pattern of Ascent in Hopkins." *Vict. Poetry*, II, 43-47.

Lukanitsch, Ruth M. "The Relationship of the Figures of Sound to the Rhythm in Certain Poems of Gerard Manley Hopkins." *DA*, XXV, 696.

McNamara, Peter L. "Motivation and Meaning in the 'Terrible Sonnets.' " *Renascence*, XVI, 78-80.

Miller, Bruce E. "On 'The Windhover.' " *Vict. Poetry*, II, 115-19.

Olney, James L. "George Herbert and Gerard Manley Hopkins: A Comparative Study in Two Religious Poets." *DA*, XXV, 1895-96.

Orr, Paul A. "The Artistic Principles of Gerard Manley Hopkins," *DA*, XXV, 2965-66.

Pendexter, Hugh. "Hopkins' 'God's Grandeur.' " *Ex.*, XXIII, Item 2.

Shea, F. X., S. J. "Another Look at 'The Windhover.' " *Vict. Poetry*, II, 219-39.
A reading of the poem with emphasis upon the literal meaning first of all.

Watson, Thomas L. "Hopkins' 'God's Grandeur.' " *Ex*, XXII, Item 47.

HOUSMAN.

Curtis, Jean-Louis. "Un gars de Shropshire." *Cahiers des saisons*, No. 35 (Fall, 1963), pp. 534-37.

Haber, Tom Burns. "A. E. Housman's Notebooks and His Posthumous Poetry." *Iowa English Yearbook*, No. 8 (Fall, 1963), pp. 55-62.

Seigel, Jules Paul. "A. E. Housman's Modification of the Flower Motif of the Pastoral Elegy." *Vict. Poetry*, II, 47-50.

HUXLEY (see also III, Cockshut, Dobrée)

Eisen, Sydney. "Huxley and the Positivists." *VS*, VII, 337-58.

Noland, Richard W. "T. H. Huxley on Culture." *The Personalist*, XLV, 94-111.

KEBLE.

Battiscombe, Georgina. *John Keble: A Study in Limitations.* . . . See VB 1963, 445.

Rev. by Josef L. Altholz in *AHR*, LXX, 233; in *Economist*, CCIX, 919; by Robert B. Martin in *Herald Trib.*, 20 Sept., p. 8; by Shildes Johnson in *LJ*, LXXXIX, 1596; by Christopher Ricks in *NY Rev. of Books*, 9 July, p. 17; by Olive J. Brose in *VS*, VIII, 188-89; in *YR*, LIV, xvi-xxvi.

KINGSLEY.

Scheverle, William H. "Henry Kingsley, A Study." *DA*, XXV, 1200-01.

KIPLING (see also III, Stewart, San Juan); HENLEY: San Juan).

Bodelsen, Carl Adolf. *Aspects of Kipling's Art.* . . . See VB 1963, 445.

Rev. by A. O. J. Cockshut in *Critical Quart.*, VI, 283-85; by Francis Léaud in *ESt*, XLV, 419-21; by J. I. M. Stewart in *Listener*, 19 Mar., pp. 483-84; by Dan Jacobson in *Manchester Guardian Weekly*, 26 Mar., p. 10; by John Gross in *NS*, LXVII, 913-14; in *TLS*, 20 Feb., pp. 137-38.

Cornell, Louis L. "Kipling in India." *DA*, XXIV, 4695-96.

Hall, Robert A., Jr. *Cultural Symbolism in Literature.* Ithaca, N.Y.: Linguistica, 1963, Pp. 169.

Includes a discussion of *Stalky and Co.*

O'Connor, Frank. *The Lonely Voice: A Study of the Short Story.* London: Macmillan, 1963. Pp. 221.

Rev. by Margaret Willy in *English*, XV, 70; by Rosalind Wade in *CR*, CCV, 164; by Jim Hunter in *S*, 17 Jan., p. 84; in *TLS*, 9 Jan., p. 28.

Includes a discussion of Kipling as short-story writer.

Rouse, John Junior. "The Literary Reputation of Rudyard Kipling: A Study of the Criticism of Kipling's Works in British Literary Periodicals from 1886 to 1960." *DA*, XXV, 1199.

Rutherford, Andrew (ed.). *Kipling's Mind and Art: Selected Critical Essays.* Stanford: Stanford Univ. Pr.; Edinburgh and London: Oliver and Boyd. Pp. x + 278.

Rev. by Gordon K. Grigsby in *CE*, XXVI, 244; by Norman Mackenzie in *Dalhousie Rev.*, XLIV, 226-30; by Douglas Hewitt in *EC*, XIV, 416-24; by Gilbert Thomas in *English*, XV, 109-10; by J. I. M. Stewart in *Listener*, 19 Mar., pp. 483-84; by K. T. Willis in *LJ*, LXXXIX, 3011; by Dan Jacobson in *Manchester Guardian Weekly*, 26 Mar., p. 10; by John Gross in *NS*, LXVII, 913; in *TLS*, 2 Apr., p. 266.

LANDOR.

Grigson, Geoffrey (ed.). *Walter Savage Landor: Poems.* London: Centaur Pr. Pp. 330.

Rev. by John Holloway in *S*, 16 Oct. p. 514; in *TLS*, 29 Oct., p. 980.

Perrine, Laurence. "Landor and Immortality." *Vict. Poetry*, II, 50-57.

LEAR.

Quennell, Peter (ed.). *Edward Lear in Southern Italy.* London: William Kimber. Pp. 212.

Rev. in *TLS*, 3 Dec., p. 1105.

LEE.

Gunn, Peter. *Vernon Lee: Violet Paget, 1856-1935.* London: Oxford Univ. Pr. Pp. xi + 244.

Rev. by Naomi Lewis in *NS*, LXVIII, 125; by Joanna Richardson in *Listener*, 23 July, p. 135; in *TLS*, 13 Aug., p. 719.

LE FANU.

Lougheed, W. E. "An Addition to the Le Fanu Bibliography." *N&Q*, n.s. XI, 224.

LIVINGSTONE (see II: Tabler).

MACAULAY.

Goulding, Daniel J. "An Analytical and Evaluative Study of the Speech Criticism of Thomas Babington Macaulay." *DA*, XXV, 2102-03.

Lamont, William M. "Macaulay, the Archbishop and the Civil War." *History Today*, XIV, 791-96.

Critique of Macaulay's treatment of Laud.

Plumb, J. H. *Men and Centuries.* Boston: Houghton, 1963. Pp. 294.

Rev. by R. R. Rea in *LJ*, LXXXIX, 106.

Includes an essay on Macaulay.

Yoder, Edwin M., Jr. "Macaulay Revisited." *SAQ*, LXIII, 542-51.

MACREADY.

Shattuck, Charles H. (ed.). *Mr. Macready Produces "As You Like It": A Prompt-Book Study.* . . . See VB 1963, 445.

Rev. by Hubert C. Heffner in *JEGP,* LXIII, 499-505; by R. Loper in *QJS,* 89-90; by Arthur Colby Sprague in *Theatre Notebook,* XVIII, 60.

Shattuck, Charles H. (ed.). *William Charles Macready's "King John."*. . . See VB 1963, 445.

Rev. by Hubert C. Heffner in *JEGP,* LXIII, 499-505; by R. Loper in *QJS,* L, 89-90.

MAURICE.

Davies, W. Merlin. *An Introduction to F. D. Maurice's Theology.* London. S. P. C. K. Pp. xii + 212.

Porter, John F., and Wolf, William J. (eds.). *Toward the Recovery of Unity: The Thought of Frederick Denison Maurice.* New York: Seabury Pr. Pp. vi + 246.

MEREDITH (see also III, Hardy).

Baylen, Joseph O., and Hogan, Patrick G., Jr. "W. T. Stead's 'Interview with George Meredith': An Unpublished Version." *Tennessee Studies in Literature,* IX, 99-116.

Stead's unpublished private memorandum of his conversation with Meredith, February 19, 1903.

Beer, Gillian. "George Meredith and *The Satirist." RES,* n.s. XV, 283-95.

On an unpublished, uncompleted play by Meredith.

Beer, Gillian. "Some Compositors' Misreadings of 'The Tragic Comedians.' " *N&Q,* n.s. XI, 229-31.

Buchen, Irving H. "The Egoists in *The Egoist:* the Sensualists and the Ascetics." *NCF,* XIX, 255-69.

Hergenhan, L. T. "Meredith's Attempts to Win Popularity: Contemporary Reaction." *St. in English Lit.,* IV, 637-51.

Concentrates on reviews of *Rhoda Fleming, Vittoria,* and *Harry Richmond.*

Hergenhan, L. T. "Meredith's Use of Revision: A Consideration of the Revisions of 'Richard Feverel' and 'Evan Harrington.' " *MLR,* LIX, 539-44.

Hergenhan, L. T. "A Note on Some of George Meredith's Contemporary Reviewers." *N&Q,* n.s. XI, 231-32.

Hergenhan, L. T. "The Reception of George Meredith's Early Novels." *NCF,* XIX, 213-35.

Includes conclusions from many neglected reviews plus a bibliography.

Ketcham, Carl H. "A Note on the Feverel Crest." *VNL,* No. 26 (Fall), p. 32.

Kruppa, Joseph E. "Meredith's Late Novels: Suggestions for a Critical Approach." *NCF,* XIX, 271-86.

Thematic interrelationships of the last three novels.

Murphy, Michael. "Meredith's 'Essay on Comedy': A Possible Source." *N&Q,* n.s. XI, 228.

Sudrann, Jean. " 'The Linked Eye and Mind': A Concept of Action in the Novels of George Meredith." *St. in English Lit.,* IV, 617-35.

Swaminathan, S. R. "Meredith's Pictures of the Comic Muse and Clara Middleton." *N&Q,* n.s. XI, 228-29.

Talon, Henri A. "Le comique, le tragique et le romanesque dans *The Ordeal of Richard Feverel. Études anglaises,* XVII, 241-61.

Thomson, Fred C. "Symbolic Characterization in 'One of Our Conquerors.' " *VNL,* No. 26 (Fall), pp. 12-14.

MILL (see also III, Cockshut, Davies, Dobrée).

Bill, Thomas Lee. "The Theory of Nature in John Stuart Mill." *DA,* XXV, 535.

Cowling, Maurice. *Mill and Liberalism.* . . . See VB 1963, 446.

Rev. by Jack Stillinger in *AHR,* LXIX, 1126-27; by John M. Robson in *Dalhousie Rev.,* XLIV, 223-26; in *Economist,* CCX, 512; in *HJ,* LXII, 110; by Maurice Cranston in *Listener,* 2 Jan., p. 446; by Gertrude Himmelfarb in *NY Rev. of Books,* 20 Feb., p. 10; by K. R. Minogue in *Philosophy,* XXXIX, 366-67; by Elie Kedourie in *S,* 9 Oct., p. 484; by Bernard Wishy in *VS,* VII, 399-400.

Ellery, John B. *John Stuart Mill.* New York: Twayne. Pp. 134.

Hall, Roland. "The Diction of John Stuart Mill." *N&Q,* n.s. XI, 30-34; 102-07; 183-88; 218-23; 307-12; 379-85; 423-29.

Mineka, Francis E. (ed.). *The Earlier Letters of John Stuart Mill, 1812-1848.* . . . See VB 1963, 446.

Rev. by David Roberts in *AHR,* LXX, 235; by David Spitz in *APSS,* CCCLVI, 227; by David Owen in *Canadian Historical Rev.,* XLV, 340-41; by Maurice Cranston in *Listener,* 2 Jan., p. 29; by Gertrude Himmelfarb in *NY Rev. of Books,* 20 Feb., p. 10; by Charles Richard Sanders in *SAQ,*

LXIII, 419-21; by William Diebold, Jr. in *SR*, 7 Mar., p. 41; in *TLS*, 16 Apr., pp. 301-03; by Jacob Viner in *TQ*, XXXIV, 98-103; by Maurice Cranston in *VS*, VII, 81-83.

Morris, John N. "Versions of the Self: Studies in English Autobiography from John Bunyan to John Stuart Mill." *DA*, XXV, 2964.

Randall, John Herman, Jr. "John Stuart Mill and the Working-Out of Empiricism." *JHI*, XXVI, 59-88.

Robson, John M. "A Note on Mill Bibliography." *TQ*, XXXIV, 93-97.

Stillinger, Jack (ed.). *The Early Draft of John Stuart Mill's "Autobiography."*. . . See VB 1962, 416.
Rev. by J. F. Burnet in *EHR*, LXXIX, 196-97.

MORRIS.

Arnot, Robert Page. *William Morris: The Man and the Myth*. London: Lawrence and Wishart. Pp. 131.
Rev. in *TLS*, 19 Nov., p. 1036.
On Morris as Socialist; written from the Marxist point of view. Includes hitherto unpublished letters.

Ellison, R. C. "An Unpublished Poem by William Morris." *English*, XV, 100-02.
Addressed to Jane Morris, written in Eddic metre; of great biographical and intrinsic interest. — O.M.

LeMire, Eugene D. "The Unpublished Lectures of William Morris. A Critical Edition, including an Introductory Survey and a Calendar and Bibliography of Morris's Public Speeches." *DA*, XXIV, 3325.

Middleton, Bernard C. *A History of the English Craft Bookbinding Technique*. New York and London: Hafner Publ. Co., 1963. Pp. 307.
Rev. by E. P. Womersley in *BSP*, LVIII, 311-13.
Includes an appendix which discusses Morris.

NEWMAN (see also III, Davies).

Altholz, Josef L. "Newman and History." *VS*, VIII, 285-94.

Apologia pro Vita Sua. Introduction by Basil Willey. London: Oxford Univ. Pr. Pp. 405.
Rev. in *TLS*, 13 Aug., p. 730.

Blehl, Vincent F., and Connolly, Francis X. (eds.). *Newman's Apologia: A Classic Reconsidered*. New York: Harcourt Brace. Pp. viii + 182.
Rev. by W. C. Heiser in *LJ*, LXXXIX, 4541.

Blehl, Vincent Ferrer (ed.). *Realizations:*

Newman's Selection of His Parochial and Plain Sermons. Foreword by Muriel Spark. London: Darton, Longman, and Todd. Pp. xix + 171.
Rev. in *TLS*, 13 Aug., p. 730.

[Buckler, William E. (ed.)] "Newman's 'Apologia': A Classic Reconsidered." *VNL*, No. 25 (Spring), pp. 24-26.
Summaries of six papers on the *Apologia* prepared by the authors: Hugo M. De Achaval, S. J.; Vincent Ferrer Blehl, S. J.; Edward E. Kelly, S. J.; Sister Mary Baylon Lenz, O. S. F.; Martin J. Svaglic; and Francis X. Connolly.

Campbell, William D. "Approaching the Venture of Faith: An Apologetical Study of the Rational Development and Experiences of a Convert Prior to the Life and Writings of John Henry Cardinal Newman." *DA*, XXV, 3134-35.

Dessain, Charles Stephen, and Blehl, Vincent Ferrer (eds.). *The Letters and Diaries of John Henry Newman*. . . . See VB 1963, 447.
Vol. XIV: *Papal Aggression, July 1850 to December 1851*. London: Nelson, 1963. Pp. xviii + 555.
Rev. in *TLS*, 27 Feb., p. 168.
Vol. XV: *The Achilli Trial, January 1852 to December 1853*. London: Nelson. Pp. xvi + 568.
Rev. in *TLS*, 30 July, p. 668.

Rowland, Sister Mary Joyce. "The Acts of the Mind in Newman's Theory of Assent." *DA*, XXIV, 4239-40.

Ryan, Alvan S. "A Matter of Unacknowledged Borrowing." *VNL*, No. 25 (Spring), pp. 26-29.
A letter to the Editor about an article on Newman.

Slavin, Howard B. "Newman's Illness in Sicily: A Review and an Interpretation." *Wiseman Rev.*, CCXXXVIII, 35-54.

Smith, T. D. Wilson. "Newman and the Teaching of History." *Wiseman Rev.*, CCXXXVIII, 147-56.

Trevor, Meriol. *Newman Today*. London: Catholic Truth Society, 1963. Pp. 24.

Trevor, Meriol. *Newman: Light in Winter*. . . . See VB 1963, 447.
Rev. by John Pick in *Books Abroad*, XXXVIII, 79; by James R. Bennett in *MP*, LXI, 318.

Trevor, Meriol. *The Pillar of the Cloud*. . . . See VB 1963, 447.
Rev. by James R. Bennett in *MP*, LXI, 318.

O'SHAUGHNESSY.

Paden, W. D. "Arthur O'Shaughnessy in the British Museum; or, The Case of the Misplaced Fusees and the Reluctant Zoologist." *VS*, VIII, 7-30.

Paden, W. D. "Arthur O'Shaughnessy: The Ancestry of a Victorian Poet." *Bull. of the John Rylands Library*, 429-47.

PATER (see also RUSKIN: Fishman, Poston).

Brzenk, Eugene J. (ed.). *Walter Pater: Imaginary Portraits: A New Collection*. With an introduction by the editor. New York: Harper and Row. Pp. 216.

> Rev. by Lawrence Poston, III, in *CE*, XXVI, 64; by Catherine A. Cox in *TQ*, XXXIV, 202-03.

Harris, Wendell V. "Pater as Prophet." *Criticism*, VI, 349-60.

Stasny, John F. "Doctor Johnson and Walter Pater on Stoicism: A Comparison of Views." *W. Va. Univ. Bull. Philological Papers*, XIV, 18-25.

Vogeler, Martha Salmon. "The Religious Meaning of *Marius the Epicurean*." *NCF*, XIX, 287-99.

PATMORE (see also III, Wright).

Shmiefsky, Marvel. " 'Principle in Art' as Criticism in the Mainstream." *VNL*, No. 26 (Fall), pp. 28-32.

> Centers about Patmore's poetic theory.

ROLFE.

Andrews, Clarence A. "Raging in the Dark — An Examination of the Life and Letters of Frederick William Rolfe, Baron Corvo." *DA*, XXIV, 4688-89.

ROSSETTIS (see also III, Wright).

Buttel, Helen. "Rossetti's 'Bridal Birth.' " *Ex*, XXIII, Item 22.

Franklin, Colin. " 'The Blessed Damozel' at Penkill." *EC*, XIV, 331-35.

> Biographical evidence to help interpret "The Blessed Damozel."

Grylls, R. Glynn. "The Reserved Rossetti Letters." *TLS*, 30 Jan., p. 96.

> 117 letters, 1868-1881, from Rossetti to Jane Morris, now first accessible at the British Museum.

Packer, Lona Mosk. *Christina Rossetti*. . . . See VB 1963, 448.

> Rev. in *Economist*, CCXI, 149; by Ralph Lawrence in *English*, XV, 110; by Philip Larkin in *Listener*, 26 Mar., p. 526; by K. T. Willis in *LJ*, LXXXIX, 858; by Paull F. Baum in *MLQ*, XXV, 224-26; by V. S. Pritchett in *NS*, LXVII, 491; by John

Smith in *Poetry Rev.*, LV, 105; briefly in *QR* (July), 359-60; by Graham Hough in *S*, 3 April, p. 453; in *TLS*, 9 April, p. 292 (and see letters by Mrs. Packer, 23 April, p. 343; H. F. Rossetti, Janet Troxell and Lucy O'Connor, 7 May, p. 402; Mrs. Packer and Virginia Surtees, 14 May, p. 415; Mrs. Troxell, 21 May, p. 435; Helen Madox Rossetti Angeli, 2 July, p. 571; Mrs. Packer, 9 July, p. 616); by Erwin Hester in *VQR*, XL, 329; by William E. Fredeman in *VS*, VIII, 71-77; by Robert L. Peters in *Western Humanities Rev.*, XVIII, 379-81.

Packer, Lona Mosk. "Christina Rossetti." *TLS*, 24 Dec., p. 1163.

> Two letters from Christina Rossetti to William Bell Scott.

Packer, Lona Mosk. "Maria Francesca to Dante Gabriel Rossetti: Some Unpublished Letters." *PMLA*, LXXIX, 613-19.

Packer, Lona Mosk (ed.). *The Rossetti-Macmillan Letters*. . . . See VB 1963, 448.

> Rev. by Ralph Lawrence in *English*, XV, 110; by Philip Larkin in *Listener*, 26 Mar., p. 526; by K. T. Willis in *LJ*, LXXXIX, 868; by John Smith in *Poetry Rev.*, LV, 105; by Graham Hough in *S*, 3 Apr., p. 453; in *TLS*, 9 Apr., p. 292; by Erwin Hester in *VQR*, XL, 331; by William E. Fredeman in *VS*, 71-77; by Robert L. Peters in *Western Humanities Rev.*, XVIII, 379-81.

Pedrick, Gale. *Life with Rossetti: or, No Peacocks Allowed*. London: Macdonald. Pp. 237.

> Rev. by Naomi Lewis in *NS*, LXVIII, 579-80; in *TLS*, 15 Oct., p. 934.
> Based on the recollections, published and unpublished, of Rossetti's assistant, Henry Treffry Dunn.

Vogel, Joseph F. "Rossetti's 'Memorial Thresholds.' " *Ex*, XXIII, Item 29.

Weatherby, Harold L. "Problems of Form and Content in the Poetry of Dante Gabriel Rossetti." *Vict. Poetry*, II, 11-19.

RUSKIN.

Bell, Quentin. *Ruskin*. . . . See VB 1963, 448.

> Rev. by P. Fontaney in *Études anglaises*, XVII, 201; by Michael Levy in *NS*, LXVII, 52-53; briefly in *QR* (Jan.), p. 120.

Bradley, John Lewis (ed.). *The Letters of John Ruskin to Lord and Lady Mount-Temple*. Columbus: Ohio State Univ. Pr. Pp. xiii + 399.

Cherry, Douglas R. "Ruskin: Unacknowledged Legislator of the Social Sciences." Contained in *Thought from the Learned Societies of Canada 1961*. Toronto: W. J.

Gage, Ltd., 1962.

Clark, Kenneth (ed.). *Ruskin Today*. London: John Murray. Pp. 362.
Rev. by Herbert Read in *Listener*, 3 Dec., p. 896; in *TLS*, 3 Dec., p. 1108.

Dearden, James. "John Ruskin's Bookplates." *Book Collector*, XIII, 335-39.
Identifies bookplates inserted in volumes formerly in Ruskin's possession.

Donald, James W. "Reason and the Idea of Man in John Ruskin." *DA*, XXV, 1192.

Fike, Francis G., Jr. "The Influence of John Ruskin Upon the Aesthetic Theory and Practice of Gerard Manley Hopkins." *DA*, XXV, 1208.

Fishman, Solomon. *The Interpretation of Art: Essays on the Art Criticism of John Ruskin, Walter Pater, Clive Bell, Roger Fry and Herbert Read*. . . . See VB 1963, 448.
Rev. by Lawrence Poston, III, in *CE*, XXV, 634; by Donald Weeks in *JAA*, XXII, 4761.

"Follies — But No Fool." *TLS*, 5 March, p. 195.
A leading article on an exhibition, "Ruskin and his Circle."

Grigson, Geoffrey. "Pope of Art." *NS*, LXVII, 222-23.
Essay responding to Arts Council's "Ruskin and His Circle."

Johnson, Wendell Stacy. " 'The Bride of Literature': Ruskin, The Eastlakes, and Mid-Victorian Theories of Art." *VNL*, No. 26 (Fall), pp. 23-28.

Poston, Lawrence S., III. "Five Victorians on Italian Renaissance Culture: A Problem in Historical Perspectives." *DA*, XXV, 484.
Ruskin, Browning, Eliot, Pater, Symonds.

Rosenberg, John D. *The Darkening Glass: A Portrait of Ruskin's Genius*. . . . See VB 1963, 448.
Rev. by Quentin Bell in *Apollo* (Aug.) p. 168; by Rachel Trickett in *EC*, XIV, 193-97; by P. Fontaney in *Études anglaises*, XVII, 79; by John L. Bradley in *MLR*, LIX, 651; by Philip Toynbee in *Observer*, 2 June.

Rosenberg, John D. (ed.). *The Genius of John Ruskin: Selections from His Writings*. New York: George Braziller; London: Allen and Unwin, 1963. Pp. 560.
Rev. by Herbert Read in *Listener*, 3 Dec., p. 896; by Francis Haskel in *NY Rev. of Books*, 2 Apr., p. 4; by Graham Hough in *S*, 2 Oct., p. 444; noticed in *TLS*, 8 Oct., p. 925.

Wise, Thomas James (ed.). *A Complete Bibliography of the Writings in Prose and Verse of John Ruskin, LL.D. With a List of the More Important Ruskiniana*. London: Dawsons. 2 vols.: pp. 329; 263.
Rev. in *TLS*, 22 Oct., p. 968.
A reprint.

RUTHERFORD (see also ELIOT: Merton).

Thomson, Patricia. "The Novels of Mark Rutherford." *EC*, XIV, 256-67.
Study of theme of married incompatibility and idealism in Rutherford's novels.

SHAW (see also III, Bentley, Brustein, Shelley, Stewart).

Barr, Alan P. "Bernard Shaw as a Religious Dramatist." *DA*, XXV, 1902-03.

Byers, William F. "The Nineteenth Century English Farce and Its Influence on George Bernard Shaw." *DA*, XXV, 4693.

DuCann, C. G. L. *The Loves of George Bernard Shaw*. . . . See VB 1963, 448.
Rev. by Marvin Mudrick in *NY Rev. of Books*, 2 Apr., p. 7.

Dukore, Bernard F. "Brecht's Shavian Saint." *QJS*, L, 136-39.

Dunbar, Janet. *Mrs. G. B. S.: A Biographical Portrait of Charlotte Shaw*. . . . See VB 1963, 448.
Rev. by Harry W. Rudman in *Books Abroad*, XXXVIII, 315.

Gassner, John. "Shaw on Ibsen and the Drama of Ideas." *English Institute Essays: Ideas in the Drama* (New York, 1964), pp. 71-100.

Geduld, Harry M. (ed.). *The Rationalization of Russia* by George Bernard Shaw. Bloomington: Indiana Univ. Pr. Pp. 134.
Rev. by John S. Reshetar, Jr. in *APSS*, CCCLVI, 211; by Irving Howe in *Book Week*, 17 May, p. 5; by Richard Ohmann in *Commonweal*, LXXX, 519; by Pat Sloan in *Science & Society*, XXVIII, 497; by P. E. Mosely in *SR*, 18 July, p. 32; in *TLS*, 7 May, p. 396.

Gollin, Richard M. "Beerbohm, Wilde, Shaw, and 'The Good-Natured Critic': Some New Letters." *Bull. New York Pub. Libr.*, LXVIII, 83-99.
The good-natured critic is Edward Rose (1849-1904): the article prints one letter from Beerbohm, one from Wilde, and twelve from Shaw.

Hales, John. "Shaw's Comedy." *DA*, XXIV, 3324.

Holt, Charles L. "The Musical Dramaturgy of Bernard Shaw: A Study in Playcrafting." *DA*, XXV, 1892.

The Independent Shavian. Vol. II, No. 3

(Spring, 1964), has items: "Mr. Bernard Shaw's Works of Fiction, Reviewed by Himself" (pp. 25, 29-32); Matlaw, Myron, "Shaw, Farleigh, and the Black Girl," an introduction to "The Black Girl Collection," a collection of drawings, water colors, engravings, and letters exchanged by Shaw and the English artist John Farleigh during the preparation of the illustrated edition of Shaw's *The Adventures of the Black Girl in Her Search for God* (pp. i-ix, special supplement); Bennett, James R., a review of Tauber, Abraham (ed.), *George Bernard Shaw on Language* (p. 28); Crompton, Louis, a review-article on Martin Meisel's *Shaw and the Nineteenth Century Theater* (pp. 34-35).

Vol. III, No. 1 (Fall, 1964) has items: Cordell, Richard A., "Shaw in the College Classroom (pp. 1-3); McDowell, Frederick P., a review-article of Geduld, Harry M. (ed.), *Bernard Shaw, The Rationalization of Russia* (pp. 4-5); Leary, Daniel J., "A Few Notes on Shaw and Tragedy" (pp. 10-11); Tepfer, John, a review of Smith, Warren S. (ed.), *The Religious Speeches of Bernard Shaw* (pp. 12-13); Nickson, Richard, a theater-review of *Arms and the Man* (p. 14).

Vol. III, No. 2 (Winter, 1964-65) has items: G. B. S., "Morris as Actor and Dramatist," from *Saturday Review*, 10 Oct., 1896, with notes by J. R. Dunlap (pp. 1-5); Dukore, Bernard F., a review of B. C. Rosset's *Shaw of Dublin* (pp. 7-8); Matlaw, Myron, a review of Eric Bentley's *The Life of the Drama* (pp. 8-9); Weissman, Philip, an excerpt from his forthcoming *Creativity in Theater: A Psychoanalytic Study* (pp. 11-13); Masumoto, Masahiko, "Shaw in Japan — A Preliminary Report" (p. 15).

Langner, Lawrence. *G. B. S. and the Lunatic.* . . . See VB 1963, 449.
　Rev. by Phoebe Adams in *AM*, CCXIII, No. 2, p. 144; in *TLS*, 24 Dec., p. 1165.

Mann, Thomas. "L'impertinence libératrice." *Cahiers des saisons*, No. 37 (Spring, 1964), pp. 167-72.

Mayne, Fred. "The Real and the Ideal: Irony in Shaw." *Southern Rev.*, I, 15-25.

McDowell, Frederick P. W. "Heaven, Hell, and Turn-of-the-Century London: Reflec-

tions on *Man and Superman.*" *Drama Survey*, II, 254-68.

McDowell, Frederick P. W. "Shaw's Increasing Stature." *Drama Survey*, III, 423-41.

Maulnier, Thierry. "De Bernard Shaw à Jean Schlumberger." *La Revue de Paris* (Mai), pp. 132-35.
　Sainte Jeanne in Paris.

Meisel, Martin. *Shaw and the Nineteenth-Century Theater.* . . . See VB 1963, 449.
　Rev. by David Morse in *Encounter*, XXII, 78; by Timothy Rogers in *English*, XV, 66-67; by Margery M. Morgan in *MLR*, LIX, 652-53; by D. Schaal in *QJS*, L, 457; by Marjorie Thompson in *Theatre Notebook*, XVIII, 135-37; by Harry Geduld in *VS*, VII, 400-01.

Nolte, William H. "GBS and HLM." *Southwest Rev.*, XLIX, 163-73.
　Contrasts Shaw and Mencken.

Ohmann, Richard M. *Shaw: The Style and the Man.* . . . See VB 1963, 449.
　Rev. by James H. Wheatley in *JEGP*, LXIII, 822-24; by Frederick P. W. McDowell in *PQ*, XLIII, 141-44; by G. S. Frazer in *VS*, VII, 317-18; by J. R. Bennett in *Western Humanities Rev.*, XVIII, 289-90.

Oppel, Horst (ed.). *Das Moderne Englishche Drama: Interpretationen.* Berlin: Erich Schmidt Verlag, 1963. Pp. 380.
　Rev. by T. M. Gang in *N&Q*, n.s. XI, 393-94.
　Three essays on Shaw and three on Yeats.

Purdom, Charles Benjamin. *A Guide to the Plays of Bernard Shaw.* . . . See VB 1963, 449.
　Rev. in *Economist*, CCVII, 61; by Jean-Claude Amalric in *Études anglaises*, XVII, 298-99; by H. A. Smith in *MLR*, LIX, 126; by Marvin Mudrick in *NY Rev. of Books*, 2 Apr., p. 7; by George Rowell in *RES*, n.s. XV, 336-37.

Rosset, B. C. *Shaw of Dublin: The Formative Years.* Foreword by Stanley Weintraub. University Park: Pennsylvania State Univ. Pr. Pp. xxiv + 388.
　Rev. by P. Moran in *LJ*, LXXXIX, 4338; by Gene Baro in *NYTBR*, 20 Sept., p. 44.

The Shaw Review, Vol. VII, No. 1 (January, 1964), has items: Nethercot, Arthur H., "A Plea for BERNARD Shaw" (pp. 2-9); Gerould, Daniel C., " 'Saint Joan' in Paris" (pp. 11-23); Ayling, Ronald, "The Ten Birthplaces of 'Saint Joan': A Letter from G.B.S." (p. 24); Brown, Jack R., "Two Notes on Shaw's 'Advice to a Young Critic': 'You Can Never Tell' and 'Arms on the Man' " (pp. 25-27); "Shaw-Script" (pp. 28-29); "A Continuing Checklist of Shaviana," compiled and edited by Stephen S. Stanton (pp. 30-34); Caro, Warren, a review of Lawrence Langner's *G.B.S. and the Lunatic* (pp. 35-36); Seabrook, Alexander, a review of Warren S. Smith's *The Religious Speeches of Bernard Shaw* (pp. 37-38); Carpenter, Charles A., a review of Martin Meisel's *Shaw and the Nineteenth-Century Theater* (pp. 38-40).

No. 2 (May, 1964) has items: Bosworth, R. F., "Shaw Recordings at the B.B.C." (pp. 42-46); Rosset, B. C., "McNulty's 'How I Robbed the Bank of Ireland' " (pp. 47-53); Weintraub, Stanley, "The Two Sides of 'Lawrence of Arabia': Aubrey and Meek" (pp. 54-57); Geduld, Harry M., "The Lineage of Lilith" (pp. 58-61); Meisel, Martin, "Cleopatra and 'The Flight into Egypt' " (pp. 62-63); Weisert, John J., "One Amongst So Many: A Minority Report from Germany" (pp. 64-65); "A Continuing Checklist of Shaviana," compiled and edited by Stephen S. Stanton (pp. 66-71); Nethercot, Arthur H., a review of C. G. L. DuCann's *The Loves of George Bernard Shaw* (pp. 72-74); Magner, Thomas F., a review of Shaw's *The Rationalization of Russia*, ed. with an intro. by Harry M. Geduld (pp. 74-76).

No. 3 (September 1964) has items: Carpenter, Charles A., "Shaw's Cross Section of Anti-Shavian Opinion" (pp. 78-86); "Two Edwardian Satires on Shaw" (pp. 87-94); Henderson, Lucille K., "Archibald Henderson" (pp. 95-104); "A Continuing Checklist of Shaviana," compiled and edited by Stephen S. Stanton (pp. 105-09); Steinhardt, Maxwell, a review of B. C. Rosset's *Shaw of Dublin* (pp. 110-12); Gerould, Daniel C., a review of George E. Wellwarth's *The Theater of Protest and Paradox: Developments in the Avant-Garde Drama* (pp. 113-116).

Smith, Warren Sylvester (ed.). *The Religious Speeches of Bernard Shaw*. University Park: Pa. State Univ. Pr., 1963. Pp. 104.
Rev. by J. A. Davidson in *Christian Century*, LXXXI, 17; by Hector Hawton in *The Humanist*, XXIV, 197; by R. W. Henderson in *LJ*, LXXXIX, 1250; by Marvin

Mudrick in *NY Rev. of Books*, 2 Apr., p. 7; by R. L. Scott in *QJS*, L, 456-57.
Stockholder, Fred E. "G. B. Shaw's German Philosophy of History and the Significant Form of His Plays." *DA*, XXV, 1221.
Tauber, Abraham (ed.). *George Bernard Shaw on Language*.... See VB 1963, 450.
Rev. by Marvin Mudrick in *NY Rev. of Books*, 2 Apr., 7; by J. D. Adams in *NYTBR*, 1 Mar., p. 2; by R. W. Wendahl in *QJS*, L, 467.
Watson, Barbara Bellow. *A Shavian Guide to the Intelligent Woman*. London: Chatto and Windus. Pp. 251.
Weintraub, Stanley. *Private Shaw and Public Shaw: A Dual Portrait of Lawrence of Arabia and G. B. S.*... See VB 1963, 450.
Rev. by Richard M. Ohmann in *SAQ*, LXIII, 139.
SPENCER (see III, Cockshut, Munro).
SPURGEON.
Spurgeon, Charles Haddon. *The Early Years*.... See VB 1963, 450.
Rev. by Patricia S. Kruppa in *VS*, VII, 393-97.
STEPHENS.
Frankenberg, Lloyd. (ed.). *James, Seumas and Jacques: Unpublished Writings of James Stephens*. New York: Macmillan. Pp. xxxii + 288.
Rev. by B. G. Loftus in *LJ*, LXXXIX, 1966.
STEVENSON (see also HENLEY: San Juan).
Kiely, Robert. *Robert Louis Stevenson and the Fiction of Adventure*. Cambridge, Mass.: Harvard Univ. Pr. Pp. ix + 285.
McKay, George L. (ed.). *A Stevenson Library: A Catalogue of a Collection of Writings By and About Robert Louis Stevenson Formed by Edwin J. Beinecke*. Vol. 6: *Addenda and Corrigenda*. New Haven, Conn.: Yale Univ. Pr.
Thomas, Dylan. *The Beach of Falesá: A Film Scenario Based on a Story of Robert Louis Stevenson*. London: Cape. Pp. 124.
Rev. in *TLS*, 30 July, p. 670.
SURTEES.
Collison, Robert L. *A Jorrocks Handbook*. London: Coole Book Service. Pp. xv + 162.
Noticed in *TLS*, 28 May, p. 461.
SWINBURNE (see also III, Wright).
The Novels of A. C. Swinburne.... See VB 1963, 450.

Rev. by David Daiches in *VS*, VII, 314-16.

Cassidy, John A. *Algernon C. Swinburne.* New York: Twayne. Pp. 186.

Lang, Cecil Y. (ed.). *New Writings by Swinburne.* Syracuse, N. Y.: Syracuse Univ. Pr. Pp. xv + 253.

Nowell-Smith, Simon. "Swinburne's *The Queen-Mother [and] Rosamond,* 1860." *Book Collector,* XIII, 357-59.
Query about publishing history of the book.

Peters, Robert L. "Swinburne and the Moral Design of Art." *Vict. Poetry,* II, 139-54.

SYMONDS.

Grosskurth, Phyllis. "The Genesis of Symonds's Elizabethan Criticism." *MLR,* LIX, 183-93.
Based on a copy of Lamb's *Specimens of English Dramatic Poets,* annotated by Symonds.

Grosskurth, Phyllis. *John Addington Symonds: A Biography.* London: Longmans. Pp. x + 370.
Rev. by C. Ricks in *NS*, LXVIII, 53; by Patrick Anderson in *S*, 10 July, pp. 50-52; in *TLS*, 16 July, p. 629 (and see letters by Phyllis Grosskurth, 6 Aug., p. 695; by Alan Bird, 8 Oct., p. 924; by L. H. Green, 22 Oct., p. 959; by Stanley Gillam, 29 Oct., p. 979; by Ian Fletcher, 5 Nov., p. 999; by Leon Edel, 3 Dec., p. 1107; by L. H. Green, 17 Dec., p. 1145).

Smith, Timothy d'Arch. "John Addington Symonds: The 'Peccant' Pamphlets." *Book Collector,* XIII, 68-70.

SYMONS (see also DOWSON: Munro; RUSKIN: Poston).

Leyris, Pierre. "Pour Arthur Symons: À propos d'une biographie." *Mercure de France,* CCCL, 3-10.

Leyris, Pierre (tr.). "Seaward Lackland." *Mercure de France,* CCCL, 11-29.

TENNYSON (see also III, Bose).

Assad, Thomas J. "Tennyson's 'Tears, Idle Tears.'" *Tulane Studies in English,* XIII, 71-83.

Brashear, William R. "Tennyson's Third Voice: A Note." *Vict. Poetry,* II, 283-86.

Bufkin, E. C. "Imagery in 'Locksley Hall.'" *Vict. Poetry,* II, 21-28.

Colbeck, Norman. "Variant Bindings on Moxon Authors." *Book Collector,* XIII, 356-57.
Bindings of *In Memoriam.*

Drew, Philip. "'Aylmer's Field': A Problem for Critics." *Listener,* 2 Apr., pp. 553; 556-57.

A perceptive analysis of one of Tennyson's "idylls of the hearth," indicating particularly well the inability of modern criticism to come to grips with the special qualities of the genre. — M.T.

Eidson, John Olin. "The First Performance of Tennyson's *Harold.*" *NEQ,* XXXVII, 387-90.
Hitherto unrecorded premiere of *Harold.*

Eidson, John Olin. "Tennyson's *The Foresters* on the American Stage." *PQ,* XLIII, 549-57.
A successful production by Augustin Daly, New York, 1892.

Eidson, John Olin. "Tennyson's First Play on the American Stage," *AL,* XXXV, 519-28.
Queen Mary opened in Philadelphia six months before its London performance.

Engbretsen, Nancy M. "The Thematic Evolution of 'The Idylls of the King.'" *VNL,* No. 26 (Fall), pp. 1-5.

Glasser, Marvin. "The Early Poetry of Tennyson and Yeats: A Comparative Study." *DA,* XXIV, 4174.

Grob, Alan. "Tennyson's *The Lotus Eaters:* Two Versions of Art." *MP,* LXII, 118-29.

Marshall, George O., Jr. *A Tennyson Handbook.* New York: Twayne Publishers, Inc., 1963. Pp. 291.
Rev. by Clyde de L. Ryals in *Vict. Poetry,* II, 215-17.

Mitchell, Charles. "The Undying Will of Tennyson's Ulysses." *Vict. Poetry,* II, 87-95.

Packer, Lona Mosk. "Sun and Shadow: The Nature of Experience in Tennyson's 'The Lady of Shalott.'" *VNL,* No. 25 (Spring), pp. 4-8.

Pitt, Valerie. *Tennyson Laureate.* . . . See VB 1963, 452.
Rev. by Joseph E. Baker in *PQ,* XLIII, 573-74; by A. Dwight Culler in *YR,* LIII, 440-43.

Poston, Lawrence, III. "The Argument of the Geraint-Enid Books in *Idylls of the King.*" *Vict. Poetry,* II, 269-75.

Püschel, Brita. *Thomas À Becket in der Literatur.* Beiträge Zur Englischen Philologie, Vol. 45: Heinrich Pöppinghaus, Bochum-Langendreer, 1963. Pp. viii + 183.
Rev. by J. C. Maxwell in *N&Q,* n.s. XI, 359-60.

Rader, Ralph Wilson. *Tennyson's Maud: The Biographical Genesis.* Berkeley: Univ. of California Pr.; London: Cambridge Univ. Pr., 1963. Pp. x + 155.

Rev. by Stephen E. Henderson in *CE*, XXVI, 64; by Gilbert Thomas in *English*, XV, 109-10; by Jerome H. Buckley in *JEGP*, LXIII, 820-22; by Christopher Ricks in *Listener*, 27 Feb., pp. 363-64; by John Killham in *MLR*, LIX, 650-51; in *TLS*, 20 Feb., p. 148; by Clyde de L. Ryals in *Vict. Poetry*, II, 133-35; by Rowland L. Collins in *VS*, VIII, 85-86.

Ricks, Christopher. "Tennyson: Three Notes." *MP*, LXII, 139-41.

Ricks, Christopher. "Tennyson's 'Hail, Briton!' and 'Tithon': Some Corrections." *RES*, n.s. XV, 53-55.

Ricks, Christopher. "Tennyson's *Maud*." *TLS*, 31 Dec., p. 1181.

Ryals, Clyde de L. *Theme and Symbol in Tennyson's Poems to 1850*. Philadelphia: University of Pennsylvania Pr.; London: Oxford University Pr. Pp. 282.
Rev. by Philip Drew in *Listener*, 15 Oct., p. 601; in *TLS*, 6 Aug., p. 698; by Lionel Stevenson in *Vict. Poetry*, II, 287-90.

Smith, Elton Edward. *The Two Voices: A Tennyson Study*. Lincoln: Univ. of Nebraska Pr. Pp. ix + 217.

Stokes, Edward. "The Metrics of *Maud*." *Vict. Poetry*, II, 97-110.
A careful analysis of the metrics reveals recurrent patterns which relate to the changing moods of the speaker.

Tennyson, Charles (ed.). *The Devil and the Lady and Unpublished Early Poems*. Bloomington: Indiana Univ. Pr. 2 vol. in one: pp. 67 and 83.
Rev. by J. R. Willingham in *LJ*, LXXXIX, 2801; by Christopher Ricks in *N Y Rev. of Books*, 11 June, p. 15.

Tennyson, Charles. "The Dream in Tennyson's Poetry." *VQR*, XL, 228-48.

Tennyson Collection: Usher Gallery, Lincoln. Lincoln: City Libraries, Museum, and Art Galleries Committee, 1963. Pp. 34.
Rev. by T. J. Brown in *Book Collector*, XIII, 237-42.

"Tennysoniana." *TLS*, 16 July, p. 640.
On a Tennyson Research Centre recently opened in the Lincoln City Library by the present Lord Tennyson.

Todd, William B. "Wise, Wrenn, and Tennyson's *Enoch Arden*." *Book Collector*, XIII, 67-68.

THACKERAY (see also II, Holloway; III, Drew, Hollingsworth; DICKENS: Johnson (Paul), Ward).

Vanity Fair. Edited with an Introduction and Notes by Geoffrey and Kathleen Tillotson.

... See VB 1963, 452.
Rev. by H.-A. Talon in *Études anglaises*, XVII, 203-04.

Dyson, A. E. "*Vanity Fair*." *Critical Quart.*, VI, 11-32.
Vanity Fair is an illustration of Thackeray's claim, as a novelist, of the right to be a "total realist," realism for him meaning "coming to terms with a radically unheroic world." Dyson insists that Thackeray must be regarded as one of the most sophisticated of ironists. Characters and events in the novel must be judged not by conventional standards, but in the context of the author's "social realism." Dyson's analysis of the two women, Amelia and Becky, is especially noteworthy. A brief resumé of Thackeray's life and the circumstances surrounding the writing and publication of *Vanity Fair* concludes the essay, which deserves a prominent place in any list of recent Thackeray studies. — M. T.

Fido, Martin. "*The History of Pendennis*, A Reconsideration." *EC*, XIV, 363-79.

Galey, Mathieu (tr.). *Le livre des Snobs*. Paris: Nouvel office d'édition.
Rev. by Pierre Arnaud in *Mercure de France*, CCCLI, 712-13.

Kock, Paul de (tr.). *Samuel Titmarsh et le grand diamant des Hoggarty*. Paris: Gallimard.
Rev. by Pierre Arnaud in *Mercure de France*, CCCLI, 712-13.
Thackeray "semble décidément revenir à la mode."

Loofbourow, John. *Thackeray and the Form of Fiction*. Princeton: Princeton Univ. Pr. Pp. vi + 236.

Loomis, Chauncey C., Jr. "Thackeray the Satirist." *DA*, XXIV, 4192.

Maître, R. "Nouvelles sources françaises de Thackeray." *Études anglaises*, XVII, 56-61.

Painting, David E. "Thackeray v. Disraeli." *QR* (Oct.), pp. 396-407.

Plunkett, P. M. "Thackeray's 'Vanity Fair.'" *Ex*, XXXIII, Item 19.

Queval, Jean (tr.). *La Rose et l'anneau*. Paris: Mercure de France.
Rev. by Pierre Arnaud in *Mercure de France*, CCCLI, 712-13.

Ray, Gordon N. "The Search for William Makepeace Thackeray." *SR*, 1 Feb., pp. 20-21; 43-44.

Stevens, Joan. "A Thackeray Error." *N&Q*, n.s. XI, 223-24.

Talon, Henri A. *Two Essays on Thackeray*. Dijon: Faculté des Lettres et des Science

Humaines. Pp. 42.
Essays on *Vanity Fair* and *Henry Esmond.*
THOMPSON.
Buchen, Irving H. "Source-Hunting versus Tradition: Thompson's 'The Hound of Heaven.'" *Vict. Poetry*, II, 111-15.
Danchin, Pierre. "Du nouveau sur Francis Thompson, Prosateur et critique." *Études anglaises*, XVII, 225-40.
Jeune, Simon. "Francis Thompson." *Revue de litt. comparée*, XXXVIII, 301-05.
TROLLOPE (see also II, Holloway; III, Mizener).
Bulgin, Randolph M. "Anthony Trollope's *The Way We Live Now*: A Study of Its Historical Background and Critical Significance." *DA*, XXIV, 4676-77.
Cadbury, William. "Character and the Mock Heroic in *Barchester Towers*." *Texas Studies in Lit. & Lang.*, V, 509-19.
Kenney, Blair Gates. "The Two Isabels: A Study in Distortion." *VNL*, No. 25 (Spring), pp. 15-17.
Trollope's Isabel Boncassen and James's Isabel Archer.
Lerner, Laurence. "Trollope: The Entertainer." *Listener*, 7 May, pp. 753-55.
Polhemus, Robert M. "The Changing World of Anthony Trollope." *DA*, XXIV, 5415.
Sadleir, Michael. *Trollope: A Bibliography.* London: Dawson. Pp. 338.
A welcome reprint of this definitive book, long unavailable.
Shaw, W. David. "Moral Drama in *Barchester Towers*." *NCF*, XIX, 45-54.
WILDE (see also III, Beebe; SHAW: Gollin).
The Ballad of Reading Gaol. Mit zwölf Holzschnitten von Erich Heckel. Hamburg: Hauswedell; New York: Ernest Rathenau. Pp. 52.
Rev. in *TLS*, 20 Aug., p. 751.
Freedman, Morris. "The Modern Tragicomedy of Wilde and O'Casey." *CE*, XXV, 518-27.
Hyde, H. Montgomery. *Oscar Wilde: The Aftermath.* . . . See VB 1963, 453.
Rev. by Margaret Willy in *English*, XV, 69; by Ian Fletcher in *MLR*, LIX, 284-85; by Thomas J. Garbáty in *VS*, VII, 401-04.
Monteiro, George. "A Contemporary View of Henry James and Oscar Wilde, 1882." *AL*, XXXV, 528-30.

When both visited Washington, D.C.
Nicholas, Brian. "Two Nineteenth-Century Utopias: The Influence of Renan's 'L'Avenir de la Science' on Wilde's 'The Soul of Man under Socialism.'" *MLR*, LIX, 361-70.
Wilson, Harry. "Epistolary Autobiography: The Letters of Oscar Wilde." *SAQ*, LXIII, 406-13.
YEATS (see also III, Stewart; SHAW: Oppel; TENNYSON: Glasser).
Adams, Hazard. "Symbolism and Yeats's *A Vision*." *JAA*, XXII, 425-36.
Allen, James L., Jr. "William Butler Yeats's One Myth." *The Personalist*, XLV, 524-32.
Brennan, Diarmuid. "As Yeats Was Going Down Grafton Street." *Listener*, 6 Feb., pp. 236-38.
Brooks, Cleanth. *The Hidden God: Studies in Hemingway, Faulkner, Yeats, Eliot, and Warren.* . . . See VB 1963, 453.
Rev. by Earl Rovit in *Books Abroad*, XXXIX, 80; by Richard Coanda in *JEGP*, LXIII, 546-47.
Byars, John A. "The Heroic Type in the Irish Legendary Dramas of W. B. Yeats, Lady Gregory, and J. M. Synge: 1903-1910." *DA*, XXIV, 3333.
Chatterjee, Bhabatosh. *The Poetry of W. B. Yeats.* . . . See VB 1963, 453.
Rev. by Frank Kermode in *RES*, n.s. XV, 119.
Clark, David R. "W. B. Yeats and the Drama of Vision." *Ariz. Q.*, XX, 127-41.
Cornwell, Ethel F. *The Still Point: Theme and Variations in the Writings of T. S. Eliot, Coleridge, Yeats, Henry James, Virginia Woolf, and D. H. Lawrence.* New Brunswick: Rutgers Univ. Pr., 1962. Pp. x + 261.
Rev. by James Benziger in *Criticism*, VI, 198-200; by J. Guiguet in *Études anglaises*, XVII, 90-91; by G. D. Klingopulos in *MLR*, LIX, 471-72.
Ellmann, Richard. "Yeats Without Analogue." *KR*, XXVI, 30-47.
Engelberg, Edward. *The Vast Design: Patterns in W. B. Yeats's Aesthetic.* Toronto: Univ. of Toronto Pr. Pp. xxxi + 224.
Rev. by Paul J. Hurley in *CE*, XXVI, 170; by Robert L. Peters in *Criticism*, VI, 386-87; by Frederic S. Colwell in *QQ*, LXXI, 446-47; by Harold Bloom in *YR*, LIII, 143-49.
Gallagher, Patrick (ed.) *The Yeats Country.*

... See VB 1963, 454.
Rev. by A. Norman Jeffares in *MLQ*, XXV, 218-22.

Gogarty, Oliver St. John. *William Butler Yeats: A Memoir*. Preface by Myles Dillon. Dublin: Dolmen Pr.; London: Oxford Univ. Pr. Pp. 27.
Rev. by Robert Greacen in *Listener*, 23 Jan., p. 162; by T. R. Henn in *MLR*, LIX, 655; by R. Ellman in *NS*, LXVII, 461; briefly in *TLS*, 21 May, p. 442.

Hurwitz, Harold M. "Yeats and Tagore." *Comparative Literature*, XVI, 55-64.
Considers mutual influences in the thirty-seven year period of friendship and correspondence.

Kersnowski, Frank L. "The Irish Scene in Yeats's Drama." *DA*, XXIV, 5409.

Kostelanetz, Anne. "Irony in Yeats's Byzantium Poems." *Tennessee Studies in Literature*, IX, 129-42.

Levin, Gerald. "The Yeats of the Autobiographies: A Man of Phase 17." *Texas Studies in Lit. and Lang.*, VI, 398-405.

Linebarger, James M. "Yeats's 'Among School Children' and Shelley's 'Defence of Poetry.'" *N&Q*, n.s. X, 375-77.

Linebarger, James M. "Yeats' Symbolist Method and the Play: *Purgatory*." *DA*, XXIV, 3750-51.

Lucas, F. L. *The Drama of Chekhov, Synge, Yeats and Pirandello*. ... See VB 1963, 454.
Rev. by W. K. Seymour in *CR*, CCV, 108-09; in *TLS*, 9 Jan., p. 28; by J. Kazantzis in *Wiseman Rev.*, CCXXXVIII, 78-80.

Malins, Edward. "Yeats and the Bell-Branch." *The Consort*, XXI (Summer).

Merritt, Robert G. "Euripides and Yeats: The Parallel Progression of Their Plays." *DA*, XXIV, 3463.

Michie, Donald M. "A Man of Genius and a Man of Talent." *Texas Studies in Lit. and Lang.*, VI, 148-54.
Dramatic collaboration of Yeats and George Moore.

Parkinson, Thomas. *W. B. Yeats: The Later Poetry*. Berkeley: Univ. of California Pr.; Cambridge: Cambridge Univ. Pr. Pp. xii + 260.
Rev. by H. C. Burke in *LJ*, LXXXIX, 262; by Harold Bloom in *YR*, LIII, 143-49.

Parks, L. C. "The Hidden Aspect of 'Sailing to Byzantium.'" *Études anglaises*, XVI, 333-44.

Parrish, Stephen Maxwell (ed.). *A Concordance to the Poems of W. B. Yeats*, programmed by James Allan Painter. ... See VB 1963, 454.
Rev. by Robert E. Knoll in *CE*, XXV, 309; by T. R. Henn in *MLR*, LIX, 285-86; in *TLS*, 23 Jan., p. 69.

Perrine, Laurence. "Yeats' 'An Acre of Grass.'" *Ex*, XXII, Item 64.

Rosenbaum, S. P. "Yeats' 'Among School Children.'" *Ex*, XXIII, Item 14.

Seiden, Irving Morton. *William Butler Yeats: The Poet as Mythmaker, 1865-1939*. ... See VB 1963, 454.
Rev. by A. Norman Jeffares in *MLQ*, XXV, 454; by John B. Vickery in *Western Humanities Rev.*, XVIII, 182-83.

Shaw, Patricia Washburn. *Rilke, Valéry, and Yeats: The Domain of the Self*. New Brunswick: Rutgers Univ. Pr. Pp. xiv + 278.
Rev. by Robert M. Adams in *NY Rev. of Books*, 22 Oct., p. 19.

Southam, B. C. "Yeats' 'Long-Legged Fly.'" *Ex*, XXII, Item 73.

Stallworthy, Jon. *Between the Lines: Yeats's Poetry in the Making*. ... See VB 1963, 454.
Rev. by Norman Nathan in *CE*, XXV, 309; by A. Norman Jeffares in *MLQ*, XXV, 218-22.

Ure, Peter. *Yeats*. Writers and Critics Series. ... See VB 1963, 454.
Rev. by W. K. Seymour in *CR*, CCV, 108-09; by V. de S. Pinto in *Critical Quart.*, VI, 186-87; briefly in *QR* (Jan.), p. 120.

Ure, Peter. *Yeats the Playwright: A Commentary on Character and Design in the Major Plays*. ... See VB 1963, 454.
Rev. by V. de S. Pinto in *Critical Quart.*, VI, 186-87; by Jon Stallworthy in *RES*, n.s. XV, 215-17.

Vendler, Helen Hennessy. *Yeats's Vision and the Later Plays*. ... See VB 1963, 454.
Rev. by V. de S. Pinto in *Critical Quart.*, VI, 186-87; by A. Norman Jeffares in *MLQ*, XXV, 218-22.

Wall, Richard J. and Fitzgerald, Roger. "Yeats and Jung: an Ideological Comparison." *Lit. and Psychology*, XII, 44-52.

Whitaker, Thomas R. *Swan and Shadow: Yeats's Dialogue with History*. Chapel Hill: Univ. of North Carolina Pr. Pp. 340.
Rev. by Robert Scholes in *Am. Scholar*, XXXIII, 137-40; by B. W. Fuson in *LJ*, LXXXIX, 4360.

The index contains in alphabetical order (1) the names of modern scholars whose books and articles are listed in the 1955-64 issues of the Victorian Bibliography, (2) the names of Victorian figures and other persons associated with titles or mentioned in comments about the works listed, and (3) certain general topics assumed to be of interest to scholars of the Victorian period. Not indexed are authors of reviews in periodicals and newspapers. I have listed all entries for an individual under one form of his name — "Doe, John A.," for instance — even though his name may appear in various forms in the Bibliography itself.

Page numbers in the index refer to the continuous pagination of this book, found at the *bottom* of each page. The pagination at the top of each page has been retained from the annual issues for purposes of cross reference. Index numbers in italics refer to annual collections of entries pertaining to Victorian authors; these collections are indicated in the bibliographies by boldface type. All other index references are in roman type.

ROBERT C. SLACK

Allen, Jeremiah Mervin, 85
Allen, Jerry, 137, 301
Allen, Louis, 8, 28, 210
Allen, Reginald, 266, 387
Allen, Richard Eilers, 60
Allen, V. L., 361
Allen, Walter Ernest, 8, 9, 385
Allen, Walter Gore, 198
Allentuck, Marcia, 196
Allingham, William, 113, *132*
Allison, Alexander, 185
Allott, Kenneth, 13, 51, 133, 172, 258, 302, 337, 374, 377
Allott, Miriam, 32, 64, 134, 167, 210, 226, 253, 265
Allt, Peter, 35
Alman, Miriam, 278
Almedingen, Edith Martha von, 115
Altholz, Josef Lewis, 198, 279, 319, 361, 391
Altick, Richard D., 53, 85, 93, 126, 155, 156, 167, 175, 184, 196, 234, 238, 293, 339
Altrincham, Lord, 149
Alvarez, Alfred, 127, 152
Ambirajan, S., 239
Amis, Kingsley, 142
Ancaster, Lord, 355
Andersen, Hans Christian, 9, 97, 139, 236
Anderson, Alan, 170
Anderson, Olive, 198, 361
Anderson, R. G., 139
Anderson, Roland F., 385
André, Robert, 351
Andreach, Robert J., 388
Andreas, Osborn, 177, 220
Andrews, Clarence, 392
Andrews, John S., 45, 60, 85, 167, 253
Andrews, Sir Linton, 15, 338
Angelo, Helena, 5
Annan, Noel, 49, 229, 374, 377
Anouilh, Jean, 355
Anson, Peter Frederick, 198, 361
Anstey, R. T., 279, 319, 361
Anstruther, Ian, 102, 319
Antonelli, E., 239
Apperley, Charles James ("Nimrod"), 191, 234, 273
Appleman, Phillip, 9, 108, 157, 198, 239, 279
Aragon, Louis, 136
Arberry, Arthur John, 99, 183, 210, 226

Archer, Mildred, 157, 279, 319
Archer, William, 85
Arents Collection, 156
Argles, Michael, 361
Aring, Charles D., 233
Aristophanes, 144
Aristotle, 63
Arlen, Sara, 149
Arlott, John, 115
Armstrong, A. MacC., 127
Armstrong, Henry Edward, 118, 201
Armstrong, Isobel, 301, 379
Armstrong, R. L., 58
Armstrong, Warren, 279
Armstrong, William A., 39, 198
Armytage, W. H. G., 13, 39, 45, 64, 74, 115, 239, 240, 279, 319
Arnault, Antoine-Vincent, 64
Arnold, Armin, 196
Arnold, Sir Edwin, 11, *13*
Arnold, J. C., 240
Arnold, Matthew, 9, 11, 12, *13*, 38, 45, 49, 50, *51*, 60, *91*, 131, *132*, 157, 167, 168, 169, 170, *172*, 176, 186, 212, *215*, *257*, 267, 290, 294, 295, *297*, 319, 335, *337*, 340, 351, 355, 374, 375, *377*
Arnold, Ralph, 240
Arnold, Thomas, 91, 127, 174, 177, *216*, 229, 255, *258*, *298*, 377, *378*
Arnot, Robert Page, 391
Arnstein, Walter L., 74, 280, 306, 319
Arthos, John, 21, 352
Arundell, Dennis, 115
Ashburnham, Lord, 318
Ashby, Sir Eric, 127
Ashby, Joseph, 240, 280
Ashby, Mabel K., 240, 280
Ashby, Michael, 280
Ashley, Robert P., 54
Ashley, Sir William, 82
Ashton, Elwyn Thoms, 45, 84
Ashworth, William, 198, 240, 280, 319
Aslin, Elizabeth, 280
Aspinwall, William H., 122
Asquith, Lady Cynthia, 14
Asquith, Lord H. H., 367
Asquith, Margot, 281
Assaad, Fawzeia Mikhail, 338
Assad, Thomas Joseph, 9, 150, 218, 228, 259, 267, 355, 380, 396
Atkin, John R., 297
Atkins, N. J., 347

Atkinson, Blanche, 30
Atkinson, Brooks, 107
Atkinson, R. F., 103
Atthill, Robin, 262
Auberon, F., 139
Auchincloss, Katharine L., 353
Auchincloss, Louis, 253
Auchmuty, J. J., 144
Auden, W. H., 99, 232
August, Eugene R., 348
Austen, Albert A., 142
Austen, Jane, 100, 171, 214, 255, 345
Austin, Alfred, *14*, 87
Austin, Deborah S., 103
Austin, Don D., 232
Austin, James C., 259, 305
Ausubel, Herman, 39, 198, 240, 280
Autret, Jean, 64, 105, 271
Avery Architectural Library, Columbia University, 270
Axton, William F., 302, 342, 383
Ayers, R. W., 59
Ayling, Ronald F., 272, 394
Aylmer, Felix, 19, 181, 182, 222, 383
Aytoun, William Edmondstoune, 45, 87, *134, 378*
Aziz, K. K., 319

Babb, Howard, 347
Babb, James T., 37
Babbage, Charles, 369
Bache, William B., 95
Bachem, Rose M., 379
Backes, James G., 350
Backstrom, Philip N., Jr., 198, 319
Bacon, J., 19
Bacon, Jean C., 73
Baden-Powell, Olave, 78, 84, 366
Badger, Kingsbury, 16, 361
Baetzhold, Howard George, 9, 39, 181
Bagehot, Walter, *14, 134*, 148, *174*, 182, 193, *216, 258*, 296, *298, 338*, 356, 375, *378*
Bagwell, Philip Sidney, 319
Bahlman, Dudley W. R., 226
Bailey, D. R., 59
Bailey, Edna Watson, 18
Bailey, Sir Edward, 280, 320
Bailey, James Osler, 57, 100, 142, 184, 307, 347
Bailey, Philip James, *14*, 16, 45, 87, 113, *298, 338*
Bailey, R. V. C., 261

Bailey, Samuel, 250
Baillie, Eileen, 115
Baines, Jocelyn, 95, 220, 261
Baird, Donald, 155, 196
Baird, Sister Mary Julian, 59
Baker, Carlos, 57
Baker, Donald Whitelaw, 45
Baker, James R., 23
Baker, Joseph E., 32, 135, 188, 315
Baker, Sir Samuel White, 320
Baker, Theodore Cardwell, 198
Baker, Wyndham, 361
Balassa, Bela A., 187
Baldanza, Frank, 31
Baldwin, Arthur Windham, 198
Balfour, Arthur James, 334
Balfour, Michael, 233
Ball, Nancy, 320
Ball, Patricia M., 355, 373
Balleine, R. G., 74
Balliet, Conrad A., 297, 339
Balston, Thomas, 115, 240
Balzac, Honoré de, 86, 188, 235
Bamford, T. W., 216
Bandet, Pierre, 28
Bandy, W. T., 238
Banham, Reyner, 350
Banim, John, 128, 168
Banks, J. A., 3, 361
Banks, Olive, 361
Bankson, Douglas Henneck, 29
Banno, Masataka, 362
Bantock, G. H., 137
Banton, Michael, 240, 280
Banville, Théodore Faullain de, 171
Barbar, W. H., 196
Barber, George S., 106
Barber, Giles, 238
Barber, R. W., 293
Barbery, Y., 218
Barbier, Carl Paul, 362
Barham, Richard Harris, *14*, 20, 31, 87, *92*, 134
Baring-Gould, Sabine, *92, 134, 217*
Barish, Evelyn, 381
Barkai, H., 189
Barkeley, Richard, 39
Barker, Felix, 3
Barker, George, 106, 273
Barker, Harley Granville, 42, 43, 191
Barker, Kathleen M. D., 373
Barker, T. C., 280, 320, 330, 362
Barlow, Hannah B., 78

Barlow, Nora, 138, 178, 342
Barmann, Lawrence F., 310, 350
Barmby, J. Goodwin, 39
Barnabus, Franklyn, 233
Barnaby, Kenneth Cloves, 198
Barnardo, Dr. Thomas John, 324
Barnes, James J., 362
Barnes, Warner, 339
Barnes, William, 185, *258, 298, 338,* 377, *378*
Barnet, Sylvan, 65
Barnett, George L., 19
Barnett, Howard A., 218
Barnett, J. H., 315
Barnett, Samuel Anthony, 138, 178, 221
Barr, Alan P., 393
Barr, D. J., 260
Barrett, George, 135
Barrett, William, 106
Barrett, Wilson, 102
Barrie, Sir James Matthew, 8, *14,* 85, *92,* 113, 114, *134,* 148, 156, *174, 217*
Barrington, Charles George, 240
Barron, Diana, 373
Barry, Dr. James, 123
Barry, James Donald, 21, 182
Bart, Barry D., 383
Barth, Max, 183
Bartle, G. F., 240, 320, 338, 362
Bartlett, Christopher John, 320, 362
Bartlett, Lynn C., 350
Bartlett, Phyllis, 23, 103, 145, 187, 230, 350
Barton, John, 117
Barton, Mary N., 238
Barzun, Jacques, 31, 353
Basden, E. B., 293
Bates, Hazel, 280
Bates, Madison, 14, 187
Bates, Ronald, 388
Bateson, F. W., 354
Bateson, Gregory, 280
Batson, Eric J., 31, 65, 353
Battiscombe, Georgina, 57, 99, 349, 389
Baudelaire, Pierre Charles, 48, 87, 238
Baum, Paull Franklin, 38, 63, 133, 150, 172, 185, 192, 215
Baumer, Franklin L., 210
Baxter, Charles, 67, 191
Bayer, Theodor A., 75
Baylen, Joseph O., 85, 141, 157, 230, 253, 280, 310, 352, 353, 362, 390
Bayley, John, 85, 137

Beach, Joseph Warren, 9
Beale, Dorothea, 120
Beales, Derek Edward Dawson, 240, 280, 320
Bealey, Frank, 115, 157
Beames, John, 240
Bearce, George Donham, Jr., 39, 240, 280, 320
Beard, Geoffrey W., 157, 259
Beard, Harry R., 39
Beardsley, Aubrey, *14, 134,* 275, 295
Beatty, C. J. P., 266, 307, 347
Beatty, Charles, 75
Beatty-Kingston, William, 208
Beaty, Jerome, 56, 98, 141, 182, 225, 265, 305
Beaumont, Ernest, 63
Beaumont, S. J., 247
Beck, Martha Ryan, 85
Beck, Warren, 68
Becker, Eugene M., 210
Becker, Werner, 146
Beckett, J. C., 157, 205, 306
Beckman, Richard, 347
Beckson, Karl E., 167
Beckwith, Frank, 217
Bédarida, François, 198
Bedient, Calvin B., 385
Beebe, Maurice, 18, 56, 227, 341, 373
Beer, Gillian, 350, 390
Beer, John, 374
Beer, Samuel H., 75
Beerbohm, Sir Max, *14,* 34, *51, 92,* 111, 114, *134,* 165, *174,* 205, 210, *217,* 248, *258,* 272, *298,* 313, *338,* 360, *378,* 393
Beesly, E. S., 160, 325, 376
Beeton, Samuel Orchart, 87
Behrman, Samuel Nathaniel, 217, 258, 271, 272
Bell, Clive, 352, 393
Bell, Enid Moberly, 115, 280, 320
Bell, F. E., 14
Bell, Sir George, 39
Bell, Gertrude, 116
Bell, Inglis, 155, 196
Bell, Margaret, 29
Bell, Marion V., 73
Bell, Martha S., 155
Bell, Peter Robert, 178, 221, 261
Bell, Quentin, 320, 352, 392
Bell, Vereen M., 210, 298, 338
Bellamy, Edward, 293

Bellas, Ralph A., 270
Bellerby, J. R., 157
Bellman, Samuel Irving, 57
Belvin, Betty J. M., 167
Bender, Todd K., 348
Bengtsson, Frans S., 52
Benians, E. A., 157, 198, 240
Benish, John Roland, 26
Benjamin, Edwin B., 19
Bennett, Arnold, 272
Bennett, Carl D., 341
Bennett, George, 280
Bennett, James R., 240, 394
Bennett, Joan, 385
Bennett, Kenneth C., Jr., 312
Bennett, Mark, 107, 108, 191
Bennett, Mary, 334
Bennett, Raymond M., 265, 306
Bennoch, Francis, 93
Benson, Sir Francis Robert, 215
Benson, Lillian Rea, 21
Bentham, Jeremy, 8, 42, 44, 84, 121,
    134, 164, 166, 202, 217
Bentinck, Lord George, 122
Bentinck, Lord William, 39
Bentley, Eric, 85, 273, 373, 394
Bentley, Nathaniel, 20
Bentley, Phyllis, 15, 93, 338
Bentley, Richard, 30, 87, 92, 202, 244
Bentwich, Norman, 210
Benziger, James, 334, 373
Bercovici, Alfred, 300
Beresford, Michael, 121
Beresford, Rosemary, 33
Berg Collection, 156
Berger, Harold L., 297
Berghaus, Erwin, 362
Bergler, Edmund, 97
Bergonzi, Bernard, 240
Bergson, Henri Louis, 185, 301
Beringouse, A. F., 85
Berkeley, George, 35
Berkelman, Robert, 316
Berkley, Humphry, 280
Berkovitz, Miriam J., 344
Berlin, Isaiah, 269
Bernad, Miguel A., 308
Bernard, Robert, 264
Bernd, Daniel W., 352
Bernstein, Aline, 158
Bernstein, Henry T., 320
Bernstein, Samuel, 115
Berol, Alfred C., 177, 238, 266

Berry, Francis, 314, 355
Berry, Minta Sue, 347
Berthrong, Merrill Gray, 115
Bertocci, Angelo P., 63
Bertram, James, 54
Bertz, Eduard, 142, 266, 306
Besant, Annie, *14*, 31, *217*, *258*, *338*,
    378
Besant, Sir Walter, *52*
Best, Geoffrey Francis Andrew, 39, 127,
    199, 240, 362
Best, Henry Digby, 213
Best, R. I., 146
Betjeman, John, 75, 127, 235, 280
Betsky, Seymour, 210
Betts, William W., 214
Beum, Robert, 275
Bevan, Bryan, 13, 175
Beveridge, Janet, 199
Bevin, Ernest, 199
Bevington, David M., 262
Bevington, Merle M., 13, 192, 218, 233,
    259
Bewick, Thomas, 321
Bewley, Marius, 173
Beyle, Marie Henri. *See* "Stendhal"
Bibby, Cyril, 60, 101, 144, 186, 229,
    268
Bicknell, John W., 293, 313
Bierman, Robert, 275
Bill, Alfred Hoyt, 253
Bill, E. G. W., 39
Bill, Thomas Lee, 390
Billiar, Donald E., 334
Billingsley, Bruce A., 293
Binns, C. T., 320
Binyon, Laurence, 355
Birch, Alan, 320
Birch, D., 19
Bird, Anthony, 362
Bird, Kenneth, 80
Birkbeck, George, 88, 128, 129
Birkenhead, Earl of, 25, 268
Birkett, Lord, 240, 275, 302
Birley, Robert, 298, 338
Bischoff, A., 143
Bishop, Edmund, 209
Bishop, Edward, 362
Bishop, George Reginald, 9
Bishop, John J., 280
Bishop, Jonathan, 94, 181, 314
Bishop, Morchard, 69, 150

Brockett, O. G., 134
Brocklehurst, J. Brian, 127
Broderick, James H., 139
Brodie, Fawn M., 340, 380
Broeker, Galen, 75
Brogan, D. W., 281
Brogan, Howard O., 100
Brogunier, Joseph, 303
Brome, Vincent, 185, 228
Bromley, John, 199, 241
Brontë, Anne, *14, 134, 174, 217, 298, 338, 379*. See also Brontës, the
Brontë, Branwell, *14, 52, 134,* 156, *217, 259, 298*. See also Brontës, the
Brontë, Charlotte, 9, *14,* 46, *52, 93, 134,* 156, *174,* 210, *217, 259, 298, 338,* 374, *379*. See also Brontës, the
Brontë, Emily, *14,* 45, *52, 93, 134, 174,* 210, *217, 298,* 335, *338,* 374, *379*. See also Brontës, the
Brontë, Patrick, *14, 134, 174, 217, 259, 298*. See also Brontës, the
Brontës, the, *14,* 38, 39, 45, *52, 93,* 113, *134,* 152, *174, 217, 259,* 295, *298, 338, 379*. See also individual Brontës
Brook, G. L., 383
Brook, Michael, 75
Brooke, Sir Charles J., 248
Brooke, Stopford Augustus, 361
Brooke, Susan, 134
Brooks, Cleanth, 45, 91, 132, 172, 357, 398
Brooks, Harold F., 232, 343
Brooks, Jean R., 343
Brooks, Roger L., 133, 172, 173, 174, 215, 233, 297, 337, 377
Brose, Olive J., 40, 158, 199, 210, 241
Brough, Robert, 87
Brougham, Henry, *93, 135,* 208, *259, 299, 339*
Broughton, Leslie Nathan, 16
Brower, Reuben A., 293
Brown, Calvin S., 188, 235
Brown, Dorothy Snodgrass, 95
Brown, Douglas, 23, 307
Brown, E. H., Phelps, 75
Brown, E. K., 133
Brown, F. J., 383
Brown, Ford K., 241, 281, 321
Brown, Ivor, 45, 116, 343, 383
Brown, Jack R., 394
Brown, Keith, 385
Brown, Lucy, 116, 158, 199

Brown, Malcolm, 27, 62
Brown, Mary, 322
Brown, Paul A., 278
Brown, R. D., 70
Brown, Samuel E., 190
Brown, T. J., 218, 267, 271, 273, 337, 340, 355
Brown, Thomas Edward, *135, 299*
Brown University Library, 231
Browne, Ray, 85
Browne, Sir Thomas, 132
Browning, D. C., 114
Browning, Elizabeth Barrett, *15,* 38, 45, 50, *52,* 88, 89, *93, 135,* 155, *175, 218, 259, 299, 339, 379*
Browning, Oscar, 45
Browning, Robert, 9, *15,* 17, 25, 38, 45, 50, 51, *52,* 73, 86, 88, 90, *93, 135,* 148, 156, *175,* 215, *218, 259,* 294, 296, *299,* 335, *339, 379,* 393
Browse, Lillian, 45, 210
Bruce, Donald, 210
Bruce, Maurice, 116, 281, 321
Bruffee, Kenneth A., 382
Brugmans, Linette F., 184, 226, 346
Brumbaugh, Thomas B., 349
Brummell, George Bryan, Beau, 205, 248
Brunel, Isambard Kingdom, 82, 164
Brunschwig, Henri, 241
Brustein, Robert, 373
Bryant, Donald C., 294
Bryson, John, 175
Brzenk, Eugene J., 147, 392
Buchan, Alastair, 216, 258, 298
Buchanan, Robert Williams, 11
Buchen, Irving H., 269, 310, 344, 390, 398
Büchner, Georg, 20
Buck, Anne M., 241, 281
Buckle, Henry Thomas, *136, 176*
Buckler, William E., 2, 14, 19, 37, 127, 133, 173, 253, 257, 337, 391
Buckley, Jerome Hamilton, 38, 51, 234, 273, 294, 314
Buckley, Vincent, 168
Buckstone, John Baldwin, 374
Budd, Kenneth, 217, 258
Buechler, John, 116
Bufkin, E. C., 396
Bugler, Gertrude, 307, 387
Buhl, Paulina E., 259
Buist, Francis, 292
Bulgin, Randolph M., 398

Cameron, Sir John, 31
Campbell, A. E., 242, 281
Campbell, Harry M., 34
Campbell, James W., 363
Campbell, Sister M. Mary Hugh, 348
Campbell, Olwen, 186
Campbell, Mrs. Patrick, 243
Campbell, Ray Hutcheson, 242, 281, 321
Campbell, William D., 391
Campbell-Bannerman, Sir Henry, 367
Campenella, Anthony P., 281
Canady, Charles E., 321
Canney, Margaret B. C., 278
Canning, Charles John, First Earl, 162, 287, 327, 330
Canning, George Rolland, Jr., 188
Canning, Stratford, 323
Cannon, Walter F., 200, 210, 253, 261
Capon, R. L., 223
Carb, Nathan R. E., Jr., 189
Cardwell, D. S. L., 75, 116
Cardwell, Edward T., 159, 201, 292
Cardwell, Margaret, 223
Cargill, Oscar, 110, 194
Carleton, William, 128, 168
Carleton, William G., 363
Carlisle, Rosalind Howard, Countess of, 161
Carlton, William J., 19, 55, 97, 139, 181, 222, 223, 262, 303, 343, 383
Carlyle, Jane Welsh, *16, 136, 176, 219, 374*
Carlyle, Thomas, 9, 11, 14, *16*, 25, 27, 47, 50, 51, 52, *54*, 65, 68, 85, 87, 88, 89, *94*, 113, 120, 128, 129, 130, 131, 132, *136*, 139, 152, 167, 169, 173, 175, *176*, 212, *219*, 230, 242, *260*, 274, 291, *300*, 314, *340*, 373, 375, 377, *380*
Carnall, Geoffrey, 133, 383
Caro, Warren, 395
Carothers, Francis B., Jr., 46
Carpenter, Charles A., Jr., 149, 191, 233, 272, 273, 313, 352, 395
Carpenter, Edward, *136*
Carpenter, James, 200, 281
Carpenter, Minnie Lindsay, 75
Carpenter, Richard C., 227, 266, 387
Carpenter, Spencer Cecil, 158
Carr, J. C., 281, 321, 363
Carr, John Dickson, 182, 225
Carr, Sister Mary Callista, 262, 302

Carr, Robert, 310
Carrington, Charles E., 25, 60, 102, 144, 157, 198, 240
Carroll, D. R., 182, 225
Carroll, Lewis, *17*, 38, *54*, 87, *95*, 113, *136*, 156, *177, 220, 260, 300, 341, 381*
Carroll, Wesley, 18
Carruthers, Clive Harcourt, 381
Carson, Mother Angela, 350
Carson, Edward, 116
Carson, R. A. G., 76
Carson, William G. B., 85
Carte, Bridget D'Oyly, 346
Carter, George Stuart, 76, 116
Carter, Harry, 281, 321
Carter, John Archer, Jr., 37, 73, 97, 186, 197, 228, 268, 275, 281, 299, 309, 321, 348
Carter, Mark Bonham, 281
Carus-Wilson, E. M., 321
Cary, Joyce, 127
Cary, Richard, 184, 339, 357
Case, Lynn M., 321
Casement, Roger, 292
Cassell, Richard A., 306, 345, 386
Cassidy, John A., 396
Casson, Allan, 182, 225, 265
Casson, L. F., 238
Cassou, Jean, 294
Cate, Hollis L., 344
Cathcart, Helen, 363
Cather, Willa, 101, 144
Cathey, Kenneth Clay, 106
Causley, Charles, 363
Caxton, Florence, 211
Cayley, Sir George, 250, 284
Cazamian, Louis, 176
Cazamian, Madeleine L., 46, 71, 127, 210
Cecchi, Emilio, 30
Cecil, Lord David, 28, 51, 63, 76, 86, 105, 266, 306, 378
Cecil, Robert, 363
Cecile, Mother, 322
Chadwick, George F., 281, 321
Chadwick, Bishop James, D.D., 288, 330
Chadwick, Owen, 4, 104, 147, 200, 229, 253, 282, 321
Chaikin, Milton, 18, 27, 57, 62, 103
Chaloner, W. H., 121, 235, 246
Chamberlain, Joseph, 79, 126, 276, 285, 326, 367
Chamberlain, Robert L., 348

Chamberlin, Edward H., 242
Chambers, J. D., 42, 242, 282
Chambers, Robert, 170, 213
Champion, Harold, 116
Champney, Basil, 64
Chamson, André, 109
Chandler, Alice K., 242
Chandler, Edmund, 147, 189, 231
Chandler, George, 200
Chandler, Jagdish, 386
Chapeau, Alphonse-Louis-Eugène, 26
Chaplin, Charles, 19
Chapman, J. K., 363
Chapman, R. W., 238
Chapman, Robert H., 353
Chapman, Ronald, 242, 282
Chappelow, Allan, 271, 312, 313, 353
Charensol, G., 253
Charles, Conrad C. P., 363
Charlier, Gustave, 15
Charlton, William, 330
Chastenet, Jacques, 242
Chatterjee, Bhabatosh, 357, 398
Chatterton, Thomas, 260
Chaucer, Geoffrey, 86, 91, 146, 188
Checkland, S. G., 76, 363
Chekhov, Anton, 86, 354, 358, 399
Cherry, Douglas R., 312, 352, 392
Chesney, Kellow, 242
Chester, Allan G., 2, 37
Chesterton, George Laval, 262
Chesterton, Gilbert Keith, 44, 109, 296
Chevenix-Trench, C. G., 4
Chevrillon, André, 187
Chewning, Harris, 29
Chiarenza, Frank J., 259
Chicago Library, University of, 262
Child, F. J., 43
Chilston, Eric Alexander Akers-Douglas, 282
Cholmondeley, Essex, 200
Cholmondeley, George James, 33
Chorley, Henry Fothergill, 55
Chorley, Katharine, 301, 341, 381
Christensen, Torben, 282, 321
Christian, Garth, 242, 321
Christian, Mildred G., 135
Christie, Albany, 28
Church, Dean R. W., *136, 177*
Churchill, Lord Randolph S., 120, 161, 204, 242, 246, 264, 304, 344
Churchill, Sir Winston S., 116, 158
Cierpial, Leo J., 311

Cirker, Blanche, 321
Civil War (American), 50, 62, 122, 208, 224, 293, 298, 310, 349, 366
Clacy, Mrs. Charles, 363
Clapham, John, 127
Clapp, B. W., 282
Clapp, Edwin R., 253
Clare, John, *17, 54, 95*
Clarendon, Lord, 250
Clark, Alexander P., 113
Clark, David R., 398
Clark, E. A. G., 242
Clark, G. Kitson, 242, 282, 321
Clark, George A., 188
Clark, George N., 363
Clark, Jeanne Gabriel, 86
Clark, Kenneth, 49, 393
Clark, M. L., 346
Clark, Ronald William, 116
Clark, William Ross, 55, 97, 262
Clarke, Arthur Charles, 116, 232
Clarke, Sir Edward, 275
Clarke, Ignatius Frederick, 127, 278
Clarke, Marcus, *136*
Clarke, Martin Lowther, 168, 210, 363
Clarke, Mary Cowden, 254
Clarke, R. O., 76
Clarke, William Kemp Lowther, 158, 200
Claudel, Paul, 189
Clay, N. L., 134
Clayton, Edward, 241, 352, 371
Clegg, Hugh Armstrong, 363
Clemens, Cyril, 227
Clemens, Samuel L., 263
Clements, Roger V., 4
Clifford, Emma, 57, 100, 184, 266
Clifford, Sir Henry, 40
Clifford, William Kingdon, 295
Cline, C. L., 103, 269
Clinton-Baddeley, V. C., 19, 262
Clipper, Lawrence J., 343
Clive, Goeffrey, 210
Clive, John, 87, 127
Clough, Arthur Hugh, 38, 45, 51, *54, 95, 136, 177, 220, 258, 260, 267, 301, 341,* 377, *381*
Coates, A. W., 242
Cobban, Alfred, 340
Cobbett, William, 55, 88, 120, 319
Cobden, Richard, *95,* 323
Coburn, Alvin Langdon, 145
Cochrane, Captain Lord, 162

Duncan-Jones, C. M., 27, 62
Duncan-Jones, E. E., 59
Duncombe, Thomas Slingsby, 367
Dunlap, Joseph R., 232, 353, 394
Dunn, Henry Treffry, 392
Dunn, Waldo Hilary, 52, 54, 265, 306, 346, 386
Dunning, E. G., 323
Dunsany, Lord, 128
Dunseath, T. K., 275
Dunsheath, Percy, 117
Dunstan, J. L., 223
Dupee, F. W., 223, 303
Dupler, Dorothy, 271
Du Pont, V., 188
Dupree, A. Hunter, 179, 221
Dupuit, Jules, 119
Dürer, Albrecht, 235
Durham, Earl of, 158
Durham, John, 201, 350
Durham University Library, 37
Durkheim, Émile, 229
Dury, George Harry, 323
Duryee, Mary Ballard, 358
Dustin, John E., 315
Duthie, E. L., 15, 52, 174
Dutton, Ralph, 41
Dwyer, F. J., 243
Dyce, William, 336
Dyos, H. J., 243, 283
Dyson, A. E., 10, 26, 91, 133, 275, 300, 397

Eagly, Robert V., 283
Earle, Peter G., 294, 380
Easson, Angus, 383
Eastlake, Sir Charles Lock, 393
Easton, John, 117
Easton, Stewart C., 364
Eaves, T. C. Duncan, 137
Ebel, Henry, 337
Ebermayer, Erich, 34
Eddleman, Floyd E., 254
Edelman, Maurice, 182
Edens, the (Emily and Frances), *21*
Edens, Walter E., 349
Edgeworth, Maria, 168
Edmindson, Mary, 140, 223
Edmonds, E. L., 283
Edward VII, 40, 74, 368
Edwardes, Allen, 340, 380
Edwardes, Michael, 106, 117, 159, 283, 323, 364

Edwards, Edward, 329, 369
Edwards, Harold Raymond, 283
Edwards, Oliver, 211
Edwards, P. D., 357
Edwards, Ralph, 118, 159, 190
Edwards, Robert Dudley, 77, 118
Edwards, Tudor, 201
Eells, John Shepard, Jr., 13, 51, 91
Eenhoorn, Michael, 187
Egan, Pierce, 11
Egerton, George, *141,* 257
Ehrenpreis, Anne Henry, 354
Eidson, John Olin, 16, 68, 396
Eigner, Edwin M., 354
Eiseley, Loren C., 18, 138, 179, 221
Eisen, Sydney, 389
Ekebald, Inga-Stina, 338
Elgar, Sir Edward, 91, 205
Elgin, Lord, 205
Eliot, Charles W., 148
Eliot, Lady Elizabeth, 201
Eliot, Emily M., 201
Eliot, George, 6, 9, 10, 11, *21,* 39, 45, 46, 49, 50, *56, 98,* 113, 132, 141, 152, 156, 157, 165, 171, 172, *182,* 187, 210, *225,* 256, *265,* 293, 294, 295, 296, *305,* 308, *344,* 374, *385,* 393
Eliot, Thomas Stearns, 24, 85, 86, 89, 92, 101, 128, 152, 168, 182, 214, 276, 302, 316, 334, 338, 355, 356, 357, 373, 378, 388, 398
Elkins, William McIntire, 56
Ellegård, Alvar, 128, 168, 179, 221, 301
Ellery, John Blaise, 27, 390
Elletson, D. H., 159
Elliott, Blanche Beatrice, 283
Elliott, Brian, 136
Elliott, Charles, 199, 241, 280
Elliott, Philip L., Jr., 150, 192, 355
Elliott, Robert C., 211
Elliott-Binns, L. E., 41
Ellis, Cuthbert Hamilton, 4, 159, 201
Ellis, Havelock, 130, *183,* 211, *226,* 263
Ellis, James D., 387
Ellison, R. C., 391
Ellmann, Richard, 34, 71, 211, 254, 272, 275, 294, 357, 398
Elsas, Madeleine, 243
Elsbree, Langdon, 345
Elsna, Hebe, 343
Elton, Lady, 151
Elton, Lord, 4, 243, 283, 323
Elwell, T. E., 144

Fetter, Frank Whitson, 244, 283
Feuchtwanger, E. J., 159
Fido, Martin, 397
Fiedler, Leslie, 354
Field, Isobel Osbourne, 233
Fielding, Henry, 110
Fielding, Kenneth Joshua, 2, 19, 20, 52, 55, 64, 98, 139, 140, 151, 181, 223, 263, 264, 303, 343, 383, 384
Fields, James T., 332, 372
Fifoot, C. H. S., 244
Fike, Francis G., Jr., 393
Filleul, Rev. L. E. F., 58
Fillon, Jane, 299
Filor, John, 277
Finberg, Alexander Joseph, 244, 323
Finberg, Hilda F., 244
Findlater, Richard, 77
Finley, I. F., 139
Finnberg, Florence Faith, 77
Finzi, John Charles, 110
Firbank, Ronald, 344
Fischer, Walther, 10
Fischler, Alexander, 307
Fish, Howard M., Jr., 17
Fisher, James, 138
Fisher, John, 201
Fisher, Marvin, 323
Fishlow, Albert, 244
Fishman, Solomon, 352, 393
Fitch, Robert E., 179
Fitton, Robert Sucksmith, 159, 201
FitzGerald, Edward, 38, 85, *99, 141,* 165, 169, *183, 226, 265, 305, 345,* 374, *386*
Fitzgerald, F. Scott, 20
Fitzgerald, Percy, 125
Fitzgerald, Roger, 399
Fixler, Michael, 194
Flanagan, John T., 30
Flanagan, Thomas J. B., 128, 168, 211, 254
Flaubert, Gustave, 87, 97, 145, 231, 263, 342, 346
Fleck, George M., 323
Fleisher, David, 339
Fleishman, Wolfgang B., 301
Fleissner, Robert F., 303, 384
Fleming, Donald, 179, 261
Fleming, Peter, 160, 244
Fletcher, Angus, 55
Fletcher, G. B. A., 143
Fletcher, Geoffrey S., 283

Fletcher, Iain, 189
Fletcher, Ian, 276, 304, 316
Fletcher, Ifan Kyrle, 294
Fletcher, Max E., 160
Fletcher, Richard M., 294
Fleury, Gabrielle, 387
Flinn, M. W., 323
Flint, John E., 201, 244
Florescu, Radu, 323
Foakes, Reginald Anthony, 128, 168, 211, 294
Foerster, Donald M., 334
Fogazzaro, Antonio, 261
Fogle, French, 65
Fogle, Stephen F., 73
Folger Library, 279
Folland, Harold F., 181
Fonblanque, Albany, 5, *22*
Fontane, Theodor, 85, 365
Fontaney, Pierre, 232
Foran, William Robert, 283
Forbes, George Hay, 289
Forbes, John Hay, 289
Forbes, John Murray, 122
Forbes, Thomas R., 283
Forbes-Robertson, Beatrice, 118, 271, 315
Forbes-Robertson, Sir Johnston, 77
Ford, Alec George, 283, 323, 365
Ford, Boris, 128, 169
Ford, Ford Madox, *22,* 38, *141,* 221, *226,* 261, *265, 306, 345, 386*
Ford, George Harry, 20, 55, 263, 305, 343, 344, 384
Ford, Grace, 283, 323
Ford, Percy, 283, 323
Ford, Richard, *141*
Forgues, Paul Émile Daurand, 78
Forker, Charles R., 192, 263
Forman, Simon, 130
Forster, E. M., 41, 77, 137, 167, 345, 385
Forster, John, 17, 19
Forsyth, Gerald, 77
Forsyth, R. A., 315, 323, 338, 374
Forter, Elizabeth Tusten, 66
Fortescue, Chichester Samuel Parkinson, 118
Foss, Kenelm, 14, 68
Foster, Brian, 272
Foster, Charles I., 244
Foster, Richard, 70, 272
Foster, Richard Jackson, 169

Glover, Willis B., Jr., 4, 41
Goddard, Henry, 78
Godden, Geoffrey Arthur, 78, 160, 245, 284, 365
Godman, Stanley, 136
Godwin, George, 367
Goethe, Johann Wolfgang von, 95, 136, 142, 355, 373
Gogarty, Oliver St. John, 399
Going, William T., 53, 134, 378
Gokhale, B. G., 324
Goldberg, Gerald Jay, 169
Goldberg, Hannah, 98
Goldberg, M. A., 100, 357
Goldfarb, Russell M., 264, 294, 304, 355, 385, 386
Goldie, Sir George, 201, 244, 364
Golding, Alfred S., 294
Goldman, Irving, 179
Goldman, Michael P., 358
Goldsmith, Richard Weinberg, 175
Goldstein, Melvin, 135, 353
Goldstone, Herbert, 175
Goldworth, Ammon, 202
Golightly, Charles Pourtales, 147
Gollan, Robin, 324
Gollin, Alfred M., 365
Gollin, Richard M., 51, 133, 137, 177, 301, 393
Gomme, Ander, 388
Gomperz, Theodor, 350
Gooch, Brison D., 118, 245
Gooch, G. P., 5, 41, 47, 62, 87, 118, 160, 202, 324
Goodheart, Eugene, 100, 139
Goodin, George, 185
Goodman, Gordon L., 160
Goodrich, Chauncey A., 294
Goodwin, John Hanchard, 229
Gopal, Ram, 324, 365
Gopal, S., 160
Gordan, John Dozier, 38, 73, 107, 140, 156, 318
Gordon, Ambrose, Jr., 306, 386
Gordon, Caroline, 345
Gordon, General Charles George, 4, 5, 83, 209, 243, 283, 323, 333
Gordon, D. J., 276, 316
Gordon, D. L., 383
Gordon, George, 263
Gordon, John D., 360
Gordon, Mary, 192
Gordon, Robert C., 95

Gordon, Scott, 5
Gordon, Walter K., 270
Gore, Catherine, 91, 281
Gore, Charles, 200
Goschen, George Joachim, 371
Gosden, Peter Henry John Heather, 245, 284
Gose, Elliott Bickley, Jr., 22, 57, 220, 347, 382
Gosse, Sir Edmund, 37, *57, 99, 142*, 146, *184*, 192, *226*, 234, 253, *266, 307, 346*
Gosse, J. S., 261
Gosse, Philip Henry, *23*, 37, 296
Gossman, Ann M., 192, 261, 313
Gossman, Norbert J., 295
Gothic, 87, 127, 227, 294, 321
Gottfried, Leon Albert, 173, 215, 337, 377
Gotthelf, Jeremias, 45
Gottshall, James K., 140, 263
Goulding, Daniel J., 389
Gow, Ronald, 66
Gower, Countess, 6
Gragg, Wilson B., 152
Graham, A. H., 245
Graham, Andrew, 160
Graham, Gerald S., 365
Graham, Hugh, 270
Graham, Thomas R., 284
Graham, W. H., 140
Grahame, Kenneth, *184, 226*
Gramont, Elisabeth, 14
Grampp, William Dyer, 202, 245, 284, 324
Grant, J. S., 61
Grant, John E., 139
Grant, Stephen Allen, 314
Granville, Lord, 307, 346
Grattan, Clinton Hartley, 324
Graubard, Stephen R., 264, 304, 344
Graver, Lawrence, 301, 341
Graves, Charles, 366
Graves, Robert, 10, 78
Graves, William L., 348
Graveson, Ronald Harry, 78
Gray, Asa, 179, 221, 342, 383
Gray, Donald J., 72, 87, 112, 154, 179, 195, 237, 254, 277, 295, 317, 359
Gray, John, 271, *346*
Gray, Malcolm, 78, 118
Gray, Richard, 245
Gray, Thomas, 19
Grayson, Laura, 379

Greaves, C. Desmond, 245
Greaves, J., 19, 139, 181
Greaves, James Pierrepont, 115
Greaves, R. W., 147
Greaves, Rose Louise, 203, 245
Green, D. J., 274
Green, David Bonnell, 57, 100, 144, 147, 152, 184, 187, 227, 234, 259, 260, 334, 341
Green, E. R. R., 118
Green, Peter, 184, 226
Green, Roger Lancelyn, 95, 217, 260, 263, 295, 301, 309
Green, Thomas Hill, 7, *23, 142,* 296, *307,* 335, *387*
Green, Thomas W., 369
Green, Vivian Hubert Howard, 105, 148, 189
Greenacre, Phyllis, 17, 54, 342, 383
Greenaway, Kate, 187
Greenberg, Clement, 275
Greenberg, Robert A., 68, 145, 197, 216, 220, 238, 265, 278, 318, 337, 370, 377
Greene, David H., 312
Greene, Graham, 261, 345
Greene, John C., 169, 179, 212, 214, 261, 301, 342
Greene, Philip L., 386
Greenfield, Joseph D., 149
Greenhalgh, M., 181
Greenleaf, W. H., 160
Greenslade, S. L., 324
Greenwall, Harry James, 78
Greenwood, E. B., 133
Greenwood, George A., 78
Greg, William Rathbone, 99
Gregg, Lyndall, 106
Gregor, Ian, 295
Gregory, Horace, 169, 212, 254, 295
Gregory, Lady, 35, 152, *266, 307,* 398
Gregory, Sir Richard, 74
Gregory, Theodore, 284
Grein, J. T., 371
Greiner, Francis J., 308
Grenander, M. E., 56
Grenberg, Bruce L., 380
Grendon, Felix, 31, 67, 107
Grennan, Joseph E., 348
Grensted, L. W., 180
Grenville, J. A. S., 118, 324, 366
Gressman, Malcolm G., 374
Greville, Charles Cavendish Fulke, 324
Grey, Earl, 125

Grey, Sir Edward, 40
Grey, Sir George, 199, 238, 251, 290
Grey Collection, Auckland City Library, 16
Gridley, Roy, 314
Grierson, Edward, 160
Grierson, Janet, 310, 350
Griffin, Alice, 31
Griffin, Ernest G., 212, 347
Griffin, Gerald, 128, 168
Griffith, Arthur, 200
Griffith, Ben W., Jr., 56, 97
Griffith, Philip Mahone, 387
Grigson, Geoffrey, 24, 314, 349, 389, 393
Grimble, Ian, 284, 324
Grimthorpe, Lord, 77
Grinnell-Milne, Duncan, 78
Grob, Alan, 396
Grob, Shirley, 384
Gronningsater, Arne Howell, 14
Gronow, Captain Rees Howell, 370
Groom, Bernard, 47, 87, 128
Grosart, A. B., *57*
Groshong, James Willard, 128
Gross, Felix, 41, 78, 118
Gross, Harvey, 374
Gross, John, 304, 343, 344, 384
Gross, Martha, 152
Gross, Seymour L., 101, 220, 261, 341
Grosskurth, Phyllis M., 354, 396
Grote, George, *346,* 363
Grotjahn, Martin, 92
Grubb, Gerald G., 19, 20, 55, 98
Grubel, Herbert G., 245
Gruber, Howard E., 262, 301
Gruber, Jacob W., 203, 245
Gruber, Valmai, 301
Grundy, J. Owen, 354
Grunfeld, Fred, 67
Grylls, R. Glynn, 78, 384, 392
Guerard, Albert Joseph, 137, 177, 178, 220, 261, 347, 387
Guerin, Wilfred L., 339
Guest, Edwin, 186
Guest, Ivor, 5, 78, 119, 160
Guetti, James L., Jr., 220
Guha, Naresh, 358
Guidi, Augusto, 59
Guillebaud, C. W., 245, 284
Gulick, Charles Adams, 38
Gullans, Charles B., 316
Gullason, Thomas Arthur, 54, 150

Hardy, Thomas, 3, 9, 22, *23*, 45, 46, 48, *57*, 73, 86, *99*, 128, 130, *142*, 156, 166, 169, 170, 171, *184*, 212, *227*, 256, *266*, 293, 294, 295, 300, 305, *307*, 314, 315, 336, 345, *346*, 374, 375, 379, *387*
Hargreaves, H. A., 273
Hargreaves, J. H., 285
Hargreaves, John Desmond, 325, 366
Harhetty, P., 285
Harkness, Bruce, 18, 212, 220, 261
Harkness, Stanley B., 16, 54
Harland, Aline, 295
Harland, Henry, 295
Harlow, Vincent, 230
Harmsworth, Geoffrey, 164, 207
Harness, William, 27, 62
Harney, George Julian, 124, 165, 207
Harper, George Graham, Jr., 184
Harper, George M., 382
Harper, James W., 259
Harris, Abram L., 62, 160, 188
Harris, Alan, 285
Harris, Arthur J., 334
Harris, C. C., Jr., 163
Harris, David, 41
Harris, Frank, 170, *185, 228*
Harris, Harold J., 354
Harris, Katharine S., 374
Harris, Markham, 22
Harris, Truett Wilson, 87
Harris, Wendell V., 254, 295, 392
Harris Public Library, 235
Harrison, Ada, 175, 218
Harrison, Brian, 325
Harrison, Frederic, *185, 228,* 293, 298, *308*, 376
Harrison, John Fletcher Clews, 87, 245, 285, 325
Harrison, Michael, 141, 182, 225, 285, 325
Harrison, Royden, 160, 203, 245, 325
Harrison, Thomas P., 95, 101, 103, 259
Harrod, Roy, 315
Hart, Francis Russell, 95, 212
Hart, Jenifer, 5, 235
Hart, John Edward, 27
Hart-Davis, Rupert, 103, 188, 315, 357, 378
Harthan, John P., 325
Hartington, Marquis of, 284, 367
Hartley, Anthony, 187
Hartley, Harold, 325

Hartman, Carl, 197
Hartman, Geoffrey H., 24, 59
Hartman, Joan E., 192
Hartwell, R. M., 160
Harwood, Thomas Franklin, 160
Harvard Library, 192, 261
Harvey, David Dow, 345, 386
Harvey, Van A., 245
Harvey, W. J., 141, 265, 305, 345
Hassing, Per Schioldborg, 203
Hastings, Sir Charles, 162, 205
Hastings, Sir Patrick, 203
Hastings, Warren, 24
Haugh, Robert F., 18, 96, 137, 177
Hauptmann, Gerhart, 149
Häusermann, H. W., 194, 236
Havard, William C., 160, 203, 245
Havelock, Sir Henry, 76
Hawes, Frances, 135
Hawker, James, 242, 321
Hawkes, Jacquetta, 212
Hawkins, Anthony Hope, 40
Hawkins, D. J. B., 147
Hawkins, Maude M., 143, 186
Hawkins, Sherman, 315
Hawthorne, Nathaniel, 22, 65, 84, 218, 259, 300, 363, 386
Hawthorne, Mrs. Nathaniel, 224
Hay, Eloise Knapp, 261, 341, 382
Hay, John, 337, 345
Hayden, Eric W., 285
Haydon, Benjamin Robert, 330
Hayek, F. A., 103
Hayter, Althea, 299, 339, 379
Hayward, John, 374
Hazen, James F., 347
Hazlitt, William, 192
Head, Francis Bond, 120, 248
Hearder, H., 78
Hearnshaw, Leslie Spencer, 366
Heasman, Kathleen J., 285, 325, 366
Heath, Frederick B., 246
Heathcote, A. W., 180
Hedman, Edwin Randolph, 78
Hegel, Georg, 48, 65, 270
Heger, Constantin, 15
Heilbrun, Carolyn G., 254, 295
Heilman, Robert B., 99, 218, 347, 387
Heimer, Jackson W., 382
Heine, Heinrich, 10, 87, 196
Heintzelman, Arthur W., 47
Heldring, E., 383
Helgesen, Moira Anne, 78

Hellstrom, Ward, 307, 387
Helm, Robert M., 285, 325
Hemans, Felicia, 11, 45
Hemingway, Ernest, 357, 398
Hemmings, F. W. J., 87
Henderson, Archibald, 31, 66, 107, 395
Henderson, Lucille K., 395
Henderson, Philip, 63, 105
Henderson, Stephen E., 192
Henderson, W. O., 5, 246, 325
Henderson-Howatt, G. M. D., 378
Hendrick, George, 68, 318
Hendy, Philip, 246
Henley, Dorothy, 161
Henley, William Ernest, 46, *58*, 86, 89, *100*, 142, *348, 388*
Henn, Thomas Rice, 47, 71
Hennock, E. P., 325
Henriques, Robert, 203
Henry, Anne W., 150
Henry, Donald R., 374
Henry, Marjorie Ruth, 93
Henry Charles Lea Library, University of Pennsylvania, 144
Henson, Janice, 272
Henty, George Alfred, *24, 388*
Herbert, George, 321
Herd, Harold, 5
Hergenhan, L. T., 350, 390
Hergesheimer, Joseph, 178
Herman, George, 348
Herman, William R., 184
Herndon, Richard J., 220, 261
Hernon, Joseph M., Jr., 366
Herodotus, 230
Herring, Jack W., 135
Herrmann, Luke, 325
Herschel, Sir John, 113, 253, 283
Hertz, Robert N., 301, 380
Herzen, Alexander, 130
Hess, M. Whitcomb, 192
Hesse, Herman, 254
Hester, Waverly E., 305
Hetherington, Hugh W., 295
Hethmon, Robert Henry, Jr., 111
Heuser, Alan, 143, 185, 228
Heussler, Robert, 325
Heuston, R. F., 366
Hewett, Osbert Wyndham, 41, 119
Hewitt, Carol B., 239
Hewitt, Margaret, 119, 161
Heyl, Edgar, 370
Heywood, C., 231, 347, 387

Hibbert, Christopher, 246, 285, 325, 366
Hicks, John H., 87, 382
Higham, Charles, 320
Higham, Norman, 366
Higher Criticism, 4
Highet, Gilbert, 212
Higonnet, René P., 79
Hill, A. C., 345
Hill, A. G., 119, 141
Hill, Alwyn S., 203
Hill, Archibald A., 24, 94, 101
Hill, Draper, 298
Hill, Gilbert M., 203
Hill, Octavia, 41
Hill, Richard, 5
Hill, Roland, 12
Hill, T. W., 19, 55, 139, 181, 223
Hill, William Thomson, 41
Hillcourt, William, 366
Hillegas, Mark Robert, 87
Hillhouse, James T., 171
Hillyer, Robert, 100
Hilton, George W., 79, 285
Hilton, Richard, 79
Hilton, William Samuel, 325
Himmelfarb, Gertrude, 179, 222, 262, 300
Hinchliff, Peter, 285, 366
Hines, Leo, 388
Hinsley, F. H., 285, 325, 366
Hinton, R. W. K., 169
Hipple, Walter J., Jr., 297
Hirsch, David H., 384
Hiscock, W. G., 381
Hitchcock, Henry Russell, 5, 87, 128, 169
Hitler, Adolf, 272, 328, 369
Hively, Robert William, 192
Hoblitzelle, Harrison, 169
Hobman, D. L., 24, 30, 41
Hobsbawm, Eric John, 79, 166, 246, 285, 326, 366, 367
Hobson, J. A., 64, *143*
Hoctor, Sister Thomas Marion, 133
Hodge, Francis, 161
Hodges, Robert R., 301, 341, 382
Hodgins, James R., 227
Hodgskin, Thomas, 5, 41, 78
Hoff, Rhoda, 263
Hoffman, Charles G., 301
Hoffman, Robert, 310
Hoffman, Russell, 387
Hoffman, Stanton de Voren, 341

Moews, Daniel D., 378
Moffatt, Robert, 288
Moffett, John, 107, 149
Mohan, Ramesh, 275
Moir, Esther, 170, 328
Moldstad, David Franklin, 22
Molloy, John I., 233
Moncure, James A., 205
Mond, Ludwig, 40, 200
Mondini, Luigi, 163
Mongan, Agnes, 122
Monjian, Mercedes C., 337
Monod, Sylvère, 98, 140, 181, 183, 223, 263, 304, 379
Montag, George E., 348
Montague, Gene, 173, 300
Monteiro, George, 337, 339, 398
Montgomery, John, 328
Moody, D. L., 330, 370
Moody, Theodore William, 122, 157, 205
Mooney, Stephen, 228
Moore, Carlisle, 17, 95, 342, 355
Moore, David C., 163, 248
Moore, Dwain Earl, 62, 146
Moore, Frank, 306
Moore, G. E., 132
Moore, George, 12, *27*, 46, *62*, 86, *103*, 114, *146*, 156, 170, *188*, 211, 227, *230, 269*, 295, *350*, 399
Moore, Jerold N., 205
Moore, John Rees, 111, 276
Moore, Katherine, 147
Moore, R. J., 369
Moore, Ruth E., 18, 96
Moore, Thomas, 147
Moore, Virginia, 35, 71, 194
Moorehead, Alan, 205, 248, 288
Moran, James, 239
Moraud, Marcel Ian, 80
Morcos, Louis, 24, 347
Mordell, Albert, 173
Morey, John H., 221
Morgan, Brian, 329
Morgan, Edward Victor, 288
Morgan, Edwin, 89
Morgan, Estelle, 296
Morgan, H. A., 145
Morgan, J., 196
Morgan, John Minter, 115
Morgan, Kenneth Owen, 329, 369
Morgan, Lady, 11, 128, 168
Morgan, Lewis H., 255

Morgan, Margery M., 42, 232, 272
Morgan, P. F., 100
Morgan Library, 217
Morison, Stanley, 369
Moritz, Harold Kenneth, 181
Morland, M. A., 130
Morley, John, 12, 24, *28*, 51, *62, 146, 188*
Morley, Malcolm, 6, 19, 55, 139, 181, 205, 223, 263, 303, 335, 343, 373, 375, 383
Morrah, Patrick, 329
Morrell, Lady Ottoline, 365
Morrell, Roy, 308, 347
Morrell, W. P., 288
Morris, Barbara, 288
Morris, Bertram, 29
Morris, David, 24
Morris, Jane, 392
Morris, John Henry, 122, 163, 205
Morris, John N., 391
Morris, John William, 17, 350
Morris, Owen James, 81
Morris, William, 9, *28, 62*, 88, *104*, 111, 120, *146*, 152, 156, *188*, 192, 197, *231, 269, 310*, 336, *350*, 362, *391*
Morse, J. Mitchell, 135
Morsiani, Yamile, 384
Mortimer, Roger, 122, 288
Morton, Arthur Leslie, 42, 163, 288, 369
Morton, Frederic, 288
Morton, James, 370
Mosely, Maboth, 369
Moser, Thomas, 54, 96, 137, 138, 178, 221, 238, 246, 299
Mosher, Thomas Bird, 298
Mosley, Leonard Oswald, 206
Moss, Arthur William, 248
Mosse, George L., 335
Mosse, Werner Eugen, 163, 206, 248, 329, 369
Mount, Charles Merrill, 81
Mount-Temple, Lady, 392
Mount-Temple, William Francis Cowper-Temple, First Baron, 392
Mowat, Charles Loch, 248, 288, 329
Moxon, Edward, 144
Moynahan, Julian, 58, 210, 224, 263
Mozley, Dorothea, 311, 351
Mozley, Harriet, 91
Mudge, Isadore Gilbert, 315
Mudrick, Marvin, 96, 178

O'Shea, W. H., 285
O'Sullivan, Vincent, 170
"Ouida" (Maria-Louise Ramé), *28*, 39, *105*, 113, *147*, *188*
Owen, Guy, Jr., 138, 221
Owen, H. P., 298
Owen, R. J., 138
Owen, Robert, 84, 117, 122, 159, 288, 369
Owen, Wilfred, 194
Owens, R. J., 141, 268
Owsley, Harriet C., 249
Oxford Movement, 4, 136, 152, 177, 210, 211, 253, 336, 364, 375
Ozy, 149, 191

Paar, H. W., 329
Packe, Michael St. John, 27, 62, 103
Packer, Lona Mosk, 148, 189, 312, 352, 354, 392, 396
Paden, William Doremus, 135, 148, 175, 192, 273, 274, 296, 392
Page, David, 135, 339
Page, Frederick, 134
Paget, George Charles Henry Victor, 249, 264, 288
Paget, Violet, 389
Paget, William, 249, 288
Paglin, M., 249
Painting, David E., 224, 397
Pakenham, Elizabeth, 206, 249
Pakenham, Pansy, 19, 55, 140, 182, 303, 343
Palgrave, Francis Turner, 268, 295
Pallette, Drew B., 272
Palliser, John, 371
Palmer, A. W., 81, 289
Palmer, David, 334
Palmer, E. H., 210
Palmer, Horsley, 158
Palmer, John Alfred, 342
Palmer, Rupert E., Jr., 219
Palmer, William, 78
Palmerston, Henry John Temple, Viscount, 84, 169, 240, 242, 282, 323, 332, 333
Palmerston, Lady, 80
Panikkar, K. M., 81
Panizzi, Anthony, 128
Pankhurst, Richard K. P., 89, 130, 230
Pannell, Charles, 122
Pantazzi, Sybille, 249, 268
Paolucci, Henry, 274

Pappe, H. O., 269
Pardoe, Julia, *28*
Pares, Richard, 81
Paris, Bernard J., 57, 305
Parish, John E., 316, 388
Park, Bruce R., 149
Parke, Ernest, 43
Parker, Dorothy E. H., 267
Parker, John William, Jr., 334
Parker, Ralph, 306
Parker, W. M., 6, 23, 296, 347
Parker, Wyman W., 370
Parkinson, Cyril Northcote, 206, 249, 289
Parkinson, Thomas, 35, 399
Parks, Lloyd C., 236, 358, 399
Parnaby, Owen W., 370
Parnell, Charles Stewart, 79, 117, 129, 164, 205, 247, 254, 285, 287, 319
Parrinder, E. G., 306
Parris, Henry, 249
Parrish, M. L., 69
Parrish, Stephen Maxfield, 173, 216, 258, 358, 399
Parrish Collection, 2, 15, 39, 384
Parrott, Thomas Marc, 48
Parry, Ann, 329
Parry, Sir Edward, 329
Parsons, Coleman O., 163
Parsons, Olive Wrenchel, 21
Parthenope, Frances, 121
Partlow, Robert B., Jr., 264
Pascal, Blaise, 165
Pascal, Roy, 170, 171
Passmore, John Arthur, 89, 171, 180
Pater, Walter, 9, 11, *28*, 40, 46, *63*, 86, 90, *105*, 132, *147*, 156, 157, *188*, *231*, 234, *270*, 305, *311*, 316, *351*, *392*
Paterson, John, 185, 227, 228, 267, 308
Patmore, Coventry, *63*, 78, *105*, 113, *147*, *189*, *231*, 266, *270*, *311*, 377, *392*
Patrick, J. Max, 60, 73
Patrick, John M., 188
Patterson, A. Temple, 329
Patterson, Jerry E., 62
Patterson, Rebecca, 135
Patteson, John Coleridge, 322
Pattison, Mark, *105*, 148, *189*
Patton, John, 267
Paul, David, 35
Paul, Rodman W., 122
Paulus, Gretchen, 89
Paxon, Omar Martin, 272

Taine, Hyppolyte Adolphe, 125, 166, 182
Talbot, Mrs. Fanny, 30, 232
Talbot, Quartus, 30
Talfourd, Thomas Noon, *68, 109,* 144
Talmon, Jacob Leib, 214, 256, 297
Talon, Henri-A., 315, 390, 397
Tamaganan, Jean, 380
Tanner, Jimmie E., 382
Tanner, Tony, 301, 342, 382
Tanzy, C. E., 136, 297
Taplin, Gardner B., 54, 94, 136, 219
Taplin, W. A., 281, 321, 363
Tappe, E. D., 83, 188, 208, 332
Tarbuck, Edward Lance, 45
Tartella, Vincent Paul, 264
Tate, Allen, 50
Tate, George, 42, 163
Taube, Myron, 235, 356
Tauber, Abraham, 354, 394, 395
Tave, Stuart M., 215
Tawney, R. H., 372
Tax, Sol, 222, 262
Taylor, A. Carey, 177, 235
Taylor, Alan John Percivale, 8, 44, 50, 73, 81, 83, 125, 166, 332
Taylor, Arthur J., 31, 67, 208
Taylor, Basil, 8
Taylor, Bayard, 31
Taylor, C. R. H., 219
Taylor, Don, 332
Taylor, Estella Ruth, 35
Taylor, F., 39
Taylor, Frank Sherwood, 125, 166
Taylor, Gordon Rattrap, 125
Taylor, Harriet, 269
Taylor, Sir Henry, *68, 109*
Taylor, J. E., 45
Taylor, Overton H., 83, 252, 291
Taylor, Philip Meadows, 45
Taylor, Robert H., 39, 114, 131
Taylor, Theodore Cooke, 78
Taylor, William, 373
Tedlock, E. W., Jr., 21
Telling, Marjorie Beach, 292
Temperley, Nicholas, 256, 292
Temple, Richard, 366
Temple, Ruth Z., 211
Templeman, William Darby, 1, 24, 36, 72, 92, 112, 308, 356
Templin, Lawrence H., 386
Tener, Robert H., 192, 193, 215, 220, 258, 338, 341, 376

Tennyson, Alfred Lord, 9, 16, 17, *32,* 38, 45, 47, 48, 51, *68,* 73, 86, 88, 90, 91, 100, *109, 150,* 152, 157, 165, 169, 170, *192,* 197, 215, *234,* 256, 267, *273,* 295, 300, *314,* 319, 336, 351, *355, 396*
Tennyson, Sir Charles, 69, 109, 110, 166, 193, 235, 355, 397
Tennyson, Emily, Lady, 32
Tennyson, Georg B., 341, 381
Tennyson-D'Eyncourt, Clara, 274
Tepfer, John, 394
Terhune, A. McKinley, 38, 99
Ternan, Ellen, 19, 181, 182
Terris, Ellaline (Lady Hicks), 8
Terrot, Charles, 166, 208
Terry, Ellen, 118, 320, 327
Terwilliger, Patricia J., 276
Texas Library, University of, 2, 156, 262, 302, 307
Thackeray, Mary Ann, 274
Thackeray, William Makepeace, 9, 19, *32,* 38, 45, 48, 49, 50, 52, *69,* 87, *110,* 113, 136, 139, *151,* 167, 171, *193,* 210, *234,* 254, 263, *274,* 293, *315,* 335, *356,* 369, 384, 385, *397*
Thale, Jerome, 16, 18, 21, 22, 64, 99, 141, 183, 225, 235, 265
Thaler, Alwin, 256
Thearle, Beatrice June, 131
Thérèse, Mother Marie, 332
Therese, Sister, S.N.D., 186
Thielicke, Helmut, 354
Thierry, Adrien, 208
Thirsk, Joan, 209
Thistlethwaite, Frank, 172, 215, 256
Thody, Philip, 136
Tholfsen, Trygve R., 125, 252
Thomas, Alfred, 231, 270, 376
Thomas, Arthur, 376
Thomas, Berte, 42
Thomas, Brandon, *33*
Thomas, Brinley, 8
Thomas, David St. John, 209, 332
Thomas, Dylan, 97, 101, 395
Thomas, Hugh, 252, 292
Thomas, J. D., 34, 180, 267, 271
Thomas, Jevan Brandon, 33
Thomas, Powell Stackhouse, 269
Thomas, W. A., 287
Thomas, W. E. S., 292
Thompson, Brooks, 292
Thompson, D., 125

White-Melville, G. J., 334
Whiteside, Thomas, 293, 333
Whiting, George Wesley, 96, 192, 233, 261
Whitla, William, 340, 380
Whitley, Alvin, 55, 100
Whitlock, Baird W., 59
Whitman, Walt, 99, 136, 147, 152, 219, 253, 340
Whitman, Wanda, 353
Whitmore, Rev. C. J., 223
Whitmore, Charles E., 33
Whitridge, Arnold, 126, 173, 293
Whittington-Egan, Richard, 209, 349
Whyte, John Henry, 126, 166, 167, 199, 209, 231
Wibberley, Leonard, 44
Wichler, Gerhard, 262
Wickenden, Thomas Douglas, 293
Wickham, Edward Ralph, 84
Wickoff, Henry, 322
Wicksteed, Philip H., 364
Wiener, Norbert, 349
Wiggins, Arch R., 373
Wilberforce, Samuel, 4, 241, 281, 321, 329
Wilbur, Richard, 309
Wilde, Allan, 385
Wilde, Oscar, 12, *34*, 38, 40, 45, 46, *70*, 85, 89, 90, *110*, 114, 134, *152*, 156, 168, 170, *194*, *235*, *275*, 296, *315*, 319, *357*, 373, 376, 393, *398*
Wilde, Richard H., 126
Wildi, Max, 35
Wiles, Anna, 83
Wiley, Elizabeth, 303
Wiley, Paul L., 346, 386
"Wilhelm." *See* Pitcher, John Charles
Wilkie, David, 125
Wilkie, J. S., 50
Wilkins, Charles T., 174, 298
Wilkins, M. S., 167
Wilkinson, D. C., 219
Wilkinson, John T., 333
Wilkinson, Rupert, 373
Willey, Basil, 50, 91, 110, 132, 168, 172, 215, 222, 262, 391
William IV, 4, 198
Williams, Bransby, 19
Williams, David, 44
Williams, George Walton, 382
Williams, Helen Maria, 219
Williams, James Eccles, 293

Williams, L. Pearce, 209
Williams, Lawrence John, 122, 163, 205
Williams, Luster J., 94
Williams, McDonald, 197
Williams, Porter, Jr., 382
Williams, R. E. T., 44, 353
Williams, R. W., 45
Williams, Raymond, 132, 172, 215, 385
Williams, Richmond Dean, 167
Williams, Sidney Herbert, 300, 341
Williams, Thomas Desmond, 77, 118
Williams, Trevor Illytd, 201, 243, 283, 322
Williams, W. A., 333
Williams, W. S., 15
Williamson, Audrey, 354
Williamson, Chilton, 8
Williamson, Eugene L., Jr., 216, 258, 338, 378
Williamson, Geoffrey, 25
Williamson, Henry, 257
Williamson, Jeffrey G., 293
Williamson, Karina, 356
Willis, Frederich, 253
Willis, Irene Cooper, 93, 379
Willoughby, John W., 219, 300, 340
Wills, Geoffrey, 45
Wills, John Howard, 18, 261, 342
Willy, Todd G., 333
Wilmot-Horton, R. J., 324, 365
Wilson, Angus, 94, 224, 336, 345
Wilson, Charles, 126, 167, 193
Wilson, Colin, 51, 149
Wilson, Edmund, 314, 354
Wilson, Edwin, 271, 313
Wilson, Francis Alexander Charles, 111, 153, 194, 236, 276, 316
Wilson, Harris, 272
Wilson, Harry, 398
Wilson, Henry Joseph, 244
Wilson, James, 5, 205
Wilson, Mardis Glen, Jr., 126
Wilson, W. G., 110
Wilson, William Carus, 174
Wimsatt, William K., 91, 132, 172
Winch, D. N., 333
Winckler, Paul A., 55
Windolph, Francis Lyman, 94
Wing, Donald G., 114, 348
Wing, George Douglas, 308, 388
Wingfield-Stratford, Esme, 45, 167
Winn, William E., 228
Winstanley, David, 120

Winsten, Stephen, 67, 108, 150
Winstone, Reece, 293
Winters, Warrington, 56, 344
Winters, Yvor, 132, 236, 276, 308, 316
Winther, Oscar O., 84, 373
Wise, Dorothy, 373
Wise, Thomas James, 37, 192, 197, 238, 253, 271, 291, 321, 393, 397
Wiseman, Cardinal, 53, *152,* 188, 219, 329
Wiseman, Nicholas, 323, 365
Wishmeyer, William Hood, 94
Wishy, Bernard, 187, 269
Witt, Marion, 35, 236
Witte, William, 177
Wittrock, Verna Dorothy, 91
Witts, R. John, 306
Wölcken, Fritz, 51
Wolf, Donald A., 259
Wolf, Joseph, 226
Wolf, William J., 390
Wolff, Michael, 157, 183, 198, 226, 239, 279, 373
Wolff, Robert Lee, 187, 268
Wollheim, Richard, 174, 217, 259
Wolseley, Garnet, 119
Wolseley, Lord, 368
Wolsky, Alexander, 180
Wong, Helene Har Lin, 91
Wood, Anthony C., 209, 253
Wood, Frederick T., 361
Wood, Mrs. Henry, 39
Wood, Herbert George, 12, 91
Wood, Margaret, 132
Wood, P. A., 162
Wood, Violet, 215, 253
Woodall, Robert, 141
Woodbridge, Homer Edwards, 354
Woodcock, George, 167, 293
Woodham-Smith, Cicil, 160, 293, 333, 373
Woodhouse, A. S. P., 375
Woodhouse, Christopher Montague, 327
Woodhowe, C. M., 293
Woodings, R. B., 384
Woodiwiss, John C., 8
Woodring, Carl R., 93
Woodruff, Douglas, 84, 126
Woodruff, Philip, 8
Woodruff, William, 167, 209
Woods, George Benjamin, 51
Woods, Thomas, 269
Woodward, Ernest Llewellyn, 293, 333

Woodward, Frances J., 92
Woodward, John, 293
Woolf, Cecil, 105, 134, 189, 231, 271, 312, 315
Woolf, Harry, 198, 239
Woolf, Leonard Sidney, 215, 257
Woolf, Virginia, 30, 31, 51, 100, 130, 172, 345, 398
Wooton, Carl, 308
Worcester College Library, 363
Wordsworth, Andrew, 84
Wordsworth, William, 14, 86, 259, 334, 345, 373, 377
Worsley, T. C., 67
Worth, Charles Frederick, 7
Worth, George John, 12, 18, 54, 69, 91, 135, 257, 264, 274, 296
Worth, Peter, 92
Wortham, Hugo, 45, 84
Wrench, Sir John Evelyn, 126, 167
Wrenn, John Henry, 397
Wright, Andrew, 196
Wright, Austin, 1, 3, 39, 74, 154, 215, 257
Wright, Charles D., 378
Wright, David, 377
Wright, Elizabeth Cox, 145, 221
Wright, Elizabeth V., 197
Wright, Esmond, 157
Wright, Frank Lloyd, 49
Wright, George T., 276, 316
Wright, Herbert G., 91, 132, 172
Wright, James A., 182
Wright, Lawrence, 209
Wright, Noel, 167
Wright, Thomas, 10
Wright, Walter F., 18, 382
Würgler, Hans, 126
Wyatt, Sibyl W., 377
Wyllie, Irvin G., 180
Wyndham, Horace, 152
Wyndham, Violet, 333, 357, 373
Wynn-Tyson, Esme, 180

Yale University Library, 145, 231, 302
Yamamoto, Bunnosuke, 100, 308
Yanko, Ann E., 304
Yarker, P. M., 39, 115, 187
Yarmolinsky, Avrahm, 24
Yarrell, William, 283
Yates, Norris W., 372
Yearly, Clifton K., Jr., 126
Yeats, A. W., 60, 229, 268

Yeats, William Butler, 3, 11, 12, 30, *34*, 45, 52, *71*, 73, 87, *110*, 113, 146, *152*, 156, 168, 169, *194*, 211, *236*, *275*, 294, 295, 310, *315*, 336, 350, *357*, *398*
Yellow Book, 141, 213, 218, 255, 257, 295, 377
Yelton, Donald C., 342
Yoder, Edwin M., Jr., 389
Yonge, Charlotte, 18, 39, *71*, 91, *111*, 113, 334
Yorks, Samuel Augustus, 110
Young, Agnes Freda, 45, 84
Young, Andrew, 315
Young, Arthur C., 99, 142, 212, 266, 306, 337, 346
Young, G. M., 85, 126, 293
Young, Howard V., Jr., 167
Young, Kenneth, 334
Young, Percy M., 91
Youngblood, Sarah Helen, 194, 358
Yü, Margaret Man Sang, 152
Yuill, W. E., 308

Zabel, Morton Dauwen, 91, 132, 172
Zale, Eric M., 311
Zall, Paul M., 229, 309
Zamwalt, Eugene E., 136
Zangler, Jules, 102, 230, 268
Zangwill, Israel, 279
Zellar, Leonard Eugene, 138
Zeltman, William, 272
Zeno, Fr., 105
Zerke, Carl Frederick, 31
Ziegler, Rev. A. F., 303
Ziegler, A. U., 140
Ziegler, Arthur P., 292
Zigerell, James, 174
Zimmerman, Paul Albert, 180, 302
Zink, David D., 297
Zola, Émile, 18, 62, 87, 103, 171, 334, 383
Zouche, Lord, 318
Zuckerman, Jerome, 342, 382
Zwerdling, Alex, 236, 276
Zwicky, Laurie Bowman, 319